A GUIDE TO TREATMENTS THAT WORK

A GUIDE TO TREATMENTS THAT WORK

Third Edition

EDITED BY

PETER E. NATHAN

JACK M. GORMAN

Oxford University Press
2007

OXFORD
UNIVERSITY PRESS

Oxford University Press, Inc., publishes works that further
Oxford University's objective of excellence
in research, scholarship, and education.

Oxford   New York
Auckland   Cape Town   Dar es Salaam   Hong Kong   Karachi
Kuala Lumpur   Madrid   Melbourne   Mexico City   Nairobi
New Delhi   Shanghai   Taipei   Toronto

With offices in
Argentina   Austria   Brazil   Chile   Czech Republic   France   Greece
Guatemala   Hungary   Italy   Japan   Poland   Portugal   Singapore
South Korea   Switzerland   Thailand   Turkey   Ukraine   Vietnam

Published by Oxford University Press, Inc.
198 Madison Avenue, New York, New York 10016

www.oup.com

Oxford is a registered trademark of Oxford University Press

Library of Congress Cataloging-in-Publication Data
A guide to treatments that work / edited by Peter E. Nathan, Jack M. Gorman.—3rd ed.
p.   ;   cm.
Includes bibliographical references and index.
ISBN 978-0-19-530414-5
1. Mental illness—Treatment—Evaluation.   I. Nathan, Peter E.   II. Gorman, Jack M.
[DNLM: 1. Mental Disorders—therapy.   2. Psychotherapy—methods. WM 400 G946 2007]
RC480.5.G85   2007
616.89'1—dc22   2006023263

1 3 5 7 9 8 6 4 2

Printed in the United States of America
on acid-free paper

For the next generation, with love:
Abigail Sara, Daniel Arthur, Emily Kathryn
Zachary John, Jennifer Margaret, Dylan Emil

With love for their devotion to
Lauren, Sara Elizabeth, Rachel Lisa, and Avi

Preface

In the absence of science, opinion prevails.

Although the reader will notice a few changes in this edition of *A Guide to Treatments That Work*, its goals and the standards by which chapter authors evaluated research on treatments remain the same in the third edition as they were in the first and second. Like its predecessors, this edition offers detailed evaluative reviews of current research on treatments for disorders for which empirically supported interventions have been developed. They are written in most instances by psychiatrists and clinical psychologists who are major contributors to that literature. Most of the chapter authors in this edition also wrote for the first two editions.

The standards by which the authors were asked to evaluate the methodological rigor of the treatment research they reviewed have not changed either. Summarized here, they are designed to enable authors and readers to assess the treatment outcome data in light of the methodological adequacy of the research studies from which the outcome data were derived. Those standards, identical to the ones that guided chapter authors in the first two editions of this book, are as follows:

The purpose of these chapters is to present the most rigorous, scientifically based evidence for the efficacy of treatments that is available. At the same time, it is clear that for some disorders there are treatments widely recognized by experienced clinicians to be useful that may not have been subjected to rigorous investigation for a variety of

reasons. Our aim is to be clear with readers what treatments are felt by a large number of experts to be valuable but have never been properly scientifically examined, and what treatments are known to be of little value.

To do this, it is useful to establish some criteria for evaluating the validity of articles in the literature that are reviewed in writing the chapters. We would like you to keep in mind the following classification when you are reviewing the literature and writing your chapter:

Type 1 Studies: These are the most rigorous and involve a randomized, prospective clinical trial. Such studies also must involve comparison groups with random assignment, blinded assessments, clear presentation of exclusion and inclusion criteria, state-of-the-art diagnostic methods, adequate sample size to offer statistical power, and clearly described statistical methods.

Type 2 Studies: These are clinical trials in which an intervention is made, but some aspects of the Type 1 study requirement are missing. For example, a trial in which a double blind cannot be maintained; a trial in which two treatments are compared but the assignment is not randomized; and a trial in which there is a clear but not fatal flaw such as a period of observation that is felt to be too short to make full judgments on treatment efficacy. Such studies clearly do not merit the same consideration as Type 1 studies but often make important contributions and generally should not be ignored.

Type 3 Studies: These are clearly methodologically limited. Generally, Type 3 studies are open treatment studies aiming at obtaining pilot data. They are highly subject to observer bias and can usually do little more than indicate if a treatment is worth pursuing in a more rigorous design. Also included in this category are case-control studies in which patients are identified and then information about treatment is obtained from them retrospectively. Such studies can, of course, provide a great deal of naturalistic information but are prone to all of the problems of uncontrolled data collection and retrospective recall error.

Type 4 Studies: Reviews with secondary data analysis can be useful, especially if the data-analytic techniques are sophisticated. Modern methods of meta-analysis attempt to account for the fact that, for example, negative studies tend to be reported at a substantially lower rate than positive outcome studies.

Type 5 Studies: Reviews without secondary data analysis are helpful to give an impression of the literature but are clearly subject to the writer's opinion and sometimes are highly biased.

Type 6 Studies: This encompasses a variety of reports that have marginal value, such as case studies, essays, and opinion papers.

We have made a few changes that we think improve the book. Three chapters have been added that review data supporting empirically based treatments for conditions for which these findings have only recently emerged. Jon E. Grant and Marc N. Potenza review current data on pharmacological and psychosocial treatments for pathological gambling and other impulse control disorders. As our society extends gambling venues in search of new revenue for local and state governments, the numbers of pathological gamblers have increased proportionately. Hence, there is a clear need for effective treatments for gambling problems; the marked increase in efforts to develop and test such treatments is reviewed in chapter 20. Lisa M. Najavits reviews the findings on psychosocial treatments for posttraumatic stress disorder in chapter 18; the dramatic recent increase in patients diagnosed with PTSD, in large part reflecting psychological casualties from the wars in Iraq and Afghanistan, has made the search for effective PTSD treatments more compelling than ever. Finally, in chapter 25, Cindy J. Aaronson, Gary P. Katzman, and coeditor Jack M. Gorman have written a comprehensive review of the efficacy of combined psychopharmacological and psychosocial treatments for the major depressive and anxiety disorders. The addition of this chapter reflects the growing use of combined treatments for many disorders for which monotherapies had previously been the rule, although in many instances evidence is lacking that combined approaches offer better outcomes than either form of treatment alone. We made room for these chapters by choosing not to include updates of second-edition chapters summarizing treatments for somatoform and factitious disorders, dissociative disorders, and sexual disorders. None of the treatments reviewed in those chapters fully met standards that established them as empirically supported.

This edition of *A Guide to Treatments That Work* testifies to the substantial evidence base underlying psychopharmacological and psychosocial treatments. Nonetheless, controversy continues over the meaning and significance of these findings. Several unresolved issues sustain this controversy. The first is whether there really are differences in efficacy among treatments, especially psychosocial treatments. Over the years, a number of meta-analyses of psychosocial treatments have failed to reflect differences in efficacy among interventions, leading to the claim (the "Dodo Bird Phenomenon") that meaningful differences in efficacy among psychosocial treatments have not been demonstrated (e.g., Stiles, Shapiro, & Elliott, 1986; Wampold et al., 1997). However, many other behavioral scientists (e.g., Chambless & Ollendick, 2001; Nathan, Stuart, & Dolan, 2000) vigorously dispute this view, pointing to data from the large and growing number of randomized clinical trials that strongly suggest that some psychosocial treatments—most of them behavioral or cognitive behavioral—do produce significantly better outcomes than others.

Another issue that encourages those who question the value of efforts to identify empirically supported treatments is the seemingly endless debate over which of two psychotherapy outcome research models—the efficacy model or the effectiveness model—captures the most crucial differences among therapy techniques and procedures and can best be relied on to provide the most accurate picture of therapy outcomes (e.g., Crits-Christoph, Wilson, & Hollon, 2005; Weisz, Weersing, & Henggeler, 2005; Westen, Novotny, & Thompson-Brenner, 2004, 2005). Critics of empirically supported treatments fault their advocates because of their supposed reliance on efficacy research, a claim supporters of empirically supported treatment heartily reject.

A third controversial issue has to do with whether common factors, including therapist variables, patient variables, and relationship variables, play a more important role in determining the outcomes of psychosocial treatments than do treatment factors (e.g., Castonguay et al., 2006; Lebow, Kelly, Knobloch-Febbers, & Moos, 2006; Smith, Barrett, Benjamin, & Barber, 2006; Stiles & Wolfe, 2006). Critics of empirically supported treatments point to data attesting to the power of common factors to affect therapeutic outcomes; advocates for empirically supported treatments acknowledge the role of both treatment factors and common factors in outcomes.

Although resolution of these issues sometimes seems as far off now as it did in 1998, when the first edition of this volume appeared, the pace of adoption of empirically supported treatments in clinical practice has nonetheless increased steadily. Research highlighted in this volume suggests that there are valid, empirically supported differences in efficacy among treatments, and increasing numbers of clinicians have responded by basing their treatment efforts accordingly.

REFERENCES

Castonguay, L. G., Holtforth, M. G., Coombs, M. M., Beberman, R. A., Kakouros, A. A., Boswell, J. F., et al. (2005). Relationship factors in treating dysphoric disorders. In L. G. Castonguay & L. E. Beutler (Eds.), *Principles of therapeutic change that work* (pp. 65–82). New York: Oxford University Press.

Chambless, D. L., & Ollendick, T. H. (2001). Empirically supported psychological interventions: Controversies and evidence. In S. T. Fiske, D. L. Schacter, & C. Zahn-Waxler (Eds.), *Annual review of psychology* (Vol. 52, pp. 685–716). Palo Alto, CA: Annual Reviews.

Crits-Christoph, P., Wilson, G. T., & Hollon, S. D. (2005). Empirically supported psychotherapies: Comment on Westen, Novotny, & Thompson-Brenner (2004). *Psychological Bulletin, 131*, 412–417.

Lebow, J., Kelly, J., Knobloch-Febbers, L. M., & Moos, R. (2006). Relationship factors in treating substance use disorders. In L. G. Castonguay & L. E. Beutler (Eds.), *Principles of therapeutic change that work* (pp. 293–318). New York: Oxford University Press.

Nathan, P. E., Stuart, S. P., & Dolan, S. L. (2000). Research on psychotherapy efficacy and effectiveness: Between Scylla and Charybdis? *Psychological Bulletin, 126*, 964–981.

Roberts, A. R., & Yeager, K. R. (Eds.). (2004). *Evidence-based treatment manual*. New York: Oxford University Press.

Smith, T. L., Barrett, M. S., Benjamin, L. S., & Barber, J. P. (2006). Relationships factors in treating personality disorders. In L. G. Castonguay & L. E. Beutler (Eds.), *Principles of therapeutic change that work* (pp. 219–238). New York: Oxford University Press.

Stiles, W. B., Shapiro, D. A., & Eliott, R. (1986). "Are all psychotherapies equivalent?" *American Psychologist, 41*, 165–180.

Stiles, W. B., & Wolfe, B. E. (2006). Relationship factors in treating anxiety disorders. In L. G. Castonguay & L. E. Beutler (Eds.), *Principles of therapeutic change that work* (pp. 155–166). New York: Oxford University Press.

Wampold, B. E., Mondin, G. W., Moody, M., Stich, F., Benson, K., & Ahn, H.-N. (1997). A meta-analysis of outcome studies comparing *bona fide* psychotherapies: Empirically, "all must have prizes." *Psychological Bulletin, 122*, 203–215.

Weisz, J. R., Weersing, V. R., & Henggeler, S. W. (2005). Jousting with straw men: Comment on Westen, Novotny, & Thompson-Brenner (2004). *Psychological Bulletin, 131*, 418–426.

Westen, D., Novotny, C. M., & Thompson-Brenner, H. (2004). The empirical status of empirically supported psychotherapies: Assumptions, findings, and report in controlled clinical trials. *Psychological Bulletin, 130*, 631–663.

Westen, D., Novotny, C. M., & Thompson-Brenner, H. (2005). EBP does not equal EST: Reply to Crits-Christoph et al. (2005) and Weisz et al. (2005). *Psychological Bulletin, 131*, 427–433.

Contents

Contributors

Aaronson, Cindy J., PhD: Assistant Clinical Professor of Psychiatry, Department of Psychiatry, Mount Sinai School of Medicine

Abikoff, Howard B., PhD: Pevaroff Cohn Professor of Child and Adolescent Psychiatry, School of Medicine, and Director, Institute for Attention Deficit Hyperactivity and Behavior Disorders, Child Study Center, New York University

Allen, Laura B., MA: Center for Anxiety and Related Disorders, Department of Psychology, Boston University

Althof, Stanley, PhD: Associate Professor of Urology, Case Western Reserve University School of Medicine

Barber, Jacques P., PhD: Professor of Psychology in Psychiatry and Associate Director, Center for Psychotherapy Research, Department of Psychiatry, University of Pennsylvania

Barlow, David H., PhD: Professor of Psychology, Research Professor of Psychiatry, and Director, Center for Anxiety and Related Disorders, Department of Psychology, Boston University

Basden, Shawnee L., MA: Center for Anxiety and Related Disorders, Department of Psychology, Boston University

Bradford, Daniel, MD: Department of Psychiatry, University of North Carolina School of Medicine

Brosse, Alisha L., MA: Department of Psychology, University of Colorado

Buysse, Daniel J., MD: Professor of Psychiatry, Department of Psychiatry, University of Pittsburgh School of Medicine and Western Psychiatric Institute and Clinic

Cowley, Deborah S., MD: Professor, Department of Psychiatry and Behavioral Sciences, University of Washington School of Medicine at Harborview Medical Center

Craighead, W. Edward, PhD: Professor and Chair, Department of Psychology, University of Colorado

Crits-Christoph, Paul, PhD: Professor of Psychology in Psychiatry and Director, Center for Psychotherapy Research, Department of Psychiatry, University of Pennsylvania School of Medicine

Dougherty, Darin D., MD: Assistant Professor of Psychiatry, Harvard Medical School at the Massachusetts General Hospital

Duterte, Emmanuelle, MD: Department of Psychiatry, MetroHealth Medical Center, Cleveland

Fairburn, Christopher G., MD: Wellcome Principal Research Fellow, Professor of Psychiatry, and Director of the Centre for Research on Eating Disorders and Obesity at the University of Oxford

Finney, John W., PhD: Director, Health Services Research and Development Center of Excellence, Center for Health Care Evaluation, VA Palo Alto Health Care System, and Consulting Professor, Department of Psychiatry and Behavioral Sciences, Stanford University School of Medicine

Foa, Edna B., PhD: Professor of Clinical Psychology in Psychiatry and Director, Center for the Treatment and Study of Anxiety, Department of Psychiatry, University of Pennsylvania School of Medicine

Franklin, Martin E., PhD: Assistant Professor of Clinical Psychology in Psychiatry and Clinical Director, Center for the Treatment and Study of Anxiety, Department of Psychiatry, University of Pennsylvania School of Medicine

Golier, Julia A., MD: Associate Professor, Traumatic Stress Studies Program, Department of Psychiatry, Mount Sinai School of Medicine and James J. Peters Veterans Administration Medical Center

Gorman, Jack M., MD: Adjunct Professor of Psychiatry, Mount Sinai School of Medicine

Grant, Jon E., JD, MD, MPH: Associate Professor, Department of Psychiatry, University of Minnesota Medical School

Greenhill, Laurence L., MD: Ruane Professor of Clinical Psychiatry, Division of Child and Adolescent Psychiatry, Columbia College of Physicians and Surgeons, Columbia University; Research Psychiatrist II, New York State Psychiatric Institute

Hinshaw, Stephen P., PhD: Professor and Chair, Department of Psychology, University of California, Berkeley

Ilardi, Stephen S., PhD: Associate Professor of Psychology, University of Kansas

Jenike, Michael A., MD: Professor of Psychiatry, Harvard Medical School at the Massachusetts General Hospital.

Katzman, Gary P., MD: Department of Psychiatry, Mount Sinai School of Medicine

Kazdin, Alan E., PhD: Director and Chair, Child Study Center, Director, Department of Child Psychiatry, Yale–New Haven Hospital, and John M. Musser Professor of Psychology and Child Psychiatry, Yale University School of Medicine

Keck, Paul E., Jr., MD: Craig and Frances Lindner Professor and Vice Chairman for Research, Department of Psychiatry, University of Cincinnati College of Medicine, and Director, General Clinical Research Center, Cincinnati VA Medical Center

Klein, Rachel G., PhD: Professor of Psychiatry, New York University School of Medicine and Child Study Center

Koenigsberg, Harold W., MD: Associate Professor of Psychiatry, Department of Psychiatry, Mount Sinai School of Medicine

Kopelowicz, Alex, MD: Associate Professor, Department of Psychiatry and Biobehavioral Sciences, David Geffen School of Medicine at UCLA

Kupfer, David J., MD: Thomas Detre Professor and Chair, Department of Psychiatry, and Professor of Neuroscience, University of Pittsburgh School of Medicine and Western Psychiatric Institute and Clinic

Legge, Juliana, MS: James J. Peters Veterans Administration Medical Center

Liberman, Robert Paul, MD: Distinguished Professor, Department of Psychiatry and Biobehavioral Sciences, David Geffen School of Medicine at UCLA

Lieberman, Jeffrey, MD: Lawrence E. Kolb Chairman of Psychiatry and Director of the Lieber Center for Schizophrenia Research at the Columbia University College of Physicians and Surgeons, and Director of the New York State Psychiatric Institute

McElroy, Susan L., MD: Professor and Director, Psychopharmacology Research Program, Department of Psychiatry, University of Cincinnati College of Medicine

McKay, James, PhD: Associate Professor of Psychology in Psychiatry, University of Pennsylvania School of Medicine, and Scientific Director, University of Pennsylvania—VA Center for Studies of Addiction and the Treatment Research Institute

Miklowitz, David J., PhD: Professor of Psychology and Psychiatry, University of Colorado, Boulder

Moos, Rudolf H., PhD: Senior Research Career Scientist, Veterans Affairs Palo Alto Health Care System, and Professor, Department of Psychiatry and Behavioral Sciences, Stanford University Medical Center

Morin, Charles M., PhD: Professor, School of Psychology, Université Laval

Moul, Douglas E., MD: Assistant Professor of Psychiatry, Department of Psychiatry, University of Pittsburgh School of Medicine and Western Psychiatric Institute and Clinic

Najavits, Lisa M., PhD: Research Psychologist, National Center for PTSD, Women's Health Sciences Division, VA Boston Healthcare System, and Professor of Psychiatry, Boston University School of Medicine

Nathan, Peter E., PhD: University of Iowa Foundation Distinguished Professor of Psychology and Public Health

Nemeroff, Charles B., MD, PhD: Reunette W. Harris Professor and Chair, Department of Psychiatry and Behavioral Sciences, Emory University School of Medicine

O'Brien, Charles P., MD, PhD: Kenneth E. Appel Professor, Vice Chair of Psychiatry, and Director of the Center for Studies of Addiction, University of Pennsylvania School of Medicine, and Director of Research, Mental Illness Research, Education, and Clinical Center, Philadelphia Veterans Affairs Medical Center

Paykina, Natalya, MA: New York State Psychiatric Institute

Potenza, Marc N., MD, PhD: Associate Professor and Director, Problem Gambling Clinic, Depart-

ment of Psychiatry, Yale University School of Medicine

Rauch, Scott L., MD: Associate Professor of Psychiatry, Harvard Medical School at the Massachusetts General Hospital

Reynolds, Charles F., III, MD: UPMC Endowed Professor of Geriatric Psychiatry, and Professor of Neurology and Neuroscience, University of Pittsburgh School of Medicine and Western Psychiatric Institute and Clinic

Roy-Byrne, Peter P., MD: Professor and Vice Chairman, Department of Psychiatry and Behavioral Sciences, University of Washington School of Medicine at Harborview Medical Center

Schatzberg, Alan F., MD: Kenneth T. Norris Jr. Professor and Chairman, Department of Psychiatry and Behavioral Sciences, Stanford University School of Medicine

Segraves, Taylor, MD, PhD: Professor of Psychiatry, Case Western Reserve School of Medicine, and Chair, Department of Psychiatry, MetroHealth Medical Center, Cleveland

Sharif, Zafar A., MD: Associate Clinical Professor of Psychiatry, Department of Psychiatry, Columbia University College of Physicians and Surgeons

Sheets, Erin S., MA: Department of Psychology, University of Colorado

Siever, Larry J., MD: Professor of Psychiatry and Director, Special Evaluation Program for Mood and Personality Disorders, Department of Psychiatry, Mount Sinai School of Medicine

Stroup, Scott, MD, MPH: Associate Professor of Psychiatry, University of North Carolina School of Medicine

Tune, Larry, MD: Professor of Psychiatry and Behavioral Sciences and Program Director, Fellowship in Geriatric Psychiatry, Emory University School of Medicine

Wilbourne, Paula L., PhD: Coordinator for Continuity of Care, Addiction Treatment Services and

Center for Health Care Evaluation, VA Palo Alto Health Care System

Wilson, G. Terence, PhD: Oscar K. Buros Professor of Psychology, Rutgers, The State University of New Jersey

Woo-Ming, Ann Marie, MD: Associate Professor of Psychiatry, Mount Sinai School of Medicine

Yehuda, Rachel, PhD: Professor and Director, Traumatic Stress Studies Program, Department of Psychiatry, Mount Sinai School of Medicine and James J. Peters Veterans Administration Medical Center

Zarate, Roberto, PhD: Research Psychologist, Pacific Clinics

Summary of Treatments
That Work

Syndrome	Treatments	Standards of Proof	References
Bipolar disorder	• *Individual and group psychoeducation* that provides information to bipolar patients and their families about the disorder, its pharmacological treatment, and treatments' side effects leads to lower rates of recurrent and greater adherence to pharmacological treatment.	• A number of Type 1 and Type 2 RCTs.	Chapter 11, pp. 309–322 (Miklowitz and Craighead)
	• *Cognitive-behavior therapy* is associated with better medication adherence and significantly fewer recurrences and rehospitalizations.	• Several Type 1 and Type 2 studies.	
	• *IPSRT (a combination of interpersonal therapy and social rhythm therapy)* demonstrated its greatest effects during a maintenance treatment period.	• A single Type 1 study.	
	• *Marital and family therapy* may be effectively combined with pharmacotherapy to reduce recurrences and improve medication adherence and family functioning.	• Four Type 1 studies.	
	• *Lithium, divalproex, carbamazepine, risperidone, olanzapine, quetiapine, ziprasidone*, and *aripiprazole* have demonstrated efficacy in the treatment of acute mania.	• Numerous Type 1 randomized, controlled clinical trials.	Chapter 12, pp. 323–350 (Keck and McElroy)

Syndrome	Treatments	Standards of Proof	References
Bipolar disorder (*cont.*)	• *Lithium, olanzapine, olanzapine-fluoxetine, quetiapine, lamotrigine, tricyclics, MAOIs, fluoxetine,* and *pramipexole* have efficacy in the treatment of acute bipolar depression.	• A number of Type 1 randomized, controlled clinical trials.	
	• *Lithium, lamotrigine, olanzapine,* and *aripiprazole* have been shown to have efficacy in relapse prevention.	• A number of Type 1 randomized, controlled clinical trials.	
Borderline personality disorder	• *Dialectical behavior therapy (DBT)* was successful in reducing rates of suicide attempt, hospitalization for suicide ideation, and overall medical risk; patients were also less likely to drop out of treatment, had fewer psychiatric emergency room visits, and few psychiatric hospitalizations.	• One Type 1 RCT and four Type 2 and Type 3 studies.	Chapter 23, pp. 641–658 (Crits-Christoph and Barber)
	• Strong evidence is emerging that supports the efficacy of the atypical antipsychotic medication *olanzepine* in reducing anger, impulsivity-aggression, possibly depression, and interpersonal sensitivity in borderline personality disorder.	• Two Type 1 studies, two Type 2 studies, and one Type 3 study.	Chapter 24, pp. 659–680 (Koenigsberg, Woo-Ming, and Siever)
Bulimia nervosa (BN)	• *Manual-based cognitive-behavioral therapy* is currently the treatment of choice for BN.	• A substantial number of well-designed (Type 1 and Type 2) studies.	Chapter 21, pp. 579–609 (Wilson and Fairburn)
	• Several different classes of *antidepressant drugs* produce significantly greater reductions in the short term for binge eating and purging in BN patients than a placebo treatment; the long-term effects of antidepressant medication on BN remain untested.	• A large number of good-to-excellent outcome studies (Type 1 and Type 2).	
	• There is little evidence that combining CBT with antidepressant medication significantly enhances improvement in the core features of BN, although it may aid in treating comorbid anxiety and depression.		

Syndrome	Treatments	Standards of Proof	References
Attention-deficit/ hyperactivity disorder (ADHD)	• Systematic combinations of *direct contingency management* plus *clinical behavior therapy* have yielded findings indicating significant improvements.	• Several Type 1 investigations.	Chapter 1, pp. 13–27 (Hinshaw, Klein, and Abikoff)
	• *Contingency management* has typically yielded large effects on behavior and academic performance, although the quality of the research findings has been limited and effects have tended not to generalize or maintain beyond the settings in which they are applied.	• Several substantial reviews of single-case experimental designs (Type 3).	
	• Psychostimulants — a group of ethylamines including *methylphenidate* and *amphetamine* — are highly effective in reducing core symptoms of ADHD in preschoolers, school-age children, adolescents, and adults. Short-term efficacy is more pronounced for behavioral rather than cognitive and learning abnormalities associated with ADHD.	• More than 225 placebo-controlled Type 1 investigations.	Chapter 2, pp. 29–70 (Paykina and Greenhill)
Conduct disorder in children	• *Parent Management Training (PMT)* with the parents of troubled children and adolescents.	• A large number of Type 1 and Type 2 RCTs of PMT over a 35-year period.	Chapter 3, pp. 71–104 (Kazdin)
	• *Multisystemic Therapy* with troubled families and their conduct-disordered adolescents.	• Multiple Type 1 RCTs of MST.	
	• *Multidimensional Treatment Foster Care Model (MTFC)* with youth in placement who are to return to their parents or more permanent foster care.	• Several Type 1 RCTs of MTFC have been completed or are in process.	
	• *Cognitive Problem-Solving Skills Training (PSST)* with impulsive, aggressive, and conduct-disordered children and adolescents.	• Several controlled clinical trials of PSST (Type 1 and Type 2) have been completed.	
	• *Anger Control Training (ACT)* youth for whom anger control is a special problem and their parents.	• Several different Type 1 and Type 2 studies of ACP have been completed.	

Syndrome	Treatments	Standards of Proof	References
Conduct disorder in children (*cont.*)	• *Functional Family Therapy (FFT)* with difficult-to-treat conduct-disordered youth and their families. • *Brief Strategic Family Therapy (BSFT)* with Hispanic families with maladaptive interactional styles.	• Type 1 and Type 2 studies of FFT spanning 30 years have produced consistent effects. • Several Type 1 and Type 2 studies of BSFT have shown improvements in child and family functioning.	
Dementia in Alzheimer's disease (AD)	• Although no cure for AD exists, the second generation of AChEs, notably, *donepezil, galantamine,* and *rivastigmine,* as well as *memantine,* appear to be promising symptomatic treatments. They offer demonstrable clinical efficacy and simpler dosing, minimal side effects, and negligible hepatotoxicity.	• For the newer AChEs: 24 Type 1 studies. • For memantine: A number of Type 1 studies	Chapter 4, pp. 105–143 (Tune)
Generalized anxiety disorder (GAD)	• The most successful psychological treatments for GAD combine *relaxation exercises and cognitive therapy* with the goal of bringing the worry process itself under the patient's control. • The pharmacological treatments of choice for GAD are *buspirone* and *antidepressants,* including SSRIs and *venlafaxine.*	• A few Type 1 and Type 2 studies • Several double-blind studies have shown buspirone to be comparable in effectiveness to the benzodiazepines, without the addictive properties of the latter drug. • Placebo-controlled trials have also shown efficacy in GAD for a number of antidepressants, including venlafaxine (4 studies), tricyclics (3), paroxetine (3), escitalopram (3), and sertraline (1).	Chapter 13, pp. 351–394 (Barlow, Allen, and Basden) Chapter 14, pp. 395–430 (Roy-Byrne and Cowley)

Syndrome	Treatments	Standards of Proof	References
Insomnia and restless legs syndrome (RLS)	• The efficacy of such *cognitive-behavioral* approaches to insomnia as *stimulus control, bed restriction,* and related approaches has been established. • *Benzodiazepine receptor agonists* are considered a first-line pharmacotherapy for primary insomnia. • For RLS, the use of *low-dose dopamine agonists* has been substantially supported.	• More than 50 clinical trials (Type 1 and Type 2) and two meta-analyses. • Substantial Type 1 clinical study data. • Several Type 1 clinical trials.	Chapter 22, pp. 611–640 (Moul, Morin, Buysse, Reynolds, and Kupfer)
Major depressive episode/Major depressive disorder (MDD)	• The first-line psychopharmacological treatment of unipolar major depression is by selective serotonin reuptake inhibitors (SSRIs)—*fluoxetine, sertraline, paroxetine, citalopram,* and *escitalopram*; serotonin norepinephrine reuptake inhibitors (SNRIs)—*venlafaxine* and *duloxetine*; as well as other compounds, including *bupropion* and *mirtazapine*. • *Behavior therapy (BT), cognitive-behavioral therapy (CBT), and interpersonal psychotherapy (IPT)* have all yielded substantial reductions in scores on the two major depression rating scales, significant decrease in percentage of patients meeting criteria for MDD posttreatment, and substantial maintenance of effects well after treatment has ended. • *Combined psychosocial and psychopharmacological treatment* for MDD is more effective than either individual treatment for chronically and recurrently depressed patients.	• A very large number of Type 1 and Type 2 studies have shown these compounds to be superior to a placebo and as effective as comparator TCAs or SSRIs in controlled trials. • At least two Type 1 or Type 2 RCTs as well as four meta-analytic reports. • Several Type 1 and Type 2 RCTs of combined treatments for MDD.	Chapter 9, pp. 271–287 (Nemeroff and Schatzberg) Chapter 10, pp. 289–307 (Craighead, Sheets, Brosse, and Ilardi) Chapter 25, pp. 681–710 (Aaronson, Katzman, and Gorman)
Obsessive-compulsive disorder (OCD)	• *Cognitive behavioral therapy* involving exposure and ritual prevention (EX/RP) is a well-established treatment for OCD in adults.	• Many Type 1 and Type 2 studies.	Chapter 15, pp. 431–446 (Franklin and Foa)

Syndrome	Treatments	Standards of Proof	References
	• *Combined treatment studies of EX/RP and SSRIs or clomipramine* have provided some advantages for the combined regimen over monotherapies, but equivocal findings have emerged as well.	• Several Type 1 and Type 2 studies.	
	• The efficacy of *CBT for pediatric OCD* has been documented in recent years.	• Several Type 1 studies.	
	• The *SRIs* have been shown repeatedly to be efficacious in the treatment of OCD.	• Overwhelming evidence of the most rigorous type.	Chapter 16, pp. 447–473 (Dougherty, Rauch and Jenike)
	• *BT*, and perhaps *CT*, may be superior to medication with respect to risks, costs, and enduring benefits.		
Panic disorder (PD) with and without agoraphobia	• *Situational in vivo exposure* has been shown to be effective for patients with PD with moderate to severe agoraphobia; *cognitive-behavioral treatments* are effective for persons with panic disorder with no more than mild agoraphobia; these treatments focus on cognitive therapy, exposure to interoceptive sensations similar to physiological panic sensations, and breathing retraining.	• A substantial number of excellent studies, largely Type 1; two large effectiveness trials (Type 1) have established successful dissemination of CBT.	Chapter 13, pp. 351–394 (Barlow, Allen, and Basden)
	• SSRIs are now considered by most experts to be the first-line pharmacological treatment for PD, affecting panic frequency, generalized anxiety, disability, and phobic avoidance.	• Eighteen Type 1 placebo-controlled trials of SSRIs for PD.	Chapter 14, pp. 395–430 (Roy-Byrne and Cowley)
Pathological gambling and other impulse control disorders	• Specific *behavioral* (e.g., *CBT*) and *pharmacological* (e.g., *naltrexone, nalmefene, lithium*) treatments significantly reduce the symptoms of pathological gambling in the short term.	• Several Type 1 and Type 2 studies.	Chapter 20, pp. 561–577 (Grant and Potenza)
	• Although long-term effects of *manual-based CBT* have been observed in several small studies, the long-term benefits of pharmacological treatment have not been adequately tested.		

Syndrome	Treatments	Standards of Proof	References
	• Several studies suggest that *CBT* is effective for trichotillomania; pharmacological treatment studies for this disorder have shown mixed results.	• Several Type 1 and Type 2 studies.	
Posttraumatic stress disorder (PTSD)	• The *SSRIs* (*fluoxetine, sertraline,* and *paroxetine*) are efficacious in reducing PTSD-specific symptoms and improving global outcome. • *Tricyclic antidepressants* (*imipramine*) and *MAOIs* (*phenelzine*) have also been found to be efficacious.	• Multiple controlled clinical trials (Type 1).	Chapter 17, pp. 475–512 (Golier, Legge, and Yehuda)
	• Several *past-* and *present-focused psychosocial treatments* are effective. Past-focused treatments emphasize repeated exposure to the memories and emotions of the event in order to diminish their impact. Present-focused treatments teach coping skills to improve functioning.	• Several Type 1 and Type 2 studies; several Type 4 meta-analyses and reports.	Chapter 18, pp. 513–530 (Najavits)
Schizophrenia	• Both the typical antipsychotic drugs, first introduced in the mid-1950s, and the atypical antipsychotic drugs, introduced in the 1970s, improve psychotic symptoms in the acute phase of the illness and reduce risk of relapse later on. The atypical antipsychotics, including *clozapine, risperidone, olanzapine, quetiapine, ziprasidone,* and *aripiprazole,* offer hope for enhanced treatment efficacy, with a reduced burden of extrapyramidal motor dysfunction.	• Hundreds of Type 1 and Type 2 studies.	Chapter 7, pp. 203–241 (Sharif, Bradford, Stroup, and Lieberman)
	• The schizophrenia PORT recommendations highlight six evidence-based, psychosocial treatments. They include *skills training, supported employment, cognitive-behavioral psychotherapy, behavior modification and social learning/token economy programs,* and *assertive community treatment.*	• Many Type 1 and Type 2 RCTs and a very large number of Type 3 studies have supported the efficacy of these treatment approaches, especially when combined with atypical antipsychotic drug treatments.	Chapter 8, pp. 243–269 (Kopelowicz, Lieberman, and Zarate)

Syndrome	Treatments	Standards of Proof	References
Sexual dysfunctions	• The efficacy of *sildenafil* as a treatment for erectile dysfunction has been demonstrated repeatedly.	• A very large number of Type 1 multiple double-blind, placebo-controlled, multicenter studies.	Chapter 19, pp. 531–560 (Duterte, Segraves, and Althof)
	• The efficacy of *psychological interventions* for erectile dysfunctions has also been established.	• A number of well-controlled (Type 1 and Type 2) investigations.	
	• *Fluoxetine, sertraline, clomipramine*, and *paroxetine* can be used to delay ejaculatory latency in men with rapid ejaculation.	• A large number of Type 1 placebo-controlled, double-blind studies.	
	• An array of *individual, conjoint*, and *group therapy* approaches employing behavioral strategies such as *stop-start* or *squeeze* techniques have evolved as the psychological treatments of choice for rapid ejaculation.	• A number of Type 1, Type 2, and Type 3 studies.	
Social phobia	• The most common treatment approaches to social phobia include *social skills training, relaxation techniques, exposure-based methods*, and *multicomponent cognitive-behavioral treatments*, with the latter two attaining the highest levels of treatment efficacy.	• A number of Type 1 studies of exposure-based methods and multicomponent cognitive-behavioral treatments.	Chapter 13, pp. 351–394 (Barlow, Allen, and Basden)
	• SSRIs are an attractive first-line treatment for social anxiety disorder (social phobia).	• Twenty-two placebo-controlled (Type 1) trials suggest that the SSRIs are effective for social phobia.	Chapter 14, pp. 395–430 (Roy-Byrne and Cowley)
Specific phobias	• The treatment of choice for specific phobias is *exposure-based procedures*, particularly in vivo exposure.	• A very large number of Type 1 studies.	Chapter 13, pp. 351–394 (Barlow, Allen, and Basden) Chapter 14, pp. 395–430 (Roy-Byrne and Cowley)
	• In general, pharmacological treatments have not proved effective for specific phobias.		
Substance use disorders	• The use of *nicotine replacement therapy* to induce and maintain smoking cessation significantly increases the abstinence rate.	• A large number of Type 1 and Type 2 controlled trials.	Chapter 5, pp. 145–177 (O'Brien and McKay)

Syndrome	Treatments	Standards of Proof	References
	• The treatment of alcoholism can now be enhanced by the opiate antagonist *naltrexone*, which reduces alcohol reward via the endogenous opioid system and results in decreased alcohol craving and reduced drinking in most randomized clinical trials in a subtype of alcoholism that responds well to the drug.	• Twenty-three Type 1 trials, including most recently results from the COMBINE multisite study.	
	• *Methadone maintenance* treatment for heroin dependence has consistently shown efficacy; the partial opiate agonist *buprenorphine* has increased treatment options for heroin dependence.	• A very large number of Type 1 and Type 2 controlled trials.	
	• Effective psychosocial treatments for the substance use disorders address not only drinking and/or drug use behavior but also patients' life contexts, sense of self-efficacy, and coping skills; included among these treatments are *cognitive-behavioral treatments*, *community reinforcement* and *contingency management approaches*, *12-step facilitation* and *12-step treatment*, and *behavioral couples* and *family treatment*.	• A large number of Type 1 and Type 2 trials.	Chapter 6, pp. 179–202 (Finney, Wilbourne, and Moos)
	• Motivational interventions, including motivational enhancement therapy, focus primarily on attempts to enhance individuals' commitment to behavior change; consistent with motivational interviewing principles, therapists who are interpersonally skilled, empathic, and less confrontational produce better patient outcomes, probably because they establish better therapeutic alliances with their patients.	• A large number of Type 1 and Type 2 trials.	

A GUIDE TO TREATMENTS THAT WORK

1

Childhood Attention-Deficit/ Hyperactivity Disorder: Nonpharmacological Treatments and Their Combination With Medication

Stephen P. Hinshaw

Rachel G. Klein

Howard B. Abikoff

Attention-deficit/hyperactivity disorder (ADHD) is a persistent disorder of childhood and adolescence that mandates early and effective intervention. Among psychosocial interventions, direct contingency management applies systematic manipulation of rewards and punishments in specialized settings. It typically yields large effects on behavior and academic performance, but (a) outcomes are often appraised through single-case experimental designs, outside the typology of clinical trials used in this volume, and (b) their effects tend not to generalize or maintain beyond the settings in which they are applied. Clinical behavior therapy involves consultation with parents and teachers regarding optimal home and school management practices. A number of Type 2 trials demonstrate the clinical value of such procedures for the behavior problems of children with ADHD as rated by parents and teachers but typically not by independent observations. Several Type 1 investigations of systematic combinations of direct contingency management plus clinical behavior therapy have yielded findings indicating significant improvements, but effects on symptoms are smaller than those found with medication. Multimodal treatment — combining intensive behavioral intervention with well-delivered pharmacological agents — does not always reveal significantly superior outcomes to medication alone, but it more consistently yields normalization of behavior patterns among children with ADHD. Further work on tailoring psychosocial interventions to ADHD-related deficits and impairments and on promoting generalized change beyond specifically targeted behaviors is urgently needed.

The prevalence, impairment, and persistence associated with attention-deficit/hyperactivity disorder (ADHD) in children provide a clarion call for the application of effective treatment strategies to youngsters with this condition (e.g., Barkley, 2006; Hinshaw, 1994, 2002). This chapter summarizes non-pharmacological intervention strategies for ADHD, the most effective of which entail behavioral approaches. We highlight at the outset that the documented efficacy of medication treatments for ADHD (Greenhill, this volume; Greenhill & Osman, 2000; Klein & Wender, 1995) provides a standard for judging other treatments (Hinshaw, 2006). Therefore, in addition to describing studies of behavioral treatments themselves, we also examine (a) comparisons of behavioral with medication treatments and (b) combinations of behavioral and pharmacological intervention strategies. The frequent co-occurrence of ADHD with aggressive and antisocial behavior patterns (Abikoff & Klein, 1992; Fergusson, Horwood, & Lloyd, 1991; Hinshaw, 1987) indicates the salience of these outcome domains; the coexistence of learning and social impairments means that these are essential outcome indicators as well. In addition, we note that ADHD has proved refractory to long-term amelioration with any treatment strategies, pharmacological or psychosocial, a point to which we return throughout the chapter.

BACKGROUND INFORMATION REGARDING ADHD

Considerable knowledge has accumulated about ADHD, a constellation of symptoms that has been described for well over a century and that has undergone many name changes over time (Barkley, 2006; Schachar, 1986). First, the constituent symptoms of this disorder fall into two main clusters: inattention-disorganization and overactivity-impulsivity (American Psychiatric Association, 2000). Because such behavior patterns are not pathological in young children, clear impairment in academic, family, interpersonal, and self-related domains must be demonstrated to justify the diagnosis. Indeed, the diagnostic criteria for ADHD in the text revision to the fourth edition of the *Diagnostic and Statistical Manual of Mental Disorders* (*DSM-IV-TR*; American Psychiatric Association, 2000) mandate the presence, from early ages, of developmentally excessive levels of the constituent behaviors that result in impairment in multiple settings (see Table 1.1). Individuals can be classified into predominantly inattentive, predominantly hyperactive-impulsive, or combined subtypes. Distinctions between inattentive-type youth versus those with inattention plus hyperactive/impulsive features have been found with respect to family history, gender distribution, and some aspects of treatment response (see Hinshaw, 1994); debate continues as to the quantitative versus qualitative

distinctiveness of these subtypes (Milich, Balentine, & Lynam, 2001).

When stringent diagnostic criteria are applied, the prevalence of childhood ADHD appears to be approximately 5–8% of school-aged children and adolescents, with a boy:girl ratio of approximately 3:1 (American Psychiatric Association, 2000). ADHD has been shown to exist across multiple cultures and in multiple nations, but precise cross-national comparisons of prevalence rates are hampered by disparate screening thresholds and diverse diagnostic criteria (Nigg, 2006).

Children with ADHD are extremely likely to show substantial impairment in key functional domains. They suffer from high rates of academic underachievement (even in the absence of formal learning disabilities), they are prone to be rejected by peers, their families are often in conflict, and they display high rates of accidental injury (see review in Hinshaw, 2002). Furthermore, prospective studies have shown that children with ADHD are at risk for persisting symptomatology and impairment into adolescence, with a substantial minority proceeding to demonstrate marked problems in young adulthood (e.g., Barkley, Fischer, Smallish, & Fletcher, 2002; Mannuzza & Klein, 1999; Weiss & Hechtman, 1993). In short, clear impairment and a highly negative course speak to the need for concerted prevention and treatment efforts.

The underlying nature of ADHD remains an area of active debate. For many years, in keeping with earlier labels of hyperactivity or hyperkinesis, basic research focused on motoric overactivity and implicated subcortical brain regions in neural models (Laufer & Denhoff, 1957). Several decades ago, focus shifted to underlying attentional processes and deficient self-regulation (e.g., Douglas, 1983). Current work capitalizes on more precise and differentiated views of executive functions and cognitive processing, with increasing recognition that children with ADHD show pronounced difficulties in response inhibition and organization of motoric output, with evidence for frontostriatal impairment (Barkley, 1997a; Nigg, 2001; Schachar, Tannock, Marriott, & Logan, 1995). Subcortical dopamine systems are strongly implicated (see Sagvolden, Aase, Johansen, & Russell, 2005). As long as basic mechanisms remain unknown, clinical evaluation must rely on observing behavioral signs, obtaining a thorough

TABLE 1.1 Diagnostic Criteria for Attention-Deficit Hyperactivity Disorder

A. Either (1) or (2):
   (1) Six (or more) of the following symptoms of **inattention** have persisted for at least 6 months to a degree that is maladaptive and inconsistent with developmental level:
      Inattention
      (a) often fails to give close attention to details or makes careless mistakes in schoolwork, work, or other activities
      (b) often has difficulty sustaining attention in tasks or play activities
      (c) often does not seem to listen when spoken to directly
      (d) often does not follow through on instructions and fails to finish schoolwork, chores, or duties in the workplace (not due to oppositional behavior or failure to understand directions)
      (e) often has difficulty organizing tasks and activities
      (f) often avoids, dislikes, or is reluctant to engage in tasks that require sustained mental effort (such as schoolwork or homework)
      (g) often loses things necessary for tasks or activities (e.g., toys, school assignments, pencils, books, or tools)
      (h) is often easily distracted by extraneous stimuli
      (i) is often forgetful in daily activities
   (2) Six (or more) of the following symptoms of **hyperactivity-impulsivity** have persisted for at least 6 months to a degree that is maladaptive and inconsistent with developmental level:
      Hyperactivity
      (a) often fidgets with hands or feet or squirms in seat
      (b) often leaves seat in classroom or in other situations in which remaining seated is expected
      (c) often runs about or climbs excessively in situations in which it is inappropriate (in adolescents or adults, may be limited to subjective feelings of restlessness)
      (d) often has difficulty playing or engaging in leisure activities quietly
      (e) is always "on the go" or often acts as if "driven by a motor"
      (f) often talks excessively
      Impulsivity
      (g) often blurts out answers before questions have been completed
      (h) often has difficulty awaiting turn
      (i) often interrupts or intrudes on others (e.g., butts into conversations or games)
B. Some hyperactive-impulsive or inattentive symptoms that caused impairment were present before age 7 years.
C. Some impairment from the symptoms is present in two or more settings (e.g., at school [or work] and at home).
D. There must be clear evidence of clinically significant impairment in social, academic, or occupational functioning.
E. The symptoms do not occur exclusively during the course of a Pervasive Developmental Disorder, Schizophrenia, or other Psychotic Disorder and are not better accounted for by another mental disorder (e.g., Mood Disorder, Anxiety Disorder, Dissociative Disorder, or a Personality Disorder).

Attention-Deficit/Hyperactivity Disorder, Combined Type: If both criteria A1 and A2 are met for the past 6 months.

Attention-Deficit/Hyperactivity Disorder, Predominantly Inattentive Type: If criterion A1 is met but criterion A2 is not met for the past 6 months.

Attention-Deficit/Hyperactivity Disorder, Predominantly Hyperactive-Impulsive Type: If criterion A2 is met but criterion A1 is not met for the past 6 months.

Source: American Psychiatric Association, 2000, *Diagnostic and statistical manual of mental disorders* (4th ed., text revision).

developmental history, and addressing both comorbid disorders and key domains of impairment.

The search for causal mechanisms has pointed to a host of potentially interacting risk factors but limited evidence for unimodal, overarching etiologies (e.g., Nigg, 2006; Tannock, 1998). Evidence is increasing for strong heritability of both dimensional and categorical conceptions of ADHD (e.g., Levy, Hay, McStephen, Wood, & Waldman, 1997). In addition, nongenetic risk factors, such as prenatal and perinatal difficulties and maternal smoking and alcohol abuse, appear to be nonspecifically linked with attentional deficits and hyperactivity (Breslau, 1995; Sprich-Buckminster, Biederman, Milberger, Faraone, & Lehman, 1993). Some investigations of high-risk, low-income samples have implicated overly stimulating parenting during infancy and toddlerhood in the later display of ADHD (E. A. Carlson,

Jacobvitz, & Sroufe, 1995), but child-rearing practices or attitudes are not likely candidates as "main effect" causes of ADHD. Indeed, birdirectional and transactional conceptions of parent-child influence are necessary (Johnston & Mash, 2001), and the clear role of coercive parenting styles in the development of aggressive and antisocial behaviors that often accompany ADHD (Anderson, Hinshaw, & Simmel, 1994; Patterson, Reid, & Dishion, 1992) implicates family intervention as a cornerstone of psychosocial treatment approaches. Still, as with nearly all other mental disorders, treatment approaches for ADHD are directed toward manifest symptoms.

It is in the classroom setting that ADHD often incurs its most harmful effects. Underfocused attention, disruptive behavior, and poor rule following place youth with ADHD at high risk for underachievement, peer rejection, decrements in motivation and effort, and lowered rates of school completion (Barkley, 2005; Hinshaw, 1994). School-based intervention is therefore a key aspect of psychosocial interventions.

In summary, ADHD is a persistent and cross-situational behavioral syndrome that yields substantial impairment. Cormorbidity with aggressive-spectrum disorders is commonplace, and associations with learning disorders as well as anxiety and mood disorders are above chance levels (Angold, Costello, & Erkanli, 1999; Jensen, Martin, & Cantwell, 1997). Prevalence of ADHD is relatively high; interacting causal factors include genetic predispositions and early biological triggers, with negative familial patterns serving as potential escalating variables. Home- and school-based intervention strategies constitute the backbone of psychosocial treatments.

HISTORICAL CONCEPTIONS OF INTERVENTION

For many decades the child guidance model and its underlying psychodynamic conceptualization held court as the primary approach for nearly all clinically referred children in the United States. Yet evidence for the efficacy of insight-oriented treatments for youngsters with ADHD is lacking. The application of behavioral, social learning approaches to youngsters specifically diagnosed as "hyperactive" began in the 1960s (e.g., Patterson, 1965). During the 1970s and 1980s, both behavioral and cognitive-behavioral interventions—with the latter promising greater durability of treatment gains through self-management training—became far more widespread. Cognitive-behavioral treatments, particularly those emphasizing the use of verbal self-instructions, have not shown clinically significant benefits for children with ADHD (Abikoff, 1991; Hinshaw, 2006). We therefore focus on systemically applied behavioral interventions, given that these are the only psychosocial treatments that have consistent empirical support for the treatment of ADHD (Pelham, Wheeler, & Chronis, 1998). A number of alternative treatments have been attempted, but consistent empirical support is lacking (Rojas & Chan, 2005).

As discussed in greater detail by Greenhill (this volume), psychopharmacological approaches to ADHD have been scientifically appraised for nearly 70 years. Stimulants were first noted to yield impressive short-term benefits for children with behavioral and emotional disturbances in the 1930s, and hundreds of controlled intervention studies have continued to document gains in core symptom areas and in domains of associated impairment when youngsters with ADHD are treated with stimulants (Campbell & Cueva, 1995; Greenhill & Osman, 2000; Swanson, McBurnett, Christian, & Wigal, 1995). However, the treatment was considered controversial for many decades (and still is in many quarters); psychosocial approaches, particularly behavioral interventions, were developed to replace it.

Developmentally, ADHD-type behaviors were viewed as under operant control, believed to result from deficient social conditioning in the child's past experience. Thus, behavioral treatments had the initial goal of instilling appropriate social behavior through conditioning principles, such as rewards for adaptive behavior and judicious punishment for negative behaviors. In addition, beneficial effects of stimulant treatment were known to disappear when treatment was interrupted. Because behavioral treatments were aimed at the acquisition of academic and social skills, the belief was that they would be free of this important shortcoming. Furthermore, combined medication and behavioral treatments were viewed as complementary, each having discrete, independent actions; consequently, their combination was hypothesized to generate optimal outcomes (see Eysenck & Rachman, 1971; Sprague & Werry, 1971). The hope was that such multimodal intervention would enable the discontinuation of stimulant treatment, related to the expression of the child's newly acquired social behaviors.

BEHAVIORAL INTERVENTIONS AND MEANS OF DETERMINING TREATMENT BENEFITS

Before appraising specific evidence regarding the documented benefits of behavioral interventions for ADHD, we discuss the different types of behavioral treatments, as well as the research designs and assessment methods used to evaluate these types of non-pharmacological treatment strategies. We note, in passing, that despite the lack of evidence for cognitive therapy procedures based on self-instruction for children with ADHD, self-management programs may still constitute an important extension of traditional reward systems. Specifically, as shown in the short-term study of Hinshaw, Henker, and Whalen (1984), when children with ADHD were trained to evaluate their own behavior while receiving reinforcement programs and were then rewarded for the accuracy of their self-evaluations, reductions in negative social behavior were effected. Thus, the potential for approaches based on problem solving and self-management to extend the benefits gained from structured contingency management programs is still worth investigating. Indeed, given the continuing problems regarding generalization and maintenance of gains from behavioral interventions, alternative approaches are worthy of study.

Direct Contingency Management and Clinical Behavior Therapy

Two types of behavioral intervention approaches for youngsters with behavior disorders are salient: (a) direct contingency management, in which intensive reward and punishment procedures are established in specialized treatment facilities, demonstration classrooms, or summer treatment programs, and (b) clinical behavior therapy procedures, in which consultation (via group or individual sessions) is provided to families and teachers, who in turn implement behavior management programs in the child's natural environment.

With direct contingency management, a variety of systematic reward and response cost procedures are implemented with frequent and intensive sched-ules of administration. The heavy reinforcement schedules implemented in specialized settings, however, may not be readily applicable in the natural environment, and effects may not be generalizable to other settings. Furthermore, gains seen under conditions of direct prompting may dissipate during periods of noncontingency. As a result, evaluation during explicitly prompted performance (e.g., in the presence of a teacher's aide who delivers strict contingencies) will yield greater estimates of efficacy than appraisal during unprompted periods. Note, however, that in the vast majority of investigations of contingency management, treatment evaluation is made during the period of active contingencies.

Clinical behavior therapy procedures involve a structured curriculum of parent and/or teacher consultation. A prototypical sequence of activities for parent training involves (a) directing positive attention to the child; (b) targeting performance goals and collecting baseline data; (c) implementing individualized, systematic, and coordinated home- and school-based reinforcement programs; (d) utilizing contingent, nonphysical punishment procedures such as time out or response cost; and (e) extending programmatic change efforts to school and neighborhood settings (e.g., Barkley, 1997b; Wells et al., 2000). Teachers receive consultation in such areas as modifying expectations, altering classroom seating patterns, individualizing reward programs, and coordinating home-school reinforcement systems. Clinical behavior therapy programs originated in the 1960s for children with oppositional or aggressive behavior patterns; during the 1970s, applications began to be targeted specifically to children with hyperactivity or ADHD (O'Leary, Pelham, Rosenbaum, & Price, 1976).

A key research issue is that the two types of behavioral treatment strategies are typically evaluated in different ways, confounding easy comparison across investigations. Specifically, direct contingency management interventions, which emanate from the applied behavior analysis tradition, often make use of single-case experimental designs (e.g., reversal or multiple-baseline) to ascertain the causal effect of specific contingencies on the dependent measures of interest, such as behavior problems and academic productivity. Such interventions are appraised nearly exclusively in specialized programs containing only youth with ADHD (or other disruptive behavior disorders), with short periods of intervention (measured in hours or days). As a result, such investigations do not fit well into the standards-of-proof framework (i.e., Type 1, Type 2, Type 3) used in the current volume. Clinical behavior therapy procedures, on the other hand, are usually implemented in home and regular-education settings and are evaluated by means of randomized, parallel-group clinical trials, with participants assigned to wait-list or contrasting treatments for periods of several months (or more). Note that we have designated most of the investigations of clinical behavior therapy that we review herein as Type 2. Although they employ random assignment to treatment condition, they have relatively short intervention periods and little or no manualization of treatment procedures. We reserve Type 1 status for the few large-scale and longer term randomized clinical trials with manualization and with at least some objective observations or other blinded outcome assessments (Abikoff, Hechtman, Klein, Weiss, et al., 2004; Barkley et al., 2000; Klein & Abikoff, 1997; MTA Cooperative Group, 1999a).

Finally, as in the second edition of this volume (Hinshaw, Klein, & Abikoff, 2002), we include a third type of behavioral intervention for ADHD, social skills training. This is an approach based on the behavioral principles of modeling, rehearsal, corrective feedback, and reinforcement, implemented in small-group therapeutic settings and designed to promote peer relationships and social cooperation. Earlier work in the field with social skills training had not focused on youth specifically diagnosed with ADHD, had embedded social skills training in multicomponent treatments, or had used single-case experimental designs. As noted below, the controlled investigation of Pfiffner and McBurnett (1997), along with others, shows that behaviorally oriented social skills training groups, incorporating copious rehearsal and reinforcement of important social skills, can yield positive outcomes for children with ADHD in the form of parent-reported outcomes.

OUTCOMES OF STUDIES OF BEHAVIORAL TREATMENTS

Our review focuses on investigations of direct contingency management, clinical behavior therapy, and social skills training for children diagnosed specifically with ADHD (or with earlier diagnostic conceptions that correspond to ADHD—e.g., attention deficit disorder with or without hyperactivity). We include designs that (a) directly compare behavioral interventions with wait-list controls, placebo treatments, or alternate psychosocial treatments; (b) contrast behavioral treatments with medication conditions; and/or (c) examine combinations of behavioral and pharmacological treatments in relation to single-treatment modalities. The comprehensive reviews of early studies in the field (see Mash & Dalby, 1979; Sprague, 1983) allow us to restrict our coverage to treatment investigations published from the year 1980 onward. Note that we exclude interventions that focus on cognitive mediational approaches, as the systematic reviews of Abikoff (1987, 1991) and Hinshaw (2000, 2006) document the lack of efficacy of these treatments for this population. Indeed, despite their initial promise, self-instructional strategies have failed to produce any significant cognitive or behavioral gains for youngsters with ADHD, even though youth rated as impulsive by teachers (who fall short of meeting diagnostic criteria for ADHD) may show some positive response (e.g., Kendall & Braswell, 1982).

Direct Contingency Management

Building on the explosion of single-case-experiment research in the 1960s and 1970s, when it was repeatedly demonstrated that specific contingencies produced strong, acute effects on observed child behavior, subsequent investigations focused on (a) comparisons of varying types of contingencies (e.g., positive vs. negative consequences) and (b) contrasts between behaviorally oriented and medication-related strategies for children with ADHD. The large number of specific reports precludes a study-by-study analysis (for a thorough review, see Pfiffner & O'Leary, 1993). We note that investigators of contingency management programs have often de-emphasized formal diagnosis; thus, results pertain to a wide range of attention-disordered and behavior-disordered children.

The prototypical investigation of direct contingency management takes place in a specialized classroom, in which all of the participating children have behavioral disorders. The teacher or "behavioral engineer" is trained to implement classroom-wide contingencies, typically incorporating (a) such positive incentives as praise or individualized reward programs for targeted behaviors (see Pfiffner, Rosen, &

O'Leary, 1985); (b) negative consequences, such as reprimands, response cost contingencies (e.g., the subtraction of earned points; see Rapport, Murphy, & Bailey, 1982), or time-out; or (c) combinations of positive and negative contingencies (e.g., Rosen, O'Leary, Joyce, Conway, & Pfiffner, 1984). The contingencies are altered over periods of hours or, at most, days; outcome measures are usually restricted to observations of on-task or disruptive classroom behavior (see Pelham, Carlson, Sams, Dixon, & Hoza, 1993, for a wider range of outcome measures). Within-subject experimental methodologies are typically employed to yield causal inferences. Given their specialized and time-restricted nature, most investigations of direct contingency management programs can best be viewed as demonstrations of the acute effects of reward and punishment procedures rather than as integrative treatments per se.

The behavioral gains yielded from these studies are often impressive (e.g., Robinson, Newby, & Ganzell, 1981). For instance, Rosen et al. (1984, Experiment 1) reported an average increase in on-task behavior (across eight subjects) from 35% during no-contingency periods to 79% during intervals of active contingent reinforcement or punishment. Importantly, academic productivity has been found to parallel the behavioral improvements in some reports (e.g., Rapport et al., 1982). The systematic work of Susan O'Leary, Linda Pfiffner, and colleagues has demonstrated that stringently implemented, individualized reward programs can yield benefit for hyperactive/disruptive youth (see Pfiffner et al., 1985), but the use of prudent, low-intensity negative consequences (e.g., brief reprimands backed up with privilege loss; response cost) is a valuable component of contingency management (Rosen et al., 1984; see also Rapport et al., 1982).

Intensive and broader applications of direct contingency management for children with ADHD can be found in the Summer Treatment Program model of Pelham, Fabiano, Gnagy, Greiner, and Hoza (2005), which has been adopted at a number of locations throughout the United States. Here, academic skills training, social skills groups, and playground and sports activities are applied in a contingency-rich environment, where five counselors work with units of 12 children during 9-hour days.

Another example of direct contingency management is the systematic, special kindergarten classroom provided by Barkley et al. (2000) for young children meeting screening criteria for both inattentive/hyperactive and aggressive behavior. In this heavily supervised, 9-month program—which featured an intensive positive and negative contingency program, as well as social skills training, anger management training, and academic readiness training—significant gains were found at the end of the school year across some outcome measures, including both adult informant reports and objective classroom observations. As discussed below, however, there was almost no maintenance of these gains in subsequent school years.

From another perspective, the experimental success of demonstrating stimulus control (i.e., improvements over baseline that remit when contingencies are removed) is tantamount to a lack of maintenance of treatment effects—that is, the absence of sustained benefits from treatment. In other words, the lack of generalized and persisting gains when contingencies are not in place enables the application of single-subject experimental studies but documents a key deficiency of direct contingency management (Pelham & Hinshaw, 1992). A parallel acuteness of effects is salient for stimulant medication treatments for children and adolescents with ADHD (Hinshaw, 2006). Providing lasting benefit is, in fact, the key treatment issue in the field.

In some early investigations, effects of behavioral manipulations appeared stronger than those from medication-related changes (Rapport et al., 1982). Yet the systematic research of Pelham and colleagues (C. L. Carlson, Pelham, Milich, & Dixon, 1992; Pelham et al., 1993) bears scrutiny. This work, conducted in intensive summer treatment program settings, demonstrates that systematic behavioral contingencies in special classroom settings produced significant benefit (compared with nonsystematic contingencies) for observed classroom behavior but did not yield significant improvement in academic productivity or accuracy. Stimulant medication, on the other hand, improved both behavioral and academic outcome domains, with an effect size approximately twice that of the behavioral contingencies (Pelham et al., 1993).

In summary, direct contingency management procedures produce significant, short-term benefits regarding core symptoms of ADHD, as rated by adults and as objectively observed, and regarding off-task and disruptive behavior patterns and some measures of academic productivity as well. These benefits, however, are largely confined to specialized settings. The lack of maintenance of behavior change and the artificiality of the settings in which contingency management has been implemented are key limitations. In addition, even intensive, systemic behavioral contingency programs show significantly weaker effects than those from stimulant medication. As noted earlier, the types of studies used to show the efficacy of direct contingency management for children with ADHD are not readily classifiable by the framework for standards of proof used in the current volume. Whereas single-case demonstrations of contingency-related effects on observed behavior are heuristic, they do not, in and of themselves, translate into comprehensive interventions for groups of youngsters in natural settings (see discussion in Kolko, Bukstein, & Barron, 1999). Incorporating the power of direct contingency management approaches into generalizable treatment strategies is a continuing challenge; investigators also need to consider the development of other types of psychosocial interventions for children with ADHD, such as those that tap the organizational difficulties inherent in this disorder.

Clinical Behavior Therapy and Social Skills Training

Table 1.2 lists key experimental investigations of clinical behavior therapy investigations for children with ADHD that have been published since the early 1980s. Between-group clinical trials are included in this table. The typical treatment period spans several months, with parent training procedures and teacher consultation sessions constituting the key clinical activities. Several recent investigations, however, have included longer intervention periods of up to 9 to 14 months. An important feature of many such programs is the establishment of a joint, home-school reward program such as a "daily report card," through which key school targets are monitored by the teacher, with home reinforcement contingent on positive teacher report and, in some cases, with response cost contingent on negative report. Several trials of social skills training—augmented by parent management training—show positive results in comparison with untreated control conditions (Frankel, Myatt, Cantwell, & Feinberg, 1997; Pfiffner & McBurnett, 1997; Tutty, Gephart, & Wurzbacher,

2003). In contrast, Antshel and Remer (2003) reported limited improvements with this approach.

The cited investigations are diverse in treatment methods and research design parameters. For example, some studies compare behavior therapy directly to medication (e.g., Klein & Abikoff, 1997, which supersedes the initial report of Gittelman et al., 1980; Firestone, Kelly, Goodman, & Davey, et al. 1981; MTA Cooperative Group, 1999a). Some evaluate combinations of medication and behavioral treatments (Firestone et al., 1981; Klein & Abikoff, 1997; MTA Cooperative Group, 1999a; Pelham et al., 1988). Still others employ either delayed treatment controls (Anastopoulos, Shelton, DuPaul, & Guevremont, 1993; Dubey, O'Leary, & Kaufman, 1983; Pfiffner & McBurnett, 1997; Pisterman et al., 1989, 1992) or alternative treatment control groups (Barkley, Guevremont, Anastopoulos, & Fletcher, 1992; Barkley et al., 2000; Dubey et al., 1983; Horn, Ialongo, Popvich, & Perdatto, 1987; Horn, Ialongo, Greenberg, Packard, & Smith-Winberry, 1990; Horn et al., 1991; Pelham et al., 1988; Sonuga-Barke, Daley, Thompson, Laver-Bradbury, & Weeks, 2001). Several investigations, in fact, perform more than one type of comparison. Furthermore, some of the clinical behavior therapy interventions include school consultation (Abikoff, Hechtman, Klein, Weiss, et al., 2004; Firestone et al., 1981; Klein & Abikoff, 1997; Pelham et al., 1988; Horn et al., 1990, 1991), and two include integrative combinations of direct contingency management and clinical behavior therapy (Barkley et al., 2000; MTA Cooperative Group, 1999a). Note that several potentially informative investigations are not included in Table 1.2 for reasons of sampling (e.g., Strayhorn & Weidman, 1989, who evaluated preventive parent-child interaction training for low-income preschoolers not designated as having ADHD) or design (i.e., within-subject investigations of Pelham, Schnedler, Bologna, & Contreras, 1980, and Pollard, Ward, & Barkley, 1983).

Despite the diversity of the reported investigations, it is apparent from Table 1.2 that clinical behavior therapy procedures often yield statistically significant benefits with regard to ADHD-related problem behavior, particularly when parents and teachers who deliver the treatments are also the informants. In several cases, the effects reveal clinical significance as well (e.g., Anastopoulos et al., 1993; Pelham et al., 1988; Pfiffner & McBurnett, 1997; Swanson et al., 2001), for at least some domains of

TABLE 1.2 Findings From Clinical Behavior Therapy Trials for ADHD From 1980 Onward

Authors	N/M Age (yr)	Behavioral Treatment	Study Design	Outcome Domains	Key Findings
Firestone et al. (1981)[a]	43/7.3	3 months: 3 individual and 6 group parent training sessions plus 2 teacher consultations	Type 2 1. BT + placebo 2. MPH 3. BT + MPH (pre-post-FU)	A. Academic achievement B. Laboratory reaction time C. Behavior ratings (P, T)	A. and B. 2 = 3 > 1 C.:[b]
Dubey et al. (1983)	37/8.4	9 weeks: weekly group parent training sessions	Type 2 1. BT 2. Parent effectiveness training 3. Delayed treatment control (pre-post-9 mo. FU)	A. Behavior ratings (P) B. Videotaped PC interaction, scored for parent and child behavior	A. 1 = 2 = 3 > 3 with 1 and 2 showing significant pre-post and pre-FU change for several scales B. No effects
Horn et al. (1987)	19/9.7	8 weeks: weekly group parent training sessions	Type 2 1. BT 2. SI 3. BT + SI (pre-post-1 mo. FU)	A. Child self-report and lab measures B. Behavior ratings (P, T) C. Classroom observations	Equivalent improvement across groups for all but 1 of 32 outcome measures[c]
Pelham et al. (1988)	30[d]/	5 months: M = 10 individual and group parent training sessions plus M = 10 teacher consultations	Type 2 1. BT + SS + MPH 2. BT + SS + placebo 3. BT + MPH 4. BT + placebo 5. SS only (not random) (pre-post)	A. Behavior ratings (P, T) B. Academic achievement C. Peer sociometrics D. Classroom observations	1 = 2 = 3 = 4; for A (parent), B, C, and D, with all 4 groups showing significant pre-post improvement (but group 5 did not). For teacher ratings, 1 and 3 improved more than 2 and 4, during periods of active medication
Pisterman et al. (1989)	46/4.2	12 weeks: 10 group parent training sessions plus 2 individual sessions	Type 2 1. BT 2. Delayed treatment control group (pre-post-3 mo. FU)	A. Videotaped PC interaction, scored for parent and child behavior B. Behavior ratings (P)	A. 1 > 2 re: child compliance and some parenting measures B. 1 = 2 re: Conners ratings[e]
Horn et al. (1990)	31/8.8	12 weeks: 12 group parent training sessions plus 3 teacher consultations	Type 2 1. BT 2. SI 3. BT + SI 4. (pre-post-8 mo. FU)	A. Child achievement, attention, and self-concept B. Behavior ratings (P, T)	No treatment differences (i.e., no group × time interactions); all groups showed gains pre-post and pre-FU[f]
Horn et al. (1991)[g]	78/7–11	12 weeks: 12 group parent training sessions plus 12 child SI consultations	Type 2 1. Placebo 2. Low-dose MPH 3. High-dose MPH 4. 1 + BT/SI 5. 2 + BT/SI 6. 3 + BT/SI (pre-post)	A. Child achievement, attention, and self-concept B. Classroom observations C. Behavior ratings (P, T)	Groups with MPH showed greater improvement with placebo; Groups 5 and 6 did not outperform 2 and 3[h]

TABLE 1.2 (continued)

Authors	N/M Age (yr)	Behavioral Treatment	Study Design	Outcome Domains	Key Findings
Barkley et al. (1992)	61/13.9	10 weeks: 8–10 weekly parent sessions	Type 2 1. Behavioral parent training 2. Problem solving and communication therapy 3. Structural family therapy (pre-post-3 mo. FU)	A. Behavior ratings (P, A) B. Family ratings (P, A) C. Videotaped P-A interaction D. Rated depression (M)	1 = 2 = 3 for all outcomes; all groups yielded pre-post improvement for A, B, and D (with maintenance at FU)[i]
Pisterman et al. (1992)	45/4.0	12 weekly group parent training sessions	Type 2 1. BT 2. Delayed treatment group (pre-post-3 mo. FU)	A. Behavior ratings (P) B. Videotaped PC interaction, scored for parent and child behavior and child attention	1 > 2, for pre-post and pre-FU comparisons regarding parent behavior and child behavior, but not child attention
Anastopoulos et al. (1993)	34/8.1	2 months: 9 sessions of parent training	Type 2 1. BT 2. Delayed treatment group (pre-post-FU)	A. Behavior ratings (P) B. Parent-reported stress, parenting efficacy, marital satisfaction	1 > 2, for pre-post comparisons regarding ADHD symptoms and some aspects of parental functioning; gains maintained at FU
Klein & Abikoff (1997)[j]	86/8.25	8 weeks: Weekly individual sessions with parents and with teacher augmented by child attendance when needed and by telephone contact	Type 1 1. BT + placebo 2. MPH 3. BT + MPH (pre-post)	A. Behavior ratings (M, T) B. Classroom observations C. Global improvement ratings (M, T, Psy) D. Academic/cognitive tests	A. [k] B. [l] C. [m] D. Few effects[n]
Pfiffner & McBurnett (1997)	27 (8–10)	Eight 90-minute sessions (weekly) for children in SS groups or parents in generalization training groups	Type 2 1. SS 2. SS + parent generalization 3. Wait list control (pre-post-4-mo. FU)	A. Behavior ratings (P, T) B. Social skills knowledge	A. 1 = 2 > 3 for parent but not teacher ratings, despite moderate effect sizes for the latter. Parent effects larger for social skills than disruptive behavior. B. 1 = 2 > 3[o]
MTA Cooperative Group (1999a)[p]	579/8.5	Integrated clinical behavior therapy and direct contingency management across 14 months, with parent, school, and child components (see text)	Type 1 1. Medication management 2. Behavioral treatment 3. Combined 1 + 2 4. Community-treated comparison (pre-post-FU)	A. ADHD symptoms (P, T, Obs) B. Oppositional symptoms (P, T, Obs) C. Internalizing (P, T, C) D. Social/peer (P, T, sociometrics) E. Family (P, C, Obs) F. Achievement	A. 1 = 3 > 2 = 4 B.-F. 3 > 4 across all 5 domains, according to at least one informant; additionally, for D., 1 > 4 (teacher) and for E., 2 > 4 (parent)

Study	N/Age	Intervention	Design	Measures	Results
Barkley et al. (2000)	158/4.8	Special day-class kindergarten program (9 mo.; see text) and 10 weekly, group parent training sessions	Type 1 1. Special class 2. Parent training 3. Combined 1 + 2 4. Regular class, no parent training 5. (pre-post–24 mo. FU; for FU, see Shelton et al., 2000)	A. Diagnostic interviews B. Parent ratings C. Teacher ratings D. Psychoeducational testing E. Clinic behavior observations F. PC interactions G. Classroom observations	No main effects or interactions of parent training. Significant effects of special class for parent ratings of adaptive behavior, multiple teacher ratings, classroom observations of externalizing behavior; but these effects not maintained at follow-up
Sonuga-Barke et al. (2001)[9]	78/3	8 weeks: Weekly individual parent training sessions at home	Type 1 1. BT 2. Parent counseling and support 3. Wait-list control (pre-post–FU)	A. ADHD Index based on clinical interview with parent and lab observation of child's ADHD behaviors B. Maternal Index based on self-ratings of well-being and self-competence	A. 1 > 2 and 3 at post and FU (found for each component of the index), with 2 = 3 B. 1 > 2 and 3 at post; with 2 = 3
Antshel & Remer (2003)	120/9.6	Eight 90-minute sessions (weekly) for children in SS groups, three parent group sessions	Type 2 1. SS + brief parent training 2. Wait list control (pre-post–3 mo. FU)	A. Social skills (P, C)	A. 1 > 2 on parent- and child-reported assertion, all other social competence measures nonsignificant
Tutty et al. (2003)[t]	110/(5–12)	Eight 50-minute group sessions, separate for parents (behavior management) and children (social skills)	Type 2 1. BSS Behavior and Social Skill 2. Treatment as usual (pre, 3 months after treatment, 6 months after treatment)	A. ADHD symptoms (P, T) B. Parental discipline (5-item scale; P)	A. 1 > 2 at 3- and 6-month FU assessments for parent but not teacher reports B. 1 > 2 at 3- and 6-month FU assessments
Abikoff, Hechtman, Klein, Weiss, et al. (2004)[s]	103/8.2	2 yrs: Weekly in 1st yr, monthly in 2nd yr. Integrated parent, child, and teacher components: parent training group (16 wks, Year 1), parent counseling (36 wks, Year 1), academic remediation (dyads, 36 wks Yr 1); individual child psychotherapy	Type 1 1. Behavioral and psychsocial Tx + medication 2. Attention control + medication 3. Medication (pre-1yr–2yr)	A. ADHD symptoms (P, T, Psy, Obs) B. ODD symptoms/conduct problems (P, T, Psy) C. Social skills (P, T, Obs) D. Academic Achievement/HW problems (P) E. Depression (C) F. Self-concept (C) G. Parenting (P)	A through G: 1 = 2 = 3; all three groups improved equivalently in all domains at 1- and 2-year assessments

(continued)

TABLE 1.2 (continued)

Note: N = number of subjects completing the investigation. BT = clinical behavior therapy; SI = self-instructional training for child; SS = social skills training for child; MPH = methylphenidate; M = mother; P = parent; T = teacher; C = child; PC = parent-child; Psy = psychiatrist; A = adolescent; PA = parent-adolescent; Obs = observations.

[a]See also Firestone, Crowe, Goodman, and McGrath (1986) for presentation of 1-year (N = 52) and 2-year (N = 30) follow-up data for subsets of this sample who remained in for assessment. At each follow-up period, no significant between-group differences were found for any outcome measure, in part because a noteworthy subgroup of parent training plus placebo subjects had "switched" to medication treatment.

[b]Results of covariance analysis are difficult to interpret, but it appears as though the medicated groups outperformed the behavior therapy plus placebo children for teacher Conners scores. MPH was individually titrated, averaging 22 mg/day. All three groups showed significant within-subject change on Metropolitan Achievement Tests and on parent- and teacher-rated behavior, but only the medicated youngsters improved on the Gates-MacGinitie Verbal Grade level score.

[c]SI treatment involved weekly group sessions for the children. One-month follow-up data showed persistence of within-subject changes across treatment groups for several outcome measures.

[d]For the 20 children in groups 1–4 who received behavior therapy, MD age was reported to be 7 years; for the 10 children in group 5, MD = 8 years. MPH dosages were fixed at 0.3 mg/kg, with most children receiving b.i.d. dosages.

[e]Immediate posttreatment gains for treated vs. delayed-treatment control group were maintained at 3-month follow-up.

[f]Pre-FU changes were found, across groups, for parent ratings only.

[g]See also Ialongo et al. (1993) for presentation of 9-month FU data, which revealed a general deterioration of performance for all groups and extremely limited evidence for groups 5 or 6 to outperform groups 2 or 3 (i.e., marginally significant finding, and only for parental ratings).

[h]Low-dose MPH = 0.4 mg/kg; high-dose = 0.8 mg/kg.

[i]When clinical significance of effects was ascertained via procedures of Jacobson and Truax (1991), only 5 to 30% improved sufficiently across treatment groups, and only 5 to 20% "recovered" (rates did not differ across treatment groups).

[j]This report supplants the partial sample report of Gittelman et al. (1980), which included the initial 61 participants. For Treatments 2 and 3, MPH was individually titrated, averaging 40.6 mg/day.

[k]For parent ratings, Treatment 3 was significantly better than Treatment 1 for 5/19 scales; no other group comparisons were significant. For teacher ratings, Treatment 3 was significantly better than Treatment 1 for 16/17 scales, Treatment 3 was significantly better than Treatment 2 for 3/17 scales, and Treatment 2 was significantly better than Treatment 1 for 11/17 scales.

[l]For classroom observations, Treatment 3 was significantly better than Treatment 1 for 9/14 codes; Treatment 3 was significantly better than Treatment 2 for 2/14 codes; and Treatment 2 was significantly better than Treatment 1 for 5/14 codes. Importantly, by the end of treatment, Treatment 3 did not differ significantly from normal classroom controls on any observational measure, reflecting normalization of behavior with combination treatment.

[m]For Clinical Global Improvement ratings by parents, 93% were rated as improved for Treatment 3, 76% for Treatment 2, and 64% for Treatment 1, with the only significant difference between 3 and 1. For ratings by teachers, respective percentages were 93%, 69%, and 57% (Treatment 3 significantly different from 1 and 2, which did not differ). By psychiatrists, respective percentages were 97%, 79%, and 50% (all three contrasts significant).

[n]Across 9 test scores (derived from WISC, WRAT, Matching Familiar Figures, and Paired Associate Test measures) × 3 treatment contrasts, only 2/27 comparisons were significant (both favoring Treatment 2 over Treatment 1: Matching Familiar Figures and Paired Associate Test). Note that psychologists who administered the tests rated participants' test behavior. Across 8 different behavior ratings × 3 treatment group contrasts, only 2/24 comparisons were significant, both favoring Treatment 2 over Treatment 1.

[o]There was modest evidence that Treatment 2 facilitated greater generalization of social skills gains to the classroom.

[p]The immediate posttreatment findings for the MTA Study are summarized in MTA Cooperative Group (1999a, 1999b). MPH dosages initially titrated through 4-week trial and maintained during monthly pharmacotherapist visits (Treatment 1 M = 37.7 mg/day, Treatment 3 M = 31.2 mg/day). With composite outcome measures (Conners et al., 2001; Swanson et al., 2001), the contrast between Treatment 3 and 2 became significant, with a small effect size (see text). See also Hinshaw et al. (2000), Jensen et al. (2001), and Owens et al. (2003) for additional moderator and mediator findings. Outcomes at 24 months (i.e., 10 months posttreatment) indicated that the superiority of the medication-management conditions for ADHD symptomatology had decreased by about 50% (MTA Cooperative Group, 2004a, 2004b); by 3 years post-random assignment, the four treatment groups were nonsignificantly different on all outcome measures (MTA Cooperative Group, 2006).

[q]Mean age not precisely specified. See Sonuga-Barke et al. (2002) for moderator findings related to maternal ADHD.

[r]Medication for ADHD varied naturalistically in both groups but did not significantly differ across conditions.

[s]The New York–Montreal Study findings are also presented in Abikoff, Hechtman, Klein, Greenfield et al. (2004) and Hechtman, Abikoff, Klein, Weiss et al. (2004); the design and rationale are discussed in Klein, Abikoff, Hechtman, and Weiss (2004). The empirical articles, each of which focuses on different outcomes, are summarized together in the table.

14

function. Overall, clinical behavior therapy procedures have received empirical support for the treatment of childhood ADHD, in terms of both core symptoms of the disorder and associated areas of impairment (see Table 1.2; see also review of Pelham et al., 1998).

The long-term, intensive, integrated behavioral program that was performed and evaluated in the multicenter MTA Study (MTA Cooperative Group, 1999a) is informative. In this clinical trial, the largest for children ever supported by the National Institute of Mental Health, 579 children, aged 7 to 9.9 years and carefully diagnosed with ADHD, combined type, were assigned randomly for 14 months of treatment to (a) medication management (MedMgt)—initial titration followed by monthly maintenance medication sessions; (b) intensive behavioral treatment (Beh); (c) combined treatment (Comb)—integrating these two systematic intervention strategies; or (d) community comparison (CC), in which the families sought services on their own from local providers. The behavioral intervention in conditions (b) and (c) was designed to be intensive and well coordinated (see Wells et al., 2000, for details). It involved 35 group and individual parent training sessions with a psychologist; biweekly teacher consultation from the same psychologist that focused on setting up a daily report card; an 8-week summer treatment program for the child (Pelham et al., 2005), and 12 weeks of paraprofessional aide intervention in the child's classroom, supervised by the psychologist. It therefore incorporated both direct contingency management and intensive clinical behavior therapy.

Treatment outcome data, obtained from parents and teachers, reveal three key findings with regard to the Beh condition (MTA Cooperative Group, 1999a). (a) For the core outcome domains of ADHD symptoms, comorbid symptoms, and school, family, and peer-related impairments, it produced gains that were comparable to those from community care. Of note, stimulant medications were used by more than two thirds of the CC participants, meaning that the Beh treatment was essentially equivalent to community-based medication treatment (see also MTA Cooperative Group (1999b) for a contrast of Beh with the medicated participants of the CC condition). (b) The benefits of Beh were significantly smaller than those from MedMgt regarding ADHD-related and oppositional-defiant symptomatology. (c) The measures revealing gains from Beh were ratings from parents and teachers, who were active participants in the behavioral intervention; objective behavior observations did not yield evidence for gains from the behavioral treatment. Overall, the long-term nature and rigor of the MTA Study add to the contention that behavioral treatments do not provide the same degree of benefit as do titrated and well-monitored pharmacological interventions for ADHD, with respect to core symptoms and associated oppositionality, even when improvement ratings are obtained from adults involved in the child's treatment.

In addition, as noted by the MTA Cooperative Group (1999b), one fourth of the participants in the Beh condition were receiving medication for ADHD by the 14-month, end-of-treatment evaluation, because of either families' dissatisfaction with progress or the clinical team's recommendation for consideration of medication. Thus, the Beh condition was not sufficiently strong to prevent medication use in a quarter of the participants assigned to it (see moderator findings below for qualification).

In secondary analyses of the MTA data, composite measures (i.e., combined parent and teacher rating scales in Swanson et al., 2001; a factor score of symptom and impairment measures in Conners et al., 2001) revealed significant superiority of Beh over CC. Furthermore, as highlighted below, the Comb treatment was found to yield significant (albeit small) incremental benefit over medication alone in these secondary analyses (again, the outcome measures were derived from informants involved in treatment delivery). Still, the combination of direct contingency management and clinical behavior therapy in the MTA provided added effects, over and above medication management alone.

Finally, behaviorally oriented *social skills training* has also received initial, empirical support in some studies (see entries for Pfiffner & McBurnett, 1997, and Tutty et al., 2003, in Table 1.2) but not all (Antshel & Remer, 2003). The sample for the investigation of Frankel et al. (1997) was a combination of youth with oppositional defiant disorder and ADHD. For this reason, it is not included in Table 1.2, but results were positive.

Limitations and Qualifications

Six key limitations and qualifications of these findings are noteworthy.

First, only four studies (New York–Montreal

Study—see Abikoff, Hechtman, Klein, Weiss, et al., 2004; kindergarten study of Barkley et al., 2000; behavior therapy–medication comparison trial of Klein & Abikoff, 1997; and the MTA Study—see MTA CooperativeGroup, 1999a) qualify as Type 1 investigations, a designation reserved for rigorous, randomized clinical trials with (a) sufficient sample sizes to yield at least moderate statistical power and (b) evaluation of multiple outcome domains that include objective measures. These stringent standards for a Type 1 designation must be kept in mind while reviewing the contents of the table.

Second, in nearly all reports, significant effects are found on parent or teacher rating scales but rarely on objectively observed behavior (e.g., Dubey et al., 1983; Klein & Abikoff, 1997; MTA Cooperative Group, 1999a). Although the best-established rating scales are well normed and treatment sensitive (see Hinshaw & Nigg, 1999), the potential for bias is real with such measures, as the adults who report on the children's behavior are the same individuals trained to implement the behavioral programs. A parent's or teacher's increased sense of efficacy or coping resulting from intervention—as well as consumer satisfaction with the interventions and treatment allegiance—may lead to better ratings of the child's behavior (Klein & Abikoff, 1997). Objective, independent assessment procedures (e.g., direct observations, sociometric appraisals from peers, tests of academic performance) are needed to provide unbiased information about children's functioning. As a case in point, in the landmark MTA Study, objective classroom observations (MTA Cooperative Group, 1999a) and peer sociometrics indicators (Hoza et al., 2005) did not reveal significant effects of randomly assigned treatment, either pharmacological or behavioral, whereas parent and teacher ratings did. On the other hand, recent findings reveal that the Beh condition from the MTA (and particularly the Comb condition) yielded improvements in an objectively coded index of parenting skill (Wells et al., 2006).

Third, the average effects of clinical behavior therapy procedures are smaller in magnitude than those from stimulant medications (Firestone et al., 1981; Horn et al., 1991; Klein & Abikoff, 1997; MTA Cooperative Group, 1999a; see also C. L. Carlson et al., 1992, and Pelham et al., 1993, from the contingency management section). Whether long-term benefits accrue from either category of treatment remains a crucial question (see the sixth point below).

Fourth, full normalization of problem behavior is rarely attained with behavior therapy programs. The analysis of Abikoff and Gittelman (1984), which includes partial data from the Klein and Abikoff (1997) investigation, is heuristic in this regard. From direct observation procedures, the main behaviors relevant to ADHD (e.g., interference, off-task, out of chair, noncompliance) did not show normalization for the behavior therapy condition, whereas medication normalized three of these four categories. Only aggressive behavior—which showed low initial levels—was brought into normative ranges with the clinical behavior therapy procedures in this trial. In addition, in other reports peer sociometric status has not been found to be normalized with behavior therapy (see Pelham et al., 1980, 1988; Hoza et al., 2005), a limitation shared by medication treatment (Whalen et al., 1989; see also Hoza et al., 2005).

Fifth, investigations of behavioral/psychosocial treatments have relied on specifically trained professionals to deliver the training. A British study suggests that this level of skill may be necessary for favorable outcomes. That is, the positive impact of a home-based parent intervention delivered by specially trained nurses (Sonuga-Barke et al., 2001) was not replicated when nonspecialist nurses were used in a subsequent trial of the same intervention (Sonuga-Barke, Thompson, Daley, & Laver-Bradbury, in press).

Sixth, analysis of long-term carryover of effects has rarely been undertaken. Investigations with any follow-through data (ranging from 1 to 24 months) have yielded only tentative evidence for significant maintenance of gains following the end of treatment. Especially pertinent in this regard is the intensive, special classroom, kindergarten intervention of Barkley et al. (2000). In this Type 1 study, both clinical behavior therapy (in the form of 10-session parent training) and systematic contingency management (9 months of a special treatment classroom) were compared and combined for young children meeting screening scale criteria for both ADHD and aggression. Results were as follows: The parent training intervention, for which attendance was low, yielded no main effects or interactions. Thus, this form of clinical behavior therapy may have limited appeal and benefit to community samples of parents of young, disruptive children who have not been clinically referred (see, however, Pisterman et al., 1989, 1992; and Sonuga-Barke et al., 2001, who did show significant gains from parent training for this age-group). In addition, whereas the intensive, 9-month classroom environment yielded posttreatment gains that were stronger than those found with a control group who received regular kindergarten education (chiefly for reports from adult informants who were aware of treatment assignment but also for some objective classroom observation codes), these benefits did not persist at 1- or 2-year follow-up (see Shelton et al., 2000). The results provide a sobering message, as it was hoped that early, intensive intervention could alter the trajectory of externalizing symptomatology. Parallel to medication, it appears that psychosocial interventions need to be maintained if gains are to persist.[1]

Incremental Effects of Combination Treatments

Can clinical behavior therapy procedures provide a boost to the effects of medication for youngsters with ADHD? Although we have mentioned relevant findings in passing, we now review this crucial issue specifically. Overall, the evidence is suggestive but not consistent.[2]

In several studies, adding direct contingency management to medication alone did not effect incremental improvement (C. L. Carlson et al., 1992; Pelham et al., 1993). On the other hand, Kolko and colleagues (1999) found at least some outcome measures for which combination interventions, in a day treatment program, were superior to medication alone. In addition, Pelham et al. (2000) studied direct contingency management implemented during intensive behavioral summer treatment programs, as part of the MTA intervention. The key finding was that during the program, while contingencies were in operation, optimally titrated medication yielded small, if any, incremental benefits over the direct contingency management alone. We also note that contingency management procedures may permit a reduction in stimulant dosage for optimal classroom behavior in specialized settings (C. L. Carlson et al., 1992; see also Horn et al., 1991; Pelham et al., 1980) and that comprehensive behavior therapy may lead to gains at lower doses than is the case with medication alone (MTA Cooperative Group, 1999a, 1999b).

With regard to clinical behavioral therapy and social skills interventions, no advantage for combination treatment over medication alone was found in

the dual-site, 2-year, randomized New York–Montreal Study (see Abikoff, Hechtman, Klein, Gallagher, et al., 2004; Abikoff, Hechtman, Klein, Weiss, et al., 2004; Hechtman, Abikoff, Klein, Greenfield, et al., 2004; Hechtman, Abikoff, Klein, Weiss, et al., 2004). In this investigation, positive responders ($N = 102$) to stimulant medication, aged 7 to 9 years, were assigned to one of three treatments for 12 months: (a) optimal-dose methylphenidate (MPH) alone; (b) MPH in combination with active parent, child, and teacher intervention; or (c) MPH in combination with an attention control intervention (mean dose of MPH = 34 mg/day). One year of maintenance "booster" therapy followed the yearlong intensive intervention phase. The psychosocial adjuncts to medication included social skills training, academic assistance, organization skills training, and individual psychotherapy for the child; parent management training and counseling for the parents; and a home-based reinforcement program for targeted school behavior. Assessments from multiple sources yielded no evidence of incremental efficacy for the psychosocial/behavioral intervention over MPH alone. In addition, multimodal treatment did not permit medication to be discontinued, as all children deteriorated when switched to placebo and had to be placed back on active medication within short intervals.[3]

Other reports, however, provide evidence for the incremental benefits of combination treatments involving clinical behavior therapy. Klein and Abikoff (1997) compared combined medication plus clinical behavior therapy to either intervention alone. First, the combined therapy ranked best across all outcome measures (adult reported as well as blinded). Second, the combined treatment was significantly superior to methylphenidate alone for some teacher rating scales, for psychiatrist and teacher global ratings of improvement, and for some objective classroom observational codes of classroom behavior. Third, only the combination condition yielded consistent normalization of key observational outcome measures. As stated by Klein and Abikoff (1997): "The study provides clear support for the potential usefulness of adding behavior therapy to methylphenidate treatment" (p. 111), at least for partial responders to medication. They noted in addition, however, that the "inconsistency in the superiority of the combined therapy over methylphenidate alone, and the marked efficacy of methylphenidate alone across multiple domains, preclude an unconditional endorsement of the combination" (p. 110). Moreover, withdrawing medication from the combined treatment regimen invariably led to clinical deterioration.

An interesting parallel to such results is found in the MTA Study (MTA Cooperative Group, 1999a). Initial outcome analyses showed that whereas combined treatment (Comb) was typically ranked best across diverse outcome measures—and that it was the only treatment significantly outperforming community control intervention for non-ADHD-symptom outcome domains—it was not significantly superior to medication management for the 19 individual outcome measures investigated. However, as noted earlier, objectively coded parent-child interactions did yield evidence for superiority of combined treatment over MedMgt or treatment as usual in the community (Wells et al., 2006). Specifically, a composite measure of positive, adaptive parenting fared best with Comb.

Furthermore, secondary analyses by Conners et al. (2001) and Swanson et al. (2001), with composite outcome measures, revealed that combination treatment significantly outperformed medication management, with a small effect size of approximately .25 for this contrast. In fact, on a categorical measure of excellent treatment response (scores on a composite ADHD/ODD rating scale measure that reflect the absence of significant symptomatology), 68% of combined treatment participants, 56% of medication management, and 34% of intensive behavioral treatment reached this criterion at the conclusion of treatment (Swanson et al., 2001). Thus, although incremental effects of multimodal (medication plus behavioral) treatments may not be large, they are sometimes significant, at least (a) when considering reports by parents and teachers who were directly involved in delivering treatment and (b) when evaluating objective indicators of positive parenting behaviors.

Along this line, the within-subject study of Pelham and colleagues (1980) complements several of the studies reported in Table 1.2. It incorporated a 5-month regimen of clinical behavior therapy (parent training plus regular-classroom teacher consultation), with 3-week-long methylphenidate probes performed at baseline and following 3 and 13 weeks of behavioral treatment. After 3 weeks of treatment, the high medication dosage yielded stronger effects than the low dosage level; but following 13 weeks, low and high medication dosages were equivalent, with both leading to normalization of behavior. The suggestion is that, over time, concerted behavioral intervention may allow a reduction in the dosage of stimulant medication that is required for optimal behavior. In the MTA Study, for example, the equivalent (and, as shown by Conners et al., 2001, and Swanson et al., 2001, better) performance of Comb relative to Med Mgt was effected with a lower average dosage of medication (31.2 mg of methylphenidate per day at treatment end point with combined vs. 37.7 mg per day with MedMgt).[4]

Moderators and Mediators of Treatment Outcome

Do any subject or family characteristics predict or moderate treatment response for behavioral treatments? The MTA Cooperative Group (1999b) found that overall study outcomes were parallel for boys versus girls with ADHD and for those with comorbid oppositional defiant or conduct disorder versus noncomorbid youth. For children in the Beh treatment, prior treatment with medication predicted the likelihood of the child's being medicated by the end of the 14-month intervention. For previously medicated children, the odds were nearly 50%; for never-mediated children, the odds were under 15%. The suggestion is that once a child is medicated, removing the medication and substituting behavioral intervention can be a difficult proposition.

Furthermore, comorbid anxiety disorder status moderated treatment response, such that ADHD/anxious children receiving the intensive behavior treatment showed more improvement than ADHD/anxious children treated in the CC (treatment as usual) condition. In fact, they showed equivalent response to ADHD/anxious children who received MedMgt or Comb (see also Jensen et al., 2001). There was also some indication of a relatively stronger response to combination treatment for low-SES MTA participants, particularly with respect to teacher-reported social skills (MTA Cooperative Group, 1999b). For the behavioral treatment, secondary analyses of Owens et al. (2003) examined combinations of moderator variables. Although no moderator variables, considered singly or together, contributed significantly to differential outcomes, the medication aspects of the MTA treatments yielded significant moderator findings. Specifically, stimulants worked optimally for children with relatively less severe baseline ADHD, particularly those with at least average IQ scores and with parents displaying low levels of baseline depressive symptomatology. Children with more difficult patterns of individual and family characteristics, then, may require even more intensive treatments.

Finally, Sonuga-Barke, Daley, and Thompson (2002) found that maternal ADHD symptomatology served as an important moderator of outcome in parent training interventions for preschoolers with ADHD. Mothers with high scores on a self-report scale of their own ADHD symptoms did not show significant benefits from the parent training intervention, whereas mothers low on this scale showed a strong benefit. Thus, parental characteristics may play a role in moderating outcome of behavioral interventions. Given the strong heritability of ADHD, this finding is clinically important.

Regarding mediators, defined as treatment-related processes that may help to explain how treatments work, Hinshaw et al. (2000) performed secondary analyses of MTA data with respect to self-reported parenting practices as potential mediators of school-based outcomes. In brief, the success of Comb for reducing teacher-reported disruptive behavior and improving teacher-reported social skills was related to the family's reduction of negative and ineffective parenting practices during the 14 months of active intervention. That is, only one subgroup of children in the MTA Study had teacher-reported levels of disruptive (ADHD and oppositional) behavior that were fully normalized at the end of treatment; this subgroup was the one receiving Comb whose parents showed substantial reductions of negative/ineffective discipline during the trial. In addition, changes in parenting fully mediated the combination treatment's ability to improve social skills in the school setting. Children of families in the unimodal treatments or the community-treated comparison group whose families showed comparable improvements in negative/ineffective discipline did not show such improvement of school behavior, however. The implication is that, with multimodal treatment, parenting practices may serve to propel significant improvements in a condition—ADHD—with substantial heritability. Considerable work remains to be done to understand additional mechanisms through which

behavioral and combined treatments provide benefit for youth with ADHD.

Summary of Findings From Contingency Management and Behavior Therapy Studies

1. Direct contingency management, provided in special classroom settings over brief time periods, yields significant and large reductions in problem behavior and, in some cases, enhancement of academic performance for youngsters with ADHD. These gains may be of such magnitude that medication treatments cannot yield much in the way of incremental gain (Pelham et al., 2000). Such gains are transitory, however, and stimulants yield stronger immediate effects than those from such classroom contingencies (C. L. Carlson et al., 1992; Pelham et al., 1993).

2. Clinical behavior therapy procedures, involving consultation with teachers and the conducting of parent management sessions, yield statistically significant improvement in child behavior as rated by parents and teachers but much less consistent benefit for directly observed behavior. In addition, gains fall short of full normalization of functioning and are significantly weaker than those from medication. Behavioral treatments can significantly enhance the gains yielded from medication, but not all investigations reveal such an incremental benefit. Although increments are typically small, children receiving combination medication/behavioral treatments are the most likely to show outcomes that reflect normalization of behavior. Some reports indicate that, while contingencies are in effect in specialized settings, behavioral programs combined with low-dosage medication yield effects that are similar to benefits from higher doses of medication.

3. Because of the importance of defiant, aggressive, and antisocial behavior patterns for the persistence and magnification of ADHD-related impairment, it is essential that treatment studies document effects for this domain. Medication effects are substantial for aggressive behavior (Hinshaw & Lee, 2000; Klein et al., 1997), and behavioral contingencies are also effective in reducing aggression.

4. The maintenance of gains from intensive behavioral intervention is not assured (Shelton et al., 2000). Medication treatments for ADHD clearly need to be continued if gains are to persist; the same

may well be true for behavioral contingencies, which are admittedly more difficult, expensive, and time-consuming to maintain.

5. As reviewed elsewhere and noted above, cognitive approaches (particularly those emphasizing self-instructional therapies) have not yielded statistically or clinically significant benefit for youth with ADHD (Abikoff, 1987, 1991; Hinshaw, 2000, 2006). The use of self-management procedures to extend the benefits of well-implemented behavioral intervention is worth further investigation.

6. Finally, behavioral treatments (particularly in combination with medication) may be particularly helpful for complex, highly comorbid cases of children with ADHD. Although they are relatively costly to implement, the benefit may be "worth it" for complex cases (see Jensen et al., 2005).

Overall, our review attests to the significant benefits of behavioral treatments for children with ADHD. At the same time, we cannot offer a "carte blanche" endorsement of nonpharmacological interventions for ADHD, as they are currently operationalized and delivered. Although benefits have been shown to accrue from well-delivered behavioral treatments, they are shown mainly from parent and teacher report; they are rarely long-lasting or clinically sufficient; and their effects, on average, are not as strong as those yielded from well-delivered medication treatment. Given the limitations of pharmacological interventions, however (see Greenhill, this volume), psychosocial/behavioral interventions may be required for families unwilling to utilize medication, for children who show an adverse response, and as an adjunct to pharmacological intervention in order to approach normalization of functioning.

How many children respond? A host of investigations of medication treatments for children with ADHD reveal that positive response to treatment occurs in 70 to 80% of children, with estimates even higher if alternative agents are tried following the clinical failure of an initial trial (see Greenhill, this volume). Nonetheless, some children with ADHD do not show significant benefit. Furthermore, some families are opposed to medicating their children for behavior disorders. A clear impetus for developing and promoting psychosocial treatments for ADHD is that a minority of afflicted children require nonpharmacological intervention.

Ascertaining the response rate of children with ADHD to behavioral treatments is more difficult.

When systematic contingencies are employed, the vast majority of children with ADHD respond. One issue, however, is whether parents and teachers are willing and motivated for the often substantial investments of time and effort required to make the environmental modifications required by clinical behavior therapy approaches. Furthermore, the strongly familial nature of this condition means that many biological parents of youth with ADHD at risk for disorganization and impulsivity are being asked to become far more regular and consistent in their parenting practices. This is a difficult task for any parent but particularly so for parents with problems in behavioral regulation themselves (see, for example, the moderator analyses of Sonuga-Barke et al., 2002). Our objective in making this statement is not to blame families for any shortcomings of behavioral interventions but to point out the clinical realities of effecting change in the most affected cases.

One means of estimating treatment response to behaviorally based intervention appears in the secondary analyses of MTA data by Swanson et al. (2001). As noted earlier, 34% of the intensive behavioral treatment group showed an "excellent response" at the end of treatment, defined as parent and teacher ratings of ADHD and oppositional symptomatology at or below the cutoff of "just a little" severity. In contrast, 68% of the combined treatment group and 56% of medication management met this criterion. Among families assigned to care from community providers the rate was only 25%, even though more than two thirds of these families received stimulant treatment. (Recall, however, that one fourth of the Beh condition participants in the MTA were receiving medication by the 14-month assessment as well.) Intensive behavioral treatment appears to yield response rates that are equivalent to or somewhat stronger than routine community care, even when such treatment includes medication (delivered and monitored in nonoptimal fashion). The additional question of how many families of children with ADHD have access to behavioral treatments, especially intensive and relatively costly ones, is a thorny but important issue, which goes beyond the scope of this chapter.

CONCLUSIONS

As we have highlighted throughout these pages, the optimal psychosocial approaches to the treatment of childhood ADHD require the application of systematic behavioral programs in home and school environments. Direct contingency management in specialized settings is a powerful treatment, but one that lacks applicability to most children with the diagnosis. Clinical behavior therapy approaches, in which parents and teachers are taught to implement regular contingencies, are effective with respect to parent- and teacher-rated outcomes but fall short of clinically sufficient benefits for the treatment of children with ADHD. The emphasis has therefore moved to more intensive and ambitious multimodal treatment programs, which explicitly target multiple functions over extended periods of time, in the hope of influencing post-treatment adjustment and functioning (see, e.g., Kazdin, 1987, who argues for a "chronic disease" model of externalizing behavior patterns, requiring long-term treatment strategies). Indeed, combinations of intensive behavioral approaches and pharmacological treatments may be required for normalization. Given the clear impairment and negative course associated with ADHD in childhood, continued efforts to improve the benefits from behavioral and combination interventions and to enhance the access to high-quality care are highly desired.

From another perspective, however, it is essential that clinicians and investigators seek to develop other types of psychosocial intervention for the distressingly persistent and pervasive problems and impairments related to ADHD. Although behavioral approaches are the only validated nonpharmacological treatments for this disorder (Pelham et al., 1998; see also Rojas & Chan, 2005), we cannot be satisfied with the rates of success for established behavioral treatments. To encourage development of additional interventions, basic science on the underlying mechanisms of the disorder will need to be coordinated with clinical science in the form of state-of-the-art intervention trials. In these, outcome measures should be specifically tailored to each individual's particular target goals (see Abikoff, 2002). Whether newer, intensive strategies (e.g., for the crucial target of organizational skills) can produce meaningful benefits remains to be demonstrated, but the effort to develop and evaluate such interventions is clearly needed.

ACKNOWLEDGMENT

Work on this chapter was supported, in part, by National Institute of Mental Health Grants R01 MH45064 and N01 MH12009 (Stephen P. Hinshaw), R01 MH35779 (Rachel G. Klein), and U01 MH50453 (Howard B. Abikoff). Address correspondence to Stephen P. Hinshaw, Department of Psychology, Tolman Hall #1650, University of California, Berkeley, CA 94720–1650. e-mail: hinshaw@ berkeley.edu.

NOTES

1. The situation with respect to medication treatment is exemplified in the follow-up findings from the MTA Study. Here, the significant advantage of medication at the end of 14 months of active treatment had been halved by the 24-month follow-up and was not present at all by the 36-month follow-up (see MTA Cooperative Group, 2004a, 2004b, in press).

2. We note, for historical reasons, a Type 3 study involving tailored combinations of medication, family therapy, tutoring, marital therapy, and individual child therapy (decided upon by careful clinical appraisal) that was undertaken nearly three decades ago (Satterfield, Cantwell, & Satterfield, 1979). Because (a) random assignment of children and families to treatment combinations was not made, (b) a control group was not utilized, and (c) only a minority of families who began the intervention were available for follow-up assessments, the attribution of decreased delinquency in adolescence (several years after the termination of treatment) to the multimodality intervention may be unwarranted (Satterfield, Satterfield, & Schell, 1987). Nonetheless, this investigation spurred the field to consider multimodal treatments for ADHD.

3. We note that during social skills training, contingent rewards were awarded at 20-minute intervals and not continuously, as is often done with direct contingency management. Yet direct contingency management was only a small part of the behavioral intervention.

4. The clinical significance of this lower dosage is not immediately apparent, however.

REFERENCES

Abikoff, H. (1987). An evaluation of cognitive behavior therapy for hyperactive children. In B. B. Lahey & A. E. Kazdin (Eds.), *Advances in clinical child psychology* (Vol. 10, pp. 171–216). New York: Plenum Press.

Abikoff, H. (1991). Cognitive training in ADHD children: Less to it than meets the eye. *Journal of Learning Disabilities, 24,* 205–209.

Abikoff, H. (2002). Matching patients to treatments. In P. S. Jensen & J. R. Cooper (Eds.), *Diagnosis and treatment of attention-deficit hyperactivity disorder: State of the science, best practices* (pp. 15–1–15–14). Kingston, NJ: Civic Research Institute.

Abikoff, H., & Gittelman, R. (1984). Does behavior therapy normalize the classroom behavior of hyperactive children? *Archives of General Psychiatry, 41,* 449–454.

Abikoff, H., Hechtman, L., Klein, R. G., Gallagher, R., Fleiss, K., Etcovitch, J., et al. (2004). Social functioning in children with ADHD treated with long-term methylphenidate and multimodal psychosocial treatment. *Journal of the American Academy of Child and Adolescent Psychiatry, 43,* 820–829.

Abikoff, H., Hechtman, L., Klein, R. G., Weiss, G., Fleiss, K., Etcovitch, J., et al. (2004). Symptomatic improvement in children with ADHD treated with long-term methylphenidate and multimodal psychosocial treatment. *Journal of the American Academy of Child and Adolescent Psychiatry, 43,* 802–811.

Abikoff, H., & Klein, R. (1992). Attention-deficit hyperactivity and conduct disorder: Comorbidity and implications for treatment. *Journal of Consulting and Clinical Psychology, 60,* 881–892.

American Psychiatric Association. (2000). *Diagnostic and statistical manual of mental disorders* (4th ed., text revision). Washington, DC: Author.

Anastopoulos, A. D., Shelton, T., DuPaul, G. J., & Guevremont, D. C. (1993). Parent training for attention-deficit hyperactivity disorder: Its impact on parent functioning. *Journal of Abnormal Child Psychology, 21,* 581–596.

Anderson, C. A., Hinshaw, S. P., & Simmel, C. (1994). Mother-child interactions in ADHD and comparison boys: Relationships to overt and covert externalizing behavior. *Journal of Abnormal Child Psychology, 22,* 247–265.

Angold, A., Costello, E. J., & Erkanli, A. (1999). Comorbidity. *Journal of Child Psychology and Psychiatry, 40,* 57–87.

Antshel, K. M., & Remer, R. (2003). Social skills training in children with attention deficit hyperactivity disorder. *Journal of Clinical Child and Adolescent Psychology, 32,* 153–165.

Barkley, R. A. (1997a). *ADHD and the nature of self-control.* New York: Guilford Press.

Barkley, R. A. (1997b). *Defiant children: A clinician's manual for parent training and assessment* (2nd ed.). New York: Guilford Press.

Barkley, R. A. (2006). *Attention deficit hyperactivity disorder: A handbook for diagnosis and treatment* (3rd ed.). New York: Guilford Press.

Barkley, R. A., Fischer, M., Smallish, L., & Fletcher, K. (2002). The persistence of attention-deficit/hyperactivity disorder into young adulthood as a function of reporting source and definition of disorder. *Journal of Abnormal Psychology, 111,* 279–289.

Barkley, R. A., Guevremont, D. C., Anastopoulos, A. D., & Fletcher, K. E. (1992). A comparison of three family therapy programs for treating family conflicts in adolescents with attention-deficit hyperactivity disorder. *Journal of Consulting and Clinical Psychology, 60,* 450–462.

Barkley, R. A., Shelton, T. L., Crosswait C., Moorehouse, M., Fletcher, K., Barrett, S., et al. (2000). Multi-method psycho-educational intervention for preschool children with disruptive behavior: Preliminary results at post-treatment. *Journal of Child Psychology and Psychiatry, 41,* 319–332.

Breslau, N. (1995). Psychiatric sequelae of low birth weight. *Epidemiologic Reviews, 17,* 96–104.

Campbell, M., & Cueva, J. E. (1995). Psychopharmacology in child and adolescent psychiatry: A review of the past seven years. *Journal of the American Academy of Child and Adolescent Psychiatry, 34,* 1124–1132.

Carlson, E. A., Jacobvitz, D., & Sroufe, L. A. (1995). A developmental investigation of inattentiveness and hyperactivity. *Child Development, 66,* 37–54.

Carlson, C. L., Pelham, W. E., Milich, R., & Dixon, J. (1992). Single and combined effects of methylphenidate and behavior therapy on the classroom performance of children with attention-deficit hyperactivity disorder. *Journal of Abnormal Child Psychology, 20,* 213–232.

Conners, C. K., Epstein J. N., March, J. S., Angold, A., Wells, K. C., Klaric, J., et al. (2001). Multimodal treatment of ADHD in the MTA: An alternative outcome analysis. *Journal of the American Academy of Child and Adolescent Psychiatry, 40,* 169–167.

Douglas, V. I. (1983). Attention and cognitive problems. In M. Rutter (Ed.), *Developmental neuropsychiatry* (pp. 280–329). New York: Guilford Press.

Dubey, D. R., O'Leary, S. G., & Kaufman, K. F. (1983). Training parents of hyperactive children in child management: A comparative outcome study. *Journal of Abnormal Child Psychology, 11,* 229–246.

Eysenck, N. T., & Rachman, S. T. (1971). The application of learning theory to child psychiatry. In T. C. Howells (Ed.), *Modern perspectives in child psychiatry* (pp. 104–169). New York: Brunner/Mazel.

Fergusson, D. M., Horwood, L. J., & Lloyd, M. (1991). Confirmatory factor models of attention deficit and conduct disorder. *Journal of Child Psychology and Psychiatry, 32,* 257–274.

Firestone, P., Crowe, D., Goodman, J. T., & McGrath, P. (1986). Vicissitudes of follow-up studies. Differential effects of parent training and stimulant medication with hyperactives. *American Journal of Orthopsychiatry, 56,* 184–194.

Firestone, P., Kelly, M. J., Goodman, J. T., & Davey, J. (1981). Differential treatment effects of parent training and stimulant medication with hyperactives. *Journal of the American Academy of Child Psychiatry, 20,* 135–147.

Frankel, F., Myatt, R., Cantwell, D. P., & Feinberg, D. T. (1997). Parent-assisted transfer of children's social skills training: Effects on children with and without attention-deficit hyperactivity disorder. *Journal of the American Academy of Child and Adolescent Psychiatry, 36,* 1056–1064.

Gittelman, R., Abikoff, H., Pollack, E., Klein, D., Katz, S., & Mattes, J. (1980). A controlled trial of behavior modification and methylphenidate in hyperactive children. In C. K. Whalen & B. Henker (Eds.), *Hyperactive children: The social ecology of identification and treatment* (pp. 221–243). New York: Academic Press.

Greenhill, L. L., & Osman, B. B. (Eds.). (2000). *Ritalin: Theory and practice* (2nd ed.). Larchmont, NY: Mary Ann Liebert.

Hechtman, L., Abikoff, H., Klein, R. G., Greenfield, B., Etcovitch, J., Cousins, L., et al. (2004). Children with ADHD treated with long-term methylphenidate and multimodal psychosocial treatment: Impact on parental practices. *Journal of the American Academy of Child and Adolescent Psychiatry, 43,* 830–838.

Hechtman, L., Abikoff, H., Klein, R. G., Weiss, G., Respitz, C., Kouri, J., et al. (2004). Academic achievement and emotional status of children with ADHD treated with long-term methylphenidate and multimodal psychosocial treatment. *Journal of the American Academy of Child and Adolescent Psychiatry, 43,* 812–819.

Hinshaw, S. P. (1987). On the distinction between attentional deficits/hyperactivity and conduct problems/aggression in child psychopathology. *Psychological Bulletin, 101,* 443–463.

Hinshaw, S. P. (1994). *Attention deficits and hyperactivity in children.* Thousand Oaks, CA: Sage.

Hinshaw, S. P. (2000). Attention-deficit hyperactivity disorder: The search for viable treatments. In P. C. Kendall (Ed.), *Child and adolescent therapy: Cognitive-behavioral procedures* (2nd ed., pp. 88–128). New York: Guilford Press.

Hinshaw, S. P. (2002). Is ADHD an impairing condition in childhood and adolescence? In P. S. Jensen & J. R. Cooper (Eds.), *Diagnosis and treatment of attention-deficit hyperactivity disorder: State of the science, best practices* (pp. 5–21). Kingston, NJ: Civic Research Institute.

Hinshaw, S. P. (2006). Attention-deficit hyperactivity disorder. In P. C. Kendall (Ed.), *Child and adolescent therapy: Cognitive-behavioral procedures* (3rd ed., pp. 46–68). New York: Guilford Press.

Hinshaw, S. P., Henker, B., & Whalen, C. K. (1984). Cognitive-behavioral and pharmacologic interventions for hyperactive boys: Comparative and combined effects. *Journal of Consulting and Clinical Psychology, 52,* 739–749.

Hinshaw, S. P., Klein, R., & Abikoff, H. (2002). Childhood attention-deficit hyperactivity disorder: Nonpharmacologic treatments and their combination with medication. In P. E. Nathan & J. Gorman (Eds.), *A guide to treatments that work* (2nd ed., pp. 3–23). New York: Oxford University Press.

Hinshaw, S. P., & Lee, S. S. (2000). Ritalin effects on aggression and antisocial behavior. In L. L. Greenhill & B. B. Osman (Eds.), *Ritalin: Theory and practice* (2nd ed., pp. 237–251). Larchmont, NY: Liebert.

Hinshaw, S. P., & Nigg, J. T. (1999). Behavior rating scales in the assessment of disruptive behavior disorders in childhood. In D. Shaffer, C. P. Lucas, & J. Richters (Eds.), *Diagnostic assessment in child and adolescent psychopathology* (pp. 91–126). New York: Guilford Press.

Hinshaw, S. P., Owens, E. B., Wells, K.C., Kraemer, H. C., Abikoff, H. B., Arnold, L. E., et al. (2000). Family processes and treatment outcome in the MTA: Negative/ineffective parenting practices in relation to multimodal treatment. *Journal of Abnormal Child Psychology, 28,* 555–568.

Horn, W. F., Ialongo, N., Greenberg, G., Packard, T., & Smith-Winberry, C. (1990). Additive effects of behavioral parent training and self-control therapy with attention deficit hyperactivity disordered children. *Journal of Clinical Child Psychology, 19,* 98–110.

Horn, W. F., Ialongo, N. S., Pascoe, J. M., Greenberg, G. A., Packard, T., Lopez, M., et al. (1991). Additive effects of psychostimulants, parent training, and self-control therapy with ADHD children. *Journal of the American Academy of Child and Adolescent Psychiatry, 30,* 233–240.

Horn, W. F., Ialongo, N., Popvich, S., & Perdatto, D. (1987). Behavioral parent training and cognitive-behavioral self-control therapy with ADD-H children: Comparative and combined effects. *Journal of Clinical Child Psychology, 16,* 57–68.

Hoza, B., Gerdes, A. C., Mrug, S., Hinshaw, S. P., Bukowski, W. M., Gold, J. A., et al. (2005). Peer-assessed outcomes in the Multimodal Treatment Study of Children with Attention Deficit Hyperactivity Disorder. *Journal of Clinical Child and Adolescent Psychology, 34,* 74–86.

Ialongo, N. S., Horn, W. F., Pascoe, J. M., Greenberg, G., Packard, T., Lopez, M., et al. (1993). The effects of a multimodal intervention with attention-deficit hyperactivity disorder children: A 9-month follow-up. *Journal of the American Academy of Child and Adolescent Psychiatry, 32,* 182–189.

Jensen, P. S., Garcia, J. A., Glied, S., Crowe, M., Schlander, M., Hinshaw, S. P., et al. (2005). Cost-effectiveness of ADHD treatments: Findings from the Multimodal Treatment Study of Children with ADHD. *American Journal of Psychiatry, 162,* 1628–1636.

Jensen, P. S., Hinshaw, S. P., Kraemer, H. C., Lenora, N., Abikoff, H. B., Conners, C. K., et al. (2001). ADHD comorbidity findings from the MTA Study: Comparing comorbid subgroups. *Journal of the American Academy of Child and Adolescent Psychiatry, 40,* 147–158.

Jensen, P. S., Martin, D., & Cantwell, D. P. (1997). Comoribidity in ADHD: Implications for research, practice, and *DSM-V. Journal of the American Academy of Child and Adolescent Psychiatry, 36,* 1065–1079.

Johnston, C., & Mash, E. J. (2001). Families of children with attention-deficit/hyperactivity disorder: Review and recommendations for future research. *Clinical Child and Family Psychology Review, 4,* 183–207.

Kazdin, A. E. (1987). Treatment of antisocial behavior in children: Current status and future directions. *Psychological Bulletin, 102,* 187–203.

Kendall, P. C., & Braswell, L. (1982). Cognitive-behavioral self-control therapy for children: A components analysis. *Journal of Consulting and Clinical Psychology, 50,* 672–689.

Klein, R. G., & Abikoff, H. (1997). Behavior therapy and methylphenidate in the treatment of children with ADHD. *Journal of Attention Disorders, 2,* 89–114.

Klein, R. G., Abikoff, H., Hechtman, L., & Weiss, G. (2004). Design and rationale of controlled study of long-term methylphenidate and multimodal psychosocial treatment in children with ADHD. *Journal of the American Academy of Child and Adolescent Psychiatry, 43,* 792–801.

Klein, R. G., Abikoff, H., Klass, E., Ganeles, D., Seese, L. M., & Pollack, S. (1997). Clinical efficacy of methylphenidate in conduct disorder with and without attention deficit hyperactivity disorder. *Archives of General Psychiatry, 54,* 1073–1080.

Klein, R. G., & Wender, P. (1995). The role of methylphenidate in psychiatry. *Archives of General Psychiatry, 52,* 429–433.

Kolko, D. J., Bukstein, O. G., & Barron, J. (1999). Methylphenidate and behavior modification in children with ADHD and comorbid ODD or CD: Main and incremental effects across settings. *Journal of the American Academy of Child and Adolescent Psychiatry, 38,* 578–586.

Laufer, M. W., & Denhoff, E. (1957). Hyperkinetic behavior syndrome in children. *Journal of Pediatrics, 50,* 463–473.

Levy, F., Hay, D. A., McStephen, M., Wood, C., & Waldman, I. (1997). Attention-deficit hyperactivity disorder: A category or a continuum? Genetic analysis of a large-scale twin study. *Journal of the American Academy of Child and Adolescent Psychiatry, 36,* 737–744.

Mannuzza, S., & Klein, R. G. (1999). Adolescent and adult outcomes of attention-deficit/hyperactivity disorder. In H. C. Quay & A. E. Hogan (Eds.), *Handbook of disruptive behavior disorders* (pp. 279–294). New York: Kluwer Academic.

Mash, E. J., & Dalby, T. (1979). Behavioral interventions for hyperactivity. In R. Trites (Ed.), *Hyperactivity: Etiology, measurement, and treatment* (pp. 161–216). Baltimore: University Park Press.

Milich, R., Balentine, A. C., & Lynam, D. R. (2001). ADHD combined type and ADHD predominantly inattentive type are distinct and unrelated disorders. *Clinical Psychology: Science and Practice, 8,* 463–488.

MTA Cooperative Group. (1999a). Fourteen-month randomized clinical trial of treatment strategies for attention-deficit hyperactivity disorder. *Archives of General Psychiatry, 56,* 1073–1086.

MTA Cooperative Group. (1999b). Moderators and mediators of treatment response in children with attention-deficit/hyperactivity disorder: The MTA Study. *Archives of General Psychiatry, 56,* 1088–1096.

MTA Cooperative Group. (2004a). National Institute of Mental Health Multimodal Treatment Study of ADHD follow-up: Changes in effectiveness of and growth after the end of treatment. *Pediatrics, 113,* 762–770.

MTA Cooperative Group. (2004b). National Institute of Mental Health Multimodal Treatment Study of ADHD follow-up: 24-month outcomes of treatment strategies for attention-deficit hyperactivity disorder. *Pediatrics, 113,* 754–761.

MTA Cooperative Group. (in press). Three-year follow-up of the NIMH MTA Study. *Journal of the American Academy of Child and Adolescent Psychiatry.*

Nigg, J. T. (2001). Is ADHD a disinhibitory disorder? *Psychological Bulletin, 127,* 571–598.

Nigg, J. (2006). *ADHD: What science can tell us about mechanisms and causes.* New York: Guilford Press.

O'Leary, K. D., Pelham, W. E., Rosenbaum, A., & Price, G. H. (1976). Behavioral treatment of hyperkinetic children. *Clinical Pediatrics, 15,* 510–515.

Owens, E. B., Hinshaw, S. P., Kraemer, H. C., Arnold, L. E., Abikoff, H. B., Cantwell, D. P., et al. (2003). Which treatment for whom for ADHD? Moderators of treatment response in the MTA. *Journal of Consulting and Clinical Psychology, 71,* 540–552.

Patterson, G. R. (1965). An application of conditioning techniques to the control of a hyperactive child. In L. P. Ullmann & L. Krasner (Eds.), *Case studies in behavior modification* (pp. 370–375). New York: Holt, Rinehart and Winston.

Patterson, G. R., Reid, J. B., & Dishion, T. J. (1992). *Antisocial boys.* Eugene, OR: Castalia.

Pelham, W. E., Carlson, C., Sams, S. E., Dixon, M. J., & Hoza, B. (1993). Separate and combined effects of methylphenidate and behavior modification on boys with attention-deficit hyperactivity disorder in the classroom. *Journal of Consulting and Clinical Psychology, 61,* 506–515.

Pelham, W. E., Fabiano, G. A., Gnagy, E. M., Greiner, A. R., & Hoza, B. (2005). The role of summer treatment programs in the context of comprehensive treatment for attention-deficit/hyperactivity disorder. In E. D. Hibbs & P. S. Jensen (Eds.), *Psychosocial treatments for children and adolescents: Empirically based strategies for clinical practice* (pp. 377–409). Washington, DC: American Psychological Association.

Pelham, W. E., Gnagy, E. M., Greiner, A., Hoza, B., Hinshaw, S. P., Swanson, J. M., et al. (2000). Behavioral versus behavioral and pharmacological treatment in ADHD children attending a summer treatment program. *Journal of Abnormal Child Psychology, 28,* 507–525.

Pelham, W. E., & Hinshaw, S. P. (1992). Behavioral intervention for attention-deficit hyperactivity disorder. In S. M. Turner, K. S. Calhoun, & H. E. Adams (Eds.), *Handbook of clinical behavior therapy* (2nd ed., pp. 259–283). New York: Wiley.

Pelham, W. E., Schnedler, R. W., Bender, M., Nilsson, D., Miller, J., Budrow, M., et al. (1988). The combination of behavior therapy and methylphenidate in the treatment of attention deficit disorder: A

therapy outcome study. In L. M. Bloomingdale (Ed.), *Attention deficit disorder* (Vol. 3, pp. 29–48). Oxford, England: Pergamon.

Pelham, W. E., Schnedler, R. W., Bologna, N. C., & Contreras, J. A. (1980). Behavioral and stimulant treatment of hyperactivity children: A therapy study with methylphenidate probes in a within-subject design. *Journal of Applied Behavior Analysis, 13,* 221–236.

Pelham, W. E., Wheeler, T., & Chronis, A. (1998). Empirically supported psychosocial treatments for attention deficit hyperactivity disorder. *Journal of Clinical Child Psychology, 27,* 190–205.

Pfiffner, L., & McBurnett, K. (1997). Social skills training with parent generalization: Treatment effects for children with attention deficit disorder. *Journal of Consulting and Clinical Psychology, 65,* 749–757.

Pfiffner, L. J., & O'Leary, S. G. (1993). School-based psychological treatments. In J. L. Matson (Ed.), *Handbook of hyperactivity in children* (pp. 234–255). Boston: Allyn and Bacon.

Pfiffner, L. J., Rosen, L. A., & O'Leary, S. G. (1985). The efficacy of an all-positive approach to classroom management. *Journal of Applied Behavior Analysis, 18,* 257–261.

Pisterman, S., McGrath, P., Firestone, P., Goodman, J. T., Webster, I., & Mallory, R. (1989). Outcome of parent-mediated treatment of preschoolers with attention deficit disorder with hyperactivity. *Journal of Consulting and Clinical Psychology, 57,* 628–635.

Pisterman, S., Firestone, P., McGrath, P., Goodman, J., Webster, I., Mallory, R., et al. (1992). The role of parent training in treatment of preschoolers with ADDH. *American Journal of Orthopsychiatry, 62,* 397–408.

Pollard, S., Ward, E., & Barkley, R. A. (1983). The effects of parent training and Ritalin on the parent-child interactions of hyperactive boys. *Child and Family Behavior Therapy, 5,* 51–69.

Rapport, M. D., Murphy, H. A., & Bailey, J. S. (1982). Ritalin vs. response cost in the control of hyperactive children: A within-subject comparison. *Journal of Applied Behavior Analysis, 15,* 205–216.

Robinson, P. W., Newby, T. J., & Ganzell, S. L. (1981). A token system for a class of underachieving hyperactive children. *Journal of Applied Behavior Analysis, 14,* 307–315.

Rojas, N. L., & Chan, E. (2005). Old and new controversies in the alternative treatment of attention-deficit hyperactivity disorder. *Mental Retardation and Developmental Disabilities Research Reviews, 11,* 116–130.

Rosen, L. A., O'Leary, S. G., Joyce, S. A., Conway, G., & Pfiffner, L. J. (1984). The importance of prudent negative consequences for maintaining the appropriate behavior of hyperactive students. *Journal of Abnormal Child Psychology, 12,* 581–604.

Sagvolden, T., Aase, H., Johansen, E. B., & Russell, V. A. (2005). A dynamic developmental theory of attention-deficit/hyperactivity disorder predominantly hyperactive/impulsive and combined subtypes. *Behavioral and Brain Sciences, 28,* 397–468.

Satterfield, J. H., Cantwell, D. P., & Satterfield, B. T. (1979). Multimodality treatment: A one-year follow-up of 84 hyperactive boys. *Archives of General Psychiatry, 36,* 965–974.

Satterfield, J. H., Satterfield, B. T., & Schell, A. M. (1987). Therapeutic interventions to prevent delinquency in hyperactive boys. *Journal of the American Academy of Child and Adolescent Psychiatry, 26,* 56–64.

Schachar, R. (1986). Hyperkinetic syndrome: Historical development of the concept. In E. A. Taylor (Ed.), *The overactive child* (pp. 19–40). London: MacKeith.

Schachar, R., Tannock, R., Marriott, M., & Logan, G. (1995). Deficient inhibitory control in attention deficit hyperactivity disorder. *Journal of Abnormal Child Psychology, 23,* 411–437.

Shelton, T. L., Barkley, R. A., Crosswait, C., Moorehouse, M., Fletcher, K., Barrett, S., et al. (2000). Multimethod psychoeducational intervention for preschool children with disruptive behavior: Two-year post-treatment follow-up. *Journal of Abnormal Child Psychology, 28,* 253–266.

Slomkowski, C., Klein, R. G., & Mannuzza, S. (1995). Is self-esteem an important outcome in hyperactive children? *Journal of Abnormal Child Psychology, 23,* 303–315.

Sonuga-Barke, E. J. S., Daley, D., Thompson, M., Laver-Bradbury, C., & Weeks, A. (2001). Parent-based therapies for preschool attention-deficit/hyperactivity disorder: A randomized controlled trial with a community sample. *Journal of the American Academy of Child and Adolescent Psychiatry, 40,* 402–408.

Sonuga-Barke, E. J. S., Daley, D., & Thompson, M. (2002). Does maternal ADHD reduce the effectiveness of parent training for preschool children's ADHD? *Journal of the American Academy of Child and Adolescent Psychiatry, 41,* 696–702.

Sonuga-Barke, E. J. S., Thompson, M., Daley, D., & Laver-Bradbury, C. (in press). Parent training for pre-school attention-deficit/hyperactivity disorder:

Is it effective as part of routine primary care? *British Journal of Clinical Psychology.*

Sprague, R. L. (1983). Behavior modification and educational techniques. In M. Rutter (Ed.), *Developmental neuropsychiatry* (pp. 404–421). New York: Guilford Press.

Sprague, R. L., & Werry, J. S. (1971). Methodology of psychopharmacological studies with the retarded. In N. R. Ellis (Ed.), *International review of research in mental retardation* (Vol. 5, pp. 147–219). New York: Academic Press.

Sprich-Buckminster, S., Biederman, J., Milberger, S., Faraone, S. V., & Lehman, B. K. (1993). Are perinatal complications relevant to the manifestation of ADD? Issues of comorbidity and familiality. *Journal of the American Academy of Child and Adolescent Psychiatry, 32,* 1032–1037.

Strayhorn, J. M., & Weidman, C. S. (1989). Reduction of attention deficit and internalizing symptoms in preschoolers through parent-child interaction training. *Journal of the American Academy of Child and Adolescent Psychiatry, 28,* 888–896.

Swanson, J. M., Kraemer, H. C., Hinshaw, S. P., Arnold, L. E., Conners, C. K., Abikoff, H. B., et al. (2001). Clinical relevance of the primary findings of the MTA: Success rates based on severity of ADHD and ODD symptoms at the end of treatment. *Journal of the American Academy of Child and Adolescent Psychiatry, 40,* 168–179.

Swanson, J. M., McBurnett, K., Christian, D. L., & Wigal, T. (1995). Stimulant medications and the treatment of children with ADHD. In T. H. Ollendick & R. J. Prinz (Eds.), *Advances in clinical child psychology* (Vol. 17, pp. 265–322). New York: Plenum Press.

Tannock, R. (1998). Attention deficit hyperactivity disorder: Advances in cognitive, neurobiological, and genetic research. *Journal of Child Psychology and Psychiatry, 39,* 65–99.

Tutty, S., Gephart, H., & Wurzbacher, K. (2003). Enhancing behavior and social skill functioning in children newly diagnosed with attention-deficit hyperactivity disorder in a pediatric setting. *Journal of Developmental and Behavioral Pediatrics, 24,* 51–57.

Weiss, G., & Hechtman, L. T. (1993). *Hyperactive children grown up* (2nd ed.). New York: Guilford Press.

Wells, K. C., Chi, T., Hinshaw, S. P., Epstein, J. N., Pfiffner, L., Nebel-Schwalm, M., et al. (2006). Treatment related changes in objectively measured parenting behaviors in the Multimodal Treatment Study of Children with ADHD. *Journal of Consulting and Clinical Psychology, 74,* 649–657.

Wells, K. C., Pelham, W. E., Kotkin, R. A., Hoza, B., Abikoff, H., Abramowitz, A., et al. (2000). Psychosocial treatment strategies in the MTA Study: Rationale, methods, and critical issues in design and implementation. *Journal of Abnormal Child Psychology, 28,* 483–505.

Whalen, C. K., Henker, B., Buhrmester, D., Hinshaw, S. P., Huber, A., & Laski, K. (1989). Does stimulant medication improve the peer status of hyperactive children? *Journal of Consulting and Clinical Psychology, 57,* 545–549.

2

Pharmacological Treatments for Attention-Deficit/ Hyperactivity Disorder

Natalya Paykina

Laurence L. Greenhill

Revised by Jack M. Gorman

More than 225 placebo-controlled Type 1 investigations demonstrate that psychostimulants — a group of ethylamines including methylphenidate and amphetamine — are highly effective in reducing core symptoms of childhood attention-deficit/hyperactivity disorder (ADHD) in pre-schoolers, school-age children, adolescents, and adults. Approximately 70% of patients respond to these medications in double-blind trials compared with 13% assigned to placebo. Short-term efficacy is more pronounced for behavioral rather than cognitive and learning abnormalities associated with ADHD. The stimulant treatment evidence base has been supplemented by two large multisite randomized controlled trials (RCTs) — the Multimodal Treatment Study of ADHD (MTA Study) and the Preschool ADHD Treatment Study (PATS) — that further support the short-term efficacy in young children. This study, plus the 1998 NIH Consensus Development Conference on ADHD, and the publication of the McMaster Evidence Based Review of ADHD Treatments (Jahad et al., 1999) emphasized the large evidence base supporting the efficacy of stimulant treatments. These medications are now available in long-duration preparations that allow for once-daily oral dosing, and they may even be sprinkled on food to accommodate children who cannot swallow pills. RCTs conducted more recently than 1998 continue to report a few key adverse events associated with stimulants — insomnia, decreased appetite, stomachache, and headache — but have not supported rarer and unexpected problems, such as visual hallucinations, cardiovascular accidents, or sudden unexpected death, reported anecdotally in the Food and Drug Administration's Adverse Event Report System (AERS) MedWatch. Although these ADHD medications have been shown to retain their efficacy for as long as 14 months, concern remains that the long-term academic and social benefits have not yet been adequately assessed. Other nonstimulant agents for which there is limited evidence of efficacy include atomoxetine, modafinil, the tricyclics, bupropion, clonidine, and venlafaxine.

Attention-deficit/hyperactivity disorder (ADHD) is a major public health problem in the United States. It is responsible for 30 to 50% of referrals to mental health services for children. The prevalence of ADHD in school-age children may be gleaned from comprehensive reviews (Bird et al., 1988; Bauermeister, Canino, & Bird, 1994; Szatmari, 1992; Visser & Lesesne, 2005; Fischer et al., 2002) and epidemiological studies conducted in Australia (Connell, Irvine, & Rodney, 1982); Norway (Vikan, 1985); the Netherlands (Verhulst, Eussen, & Berden, 1992); Ontario, Canada (Szatmari et al., 1989); Mannheim, Germany (Esser, Schmidt, & Woerner, 1996); New Zealand (Anderson, Williams, McGee, & Silva, 1987);

Pittsburgh, Pennsylvania (Costello, 1989); Puerto Rico (Bird et al., 1988); East London (Taylor, Sandberg, Thorley, & Rutter, 1991); and the Great Smoky Mountain area of rural North Carolina. Rates for ADHD range between 2.0 and 6.3% (Szatmari et al., 1989), whereas ADD (attention deficit disorder) shows a wider range, between 2.2 and 12.6% (Velez, Johnson, & Cohen, 1989). Using families identified in the National Comorbity Study, (Kessler et al., 2006) estimated that prevalence of ADHD in adults, aged 18 to 44, was 4.4% in the United States.

Fortunately, ADHD responds to both psychosocial and psychopharmacological treatments (Richters et al., 1995). Between 2 and 2.5% of all school-age children in North America receive some pharmacological intervention for hyperactivity (Bosco & Robin, 1980), more than 90% being treated with the psychostimulant methylphenidate (MPH; Greenhill, 1995; Wilens & Biederman, 1992). If all ADHD medication treatments are included, approximately 4 million individuals—2.5 million under 18 years of age and 1.5 million over 18—in the United States take pills every day to reduce the ADHD symptoms. Estimates (Swanson, Lerner, & Williams, 1995) suggest that, from 1990 to 1993, the number of outpatient visits for ADHD increased from 1.6 to 4.2 million per year, and the amount of MPH manufactured increased from 1,784 to 5,110 kg per year.

Psychostimulants can reduce the core ADHD symptoms within 30 minutes of administration, when the proper dose is given to a responder. This rapid and robust response explains, to some degree, why published drug research on childhood ADHD in the past four decades has focused mainly on stimulants (Vitiello & Jensen, 1995). Rather than explore new compounds, academic researchers have relied on either methylphenidate or the amphetamines to study response patterns, adverse events, the determination of "normalization" during drug treatment, and patient characteristics among nonresponders.

This chapter updates previous reviews of the ADHD medication treatments that work. As with other chapters in this volume, the study classification system based on published evidence will be used to guide the reader, as shown below. Unlike in other chapters, a thorough description of the *Diagnostic and Statistical Manual of Mental Disorder–IV–TR* (American Psychiatric Association, 2000) syndrome of ADHD, its principal diagnostic criteria, and information on incidence, prevalence, and epidemiology will not be given because they are well covered elsewhere (see Hinshaw, Klein, & Abikoff, this volume). Instead, the chapter will include (a) a brief historical perspective on ADHD drug treatment studies, using Type 5 reviews to highlight conceptual notions driving drug research; (b) an updated description of current psychopharmacological treatments of choice, supported by recently published Type 1 randomized controlled trials (RCTs) on new long-duration stimulant formulations; and (c) a perspective on controversies surrounding the safety of ADHD psychopharmacological interventions.

HISTORICAL PERSPECTIVE: PHARMACOLOGICAL INTERVENTIONS FOR ADHD

In 1937, Bradley, looking for a new treatment for headaches, serendipitously observed that disturbed children and adolescents responded to benzedrine, a racemic form of amphetamine. This treatment had a dramatic calming effect, while simultaneously producing an increase in academic productivity and a "zest for work." Bradley published other Type 6 studies reporting the improvement of children during amphetamine treatment (Bradley, 1941; Bradley & Bowen, 1941). The earliest investigations of these drugs suggested that psychostimulants operated by stabilizing cortical circuits as shown by their ability to increase the seizure threshold (Laufer, Denhoff, & Solomon, 1957). These medications also decreased oppositional behavior in boys with conduct disorder attending a residential school (Eisenberg et al., 1961) and reliably reduced the target symptoms of ADHD as measured by parents and teachers (Conners, Eisenberg, & Barcai, 1967). However, these early protocols lacked uniform diagnostic criteria, reliability measures, and multiple observers, so they must be judged Type 2 studies. Since then, more carefully designed, placebo-controlled studies have demonstrated that both dextroamphetamine (DEX) and MPH produce statistically significant and clinically meaningful reductions in ADHD symptoms within 1 hour of taking an effective dose. Starting in 1977 (Barkley, 1977), a series of Type 5 literature reviews summarized these studies. Wilens and Biederman's (1992) MEDLINE search retrieved more than 990 psychostimulant treatment studies published between 1982 and 1991. Further verification appeared in a Type 4 meta-analysis (Swanson, 1993) that analyzed the reviews, concluding that the most marked effects of stimulants can be observed on teacher measures of classroom behavior (with effect sizes ranging from 0.63 to 0.85) and that lesser effect sizes (in the range of 0.19 to 0.47) can be identified on measures of intelligence or academic achievement. The effect sizes observed on teacher ratings would satisfy rigorous Phase III, premarketing, investigational new drug applications to the Food and Drug Administration (FDA). A small sample of frequently-cited reviews appears in Table 2.1.

The psychostimulants MPH and DEX produced significant reductions in task-irrelevant activity and classroom disturbance (Barkley, 1977; Jacobvitz, Sroufe, Stewart, & Leffert, 1990), with robust responses occurring in between 65 and 75% of the 4,777 ADHD subjects treated (Wilens & Biederman, 1992). This review included 4 preschool, 96 school-age, 6 adolescent, and 6 adult controlled studies. More recent

Type 4 meta-analyses verified these findings and included "A Review of Therapies for Attention Deficit Hyperactivity Disorder" by the Canadian Coordinating Office for Health Technology Assessment (Pelham, Hoffman, Lock, & SUNY CONCERTA Study Group, 2000a), "The Treatment of Attention Deficit Hyperactivity Disorder: An Evidence Report," contracted to the McMaster University Evidence-Based Practice Center by the Agency for Health Care Research and Quality (1998), and others (Campbell & Ewing, 1990; Leech, Richardson, Goldschmidt, & Day, 1999).

The large Type 5 reviews touch on diverse types of responses to stimulants, including the best methods of determining the optimal stimulant dose to reduce ADHD behaviors (Barkley, 1977, 1982; DuPaul & Barkley, 1990), the mechanisms of action (Solanto, 1984), whether stimulant response is diagnostically specific (R. Gittelman, 1980), and the ability of these medications to enhance other therapies

TABLE 2.1 Selected Reviews of Psychostimulant Treatments: School-Age Children

Study (Year)	Type	Drugs	No. Studies	Subjects	Response Rate %	Placebo Response %	References
Barkley (1977)	3	DEX	15	915	74	29	159
		MPH	14	866	77	23	
		PEM	2	105	73	27	
		PL	8	417	39	—	
Gittelman[a] (1987)	3	MPH	25	777	N/A	N/A	82
		PEM	1	20	N/A	N/A	
Hinshaw (1991)	3	MPH	10	187	Situation[b]	N/A	82
Jacobvitz (1990)	4	MPH	136	N/A	N/A	N/A	175
Wilens & Biederman (1992)	3	MPH	37	1,113	73	222	121
Schachar (1993)	4	MPH	18	531	Resp.	26 attrition	88
Greenhill (1995)	3	MPH	15	236	70	20	229
		SR	7	181	75	20	
		DEX	2	2	High	Low	
		PEM	1	22	75	20	
Spencer (1996)	3	MPH	133	N/A	70	N/A	202
		DEX	22	N/A			
		PEM	6	N/A			
Jadad (1999) (78 studies)	3	MPH	56	N/A	N/A	N/A	116
		SR	N/A				
		DEX	18				
		PEM	5				

Resp. = Only responders included in Schachar et al.'s examination of long-term stimulant treatment. [a] = author of both reviews is Rachel Klein, Ph.D. [b] = Hinshaw's review focuses on aggression and reports different rates depending on age and setting. N/A = Information not given in the review.

Based on Wilens et al., 1992.

(K. Gittelman, 1987). In addition, dosing methods, paradoxical stimulant effects, and whether stimulants improve academic performance (DuPaul & Barkley, 1990; Jacobvitz et al., 1990) are addressed.

Dosing methods and dose-response issues were considered in the seminal paper by Sprague and Sleator (1977), which reported dissociation of cognitive and behavioral MPH responses in ADHD children. Using weight-adjusted doses, they found that children responded optimally to a memory task at a low dose (0.3 mg/kg) but required higher doses (1.0 mg/kg) to attain optimal behavioral control in the classroom. This paper established the customary weight-adjusted MPH dosing standard that would permeate the ADHD drug-treatment literature until the present and also raised the question whether MPH doses optimized for behavior might not be best for learning.

Reviews of pre-1990 drug studies (Jacobvitz et al., 1990; Wilens & Biederman, 1992) concluded that there was no diagnostically specific positive response to stimulants for ADHD children. No differences in response were found between stimulant-treated ADHD children, stimulant-treated normal children, or clinically referred non-ADHD children (Rapoport et al., 1980). Also rejected was the notion that ADHD children show a "paradoxical" slowdown response to stimulants. Rather, the literature shows a decrease in aimless activity, an increase in attention, and an elevation in heart rate and blood pressure.

These reviews also grappled with the question of whether stimulants, so successful in short-term trials, lead to long-term improvements. ADHD follow-up studies (Barkley, Fischer, Edelbrock, & Smallish, 1990; Mannuzza, Klein, Bessler, Malloy, & LaPadula, 1993; Weiss & Hechtman, 1993) have demonstrated that ADHD core symptoms continue into late adolescence and even into adult life. No stimulant benefit has been shown to persist when children are treated over the years, as indicated in the 2-year posttreatment follow-up reports of the National Institute of Mental Health (NIMH) MTA Study (Jensen, Arnold, Severe, Vitiello, & Hoagwood, 2004). Though ADHD symptom reduction was greatest in the two stimulant-treated groups at the end of the 14-month treatment, all four groups had equal but limited benefit at 24 and 36 months after randomization. Although evidence for short-term gains in arithmetic performance exists (Pelham, Bender, Caddell, Booth, & Moorer, 1985), other evidence (Charles, Schain, & Guthrie, 1979) points to a lack of differences in long-term academic achievement between treated and untreated ADHD children.

Despite the breadth and depth of the stimulant treatment literature showing robust evidence of a powerful "treatment that works," most long-term studies continue to present stiff challenges. Randomization cannot be maintained over years, so that drift and loss of control over selection biases are the case with long-term follow-up programs. Observations lasting years lose random assignment, fail to maintain checks on treatment adherence, and experience variable attrition rates. Studies continue to use global improvement rather than objective measures of cognitive skills to optimize individual medication doses. No mention is made of whether the time of dosing is synchronized. The majority of drug studies covered by reviews in Table 2.1 lasted 6 weeks or less, which is too brief to generalize to typical medication treatments, which average 3 years. Since no common definition of a categorical treatment responder has been established it has been difficult to interpret meta-analytic research looking across studies for identical response patterns in children.

LARGE RANDOMIZED CONTROLLED TRIALS OF STIMULANT MEDICATION

Generalizability and statistical power were limited in earlier ADHD treatment studies because they were conducted at one site, often with a clinical population with local characteristics. A new era in ADHD treatment studies was ushered in during the early 1990s when clinical trial science was applied to the ADHD field. First the NIMH, and then the pharmaceutical industry, began to employ multisite clinical trial designs to determine the safety and efficacy of stimulants. This allowed investigators to recruit subjects from several performance sites to obtain the necessary sample size needed to make estimates of the efficacy of the drug. Duration of stimulant drug exposure became a key design feature in these large multisite clinical trials, because ADHD is a chronic disorder lasting many years constituting maintenance treatment as the main component of care. However, only 22 published stimulant studies lasted longer than 3 weeks (Schachar & Tannock, 1993). The few long-duration stimulant studies published before the 1990s had been constrained by their retrospective methods, lack of standard outcome measures, restrictive inclusion criteria that rejected patients with comorbid disorders, irregular prescribing patterns (Sherman, 1991), and lack of compliance measures (Richters et al., 1995).

The MTA Study was designed to address most of the shortcomings of the pre-1990 ADHD treatment trials. It established a standard in size, diagnostic rigor, quality control, use of standardized measures, parallel design, and randomization that was followed by the large pharmaceutical stimulant trials taking place between 1998 and 2005. The MTA Study did this by recruiting almost 600 children with ADHD from seven performance sites in the United States and Canada using uniform diagnostic criteria, randomized these subjects to different treatments, and then maintained them for 14 months on those treatments employing intent-to-treat methods not previously used for this population. The study goal was to compare the relative effectiveness of four randomly assigned 14-month treatments: algorithmic medication management (MedMgt), behavioral treatment (Beh), combination (Comb), and community comparison group (CC) receiving treatment as usual (Arnold et al., 1997). The study questions included the following: (a) Do Beh and MedMgt treatments result in comparable levels of improvement over time? (b) Do participants assigned to Comb show greater improvement over time than those assigned to either MedMgt or to Beh? (c) Do participants assigned to any of the three MTA intensive treatments show greater improvement over time than those assigned to treatment as usual in the community (CC)? Assessment points for measured outcomes were evaluated in multiple domains before, during, and at the end of treatment (with Comb and MedMgt subjects on medication at time of assessment).

Children randomized to medication management alone (MedMgt, $N = 144$) or to combined treatment (Comb, $N = 145$) began treatment with a 28-day, double-blind, placebo-controlled titration to identify each child's optimal MPH dose. Due to its 3- to 4-hour duration of action, immediate-release methylphenidate (IR-MPH) and placebo were administered three times daily (Greenhill et al., 1996; Greenhill, Perel, et al., 2001). Medication conditions were switched daily to reduce error variance. Parents and teachers rated ADHD symptoms and impairment daily. During titration, a repeated-measures ANOVA revealed a main effect of MPH/placebo dose with greater effects on teacher's ratings ($F(3) = 100.6$, $N = 223$, $p = .0001$; effect sizes 0.8 to 1.3) than on parent's ratings ($F(3) = 55.61$, $N = 253$, $p = .00001$; effect sizes 0.4 to 0.6). Dose did not interact with between-subjects factors (period, dose order, comorbid diagnosis, site or treatment group). Drug-related adverse events were reported more often by parents than by teachers, who rated irritability highest on placebo. The distribution of the best MPH starting doses determined during titration (10 to 50 mg/day), response rate (77%), and adverse event profile across six sites and multiple subgroups suggest that MPH titration in office practice should explore MPH's full dosage range in 7- to 10-year-old children over 25 kg in weight. Parent weekend symptom ratings showed daytime drug effects, but not as clearly as weekday after-school ratings. Nonresponders to MPH were older, had less severe symptoms, and were medication naive. Thus, the MTA controlled multisite titration trial using daily dose switches replicated the published, single-site MPH trial effect sizes and adverse event rates (Spencer, Biederman, Wilens, et al., 1996).

Data were analyzed through intent-to-treat random-effects regression. All four groups at 14 months (end of the active treatment period) showed sizable reductions in symptoms over time, with significant differences among them in degrees of change. For ADHD symptoms, children in the combined and medication management groups showed significantly greater improvement than those given intensive behavioral treatment or community care. However, combined and medication management treatments did not differ significantly for ADHD symptoms. Although, as measured by teacher-rated social skills, parent-child relations, and reading achievement, combined treatment proved significantly better than other treatments at reducing symptom scores for internalizing symptoms. The MTA Study medication strategies were superior to treatment as usual in the community, despite the fact that two thirds of community-treated subjects received medication during the study period. The combined treatment did not yield significantly greater benefits than medication management for core ADHD symptoms, but it may have provided modest additional advantages for non-ADHD-symptom and positive functioning outcomes.

The MTA is the largest and most methodologically sophisticated randomized multisite pediatric ADHD treatment study to date that includes monomodal and combined treatments. These therapeutic methods had been previously shown effective in simpler two-arm (active vs. placebo) controlled studies (Pelham, 1989; Pelham & Murphy, 1986). Due to its size, the MTA Study was able to address comparative treatment questions. It concluded that stimulant medication efficacy can be realized across diverse settings and patient groups, is more effective than behavioral modification for core ADHD symptoms, and can be maintained during chronic therapy lasting more than a year.

The MTA replicated findings from smaller long-duration stimulant trials—the 102-child New York/Montreal Study (Klein, Abikoff, Hechtman, & Weiss, 2004), the 91-child Toronto study (Schachar, Tannock, Cunningham, & Corkum, 1997), and the 62-child Gillberg (Gillberg et al., 1997) study. Collectively, these smaller multisite studies show a persistence of medication effects over time. Within-subject effect sizes reported 12 to 24 months following the MPH treatment resembled those previously reported in short-duration studies (Elia, Borcherding, Rapoport, & Keysor, 1991; Thurber & Walker, 1983). Domain of greatest improvement differs among studies, with some (Gillberg et al., 1997) showing greater effects at home and another (Schachar et al., 1997) showing greater effects at school. The total mean MPH daily doses reported by three long-duration studies ranged between 33 and 37.5 mg. The one DEX study reported a mean dose half of this level, agreeing with the general ratio of DEX to MPH doses. Persistent stimulant drug side effects and assignment to placebo treatment were associated with dropout. Fortunately, attrition from placebo assignment was slow, allowing ample time for standard 8-week efficacy trials to be conducted.

DIAGNOSIS OF ADHD

Treatment with stimulants is indicated when there is a diagnosis of ADHD. However, the ADHD diagnosis has been controversial because there are no confirmatory laboratory tests. The diagnosis is further complicated because its criteria have been revised four times over the past 25 years. The most recent criteria appear in the DSM-IV-TR (APA, 2000). ADHD covers two symptom domains (inattention and hyperactivity-impulsivity) and is subdivided into predominantly inattentive, predominantly hyperactive-impulsive, and combined subtypes (APA, 2000).

Guidelines for making the ADHD diagnosis in the office practice context have been published by the American Academy of Pediatrics (2001) and the American Academy of Child and Adolescent Psychiatry (AACAP, 2006). Because ADHD is so prevalent, the AACAP recommends that screening for ADHD should be part of any patient's mental health assessment. This can be accomplished by asking questions about inattention, impulsivity, and hyperactivity, and whether such symptoms cause impairment. Alternatively, parents and teachers can be asked to fill out rating scales containing DSM–IV symptoms of ADHD prior to interviewing the patient. A positive screen on a rating scale, however, does not make a definitive diagnosis of ADHD.

Because there are no laboratory tests, the diagnosis of ADHD must be established by history taken from multiple informants, including the child, the parents, and the teacher. The clinician should address each of the five major DSM-IV criteria, including age of onset (before 7), requirement for impairment in a minimum of two settings, 6-month duration of symptoms, and a differential diagnosis ruling out other diagnostic conditions that can cause a patient to experience inattention, overactivity, or impulsivity. The confirmation depends on specific symptom criteria encompassing the type, duration, severity, and frequency of ADHD problems. The patient must experience at least six out of nine ADHD symptoms in either or both inattention and hyperactivity-impulsivity symptom lists, giving positive endorsement only if the symptom occurs often (at least half of the time). The symptoms must start in childhood and have a chronic course.

A physical examination and medical history should be carried out during the diagnostic evaluation. If the patient's medical examination and history are unremarkable, no additional laboratory or neurological testing is required (AACAP, 2006). Similarly, no routine psychological testing is needed for the evaluation of ADHD unless the patient's history suggests low achievement in reading, language, writing, or mathematics "relative to the patient's intellectual ability beyond that accounted for by the ADHD symptoms themselves" (AACAP, 2006).

The next diagnostic procedure includes an interview of the child or adolescent to determine if other psychiatric disorders are present that account for the impairment. Whereas it is helpful to interview a pre-school or school-age child with the parent present, older children and adolescents should be interviewed alone because they are more likely to discuss symptoms of substance use, suicidal ideation or behavior, or depression with the parent absent. Because ADHD behaviors in youth are often attenuated during the first few visits with a clinician, the child interview serves another purpose besides confirming the diagnosis of ADHD.

Since a majority of children with ADHD also suffer from at least one other Axis I psychiatric disorder (Biederman, Newcorn, & Sprich, 1991), the clinician should make inquiries about symptoms of oppositional defiant disorder, conduct disorder, depression, anxiety disorders, tic disorders, substance use disorders, and mania. Symptoms of these disorders are captured by parent symptom checklists (Achenbach CBCL) and rating scales (Swanson, Nolan, and Pelham Rating Scale, Version IV [SNAP–IV]). In addition, the clinician should obtain information about the family history, patient's prenatal history, developmental milestones, and medical history.

USE OF PSYCHOSTIMULANTS IN CHILDREN YOUNGER THAN 6 YEARS

The signs and symptoms of ADHD, such as particularly pronounced motor activity, excessive climbing, aggressivity, and destructiveness, may be evident before age 3. These signs can disrupt family life and make nursery school attendance impossible. Campbell found that many hyperactive preschoolers did not "grow out of" this behavior but maintained their hyperkinesis when in grade school (Campbell, Endman, & Bernfield, 1977). More recently, Lahey and his colleagues conducted an 8-year follow-up study in 118 children, aged 4 to 6 years, who initially met *DSM-IV* criteria for ADHD. The study finding was that 81% of children with ADHD combined type and 73.9% of those with predominantly hyperactive subtype continued to meet criteria for any ADHD subtype, (Lahey, Pelham, Loney, Lee, & Willcutt, 2005). Even though these early ADHD symptoms resemble the behaviors among older ADHD patients, the diagnostic manuals give little guidance about the validity of the ADHD diagnosis in the preschool

years. School-age norms gathered on standard teacher global rating forms, such as the Conners Teacher Questionnaire (CTQ), have not included preschoolers in the past (Conners, personal communication).

Until recently, there were only a handful of small, single-site, published studies addressing stimulant treatment in preschoolers. For the amphetamines, there is only one single-case intensive study suggesting that dextroamphetamine reduces temper outbursts in a toddler (Speltz, Varley, Peterson, & Beilke, 1988). MPH treatment studies have found that the drug ameliorates mother-child interactions (Barkley, 1988) in a linear dose-response fashion, perhaps related to increasing child compliance and decreased symptomatic intensity. No pharmacokinetic studies have been done in this age-group to determine if younger children metabolize psychostimulants differently than older children.

A comprehensive review of preschool stimulant treatment studies (Connor, 2002) identified nine controlled studies ($N = 206$) of stimulants in children under age of 6 (Barkley, 1988; Barkley, Karlsson, Strzelecki, & Murphy, 1984; Conners, 1975; Mayes, Crites, Bixler, Humphrey, & Mattison, 1994; Musten, Firestone, Pisterman, Bennett, & Mercer, 1997; Schleifer et al., 1975; Handen, Feldman, Lurier, & Murray, 1999). MPH doses ranged from 2.5 to 30 mg/day (0.15 to 1.0 mg/kg/day). Most of the studies showed MPH efficacy at weight-adjusted doses comparable to those reported for older school-age children, producing improvements in structured situations but not in free play (Schleifer et al., 1975). These studies, particularly if they involved preschoolers with developmental delays, suggested that stimulants may produce higher rates of side effects than those reported in school-age children, including tearfulness and irritability that would be expected in school-age children (Handen et al., 1999). This suggests that preschoolers with ADHD should be started on low MPH doses.

Interpretations of these early data are difficult because of methodological differences among the nine studies, which utilized very different inclusion/exclusion criteria, diagnostic definition, ratings forms, and study designs, thus making a meta-analysis impossible. However, even without conclusive data, the FDA package insert instructions warn against using MPH in children younger than age 6. In spite of these warnings, there has been a 180% increase since 1996 in the prescriptions of MPH for preschoolers. Clearly, more controlled data are needed.

To address the lack of methodologically sound data on the safety and efficacy of MPH in preschool ADHD children, the NIMH launched a randomized, placebo-controlled, six-performance-site controlled trial of methylphenidate, the Preschool ADHD Treatment Study (PATS). This study recruited 303 randomized children; 279 of their parents were entered into a 10-week course of parent training. Afterward, only 183 families agreed to then enter the PATS medication protocol. Of these, 165 families were randomized into a double-blind, placebo-controlled, crossover design dose-optimization study that began with a 1-week, open, stepwise safety phase exposing all the preschoolers to the drug before their entry into the double-blind protocol. Then the children were given medication (placebo, 1.25 mg, 2.5 mg, 5 mg, or 7.5 mg) capsules three times a day, and the dose was switched each week. Blind raters selected the MPH dose for each child that produced the best compromise between lowering ADHD symptoms without creating large adverse events (Kollins et al., 2006). The mean "best" total daily MPH dose for all the preschoolers as determined by the raters was 14 mg, or 0.75 mg/kg/day, which was lower than the mean 1.0 mg/kg/day MPH dose reported by the MTA Study (Greenhill et al., 2006a).

On their "best" dose, the 165 preschoolers in the PATS study showed a significant decrease in ADHD symptoms compared with their response to placebo. A subset of 114 children was then randomized to a double-blind, parallel design study, with half randomized to their best MPH dose and the other half to placebo. The teacher reports showed significant continued improvements for those on MPH. However, 11% of PATS subjects discontinued the trial because of MPH-associated adverse events, which is far more than the 2% of subjects who stopped the MTA Study for similar reasons. The preschool group showed a significantly higher rate of irritability, decreased appetite, delay in sleep onset, and proneness to crying in the MPH condition than they did on placebo (T. Wigal et al., 2006). An open pharmacokinetic pilot study done on a small subset of PATS patients suggested that preschoolers with ADHD show significantly lower MPH clearance than do school-age children even when corrected for weight (T. Wigal et al., 2006).

USE OF PSYCHOSTIMULANTS IN THE TREATMENT OF ADULTS WITH ADHD

Until recently, the prevalence and severity of ADHD in adults, as well as indications for treatment, were not clear. Contrary to the assumption that children outgrow their childhood problems, ADHD symptoms persist into adulthood. From 2% (Mannuzza et al., 1993) to 27% of patients (Barkley, Fischer, Smallish, & Fletcher, 2002) are estimated to continue having the disorder into the adult life range. Epidemiological studies using a two-stage probability sample screen of 3,199 individuals, aged 19 to 44 years, estimated the point prevalence of adult ADHD to be 4.4% (Kessler et al., 2006).

As ADHD problems from childhood onset persist into adolescence, the impairment from the disorder continues. Almost 30% of ADHD adolescents fail a course in school; 46% are suspended; and most have difficulties taking notes, planning assignments, writing, and transitioning from homework to self-motivated study, resulting in academic underachievement. As adults, patients with childhood histories of ADHD have problems with money management and self-regulation, and show impulse-based addictions, including gambling, sex bingeing, video game playing, increased rates of substance use disorders, and spending long periods of time in internet chat groups.

If adolescents with ADHD begin to smoke, they have much more difficulty stopping. Substance use disorders are also high in adults who had suffered from ADHD as children, ranging from 18% (Mannuzza, Klein, & Moulton, 2002) to 43% (Barkley et al., 2002). When the adolescents begin to drive, they are more apt to have their license suspended, gather more speeding violations, be more involved in vehicle accidents where they are at fault, and experience more damage to themselves and to their vehicles (Barkley, Guevremont, Anastopoulos, DuPaul, & Shelton, 1993; Barkley, Murphy, & Kwasnik, 1996). In his Milwaukee follow-up study, Barkley reported that 40% of children with ADHD continue to have impairing ADHD as adults. If they also had childhood comorbid conduct disorder, their rates of other disorders in adulthood greatly increase, including depression (27% more than ADHD children without conduct disorder) and substance use/abuse disorders (up 24%), and 21% have personality disorders, particularly antisocial personality disorder (up to 25%; Fischer, Barkley, Smallish, & Fletcher, 2002).

As adults, patients with childhood histories of ADHD continue to have problems (Barkley et al., 1990; Biederman et al., 1996; Weiss, Hechtman, Milroy, & Perlman, 1985; Mannuzza, Klein, Bessler, Malloy, & LaPadula, 1998). Between 66 and 85% were reported to suffer from at least one impairing symptom of ADHD. Although 80% of parents report that their older adolescents show persistence of ADHD symptoms from childhood, including impulsiveness, easy distractibility, inattentiveness, easily bored attitude, and restlessness, other types of impairments are also noted during interviews with the parents. Compared with controls, the index group report fewer years of education completed, a higher incidence of antisocial personality disorder, lower scores on clinician-rated global assessment rating scales, more complaints of restlessness, as well as sexual and interpersonal problems.

The first stimulant treatment studies of adults with ADHD did not show the high response rates seen in children. Mattes and Boswell (Mattes, Boswell, & Oliver, 1984) reported little benefit from MPH, but others have found robust effects (Ratey, Greenberg, & Lindem, 1991; Wender, Reimherr, & Wood, 1981). As a result, other drugs have been tested in adults with ADHD symptoms, including fluoxetine (Sabelsky, 1990), nomifensine (Shekim, Masterson, Cantwell, Hanna, & McCracken, 1989), pargyline (Wender, Wood, Reimherr, & Ward, 1994), bupropion (Wender & Reimherr, 1990), the monoamine oxidase (MAO) inhibitor selegiline (Ernst et al., 1995), and the long-acting methamphetamine compound Desoxyn Gradumets (Wender, 1994). Whereas the nicotinic analog ABT 418 significantly reduced ADHD symptoms (Pelham et al., 2000), the antinarcoleptic modafinil (Provigil) failed to separate from placebo in multisite controlled trials of three doses (100, 200, and 400 mg; Cephalon Press Release, July 31, 2000). Wilens and Biederman (1992) pointed out that the initial studies of stimulant-treated adults were inconclusive due to the low stimulant dosages used, the high rate of comorbid disorders in the patients, and/or the lack of a clear

childhood ADHD history. A number of these studies used self-report outcome measures, even though adult ADHD patients appear to be unreliable reporters of their own behaviors. When the clinicians served as reporters, and weight-adjusted doses of stimulants were used, the adult response rates were just as elevated as those in school-age children.

The efficacy of methylphenidate (Spencer et al., 1995), mixed salts of amphetamine (MSA; Spencer et al., 2001), and atomoxetine (ATX; Michelson et al., 2003) has been established by double-blind, placebo-controlled, randomized controlled trials. MPH's efficacy was shown in a 7-week, double-blind comparison of MPH (1 mg/kg/dose) and placebo carried out in 23 adult ADHD patients; 78% showed improvement on MPH versus 4% who responded to placebo (Spencer et al., 1995). The MPH response was independent of gender, comorbidity, or family history of psychiatric disorders. Treatment was generally well tolerated at the target dose of 1.0 mg/kg; side effects included loss of appetite, insomnia, and anxiety. MSA efficacy was also ascertained in a 7-week, randomized, double-blind, placebo-controlled trial for 27 adults meeting *DSM–IV* criteria for ADHD of childhood onset with symptoms persistent into adulthood (Spencer et al., 2001). MSA treatment with a mean bid dose of 54 mg was associated with a 42% drop in ADHD symptom severity, and improvement seen in the 1st week. Finally, atomoxetine treatment was associated with a significant improvement in ADHD symptoms as compared with placebo over a 10-week study period (Michelson et al., 2003; Spencer et al., 2001). A chart review study reported that 32 adult ADHD patients demonstrated a positive response to treatment with tricyclics (Wilens, Biederman, Mick, & Spencer, 1994).

Thus far, the FDA has approved only atomoxetine and extended-release mixed salts of amphetamine for treatment of adults with ADHD. However, Barkley (DuPaul & Barkley, 1990) and Wender et al. (1994) recommended a number of medications that can be used safely to treat ADHD in adults. These include MPH, 5 to 20 mg tid; DEX, 5 mg tid to 20 mg bid; methamphetamine (Desoxyn Gradumets), 5 to 25 mg once in the morning; bupropion (Wellbutrin), 100 mg bid to 100 mg tid; and selegiline (Eldepryl), 5 mg bid only. Clinicians should be cautious about prescribing psychostimulants for adults with comorbid substance abuse disorder. In these patients, it is preferable to use drugs with lower abuse potential, such as pemoline (PEM) or tricyclic antidepressants.

CURRENT PSYCHOPHARMACOLOGICAL AGENTS: EFFICACY AND UTILITY

Three groups of stimulants are currently approved by the FDA for ADHD treatment in children. These are available in both brand and generic, and in immediate-release (short-duration) and long-duration formulations: the amphetamines (Adderall®, Dextrostat, and Dexedrine), the methylphenidates (Concerta®, Metadate-ER®, Metadate-CD®, methylphenidate, Methylin, Ritalin®, Ritalin-SR®, Ritalin-LA®, and Focalin®), and magnesium pemoline (Cylert®). Characteristics of these stimulants can be found in Table 2.2. Dextroamphetamine (DEX) and methylphenidate (MPH) are structurally related to the catecholamines (dopamine [DA] and norepinephrine [NE]) The term *psychostimulant* used for these compounds refers to their ability to increase CNS activity in some but not all brain regions.

Compared with placebo, psychostimulants have a significantly greater ability to reduce ADHD symptoms, such as overactivity (e.g., fidgetiness and off-task behavior during direct observation), and to eliminate behavior that causes disruptions in the classroom (e.g., constant requests of the teacher during direct observation; Jacobvitz et al., 1990). In experimental settings, stimulants have been shown to improve child behavior during parent-child interactions (Barkley & Cunningham, 1979) and problem-solving activities with peers (Whalen et al., 1989). The behavior of children with ADHD has a tendency to elicit negative, directive, and controlling behavior from parents and peers (Campbell, 1973). When these children are placed on stimulants, their mothers' rate of disapproval, commands, and control diminishes to the extent seen in mothers' of non-ADHD children (Barkley & Cunningham, 1979; Barkley et al., 1984; Humphries, Kinsbourne, & Swanson, 1978). In the laboratory, stimulant-treated ADHD children demonstrate major improvements during experimenter-paced continuous performance tests (Halperin, Matier, Bedi, Sharma, & Newcorn, 1992), paired-associate learning, cued and free recall, auditory and reading comprehension, spelling recall, and arithmetic computation (Pelham & Bender,

1982; Stephens, Pelham, & Skinner, 1984). Some studies show correlations between plasma levels of MPH and performance on a laboratory task (Greenhill, 1995), but plasma levels rarely correlate with clinical response. Likewise, hyperactive conduct-disordered children and preadolescents observed in structured and unstructured school settings show reductions in aggressive behavior when treated with stimulants (Hinshaw, 1991). Stimulants can also reduce the display of covert antisocial behaviors such as stealing and property destruction (Hinshaw, Heller, & McHale, 1992).

No single theory explains the psychostimulant mechanism of action on the central nervous system that ameliorates ADHD symptoms. The medication effect based on a single neurotransmitter has been discounted (Zametkin & Rapoport, 1987), as well as its ability to correct the ADHD child's under- or over-aroused central nervous system (Solanto, 1984). More recently, a two-part theory of stimulant action has been postulated (McCracken, 1991) in which stimulants increase DA release, producing enhanced autoreceptor-mediated inhibition of ascending DA neurons, while simultaneously increasing adrenergic-mediated inhibition of the noradrenergic-locus coeruleus via epinephrine activity. This theory awaits confirmation from basic research in animals and imaging studies in humans. To date, brain imaging has revealed few consistent psychostimulant effects on glucose metabolism. Although some studies in ADHD adults using positron emission tomography (PET) and [^{18}F]fluorodeoxyglucose show that stimulants lead to increased brain glucose metabolism in the striatal and frontal regions (Ernst & Zametkin, 1995), others (Matochik et al., 1993; 1994) are unable to find a change in glucose metabolism during acute and chronic stimulant treatment. Psychostimulants are thought to release catecholamines and block their reuptake.

Methylphenidate, like cocaine, has affinity for the dopamine transporter (DAT), and DAT blockade is now regarded as the putative mechanism for psychostimulant action in the human central nervous system. PET scan data show that [^{11}C]methylphenidate concentration in brain is maximal in striatum, an area rich in dopamine terminals where DAT resides (Volkow et al., 1995). These PET scans reveal a significant difference in the pharmacokinetics of [^{11}C]methylphenidate and [^{11}C]cocaine (Volkow et al., 1995). Although both drugs display rapid uptake into striatum,

TABLE 2.2 Stimulant Drugs and Their Doses

Medication	Duration of Action	Pediatric Starting Dose	Adult Starting Dose
d-Methylphenidate — Focalin (Novartis)	6 hours (2)	2.5 mg A.M./5 mg A.M.	5 mg A.M./20 mg A.M.
d,l-Methylphenidate			
Short-term (immediate release)	3–5 hours	5 mg tid/10 mg tid	10 mg bid/20 mg tid
Average generic price			35.40
Ritalin (Novartis			75.00
Methylin oral		5 mg tid/10 mg tid	10 mg bid/20 mg tid
Methylin chewable tablets		5 mg tid/10 mg tid	10 mg bid/20 mg tid
Intermediate-acting	3–8 hours		
Metadate ER	Single pulse	10 mg bid/30 mg A.M.	10 mg bid/80 mg A.M.
Methylin ER	Single pulse	10 mg bid/30 mg A.M.	10 mg bid/80 mg A.M.
Ritalin-SR	Single pulse	20 mg A.M./40 mg A.M.	20 mg A.M./80 mg A.M.
Long-acting	8–12 hours		
Metadate CD (Celltech)	8–10 hours; dual pulse	10 mg A.M./30 mg A.M.	20 mg A.M./80 mg A.M.
Concerta (McNeil)	8–12 hours; ascending single pulse	18 mg in A.M./36 mg A.M.	18 mg A.M./72 mg A.M.
Ritalin LA (Novartis)	8–10 hours; dual pulse	10 mg A.M./30 mg A.M.	10 mg A.M./80 mg A.M.
Daytrana (Noven-Shire)	10–12 hours; transdermal single pulse	10 mg patch qd × 9 hours, off 15 hours; 30 mg patch qd × 9 hours, off 15 hours	10 mg patch qd × 9 hours, off 15 hours; 60 mg patches qd × 9 hours, off 15 hours
d-Amphetamine	4–6 hours	10 mg bid/5 mg tid	
Dextrostat generic price		5 mg bid/10 mg bid	5 mg bid/15 mg bid
Dexedrine (Glaxo SmithKline)		5 mg bid/10 mg bid	5 mg bid/15 mg bid
Long duration	6–8 hours		
Dexedrine spansules (Glaxo SmithKline)		5 mg A.M./15 mg A.M.	5 mg A.M./30 mg A.M.
Amphetamine mixed salts			
Generic	4–6 hours	5 mg bid/10 mg bid	5 mg bid/15 mg bid
Adderall (Shire)		5 mg bid/10 mg bid	5 mg bid/10 mg bid
Adderall XR	8–10 hours; dual pulse	5 mg A.M./30 mg A.M.	5 mg A.M./60 mg A.M.
Atomoxetine	24 hours	0.5 mg/kg/day/1.2 mg/kg/day, both bid	0.5 mg/kg/day/1.2 mg/kg/day, both bid

MPH is more slowly cleared from brain. The authors speculate that this low reversal of binding to the DAT means that MPH is not as reinforcing as cocaine and, therefore, does not lead to as much self-administration. More recently, the same authors (Volkow et al., 2001) showed that therapeutic doses of oral MPH significantly increase extracellular dopamine in the human brain: "Because DA decreases background firing rates and increases signal-to-noise in target neurons, we postulate that the amplification of weak DA signals in subjects with ADHD by methylphenidate would enhance task-specific signaling, improving attention and decreasing distractibility" (p. 1).

One of the most important findings in the stimulant treatment literature is the high degree of short-term efficacy for *behavioral* targets, with weaker effects for *cognition and learning*. Conners (personal communication, 1993) notes that 0.8, 1.0, and 0.9 effect sizes are reported for behavioral improvements in Type 4 meta-analytic reviews of stimulant drug actions (Kavale, 1982; Ottenbacher & Cooper, 1983; Thurber & Walker, 1983). These behavioral responses to stimulant treatment, when compared with placebo, resemble the treatment efficacy of antibiotics. Less powerful effects are found in laboratory measures of cognitive changes, in particular on the continuous performance task, for which effect sizes of these medications range between 0.6 and 0.5 for omissions and commissions, respectively, in a within-subject design (Milich, Licht, Murphy, & Pelham, 1989), and 0.6 and 1.8 in a between-subject study (Schechter & Keuezer, 1985).

Psychostimulants continued to show behavioral efficacy in the Type 1 RCTs published over the last 10 years (see Table 2.3). These modern-day controlled trials have matured with the field and now utilize multiple-dose conditions with multiple stimulants (Elia et al., 1991), parallel designs (Spencer et al., 1995), and normalization as a common definition of response (Abikoff & Gittelman, 1985; Rapport, Denney, DuPaul, & Gardner, 1994). These studies assess psychostimulants in special ADHD populations, including adolescents (Klorman et al., 1990), adults (Spencer et al., 1995), mentally retarded children (Horn et al., 1991), ADHD subjects with anxiety disorders and internalizing disorders, as well as ADHD subjects with tic disorders (Gadow, Sverd, Sprafkin, Nolan, & Ezor, 1995). As shown in Table 2.3, 70% of ADHD subjects respond to stimulants and less than 13% respond to placebo (Greenhill, Swanson et al., 2001a).

Studies have also attempted to learn more about stimulant nonresponders. Some drug trials (Douglas, Barr, Amin, O'Neill, & Britton, 1988) report a 100% response rate in small samples in which multiple MPH doses are used. Others find that a trial involving two stimulants effectively lowers the nonresponse rate. Elia and colleagues (1991) reduced the 32% nonresponse rate to a single psychostimulant to less than 4% when two stimulants, DEX and MPH, were titrated sequentially in the same subject. However, the rate of medication nonresponse might be higher if children with comorbidity are included in the sample. Finally, a few studies have used the double-blind or single-blind placebo discontinuation models to determine if the child continues to respond to stimulants after being treated for 1 year or more. One study found that 80% of ADHD children relapsed when switched single blind from MPH to a placebo after 8 months of treatment (H. Abikoff, personal communication, 1994). Even so, these observations about the "rare nonresponder" do not address the rate of placebo response. Few, if any, of the current

RCTs are parallel designs, which can evaluate if placebo response emerges at some point over the entire drug trial. Few treatment studies prescreen for placebo responders, so the numbers of actual medication responders in any sample of ADHD children might be closer to 55%, not the 75 to 96% often quoted. Furthermore, these estimates apply to group effects and do not inform the clinician about the individual patient.

Stimulant Drugs: General Features

Psychopharmacological treatment of ADHD should begin with medications approved by the FDA. These medications have been tested for short-term efficacy and safety in at least two different RCTs. Including generic preparations, 10 racemic (d-, l-) methylphenidate, 2 d-methylphenidate, 2 dextroamphetamine, 3 mixed salts of amphetamine, and 1 atomoxetine medications have been approved for children, aged 6 to 12 years (see Table 2.2). Of these preparations, extended-release mixed salts of amphetamine (Adderall XR) and atomoxetine also have been separately approved for the ADHD treatment in adults.

Stimulants show high effect sizes, compared with placebo, in their ability to reduce ADHD symptoms. Meta-analyses of 62 three-month (or less) methylphenidate RCTs revealed large effect sizes (0.8 standard deviations) using teacher ratings and moderate effect sizes (0.5 standard deviations) using parent ratings (Schachter, Pham, King, Langford, & Moher, 2001). Six MPH treatment RCTs involving adults with ADHD ($N = 140$) reported large effect sizes (0.9) when patients were rated by their physicians (Faraone, Spencer, Aleardi, Pagano, & Biederman, 2004).

Methylphenidate, or methyl a-phenyl-2-piperidineacetate hydrochloride, forms the active ingredient of the majority of stimulant medications prescribed in the United States. With the exception of the two d-methylphenidate (Focalin, Focalin-XR) products, MPH is a racemic mixture composed of the d- and l-threo enantiomers. The d-threo enantiomer is more pharmacologically active than the l-threo enantiomer. MPH is thought to block the reuptake of dopamine and norepinephrine (NE) into the presynaptic neuron in the central nervous system and increase the concentration of these neurotransmitters in the interneuronal space. After the immediate-release tablet is swallowed, MPH absorption into the

TABLE 2.3 Type 1 Studies Showing Efficacy in ADHD Drug Treatments (N=1702)

Study (Year)	N	Age Range	Design	Drug (Dose)	Duration	Response	Comment
Abikoff & Gittelman (1985)	28	6–12	ADHD Controls	MPH (PB, 41 mg)	8 weeks	80.9%	ADHD kids normalized
Abikoff (1998)	103	6–12	ADHD	MPH tid (33.7 mg)	2 years	100% 2.7 SD	Multisite, multimodal study; all children on MPH
Barkley et al. (1989)	74	6–13	Xover 37 agg 37 nonagg	MPH (PB, 0.3, 0.5)	4 weeks	80%	Aggression responsive to MPH
Barkley et al. (1991)	40	6–12	Xover 23 ADHD 17 ADHD-W	MPH bid (5, 10, 15 bid) PB bid	6 weeks	ADHD 95% ADHD-W 76%	Fewer ADHD-W respond, need low dose
Castellanos et al. (1997)	20	6–13	Xover	MPH 45 mg bid DEX 22.5 mg bid	9 weeks	ADHD + TS	Tics dose-related at high doses
Douglas et al. (1988)	19	7–13	Xover	MPH (PB, 0.15, 0.3, 0.6)	2 weeks	100%	Linear D/R relationships
Douglas et al. (1995)	17	6–11	Xover	MPH (0.3, 0.6, 0.9) PB	4 weeks	behavior 70%	No cognitive toxicity at high doses, linear D/R curves
DuPaul & Rapport (1993)	31	6–12	Xover 31 ADHD 25 normals	MPH (20 mg) PB bid	6 weeks	behavior 78% attention 61%	MPH can normalize classroom behavior; 25% of ADHD subjects didn't normalize academics
DuPaul et al. (1994)	40	6–12	Xover 12 high ANX 17 mid ANX 11 low ANX	MPH (5, 10, 15 mg) PB single dose	6 weeks	high 68% nor mid 70% nor low 82% nor	25% in internalizing group deteriorated on meds ADHD; subjects with comorbid int disorders less to be normalized or to respond to MPH
Elia et al. (1991)	48	6–12	Xover	MPH (0.5; 0.8, 1.5) PB bid DEX (0.25, 0.5, 0.75)	6 weeks	MPH 79% DEX 86%	Response rate for two stimulants = 96%
Gadow et al. (1995)	34	6–12	Xover ADHD + tic disorder	MPH (0.1, 0.3, 0.5) PB bid	8 weeks	100% MPH	No nonresponders to behavior; MD's motor tic ratings show 2 min increases on drug; Only shows effects of 8 weeks treatment

(continued)

TABLE 2.3 (continued)

Study (Year)	N	Age Range	Design	Drug (Dose)	Duration	Response	Comment
Gillberg et al. (1997)	62	6–12	Parallel	AMP (17 mg) PB bid	60 weeks	70% respond 27–40% impr	No dropouts but only 25% placebo groups at 15-month assessment
Greenhill et al. (2001)	277	6–12	Parallel	Metadate-CD Placebo	3 weeks	70% respond	Mean total daily dose 40 mg. FDA registration
Klein et al. (1997)	84	6–15	Parallel	MPH bid (1.0)	5 weeks	MPH 59–78% PB 9–29%	MPH reduced ratings of antisocial behaviors
Klorman et al. (1990)	48	12–18	Xover	MPH tid (0.26) PB bid	6 weeks	MPH 60%	Less med benefits for adolescents
MTA (1999)	579	7–9	Parallel	MPH tid (< 0.8)	4 weeks (14 months)	MPH 77% DEX 10% None 13%	Titration Trial for multisite, multimodal study, full study data for 288 on 38.7 mg MPH
Musten et al. (1997)	31	4–6	Xover	MPH bid (0.3, 0.5)	3 weeks	MPH > NA	MPH improves attention in preschoolers
Pelham et al. (1990)	22	8–13	Xover	MPH 10 bid; PB bid; DEX span 10 mg PEM 56.25 daily	24 days	Stim 68%	DEX Span, PEM best for behavior 27% did best on DEX; 18% on SR; 18% on PEM; 5% on MPH bid.
Pelham et al. (1995)	28	5–12	Xover	PEM (18.75, 37.5, 75, 112.5 mg) PB OD	7 weeks	PEM resp 89% PB resp 0%	PEM dose ≥ 37.5 mg/day lasts 2–7 hours. Efficacy and time course = MPH
Rapport et al. (1988)	22	6–10	Xover	MPH (PB, 5, 10, 15 mg)	5 weeks	72%	MPH response same in home and school
Rapport et al. (1994)	76	6–12	Xover	MPH (5,10, 15, 20 mg) PB bid	5 weeks	94% beh 53% att	MPH normalizes behavior > academics. Higher doses better, linear D/R curve
Schachar et al. (1997)	91	6–12	Parallel	MPH (33.5 mg) PB bid	52 weeks	0.7 SD effect size	15% side effects: affective, overfocusing led to dropouts

Study	N	Age	Design	Medication (dose)	Duration	Response	Comments
Spencer et al. (1995)	23	18–60	Xover	MPH (1 mg/kg/d)	7 weeks	78% PB 4%	MPH at 1 mg/kg/d produces improvement in adults equivalent to that seen in kids
Swanson et al. (1998)	29	7–14	Xover	Adderall (5, 10, 15, 20, PB, MPH)	7 weeks	100%*	Adderall peaks at 3 hr, MPH at 1.5 hr
Tannock et al. (1995)	40	6–12	Xover	MPH (0.3, 0.6) 17 ADHD-Anx	2 weeks	70%	Activity level better in both groups; working memory not improved in anxious kids
Tannock et al. (1995)	28	6–12	Xover	MPH (0.3, 0.6, 0.9) PB	2 weeks	70% 70%	Effects on behavior D/R curve linear, but effects on resp inhibition U-shaped suggest adjust dose on obj measures
Taylor et al. (1987)	38	6–10	Xover	MPH (PB 0.2–1.4)	6 weeks	58%	Severe ADHD symptoms, better response
Whalen et al. (1989)	25	6.3–12	Xover	MPH (PB, 0.3, 0.5)	5 weeks	48–72%	MPH helps, not normalizes, peer status
Wolraich et al. (2001)	277	6–12	Parallel	Concerta 36 mg Placebo MPH tid	4 weeks	62%	Concerta rated effective by teachers and parents

Doses listed as mg/kg/dose, and medication is given twice daily unless otherwise stated.

Abbreviations: PB = placebo; Xover = crossover design; Anx = anxiety; MPH = methylphenidate; DEX = dextroamphetamine; AMP = d,l-amphetamine (Adderall); mg/kg/d = dosage in milligram/kilogram/day; Agg = aggression; ADHD-W = ADD without hyperactivity; sx = symptoms; obj = objective; resp = response.

systemic circulation is rapid, so that effects on behavior can be seen within 30 minutes. Plasma concentration reaches a peak by 90 minutes, with a mean half-life of about 3 hours and a 3- to 5-hour duration of action. Most children taking one immediate-release methylphenidate dose just after breakfast will require a second dose at lunch (which for young children must be given by the school nurse), and a third dose after coming home from school in the afternoon to prevent loss of effectiveness and rebound crankiness and tearfulness. Long-duration preparations have been developed in the past decade to overcome the need for multiple daily MPH doses, and these preparations are now the mainstay of practice.

In humans, MPH is metabolized extrahepatically via de-esterification to alpha-phenyl-piperdine acetic acid (PPA, ritalinic acid), an inactive metabolite. About 90% of radiolabeled MPH is recovered from the urine.

IR-MPH tablets are often used in clinical practice to provide a boost in the morning for certain long-duration forms, such as OROS-MPH, or to smooth withdrawal in the late afternoon. When used as the main ADHD treatment, IR-MPH should be initiated at low doses, 5 mg in the morning for children and 10 mg for adults. The IR-MPH dose should be increased every 3 days by adding a noontime and an afternoon dose until the three-times-daily schedule is achieved. Dosage should be increased through the recommended range up to 20 mg three times daily, which is a total daily dose (TDD) of 60 mg.

A myriad of RCTs (Schachter et al., 2001) plus a half century of use in the community have supported MPH's safety and efficacy for the treatment of ADHD in youth (American Academy of Child and Adolescent Psychiatry, 2002). Investigators in the NIMH MTA Study identified IR-MPH to be the most effective initial treatment strategy for their trial that randomized 579 children, aged 7 to 10 years, with ADHD combined type, to MPH alone (MED), behavior therapy alone (BEH), combination (COMB), or community care (CC; Jensen, Arnold, et al., 1999a). A double-blind, placebo-controlled titration protocol was used to titrate each MTA subject to his or her "best" IR-MPH dose, which was given in a three-times-per-day dosing schedule (Greenhill, Swanson, et al., 2001a). Similar methods were used in the NIMH PATS randomized clinical trial of IR-MPH in 165 preschool children with ADHD, aged 3 to 5.5 years (Greenhill, 2001). Both studies showed a response rate of better than 75% for those exposed to IR-MPH. However, the mean "best" IR-MPH TDD varied by age, with preschoolers in the PATS doing best on 14.4 ± 0.75 mg/day (0.75 mg/kg/day) and school-age children in the MTA optimally improving on 31.2 ± 0.55 mg/day (0.95 mg/kg/day). Immediate-release MPH effect sizes and optimal daily doses were greater in school-age children (1.2 for teachers, 0.8 for parents at 30 mg/day) than in preschoolers (0.8 for teachers, 0.5 for parents at 14 mg/day).

Short- and long-duration MPH preparations demonstrate the same adverse event profile during placebo-controlled randomized clinical trials. These include delay in sleep onset, appetite loss, weight decrease, headache, abdominal pain, and new-onset tics. Other adverse effects reported as infrequent are nausea, abdominal pain, dryness of the throat, dizziness, palpitations, headache, akathesia, dyskinesia, and drowsiness. Rare but serious adverse events include angina, tachycardia, urticaria, fever, arthalgia, exfoliative dermatitis, erythemia multiforme, and thrombocytopenic purpura. Also rare are tactile hallucinations, formication, phobias of insects, leucopenia, anemia, eosinophilia, transiently depressed mode, sudden unexpected death, and hair loss. Neuroleptic malignant syndrome (NMS) has been reported very rarely and only when MPH is used in combination with drugs that are associated with NMS.

MPH interacts with few medications, including monoamine oxidase inhibitors (isocarboxazid, phenelzine, selegiline, and tranylcyromine), as well as antibiotics with MAO-inhibiting activity (linezolid), leading to blood pressure elevations and increase in MPH serum concentrations. Furthermore, phenytoin, phenobarbital, tricyclic antidepressants, and warfarin increase the MPH serum concentrations. The effects of centrally acting antihypertensives (guanadrel, methyldopa, and clonidine) can be reduced by MPH. NMS has been reported in patients treated with both venlafaxine and MPH.

Despite the IR-MPH effectiveness, its short, 3- to 5-hour duration of action means that a midday dosing in school is necessary, which might expose children to peer ridicule. The short duration of action also requires administration by nonfamily members when children participate in after-school programs. Long-duration MPH preparations address these problems with a once-daily dosing formulation and have become a mainstay of clinical practice in the United States (Biederman, Lopez, Boellner, & Chandler,

2002; Greenhill, Findling, & Swanson, 2002; Greenhill, Muniz, Ball, Levine, Pestreich, & Jiang, 2006b; McCracken, Biederman, et al., 2003; Pelham, Aronoff, et al., 1999; Wolraich, Greenhill, et al., 2001) ; . A methylphenidate transdermal patch (Findling, Biederman, Wilens, Spencer, McGough, Lopez, & Tulloch, 2005) has been approved for pediatric population. Unlike the short-duration stimulants, these newer formulations' efficacy has been firmly established in FDA registration trials, which were multi-center and used rigorous, double-blind, placebo-controlled designs. Although most of them use MPH as the active ingredient, they differ in the number and shape of the MPH pulses released into the circulation. They include the older single-pulse MPH drugs, such as Ritalin SR, newer dual-pulse beaded MPH products such as Metadate-CD, Ritalin LA, and Focalin-XR, as well as the complex release formulations, such as OROS-MPH (Concerta).

Single-pulse sustained-release, long-duration MPH formulations (Ritalin-SR, Metadate-ER) use a wax-matrix to prolong delivery. They display a slower onset of action than immediate-release MPH, produce lower serum concentrations, and have 6- to 8-hour duration of action (Birmaher, Greenhill, Cooper, Fried, & Maminski, 1989). Clinicians regard these as less effective in practice than the immediate-release or the dual-pulse, beaded MPH or OROS preparations. To compensate for reduced effectiveness and slow onset of action, clinicians should administer them twice daily or supplement them with an immediate-release tablet in the morning. Metadate ER and Methylin ER are referred to as "branded generics" because they are copies of Ritalin-ER.

The beaded MPH products use an extended-release formulation with a bimodal release profile. In Ritalin-LA, this is created using a proprietary Spheroidal Oral Drug Absorption System (SODAS) technology. MPH products using SODAS technology (Ritalin-LA and Focalin XR) may help young children who have difficulty swallowing pills. The capsule can be opened, and the tiny medication spheres can be sprinkled into a small amount of cold applesauce. Ritalin LA uses the SODAS technology that encloses the active IR-MPH into a bead. Each bead-filled Ritalin LA capsule contains half the dose of immediate-release MPH beads and half of an enteric-coated, delayed-release beads, thus providing a two-pulse release system that mimics the use of IR-MPH given in two doses 4 hours apart. Ritalin LA

10-, 20-, 30-, and 40-mg capsules provide the same amount of methylphenidate in a single dose as twice-daily IR-MPH dosages of 5, 10, 15, or 20 mg. Ritalin LA given once daily exhibits a lower second peak concentration (Cmax2), higher interpeak minimum concentrations (Tminip), and less peak-to-peak trough fluctuations in serum concentration of MPH than IR-MPH tablets administered 4 hours apart. This may be due to an earlier onset and more prolonged absorption of the delayed-release beads. The efficacy of Ritalin LA in the ADHD treatment was established in one controlled trial of children aged 6 to 12 who met DSM–IV criteria for ADHD.

Dexmethylphenidate hydrochloride (Focalin) is the d-threo-enantiomer of racemic MPH. The drug's plasma concentrations increase rapidly after ingestion, reaching a maximum in the fasted state at about 1 to 1.5 hours postdose (Quinn et al., 2004; S. Wigal et al., 2004). Plasma d-MPH levels were comparable to those achieved following single racemic IR-MPH doses given as capsules in twice the total milligram amount. D-MPH (5, 10, or 20 mg/day total dose), d-threo-MPH HCL (10, 20, or 40 mg/day total dose), and placebo, all administered twice daily, were compared in a multicenter, 4-week, parallel group study of 132 patients. Patients treated with d-MPH showed a statistically significant improvement in SNAP–IV teacher-rated symptom scores from baseline over patients who received placebo.

Focalin XR (d-MPH) is an extended-release formulation of d-MPH with a bimodal release utilizing the proprietary SODAS technology similar to that of Ritalin-LA. Each bead-filled Focalin XR capsule contains half the dose as immediate-release beads and half as enteric-coated, delayed-release beads. Focalin XR 5-, 10-, and 20-mg capsules provide in a single dose the same amount of d-MPH as dosages of 2.5, 5, or 10 mg of Focalin given twice daily. After administration of Focalin XR, the first peak, on average, was 45% higher in females, even though pharmacokinetics d-MPH parameters were similar for males and females. Focalin XR effectiveness was shown in a randomized, double-blind, placebo-controlled parallel-group study of 103 pediatric patients, aged 6 to 17. Using mean change scores from baseline on teacher-rated Conners ADHD/DSM–IV scales (CADS–T), the study reported significantly greater decreases in ADHD scores for youth on the active Focalin XR than on placebo (Greenhill, Muniz, et al., 2006). The medication effectiveness for adult ADHD was reported in a 5-week, randomized, double-blind, parallel-group, placebo-controlled study of 221 adults, aged 18 to 60, who met ADHD criteria on the *DSM–IV* Attention Deficit/Hyperactivity Disorder Rating Scale (*DSM–IV* ADHD RS). Signs and symptoms of ADHD were substantially reduced for adults on 20, 30, or 40 mg of Focalin XR than for those randomized to placebo.

The OROS-MPH caplet uses an osmotic delivery system to produce the ADHD symptom reduction for up to 12 hours (Swanson et al., 2004; Wolraich et al., 2001). The caplet is coated with IR-MPH for immediate action. The long-duration component is delivered by an osmotic pump (OROS) that gradually releases the drug over a 10-hour period, producing slightly ascending MPH serum concentrations. Taken once daily, it mimics the serum concentrations produced by taking IR-MPH three times daily, but with less variation (Modi, Wang, Noveck, & Gupta, 2000). Other long-duration preparations using the beaded dual-pulse technology have claimed greater efficacy than OROS-MPH for controlling ADHD symptoms in the early morning hours (Swanson et al., 2004). Two double-blind, placebo-controlled, randomized clinical trials have tested the efficacy and safety of OROS-MPH compared with the IR-MPH for ADHD children (Swanson et al., 2003; Wolraich et al., 2001), and both found equal efficacy. Another multisite trial showed similar efficacy of Concerta over placebo as MPH in adolescents, when the upper dose range of Concerta was extended to 72 mg per day (Wilens et al., 2006). The results show that once-daily OROS-MPH dosing matches MPH in the robust reductions of ADHD symptoms . Low placebo response rates are similar to the rates reported in the MTA Study. In addition, OROS-MPH has been demonstrated in a small study (N = 6) to have a longer duration for reducing ADHD-induced driving impairments in the evening than IR-MPH given three times daily (Cox, Merkel, Penberthy, Kovatchev, & Hankin, 2004).

Short-duration branded MPH generics have been formulated for young children who have difficulty swallowing pills or capsules. Methylin chewable tablets show peak plasma MPH concentrations in 1 to 2 hours (T_{max}), with a mean peak concentration (C_{max}) of 10 mg/ml after a 20-mg chewable tablet. High-fat meals delay the peak by 1 hour (1.5 hours, fasted, and 2.4 hours, fed), similar to what is seen with an IR-MPH tablet. Methylin chewable tablets are available in 2.5-, 5-, and 10-mg doses. The Methylin Oral Solution is available in 5 mg/5 cc and 10 mg/5cc strength. There have been no large-scale clinical trials published using Methylin chewable or oral solution.

In the transdermal MPH preparations (Daytrana), MPH is steadily absorbed after application of the patch, but it does not reach peak concentration until 7 to 9 hours later, with no noticeable action for the first two hours. Chronic dosing with the patch results in higher peak MPH levels than are equivalent to the OROS-MPH doses suggesting increased absorption. Duration of MPH action for a 9-hour wear period is about 11.5 hours. A double-blind, placebo-controlled, crossover study conducted in a laboratory classroom showed significantly lower ADHD symptom scores and higher math test ratings on active versus placebo patch for postdose hours 2 through 9 (McGough et al., 2006). Transdermal MPH (Daytrana) appears to be as effective as other long-duration MPH preparations, but adverse effects, such as anorexia, insomnia, and tics, occur more frequently with the patch, and mild skin reactions are common.

Amphetamines are manufactured in the dextro isomer, as in dextroamphetamine (Dexedrine, Dextrostat), or in racemic forms, with mixtures of *d*- and *l*-amphetamine (Adderall or Adderall XR). Efficacy of these amphetamine products resembles that of the MPH products for controlling overactivity, inattention, and impulsivity in ADHD patients. Some children who have severe adverse events associated with MPH may respond without such problems when taking amphetamine products. Absorption is rapid, and the drug's plasma levels peak 3 hours after oral administration. All amphetamines are metabolized hepatically. Acidification of the urine increases urinary output of amphetamines. Taking the medication with ascorbic acid or fruit juice decreases absorption of amphetamine, whereas alkalinizing agents such as sodium bicarbonate increase it (Vitiello, 2006). Acidification of the urine increases excretion (American Academy of Child and Adolescent Psychiatry, 2002; Vitiello, 2006). Effects of dextroamphetamine can be seen within 1 hour of ingestion, and the duration of action lasts up to 5 hours, somewhat longer than that of MPH. Nevertheless, twice-daily administration is needed to extend the effectiveness of the immediate release preparation throughout the school day. Adderall and Adderall XR are amphetamine salt mixtures. Adderall XR is a dual-pulse capsule preparation that includes both immediate-release and extended-release beads. There is no evidence that these mixed amphetamine salts offer any advantage over MPH or dextroamphetamine, but some patients can respond to one and not to another.

ADVERSE EVENTS WITH STIMULANTS

Common adverse events frequently reported during stimulant use include delay of sleep onset, headache, appetite decrease, and weight loss. Infrequently observed adverse events include emotional lability and tics. All stimulant products carry a warning in the package insert that they should be used with care in patients with a history of drug dependence or alcoholism. In addition, there is a warning about sudden death that may be associated with preexisting cardiac abnormalities or other serious heart problems. For adults, the warning includes sudden death and also extends to stroke and myocardial infarction. In addition, adults are warned that they should be cautious taking stimulants if they have preexisting hypertension, heart failure, recent myocardial infarction, or ventricular arrhythmia. Those with preexisting psychotic and bipolar psychiatric illness are cautioned against taking stimulants. Additionally, children are warned about stimulants' ability to slow growth rates and lower the convulsive threshold.

Clinical benefits associated with stimulant use have had to be weighed against reports of serious, unexpected adverse events in populations taking stimulants for ADHD treatment. These concerns arose from a series of reviews conducted by the FDA of cardiovascular and psychiatric adverse events associated with use of approved stimulant medications. On June 30, 2005, the agency began this review by examining the passive surveillance reports concerning treatment with OROS-MPH (Concerta) (http://www.fda.gov/ohrms/dockets)/ac/05/slides/2005–4152s2.html). The review uncovered 135 adverse events, including 36 psychiatric adverse events and 20 cardiovascular events. In particular, the reports documented 12 instances of tactile and visual hallucinations (classified under "psychosis") on OROS-MPH, the same clinical phenomena seen in cases of delirium. These OROS-MPH adverse event reports represent 135 per 1.3 million cases, and thus seem to be rare unexpected adverse events.

More worrisome were reports of 20 cases of sudden unexpected death (14 children and 6 adults) and 12 cases of stroke in patients taking mixed salts of amphetamine (Adderall XR). This led to Health Canada suspending the sales of Adderall XR (http://www.hc-sc.gc.ca/ahc-asc/media/advisories-avis/2005/2005_01_e.html). The deaths occurred in 5 patients with preexisting structural heart defects, and the rest of the victims had "family history of ventricular tachycardia, association of death with heat exhaustion, dehydration and near-drowning, very rigorous exercise, fatty liver, heart attack, and type 1 diabetes mellitus." (*http://www.fda.gov/cder/drug/advisory/adderall.htm*). Pliszka et al. (2006) notes that the rate of sudden unexpected death (SUD) on mixed salts of amphetamine is estimated at 0.5 per 100,000 patient-years, the rate on MPH is estimated at 0.19 per 100,000 patient-years, whereas the rate of SUD in the general population has been estimated at 1.3 to 8.5 per 100,000 patient-years (Liberthson, 1996). However, patients with preexisting heart disease should be referred to a cardiologist before initiating stimulant treatment.

In summary, serious unexpected cardiac or psychiatric adverse events associated with stimulants have been known for years and are extremely rare. The rates of cardiac adverse effects are too low to prove a causal association with stimulants in patients with no history of previous heart disease. Routine EKGs and echocardiograms are not indicated before starting a patient on stimulants who has an unremarkable history and physical examination. It is advised that the physician prescribing stimulants first asks patients and their families for a history of structural heart disease, and/or if they have consulted previously with a cardiologist. Known cardiac problems that raise a caution about using stimulants include postoperative tetralogy of Fallot, cardiac artery abnormalities, and obstructive subaortic stenosis. Clinicians should be alert if the patient has hypertension or complains of syncope, arrhythmias, or chest pain, as these symptoms may indicate hypertrophic cardiomyopathy, which has been associated with sudden unexpected death.

Growth slowdown is another infrequent psychostimulant adverse reaction. Psychostimulant-induced reductions in growth velocity have been the most consistently researched long-term side effect for this type of medication (Greenhill, 1984). Even with the many studies in this area (Greenhill, 1981), myriad methodological difficulties prevent an easy interpretation. Few studies employ the optimal controls needed, which include untreated ADHD children, a psychiatric control group, and an ADHD group treated with a class of medications other than stimulants. Studies differ in quality of compliance measures, whether the children are off stimulants on weekends, and whether the stimulants are used through the summer. One large controlled study (Gittelman-Klein, Landa, Mattes, & Klein, 1988) reported growth rate reductions among a subgroup of children, but growth resumed immediately when treatment was interrupted (Safer, Allen, & Barr, 1975). Most recently, growth slowing for height and weight was reported for children with ADHD, aged 7 to 10, treated with MPH at mean doses of 30 mg/kg/day in the MTA Study (Swanson et al., 2002). School-age children grew 1.0 cm less per year and gained 2.5 kg less than predicted from Centers for Disease Control growth charts. Similar effects were observed for preschool children (Swanson et al., 2006), who grew 1.5 cm less height and gained 2.5 kg less than predicted while treated with mean MPH doses of 14 mg/kg/day. Safer and Allen (Safer, Allen, & Barr, 1972; 1975; Safer & Allen, 1973) first reported that treatment for 2 or more years with MPH and DEX could produce decrements in weight velocity on age-adjusted growth rate chars; stopping the medication produced a quick return to baseline growth velocities. Dextroamphetamine, with a half-life two to three times that of MPH, produces more sustained effects than MPH on weight velocity, as well as suppressing mean sleep-related prolactin concentrations (Greenhill, 1981). In MPH-treated ADHD children, followed for 2 to 4 years, dose-related decreases in weight velocity were seen (Gittelman-Klein et al., 1988; Satterfield, Cantwell, Schell, & Blaschke, 1979), with some tolerance of the suppressive effect developing in the 2nd year. Hechtman, Weiss, Perlman, and Amsel (1984) reported growth slowdown in untreated ADHD children, suggesting that there may be differential growth associated with the ADHD disorder itself. Spencer, Biederman, Harding, and colleagues (1996b) also detected similar different growth rates for ADHD children that could be associated with the disorder itself and not with stimulant treatment alone.

The actual psychostimulant mechanism for any growth slowdown is unknown. Early theories attributed the drug's putative growth-suppressant action on its effects on growth hormone or prolactin, but research studies on 13 children treated for 18 months with 0.8 mg/day of DEX (Greenhill et al., 1981) and on 9 children treated for 12 months on 1.2 mg/kg/day of MPH (Greenhill et al., 1984) failed to demonstrate a consistent change in growth hormone release. The most parsimonious explanation for this drug effect is the medication's suppression of appetite, leading to reduced caloric intake. No study, however, has collected the standardized diet diaries necessary to track calories consumed by ADHD children on psychostimulants (Greenhill et al., 1981). In any case, the growth effects of MPH appear to be minimal. Satterfield et al. (1979) followed 110 children and found decreases in height velocity during the 1st year of psychostimulant treatment, but this reversed during the 2nd year of treatment. An initial growth loss during MPH treatment was seen in 65 children followed to age 18, but these children "caught up" during adolescence and reached heights predicted from their parents' heights (Gittelman & Mannuzza, 1988). These results confirm the observations by Roche, Lipman, Overall, and Hung (1979) that psychostimulants have mild and transitory effects on weight and only rarely interfere with height acquisition. Height and weight should be measured at 6-month intervals during stimulant treatment and recorded on age-adjusted growth forms to determine the presence of a drug-related reduction in height or weight velocity. If such a decrement is discovered during maintenance therapy with psychostimulants, a reduction in dosage or change to another class of medication is advisable.

Two major reviews (Faraone, Biederman, Morley, & Spencer, 2006; Poulton, 2005) have concluded that stimulant treatment most likely slows height acquisition in children, at least during the first 1 to 3 years of treatment. Patients followed in the MTA Study showed significantly less height acquisition over the first 2 years if they had been randomized to the stimulant treatment arms versus the nonstimulant arms (MTA Cooperative Group, 2004). The PATS study subjects grew 1.30 cm less and gained 1.3 kg less than predicted by the Centers for Disease Control growth norms (Swanson et al., 2006). Interestingly, youth with ADHD in both the PATS and the MTA studies began treatment larger than average. Thus, clinicians may not observe growth slowdown as often as predicted because the ADHD-treated children do not slow down in height acquisition to become shorter than average. There is also evidence that even if height acquisition is reduced during the 1st year of stimulant treatment, these effects attenuate after that time (Faraone et al., 2006). Pliszka et al. (2006) found that amphetamine more than MPH affected the rate of weight acquisition, but neither had significant effects on the rate of height acquisition. The AACAP guidelines (2006) for ADHD recommend that no change in treatment should occur until the patient has a change in height or weight percentile that crosses two percentile lines on the Centers for Disease Control chart. If this happens, the clinician can reduce the dose, switch to another ADHD medication, or temporarily stop stimulant treatment.

The most common adverse events associated with stimulant discontinuation in controlled trials (Focalin XR) included twitching (e.g., motor and vocal tics), anorexia, insomnia, and tachycardia, with reported incident rates of approximately 1%. Motor or vocal tics have been reported in as many as 1% of children taking MPH (Ickowicz, Tannock, Fulford, Purvis, & Schachar, 1992). A controlled MPH trial in ADHD children with chronic tic disorder (Gadow et al., 1995) reported significant improvement in ADHD symptoms for all subjects without consistent worsening or increase in tic frequency. However, the total daily MPH doses did not exceed 20 mg/day. These low doses and the short 8-week study do not resemble the higher doses or longer treatment duration found in clinical practice, where tics may appear after several months of MPH administration. The clinical literature has held that MPH lowers the seizure threshold, although MPH treatment of ADHD patients with seizures shows no change in seizure frequency (Klein, 1995).

Several clinical conditions have been worsened by stimulant treatment, including florid psychosis, mania, concurrent substance abuse, Tourette's syndrome, and eating disorders. More recently, structural cardiac lesions and hypertensive states were added as contraindications for using stimulants to treat ADHD.

The Controversy and Politics of Stimulant Treatments for Children With ADHD

Even though the psychostimulants are the most widely researched, clinically effective, and commonly prescribed treatments for ADHD, their use in children has become the focus of a major controversy. This is related to their classification as drugs of abuse, which makes for concern about their administered to young children to treat a condition that has no readily available laboratory test validating the diagnosis. A 1998 Consensus Development Conference (Kupfer et al., 2000) on ADHD sponsored by the National Institutes of Health concluded that stimulants were effective in reducing the defining ADHD pediatric symptoms in the short term but indicated that the controversy about their use demanded serious consideration. Also noted were the lack of evidence for the long-term benefit and safety; the considerable risks of treatment; the wide variation in prescribing practices among practitioners; and the absence of evidence regarding the appropriate ADHD diagnostic threshold above which the benefits of psychostimulant therapy outweigh the risks.

The Consensus Development Conference's conclusions were much less sanguine than a similar report published the same year by the Council on Scientific Affairs of the American Medical Association. After reviewing hundreds of trials involving thousands of patients, the council concluded that "the risk-benefit ratio of stimulant treatment in ADHD must be evaluated and monitored on an on-going basis in each case, but in general is highly favorable" (Goldman, Genel, Bazman, & Slanetz, 1998, p. 1106).

Stimulant Medications in Practice

Currently, more than 85% of psychostimulant prescriptions in the United States are written for MPH (Safer, Zito, & Fine, 1996; Williams & Swanson, 1996). The rate of MPH prescription writing increased fourfold from 1990 to 1995. The indications, pharmacology, adverse effects, and usage directions for MPH are frequently highlighted in reviews (Dulcan, 1990; Greenhill, 1995; Wilens & Biederman, 1992). MPH has become the "first-line" psychostimulant for ADHD, followed by DEX and PEM (Richters et al., 1995). Within the group of stimulants, practitioners order MPH first, DEX second, and PEM third. However, the popularity of MPH as the first choice in psychostimulants is not supported by the literature. DEX and PEM have identical efficacy to MPH (Arnold, Christopher, Huestis, & Smeltzer, 1978; Elia et al., 1991; Pelham et al., 1990; Vyborova, Nahunek, Drtilkova, Balastikova, & Misurec, 1984; Winsberg, Press, Bialer, & Kupietz, 1974). Arnold noted (Greenhill et al., 1996) that of the 141 subjects in these studies, 50 responded better to DEX, and only 37 better to MPH.

Outpatient visits devoted to ADHD increased from 1.6 to 4.2 million per year during the years 1990–1993 (Swanson et al. 1995a); by 1995, these figures had climbed to 2 million visits and 6 million stimulant drug prescriptions (Jensen, Kettle, et al., 1999b). During those visits, 90% of the children were given prescriptions, 71% of which were for MPH. Its production in the United States increased from 1,784 to 5,110 kg during the same time period, so that more than 10 million prescriptions for MPH were written in 1996 (Vitiello & Jensen, 1997). It has been estimated that 2.8% of U.S. youth, aged 5 to 18, were prescribed stimulants in 1995 (Goldman et al., 1998). However, specific epidemiological surveys suggest that 12-month prescription rates for the school-age group—aged 6 to 12 years—may be higher, ranging between 6% urban (Safer et al., 1996) and 7% rural (Angold, Erkanli, Egger, & Costello, 2000) and extending up to 10% in some communities (LeFever, Dawson, & Morrow, 1999).

Psychostimulant use has increased fivefold since 1989, and this has raised concerns at the U.S. Drug Enforcement Administration (DEA)—which regulates their production—about the risk of abuse and diversion. Production of MPH has tripled over a 10-year period, and 90% of U.S.-produced MPH is used in the United States. Increased MPH use could mean increases in ADHD prevalence, a change in the ADHD diagnosis, improved recognition of ADHD by physicians, broadened indications for use, or an increase in drug diversion and prescription for profit or abuse (Goldman et al., 1998). Analyses of managed-care data sets reveals a 2.5-fold increase in prescribing in the 1990–1995 time period, accounted for by longer durations of treatment, inclusion of girls and patients with predominantly inattention subtype, and treatment of high school students (Safer et al., 1996). An epidemiologically based survey in four different communities found that only one eighth of diagnosed ADHD children received adequate stimulant treatment (Jensen, Kettle, et al., 1999b); another survey in rural North Carolina found many school-age children taking stimulants did not meet *DSM-IV* criteria for ADHD (Angold et al., 2000).

Because of hepatotoxicity reports by the FDA during postmarketing surveillance, 1975–1990, PEM is now not recommended as a first-line ADHD treatment (Burns, Hoagwood, & Mrazek, 1999). As a result of manufacturer's warning letters, sales of PEM declined between 1996 and 1999, and it has been taken off formulary in various parts of the United Kingdom. Practitioners are advised to obtain informed consent from parents using a form attached to the package insert before initiating treatment, and to monitor liver function via biweekly blood tests. However, ADHD children, especially those with needle phobias, may refuse the tests. Furthermore, PEM is more expensive than the other psychostimulants. For these reasons, practitioners are reluctant to prescribe this otherwise effective medication. Pelham's RCT (Pelham et al., 1995b) comparing four doses of once-daily PEM with a placebo showed a 72% rate of response for PEM in daily doses of 37.5 mg.

Stimulant responsiveness and rates of side effects were originally thought to be affected by the presence of comorbid anxiety symptoms. Pliszka (1989) used MPH (0.25 to 0.4 mg/kg and 0.45 to 0.70 mg/kg) and placebo to treat ADHD in 43 subjects for 4 weeks. The 22 ADHD subjects comorbid for anxiety (the ADHD plus ANX group) showed less efficacy when active stimulant treatment was compared with placebo, as judged by teachers' global ratings, with no increase in side effects. This might be explained by strong placebo response in this group. Tannock, Ickowicz, and Schachar (1995) reported that ADHD children, some with ($N = 18$) and some without ($N = 22$) comorbid anxiety symptoms, treated in a double-blind, randomized, crossover design with three MPH doses (0.3, 0.6, and 0.9 mg/kg), showed equal decreases in motor activity. However, the group with comorbid anxiety did poorer on a serial addition task and had a differential heart rate response to MPH. DuPaul, Barkley, and McMurray (1994) found that 40 children with ADHD and comorbid anxiety were less likely to respond to MPH and showed more side effects for three doses of MPH (5, 10, and 15 mg). Although, the study did not collect ratings for anxiety symptoms, so the direct effect of MPH on such symptoms was not recorded. More recent data do not support these early impressions. A controlled study (Gadow et al., 1995) that tested the MPH effects in children with comorbid symptoms found equally good response in those with and without the anxiety disorder. These divergent data leave open the question of whether comorbid anxiety symptoms predict poor response to stimulant treatment.

Predicting the individual drug response in ADHD children is difficult. While pretreatment patient characteristics (i.e., young age, low rates of anxiety, low severity of disorder, and high IQ) may predict a good response to methylphenidate on global rating scales (Buitelaar, Van der Gaag; Swaab-Barneveld, & Kuiper, 1995), most research shows that neurological, physiological, or psychological measures of functioning have not been identified as reliable predictors of response to psychostimulants (Pelham & Milich, 1991; Zametkin & Rapoport, 1987). Once a child responds, there is no universally agreed-upon criterion for how much the symptoms must change before the clinician stops increasing the dose. Furthermore, there is no standard for the outcome measure. For example, should global ratings alone be used, or should they be combined with more "objective" academic measures such as percentage correct or percentage completed lists of math problems? Some have advocated a 25% reduction of ADHD symptoms, whereas others have suggested that the dose should continue to be adjusted until the child's behavior and classroom performance are normalized.

The concept of *normalization* has helped standardize the definition of a categorical responder across domains and across studies. Studies now determine whether the improvement from treatment is clinically meaningful using normal classroom controls, instead of just being statistically significant. Treatment was noted to remove differences between ADHD children and nonreferred classmates on measures of activity and attention (Abikoff & Gittelman, 1985), but not for positive peer nominations (Whalen et al., 1989). Further advances occurred when investigators used statistically derived definitions of clinically meaningful change during psychotherapeutic treatment (Jacobson & Truax, 1991). Rapport and colleagues (1994) used this technique to calculate reliable change and normalization on the Abbreviated Conners Teacher Rating Scale (ACTRS) using national norms. They determined that a child would be normalized when his or her ACTRS score fell closer to the mean of the normal population than to the mean of the ADHD population. Using this technique in a controlled trial of four MPH doses in ADHD children, they found that MPH normalized behavior and, to a lesser extent, academics (94% vs. 53%). Similarly, DuPaul and colleagues (DuPaul & Rapport, 1993) found that MPH normalized behav-

ior for all ADHD children treated, but only 75% of the ADHD children normalized for academics. In another study, the same group (DuPaul et al., 1994) reported that normalization in behavior and academics occurred less often when ADHD subjects were comorbid for high levels of internalizing disorders. Swanson applied this approach to the cumulative-distribution curves of the SNAP–IV parent and teacher ratings at the end of the MTA Study and found that 88% of classroom controls, 65% of ADHD children treated with combined treatment, and 55% of ADHD children treated with MTA medication strategies had mean symptom scores of 1 or less, equivalent to a "normal" response on those scales.

LIMITATIONS OF STIMULANTS FOR THE TREATMENT OF ADHD

Although 3- to 7-month treatment studies carried out in groups of ADHD children (Schachar & Tannock, 1993) show impressive reductions in ADHD symptoms, clinicians must manage individual treatments over years. Although psychostimulants produce moderate to marked short-term improvement in motor restlessness, on-task behavior, compliance, and classroom academic performance (DuPaul & Barkley, 1990), these effects have been demonstrated convincingly only in short-term studies. When examined over periods greater than 6 months, these medications fail to maintain academic improvement (Gadow, 1991) or to improve the social problem-solving deficits that accompany ADHD. Many of the long-term studies reporting lack of academic improvement have been uncontrolled, with many of the children followed not taking stimulants consistently, so it is not possible to draw conclusions about whether stimulant treatment reverses academic failure over time. Although there are more than 100 controlled studies of stimulant efficacy in the literature, only 18 studies lasted as long as 3 months, according to a recent authoritative review (Schachar & Tannock, 1993). Because literally 4 million psychostimulant prescriptions were written in 1994 and because the duration of treatment extends from first grade through college, there is growing interest in showing that stimulant treatment is effective over the long run. A dual-site multimodal treatment study (Abikoff et al., 2004) treated children over 2 years and found that medication-alone treatment is as effective as combination treatment involving medication plus psychosocial interventions. However, that study did not have a no-medication group. Concern over drawing long-term conclusions from short-term benefits in the psychostimulant literature became one of the driving forces behind the implementation of the 14-month NIMH MTA Study (Richters et al., 1995). This study attempted to address long-term stimulant use by including a no-medication psychosocial-treatment-only-arm in a sample of 576 children with ADHD.

Other caveats have been expressed about the use of psychostimulants for ADHD treatment in children. First, the behavioral benefits from a single psychostimulant dose last only a few hours during its absorption phase (Perel, Greenhill, Curran, Feldman, & Puig-Antich, 1991) and are often gone by the afternoon if the medication is administered in the morning. Second, even with the new understanding about the relatively small numbers of nonresponders (Elia et al., 1991), a small number of children improve but experience unmanageable side effects. Approximately 25% of ADHD children are not helped by the first psychostimulant given or experience side effects so bothersome that meaningful dose adjustments cannot be made (DuPaul & Barkley, 1990). Third, the indications for choosing a particular psychostimulant and the best methods for adjusting the dose remain unclear, and this may prove confusing to the clinician and family. Although MPH is regarded as the drug of choice for ADHD treatment, controlled treatment studies show no particular advantage of this medication over DEX. Fourth, many treatment studies are troubled by methodological problems, including failure to control for prior medication treatment and inappropriately short washout periods.

In addition to widely accepted short-term side effects of stimulants, other concerns have been more theoretical but are still controversial. A few studies have reported dissociation of cognitive and behavioral responses to MPH (Sprague & Sleator, 1977), or that the response to MPH treatment may be diminished by the presence of comorbid internalizing disorders (Pliszka, 1989; Tannock, Schachar, & Logan, 1993). There has also been the concern that children treated with stimulants may develop negative self-attributions, coming to believe that they are incapable of functioning without the medication. In addition, investigators have sometimes found that stimulant effects may be influenced by the patient's IQ or age (Buitelaar et al., 1995; Pliszka, 1989).

Fifth, some have speculated that dose-response measures of academic performance in stimulant-treated ADHD children may be influenced by state-dependent learning (Pliszka, 1989; Swanson & Kinsbourne, 1976). Sixth, the possibility that stimulant medication response may be related to the presence of minor physical anomalies, neurological soft signs, or metabolic/nutritional status has yet to be explored.

The practitioner may find it difficult to cull specific guidelines about dosing the individual patient from these studies. There is no universally agreed-upon method for dosing with these medications: Some practitioners use the child's weight as a guideline (dose-by-weight method), and others titrate individual response through the approved dose range until clinical response occurs or side effects limit further dose increases (stepwise-titration method). Rapport, DuPaul, and Kelly (1989) have shown that there is no consistent relationship between weight-adjusted MPH doses and behavioral responses, calling into question the widely accepted practice in research of standardizing MPH doses by weight adjustment. Some ADHD children experience dose responses that can be conceptualized as a simple linear function (Gittelman & Kanner, 1986), whereas others show curvilinear patterns. These relationships may vary in the same child, one type for cognitive performance and another type for behavioral domain (Sprague & Sleator, 1977). Adverse reactions to medications show the same variability and may appear unpredictably during different phases of the medication absorption or metabolic phases. Although long-term adverse reactions, such as inhibition of linear growth in children, have been shown to resolve by adult life, no long-term, prospective studies maintaining adolescents on psychostimulants through the critical period when their long bone epiphyses fuse have been published. Therefore, the final evidence remains to be gathered to show that continuously treated adolescents will reach the final height predicted from their parents' size (Greenhill, 1981).

NONSTIMULANT MEDICATION TREATMENTS FOR ADHD

Because of the controversy surrounding the use of scheduled drugs in children, clinicians and parents may prefer nonstimulant medications for ADHD treatment. Besides the controversy, other problems face the family using stimulants for ADHD. Short-acting stimulants require cooperation from the school personnel for midday dosing, and this may not always be possible. Stimulants, which cause insomnia, cannot be given too late in the day. MPH's attention-enhancing effects, which last only 3 to 4 hours, are often needed in the late evening to help school-age children with their homework but may result in delayed sleep onset and insomnia. Adverse effects, including severe weight loss, headaches, insomnia, and tics, can occur. March, Conners, Erhardt, and Johnson (1994) suggested that a nonstimulant may be used when there is an unsatisfactory response to two different stimulants; this recommendation is in congruence with the studies of Elia et al. (1991). Other ADHD treatment parameters as well as the Texas Children's Medication Algorithm Program (C-MAP) recommend the use of nonstimulants when stimulants cannot be used because of inadequate response, unwanted side effects, or parental preference (Pliszka et al., 2000). Type 1 studies of alternative medications have appeared since 1996. These are listed in Table 2.4.

Atomoxetine (ATX) is a selective norepinephrine reuptake inhibitor. It is the first drug to be approved by the FDA to treat ADHD both in children and in adults, because of its efficacy in randomized controlled trials (Michelson et al., 2001; Michelson et al., 2002; Michelson et al., 2003; Michelson et al., 2004). It is neither a controlled substance nor a stimulant. It is rapidly absorbed, with peak serum concentrations occurring in 1 hour without food and 3 hours with food. The drug undergoes hepatic metabolism with CYP2D6 isozyme and then is glucuronidated and excreted in urine. Plasma elimination half-life averages 5 hours for most patients, although 5 to 10% of patients have a polymorphism for the allele that codes for CYP2D6 and show ATX half-life as long as 24 hours. The pharmacodynamics differ from the pharmacokinetics in that the duration of action in reducing ADHD symptoms lasts much longer than the pharmacokinetic half-life, so once-daily dosing can manage ADHD symptoms. It also can be given in the evening, whereas stimulants cannot. Its value as a treatment is for patients who have not responded to or cannot tolerate stimulants, or for those who do not want treatment with a schedule II stimulant ("Atomoxetine for ADHD," 2003) .

The effect size in reducing ADHD symptoms was calculated to be 0.7, which means a medium effect size. This was borne out by significantly higher response rates in patients randomized to double-blind, placebo-controlled treatment with immediate-release stimulants (0.91) versus those randomized to once-daily ATX (0.62; Faraone, Spencer, Aleardi, Pagano, & Biederman, 2003) .In practice, some clinicians have been concerned by low numbers of ADHD children responding to ATX, which is available in 10-, 18-, 25-, 40-, and 60-mg capsules. Youth weighing 70 kg or less should be started at 0.5 mg/kg/day in divided doses and increased after 1 week to a target dose of 1.2 mg/kg/day to limit adverse events. The maximum dose is 1.4 mg/kg/day, or 100 mg, whichever is less. Patients with hepatic dysfunction should take half the usual dose.

ATX and monoamine oxidase inhibitors should not be used together or within 2 weeks of each other. The initial dose of ATX should not be increased rapidly if the patient is taking a potent CYP2D6 inhibitor, such as fluoxetine (Prozac). Somnolence, nausea, decreased appetite, and vomiting have occurred in children on ATX, particularly when the dose is increased from initial to top levels within 3 days. Slow metabolizers displayed higher rates of decreased appetite. Two warnings have been added to the ATX package insert instructions. The first warning was added on December 17, 2004. Based on reports by two patients (one adult, one child), the FDA required that patients developing jaundice or dark urine should stop ATX. The second warning was added in September 2005. Lilly Pharmaceuticals reported that 5 of 1,800 youth in ATX trials spontaneously reported suicidal ideation, whereas none randomized to placebo made such reports. The FDA required that ATX's label carry a black-box warning about its possible association with suicidality. It is noteworthy that both warnings are based on spontaneous reports, not systematically elicited adverse events.

Bupropion, an antidepressant with noradrenergic activity, has been reported to be effective for some of the ADHD symptoms in placebo-controlled trials (Casat, Pleasants, Schroeder, & Parler, 1989; Clay, Gualtieri, Evans, & Guillian, 1988; Simeon, Ferguson, & Van Wyck, 1986). Barrickman and colleagues (1995) concluded that bupropion was equivalent to MPH in the treatment of 15 children with ADHD, who had equal improvements for both medications on the CGI, Conners teacher and parent ratings, the continuous performance test, and ratings of anxiety and depression. The study shows an order effect, which suggests a carryover from one drug condition to the next. Also, subjects were not placed on pla-

TABLE 2.4 Studies (Arranged by Drug) of Alternative Medications for ADHD

Study (Year)	N	Age Range	Design	Drug (Dose)	Duration	Response	Comment
Simeon et al. (1986)	17	7–13	Single-blind	Bupropion (135 mg/d)	8 weeks	70% improve	CGI, Conners Rating Scales
Casat et al. (1987)	30	6–12	DB parallel	Bupropion (150–250 mg/d)	4 weeks	Mod improve	Teacher, CGI improved
Clay et al. (1988)	33	6–12	DB parallel	Bupropion (5.3 mg/kg/d)	3 weeks	Mod improve	Teacher, parent, CGI improve
Spencer et al. (1993)	4	7–12	Open-L	Bupropion (75–225 mg/d)	1 week–2 months	50% improve	Increased tics, so stopped BPR
Jacobsen et al. (1994)	1	7	Open-L	Bupropion (75 mg tid)	4 weeks	Mod improve	Increased compulsions, so stopped BPR
Barrickman et al. (1995)	15	7–17	Xover	Bupropion (3.3 mg/kg/d) MPH (0.7 mg/kg/d)	6 weeks	BPR = MPH	CGI, IOWA-Conners, CDI, CMAS, CPT. No placebo group; order effects
McCormick et al. (1994)	10	6–12	Xover	Buspirone (10 mg/d) PB	6 weeks	BPR > PB	Teacher ratings better
Quiason et al. (1991)	1	8	Open-L	Buspirone (15 mg tid)	10 days	Improved	Decreased aggression
Hunt et al. (1985)	10	11.6	Open	Clonidine	12 weeks	70% improve	Observers disagree about improvement
Ernst et al. (1995)	36	37.6	Xover	l-Deprenyl (20 mg, 60 mg)	6 weeks	PB = active	High-dose l-deprenyl decreased p-HVA
Castellanos (1996) (Review)	12	6–12	1 Xover	CMI	3 weeks	N/A	CMI > MPH for depressive symptoms
	55	3–39	5 Open	Fluoxetine	6 weeks–3 months	Improvement	All open studies
Barrickman et al. (1991)	22	7–15	Open	Fluoxetine (20–60 mg)	6 weeks	58% improve	19 completers

Study	N	Age	Study type	Drug (dose)	Duration	Improvement	Comments
Chappell et al. (1995)	10	8–16	Open	Guanfacine (1.5 mg/d)	4–20 weeks	Improve tics 40% ADHD	ADHD + Tourette's patients 40% behavior improve
Hunt et al. (1995)	13	8–17	Open	Guanfacine (0.5–4.0 mg)	4 weeks	Improve	Compares baseline versus end point
Conners et al. (1995)	17	N/A	Xover	Nicotine patch 11 nonsmoke 6 smokers	3 sessions (7 mg patch) (21 mg patch)	Improve	Improved CGI, reaction time
Hinton et al. (1995)	10	N/A	Xover	Nicotine patch A-B-A	3 sessions (7 mg patch)	Improve	Improve deficits in timing accuracy
Castellanos (1996) (Review)	1	24	1 Open	Sertraline	N/A	Improvement	Temper, distractibility improved
Spencer et al. (1998)	22	adults (76 mg/d)	Xover	Tomoxetin 10% placebo	6 weeks	52% active	Found mild appetite suppression for this NE reuptake inhibitor
Pleak & Gormly (1995)	1	11	Open-L	Venlafaxine (75 mg tid)	6 weeks	Improved	Diastolic blood pressure increases on doses over 100 mg twice daily
Wilens et al. (1995)	2	45–48	Open	Venlafaxine (18.75 tid–75 bid)	2 months	Improved	52–60% reduction of ADHD symptoms
Reimherr et al. (1995)	20	35	Open	Venlafaxine (50–150 mg/d)	N/A	40% improved	8 patients unable to tolerate lowest dose
Adler et al. (1995)	12	19–59	Open	Venlafaxine (110.4 mg/d)	8 weeks	49.6% improve	4 dropped: sedation
Hornig-Rohan & Amsterdam (1995)	17	43	Open	Venlafaxine (N/A)	N/A	80% improve	Small samples, some on multiple meds
Luh (1995)	15	8–17	Open	Venlafaxine (12.5–75 mg)	5 weeks	50% improve	Well tolerated
Derivan et al. (1995)	25	6–15	Open PK	Venlafaxine	6 weeks	Significant	AUC, clearance kids > adults

Studies arranged alphabetically by drug generic name. Most studies open or letters (see "L" added to study type column).

55

cebo in the crossover, so the study is not placebo controlled. The multisite, double-blind, placebo-controlled trial of bupropion revealed that teachers could detect a reduction of ADHD symptoms at a significant level, but parents could not (Conners et al., 1996). This suggests that bupropion is a second-line agent for ADHD treatment.

Clonidine (CLON) is an alpha-2 presynaptic receptor agonist indicated for adult hypertension. The drug has been touted as a nonstimulant treatment for aggressive ADHD children although much of its popularity among practitioners and families may be based on its sedating effects useful for counteracting stimulant-related insomnia (Wilens, Biederman, & Spencer, 1994b). However, a recent review (Swanson, Flockhart et al., 1995) reveals that there was a fivefold increase in physicians writing CLON prescriptions for ADHD children from 1990 to 1995. Safety and efficacy issues have not been addressed in this age-group. Only one small controlled study of 10 ADHD children (Hunt, Minderaa, & Cohen, 1985) suggested that CLON may be effective for ADHD treatment, with reductions in hyperactivity and aggression. Another review (Williams & Swanson, 1996) showed that publications mentioned only 124 CLON-treated children, 42 with ADHD, 74 with Tourette's Syndrome, and 8 with early infantile autism. Improvements averaged 22.9% for parent ADHD ratings in the five published studies (Williams & Swanson, 1996). Connor conducted a pilot study comparing methylphenidate, clonidine, and methylphenidate-clonidine combination in 24 ADHD children comorbid with aggression and either oppositional-defiant or conduct disorders (Connor, Barkley, & Davis, 2000). Although all groups showed improvement, the group on clonidine showed a decrease in fine motor speed. Connor, in reviewing this clonidine study and others in a meta-analysis, concluded that clonidine has a moderate effect size of 0.56 on ADHD symptoms in children and adolescents with ADHD and those comorbid with conduct disorder, developmental delay, and tic disorders (Connor, Fletcher, & Swanson, 1999). Although Connor concluded that clonidine may be an effective second-tier treatment for ADHD symptoms, its clinical use is associated with many side effects. This was seconded by reports coming into the FDA's Post Marketing Surveillance MEDWATCH system, whereby 23 children treated simultaneously with CLON and MPH have been reported for drug reactions, including heart rate and blood pressure abnormalities. Among that group, 4 experienced severe adverse effects, including death (Swanson et al., 1995ab). Guanafacine, a similar alpha-2 presynaptic agonist, has been studied in two open trials involving 23 children (Chappell et al., 1995; Hunt, Arnsten, & Asbell, 1995), but no efficacy or safety data are available.

Modafinil, a nonstimulant with no cardiovascular effects, is used for the treatment of narcolepsy and fatigue among patients with multiple sclerosis and those who are shift workers. It has also been used off-label for ADHD treatment. The mechanism of action has not been determined. Some claim that it may inhibit sleep-promoting neurons by blocking norepinephrine uptake ("New Indications," 2004). It was found to be equivalent to 600 mg of caffeine (approximately 6 cups of coffee) in maintaining alertness and performance in sleep-deprived normal volunteers (Wesensten et al., 2002). Recent reports of Stevens-Johnson syndrome and visual hallucinations emerged from large sponsor-supported registration trials, after which the manufacturer withdrew its FDA application for a new indication for ADHD treatment.

Selective serotonin reuptake inhibitors (SSRIs) enjoy a reputation for high efficacy and low adverse event reporting in adults with major depressive disorder. Castellanos (1996) found no signs of efficacy for SSRIs in the treatment of ADHD symptoms in children in the seven studies ($N = 68$) he reviewed.

MONITORING TREATMENT

The AACAP Practice Parameters recommend that during a psychopharmacological intervention for ADHD, the patient should be monitored for treatment-emergent side effects. The effectiveness of regular monthly visits and dose adjustments based on tolerability and lingering ADHD symptoms was shown in the MTA Study. Those assigned medication management by NIMH protocol had significantly lower ADHD symptom scores than those followed by providers in the community. When compared, children in the MTA Study had five times the rate of appointments, increased feedback from the teacher to the provider, and higher mean MPH total daily doses. Monitoring can be done through direct visits between patient and provider, by phone calls with the patient and family, or even by e-mail contact. Teacher input should be sought at least once in the fall and once in the spring for patients attending primary, middle, or high school. Monitoring should also follow a predetermined plan that is worked out with the patient, and if a child, with the parents as well. Generally, the schedule of monitoring visits should be weekly during the initial dose adjustment phase and then should become monthly for the first few months of maintenance. After that, visits can be regularly scheduled but less frequent. During monitoring visits, the clinician should collect information about the exact dose used and the administration schedule for the stimulants, including times of days. The clinicians should ask about skipped doses. Questions about common and less common, as well as acute and long-term side effects should also be raised by the clinician. At that point, family and clinician should agree whether the patient is to be continued on the same stimulant dose or started on another dose. A new prescription should be written and a new appointment scheduled. The patient should leave with a prescription, a plan for administration, and possible schedule for telephone contact.

The practitioner and family should agree on the pattern of stimulant treatment. The choice lies between continuous daily administration of stimulant medications or treatment only for schooldays, with weekends and holidays off drug. Those patients with more impairing ADHD symptoms will benefit from treatment with stimulants 365 days per year. Patients should have their need for continued treatment with stimulant medication verified once per year through a brief period of medication discontinuation. This should be planned for a part of the school year when academic testing is not in progress. Strategies for maintaining adherence to treatment are a key component of monitoring. These include the option to adjust stimulant doses to reduce treatment-emergent adverse events. When an adverse event occurs, the practitioner would do well to assess the impairment induced. Some adverse events may not interfere with the child's health or cause significant interruption of routine. If the adverse event worsens, then dose reduction is indicated. If the dose reduction helps the adverse event but results in an increase of ADHD symptoms, then the clinician may want to consider switching to another stimulant.

The AACAP Practice Parameters suggest that adjunctive pharmacotherapy can be used to deal with a troublesome adverse event when the stimulant treatment is particularly helpful. Stimulant-induced delay of sleep onset may benefit from the use of antihistamines, clonidine, or a bedtime dose of 3 mg melatonin (Tjon Pian Gi, Broeren, Starreveld, & Versteegh, 2003). Gadow and his colleagues (1999) found that ADHD children comorbid for tic disorders often show a decrease in tic frequency when placed on a stimulant.

CHOICE OF MEDICATION

An international consensus statement (Kutcher et al., 2004), the AACAP ADHD Practice Parameters (2006), the Texas Medication Algorithm Project (Pliska et al., 2006), and the American Academy of Pediatrics (2001) all recommend stimulant medications as the first line of treatment. Direct comparisons of MPH and atomoxetine in a double-blind, randomized, multisite trial (Buitelaar et al., 2006; Michelson, 2004; Newcorn et al., in press) have shown a decided benefit for MPH and confirm the Faraone et al. meta-analysis (2003), which suggested the MPH effect size (0.91) was greater than that of atomoxetine (0.62). However, atomoxetine might take precedent if the family had an aversion to stimulants or the patient had comorbid anxiety, suffered from chronic motor tics, or was an adolescent or adult with a substance abuse problem. The AACAP treatment should begin with either an amphetamine or an MPH-based stimulant in long-duration formulation. The specific drug can be chosen based on its rapidity of onset, duration of action, and effectiveness in the specific patient under treatment. Short-acting stimulants can be used at first for small children or preschoolers if there is no long-acting preparation available in a low enough dose. Dual-pulse MPH and amphetamine products (see Table 2.2) have strong effects in the morning and early afternoon but wear off by late afternoon. These drugs work best for children with academic problems at the beginning and middle of the school day, for those whose appetite is strongly suppressed, and for those who have delay of sleep onset during stimulant treatment. Because transdermal stimulants are reported to have higher-than-average numbers of adverse events, orally administered stimulants should be used first. Atomoxetine should be employed only if the family does not want treatment with a controlled substance, or if the patient fails full dose range trials of both a long-duration methylphenidate and a long-duration amphetamine preparation. The AACAP Practice Parameters for ADHD (2006) wisely point out that none of the extant practice guidelines should be interpreted as justification for requiring a patient to be a treatment failure (or experience adverse events) with one agent before allowing the trial of another.

CONCLUSIONS

Psychostimulant medications have become a mainstay in the American treatment of ADHD, primarily based on their proven efficacy during short-term controlled studies. In fact, the majority of children with ADHD will respond to either MPH or DEX, so that nonresponders are rare (Elia et al., 1991). Although the long-term response of ADHD children to psychostimulants has not been examined in a controlled study much longer than 24 months (Jacobvitz et al., 1990), anecdotal reports suggest that patients relapse when their medication is withdrawn and respond when it is restarted. Optimal treatment involves initial titration to optimize dose, followed by regular appointments and a clinician who remains in frequent contact with the teacher or school (Greenhill, Swanson, et al., 2001a).

Stimulants continue to be a mainstay of the child psychiatry practice. The effects of psychostimulants are rapid, dramatic, and normalizing. The risk of long-term side effects remains low, and no substantial impairments have emerged to lessen the remarkable therapeutic benefit-to-risk ratio of these medications. More expensive and demanding treatments, including behavior modification and cognitive behavioral therapies, have, at best, only equaled treatment with psychostimulants. The combination of behavioral and medication therapies is only slightly more effective in reducing ADHD symptoms than medication alone (MTA Cooperative Group, 1999). The NIMH MTA Follow-Up Study will test whether combined treatment results in better long-term functioning and decreased appearance of comorbid conditions than monomodal treatment with psychostimulants alone.

Although psychostimulant treatment research has flourished, there is ample opportunity for more studies. Not all patients respond to psychostimulants, in particular, patients with comorbid psychiatric disorders. It is also important to determine medication effects on the acquisition of social skills in ADHD children (Hinshaw, 1991). The aim of the new psychopharmacological studies will be to target populations with comorbid disorders (e.g., the child with ADHD and comorbid anxiety disorder) and to examine differential responses to medications in these patients versus patients without the additional psychiatric diagnoses.

REFERENCES

Abikoff, H. & Gittelman, R. (1985). Hyperactive children treated with stimulants. Is cognitive training a useful adjunct? *Archives of General Psychiatry, 42,* 953–961.

Abikoff, H., & Hechtman, L. (1998). *Multimodal treatment for children with ADHD: Effects on ADHD and social behavior and diagnostic status.* Unpublished manuscript.

Abikoff, H., Hechtman, L., Klein, R. G., Weiss, G., Fleiss, K., Etcovitch, J., et al. (2004). Symptomatic improvement in children with ADHD treated with long-term methylphenidate and multimodal psychosocial treatment. *Journal of the American Academy of Child and Adolescent Psychiatry, 43,* 802–811.

Adler, L., Resnick, S., Kunz, M., & McDevinsky, O. (1995). Open-label trial of venlafaxine (Effexor) in attention deficit disorder. *Psychological Bulletin, 31,* 544.

American Academy of Child and Adolescent Psychiatry (2002). Practice parameter for the use of stimulant medications in the treatment of children, adolescents, and adults. *Journal of the American Academy of Child and Adolescent Psychiatry, 41,* 26S-49S.

American Academy of Child and Adolescent Psychiatry (2006). Practice parameter for the assessment and treatment of attention-deficit/hyperactivity disorder. *Journal of the American Academy of Child and Adolescent Psychiatry.*

American Academy of Pediatrics (2001). Clinical practice guideline: treatment of the school-aged child with attention-deficit/hyperactivity disorder. *Pediatrics, 108,* 1033–1044.

American Psychiatric Association (2000). *Diagnostic and statistical manual of mental disorders* (4th ed.; DSM-IV-TR). Washington, DC: Author.

Anderson, J. C., Williams, S., McGee, R., & Silva, P. A. (1987). DSM-III disorders in preadolescent children: Prevalence in a large sample from the general population. *Archives of General Psychiatry, 44,* 69–76.

Angold, A., Erkanli, A., Egger, H. L., & Costello, E. J. (2000). Stimulant treatment for children: a community perspective. *Journal of the American Academy of Child and Adolescent Psychiatry, 39*, 975–984.

Arnold, L. E., Abikoff, H. B., Cantwell, D. P., Conners, C. K., Elliott, G., Greenhill, L. L., et al. (1997). National Institute of Mental Health Collaborative Multimodal Treatment Study of Children with ADHD (the MTA): Design challenges and choices. *Archives of General Psychiatry, 54*, 865–870.

Arnold, L. E., Christopher, J., Huestis, R., & Smeltzer, D. J. (1978). Methylphenidate vs dextroamphetamine vs caffeine in minimal brain dysfunction: Controlled comparison by placebo washout design with Bayes' analysis. *Archives of General Psychiatry, 35*, 463–473.

Atomoxetine (Strattera) for ADHD (2003). *Medical Letter on Drugs and Therapeutics, 45*, 11.

Barkley, R. A. (1977). A review of stimulant drug research with hyperactive children. *Journal of Child Psychology and Psychiatry, 18*, 137–165.

Barkley, R. A. (1982). *Hyperactive children: A handbook for diagnosis and treatment.* New York: Guilford Press.

Barkley, R. A. (1988). The effects of methylphenidate on the interactions of preschool ADHD children with their mothers. *Journal of the American Academy of Child and Adolescent Psychiatry, 27*, 336–341.

Barkley, R. A. & Cunningham, C. E. (1979). The effects of methylphenidate on the mother-child interactions of hyperactive children. *Archives of General Psychiatry, 36*, 201–208.

Barkley, R. A., DuPaul, G. J., & McMurray, M. B. (1991). Attention deficit disorder with and without hyperactivity: Clinical response to three dose levels of methylphenidate. *Pediatrics, 87*, 519–531.

Barkley, R. A., Fischer, M., Edelbrock, C. S., & Smallish, L. (1990). The adolescent outcome of hyperactive children diagnosed by research criteria: I. An 8-year prospective follow-up study. *Journal of the American Academy of Child and Adolescent Psychiatry, 29*, 546–557.

Barkley, R. A., Fischer, M., Smallish, L., & Fletcher, K. (2002). The persistence of attention-deficit/hyperactivity disorder into young adulthood as a function of reporting source and definition of disorder. *Journal of Abnormal Psychology, 111*, 279–289.

Barkley, R. A., Guevremont, D. C., Anastopoulos, A. D., DuPaul, G. J., & Shelton, T. L. (1993). Driving-related risks and outcomes of attention deficit hyperactivity disorder in adolescents and young adults: A 3- to 5-year follow-up survey. *Pediatrics, 92*, 212–218.

Barkley, R. A., Karlsson, J., Strzelecki, E., & Murphy, J. V. (1984). Effects of age and Ritalin dosage on the mother-child interactions of hyperactive children. *Journal of Consulting and Clinical Psychology, 52*, 750–758.

Barkley, R. A., McMurray, M. B., Edelbrock, C. S., & Robbins, K. (1989). The response of aggressive and nonaggressive ADHD children to two doses of methylphenidate. *Journal of the American Academy of Child and Adolescent Psychiatry, 28*, 873–881.

Barkley, R. A., Murphy, K. R., & Kwasnik, D. (1996). Motor vehicle driving competencies and risks in teens and young adults with attention deficit hyperactivity disorder. *Pediatrics, 98*, 1089–1095.

Barrickman, L. L., Perry, P. J., Allen, A. J., Kuperman, S., Arndt, S. V., Herrmann, K. J., et al. (1995). Bupropion versus methylphenidate in the treatment of attention-deficit hyperactivity disorder. *Journal of the American Academy of Child and Adolescent Psychiatry, 34*, 649–657.

Barrickman, L., Noyes, R., Kuperman, S., Schumacher, E., & Verda, M. (1991). Treatment of ADHD with fluoxetine: A preliminary trial. *Journal of the American Academy of Child and Adolescent Psychiatry, 30*, 762–767.

Bauermeister, J. J., Canino, G., & Bird, H. (1994). Epidemiology of disruptive behavior disorders. *Child and Adolescent Psychiatric Clinics of North America, 3*, 177–194.

Biederman, J., Faraone, S., Milberger, S., Guite, J., Mick, E., Chen, L., et al. (1996). A prospective 4-year follow-up study of attention-deficit hyperactivity and related disorders. *Archives of General Psychiatry, 53*, 437–446.

Biederman, J., Lopez, F. A., Boellner, S. W., & Chandler, M. C. (2002). A randomized, double-blind, placebo-controlled, parallel-group study of SLI381 (Adderall XR) in children with attention-deficit/hyperactivity disorder. *Pediatrics, 110*, 258–266.

Biederman, J., Newcorn, J., & Sprich, S. (1991). Comorbidity of attention deficit hyperactivity disorder with conduct, depressive, anxiety, and other disorders. *American Journal of Psychiatry, 148*, 564–577.

Bird, H. R., Canino, G., Rubio-Stipec, M., Gould, M. S., Ribera, J., Sesman, M., et al. (1988). Estimates of the prevalence of childhood maladjustment in a community survey in Puerto Rico: The use of combined measures. *Archives of General Psychiatry, 45*, 1120–1126.

Birmaher, B., Greenhill, L. L., Cooper, T. B., Fried, J., & Maminski, B. (1989). Sustained release methylphenidate: Pharmacokinetic studies in ADDH males.

Journal of the American Academy of Child and Adolescent Psychiatry, 28, 768–772.

Bosco, J. & Robin, S. (1980). Hyperkinesis: Prevalence and treatment. In C. Whalen & B. Henker (Eds.), *Hyperkinetic children: The social ecology of identification and treatment* (pp. 173–186). New York: Academic Press.

Bradley, C. (1937). The behavior of children receiving benzedrine. *American Journal of Psychiatry, 94,* 577–585.

Bradley, C. (1941). The behavior of children receiving benzedrine. *American Journal of Orthopsychology, 11,* 92–103.

Bradley, C. & Bowen, M. (1941). Amphetamine (benzedrine) therapy of children's behavior disorders. *American Journal of Orthopsychology, 11,* 92–103.

Buitelaar, J. K., Michelson, D., Danckaerts, M., Gillberg, C., Spencer, T. J., Zuddas, A., et al. (2006). A randomized, double-blind study of continuation treatment for attention-deficit/hyperactivity disorder after 1 year. *Biological Psychiatry.* In press.

Buitelaar, J. K., Van der Gaag, R. J., Swaab-Barneveld, H., & Kuiper, M. (1995). Prediction of clinical response to methylphenidate in children with attention-deficit hyperactivity disorder. *Journal of the American Academy of Child and Adolescent Psychiatry, 34,* 1025–1032.

Burns, B. J., Hoagwood, K., & Mrazek, P. J. (1999). Effective treatment for mental disorders in children and adolescents. *Clinical Child and Family Psychology Review, 2,* 199–254.

Campbell, S. (1973). Mother-child interaction in reflective, impulsive, and hyperactive children [Abstract]. *Developmental Psychology, 8,* 341–349.

Campbell, S. B., Endman, M., & Bernfield, G. (1977). A three-year follow-up of hyperactive preschoolers into elementary school. *Journal of Child Psychology and Psychiatry, 18,* 239–249.

Campbell, S. B. & Ewing, L. (1990). Follow-up of hard-to-manage preschoolers: Adjustment at age 9 and predictors of continuing symptoms [Abstract]. *Journal of Child Psychology and Psychiatry and Allied Disciplines, 31,* 871–889.

Casat, C. D., Pleasants, D. Z., Schroeder, D., & Parler, D. (1989). Buproprion in children with attention deficit disorder. *Psychopharmacology Bulletin, 25,* 198–201.

Casat, C. D., Pleasants, D. Z., & Van Wyck, F. J. (1987). A double-blind trial of bupropion in children with attention deficit disorder. *Psychopharmacology Bulletin, 23,* 120–122.

Castellanos, F. X. (1996). *SSRIs in ADHD.* Unpublished manuscript.

Castellanos, F. X., Giedd, J. N., Elia, J., Marsh, W. L., Ritchie, G. F., Hamburger, S. D., et al. (1997). Controlled stimulant treatment of ADHD and comorbid Tourette's syndrome: Effects of stimulant and dose. *Journal of the American Academy of Child and Adolescent Psychiatry, 36,* 589–596.

Chappell, P. B., Riddle, M. A., Scahill, L., Lynch, K. A., Schultz, R., Arnsten, A., et al. (1995). Guanfacine treatment of comorbid attention-deficit hyperactivity disorder and Tourette's syndrome: Preliminary clinical experience. *Journal of the American Academy of Child and Adolescent Psychiatry, 34,* 1140–1146.

Charles, L., Schain, R. J., & Guthrie, D. (1979). Long-term use and discontinuation of methylphenidate with hyperactive children. *Developmental Medicine in Child Neurology, 21,* 758–764.

Clay, T., Gualtieri, C., Evans, P., & Guillian, C. (1988). Clinical and neurophysiological effects of the novel antidepressant buproprion. *Psychological Bulletin, 24,* 143–148.

Connell, H., Irvine, L., & Rodney, J. (1982). Psychiatric disorder in Queensland primary school children. *Australian Pediatrics, 18,* 177–180.

Conners, C., Levin, E., March, J., Sparrow, E., & Erhardt, D. (1995). Neurocognitive and behavioral effects of nicotine in adult attention-deficit hyperactivity disorder (ADHD). *Psychopharmacology Bulletin, 31,* 559.

Conners, C. K. (1975). Controlled trial of methylphenidate in preschool children with minimal brain dysfunction [Abstract]. *International Journal of Mental Health, 4,* 61–74.

Conners, C. K., Casat, C. D., Gualtieri, C. T., Weller, E., Reader, M., Reiss, A., et al. (1996). Bupropion hydrochloride in attention deficit disorder with hyperactivity. *Journal of the American Academy of Child and Adolescent Psychiatry, 35,* 1314–1321.

Conners, C. K., Eisenberg, L., & Barcai, A. (1967). Effect of dextroamphetamine on children: Studies on subjects with learning disabilities and school behavior problems. *Archives of General Psychiatry, 17,* 478–485.

Connor, D. F. (2002). Preschool attention deficit hyperactivity disorder: A review of prevalence, diagnosis, neurobiology, and stimulant treatment. *Journal of Developmental and Behavioral Pediatrics, 23,* S1–S9.

Connor, D. F., Barkley, R. A., & Davis, H. T. (2000). A pilot study of methylphenidate, clonidine, or the combination in ADHD comorbid with aggressive oppositional defiant or conduct disorder. *Clinical Pediatrics, 39,* 15–25.

Connor, D. F., Fletcher, K. E., & Swanson, J. M. (1999). A meta-analysis of clonidine for symptoms of attention-deficit hyperactivity disorder. *Journal of the American Academy of Child and Adolescent Psychiatry, 38,* 1551–1559.

Costello, E. J. (1989). Child psychiatric disorders and their correlates: A primary care pediatric sample. *Journal of the American Academy of Child and Adolescent Psychiatry, 28,* 851–855.

Cox, D. J., Merkel, R. L., Penberthy, J. K., Kovatchev, B., & Hankin, C. S. (2004). Impact of methylphenidate delivery profiles on driving performance of adolescents with attention-deficit/hyperactivity disorder: A pilot study. *Journal of the American Academy of Child and Adolescent Psychiatry, 43,* 269–275.

Derivan, A., Aquir, L., Preskorn, S., D'Amico, D., & Troy, S. (1995). A study of venlafaxine in children and adolescents with conduct disorder [Abstract]. In *Proceedings of the Annual Meeting of the American Academy of Child and Adolescent Psychiatry, 11,* 128.

Douglas, V. I., Barr, R. G., Amin, K., O'Neill, M. E., & Britton, B. G. (1988). Dose effects and individual responsivity to methylphenidate in attention deficit disorder. *Journal of Child Psychology and Psychiatry, 29,* 453–475.

Douglas, V. I., Barr, R. G., Desilets, J., & Sherman, E. (1995). Do high doses of stimulants impair flexible thinking in attention-deficit hyperactivity disorder? *Journal of the American Academy of Child and Adolescent Psychiatry, 34,* 877–885.

Dulcan, M. (1990). Using psychostimulants to treat behavior disorders of children and adolescents. *Journal of Child and Adolescent Psychopharmacology, 1,* 7–20.

DuPaul, G. J. & Barkley, R. A. (1990). Medication therapy. In R. A. Barkley (Ed.), *Attention deficit hyperactivity disorder: A handbook for diagnosis and treatment* (2nd ed., pp. 573–612). New York: Guilford Press.

DuPaul, G. J., Barkley, R. A., & McMurray, M. B. (1994). Response of children with ADHD to methylphenidate: Interaction with internalizing symptoms. *Journal of the American Academy of Child and Adolescent Psychiatry, 33,* 894–903.

DuPaul, G. J. & Rapport, M. D. (1993). Does methylphenidate normalize the classroom performance of children with attention deficit disorder? *Journal of the American Academy of Child and Adolescent Psychiatry, 32,* 190–198.

Eisenberg, L., Lachman, R., Molling, P., Lockner, A., Mizelle, J., & Conners, C. (1961). A psychopharmacological experiment in a training school for de-linquent boys: Methods, problems and findings. *American Journal of Orthopsychology, 33,* 431–447.

Elia, J., Borcherding, B. G., Rapoport, J. L., & Keysor, C. S. (1991). Methylphenidate and dextroamphetamine treatments of hyperactivity: Are there true nonresponders? *Psychiatry Research, 36,* 141–155.

Ernst, M., Liebenauer, L., Jons, P., Murphy, D., & Zametkin, A. (1995). L-Deprenyl on behavior and plasma monoamine metabolites in hyperactive adults [Abstract]. *Psychopharmacology Bulletin, 31,* 565.

Ernst, M. & Zametkin, A. (1995). The interface of genetics, neuroimaging, and neurochemistry in attention-deficit hyperactivity disorder. In F. Bloom & D. Kupfer (Eds.), *Psychopharmacology: The fourth generation of progress* (4th ed., pp. 1643–1652). New York: Raven Press.

Esser, G., Schmidt, M., & Woerner, W. (1996). Epidemiology and course of psychiatric disorders in school-age children—results of a longitudinal study. *Journal of Child Psychology and Psychiatry, 31,* 243–253.

Faraone, S. V., Biederman, J., Morley, C., & Spencer, T. J. (2006). *The effects of stimulants on height and weight: A review of the literature.* Manuscript in preparation.

Faraone, S. V., Spencer, T., Aleardi, M., Pagano, C., & Biederman, J. (2004). Meta-analysis of the efficacy of methylphenidate for treating adult attention-deficit/hyperactivity disorder. *Journal of Clinical Psychopharmacology, 24,* 24–29.

Faraone, S. V., Spencer, T. J., Aleardi, M., Pagano, C., & Biederman, J. (2003). *Comparing the efficacy of medications used for ADHD using meta-analysis.* Paper presented at the 15th Annual Meeting of the American Psychiatric Association, San Francisco, CA.

Findling, R. L., Biederman, J., Wilens, T. E., Spencer, T. J., McGough, J. J., Lopez, F. A., et al. (2005). Short- and long-term cardiovascular effects of mixed amphetamine salts extended release in children. *Journal of Pediatrics, 147,* 348–354.

Fischer, M., Barkley, R. A., Smallish, L., & Fletcher, K. (2002). Young adult follow-up of hyperactive children: Self-reported psychiatric disorders, comorbidity, and the role of childhood conduct problems and teen CD. *Journal of Abnormal Child Psychology, 30,* 463–475.

Gadow, K. (1991). Effects of stimulant drugs on academic performance in hyperactive and learning disabled children. *Journal of Learning Disorders, 16,* 190–199.

Gadow, K. D., Sverd, J., Sprafkin, J., Nolan, E. E., & Ezor, S. N. (1995). Efficacy of methylphenidate for attention-deficit hyperactivity disorder in children with tic disorder. *Archives of General Psychiatry, 52,* 444–455.

Gadow, K. D., Sverd, J., Sprafkin, J., Nolan, E. E., & Grossman, S. (1999). Long-term methylphenidate therapy in children with comorbid attention-deficit hyperactivity disorder and chronic multiple tic disorder. *Archives of General Psychiatry, 56,* 330–336.

Gillberg, C., Melander, H., von Knorring, A. L., Janols, L. O., Thernlund, G., Hagglof, B., et al. (1997). Long-term stimulant treatment of children with attention-deficit hyperactivity disorder symptoms: A randomized, double-blind, placebo-controlled trial. *Archives of General Psychiatry, 54,* 857–864.

Gittelman, K. (1987). Pharmacotherapy of childhood hyperactivity: An update. In H. Y. Meltzer (Ed.), *Psychopharmacology: The third generation of progress* (3rd ed., pp. 1215–1224). New York: Raven Press.

Gittelman, R. (1980). Drug treatment of child psychiatric disorders. In D. F. Klein, R. Gittelman, F. Quitkin, & A. Rifkin (Eds.), *Diagnosis and Drug Treatment of Psychiatric Disorders* (2nd ed.; pp. 590–756). Baltimore: Williams & Wilkins.

Gittelman, R. & Kanner, A. (1986). Psychopharmacotherapy. In H. Quay & J. Werry (Eds.), *Psychopathological disorders of childhood* (3rd ed., pp. 455–495). New York: Wiley.

Gittelman, R. & Mannuzza, S. (1988). Hyperactive boys almost grown up: 3. Methylphenidate effects on ultimate height. *Archives of General Psychiatry, 45,* 1131–1134.

Gittelman-Klein, R., Landa, B., Mattes, J. A., & Klein, D. F. (1988). Methylphenidate and growth in hyperactive children. *Archives of General Psychiatry, 45,* 1127–1130.

Goldman, L., Genel, M., Bazman, R., & Slanetz, P. (1998). Diagnosis and treatment of attention-deficit/hyperactivity disorder [Abstract]. *Journal of the American Medical Association, 279,* 1100–1107.

Greenhill, L. (1995). Attention-deficit hyperativity disorder: The stimulants. *Child and Adolescent Psychiatric Clinics, 4,* 123–168.

Greenhill, L., Swanson J. M., Vitiello, B., Davies, M., Clevenger, W., Wu, M., et al. (2001a). Determining the best dose of methylphenidate under controlled conditions: Lessons from the MTA titration. *Journal of the American Academy of Child and Adolescent Psychiatry, 40,* 180–187.

Greenhill, L. L. (1981). Stimulant-relation growth inhibition in children: A review. In M.Gittelman (Ed.), *Strategic interventions for hyperactive children* (pp. 39–63). Armonk, NY: Sharpe.

Greenhill, L. L. (1984). Stimulant related growth inhi-

bition in children: A review. In B. Shopsin (Ed.), *The psychobiology of childhood* (pp. 135–157). New York: SP Medical and Scientific Books.

Greenhill, L. L. (2001). Preschool ADHD treatment study (PATS): Science and controversy. *The Economics of Neuroscience, 3,* 49–53.

Greenhill, L. L., Abikoff, H. B., Arnold, L. E., Cantwell, D. P., Conners, C. K., Elliott, G., et al. (1996). Medication treatment strategies in the MTA Study: Relevance to clinicians and researchers. *Journal of the American Academy of Child and Adolescent Psychiatry, 35,* 1304–1313.

Greenhill, L. L., Abikoff, H. B., Arnold, L. E., Cantwell, D. P., Conners, C. K., Elliott, G., et al. (1996). Medication treatment strategies in the MTA Study: Relevance to clinicians and researchers. *Journal of the American Academy of Child and Adolescent Psychiatry, 35,* 1304–1313.

Greenhill, L. L., Findling, R. L., & Swanson, J. M. (2002). A double-blind, placebo-controlled study of modified-release methylphenidate in children with attention-deficit/hyperactivity disorder. *Pediatrics, 109,* e39.

Greenhill, L. L., Kollins, S., Abikoff, H., McCracken, J. T., Riddle, M., Swanson, J., et al. (2006). Efficacy and safety of immediate-release methylphenidate for preschoolers with ADHD. *Journal of the American Academy of Child and Adolescent Psychiatry, 45,* 1284–1293.

Greenhill, L. L., Muniz, R., Ball, R. R., Levine, A., Pestreich, L., & Jiang, H. (2006b). Efficacy and safety of dexmethylphenidate extended-release capsules in children with attention-deficit/hyperactivity disorder. *Journal of the American Academy of Child and Adolescent Psychiatry, 45,* 817–823.

Greenhill, L. L., Perel, J. M., Rudolph, G., Feldman, B., Curran, S., Puig-Antich, J., et al. (2001). Correlations between motor persistence and plasma levels in methylphenidate-treated boys with ADHD. *International Journal of Neuropsychopharmacology, 4,* 207–215.

Greenhill, L. L., Puig-Antich, J., Chambers, W., Rubinstein, B., Halpern, F., & Sachar, E. J. (1981). Growth hormone, prolactin, and growth responses in hyperkinetic males treated with d-amphetamine. *Journal of the American Academy of Child and Adolescent Psychiatry, 20,* 84–103.

Greenhill, L. L., Puig-Antich, J., Novacenko, H., Solomon, M., Anghern, C., Florea, J., et al. (1984). Prolactin, growth hormone and growth responses in boys with attention deficit disorder and hyperactivity treated with methylphenidate. *Journal of the American Academy of Child and Adolescent Psychiatry, 23,* 58–67.

Halperin, J. M., Matier, K., Bedi, G., Sharma, V., & Newcorn, J. H. (1992). Specificity of inattention, impulsivity, and hyperactivity to the diagnosis of attention-deficit hyperactivity disorder. *Journal of the American Academy of Child and Adolescent Psychiatry, 31,* 190–196.

Handen, B. L., Feldman, H. M., Lurier, A., & Murray, P. J. H. (1999). Efficacy of methylphenidate among preschool children with developmental disabilities and ADHD. *Journal of the American Academy of Child and Adolescent Psychiatry, 38,* 805–812.

Hechtman, L., Weiss, G., Perlman, T., & Amsel, R. (1984). Hyperactives as young adults: Initial predictors of adult outcome. *Journal of the American Academy of Child Psychiatry, 23,* 250–260.

Hinshaw, S. (1991). Effects of methylphenidate on aggressive and antisocial behavior [Abstract]. *Proceedings of the American Academy of Child and Adolescent Psychiatry, 7,* 31–32.

Hinshaw, S. P., Heller, T., & McHale, J. P. (1992). Covert antisocial behavior in boys with attention-deficit hyperactivity disorder: External validation and effects of methylphenidate. *Journal of Consulting and Clinical Psychology, 60,* 274–281.

Hinton, S., Conners, C., Levin, E., & Meck, W. (1995). Nicotine and attention-deficit disorder: Effects on temporal generalization [Abstract]. *Psychopharmacology Bulletin, 31,* 579.

Horn, W. F., Ialongo, N. S., Pascoe, J. M., Greenberg, G., Packard, T., Lopez, M., et al. (1991). Additive effects of psychostimulants, parent training, and self-control therapy with ADHD children. *Journal of the American Academy of Child and Adolescent Psychiatry, 30,* 233–240.

Hornig-Roher, M. & Amsterdam, J. (1995). Venlafaxine verus stimulant therapy in patients with dual diagnosis of attention deficit disorder and depression [Abstract]. *Psychological Bulletin, 3,* 580.

Humphries, T., Kinsbourne, M., & Swanson, J. (1978). Stimulant effects on cooperation and social interaction between hyperactive children and their mothers. *Journal of Child Psychology and Psychiatry, 19,* 13–22.

Hunt, R. D., Arnsten, A. F., & Asbell, M. D. (1995). An open trial of guanfacine in the treatment of attention-deficit hyperactivity disorder. *Journal of the American Academy of Child and Adolescent Psychiatry, 34,* 50–54.

Hunt, R. D., Minderaa, R. B., & Cohen, D. J. (1985). Clonidine benefits children with attention deficit disorder and hyperactivity: Report of a double-blind placebo-crossover therapeutic trial. *Journal of*

the American Academy of Child and Adolescent Psychiatry, 24, 617–629.

Ickowicz, A., Tannock, R., Fulford, P., Purvis, K., & Schachar, R. (1992). Transient tics and compulsive behaviors following methylphenidate: Evidence from a placebo-controlled double-blind clinical trial. *American Academy of Child and Adolescent Psychiatry, Scientific Proceedings of the Annual Meeting, 8,* 70.

Jacobsen, L. K., Chappell, P., & Woolston, J. L. (1994). Bupropion and compulsive behavior. *Journal of the American Academy of Child and Adolescent Psychiatry, 33,* 143–144.

Jacobson, N. S. & Truax, P. (1991). Clinical significance: A statistical approach to defining meaningful change in psychotherapy research. *Journal of Consulting and Clinical Psychology, 59,* 12–19.

Jacobvitz, D., Sroufe, L. A., Stewart, M., & Leffert, N. (1990). Treatment of attentional and hyperactivity problems in children with sympathomimetic drugs: A comprehensive review. *Journal of the American Academy of Child and Adolescent Psychiatry, 29,* 677–688.

Jahad, A., Boyle, M., Cunningham, C., Kim, M., & Shcachar, R. (1999). *Treatment of Attention-Deficit/Hyperactivity Disorder, AHRQ Publication No. 00-E005.* Rockville, MD: Agency for Healthcare Research and Quality, U.S. Department of Health and Human Services.

Jensen, P. S., Arnold, L. E., Richters, J. E., Severe, J. B., Vereen, D., Vitiello, B., et al. (1999). Moderators and mediators of treatment response for children with attention-deficit/hyperactivity disorder: The multimodal treatment study of children with attention-deficit/hyperactivity disorder. *Archives of General Psychiatry, 56,* 1088–1096.

Jensen, P. S., Arnold, L. E., Severe, J. B., Vitiello, B., & Hoagwood, K. (2004). National Institute of Mental Health Multimodal Treatment Study of ADHD follow-up: 24-month outcomes of treatment strategies for attention-deficit/hyperactivity disorder. *Pediatrics, 113,* 754–761.

Jensen, P. S., Kettle, L., Roper, M. T., Sloan, M. T., Dulcan, M. K., Hoven, C., et al. (1999). Are stimulants overprescribed? Treatment of ADHD in four U.S. communities. *Journal of the American Academy of Child and Adolescent Psychiatry, 38,* 797–804.

Kavale, K. (1982). The efficacy of stimulant drug treatment for hyperactivity: A meta-analysis. *Journal of Learning Disabilities, 15,* 280–289.

Kessler, R., Adler, L., Barkley, R., Biederman, J., Conners, C. K., Demler, O., et al. (2006). The prevalence and correlates of adult ADHD in the United

States: Results from the national comorbidity survey replication. *American Journal of Psychiatry, 4,* 716–723.

Klein, R. G. (1995). The role of methylphenidate in psychiatry. *Archives of General Psychiatry, 52,* 429–433.

Klein, R. G., Abikoff, H., Hechtman, L., & Weiss, G. (2004). Design and rationale of controlled study of long-term methylphenidate and multimodal psychosocial treatment in children with ADHD. *Journal of the American Academy of Child and Adolescent Psychiatry, 43,* 792–801.

Klein, R. G., Abikoff, H., Klass, E., Ganeles, D., Seese, L. M., & Pollack, S. (1997). Clinical efficacy of methylphenidate in conduct disorder with and without attention deficit hyperactivity disorder. *Archives of General Psychiatry, 54,* 1073–1080.

Klorman, R., Brumaghim, J. T., Fitzpatrick, P. A., & Borgstedt, A. D. (1990). Clinical effects of a controlled trial of methylphenidate on adolescents with attention deficit disorder. *Journal of the American Academy of Child and Adolescent Psychiatry, 29,* 702–709.

Kollins, S., Greenhill, L., Swanson, J., Wigal, S., Abikoff, H., McCracken, J., et al. (2006). Rationale, design and methods of the Preschool ADHD Treatment Study. *Journal of the American Academy of Child and Adolescent Psychiatry, 45,* 1275–1283.

Kupfer, D. J., Baltimore, R. S., Berry, D. A., Breslau, N., Ellinwood, E. H., Ferre, J., et al. (2000). National Institutes of Health Consensus Development Conference Statement: Diagnosis and treatment of attention-deficit/hyperactivity disorder (ADHD). *Journal of the American Academy of Child and Adolescent Psychiatry, 39,* 182–193.

Lahey, B. B., Pelham, W. E., Loney, J., Lee, S. S., & Willcutt, E. (2005). Instability of the *DSM-IV* subtypes of ADHD from preschool through elementary school. *Archives of General Psychiatry, 62,* 896–902.

Laufer, M. W., Denhoff, E., & Solomon, G. (1957). Hyperkinetic impulse disorder in children's behavior problems. *Psychosomatic Medicine, 19,* 38–49.

Leech, S. L., Richardson, G. A., Goldschmidt, L., & Day, N. L. (1999). Prenatal substance exposure: Effects on attention and impulsivity of 6-year-olds. *Neurotoxicology and Teratology, 21,* 109–118.

LeFever, G. B., Dawson, K. V., & Morrow, A. L. (1999). The extent of drug therapy for attention deficit-hyperactivity disorder among children in public schools. *American Journal of Public Health, 89,* 1359–1364.

Liberthson, R. R. (1996). Current concepts: Sudden death from cardiac causes in children and young adults. *New England Journal of Medicine, 334,* 1039–1044.

Luh, J., Pliszka, S. R., Olvera, R., & Taton, R. (1995). An open trial of venlafaxine in the treatment of ADHD [Abstract]. *Proceedings of the Annual Meeting of the American Academy of Child and Adolescent Psychiatry, 11,* 122.

Mannuzza, S., Klein, R. G., Bessler, A., Malloy, P., & LaPadula, M. (1993). Adult outcome of hyperactive boys: Educational achievement, occupational rank, and psychiatric status. *Archives of General Psychiatry, 50,* 565–576.

Mannuzza, S., Klein, R. G., Bessler, A., Malloy, P., & LaPadula, M. (1998). Adult psychiatric status of hyperactive boys grown up. *American Journal of Psychiatry, 155,* 493–498.

Mannuzza, S., Klein, R. G., & Moulton, J. L., III (2002). Young adult outcome of children with "situational" hyperactivity: A prospective, controlled follow-up study. *Journal of Abnormal Child Psychology, 30,* 191–198.

March, J., Conners, C. K., Erhardt, D., & Johnson, H. (1994). Pharmacotherapy of attention-deficit hyperactivity disorder. *Annals of Drug Therapy, 2,* 187–213.

Matochik, J. A., Liebenauer, L. L., King, A. C., Szymanski, H. V., Cohen, R. M., & Zametkin, A. J. (1994). Cerebral glucose metabolism in adults with attention deficit hyperactivity disorder after chronic stimulant treatment. *American Journal of Psychiatry, 151,* 658–664.

Matochik, J. A., Nordahl, T. E., Gross, M., Semple, W. E., King, A. C., Cohen, R. M., et al.. (1993). Effects of acute stimulant medication on cerebral metabolism in adults with hyperactivity. *Neuropsychopharmacology, 8,* 377–386.

Mattes, J. A., Boswell, L., & Oliver, H. (1984). Methylphenidate effects on symptoms of attention deficit disorder in adults. *Archives of General Psychiatry, 41,* 1059–1063.

Mayes, S. D., Crites, D. L., Bixler, E. O., Humphrey, F. J., & Mattison, R. E. (1994). Methylphenidate and ADHD: Influence of age, IQ and neurodevelopmental status. *Developmental Medicine and Child Neurology, 36,* 1099–1107.

McCormick, L., Rizzuo, G., & Knickes, H. (1994). A pilot study of buspirone in ADHD. *Archives of General Psychiatry, 3,* 68–70.

McCracken, J. T. (1991). A two-part model of stimulant action on attention-deficit hyperactivity disorder in children. *Journal of Neuropsychiatry and Clinical Neuroscience, 3,* 201–209.

McCracken, J. T., Biederman, J., Greenhill, L. L., Swanson, J. M., McGough, J. J., Spencer, T., et al.

(2003). Analog classroom assessment of a once-daily mixed amphetamine formulation, SLI381 (Adderall XR), in children with ADHD. *Journal of the American Academy of Child and Adolescent Psychiatry, 42,* 673–683.

McGough, J. J., McBurnett, K., Bukstein, O., Wilens, T. E., Greenhill, L., Lerner, M., et al. (2006). Once-daily OROS methylphenidate is safe and well tolerated in adolescents with attention-deficit/hyperactivity disorder. *Journal of Child and Adolescent Psychopharmacology, 16,* 351–356.

McMaster University Evidence-Based Practice Center (1998). *The treatment of attention-deficit/hyperactivity disorder: An evidence report.* Contract 290–97–0017. [Abstract].

Michelson, D. (2004). *Results from a double-blind study of atomoxetine, OROS methylphenidate, and placebo.* Paper presented at the 51st Annual Meeting of the American Academy of Child and Adolescent Psychiatry, Washington, DC.

Michelson, D., Adler, L., Spencer, T., Reimherr, F. W., West, S. A., Allen, A. J., et al. (2003). Atomoxetine in adults with ADHD: Two randomized, placebo-controlled studies. *Biological Psychiatry, 53,* 112–120.

Michelson, D., Allen, A. J., Busner, J., Casat, C., Dunn, D., Kratochvil, C., et al. (2002). Once-daily atomoxetine treatment for children and adolescents with attention deficit hyperactivity disorder: A randomized, placebo-controlled study. *American Journal of Psychiatry, 159,* 1896–1901.

Michelson, D., Buitelaar, J. K., Danckaerts, M., Gillberg, C., Spencer, T. J., Zuddas, A., et al. (2004). Relapse prevention in pediatric patients with ADHD treated with atomoxetine: A randomized, double-blind, placebo-controlled study. *Journal of the American Academy of Child and Adolescent Psychiatry, 43,* 896–904.

Michelson, D., Faries, D., Wernicke, J., Kelsey, D., Kendrick, K., Sallee, F. R., et al. (2001). Atomoxetine in the treatment of children and adolescents with attention-deficit/hyperactivity disorder: A randomized, placebo-controlled, dose-response study. *Pediatrics, 108,* e83.

Milich, R., Licht, B. G., Murphy, D. A., & Pelham, W. E. (1989). Attention-deficit hyperactivity disordered boys' evaluations of and attributions for task performance on medication versus placebo. *Journal of Abnormal Psychology, 98,* 280–284.

Modi, N. B., Wang, B., Noveck, R. J., & Gupta, S. K. (2000). Dose-proportional and stereospecific pharmacokinetics of methylphenidate delivered using an osmotic, controlled-release oral delivery system. *Journal of Clinical Pharmacology, 40,* 1141–1149.

MTA Cooperative Group (1999). 14-month randomized clinical trial of treatment strategies for attention deficit hyperactivity disorder. *Archives of General Psychiatry, 56,* 1073–1086.

MTA Cooperative Group (2004). National Institute of Mental Health Multimodal Treatment Study of ADHD follow-up: Changes in effectiveness and growth after the end of treatment. *Pediatrics, 113,* 762–769.

Musten, L. M., Firestone, P., Pisterman, S., Bennett, S., & Mercer, J. (1997). Effects of methylphenidate on preschool children with ADHD: Cognitive and behavioral functions. *Journal of the American Academy of Child and Adolescent Psychiatry, 36,* 1407–1415.

New Indications for Modafinil (Provigil). (2004). *Medical Letter on Drugs and Therapeutics, 46,* 34–35.

Newcorn, J., Michelson, D., Kratochvil, C., Allen, A. J., Ruff, D., & Moore, P. (2006). Low-dose atomoxetine for maintenance treatment of ADHD. *Pediatrics.* In press.

Ottenbacher, K. J. & Cooper, H. M. (1983). Drug treatment of hyperactivity in children. *Developmental Medicine and Child Neurology, 25,* 358–366.

Pelham, W. (1989). Behavior therapy, behavioral assessment and psychostimulant medication in the treatment of attention deficit disorders: An interactive approach. In J. Swanson & L. Bloomingdale (Eds.), *Attention deficit disorder: Vol. 4, Emerging trends in the treatment of attention and behavioral problems in children* (pp. 169–195). London: Pergamon.

Pelham, W. & Bender, M. E. (1982). Peer relationships in hyperactive children: Description and treatment. In K. D. B. I. Gadow (Ed.), *Advances in learning and behavioral disabilities* (pp. 365–432). Greenwich, CT: JAI Press.

Pelham, W. & Murphy, H. (1986). Behavioral and pharmacological treatment of hyperactivity and attention deficit disorders. In M. Hersen & J. Breuning (Eds.), *Pharmacological and behavioral treatment: An integrative approach* (pp. 108–147). New York: Wiley.

Pelham, W. E., Aronoff, H. R., Midlam, J. K., Shapiro, C. J., Gnagy, E. M., Chronis, A. M., et al. (1999). A comparison of ritalin and adderall: Efficacy and time-course in children with attention-deficit/hyperactivity disorder. *Pediatrics, 103,* e43.

Pelham, W. E., Bender, M. E., Caddell, J., Booth, S., & Moorer, S. H. (1985). Methylphenidate and children with attention deficit disorder: Dose effects on classroom academic and social behavior. *Archives of General Psychiatry, 42,* 948–952.

Pelham, W. E., Greenslade, K. E., Vodde-Hamilton, M., Murphy, D. A., Greenstein, J. J., Gnagy, E. M., et al. (1990). Relative efficacy of long-acting stimulants on children with attention deficit-hyperactivity disorder: Comparison of standard methylphenidate, sustained-release methylphenidate, sustained-release dextroamphetamine, and pemoline. *Pediatrics, 86,* 226–237.

Pelham, W. E., Hoffman, M. T., Lock, T., & SUNY CONCERTA Study Group (2000). *Evaluation of once-a-day OROS methylphenidate HCl (MPH extended-release tablet versus MPH tid in children with ADHD in natural school settings* [Abstract]. Paper presented at the Pediatric Academic Societies and American Academy of Pediatrics Joint Meeting, Boston, MA.

Pelham, W. E. & Milich, R. (1991). Individual differences in response to Ritalin in classwork and social behavior. In L. L.Greenhill & B. Osman (Eds.), *Ritalin: Theory and patient management* (pp. 203–222). New York: Mary Ann Liebert.

Pelham, W. E., Swanson, J. M., Furman, M. B., & Schwindt, H. (1995). Pemoline effects on children with ADHD: A time-response by dose-response analysis on classroom measures. *Journal of the American Academy of Child and Adolescent Psychiatry, 34,* 1504–1513.

Perel, J. M., Greenhill, L. L., Curran, S., Feldman, B., & Puig-Antich, J. (1991). Correlates of pharmacokinetics and attentional measures in methylphenidate-treated hyperactive children. *Clinical Pharmacology and Therapy, 49,* 160–161.

Pleak, R. R. & Gormly, L. J. (1995). Effects of venlafaxine treatment for ADHD in a child. *American Journal of Psychiatry, 152,* 1099.

Pliszka, S. R. (1989). Effect of anxiety on cognition, behavior, and stimulant response in ADHD. *Journal of the American Academy of Child and Adolescent Psychiatry, 28,* 882–887.

Pliszka, S. R., Greenhill, L. L., Crismon, M. L., Sedillo, A., Carlson, C., Conners, C. K., et al. (2000). The Texas Children's Medication Algorithm Project: Report of the Texas Consensus Conference Panel on Medication Treatment of Childhood Attention-Deficit/Hyperactivity Disorder. Part II: Tactics. Attention-deficit/hyperactivity disorder. *Journal of the American Academy of Child and Adolescent Psychiatry, 39,* 920–927.

Pliszka, S. R., Matthews, T. L., Braslow, K. J., & Watson, M. A. (2006). Comparative effects of methylphenidate and mixed salts amphetamine on height and weight in children with attention-deficit/hyperactivity disorder. *Journal of the American Academy of Child and Adolescent Psychiatry, 45,* 520–526.

Poulton, A. (2005). Growth on stimulant medication; clarifying the confusion: A review. *Archives of Disease in Childhood, 90,* 801–806.

Quiason, N., Ward, D., & Kitchen, T. (1991). Buspirone for aggression. *Journal of the American Academy of Child and Adolescent Psychiatry, 30,* 1026.

Quinn, D., Wigal, S., Swanson, J., Hirsch, S., Ottolini, Y., Dariani, M., et al. (2004). Comparative pharmacodynamics and plasma concentrations of d-threomethylphenidate hydrochloride after single doses of d-threo-methylphenidate hydrochloride and d,l-threo-methylphenidate hydrochloride in a double-blind, placebo-controlled, crossover laboratory school study in children with attention-deficit/hyperactivity disorder. *Journal of the American Academy of Child and Adolescent Psychiatry, 43,* 1422–1429.

Rapoport, J. L., Buchsbaum, M. S., Weingartner, H., Zahn, T. P., Ludlow, C., & Mikkelsen, E. J. (1980). Dextroamphetamine: Its cognitive and behavioral effects in normal and hyperactive boys and normal men. *Archives of General Psychiatry, 37,* 933–943.

Rapport, M. D., Denney, C., DuPaul, G. J., & Gardner, M. J. (1994). Attention deficit disorder and methylphenidate: Normalization rates, clinical effectiveness, and response prediction in 76 children. *Journal of the American Academy of Child and Adolescent Psychiatry, 33,* 882–893.

Rapport, M. D., DuPaul, G. J., & Kelly, K. L. (1989). Attention deficit hyperactivity disorder and methylphenidate: The relationship between gross body weight and drug response in children. *Psychopharmacology Bulletin, 25,* 285–290.

Rapport, M. D., Stoner, G., DuPaul, G. J., Kelly, K. L., Tucker, S. B., & Schoeler, T. (1988). Attention deficit disorder and methylphenidate: A multilevel analysis of dose-response effects on children's impulsivity across settings. *Journal of the American Academy of Child and Adolescent Psychiatry, 27,* 60–69.

Ratey, J. J., Greenberg, M. S., & Lindem, K. J. (1991). Combination of treatments for attention deficit hyperactivity disorder in adults. *The Journal of Nervous and Mental Disease, 179,* 699–701.

Reimherr, F., Hedges, D., Strong, R., & Wender, P. (1995). An open trial of venlafaxine in adult patients with ADHD. *Psychological Bulletin, 31,* 609–614.

Richters, J. E., Arnold, L. E., Jensen, P. S., Abikoff, H., Conners, C. K., Greenhill, L. L., et al. (1995). NIMH collaborative Multisite Multimodal Treatment Study of Children with ADHD. I. Background and rationale. *Journal of the American*

Academy of Child and Adolescent Psychiatry, 34, 987–1000.

Roche, A. F., Lipman, R. S., Overall, J. E., & Hung, W. (1979). The effects of stimulant medication on the growth of hyperactive children. *Pediatrics, 63,* 847–849.

Sabelsky, D. (1990). Fluoxetine in adults with residual attention deficit disorder and hypersomnolence. *Journal of Neuropsychiatry and Clinical Neuroscience, 2,* 463–464.

Safer, D., Allen, R., & Barr, E. (1972). Depression of growth in hyperactive children on stimulant drugs. *New England Journal of Medicine, 287,* 217–220.

Safer, D. J. & Allen, R. P. (1973). Factors influencing the suppressant effects of two stimulant drugs on the growth of hyperactive children. *Pediatrics, 51,* 660–667.

Safer, D. J., Allen, R. P., & Barr, E. (1975). Growth rebound after termination of stimulant drugs. *Journal of Pediatrics, 86,* 113–116.

Safer, D. J., Zito, J. M., & Fine, E. M. (1996). Increased methylphenidate usage for attention deficit disorder in the 1990s. *Pediatrics, 98,* 1084–1088.

Satterfield, J. H., Cantwell, D. P., Schell, A., & Blaschke, T. (1979). Growth of hyperactive children treated with methylphenidate. *Archives of General Psychiatry, 36,* 212–217.

Schachar, R. & Tannock, R. (1993). Childhood hyperactivity and psychostimulants: A review of extended treatment studies. *Journal of Child and Adolescent Psychopharmacology, 3,* 81–97.

Schachar, R. J., Tannock, R., Cunningham, C., & Corkum, P. V. (1997). Behavioral, situational, and temporal effects of treatment of ADHD with methylphenidate. *Journal of the American Academy of Child and Adolescent Psychiatry, 36,* 754–763.

Schachter, H. M., Pham, B., King, J., Langford, S., & Moher, D. (2001). How efficacious and safe is short-acting methylphenidate for the treatment of attention-deficit disorder in children and adolescents? A meta-analysis. *Canadian Medical Association Journal, 165,* 1475–1488.

Schechter, M. & Keuezer, E. (1985). Learning in hyperactive children: Are there stimulant-related and state-dependent effects? *Journal of Clinical Pharmacology, 25,* 276–280.

Schleifer, M., Weiss, G., Cohen, N., Elman, M., Cvejic, H., & Kruger, E. (1975). Hyperactivity in preschoolers and the effect of methylphenidate. *American Journal of Orthopsychiatry, 45,* 38–50.

Shekim, W. O., Masterson, A., Cantwell, D. P., Hanna, G. L., & McCracken, J. T. (1989). Nomifensine maleate in adult attention deficit disorder. *Journal of Nervous and Mental Disease, 177,* 296–299.

Sherman, M. (1991). Prescribing practice of methylphenidate: The Suffolk County study. In B. Osman & L. L. Greenhill (Eds.), *Ritalin: Theory and patient management* (pp. 401–420). New York: Mary Ann Liebert.

Simeon, J. G., Ferguson, H. B., & Van Wyck, F. J. (1986). Bupropion effects in attention deficit and conduct disorders. *Canadian Journal of Psychiatry, 31,* 581–585.

Solanto, M. V. (1984). Neuropharmacological basis of stimulant drug action in attention deficit disorder with hyperactivity: A review and synthesis. *Psychological Bulletin, 95,* 387–409.

Speltz, M. L., Varley, C. K., Peterson, K., & Beilke, R. L. (1988). Effects of dextroamphetamine and contingency management on a preschooler with ADHD and oppositional defiant disorder. *Journal of the American Academy of Child and Adolescent Psychiatry, 27,* 175–178.

Spencer, T., Biederman, J., Steingard, R., & Wilens, T. (1993). Bupropion exacerbates tics in children with attention-deficit hyperactivity disorder and Tourette's syndrome. *Journal of the American Academy of Child and Adolescent Psychiatry, 32,* 211–214.

Spencer, T., Biederman, J., Wilens, T., Faraone, S., Prince, J., Gerard, K., et a. (2001). Efficacy of a mixed amphetamine salts compound in adults with attention-deficit/hyperactivity disorder. *Archives of General Psychiatry, 58,* 775–782.

Spencer, T., Biederman, J., Wilens, T., Harding, M., O'Donnell, D., & Griffin, S. (1996). Pharmacotherapy of attention-deficit hyperactivity disorder across the life cycle. *Journal of the American Academy of Child and Adolescent Psychiatry, 35,* 409–432.

Spencer, T., Biederman, J., Wilens, T., Prince, J., Hatch, M., Jones, J., Harding, M., Faraone, S. V., & Seidman, L. (1998). Effectiveness and tolerability of tomoxetine in adults with attention deficit hyperactivity disorder. *American Journal of Psychiatry, 155,* 693–695.

Spencer, T., Wilens, T., Biederman, J., Faraone, S. V., Ablon, J. S., & Lapey, K. (1995). A double-blind, crossover comparison of methylphenidate and placebo in adults with childhood-onset attention-deficit hyperactivity disorder. *Archives of General Psychiatry, 52,* 434–443.

Spencer, T. J., Biederman, J., Harding, M., O'Donnell, D., Faraone, S. V., & Wilens, T. E. (1996). Growth deficits in ADHD children revisited: evidence for disorder-associated growth delays? *Journal of the American Academy of Child and Adolescent Psychiatry, 35,* 1460–1469.

Sprague, R. L. & Sleator, E. K. (1977). Methylphenidate in hyperkinetic children: Differences in dose
effects on learning and social behavior. *Science,
198*, 1274–1276.

Stephens, R. S., Pelham, W. E., & Skinner, R. (1984).
State-dependent and main effects of methylphenidate and pemoline on paired-associate learning
and spelling in hyperactive children. *Journal of
Consulting and Clinical Psychology, 52*, 104–113.

Swanson, J. (1993). Effect of stimulant medication on
hyperactive children: A review of reviews. *Excep-
tional Child, 60*, 154–162.

Swanson, J., Flockhart, D., Udrea, D., Cantwell, D.,
Conner, D., & Williams, L. (1995). Clonidine in
the treatment of ADHD: Questions about the
safety and efficacy. *Journal of Child and Adolescent
Psychopharmacology, 5*, 301–305.

Swanson, J., Greenhill, L., Wigal, T., Kollins, S., Stehli-
Nguyen, Davies, M., et al. (2006). Stimulant-
related reductions of growth rates in the PATS.
*Journal of the American Academy of Child and Ado-
lescent Psychiatry, 45*, 1304–1313.

Swanson, J., Gupta, S., Lam, A., Shoulson, I., Lerner,
M., Modi, N., et al. (2003). Development of a new
once-a-day formulation of methylphenidate for the
treatment of attention-deficit/hyperactivity disorder: Proof-of-concept and proof-of-product studies.
Archives of General Psychiatry, 60, 204–211.

Swanson, J. M., Gupta, S., Williams, L., Agler, D., Lerner, M., & Wigal, S. (2002). Efficacy of a new pattern of delivery of methylphenidate for the treatment of ADHD: Effects on activity level in the
classroom and on the playground. *Journal of the
American Academy of Child and Adolescent Psychiatry, 41*, 1306–1314.

Swanson, J. M. & Kinsbourne, M. (1976). Stimulant-
related state-dependent learning in hyperactive
children. *Science, 192*, 1354–1357.

Swanson, J. M., Lerner, M., & Williams, L. (1995b).
More frequent diagnosis of attention deficit-hyperactivity disorder. *New England Journal of Medicine, 333*, 944.

Swanson, J. M., Wigal, S., Greenhill, L. L., Browne,
R., Waslik, B., Lerner, M., et al. (1998). Analog
classroom assessment of Adderall in children with
ADHD. *Journal of the American Academy of Child
and Adolescent Psychiatry, 37*, 519–526.

Swanson, J. M., Wigal, S. B., Wigal, T., Sonuga-Barke,
E., Greenhill, L. L., Biederman, J., et al. (2004). A
comparison of once-daily extended-release methylphenidate formulations in children with attention-
deficit/hyperactivity disorder in the laboratory school

(the Comacs Study). *Pediatrics, 113*, e206–e216.

Szatmari, P. (1992). The epidemiology of attention-
deficit hyperactivity disorders. *Child and Adolescent Psychiatric Clinics, 1*, 361–371.

Szatmari, P., Offord, D. R., & Boyle, M. H. (1989). Ontario Child Health Study: Prevalence of attention
deficit disorder with hyperactivity. *Journal of Child
Psychology and Psychiatry, 30*, 219–230.

Tannock, R., Ickowicz, A., & Schachar, R. (1995). Differential effects of methylphenidate on working
memory in ADHD children with and without
comorbid anxiety. *Journal of the American Academy of Child and Adolescent Psychiatry, 34*, 886–
896.

Tannock, R., Schachar, R., & Logan, G. (1995). Methylphenidate and cognitive flexibility: Dissociated
dose effects in hyperactive children. *Journal of Abnormal Child Psychology, 23*, 235–266.

Tannock, R., Schachar, R., & Logan, R. (1993). Methylphenidate and working memory: Differential effects in attention-deficit hyperactivity disorder
(ADHD) with and without memory. *AACAP, Scientific Proceedings of the Annual Meeting, 9*, 42.

Taylor, E., Sandberg, S., Thorley, G., & Rutter, M.
(1991). The epidemiology of childhood hyperactivity. In E.Taylor & M.Rutter (Eds.), *Child psychiatry* (pp. 1–122). London: Oxford University Press.

Taylor, E., Schachar, R., Thorley, G., Wieselberg,
H. M., Everitt, B., & Rutter, M. (1987). Which
boys respond to stimulant medication? A controlled
trial of methylphenidate in boys with disruptive behaviour. *Psychological Medicine, 17*, 121–143.

Thurber, S. & Walker, C. E. (1983). Medication and
hyperactivity: A meta-analysis. *The Journal of General Psychology, 108*, 79–86.

Tjon Pian Gi, C. V., Broeren, J. P., Starreveld, J. S., &
Versteegh, F. G. (2003). Melatonin for treatment
of sleeping disorders in children with attention
deficit/hyperactivity disorder: A preliminary open
label study. *European Journal of Pediatrics, 162*,
554–555.

Velez, C. N., Johnson, J., & Cohen, P. (1989). A longitudinal analysis of selected risk factors for childhood psychopathology. *Journal of the American
Academy of Child and Adolescent Psychiatry, 28*,
861–864.

Verhulst, F., Eussen, M., & Berden, G. (1992). Pathways of problem behaviors from childhood to adolescence. *Journal of the American Academy of
Child and Adolescent Psychiatry, 32*, 388–392.

Vikan, A. (1985). Psychiatric epidemiology in a sample
of 1510 ten-year-old children: I. Prevalence. *Journal of Child Psychology and Psychiatry, 26*, 55–75.

Visser, S. N. & Lesesne, C. A. (2005). Mental health in the United States: prevalence of diagnosis and medication treatment for attention-deficit/hyperactivity disorder—United States, 2003. *Morbidity and Mortality Weekly Report, 54*, 842–847.

Vitiello, B. (2006). Research in child and adolescent psychopharmacology: recent accomplishments and new challenges. *Psychopharmacology (Berlin)*. In press.

Vitiello, B. & Jensen, P. S. (1995). Developmental perspectives in pediatric psychopharmacology. *Psychopharmacology Bulletin, 31*, 75–81.

Vitiello, B. & Jensen, P. S. (1997). Medication development and testing in children and adolescents: Current problems, future directions. *Archives of General Psychiatry, 54*, 871–876.

Volkow, N. D., Ding, Y. S., Fowler, J. S., Wang, G. J., Logan, J., Gatley, J. S., et al. (1995). Is methylphenidate like cocaine? Studies on their pharmacokinetics and distribution in the human brain. *Archives of General Psychiatry, 52*, 456–463.

Volkow, N. D., Wang, G., Fowler, J. S., Logan, J., Gerasimov, M., Maynard, L., (2001). Therapeutic doses of oral methylphenidate significantly increase extracellular dopamine in the human brain. *Journal of Neuroscience, 21*, RC121.

Vyborova, L., Nahunek, K., Drtilkova, I., Balastikova, B., & Misurec, J. (1984). Intraindividual comparison of 21-day application of amphetamine and methylphenidate in hyperkinetic children. *Activas Nervosa Superior, 26*, 268–269.

Weiss, G. & Hechtman, L. (1993). *Hyperactive children grown up.* New York: Guilford Press.

Weiss, G., Hechtman, L., Milroy, T., & Perlman, T. (1985). Psychiatric status of hyperactives as adults: A controlled prospective 15-year follow-up of 63 hyperactive children. *Journal of the American Academy of Child and Adolescent Psychiatry, 24*, 211–220.

Wender, P. (1994). *Attention deficit/hyperactivity disorder in adults.* Presentation at Grand Rounds, New York State Psychiatric Institute, New York.

Wender, P., Wood, D., Reimherr, F., & Ward, M. (1994). An open trial of pargyline in the treatment of adult attention deficit disorder, residual type. *Psychiatry Research, 9*, 329–336.

Wender, P. H. & Reimherr, F. W. (1990). Bupropion treatment of attention-deficit hyperactivity disorder in adults. *American Journal of Psychiatry, 147*, 1018–1020.

Wender, P. H., Reimherr, F. W., & Wood, D. R. (1981). Attention deficit disorder ("minimal brain dysfunction") in adults: A replication study of diagnosis and drug treatment. *Archives of General Psychiatry, 38*, 449–456.

Wesensten, N. J., Belenky, G., Kautz, M. A., Thorne, D. R., Reichardt, R. M., & Balkin, T. J. (2002). Maintaining alertness and performance during sleep deprivation: Modafinil versus caffeine. *Psychopharmacology (Berlin), 159*, 238–247.

Whalen, C. K., Henker, B., Buhrmester, D., Hinshaw, S. P., Huber, A., & Laski, K. (1989). Does stimulant medication improve the peer status of hyperactive children? *Journal of Consulting and Clinical Psychology, 57*, 545–549.

Wigal, S., Swanson, J. M., Feifel, D., Sangal, R. B., Elia, J., Casat, C. D., et al. (2004). A double-blind, placebo-controlled trial of dexmethylphenidate hydrochloride and d,l-threo-methylphenidate hydrochloride in children with attention-deficit/hyperactivity disorder. *Journal of the American Academy of Child and Adolescent Psychiatry, 43*, 1406–1414.

Wigal, T., Greenhill, L., Chuang, S., McGough, J., Vitiello, B., Skrobala, A., et al. (2006). Safety and tolerability of methylphenidate in preschool children with ADHD. *Journal of the American Academy of Child and Adolescent Psychiatry, 45*, 1294–1303.

Wilens, T., Biederman, J., Mick, E., & Spencer, T. (1994a). Treatment of adult attention-deficit hyperactivity disorder (ADHD) with tricyclic antidepressants: Clinical experience with 23 patients. *AACAP, Scientific Proceedings of the Annual Meeting, 9*, 45.

Wilens, T. E. & Biederman, J. (1992). The stimulants. *Psychiatric Clinics of North America, 15*, 191–222.

Wilens, T. E., Biederman, J., & Spencer, T. (1994b). Clonidine for sleep disturbances associated with attention-deficit hyperactivity disorder. *Journal of the American Academy of Child and Adolescent Psychiatry, 33*, 424–426.

Wilens, T. E., Biederman, J., & Spencer, T. J. (1995). Venlafaxine for adult ADHD. *American Journal of Psychiatry, 152*, 1099–1100.

Wilens, T. E., McBurnett, K., Bukstein, O., McGough, J., Greenhill, L., Lerner, M., et al. (2006). Multisite controlled study of OROS methylphenidate in the treatment of adolescents with attention-deficit/hyperactivity disorder. *Archives of Pediatrics and Adolescent Medicine, 160*, 82–90.

Williams, L. & Swanson, J. (1996). *Some aspects of the efficacy and safety of clonidine in children with ADHD.* Unpublished manuscript.

Winsberg, B. G., Press, M., Bialer, I., & Kupietz, S. (1974). Dextroamphetamine and methylphenidate in the treatment of hyperactive-aggressive children. *Pediatrics, 53,* 236–241.

Wolraich, M. L., Greenhill, L. L., Pelham, W., Swanson, J., Wilens, T., Palumbo, D., et al. (2001). Randomized, controlled trial of OROS methylphenidate once a day in children with attention-deficit/ hyperactivity disorder. *Pediatrics, 108,* 883–892.

Zametkin, A. J. & Rapoport, J. L. (1987). Neurobiology of attention deficit disorder with hyperactivity: Where have we come in 50 years? *Journal of the American Academy of Child and Adolescent Psychiatry, 26,* 676–686.

3

Psychosocial Treatments for Conduct Disorder in Children and Adolescents

Alan E. Kazdin

Antisocial and aggressive behavior in children (conduct disorder) is extremely difficult to treat in light of the stability of the problem, untoward long-term prognosis, and the diverse domains of dysfunction in the child, parent, and family with which the problem is associated. Significant advances have been made in treatment. Seven treatments with strong evidence in their behalf with children and adolescents are reviewed and include parent management training, multisystemic therapy, multidimensional treatment foster care, cognitive problem-solving skills training, anger control training, functional family therapy, and brief strategic family therapy. *Parent management training* is directed at altering parent-child interactions in the home, particularly those interactions related to child-rearing practices and coercive interchanges. *Multisystemic therapy* focuses on the individual, family, and extrafamilial systems and their interrelations as a way to reduce symptoms and to promote prosocial behavior. The *multidimensional treatment foster care model* focuses on youth who are in placement and who are to return to their parents or more permanent foster care. Behavioral treatments in the placement and in the setting to which the child is returned are part of a comprehensive effort to integrate treatment and community life. *Cognitive problem-solving skills training* focuses on cognitive processes that underlie social behavior and response repertoires in interpersonal situations. Also cognitively based, *anger control training* includes problem-solving skills training in the context of groups in the schools. The program has an additional component that includes parent management training. *Functional family therapy* utilizes principles of systems theory and behavior modification for altering interaction, communication patterns, and problem solving among family members. *Brief strategic family therapy* focuses on the structure of the family and concrete strategies that can be used to promote improved patterns of interaction. This treatment has been developed with Hispanic children and adolescents and has integrated culturally pertinent issues to engage the families. Questions remain about the long-term impact of various treatments, the persons for whom one or more of these treatments is well suited, and how to optimize therapeutic change. Even so, the extensive evidence indicates that there are several viable treatments for conduct disorder. Disseminating these to professionals and children and families remains a key challenge.

Antisocial behaviors in children refer to a variety of acts that reflect social rule violations and actions against others. Such behaviors as fighting, lying, and stealing are seen in varying degrees in most children over the course of development. *Conduct disorder* (CD) refers to antisocial behavior that is clinically significant and clearly beyond the realm of "normal" functioning. The extent to which antisocial behaviors are sufficiently severe to constitute CD depends on several characteristics of the behaviors, including

71

their frequency, intensity, and chronicity, whether they are isolated acts or part of a larger syndrome with other deviant behaviors, and whether they lead to significant impairment of the child, as judged by parents, teachers, or others.

The significance of CD as a clinical and social problem derives from several factors (Hill & Maughan, 2001; Rutter, Giller, & Hagell, 1998; Stoff, Breiling, & Maser, 1997). The behaviors that constitute CD are among the most frequent bases of clinical referral in child and adolescent treatment services and encompass from one third to one half of referral cases. Moreover, children with CD often traverse multiple social services in childhood, adolescence, and adulthood (e.g., special education, mental health, juvenile justice). This contributes to the fact that CD is one of the most costly mental disorders in the United States (Robins, 1981). The estimated cost for a child with CD is $10,000 to $14,000 per year for social services over the course of childhood and adolescence (Knapp, Scott, & Davies, 1999; Scott, Knapp, Henderson, & Maughan, 2001). These costs are 10 times greater than for a child without the diagnosis.

Fortunately, significant advances have been made in developing effective interventions, in relation to both treatment and prevention (see Kazdin & Weisz, 2003; Lutzker, 2006; Nock, 2003; Weisz, 2004). This chapter reviews significant advances in psychosocial treatments. The treatments were selected because they have been carefully evaluated in controlled clinical trials (Type 1 and 2 studies) with children and adolescents.[1] The chapter describes and evaluates the underpinnings, techniques, and evidence in behalf of these treatments. Limitations of the current evidence and research priorities are also examined.

CHARACTERISTICS OF CONDUCT DISORDER: OVERVIEW

Descriptive Features: Diagnosis and Prevalence

Conduct disorder reflects a persistent pattern of behavior in which the rights of others and age-appropriate social norms are violated. Isolated acts of physical aggression, destruction of property, stealing, and fire setting are sufficiently severe to warrant concern and attention in their own right. Although these behaviors may occur in isolation, several of these are likely to appear together as a constellation or syndrome and form the basis of a clinical diagnosis. For example, in the *Diagnostic and Statistical Manual of Mental Disorders* (*DSM-IV*; American Psychiatric Association, 1994), the diagnosis of conduct disorder is reached if the child shows at least 3 of the 15 symptoms within the past 12 months, with at least 1 symptom evident within the past 6 months. The symptoms include bullying others, initiating fights, using a weapon, being physically cruel to others or to animals, stealing items of nontrivial value, stealing while confronting a victim, fire setting, destroying property, breaking into others' property, staying out late, running away, lying, and truancy.[2]

Using these diagnostic criteria or criteria from prior versions of the *DSM*, the prevalence of the disorder among community samples of school-age youth is approximately 2 to 6% (see Zoccolillo, 1993). Lifetime prevalence rate is approximately 9.5% (Nock, Kazdin, Hiripi, & Kessler, 2006). One of the most frequent findings is that boys show approximately three to four times higher rates of CD than girls. Rates of CD tend to be higher for adolescents (approximately 7% for youths aged 12 to 16) than for children (approximately 4% for children aged 4 to 11 years; Offord, Boyle, & Racine, 1991). The higher prevalence rate for boys is associated primarily with childhood-onset CD; the boy-to-girl ratio evens out for adolescent-onset CD. Characteristic symptom patterns tend to differ as well. Child-onset conduct problems tend to reflect aggressive behavior, whereas adolescent-onset problems tend to reflect delinquent behavior (theft, vandalism).

The prevalence rates underestimate the extent of the problem. The criteria for delineating individual symptoms and the diagnosis are recognized as being somewhat arbitrary. Youths who approximate but fail to meet the diagnosis, sometimes referred to as subsyndromal, often are significantly impaired (Angold, Costello, Farmer, Burns, & Erkanli, 1999). It is likely that CD is better represented as a continuum or set of continua based on the number, severity, and duration of symptoms and degree of impairment rather than as a condition achieved by a particular cutoff (Boyle et al., 1996; Offord et al., 1992). Individuals who miss the cutoff criteria for the diagnosis are likely to show impairment and poor long-term prognoses, although to a lesser extent as a function of the degree of dysfunction.

The general pattern of conduct-disordered behavior has been studied extensively using varied populations (e.g., clinical referrals and delinquent samples) and defining criteria (Kazdin, 1995b; Stoff et al., 1997). There is widespread agreement and evidence that a constellation of antisocial behaviors can be identified and has correlates related to child, parent, and family functioning. Moreover, antisocial behaviors included in the constellation extend beyond those included in the diagnosis (e.g., substance abuse, associating with delinquent peers).

Onset and Long-Term Clinical Course

Conduct disorder is not a homogeneous disorder. Given the diagnostic criteria mentioned previously, more than 32,000 distinct symptom profiles can be identified that would qualify children for the diagnosis. Thus, many children might meet diagnostic criteria for the disorder but not share any of the symptoms. It is unlikely that CD results from a single cause or simple set of antecedents. Current research has focused on different ways of subtyping youth (e.g., Patterson, Reid, & Dishion, 1992), identifying different life courses (e.g., Moffitt & Caspi, 2005), and key personality traits or styles (e.g., Frick & Morris, 2004) that might delineate youth with CD and permit finer grained analyses of the disorder. In addition, extensive research has focused on characteristics, events, and experiences that influence the likelihood (increase the risk) of CD. Table 3.1 highlights several factors that predispose children and adolescents to CD that have been identified in the context of clinically referred and adjudicated youths.

Merely enumerating risk factors is misleading without conveying some of the complexities of how they operate. These complexities have direct implications for interpreting the findings, for understanding the disorder, and for identifying at-risk children for preventive interventions. First, risk factors tend to come in "packages." Thus, at a given point in time several factors may be present, such as low income, large family size, overcrowding, poor housing, poor parental supervision, parent criminality, and marital discord, to mention a few (Kazdin, 1995b). Second, over time, several risk factors become interrelated, because the presence of one factor can lead to the accumulation of other risk factors. For example, early aggression can lead to poor peer relations, aca-demic dysfunction, and dropping out of school, which further increase risk for CD.

Third, risk factors may interact with (i.e., be moderated or influenced by) each other and with other variables such as age, sex, and ethnicity of the child. For example, marital discord and separation appear to serve as risk factors primarily when they occur early in the child's life (e.g., within the first 4 or 5 years; Wadsworth, 1979). How risk factors exert impact in childhood and why some periods of development are sensitive to particular influences underscore the importance of understanding "normal" developmental processes.

Gene-environment interactions in relation to risk convey recent advances in understanding the emergence of antisocial behavior. Individuals with a history of abuse and a particular genetic polymorphism (related to the metabolism of serotonin) are at much greater risk for antisocial behavior (Caspi et al., 2002). Among boys with the allele and maltreatment, 85% developed some form of antisocial behavior (diagnosis of CD, personality assessment of aggression, symptoms of adult personality disorder, or court conviction of violent crime) by the age of 26. Replication and extension of these effects to family adversity have underscored the critical role of gene-environment interactions in antisocial outcomes (Foley et al., 2004; Jaffee et al., 2005).

No single characteristic or factor seems to be necessary or sufficient for the onset of the disorder. Even though some risk factors are more important than others, the accumulation of factors (i.e., number present) itself is important. One or two risk factors may not increase risk very much. With several risk factors, however, the likelihood of the outcome may increase sharply (e.g., Rutter et al., 1998; Sanson, Oberklaid, Pedlow, & Prior, 1991). Even with the presence of multiple risk factors, the outcome is not determined. Some individuals at high risk may not show any dysfunction (Werner & Smith, 1992).

Longitudinal studies have consistently shown that CD identified in childhood predicts a continued course of social dysfunction, problematic behavior, and poor school adjustment. We have known for some time that antisocial child behavior predicts multiple problems in adulthood 30 years later (Robins, 1966). Youths who are referred for their antisocial behavior, compared with youths with other clinical problems or matched "normal" controls, are likely to show psychiatric and physical symptoms,

TABLE 3.1 Factors That Place Youths at Risk for the Onset of Conduct Disorder

Child Factors

Difficult Child Temperament. A more difficult child temperament (on a dimension of "easy-to-difficult"), as characterized by more negative mood, lower levels of approach toward new stimuli, and less adaptability to change.

Neuropsychological Deficits and Difficulties. Deficits in diverse functions related to language (e.g., verbal learning, verbal fluency, verbal IQ), memory, motor coordination, integration of auditory and visual cues, and "executive" functions of the brain (e.g., abstract reasoning, concept formation, planning, control of attention).

Subclinical Levels of Conduct Disorder. Early signs (e.g., elementary school) of mild ("subclinical") levels of unmanageability and aggression, especially with early age of onset, multiple types of antisocial behaviors, and multiple situations in which they are evident (e.g., at home, school, the community).

Hyperactive, Impulsive, Oppositional-Defiant Disorder. One of these disorders increases risk.

Academic and Intellectual Performance. Academic deficiencies and lower levels of intellectual functioning.

Poor Bonding and Attachment to Conventional Values. Little connection to family life and schoolwork or to others who are bonded to these values.

Parent and Family Factors

Prenatal and Perinatal Complications. Pregnancy- and birth-related complications, including maternal infection, prematurity and low birth weight, impaired respiration at birth, and minor birth injury.

Psychopathology and Criminal Behavior in the Family. Past or current criminal behavior, antisocial personality disorder, and alcoholism of the parent.

Untoward and Coercive Parent-Child Interaction. Harsh (e.g., severe corporal) punishment, inconsistent punishment, and coercive interchanges increase risk.

Poor Monitoring of the Child. Poor supervision, lack of monitoring of whereabouts, and few rules about where youth can go and when they can return.

Poor Quality of the Family Relationships. Less parental acceptance of their children, less warmth, affection, and emotional support, and less attachment.

Early Marriage. Teen marriage of the child's mother

Marital Discord. Unhappy marital relationships, interpersonal conflict, and aggression of the parents.

Large Family Size. More children in the family.

Sibling With Antisocial Behavior. Presence of a sibling, especially an older brother, with antisocial behavior.

Few Family Activities. Little involvement of the family in activities (e.g., recreation, religious) together

Socioeconomic Disadvantage. Poverty, overcrowding, unemployment, receipt of social assistance ("welfare"), and poor housing.

School-Related Factors

Characteristics of the Setting. Attending schools where there is little emphasis on academic work, little teacher time spent on lessons, infrequent teacher use of praise and appreciation for school work, little emphasis on individual responsibility of the students, poor working conditions for pupils (e.g., furniture in poor repair), unavailability of the teacher to deal with children's problems, and low teacher expectancies.

Note: The list of risk factors highlights major influences. The number of factors, their influence, and their interactions are more complex than the summary statements noted here. For a more detailed discussion, other sources can be consulted (e.g., Hill & Maughan, 2001; Kazdin, 1995b; Rutter et al., 1998).

criminal behavior, and problems of social adjustment in adulthood. Even though CD portends a number of other significant problems, not all antisocial children suffer impairment as adults. Among the most severely antisocial children, less than 50% become antisocial adults (Robins, 1978). If diverse diagnoses are considered, rather than serious antisocial behavior alone, the picture of impairment in adulthood is much worse. Among youths referred for antisocial behavior, 84% received a diagnosis of some psychiatric disorder as adults (Robins, 1966).

Additional longitudinal studies have replicated and extended these early findings (e.g., Fergusson, Horwood, & Ridder, 2005; Moffitt, Caspi, Rutter, & Silva, 2001). Moreover, the scope of physical as well as psychiatric consequences also has been elaborated. For example, many children with CD have been subjected to abusive parenting practices, which predict higher morbidity and mortality rates from serious disease (e.g., heart attack, cancer, respiratory illness) in adulthood (Krug, Dahlberg, Mercy, Zwi, & Lozano, 2002). In short, the scope of consequences, suffering, and impairment over the life course is quite astounding. Beyond what CD youth suffer as they move to adolescence and adulthood, the suffering of the victims of their acts (e.g., criminal activity, domestic violence) is enormous as well.

The Scope of Dysfunction

If one were to consider "only" the symptoms of CD and the persistence of impairment, the challenge of identifying effective treatments would be great enough. However, the presenting characteristics of children and their families usually raise other considerations that are central to treatment. Consider characteristics of children, families, and contexts that are associated with CD, as a backdrop for later comments on treatment.

Child Characteristics

Children who meet criteria for CD are likely to meet criteria for other disorders as well. The coexistence of two or more disorders is referred to as *comorbidity*. In general, diagnoses involving disruptive or externalizing behaviors (CD, oppositional defiant disorder [ODD], and attention-deficit/hyperactivity disorder [ADHD]) often go together. In studies of community and clinic samples, a large percentage of youth with CD or ADHD (e.g., 45 to 70%) also meet criteria for the other disorder (e.g., Fergusson, Horwood, & Lloyd, 1991; Offord et al., 1991). The co-occurrence of CD and ODD is common as well. Among clinic-referred youths who meet criteria for CD, 84 to 96% also meet concurrent diagnostic criteria for ODD (see Hinshaw, Lahey, & Hart, 1993).[3] CD is sometimes comorbid with anxiety disorders and depression (Nock et al., 2006).

Several other associated features of CD are relevant to treatment. For example, children with CD are also likely to show academic deficiencies, as reflected in achievement level, grades, being left behind in school, early termination from school, and deficiencies in specific skill areas such as reading. Youths with the disorder are likely to evince poor interpersonal relations, as reflected in diminished social skills in relation to peers and adults and higher levels of peer rejection. They are likely to show deficits and distortions in cognitive problem-solving skills, attributions of hostile intent to others, and re-sentment and suspiciousness. Clearly, CD is pervasive in the scope of characteristics that are affected.

Parent and Family Characteristics

Several parent and family characteristics are associated with CD (see Rutter et al., 1998; Stoff et al., 1997). Criminal behavior and alcoholism are two of the stronger and more consistently demonstrated parental characteristics. Harsh, lax, erratic, and inconsistent parent disciplinary practices and attitudes often characterize the families of CD children. Dysfunctional relations are also evident, as reflected in less acceptance of their children, less warmth, affection, and emotional support, and less attachment, compared with parents of nonreferred youths. Less supportive and more defensive communications among family members, less participation in activities as a family, and more clear dominance of one family member are also evident. In addition, unhappy marital relations, interpersonal conflict, and aggression characterize the parental relations of antisocial children. Poor parental supervision and monitoring of the child and knowledge of the child's whereabouts also are associated with CD.

Contextual Conditions

CD is associated with a variety of untoward living conditions such as large family size, overcrowding, poor housing, and disadvantaged school settings (see Kazdin, 1995b). Many of the untoward conditions in which families live place stress on the parents or diminish their threshold for coping with everyday stressors. The net effect can be evident in strained parent-child interactions in which parent behavior inadvertently sustains or exacerbates child antisocial and aggressive behavior (e.g., Dumas & Wahler, 1985; Patterson, Capaldi, & Bank, 1991).

Quite often the child's dysfunction is embedded in a larger context that cannot be neglected in conceptual views about the development, maintenance, and course of CD or in the actual delivery of treatment. For example, at an outpatient clinical service where I work (Yale Parenting Center and Child Conduct Clinic), it is likely that a family referred for treatment will experience a subset of these characteristics: financial hardship (unemployment, significant debt, bankruptcy), untoward living conditions (dangerous neighborhood, small living quarters), transportation obstacles (no car or car in frequent repair, state-provided taxi service), psychiatric impairment of one of the parents, stress related to significant others (former spouses, boyfriends, or girlfriends), and adversarial contact with an outside agency (schools, youth protective services, and the courts). CD is conceived as a dysfunction of children and adolescents. The accumulated evidence regarding the symptom constellation, risk factors, and course over the life span attests to the heuristic value of focusing on characteristics of the child. At the same time, there is a child-parent-family-context gestalt that includes multiple and reciprocal influences that affect each participant (child and parent) and the systems in which they operate (family, school). The multiplicity of the domains encompassed by CD has served as the basis for many treatments that involve packages of interventions that target key domains of the child, parent, and family and the systems and contexts in which they operate.

EVIDENCE-BASED TREATMENTS

Overview of Child and Adolescent Therapy Research

The context for examining psychosocial treatments for CD is the broader child and adolescent therapy literature (see Kazdin, 2000b). There has been remarkable progress in research in the quantity and quality of the evidence. As of the year 2000, approximately 1,500 controlled outcome studies could be identified (e.g., Kazdin, 2000a), a number that now is likely to be closer to 2,000. Although meta-analytic reviews include only a small portion of the studies, the reviews have consistently concluded that treatments for children are effective in producing medium to large effects (see Weisz, 2004).[4] Evidence-based treatments (EBTs) have been identified for several problem domains, including child anxiety, depression, CD, ODD, and ADHD, to mention a few (Christophersen & Mortweet, 2001; Kazdin & Weisz, 2003; Lonigan & Elbert, 1998).

Many different treatments have been applied to youths with CD, including variations of psychotherapy, pharmacotherapy, psychosurgery, home-, school-, and community-based programs, residential and hospital treatment, and social services (e.g., Brandt,

2006; Kazdin & Weisz, 2003; Nock, 2003; Weisz, 2004). Several treatments now have solid evidence in their behalf, and these are highlighted here. The outcome data for these treatments derive primarily from randomized, controlled clinical trials (Type 1 studies). In highlighting the approaches, the purpose is not to convey that these are the only promising treatments. Yet these are clearly among the most well developed in relation to the number of controlled clinical trials and replications across investigators and samples.

Parent Management Training

Background and Characteristics of Treatment

Parent management training (PMT) refers to procedures in which parents are trained to alter their child's behavior in the home (Kazdin, 2005). The parents meet with a therapist or trainer, who teaches them to use specific procedures to alter interactions with their child, to promote prosocial behavior, and to decrease deviant behavior. Training is based on the general view that conduct problem behavior is inadvertently developed and sustained in the home by maladaptive parent-child interactions. There are multiple facets of parent-child interaction that promote aggressive and antisocial behavior. These patterns include directly reinforcing deviant behavior, frequently and ineffectively using commands and harsh punishment, and failing to attend to appropriate behavior (Patterson, 1982; Patterson et al., 1992; Reid et al., 2002). Influences are bidirectional, so that the child influences the parent as well (see Wahler & Dumas, 1986).

Among the many interaction patterns, those involving coercion have received the greatest attention (Patterson et al., 1992; Reid, Patterson, & Snyder, 2002). Coercion refers to deviant behavior on the part of one person (e.g., the child), which is reinforced by another person (e.g., the parent). Aggressive children are inadvertently reinforced for their aggressive interactions and their escalation of coercive behaviors, as part of the discipline practices that sustain aggressive behavior. The critical role of parent-child discipline practices has been supported by correlational research, relating specific discipline practices to child antisocial behavior, and by experimental research showing that directly altering these practices reduces antisocial child behavior (see Dishion, Patterson, & Kavanagh, 1992; Snyder & Stoolmiller, 2002).

PMT alters the pattern of interchanges between parent and child so that prosocial, rather than coercive, behavior is directly reinforced and supported within the family. This requires developing several different parenting behaviors, such as establishing the rules for the child to follow, providing positive reinforcement for appropriate behavior, delivering mild forms of punishment to suppress behavior, negotiating compromises, and other procedures. These parenting behaviors are systematically and progressively developed within the sessions in which the therapist shapes (develops through successive approximations) parenting skills. The programs that parents eventually implement in the home also serve as the basis for the focus of the sessions in which the procedures are modified and refined.

Although many variations of PMT exist, several common characteristics can be identified. First, treatment is conducted primarily with the parent(s), who implement several procedures in the home. The parents meet with a therapist, who teaches them to use specific procedures to alter interactions with their child, to promote prosocial behavior, and to decrease deviant behavior. There usually is little direct intervention of the therapist with the child. With young children, the child may be brought into the session to help train both parent and child how to interact and especially to show the parent precisely how to deliver antecedents (prompts) and consequences (reinforcement, time out from reinforcement). Older youths may participate to negotiate and to develop behavior-change programs in the home. Second, parents are trained to identify, define, and observe problem behaviors in new ways. Careful specification of the problem is essential for delivering reinforcing or punishing consequences and for evaluating if the program is achieving the desired goals. Third, the treatment sessions cover social learning principles and the procedures that follow from them, including positive reinforcement (e.g., the use of social praise and tokens or points for prosocial behavior), mild punishment (e.g., use of time out from reinforcement, loss of privileges), negotiation, and contingency contracting. Fourth, the sessions provide opportunities for parents to see how the techniques are implemented, to practice using the techniques, and to review the behavior-change programs

in the home. The immediate goal of the program is to develop specific skills in the parents. As the parents become more proficient, the program can address the child's most severely problematic behaviors and encompass other problem domains (e.g., school behavior). Over the course of treatment, more complex repertoires are developed, both in the parents and in the child. Finally, child functioning at school is usually incorporated into the program. Parent-managed reinforcement programs for child deportment and performance at school, completion of homework, and activities on the playground often are integrated into the behavior-change programs. If available, teachers can play an important role in monitoring or providing consequences for behaviors at school.

Overview of the Evidence

Over the past 35 years, several randomized, controlled studies of PMT have been completed with youths varying in age and degree of severity of dysfunction (e.g., oppositional, CD, delinquent youth; Kazdin, 2005; Sanders, Markie-Dadds, & Turner, 2003). It is important to note that the evidence extends well beyond a handful of isolated Type 1 studies. Several investigators have completed programmatic research on PMT that has contributed enormously to developing the treatment, assessing factors that contribute to change, evaluating follow-up, and replicating treatment effects across multiple samples.[5]

Treatment effects have been evident in marked improvements in child behavior on a wide range of measures, including parent and teacher reports of deviant behavior, direct observation of behavior at home and at school, and institutional (e.g., school, police) records. The effects of treatment have also been shown to bring problematic behaviors of treated children within normative levels of their peers who are functioning adequately in the community. Follow-up assessment has shown that the gains are often maintained 1 to 3 years after treatment. Longer follow-up assessment is rarely conducted, although one program reported maintenance of gains 10 to 14 years later (Forehand & Long, 1988; Long, Forehand, Wierson, & Morgan, 1994).

The impact of PMT can be relatively broad. The effects of treatment are evident for child behaviors that have not been focused on directly as part of training. Also, siblings of children referred for treatment improve, even though they are not directly focused on in treatment. This is an important effect because siblings of children with CD are at risk for severe antisocial behavior. In addition, maternal psychopathology, particularly depression, decreases systematically following PMT (see Kazdin, 2005). These changes suggest that PMT alters multiple aspects of dysfunctional families.

Several characteristics of the treatment contribute to outcome. Duration of treatment appears to influence outcome. Brief and time-limited treatments (e.g., less than 10 hours) are less likely to show benefits with clinical populations. More dramatic and durable effects have been achieved with protracted or time-unlimited programs extending up to 50 or 60 hours of treatment (see Kazdin, 2005). Second, specific training components, such as providing parents with in-depth knowledge of social learning principles and utilizing time out from reinforcement in the home, enhance treatment effects. Third, families characterized by many risk factors associated with childhood dysfunction (e.g., socioeconomic disadvantage, marital discord, parent psychopathology, poor social support) tend to show fewer gains in treatment than families without these characteristics and to maintain the gains less well (e.g., Dadds & McHugh, 1992; Dumas & Wahler, 1983; Webster-Stratton, 1985), but this is not always the case (Kazdin & Whitley, 2006). Socioeconomic disadvantage and maternal mental health problems are the more well studied factors that attenuate responsiveness of the child to PMT (Reyno & McGrath, 2006). Efforts to address parent and family stress and dysfunction during PMT have led to improved effects of treatment outcome for the child in some studies (e.g., Dadds, Schwartz, & Sanders, 1987; Griest et al., 1982; Kazdin & Whitley, 2003) but not in others (Webster-Stratton, 1994). Much more work is needed on the matter given the prominent role of parent and family dysfunction among many youths referred for treatment.

One promising line of work has focused on implementation of PMT in community rather than clinic settings. The net effect is to bring treatment to those persons least likely to come to, or remain in, treatment. In one study, for example, when PMT was delivered in small parent groups in the community, the effectiveness surpassed what was achieved with clinic-based PMT. Also, community-based treatment was considerably more cost-effective (Cunningham, Bremner, & Boyle, 1995).

Research on processes in treatment represents a related and important advance. A series of studies on therapist-parent interaction within PMT sessions has identified factors that contribute to parent resistance (e.g., parent saying, "I can't," "I won't"). The significance of this work is in showing that parents' reactions in therapy relate to their discipline practices at home, that changes in resistance during therapy predict changes in parent behavior, and that specific therapist ploys (e.g., reframing, confronting) can help overcome or contribute to resistance (Patterson & Chamberlain, 1994). The therapeutic alliance of the parent and therapist also relates to improved parenting practices and therapeutic change of the children (Kazdin, Marciano, & Whitley, 2005; Kazdin, Whitley, & Marciano, in press). Children of parents with a strong alliance early in treatment, controlling for severity of parent and child impairment, do better at the end of treatment. The alliance is a predictor of change; it is not clear through what mechanism alliance may operate (e.g., increased parent compliance).

Overall Evaluation

The extensive outcome evidence makes PMT the most well investigated and established of the EBTs for conduct problem children. The outcome evidence is bolstered by related lines of work. First, the study of family interaction processes that contribute to antisocial behavior in the home and evidence that changing these processes alters child behavior provide a strong empirical base for treatment. Second, the procedures and practices that are used in PMT (e.g., various forms of reinforcement and punishment practices) have been widely and effectively applied outside the context of CD. For example, the procedures have been applied with parents of children with autism, language delays, developmental disabilities, medical disorders for which compliance with special treatment regimens is required, and with parents who physically abuse or neglect their children (see Kazdin, 2001). Third, a great deal is known about the procedures and the parameters that influence the reinforcement and punishment practices that form the core of PMT. Consequently, very concrete recommendations can be provided to change behavior and to alter programs when behavior change has not occurred (Kazdin, 2005). Treatment manuals and training materials for PMT are available for parents and therapists (e.g., Barkley, 1997; Cavell, 2000; Forehand & McMahon, 1981; Kazdin, 2005; Sanders & Dadds, 1993; Webster-Stratton, 2000) to learn about the treatments.

Several limitations of PMT can be identified as well. First, as with any treatment (e.g., aspirin, chemotherapy), not everyone responds. PMT makes several demands on the parents, such as mastering educational materials that convey major principles underlying the program, systematically observing deviant child behavior and implementing specific procedures at home, attending weekly sessions, and responding to frequent telephone contacts made by the therapist. For some families, the demands may be too great to continue in treatment. Second, perhaps the greatest limitation or obstacle in using PMT is that there are few training opportunities for professionals to learn the approach. Training programs in child psychiatry, clinical psychology, and social work are unlikely to provide exposure to the technique, much less opportunities for formal training. PMT requires mastery of social learning principles and multiple procedures that derive from them (Cooper, Heron, & Heward, 1987; Kazdin, 2001). Finally, PMT has been applied primarily to parents of children. Although treatment has been effective with delinquent adolescents (Bank, Marlowe, Reid, Patterson, & Weinrott, 1991) and younger adolescents with conduct problems who have not yet been referred for treatment (Dishion & Andrews, 1995), some evidence suggests that treatment is more effective with preadolescent youths (see Dishion & Patterson, 1992). Parents of adolescents may less readily change their discipline practices and also have higher rates of dropping out of treatment. The importance and special role of peers in adolescence and greater time that adolescents spend outside the home suggest that the principles and procedures may need to be applied in novel ways. At this point, few PMT programs have been developed specifically for adolescents, and so conclusions about the effects for youths of different ages must be tempered. On balance, PMT is probably the most well studied treatment for oppositional, aggressive, and antisocial behavior.

Multisystemic Therapy

Background and Characteristics of Treatment

Multisystemic therapy (MST) is a family-systems-based approach to treatment (Henggeler & Lee, 2003; Henggeler, Schoenwald, Borduin, Rowland, & Cunningham, 1998). Family approaches maintain that clinical problems of the child emerge within the context of the family and focus on treatment at that level. MST expands on that view by considering the family as only one, albeit a very important, system. The child is embedded in multiple systems, including the family (immediate and extended family members), peers, schools, neighborhood, and so on. Also, within a given system, different subsystem issues may be relevant. For example, within the context of the family, some tacit alliance between one parent and child may contribute to disagreement and conflict over discipline between the parents. Treatment may be required to address the alliance and sources of conflict in an effort to alter child behavior. Child functioning at school may involve limited and poor peer relations; treatment may address these areas as well. Finally, the systems approach entails a focus on the individual's own behavior insofar as it affects others. Individual treatment of the child or parents may be included in treatment. Many different treatment techniques are used to address the multiple foci of the case. Thus, MST can be viewed as a package of interventions that are deployed with children and their families. Treatment procedures are used "as needed" to address individual, family, and system issues that may contribute to problem behavior. The conceptual view focusing on multiple systems and their impact on the individual serves as a basis for selecting multiple and quite different treatment procedures.

Several family therapy techniques (e.g., joining, reframing, enactment, paradox, and assigning specific tasks) are used to identify problems, increase communication, build cohesion, and alter how family members interact. The goals of treatment are to help the parents develop behaviors of the adolescent, to overcome marital difficulties that impede the parents' ability to function as parents, to eliminate negative interactions between parent and child, and to develop or build cohesion and emotional warmth among family members. MST draws on many other techniques as needed, such as PMT, problem-solving skills training, and marital therapy, to alter parent-child interactions at home, the response repertoire of the child, and marital communication, respectively. In some cases, practical advice and guidance are also given to address parenting issues (e.g., involving the adolescent in prosocial peer activities at school, restricting specific activities with a deviant peer group). Although MST includes distinct techniques from other approaches, it is not a mere amalgamation of them. The focus of treatment is on interrelated systems and how they affect each other. Domains are addressed in treatment (e.g., parent unemployment) if they raise issues for one or more systems (e.g., parent stress, increased alcohol consumption) and affect how the child is functioning (e.g., marital conflict, child-discipline practices). In any given case, multiple interventions are likely to be applied.

Overview of the Evidence

A large number of Type 1 studies have evaluated MST, primarily with delinquent and substance-dependent youths with arrest and incarceration histories including violent crime (e.g., manslaughter, aggravated assault with intent to kill; Henggeler & Lee, 2003). MST is superior in reducing delinquency, drug use, and emotional and behavioral problems and increasing school attendance and family functioning, in comparison to other procedures, including "usual services" provided to such youths (e.g., probation, court-ordered activities that are monitored such as school attendance), individual counseling, and community-based eclectic treatment (e.g., Borduin et al., 1995; Brown, Henggeler, Schoenwald, Brondino, & Pickrel, 1999; Henggeler, Pickrel, & Brondino, 1999; Ogden & Halliday-Boykins, 2004; Rowland et al., 2005). Follow-up examinations of MST up to 15 years later have shown that MST youths have lower arrest rates, repeat offenses, and rates of conviction relative to youths who receive other services (see Henggeler et al., 1998; Henggeler, Clingempeel, Brondino, & Pickrel, 2002; Schaeffer & Borduin, 2005). Further, MST results in lower rates of youths dropping out of treatment, relative to usual community services (Henggeler, Pickrel, Brondino, & Crouch, 1996). A cost-benefit analysis by the Washington State Institute on Public Policy found that the effects of MST result in net monetary bene-

fits (benefits of program minus cost of program) of more than $30,000 per participant when considering only taxpayer benefits, and more than $130,000 when considering victim benefits along with taxpayer benefits (Aos, Phipps, Barnoski, & Leib, 2001).

Efforts to evaluate different moderators of treatment outcome reflect other strengths of MST research. For example, therapist adherence to the MST treatment protocol has been related to both improvements in family relations and decreases in delinquent peer affiliation, which, in turn, are associated with decreases in delinquent behavior (Huey, Henggeler, Brondino, & Pickrel, 2000). Therapist adherence to MST is influenced by referral type (lower ratings for youths referred for both criminal offenses and substance abuse, relative to youths referred for either offenses or abuse), lower adherence is related to greater pretreatment arrests and school suspensions, and higher ratings are related to greater family educational disadvantage, caregiver-therapist ethnic and gender match, and African American ethnicity (Schoenwald, Halliday-Boykins, & Henggeler, 2003; Schoenwald, Letourneau, & Halliday-Boykins, 2005). A positive ethnic match (therapist and caregiver matched on ethnicity) is related to greater symptom reduction, greater length of treatment (i.e., more treatment retention), and increases in the likelihood of case termination due to the meeting of treatment goals (Halliday-Boykins, Schoenwald, & Letourneau, 2005). Evaluation of adherence and other moderators of treatment reflect important lines of work.

Overall Evaluation

Several controlled outcome studies are consistent in showing that treatment leads to change in adolescents and that the changes are sustained. A strength of the studies is that many of the youths who are treated are quite severely impaired (delinquent adolescents with history of arrest). Another strength is the conceptualization of CD as a problem involving multiple domains of dysfunction within and between individual, family, and extrafamilial systems. MST begins with the view that many different domains are likely to be relevant; they need to be evaluated and then addressed as needed in treatment.

Recent evidence has identified predictors and correlates of critical components of the treatment. Identifying these factors may lead to future research identifying the most important ingredients of MST that lead to change in problems with CD. Indeed, this recent work relates directly to perhaps the greatest challenges in employing MST:deciding what treatments to use in a given case, and monitoring the integrity or adherence to the MST protocol. Consultation with MST therapists and means to evaluate quality of treatment delivery (Schoenwald, Sheidow, & Letourneau, 2004) are important components to guide implementation and dissemination of MST. Detailed description of the treatment and key principles of delivery are readily available (Henggeler et al., 1998; http://www.mstservices.com).

There remain important challenges for the approach. First, treatment is guided by broad principles, and moving from the principles to specific action plans within the session is not entirely straightforward. However, several illustrations are available (Henggeler et al., 1998). Second, the administration of MST is demanding in light of the need to provide several different interventions in a high-quality fashion. Individual treatments alone are difficult to provide; multiple combinations of different treatments invite all sorts of challenges (e.g., therapist training, ensuring treatments of high quality, strength, and integrity). Third, and related, MST is intensive. In some projects, therapists are available 24 hours a day, 7 days a week. Sometimes a team of therapists is involved rather than merely one therapist. It may be the case that this model of treatment delivery is precisely what is needed for clinical problems that are multiply determined, protracted, and recalcitrant to more abbreviated interventions.

Overall, MST is an EBT with excellent evidence in its behalf. The outcome studies have included youths with different types of problems (sexual offenses, drug use). Moreover, recent evidence suggests MST effects may extend to other serious problem domains (e.g., acute psychiatric crises, suicide attempts; Huey et al., 2005; Sheidow et al., 2004). Thus, the model of providing treatment may have broad applicability across multiple problem domains among seriously disturbed children.

Multidimensional Treatment Foster Care Model

Background and Characteristics of Treatment

Multidimensional Treatment Foster Care (MTFC) is a community-based treatment program (Chamber-

lain & Smith, 2003, 2005). It began as an alternative to institutional, residential, and group care placements for youths with severe and chronic delinquent behavior and has since been extended to work with children and adolescents, referred from either mental health or child welfare service systems.

The goals of the program are to provide opportunities for youth to live successfully in their communities while at the same time providing them with intensive supervision, support, and skill development, and to prepare their parents (or other aftercare resource) to provide effective parenting. (Approximately 85% of the youths return to their families; the remaining 15% return to long-term foster care or residential placement.) The youths begin treatment while they are out of their homes. They are placed individually in a foster home and are provided with intensive support and treatment in that setting. Individual placement is important and departs from many programs where several antisocial youth might be placed together in one setting. Evidence that group-based treatments for youth with CD can make them worse has fostered concern about many programs (Dishion, McCord, & Poulin, 1999; Feldman, Caplinger, & Wodarski, 1983; Mager, Millich, Harris, & Howard, 2005; O'Donnell, 1992). Once the foster program is in place, PMT is provided to the parents (biological or other) to whom the child will return after foster care placement.

In foster placement (e.g., 6 to 9 months), several interventions are provided, including family and individual therapy, skill training, academic support, case management, and medication, as needed. The interventions are provided across home, school, and the community. The foster setting is designed both to change behavior of the youths and to prepare them for return to their families or placement in a different home. Four key elements of treatment provide youths with the following:

1. A reinforcing environment where they are mentored and encouraged to perform specific behaviors that will increase their skills;
2. Daily structure that includes clear expectations, limits, and consequences;
3. Close supervision and monitoring of the youth's whereabouts; and
4. Prosocial peer contacts and support rather than associations with delinquent peers.

Each child is supervised by a team involving a case manager, individual therapist for the child, family therapist for the aftercare parents, behavioral support specialist, and psychiatrist, who conducts the treatment intervention. The team facilitates implementing and coordinating interventions, which are implemented across multiple settings (i.e., foster care setting where the child is placed, school, family home to which the child returns, and community). The overall conceptual focus of treatment is social learning, that is, providing learning experiences in the context of a positive interpersonal environment and various systems (home, community, school). Foster parents are trained to implement behavioral programs and focus on such behaviors as getting up on time, attending school, positive behavior in class and at home, following directions, maturity, and positive attitude. Interventions are those that constitute PMT, highlighted earlier in the chapter (e.g., clear goals, feedback, praise, points, response cost). Parents to whom the child returns also receive PMT. They are gradually exposed to the child under supervision before the child is returned home to oversee the practices of the parents in light of their PMT. Parents visit the foster setting, and the child visits the home of the biological parents. The gradual exposure to the home environment ensures that the transition will be smooth when the child is placed and that the biological parents have the skills and new ways of interacting to sustain and foster gains in their child.

Overview of the Evidence

Several randomized trials (Type 1) have been completed and are in process with youth referred from multiple sources, including child welfare and mental health services, as noted previously (see Chamberlain & Smith, 2003, 2005, for reviews). The samples usually include individuals with comorbid disorders, a history of trauma and abuse, and prior treatments and multiple placements. Those with the most severe conduct problems have included youth referred from juvenile justice departments (aged 12 to 17), who have been involved in serious and frequent offending, and who are mandated by the courts for out-of-home placement.

The outcome studies have shown that the MTFC program leads to significant reductions in crime and delinquent behavior relative to treatment as usual. In the first outcome trial, delinquent youths were studied and randomly assigned to MTFC or treatment as usual (Chamberlain & Reid, 1998). In the case of chronically delinquent youths, treatment as usual consists of group care placement, as determined by parole or probation officers. The program includes individual, group, and family therapy, although these can vary in conceptual approach and degree across settings. This initial study and others that followed (e.g., Eddy, Bridges-Whaley, & Chamberlain, 2004; Eddy & Chamberlain, 2001) conveyed strong benefits of the MTFC program compared with control conditions. The benefits were reflected on important outcome measures, including the extent to which youths run away, records and self-report of criminal activity, arrest rates, and days spent in locked settings (e.g., state training schools; Chamberlain & Smith, 2003, 2005). The positive outcomes 1 year following treatment have been shown to be mediated by the quality of parent's use of PMT skills and by posttreatment association of youths with delinquent peers. In a recent Type 1 study of delinquent girls, MTFC was compared with group care; the greater effects of treatment were evident on fewer days in locked care and reduced caregiver reported delinquency at the 12-month follow up (Leve, Chamberlain, & Reid, 2005).

Monetary costs of the MTFC program for treating individuals from the juvenile justice system are approximately one-third less than placement and treatment in group care (treatment as usual; Chamberlain & Smith, 2003). A cost-effectiveness evaluation by the Washington State Institute for Public Policy (Aos, Phipps, Barnoski, & Leib, 1999) estimated that MTFC model saves taxpayers approximately $44,000 per participant in criminal justice and avoided victim costs. For every dollar spent on MTFC, approximately $23.00 of taxpayer benefits were estimated when compared with more commonly used programs.

Overall Evaluation

The evidence in behalf of the program is impressive in light of the repeated replications, application to severely impaired youth, and extensions to multiple samples drawn from different types of agencies. Also, the interventions that are used receive empirical support well beyond the specific studies that have evaluated the model. The program relies heavily on PMT, within the foster home and the home to which the child will be returned. The integration of the program into the community is critically important. For example, school behavior and activities are carefully monitored and incorporated into behavioral programs of the child.

The intensive effort required to implement treatment is noteworthy. For example, the team includes a case manager who can oversee more than one case (e.g., approximately 10 families). The case manager coordinates all facets of treatment. The demands can be great, as the manager provides daily telephone contact, supervises weekly foster parent meetings, and is available 24 hours a day.

Overall, this is a well-developed program. It draws on two literatures at least in relation to EBTs. First, the evidence for this program is solid in its own right. This literature continues to emerge in replications extending to programs in many states in the United States and to other countries. Second, PMT is pivotal to the foster and biological parent facets of the intervention. The strong PMT literature, much of which has emanated from the same center (in Oregon) from which this intervention emerged, provides further evidence underpinning this treatment program.

Cognitive Problem-Solving Skills Training

Background and Characteristics of Treatment

Cognitive processes refer to a broad class of constructs that pertain to how the individual perceives, codes, and experiences the world. Individuals who engage in aggressive behavior show distortions and deficiencies in various cognitive processes. These distortions and deficiencies are not merely reflections of intellectual functioning. Several cognitive processes have been studied. Examples include generating alternative solutions to interpersonal problems (e.g., different ways of handling social situations), identifying the means to obtain particular ends (e.g., making friends) or consequences of one's actions (e.g., what could happen after a particular behavior); making attributions to others of the motivation of their actions; perceiving how others feel; and expectations of the effects of one's own actions (Lochman, Powell, Whidby, & FitzGerald, 2006; Shirk, 1988; Spivack & Shure, 1982). Deficits and distortion among these processes relate to teacher ratings of disruptive behavior, peer evaluations, and direct assessment of overt behavior (e.g., Lochman & Dodge, 1994; Rubin, Bream, & Rose-Krasnor, 1991).

An example of cognitive processes implicated in CD can be seen in the work on attributions and aggressive behavior. Aggression is not merely triggered by environmental events, but rather through the way in which these events are perceived and processed. The processing refers to the child's appraisals of the situation, anticipated reactions of others, and self-statements in response to particular events. Attribution of intent to others represents a salient cognitive disposition critically important to understanding aggressive behavior. Aggressive children and adolescents tend to attribute hostile intent to others, especially in social situations where the cues of actual intent are ambiguous (see Crick & Dodge, 1994). Understandably, when situations are initially perceived as hostile, children are more likely to react aggressively. Although many studies have shown that children with CD experience various cognitive distortions and deficiencies, the specific contribution of these processes to CD, as opposed to risk factors with which they may be associated (e.g., untoward living conditions, low IQ) has not been established. Nevertheless, research on cognitive processes among aggressive children has served as a heuristic base for conceptualizing treatment and for developing specific treatment strategies (Kendall, 2006).

Problem-solving skills training (PSST) consists of developing interpersonal cognitive problem-solving skills. Although many variations of PSST have been applied to conduct problem children, several characteristics usually are shared. First, the emphasis is on how children approach situations, that is, the thought processes in which the child engages to guide responses to interpersonal situations. The children are taught to engage in a step-by-step approach to solve interpersonal problems. They make statements to themselves that direct attention to certain aspects of the problem or tasks that lead to effective solutions. Second, the behaviors (solutions to the interpersonal problems) that are selected are important as well. Prosocial behaviors are fostered through modeling and direct reinforcement as part of the problem-solving process. Third, treatment utilizes structured tasks involving games, academic activities, and stories. Over the course of treatment, the cognitive problem-solving skills are increasingly applied to real-life situations. Fourth, therapists play an active role in treatment. They model the cognitive processes by making verbal self-statements, apply the sequence of statements to particular problems, provide cues to prompt use of the skills, and deliver feedback and praise to develop correct use of the skills. Finally, treatment usually combines several different procedures, including modeling and practice, role playing, and reinforcement and mild punishment (loss of points or tokens). These are deployed in systematic ways to develop increasingly complex response repertoires of the child.

Overview of the Evidence

Several controlled clinical trials (Type 1 and 2 studies) have been completed with children and adolescents with impulsive, aggressive, and antisocial behavior (see Baer & Nietzel, 1991; Durlak, Furhman, & Lampman, 1991; Sukhodolsky, Kassinove, & Gorman, 2004, for reviews). Cognitively based treatments have significantly reduced aggressive and antisocial behavior at home, at school, and in the community. At follow-up, these gains have been evident up to 1 year later. Many early studies in the field (e.g., 1970s through 1980s) focused on impulsive children and nonpatient samples. Since that time, several additional (Type 1 and 2) studies have shown treatment effects with inpatient and outpatient cases. For example, in Type 1 studies with inpatient children, those who received PSST performed significantly better at the end of treatment than those who received relationship therapy (Kazdin, Bass, Siegel, & Thomas, 1989; Kazdin, Esveldt-Dawson, French, & Unis, 1987). The literature has expanded greatly since then in support of treatment (see Kazdin, 1995b; Kendall, 2006; Pepler & Rubin, 1991).

The strength of the evidence in the context of treatment for referred cases stands on its own in support of PSST as a promising treatment for CD. Evidence outside the context of treatment is quite pertinent to the evaluation of this intervention. PSST has been studied for a period spanning close to three decades in a very well developed program of research (see Shure, 1997, 1999). In one of the reports, PSST was provided in the classrooms of economically disadvantaged elementary school children. Those who received the training, unlike those who did not, showed decreases in disruptive student behavior and increases in positive, prosocial behavior. Although the effects were evident when training was conducted for 1 year (kindergarten), the impact was greater when training was continued for 2 years (kindergarten and first grade). Either way, the benefits of the intervention were still evident at least up to 2 years after the program ended. The program is noteworthy because it can be implemented on a large scale in the schools and used to improve outcomes of children who are at high risk for academic, social, emotional, and behavioral problems.

In the context of treatment, there is only sparse evidence that addresses the child, parent, family, contextual, or treatment factors that influence treatment outcome. Evidence suggests that older children (greater than 10 to 11 years of age) profit more from treatment than younger children, perhaps due to their cognitive development (Durlak et al., 1991). Younger children can participate in and profit from cognitively based treatments, although materials may need to be altered as a function of age (Doherr, Reynolds, Wetherly, & Evans, 2005). More generally, the basis for differential responsiveness to treatment as a function of age has not been well tested. Children with CD who show comorbid diagnoses, academic delays and dysfunction, and lower reading achievement and who come from families with high levels of impairment (parent psychopathology, stress, and family dysfunction) respond less well to treatment than do children with less dysfunction in these domains (Kazdin, 1995a; Kazdin & Crowley, 1997). These child, parent, and family characteristics may influence the effectiveness of several different treatments for CD rather than PSST in particular. Much further work is needed to evaluate factors that contribute to responsiveness to treatment.

Overall Evaluation

There are features of PSST that make it an extremely promising approach. First, several controlled outcome studies with clinic samples have shown that cognitively based treatment leads to therapeutic change. Second, basic research in developmental psychology continues to elaborate the relation of maladaptive cognitive processes among children and adolescents and conduct problems that serve as underpinnings of treatment (Crick & Dodge, 1994; Lochman et al., 2006). Finally, and on a more practical level, many versions of treatment are available in manual form (e.g., Bourke & Van Hasselt, 2001; Feindler, & Ecton, 1986; Finch, Nelson, & Ott, 1993; Friedberg & McClure, 2002; Larson & Lochman, 2002; McGuire, 2000; Shure, 1992, 1996) to facilitate further evaluation and refinement in research and application in clinical practice.

Critical questions remain to be addressed in research. Primary among these is the role of cognitive processes in clinical dysfunction. Evidence is not entirely clear in showing that a specific pattern of cognitive processes characterizes children with conduct problems, rather than adjustment or externalizing problems more generally. Also, although evidence has shown that cognitive processes change with treatment, evidence has not established that change in these processes mediates or is responsible for improvements in treatment outcome. Thus, the basis for therapeutic change has yet to be established. Although central questions about treatment and its effects remain to be resolved, PSST is highly promising in light of its effects in several controlled outcome studies with children with CD.

Anger Control Training

Background and Characteristics of Treatment

The Anger Control Training program has developed and evolved over the years and includes two main programs—the Anger Coping Program (ACP) and the Coping Power Program (CPP; Lochman, Barry, & Pardini, 2003; Lochman et al., 2006). The ACP is delivered to children in a group and draws on anger management training, as well as cognitive problem skills training models of aggression and intervention. Key concepts discussed in the context of PSST apply to the ACP. The CPP includes the prior component but adds to that a parent program that relies on PMT delivered in group format.

Although key components of PSST and PMT are central to this program, there are unique features as well. For example, within the cognitively based program for the children, attention is given to anger management and skills not usually included in PSST (e.g., relaxation training, social skills training). Similarly, within the PMT training, additional techniques are included beyond those that alter child-parent interaction discipline and monitoring practices. Within the sessions for parents, family communication and stress management in the home are covered as well. A third component has been added to treatment that includes several teacher in-service meetings and ongoing teacher consultation.

The most well developed and researched component is the ACP, which includes approximately 18 sessions that cover self-instruction, steps for problem solving, self-control and anger management, and toward the end of treatment a review of videotapes to manage problems in different contexts (e.g., school, other children). Children make and view videos, write scripts, and enact them to convey appropriately coping with anger and solving interpersonal problems. The program is provided to elementary school children in the classroom who are identified as aggressive.

Overview of the Evidence

Several types of studies (Type 1 and 2) have been completed in support of the ACP. Comparisons have included variations of the program with components deleted or added to understand and augment treatment effects. Early Type 1 research showed that the ACP program reduced aggression greater than did no treatment (e.g., Lochman, Burch, Curry, & Lampron, 1984; Lochman, Lampron, Gemmer, Harris, & Wycoff, 1989). Follow-up of the program 3 years after treatment (when youths were on average 15 years old) has been favorable. Youths who had received the ACP exhibited lower levels of substance use (alcohol and marijuana or other drugs; Lochman, 1992). Interestingly, the youths with the greatest improvements were those who initially showed greater comorbidity, peer rejection, and deficits in problem-solving skills. The CPP is less well studied only because it reflects a more recent evolution from this research program. Type 1 trials support the effects of the program with both child and parent components compared with no treatment. In one of the studies fourth- and fifth-grade boys rated high in aggression showed lower rates of delinquency and parent-rated substance use 1 year following treatment (Lochman & Wells, 2002).

Overall Evaluation

The evidence for this program is quite favorable. Also, the evidence for PSST and and that for ACP complement each other—they share many of the interventions related to problem-solving skills training. ACP is a school-based program. Among the interventions discussed in this chapter, none has been developed, implemented, and evaluated in the schools in quite this way for the treatment of children with aggression. As mentioned previously, group treatment programs for antisocial youth have often been found to produce negative outcomes, a finding attributed to the socialization and connection that group members have with peers who further foster antisocial behavior, in citations noted previously. The ACP has not shown such effects; group anger control training does not lead to worse outcomes than no treatment. Just the opposite. This is encouraging and raises important questions about when and under what circumstances group processes and peer connections can be problematic.

Functional Family Therapy

Background and Characteristics of Treatment

Functional family therapy (FFT) reflects an integrative approach to treatment that relies on systems, behavioral, and cognitive views of dysfunction (Alexander, Holtzworth-Munroe, & Jameson, 1994; Alexander & Parsons, 1982; Sexton & Alexander, 1999). Clinical problems are conceptualized from the standpoint of the functions they serve in the family as a system, as well as for individual family members. Problem behavior evident in the child is assumed to be the way in which some interpersonal functions (e.g., intimacy, distancing, and support) are met among family members. Maladaptive processes within the family are considered to preclude a more direct means of fulfilling these functions. The goal of treatment is to alter interaction and communication patterns in such a way as to foster more adaptive functioning. Treatment is also based on learning theory and focuses on specific stimuli and responses that can be used to produce change. Social learning concepts and procedures, such as identifying specific behaviors for change, reinforcing new adaptive ways of responding, and evaluating and monitoring change, are included in this perspective. Cognitive processes refer to the attributions, attitudes, assumptions, expectations, and emotions of the family. Family members may begin treatment with attributions that focus on blaming others or themselves. New perspectives may be needed to help serve as the basis for developing new ways of behaving.

The underlying rationale emphasizes a family systems approach. Specific treatment strategies draw on findings that underlie PMT in relation to maladaptive and coercive parent-child interactions, discussed previously. FFT views interaction patterns from a broader systems view that focuses also on communication patterns and their meaning. As an illustration of salient constructs, research underlying FFT has found that families of delinquents show higher rates of defensiveness in their communications, in both parent-child and parent-parent interactions, blaming, and negative attributions, and also lower rates of mutual support than do families of nondelinquents (see Alexander & Parsons, 1982). Improving these communication and support functions is a goal of treatment.

FFT requires that the family see the clinical problem from the relational functions it serves within the family. The therapist points out interdependencies and contingencies between family members in their day-to-day functioning and with specific reference to the problem that has served as the basis for seeking treatment. Over the course of treatment, the family is encouraged to see alternative ways of viewing the problem; in doing so, the incentive for the family to interact more constructively is increased.

The intervention is administered across three reciprocal and interdependent phases (Sexton & Alexander, 2002). The first, engagement and motivation, has a primary aim of increasing the perception of the intervention's credibility within the family, which includes fostering an expectation of change, and establishing the alliance between therapist and family members. This is accomplished, in part, through therapists' reframing negative themes of presenting problems into positive themes, to develop a family-focused perception of the maladaptive behaviors and emotions that may be present within the family. The second phase, behavior change, aims to identify targets of change for each family member, with the idea that changes be tailored to the unique characteristics of the family member, as well as be appropriate for the cultural and contextual underpinnings of the family. Foci of behavior change are expected to encompass cognitive, interactive, and emotional domains of functioning. The last phase, generalization, aims to apply the changes observed in the second phase to other problem areas and/or situations in the family system. The primary goal in this phase is for treatment to foster the family's ability to maintain changes observed in treatment, and prevent relapses in dysfunction. Finally, over the course of treatment, all family members meet in sessions. The focus of treatment is to identify consistent patterns of behavior and the range of functions they serve and messages they send. As mentioned previously, a number of specific techniques that can be used to focus on relations in therapy are used.

Overview of the Evidence

Several Type 1 studies have evaluated FFT and have focused on populations that are difficult to treat, including adjudicated delinquent and multiple offender delinquent adolescents (see Alexander et al., 1994; Alexander, Sexton, & Robbins, 2000). The studies have produced relatively clear effects. FFT has led to greater change than other treatment techniques (e.g., client-centered family groups, psychodynamically oriented family therapy) and various control conditions (e.g., group discussion and expression of feeling, no-treatment control groups). Treatment outcome is reflected in improved family communication and interactions and lower rates of referral to and contact of youth with the courts. Moreover, at 5-year follow-up, FFT youths evidence lower recidivism rates as adults than do those who received probation services as usual (Gordon, Graves, & Arbuthnot, 1995).

Research has examined processes in therapy to identify in-session behaviors of the therapist and how these influence responsiveness among family members (Alexander, Barton, Schiavo, & Parsons, 1976; Newberry, Alexander, & Turner, 1991). For example, providing support and structure and reframing (recasting the attributions and bases of a problem) influence family member responsiveness and blaming of others. The relations among such variables are complex insofar as the impact of various type of statements (e.g., supportive) can vary as a function of gender of the therapist and family member. Evidence of changes in processes proposed to be critical to FFT (e.g., improved communication in treatment, more spontaneous discussion) supports the conceptual view of treatment.

Overall Evaluation

Several noteworthy points can be made about FFT. First, the outcome studies indicate that FFT can alter conduct problems among delinquent youth who vary in severity and chronicity of antisocial behavior

(e.g., youths with status offenses; others with multiple offenses and who have served in maximum-security wards). The studies spanning more than 30 years have produced consistent effects. Second, cost-effectiveness analyses have shown FFT to surpass alternatives such as detention and residential treatment for delinquents (Sexton, in press). Third, the evaluation of processes that contribute to family member responsiveness within the sessions, as well as to treatment outcome, represents a line of work rarely seen among treatment techniques for children and adolescents. Some of this process work has extended to laboratory (analogue) studies to examine more precisely how specific types of therapist statements (e.g., reframing) can reduce blaming among group members (e.g., Morris, Alexander, & Turner, 1991; Sexton & Alexander, 1999). Fourth, treatment manuals have been provided (Alexander & Parsons, 1982, Sexton, in press); Internet sources are also available (Functional Family Therapy, 2003).

On balance, the treatment has several features in its favor. The evidence includes many studies. The samples included in the studies have been severely impaired delinquent youth. Extending FFT to clinically referred youths, youths with comorbid diagnoses, and families of such youth would be worthwhile. Clinical samples are not necessarily any more recalcitrant to treatment. Yet delinquency and CD, despite overlap of selected characteristics, are not the same designations, and generalization from one population to another is not assured. As with other treatment packages reviewed in this chapter, it is not clear if all the treatments that constitute the FFT "package" are needed or are needed for some, most, or all of the cases.

Brief Strategic Family Therapy

Background and Characteristics of Treatment

Brief strategic family therapy (BSFT) has emerged from a programmatic series of studies with Hispanic youths (see Coatsworth, Szapocznik, Kurtines, & Santisteban, 1997; Robbins, Schwartz, & Szapocznik, 2004; Robbins et al., 2003; Szapocznik & Kurtines, 1989). The program has systematically evaluated children (aged 6 to 11), early adolescents (12 to 14), and adolescents (13 to 18) and included youths from varied backgrounds (e.g., Cuban, Nicaraguan,

Colombian, Honduran, and Puerto Rican). Although the groups vary widely, the approach is based on the view that as a group Hispanics show more family orientation and shared values and many immigration and acculturation experiences that make the grouping meaningful (Santisteban et al., 2003). The youths have included those referred for externalizing behaviors such as CD, drug abuse, and a broader range of problems as well.

BSFT views child behavior within the context of the family system. Integrated into a family approach is a cultural frame of reference that draws from the study of Hispanic families. Among the key foci of this frame of reference are the importance of strong family cohesion, parental control, and communication issues that may arise from cultural and intergenerational conflicts (e.g., individualism of the adolescent vs. family ties). Both family and individual behavior are considered as interdependent and interactive. Individuals are jointly responsible for the state of the family system and for the changes that are to be made in treatment. Patterns of interaction, conceptualized as the structure of the family system, are identified as the likely bases for maladaptive functioning. Thus a child's "problem" brought to treatment is reconceptualized as dysfunction in relation to the family. Persistent maladaptive behavior in one or more family members must in some way be maintained by the family.

Treatment focuses on strategies that can be used to alter interaction patterns. The focus is on providing concrete and direct changes in the family situation to promote improved interactions. This is distinguished from more traditional strategies that have focused on insight and understanding. The treatment sessions are problem focused whenever possible. The therapist identifies what can be altered within the family to promote change. Formal assessment is provided by a set of family tasks (e.g., planning a menu, discussing a prior family argument) that allow the therapist to identify areas of focus. Structure of the family, alliance, conflict resolution, roles (e.g., patient, model child), and flexibility of the family are some of the dimensions that are examined in assessment and focused on in treatment. During treatment, the therapist challenges interaction patterns, reformulates (reframes) ways of considering interaction and communication patterns, and encourages new ways of interacting to break up established sequences.

Overview of the Evidence

There have been several studies (Type 1 and 2) to develop and evaluate the intervention with youths referred for diverse problems. The results have shown improvements in child and family functioning as a result of treatment when compared with other treatment and control (e.g., minimal contact conditions) across several studies (see Coatsworth et al., 1997; Muir, Schwartz, & Szapocznik, 2004; Szapocznik & Kurtines, 1989). For example, a recent trial (Type 1) of clinically referred adolescents showed that BFST led to greater reductions in parent-reported conduct problems and delinquency, marijuana use, and improved family functioning relative to a group treatment control condition (Santisteban et al., 2003). Although the outcome focus of treatment emphasizes child and adolescent behavior, changes in the family are viewed as critical as well. Comparisons early in this program of research showed that even when two interventions (BFST and psychodynamic therapy) were equally effective in reducing symptoms, BFST also improves family functioning (Szapocznik et al., 1989).

Conceptually interesting findings have been obtained in the context of the outcome studies. For example, family therapy is usually conceptualized as an intervention in which the entire family is seen in treatment. Szapocznik and his colleagues have argued that family therapy is a way of conceptualizing problems and interventions. Seeing the entire family or most members may not necessarily be important. Indeed, a controlled comparison found that seeing the individual is as effective as seeing the entire family, when these two variants of family therapy are compared (Szapocznik, Kurtines, Foote, Perez-Vidal, & Hervis, 1986). The research has focused as well on engaging the family so that they remain in treatment. Special attention to the family early in treatment in an effort to address family and cultural barriers to treatment participation, evaluated in randomized controlled trials, has significantly reduced dropping out of treatment (e.g., Santisteban et al., 1996; Szapocznik et al., 1988).

Overall Evaluation

Overall BFST has been studied in a well-developed program of research that has been restricted primarily to a particular research center and set of investigators. Treatment has been replicated in several studies and with children presenting diverse clinical problems. The research program is unique in directly developing a treatment sensitive to critical cultural issues and developing methods to assess these issues. The program has been extended to African American families and to other clinical problems than conduct problems (e.g., substance use, prevention of HIV). Apart from the accomplishments of the studies in relation to BFST, the broader approach of assessing and studying cultural features of families and then integrating these features into therapy may reflect a model for developing ethnically relevant and sensitive treatment. There has been very little attention to ethnic issues in trials of psychotherapy with children and adolescents, and this program has been exemplary.

GENERAL COMMENTS

Clearly, advances have been made in identifying EBTs for youth with conduct problems. The treatments highlighted previously encompass young children through adolescents and a range of severity from oppositional and noncompliance to serious antisocial and criminal behavior. The research has included youths referred clinically, as well as from the courts, child welfare and protective services, and various agencies where such children may reside (e.g., foster care). Occasionally critical evaluations of EBTs note that perhaps the participants are not like "real" patients referred for treatment, or perhaps they do not have serious or multiple disorders. Plainly the concern is flatly incorrect in relation to EBTs of CD. The treatments (e.g., PMT, MST, MTFC) include cases with all sorts of serious child, parent, family, and social problems. In terms of psychiatric diagnosis, our own studies show that comorbidity is the rule rather than the exception in our trials, with some children meeting criteria for five or six psychiatric disorders (e.g., Kazdin & Whitley, 2006).

There are now multiple treatments available for youth with CD. Extending these to professionals and families in need is not the only task remaining, as I note in the sections that follow, but it is likely to be the most daunting. Some of the treatments (e.g., MST, FFT, BSFT) have been well established for some time (e.g., 20 to 35 years). More recent evidence makes the case stronger and better, and the

movement toward EBTs perhaps gives new emphasis. Even so, these treatments are rarely taught in graduate school or advanced training among those professions involved in treatment of children and families (clinical psychology, child psychiatry, social work, and nursing). This is especially stark for PMT, which emerged from several research centers, whereas most of the other treatments came from a single investigative team. Demonstrating effective treatments will not be sufficient to improve patient care. Getting the treatments out to those who administer or seek treatment is a huge task.

LIMITATIONS OF WELL-INVESTIGATED TREATMENTS

Each treatment reviewed has randomized controlled trials (Type 1 studies) in its behalf, includes replications of treatment effects, focuses on youths whose aggressive and antisocial behavior has led to impairment and referral to social services (e.g., clinics, hospitals, courts), and has assessed outcome over the course of follow-up, at least up to a year, but occasionally longer. Even though these treatments have made remarkable gains, they also bear limitations worth highlighting.

Impact of Treatment

The criteria for identifying and establishing treatments as evidence based have enormous implications for what can be stated about the treatments and their effects. The criteria require demonstrating that treatment is better than no treatment or treatment as usual. "Better than" means statistically significantly different on some outcome measures. There are separate issues here raised by the limits of statistical significance. First, demonstrating statistically significant differences is not very stringent. Research in adult therapy has shown that almost any active treatment is better (statistically) than no treatment. Expectations, attention, and the common factors associated with coming to therapy alone can produce such a difference. Indeed, active "fake" treatments in which the patient engages in some activities not considered on a priori grounds to have therapeutic value can generate such a difference and surpass the effects of no treatment (Grissom, 1996). Moreover, as the "fake" treatment increasingly resembles the veridical treatment in terms of structure, components, and expectations for change generated in the client, the less likely there is to be a difference between treatment and the control condition (Baskin, Tierney, Minami, & Wampold, 2003). Thus, a difference of treatment versus no treatment in a Type 1 study of therapy says little about whether the specific features of that therapy are responsible for the difference or treatment effect.

Second, statistical significance has no necessary bearing on the practical impact of treatment on the patient. For example, a statistically significant difference favoring one treatment over another on some measure of anxiety may not reflect genuine differences or improvements on patient anxiety or functioning in everyday life. Similarly, indices of magnitude of effect (e.g., d, r, $\hat{a}$) are excellent supplements to statistical significance for purposes of research. Yet strength of an effect from a statistical standpoint (e.g., in standard deviation units) may have no bearing on the impact of treatment on patients (Blanton & Jaccard, 2006; Kazdin, 2006a). Indeed, effect size can be quite large in cases where impact on the patient is nugatory.

In an effort to redress the limits of statistical significance, clinical significance has been added to evaluate treatments. *Clinical significance* refers to a set of indices designed to evaluate whether impact of treatment translates to meaningful changes in the patient (Kazdin, 2001; Kendall, 1999). Among the indices of clinical significance are return of "symptom" to normative levels of functioning, no longer meeting criteria for psychiatric diagnosis, and making large changes on key scales from pre- to posttreatment. These are all designed to evaluate impact that is important. A difficultly is that none of these indices has been validated in relation to clinical impact on functioning of the patient in everyday life. It is not difficult to show in principle how measures of clinical significance have no necessary relation to patient functioning (Kazdin, 2001).

Overall, evidence suggests that children receiving one of the treatments reviewed earlier make marked changes. Even so, interpretation of the impact of treatment on everyday functioning is not clear. Part of the problem stems from the focus of treatment. In some cases, complete elimination of the behavior (e.g., fire setting, cruelty to animals, brandishing a weapon) would provide clear evidence that treatment had significant impact. Yet, more commonly, changes

in such behaviors as rule breaking, getting into trouble, and arguing are less readily interpretable because the changes may be a matter of degree and because changes on the usual parent and teacher ratings do not automatically translate to actual functioning in everyday situations. In some of the studies reviewed previously, the outcome measures have included rearrest and reincarceration rates among adjudicated delinquents. These measures convey significant impact of treatment on outcomes well beyond the usual rating scales.

Limited Assessment of Outcome Domains

The prior comments emphasize the research criteria (e.g., statistical significance) for deciding whether treatment will qualify as evidence based. It is worth distinguishing as a separate issue the constructs and measures used to evaluate the impact of treatment. In the majority of child therapy studies, child symptoms are the exclusive focus of outcome assessment. Other domains such as prosocial behavior, peer relations, and academic functioning are neglected, even though they relate to concurrent and long-term adjustment. Perhaps the greatest single deficit in the evaluation of treatment is absence of attention to impairment. Impairment reflects the extent to which the individual's functioning in everyday life is impeded. School and academic functioning, peer relations, and participation in activities are some of key areas of functioning. Impairment can be distinguished from symptoms insofar as individuals with similar levels of symptoms, diagnoses, and patterns of comorbidity are likely to be distinguishable based on their ability to function adaptively. Indeed, impairment is associated with significant disturbance whether or not youths meet criteria for psychiatric diagnosis (Angold et al., 1999). Understandably, referral to clinical services is more likely to be related to impairment in everyday life rather than to meeting criteria for a psychiatric disorder (e.g., Bird et al., 1990). Treatment may significantly reduce symptoms, but is there any change or reduction in impairment? The impact of treatment on impairment is arguably as important as the impact on the CD symptoms.

Beyond child functioning, parent and family functioning may also be relevant as outcome domains of child and adolescent therapy. Parents and family members of youths with CD often experience dysfunction (e.g., psychiatric impairment, high levels of stress in the home, marital conflict). Also, the problem behaviors of the child often are part of complex, dynamic, and reciprocal influences that affect all relations in the home. Consequently, parent and family functioning and the quality of life for family members are relevant outcomes and may be appropriate goals for treatment. Parent dysfunction (e.g., depression, symptoms across diverse disorders) and perceived stress and family relations improve with child treatment, even though these are not focused on directly (Kazdin & Wassell, 2000). The impact of improved parent and child functioning on the long-term course of child CD has yet to be evaluated.

Long-Term Outcomes

Promising treatments have included follow-up assessment, usually up to a year after treatment. Yet CD has a poor long-term prognosis, so it is especially important to identify whether treatment has enduring effects. Also, in evaluating the relative merit of different treatments, follow-up data play a critical role. When two (or more) treatments are compared, the treatment that is more (or most) effective immediately after treatment is not always the one that proves to be the most effective in the long run (Kazdin, 2000b).

The study of long-term effects of treatment is difficult in general, but the usual problems are exacerbated by focusing on CD. Among clinic samples, families of children diagnosed with CD have high rates of dropping out during treatment and during the follow-up assessment period due in part to the many parent and family factors (e.g., socioeconomic disadvantage, stress) often associated with conduct problems and attrition (Kazdin, 1996). As the sample size decreases over time, conclusions about the impact of treatment become increasingly difficult to draw.

Another problem that interferes with long-term follow-up is having a control group or a way of estimating what improvements would have occurred without treatment over the follow-up period. It is quite possible that improvements evident in the long run (e.g., 15 years later) would have been found in the no-treatment group or alternative-treatment group. Indeed, the group that received the special treatment could even show fewer gains than a control condition. For example, there are long-term studies of patients seen in PMT, as referred to previously, but the design (absence of a comparison group) does not permit one to conclude that treatment had any influence on the status of patients at the time of follow-up. There are statistical options to estimate long-term gains with treatment in a quasi-experimental (Type 2) fashion (e.g., propensity analysis; D'Agostino, 1998). Such analyses to inform the long-term effects of EBT, to my knowledge, have yet to be used.

Notwithstanding the obstacles, some studies have been able to obtain follow-up to evaluate the long-term maintenance of change. Among the treatments I have reviewed, MST has provided evidence attesting to the effects of treatment 10 to 15 years after treatment and when youths were in their late 20s (Henggeler et al., 1998; Schaeffer & Borduin, 2005). FFT has shown that recidivism is reduced up to 5 years after treatment (Gordon et al., 1995). Evaluation of the long-term effects of treatment remains a high priority for treatment research, perhaps especially so among problems such as CD that have a long-term course. Yet many child problems (e.g., ODD, ADHD, depression) are now known to have long-term courses or predict untoward outcomes in adulthood. Whether treatment effects obtained in childhood continue or whether they prevent the emergence of other disorders in adulthood remain to be elaborated.

GENERAL COMMENTS

Even among the most well investigated treatments, several critical questions remain. Yet it is important to place these treatments in perspective. The most commonly used treatments in clinical practice consist of "traditional" approaches, including psychodynamic, relationship, play, and family therapies (other than those mentioned above; Kazdin, Siegel, & Bass, 1990). These treatments have rarely been tested in controlled outcome studies to show that they achieve therapeutic change in referred (or nonreferred) samples of youth with conduct problems.

One genre of psychosocial interventions is worth mentioning in passing. Occasionally, interventions are advocated and implemented such as sending youths with CD to a camp out in the country where they learn how to "rough it," to assume responsibility (e.g., take care of horses), or to experience military (e.g., basic training) regimens. The conceptual bases of such treatments and supportive research on the processes involved in the onset or maintenance of CD are rarely provided. On the one hand, developing treatments that emerge outside of the mainstream of the mental health professions is to be encouraged precisely because traditional treatments have not resolved the problem. On the other hand, this genre of intervention tends to eschew evaluation. Evaluation is key because well-intentioned and costly interventions can have little or no effect on youths they serve (Weisz, Walter, Weiss, Fernandez, & Mikow, 1990) and sometimes may actually increase antisocial behavior (Lundman, 1984).

FUTURE DIRECTIONS

Randomized controlled trials of treatment and further study to establish EBTs can only go so far in answering key questions that will improve patient care. These studies need to be supplemented with other foci to advance both our understanding of treatment and the impact of treatment on patients. Three lines of work to address these goals are highlighted here.

Focus on Mechanisms of Therapeutic Change

The interest in EBT has narrowed the focus of therapy research to address primarily two questions: Is a treatment "efficacious" (beneficial in controlled settings)? Can the treatment be transported to clinical settings? We would like to have a broad set of questions answered about therapy. For a given treatment, we would like to know the following:

1. What is the impact of treatment relative to no treatment?
2. What components contribute to change?
3. What treatments can be added (combined treatments) to optimize change?
4. What parameters can be varied to influence (improve) outcome?
5. How effective is this treatment relative to other treatments for this problem?
6. What patient, therapist, treatment, and contextual factors influence (moderate) outcome?
7. What processes within or during treatment influence, cause, and are responsible for outcome?

8. To what extent are treatment effects generalizable across problem areas, settings, and other domains?
9. What facets of treatment, training, organizations, and service delivery facilitate or moderate effective adoption and implementation of treatment?

Among the highest priorities is understanding why treatment works, that is, the mechanisms of change (i.e., question 7). The study of mechanisms of treatment is probably the best short-term and long-term investment for improving clinical practice and patient care. In studying mechanisms, it is critical to distinguish cause and mechanisms of therapeutic change. By *cause*, I mean what led to change—a demonstration that some intervention led to some outcome. By *mechanisms*, I refer to those processes or events that account for the change. *Mediator* is often used as the term intended to signify a cause or mechanism of change and distinguished from *moderator*, as evident in the now classic paper by Baron and Kenny (1986). For this discussion, I retain *mechanism* as the term. Mediator analyses raise multiple issues and may identify factors that do not explain why treatment works, a topic beyond the scope of this chapter (Baron & Kenny, 1986; Kazdin & Nock, 2003; Kraemer, Stice, Kazdin, Offord, & Kupfer, 2001). A randomized controlled clinical trial (e.g., comparing treatment vs. no treatment) can establish a causal relation between an intervention and therapeutic change. However, demonstrating a causal relation does not necessarily explain *why* the relation was obtained. Thus, we may know *that* the intervention caused the change but not understand *why* (the basis for the cause or the mechanism) the intervention led to change.

As an example, consider cognitive therapy (CT) for the treatment of unipolar depression among adults. By all counts, this treatment is evidence based and then some in light of the range of trials, replications, and comparisons (Hollon & Beck, 2004). Why does CT work, that is, through what mechanisms? In fact, little can be stated as to why treatment works. The conceptual model has emphasized changes in various cognitions. However, it is not obvious, clear, or established that changes in cognitions are the basis for therapeutic change. Indeed, suitable studies are rarely done. Designs are needed in which processes and symptom changes are evaluated at multiple points over the course of treatment (Kazdin, 2006b). Some studies have demonstrated that changes in cognitions during treatment predict symptom change (DeRubeis et al., 1990; Kwon & Oei, 2003), yet it has not been clear in such studies whether symptom change *preceded* rather than followed changes in cognition. In general, there is a firm basis for stating that CT can change depression but little empirical basis for stating why.

Similarly, decades of research have focused on the therapeutic alliance or other facets of the therapeutic relationship (e.g., Norcross, 2002; Orlinsky, Rønnestad, & Willutzki, 2004). A commonly held view is that the alliance leads to and is responsible for improvement in symptoms. Unfortunately, in the majority of studies, the time line has not been established that demonstrates that a positive relationship or alliance precedes therapeutic change. To show the temporal relation, one must show that alliance has changed and symptoms have not but eventually change later. Most studies have not assessed symptoms and alliance repeatedly and at the same point in time during treatment to establish their temporal relation, although there are important exceptions (Barber, Connolly, Crits-Christoph, Gladis, & Siqueland, 2000). Another issue yet to be resolved is clarification of how relationship factors operate if they do lead to symptom change (e.g., how does alliance reduce obsessions or stress?). Specifying what the relationship does or how it operates to alter this or that in the client requires noting the steps and putting empirical meat on a conceptual skeleton.

The previous examples convey what we do not know from two areas where mechanisms have been discussed but not established. A promising example of what to look forward to is evident in the treatment of fear in adults. The treatment of fear and anxiety in adults has profited from basic animal research over a period spanning decades. More recently, work focusing on the conditioning of fear and the biological underpinnings of extinction has elaborated mechanisms of action to improve treatment. Conditioning and extinction of fear depend on a particular protein in the brain (the N-methyl-D-asparatate receptor in the amygdala; Davis, Myers, Ressler, & Rothbaum, 2005). Animal research (rats) shows that blocking the receptor blocks extinction; improving the activity of this receptor improves extinction. Efforts to improve activity of this receptor among humans receiving exposure-based therapy for fear of heights (acrophobia) improves the effects of treatment (Ressler et al., 2004). This is promising work that shows how understanding mechanisms can improve treatment outcomes.

Making Moderators Useful

We have known for many years that a critical question of psychotherapy is not what technique is effective, but rather what technique works for whom, under what conditions, as administered by what type of therapists (Kiesler, 1971; question 6 from the prior list). Stated in more contemporary terms, what are the moderators of treatment, that is, those characteristics that influence the effects of treatment. In the case of CD, several studies have looked at who responds to treatment, mostly in the context of PMT. As mentioned previously, evidence suggests that risk factors for onset of CD and poor long-term prognosis (e.g., early onset, severe aggressive behavior, family adversity) also influence responsiveness to treatment. Children and families with adversity in one or more of these characteristics tend to respond less well to treatment than those without these characteristics or less adverse degrees.

The ways in which moderators are studied have not been very helpful in making decisions about treatment or directing patients to the appropriate intervention. First, one might be able to identify children who respond less well to treatment. For example, in a recent study of moderators, we found that families who experienced barriers to participation in treatment responded significantly less well to treatment (showed less change) than those who experience fewer or no such barriers (Kazdin & Whitley, 2006). Barriers to treatment participation moderated treatment. The finding does not help in decision making about treatment. The families of children with CD with high barriers still showed therapeutic change. Indeed, the effect sizes for these families was 1.24 (Cohen's *d*), which is large. Even though a variable moderates treatment, this does not necessarily mean individuals with the moderators who respond less well will not respond to treatment.

Second, when moderators operate and we identify a group less likely to respond, we do not know whether the group would respond better to another treatment. For example, we may find that children who have multiple disorders in addition to CD and a heavy genetic loading for CD do not respond to

PMT or MST. This may be important, but we do not know if that is a strong basis to refer such children to another treatment. It may well be that a moderator for one treatment has broad generality and would impede the effects of any one treatment.

The study of moderators is extremely important. One way to make treatment more effective is to identify interventions that work. Another way is to have better triage, that is, to direct patients to treatments from which they are likely to profit and away from those likely to exert little control. Better triage increases the overall impact of all treatments on the target population by reducing the rate of misassigning patients to inappropriate treatment. The difficulty is that studies of moderators are not designed to help with decision making. We need a different kind of moderator research on therapy. That research would examine the extent to which moderators apply to specific treatments rather than treatments in general and would propose treatment algorithms or probabilities to which patients with various characteristics would be likely to respond. Such research could greatly improve the effects of treatment by reducing the failure rates from misapplied treatments.

New Ways of Delivering Treatment

Several EBTs have been identified for CD. There remain questions about these treatments (e.g., mechanisms of actions, moderators), but we already know enough to be of great help to those in need. The need for treatment among youths (e.g., in the United States) is enormous. Estimates still place one in five individuals in the community (children, adolescents, and adult) as meeting criteria for a psychiatric diagnosis. Among the 70 million children in the United States, 14 million (20%) would meet criteria. This is a conservative estimate because those who do not meet criteria (e.g., for CD or depression) can be significantly impaired.

Consider the plight of children with clinical diagnoses in need of treatment. Estimates suggest that 67% of the children in need do not receive treatment (U.S. Congress, 1991). Dropout rates (premature termination) for therapy are 40 to 60% for children, adolescents, and adults (Kazdin, 1996); for ease of calculation, let us take 50%. Out of 100 children in need, approximately 33 will receive treatment (100 minus 67 from above). Of these, approximately 50%

will drop out early. Now we have, let us say, 17 children who are receiving treatment. Leave aside for the moment that the chance of these children receiving an EBT is well below the likelihood of finding life on Pluto. I wish to underscore another point—treatments are not reaching the group in need.

Novel methods of delivering treatment need to be pursued. They are, and some advances can be identified already. Therapies are completed by self-help manuals, telephone, mail, Internet and computer, videotapes and DVDs. Not all the applications are effective, but many of them are. For example, I highlighted PMT as one of the most well studied interventions for CD. Materials are available that can help disseminate treatment. In a programmatic series of studies (Type 1) with young conduct problem children (3 to 8 years), Webster-Stratton and her colleagues have developed and evaluated videotaped materials to present PMT to parents; treatment can be self-administered in individual or group format supplemented with discussion (see Webster-Stratton & Reid, 2003). Similarly, Gordon (2000; Kacir & Gordon, 1999) has developed a set of self-administered videos for low socioeconomic status families. For both programs mentioned here, controlled studies have shown changes at posttreatment and follow-up assessments with variations of videotaped treatment. The potential for extension of PMT is readily available.

Apart from means of delivering treatment, novel models are needed. For example, the notion of stepped care has been introduced in psychotherapy to suggest that minimal treatments be used first before one moves to more intensive, time-consuming, and costly treatments (Haaga, 2000). Are there low-cost and brief interventions that might be applied to children with CD? Even if such interventions are effective with only a small number of individuals, their ease of dissemination and relatively low cost may make them worthwhile. Promising lines of work indicate that in the case of treatment for adults, therapeutic gains often are rapid, a phenomenon called *sudden therapeutic gains* (Tang & DeRubeis, 1999). In our own work we have found that many of the families with CD children who drop out of treatment early have made large gains (Kazdin & Wassell, 1998). Not all children in need of treatment will need individual sessions of therapy over a course of months. Research is needed to elaborate a portfolio of treatments that vary in cost, ease of administration, and therapeutic effort. There are effective models for this kind of work. For example, in medicine a standard generic antibiotic is given and is usually effective for common varieties of bacterial infections; a much more powerful one is sometimes needed when the individual does not initially respond. Graded interventions and interventions that vary in ease of disseminability would greatly improve the reach and impact of effective treatments. A stepped approach to care may be especially important for CD because many of the interventions reviewed previously include several treatment techniques; some involve a research team (rather than one clinician), and one or more individuals are available 24 hours a day for 7 days a week. EBTs are not disseminated widely, but some of them perhaps cannot be in relation to the mental health service needs of children.

CONCLUSIONS

Many types of treatment have been applied to CD. Seven treatments with the strongest evidence to date were detailed and included parent management training, multisystemic therapy, multidimensional treatment foster care, cognitive problem-solving skills training, anger control training, functional family therapy, and brief strategic family therapy. *Parent management training* is directed at altering parent-child interactions in the home, particularly those interactions related to child-rearing practices and coercive interchanges. *Multisystemic therapy* focuses on the individual, family, and extrafamilial systems and their interrelations as a way to reduce symptoms and promote prosocial behavior. Multiple treatments (e.g., PSST, PMT, family therapy) are used in combination to address domains that affect the child. The *Multidimensional treatment foster care model* focuses on youth who are in placement and who are to return to their parents or more permanent foster care. Behavioral treatments in the placement and the home to which the child is returned are part of a comprehensive effort to integrate treatment and community life. *Cognitive problem-solving skills training* focuses on cognitive processes that underlie social behavior and response repertoires in interpersonal situations. The intervention is provided in the context of individual therapy for the child. Also cognitively based, *Anger Control Training* includes problem-solving skills training in the context of groups in

the schools. The program has an additional component that includes PMT as a key addition. *Functional family therapy* utilizes principles of systems theory and behavior modification for altering interaction, communication patterns, and problem solving among family members. *Brief strategic family therapy* focuses on the structure of the family and concrete strategies that can be used to promote improved patterns of interaction. This treatment has been developed with Hispanic children and adolescents and has integrated culturally pertinent issues to engage the families.

Evidence in behalf of these treatments was reviewed. All the treatments have Type 1 studies and follow-up data in their behalf. PMT and MST have a large number of replications across many setting. PMT enjoys replication across many investigators and perhaps has the longest running history of Type 1 studies of the treatments reviewed in this chapter. Although the other treatments are not as well researched, they are very well studied. There is now a strong cadre of interventions for use with children referred for CD, spanning the full range of severity.

What is striking about the treatments is that there is a strong emphasis on the family; most of the treatments explicitly focus on parents and family interaction in some way. The evidence does not establish that the family is the only or best way to intervene. At the same time, a striking feature of CD among those who treat clinically referred cases is the significant parent, family, and contextual influences in which the child's function is embedded. This too does not mean that the child's problem is caused by these influences, but it does mean that with any intervention, it is difficult and perhaps not even possible to ignore the parent and family. Indeed, parent functioning, stress, and perceptions about treatment strongly influence whether children come to, remain in, and profit from therapy. Consequently, engaging the family in special ways to participate in treatment and directly addressing parent and family functioning are high-priority foci. Better assessment and diagnosis of parent, family, and contextual factors are needed to provide a systematic way of identifying whether multiple foci and which foci are optimal for a particular child or type of child-parent-family-context gestalt. At this point in time the broad foci on children, parents, and families and the use of multiple techniques have not really been justified empirically. The need to do the empirical tests goes beyond our thirst for understanding; the mental health needs of children mean that comprehensive, all-inclusive treatments, whether evidence based or not, will not be served by such treatments.

We cannot yet say that one intervention can ameliorate CD and overcome the poor long-term prognosis. On the other hand, much can be said. Much of what is practiced in clinical settings is based on psychodynamically oriented treatment, general relationship counseling, various forms of family therapy (other than those reviewed above), and group therapy (with all antisocial youths as members). These and other procedures, alone and in various combinations in which they are often used, have not been evaluated carefully in controlled trials. Of course, absence of evidence is not tantamount to ineffectiveness. At the same time, effective treatments are available. A very persuasive argument is needed to justify administration of treatments that have neither basic research on their conceptual underpinnings in relation to CD nor outcome evidence from controlled clinical trials on their behalf.

Even considering only the EBTs for CD, important questions remain unanswered. The short- and long-term impact on children and the extent to which the changes materially alter their everyday lives are not clear from current research. Further development of treatments clearly is needed. Apart from treatment studies, further progress in understanding the nature of CD is likely to have very important implications for improving treatment outcome. Improved triage of patients to treatments that are likely to work will require understanding of characteristics of children, parents, and families that will make them more or less amenable to current treatments. Perhaps most important, research is needed that attempts to understand the bases of therapeutic change. Understanding the change process is the best long-term investment in developing effective treatments for clinical use.

ACKNOWLEDGMENT

Completion of this chapter was facilitated in part by support from the National Institute of Mental Health (MH59029). Correspondence should be directed to Alan E. Kazdin, Child Study Center, Yale University School of Medicine, 230 S. Frontage Road, New Haven, CT 06520–7900.

NOTES

1. *Children* will be used to refer to both children and adolescents. When pertinent to the discussion, a distinction will be made and referred to accordingly.

2. In this chapter, I refer to conduct disorder or CD as antisocial and aggressive behavior where the children's functioning is impaired, whether or not they meet criteria for the diagnosis. When children meet the criteria, this will be so noted in the text. The cut point that delineates whether someone has or does not have the disorder (meets the diagnostic criteria) cannot be defended empirically, and hence it is more useful to encompass broader samples of individuals with aggressive and antisocial behavior.

3. In *DSM-IV*, if the child meets criteria for CD, ODD is not diagnosed, because the former is likely to include many symptoms of the latter. Yet invoking and evaluating the criteria for these diagnoses ignoring this consideration has been useful in understanding the relation and overlap of these diagnoses.

4. Medium-to-large effects refers to effect sizes that reflect the amount of changes on measures in standard deviation units. Small, medium, and large effect size estimates as .20, .50, and .80 (Cohen, 1988) can be used as a guide to evaluate the impact of treatment. As noted later in this chapter, effect sizes have no necessary relation or bearing to clinical importance or impact of the outcome on client functioning.

5. Key researchers with programs of PMT in relation to oppositional and CD research include Eyberg (University of Florida), Forehand (University of Georgia, University of Vermont), Patterson (Oregon Social Learning Research Center), Webster-Stratton (University of Washington), and Wahler (University of Tennessee). Samples of this work are cited in the chapter. Various compendiums include reviews of several of these researchers (Hibbs & Jensen, 2005; Kazdin & Weisz, 2003; Reid et al., 2002). Many other researchers use variations of PMT for other clinical problems (e.g., ADHD, autism).

REFERENCES

Alexander, J. F., Barton, C., Schiavo, R. S., & Parsons, B. V. (1976). Systems-behavioral intervention with families of delinquents: Therapist characteristics, family behavior, and outcome. *Journal of Consulting and Clinical Psychology, 44,* 656–664.

Alexander, J. F., Holtzworth-Munroe, A., & Jameson, P. B. (1994). The process and outcome of marital and family therapy research: Review and evaluation. In A. E. Bergin & S. L. Garfield (Eds.), *Hand-*

book of psychotherapy and behavior change (4th ed., pp. 595–630). New York: Wiley.

Alexander, J. F., & Parsons, B. V. (1982). *Functional family therapy*. Monterey, CA: Brooks/Cole.

Alexander, J. F., Sexton, T. L., and Robbins, M. S. 2000. The developmental status of family therapy in family psychology intervention science. In H. Liddle, D. Santisteban, R. Levant, & J. Bray (Eds.), *Family psychology intervention science*. Washington, DC: American Psychological Association.

American Psychiatric Association. (1994). *Diagnostic and statistical manual of mental disorders* (4th ed.). Washington, DC: Author.

Angold, A., Costello, E. J., Farmer, E. M., Burns, B. J., & Erkanli, A. (1999). Impaired but undiagnosed. *Journal of the American Academy of Child and Adolescent Psychiatry, 38*, 129–137.

Aos, S., Phipps, P., Barnoski, R., & Leib, R. (1999). *The comparative costs and benefits of programs to reduce crime: A review of national research findings with implications for Washington state*. Olympia, WA: Washington State Institute for Public Policy.

Aos, S., Phipps, P., Barnoski, R., & Leib, R. (2001). *The comparative costs and benefits of programs to reduce crime, Version 4.0*. Olympia, WA: Washington State Institute for Public Policy.

Baer, R. A., & Nietzel, M.T. (1991). Cognitive and behavioral treatment of impulsivity in children: A meta-analytic review of the outcome literature. *Journal of Clinical Child Psychology, 20*, 400–412.

Bank, L., Marlowe, J. H., Reid, J. B., Patterson, G. R., & Weinrott, M. R. (1991). A comparative evaluation of parent-training interventions for families of chronic delinquents. *Journal of Abnormal Child Psychology, 19*, 15–33.

Barber, J. P., Connolly, M. B., Crits-Christoph, P., Gladis, L., & Siqueland, L. (2000). Alliance predicts patients' outcome beyond in-treatment change in symptoms. *Journal of Consulting and Clinical Psychology, 68*, 1027–1032.

Barkley, R. A. (1997). *Defiant children: A clinician's manual for parent training* (2nd ed.). New York: Guilford Press.

Baron, R. M., & Kenny, D. A. (1986). The moderator-mediator variable distinction in social psychological research: Conceptual, strategic, and statistical considerations. *Journal of Personality and Social Psychology, 51*, 1173–1182.

Baskin, T. W., Tierney, S. C., Minami, T., & Wampold, B. E. (2003). Establishing specificity in psychotherapy: A meta-analysis of structural equivalence of placebo controls. *Journal of Consulting and Clinical Psychology, 71*, 973–979.

Bird, H. R., Yager, T. J., Staghezza, B., Gould, M. S., Canino, G., & Rubio-Stipec, M. (1990). Impairment in the epidemiological measurement of psychopathology in the community. *Journal of the American Academy of Child and Adolescent Psychiatry, 29*, 796–803.

Blanton, H., & Jaccard, J. (2006). Arbitrary metrics in psychology. *American Psychologist, 61*, 27–41.

Borduin, C. M., Mann, B. J., Cone, L. T., Henggeler, S. W., Fucci, B. R., Blaske, D. M., et al. (1995). Multisystemic treatment of serious juvenile offenders: Long-term prevention of criminality and violence. *Journal of Consulting and Clinical Psychology, 63*, 569–578.

Bourke, M. L., & Van Hasselt, V. B. (2001). Social problem-solving skills training for incarcerated offenders: A treatment manual. *Behavior Modification, 25*, 163–188.

Boyle, M. H., Offord, D. R., Racine, Y., Szatmari, P., Fleming, J. E., & Sanford, M. (1996). Identifying thresholds for classifying childhood psychiatric disorder: Issues and prospects. *Journal of the American Academy of Child and Adolescent Psychiatry, 35*, 1440–1448.

Brandt, D. E. (2006). *Delinquency, development, and social policy*. New Haven, CT: Yale University Press.

Brown, T. L., Henggeler, S. W., Schoenwald, S. K., Brondino, M. J., & Pickrel, S. G. (1999). Multisystemic treatment of substance abusing and dependent delinquents: Effects on school attendance at posttreatment and 6-month follow-up. *Children's Services: Social Policy, Research, and Practice, 2*, 81–93.

Caspi, A., McClay, J., Moffitt, T. E., Mill, J., Martin, J., Craig, I., et al. (2002, August 2). Role of genotype in the cycle of violence in maltreated children. *Science, 297*, 851–854.

Cavell, T. A. (2000). *Working with aggressive children: A practitioner's guide*. Washington, DC: American Psychological Association.

Chamberlain, P., & Reid, J. B. (1998). Comparison of two community alternatives to incarceration for chronic juvenile offenders. *Journal of Consulting and Clinical Psychology, 66*, 624–633.

Chamberlain, P., & Smith, D. K. (2003). Antisocial behavior in children and adolescents: The Oregon Multidimensional Treatment Foster Care Model. In A. E. Kazdin & J. R. Weisz (Eds.), *Evidence-based psychotherapies for children and adolescents* (pp. 282–300). New York: Guilford Press.

Chamberlain, P., & Smith, D. K. (2005). Multidimensional Treatment Foster Care: A community solution for boys and girls referred from juvenile justice. In E. D. Hibbs & P. S. Jensen (Eds.),

Psychosocial treatments for child and adolescent disorders: Empirically based strategies for clinical practice (2nd ed., pp. 557–574). Washington, DC: American Psychological Association.

Christophersen, E. R., & Mortweet, S. L. (2001). *Treatments that work with children: Empirically supported strategies for managing childhood problems.* Washington, DC: American Psychological Association.

Coatsworth, J. D., Szapocznik, J., Kurtines, W., & Santisteban, D. A. (1997). Culturally competent psychosocial interventions with antisocial problem behavior in Hispanic youths. In D. M. Stoff, J. Breiling, & J. D. Maser (Eds.), *Handbook of antisocial behavior* (pp. 395–404). New York: Wiley.

Cohen, J. (1988). *Statistical power analysis for the behavioral sciences* (2nd ed.). Hillsdale, NJ: Erlbaum.

Cooper, J. O., Heron, T. E., & Heward, W. L. (1987). *Applied behavior analysis.* Columbus, OH: Merrill.

Crick, N. R., & Dodge, K. A. (1994). A review and reformulation of social information processing mechanisms in children's social adjustment. *Psychological Bulletin, 115,* 74–101.

Cunningham, C. E., Bremner, R., & Boyle, M. (1995). Large group community-based parenting programs for families of preschoolers at risk for disruptive behaviour disorders: Utilization, cost effectiveness, and outcome. *Journal of Child Psychology and Psychiatry, 36,* 1141–1159.

Dadds, M. R., & McHugh, T. A. (1992). Social support and treatment outcome in behavioral family therapy for child conduct problems. *Journal of Consulting and Clinical Psychology, 60,* 252–259.

Dadds, M. R., Schwartz, S., & Sanders, M. R. (1987). Marital discord and treatment outcome in behavioral treatment of child conduct disorders. *Journal of Consulting and Clinical Psychology, 55,* 396–403.

D'Agostino, R. B., Jr. (1998). Tutorial in biostatistics: Propensity score methods for bias reduction in the comparison of a treatment to a non-randomized control group. *Statistics in Medicine, 17,* 2265–2281.

Davis, M. R., Myers, K. M., Ressler, K. J., & Rothbaum, B. O. (2005). Facilitation of extinction of conditioned fear by D-cycloserine. *Current Directions in Psychological Science, 14,* 214–219.

DeRubeis, R. J., Evans, M. D., Hollon, S. D., Garvey, M. J., Grove, W. M., & Tuason, V. B. (1990). How does cognitive therapy work? Cognitive change and symptom change in cognitive therapy and pharmacotherapy for depression. *Journal of Consulting and Clinical Psychology, 58,* 862–869.

Dishion, T. J., & Andrews, D. W. (1995). Preventing escalation in problem behaviors with high-risk young adolescents: Immediate and 1-year outcomes. *Journal of Consulting and Clinical Psychology, 63,* 538–548.

Dishion, T. J., McCord, J., & Poulin, F. (1999). When interventions harm: Peer groups and problem behavior. *American Psychologist, 54,* 755–764.

Dishion, T. J., & Patterson, G. R. (1992). Age effects in parent training outcomes. *Behavior Therapy, 23,* 719–729.

Dishion, T. J., Patterson, G. R., & Kavanagh, K. A. (1992). An experimental test of the coercion model: Linking theory, measurement, and intervention. In J. McCord & R. E. Tremblay (Eds.), *Preventing antisocial behavior* (pp. 253–282). New York: Guilford Press.

Doherr, L., Reynolds, S., Wetherly, J., & Evans, E. H. (2005). Young children's ability to engage in cognitive tasks: Associations with age and educational experience. *Behavioural and Cognitive Psychotherapy, 33,* 201–215.

Dumas, J. E., & Wahler, R. G. (1983). Predictors of treatment outcome in parent training: Mother insularity and socioeconomic disadvantage. *Behavioral Assessment, 5,* 301–313.

Dumas, J. E., & Wahler, R. G. (1985). Indiscriminate mothering as a contextual factor in aggressive oppositional child behavior: "Damned if you do and damned if you don't." *Journal of Applied Behavior Analysis, 13,* 1–17.

Durlak, J. A., Fuhrman, T., & Lampman, C. (1991). Effectiveness of cognitive-behavioral therapy for maladapting children: A meta-analysis. *Psychological Bulletin, 110,* 204–214.

Eddy, J. M., Bridges-Whaley, R., & Chamberlain, P. (2004). The prevention of violent behavior by chronic and serious male juvenile offenders: A 2-year follow-up of a randomized clinical trial. *Journal of Emotional and Behavioral Disorders, 12,* 2–8.

Eddy, J. M., & Chamberlain, P. (2001). Family management and deviant peer association as mediators of the impact of treatment condition on youth antisocial behavior. *Journal of Consulting and Clinical Psychology, 68,* 857–863.

Feindler, E. L., & Ecton, R. B. (1986). *Adolescent anger control: Cognitive-behavioral techniques.* Elmsford, NY: Pergamon.

Feldman, R. A., Caplinger, T. E., & Wodarski, J. S. (1983). *The St. Louis conundrum: The effective treatment of antisocial youths.* Englewood Cliffs, NJ: Prentice-Hall.

Fergusson, D. M., Horwood, L. J., & Lloyd, M. (1991). Confirmatory factor models of attention deficit and conduct disorder. *Journal of Child Psychology and Psychiatry, 32,* 257–274.

Fergusson, D. M., Horwood, L. J., & Ridder, E. M. (2005). Show me the child at seven: The consequences of conduct problems in childhood for psychosocial functioning in adulthood. *Journal of Child Psychology and Psychiatry, 46,* 837–849.

Finch, A. J., Jr., Nelson, W. M., & Ott, E. S. (1993). *Cognitive-behavioral procedures with children and adolescents: A practical guide.* Needham Heights, MA: Allyn and Bacon.

Foley, D., Wormley, B., Silberg, J., Maes, H., Hewitt, J., Eaves, L., et al. (2004). Childhood adversity, MAOA genotype, and risk for conduct disorder. *Archives of General Psychiatry, 61,* 738–744.

Forehand, R., & Long, N. (1988). Outpatient treatment of the acting out child: Procedures, long-term follow-up data, and clinical problems. *Advances in Behaviour Research and Therapy, 10,* 129–177.

Forehand, R., & McMahon, R. J. (1981). *Helping the noncompliant child: A clinician's guide to parent training.* New York: Guilford Press.

Frick, P. J., & Morris, A. S. (2004). Temperament and developmental pathways to severe conduct problems. *Journal of Clinical Child and Adolescent Psychology, 33,* 54–68.

Friedberg, R. D., & McClure, J. M. (2002). *Clinical practice of cognitive therapy with children and adolescents: The nuts and bolts.* New York: Guilford Press.

Functional Family Therapy. (2003). CSS — Clinical service system. Retrieved September 27, 2006, from http://www.fftinc.com

Gordon, D. A. (2000). Parent training via CD-ROM: Using technology to disseminate effective prevention practices. *Journal of Primary Prevention, 21,* 227–251.

Gordon, D. A., Graves, K., & Arbuthnot, J. (1995). The effect of functional family therapy for delinquents on adult criminal behavior. *Criminal Justice and Behavior, 22,* 60–73.

Griest, D. L., Forehand, R., Rogers, T., Breiner, J., Furey, W., & Williams, C. A. (1982). Effects of parent enhancement therapy on the treatment outcome and generalization of a parent training program. *Behaviour Research and Therapy, 20,* 429–436.

Grissom, R. J. (1996). The magical number .7 +/– .2: Meta-meta-analysis of the probability of superior outcome in comparisons involving therapy, placebo, and control. *Journal of Consulting and Clinical Psychology, 64,* 973–982.

Haaga, D. A. F. (2000). Introduction to the special section on stepped-care models in psychotherapy. *Journal of Consulting and Clinical Psychology, 68,* 547–548.

Halliday-Boykins, C. A., Schoenwald, S. K., & Letourneau, E. J. (2005). Caregiver-therapist ethnic similarity predicts youth outcomes from an empirically based treatment. *Journal of Consulting and Clinical Psychology, 73,* 808–818.

Henggeler, S. W., Clingempeel, W. G., Brondino, M. J., & Pickrel, S. G. (2002). Four-year follow-up of multisystemic therapy with substance-abusing and substance-dependent juvenile offenders. *Journal of the American Academy of Child and Adolescent Psychiatry, 41,* 868–874.

Henggeler, S. W., & Lee, T. (2003). Multisystemic treatment of serious clinical problems. In A. E. Kazdin & J. R. Weisz (Eds.), *Evidence-based psychotherapies for children and adolescents* (pp. 301–322). New York: Guilford Press.

Henggeler, S. W., Pickrel, S. G., & Brondino, M. J. (1999). Multisystemic treatment of substance-abusing and dependent delinquents: Outcomes, treatment fidelity, and transportability. *Mental Health Services Research, 1,* 171–184.

Henggeler, S. W., Pickrel, S. G., Brondino, M. J., & Crouch, J. L. (1996). Eliminating (almost) treatment dropout of substance abusing or dependent delinquents through home-based multisystemic therapy. *American Journal of Psychiatry, 153,* 427–428.

Henggeler, S. W., Schoenwald, S. K., Borduin, C. M., Rowland, M. D., &. Cunningham, P. B. (1998). *Multisystemic treatment of antisocial behavior in children and adolescents.* New York: Guilford Press.

Hibbs, E. D., & Jensen, P. S. (Eds.). (2005). *Psychosocial treatments for child and adolescent disorders: Empirically based strategies for clinical practice* (2nd ed.). Washington, DC: American Psychological Association.

Hill, J., & Maughan, B. (Eds.). (2001). *Conduct disorders in childhood and adolescence.* Cambridge, England: Cambridge University Press.

Hinshaw, S. P., Lahey, B. B., & Hart, E. L. (1993). Issues of taxonomy and comorbidity in the development of conduct disorder. *Development and Psychopathology, 5,* 31–49.

Hollon, S. D., & Beck, A. T. (2004). Cognitive and cognitive behavioral therapies. In M. J. Lambert (Ed.), *Bergin and Garfield's handbook of psychotherapy and behavior change* (5th ed., pp. 447–492). New York: Wiley.

Huey, S. J., Henggeler, S. W., Brondino, M. J., & Pickrel, S. G. (2000). Mechanisms of change in multisystemic therapy: Reducing delinquent behavior through therapist adherence and improved family and peer functioning. *Journal of Consulting and Clinical Psychology, 68,* 451–467.

Huey, S. J., Henggeler, S. W., Rowland, M. D., Halliday-Boykins, C. A., Cunningham, P. B., Pickrel, S. G., et al. (2005). Multisystemic therapy effects on attempted suicide by youths presenting psychiatric emergencies. *Journal of American Academy of Child and Adolescent Psychiatry, 43,* 183–190.

Jaffee, S. R., Caspi, A., Moffitt, T. E., Dodge, K., Rutter, M., Taylor, A., et al. (2005). Nature × nurture: Genetic vulnerabilities interact with physical maltreatment to promote behavior problems. *Development and Psychopathology, 17,* 67–84.

Kacir, C. D., & Gordon, D. A. (1999). Parenting adolescents wisely: The effects of an interactive video-based parent training program in Appalachia. *Child and Family Behavior Therapy, 21,* 1–22.

Kazdin, A. E. (1995a). Child, parent, and family dysfunction as predictors of outcome in cognitive-behavioral treatment of antisocial children. *Behaviour Research and Therapy, 33,* 271–281.

Kazdin, A. E. (1995b). *Conduct disorder in childhood and adolescence* (2nd ed.). Thousand Oaks, CA: Sage.

Kazdin, A. E. (1996). Dropping out of child therapy: Issues for research and implications for practice. *Clinical Child Psychology and Psychiatry, 1,* 133–156.

Kazdin, A. E. (2000a). Developing a research agenda for child and adolescent psychotherapy research. *Archives of General Psychiatry, 57,* 829–835.

Kazdin, A. E. (2000b). *Psychotherapy for children and adolescents: Directions for research and practice.* New York: Oxford University Press.

Kazdin, A. E. (2001). *Behavior modification in applied settings* (6th ed.). Belmont, CA: Wadsworth/Thomson Learning.

Kazdin, A. E. (2005). *Parent management training: Treatment for oppositional, aggressive, and antisocial behavior in children and adolescents.* New York: Oxford University Press.

Kazdin, A. E. (2006a). Arbitrary metrics: Implications for identifying evidence-based treatments. *American Psychologist, 61,* 42–49.

Kazdin, A. E. (2006b). Mechanisms of change in psychotherapy: Advances, breakthroughs, and cutting-edge research (do not yet exist). In R. R. Bootzin & P. M. McKnight (Eds.), *Strengthening research methodology: Psychological measurement and eval-uation* (pp. 77–101). Washington, DC: American Psychological Association.

Kazdin, A. E., Bass, D., Siegel, T., & Thomas, C. (1989). Cognitive-behavioral treatment and relationship therapy in the treatment of children referred for antisocial behavior. *Journal of Consulting and Clinical Psychology, 57,* 522–535.

Kazdin, A. E., & Crowley, M. (1997). Moderators of treatment outcome in cognitively based treatment of antisocial behavior. *Cognitive Therapy and Research, 21,* 185–207.

Kazdin, A. E., Esveldt-Dawson, K., French, N. H., & Unis, A. S. (1987). Problem-solving skills training and relationship therapy in the treatment of antisocial child behavior. *Journal of Consulting and Clinical Psychology, 55,* 76–85.

Kazdin, A. E., Marciano, P. L., & Whitley, M. (2005). The therapeutic alliance in cognitive-behavioral treatment of children referred for oppositional, aggressive, and antisocial behavior. *Journal of Consulting and Clinical Psychology, 73,* 726–730.

Kazdin, A. E., & Nock, M. K. (2003). Delineating mechanisms of change in child and adolescent therapy: Methodological issues and research recommendations. *Journal of Child Psychology and Psychiatry, 44,* 1116–1129.

Kazdin, A. E., Siegel, T., & Bass, D. (1990). Drawing upon clinical practice to inform research on child and adolescent psychotherapy. *Professional Psychology: Research and Practice, 21,* 189–198.

Kazdin, A. E., & Wassell, G. (1998). Treatment completion and therapeutic change among children referred for outpatient therapy. *Professional Psychology: Research and Practice, 29,* 332–340.

Kazdin, A. E., & Wassell, G. (2000). Therapeutic changes in children, parents, and families resulting from treatment of children with conduct problems. *Journal of the American Academy of Child and Adolescent Psychiatry, 39,* 414–420.

Kazdin, A. E., & Weisz, J. R. (Eds.). (2003). *Evidence-based psychotherapies for children and adolescents.* New York: Guilford Press.

Kazdin, A. E., & Whitley, M. K. (2003). Treatment of parental stress to enhance therapeutic change among children referred for aggressive and antisocial behavior. *Journal of Consulting and Clinical Psychology, 71,* 504–515.

Kazdin, A. E., & Whitley, M. K. (2006). Comorbidity, case complexity, and effects of evidence-based treatment for children referred for disruptive behavior. *Journal of Consulting and Clinical Psychology, 74,* 455–467.

Kazdin, A. E., Whitley, M., & Marciano, P. L. (2006). Child-therapist and parent-therapist alliance and therapeutic change in the treatment of children referred for oppositional, aggressive, and antisocial behavior. *Journal of Child Psychology and Psychiatry, 47,* 436–445

Kendall, P. C. (Ed.). (1999). Special section: Clinical significance. *Journal of Consulting and Clinical Psychology, 67,* 283–339.

Kendall, P. C. (Ed.). (2006). *Child and adolescent therapy: Cognitive-behavioral procedures* (3rd ed.). New York: Guilford Press.

Kiesler, D. J. (1971). Experimental designs in psychotherapy research. In A. E. Bergin & S. L. Garfield (Eds.), *Handbook of psychotherapy and behavior change: An empirical analysis* (pp. 36–74). New York: Wiley.

Knapp, M., Scott, S., & Davies, J. (1999). The cost of antisocial behaviour in younger children. *Clinical Child Psychology and Psychiatry, 4,* 457–473.

Kraemer, H. C., Stice, E., Kazdin, A. E., Offord, D. R., & Kupfer, D. J. (2001). How do risk factors work together? Mediators, moderators, independent, overlapping, and proxy-risk factors. *American Journal of Psychiatry, 158,* 848–856.

Krug, E. G., Dahlberg, L. L., Mercy, J. A., Zwi, A. B., & Lozano, R. (2002). *World report on violence and health.* Geneva, Switzerland: World Health Organization.

Kwon, S., & Oei, T. P. S. (2003). Cognitive processes in a group cognitive behavior therapy of depression. *Journal of Behavior Therapy and Experimental Psychiatry, 34,* 73–85.

Larson, J., & Lochman, J. E. (2002). *Helping school children cope with anger: A cognitive-behavioral intervention.* New York: Guilford Press.

Leve, L. D., Chamberlain, P., & Reid, J. B. (2005). Intervention outcomes for girls referred from juvenile justice: Effects on delinquency. *Journal of Consulting and Clinical Psychology, 73,* 1181–1185.

Lochman, J. E. (1992). Cognitive-behavioral interventions with aggressive boys: Three-year follow-up and preventive effects. *Journal of Consulting and Clinical Psychology, 60,* 426–432.

Lochman, J. E., Barry, T. D., & Pardini, D. A. (2003). Anger control training for aggressive youth. In A. E. Kazdin & J. R. Weisz (Eds.), *Evidence-based psychotherapies for children and adolescents* (pp. 263–281). New York: Guilford Press.

Lochman, J. E., Burch, P. P., Curry, J. F., & Lampron, L. B. (1984). Treatment and generalization effects of cognitive-behavioral and goal setting interventions with aggressive boys. *Journal of Consulting and Clinical Psychology, 52,* 915–916.

Lochman, J. E., & Dodge, K. A. (1994). Social-cognitive processes of severely violent, moderately aggressive, and nonaggressive boys. *Journal of Consulting and Clinical Psychology, 62,* 366–374.

Lochman, J. E., Lampron, L. B., Gemmer, T. C., Harris, S. R., & Wycoff, G. M. (1989). Teacher consultation and cognitive-behavioral interventions with aggressive boys. *Psychology in the Schools, 26,* 179–188.

Lochman, J. F., Powell, N. R., Whidby, J. M., & Fitz-Gerald, D. P. (2006). Aggressive children: Cognitive-behavioral assessment and treatment. In P. C. Kendall (Ed.), *Child and adolescent therapy: Cognitive-behavioral procedures* (3rd ed., pp. 33–81). New York: Guilford Press.

Lochman, J. E., & Wells, K. C. (2002). The Coping Power Program for preadolescent aggressive boys and their parents: Outcome effects at the 1-year follow-up. *Journal of Consulting and Clinical Psychology, 72,* 571–578.

Long, P., Forehand, R., Wierson, M., & Morgan, A. (1994). Does parent training with young noncompliant children have long-term effects? *Behaviour Research and Therapy, 32,* 101–107.

Lonigan, C. J., & Elbert, J. C. (1998). Special issue on empirically supported psychosocial interventions for children. *Journal of Clinical Child Psychology, 27,* 138–226.

Lundman, R. J. (1984). *Prevention and control of juvenile delinquency.* New York: Oxford University Press.

Lutzker, J. R. (Ed.). (2006). Preventing violence: Research and evidence-based intervention strategies. Washington, DC: American Psychological Association.

Mager, W., Millich, R., Harris, M. J., & Howard, A. (2005). Intervention groups for adolescents with conduct problems: Is aggregation harmful or helpful? *Journal of Abnormal Child Psychology, 33,* 349–362.

McGuire, J. (2000). *Thinkfirst: Outline programme manual case managers' manual and supplements.* London: Home Office Communications Unit.

Moffitt, T. E., & Caspi, A. (2005). Life-course persistent and adolescence-limited antisocial males: Longitudinal followup to adulthood. In D. M. Stoff & E. J. Susman (Eds.), *Developmental psychobiology of aggression* (pp. 161–186). New York: Cambridge University Press.

Moffitt, T. E., Caspi, A., Rutter, M., & Silva, P. A. (2001). *Sex differences in antisocial behaviour: Conduct disorder, delinquency, and violence in the Dunedin Longitudinal Study.* New York: Cambridge University Press.

Morris, S. M., Alexander, J. F., & Turner, C. W. (1991). Do reattributions reduce blame? *Journal of Family Psychology, 5,* 192–203.

Muir, J. A., Schwartz, S. J., & Szapocznik, J. (2004). A program of research with Hispanic and African American families: Three decades of intervention development and testing influenced by the changing cultural context of Miami. *Journal of Marital and Family Therapy, 30,* 285–303.

Newberry, A. M., Alexander, J. F., & Turner, C. W. (1991). Gender as a process variable in family therapy. *Journal of Family Psychology, 5,* 158–175.

Nock, M. K. (2003). Progress review of the psychosocial treatment of child conduct problems. *Clinical Psychology: Science and Practice, 10,* 1–28.

Nock, M. K., Kazdin, A. E., Hiripi, E., & Kessler, R. C. (2006). Prevalence, subtypes, and correlates of *DSM-IV* Conduct Disorder in the National Comorbidity Survey Replication. *Psychological Medicine, 36,* 699–710.

Norcross, J. C. (Ed.). (2002). *Psychotherapy relationships that work: Therapist contributions and responsiveness to patients.* New York: Oxford University Press.

O'Donnell, C. R. (1992). The interplay of theory and practice in delinquency prevention: From behavior modification to activity settings. In J. McCord & R. E. Tremblay (Eds.), *Preventing antisocial behavior* (pp. 209–232). New York: Guilford Press.

Offord, D. R., Boyle, M. H., & Racine, Y. A. (1991). The epidemiology of antisocial behavior. In D. J. Pepler & K. H. Rubin (Eds.), *The development and treatment of childhood aggression* (pp. 31–54). Hillsdale, NJ: Erlbaum.

Offord, D. R., Boyle, M. H., Racine, Y. A., Fleming, J. E., Cadman, D. T., Blum, H. M., et al. (1992). Outcome, prognosis, and risk in a longitudinal follow-up study. *Journal of the American Academy of Child and Adolescent Psychiatry, 31,* 916–923.

Ogden, T., & Halliday-Boykins, C. A. (2004). Multisystemic treatment of antisocial adolescents in Norway: Replication of clinical outcomes outside of the US. *Child and Adolescent Mental Health, 9,* 77–83.

Orlinsky, D. E., Rønnestad, M. H., & Willutzki, U. (2004). Fifty years of psychotherapy process-outcome research: Continuity and change. In M. J. Lambert (Ed.), *Bergin and Garfield's handbook of psychotherapy and behavior change* (5th ed., pp. 307–389). New York: Wiley.

Patterson, G. R. (1982). *Coercive family process.* Eugene, OR: Castalia.

Patterson, G. R., Capaldi, D., & Bank, L. (1991). An early starter model for predicting delinquency. In D. J. Pepler & K. H. Rubin (Eds.), *The development and treatment of childhood aggression* (pp. 139–168). Hillsdale, NJ: Erlbaum.

Patterson, G. R., & Chamberlain, P. (1994). A functional analysis of resistance during parent training therapy. *Clinical Psychology: Science and Practice, 1,* 53–70.

Patterson, G. R., Reid, J. B., & Dishion, T. J. (1992). *Antisocial boys.* Eugene, OR: Castalia.

Pepler, D. J., & Rubin, K. H. (Eds.). (1991). *The development and treatment of childhood aggression.* Hillsdale, NJ: Erlbaum.

Reid, J. B., Patterson, G. R., & Snyder, J. (Eds.). (2002). *Antisocial behavior in children and adolescents: A developmental analysis and model for intervention.* Washington, DC: American Psychological Association.

Ressler, K. J., Rothbaum, B. O., Tannenbaum, L., Anderson, P., Graap, K., Zimand, E., Hodges, L., & Davis, M. (2004). Cognitive enhancers as adjuncts to psychotherapy. Use of D-cycloserine in phobic individuals to facilitate extinction of fear. *Archives of General Psychiatry, 61,* 1136–1144.

Reyno, S. M., & McGrath, P. J. (2006). Predictors of parent training efficacy for child externalizing behavior problems—a meta-analytic review. *Journal of Child Psychology and Psychiatry, 47,* 99–111.

Robbins, M. S., Schwartz, S., & Szapocznik, J. (2004). Structural ecosystems therapy with Hispanic adolescents exhibiting disruptive behavior disorders. In J. R. Ancis (Ed.), *Culturally responsive interventions: Innovative approaches to working with diverse populations* (pp. 71–99). New York: Brunner-Routledge.

Robbins, M. S., Szapocznik, J., Santisteban, D. A., Hervis, O., Mitrani, V. B., & Schwartz, S. J. (2003). Brief Strategic Family Therapy for Hispanic youth. In A. E. Kazdin & J. R. Weisz (Eds.), *Evidence-based psychotherapies for children and adolescents* (pp. 407–424). New York: Guilford Press.

Robins, L. N. (1966). *Deviant children grown up.* Baltimore: Williams and Wilkins.

Robins, L. N. (1978). Sturdy childhood predictors of adult antisocial behavior: Replications from longitudinal studies. *Psychological Medicine, 8,* 611–622.

Robins, L. N. (1981). Epidemiological approaches to natural history research: Antisocial disorders in children. *Journal of the American Academy of Child Psychiatry, 20,* 566–580.

Rowland, M. D., Halliday-Boykins, C. A., Henggeler, S. W., Cunningham, P. B., Lee, T. G., Kruesi, M. J., et al. (2005). A randomized trial of multisystemic therapy with Hawaii's Felix class youths. *Journal of Emotional and Behavioral Disorders, 13,* 13–23.

Rubin, K. H., Bream, L. A., & Rose-Krasnor, L. (1991). Social problem solving and aggression in childhood. In D. J. Pepler & K. H. Rubin (Eds.), *The development and treatment of childhood aggression* (pp. 219–248). Hillsdale, NJ: Erlbaum.

Rutter, M., Giller, H., & Hagell, A. (1998). *Antisocial behavior by young people.* New York: Cambridge University Press.

Sanders, M. R., & Dadds, M. R. (1993). *Behavioral family intervention.* Needham Heights, MA: Allyn and Bacon.

Sanders, M. R., Markie-Dadds, C., & Turner, K. M. T. (2003). Theoretical, scientific, and clinical foundations of the Triple P-Positive Parenting Program: A population approach to the promotion of parenting competence. *Parenting Research and Practice* (Monograph 1), 1–24.

Sanson, A., Oberklaid, F., Pedlow, R., & Prior, M. (1991). Risk indicators: Assessment of infancy predictors of pre-school behavioural maladjustment. *Journal of Child Psychology and Psychiatry, 32,* 609–626.

Santisteban, D. A., Coatsworth, J. D., Perez-Vidal, A., Kurtines, W. M., Schwartz, S. J., LaPerriere, A., et al. (2003) Efficacy of brief strategic family therapy in modifying Hispanic adolescent behavior problems and substance use. *Journal of Family Psychology, 17,* 121–133.

Santisteban, D. A, Szapocznik, J., Perez-Vidal, A., Kurtines, W. H, Murray, E. J., & LaPerriere, A. (1996). Efficacy of intervention for engaging youth and families into treatment and some variables that may contribute to differential effectiveness. *Journal of Family Psychology, 10,* 35–44.

Schaeffer, C. M., & Borduin, C. M. (2005). Long-term follow-up to a randomized clinical trial of multisystemic therapy with serious and violent juvenile offenders. *Journal of Consulting and Clinical Psychology, 73,* 445–453.

Schoenwald, S. K., Halliday-Boykins, C. A., & Henggeler, S. W. (2003). Client-level predictors of adherence to MST in community service settings. *Family Process, 42,* 345–359.

Schoenwald, S. K., Letourneau, E. J., & Halliday-Boykins, C. A. (2005). Predicting therapist adherence to a transported family-based treatment for youth. *Journal of Clinical Child and Adolescent Psychology, 34,* 658–670.

Schoenwald, S. K., Sheidow, A. J., & Letourneau, E. J. (2004). Toward effective quality assurance in evidence-based practice: Links between expert consultation, therapist fidelity, and child outcomes. *Journal of Clinical Child and Adolescent Psychology, 33,* 94–104.

Scott, S., Knapp, M., Henderson, J., & Maughan, B. (2001). Financial cost of social exclusion: Follow up study of antisocial children into adulthood. *British Medical Journal, 323,* 191–194.

Sexton, T. L. (in press). *Functional family therapy.* Las Vegas, NV: The Family Project.

Sexton, T. L., & Alexander, J. F. (1999). *Functional family therapy: Principles of clinical intervention, assessment, and implementation.* Henderson, NV: RCH Enterprises.

Sexton, T. L., & Alexander, J. F. (2002). Functional family therapy for at-risk adolescents and their families. In F. W. Kaslow & T. Patterson (Eds.), *Comprehensive handbook of psychotherapy: Cognitive-behavioral approaches* (Vol. 2, pp. 117–140). New York: Wiley.

Sheidow, A. J., Bradford, W. D., Henggeler, S. W., Rowland, M. D., Halliday-Boykins, C., Schoenwald, S. K., et al. (2004). Treatment costs for youths receiving multisystemic therapy for hospitalization after a psychiatric crisis. *Psychiatric Services, 55,* 548–554.

Shirk, S. R. (Ed.). (1988). *Cognitive development and child psychotherapy.* New York: Plenum Press.

Shure, M. B. (1992). *I Can Problem Solve (ICPS): An interpersonal cognitive problem solving program.* Champaign, IL: Research Press.

Shure, M. B. (1996). *Raising a thinking child: Help your young child to resolve everyday conflicts and get along with others.* New York: Pocket Books.

Shure, M. B. (1997). Interpersonal cognitive problem solving: Primary prevention of early high-risk behaviors in the preschool and primary years. In G. W. Albee & T. P. Gulotta (Eds.), *Primary prevention works* (pp. 167–188). Thousand Oaks, CA: Sage.

Shure, M. B. (1999). *Preventing violence the problem-solving way.* Juvenile Justice Bulletin, April, 1–11. Publication of the U.S. Department of Justice, Office of Juvenile Justice and Delinquency Prevention, Washington, DC.

Snyder, J., & Stoolmiller, M. (2002). Reinforcement and coercion mechanisms in the development of antisocial behavior: The family. In J. B. Reid, G. R. Patterson, & J. Snyder (Eds.), *Antisocial behavior in children and adolescents: A developmental analysis and model for intervention* (pp. 65–100). Washington, DC: American Psychological Association.

Spivack, G., & Shure, M. B. (1982). The cognition of social adjustment: Interpersonal cognitive problem solving thinking. In B. B. Lahey & A. E. Kazdin (Eds.), *Advances in clinical child psychology* (Vol. 5, pp. 323–372). New York: Plenum Press.

Stoff, D. M., Breiling, J., & Maser, J. D. (Eds.). (1997). *Handbook of antisocial behavior.* New York: Wiley.

Sukhodolsky, D. G., Kassinove, H., & Gorman, B. S. (2004). Cognitive-behavioral therapy for anger in children and adolescents: A meta-analysis. *Aggression and Violent Behavior, 9,* 247–269.

Szapocznik, J., & Kurtines, W. M. (1989). *Breakthroughs in family therapy with drug-abusing problem youth.* New York: Springer.

Szapocznik, J., Kurtines, W. H., Foote, F. H., Perez-Vidal, A., & Hervis, O. (1986). Conjoint versus one person family therapy: Further evidence for the effectiveness of conducting family therapy through one person. *Journal of Consulting and Clinical Psychology, 54,* 395–397.

Szapocznik, J., Perez-Vidal, A., Brickman, A., Foote, F. H., Santisteban, D. A., Hervis, O., et al. (1988). Engaging adolescent drug abusers and their families into treatment: A strategic structural systems approach. *Journal of Consulting and Clinical Psychology, 56,* 552–557.

Szapocznik, J., Rio, A., Murray, E., Cohen, R., Scopetta, M., Rivas-Vasquez, A., et al. (1989). Structural family versus psychodynamic child therapy for problematic Hispanic boys. *Journal of Consulting and Clinical Psychology, 57,* 571–578.

Tang, T. Z., & DeRubeis, R. J. (1999). Sudden gains and critical sessions in cognitive-behavioral therapy for depression. *Journal of Consulting and Clinical Psychology, 67,* 894–904.

U.S. Congress, Office of Technology Assessment. (1991). *Adolescent health* (OTA-H-468). Washington, DC: U.S. Government Printing Office.

Wadsworth, M. (1979). *Roots of delinquency: Infancy, adolescence and crime.* New York: Barnes and Noble.

Wahler, R. G., & Dumas, J. E. (1986). Maintenance factors in coercive mother-child interactions: The compliance and predictability hypotheses. *Journal of Applied Behavior Analysis, 19,* 13–22.

Webster-Stratton, C. (1985). Predictors of treatment outcome in parent training for conduct disordered children. *Behavior Therapy, 16,* 223–243.

Webster-Stratton, C. (1994). Advancing videotape parent training: A comparison study. *Journal of Consulting and Clinical Psychology, 62,* 583–593.

Webster-Stratton, C. (2000). *How to promote social and academic competence in young children.* London: Sage.

Webster-Stratton, C., & Reid, M. J. (2003). The Incredible Years Parents, Teachers, and Children Training Series: A multifaceted treatment approach for young children with conduct problems. In A. E. Kazdin & J. R. Weisz (Eds.), *Evidence-based psychotherapies for children and adolescents* (pp. 224–240). New York: Guilford Press.

Weisz, J. R. (2004). *Psychotherapy for children and adolescents: Evidence-based treatments and case examples.* Cambridge, England: Cambridge University Press.

Weisz, J. R., Walter, B. R., Weiss, B., Fernandez, G. A., & Mikow, V. A. (1990). Arrests among emotionally disturbed violent and assaultive individuals following minimal versus lengthy intervention through North Carolina's Willie M. Program. *Journal of Consulting and Clinical Psychology, 58,* 720–728.

Werner, E. E., & Smith, R. S. (1992). *Overcoming the odds: High risk children from birth to adulthood.* Ithaca, NY: Cornell University Press.

Zoccolillo, M. (1993). Gender and the development of conduct disorder. *Development and Psychopathology, 5,* 65–78.

4

Treatments for Dementia

Larry Tune

Dementia refers to a large number of disorders characterized by global cognitive deficits, including impairments of recent memory, and one or more of the following: aphasia, apraxia, agnosia, and disturbance of executive functioning. The most common dementias are Alzheimer's disease (AD), vascular dementia, dementia due to general medical conditions (including HIV dementia), head trauma, Parkinson's disease (PD), Huntington's disease, Pick's disease, Creutzfeldt-Jakob disease, substance-induced persisting dementia, and multiple etiologies. Alzheimer's disease, alone or in combination with other conditions (e.g., stroke), is easily the most common. With the exception of dementia associated with Parkinson's disease, the remaining syndromes are either so rare or heterogeneous that it is difficult to find well-controlled studies that would meet diagnostic and clinical design criteria for standards defined for this book. The focus of this chapter is on therapeutic interventions for Alzheimer's disease. Innumerable articles investigating patient populations defined as "geropsychiatric" or "gerontopsychiatric" have been excluded. Following this discussion, there is a brief review of therapeutic interventions for Parkinson's disease.

ALZHEIMER'S DISEASE

Alzheimer's disease accounts for approximately 70% of all patients suffering with dementia and affects approximately 2.5 million individuals in North America over the age of 65. Mortimer, Ebbitt, Jun, and Finch (1992) found an incidence of 1% per year in the elderly. The prevalence increases with age. Approximately 10% of all patients over the age of 65 are demented, and 33 to 50% of adults over the age of 84 suffer from dementia.

The study of therapeutic interventions in AD has been affected both by our increased understanding of the pathophysiology of AD and by progressive refinement in diagnostic criteria. Clinicopathologic studies have shown a clinical diagnostic accuracy of approximately 90%. However, recent studies have shown that the more we understand about Alzheimer's disease, the more complicated the story becomes. For example, approximately one third of autopsy-confirmed AD cases have coexisting "Lewy body dementia" with associated clinical findings of extrapyramidal symptoms and fluctuating levels of consciousness (Thal, 1994).

Other issues critical to the investigation of any drug for AD include the myriad rating instruments used to measure clinical outcome (in the accompanying tables, more than 200 separate measures were used to assess clinical outcome), the absence of clinical diagnostic markers, the absence of compelling animal models for AD, and the variability in the course of illness. This is a slow, variably progressive illness in a patient population with markedly heterogeneous premorbid cognitive abilities. Most clinical trials are of relatively short duration and emphasize short-term clinical improvement as the principal outcome measure. Until recently, most investigations have excluded the possibility of slowing the rate of progression of illness. Several recent studies have focused on change in the rate of clinical deterioration, but most of these are studies of relatively short duration.

The choice of study design must be carefully considered. Three basic designs — crossover studies, randomized control parallel design, and enrichment designs (e.g., see U.S. multicenter tacrine study; Davis et al., 1992) — have all been used. All of these designs could satisfy criteria for Type 1 studies. Each has significant strengths and weaknesses, particularly the long-term studies.

Vasodilators and Metabolic Enhancement Strategies

Most early clinical trials focused on the potential roles of vasodilators or (more recently) metabolic enhancers (Tables 4.1 and 4.2) in the treatment of AD. By far the most popular of these was dihydroergotoxine mesylate (Hydergine). Hydergine is one of the drugs currently approved for use in dementia (actually for use in "idiopathic decline in mental capacity"). Despite its long (more than 40 years) and frequent use, its utility in the management of dementia is still in doubt.

Many small, double-blind investigations showed significant improvement in patients with dementia. Most of these early investigations suffered from several critical flaws, including poor diagnostic criteria and outcome measures that did not focus specifically on cognition (for full review, see Hollister & Yesavage, 1984; Olin, Schneider, Novit, & Luczak, 2000). One investigation found that two ergot derivatives, nicergoline and ergoloid mesylate, were moderately effective in the management of mild to moderate dementia (Battaglia, Bruni, Ardia, & Sacchetti, 1989).

Nootropic agents (e.g., piracetam, oxiracetam, aniracetam, pyrrolidone), derivatives of the excitatory amino acid neurotransmitter GABA, have been extensively investigated in the treatment of dementing illnesses. Animal studies have repeatedly shown these nootropic compounds to facilitate learning and memory performance in animals. Although the exact mechanism of action is unclear, they are thought to serve as neuroprotective agents in the central nervous system (CNS) circulation. Table 4.2 summarizes several Type 2 and Type 3 studies of piracetam, oxiracetam, and vinpocetine. Most studies have failed to show significant clinical improvement with these drugs. One lingering experimental question is whether long-term nootropic administration might affect the progression of disease (e.g., see Croisile, Trillet, Fondarai, Laurent, Mauguiere, &Billardon, 1993).

Cholinergic Augmentation Strategies

The newer therapeutic approaches have followed our understanding of the pathophysiology of AD. The first of these, and by far the most extensively studied, focuses on selective impairments in cholinergic neurotransmission, which were first identified in 1976 (Tables 4.3 through 4.6). These cholinergic strategies have attempted to potentiate cholinergic neurotransmission in one of several ways: cholinergic precursor loading, acetylcholinesterase inhibition, and direct or indirect central cholinergic stimulation.

Precursor loading strategies are based on demonstrations that peripheral administration enhances brain acetylcholine levels in animal models. Few of the existing human studies, most of which involved lecithin or choline administration, show convincing clinical efficacy (Tables 4.6 and 4.7, respectively). We found one Type 1 study (with significant improvement from bethanechol), eight Type 2 studies (five showing improvement), and two Type 3 studies (with one showing improvement). Two studies (one each of Types 2 and 3) of nicotinic agonists showed clinical improvement. Overall, the effects of this treatment strategy have been mixed. Many have suffered either from poor study design or from small sample size.

Of these cholinergic augmentation strategies, the use of acetylcholinesterase inhibitors (Tables 4.3 through 4.5, respectively) has provided the most impressive data, and four drugs in this class have been approved by the FDA for the treatment of Alzheimer's disease. The earliest studies focused on physostigmine. Physostigmine proved to be a difficult investigational compound, largely because of its relatively brief half-life ($T\frac{1}{2} = 30$ min following oral ingestion) and high rate of side effects. However, Thal, Fuld, Masur, and Sharpless (1983) showed that the

TABLE 4.1 Hydergine[a]

Authors	Design	N	Outcome Measures	Length of Study	Measure Results
Thompson et al. (1990)	DB, PC, random parallel group	80	DSY, WMS, SCAGS, IPSCE, GERRI	24 weeks	No significant improvement
Rouy et al. (1989)	DB, PC, random parallel group	97	SCAGS, NOISE	6 months	Significant improvement on SCAGS
Thienhaus et al. (1987)	DB, PC, random parallel group	41	IPSCE, GDS, BSRT, DSY, ZVT	12 weeks	Significant improvement on memory section of IPSCE
van Loveren-Huyben et al. (1984)	DB, PC, random parallel group	58	BDT, DS, DSY, SCAGS, BVRT, TMT, LT	24 weeks	Significant improvement on SCAGS
Hollingsworth (1980)	DB, PC, random parallel group	60	SCAGS, MSCL	3 months	Significant improvement on SCAGS
Matejcek et al. (1979)	DB, PC, random parallel group	16	EEG, SCAGS	12 weeks	Significant improvement on EEG only
Novo et al. (1978)	DB, PC, random parallel group	34	SCAGS, PNRS	16 weeks	Significant improvement on SCAGS and PNRS
Soni & Soni (1975)	DB, PC, random parallel group	78	CS	9 months	Significant improvement at 3-month evaluation only
Thibault (1974)	DB, PC, random parallel group	48	ADL, psychological, and physical states	12 weeks	Significant improvement on all three scales
Rechman (1973)	DB, PC, random crossover and parallel group	43, 60	CS	16 and 12 weeks	Significant improvement on parallel group study only
McConnachie (1973)	DB, PC, random parallel group	58	ADL, physical, mood, and motor activity scales	12 weeks	Significant improvement in all but ADL
Jennings (1972)	DB, PC, random parallel group	50	CSCL, MSCL	12 weeks	Significant improvement on CSCL
Banen (1972)	DB, PC, random parallel group	78	Subtests from WAIS	12 weeks	No significant improvement on WAIS subtests
Triboletti & Ferri (1969)	DB, PC, random parallel group	59	MSCL, "in-house" rating scales	12 weeks	Significant improvement on one subtest of MSCL

All studies were Type 1.

[a]Refer to "List of Acronyms," pp. 131–134, for definitions of abbreviations.

improvement in memory performance following multiple doses of physostigmine could persist up to 36 hours.

Several investigations have used longer acting cholinesterase inhibitors. Tacrine hydrochloride alone or in combination with lecithin was the first of four AChEs to be approved by the FDA. Four Type 1 studies showed that tacrine provides a modest, clinically significant effect. Three of nine Type 2, and three of four Type 3 studies report similar findings. Most of the Type 2 and 3 studies involve relatively small samples and are of relatively short duration. None of these has demonstrated a clear effect on the course of illness. Of particular interest is the U.S. multicenter tacrine study (Davis et al., 1992), which utilized a novel enrichment strategy combining aspects of both crossover and parallel design studies. All patients were initially treated with tacrine. Those

TABLE 4.2 Nootropics[a]

Authors	Drug	Type	Design	N	Outcome Measures	Length of Study	Measure Results
Ruther et al. (1994)	Cerebrolysin	1	DB, PC, random parallel group	120	MMSE, SCAGS, CGI, ADL, TMT	4 weeks	Significant improvement on CGI, TMT
Croisile et al. (1993)	Piracetam	2	DB, PC, random parallel group	33	MMSE, DS, AB, VVLT, SS, CFT	1 year	No significant improvement
Green et al. (1992)	Oxiracetam	2	DB, PC, random parallel group	24	BSRT, BVRT, BNT, COWGT, TT, BDT, ROCF	3 months	No significant improvement
Bottini et al. (1992)	Oxiracetam	2	DB, PC, random parallel group	58	QOL, RT, COWGT, SS, RPMT, TT, DS, WLL	12 weeks	Significant improvement on QOL, SS, RPM, COWGT
Villardita et al. (1987)	Oxiracetam	2	DB, PC, random cross-over	40	MMSE, ACPT, VCPT, WLL, LM, DS, BTT, VFT, RCFT, RPMT, LAS, MC, GS, IADL	90 days	Significant improvement on MMSE, ACPT, BTT, VFT, IADL
Sourander et al. (1987)	Aniracetam	2	DB, PC, random parallel group	44	FTT, TMT, BD, DS, SM, BVRT, SCAGS, PB, SVT, HP, VPM, OM, TG, WLL, SM, CN, SIM, ASMC, OR	3 months	Significant improvement on WLL only

Reference	Treatment		Design	n	Tests	Duration	Results
Growden et al. (1986)	Piracetam and physostigmine	2	DB, PC, random crossover	18	BPDP, DS, BS, SR, BNT, VFT, PWT, AF	2 to 8 weeks	No significant improvement
R. C. Smith et al. (1984)	Lecithin and piracetam plus lecithin	2	DB, PC, random crossover	11 & 11	BSRT, AST, DRS, PMSE	10 and 6 months	No significant improvement on lecithin; improvement on BSRT in 8/11 piracetam + lecithin
Clauss et al. (1991)	Pramiracetam	3	SB, dose finding and DB, PC, random crossover	10	ADAS-Cog, BSRT, DS, VFT, LM, VSRT	5 and 4 weeks	Significant improvement on part of VSRT
Sinforiani et al. (1990)	Acetyl-L-carnitine and piracetam	3	SB, open label	12 & 12	DS, DSY, BTT, GS, VFT, WLL	2 week IV and 90 day oral	No significant improvement for piracetam
Falsaperla et al., (1990)	Oxiracetam and selegiline	3	SB, random parallel group	40	BRS, RMT, DS, SR, VFT, GS	90 days	Significant improvement on all tests with oxiracetam
Thal, Salmon, et al. (1989)	Vinpocetine	3	Open label pilot study	19	VFT, BSRT, COWGT, BNT, CCSE, CGI	52 weeks	No significant improvement
Heiss et al. (1988)	Piracetam in Alzheimer's disease and MID	3	Open label	9 & 7	RCGM in PET	2 weeks	Increase in RCGM in AD but not MID
Branconnier et al. (1983)	Pramiracetam	3	Open label	32	BSRT, VFT, RMPT, SCAGS	4 weeks	Significant improvement on SCAGS
Delwaide et al.[b] (1980)	Piracetam, lysin-vasopressin, and physostigmine	3	DB, crossover	13	AVLT	Acute injection	Significant improvement with piracetam and lysin-vasopressin

[a] Refer to "List of Acronyms," pp. 131–134, for definitions of abbreviations.
[b] See also Table 4.4.

TABLE 4.3 Cholinesterase Inhibitors: Tacrine[a]

Authors	Drug	Type	Design	N	Outcome Measures	Length of Study	Measure Results
Knapp et al. (1994)	Tacrine	1	DB, PC, random parallel group	263	CIBC, ADAS-Cog, FCCA	30 weeks	Significant difference on CIBC, ADAS-Cog, FCCA
Sahakian & Coull (1993)[b]	Tacrine	1	DB, PC, random cross-over	89	MMSE, AMTS, ADL, RNCP, KOL, CANTAB	30 weeks	Significant effect on MMSE, AMTS, CANTAB-attention
Wilcock et al. (1993)	Tacrine	1	DB, PC, random cross-over	79	MMSE, ADAS-NCog, FLS, ADL, KOL, LMT, DS, IADL, CAMCOG	24 weeks	Significant improvement on KOL & CAMCOG
Farlow et al. (1992)	Tacrine	1	DB, PC, random parallel group	468	ADAS-Cog, CL-CGIC, CG-CGIC, MMSE, PDS, ADAS, ADAS-NCog	12 weeks	Significant improvement on ADAS-Cog, CL-CGIC, CG-CGIC
Maltby et al. (1994)	Tacrine and lecithin	2	DB, PC, random parallel group	41	MMSE, V&V SRT, WNA, LPRS, IADL	36 weeks	No significant difference between groups
Minthon et al. (1993)	Tacrine and lecithin	2	DB, PC, random cross-over	17	VOCT, KBD, VL, DS, RT, CFF, EEG, rCBF	26 weeks	6 patients classified as responders
Schneider et al. (1993)[c]	L-Deprenyl and tacrine or physostigmine	2	DB, PC, random cross-over	10	ADAS-Cog, MMSE	8 weeks	Significant improvement on ADAS-Cog in those receiving drug first
Gustafson (1993)[d]	Physostigmine, tacrine, and lecithin	2	DB, PC, random cross-over	10 & 17	rCBF, EEG, OBS-DS, OBS-CS, CGI, RR	2-hr IV (P) 26 weeks (T&L)	No significant improvement compared with placebo
Davis et al. (1992)	Tacrine	2	DB, PC, random parallel group	215	ADAS, CGIC, MMSE, PDS, IADL, PSMS	14 weeks	Smaller decline in ADAS-Cog

Study	Drug		Design	Measures	N	Duration	Result
Molloy et al. (1991)	Tacrine	2	DB, PC, random crossover	MMSE, MSQ, VFT, PWT, DS, LMT, CST, BVRT, BI, LS	34	9 weeks	No significant difference between groups
Weinstein et al., (1991)	Tacrine and lecithin	2	DB, PC, random parallel group	CAMCOG, IDDD	12	12 weeks	No significant difference between groups
Chatellier & Lacomblez (1990)	Tacrine and lecithin	2	DB, PC, random crossover	MMSE, SGRS, MDS, LC, PVAS	67	8 weeks	Significant improvement on PVAS
Fitten et al. (1990)[e]	Tacrine and lecithin	2	DB, PC, random crossover	MMSE, FOM, DS, TMT, NLT, ADL, IADL, NOSIE, GDS, COWGT, GERRI, ADAS	10 & 6	3 weeks and 10 weeks	3 weeks, no significant improvement; 10 weeks, mild improvement in some
Gauthier et al. (1990)	Tacrine and lecithin	2	DB, PC, random crossover	MMSE, RDRS-II, HDS	52	20 weeks	Significant improvement on MMSE
Summers et al. (1986)	Tacrine	2	DB, PC, random crossover	GAS, NLT, OT	17	6 weeks	Significant improvement on GAS, NLT, OT
Alhainen & Rickkinen (1993)	Tacrine	3	Pilot responder discrimination	QEEG, MMSE, ADAS-Cog, BRST, HVR, VFT, DS, TMT	25	7 weeks	Significant improvement on MMSE, TMT
Mellow et al. (1993)	Tacrine and TRH	3	Pilot SB, PB, crossover	BSRT, VFT, DS, PMT	6	Acute 2 days	Significant improvement on VFT
Kaye et al. (1982)[f]	Tacrine and lecithin	3	PC random crossover	SLT, BSRT, FR-subjects diagnosed with PDD	10	Acute 3 doses	No significant improvement
Summers & Viesselman (1981)	Tacrine	3	Pilot—1, 6, 24 hour post-IV	OT, NLT	12	Acute 1-hr IV	Significant improvement on OT in 6 of 12

[a] Refer to "List of Acronyms," pp. 131–134, for definitions of abbreviations.

[b] See also Eagger et al., 1991, 1992; Eagger, Levy, & Sahakain, 1992; for papers evaluating the same population.

[c] See also Table 4.9.

[d] See also Gustafson et al., 1987, for evaluation of the same population.

[e] See also Perryman & Fitten, 1993, for evaluation of the same population.

[f] See also Table 4.11.

TABLE 4.4 Cholinesterase Inhibitors: Physostigmine[a]

Authors	Drug	Type	Design	N	Outcome Measures	Length of Study	Measure Results
Gustafson (1993)[b]	Physostigmine, tacrine, and lecithin	2	DB, PC, random crossover	10 & 17	rCBF, EEG, OBS-DS, OBS-CS, CGI, RR	2-hr IV (P), 26 weeks (T&L)	No significant improvement compared with placebo
Sano et al. (1993)	Physostigmine	2	DB, PC, random crossover	29	BSRT	12 weeks	Significant difference on BSRT-Total Recall/ Intrusions
Schneider et al. (1993)[c]	L-Deprenyl and tacrine or physostigmine	2	DB, PC, random crossover	10	ADAS-Cog, MMSE	8 weeks	Significant important on ADAS-Cog in those receiving drug first
Sevush et al. (1991)	Physostigmine	2	DB, PC, random crossover	8	AVLT, DS, VFT	3 weeks	Significant improvement on AVLT
Harrell, Callaway, et al. (1990)	Physostigmine	2	DB, PC, random crossover	20	BSRT, COWGT, PRT, FTT	8 weeks	No significant improvement except for responder subgroup
Jenike et al. (1990)	Physostigmine	2	DB, PC, random crossover	12	DRST, BSRT, ADAS	8 days	No significant difference between groups
Thal, Salmon et al. (1989)	Physostigmine	2	DB, PC, random parallel group	16	BSRT, BICMT, MDS	12 weeks	Significant improvement on BSRT in 7/10 physostigmine subjects
Stern et al. (1988)	Physostigmine	2	DB, PC, random crossover	14	BSRT	36 weeks	Significant improvement compared with placebo
Stern et al. (1987)	Physostigmine	2	DB, PC, random crossover	22	BSRT, WAIS-R, WMS, RDT, mMMSE, CWAT, VFT	2 weeks	Significant improvement on WAIS-R Digit Span Subtest
Beller et al. (1985)	Physostigmine	2	DB, PC, random crossover	8	BSRT	8 days	Significant improvement on highest dose
Mohs et al. (1985)	Physostigmine	2	DB, PC, crossover	12	ADAS	6–10 days	Significant improvement in 3 subjects
Schwartz & Kohlstaedt (1986)	Physostigmine and lecithin	2	DB, PC, random crossover, & replication	11	BSRT	Acute injections	No significant improvement

112

Study	Drug	Design		n	Test	Duration	Outcome
Sullivan et al. (1982)	Physostigmine	DB, PC, random crossover	2	12	VPAL, NVPAL, BPDP, VRMT	Acute 30-min IV	No significant improvement
Davis & Mohs (1982)	Physostigmine	DB, PC, random crossover	2	10	DS, FFT, BSRT	Acute 30-min IV	Significant improvement in 8 subjects
Peters & Levin (1979)	Physostigmine and lecithin	DB, PC, random crossover	2	5	BSRT	Acute subQ injection	No significant improvement compared with baseline
Bierer et al. (1994)	Physostigmine and clonodine	SB, PC, random crossover	3	10	ADAS	2 weeks	No significant improvement
Beller et al. (1988)	Physostigmine	Open-label follow-up	3	5	BSRT	17 months to 3 years	4/5 BSRT scores at end same as at start
Thal et al. (1986)	Physostigmine	DB, PC, crossover, open-label follow-up	3	16 & 10	BSRT	1 week and 4–18 months	Significant improvement for responders
Muramoto et al. (1984)	Physostigmine	DB, SB, PC, random crossover	3	6	Figure copying	Acute injections	Significant improvement in 3/6 subjects
Wettstein (1983)	Physostigmine and lecithin	DB, PC, random crossover	3	8	Self-designed test battery	12 weeks	No significant improvement
Jotkowitz (1983)	Physostigmine	SB, PC, crossover	3	10	BRS	Up to 10 months	No significant improvement
Thal et al. (1983)	Physostigmine and lecithin	Open label, DB, PC, crossover	3	8	BSRT	6 days for each	Significant improvement in 6 of 8
Ashford et al. (1981)	Physostigmine	DB, PC, random crossover	3	6	BWLLT, BVRT subjects diagnosed with PDD	Acute 30-min IV	No significant improvement
Christie et al. (1981)[c]	Physostigmine and arecoline	DB, PC, random crossover	3	11 & 7	SPT	Acute 30-min IV	Significant improvement in both groups
Delwaide et al. (1980)[d]	Piracetam, lysin-vasopressin, and physostigmine	DB, crossover	3	13	AVLT	Acute injection	No significant improvement with physostigmine
Muramoto et al. (1979)	Physostigmine	DB, PC, case study	3	1	Figure copying, BSRT	Acute subQ injection	Significant improvement on figure copying

[a] Refer to "List of Acronyms," pp. 131–134, for definitions of abbreviations.
[b] See also Gustafson et al., 1987.
[c] See also Table 4.9.
[d] See also Table 4.2.

TABLE 4.5a Cholinesterase Inhibitors: Velnacrine[a]

Authors	Drug	Type	Design	N	Outcome Measures	Length of Study	Measure Results
Antuona (1995)	Velnacrine	1	DB, PC, random parallel group	449	ADAS-Cog, CGIC	24 weeks	Significantly less deterioration on ADAS-Cog and CGIC
Murphy et al. (1991)	Velnacrine maleate	1	DB, PC, random parallel group	105	ADAS-Cog, CGI, IADL, PGIR, ADAS-NCog	15 weeks	No significant improvment
Ebmeier et al. (1992)	Velnacrine	2	DB, PC, random parallel group (SPECT)	12 and 21	ORT, WRT, SPECT	Single dose	Significant improvement on WRT and increase in frontal SPECT
Sigfried (1993)	Velnacrine	3	DB, PC, random crossover	35	ADAS-Cog, IWRT, CGII, CRTT	3 weeks	Significant improvement on ADAS-Cog, IWRT
Dal-Bianco et al. (1991)	Galanthamine	3	Open label	18	Neuropsychological battery	2–6 months	No significant improvement

[a]Refer to "List of Acronyms," pp. 131–134, for definitions of abbreviations.

patients showing a response in the open trial, following a drug washout period, participated in a randomization trial investigating either tacrine or placebo in a double-blind, parallel group study.

Schneider and Tariot (1994) reviewed the clinical trials involving tacrine and found that individualized dosing produced greater clinical results. Clinical response occurred at higher doses (>120 mg/day). Unfortunately, adequate dosing (>120 mg/day) often resulted in significant hepatotoxicity (approximately 30% of patients). Because this drug is rarely prescribed, treatment strategy must be diligently monitored with weekly determinations of hepatic enzymes. In fact, this drug has been almost entirely replaced by the three newer AChEs, donepezil, rivastigmine, and galantamine.

The efficacy and safety of donepezil, rivastigmine, and galantamine have been established by multiple Type 1 studies that have been reviewed in detail (Delagarza, 2003; Kaduszkiewicz, Zimmermann, Beck-Bornholdt, & van den Bussche, 2005; Lanctot et al., 2003). In a systematic review, Kaduszkiewicz et al. (2005) found 22 Type 1 publications involving clinical trials of one of these three AChEs compared with placebo (12 for donepezil, and 5 each for rivastigmine and galantamine). The duration of these studies ranged from 6 weeks to 3 years. In almost all of these trials (19/22), active drug was significantly better than placebo. However, the improvement was characterized as "rather moderate." In their meta-analysis of 24 Type 1 studies of at least one of the three AChEs, Lanctot et al. (2003) reported a 9% difference between drug and placebo on global response and a number needed to treat (NNT) of 12. The most common adverse effects of these drugs are nausea, anorexia, vomiting and diarrhea, although these are generally mild and dissipate quickly with continued use (Delagarza, 2003). Very few studies have compared the three currently used AChEs and there is a general consensus that they are of similar efficacy. One study did find a slightly higher response to donepezil than galantamine (R. W. Jones, Passmore, & Wetterberg, 2002), and another found equal efficacy for donepezil and rivastigmine (Wilkinson et al., 2002). Donepezil can be administered once daily, whereas galantamine and rivastigmine both require twice-daily dosing.

One of the more novel cholinergic strategies is a procholinergic strategy using high-dose infusions of thyrotropin in conjunction with physostigmine (Mellow, Aronson, Giordani, & Berent, 1993). One Type 1 study investigating 4-aminopyridine showed no appar-

TABLE 4.5b Second-Generation Cholinesterase Inhibition[a]

Authors	Drug	Type	Design	N	Outcome Measures	Length of Study	Results
Rogers et al. (1998a)	Donepezil	1	DB, PC, randomized parallel	468	ADAS — Cog; CIBIC Plus MMSE, CDR-SB	12 weeks	Significant improvement in cognition, global function
Rodgers (1998b)	Donepezil	1	DB, PC, randomized parallel	473	ADAS — Cog; CIBIC Plus MMSE, CDR-SB	24 weeks	Significant improvement in cognition, global function
Burns et al. (1999)	Donepezil	1	DB, PC, randomized parallel	647	ADAS — Cog; CIBIC Plus MMSE, CDR-SB	24 weeks	Significant improvement in cognition, global function, ADCs
Corey-Bloom et al. (1998)	Rivastigmine	1	DB, PC, randomized parallel	699	ADAS — Cog; CIBIC Plus MMSE	26 weeks	Significant improvement in cognition, global function
Rosler et al. (1999)	Rivastigmine	1	DB, PC, randomized parallel	725	ADAS — Cog; CIBIC Plus MMSE	26 weeks	Significant improvement in cognition, global function
Agid et al. (1998)	Rivastigmine	1	DB, PC, randomized parallel	402	CIBIC, MMSE	5 months	Significant improvement in cognition, global function, ADC, behavior
Tariot et al. (2000)	Galantamine	1	DB, PC, randomized parallel	978	ADAS — Cog; CIBIC, DAD	6 months	Significant improvement in cognition, global function
Raskind et al. (2000)	Galantamine	1	DB, PC, randomized parallel	636	ADAS — Cog; CIBIC, DAD	6 months	Significant improvement in cognition, global function

[a]Refer to "List of Acronyms," pp. 131–134, for definitions of abbreviations.

ent therapeutic benefit (see "Other Treatment Strategies" section). Asthana and colleagues (1995) found that continuous intravenous infusion of physostigmine resulted in significant short-term improvement in five of nine patients with mild-to-moderate AD.

The most exciting noncholinergic strategy focuses on reducing the accumulation of amyloid protein or the degradation of tau protein. Amyloid plaque is an insoluble, fibrillary component of the senile plaques first described by Alzheimer in 1907. Amyloid protein accumulation is thought by many to be the central lesion in many forms of AD.

A number of studies have used antiamyloid treatment strategies (Table 4.8). One approach has been to focus on the possible role of nonsteroidal antiinflammatory drugs (NSAIDs) as a means of primary prevention. A second strategy, summarized below, involves treatment with estrogen-like compounds. Breitner (1996) reviewed 15 observation studies examining the role of either glucocorticoids or NSAIDs as a means of delaying the onset or halting the progression of AD. Of these studies, 14 of 15 suggested that both strategies are effective, decreasing the risk of developing AD or delaying the onset of AD in pa-

TABLE 4.6 Lecithin and Tacrine[a]

Authors	Drug	Type	Design	N	Outcome Measures	Length of Study	Measure Results
Maltby et al. (1994)	Tacrine and lecithin	2	DB, PC, random parallel group	41	MMSE, V&V SRT, WNA, LPRS, IADL	35 weeks	No significant difference between groups
Minthon et al. (1993)	Tacrine and lecithin	2	DB, PC, random cross-over	17	VOCT, KBD, VL, DS, RT, CFF, EEG, rCBF	26 weeks	6 patients classified as responders
Gustafson (1993)[b]	Physostigmine, tacrine, and lecithin	2	DB, PC, random cross-over	10 & 17	rCBF, EEG, OBS-DS, OBS-CS, CGI, RR	2-hr IV (P), 26 weeks (T&L)	No significant improvement compared with placebo
Weinstein et al. (1991)[b]	Tacrine and lecithin	2	DB, PC, random parallel group	12	CAMCOG, IDDD	12 weeks	No significant difference between groups
Lampe et al. (1990)	TRH and lecithin	2	DB, PC, random cross-over	8	VFT, TMT, BSRT, BVRT	2 weeks	Significant improvement on part of BSRT
Chatellier & Lacomblez[b] (1990)	Tacrine and lecithin	2	DB, PC, random cross-over	67	MMSE, SGRS, MDS, LC, PVAS	8 weeks	Significant improvement on PVAS
Fitten et al. (1990)[b]	Tacrine and lecithin	2	DB, PC, random cross-over	10 & 6	MMSE, FOM, DS, TMT, NLT, OT, ADL, IADL, NOSIE, GDS, COWGT, GERRI, ADAS	3 weeks and 10 weeks	3 weeks, no significant improvement; 10 weeks, mild improvement in some
Gauthier et al. (1990)[b]	Tacrine and lecithin	2	DB, PC, random cross-over	52	MMSE, RDRS-II, HDS	20 weeks	Significant improvement on MMSE
Heyman et al. (1987)	Lecithin	2	DB, PC, random parallel group	37	MMSE, AST, VFT, BSRT, VSRT, SMT	6 months	No significant improvement
Jenike et al. (1986)[c]	Lecithin and ergoloid mesylates	2	DB, PC, random cross-over	7	DRS, DRST	10 weeks	No significant improvement
Schwartz & Kohlstaedt (1986)	Physostigmine and lecithin	2	DB, PC, random cross-over, and replication	11	BSRT	Acute injections	No significant improvement
Little et al. (1985)	Lecithin	2	DB, PC, random parallel group	51	PWT, VFT, OR, KT, IL CA, DCT	6 months	No significant improvement

Study	Treatment		Design	N	Tests	Duration	Results
D. E. Smith et al. (1984)[d]	Lecithin and piracetam plus lecithin	2	DB, PC, random crossover	11 & 11	BSRT, AST, DRS, PMSE	10 months and 6 months	No significant improvement on lecithin; improvement on BSRT in 8/11 piracetam + lecithin
Weintraub et al. (1983)	Lecithin	2	DB, PC, random crossover	13	DRS	6 months	No significant improvement
Brinkman et al. (1992)	Lecithin	2	DB, PC, random crossover	10	BSRT	6 weeks	No significant improvement
Sullivan et al. (1982)	Lecithin	2	DB, PC, random crossover	18	VPAL-NVPAL, BPDP, VRMT	16 weeks	No significant improvement
Hyman, Eslinger, & Damasio (1982)	Lecithin	2	DB, PC, random crossover	18	MMSE, DS, VFT, AST	8 weeks	No significant improvement
Pomara et al. (1982)	Lecithin	2	DB, PC, random crossover	5	BSRT	4 weeks	No significant improvement
Dysken et al. (1982)	Lecithin	2	DB, PC, random crossover	10	WRT, WLL, PALT	4 weeks	No significant improvement
Vroulis et al. (1981)	Lecithin	2	DB, PC, random crossover	18	BSRT, AST, DRS, IMCI	4–16 weeks	No significant improvement; slight improvement in 8/15
Peters & Levin (1979)[b]	Physostigmine and lecithin	2	DB, PC, random crossover	5	BSRT	Acute subQ injection	No significant improvement compared with baseline
Etienne et al. (1981)	Lecithin	2	DB, PC, crossover	11	WMS, FRT	3 months	No significant improvement
Thal et al. (1983)[b]	Physostigmine and lecithin	3	Open label and DB, PC, crossover	8	BSRT	6 days for each	Significant improvement in 6 of 8
Wettstein (1983)[b]	Physostigmine and lecithin	3	DB, PC, and Xover	8	Self-designed test battery	12 weeks	No significant improvement
Kaye et al. (1982)[c]	Tacrine and lecithin	3	PC, random crossover	10	SLT, BSRT, FR; subjects diagnosed with PDD	Acute 3 doses	No significant improvement

[a]Refer to "List of Acronyms," pp. 131–134, for definition of abbreviations.
[b]See also Table 4.3.
[c]See also Table 4.1.
[d]See also Table 4.2.

TABLE 4.7 Muscarinic/Cholinergic Agonists[a]

Authors	Drug	Type	Design	N	Measures	Length of Study	Measure Results
Harbaugh et al. (1989)	Bethanechol chloride muscarinic agonist	1	DB, PC, random cross-over	49	DS, DSY, BDT, WMS, TMT, BSRT, VFT, BNT, MMSE	24 weeks	Significant improvement on MMSE only
Wilson et al. (1995)	Nicotine patches	2	DB, PC, random cross-over	6	DMTS, DRS, RAT	3 weeks	Significant improvement on RAT
Soncrant et al. (1993)	Arecoline muscarinic/cholinergic agonist	2	Open label and DB, PC, random crossover	9	BSRT, COWGT, VFT, DS, BVRT, VCRMT, VBCRMT, SCWIT, TT, ERDT, CALC	Approximately 2 weeks for each	Significant improvement on part of BSRT; 6/9 were responders on BSRT
Raffaele, Berardi, Asthana, et al. (1991)	Arecoline muscarinic/cholinergic agonist	2	Open label and DB, PC, random crossover	8	BSRT	Approximately 2 weeks for each	Significant improvement in open label but not on double-blind
Penn et al. (1988)	Bethanechol chloride muscarinic agonist	2	DB, PC, random cross-over, and escalating dose	10 & 8	MMSE, COWGT, BSDL, BSRT	24 weeks	No significant improvement in either study
Tariot et al. (1988)	Arecoline muscarinic/cholinergic agonist	2	DB, PC, random parallel group	12	PRT, VFT, BSRT	Acute 2-hr infusions	No significant difference between groups
Mouradian et al. (1988)	RS-86 muscarinic agonist	2	DB, PC, random cross-over	7	DS, PMT, VFDT, RF, DL, WLL, RT, LMT, SM	2 weeks	No significant improvement
Davis et al. (1987)	Oxo-tremorine	2	DB, PC, random cross-over	7	WRT	Acute	No significant improvement
Hollander et al. (1987)	RS-86 muscarinic agonist	2	DB, PC, random cross-over	12	ADAS	3 weeks	6/12 had >10% improvement on ADAS
Bruno et al. (1986)	RS-86 muscarinic agonist	2	DB, PC, random cross-over	8	IMPP, PMT, VFDT, RF, DL, WLL, RT	3 weeks	No significant improvement

Study	Drug		n	Tests	Duration	Results
Wettstein & Spiegel (1984)	RS-86 muscarinic agonist	2	6 & 17	MMSE, WRT, PRT, WLL, VT, CP	12 and 18 weeks	Significant improvement on VT in Study 1; No significant results in Study 2
Thal et al. (1981)	Choline chloride	2	7	WLL, CP, VFT, CR, PB	12 weeks	No significant improvement
Caamano et al. (1994)	CDP-choline	3	20	MMSE, BCRS, FAST, TCD	4 weeks	Significant improvement in MMSE of EOAD subset
G. M. M. Jones et al. (1992)	Nicotine	3	70 (24 AD)	RVIP, DRMLO, CFF, FTT, DS	Acute injection	Significant improvement on parts of RVIP, DRMLO, CFF
Raffaele, Berardi, Morris, et al. (1991)	Arecoline muscarinic/cholinergic agonist	3	15	BSRT, ERDT	Acute 30-min injection	No significant improvement
Sahakian et al. (1989)	Nicotine	3	21	DS, FTT, CFF	Acute 7 day	Significant improvement on FTT, CFF
Newhouse et al. (1988)	Nicotine	3	6	COWGT, WLL	Acute 4 day	Significant decrease in intrusions
Harbaugh et al. (1984)	Bethanechol chloride muscarinic agonist	3	4	Subjective family response	8 months	Subjective improvement only during drug periods
Christie et al. (1981)[b]	Physostigmine and arecoline	3	11 & 7	SPT	Acute 30-min IV	Significant improvement in both groups
Renvoize & Jerram (1979)	Choline chloride	3	18	BRS	2 months	No significant improvement
Ferris et al. (1979)	Choline chloride	3	14	26 cognitive tests	4 weeks	No significant improvement
C. M. Smith et al. (1978)	Choline bitartate salt	3	10	RPMT, DS	1 month	No significant improvement

Notes on study design (column before n): DB, PC, random crossover, and parallel group; DB, PC, random crossover; Open label; SB, PC, crossover; Open label; SB, PC, crossover; SB, PC, crossover; SB, PC, crossover pilot study; DB, PC, random crossover; DB, PC, parallel group; Open label; DB, PC, crossover

[a] Refer to "List of Acronyms," pp. 131–134, for definitions of abbreviations.
[b] See also Table 4.4.

119

TABLE 4.8 Nonsteroidal Anti-Inflammatory Drugs[a]

Authors	Drug	Type	Design	N	Outcome Measures	Length of Study	Measure Results
Rogers et al. (1993)	Indomethicin	2	DB, PC, random parallel group	28	MMSE, ADAS, BNT, TT	6 months	Significant differences across all measures
Rich et al. (1995)	NSAIDs	3	Chart review of Alzheimer's Disease Research Center	210	Duration of illness, MMSE, VFT, BNT, TT, BVRT, BDT, RNT, DRST, GIFT, PGDRS	1 year	Less decline on VFT, DRST, orientation subscale of PGDRS
Andersen et al. (1995)	NSAIDs	3	Chart review of dementia study	6,258	Relative risk for Alzheimer's disease	NA	RR .38 for NSAID users
Breitner et al. (1994)	NSAIDs, steroid/ACTH, or aspirin	3	Co-twin control	50 pairs	Age of onset of Alzheimer's disease	NA	Odds ratios for all drugs were below 1. Best for steroid/ACTH
Canadian Study of Health and Aging (1994)	NSAIDs and arthritis	3	Chart review of dementia study	793	Odds ratios of risk factors for Alzheimer's disease	NA	OR for NSAID and arthritis groups significant below 1

[a]Refer to "List of Acronyms," pp. 131–134, for definitions of abbreviations.

tient populations for which these drugs are regularly administered for other purposes (e.g., NSAIDs for treatment of arthritis or leprosy, for which the rate of AD neuropathology is significantly less than for controls). One twin study (Breitner et al., 1994) has suggested that NSAIDs reduce the risk of AD. Table 4.8 lists several of the important studies (Types 2, 3).

Again, although most of these studies lack the scientific rigor of Type 1 clinical trials, all of these mainly retrospective studies suggested a role for NSAIDs in either reducing risk or slowing progression of AD. For example, McGeer, McGeer, Rogers, and Sibley (1990) reviewed 7,490 charts of patients treated with NSAIDs and who suffered from AD. The overall rate of AD was 6 to 12 times lower in NSAID patients than would have been predicted in this population. Unfortunately, this enthusiasm has been blunted by prospective trials that failed to find any benefit for anti-inflammatory drugs as treatments of AD (Scharf, Mander, Ugoni, Vajda, & Christophidis, 1999; Aisen et al., 2000).

Catecholamine Enhancement in Alzheimer's Disease

Several groups have investigated the other neurotransmitter abnormalities associated with AD, particularly the catecholamines. Although less compelling than the marked reductions in cholinergic neurotransmission, levels of norepinephrine and serotonin, but not dopamine, are diminished in postmortem studies of AD patients. With a few exceptions, most treatment strategies have studied the inhibition of monoamine oxidase (MAO), a major catecholaminergic (monoaminergic) degradative enzyme. Monoamine oxidase B inhibitors have been investigated on the assumption that (a) monoaminergic systems are directly involved in the pathophysiology of AD, (b) intact monoaminergic systems facilitate the effects of cholinergic medications in AD, and (c) they may affect the deposition of amyloid in patients with AD. Most published reports show clear improvements in agitation and depression, along with many measures of cognition (Table 4.9). Although enthusiasm among clinicians has been dampened by concerns about side effects and the requirement that patients remain on a tyramine-free diet while on MAO inhibitors, the final story will have to await results of ongoing clinical trials.

Memantine, a drug that may work by decreasing the activity of the neurotransmitter glutamate, was recently approved for the treatment of moderate to severe AD. In a Type 1 study (Reisberg et al., 2003) memantine was compared with placebo for 28 weeks. Memantine was statistically significantly better on a last observation carried forward basis on the Severe Impairment Battery and on the Alzheimer's Disease Cooperative Study Activities of Daily Living Inventory (ADCS-ADLsev) and superior at a trend level ($p < .06$) on the Clinician's Interview-Based Impression of Change Plus Caregiver Input (CIBIC-Plus) scale. On the Severe Impairment Battery based on a predetermined definition 29% of patients treated with memantine and 10% of patients treated with placebo met response criteria, a significant difference.

Neuropeptide-Based Treatment Strategies

Animal studies have shown that neuropeptide treatments enhance performance on a wide variety of experimental tasks. Based on these findings, several neuropeptides have been investigated as potential treatments for AD. The most extensively studied of these are naloxone (Table 4.10), vasopressin (Table 4.11), adrenocorticotropic hormone (ACTH), and somatostatin (for review of ACTH and somatostatin, see Thal, 1994). Naloxone has been shown to have direct facilitatory effects on memory performance in animals. Unfortunately, most investigations with either naloxone (administered intravenously) or naltrexone, a long-acting, orally active opiate antagonist, have not shown any benefit for AD patients. In addition to animal data showing improvements in maze learning and amnesia induced by electroconvulsive therapy (ECT), postmortem samples from AD patients have revealed small decreases in hippocampal vasopressin levels. Most clinical studies, including one Type 1 multicenter trial, failed to demonstrate significant improvements in AD.

Novel Treatment Strategies

Acetyl-L-Carnitine/Membrane Stabilizing Agents

One of the more interesting new treatment strategies involves the use of acetyl-L-carnitine hydrochloride and other membrane "stabilizing" agents (e.g., phos-

TABLE 4.9 Monoamine Oxidase Inhibitors[a]

Authors	Drug	Type	Design	N	Outcome Measures	Length of Study	Measure Results
Dysken et al. (1992)	Milacemide	1	DB, PC, random parallel group	228	CGI, WMS, VS, IADL, VFT	9 weeks	No significant improvement
Mangoni et al. (1991)	L-Deprenyl	1	DB, PC, random parallel group	119	BRS, DS, SS, VFT, DT, TPAT	3 months	Significant improvement on BRS, DS, SS, VFT, DT, TPAT
Marin et al. (1995)	L-Deprenyl and physostigmine	2	DB, PC, random cross-over	17	DS, VFT, WLL, CP, WR, WRT	8 weeks	No significant improvement
Burke et al. (1993)	L-Deprenyl	2	DB, PC, random parallel group	39	CDR, MMSE, BRS, GERRI	First 2 months of 15-month trial	No significant improvement over first 2 months of study
Schneider et al. (1993)[b]	L-Deprenyl and tacrine or physostigmine	2	DB, PC, random cross-over	10	ADAS-Cog, MMSE	8 weeks	Significant improvement on ADAS-Cog in those receiving drug first
Finali et al. (1991)	L-Deprenyl	2	DB, PC, random cross-over	19	WLL, R-AVL	6 months	Significant improvement on some R-AVL parameters
Piccinin, Finali, & Piccirilli (1990)	L-Deprenyl	2	DB, PC, random cross-over	20	TT, VFT, DS, AVLT, 7/24 Test, LC, TMT, PCT	6 months	Significant improvement on VFT, DS, LC, part of 7/24 test
Tariot, Cohen, et al. (1987)	L-Deprenyl	2	DB, PC, serial treatment	17	BPRS, BSRT, VFT, CPT, VT	8 weeks	Significant improvement on BPRS, BSRT on 10-mg dose
Tariot, Sunderland, et al. (1987)	L-Deprenyl	2	DB, PC, serial treatment	17	BSRT, VT, VFT, CPT	12 weeks	Significant improvement on free recall on BSRT
Goad et al. (1991)	Selegiline	3	Open label	8	MMSE	8 weeks	Clinically significant improvement recall and orientation
Schneider et al. (1991)	L-Deprenyl	3	Open label	14	MMSE, BSRT, COWGT, DS, NC	4 weeks	Significant improvement on BSRT
Falsaperla, Preti, & Oliani (1990)	Selegiline and oxiracetam	3	SB, random parallel group	40	BRS, RMT, DS, SR, VFT, GS	90 days	Significant improvement on all tests with selegiline
Campi, Todeschini, & Scarzella (1990)	Selegiline and acetyl-L-carnitine	3	SB, random parallel group	40	BRS, RMT, DS, SR, VFT, GS	90 days	Significant improvement on all tests with selegiline
Monteverde et al. (1990)	Selegiline and phosphatidylserine	3	SB, PC, random cross-over	40	BRS, RMT, DS, SR, VFT, GS	90 days	Significant improvement on all tests with selegiline

[a]Refer to "List of Acronyms," pp. 131–134, for definitions of abbreviations.
[b]See also Tables 4.3 and 4.4.

122

TABLE 4.10 Naloxone/Naltrexone[a]

Authors	Drug	Type	Design	N	Outcome Measures	Length of Study	Measure Results
Henderson et al. (1989)	Naloxone	2	DB, PC, random crossover	54	MMSE, DS, FTT, VRT, VMT, VFT, BNT, modified TT, DSY	Acute injections	Significant improvement on intrusions in VMT
Tariot et al. (1986)	Naloxone	2	DB, PC, random crossover	12	COWGT, DS, BSRT, FTT, DSY, DYN, VT	Acute 3 day	No significant improvement
Hyman et al. (1982)	Naltrexone	2	DB, PC, random crossover	17	OR, DS, COWGT, VL, VMT, NC	6 weeks	No significant improvement
Pomara et al. (1985)	Naltrexone	2	DB, PC, random crossover	10	DS, TT, VFT, FTT, WLL, CNFN	Acute 4 injections	Significant improvement on TT
Tennant (1987)	Naltrexone	3	Open label and DB, PC, random crossover	6 & 3	MMSE, BRS	6 weeks	Significant improvement on MMSE, BRS
Knopman & Hartman (1986)	Naltrexone	3	Open label	10	AVLT, VFT, SD, WMS	6 weeks	Significant improvement on AVLT
Serby et al. (1986)	Naltrexone	3	Open label and DB for responders	9 & 2	BSRT, PMT, NYUMT	2 weeks each	No significant improvement
Steiger et al. (1985)	Naloxone	3	DB, PC, random crossover	16	BCRS	2 months	No significant improvement
Panella & Blass (1984)	Naloxone	3	DB, PC, random crossover	12	MMSE, MSQ, DS, BRS	Acute injections	No significant improvement
Reisberg et al. (1983a)	Naloxone	3	DB, PC, random crossover	7	BCRS, DSY, FTT, VFT, DS, PS	Acute injections	Significant improvement in all but VFT and PS
Reisberg et al. (1983b)	Naloxone	3	Open label	5	BCRS, DSY, FTT, VFT, DS, PS	Acute injections	Clinical improvement in 3/5

[a]Refer to "List of Acronyms," pp. 131–134, for definitions of abbreviations.

123

TABLE 4.11 Vasopressin[a]

Authors	Drug	Type	Design	N	Outcome Measures	Length of Study	Measure Results
Wolters et al. (1990)	Deglycin amide-arginine-vasopressin	1	DB, PC, random parallel group	115	SCAGS, BCRS, IADL, GAS, SLT, COC, VFT, MPM, SR, VR, MCGBRS	84 days	No significant improvement
Peabody, Davis, et al., (1986)	Desamino-D-arginine-vasopressin	2	DB, PC, random parallel group	14	BSRT, LM, SV	4 weeks	No significant improvement on cognitive scales
Peabody et al. (1985)	Deglycin amide-arginine-vasopressin	2	DB, PC, random parallel group	17	BSRT, WLL	1 week	Significant improvement on parts of BSRT
Chase et al. (1982)	Lysine vasopressin	2	DB, PC, random parallel group	16	RT, TR, MPP, WLL, PMT, RF	10 days	Significant improvement on RT
Durso et al. (1982)	Lysine vasopressin	2	DB, PC, random parallel group	17	WLL, BSRT, PWT, SR, PMT, RT, RF, TR	10 days	Significant improvement on RT
Tinklenberg et al. (1982)	Deglycin amide-arginine-vasopressin	3	SB, PC, parallel group	11	BSRT, WLL	10 days	No significant improvement
Kaye et al. (1982)[b]	Desamino-D-arginine-vasopressin	3	SB, PC, crossover	7	WMS, BSRT, WLL, VFT	1 month	Significant improvement on VFT
Tinklenberg et al. (1981)	Desamino-D-arginine-vasopressin	3	DB, PC, random parallel group	7	BSRT, PWT	1–2 weeks	No significant improvement
Weingartner et al. (1981)	Desamino-D-arginine-vasopressin	3	DB, PC, random crossover	7	VFT, WLL	Acute	Significant improvement on VFT

[a]Refer to "List to Acronyms," pp. 131–134, for definitions of abbreviations.
[b]See also Tables 4.3 and 4.6.

phatidyl serine) as primary prevention strategy to slow the disease progression (Tables 4.12 and 4.13). Alzheimer's disease has been associated with disturbances in membrane phospholipid turnover (Pettegrew, 1989) and membrane oxidative metabolism. Animal studies show that carnitine acts as a carrier of fatty acids from the cytosol into the mitochondrial matrix, in which they can be subjected to beta oxidation. Carnitine increases the activity of acetyl-CoA and choline acetyltransferase and in this way may have cholinomimetic effects. It also normalizes alterations in membrane and energy metabolism and increases both the levels and utilization of nerve growth factor (NGF) in the CNS.

Several open clinical trials (Type 2 studies without placebo controls) have been conducted. Of the 22 trials reviewed in Calvani, Carta, Caruso, Benedetti, and Iannuccelli, (1992), clinical improvement was found in 7 trials compared with the placebo, and four of 7 trials showed substantial improvement. Thal, Carta, et al. (1996), in a double-blind, randomized, placebo-controlled trial (Type 1), parallel design study found significant clinical improvements on disability, attention, and apraxia over a 1-year period. They found that a subgroup of younger AD patients might benefit from this therapy, whereas older patients actually did poorer. Overall, there was little difference between the AD patients and the placebo controls. Both Type 1 studies of phosphatidyl serine, as well as two of four Type 2 studies, and one of two Type 3 studies, found modest positive effects.

Estrogen Replacement

The second of the antiamyloid strategies, based on (a) the preclinical observation that estrogen administration influences cholinergic function and increases binding sites of hypothalamic nicotinic acetylcholine receptors in rats, (b) data suggesting that estrogen has a clear role in diminishing amyloid deposition and (c) preclinical data showing that estrogen promotes neurogenesis within the subgranular layer of the dentate gyrus of the hippocampus, estrogen replacement strategies have recently gained attention. Estrogen administration has been associated with modest improvements in measures of attention, memory, and concentration in pre- and postmenopausal women. Several small open trials (Fillit et al., 1986; Honjo et al., 1989; Ohkura et al., 1995) have found that estrogen replacement therapy improves psychometric test

performance, as well as cortical cerebral blood flow and electroencephalogram (EEG) activity in patients with AD. Table 4.14 presents estrogen data to date.

Several studies promoted enthusiasm for this strategy. Tang et al. (1996) followed a large cohort of elderly females prospectively (5 years) to assess the role of estrogen replacement therapy (ERT) in delaying/ameliorating AD. Estrogen demonstrated significant effects in both domains. Schneider, Farlow, and Henderson (1996) reported on a 30-week, randomized, double-blind, placebo-controlled multicenter investigation of 343 female patients with AD. Women receiving ERT in addition to tacrine showed significantly greater improvement in AD symptoms than did patients receiving a placebo or tacrine alone. This suggests that prior, or continuing, treatment with estrogen may enhance response to tacrine in AD patients. However, two recent double-blind, placebo-controlled trials (Mulnard et al., 2000; Henderson, Paganini-Hill, Miller, et al., 2000) reveal no significant effect of estrogen therapy on disease progression in mild to moderate Alzheimer's disease. In fact, data from the Women's Health Initiative Memory Study suggested that estrogen plus progestin may lead to greater decline in cognitive function (Rapp et al., 2003) and increased risk for dementia (Shumaker et al., 2003) than placebo.

Other Treatment Strategies

A vast array of interventions have been tried for AD patients. The use of vitamin E was supported from the results of the Alzheimer's Disease Cooperative Study (Sano et al., 1997), which compared 10 mg of the MAO inhibitor selegiline given once daily, 1000 IU of vitamin E given twice daily, and placebo. Both selegiline and vitamin E were superior to placebo in delaying disability and nursing home placement. Many other strategies have been unconvincing, either because of limitations in study design or because the rationale was weak. They are summarized in Table 4.15. These unsuccessful strategies have included carbon dioxide, carbonic anhydrous inhibitors, hyperbolic oxygen, and vasodilators (papaverine, cyclandelate, isosuprine, cinnizarine).

Summary for the Treating Clinician

Although no cure exists for AD, the most promising, symptomatic treatments for AD subjects are the

TABLE 4.12 Acetyl-L-Carnitine[a]

Authors	Drug	Type	Design	N	Outcome Measures	Length of Study	Measure Results
Spagnoli et al. (1991)	Acetyl-L-carnitine	1	DB, PC, random parallel group	130	SBI, BRS, BICMT, RPMT, VJMCT, VSMD, PRMT, SVL, BTT, TT, WAT, IBAT, GCAT, FAT	1 year	Significant decrease in deterioration on BRS, RPM, BSMD, IBAT
Pettegrew et al. (1995)	Acetyl-L-carnitine	2	DB, PC, parallel groups (3)	33	MMSE, ADAS	1 year	Significantly less deterioration on MMSE
Sano et al. (1992)	Acetyl-L-carnitine	2	DB, PC, random parallel group	30	BSRT, mMMSE, WMS, BVRT, VFT, cancellations	6 months	Significant difference on VFT, DS, cancellations
Passeri et al. (1990)	Acetyl-L-carnitine	2	DB, PC, random parallel group	60	MMSE, BRS, RCFT, VFT, CT, TPBT	3 months	Significant improvement on BRS, RCFT, CT, VFT, TPBT
Rai et al. (1990)	Acetyl-L-carnitine	2	DB, PC, random parallel group	20	KOL, DCT, NLT, VFT	24 weeks	No significant difference
Urakami et al. (1993)	Nebracetam fumarate	3		9	MMSE, GBS, HWDS	8 weeks	Significant improvement on GBS, HWDS
Sinforiani et al. (1990)	Acetyl-L-carnitine and piracetam	3	SB, open label	12 & 12	DS, DSY, BTT, GS, VFT, WLL	2-week IV and 90-day oral	Significant improvement on DSY, GS for ALC
Campi et al. (1990)	Acetyl-L-carnitine and selegiline	3	SB, random parallel group	40	BRS, RMT, DS, SR, VFT, GS	90 days	Significant improvement for selegiline on all measures
Bellagamba et al. (1990)	Acetyl-L-carnitine	3	DB, PC, random parallel group	35	DSY, RCFT, RPMT, and others	3 months	Significant improvement on DSY, RCFT, RPMT

[a]Refer to "List of Acronyms," pp. 131–134, for definitions of abbreviation.

[b]See also Table 4.4.

126

TABLE 4.13 Membrane Stabilizing Agents[a]

Authors	Drug	Type	Design	N	Outcome Measures	Length of Study	Measure Results
Crook et al. (1991)	Phosphatidylserine	1	DB, PC, random parallel group	149	FRT, NFA, TNR, MOR	12 weeks	Significant improvement on FRT, NFA
Amaducci & the SMID Group (1988)	Phosphatidylserine	1	DB, PC, random parallel group	142	DRS, RMT, SR, DS, BTT, TT, ST, CASE	3 months with 21-month follow-up	Significant improvement on ST, BTT, and BDS subscale
Flicker et al. (1991)	Ganglioside GM$_1$	2	DB, PC, random crossover	12	DS, TNR, DSY, BDT, FTT, ORT, SLT, MMSE, JLO	15 weeks	No significant improvement
Crook, Petrie, et al. (1992)	Phosphatidylserine	2	DB, PC, random parallel group	51	CGI, CRS, MAC-P	12 weeks	Significant difference on 2 CGI variables, 3 CRS variables
Ala et al. (1990)	Ganglioside GM$_1$	2	DB, PC, random parallel group	46	MMSE, BCRS, VFT, PB, LC, DSY, BSRT, RCFT, CD	12 weeks	No significant improvement
Delwaide et al. (1986)	Phosphatidylserine	2	DB, PC, random parallel group	35	CS, PRS	6 weeks	Significant improvement on PRS
Heiss et al. (1994)	Phosphatidylserine, pyritinol, cognitive training	3	Open label 4 parallel group combination of three "drugs"	70	MMSE, FTT, PMT, VMT, VFT, TT, RT, OT, IPT, QEEG, PET	6 months	No significant difference among the 4 groups
Monteverde et al. (1990)	Phosphatidylserine and selegiline	3	SB, PC, random crossover	40	BRS, RMT, DS, SR, VFT, GS	90 days	Significant improvement on subscales of BRS and RMT for P-serine

[a]Refer to "List of Acronyms," pp. 131–134, for definitions of abbreviations.

127

TABLE 4.14 Estrogen[a]

Authors	Drug	Type	Design	N	Outcome Measures	Length of Study	Measure Results
Hagino et al. (1995)	Estrogen replacement therapy	3	Open label	15 & 7	MMSE, HWDS, GBS	6 weeks and 5–28 months	Significant improvement on MMSE, HDS, GBS in Study 1 and in some subjects in Study 2
Ohkura et al. (1995)	Estrogen replacement therapy	3	Open label, case study	7	MMSE, HWDS, GBS	5–45 months	Nonsignificant improvement on MMSE and HDS in 4 cases
Weis (1987)	Estrogen and nalmefene	3	Open label	5	GDS, MMSE, BSRT, TMT, VFT, BCRS	4 weeks	No significant improvement
Brenner et al. (1994)	Estrogen replacement therapy	2	Population-based case control	107 AD, 120 cntr.	Adjusted odds ratios of estrogen replacement therapy and AD	Followed for 6 years	No association between ERT and AD
Henderson et al. (1994)	Estrogen replacement therapy	3	Population-based case control	143 AD, 92 cntr.	Likelihood of developing AD in controls and comparison of MMSE scores	NA	Significant difference in risk and MMSE scores favoring ERT
Barrett-Conner & Kritz-Silverstein (1993)	Estrogen replacement therapy	1	Population-based case control	800	Adjusted odds ratio of ERT and cognitive function (BSRT, WMS, MMSE, BRS, TMT, VFT)	Followed for 15 years	No significant effect of estrogen on cognitive function
Honjo et al. (1989)	Estrogen replacement therapy	3	Open label, parallel group	7	JST, HWDS	6 weeks	Significant improvement on JST
Fillit et al. (1986)	Estrogen replacement therapy	3	Open label	7	GDS, BRS, WAIS, MMSE, RMT, DRS	6 weeks	Significant improvement in three subjects
Mulnard et al. (2000)	Estrogen replacement therapy	1	DB, PC	120	CG1C, CDR	1 year	No effect on sentinel events
Henderson et al. (2000)			DB, PC, parallel group	42	ADAS-Cog, CGIC, Caregiver function status	16 weeks	No effect on outcome measures

[a]Refer to "List of Acronyms," pp. 131–134, for definitions of abbreviations.

TABLE 4.15 Other Interventions[a]

Authors	Drug	Type	Design	N	Outcome Measures	Length of Study	Measure Results
Scherder et al. (1995)	Trans-Q electrical nerve stimulation	2	DB, PC, random parallel group	16	DS, VMS, VFT, EWT, FRT, PRT	6 weeks	Significant effect on recognition in EWT and on FRT, PRT
Saletu et al. (1992)	Denbufylline in AD and MID	2	DB, PC, random parallel group	45 and 51	EEG mapping, CGI, MMSE, DSY, TMT, DS, SCAGS	12 weeks	Significant improvement on CGI, MMSE, DSY, SGAGS
Tollefson (1990)	Nimodepine	1	DB, PC, random parallel group	227	BSRT, VFT, FT, CGI, ADL, RAGS, SRT, SDMT, FLNT	12 weeks	Significant improvement on parts of the BSRT
Saletu et al. (1994)	Nicergoline in SDAT and Multi-infarct dementia	1	DB, PC, random parallel group	112	CGI, MMSE, SCAGS	8 weeks	Significant improvement on CGI & MMSE for both SDAT & MID
Battaglia et al. (1989)	Nicergoline	1	DB, PC, random parallel	315	SCAGS	6 months	Significant improvement on SCAGS
Nicergoline Study Group (1990)	Nicergoline and ergoloid mesylates	3	SB placebo followed by DB, parallel group	73 and 73	SCAGS, PP	7 months	Significant improvement on SCAGS, PP for both groups
Miller, Fong, & Tinklenberg (1993)	ORG 2766 ACTH 4-9 analog	2	DB, PC, random parallel group	40	BSRT, MMSE, DSY, ADAS, GDS, RT, PTT	16 weeks	Significant improvement on RT
Kragh-Sorensen et al. (1986)	ORG 2766 ACTH 4-9 analog	2	DB, PC, random parallel group	156	SCAGS, GAGS, LPRS, BRS	4 weeks	Significant improvement on SCAGS, LPRS & GAGS at varied doses
Soininen et al. (1985)	ORG 2766 ACTH 4-9 analog	2	DB, PC, random parallel group	77	SCAGS, GPIE, LPRS, GAS	6 months	No significant improvement
Ferris et al. (1982)	L-Dopa	3	DB, PC, random crossover group	56	BSRT	16 weeks	No significant improvement
Branconnier et al. (1979)	ACTH 4-10	2	DB, PC, random crossover	18	SPPT, BGT, RT, WMS	Acute injection	No significant improvement
Davidson et al. (1988)	4-Aminopyridine	2	DB, PC, random crossover	14	ADAS	4 weeks	No significant improvement
D. F. Smith et al. (1984)	Tryptophan	2	DB, PC, random crossover	28	PGRS, GRS	4 weeks	No significant improvement
Cutler et al. (1985)	Zimeldine	2	DB, PC, random crossover	4	RT, OM, WLL	23 weeks	No significant improvement
Dehlin et al. (1985)	Alaproclate	2	DB, PC, random parallel group	40	GBS, CGI, CPRS	8 weeks	Significant improvement on subtest of GBS
Meador et al. (1993)	Thiamine 1 DB and 1 SB experiment	2 and 3	DB and SB, PC, random crossover	18 and 28	ADAS, MMSE, CGI	8 weeks	Significant improvement on ADAS in 13 DB subjects
Nolan et al. (1991)	Thiamine	2	DB, PC, random parallel group	15	BNT, MMSE, WLL	1 year	No significant improvement

(continued)

TABLE 4.15 (continued)

Authors	Drug	Type	Design	N	Outcome Measures	Length of Study	Measure Results
Blass et al. (1988)	Thiamine	2	DB, PC, random crossover	16	MMSE	6 months	Significant improvement on MMSE
Adolfsson et al. (1982)	Levodopa	2	DB, PC, random parallel group	37	DS, SM, FOM, BGT, RT, FTT	10 weeks	No significant improvement
Lebowitz & Crook (1991)	Guanfacine	1 and 2	DB, SB, PC, random parallel group	160 and 40	MAC-S, MAC-CGI, MAC-P, LM, BVRT, PAT	4 weeks	No significant improvement
Crook, Wilner, et al. (1992)	Guanfacine	2	DB, PC, random parallel group	29	CGI, CRS, MAC-F, ALT, LMT, BVRT	13 weeks	No significant improvement
Schlegel et al. (1989)	Guanfacine	2	DB, PC, random crossover	5	PMT, SM, VFT, DS, BVRT	4 weeks	No significant improvement
Mouradian et al. (1991)	Somatostatin (Octreotide)	2	DB, PC, random crossover	14	ADAS, BSRT, DS, SM, VFT, RVL, LMT	Acute injections and IV	No significant improvement
McLachlan et al. (1991)	Desferri-oxamine	2	DB, PC, random parallel group	48	ADL, VHB	24 months	Significant decrease in rate of decline of ADL
Mellow et al. (1989)	Thyrotropin-releasing hormone	2	DB, PC, random crossover	10	VT, VFT, PRT, BSRT	Acute 3 day	No significant improvement on cognition
Lampe et al. (1990)	TRH and lecithin	2	DB, PC, random crossover	8	VFT, TMT, BSRT, BVRT	2 weeks	Significant improvement on part of BSRT
Peabody et al. (1986)	Thyrotropin-releasing hormone	3	DB, PC, crossover	4	DS, BSRT, TET, ZVT	Acute injection	No significant improvement
Imagawa (1990)	Coenzyme Q_{10}, vitamin B_6, and iron	3	Open label	27	HWDS	8 weeks	Significant improvement on HWDS
Mohr et al. (1986)	THIP	2	DB, PC, random crossover	6	SR, VFDT, WLL, PMT, RT, RF	2 weeks	No significant improvement
Mohr et al. (1989)	Clonidine	2	DB, PC, random crossover	8	SM, VFT, DS, OP, VL	~4 weeks	No significant improvement
Ihl et al. (1989)	Tenilsetam	3	Open label	12	RT, SLT, CGI, FJT(?)	3 months	Significant improvement on FJT and RT
Fleischhacker et al. (1986)	Memantine	3	SB, PC, random parallel group	20	FPB, PGRS, SCAGS, CGI, SKT	5 weeks	No significant improvement
Sano et al. (1997)	Vitamin E, vitamin E and selegeline, selegeline		DB, PC	341	CDR, MMSE, ADAS-Cog	2 years	Vitamin E reduced risk of institutionalization

Refer to "List of Acronyms," pp. 131–134, for definitions of abbreviations.

TABLE 4.16 Dementia in Parkinson's Disease[a]

Authors	Drug	Type	Design	N	Measures	Length of Study	Measure Results
Sano et al. (1990)	Piracetam	2	DB, PC, random crossover	20	mMMSE, BSRT, VFT, RT, CPT	24 weeks	No significant improvement
Garcia et al. (1982)	Lecithin	2	DB, PC, random parallel group	16	VOCT, BDT, RPMT, DSY, VFT, OR	9 weeks	No significant differences between groups
Barbeau (1980)	Lecithin	3	Open label	10	KBD	3 months	Improvement in KBD

[a]Refer to "List of Acronyms," pp. 131–134, for definitions of abbreviations.

AChEs and memantine. The second generation of AChEs, notably donepezil, galantamine, and rivastigmine, as well as memantine, offer demonstrable clinical efficacy and simpler dosing, minimal side effects, and negligible hepatotoxicity. At this time there are no convincing "head-on" comparisons among these three compounds. The clinical effects are very likely due to a class effect. At the current time, it is hard to advocate one over another.

Combination trials of NSAIDs and/or estrogen replacement with AChEs are now under way. These combinations are now not approved interventions, but these trials are likely to soon change this recommendation.

DEMENTIA ASSOCIATED WITH PARKINSON'S DISEASE

Dementia is common in Parkinson's disease, but the exact pathophysiology, especially the relationship among Alzheimer's disease, Parkinson's dementia, and Lewy body dementia, has yet to be fully understood. Dementia is common in Parkinson's disease, affecting approximately 30% of all PD patients (Koller & Megaffin, 1994; Pollack & Hornabrook, 1966). Age and duration of illness appear to be significant risk factors in the development of dementia. Mayeux, Chen, and Mirabello (1990) found that the incidence rate of dementia was 69/1,000 population per years of follow-up, and that the risk of dementia as a function of age in this group reached 65% by age 85 (Koller & Megaffin, 1994). This resulted in an age-specific prevalence of 21% in patients whose other PD symptoms occurred after age 70. This dementia may be genetically determined. Marder, Flood, and

Cote (1990) found that the risk of dementia among first-degree relatives of demented patients with PD was sixfold greater than in relatives of nondemented PD patients.

Table 4.16 summarizes a limited experience with treatments for the dementia associated with PD. Both piracetam and phosphatidylserine have been tried in Type 1 studies without success. Two Type 3 studies — open clinical trials with a small number of subjects — have both proposed that the coadministration of lecithin with sinemet resulted in improved performance in measures of cognitive performance. One encouraging note is that many of the ongoing trials mentioned earlier in this chapter for AD subjects have now been extended to patients with Lewy body dementia and dementia associated with Parkinson's disease.

List of Acronyms

AB	Aphasia battery
ACPT	Auditory Continuous Performance Test
ACTH	adrenocorticotropic hormone
AD	Alzheimer's disease
ADAS	Alzheimer's Disease Assessment Scale
ADAS-Cog	Alzheimer's Disease Assessment Scale — Cognitive Scale
ADAS-NCog	Alzheimer's Disease Assessment Scale — Noncognitive Scale
ADL	activities of daily living
AF	attentional focusing
AMTS	Abbreviated Mental Test score
ASMC	automatic speech and mental control
AST	Aphasia Screening Test
AVLT	Auditory Verbal Learning Test

BCRS	Brief Cognitive Rating Scale		CWAT	Controlled Word Association Test
BDT	Block Design subtest of the Wechsler Adult Intelligence Test		DAT	dementia of the Alzheimer type
			DB	double blind
BGT	Bender-Gestalt Test		DCT	Digit Copy Test
BI	Barthal Index		DL	dichotic listening
BICMT	Blessed Information-Concentration-Memory Test		DMTS	delayed matching to sample
			DRMLO	delayed response matching to location order
BNT	Boston Naming Test			
BPDP	Brown-Peterson Distractor Paradigm		DRS	Dementia Rating Scale
BPRS	Brief Psychiatric Rating Scale		DRST	Delayed Recognition Span Test
BRS	Blessed-Roth Scale		DS	Digit Span subtest of the Wechsler Adult Intelligence Test
BS	block span			
BSDL	Benton Serial Digit Learning		DSY	Digit Symbol subtest of the Wechsler Adult Intelligence Test
BSRT	Buschke Selective Reminding Task			
BTT	block-tapping task		DYN	dynometry
BVRT	Benton Visual Retention Test		EEG	electroencephalogram
BWLLT	Buschke Word List Learning Test		EOAD	early-onset Alzheimer's disease
CA	cube analysis		ERDT	Extended Range Drawing Test
CALC	calculations		ERT	estrogen replacement therapy
CAMCOG	Cambridge Cognitive Examination		EWT	Eight Word Test
CANTAB	Cambridge Neuropsychological Test Automated Battery		FAST	functional assessment stages
			FAT	Finger Agnosia Test
CASE	Clifton Assessment Scale for the Elderly		FCCA	Final Comprehensive Consensus Assessment
CCSE	Cognitive Capacity Screening Examination		FFT	Famous Faces Test
			FLNT	First and Last Names Test
CD	clock drawing		FLS	Functional Life Scale
CDR	Clinical Dementia Rating Scale		FOM	Fuld Object Memory
CFF	critical flicker fusion		FPB	Funktionspsychose-Skala-B
CFT	Complex Figure Test		FR	free recall of random and related words
CG-CGIC	Caregiver-Rated Clinical Global Impression of Change			
			FRT	Facial Recognition Test
CGI	clinical global impression		FTT	finger-tapping task
CGIC	clinical global impression — change		GAS	Global Assessment Scale
CGII	clinical global impression of improvement		GBS	Gottfries, Brane, and Steen Scale Test
			GCAT	Geometrical Constructive Apraxia Test
CIBC	clinician interview-based impression		GDS	Global Deterioration Scale
CL-CGIC	clinician-rated clinical global impression of change		GERRI	Geriatric Evaluations by Relatives Rating Instrument
CN	color naming		GIFT	Gollin Incomplete Figures Test
CNFN	confrontation naming		GPIE	General Psychiatric Impression — Elderly
COC	cross-out concentration			
COWGT	Controlled Oral Word Generation Test		GRS	Gerontopsychiatric Rating Scale
			GS	Gibson Spiral
CP	constructional praxis		HDS	Hierarchic Dementia Scale
CPRS	Comprehensive Psychopathological Rating Scale		HP	hand positions
			HVR	Halton's Visual Reproductions
CPT	continuous performance task		HWDS	Hasegawa's Dementia Scale
CR	category recognition		IADL	instrumental activities of daily living
CRTT	choice reaction time task		IBAT	Ideomotor and Buccal-Facial Apraxia Test
CS	Crichton Scale			
CSCL	Clinical Status Checklist		IDDD	Interview for Deterioration in Daily life in Dementia
CST	Color Slide Test			
CT	Corsi's Test		IL	incomplete letters

IMCI	Information-Memory-Concentration Instrument	PB	pegboard
IMPP	immediate memory for prose passages	PC	placebo-controlled
IPSCE	Inventory of Psychic and Somatic Complaints in the Elderly	PCT	Picture Cancellation Task
		PDD	primary degenerative dementia
IPT	Incomplete Picture Task	PDS	Progressive Deterioration Scale
IWRT	Immediate Word Recognition Task	PET	positron-emission tomography
JLO	judgment of line orientation	PGDRS	Psychogeriatric Dependency Rating Scales
JST	Japanese Screening Test		
KBD	Koh's Block Design	PGRS	Plutchik Geriatric Rating Scale
KOL	Kendrick Object Learning	PMSE	Pfeifer Mental Status Exam
KT	Kew Tests	PMT	Picture Memory Task
LAS	Luria Alternating Series	PNRS	Plutchnik Nurse's Rating Scale
LC	letter cancellation	PP	Polarity Profile
LM	letter matching	PRMT	Prose Memory Test
LMT	Logical Memory test of the Wechsler Adult Intelligence Test	PRS	Peri Scale
		PRT	Picture Recognition Task
LPRS	London Psychogeriatric Rating Scale	PS	perceptual speed
LS	Lawton Scale	PSMS	Physical Self-Maintenance Scale
LT	Labyrinth Test	PTT	Pursuit Tracking Task
MAC-CGI	Memory Assessment Clinics Clinical Global Improvement Scale	PVAS	Physician Visual Analogue Scale
		PWT	Paired Words Test
MAC-P	Memory Assessment Clinics Psychiatric Rating Scale	QEEG	Quantitative EEG
		RAGS	relative's assessment of global symptomatology
MAC-S	Memory Assessment Clinics Self-Rating Scale	RAT	Repeated Aquisition Task
		RAVL	Rey Auditory Verbal Learning Test
MC	mental control	rCBF	regional cerebral blood flow
MCGBRS	Modified Crighton Geriatric Behavior Rating Scale	RCFT	Rey Complex Figure Test
		RCGM	regional cerebral glucose metabolism
MDS	Mattis Dementia Scale	RDRS-II	Rapid Disability Rating Scale II
mMMSE	Modified Mini-Mental State Exam	RDT	Rosen Drawing Test
MMSE	Mini-Mental State Exam	RF	recurring figures
MOR	misplaced object recall	RMPT	Roadmap Test
MPM	Modified Progressive Matrices	RMT	Randt Memory Test
MPP	memory for prose passages	RNCP	Rosen Noncognitive Portion
MSCL	Mental Status Checklist	RNT	Responsive Naming Test
MSQ	Mental Status Questionnaire	RPMT	Raven's Progressive Matrices Test
NC	number cancellation	RR	relative reports
NFA	name-face association	RT	reaction time
NLT	Name Learning Test	RVIP	raid visual information processing
NOSIE	Nurse's Observation Scale for In-Patients	SB	single blind
		SBI	spontaneous behavior interview
NSAID	nonsteroidal anti-inflammatory drug	SCAGS	Sandoz Clinical Assessment-Geriatric Scale
NVPAL	nonverbal paired-associate learning		
NYUMT	New York University Memory Task	SCWIT	Stroop Color Word Interference Test
OBS-CS	Organic Brain Syndrome — Confusion Scale	SDAT	senile dementia of the Alzheimer's type
OBS-DS	OBS Disorientation Scale	SDMT	Symbol Digit Modality Test
OM	object memory	SGRS	Stockton Geriatric Rating Scale
OP	object placement	SIM	Similarities subtest of the Wechsler Adult Intelligence Test
OR	orientation		
ORT	Object Recognition Task	SKT	Syndrom-Kurztest
OT	Orientation Test	SLT	shopping-list task
PALT	Paired Associates Learning Test	SM	sentence memory

SMT	Spatial Memory Test
SPECT	single-photon emission computed tomography
SPPT	Sperling's Perceptual Trace
SPT	Shepard Picture Test
SR	story recall
SRT	Standardized Roadmap Test
SS	short story
ST	Set Test
SV	sentence verification
SVL	supraspan verbal learning
SVT	Serial Visuographic Task
T & L	tacrine and lecithin
TCD	transcranial Doppler ultrasonography
TET	Time Estimation Task
TG	trigrams
THIP	4,5,6,7-tetrahydroisozalolo(5, 4-c)pyridin-3-ol
TMT	Trail Making Test
TNR	telephone number recall
TPBT	Toulouse-Pieron Barrage Test
TR	tachistoscopic recognition
TRH	thyrotropin-releasing hormone
TT	Token Test
V&V SRT	Visual and Verbal Selective Reminding Tasks
VCPT	Visual Continuous Performance Test
VCRMT	Visual Continuous Recognition Memory Task
VFDT	Visual Form Discrimination Test
VFT	Verbal Fluency Test
VJ	verbal judgment
VL	verbal learning
VMS	Visual Memory Span from WMS
VMT	Visual Memory Task
VOCT	vocabulary test
VPAL	verbal paired-associate learning
VPM	visual pattern matching
VR	visual recognition
VRMT	Verbal Recognition Memory Test
VRT	verbal reproduction task
VSMD	visual search on matrices of digits
VSRT	verbal selective reminding task
VST	visuomotor task
VT	vigilance task
VVLT	Visuo-Verbal Learning Test
WAIS-R	Wechsler Adult Intelligence Scale — Revised
WAT	word association test
WLL	word list learning
WMS	Wechsler Memory Scale
WNA	Walsh neuropsychological approach
WR	word recall
WRT	word recognition task
ZVT	Zahlen Verbindungs Test

REFERENCES

Adolfsson, R., Brane, G., et al. (1982). A double-blind study with levodopa in dementia of Alzheimer type. In S. Corkin, (Ed.), *Alzheimer's disease: A report of progress in research.* New York: Raven Press.

Agid, Y., Dubois, B., Anand, R., et al. (1998). Efficacy and tolerability of rivastigmine in patients with dementia of the Alzheimer type. *Current Therapeutic Research — Clinical and Experimental, 59,* 837–845.

Aisen, P. S., Davis, K. L., Berg, J. D., Schafer, K., Campbell, K., Thomas, R. G., et al. (2000). A randomized controlled trial of prednisone in Alzheimer's disease: Alzheimer's Disease Cooperative Study. *Neurology, 54,* 588–593.

Ala, T., Remero, S., et al. (1990). GM-1 treatment of Alzheimer's disease: A pilot study of safety and efficacy. *Archives of Neurology, 47,* 1126–1130.

Alhainen, K., & Rickkinen, P. J. (1993). Discrimination of Alzheimer's patients responding to cholinesterase inhibitors. *Acta Neurologica Scandinavica, 149,* 16–21.

Amaducci, L., & the SMID Group. (1988). Phosphaditylserine in the treatment of Alzheimer's disease: Results of a multicenter study. *Psychopharmacology Bulletin, 24,* 130–134.

American Psychiatric Association. (1994). *Diagnostic and statistical manual of mental disorders* (4th ed.). Washington, DC: Author.

Andersen, K., Launer, L. J., et al. (1995). Do nonsteroidal anti-inflammatory drugs decrease the risk for Alzheimer's disease. *Neurology, 45,* 1441–1445.

Antuona, P. G. (1995). Effectiveness and safety of velnacrine for the treatment of Alzheimer's disease: A double-blind, placebo controlled study. *Archives of Internal Medicine, 155,* 1766–1772.

Ashford, J. W., Soldinger, S., et al. (1981). Physostigmine and its effect on six patients with dementia. *American Journal of Psychiatry, 138,* 829–830.

Asthana, S., Raffaele, K. C., Bernardi, A., Grieg, N. H., Haxby, J. V., Schapiro, M. B., et al. (1995). Treatment of Alzheimer's disease by continuous infusion of physostigmine. *Alzheimer's Disease and Associated Disorders, 9,* 223–232.

Banen, D. M. (1972). An ergot preparation (Hydergine) for relief of symptoms of cerebrovascular insufficiency. *Journal of the American Geriatric Society, 24,* 22–24.

Barbeau, A. (1980). Lecithin in Parkinson's disease. *Journal of Neural Transmission, 16*(Suppl.), 187–193.

Barrett-Conner, E., & Kritz-Silverstein, D. (1993). Estrogen replacement therapy and cognition in older women. *Journal of the American Medical Association, 269,* 2637–2641.

Battaglia, A., Bruni, G., Ardia, Al, & Saccheti, G. (1989). Nicergoline in mild to moderate dementia: A multicenter, double-blind, placebo-controlled study. *Journal of the American Geriatrics Society, 37,* 295–302.

Bellagamba, G., Postacchini, D., et al. (1990). Acetyl-L-carnitine activity in senile dementia Alzheimer type. *Neurobiology of Aging, 11,* 345.

Beller, S. A., Overall, J. E., Rhoades, H. M., & Swann, A. C. (1988). Long-term outpatient treatment of senile dementia with oral physostigmine. *Journal of Clinical Psychiatry, 49,* 400–404.

Beller, S. A., Overall, J. E., & Swann, A. C. (1985). Efficacy of oral physostigmine in primary degenerative dementia: A double-blind study of response to different dose levels. *Psychopharmacology, 87,* 147–151.

Bierer, L. M., Aisen, P. S., et al. (1994). A pilot study of clonidine plus physostigmine in Alzheimer's disease. *Dementia, 5,* 243–246.

Blass, J. P., Gleason, P., et al. (1988). Thiamine and Alzheimer's disease: A pilot study. *Archives of Neurology, 45,* 833–835.

Bottini, G., Vallar, G., et al. (1992). Oxiracetam in dementia: A double-blind, placebo-controlled study. *Acta Neurologica Scandinavica, 86,* 237–241.

Branconnier, R. J., Cole, J. O., et al. (1983). The therapeutic efficacy of pramiracetam in Alzheimer's disease: Preliminary observations. *Psychopharmacology Bulletin, 19,* 726–730.

Branconnier, R. J., Cole, J. O., & Gardos, G. (1979). ACTH 4–10 in the amelioration of neuropsychological symptomatology associated with senile organic brain syndrome. *Psychopharmacology, 61,* 161–165.

Breitner, J. C. S. (1996). Inflammatory processes and anti-inflammatory drugs in Alzheimer's disease: A current appraisal. *Neurobiology of Aging, 17,* 789–794.

Breitner, J. C., Gau, B. A., Welsh, K. A., Plassman, B. L., McDonald, W. M., Helms, M. J., et al. (1994). Inverse association of anti-inflammatory treatments and Alzheimer's disease: Initial results of a co-twin control study. *Neurology, 44,* 227–232.

Brenner, D. E., Kukull, W. A., et al. (1994). Postmenopausal estrogen replacement therapy and the risk of Alzheimer's disease: A population-based case-control study. *American Journal of Epidemiolgy, 140,* 262–267.

Brinkman, S. D., Pomara, N., et al. (1992). A dose-ranging study of lecithin in the treatment of primary degenerative dementia (Alzheimer disease). *Journal of Clinical Pharmacology, 2,* 281–285.

Bruno, G., Mohr, E., et al. (1986). Muscarinic agonist therapy of Alzheimer's disease: A clinical trial of RS-86. *Archives of Neurology, 43,* 659–661.

Burke, W. J., Ranno, A. K., et al. (1993). L-Deprenyl in the treatment of mild dementia of the Alzheimer type: Preliminary results. *Journal of the American Geriatric Society, 41,* 367–370.

Burns, A., Russell, E., & Page, S. (1999). New drugs for Alzheimer's disease. *British Journal of Psychiatry, 174,* 476–479.

Caamano, J., Gomez, M. J., et al. (1994). Effects of CDP-choline on cognition and cerebral hemodynamics in patients with Alzheimer's disease. *Methods and Findings in Experimental and Clinical Pharmacology, 16,* 211–218.

Calvani, M., Carta, A., Caruso, G., Benedetti, N., Iannuccelli, M. (1992). Action of acetyl-L-carnitine in neurodegeneration and Alzheimer's disease. *Annals of the New York Academy of Sciences, 663,* 483–486.

Campi, N., Todeschini, G. P., & Scarzella, L. (1990). Selegiline versus acetyl-L-carnitine in the treatment of Alzheimer-type dementia. *Clinical Therapeutics, 12,* 306–314.

Canadian Study of Health and Aging. (1994). The Canadian Study of Health and Aging: Risk factors for Alzheimer's disease in Canada. *Neurology, 44,* 2073–2080.

Chase, T. N., Durso, R., et al. (1982). Vasopressin treatment of cognitive deficits in Alzheimer's disease. In S. Corkin, (Ed.), *Alzheimer's disease: A report of progress in research.* New York: Raven Press.

Chatellier, G., & Lacomblez, L. (1990). Tacrine (tetrahydroaminoacridine: THA) and lecithin in senile dementia of the Alzheimer type: A multicenter trial. *British Medical Journal, 300,* 495–499.

Christie, J. E., Shering, A., et al. (1981). Physostigmine and arecoline: Effects of intravenous infusions in Alzheimer presenile dementia. *British Journal of Psychiatry, 138,* 46–50.

Clauss, J. J., Ludwig, C., et al. (1991). Nootropic drugs in Alzheimer's disease: Symptomatic treatment with pramiracetam. *Neurology, 41,* 570–574.

Corey-Bloom, J., Anand, R., Veach, J., et al. (1998). A randomized trial evaluating the efficacy and safety of ENA 713 (rivastigmine tartrate), a new acetylcholinesterase inhibitor, in patients with mild to moderate severe Alzheimer's disease. *Internation-*

al Journal of Geriatric Psychopharmacology, 1, 55–65.

Croisile, B., Trillet, M., Fondarai, J., Laurent, B., Mauguiere, F., & Billardon, M. (1993). Long-term and high-dose piracetam treatment of Alzheimer's disease. *Neurology, 43,* 301–305.

Crook, T., Petrie, W., et al. (1992). Effects of phosphatidylserine in Alzheimer's disease. *Psychopharmacology Bulletin, 28,* 61–66.

Crook, T., Wilner, E., et al. (1992). Noradrenergic intervention in Alzheimer's disease. *Psychopharmacology Bulletin, 28,* 67–70.

Crook, T. H., Tinklenberg, J., et al. (1991). Effects of phosphatidylserine on age-associated memory impairment. *Neurology, 41,* 644–649.

Cutler, N. R., Haxby, J., et al. (1985). Evaluation of zimeldine in Alzheimer's disease: Cognitive and biochemical measures. *Archives of Neurology, 42,* 744–748.

Dal-Bianco, P., Maly, J., et al. (1991). Galanthamine treatment in Alzheimer's disease. *Journal of Neural Transmission, 33*(Suppl.), 59–63.

Davidson, M., Zemishlany, Z., et al. (1988). 4-Aminopyridine in the treatment of Alzheimer's disease. *Biological Psychiatry, 23,* 485–490.

Davis, K. L., Hollander, E., et al. (1987). Induction of depression with oxotremorine in patients with Alzheimer's disease. *American Journal of Psychiatry, 144,* 468–471.

Davis, K. L., & Mohs, R. C. (1982). Enhancement of memory processes in Alzheimer's disease with multiple-dose intravenous physostigmine. *American Journal of Psychiatry, 139,* 1421–1424.

Davis, K. L., Thal, L. J., Gamzu, E. R., Davis, C. S., Woolson, R. F., Gracon, S. I., et al. (1992). A double-blind, placebo-controlled multicenter study of tacrine for Alzheimer's disease. *New England Journal of Medicine, 327,* 1253–1259.

Dehlin, O., Hedenrud, B., et al. (1985). A double-blind comparison of alaproclate and placebo in the treatment of patients with senile dementia. *Acta Psychiatrica Scandinavica, 71,* 190–196.

Delagarza, V. W. (2003). Pharmacologic treatment of Alzheimer's disease: An update. *American Family Physician, 68,* 1365–1372.

Delwaide, P. J., Devoitille, A. R., & Ylieff, M. (1980). Acute effects of drugs on memory of patients with senile dementia. *Acta Psychiatrica Belgica, 80,* 748–754.

Delwaide, P. J., Gyselynck-Mambourg, A. M., et al. (1986). Double-blind randomized controlled study of phosphatidylserine in senile demented patients. *Acta Neurologica Scandinavica, 73,* 136–140.

Durso, R., Fedio, P., et al. (1982). Lysine vasopressin in Alzheimer disease. *Neurology, 32,* 674–677.

Dysken, M. W., Fovall, P., et al. (1982). Lecithin administration in Alzheimer dementia. *Neurology, 32,* 1203–1204.

Dysken, M. W., Mendels, J., et al. (1992). Milacemide: A placebo-controlled study in senile dementia of the Alzheimer type. *Journal of the American Geriatric Society, 40,* 503–506.

Eagger, S. A., et al. (1991). Tacrine in Alzheimer's disease. *Lancet, 337,* 989–992.

Eagger, S. A., et al. (1992). Tacrine in Alzheimer's disease: Time course of changes in cognitive function and practice effects. *British Journal of Psychiatry, 16,* 36–40.

Eagger, S. A., Levy, R., & Sahakain, B. J. (1992). Tacrine in Alzheimer's disease. *Acta Neurologica Scandinavica, 139*(Suppl.), 75–80.

Ebmeier, K. P., Hunter, R., et al. (1992). Effects of a single dose of the acetylcholinesterase inhibitor velnacrine on recognition memory and regional cerebral blood flow in Alzheimer's disease. *Psychopharmacology, 108,* 103–109.

Etienne, P., Dastoor, D., et al. (1981). Alzheimer's disease: Lack of effect of lecithin treatment for 3 months. *Neurology, 31,* 1552–1554.

Falsaperla, A., Preti, P. A. M., & Oliani, C. (1990). Selegiline versus oxiracetam in patients with Alzheimer-type dementia. *Clinical Therapeutics, 12,* 376–384.

Farlow, M., Gracon, S. I., et al. (1992). A controlled trial of tacrine in Alzheimer's disease. *Journal of the American Medical Association, 268,* 2523–2529.

Ferris, S., Mann, J. J., Stanley, M., et al. (1981). Central amine metabolism in Alzheimer's disease: In vivo relationship to cognitive performance. *Neurobiology of Aging, 2,* 57–60.

Ferris, S. H., Sathananthan, G., et al. (1979). Long-term choline treatment of memory-impaired elderly patients. *Science, 205,* 1039–1040.

Fillit, H., Weinreb, H., Cholst, I., Luine, V., McEwen, B., Amador, R., et al. (1986). Observations in a preliminary open trial of estradiol therapy for senile dementia-Alzheimer's type. *Psychoneuroendocrinology, 11,* 337–345.

Finali, G., Piccirilli, M., et al. (1991). L-Deprenyl therapy improves verbal memory in amnesic Alzheimer's patients. *Clinical Neuropharmacology, 14,* 523–536.

Fitten, L. J., Perryman, K. M., et al. (1990). Treatment of Alzheimer's disease with short- and long-term oral THA and lecithin: A double-blind study. *American Journal of Psychiatry, 147,* 239–242.

Fleischhacker, W. W., Buchgeher, A., & Schubert, H. (1986). Memantine in the treatment of senile dementia of the Alzheimer type. *Progress in Neuro-Psychopharmacology and Biological Psychiatry, 10*, 87–93.

Flicker, C., Ferris, S. H., & Reisberg, B. (1991). Mild cognitive impairment in the elderly: Predictors of dementia. *Neurology, 41*, 1006–1009.

Garcia, C. A., Tweedy, J. R., et al. (1982). Lecithin and Parkinsonian dementia. In S. Corkin, (Ed.), *Alzheimer's disease: A report of progress in research.* New York: Raven Press.

Gauthier, S., Bouchard, R., et al. (1990). Tetrahydroaminoacridine-lecithin combination treatment in patients with intermediate stage Alzheimer's disease. *New England Journal of Medicine, 322*, 1272–1276.

Goad, D. L., Davis, C. M., et al. (1991). The use of selegline in Alzheimer's patients with behavior problems. *Journal of Clinical Psychiatry, 52*, 342–345.

Green, R. C., Goldstein, F. C., et al. (1992). Treatment trial of oxiracetam in Alzheimer's disease. *Archives of Neurology, 49*, 1135–1136.

Growden, J. H., Corkin, S., et al. (1986). Piracetam combined with lecithin in the treatment of Alzheimer's disease. *Neurobiology of Aging, 7*, 296–276.

Gustafson, L. (1993). Physostigmine and tetrahydroaminoacridine treatment of Alzheimer's disease. *Acta Neurologica Scandinavica, 149*, 39–41.

Gustafson, L., Edvinson, L., et al. (1987). Intravenous physostigmine treatment of Alzheimer's disease evaluated by psychometric testing, regional cerebral blood flow (rCBF) measurement, and EEG. *Psychopharmacology, 93*, 31–35.

Hagino, N., Ohkura, T., et al. (1995). Estrogen in clinical trials for dementia of Alzheimer type. In I. Hanin, M. Yoshida, & A. Fisher (Eds.), *Alzheimer's and Parkinson's diseases: Recent developments.* New York: Plenum Press.

Harbaugh, R. E., Reeder, T. M., et al. (1989). Intracerebroventricular bethanechol chloride infusion in Alzheimer's disease: Results of a collaborative double-blind study. *Journal of Neurosurgery, 71*, 481–486.

Harbaugh, R. E., Roberts, D. W., et al. (1984). Preliminary report: Intracranial cholinergic drug infusion in patients with Alzheimer's disease. *Neurosurgery, 15*, 514–518.

Harrell, L. E., Callaway, R., et al. (1990). The effect of long-term physostigmine administration in Alzheimer's disease. *Neurology, 40*, 1350–1354.

Harrell, L. E., Jope, R. S., et al. (1990). Biological and neuropsychological characterization of physostigmine responders and nonresponders in Alzheimer's disease. *Journal of the American Geriatric Society, 38*, 113–122.

Heiss, W. D., Hebold, I., et al. (1988). Effect of piracetam on cerebral glucose metabolism in Alzheimer's disease as measured by positron emission tomography. *Journal of Cerebral Blood Flow and Metabolism, 8*, 613–617.

Heiss, W. D., Kessler, J., et al. (1994). Long-term effects of phosphatidylserine, pyritinol, and cognitive training in Alzheimer's disease: A neuropsychological, EEG, and PET investigation. *Dementia, 5*, 88–98.

Henderson, V. W., Paganini-Hill, A., et al. (1994). Estrogen replacement therapy in older women: Comparisons between Alzheimer's disease cases and nondemented control subjects. *Archives of Neurology, 51*, 896–900.

Henderson, V. W., Paganini-Hill, A., Miller, B. L., Elble, R. J., Reyes, P. F., Shoupe, D., et al. (2000). Estrogen for Alzheimer's disease in women: Randomized, double-blind, placebo-controlled trial. *Neurology, 54*, 295–301.

Henderson, V. W., Roberts, E., et al. (1989). Multicenter trial of naloxone in Alzheimer's disease. *Annals of Neurology, 25*, 404–406.

Heyman, A., Schmechel, D., et al. (1987). Failure of long-term high-dose lecithin to retard progression of early-onset Alzheimer's disease. *Journal of Neural Transmission, 24*(Suppl.), 279–286.

Hollander, E., Davidson, M., et al. (1987). RS 86 in the treatment of Alzheimer's disease: Cognitive and biological effects. *Biological Psychiatry, 22*, 1067–1078.

Hollingsworth, S. W. (1980). Response of geriatric patients from the satellite nursing homes of Maricopa County to Hydergine therapy: A double-blind study. *Current Therapeutic Research, 27*, 401–410.

Hollister, L. E., & Yesavage, J. (1984). Ergoloid mesylates for senile dementias: Unanswered questions. *Annals of Internal Medicine, 100*, 894–898.

Honjo, H., Ogino, Y., Naitoh, K., Ruabe, M., Kitawaki, J., Yasuda, J., et al. (1989). In vivo effects by estrone sulfate on the central nervous system: Senile dementia (Alzheimer's type). *Journal of Steroid Biochemistry, 34*, 521–525.

Hyman, B., Eslinger, P. J., & Damasio, A. R. (1982). Effect of naltrexone on senile dementia of the Alzheimer type. *Journal of Neurology, Neurosurgery, and Psychiatry, 49*, 1321–1322.

Ihl, R., Perisic, I., & Dierks, T. (1989). Effects of 3 months of treatment with tenilsetam in patients suffering from dementia of the Alzheimer type (DAT). *Journal of Neural Transmission, 1*(Sec. P-D), 84–85.

Imagawa, M. (1990). Therapy with a combination of co-enzyme Q10, vitamin B6 and iron for Alzheimer's disease and senile dementia of the Alzheimer type. In K. Iqbal, D. R. C. McLachlan, et al. (Eds.), *Alzheimer's disease: Basic mechanisms, diagnosis and therapeutic strategies.* New York: Wiley.

Imagawa, M. (1992). Coenzyme Q, iron, and vitamin B-6 in genetically confirmed Alzheimer's disease. *Lancet, 340,* 671.

Jenicke, M. A., Albert, M. S., et al. (1986). Combination therapy with lecithin and ergoloid mesylates for Alzheimer's disease. *Journal of Clinical Psychiatry, 47,* 249–251.

Jenicke, M. A., Albert, M. S., et al. (1990). Oral physostigmine treatment for patients with presenile and senile dementia of the Alzheimer type: A double-blind placebo-controlled trial. *Journal of Clinical Psychiatry, 51,* 3–7.

Jennings, W. G. (1972). An ergot alkaloid preparation (Hydergine) versus placebo for treatment of symptoms of cerebrovascular insufficiency: Double-blind study. *Journal of the American Geriatric Society, 20,* 407–412.

Jones, G. M. M., Sahakian, B. J., et al. (1992). Effects of acute subcutaneous nicotine on attention, information processing and short-term memory in Alzheimer's disease. *Psychopharmacology, 108,* 485–494.

Jones, R. W., Passmore, P., & Wetterberg, P. (2002, April). *First head-to-head study comparing the tolerability and the efficacy of donepezil and galantamine in Alzheimer's disease.* Paper presented at the Seventh International Geneva/Springfield Symposium on Advances in Alzheimer Therapy (AAT), Geneva, Switzerland.

Jotkowitz, S. (1983). Lack of clinical efficacy of chronic oral physostigmine in Alzheimer's disease. *Annals of Neurology, 14,* 690–691.

Kaduszkiewicz, H., Zimmermann, T., Beck-Bornholdt, H. P., & van den Bussche, H. (2005). Cholinesterase inhibitors for patients with Alzheimer's disease: Systematic review of randomized clinical trials. *British Medical Journal, 331,* 321–337.

Kaufer, D. I., Cummings, J., & Christine, D. (1996). Effect of tacrine on behavioral symptoms in Alzheimer's disease: An open label study. *Journal of Geriatric Psychiatry and Neurology, 9,* 1–6.

Kaye, W. H., Weingartner, H., et al. (1982). Cognitive effects of cholinergic and vasopressinlike agents in patients with primary degenerative dementia. In S. Corkin, (Ed.), *Alzheimer's disease: A report of progress in research.* New York: Raven Press.

Knapp, M. J., Knopman, D. S., et al. (1994). A 30-week randomized controlled trial of high-dose tacrine in patients with Alzheimer's disease. *Journal of the American Medical Association, 271,* 985–991.

Knopman, D. S., & Hartman, M. (1986). Cognitive effects of high-dose naltrexone in patients with probable Alzheimer's disease. *Journal of Neurology, Neurosurgery, and Psychiatry, 49,* 1321–1322.

Knopman, D., Schneider, L., Davis, K., et al. (1996). Long term tacrine (Cognex) treatment: Effects on nursing home placement and mortality, Tacrine Study Group. *Neurology, 47,* 166–177.

Koller, W., & Megaffin, B. B. (1994). Parkinson's disease and Parkinsonism. In C. E. Coffey & J. L. Cummings (Eds.), *Textbook of geriatric neuropsychiatry* (pp. 433–456). Washington, DC: American Psychiatric Press.

Kragh-Sorensen, P., Olsen, R. B., et al. (1986). Neuropeptides: ACTH-peptides in dementia. *Progress in Neuro-Psychopharmacology and Biological Psychiatry, 10,* 479–492.

Lampe, T. H., Norris, J., et al. (1990). Therapeutic potential of thyrotropin-releasing hormone and lecithin co-administration in Alzheimer's disease. In K. Iqbal, D. R. C., McLachlan, et al. (Eds.), *Alzheimer's disease: Basic mechanisms, diagnosis, and therapeutic strategies.* New York: Wiley.

Lampe, T. H., Norris, S. C., Risse, E., et al. (1991). Therapeutic potential of thyrotropin-releasing hormone and lecithin coadministration in Alzheimer's disease. In K. Equable, D. R. C. McLachlan, B. Winblad, & H. M. Wisniewski (Eds.), *Alzheimer's disease: Basic mechanisms, diagnosis, and therapeutic strategies* New York: Wiley.

Lanctot, K. L., Herrmann, N., Yau, K. K., Kahn, L. R., Liu, B. A., LouLou, M. M., et al. (2003). Efficacy and safety of cholinesterase inhibitors in Alzheimer's disease: A meta-analysis. *Canadian Medical Association Journal, 169,* 557–564.

Lebowitz, B., & Crook, T. (1991). Treatment of adult-onset cognitive disorders: Results of multicenter trials. *Psychopharmacology Bulletin, 27,* 41–46.

Little, A., Levy, R., et al. (1985). A double-blind, placebo-controlled trial of high-dose lecithin in Alzheimer's disease. *Journal of Neurology, Neurosurgery, and Psychiatry, 48,* 736–742.

Maltby, N., Broe, G. A., et al. (1994). Efficacy of tacrine and lecithin in mild to moderate Alzheimer's disease: Double blind trial. *British Medical Journal, 308,* 879–883.

Mangoni, A., Grassi, M. P., et al. (1991). Effects of a MAO-B inhibitor in the treatment of Alzheimer's disease. *European Neurology, 31,* 100–107.

Marder, K., Flood, P., & Cote, L. (1990). A pilot study of risk factors for dementia in Parkinson's disease. *Movement Disorders, 5,* 156–161.

Marin, D. B., Bierer, L. M., et al. (1995). L-Deprenyl and physostigmine for the treatment of Alzheimer's disease. *Psychiatry Research, 58*, 181–189.

Matejcek, M., Knor, K., et al. (1979). Electroencephalographic and clinical changes in geriatric patients treated 3 months with alkaloid preparation. *Journal of the American Geriatric Society, 27*, 198–202.

Mayeux, R., Chen, J., & Mirabello, E. (1990). An estimate of the incidence of dementia in idiopathic Parkinson's disease. *Neurology, 40*, 1513–1517.

McConnachie, R. W. (1973). A clinical trial comparing "Hydergine" with placebo in the treatment of cerebrovascular insufficiency in elderly patients. *Current Medical Research and Opinion, 1*, 463–468.

McGeer, P. L., McGeer, E., Rodgers, J., & Sibley, J. (1990). Anti-inflammatory drugs and Alzheimer's disease. *Lancet, 335*, 1037.

McLachlan, D. R. C., Dalton, A. J., et al. (1991). Intramuscular desferrioxamine in patients with Alzheimer's disease. *Lancet, 337*, 1304–1308.

Meador, K., Loring, D., et al. (1993). Preliminary findings of high-dose thiamine in dementia of the Alzheimer type. *Journal of Geriatric Psychiatry and Neurology, 6*, 222–229.

Mellow, A. M., Aronson, S. M., Giordani, B., & Berent, S. (1993). A peptide enhancement strategy in Alzheimer's disease: Pilot study with TRH-physostigmine infusions. *Biological Psychiatry, 34*, 271–273.

Mellow, A. M., Sunderland, T., et al. (1989). Acute effects of high-dose thyrotropin releasing hormone infusions in Alzheimer's disease. *Psychopharmacology, 98*, 403–407.

Miller, T. P., Fong, K., & Tinklenberg, J. R. (1993). An ACTH 4–9 analog (ORG 2766) and cognitive performance: High-dose efficacy and safety in dementia of the Alzheimer's type. *Biological Psychiatry, 33*, 307–309.

Minthon, L., Gustafson, L., et al. (1993). Oral tetrahydroaminoacridine treatment of Alzheimer's disease evaluated clinically by regional cerebral blood flow and EEG. *Dementia, 4*, 32–42.

Mohr, E., Bruno, G., et al. (1986). GABA-agonist therapy for Alzheimer's disease. *Clinical Neuropharmacology, 9*, 257–263.

Mohr, E., Schlegel, J., et al. (1989). Clonidine treatment of Alzheimer's disease. *Archives of Neurology, 46*, 376–378.

Mohs, R. C., Davis, B. M., et al. (1985). Oral physostigmine treatment of patients with Alzheimer's disease. *American Journal of Psychiatry, 142*, 28–33.

Molloy, D. W., Guyatt, G. H., et al. (1991). Effect of tetrahydroaminoacridine on cognition, function and behavior in Alzheimer's disease. *Canadian Medical Association Journal, 144*, 29–34.

Monteverde, A., Gnemmi, P., et al. (1990). Selegiline in the treatment of mild to moderate Alzheimer-type dementia. *Clinical Therapeutics, 12*, 315–322.

Mortimer, J. A., Ebbitt, B., Jun, S. P., & Finch, M. D. (1992). Predictors of cognitive and functional progression in patients with probable Alzheimer's disease. *Neurology, 42*, 1689–1696.

Mouradian, M. M., Mohr, E., et al. (1988). No response to high-dose muscarinic agonist therapy in Alzheimer's disease. *Neurology, 38*, 606–608.

Mouradian, M. M., Thin, J., et al. (1991). Somatostatin replacement therapy for Alzheimer disease. *Annals of Neurology, 30*, 610–613.

Mulnard, R. A., Cotman, C. W., Kawas, C., van Dyck, C. H., Sano, M., Doody, R., et al. (2000). Estrogen replacement therapy for treatment of mild to moderate Alzheimer disease: A randomized controlled trial. *Journal of the American Medical Association, 283*, 1007–1015.

Muramoto, O., Sugishia, M., et al. (1979). Effect of physostigmine on constructional and memory tasks in Alzheimer's disease. *Archives of Neurology, 36*, 501–503.

Muramoto, O., Sugishia, M., & Ando, K. (1984). Cholinergic system and constructional praxis: A further study of physostigmine in Alzheimer's disease. *Journal of Neurology, Neurosurgery, and Psychiatry, 47*, 485–491.

Murphy, M. F., Hardiman, S. T., et al. (1991). Evaluation of HP 029 (velnacrine maleate) in Alzheimer's disease. *Annals of the New York Academy of Sciences, 640*, 253–262.

Newhouse, P. A., Sunderland, T., et al. (1988). Intravenous nicotine in Alzheimer's disease: A pilot study. *Psychopharmacology, 95*, 171–175.

Nicergoline Study Group. (1990). A double-blind randomized study of two ergot derivatives in mild to moderate dementia. *Current Therapeutic Research, 48*, 597–612.

Nolan, K. A., Black, R. S., et al. (1991). A trial of thiamine in Alzheimer's disease. *Archives of Neurology, 48*, 81–83.

Novo, F. P., Ryan, R. P., & Frazier, E. L. (1978). Dihydroergotexine mesylate in the treatment of symptoms of idiopathic cerebral dysfunction in geriatric patients. *Clinical Therapeutics, 1*, 359–369.

Ohkura, T., Isse, K., Akazawa, K., Hamamoto, M., Yaoi, Y., Hagino, N. (1995). Long-term estrogen replacement therapy in female patients with dementia of the Alzheimer type: Seven case reports. *Dementia, 6*, 99–107.

Ohlin, J., Schneider, L., Novit, Al, Luczak, S. (2000). Hydergine for dementia. *Cochrane Database System Review, 2,* CD000359.

Panella, J. J., & Blass, J. P. (1984). Lack of clinical benefit for naloxone in a dementia day hospital. *Annals of Neurology, 15,* 306–307.

Passeri, M., Cucinotta, D., et al. (1990). Acetyl-L-carnitine in the treatment of mildly demented elderly patients. *International Journal of Clinical Pharmacology Research, 10,* 75–79.

Peabody, C. A., Davis, H., et al. (1986). Desamino-D-arginine-vasopressin (DDAVP) in Alzheimer's disease. *Neurobiology of Aging, 7,* 301–303.

Peabody, C. A., Deblois, T. E., & Tinklenberg, J. R. (1986). Thyrotropin-releasing hormone (TRH) and Alzheimer's disease. *American Journal of Psychiatry, 143,* 262–263.

Peabody, C. A., Thiemann, O., et al. (1985). Desglycinamide-9-arginine-8-vasopressin (DGAVP, Organon 5667) in patients with dementia. *Neurobiology of Aging, 6,* 95–100.

Penn, R. D., Martin, E. M., et al. (1988). Intraventricular bethanechol infusion for Alzheimer's disease: Results of double-blind and escalating-dose trials. *Neurology, 38,* 219–222.

Perryman, K. M., & Fitten, L. J. (1993). Delayed matching-to-sample performance during a double-blind trial of tacrine (THA) and lecithin in patients with Alzheimer's disease. *Life Sciences, 53,* 479–486.

Peters, B. H., & Levin, H. S. (1979). Effects of physostigmine and lecithin on memory in Alzheimer's disease. *Annals of Neurology, 6,* 219–221.

Pettegrew, J. W. (1989). Molecular insights into Alzheimer's disease. *Annals of the New York Academy of Sciences, 568,* 5–28.

Pettegrew, J. W., Klunk, W. E., et al. (1995). Clinical and neurochemical effects of acetyl-L-carnitine in Alzheimer's disease. *Neurobiology of Aging, 16,* 1–4.

Piccinin, G. L., Finali, G., & Piccirilli, M. (1990). Neuropsychological effects of L-deprenyl in Alzheimer's type dementia. *Clinical Neuropharmacology, 13,* 147–163.

Pollack, M., & Hornabook, R. W. (1966). The prevalence, natural history, and dementia of Parkinson's disease. *Brain, 89,* 429–448.

Pomara, N., Goodnick, P. J., et al. (1982). A dose-response study of lecithin in the treatment of Alzheimer's disease. In S. Corkin, (Ed.), *Alzheimer's disease: A report of progress in research.* New York: Raven Press.

Pomara, N., Roberts, R., et al. (1985). Multiple, single dose naltrexone administrations fail to affect overall cognitive functioning and plasma cortisol in individuals with probable Alzheimer's disease. *Neurobiology of Aging, 6,* 233–236.

Raffaele, K. C., Berardi, A., Asthana, S., et al. (1991). Effects of long-term continuous infusion of the muscarinic cholinergic agonist arecoline on verbal memory in dementia of the Alzheimer's type. *Psychopharmacology, 27,* 315–319.

Raffaele, K. C., Berardi, A., Morris, P. P., et al. (1991). Effects of acute infusion of the muscarinic cholinergic agonist arecoline on verbal memory and visuo-spatial function in dementia of the Alzheimer's type. *Progress in Neuro-Psychopharmacology and Biological Psychiatry, 15,* 643–648.

Rai, G., Wright, G., et al. (1990). Double-blind, placebo controlled study of acetyl-L-carnitine in patients with Alzheimer's dementia. *Current Medical Research and Opinion, 11,* 638–647.

Rapp, S. R., Espeland, M. A., Shumaker, S. A., Henderson, V. W., Brunner, R. L., Manson, J. E., et al. (2003) Effect of estrogen plus progestin on global cognitive function in postmenopausal women: The Women's Health Initiative Memory Study: A randomized controlled trial. *Journal of the American Medical Association. 289,* 2717–2719.

Raskind, M. A., Peskind, E. R., Wessel, T., et al. (2000). Galantamine in AD: A 6-month randomized, placebo-controlled trial with a 6-month extension. *Neurology, 54,* 2261–2268.

Rechman, S. A. (1973). Two trials comparing "Hydergine" with placebo in the treatment of patients suffering from cerebrovascular insufficiency. *Current Medical Research and Opinion, 1,* 456–462.

Reisberg, B., Doody, R., Stoffler, A., Schmitt, F., Ferris, S., Mobius, H. J., et al. (2003). Memantine in moderate-to-severe Alzheimer's disease. *New England Journal of Medicine, 348,* 1333–1341.

Reisberg, B., Ferris, S. H., et al. (1983a). Effects of naloxone in senile dementia: A double-blind trial. *New England Journal of Medicine, 308,* 721–722.

Reisberg, B., Ferris, S. H., et al. (1983b). Naloxone effects on primary degenerative dementia (PDD). *Psychopharmacology Bulletin, 19,* 45–47.

Renvoize, E. B., & Jerram, T. (1979). Choline in Alzheimer's disease. *New England Journal of Medicine, 301,* 330.

Rich, J. B., Rasmusson, D. X., et al. (1995). Nonsteroidal anti-inflammatory drugs in Alzheimer's disease. *Neurology, 45,* 51–55.

Rodgers, S., Friedhof, L., & the Donepezil Study Group. (1996). The efficacy and safety of donepezil in patients with Alzheimer's disease: Results of a U.S. multicenter, randomized, double-blind, placebo-controlled trial. *Dementia, 7,* 293–303.

Rogers, L., Kirby, L. C., et al. (1993). Clinical trial of indomethacin in Alzheimer's disease. *Neurology, 43,* 1609–1611.

Rogers, S. L., Doody, R. S., Mohs, R. C., et al. (1998a). Donepezil improves cognition and global function in Alzheimer's disease: A 15-week, double-blind, placebo-controlled study. *Archives of Internal Medicine, 158,* 1021–1031.

Rogers, S. L., Farlow, M. R., Doody, R. S., et al. (1998b). A 24-week, double-blind, placebo-controlled trial of donepezil in patients with Alzheimer's disease. *Neurology, 50,* 136–145.

Rosler, M., Anand, R., Cicin-Sain, A., et al. (1999). Efficacy and safety of rivastigmine in patients with Alzheimer's disease: International randomized controlled trial. *British Medical Journal, 318,* 633–640.

Rouy, J. M., Douillon, A. M., et al. (1989). Ergoloid mesylates ("Hydergine") in the treatment of mental deterioration in the elderly: A 6-month double-blind, placebo-controlled trial. *Current Medical Research and Opinion, 11,* 380–389.

Ruther, E., Ritter, R., et al. (1994). Efficacy of the peptidic nootropic drug cerebrolysin in patients with senile dementia of the Alzheimer type (SDAT). *Pharmacopsychiatrist, 27,* 32–40.

Sahakian, B. J., & Coull, J. T. (1993). Tetrahydroaminoacridine (THA) in Alzheimer's disease: An assessment of attentional and mnemonic function using CANTAB. *Acta Neurologica Scandinavica, 149,* 29–35.

Sahakian, B., Jones, G., et al. (1989). The effects of nicotine on attention, information processing, and short-term memory in patients with dementia of the Alzheimer type. *British Journal of Psychiatry, 154,* 797–800.

Saletu, B., Anderer, P., et al. (1992). EEG mapping and psychopharmacological studies with denbufylline in SDAT and MID. *Biological Psychiatry, 32,* 668–681.

Saletu, B., Paulus, E., et al. (1994). Nicergoline in senile dementia of Alzheimer type and multi-infarct dementia: A double-blind, placebo-controlled, clinical and EEG/ERP mapping study. *Psychopharmacology, 117,* 385–395.

Sano, M., Bell, K., et al. (1992). Double-blind parallel design pilot study of acetyl levocarnitine in patients with Alzheimer's disease. *Archives of Neurology, 49,* 1137–1141.

Sano, M., Bell, K., et al. (1993). Safety and efficacy of oral physostigmine in the treatment of Alzheimer disease. *Clinical Neuropharmacology, 16,* 61–69.

Sano, M., Ernesto, C., Thomas, R. G., et al. (1997). A controlled trial of selegiline, alpha-tocopherol, or both as treatment of Alzheimer's disease: The Alzheimer's Disease Cooperative Study. *New England Journal of Medicine, 336,* 1216–1222.

Sano, M., Stern, Y., et al. (1990). A controlled trial of piracetam in intellectually impaired patients with Parkinson's disease. *Movement Disorders, 5,* 230–234.

Scharf, S., Mander, A., Ugoni, A., Vajda, F., Christophidis, N. (1999). A double-blind, placebo-controlled trial of diclofenac/misoprostol in Alzheimer's disease. *Neurology, 53,* 197–201.

Scherder, E. J. A., Bouma, A., & Steen, A. M. (1995). Effects of short-term transcutaneous electrical nerve stimulation on memory and affective behaviour in patients with probable Alzheimer's disease. *Behavioural Brain Research, 67,* 211–219.

Schlegel, J., Mohr, E., et al. (1989). Guanfacine treatment of Alzheimer's disease. *Clinical Neuropharmacology, 12,* 124–128.

Schneider, L. S., Farlow, M. R., & Henderson, V. W. (1996). Effects of estrogen replacement therapy on response to tacrine in patients with Alzheimer's disease. *Neurology, 46,* 1580–1584.

Schneider, L. S., & Olin, J. T. (1994). Overview of clinical trials of Hydergine in dementia. *Archives of Neurology, 51,* 787–798.

Schneider, L., Olin, J. T., & Pawluczyk, S. (1993). A double-blind crossover pilot study of L-deprenyl (selegiline) combined with cholinesterase inhibitor in Alzheimer's disease. *American Journal of Psychiatry, 150,* 321–333.

Schneider, L. S., Pollock, V. E., et al. (1991). A pilot study of low-dose L-deprenyl in Alzheimer's disease. *Journal of Geriatric Psychiatry and Neurology, 4,* 143–148.

Schneider, L. S., & Tariot, P. N. (1994). Emerging drugs for Alzheimer's disease. *Medical Clinics of North America, 78,* 911–934.

Schwartz, A. S., & Kohlstaedt, E. V. (1986). Physostigmine in Alzheimer's disease: Relationship to dementia severity. *Life Sciences, 38,* 1021–1028.

Serby, M., Resnick, R., et al. (1986). Naltrexone and Alzheimer's disease. *Progress in Neuro-Psychopharmacology and Biological Psychiatry, 10,* 587–590.

Sevush, S., Guterman, A., & Villalon, A. V. (1991). Improved verbal learning after outpatient oral physostigmine therapy in patients with dementia of the Alzheimer type. *Journal of Clinical Psychiatry, 52,* 300–303.

Shumaker, S. A., Legault, C., Rapp, S. R., Thal, L., Wallace, R. B., Ockene, J. K., et al (2003). Estrogen plus progestin and the incidence of dementia and mild cognitive impairment in postmentopausal women: The Women's Health Initiative Memory Study: A randomized control trial. *Journal of the American Medical Association, 289,* 2651–2662.

Sigfried, K. R. (1993). Pharmacodynamic and early clinical trials with velnacrine. *Acta Neurologica Scandinavica, 149,* 26–28.

Sinforiani, E., Iannuccelli, M., et al. (1990). Neuropsychological changes in demented patients treated with acetyl-L-carnitine. *International Journal of Clinical Pharmacology Research, 10,* 69–74.

Smith, C. M., Swase, M., et al. (1978). Choline therapy in Alzheimer's disease. *Lancet, 2,* 318.

Smith, D. E., Stromgren, E., et al. (1984). Lack of effect of tryptophan treatment in demented gerontopsychiatric patients. *Acta Psychiatrica Scandinavica, 70,* 470–477.

Smith, R. C., Vroulis, G., et al. (1984). Comparison of therapeutic response to long-term treatment with lecithin versus piracetam plus lecithin in patients with Alzheimer's disease. *Psychopharmacology Bulletin, 20,* 542–545.

Soininen, H., Koskinen, T., et al. (1985). Treatment of Alzheimer's disease with a synthetic ACTH49 analog. *Neurology, 35,* 1348–1351.

Soncrant, T. T., Raffaele, K. C., et al. (1993). Memory improvement without toxicity during chronic, low dose intravenous arecoline in Alzheimer's disease. *Psychopharmacology, 112,* 421–427.

Soni, S. D., & Soni, S. S. (1975). Dihydrogenated alkaloids of ergotexine in non-hospitalised elderly patients. *Current Medical Research and Opinion, 3,* 464–468.

Sourander, L. B., Portin, R., et al. (1987). Senile dementia of the Alzheimer type treated with aniracetam: A new nootropic agent. *Psychopharmacology, 91,* 90–95.

Spagnoli, A., Lucca, U., et al. (1991). Long-term acetyl-L-carnitine treatment in Alzheimer's disease. *Neurology, 41,* 1726–1732.

Steiger, W. A., Mendelson, M., et al. (1985). Effects of naloxone in treatment of senile dementia. *Journal of the American Geriatric Society, 33,* 155.

Stern, Y., Sano, M., & Mayeux, R. (1987). Effects of oral physostigmine in Alzheimer's disease. *Annals of Neurology, 22,* 306–310.

Stern, Y., Sano, M., & Mayeux, R. (1988). Long-term administration of oral physostigmine in Alzheimer's disease. *Neurology, 38,* 1837–1841.

Sullivan, E. V., Shedlack, K. J., et al. (1982). Physostigmine and lecithin in Alzheimer's disease. In S. Corkin, (Ed.), *Alzheimer's disease: A report of progress in research.* New York: Raven Press.

Summers, W. K., Majovski, L. V., et al. (1986). Oral tetrahydroaminoacridine in long-term treatment of senile dementia, Alzheimer type. *New England Journal of Medicine, 315,* 1241–1245.

Summers, W. K., & Viesselman, J. O. (1981). Use of THA in treatment of Alzheimer-like dementia: pilot study in 12 patients. *Biological Psychiatry, 16,* 145–153.

Tang, M. X., Jacobs, D., Stern, Y., Marder, K., Schofield, P., Gurland, B., et al. (1996). Effect of estrogen during menopause on risk and age at onset of Alzheimer's disease. *Lancet, 348,* 429–432.

Tariot, P. N., Cohen, R. M., et al. (1987). L-Deprenyl in Alzheimer's disease: Preliminary evidence for behavioral change with monoamine oxidase B inhibitors. *Archives of General Psychiatry, 44,* 427–433.

Tariot, P. N., Cohen, R. M., et al. (1988). Multiple-dose arecoline infusions in Alzheimer's disease. *Archives of General Psychiatry, 45,* 901–905.

Tariot, P. N., Solomon, P. R., Morris, J. C., et al. (2000). A 5 month, randomized, placebo-controlled trial of galantamine in AD. *Neurology, 54,* 2269–2276.

Tariot, P. N., Sunderland, T., et al. (1986). Naloxone and Alzheimer's disease: Cognitive and behavioral effects of a range of doses. *Archives of General Psychiatry, 43,* 727–732.

Tariot, P. N., Sunderland, T., et al. (1987). Cognitive effects of L-deprenyl in Alzheimer's disease. *Psychopharmacology, 91,* 489–495.

Tennant, F. S. (1987). Preliminary observations on naltrexone for the treatment of Alzheimer's type dementia. *Journal of the American Geriatric Society, 35,* 369–370.

Thal, L. (1994). Future directions for research in Alzheimer's disease. *Neurobiology of Aging, 15*(Suppl. 2), S71–S72.

Thal, L. J., Carta, A., Clarke, W. R., Ferris, S. H., Friedland, R. P., Petersen, R. C., et al. (1996). A 1-year multicenter placebo-controlled study of acetyl-L-carnitine in patients with Alzheimer's disease. *Neurology, 47,* 705–711.

Thal, L. J., Fuld, P. A., Masure, D. M., & Sharpless, N. S. (1983). Oral physostigmine and lecithin improve memory in Alzheimer's disease. *Annals of Neurology, 13,* 491–496.

Thal, L. J., Masur, D. M., et al. (1986). Acute and chronic effects of oral physostigmine and lecithin in Alzheimer's disease. *Progress in Neuro-Psychopharmacology and Biological Psychiatry, 10,* 627–636.

Thal, L. J., Masur, D. M., et al. (1989). Chronic oral physostigmine without lecithin improves memory in Alzheimer's disease. *Journal of the American Geriatric Society, 37,* 42–48.

Thal, L. J., Rosen, W., et al. (1981). Choline chloride fails to improve cognition in Alzheimer's disease. *Neurobiology of Aging, 2,* 205–208.

Thal, L. J., Salmon, D. P., et al. (1989). The safety and lack of efficacy of vinpocetine in Alzheimer's disease. *Journal of the American Geriatric Society, 37,* 515–520.

Thibault, A. (1974). A double-blind evaluation of "Hydergine" and placebo in the treatment of patients with organic brain syndrome and cerebral arteriosclerosis in a nursing home. *Current Medical Research and Opinion, 2,* 482–487.

Thienhaus, O. J., Wheeler, B. G., et al. (1987). A controlled double-blind study of high-dose dihydroergotexine mesylate (Hydergine) in mild dementia. *Journal of the American Geriatric Society, 35,* 219–223.

Thompson, T. L., Filly, C. M., et al. (1990). Lack of efficacy of Hydergine in patients with Alzheimer's disease. *New England Journal of Medicine, 323,* 445–448.

Tinklenberg, J. R., Pfefferbaum, A., & Berger, P. A. (1981). l-Desamino-D-arginine vasopressin (DDAVP) in cognitively impaired patients. *Psychopharmacology Bulletin, 17,* 206–207.

Tinklenberg, J. R., Pigache, R., et al. (1982). Desglycinamide-9-arginine-8-vasopressin (DGAVP, Organon 5667) in cognitively impaired patients. *Psychopharmacology Bulletin, 18,* 202–204.

Tollefson, G. D. (1990). Short-term effects of the calcium channel blocker nimodepine (Bay-e-9736) in the management of primary degenerative dementia. *Biological Psychiatry, 27,* 1133–1142.

Triboletti, F., & Ferri, H. (1969). Hydergine for treatment of symptoms of cerebrovascular insufficiency. *Current Therapeutic Research, 11,* 609–620.

Urakami, K., Shimomura, T., et al. (1993). Clinical effect of WEB 1881 (nebracetam fumarate) on patients with dementia of the Alzheimer type and study of its clinical pharmacology. *Clinical Neuropharmacology, 16,* 347–358.

Van Dyck, C. H., Newhouse, P., Falk, W. E., et al. (2000). Extended-release physostigmine in Alzheimer disease: A multicenter, double-blind, 12-week study with dose enrichment. *Archives of General Psychiatry, 57,* 157–164.

van Loveren-Huyben, C. M. S., Engelaar, H. F. J. W., et al. (1984). Double-blind clinical and psychologic study of ergoloid mesylates (Hydergine) in subjects with senile mental deterioration. *Journal of the American Geriatric Society, 32,* 584–588.

Villardita, C., Parini, J., et al. (1987). Clinical and neuropsychological study with oxiracetam versus placebo in patients with mild to moderate dementia. *Journal of Neural Transmission, 24*(Suppl.), 293–298.

Vroulis, G. A., Smith, R. C., et al. (1981). The effects of lecithin on memory in patients with senile dementia of the Alzheimer's type. *Psychopharmacology Bulletin, 17,* 127–129.

Weingartner, H., Kaye, W., et al. (1981). Vasopressin treatment of cognitive dysfunction in progressive dementia. *Life Sciences, 29,* 2721–2726.

Weinstein, H. C., Teunisse, S., & van Gool, W. A. (1991). Tetrahydroaminoacridine and lecithin in the treatment of Alzheimer's disease. *Journal of Neurology, 238,* 34–38.

Weintraub, S., Mesulam, M. M., et al. (1983). Lecithin in the treatment of Alzheimer's disease. *Archives of Neurology, 40,* 527–528.

Weis, B. L. (1987). Failure of nalmefene and estrogen to improve memory in Alzheimer's disease. *American Journal of Psychiatry, 144,* 386–387.

Wettstein, A. (1983). No effect from double-blind trial of physostigmine and lecithin in Alzheimer's disease. *Annals of Neurology, 13,* 210–212.

Wettstein, A., & Spiegel, R. (1984). Clinical trials with the cholinergic drug RS 86 in Alzheimer's disease (AD) and senile dementia of the Alzheimer type (SDAT). *Psychopharmacology, 84,* 572–573.

Wilcock, G. K., Surmon, D. J., et al. (1993). An evaluation of the efficacy and safety of tetrahydroaminoacridine (THA) without lecithin in the treatment of Alzheimer's disease. *Age and Aging, 22,* 316–324.

Wilkinson, D. G., Passmore, A. P., Bullock, R., Hopker, S. W., Smith, R., Potocnik, F. C., et al. (2002). A multinational, randomized, 12-week, comparative study of donepezil and rivastigmine in patients with mild to moderate Alzheimer's disease. *International Journal of Clinical Practice, 56,* 441–446.

Wilson, A. L., Langley, L. K., et al. (1995). Nicotine patches in Alzheimer's disease: Pilot study on learning, memory and safety. *Pharmacology, Biochemistry and Behavior, 51,* 509–514.

Wolters, E. C., Riekkinen, P., et al. (1990). DGAVP (Org 5667) in early Alzheimer's disease patients: An international double-blind, placebo-controlled multicenter trial. *Neurology, 40,* 1099–1101.

5

Psychopharmacological Treatments for Substance Use Disorders

Charles P. O'Brien

James McKay

The treatment of substance abuse with pharmacological agents is well established, although most experts agree that, to be successful, medication interventions must be combined with psychosocial therapies. A large number of Type 1 and Type 2 controlled trials have shown that the use of nicotine replacement therapy to induce and maintain smoking cessations significantly increases the abstinence rate. Bupropion, which is also an antidepressant, has been found in controlled trials to significantly increase the smoking abstinence rate measured at intervals up to 12 months after beginning of treatment. Trials with novel agents such as the cannabinoid receptor antagonist rimonabant and varenicline, a nicotine receptor partial agonist, have been reported at meetings but have not yet appeared in print. The treatment of alcoholism can now be enhanced by three totally different types of medications: disulfiram, which works when compliance is assured; naltrexone, which reduces alcohol reward via the endogenous opioid system and results in decreased alcohol craving and reduced drinking in most randomized clinical trials; and acamprosate, which reduces post-alcohol excitability and has been effective in European trials but less so in U.S. trials. A depot version of the opiate antagonist naltrexone was approved by the FDA in 2006. It gives therapeutic blood levels for at least 30 days and should greatly improve compliance, thus making naltrexone more useful for the treatment of both opiate addiction and alcoholism. Methadone maintenance treatment for heroin dependence has consistently shown efficacy, and the treatment options have been increased by the availability of the partial opiate agonist buprenorphine. Buprenorphine is unique in that it can be used for the treatment of opiate addiction by qualified physicians in their offices rather than requiring enrollment in a highly regulated methadone treatment program. There are as yet no FDA-approved medications for the treatment of stimulant addiction, which includes cocaine and methamphetamine. There are recent double-blind, placebo-controlled clinical trials of several medications that have been found effective against cocaine addiction and are currently in multi-site trials to confirm efficacy.

Substance use disorders affect virtually every sector of society. As a group they are among the most common of all mental disorders. Household surveys have found a lifetime prevalence rate of 15 to 18% and a 6-month prevalence rate of 6 to 7% (Myers et al., 1984; Robins et al., 1984). These rates do not include nicotine addiction, the most devastating and difficult to treat of all the addictive disorders. Although rates of cigarette smoking in the United States have declined, smokers unable to quit on their own are among the most difficult patients presenting for treatment. Many individuals have multiple addictions; for example, alcoholics frequently are addicted to both cocaine and nicotine. There is also a good deal of overlap with other mental disorders such as anxiety and affective disorders. There are common properties among the disorders produced by the major drugs of abuse, but there are also important differences, particularly in treatment approaches. Thus, a chapter on treatment of substance use disorders must consist of four distinct reviews focusing on the major drugs or drug categories: nicotine, alcohol, stimulants (cocaine, methamphetamine), and opioids (heroin). Other drugs such as cannabinoids, hallucinogens, ecstasy, and minor tranquilizers may also be abused, but they account for a relatively small proportion of patients needing treatment, and there are no effective medications currently available. An antagonist at the cannabinoid receptor (CB-1) has recently been tested in clinical trials, but no published results are available. Based on preclinical data, this antagonist may eventually prove useful in the treatment of marijuana dependence, as well as other appetitive disorders such as obesity and smoking.

The features that define substance use disorders include compulsive use of the substance in spite of interference with normal activities and adverse effects on health. Terminology in this area is confusing because the *Diagnostic and Statistical Manual of Mental Disorders (DSM-IV)* describes two kinds of "dependence." The diagnosis of dependence is the overall label for the syndrome produced by compulsive drug use, and it may or may not include "physiological dependence." There is no justification for distinguishing "physiological" from "not physiological" because in the absence of the signs of classic drug withdrawal (tremors, vomiting, etc.), we now recognize major changes in brain physiology that may be evident only in the patient's behavior. Tolerance and physiological dependence were emphasized in previous definitions of addiction, but modern research has shown that these are simply normal adaptive reactions to the use of many substances, including ordinary medications such as those used in the treatment of hypertension. Tolerance is simply a reduced effect with repeated use of a drug, and physiological dependence refers to a state demonstrated by the appearance of physiological rebound symptoms when a drug to which the body had become adapted is suddenly withdrawn. Although tolerance and physiological dependence are often present and will influence the course of treatment, these are not essential features of addiction ("dependence" in the official diagnostic sense).

SUCCESS OF TREATMENT

In this chapter we define successful treatment as significant improvement in the ability to function according to one's societal role. Total abstinence from the addicting substance is the accepted goal of treatment, but this is not often achieved. Significant reduction in substance use, such that function in society is improved, can be measured as a partial treatment success. In the case of opiate addiction, transfer to a stable maintenance medication, albeit similar in some ways to heroin, is considered successful treatment provided that the person is able to refrain from socially and personally harmful behavior. This definition of success is commonly utilized for other chronic disorders such as arthritis or diabetes; it therefore is a pragmatic and medically acceptable definition based on functional capacity.

DETOXIFICATION

Detoxification is simply the removal of a drug from the body. This usually occurs because of metabolism by the liver and excretion via the kidneys. If the intake of the drug is gradually lowered, detoxification can be accomplished with little risk or discomfort as the body adapts to the absence of the drug. Detoxification is often confused with treatment. In reality detoxification is, at best, the first step in treatment. Detoxification from sedatives such as alcohol can be dangerous because of medical complications during withdrawal, but these are readily treated in any medical facility. Treatment of the addiction involves a process of rehabilitation to reduce the probability of relapse and lengthen the time that the person is no longer using the drug of abuse. There is no evidence that rapid detoxification under general anesthesia is any more effective in the long term than less heroic and expensive means. Although some interesting research has been done on novel ways to achieve detoxification, for the purposes of this chapter we will emphasize long-term, relapse prevention treatment.

PSYCHOACTIVE AGENTS IN THE TREATMENT OF ADDICTION

One might reasonably ask whether medications are ever justified in the treatment of a disorder that involves excessive use of drugs. Although there is controversy about this on philosophical grounds, empirical studies clearly show the benefits of medications when they are indicated. In addition to treatment of the addictive disorder itself, psychoactive medications are often indicated for accompanying psychiatric disorders. One school of thought that had many proponents in the past was that addicts were all more or less alike and all had to be treated by "getting at the underlying problem" and insisting on strict freedom from all chemicals. In that earlier era, nicotine and caffeine were not usually thought of as chemicals, but all psychoactive medications prescribed by physicians were avoided. Subsequent data, however, have demonstrated that all addicts are not alike. Even within a single drug category such as alcohol, there are alcoholics with different needs requiring different kinds of treatment. Heredity has also been found to have a major influence on risk of addiction, and recent data suggest that treatment response is also influenced (Oslin et al., 2003). The concept of patient-treatment matching has become popular despite a relative paucity of replicated, empirical findings.

NICOTINE DEPENDENCE

Cessation of smoking may be very difficult even for smokers who strongly desire to quit, and subsequent resumption of smoking, despite long periods of abstinence, is common. Those who begin smoking prior to age 21 are less likely to succeed in smoking cessation programs. Most smokers are nicotine dependent and experience a variable withdrawal syndrome when regular administration of nicotine is stopped. The nicotine withdrawal syndrome consists of irritability, impatience, hostility, anxiety, dysphoric or depressed mood, difficulty concentrating, restlessness, decreased heart rate, and increased appetite or weight gain.

Nicotine administration can block these withdrawal symptoms whether given intravenously, by absorption though the mucosal membranes of the mouth (chewing gum), by absorption through the skin (patch), or via nasal spray. However, the peak nicotine levels associated with the psychoactive effects of smoking are not achieved by chewing gum or by patch administration. The widespread availability of nicotine patch and chewing gum as over-the-counter medications has enabled many smokers to give up tobacco as a source of nicotine and thus avoid the serious health risks of tobacco smoke. Most smokers can then gradually reduce their nicotine dependence over several days to several weeks. Craving for the psychoactive effects continues, however, and relapses to smoking over the ensuing months are common. Table 5.1 summarizes some significant studies and reviews showing stable, confirmed abstinence rates at 6 and 12 months. The preponderance of controlled studies show that in addicted smokers who are motivated to quit and remain abstinent, the use of the nicotine patch or chewing gum significantly increases the abstinence rate. Current research involves efforts to enhance the success rate of these nicotine delivery systems using behavior therapy.

The association of smoking and depression has prompted the use of antidepressant medication in conjunction with nicotine replacement in programs for treatment of smoking addiction. Fluoxetine and other antidepressants are often recommended for depressed smokers and for those attempting to quit whose symptoms meet diagnostic criteria for depression. A specific antidepressant, bupropion, has been found to reduce smoking relapse even in nondepressed smokers. Placebo-controlled studies (Hurt et al., 1997; Jorenby et al., 1999) of bupropion showed significantly improved abstinence rates (Table 5.1). It is not clear whether bupropion inhibits nicotine craving, but there is evidence that it reduces withdrawal symptoms (Shiffman et al., 2000). Other medications in clinical trials include the cannabinoid receptor antagonist rimonabant and the nicotine receptor partial agonist varenicline. Verbal reports of success have been presented at meetings, but no published papers are yet available for these two medications. Other recent research has focused on genetic variance as a predictor of treatment response (Berrettini & Lerman, 2005). Alleles of the dopamine D2 receptor and the mu opiate receptor have been

TABLE 5.1 Treatment of Nicotine Use Disorder: Nicotine Replacement

Authors	Study Class	N	Treatment Length	Follow-up Length	Results	Comments
					Double-Blind, Placebo-Controlled Trials	
Fiore, Smith, et al. (1994)	4	5,098 17 studies	4 weeks or longer	6 months	Abstinence rates End of treatment / 6 months Nicotine patch 27% / 22% Placebo 13% / 9%	Excellent review; counseling added modestly to nicotine patch results.
Imperial Cancer Fund General Practice Research Group (1993)	1	1,686	12 weeks	—	Cessation rates Nicotine patch 19.4% Placebo patch 11.7%	No additional effect of detailed written supporting material.
Fiore, Kenford, et al. (1994)	1	Study 1 = 88 Study 2 = 112	8 weeks 6 weeks	6 months	Posttreatment Nicotine / Placebo 1. 22-mg patch 8 weeks 59% / 40% 2. 22-mg 4 weeks, then 37% / 20% 11 mg 2 weeks 6 months / Follow-up Study 1 34% / 21% Study 2 18% / 7%	Higher dose patch for 8 weeks shows somewhat better results.
Richmond et al. (1994)	1	313	5 weeks	6 months	Abstinence Rates 3 months / 6 months Nicotine patch 48% / 33% Placebo patch 21% / 14%	

148

Nicotine Patch Plus Nicotine Gum

Reference	No.	N	Duration	Follow-up	Description	Abstinence Rates			Comments
						12 weeks	24 weeks	52 weeks	
Kornitzer et al. (1995)	1	374	12 weeks	12 months	1. Nicotine patch + nicotine gum 2. Nicotine patch + placebo gum 3. Placebo patch + nicotine gum				This study suggests that the flexibility of nicotine gum adds significantly to the results of the patch alone.
					1.	34.2%	27.5%	18.1%	
					2.	22.7%	15.3%	12.7%	
					3.	17.3%	14.7%	13.3%	
Nicotine Nasal Spray									
Croghan et al. (2003)	2	1,384	6 weeks	6 months	Open comparison of spray, patch, and combination. At 6 weeks, abstinence rate: patch, 21.1; spray 13.6; combination 27.1				At 6-mo. follow-up, there was no difference among 3 groups
Bupropion									
Hurt et al. (1997)	1	615	7 weeks	12 months					150- and 300-mg dose significantly more effective than placebo; 100 mg not effective. Less weight gain. Long-term relapse a problem
Jorenby et al. (1999)	1	893	9 weeks	12 months					Comparison of placebo, nicotine patch, bupropion, bupropion + patch. Bupropion significantly more effective than patch alone and placebo. Best result with patch + bupropion at 12 months

found to be markers of treatment response in nicotine-dependent individuals.

ALCOHOL DEPENDENCE (ALCOHOLISM)

Medications that have been evaluated as treatments for alcoholism include antidipsotropic agents, serotonergic antidepressants and anxiolytic agents, and agents that purportedly block the reinforcing effects of alcohol at the neurotransmitter level (O'Brien, 2005). In 2004 the FDA approved a novel medication, acamprosate, for prevention of alcoholism relapse, and in 2006 a new delivery system for naltrexone was approved, a depot formulation. Studies of these agents are described in Table 5.2.

Antidipsotropic Medications

Antidipsotropic medications are agents that produce an unpleasant reaction when alcohol is consumed, thereby acting as a deterrent to drinking (Fuller, 1995). The studies presented in Table 5.2 indicate that, overall, disulfiram provided orally or through implants is not more effective than placebo in reducing drinking. Similar conclusions were also reached in another recent review (Suh, Pettinati, Kampman, & O'Brien, 2006). However, there is evidence that disulfiram may reduce further drinking in older patients who have relapsed but have good motivation and at least moderate social stability. Disulfiram may also be more effective in preventing relapse when it is used in treatment interventions that include contracts that specify disulfiram ingestion will be monitored by a significant other (Azrin, Sisson, Meyers, & Godley, 1982; O'Farrell, Cutter, & Floyd, 1985). Since poor compliance is a major obstacle to the effectiveness of disulfiram treatment, this sort of behavioral contracting may be an important component of treatment with this agent. However, the side effects of disulfiram and potential danger of disulfiram-ethanol reactions contraindicate its use in patients with a wide array of medical and psychiatric conditions and in pregnant women (Fuller, 1995; Schuckit, 1996).

Serotonergic Agents

Serotonin appears to play an important neurochemical role in the modulation of mood and impulse control, and may therefore influence the development and maintenance of alcohol use disorders. Because studies have suggested that individuals with alcohol use disorders may have low levels of serotonin (Gorelick, 1989; Kranzler & Anton, 1994; Roy, Virkkunen, & Linnoila, 1990), a number of serotonergic drugs have been evaluated as possible treatments for alcoholism. The agents that have received the greatest attention are selective serotonin reuptake inhibitors (SSRIs), such as fluoxetine and sertraline, and buspirone, a serotonin 1A receptor partial agonist. Studies of SSRIs presented in Table 5.2 indicate that these agents may lead to short-term reductions in alcohol consumption in heavy drinkers. However, studies that have been done with alcoholics in psychosocial treatment programs have yielded mixed findings (Pettinati & Rabinowitz, 2005). On the other hand, a study with alcoholics who had comorbid major depression found that fluoxetine reduced both alcohol use and depression levels (Cornelius et al., 1997). It also appears that buspirone may be an effective treatment for alcoholics who have comorbid anxiety disorders. Finally, several studies suggest that tricyclic antidepressants may reduce both depression and alcohol use in patients with major depression (Mason, Kocsis, Ritvo, & Cutler, 1996; McGrath et al., 1996).

The efficacy of two serotonin receptor antagonists, ritanserin and ondansetron, has been examined in several studies. Ritanserin, a 5HT2 receptor antagonist, does not appear to be an effective treatment for alcohol use disorders (B. A. Johnson et al., 1996). However, ondansetron, a 5HT3 receptor antagonist, produced better alcohol use outcomes than placebo in patients with early-onset alcoholism (i.e., prior to age 25) who were receiving cognitive-behavioral therapy, when used alone (B. A. Johnson, Roache, J. D., Javors, M. A. DiClemente, C. C., Cloninger, C. R., Prihoda, T. J., et al., 2000) or in combination with naltrexone (B. A. Johnson, Ait-Daoud, & Priholda, 2000). Topiramate, an anticonvulsant medication, was reported in a single controlled trial to reduce alcohol drinking and improve the results of rehabilitation (B. A. Johnson et al., 2004).

Opioid Antagonists

Clinical trials of naltrexone, a generic medication, have been supported by the National Institutes of Health (NIH) and other national research agencies

TABLE 5.2 Medications for Alcohol Dependence

Author	Study Class	N	Treatment Length	Follow-up Length	Results	Comments
Antidipsotropic medications						
Oral disulfiram						
Baekland et al. (1971)	2	232	26 weeks	—	Patients who had a better response to disulfiram were older, had longer histories of heavy drinking, were less likely to be depressed, and had higher motivation and AA contact.	Subjects were participants in an outpatient clinic.
Gerrein et al. (1973)	2	49	8 weeks	—	Better attendance and abstinence rates in supervised disulfiram, compared to nonsupervised and no disulfiram.	Statistical significance of abstinence results not provided.
Fuller & Roth (1979)	1(N)	128	12 months	—	Continuous abstinence rates higher in disulfiram than placebo (23% vs. 12%), but not statistically significant.	Outcomes similar for 1-mg and 250-mg disulfiram conditions.
Fuller et al. (1986)	1	605	12 months	—	No differences between disulfiram and placebo in total abstinence, time to first drink, psychosocial functioning.	Disulfiram was effective for patients who drank and completed all assessments.
Chick et al. (1992)	2	126	26 weeks	—	Supervised disulfiram (200 mg/day) produced better outcomes on most drinking measures than placebo.	Patients in control condition were told they were receiving placebo.
Carroll et al. (1998)	1	122	12 weeks	—	Disulfiram (modal dose 261 mg/day) produced longer durations of alcohol and cocaine abstinence and better retention than placebo.	Subjects had comorbid alcohol abuse/dependence and cocaine dependence, and received one of three manualized, weekly outpatient therapies.
Implanted disulfiram						
Johnsen et al. (1987)	2(N)	21	—	20 weeks	No differences between disulfiram and placebo in self-reported drinking or liver function measures.	Wound complications in 30% of disulfiram implant group.
Johnsen & Morland (1991)	1	76	—	300 days	Disulfiram implants (1 g) did not produce better drinking outcomes than placebo implants, although improvements were observed in both conditions.	Subjects in both conditions were told they were receiving disulfiram.
Serotonergic agents						
SSRIs						
Naranjo et al. (1987)	1	39	12 weeks	—	Citalopram (40 mg/day) produced better drinking outcomes than 20 mg/day or placebo.	Subjects were male heavy drinkers; non-treatment-seeking.
Naranjo et al. (1989)	1	29	7 weeks	—	Viqualine (200 mg/day) produced better drinking outcomes than placebo. 100 mg/day was ineffective.	Subjects were male heavy drinkers; non-treatment-seeking.
Gorelick & Paredes (1992)	1	20	4 weeks	—	Small advantage to fluoxetine (80 mg/day) over placebo in first week, but not in Weeks 2–4.	Study conducted on an inpatient research ward where alcohol was available.

(continued)

TABLE 5.2 (continued)

Author	Study Class	N	Treatment Length	Follow-up Length	Results	Comments
Naranjo et al. (1990)	1	29	4 weeks	—	Fluoxetine (60 mg/day) reduced number of drinks consumed, but not days abstinent. 40 mg/day was ineffective.	Subjects were male heavy drinkers; non-treatment-seeking.
Naranjo et al. (1992)	1	16	4 weeks	—	Citalopram (40 mg/day) increased abstinent days and decreased number drinks consumed, compared to placebo.	Alcohol-dependent subjects.
Kranzler et al. (1995)	1	101	12 weeks	—	Fluoxetine (60 mg/day) was no better than placebo in reducing alcohol consumption.	Subjects were alcohol-dependent outpatients also receiving relapse prevention.
Cornelius et al. (1997)	1	51	12 weeks	—	Fluoxetine (mean of 25 mg/day) produced lower total alcohol consumption and greater reductions in depressive symptoms than placebo.	Subjects had comorbid alcohol dependence and major depression and also received two therapy sessions per week.
Angelone et al. (1998)	1	81	16 weeks	—	Fluvoxamine (150 mg/day) and citalopram (20 mg/day) both produced higher rates of continuous abstinence than placebo but did not differ from each other. Only citalopram reduced craving.	Subjects were hospitalized for 3 weeks prior to baseline and received 8 weeks of daily outpatient cognitive behavioral therapy (CBT), followed by 8 weeks of weekly CBT.
Buspirone						
Bruno (1989)	2	50	8 weeks	—	Buspirone (20 mg/day) produced better retention than placebo. Comparisons of drinking outcomes not done due to high dropout rate in placebo condition.	Subjects were outpatients with mild to moderate alcohol abuse.
Tollefson et al. (1992)	1	51	24 weeks	—	Buspirone (30 or 60 mg/day) produced better drinking outcomes than placebo on a subjective, global measure.	Standardized measures of drinking outcomes not included. Subjects were abstinent alcoholics with comorbid anxiety disorder.
Malcolm et al. (1992)	1	67	26 weeks	—	Buspirone (45–60 mg/day) did not produce better outcomes than placebo on any drinking measures.	Subjects were anxious, alcohol-dependent male veterans.
Kranzler et al. (1994)	1	61	12 weeks	—	Buspirone (up to 52 mg/day) produced better drinking outcomes than placebo.	Subjects were alcohol-dependent with comorbid anxiety disorder and were in outpatient treatment.
Serotonin receptor antagonists						
Johnson et al. (1996)	1	423	12 weeks	—	Retanserin (2.5 or 5 mg/day) did not produce better outcomes on any of drinking, craving, or clinical status outcome measures.	Subjects also received weekly individual manual-guided cognitive behavioral therapy.

Reference		N	Duration	Follow-up	Results	Comments
Johnson et al. (2000)	1	271	12 weeks	—	Ondansetron at three dose levels (1 µg/kg, 4 µg/kg, 16 µg/kg, 2 ×/day) produced fewer drinks per day than placebo, and 4 µg/kg dose produced more abstinent days than placebo. These results were obtained only in early-onset (<25-year-old) drinkers.	Subjects also received weekly group manual-guided cognitive behavioral therapy.
Johnson et al. (2000)	?	21	8 weeks	—	Ondansetron (4 µg/kg, 2 ×/day) plus naltrexone (25 mg, 2 ×/day) produced fewer drinks/day and drinks/drinking day than placebo in patients with early-onset alcoholism.	Subjects also received weekly group manual-guided cognitive behavioral therapy.
Acamprosate						
Lhuitre et al. (1985)	1	85	90 days	—	Acamprosate produced lower rate of relapse than placebo.	—
Lhuitre et al. (1990)	1	365	90 days	—	Acamprosate condition had lower liver enzyme values during follow-up than placebo.	—
Paille et al. (1995)	1	538	12 months	6 months	Drinking outcomes consistently best in high-dose acamprosate (2 g/day), followed by low-dose (1.3 g/day) and placebo.	Subjects also received supportive outpatient therapy as required.
Whitworth et al. (1996)	1	455	12 months	—	Complete abstinence rates and days of abstinence favored acamprosate over placebo.	—
Sass et al. (1996)	1	272	48 weeks	48 weeks	Drinking outcomes consistently favored acamprosate over placebo. Effect of acamprosate persisted during the posttreatment follow-up period.	Subjects were also offered outpatient therapy with a behavioral orientation during the study period.
Pelc et al. (1997)	1	188	90 days	—	Acamprosate conditions (1332 and 1998 mg/day) had better outcomes on all drinking measures than placebo, and there were trends toward stronger effects at the higher dose.	Subjects entered the study following a 14-day inpatient detoxification and received supportive counseling as needed during the trial.
Poldrugo (1997)	1	246	6 months	6 months	Acamprosate (1332 or 1998 mg/day, depending on weight) produced higher abstinence rates and better retention than placebo. Similar abstinence results were obtained in the posttreatment follow-up.	Subjects entered the study following brief inpatient detoxification and received comprehensive outpatient treatment that included active linking to recovering alcoholics in the community.
Besson et al. (1998)	1	118	360 days	360 days	Acamprosate (1332 or 1998 mg/day, depending on weight) produced more abstinent days and higher abstinence rates than placebo during the trial. The best results were in patients in the acamprosate condition who also took disulfiram. Low follow-up rates in the posttreatment phase precluded analysis.	Subjects entered the study following brief inpatient detoxification and received routine outpatient counseling provided by attending physicians.
Tempesta et al. (2000)	1	330	6 months	3 months	Acamprosate (1998 mg/day) produced more abstinent days and higher abstinence rates than placebo, as well as less severe relapses. Results in the posttreatment follow-up also favored acamprosate but were not significant.	Subjects entered the study following brief inpatient detoxification and received supportive outpatient counseling (1–2 sessions/wk).

(continued)

TABLE 5.2 (continued)

Author	Study Class	N	Treatment Length	Follow-up Length	Results	Comments
Chick et al. (2000b)	1	581	24 weeks	4 weeks	Acamprosate (1998 mg/day) did not produce better drinking outcomes than placebo, either in the full sample or in subgroup analyses.	Subjects entered the study within 5 weeks of detoxification and received usual psychosocial outpatient care during the trial.
Opioid antagonists Naltrexone						
Volpicelli et al. (1990, 1992)	1	70	12 weeks	—	Less craving, fewer days drinking, lower relapse rate in naltrexone (50 mg/day) group, compared to placebo. Subjects who drank at all were much less likely to progress to full relapse if they received naltrexone.	Subjects were male veterans in an intensive day hospital rehabilitation program.
O'Malley et al. (1992)	1	97	12 weeks	(see below)	Fewer days drinking, longer time to first relapse in naltrexone (50 mg/day) group, compared to placebo.	Subjects also received coping skills or supportive therapy.
O'Malley et al. (1996a)	1	97	—	26 weeks	Naltrexone led to higher abstinence rates in Month 1 (but not 2–6), lower relapse rate over all 6 months, compared to placebo.	Among subjects who drank at all, best outcomes were in naltrexone/coping-skills group.
Volpicelli et al. (1997)	1	97	12 weeks	—	On intent-to-treat analysis, rates of relapse and days drinking were not significantly different in naltrexone (50 mg/day) and placebo groups. However, among patients who drank at all, those who received naltrexone were less likely to have full relapses.	Subjects also received outpatient counseling; 2 x/week in first month, 1 x/week in Months 2 and 3.
Oslin et al. (1997)	1	44	12 weeks	—	Naltrexone (50 mg/day) did not produce higher abstinence rates than placebo. However, among patients who drank at all, those who received naltrexone were less likely to have full relapses.	Subjects were all over 50 years of age and received weekly group therapy and case management.
Kranzler et al. (1998)	1	20	4 weeks	4 weeks	Injectable, sustained-release naltrexone (206 mg) produced fewer heavy drinking days during injection and follow-up periods than placebo injection.	Subjects also received individual coping-skills therapy (weekly, for 8 weeks).
Hersh et al. (1998)	1	64	8 weeks	—	Naltrexone (50 mg/day) did not produce better alcohol or cocaine use outcomes than placebo.	Subjects had comorbid alcohol and cocaine abuse/dependence. They also received manualized relapse prevention therapy (up to 12 ind. sessions over 8 weeks).
Anton et al. (1999)	1	131	12 weeks	—	Naltrexone (50 mg/day) produced less drinking, longer time to relapse, more time between relapses, and greater resistance to and control over alcohol-related thoughts and urges than placebo.	Subjects were abstinent a minimum of 5 days prior to study entry and received manualized cognitive behavioral therapy (weekly).

154

Study		N	Duration	Follow-up	Results	Comments
Knox & Donovan (1999)	2	122	3 weeks	6 months	This study is severely flawed in that treatment was limited to a 3-wk inpatient stay, and then outpatient care was optional. No difference between naltrexone and placebo at 6-month follow-up.	Treatment of a chronic disorder by brief inpatient treatment with optional follow-up care is difficult to rationalize.
Kranzler et al. (2000)	1	183	12 weeks	—	Naltrexone (50 mg/day), nefazodone (200 mg/day), and placebo did not differ on drinking outcomes. Naltrexone did produce more adverse neuropsychiatric and gastrointestinal effects, poorer compliance, and greater treatment attrition.	Subjects were abstinent a minimum of 3 days prior to study entry and received manualized individual cognitive behavioral therapy (weekly).
Chick et al. (2000a)	1	175	12 weeks		In compliant patients, the naltrexone group consumed less alcohol, had less craving, and had improved liver function. For total sample, no difference in drinking, but improved liver function in the naltrexone group.	Very little counseling involved in this study.
Morris et al. (2001)	1	111	12 weeks		Significantly fewer relapses and less consumption of alcohol in group randomized to naltrexone.	—
Latt et al. (2001)	1	107	12 weeks		Naltrexone significantly reduced relapse rates. The effect was most marked in the first 6 weeks.	This study was specifically designed to test naltrexone in a primary-care practice without formal psychotherapy.
Krystal et al. (2001)	1	627	3 months & 12 months		No difference between naltrexone and placebo for 3 months or 12 months. Secondary analyses including medication compliance also found no effect.	This is the largest and longest study of naltrexone in alcoholism. It is the first multiclinic trial with 15 VA clinics involved. Counseling was once weekly for 16 weeks; 12-step facilitation.
Nalmefene						
Mason et al. (1994)	1	21	12 weeks	—	Nalmefene (40 mg) led to lower rates of relapse and more abstinent days than nalmefene (10 mg) or placebo. Both nalmefene conditions led to reductions in drinks per drinking day.	Subjects were alcohol-dependent, with no other substance dependence or major psychiatric disorders. Psychosocial treatment was not provided.
Mason et al. (1999)	1	105	12 weeks	—	Nalmefene (20 and 80 mg/day conditions) produced lower rates of relapse to heavy drinking and fewer number of relapses than placebo. Outcomes did not differ between the two doses.	Subjects were abstinent an average of 2 weeks prior to randomization and received manualized individual cognitive behavioral therapy (weekly).

rather than a pharmaceutical company. Most trials have shown significantly less drinking in the alcoholics randomized to naltrexone compared with placebo, but not necessarily complete abstinence (Table 5.2). A reading of the 22 Type 1 trials of naltrexone in the treatment of alcoholism suggests that there is a subtype of alcoholism that responds well to naltrexone, whereas some alcoholics do not respond at all. Factors that have been reported to increase the likelihood of a response are high alcohol craving, strong family history of alcoholism, tendency to report euphoria from alcohol drinking, and, of course, adherence to medication regimen (O'Brien, 2005). A retrospective study of genotypes of alcoholics in clinical trials found that an allele of the mu opiate receptor predicted poor outcome when randomized to placebo but excellent outcome when receiving naltrexone (Oslin et al., 2003). This allele was also associated with a greater stimulation response to alcohol in the laboratory (Ray & Hutchison., 2004) and increased risk of alcoholism (Bart et al., 2005), as well as heroin addiction (Bart et al., 2004). This raises the future prospect of a genetic test to aid in the selection of medication for alcoholism.

A major step forward in the use of naltrexone for the treatment of both alcoholism and heroin addiction is the development of a depot formulation. Treatment adherence has been a major determinant of treatment success with this medication (Volpicelli et al., 1997). Three different formulations of depot naltrexone have been studied in clinical trials, and one product received FDA approval in 2006 (Garbutt et al., 2005). In a large clinical trial among alcoholics, therapeutic levels were maintained for 30 to 40 days following injection. The medication was well tolerated, and most alcoholics remained in the trial for 6 months. This new treatment option could have a major impact on the treatment of both alcoholism and opiate addiction.

Acamprosate

Calcium bisacetyl homotaurine (acamprosate) has shown consistent efficacy in European clinical trials in improving treatment retention and decreasing drinking in alcoholics following initial detoxification. Nine of the 10 European studies of acamprosate presented in Table 5.2 have generated positive findings during the treatment phase, and some of these stud-

ies have indicated the effects of acamprosate persist to some degree in posttreatment follow-up periods. Although the actions of acamprosate are not entirely clear, it appears that it lowers neuronal excitability by reducing the postsynaptic efficacy of excitatory amino acid (EAA) neurotransmitters such as glutamate. This leads to reports of less anxiety and alcohol craving and fewer episodes of drinking. The first study in the United States (Mason, Goodman, Chabac, & Lehert, 2006) failed to show an overall effect on days abstinent, but after controlling for baseline variables and treatment exposure, those randomized to acamprosate had a significantly greater percentage of days abstinent. Acamprosate was approved by the FDA in 2004 and is currently in clinical use.

In 2006 an important trial was published by a group of investigators supported by the National Institute on Alcoholism and Alcohol Abuse (NIAAA) involving 1,383 recently abstinent alcoholics (Anton et al., 2006). The study had a complex design consisting of eight groups to which the patients were randomized for 16 weeks of treatment. Groups received either naltrexone 100 mg/day, acamprosate 3 g/day, the combination of both medications, placebo with or without a combined behavioral intervention, or behavioral intervention only with no pills. Although retention and adherence to the protocol were good and approximately equal for all groups, outcome at 16 weeks showed a significant advantage for medical management with naltrexone and combined behavioral intervention alone or together with naltrexone. No advantage was found for acamprosate as measured by reduction in drinking whether alone or combined with behavioral intervention. This study was the most recent among many showing that naltrexone significantly reduces heavy drinking in many but not all patients. Acamprosate, despite numerous positive trials in Europe, did not show a significant overall benefit in this study. This variability in efficacy suggests that more work is needed in selecting which patients are most likely to respond to naltrexone and which are most likely to respond to acamprosate. There are also considerable differences in the patient populations studied in the United States when compared with those studied in Europe. Another conclusion that one can draw from this study is that alcoholism can be treated in general health care settings with medication and minimal psychosocial interventions. This may become even more practical with the availability of an extended release delivery system for naltrexone permitting once-monthly injections.

Another promising agent with a different mechanism of action is the anticonvulsant topiramate. B. A. Johnson and colleagues (2004) found increased abstinence and improved rehabilitation in a Type 1 trial among alcoholics. This medication is being investigated further in a multisite trial among alcoholics. It has also shown efficacy for cocaine dependence and thus could be useful in those abusing both cocaine and alcohol (Kampman et al., 2004).

STIMULANT DEPENDENCE

Most efforts to identify medications that would be effective in treating patients with cocaine use disorders have been directed toward finding agents that either correct alterations in neurochemical substrates brought on by chronic cocaine use or block the reinforcing effects of cocaine (Kleber, 1995). Although reports of several Type 1 trials published in recent years have shown a significant effect in reducing cocaine use, replication has not yet occurred. Multisite trials are currently under way for modafinil and baclofen, two medications that have shown efficacy in smaller trials. (See Table 5.3.)

Methamphetamine abuse has reached epidemic proportions in parts of the western United States, and so far no medication has been found useful in the treatment of this disorder.

Antidepressants

Stimulant abusers frequently report anhedonia following cessation of cocaine or methamphetamine use, and dysphoria and/or depression may play a role in the onset and maintenance of drug use. These observations have raised the possibility that antidepressant medications may reduce cocaine use in cocaine-dependent patients. Early studies with desipramine were promising, but when more severe cocaine addicts were treated, results were disappointing (Arndt, Dorozynsky, Woody, McLellan, & O'Brien, 1992). Studies of tricyclic antidepressants indicate that these agents do not improve retention but may lead to reduced cocaine use in some patients, particularly those with less severe cocaine abuse (Carroll

et al., 1994; Nunes et al., 1995). Furthermore, one study reported improvement in cocaine abstinence in patients abusing both opioids and cocaine (Oliveto, Feingold, Schottenfeld, Jatlow, & Kosten, 1999). Initial studies of fluoxetine and gepirone found no evidence that these agents were more effective than placebo in improving retention or reducing cocaine use.

Dopaminergic Agents

Several agents with dopamine agonist properties that appear to relatively quickly counteract alterations in the dopamine system caused by chronic use of cocaine have been evaluated as adjuncts to detoxification and aids in initial treatment (e.g., amantadine, bromocriptine, methylphenidate, and diethylpropion). However, none of these agents has shown consistent evidence of effectiveness in reducing cocaine use. Another line of medications research has focused on identifying agents that block the dopamine-mediated reinforcing effects of cocaine. Unfortunately, most of these agents (e.g., neuroleptics) have serious side effects and are not likely to lead to high compliance on the part of cocaine abusers. However, one study reported that flupenthixol, which has antidepressant effects at low doses and neuroleptic effects at high doses, may be effective in reducing cocaine use (Gawin, Allen, & Humblestone, 1989).

Other Agents

Buprenorphine, an opioid agonist/antagonist that has been shown in animal models to selectively reduce cocaine self-administration, has not been more effective than methadone in reducing cocaine use in patients who are dependent on both cocaine and opioids, with the exception of male patients in one study (Oliveto et al., 1999). Carbamazepine, an anticonvulsant agent, has been evaluated as a treatment for cocaine abuse because it reverses cocaine-induced kindling in an animal model and dopamine receptor supersensitivity that can result from long-term cocaine use (Kleber, 1995). Multiple double-blind studies, however, have found no difference between carbamazepine and placebo in treatment retention or cocaine use outcomes.

Three studies have evaluated medications that have traditionally been used to treat other types of

TABLE 5.3 Medications for Cocaine Dependence

Authors	Class	N	Treatment Length	Follow-up Length	Results	Comments
Antidepressants						
Desipramine						
Gawin, Kleber, et al. (1989)	1	72	6 weeks	—	Desipramine (2.5 mg/kg) produced better cocaine use outcomes and lower craving than lithium or placebo.	Subjects were cocaine dependent and received weekly psychotherapy.
Levin & Lehman (1991)	4	200	12–168 days	—	Retention in treatment: desipramine no better than placebo. Reducing cocaine use during trial: desipramine better than placebo.	In meta-analysis, only 2 of 6 studies found advantage to desipramine in reducing cocaine use.
Weddington et al. (1991)	2	54	12 weeks	—	Trend indicated desipramine (200 mg/day) was associated with higher early dropout rate than amantadine or placebo. No group differences in cocaine use or craving.	Subjects in this single-blind study also received outpatient psychotherapy (2 ×/week). Dosage of desipramine may have been subtherapeutic.
Arndt et al. (1992)	1	59	12 weeks	26 weeks	Desipramine (250–300 mg/day) associated with higher dropout rate and worse cocaine use outcomes at 3- and 6-month follow-up than placebo. No group differences in cocaine use during the 12-week treatment phase.	Subjects were methadone-maintained male veterans who also met *DSM-III* criteria for cocaine abuse.
Kolar et al. (1992)	2	22	12 weeks	—	Desipramine (200 mg/day) produced better retention rates and higher abstinence rates at the end of the trial than amantadine or placebo.	Subjects were methadone maintenance patients who also met *DSM-III-R* criteria for cocaine dependence.
Kosten et al. (1992)	1	94	12 weeks	—	Desipramine (150 mg/day) did not produce better retention or cocaine urine toxicology results than amantadine or placebo but was associated with greater reductions in money spent for cocaine in weeks 2 and 4 than placebo.	Subjects were methadone maintenance patients who also met *DSM-III-R* criteria for cocaine dependence.
Carroll et al. (1994)	1	97	12 weeks	12 months	No differences in cocaine use between desipramine and placebo group during the 12-month follow-up from the above study.	Differences favoring relapse prevention over clinical management emerged in months 6–12.
Rawson et al. (1994)	1	99	16 weeks	10 weeks	No differences between desipramine (200 mg/day) and placebo on any outcome measures.	Subjects also received a 26-week outpatient treatment package.
Oliveto et al. (1999)	1	189	13 weeks	—	Desipramine (150 mg/day) increased cocaine abstinence more rapidly than placebo in both men and women.	Subjects were opioid dependent and reported regular cocaine use.
Imipramine						
Nunes et al. (1995)	1	113	12 weeks	—	Imipramine (150–300 mg/day) produced greater reductions in craving, cocaine euphoria, and depression, and also a trend ($p < .09$) toward higher rates of 3 consecutive cocaine-free weeks than placebo. Imipramine effect was greater among nasal users.	Subjects also received weekly individual counseling.

Fluoxetine

Study		N	Duration	Follow-up	Results	Comments
Grabowski et al. (1995)	1	155	12 weeks	—	Retention was lowest in high-dose fluoxetine (40 mg/day), followed by low-dose (20 mg), and placebo. No group differences in cocaine use outcomes.	Subjects also received 1 hour of behaviorally oriented therapy per week and visited the clinic at least one other time per week.
	1(N)	21	8 weeks	—	Fluoxetine (20 mg/day) produced better cocaine outcomes than placebo in weeks 3 and 4, but not in the other 6 weeks.	Subjects were methadone maintenance patients who were also cocaine dependent.
Schmitz et al. (2001)	1	68	12 weeks	—	Fluoxetine (40 mg/day) produced worse cocaine outcomes than placebo in weeks 1–6; no difference in weeks 7–12.	Subjects had major depression in addition to cocaine dependence. All received individual CBT for depression and drug addiction.

Nefazodone

Study		N	Duration	Follow-up	Results	Comments
Ciraulo et al. (2005)	1	69	8 weeks	—	Nefazadone (400 mg/day) produced greater decreases in cocaine use than placebo but also had worse cocaine severity at baseline.	Subjects had cocaine dependence and Hamilton Depression scores of 12 or higher. All received individual counseling.

Gepirone

Study		N	Duration	Follow-up	Results	Comments
Jenkins et al. (1992)	1	41	12 weeks	—	No differences were found between gepirone (16 mg/day) and placebo on any outcome measures.	Subjects all received 1 week of inpatient treatment at start of study, followed by outpatient therapy.

Dopaminergic Agents: Agonists

Amantadine

Study		N	Duration	Follow-up	Results	Comments
Tennant & Sagherian (1987)	1	14	10 days	—	Amantadine (100 mg/day) led to greater retention and lower withdrawal scores during detoxification than bromocriptine.	Subjects were cocaine dependent and participating in an outpatient detoxification program.
Gawin, Morgan, et al. (1989)	2	10	1 day	—	Amantadine (300 mg) did not result in reduced craving, compared with placebo.	Subjects were severe cocaine abusers in outpatient treatment.
Giannini et al. (1989)	1	30	30 days	—	Amantadine (100 mg/6 hr) led to lower ratings of psychiatric symptoms than placebo early in withdrawal.	No measures of cocaine use were included in the study.
Weddington et al. (1991)	2	54	12 weeks	—	Amantadine (400 mg/day) did not produce better outcomes (retention, cocaine use) than placebo.	Subjects in this single-blind study also received outpatient psychotherapy (2 ×/week).
Kolar et al. (1992)	2	22	12 weeks	—	Amantadine (200 mg/day) did not produce better outcomes (retention, cocaine use) than placebo.	See above.
Kosten et al. (1992)	1	94	12 weeks	—	Amantadine (300 mg/day) did not produce better retention or cocaine urine toxicology results than placebo but was associated with greater reductions in money spent for cocaine in weeks 2 and 4.	See above.
Alterman et al. (1992)	1	42	10.5 days	2 weeks	Amantadine (200 mg/day) produced higher rates of cocaine-free urines at 2 and 4 weeks postbaseline.	Subjects were cocaine-dependent male veterans in a day hospital program being detoxified.

(continued)

159

TABLE 5.3 (continued)

Authors	Class	N	Treatment Length	Follow-up Length	Results	Comments
Kampman et al. (2000)	1	61	8 weeks	—	Effect favoring amantadine over placebo on cocaine use outcomes in patients with severe cocaine withdrawal at baseline.	Subjects were cocaine dependent and in outpatient treatment.
Shoptaw et al. (2002)	1	69	16 weeks	—	Amantadine (200 mg/day) produced better retention and better cocaine use outcomes on some but not all measures at 8 and 16 weeks.	Subjects were cocaine dependent and received group counseling (3x/week).
Methylphenidate						
Gawin et al. (1985)	3	5	2–5 weeks	—	Methylphenidate (up to 100 mg/day) appeared to increase cocaine use.	Patients did not have attention deficit disorder.
Grabowski et al. (1997)	1	24	11 weeks	—	Methylphenidate (5 mg + 20 mg sustained release) produced similar cocaine use outcome to placebo.	Patients were cocaine dependent and received manualized behavioral treatment (1 hr/week).
Diethylpropion						
Alim et al. (1995)	?	50	2 weeks	—	Diethylpropion (25–75 mg/day) did not produce better craving outcomes than placebo.	Patients received medication while on an inpatient unit.
Dopaminergic Agents: Antagonists						
Flupenthixol						
Gawin, Allen, et al. (1989)	3	10	not specified	up to 62 weeks	Flupenthixol decanoate (10 or 20 mg every 2–4 weeks) appeared to enhance retention and abstinence rates.	Subjects in this open trial were poor prognosis crack smokers who were cocaine dependent.
Khalsa et al. (1994)	1	63	6 weeks	—	Flupenthixol and desipramine were both superior to placebo in retention, cocaine use, cocaine craving. No comparisons of the two active drugs were provided.	Patients in this preliminary report were crack cocaine users receiving minimal psychotherapy.
Other Agents						
Buprenorphine						
Strain et al. (1994b)	1	164	26 weeks	—	Buprenorphine (8 mg/day) and methadone did not differ on rates of cocaine-positive urines.	Patients were new admissions to an opioid treatment program.
Strain et al. (1994a)	1	51	26 weeks	—	Buprenorphine (11 mg/day) and methadone did not differ on rates of cocaine-positive urines.	Patients were new admissions to an opioid treatment program who were using cocaine prior to admission.
Oliveto et al. (1999)	1	189	13 weeks	—	Buprenorphine (12 mg/day) increased cocaine abstinence more rapidly than methadone (65 mg/day) in men, whereas the opposite effect was obtained in women.	Subjects were opioid dependent and reported regular cocaine use.

Medication / Study		N	Duration		Results	Notes
Carbamazepine						
Cornish et al. (1995)	1	82	10 weeks	—	Carbamazepine (200 mg) and placebo did not differ on retention, rates of cocaine-positive urines, or craving.	Patients were male, cocaine-dependent new admissions to a VA outpatient program.
Montoya et al. (1995)	1	62	8 weeks	—	Carbamazepine (600 mg) and placebo did not differ on retention or rates of cocaine-positive urines.	Patients were cocaine dependent and also received individual counseling 2 ×/week.
Disulfiram						
Carroll et al. (1998)	1	122	12 weeks	—	Disulfiram (modal dose 261 mg/day) produced longer durations of alcohol and cocaine abstinence and better retention than placebo.	Subjects had comorbid alcohol abuse/dependence and cocaine dependence and received one of three manualized, weekly outpatient therapies.
Petrakis et al. (2000)	1	67	12 weeks	—	Disulfiram (250 mg/day) produced greater decreases in the quantity and frequency of cocaine use than placebo. Alcohol use was minimal in both conditions.	Patients had comorbid cocaine and opioid dependence and had been on methadone for at least 3 months prior to study entry.
Carroll et all. (2004)	1	121	12 weeks	—	Disulfiram (250 mg/day) produced greater reductions in cocaine use than placebo. The effect was stronger in patients who were not alcohol dependent.	Patients received either CBT or IPT therapy, manualized, and delivered in individual sessions.
Propranolol						
Kampman et al. (1999)	1	65	7 weeks	—	Propranolol (100 mg/day) produced better retention than placebo control, but no difference on cocaine use outcomes.	Patients were primary cocaine dependent and received 2 hr/week of individual therapy.
Kampman et al. (2001)	1	108	8 weeks	—	No main effect for propranolol vs. placebo on cocaine outcomes. However, patient with more severe cocaine withdrawal symptoms had better retention and cocaine use outcomes on propranolol, relative to placebo.	

TABLE 5.3 (continued)

Authors	Class	N	Treatment Length	Follow-up Length	Results	Comments
Naltrexone						
Hersh et al. (1998)	1	64	8 weeks	—	Naltrexone (50 mg/day) did not produce better alcohol or cocaine use outcomes than placebo.	Subjects had comorbid alcohol and cocaine abuse/dependence. They also received manualized relapse prevention therapy (up to 12 sessions over 8 weeks).
Schmitz et al. (2001)	1	85	12 weeks	—	Combination of naltrexone (50 mg/day) and relapse prevention produced best cocaine use outcomes in a 2×2 design (Nal vs. placebo $\times$ RP vs. drug counseling).	Subjects were cocaine dependent and had achieved initial abstinence during intake and detoxification phase.
Modafinil						
Dackis et al. (2005)	1	62	8 weeks	—	Modafinil (400 mg/day) produced better cocaine use outcomes than placebo.	Subjects were cocaine-dependent patients free of significant medical or psychiatric problems. All received twice-a-week cognitive behavioral therapy.
Topiramate						
Kampman et al. (2004)	2	40	13 weeks	—	Topiramate (200 mg/day) produced better cocaine use outcomes than placebo, after the initial 8-week titration period.	—
Baclofen						
Shoptaw et al. (2003)	1	70	16 weeks	—	Baclofen (20 mg/tid) produced greater reductions in cocaine use than placebo. Results were stronger for patients with more severe cocaine use at baseline.	Subjects were cocaine-dependent patients receiving 3x/weekly cognitive-behavioral group therapy.
Ritanserin						
Cornish et al. (2001)	1	80	4 weeks	—	Ritanserin (10 mg/day) did not produce better cocaine use outcomes than placebo.	Participants were cocaine-dependent patients in outpatient treatment.

162

substance abuse. In two studies, disulfiram was more effective than placebo in decreasing cocaine use, even in patients without alcohol use disorders (Carroll, Nich, Ball, McCance, & Rounsaville, 1998; Petrakis et al., 2000). Carroll and colleagues later (2004) replicated this work, showing decreased cocaine use in patients not comorbid for alcohol abuse. In contrast, naltrexone did not produce better cocaine use outcomes in patients with comorbid alcohol and cocaine use disorders (Hersh, Van Kirk, & Kranzler, 1998). Propranolol in a Type 1 trial was found to reduce cocaine use in severely addicted patients with significant cocaine withdrawal symptoms (Kampman et al., 2001).

Three kinds of medications have shown promise in small trials. Modafinil, a medication used to treat narcolepsy, was found to reduce cocaine euphoria (Dackis et al., 2003; Donovan et al., 2005; Malcolm, Book, Moak, DeVane, & Czepowicz, 2002) and to reduce cocaine use in a Type 1 trial (Dackis, Kampman, Lynch, Pettinati, & O'Brien, 2005). A multisite trial is currently under way. Baclofen, a GABA beta receptor agonist, was reported to reduce cocaine use (Shoptaw et al., 2003), and it too is being studied in a multisite trial. Another GABA active medication, vigabatrin, was reported to reduce stimulant use (Brodie, Figueroa, Laska, & Dewey, 2005), but it is not available in the United States due to side effects. Topiramate, another anticonvulsant medication, has been reported to reduce cocaine use in a Type 1 trial (Kampman et al., 2004).

In summary, although there is as yet no FDA-approved medication for cocaine addiction, several drugs that are approved for other purposes can be considered at this time. These include modafinil, baclofen, disulfiram, topiramate, and propranolol. All have shown some benefits in controlled trials, but definitive conclusions await the results of larger, multisite trials.

There is an active search at present to find medications that can aid in the treatment of persons devastated by methamphetamine addiction. Naturally, those medications that appear to have some efficacy for cocaine addiction are being tested, but results are not yet available. Future research efforts should also continue to examine the joint impact of psychosocial and psychopharmacological interventions because there is evidence that psychosocial treatments can reduce cocaine use (Alterman et al., 1994; Carroll et al., 1994; Higgins et al., 1993; McKay et al., 1998).

Preclinical evidence has shown that there are per-

sistent changes in brain reward systems after cessation of chronic stimulant use. This suggests that there are biological factors that continue after cessation of drug use and may increase the probability of relapse (Koob, 1992). Evidence of postcocaine conditioned responses has been demonstrated in human studies showing craving and autonomic nervous system arousal in response to cocaine-related cues (Childress, McLellan, Ehrman, & O'Brien, 1987; O'Brien et al., 1988). Using modern brain imaging techniques, reflex changes in limbic brain activity have been reported in drug-free former cocaine addicts shown cues related to their former drug use (Childress et al., 1999). This phenomenon has been used to screen new medications that might diminish this conditioned craving effect (Berger et al., 1996; Robbins, Ehrman, Childress, & O'Brien, 1992). It seems reasonable to hope that medications will ultimately be found that can ameliorate these biological effects of chronic stimulant use and augment the effects of psychosocial interventions.

OPIOID DEPENDENCE

Although the history of opiate addiction in the United States goes back more than 100 years, most of the societal response has been legal rather than medical. Physicians are heavily restricted in their ability to deal with opiate addiction as a medical problem. Most treatment consists only of detoxification, that is, removal of the drug from the body by metabolism while withdrawal symptoms are being treated by another medication. In reality, detoxification is simply a first step in a long-term relapse prevention program. Two medical approaches to aid in detoxification are available. One is the use of an opioid agonist in gradually decreasing doses over 5 to 10 days. This permits a smooth, comfortable detoxification for most patients. A long-acting medication such as methadone or buprenorphine is preferable because it permits a smooth transition to the drug-free state. A second option is the use of a drug that blocks certain aspects of the withdrawal syndrome, such as clonidine or lofexidine.

Methadone

Some opioid addicts are able to detoxify and remain drug free, but the majority relapse, even after intensive psychotherapy. More important, many heroin addicts will not even consider a drug-free treatment approach or entry into a therapeutic community. Maintenance treatment using methadone (Table 5.4a), which was developed in the 1960s, consists of transferring the patient from heroin, a short-acting opiate that must be taken by injection two to four times daily, to methadone, a long-acting opioid that need be taken only once daily by mouth. The changes produced by transfer to a long-acting opioid are significant. The treatment requires relatively little effort on the part of the patient, giving it wide appeal. This appeal is important from a public health perspective because infections such as HIV and resistant tuberculosis threaten the general public as well as substance abusers.

Initially, most heroin addicts have poor motivation to change their lives. When first introduced to methadone treatment, they still want to get "high" and mix other drugs with prescribed medication. With appropriate counseling in a structured program, the patient can make the transition from thinking like a street addict to behaving like a productive citizen. Methadone substitutes for heroin, reduces drug-seeking behavior, and blocks opiate withdrawal symptoms. It stabilizes physiological systems because of its long duration of action in contrast to the short action of heroin, which produces ups and downs (Kreek, 1992). Typically patients continue to use some heroin during the first few weeks or months on methadone. Methadone does not block the effects of heroin, but it produces cross-tolerance to heroin and all similar drugs. Thus, the effects of usual doses of heroin are diminished, and over time the typical patient decreases heroin use further and then stops. The evidence shows that the improvement in all areas of function shown by methadone patients is produced by a combination of medication (methadone) and psychosocial intervention. When methadone dose is held constant at a level adequate for most patients (60 mg), there is an orderly relationship between the "dose" of psychotherapy and the outcome of treatment (McLellan et al., 1993). Some improvement is seen with methadone alone, but with increments in psychosocial interventions, there is significantly greater improvement as measured by illicit drug use, psychiatric symptoms, family problems, and employment. Other studies have demonstrated that patients on methadone become healthier and

have lower rates of exposure to infections, including HIV (Metzger et al., 1993).

The physiological stability produced by methadone is demonstrated in several ways. Patients report fewer sleep problems and less depression. Males report improved sexual performance. While on heroin, they were in and out of withdrawal, and when they found time for sex, they frequently experienced premature ejaculations. On methadone, although sexual arousal and orgasm were reported to be slowed, the patients reported that sex was more satisfying (Mintz, O'Brien, & Goldschmidt, 1974). Women report irregular menses while on heroin, but on methadone there is at first a suppression of menstruation and then, after about 6 to 12 months, a resumption of regular cycling. A similar stabilization is noted in the hypothalamic-pituitary-adrenal axis. Women can conceive while on methadone, and the babies are born physically dependent on the opioid. While on methadone, expectant mothers can receive good prenatal care, and the withdrawal syndrome in newborns is readily treated. Although it would be preferable to have women drug free during pregnancy, babies born to methadone-treated mothers are significantly healthier than babies born of mothers using street heroin.

Brief maintenance (extended detoxification) as defined by federal methadone regulations is up to 180 days of methadone treatment. This is enough time to give some patients a stable period during which they can organize their lives and become engaged in psychotherapy. Six months is too short for most patients, however, and the duration of methadone treatment should be determined by the patient's needs and not by an arbitrary time limit. Some patients require several years of stable methadone maintenance before they can be gradually detoxified by decreasing the dose of methadone. Many others require indefinite maintenance on this medication. For these patients, methadone should be considered as a kind of "hormone replacement therapy" analogous to thyroxine for patients with hypothyroidism or prednisone for patients with Addison's disease. The endogenous opioid system is so complicated that a simple diagnostic test has not yet been devised that could demonstrate a primary or secondary deficiency state, if one existed. Some data measuring spinal fluid or plasma endogenous opioids from addicts do exist, however, but they are limited to individual pep-

TABLE 5.4a Medications for Heroin Dependence: Methadone

Authors	Study Class	N	Treatment Length	Follow-up Length	Results	Comments
Dole et al. (1969)	2	32	12 months	6 months	18 of 20 nonmethadone heroin users were reincarcerated vs. only 3 to 12 in methadone group. Use of heroin mainly limited to first 3 months on methadone.	Earliest methadone controlled trial randomized but not blinded.
Gunne & Gronbladh (1984)	2	34	24 months	5 years	At follow-up, 12 of 17 patients assigned to methadone were no longer using illegal drugs, while only 1 of 17 in control groups was doing well at follow-up.	Random assignment but not blinded.
Stimmel et al. (1977)	3	335	Variable	6 years	At follow-up after detoxification from methadone, 83% of those who completed treatment were narcotic free. Including all patients, 35% were narcotic free.	This study shows high abstinence rates for patients judged ready to detoxify from methadone.
Anglin et al. (1989)	3	99	–	2 years	Former patients followed after closing of methadone program; 54% returned to addiction, and incarceration rate was double that of comparison group.	This was not a typical outcome study, but it documented the social and economic loss when methadone treatment is cut off.
Newman & Whitehill (1979)	1	100	2.5 years	2.5 years	60% of maintenance patients remained in treatment for 2.5 years. Only 20% of detoxified patients remained in treatment for 60 days and none for entire study.	Study was a controlled randomized trial, but drug-placebo differences were so great that patients all knew their assignment.

tides and do not give a clear picture of the overall system (O'Brien, 1993). There are also data from nonaddict populations showing that the system can be congenitally hyperactive, resulting in babies born with stupor and respiratory depression that is reversed by opiate antagonists such as naloxone or naltrexone (Myer, Morris, Brase, Dewey, & Zimmerman, 1990). It is theoretically possible, therefore, that other individuals could be born with congenitally low endogenous opioids, possibly giving them a lower threshold for pain and making them more vulnerable to becoming opioid addicts. It is also possible, but not clearly demonstrated, that years of taking exogenous opiates, such as heroin, could suppress the production of endogenous opioids and create a need for lifetime methadone as "hormone replacement." This would explain why many former opioid addicts are unable to remain free of exogenous opioids despite apparently good motivation.

A hypothetical derangement of the endogenous opioid system would also be consistent with data demonstrating a protracted opioid withdrawal syndrome (Martin & Jasinski, 1969). Although the acute opioid withdrawal syndrome diminishes in a matter of 5 to 10 days whether or not treatment is received, a more subtle withdrawal syndrome lasting 6 months has been described under controlled inpatient conditions. Symptoms consist of sleep disturbance and dysphoria with accompanying disturbances in appetite, blood pressure, and cortisol rhythms. These symptoms would be expected to increase the probability of heroin use if the patient were in an environment where opiates were available.

Despite overwhelming evidence demonstrating efficacy (Table 5.4a), methadone remains a controversial treatment (IOM Report, 1990). Methadone produces clear functional improvement, but not a cure. The patient remains physically dependent on a synthetic replacement medication and is capable of functioning normally. The general public expects methadone patients to be stuporous, but this is not the case for a properly regulated methadone patient. Tolerance develops to the sedating effects of opioids, and patients receiving methadone are quite alert (Zacny, 1995) and capable of operating motor vehicles and performing complex tasks such as teaching school or practicing law or medicine. Approximately 120,000 patients in the United States are receiving methadone as treatment for heroin addiction at present. Good programs, which have adequate counsel-

ing staff and use adequate doses of methadone, have success rates of 60 to 70% as defined by significant improvement in functional status. This is remarkable considering that the typical patient arrives with little motivation for change and numerous problems. Unfortunately, methadone programs are generally underfunded, and some programs do little more than dispense methadone. This can be of some benefit, but the full impact of methadone treatment requires a structured counseling/psychotherapy program. Eventually, frequent counseling sessions become unnecessary, and patients can be trusted to take methadone at home. Legal requirements permit only limited doses to be prescribed for use at home, even for patients who have demonstrated their trustworthiness. An exception is "medical maintenance" that requires only monthly visits but is available in only a few experimental programs (Novick, Pascarelli, & Joseph, 1988).

During the 1990s, heroin in the United States became cheaper, with historically high purity. Thus, the average street heroin addict is likely to have a higher level of physiological dependence. This has necessitated higher doses of methadone to prevent withdrawal and produce sufficient cross-tolerance to counter the effects of very potent heroin. Although very few treatment outcome studies have been done under these new circumstances, anecdotal evidence suggests that methadone treatment may be less effective or at least more difficult in the era of cheap and potent heroin.

Buprenorphine

Buprenorphine (Table 5.4b) belongs to another class of medications called *partial agonists*. It was originally approved for the treatment of pain but has also shown good efficacy as a maintenance drug in several clinical trials among heroin addicts. As a partial mu opiate agonist, buprenorphine activates opiate receptors, producing effects similar to those of heroin and methadone, but there is a "ceiling" such that higher doses produce no greater effect. In studies so far, overdose from buprenorphine alone has occurred rarely, if at all, but the drug can be lethal when mixed with benzodiazepines in high doses. If heroin or other opioids are taken, their effects are attenuated or blocked by the presence of buprenorphine. Buprenorphine was approved for treatment of opiate addiction in the United States in 2002. A unique aspect

TABLE 5.4b Medications for Heroin Dependence: Buprenorphine

Authors	Study Class	N	Treatment Length	Follow-up Length	Results	Comments
Mello & Mendelson (1980)	1	10	14 days	—	This inpatient experiment showed that buprenorphine 8 mg daily suppressed heroin self-administration 69–98%.	Buprenorphine suppresses heroin use.
Bickel et al. (1988)	1	45	90 days	—	Detoxification, methadone vs. buprenorphine, method was more effective in blocking opiate effects in lab, but use of street opiates not different.	No clinical difference between methadone and buprenorphine.
R. E. Johnson et al. (1992)	1	162	6 months	—	Buprenorphine 8 mg was compared to methadone 20 mg and methadone 60 mg. Low-dose methadone had lower retention rates than the other two groups. There was a trend for buprenorphine groups to have a higher percentage of opiate-free urines. There were no differences in urines positive for cocaine metabolites.	—
Bickel & Amass (1995)	5	n/a	—	—	This is an excellent, up-to-date review describing pros and cons of buprenorphine medication for opiate addiction.	—
Ling et al. (1998)	1	736	16 weeks	—	Double-blind comparison of 1, 4, 8, 16 mg buprenorphine. 8 and 16 mg were significantly better than 1 mg.	8 to 16 mg appear to be optimal doses, but higher doses may be necessary in era of potent heroin.
Ling et al. (1996)	1	225	52 weeks	—	Double-blind comparison of 8 mg buprenorphine vs. 30 mg and 80 mg methadone. Performance of 80-mg methadone group was better than low-dose methadone or 8-mg buprenorphine.	—
R. E. Johnson et al. (2000)	2	220	17 weeks	—	Randomized, not blinded comparison of LAAM, buprenorphine 16–32 mg, methadone 60–100 mg, and methadone 20 mg. Low-dose methadone significantly less effective than LAAM, buprenorphine, or high-dose methadone.	Low-dose methadone significantly less effective. Other 3 groups about equal.
Krook et al. (2002)	1	106	12 weeks	—	Buprenorphine (16 mg) produced larger decreases in opiate and other drug use, and longer retention than placebo.	Subjects did not receive any psychosocial treatment.
Fudala et al. (2003)	1	326	4 weeks	—	Random assignment, buprenorphine, buprenorphine/Nalox, placebo. Study terminated early due to clear efficacy of buprenorphine over placebo, negative urines, 17.8%, 20.7% versus 5.8% for placebo.	Study was office based, not research centers.
Montoya et al. (2004)	1	200	13 weeks	—	Dose of buprenorphine 2, 8, 16, or 16 every other day, versus placebo: significantly decreased opiate and cocaine use in the 8- and 16-mg dose groups.	Authors believe effect on cocaine use independent of effect on opiate use.

is that it can be prescribed in a doctor's office, thus eliminating the need to attend a strictly controlled methadone clinic. In order to legally prescribe buprenorphine, physicians must take a formal course on the drug to obtain a special license, and they are limited to 30 patients on this medication at any one time. The results of clinical trials are roughly similar to those involving methadone, although heroin addicts with a high degree of physical dependence may require the full agonist benefits of methadone (R. E. Johnson et al., 2000). The upper limit of buprenorphine effects is equivalent to about 40 mg of methadone. Based on experience from clinical trials, some heroin addicts prefer methadone, and others state that they feel the most stable and alert on buprenorphine. As with the treatment of other diseases, it is helpful for the clinician to have a selection of medications from which to choose.

Opioid Antagonist Treatment

The discovery of specific opiate receptor antagonists in the early 1970s gave rise to hopes for the "perfect" medication for the treatment of heroin addiction. Naltrexone (Table 5.4c) seemed to be the answer because it specifically blocks mu opiate receptors and, to a lesser extent, κ receptors and σ receptors (Raynor et al., 1994), and it has little or no direct or agonist effects of its own. Naltrexone and its short-acting analog naloxone have high affinity for opiate receptors and will displace drugs like morphine or methadone, resulting in the sudden onset of withdrawal symptoms when given to people who are opioid dependent. If the heroin addict is first detoxified so that opiate receptors are gradually evacuated, naltrexone will bind to the receptors and prevent subsequent injections of heroin from having an effect. Numerous clinical trials showed that naltrexone was effective in blocking opiate receptors and safe; thus, it was approved by the FDA in 1983. Unfortunately, naltrexone is a very underutilized medication in the treatment of heroin addiction. Unlike methadone, it has no positive psychoactive effects. Few street heroin addicts show any interest in this type of treatment, and few programs encourage patients to try it. Opioid antagonists are more complicated to prescribe than methadone, and most physicians have not been trained in their use. Opioid-dependent health care workers such as physicians, pharmacists, and nurses often do well on naltrexone because it enables them to return to work with no risk of relapse even though they work in areas with high drug availability. There is also evidence that naltrexone is helpful in preventing relapse in probationers who have a conditional release from prison after drug-related crimes (Brahen, Henderson, Copone, & Kordal, 1984; Cornish et al., 1997).

Experience with naltrexone demonstrates that blocking opiate receptors does not impair normal function for most people. Studies in animals have implicated opiate receptors in a wide variety of functions such as control of appetite, sexual behavior, and, of course, pain perception. Occasionally, normal volunteers given naltrexone report dysphoria or depression, but most former heroin addicts have few symptoms related to the antagonist. Some have remained on naltrexone for up to 20 years with no apparent change in appetite or pain perception and no impairment of ability to experience pleasure from sources such as sex or music. The recent approval of depot naltrexone should have an immediate positive effect on the treatment of heroin addiction. Although the cost of monthly injections will likely be an issue, it will be far less than the costs of drug-related crime and imprisonment.

CONCLUSIONS

The studies reviewed in this chapter indicate that, at this time, there are medications with at least some degree of efficacy in the treatment of nicotine, alcohol, and opiate use disorders. Several medications approved for other indications have shown efficacy for cocaine addiction. Methamphetamine addiction is the target of intense clinical research at present, and a medication that aids in the treatment of this difficult addiction will likely be discovered in the future. In addition, medications aimed at the treatment of drug craving are beginning to appear (O'Brien, 2005). Long-term psychosocial interventions should generally be used in conjunction with pharmacotherapy when treating substance use disorders to facilitate retention and compliance and to address the myriad of psychological and social problems that often accompany addiction (O'Brien, 1996). It is also important to treat comorbid psychiatric disorders, particularly when they are either preexisting or independent of the substance use disorder. Additional studies are needed to examine issues such as the

TABLE 5.4c Medications for Heroin Dependence: Naltrexone

Authors	Study Class	N	Treatment Length	Follow-up Length	Results	Comments
Hollister (1978)	1	192	9 months	–	Very high dropout rates in both groups. No significant differences.	Multiclinic trial.
Greenstein et al. (1984)	3	327	6 months or longer	6 months	Few side effects, multiple treatment episodes, no evidence of increased nonopiate use, 1/3 of patients opiate free at 6-month follow-up.	–
Washton et al. (1984)	3	114	6 months	12–18 months	All patients successfully detoxified and began naltrexone, 61% completed 6-month treatment; at 12–18 month follow-up, 64% still opiate free.	Shows excellent results with middle-class opiate addicts.
Ling & Wesson (1984)	3	60	6 months	Variable	Physicians and other health professionals. Average duration of naltrexone 6 months. All patients rated as much or moderately improved at 6 months.	Excellent results for health care workers.
Tennant et al. (1984)	3	160	51 days (mean)	–	Mean treatment length: 51 days; 29.5% dropped out in first week. Better results with those completely detoxified before starting naltrexone.	–
Judson et al. (1981)	2	119	12 months	End of treatment	60 mg vs. 120 mg thrice weekly. No difference between the two groups. Dramatic decrease in craving by end of first week.	Double-blind, two-dose comparison. No placebo group.
Gerra et al. (1995)	1	152	3 months	6 months	Double-blind, placebo-controlled 3 months of daily medication: clonidine only, clonidine and naltrexone, clonidine and naloxone; placebos. Better results with longer duration of naltrexone treatment.	Consistent with prior studies showing high dropout rate, but good results for patients who remain longer.
Shufman et al. (1994)	2	32	3 months	–	Fewer heroin-positive urine tests, more drug-free patients, more improvement in psychological parameters in naltrexone group.	Small sample size.
Azatian et al. (1994)	6	68	7 weeks	–	Open study, only 3 of 44 inpatient detox subjects succeeded in entering maintenance phase. A total of 27 of 68 entered maintenance and all discontinued by 50 days.	No control group, high early dropout rate.
Lerner et al. (1992)	1	31	–	2 months	Craving reduced in naltrexone group; reports of euphoria blocked when opiates used, but no evidence of reduced drug use as compared with placebo.	–
Cornish et al. (1997)	1	51	6 months	6 months	All participants volunteers from federal probation. Those randomized to control group received equivalent counseling, but no placebo. 52% completion in naltrexone vs. 33% for controls. Opioid use 8% in naltrexone vs. 30% for controls. Only 26% of naltrexone groups were reincarcerated vs. 56% for controls.	Demonstrates potential usefulness of naltrexone in a parole population.
Comer et al. 2005	1	60	2 months	–	Depot naltrexone, Biotek version, placebo, 192 or 384 mg depot naltrexone per month; treatment retention, dose related, 39, 60, 69% retention, positive urines varied according to dose.	Minimal side effects.

169

long-term efficacy and effectiveness of existing and new medications, matching subgroups of patients to particular medications, and potential dangers associated with severe relapse while on medications (Schuckit, 1996).

REFERENCES

Alterman, A. I., Droba, M., Antelo, R. E., Cornish, J. W., Sweeney, K. K., Parikh, G. A., et al. (1992). Amantadine may facilitate detoxification of cocaine addicts. *Drug and Alcohol Dependence, 31,* 19–29.

Alterman, A. I., O'Brien, C. P., McLellan, A. T., August, D. S., Snider, E. C., Droba., M., et al. (1994). Effectiveness and costs of inpatient versus day hospital cocaine rehabilitations. *Journal of Nervous and Mental Disease, 182,* 157–163.

American Psychiatric Association. (2000). *Diagnostic and statistical manual of mental disorders* (4th ed., text revision). Washington, DC: Author.

Angelone, S. M., Bellini, L., Di Bella, D., & Catalano, M. (1998). Effects of fluvoxamine and citalopram in maintaining abstinence in a sample of Italian detoxified alcoholics. *Alcohol and Alcoholism, 33,* 151–156.

Anglin, M. D., Speckart, G. R., Booth, M. W., & Ryan, T. M. (1989). Consequences and costs of shutting off methadone. *Addictive Medicine, 14,* 307–326.

Anton, R. F., Moak, D. H., Waid, L. R., Latham, P. K., Malcolm, R. J., & Dias, J. K. (1999). Naltrexone and cognitive behavioral therapy for the treatment of outpatient alcoholics: Results of a placebo-controlled trial. *American Journal of Psychiatry, 156,* 1758–1764.

Anton, R. F., O'Malley, S. S., Ciraulo, D. A., Cisler, R. A., Couper, D., Donovan, D. M., et al. for the COMBINE Study Research Group. (2006). Combined pharmacotherapies and behavioral interventions for alcohol dependence—The COMBINE Study: A randomized controlled trial. *Journal of the American Medical Association, 295,* 2003–2017.

Arndt, I. O., Dorozynksy, L., Woody, G. E., McLellan, A. T., & O'Brien, C. P. (1992). Desipramine treatment of cocaine dependence in methadone-maintained patients. *Archives of General Psychiatry, 49,* 888–893.

Azatian, A., Papiasvilli, A., & Joseph, H. (1994). A study of the use of clonidine and naltrexone in the treatment of opioid addiction in former USSR. *Journal of Addictive Disease, 13,* 35–52.

Azrin, N. H., Sisson, R. W., Meyers, R., & Godley, M. (1982). Alcoholism treatment by disulfiram and community reinforcement therapy. *Journal of Behavioral Therapy and Experimental Psychiatry, 13,* 105–112.

Bart, G., Heilig, M., LaForge, K. S., Pollak, L., Leal, S. M., Ott, J., et al. (2004). Substantial attributable risk related to a functional mu-opioid receptor gene polymorphism in association with heroin addiction in central Sweden. *Molecular Psychiatry, 9,* 547–549.

Bart, G., Kreek, M. J., Ott. J., LaForge, K. S., Proudnikov, D., Pollak, L., et al. (2005). Increased attributable risk related to a functional mu-opioid receptor gene polymorphism in association with alcohol dependence in central Sweden. *Neuropsychopharmacology, 30,* 417–422.

Berger, S. P., Hall, S., Michalian, J. D., Reid, M. S., Crawford, C. A., Delucchi, K., et al. (1996). Haloperidol antagonism of cue-elicited cocaine craving. *Lancet, 347,* 504–508.

Berrettini, W. H., & Lerman, C. E. (2005). Pharmacotherapy and pharmacogenetics of nicotine dependence. *American Journal of Psychiatry, 162,* 1441–1451.

Besson, J., Aeby, F., Kasas, A., Lehert, P., & Potgieter, A. (1998). Combined efficacy of acamprosate and disulfiram in the treatment of alcoholism: A controlled study. *Alcoholism: Clinical and Experimental Research, 22,* 573–579.

Bickel, W. K., & Amass, L. (1995). Buprenorphine treatment of opioid dependence: A review. *Experimental and Clinical Psychopharmacology, 3,* 477–489.

Bickel, W. K., Stitzer, M. L., Bigelow, G. E., Liebson, I. A., Jasinski, D. R., & Johnson, D. E. (1988). A clinical trial with buprenorphine: Comparison with methadone in the detoxification of heroin addicts. *Clinical Pharmacological Therapy, 43,* 72–78.

Brahen, L. S., Henderson, R. K., Copone, T., & Kordal, N. (1984). Naltrexone treatment in a jail work-release program. *Journal of Clinical Psychiatry, 45,* 49–52.

Brodie, J. D., Figueroa, E., Laska, E. M., & Dewey, S. L. (2005). Safety and efficacy of gamma-vinyl GABA (GVG) for the treatment of methamphetamine and/or cocaine addiction. *Synapse, 55,* 122–125.

Bruno, F. (1989). Buspirone in the treatment of alcoholic patients. *Psychopathology, 22*(Suppl. 1), 49–59.

Carroll, K. M., Fenton, L. R., Ball, S. A., Nich, C., Frankforter, T. L., Shi, J. et al. (2004). Efficacy of disulfiram and cognitive behavior therapy in cocaine-dependent outpatients: A randomized placebo-controlled trial. *Archives of General Psychiatry, 61,* 264–272.

Carroll, K. M., Nich, C., Ball, S. A., McCance, E., & Rounsaville, B. J. (1998). Treatment of cocaine and alcohol dependence with psychotherapy and disulfiram. *Addiction, 93,* 713–727.

Carroll, K. M., Rounsaville, B. J., Nich, C., Gordon, L. T., Wirtz, P. W., & Gawin, F. H. (1994). One year follow-up of psychotherapy and pharmacotherapy for cocaine dependence: Delayed emergence of psychotherapy effects. *Archives of General Psychiatry, 51,* 989–997.

Chick, J., Gough, K., Falkowski, W., Kershaw, P., Hore, B., Mehta, B., et al. (1992). Disulfiram treatment of alcoholism. *British Journal of Psychiatry, 161,* 84–89.

Chick, J., Howlett, H., Morgan, M. Y., & Ritson, B. (2000). United Kingdom Multicentre Acamprosate Study (UKMAS): A 6-month prospective study of acamprosate versus placebo in preventing relapse after withdrawal from alcohol. *Alcohol and Alcoholism, 35,* 176–187.

Childress, A. R., McLellan, A. T., Ehrman, R., & O'Brien, C. P. (1987). Extinction of conditioned responses in abstinent cocaine or opioid users [Monograph]. *Problems of Drug Dependence, 76,* 189–195.

Childress, A. R., Mozley, P. D., McElgin, W., Fitzgerald, J., Reivich, M., & O'Brien, C. P. (1999). Limbic activation during cue-induced cocaine craving. *American Journal of Psychiatry, 156,* 11–18.

Ciraulo, D. A., Knapp, C., Rotrosen, J., Sarid-Segal, O., Ciraulo, A. M., LoCastro, J., et al. (2005). Nefazodone treatment of cocaine dependence with comorbid depressive symptoms. *Addiction, 100,* 23–31.

Comer, S. D., Sullivan, M. A., Yu, W., Rothenberg, J. L., Kleber, H. D., Kampman, K., et al. (2005). Injectable, sustained-release naltrexone for the treatment of opioid dependence: A randomized, placebo-controlled trial. *Archives of General Psychiatry, 62,* 210–218.

Cornelius, J. R., Salloum, I. M., Ehler, J. G., Jarrett, P. J., Cornelius, M. D., Perel, J. M., et al. (1997). Fluoxetine in depressed alcoholics: A double-blind, placebo-controlled trial. *Archives of General Psychiatry, 54,* 700–705.

Cornish, J. W., Maany, I., Fudala, P. J., Ehrman, R. N., Robbins, S. J., & O'Brien, C. P. (2001). A randomized, double-blind, placebo-controlled study of ritanserin pharmacotherapy for cocaine dependence. *Drug Alcohol Dependence, 61,* 183–189.

Cornish, J. W., Maany, I., Fudala, P. J., Neal, S., Poole, S. A., Volpicelli, P., et al. (1995). Carbamazepine treatment for cocaine dependence [Monograph]. *Drug and Alcohol Dependence, 38,* 221–227.

Cornish, J. W., Metzger, D., Woody, G. E., Wilson, D., McLellan, A. T., Vandergrift, B., et al. (1997). Naltrexone pharmacotherapy for opioid dependent federal probationers. *Journal of Substance Abuse Treatment, 14,* 167–174.

Croghan, G. A., Sloan, J. A., Croghan, I. T., Novotny, P., Hurt, R. D., DeKrey, W. L., et al. (2003). Comparison of nicotine patch alone versus nicotine nasal spray alone versus a combination for treating smokers: A minimal intervention, randomized multicenter trial in a nonspecialized setting. *Nicotine Tobacco Research, 5,* 181–187.

Dackis, C. A., Kampman, K. M., Lynch, K. G., Pettinati, H. M., & O'Brien, C. P. (2005). A double-blind, placebo-controlled trial of modafinil for cocaine dependence. *Neuropsychopharmacology, 30,* 205–211.

Dackis, C. A., Lynch, K. G., Yu, E., Samaha, F. F., Kampman, K. M., Cornish, J. W., et al. (2003). Modafinil and cocaine: A double-blind, placebo-controlled drug interaction study. *Drug and Alcohol Dependence, 70,* 29–37.

Dole, V. P., Robinson, J. W., Orraca, J., Towns, E., Searcy, P., & Caine, E. (1969). Methadone treatment of randomly selected criminal addicts. *New England Journal of Medicine, 280,* 1372–1375.

Donovan, J. L., DeVane, C. L., Malcolm, R. J., Mojsiak, J., Chiang, C. N., Elkashef, A., et al. (2005). Modafinil influences the pharmacokinetics of intravenous cocaine in healthy cocaine-dependent volunteers. *Clinical Pharmacokinetics, 44,* 753–765.

Fiore, M. C., Kenford, S. L., Jorenby, D. E., Wetter, D. W., Smith S. S., & Baker, T. B. (1994). Two studies of the clinical effectivness of the nicotine patch with different counseling treatments. *Chest, 105(2),* 524–533.

Fiore, M. C., Smith, S. S., Jorenby, D. E., & Baker, T. B. (1994). The effectiveness of the nicotine patch for smoking cessation: A meta-analysis. *Journal of the American Medical Association, 271,* 1940–1947.

Fudala, P. J., Bridge, T. P., Herbert, S., Williford, W. O., Chiang, C. N., Jones, K., et al. (2003). Office-based treatment of opiate addiction with a sublingual-tablet formulation of buprenorphine and naloxone. *New England Journal of Medicine, 349,* 949–958.

Fuller, R. K. (1995). Antidipsotropic medications. In R. K. Hester & W. R. Miller (Eds.), *Handbook of alcoholism treatment approaches: Effective alternatives* (2nd ed., pp. 123–133). Needham Heights, MA: Allyn and Bacon.

Fuller, R. K., Branchey, L., Brightwell, D. R., Derman, R. M., Emrick, C. D., Iber, F. L., et al. (1986). Disulfiram treatment of alcoholism: A Veterans Administration cooperative study. *Journal of the American Medical Association, 256,* 1449–1455.

Garbutt, J. C., Kranzler, H. R., O'Malley, S. S., Gastfriend, D. R., Pettinati, H. M., Silverman, B. L., et al. (2005). Efficacy and tolerability of long-acting injectable naltrexone for alcohol dependence: A randomized controlled trial. *Journal of the American Medical Association, 293,* 1617–1625.

Gawin, F. H., Allen, D., & Humblestone, B. (1989). Outpatient treatment of "crack" cocaine smoking with flupenthixol deconoate: A preliminary report. *Archives of General Psychiatry, 46,* 322–325.

Gawin, F. H., Kleber, H. D., Byck, R., Rounsaville, B. J., Kosten, T. R., Jatlow, P. I., et al. (1989). Desipramine facilitation of initial cocaine abstinence. *Archives of General Psychiatry, 46,* 117–121.

Gawin, F. H., Morgan, C., Kosten, T. R., & Kleber, H. D. (1989). Double-blind evaluation of the effect of acute amantadine on cocaine craving. *Psychopharmacology, 97,* 402–403.

Gawin, F. H., Riordan, C., & Kleber, H. (1985). Methylphenidate treatment of cocaine abusers without attention deficit disorder: A negative report. *American Journal of Drug and Alcohol Abuse, 11,* 193–197.

Gerra, G., Marcato, A., Caccavari, R, Fontanesi, B., Delsignore, R., Fertonani, G., et al. (1995). Clonidine and opiate receptor antagonists in the treatment of heroin addiction. *Journal of Substance Abuse Treatment, 12,* 35–41.

Giannini, A. J., Folts, D. J., Feather, J. N., & Sullivan, B. S. (1989). Bromocriptine and amantadine in cocaine detoxification. *Psychiatry Research, 29,* 11–16.

Gorelick, D. A. (1989). Serotonin reuptake blockers and the treatment of alcoholism. In M. Galanter (Ed.), *Recent developments in alcoholism* (pp. 267–281). New York: Plenum Press.

Gorelick, D. A., & Paredes, A. (1992). Effect of fluoxetine on alcohol consumption in male alcoholics. *Alcoholism: Clinical and Experimental Research, 16,* 261–265.

Grabowski, J., Rhoades, H., Elk, R., Schmitz, J., Davis, C., Creson, D., et al. (1995). Fluoxetine is ineffective for treatment of cocaine dependence or concurrent opiate and cocaine dependence: Two placebo-controlled, double blind trials. *Journal of Clinical Psychopharmacology, 15,* 163–174.

Grabowski, J., Rhoades, H., Silverman, P., Schmitz, J. M., Stotts, A., Creson, D. et al. (2000). Risperidone for the treatment of cocaine dependence: Randomized, double-blind trial. *Journal of Clinical Psychopharmacology, 20,* 305–310.

Grabowski, J., Roache, J. D., Schmitz, J. M., Rhoades, H., Creson, D., & Korszun, A. (1997). Replacement medication for cocaine dependence: Methylphenidate. *Journal of Clinical Psychopharmacology, 17,* 485–488.

Greenstein, R. A., Arndt, I. C., McLellan, A. T., O'Brien, C. P., & Evans, B. (1984). Naltrexone: A clinical perspective. *Journal of Clinical Psychiatry, 45,* 25–28.

Gunne, L., & Gronbladh, L. (1984). The Swedish methadone maintenance program. In G. Servan (Ed.), *Social and medical aspects of drug abuse* (pp. 205–213). Jamaica, NY: Spectrum.

Hersh, D., Van Kirk, J. R., & Kranzler, H. R. (1998). Naltrexone treatment of comorbid alcohol and cocaine use disorders. *Psychopharmacology, 139,* 44–52.

Higgins, S. T., Budney, A. J., Bickel, W. K., Hughes, J. R., Goerg, F. & Badger, G. (1993). Achieving cocaine abstinence with a behavioral approach. *American Journal of Psychiatry, 150,* 763–769.

Hollister, L. (1978). Clinical evaluation of naltrexone treatment for opiate-dependent individuals. *Archives of General Psychiatry, 35,* 335–340.

Hurt, R. D., Sachs, D. P. L., Glover, E. D., Offord, K. P., Johnston, J. A., Dale, L. C., et al. (1997). A comparison of sustained-release bupropion and placebo for smoking cessation. *New England Journal of Medicine, 337,* 1195–1202.

Imperial Cancer Fund General Practice Research Group. (1993). Effectiveness of a nicotine patch in helping people stop smoking: Results of a randomized trial in general practice. *British Medical Journal, 306,* 1304–1308.

Jenkins, S. W., Warfield, N. A., Blaine, J. D., Cornish, J., Ling, W., Rosen, M. I., et al. (1992). A pilot study of gepirone vs. placebo in the treatment of cocaine dependency. *Psychopharmacology Bulletin, 28,* 21–26.

Johnsen, J., & Morland, J. (1991). Disulfiram implant: A double-blind placebo controlled follow-up on treatment outcome. *Alcoholism: Clinical and Experimental Research, 15,* 532–536.

Johnson, B. A., Ait-Daoud, N., Akhtar, F. Z., & Ma, J. Z. (2004). Oral topiramate reduces the consequences of drinking and improves the quality of life of alcohol-dependent individuals: A randomized controlled trial. *Archives of General Psychiatry, 61,* 905–912.

Johnson, B. A., Ait-Daoud, N. & Priholda, T. J. (2000). Combining ondansetron and naltrexone effectively treats biologically predisposed alcoholics: From hypotheses to preliminary clinical evidence. *Alcoholism: Clinical and Experimental Research, 24,* 737–742.

Johnson, B. A., Jasinski, D. R., Galloway, G. P., Kranzler, H., Weinrieb, R., Anton, R. F., et al. (1996). Ritanserin in the treatment of alcohol dependence: A multi-center clinical trial. *Psychopharmacology, 128,* 206–215.

Johnson, B. A., Roache, J. D., Javors, M. A., DiClemente, C. C., Cloninger, C. R., Prihoda, T. J., et al. (2000). Ondansetron for reduction of drinking among biologically predisposed alcohol patients: A randomized controlled trial. *Journal of the American Medical Association 28,* 963–971.

Johnson, R. E., Chutuape, M. A., Strain, E. C., Walsh, S. L., Stitzer, M. L. & Bigelow, G. E. (2000). A comparison of levomethadyl acetate, buprenorphine, and methadone for opioid dependence. *New England Journal of Medicine, 343,* 1290–1297.

Johnson, R. E., Jaffe, J. H., & Fudala, P. J. (1992). A controlled trial of buprenorphine treatment for opioid dependence. *Journal of the American Medical Association, 267),* 2750–2755.

Jorenby, D. E., Leschow, S. J., Nides, M. A., Rennard, S. I., Johnston, J. A., Hughes, A. R., et al. (1999). A controlled trial of sustained-release bupropion, a nicotine patch, or both for smoking cessation. *New England Journal of Medicine, 340,* 685–691.

Judson, B. A., Carney, T. M., & Goldstein, A. (1981). Naltrexone treatment of heroin addiction: Efficacy and safety in a double-blind dosage comparison. *Drug and Alcohol Dependence, 7,* 325–346.

Kampman, K. M., Pettinati, H., Lynch, K. G., Dackis, C., Sparkman, T., Weigley, C. et al. (2004). A pilot trial of topiramate for the treatment of cocaine dependence. *Drug and Alcohol Dependence, 75,* 233–240.

Kampman, K. M., Rukstalis, M., Ehrman, R., McGinnis, D. E., Gariti, P., Volpicelli, J. R., et al. (1999). Open trials as a method of prioritizing medications for inclusion in controlled trials for cocaine dependence. *Addictive Behaviors, 24,* 287–291.

Kampman, K. M., Volpicelli, J. R., Alterman, A. I., Cornish, J., & O'Brien, C. P. (2000). Amantadine in the treatment of cocaine-dependent patients with severe withdrawal symptoms. *American Journal of Psychiatry, 157,* 2052–2054.

Kampman, K. M., Volpicelli, J. R., Mulvaney, F., Alterman, A. I., Cornish, J., Gariti, P., et al. (2001). Effectiveness of propranolol for cocaine dependence treatment may depend on cocaine withdrawal symptom severity. *Drug and Alcohol Dependence, 61,* 69–78.

Khalsa, E., Jatlow, P., & Gawin, F.(1994). Flupenthixol and desipramine treatment of crack users: Double-blind results. *NIDA Research Monograph, 141,* 438.

Kleber, H. D. (1995). Pharmacotherapy, current and potential, for the treatment of cocaine dependence. *Clinical Neuropharmacology, 15,* S96–S109.

Knox, P. C., & Donovan, D. M. (1999). Using naltrexone in inpatient alcoholism treatment. *Journal of Psychoactive Drugs, 31,* 373–388.

Kolar, A. F., Brown, B. S., Weddington, W. W., Haertzen, C. C., Michaelson, B. S., & Jaffe, J. H. (1992). Treatment of cocaine dependence in methadone maintenance clients: A pilot study comparing the efficacy of desipramine and amantadine. *International Journal of the Addictions, 27,* 849–868.

Koob, G. F. (1992). Neurobiological mechanisms in cocaine and opiate dependence. In C. P. O'Brien & J. Jaffe (Eds.), *Addictive states* (pp. 79–92). New York: Raven Press.

Kornitzer, M., Boutsen, M., Dramaix, M., Thijs, J., & Gustavsson, G. (1995). Combined use of nicotine patch and gum in smoking cessation: A placebo-controlled clinical trial. *Preventive Medicine, 24,* 41–47.

Kosten, T. R., Morgan, C. M., Falcione, J., & Schottenfeld, R. S. (1992). Pharmacotherapy for cocaine-abusing methadone-maintained patients using amantadine or desipramine. *Archives of General Psychiatry, 49,* 894–898.

Kranzler, H. R., & Anton, R. F. (1994). Implications of recent neuropsychopharmacologic research for understanding the etiology and development of alcoholism. *Journal of Consulting and Clinical Psychology, 62,* 1116–1126.

Kranzler, H. R., Burleson, J. A., Del Boca, F. K., Babor, T. F., Korner, P., Brown, J.,et al. (1994). Buspirone treatment of anxious alcoholics: A placebo-controlled trial. *Archives of General Psychiatry, 51,* 720–731.

Kranzler, H. R., Burleson, J. A., Korner, P., Del Boca, F. K., Bohn, M. J., Brown, J.,et al. (1995). Placebo-controlled trial of fluoxetine as an adjunct to relapse prevention in alcoholics. *American Journal of Psychiatry, 152,* 391–397.

Kranzler, H. R., Modesto-Lowe, V., & Nuwayser, E. S. (1998). Sustained-release naltrexone for alcoholism treatment: A preliminary study. *Alcoholism: Clinical and Experimental Research, 22,* 1074–1079.

Kranzler, H. R., Modesto-Lowe, V., & Van Kirk, J. (2000). Naltrexone vs. nefazodone for treatment of alcohol dependence: A placebo-controlled trial. *Neuropsychopharmacology, 22,* 493–503.

Kreek, M. J. (1992). Rationale for maintenance pharmacotherapy of opiate dependence. In C. P. O'Brien

& J. H. Jaffe (Eds.), *Addictive states* (pp. 205–330). New York: Raven Press.

Krook, A. L., Brors, O., Dahlberg, J., Grouff, K., Magnus, P., Roysamb, E. et al. (2002). A placebo-controlled study of high dose buprenorphine in opiate dependents waiting for medication-assisted rehabilitation in Oslo, Norway. *Addiction, 97,* 533–542.

Krystal, J. H., Cramer, J. A., Krol, W. F., Kirk, G. F., Rosenheck, R. A. & Veterans Affairs Cooperative Study 425 Group. (2001). Naltrexone in the treatment of alcohol dependence. *New England Journal of Medicine, 345,* 1734–1739.

Lerner, A., Sigal, M., Bacalu, E., Shiff, R., Burganski, I., & Gelkopf, M. (1992). A naltrexone double blind placebo controlled study in Israel. *Israel Journal of Psychiatry and Related Sciences, 29,* 36–43.

Levin, F. R., & Lehman, A. F. (1991). Meta-analysis of desipramine as an adjunct in the treatment of cocaine addiction. *Journal of Clinical Psychopharmacology, 11,* 374–378.

Lhuintre, J. P., Moore, N. D., Saligaut, C., Boismare, F., Daoust, M., Chretien, P., et al. (1985). Ability of calcium bis acetyl homotaurinate, a GABA agonist, to prevent relapse in weaned alcoholics. *Lancet, 1,* 1014–1016.

Lhuintre, J. P., Moore, N. D., Tran, G., Steru, L., Lancrenon, S., Daoust, M., et al. (1990). Acamprosate appears to decrease alcohol intake in weaned alcoholics. *Alcohol and Alcoholism, 25,* 613–622.

Ling, W., Charuvastra, C., Collins, J. F., Batki, S., Brown, L. S., Kintaudi, P., et al. (1998). Buprenorphine maintenance treatment of opiate dependence: A multicenter, randomized clinical trial. *Addiction, 93,* 475–486.

Ling, W., & Wesson, D. R. (1984). Naltrexone treatment for addicted health-care professionals: A collaborative private practice. *Journal of Clinical Psychiatry, 34,* 46–52.

Ling, W., Wesson, D. R., Charuvastra, C., & Klett, C. J. (1996). A controlled trial comparing buprenorphine and methadone maintenance in opioid dependence. *Archives of General Psychiatry, 53,* 401–407.

Malcolm, R., Anton, R. F., Randall, C. L., Johnston, A., Brady, K., & Thevos, A. (1992). A placebo-controlled trial of buspirone in anxious inpatient alcoholics. *Alcoholism: Clinical and Experimental Research, 16,* 1007–1013.

Malcolm, R., Book, S. W., Moak, D., DeVane, L., & Czepowicz, V. (2002). Clinical applications of modafinil in stimulant abusers: Low abuse potential. *American Journal on Addictions, 11,* 247–249.

Martin, W. R., & Jasinski, D. (1969). Psychological parameters of morphine in man-tolerance, early abstinence, protracted abstinence. *Journal of Psychiatric Research, 7,* 9–16.

Mason, B. J., Goodman, A. M., Chabac, S., & Lehert, P. (2006). Effect of oral acamprosate on abstinence in patients with alcohol dependence in a double-blind, placebo-controlled trial: The role of patient motivation. *Journal of Psychiatric Research, 40,* 383–393.

Mason, B. J., Kocsis, J. H., Ritvo, E. C., & Cutler, R. B. (1996). A double-blind, placebo-controlled trial of desipramine for primary alcohol dependence stratified on the presence or absence of major depression. *Journal of the American Medical Association, 275,* 761–767.

Mason, B. J., Ritvo, E. C., Morgan, R. O., Salvato, F. R., Goldberg, G., Welch, B., et al. (1994). A double-blind, placebo-controlled pilot study to evaluate the efficacy and safety of oral nalmefene HCl for alcohol dependence. *Alcoholism: Clinical and Experimental Research, 18,* 1162–1167.

Mason, B. J., Salvato, F. R., Williams, L. D., Ritvo, E. C., & Cutler, R. B. (1999). A double-blind, placebo-controlled study of oral nalmefene for alcohol dependence. *Archives of General Psychiatry, 56,* 719–724.

McGrath, P. J., Nunes, E. V., Stewart, J. W., Goldman, D., Agosti, V., Ocepek-Welikson, K., et al. (1996). Imipramine treatment of alcoholics with primary depresssion: A placebo-controlled clinical trial. *Archives of General Psychiatry, 53,* 232–240.

McKay, J. R., Alterman, A. I., McLellan, A. T., Boardman, C., Mulvaney, F., & O'Brien, C. P. (1998). Random versus nonrandom assignment in the evaluation of treatment for cocaine abusers. *Journal of Consulting and Clinical Psychology, 66,* 697–701.

McLellan, A. T., Arndt, I. O., Metzger, D., Woody, G., & O'Brien, C. P. (1993). The effects of psychosocial services in substance abuse treatment. *Journal of the American Medical Association, 269,* 1959–1993.

Mello, N. K., & Mendelson, J. H. (1980). Buprenorphine suppresses heroin use by heroin addicts. *Science, 207,* 657–659.

Metzger, D. S., Woody, G. E., McLellan, A. T., O'Brien, C. P., Druley, P., Navaline, H., et al. (1993). Human immunodeficiency virus seroconversion among in- and out-of-treatment drugs users: An 18 month prospective follow-up. *Journal of AIDS, 6,* 1049–1056.

Mintz, J., O'Brien, C. P., & Goldschmidt, J. (1974). Sexual problems of heroin addicts when drug free, on heroin, and on methadone. *Archives of General Psychiatry, 31*, 700–703.

Montoya, I. D., Gorelick, D. A., Preston, K. L., Schroeder, J. R., Umbricht, A., Cheskin, L. J., et al. (2004). Randomized trial of buprenorphine for treatment of concurrent opiate and cocaine dependence. *Clinical Pharmacology and Therapeutics, 75*, 34–48.

Montoya, I. D., Levin, F. R., Fudala, P. J., & Gorelick, D. A. (1995). Double-blind comparison of carbamazepine and placebo for the treatment of cocaine. *Drug and Alcohol Dependence, 39*, 213–219.

Myer, E. C., Morris, D. L., Brase, D. A., Dewey, W. L., & Zimmerman, A. W. (1990). Naltrexone therapy of apnea in children with elevated cerebrospinal fluid b-endorphin. *Annals of Neurology, 27*, 75–80.

Myers, J. K., Weissman, M. M., Tischler, G. L., Holzer, C. E., Leaf, P. J., Orvaschel, H., et al. (1984). Six month prevalence of psychiatric disorders in three communities 1980–1982. *Archives of General Psychiatry, 41*, 959–967.

Naranjo, C. A., Sellers, E. M., Sullivan, J. T., Woodley, D. V., Kadlec, K., & Sykora, J. (1987). The serotonin uptake inhibitor citalopram attenuates ethanol intake. *Clinical Pharmacology and Therapeutics, 41*, 266–274.

Newman, R. G., & Whitehill, W. G. (1979). Double-blind comparison of methadone and placebo maintenance treatment of narcotic addicts in Hong Kong. *Lancet, 2*, 485–488.

Novick, D. M., Pascarelli, E. F., & Joseph, H. (1988). Methadone maintenance patients in general medical practice: A prelminary report. *Journal of the American Medical Association, 259*, 3299–3302.

Nunes, E. V., McGrath, P. J., Quitkin, F. M., Ocepek-Welikson, K., Stewart, J. K. W., Koenig, T., et al. (1995). Imipramine treatment of cocaine abuse: Possible boundaries of efficacy. *Drug and Alcohol Dependence, 39*, 185–195.

O'Brien, C. P. (1993). Opioid addiction. In A. Herz (Ed.), *Handbook of experimental pharmacology* (Vol. 104/II pp. 803–823). Berlin: Springer-Verlag.

O'Brien, C. P. (1996). Recent developments in the pharmacotherapy of substance abuse. *Journal of Consulting and Clinical Psychology, 64*, 677–686.

O'Brien, C. P. (2005). Anti-craving (relapse prevention) medications: Possibly a new class of psychoactive medication. *American Journal of Psychiatry, 162*, 1423–1431.

O'Brien, C. P., Childress, A. R., Arndt, I. O., McLellan, A. T., Woody, G. E., & Maany, I. (1988). Pharmacological and behavioral treatments of cocaine dependence: Controlled studies. *Journal of Clinical Psychiatry, 49*, 17–22.

O'Farrell, J. J., Cutter, H. S. G., & Floyd, F. J. (1985). Evaluating behavioral marital therapy for male alcoholics: Effects on marital adjustment and communication from before to after therapy. *Behavior Therapy, 16*, 147–167.

Oliveto, A. H., Feingold, A., Schottenfeld, R., Jatlow, R., & Kosten, T. R. (1999). Desipramine in opioid-dependent cocaine abusers maintained on buprenorphine. *Archives of General Psychiatry, 56*, 812–820.

O'Malley, S. S., Jaffe, A. J., Chang, G., Schottenfeld, R. S., Meyer, R. E., & Rounsaville, B. J. (1992). Naltrexone and coping skills therapy for alcohol dependence. *Archives of General Psychiatry, 49*, 881–887.

Oslin, D., Liberto, J. G., O'Brien, J., Krois, S., & Norbeck, J. (1997). Naltrexone as an adjunctive treatment for older patients with alcohol dependence. *American Journal of Geriatric Psychiatry, 5*, 324–332.

Oslin, D. W., Berrettini, W., Kranzler, H., Pettinati, H., Gelernter, J., Volpicelli, J.et al. (2003). A functional polymorphism of the mu opioid receptor gene is associated with naltrexone response in alcohol dependent patients. *Neuropsychopharmacology, 28*, 1546–1552.

Paille, F. M., Guelfi, J. D., Perkins, A. C., Royer, R. J., Steru, L., & Parot, P. (1995). Double-blind randomized multicentre trial of acamprosate in maintaining abstinence from alcohol. *Alcohol and Alcoholism, 30*, 239–247.

Pelc, I., Verbanck, P., Le Bon, O., Gavrilovic, M., Lion, K., & Lehert, P. (1997). Efficacy and safety of acamprosate in the treatment of detoxified alcohol-dependent patients: A 90-day placebo-controlled dose-finding study. *British Journal of Psychiatry, 171*, 73–77.

Petrakis, I. L., Carroll, K. M., Nich, C., Gordon, L. T., McCance-Katz, E. F., Frankforter, T.,et al. (2000). Disulfiram treatment for cocaine dependence in methadone-maintained opioid addicts. *Addiction, 95*, 219–228.

Pettinati, H. M., & Rabinowitz, A. R. (2005). Recent advances in the treatment of alcoholism. *Clinical Neuroscience Research, 5*, 151–159.

Poldrugo, F. (1997). Acamprosate treatment in a long-term community-based alcohol rehabilitation programme. *Addiction, 92*, 1537–1546.

Rawson, R. A., Shoptaw, M. J., & Minsky, S. (1994). Effectiveness of desipramine in treating cocaine dependence. *NIDA Research Monograph, 153*, 494.

Ray, L. A., & Hutchison, K. E. (2004). A polymorphism of the mu-opioid receptor gene (OPRM1) and sensitivity to the effect of alcohol in humans. *Alcoholism: Clinical and Experimental Research, 28,* 1789–1795.

Raynor, K., Kong, H., Chen, Y., Yasuda, K., Yu, L., Bell, G. I., et al. (1994). Pharmacological characterization of the cloned k-, d- and m-opioid receptors. *Molecular Pharmacology., 45,* 330–334.

Richmond, R. L., Harris, K., & de Almeida Neta, A. (1994). The transdermal nicotine patch: Results of a randomized placebo-controlled trial. *Medical Journal of Australia 161,* 130–135.

Robbins, S., Ehrman, R., Childress, A. R., & O'Brien, C. P. (1992). Using cue reactivity to screen medications for cocaine abuse: Amantadine hydrochloride. *Addictive Behaviors, 17,* 491–499.

Robins, L. N., Helzer, J. E., Weissman, M. M., Orvaschel, H., Gruenberg, E., Burke, J. D., et al. (1984). Lifetime prevalence of specific psychiatric disorders in three sites. *Archives of General Psychiatry, 41,* 949–958.

Roy, A., Virkkunen, M., & Linnoila, M. (1990). Serotonin in suicide, violence, and alcoholism. In E. F. Coccaro & D. L. Murphy (Eds.), *Serotonin in major psychiatric disorders* (pp. 187–208). Washington, DC: American Psychiatric Press.

Sass, H., Soyka, M., Mann, K., & Zieglgansberger, W. (1996). Relapse prevention by acamprosate: Results from a placebo controlled study in alcohol dependence. *Archives of General Psychiatry, 53,* 673–680.

Schmitz, J. M., Averill, P., Stotts, A. L., Moeller, F. G., Rhoades, H. M., & Grabowski, J. (2001). Fluoxetine treatment of cocaine-dependent patients with major depressive disorder. *Drug and Alcohol Dependence, 63,* 207–214.

Schuckit, M. A. (1996). Recent developments in the pharmacotherapy of alcohol dependence. *Journal of Consulting and Clinical Psychology, 64,* 669–676.

Shiffman, S., Johnson, J. A., Khayrallah, M., Elash, C. A., Gwaltney, C. J., Paty, J. A., et al. (2000). The effect of bupropion on nicotine craving and withdrawal. *Psychopharmacology, 148,* 33–40.

Shoptaw, S., Kintaudi, P. C., Charuvastra, C. & Ling, W. (2002). A screening trial of amantadine as a medication for cocaine dependence. *Drug and Alcohol Dependence, 66,* 217–224.

Shoptaw, S., Yang, X., Rotheram-Fuller, E. J., Hsieh, Y. C., Kintaudi, P. C., Charuvastra, V. C., et al. (2003). Randomized placebo-controlled trial of baclofen for cocaine dependence: Preliminary effects for individuals with chronic patterns of cocaine use. *Journal of Clinical Psychiatry, 64,* 1440–1448.

Shufman, E. N., Porat, S., Witztum, E., Gandacu, D., Bar-Hamburger, R., & Ginath, U. (1994). The efficacy of naltrexone in preventing reabuse of heroin after detoxification. *Biological Psychiatry, 35,* 935–945.

Stimmel, B., Goldberg, J., Rotkopf, E., & Cohen, M. (1977). Ability to remain abstinent after methadone detoxification: A six-year study. *Journal of the American Medical Association, 237,* 1216–1220.

Strain, E. C., Stitzer, M. L., Liebson, I. A., & Bigelow, G. E. (1994a). Buprenorphine versus methadone in the treatment of opioid-dependent cocaine users. *Psychopharmacology, 116,* 401–406.

Strain, E. C., Stitzer, M. L., Liebson, I. A., & Bigelow, G. E. (1994b). Comparison of buprenorphine and methadone in the treatment of opioid dependence. *American Journal of Psychiatry, 151,* 1025–1030.

Suh, J. J., Pettinati, M. H., Kampman, K. M., & O'Brien, C. P. (2006). The status of disulfiram: A half of a century later. *Journal of Clinical Psychopharmacology, 26,* 290–302.

Tempesta, E., Janiri, L., Bignamini, A., Chabac, S., & Potgieter, A. (2000). Acamprosate and relapse prevention in the treatment of alcohol dependence: A placebo-controlled study. *Alcohol and Alcoholism, 35,* 202–209.

Tennant, F. S., Rawson, R. A., Cohen, A. J., & Mann, A. (1984). Clinical experience with naltrexone in suburban opioid addicts. *Journal of Clinical Psychiatry, 34*(9 sec. 2), 42–45.

Tennant, F. S., & Sagherian, A. A. (1987). Double-blind comparison of amantadine and bromocriptine for ambulatory withdrawal from cocaine dependence. *Archives of Internal Medicine, 147,* 109–112.

Tollefson, G. D., Montague-Clouse, J., & Tollefson, S. L. (1992). Treatment of comorbid generalized anxiety in a recently detoxified alcohol population with a selective serotonergic drug (buspirone). *Journal of Clinical Psychopharmacology, 12,* 19–26.

Volpicelli, J. R., Alterman, A. I., Hayashida, M., & O'Brien, C. P. (1992). Naltrexone in the treatment of alcohol dependence. *Archives of General Psychiatry, 49,* 876–880.

Volpicelli, J. R., Clay, K. L., Rhines, J. S., Volpicelli, L. A., Alterman, A. I., & O'Brien, C. P. (1997). Naltrexone and alcohol dependence: Role of subject compliance. *Archives of General Psychiatry, 54,* 737–742.

Washton, A. M., Pottash, A. C., & Gold, M. S. (1984). Naltrexone in addicted business executives and physicians. *Journal of Clinical Psychiatry, 34*(9 sec. 2), 39–41.

Weddington, W. W., Brown, B. S., Haertzen, C. A., Hess, J. M., Mahaffey, J. R., Kolar, A. F., et al.

(1991). Comparison of amantadine and desipramine combined with psychotherapy for treatment of cocaine dependence. *American Journal of Drug and Alcohol Abuse, 17,* 137–152.

Whitworth, A. B., Fischer, F., Lesch, O. M., Nimmerichter, A., Oberbauer, H., Platz, T., et al. (1996). Comparison of acamprosate and placebo in long-term treatment of alcohol dependence. *Lancet, 347,* 1438–1442.

Zacny, J. C. (1995). A review of the effects of opioids on psychomotor and cognitive functioning in humans. *Experimental and Clinical Psychopharmacology, 3,* 432–466.

6

Psychosocial Treatments
for Substance Use Disorders

John W. Finney
Paula L. Wilbourne
Rudolf H. Moos

Our review of the literature indicates that among the most effective treatments for alcohol and illicit drug use disorders are cognitive-behavioral treatments, community reinforcement and contingency management approaches, 12-step facilitation and 12-step treatment, behavioral couples and family treatment, and motivational enhancement interventions. Most of these treatment modalities address not only drinking and/or drug use behavior but also patients' life contexts, sense of self-efficacy, and coping skills; motivational interventions focus primarily on attempts to enhance individuals' commitment to behavior change. Consistent with motivational interviewing principles, therapists who are interpersonally skilled, empathic, and less confrontational produce better patient outcomes, probably because they establish better therapeutic alliances with their patients.

An effective strategy for many patients may be to provide lower intensity treatment for a longer duration—that is, treatment sessions spread at a lower rate over a longer period to match better the chronic, relapsing nature of many individuals' substance use disorders. At this point, it seems wise to restrict brief interventions as a stand-alone treatment to patients with mild to moderate disorders. Longer term interventions and treatment in inpatient or residential settings should be reserved for patients with more severe, treatment-resistant substance use disorders, fewer social resources, more concomitant medical/psychiatric disorders, and a desire for longer term and/or residential treatment.

Substance use disorders are the "number one health problem" in the United States, according to a report from the Robert Wood Johnson Foundation (2001). In 2001–2002, 7.35% of persons 18 and older in the United States met criteria for an alcohol use disorder (AUD; abuse and/or dependence), .9% for an illicit drug use disorder (DUD), and 1.1% for both an alcohol and drug use disorder (Stinson et al., 2005). Thus, more than 9% of Americans met criteria for a substance use disorder. Substance use disorders (SUDs) have well-known deleterious effects on physical health, work, psychological functioning, social relationships, and premature mortality. For example, illicit drug use and excessive or hazardous alcohol use contribute to the deaths of more than 100,000 Americans each year (Mokdad, Marks, Stroup, & Gerberding, 2004). In addition to these substantial personal and social costs, the economic costs of substance use disorders in the United States are estimated to total $414 billion annually, with alcohol-related costs alone approaching $166 billion a year (Robert Wood Johnson Foundation, 2001).

Although many persons experiencing substance use–related problems improve without treatment

(Cunningham, 1999; L. C. Sobell, Ellingstad, & Sobell, 2000), others turn to formal treatment services, usually after their own attempts to change their substance use behavior have failed. Almost 6.1% of the persons with an alcohol use disorder had sought treatment in 2001–2002, as had 15.6% of those with a drug use disorder, and 21.8% of those with co-occurring alcohol and drug use disorders (Stinson et al., 2005). Nearly 1.7 million Americans were admitted to publicly funded substance use disorder treatment programs in 2003 (National Institute on Drug Abuse, 2005).

Given the costs of substance use disorders and the centrality of treatment as a societal response, considerable research has focused on the "efficacy" (effects under "ideal" research conditions) and, to a lesser extent, the "effectiveness" (effects when delivered routinely in "real-life" clinical settings) of SUD treatment. The "mesa grande" (Miller & Wilbourne, 2002) database now includes almost 600 comparative studies of alcohol treatment (psychosocial and pharmacological) reported through 2004, the great majority of which have employed random assignment to treatment conditions. Likewise, Prendergast, Podus, Chang, and Urada (2002) reviewed 78 comparative trials of different psychosocial techniques and modalities for treating drug use disorders, and a number of new trials have been reported since that review.

Almost all studies of SUD treatment assume that the outcome of treatment is a function of patients' characteristics at intake, especially the severity and chronicity of the substance use disorder and other aspects of psychosocial impairment, and characteristics of the treatment itself. From a broader perspective, however, treatment outcome also is influenced by life context factors (e.g., stressors, social support for drinking/using and for abstinence) prior to intake and those that occur during and after treatment (Moos, Finney, & Cronkite, 1990). To preview one conclusion of our review, many of the efficacious/effective SUD treatment modalities are those that help patients shape and adapt to their life circumstances.

In this review, we first consider modalities of SUD treatment that are supported by research evidence. Following that, we consider evidence on matching patients to SUD treatment modalities. Later sections cover research on therapists' characteristics/styles and the therapeutic alliance, the duration and amount of treatment, and various settings of SUD treatment. We conclude by briefly considering some characteristics of existing research that place limits on our ability to identify "evidence-based treatment practices," but we then summarize what current research indicates are the "treatments that work."

EFFICACY/EFFECTIVENESS OF TREATMENT MODALITIES FOR SUBSTANCE USE DISORDERS

Although some research has focused on psychosocial treatment modalities for patients with mixed substance use disorders, a great deal still focuses separately on treatment modalities for either alcohol use disorders or illicit drug use disorders, with more studies having been done of alcohol than of drug treatment. However, because many of the same modalities have been evaluated in separate alcohol and drug treatment trials, we integrate our review of these two bodies of research.

Table 6.1 provides the rankings for 15 psychosocial treatment modalities for alcohol use disorders that had three or more studies addressing their effectiveness in each of the "box-score" reviews by Holder, Longabaugh, Miller, and Rubonis (1991), Finney and Monahan (1996), Miller, Andrews, Wilbourne, and Bennett (1998), and Miller and Wilbourne (2002). Box-score reviews determine modality effectiveness from the proportion of relevant studies that found a significant treatment effect on one or more outcome variables favoring a particular modality. Although there is variation in the rankings of some modalities across the reviews, some modalities were consistently highly ranked.

We use the modalities identified as effective in Table 6.1 as a point of departure. However, findings in Table 6.1 are limited not only by their alcohol focus but also by the fact that any modality included must have had three extant studies before 1991, the year the earliest review was published. Accordingly, we integrate the findings on highly ranked modalities in Table 6.1 with results of studies of the same modalities for individuals with drug use disorders, as well more recent studies of alcohol treatment modalities. Our conclusions regarding evidence-based treatments are based on studies that typically met criteria for either a Type 1 study (e.g., random assign-

TABLE 6.1 Rankings by Effectiveness Indices of 15 Psychosocial Treatment Modalities Having Three or More Studies in Holder et al. (1991), Finney and Monahan (1996), Miller et al. (1998), and Miller and Wilbourne (2002)

Modality	Holder et al. (1991)	Finney & Monahan (1996)	Miller et al. (1998)	Miller & Wilbourne (2002) Clinical Samples
Social skills training	1	2	2	1
Self-control training	2	10	6	8
Brief motivational counseling	3	7	1	3*
Marital therapy, behavioral	4	3	5	4
Community reinforcement	5.5	1	3	2
Stress management training	5.5	5	11	10
Aversion, covert sensitization	7	8.5	8	7
Marital therapy, other	8	4	10	11
Cognitive therapy	9.5	11	7	5
Hypnosis	9.5	15	12	12
Aversion, electric shock	11	8.5	9	9
Aversion, nausea	12	6	4	6
Confrontational interventions	13	13	12	13
Educational lectures/films	14	12	15	14
General counseling	15	14	14	15

*Brief interventions and motivational enhancement were separated as modalities for the first time in Miller and Wilbourne (2002), with brief interventions ranked first in effectiveness among 46 behavioral and pharmacological modalities, and motivational enhancement ranked 11th. The average of these two rankings (5.5) was the third-highest rank for the 15 modalities with three or more studies across all four reviews.

ment to treatment conditions, state-of-the art diagnostic procedures, adequate statistical power, appropriate statistical analyses) or, more frequently, a Type 2 study (i.e., studies that did not include one or more of the criteria of a Type 1 study but were of adequate methodological quality overall).

For the most part, the modalities that have empirical support across the reviews in Table 6.1 and in other studies focus on enhancing clients' skills in coping with everyday life circumstances (including situations that put them at risk for substance use), on improving the match between patients' abilities and environmental demands, and/or on enhancing patients' motivation for behavior change. The modalities include cognitive-behavioral interventions, such as social skills training, environmentally oriented interventions, such as the community reinforcement approach, behaviorally oriented couples and family therapy, contingency management interventions, and motivational interventions. In addition, 12-step facilitation and 12-step treatment, which combine cognitive and behavioral elements with social environment changes, also have empirical support from more recent studies.

Cognitive-Behavioral Treatments

These treatments include social skills training, self-control training, and stress management training. They focus primarily on enhancing clients' self-efficacy and skills in coping with everyday life circumstances (including relapse-inducing situations) and on improving the match between patients' abilities and environmental demands. The most highly ranked of these in Table 6.1 is social skills training, which focuses on developing assertion and communication skills. After an initial assessment to identify skill deficits, patients learn how to initiate social interactions, express their thoughts and feelings, respond appropriately to criticism from others, refuse drugs and alcohol, and so on. Treatment is often in a group format, so that patients can role-play, receive feedback, and model the behavior of others. Social skills training has been shown to be effective when applied alone (Eriksen, Bjornstad, & Gotestam, 1986; Monti, Gulliver, & Myers, 1994) or, as is common in more recent studies, when applied with other interventions, such as coping skills training (see Monti et al., 1997; Monti & O'Leary, 1999).

Community Reinforcement Approach

The community reinforcement approach (CRA), which seeks to make a sober lifestyle more rewarding than substance use, employs familial, social, recreational, and vocational rewards to assist in the recovery process. CRA emphasizes behavioral skills training to help clients develop communication, problem-solving, and drink-refusal skills. In addition, it emphasizes the development of job skills, social and recreational counseling to identify new sources of social activities, and functional analysis to identify external triggers and high-risk situations for substance use, and to specify alternative behaviors that enable clients to attain positive feelings comparable to those that accompany substance use. The taking of Antabuse while being monitored by another person (usually the spouse) is an optional component of CRA and may be a useful deterrent to impulsive drinking.

Although there are variations in the specific components included in CRA, it has retained a core, broad-spectrum focus on monitoring patients' sobriety, developing more supportive family and work settings, allowing individuals to experience the consequences of their substance use, and promoting rewarding activities to substitute for substance use. Recent studies and reviews have confirmed those of earlier investigations and concluded that CRA is more effective than usual care, especially when it includes abstinence-based incentives and Antabuse monitoring and social reinforcement for pill taking (Higgins, Alessi, & Dantona, 2002; Miller, Meyers, Tonigan, & Grant, 2001; J. E. Smith, Meyers, & Delaney, 1998; J. E. Smith, Meyers, & Miller, 2001).

Contingency Management

Contingency management (CM) treatment, like CRA, is based on the principle that behaviors that are reinforced are more likely to be repeated, but its focus typically is limited to the treatment setting, not patients' broader social environments. In CM, a contingency that is met (e.g., a series of drug-free urine screens) is reinforced by providing something of value to the patient (e.g., a voucher to purchase specified items). Based on a meta-analysis of findings from 30 randomized trials of voucher-based contingency management interventions for individuals with substance use disorders, Lussier, Heil, Mongeon,

Badger, and Higgins (2006) concluded that CM was superior to control conditions on abstinence outcomes. Voucher delivery that immediately followed meeting a contingency (e.g., demonstrated abstinence) and higher value vouchers were associated with stronger treatment effects (larger effect sizes). CM also was shown to be efficacious in enhancing treatment attendance and medication compliance, mechanisms that may account for its positive effects on patient outcomes (see also Higgins et al., 2002).

Similarly, a meta-analytic review of CM interventions that included, but were not limited to, voucher-based reinforcements also concluded that CM was effective (Prendergast, Podus, Finney, Greenwell, & Roll, in press). However, outcomes in many CM trials have been assessed during or at the end of the intervention; only 20% of the drug/alcohol studies reviewed by Prendergast et al. (2006) included posttreatment follow-ups. Follow-up in only one study occurred at 12 months after CM ended; the others occurred at less extended points. Thus, although CM has been consistently shown to be efficacious in reducing substance use during treatment, more research is needed to determine its longer term effects when intervention contingencies are no longer reinforced. Combining CM with some other form of therapy, such as cognitive-behavioral treatment (Budney, Moore, Rocha, & Higgins, 2006), may help maintain initial patient gains under CM.

Behaviorally Oriented Couples and Family Therapy

Behavioral couples- and family-based treatments typically begin with a thorough assessment of the alcoholic patient's drinking behavior and of the marital relationship. Interventions to address drinking include behavioral contracts and Antabuse contracts. Marital interventions focus on improving the relationship and resolving marital conflicts and problems, using such procedures as increasing caring behaviors, planning joint recreational activities, enhancing communication skills, and developing behavioral change agreements. Substantial evidence supports the efficacy/effectiveness of these treatments (e.g., O'Farrell, Choquette, Cutter, Brown, & McCourt, 1993, O'Farrell, Choquette, & Cutter, 1998; O'Farrell & Fals-Stewart, 2001; Stanton & Shadish, 1997).

Motivational Enhancement and Motivational Interviewing

Brief interventions based on motivational interviewing principles, motivational interviewing, and motivational enhancement therapies have accumulated considerable evidence of effectiveness as alcohol treatments, as indicated in the reviews listed in Table 6.1. Typically, all of these interventions are provided in four or fewer sessions and rely on activating or enhancing clients' existing resources and personal strengths, and assume that clients can then make behavior changes on their own. All have made use of normative feedback of objective assessment results to assist clients in perceiving the discrepancy between their own behavior and that of most other people. These interventions are based on the assumptions that empathy from the therapist/interventionist, an egalitarian relationship between client and therapist, and the instillation of hope increase the likelihood of positive behavior change, whereas an authoritarian stance, confrontation, and highly directive methods decrease the likelihood of such change. Brief interventions, not all of which have employed motivational principles, are discussed in a later section on treatment duration, intensity, and setting. Here we focus on motivational interviewing and motivational enhancement as a class of psychosocial treatments.

Motivational interviewing (MI) is defined much more by style and manner of interacting with clients to facilitate choices about change than by the length of treatment. Nevertheless, the duration of MI delivery typically ranges from as little as a single 30-minute session to as much as four 60-minute sessions. MI is a client-centered yet directive intervention in which therapists have an accepting, empathic, and egalitarian style of interaction. It is defined by four core principles: (a) empathizing with the client's perspective, (b) developing discrepancies between the client's substance use and outcomes that the client desires, (c) rolling with client resistance to change, and (d) supporting the client's sense of self-efficacy to change his or her behavior.

Overall, MI seeks to help clients resolve their ambivalence about change, reinforce client statements about reasons for change, and strengthen clients' commitment to changing their substance use behavior (Miller & Rollnick, 2002). Motivational interviewing can be used as a stand-alone intervention, conducted at the beginning of a treatment episode, or provided to individuals who are contemplating changes in their substance use. A recent meta-analysis by Hettema, Steele and Miller (2005; see earlier reviews by Burke, Arkowitz, & Menchola, 2003; Dunn, DeRoo, & Rivara, 2001) found significant effect sizes indicating the superiority of MI to various comparison conditions in studies of both alcohol ($N = 31$ studies) and drug use disorder ($N = 13$ studies) treatment.

A four-session intervention using the principles of MI and normative assessment feedback, designated Motivational Enhancement Therapy (MET), was developed for Project MATCH. Project MATCH (Project MATCH Research Group, 1997a) randomly assigned more than 1,700 individuals with alcohol use disorders to receive 12 sessions of 12-step facilitation treatment (TSF), 12 sessions of cognitive-behavioral treatment (CBT), or 4 sessions of motivational enhancement therapy (MET), all over a 12-week period, either as stand-alone outpatient treatment or as aftercare. On the primary outcomes of drinks per drinking day and percent days abstinence, MET was as efficacious as the other two more intensive treatments. Similarly, in a randomized trial involving more than 700 individuals with alcohol problems in the United Kingdom, 3 sessions of motivational enhancement over a 12-week period were just as effective at a 12-month follow-up as 9 sessions of social behavior and network therapy (UKATT Research Team, 2005).

In a review of motivational interventions, Ashton (2005) observed that "clearly, there is something here which works most of the time and more consistently and at less cost than the usual alternatives" (p. 29). However, he cites the need for more research to determine what that "something" is and points to evidence that motivational interviewing is best directed at individuals who are contemplating changing their substance use behavior. Persons who are already committed to change may be "set back" by the consideration of positive aspects of substance use that is often a component of a motivational intervention.

Twelve-Step (Facilitation) Treatment

Traditional 12-step treatment is based in part on principles of Alcoholics Anonymous (AA) and the "disease model" of addiction. Disease model and 12-

step approaches try to help patients reduce their denial and accept their powerlessness over substances, acknowledge that they have a progressive disease and understand that recovery is a lifelong process, surrender control to a higher power, work a recovery program, and facilitate identification with people in recovery and a commitment to attend 12-step self-help group meetings.

An important development in the SUD treatment research field over the past decade is a series of studies that indicates that the efficacy and effectiveness of 12-step treatment approaches, and of interventions to facilitate 12-step treatment, are at least as strong as is the case for cognitive-behavioral interventions. For example, Project MATCH (Project MATCH Research Group, 1997a), which was described earlier, found no overall main effect of treatment in either its outpatient or its aftercare arm on two primary drinking-related outcome variables (drinks per drinking day and percent days abstinent) over a 12-month follow-up period. However, 12-step facilitation patients were functioning somewhat better with respect to several secondary outcome variables, including abstinence.

A naturalistic, multisite evaluation focused on more than 3,000 Department of Veterans Affairs inpatients who received traditional 12-step, cognitive-behavioral, or mixed 12-step and cognitive-behavioral treatment under "normal" conditions of treatment delivery. At a 1-year follow-up, there were no differences among the three groups on 9 of 11 outcome criteria (Ouimette, Finney, & Moos, 1997). Patients in 12-step programs were significantly more likely than cognitive-behavioral patients to abstain from alcohol and other drugs in the 3 months prior to follow-up, and mixed program patients were more likely to be unemployed than patients in the other two groups. Additional analyses suggested that the effect of 12-step treatment on abstinence may have been mediated by patients' involvement in 12-step self-help groups (Humphreys, Huebsch, Finney, & Moos, 1999).

The findings from the two studies above that favored 12-step facilitation or 12-step treatment on only one or two of an array of assessed outcomes are offset by findings of studies of cocaine abuse treatment by Wells, Peterson, Gainey, Howkins, and Catalano (1994) and Maude-Griffin et al. (1998) that yielded better results for cognitive-behavioral treatment than for 12-step treatment on one of several outcomes. On

the other hand, Brown, Seraganian, Tremblay, and Annis (2002), in a randomized trial of 12-step facilitation and relapse prevention aftercare sessions for SUD patients, found no difference between the two groups on any outcome. Finally, to further balance findings, a comparison of the effects of 12-step treatment versus cognitive-behavioral Self-Management and Recovery Training (SMART) for persons with co-occurring serious mental illness and substance use disorders (Brooks & Penn, 2003) found one treatment to be superior on some outcomes and the other to be superior on different outcomes. Again, the overall pattern of results to date can be most succinctly summarized as indicating the general equivalence of treatments guided by 12-step principles to cognitive-behavioral treatments, the latter having had much earlier empirical support of efficacy.

Other Common Psychosocial Alcohol and Drug Treatment Approaches

A noteworthy feature of Table 6.1 is the low effectiveness rankings of many of the prevalent alcohol treatment approaches in the United States — educational films, confrontational interventions, and general counseling. These interventions also are applied in many drug treatment programs. However, it is difficult to think of education as a complete treatment in itself, rather than a component of a multimodal approach. Confrontational interventions consistently fare poorly, perhaps because many individuals react negatively to pervasive criticism, although Polcin (2003) argues that when confrontation occurs in a supportive context it may be perceived as helpful and be effective. As a case in point, in a recent study of motivational interviewing, when therapist confrontation occurred in the context of an empathic, accepting, and egalitarian relationship between interpersonally skilled therapists and their clients, it was positively associated with the client's participation in treatment (Moyers, Miller, & Hendrickson, 2005). Finally, although alcohol counseling has been an ineffective, relatively unstructured attention-control condition in many studies, manual-guided individual and group drug counseling was shown to be more efficacious than cognitive therapy or supportive-expressive therapy in a study of treatment for cocaine abuse (Crits-Christoph et al., 1999). A partial mediator of the superior effect of counseling appeared to be its enhancement of patients' involvement in 12-step activities (Crits-Christoph et al., 2003).

Another well-known SUD psychosocial treatment modality is the therapeutic community (TC). TCs typically provide a comprehensive approach, although there are variations for different populations, such as prisoners and mentally ill persons with substance use disorders, different prescribed durations of treatment, and different settings (e.g., day treatment). However, residential TC treatment is still prototypical (De Leon, 2000). Modern concept-based TCs employ a structured, supportive, milieu-oriented approach. The treatment is based on a social learning approach, and clients are expected to focus on "right living" and to be guided by such values as honesty, responsible concern for others, and a strong work ethic (De Leon, 2000). Clients work their way up through various jobs of increasing responsibility. Rehabilitation includes efforts to improve clients' self-concepts and address psychological and social problems that are associated with their drug abuse.

Better outcomes for patients treated in TCs versus other comparison conditions have been found in several studies (e.g., De Leon, Sacks, Staines, & McKendrick, 2000); Prendergast et al. (2002) reported a significant positive effect size for TCs relative to various control conditions in a meta-analysis of eight studies. It should be noted, however, that a recent Cochrane Collaboration review of seven studies (L. A. Smith, Gates, and Foxcroft, 2006) concluded that the effectiveness of TCs has not been shown to be superior to other forms of *residential* SUD treatment. We consider evidence regarding the relative effectiveness of inpatient/residential versus outpatient treatment in a later section of this chapter.

Finally, the Matrix Model is another SUD treatment approach that has been gaining prominence as a treatment for stimulant abuse. Typically a 16-week outpatient treatment program, the Matrix Model combines relapse prevention, facilitation of 12-step group involvement, family systems treatment, and education delivered in a group context. In addition, the model includes a nonconfrontational approach with individual counseling and physiological monitoring of drug use (Obert et al., 2000); a briefer (six-session) variant has been developed for "hazardous users" (Obert, Rawson, & Miotto, 1997). Because of a lack of rigorous research to date, the empirical support for its efficacy/effectiveness is not strong, consisting of such findings as an association between time

in Matrix treatment and better outcomes (Rawson et al., 1995; Shoptaw, Rawson, McCann, & Obert, 1994). A CSAT-funded, multisite, randomized clinical trial is under way that should provide more solid evidence of the effectiveness of this approach.

Conclusions

Overall, among the most effective treatments for alcohol and drug use disorders are cognitive-behavioral treatments, community reinforcement and contingency management approaches, 12-step facilitation and 12-step treatment, and behavioral couples and family treatment. Importantly, each of these treatments relies on elements of one or more of four underlying psychological theories about the development, maintenance, and cessation of substance use: social learning theory, stress and coping theory, behavioral economics and behavioral choice theory, and social control theory (for a brief description of these theories, see Moos, 2006).

Cognitive-behavioral treatments are based on social learning theory, which posits that substance use is maintained in part by the substance-specific attitudes and behaviors of the adults and peers who serve as an individual's role models; on stress and coping theory, which suggests that stressors are most likely to impel substance use among individuals with inadequate coping skills who try to avoid experiencing distress and alienation; and on the idea that an individual's cognitions, emotions, and behaviors all interact to determine his or her risk of relapse. Community reinforcement and contingency management approaches are based on behavioral economics or behavioral choice theory, which assumes that the key aspect of the social context is involvement in traditional activities, such as educational, work, social, and religious pursuits, that provide rewards to substitute for substance use and shield individuals from exposure to substances and opportunities to use them.

Twelve-step facilitation and 12-step treatment focus on aspects of social learning and social control theories, which emphasize the importance of strong bonds with family, school, work, religion, and other aspects of traditional society to motivate individuals to engage in responsible behavior. Effective models of couples and family therapy highlight the importance of abstinent role models, rewards for abstinence, and the development of rewards that can substitute for those from substance use. It is plausible to assume that the effectiveness of these treatments rests in part on the fact that they follow the key theories that have been used to explain the development and maintenance of substance use.

Motivational interventions also have substantial evidence of effectiveness, are derived from humanistic psychology tradition, and focus on the individual and marshaling his or her resources for change. Given their distinctive focus, motivational interventions can increase individuals' readiness to change and, perhaps, enter treatment and have the potential to augment the effects of other treatment modalities (e.g., Baer, Kivlahan, & Donovan, 1999; Rohsenow et al., 2004).

MATCHING PATIENTS TO EFFECTIVE TREATMENT MODALITIES

Less severely impaired patients seem to respond better to less structured treatment modalities, whereas those who have more severe and chronic disorders seem to need more structure. In this vein, Mattson and her colleagues (1994) concluded that relationship-oriented treatment, which tends to be less structured, is more effective for patients who are functioning better, that is, those with weaker urges to drink, good role-playing skills, and less sociopathy and psychiatric severity. In contrast, the more structured cognitive-behavioral approaches seem to be more effective for patients who have severe psychiatric disorders or who have antisocial personality disorders (see also Rosenblum et al., 2005). Communication skills training, which also is relatively structured, is particularly effective for patients who have less education and are more anxious, perhaps because the new interpersonal abilities such patients develop help them initiate and sustain new social interactions.

Moreover, scattered research indicates that patients who have fewer personal or social resources may improve more when they receive treatment that substitutes for or attempts to increase these resources. For example, compared with married patients, most of whom had some family support, unmarried patients may benefit more from broad-spectrum CRA treatment because it provides an essential source of support for these individuals with fewer social resources (Azrin, Sisson, Meyers, & Godley, 1982). Similarly, because it focuses more on compensating for patients' lack of resources, CBT may work better

than motivational interviewing for patients who have trouble expressing their feelings and those who have less network support for abstinence (Rosenblum et al., 2005). In addition, CBT may be better than TSF for patients with major depressive disorders (Maude-Griffin et al., 1998). However, CBT requires a reasonable level of cognitive ability: Patients who are more adept at abstract reasoning may do better in CBT than in TSF, and, more generally, patients with neuropsychological impairments may benefit less from skills training because of their greater difficulty in learning and recalling new information (Maude-Griffin et al., 1998; D. E. Smith & McCrady, 1991). Finally, when a personal resource matches an emphasis in treatment, patients may respond better to that treatment. Thus, African American clients who had stronger religious beliefs fared better following TSF than CBT (Maude-Griffin et al., 1998).

Although these findings are of interest, their potential importance is diminished by the fact that Project MATCH yielded relatively little evidence of patient-treatment matching effects. Sixteen a priori hypotheses selected on the basis of prior research evidence and theoretical support were examined with respect to two primary drinking outcome variables in each of the two arms of the studies (64 contrasts overall). However, only one was statistically significant. Contrary to expectation, there was little difference in outcome by treatment condition among outpatients with greater psychiatric impairment. Among those lower in psychiatric severity, however, TSF patients experienced better outcomes than did patients in CBT and MET (Project MATCH Research Group, 1997a). Analyses of secondary hypotheses indicated that patients high in anger had better outcomes after MET treatment, whereas those lower in anger had better outcomes in CBT and TSF at 1- and 3-year follow-ups (Project MATCH Research Group, 1998a). Patients with more symptoms of alcohol dependence had better 1-year outcomes following TSF; patients low in dependence fared better in CBT (Project MATCH Research Group, 1997b). It was also found that patients who had high support for drinking had better outcomes following TSF than did patients in MET, an effect apparently mediated, at least in part, by TSF patients' greater involvement in Alcoholics Anonymous (Longabaugh, Wirtz, Zweben, & Stout, 1998).

Several of these findings are consistent with the idea that a treatment that specifically targets a problem is likely to do better with patients who have that problem. Thus, MET does better with patients who are high on anger, and TSF does better with patients who are more alcohol dependent and those whose networks support drinking. TSF also does better with patients who are low on psychiatric severity, perhaps because it does not target psychiatric symptoms as much as CBT does. The finding that MET worked better than TSF or CBT for patients high in anger was mediated, in an analysis of data from one Project MATCH site, by the lower level of directiveness exhibited by therapists in MET than in the other two conditions (Karno & Longabaugh, 2004). Further analyses indicated that across the three Project MATCH treatment conditions, therapist directiveness interacted with patient anger and reactance, suggesting again that treatments that target patients' specific problems have better results (Karno & Longabaugh, 2005a, 2005b).

Although some scattered matching findings have emerged, the lack of more supportive evidence for patient-treatment modality interaction effects in a rigorous multisite trial like Project MATCH is disconcerting. A review by Moyer, Finney, Elworth, and Kraemer (2001) found that more than 20% of the variance in the number of significant patient-treatment interaction effects found in 54 alcohol treatment studies could be accounted for by the number of tests for interaction effects conducted. The extent to which Type I error (rejecting a true null hypothesis) apparently has contributed to findings regarding patient-treatment matching effects, in combination with the largely negative findings of Project MATCH, raises questions about some of the findings in other studies of matching patients to alcohol treatment modalities.

On the other hand, some significant patient-treatment interaction effects did emerge from Project MATCH. In addition, Project MATCH tested hypotheses regarding only three treatment modalities that may not have been as distinctive as would be desired for a study of patient-treatment matching (McClelland & Judd, 1993). For example, each of the psychosocial modalities was delivered by a therapist in individual sessions with clients. Other types of patient-treatment matching have some support. For example, some evidence suggests that overall patient severity can be used to match patients to different settings of treatment, a topic we discuss in a later section. Likewise, research supports the idea of matching ancillary services to patients' problems or needs (e.g., in social, psychiatric, and employment domains) as a way of improving substance use–related outcomes in SUD treatment programs (Friedmann, Hendrickson, Gerstein, & Zhang, 2004; McLellan et al., 1997, 1998). Finally, the work of Karno and Longabaugh (2005a, 2005b) on therapist directiveness suggests the potential value of focusing on interactions between patient factors and therapists' characteristics and style as another way of improving the overall effectiveness of SUD treatment.

THERAPISTS' CHARACTERISTICS AND THE THERAPIST-CLIENT RELATIONSHIP

Therapists' characteristics and style, and the therapist-client relationship or "therapeutic alliance," may well have a stronger impact on treatment outcome than the particular type of treatment therapists apply. In fact, substantial differences among therapists have been found with respect to patient retention and outcomes (Luborsky et al., 1986; Najavits & Weiss, 1994).

Therapist Characteristics and Style

A few studies have attempted to determine why patient outcomes differ across therapists (for reviews, see Haaga, Hall, & Haas, 2006; Lebow, Kelly, Knobloch-Fedders, & Moos, 2006; Najavits & Weiss, 1994). In general, therapist differences were not attributable to variation in the characteristics of patients being treated or to therapists' training, treatment orientation, experience, or recovery status. Although certain therapist characteristics were associated with better patient outcomes only when providing particular treatment modalities (see Project MATCH Research Group, 1998b), most studies considered in the reviews above found that patients of therapists who were more interpersonally skilled, less confrontational, and/or more empathic experienced better outcomes. Although such findings are supportive of the motivational interviewing approach discussed earlier as a treatment modality, proponents of all the major treatment modalities emphasize the importance of developing a good patient-therapist alliance.

Therapeutic Alliance

Following Hatcher and Barends (1996), the therapeutic alliance can be defined as "the collaborative relationship between clients and therapist; it reflects their emotional bond, the therapist's empathy for the client, and a shared presumption about the tasks and goals of treatment" (Lebow et al., 2006, p. 294). In the Project MATCH outpatient arm, stronger therapeutic alliances, as rated by therapists and patients, were associated with better patient outcomes: fewer drinks on drinking days and a higher proportion of abstinent days (Connors, Carroll, DiClemente, Longabaugh, & Donovan, 1997). However, in the aftercare arm, only therapists' ratings of a more positive alliance were associated with one outcome: a higher proportion of abstinent days. Likewise, Joe, Simpson, Greener, and Rowan-Szal (1999) reported that therapists' perceptions of a more positive therapeutic alliance were predictive of less patient cocaine use at 3- and 6-month follow-ups. Similar findings emerged for both patient and therapist ratings of alliance in Belding, Iguchi, Morral, and McLellan's (1997) study of opioid-dependent patients in methadone treatment, and for observer ratings of the therapeutic alliance in Fenton, Cecero, Nich, Frankforter, and Carroll's (2001) study of patients with co-occurring cocaine and alcohol use disorders.

A potential mechanism linking therapeutic alliances to patient outcomes is enhanced retention in treatment. A stronger initial therapeutic alliance was linked to greater attendance during the first two months of DUD treatment by Joe et al. (1999) and to overall length of treatment by Simpson, Joe, and Rowan-Szal (1997). Among couples in marital therapy for AUDs, a better treatment alliance was related to better attendance and to completing treatment (Raytek, McCrady, Epstein, & Hirsch, 1999). Psychiatric symptoms may moderate the relationship between therapeutic alliance and treatment attendance (Petry & Bickel, 1999), with a stronger relationship among patients with moderate to severe psychiatric symptoms. In this vein, patients with antisocial personality disorder who felt they had a positive relationship with their therapist relatively early in treatment had better outcomes with respect to drug use and employment (Gerstley et al., 1989).

Overall, the quality of the therapeutic alliance appears to be an important factor in accounting for patient outcomes. However, more research is needed to determine the personal and treatment factors that explain when and why therapists' and patients' perceptions of the relationship are and are not related to patients' outcomes.

DURATION AND AMOUNT OF TREATMENT

In this section, we consider the effectiveness of brief interventions, longer versus shorter stays in inpatient/residential treatment, aftercare or continuing care participation, and medical management versus more intensive psychosocial treatment as investigated in a recent study of combined pharmacological and psychosocial alcohol treatment.

Brief Interventions

Brief interventions (BIs) can range from several minutes in length to as many as three or four sessions. A BI can be as straightforward as simply advising a patient to cut back or abstain from substance use. However, Miller and Sanchez (1993) offered the acronym FRAMES to identify what they believed were the six "active ingredients" of empirically supported brief interventions to change substance use behavior: Feedback of personal risk or impairment, emphasis on personal Responsibility for change, clear Advice to change, a Menu of alternative change options, therapeutic Empathy, and enhancement of patients' Self-efficacy or optimism. As noted earlier, many, but not all (see Copeland, Swift, Roffman, & Stephens, 2001), brief interventions are guided by motivational interviewing principles (e.g., therapist empathy, feedback, assumption that responsibility for change rests with the client) that partially overlap with the FRAMES ingredients.

Reviews of predominantly Type 1 and Type 2 studies have consistently concluded that brief interventions are more efficacious than no treatment for persons with heavy drinking and/or moderate alcohol problems, and as efficacious as more extensive treatment (e.g., Bien, Miller, & Tonigan, 1993; Marijuana Treatment Project Research Group, 2004; Moyer, Finney, Swearingen, & Vergun, 2002; Wilk et al., 1997). Moreover, among alcohol treatment modalities with three or more studies reviewed by Miller and Wilbourne (2002), brief interventions had the highest effectiveness score. The finding held even when studies were restricted to those of "clinical populations," defined as "people seeking treatment for alcohol problems" (although not necessarily presenting for treatment at specialized programs or facilities).

Several points should be kept in mind when considering this evidence, however. First, as Jonson, Hermansson, Ronnberg, Gyllen-Hammar, and Forsberg (1995) noted, "brief" (in terms of number of sessions) interventions in some of the studies have been considered to be more extended interventions in other studies. Moreover, a brief intervention is not necessarily all the treatment received by individuals assigned to that treatment condition. As an example, Monahan and Finney (1996) calculated that the average patient in the single-session "advice" condition in the well-known study by Edwards et al. (1977) actually received more than 30 hours of assessment and treatment during the year that other participants were receiving extended "treatment."

Also, brief interventions (in terms of number of sessions) may be provided over a somewhat extended period. For example, Bien et al. (1993) note that some BIs include follow-up sessions. More concretely, the three and four planned sessions of brief motivational enhancement in the UKATT trial (UKATT Research Team, 2005) and Project MATCH (Project MATCH Research Group, 1997a), respectively, were provided over a 12-week period. Finally, in the review by Miller and Wilbourne (2002), brief interventions benefited from an effectiveness scoring system that provided points if a brief intervention was not significantly inferior to a more extensive intervention, and that assigned modalities that were shown to be superior to a no-treatment control condition more points than modalities that were shown to be more effective than another treatment. Studies of brief interventions, especially those conducted in medical settings, are more likely to have no-treatment control conditions (e.g., see Wilk et al., 1997) than studies of more intensive/extensive treatment modalities.

Even with these caveats in mind, the evidence supporting the effectiveness of low-cost brief interventions is impressive. The studies of brief interventions have been conducted most often with clients of low to moderate severity in terms of their alcohol use disorders. Individuals with mild abuse to moderate dependence make up the largest segment of individuals with alcohol-related problems. Research is needed to examine the effectiveness of brief interventions among patient populations that vary more substantially in severity. Brief interventions continue to be untested in the most severely dependent populations. Their use in these populations may be most sensible in a stepped care model that provides more intense care for individuals who do not respond to an initial brief intervention (Breslin, Sobell, Sobell, Buchan, & Cunningham, 1997; M. B. Sobell & Sobell, 2000).

At present, however, clients with problems ranging from substance abuse to moderate alcohol dependence, who have positive life contexts and do not have severe skills deficits, appear to be the best candidates for brief interventions. There also is some indication that brief interventions may be less effective for persons who have failed to respond to previous advice to reduce their alcohol consumption (Bien et al., 1993). Finally, to begin to disentangle the effects of modality, intensity, and duration, studies are needed that compare fewer versus more sessions of both motivational and other treatments (e.g., CBT), provided over shorter and longer periods.

Length of Stay in Inpatient/ Residential Treatment

Miller and Hester (1986) and Mattick and Jarvis (1994) reviewed several randomized Type 1 and Type 2 trials comparing different lengths of inpatient or residential treatment for alcohol use disorders and concluded there was no benefit to more extended treatment. Recent randomized trials of varying planned lengths of residential SUD treatment (e.g., 3 versus 6, and 6 versus 12 months, McCusker et al., 1995, 1997; 10 months of planned residential treatment followed by 2 months of planned outpatient care versus 6 months of planned residential treatment followed by 6 months of planned outpatient care, Nemes, Wish, & Messina, 1999) likewise have not found longer planned residential treatment durations to be superior to shorter planned durations. These findings stand in contrast to those of many correlational studies that have found longer stays in inpatient/residential treatment to be associated with better patient outcomes (e.g., Condelli & Hubbard, 1994; Simpson, Joe, & Brown, 1997).

There are at least three possible explanations for the discrepancy in the results of randomized trials and correlational studies. First, in randomized trials, clients who are directed to attend a specified amount of treatment may or may not comply with these directions. The lack of differences in outcomes between groups may reflect the fact that the dose of treatment in longer and shorter treatments was not as discrete as it was intended to be. Second, positive correlations between duration of residential treatment and patient improvement may reflect the effects of the characteristics of patients who self-select longer treatment on improved outcomes, not the effects of longer treatment. Patient characteristics tend to be equated in groups in randomized trials that have different planned treatment durations. Finally, positive correlations between length of treatment and outcome also may reflect a dynamic interaction between patients and treatment in which patients with certain characteristics stay in treatment longer but, as a result of longer treatment, change in ways that are conducive to improved functioning and remaining in treatment even longer. In this sense, naturalistic correlational designs may be more likely to mirror real-life phenomena, as they combine the effects of patients' motivation and the effects of treatment, which, in psychosocial treatments, are inextricably linked.

Whatever factors may account for discrepancies between the results of randomized trials and naturalistic correlational studies, the absence of main effects favoring longer residential treatments in randomized trials indicates that merely assigning patients to longer treatment, without regard to their motivation, will not improve outcome for patients in general. In combination with correlational findings, results of RCTs do suggest that enabling clients to remain in treatment when they choose to is associated with improved outcomes. In addition, it may be that beneficial effects of assigned longer stays in inpatient/residential treatment apply to more impaired patients with fewer social resources (e.g., Moos & Moos, 1995; Simpson, Joe, Fletcher, Hubbard, & Anglin, 1999). For example, Welte, Hynes, & Sokolow (1981) found no relationship between length of stay and outcome for higher social stability patients; in contrast, for patients with lower social stability, those with longer stays had better outcomes. This finding is conceptually similar to a finding that community reinforcement treatment was more effective for unmarried patients (Azrin et al., 1982).

Continuing Care Following an Acute Treatment Episode

Most clinicians recommend additional outpatient treatment to maintain or enhance the therapeutic gains achieved during inpatient/residential or intensive outpatient (e.g., day hospital) treatment. Outpatient treatment attempts to provide the ongoing support needed to continue a course of sobriety or to limit the course of a lapse. Supporting these recommendations are a number of naturalistic studies finding that longer periods of continuing care are associated with better patients outcomes (e.g., Moos, Finney, & Moos, 2000; Moos & Moos, 2003; Ouimette, Moos, & Finney, 1998). Although a review by McKay (2001) concluded that in only three of seven randomized clinical trials did continuing care demonstrate better patient outcomes than no continuing care, the results of more recent randomized trials have been more consistent in finding greater improvement for continuing care patients (Brooner et al., 2004; Dennis, Scott, & Funk, 2003; Lash, Burden, Monteleone, & Lehmann, 2004; Lash et al., 2005; Sannibale et al., 2003).

One reason that more consistent positive findings may have emerged in later studies is that more active efforts were made to engage and retain patients in continuing care. For example, Lash et al. (2004, 2005) used prompting and social reinforcement, in addition to contracting with patients, to foster continuing care attendance. An earlier study (Gilbert, 1988) also used active approaches for fostering aftercare but did not find positive effects. However, a sizable proportion of the patients in the no-aftercare condition received aftercare from other sources and/or participated in self-help groups. Overall, active efforts to enhance aftercare attendance appear to have positive effects. Telephone-based continuing care, which can be more active than relying on patients to come in to a treatment setting, is a promising form of treatment delivery (McKay et al., 2004; McKay, Lynch, Shepard, & Pettinati, 2005). More research is needed to evaluate its efficacy and effectiveness.

Medical Management and Psychosocial Treatment in the COMBINE Study

As this chapter was being completed, initial results were published (Anton et al., 2006) of a National

Institute on Alcohol Abuse and Alcoholism–funded, randomized, multicenter trial of pharmacological treatment (naltrexone, acamprosate) combined with either medical management (MM) delivered in 9 sessions by a health care provider, or MM plus up to 20 individual sessions of a combined behavioral intervention (CBI) that included motivational interviewing, cognitive-behavioral therapy, and 12-step facilitation provided by a trained psychotherapist. Two primary outcomes (percent days abstinent and having at least one heavy drinking episode) were assessed at the end of treatment and at a 1-year follow-up for nine study groups that received different combinations of pharmacological (or placebo) and psychosocial treatment over 16 weeks.

There was no superiority (no main effect) at the end of treatment or at the 1-year follow-up for MM plus CBI versus MM only for participants collapsed across groups receiving one or the other medication, both medications, or placebo, on either outcome variable at either assessment point. At the end of treatment, individuals randomly assigned to a ninth group that received CBI only (no pills and no MM) did not differ from the group receiving MM plus placebo, but they were significantly more likely to have at least one heavy drinking day than the group that received CBI plus MM plus placebo. There was no significant difference at 1-year follow-up. The poorer earlier outcomes for CBI-only may reflect the absence of MM, the absence of a placebo effect, or participants' disappointment at not receiving pills after signing up for a medication trial.

Overall, the results indicate that adding a comprehensive, individualized psychosocial treatment to relatively intensive medical management yielded no better outcomes than MM alone. In this regard, MM was a more complex and extensive intervention than is typically provided in primary care settings. Guided by an intervention manual, MM providers not only developed a medication adherence plan in collaboration with the client and discussed how to cope with adverse "medication" effects but they also reviewed and monitored the client's drinking behavior, negative consequences, and general functioning, recommended abstinence, and encouraged attendance at self-help groups, such as AA (Pettinati et al., 2005). Participants who had a "full dose" of MM received more than 200 minutes (a 45-minute initial session followed by eight 20-minute sessions) of the intervention. Nevertheless, the percentage of abstinent days at the 1-year follow-up, which ranged from 59% to 69% across the nine COMBINE groups, is lower than that in any of five major psychosocial treatment trials examined by Miller, Walters, and Bennett (2001), including the 74% days abstinent at 1 year for outpatients who had received one of three psychosocial treatments in Project MATCH.

The only significant, but small, medication (versus placebo) main effect was for naltrexone in reducing the likelihood of having at least one heavy drinking day during the 16-week treatment period (68.2% vs. 71.4%). Combined with no main effects for acamprosate, these results suggest that it may be difficult for medication effects to emerge when a relatively intensive psychosocial intervention (such as MM) also is provided.

The COMBINE Study findings need to be placed in the context of the characteristics of the participants and the extent of their participation. Of more than 4,965 volunteers seeking treatment for alcohol dependence, only 1,383 (28%) participated in the trial. It is not clear how many were excluded because of not meeting criteria for alcohol dependence, and how many were excluded because they had more complicated conditions (e.g., history of substance use other than nicotine or cannabis). Moreover, across the nine study groups, between 27% and 43% of participants discontinued medication (or placebo), and between 14 and 29% discontinued all treatment. Between 36% and 50% of the participants were married, 69 to 80% were employed, and 64 to 74% had more than a high school education. Thus, many participants were higher functioning individuals than typically present for treatment at specialty alcohol programs, especially public sector and nonprofit programs. How similar COMBINE participants are to patients with alcohol dependence who are likely to receive pharmacotherapy in primary-care settings is not clear.

Overall, the findings suggest that similar patients who are receiving a medication, such as naltrexone, do not obtain added benefit on alcohol-related outcomes from a psychosocial intervention more intensive than MM over the course of a 4-month medication period. However, more psychosocial (and/or pharmacological) treatment over a longer period may be needed for initial nonresponders and to reduce decay in during-treatment gains on alcohol-related outcomes.

Summary

These reviews and studies indicate that an effective strategy may be to provide lower intensity treatment for a longer duration — that is, treatment sessions at a lower rate spread over a longer period (see McKay, 2006; Moos, Finney, Ouimette, & Suchinsky, 1999; Moos & Moos, 2003). The effectiveness of this strategy is suggested by the positive findings for outpatient care following inpatient treatment and for brief interventions that incorporated extended follow-up contacts with patients. More extended treatment may improve patient outcomes by providing patients with ongoing support and monitoring, and the potential to discuss and resolve problems prior to the occurrence of a full-blown relapse. In this vein, brief interventions may be most effective for relatively healthy patients who have intact community support systems, and medical management may be all the psychosocial intervention needed while patients are receiving an effective medication for a substance use disorder. Patients who have severe alcohol and/or drug dependence, concomitant psychiatric disorders, and/or deficient social resources appear to be appropriate candidates for longer (and more intensive) treatment to address their multiple disorders.

TREATMENT SETTING

Choosing the setting of treatment is an important decision for treatment providers and patients, given the extent to which the setting drives treatment cost. Prompted by the cost differential between inpatient and outpatient treatment, three reviews of the literature on the relative effectiveness of alcohol treatment in these two types of settings were published in the 1980s (Annis, 1986; Miller & Hester, 1986; Saxe, Dougherty, Esty, & Fine, 1983). After examining controlled studies employing either random assignment to treatment setting or matching inpatients and outpatients on pretreatment variables, each of these reviews concluded there was no evidence for the overall superiority of inpatient over outpatient treatment, although they noted that some evidence suggested more severely impaired patients might be treated more effectively in inpatient or residential settings.

In a more recent box-score review of 14 relevant studies of the Type 1 and 2 varieties by Finney,

Hahn, and Moos (1996), 5 studies found inpatient alcohol treatment significantly superior to outpatient treatment on at least one drinking-related outcome variable, and 2 found day hospital treatment superior to inpatient treatment. In all but one instance in which a significant effect emerged, patients in the "superior" setting received more intensive treatment. A subsequent meta-analysis of effect sizes yielded an average positive effect of inpatient treatment across studies that was significant, although small, at 3-month follow-ups, but no longer significant at 6- and 12-month follow-ups (Finney & Moos, 1996; cf. Mattick & Jarvis, 1994). Likewise, Rychtarik et al. (2000) found no differences over an 18-month follow-up interval on primary outcome variables for patients with AUDs randomly assigned to inpatient, intensive outpatient, and standard outpatient treatment. Similarly, in a randomized trial of patients with substance use disorders (Greenwood, Woods, Guydish, & Bein, 2001; Guydish, Werdegard, Sorenson, Clark, & Acampora, 1998; Guydish, Sorensen, Chan, Werdegar, Bostrom, & Acampora, 1999), those receiving residential treatment were less likely to relapse and to have fewer social problems and psychiatric symptoms at a 6-month follow-up than patients receiving day treatment, but there were no differences on eight other outcomes at that point. Patients treated in the two settings did not differ on any outcome assessed at 12- and 18-month follow-ups (see also Schneider, Mittelmeier, & Gadish, 1996).

Because patients who are clinically judged to need inpatient or residential care cannot ethically be randomized to inpatient or outpatient care, many of the studies comparing inpatient/residential and outpatient treatment have necessarily focused on patients considered eligible for treatment in outpatient settings (Finney & Moos, 1996); thus, their conclusions are limited to this patient population. The relative efficacy of inpatient/residential versus outpatient treatment for more impaired patients has been examined primarily in naturalistic studies of patient–treatment setting matching.

Aspects of hypothesized patient–treatment setting matches have been captured in the American Society of Addiction Medicine (ASAM) Patient Placement Criteria (PCC; Gastfriend, Rubin, Sharon, Turner, Anton, Donovan, et al., 2003). The criteria attempt to match patients to one of five levels of care: (a) early intervention, (b) outpatient treatment, (c) intensive outpatient/partial hospitalization treatment,

(d) residential/inpatient treatment, or (e) medically managed intensive inpatient treatment. Placement decisions are based on a comprehensive assessment of patients' standing on six dimensions: (a) acute intoxication and/or withdrawal potential, (b) biomedical conditions and complications, (c) emotional/behavioral conditions or complications, (d) readiness to change, (e) relapse/continued use potential, and (f) recovery environment. Although the rationales for PCC patient–treatment setting matches are generally compelling and some research has supported them (for a review, see Gastfriend et al., 2003), the body of relevant research is still small.

Although not guided by the PCC, other studies of patient–treatment setting matching also have shown that more severely impaired patients do better in inpatient or residential treatment. For example, in their randomized trial, Rychtarik et al. (2000) found that patients who were high in alcohol involvement did better following inpatient rather than outpatient treatment; patients who were low in alcohol involvement fared better with outpatient than with inpatient care. Similarly, patient with lower cognitive functioning had better outcomes following inpatient than outpatient treatment, but there was no support for the hypothesis that persons from environments that promote excessive drinking benefit more from a residential stay (probably because the characteristics of the environment to which patients eventually return are more important than the setting of treatment). Other studies by McKay et al. (2002), Moos et al. (2000), Magura et al. (2003), Melnick, De Leon, Thomas, and Kressel (2001), Pettinati et al. (1999), and Simpson et al. (1999) found that patients with greater substance use severity, psychiatric impairment, and/or fewer social resources tend to benefit more from an initial episode of inpatient or residential treatment rather than outpatient treatment, especially if followed by continuing outpatient care. Most of these studies did not employ random assignment to treatment.

Overall, we believe that the best approaches for treatment providers now are those recommended in previous reviews: (a) provide outpatient treatment for most individuals with sufficient social resources and no serious medical or psychiatric impairment; (b) use less costly intensive outpatient treatment options for patients who have not responded to brief interventions or for whom a more intensive intervention seems warranted, but who do not need the structured environment of a residential setting; and (c) retain residential options for those with few social resources and/or environments that are serious impediments to recovery, and inpatient treatment options for individuals with serious medical or psychiatric conditions.

Although it is very important from a cost perspective, the setting of treatment for substance use disorders is a distal variable in relation to patients' posttreatment functioning. Other treatment variables, such as the treatment modality, therapists' characteristics, the amount and duration of treatment, and the degree of support and structure provided in treatment, should have a more direct impact on patient posttreatment functioning. Treatment setting can affect duration and amount of treatment (Finney et al., 1996), however, and residential settings may attract some patients (e.g., homeless individuals) who would not enter outpatient treatment. A recent study by Milby, Schumacher, Wallace, Freedman, and Vuchinich (2005) supports the beneficial effects of providing homeless patients a place to stay while undergoing SUD treatment.

DISCUSSION

Our primary objective here is to review and discuss our conclusions regarding "what works" in treatment for substance use disorders. Before doing so, however, we first focus on problems in existing research that place some limitations on our ability to draw conclusions about effectiveness and relative effectiveness of different treatments.

Limitations in Identifying Best Practices From Existing Research

We have arrived at conclusions regarding empirically supported treatment modalities, in part, based on the results of comprehensive box-score reviews, such as those summarized in Table 6.1, that consider many treatment modalities. As noted earlier, box-score reviews use the proportion of relevant studies that have found a particular treatment approach to be significantly better than some alternative as the index of treatment effectiveness. However, box-score reviews suffer from the fact that, because of ethical concerns about providing no treatment to persons with substance use disorders, most studies of psychosocial treatment modalities are comparisons of alternative treatments (see Swearingen et al., 2003). Consequently, the strength of the competition against which different modalities are pitted varies from study to study. If two highly effective modalities were consistently pitted against only each other in studies, each would be found to be "ineffective" in a box-score review (see Finney, 2000). Finney and Monahan (1996) adjusted their box-score effectiveness ratings for the strength of the competition, but those competition ratings, themselves, were box-score indices.

Another problem involves studies with low statistical power (due primarily to small patient samples) to detect treatment effects. Although Moyer, Finney, and Swearingen (2002) found that statistical power of alcohol treatment studies has increased over time, the average statistical power of comparative studies reported between 1970 and 1998 was .54. In other words, studies had just over a 50–50 chance, on average, of detecting a medium-sized difference between treatment conditions at a statistically significant level. Low power can contribute to "no-difference" findings that may have been detected as significant treatment effects in larger, more powerful studies.

A methodological problem with contrasting implications for finding statistically significant treatment effects is that many studies examine multiple outcome variables assessed at multiple follow-up points. There typically is no correction in box-score reviews for the number of tests for SUD treatment effects that were conducted, so some reported statistically significant treatment effects are due to chance. Baldwin, Murray, and Shadish (2005) have highlighted another factor that has contributed to an overestimate of the number of statistically significant treatment effects—the common application of inappropriate statistical analyses that ignore the fact that some SUD treatments were delivered to groups of patients, rather than to individual patients. All these factors raise questions about the rankings of treatment modalities in box-scores reviews, such as those summarized in Table 6.1, that are based on finding at least one statistically significant treatment effect.

An alternative to box-score reviews that addresses some, but not all, of these concerns is to conduct meta-analyses based on effect sizes. Effect sizes index the *magnitude* of treatment effects across studies, not their statistical significance in individual studies. Also, syntheses based on effect sizes are less likely than box-score approaches to be distorted by low power and multiple tests for treatment effects. Finally, as illustrated by Baldwin et al. (2005), meta-analyses can make assumptions about and adjust for group delivery of treatment in estimating treatment effects, although their review is the only one, to our knowledge, that has done so. However, meta-analyses often address the issue of multiple, varying comparison conditions in studies of different treatment modalities by narrowing their focus to a specific pair of treatment conditions or treatment and control conditions (e.g., inpatient vs. outpatient treatment, brief intervention vs. more extended treatment, medication vs. placebo). Thus, they typically do not provide the kind of comprehensive evaluation of treatment effectiveness that has been attempted in some box-score reviews.

Even with their limitations, box-score reviews of the results of a large number of studies can reveal important general patterns. However, because of the typically small number of studies of individual treatment modalities, patterns of findings across studies can change over time as more studies are considered. Moreover, all types of quantitative syntheses can obscure important differences across studies, such as variation in treatment implementation (therapist characteristics, duration and amount of treatment, and treatment setting) and in patient characteristics, that should be considered in evaluating overall effectiveness. These are issues that treatment providers and health care system leaders should keep in mind as they attempt to make sense of research findings and to gauge how the findings of individual studies and research syntheses should be used to shape clinical practice.

What Works in SUD Treatment

These limitations notwithstanding, the reviews and studies we have considered point to the effectiveness of cognitive-behavioral interventions (see also DeRubeis & Crits-Christoph, 1998). Many of the treatment modalities with evidence of effectiveness (e.g., the community reinforcement approach, behavioral marital therapy, and social skills training) address not only drinking and/or drug use behavior but also patients' life contexts and their ability to cope with life contexts. This broad-spectrum approach may be necessary to achieve positive outcomes with many patients whose substance use disorders have produced, and are perpetuated by, deficits in coping skills and problems in multiple life areas. Likewise, 12-step treatment is a broad-spectrum approach that focuses not only on abstinence from substance use but also on changing recipients' beliefs (e.g., disease model and spiritual beliefs), modeling coping skills (Snow, Prochaska, & Rossi, 1994), and providing social support for recovery in the form of 12-step self-help groups and sponsors. Finally, motivational interventions also have considerable support regarding their equivalent effectiveness to other empirically supported modalities (e.g., cognitive-behavioral treatment) even when provided at lower doses. Motivational interviewing seems especially effective with individuals who are still ambivalent about changing their substance use.

For all these treatment modalities, more research is needed to identify their "active ingredients" and "mechanisms of change." For example, McCrady and Nathan (2006) also point to increasing/maintaining patient motivation, teaching coping skills, and restructuring individuals' social environments as general principles for changing substance use behavior. In their view, these change processes likely exert their effects by changing patients' perceptions of social norms regarding substance use, and by increasing patients' sense of self-efficacy for not drinking or using in relapse-inducing situations. In addition, research is needed to establish the effectiveness in real-life situations of treatment modalities that have been demonstrated to be efficacious when delivered under ideal research conditions. For treatments that have been identified as effective, more research is needed to identify how best to implement them in routine care (e.g., Morgenstern, Blanchard, Morgan, Labouvie, & Hayaki, 2001; Sorensen et al., 1988; Sorenson & Midkiff, 2000).

Regardless of the treatment modality applied, therapists are likely to have a significant impact on patients' posttreatment functioning. The few studies of therapist effects, combined with the substantial research literature on motivational interviewing, suggest that therapists who are interpersonally skilled, empathic, and less confrontational produce better patient outcomes, probably because they establish better therapeutic alliances with their patients in many cases.

On the issue of duration and amount of treatment, an effective strategy for many patients may be to provide lower intensity treatment for a longer duration—that is, treatment sessions spread at a lower rate over a longer period. Extended treatment can provide both care and less-intensive monitoring that is matched to the chronic, relapsing nature of many individuals' substance use disorders. Although more research is needed, it seems wise at this point to restrict brief interventions as a stand-alone treatment to patients with mild to moderate disorders. Longer term interventions, and treatment in inpatient or residential settings, should be reserved for patients with more severe, treatment-resistant substance use disorders, fewer social resources, more concomitant medical or psychiatric disorders, and a desire for longer term and/or residential treatment.

Overall, an ideal SUD treatment system at the level of a community or of a health care organization (see Humphreys & Tucker, 2002) would provide easy access to diverse evidence-based interventions across a full continuum of care with respect to intensity, duration, setting, and ancillary services, as needed and appropriate throughout the course of individuals' substance use disorders. Such a system would be able to effectively assist and monitor persons with different levels of substance use severity, co-occurring problems, motivational levels, and treatment preferences through periods of lapse, relapse, remission, and recovery.

ACKNOWLEDGMENTS

Preparation of this revised chapter was supported in part by the Department of Veterans Affairs Quality Enhancement Research Initiative and by NIAAA Grant AA15685. The views expressed are those of the authors and do not necessarily reflect those of the Department of Veterans Affairs. We thank Daniel Kivlahan for his helpful comments.

REFERENCES

Annis, H. M. (1986). Is inpatient rehabilitation cost effective? Con position. *Advances in Alcohol and Substance Abuse, 5,* 175–190.

Anton, R. F., O'Malley, S. S., Ciraulo, D. A., Cisler, R. A., Couper, D., Donovan, D. M., et al. (2006). Combined pharmacotherapies and behavioral interventions for alcohol dependence: The COMBINE Study: A randomized controlled trial. *Journal of the American Medical Association, 295,* 2003–2017.

Ashton, M. (2005). The motivational hallo. *Drug and Alcohol Findings, 13*, 23–30.

Azrin, N. H. (1976). Improvements in the community-reinforcement approach to alcoholism. *Behavior Research and Therapy, 14*, 339–348.

Azrin, N. H., Sisson, R. W., Meyers, R., & Godley, M. (1982). Alcoholism treatment by disulfiram and community reinforcement therapy. *Journal of Behavior Therapy and Experimental Psychiatry, 13*, 105–112.

Baer, J. S., Kivlahan, D. R., & Donovan, D. M. (1999). Integrating skills training and motivational therapies: Implications for the treatment of substance dependence. *Journal of Substance Abuse Treatment, 17*, 37–44.

Baldwin, S. A., Murray, D. M., & Shadish, W. R. (2005). Empirically supported treatments or Type I errors? Problems with the analysis of data from group-administered treatments. *Journal of Consulting and Clinical Psychology, 73*, 924–935.

Belding, M. A., Iguchi, M. Y., Morral, A. R., & McLellan, A. T. (1997). Assessing the helping alliance and its impact in the treatment of opiate dependence. *Drug and Alcohol Dependence, 48*, 51–59.

Bien, T. H., Miller, W. R., & Tonigan, J. S. (1993). Brief interventions for alcohol problems: A review. *Addiction, 88*, 315–336.

Breslin, F. C., Sobell, M. B., Sobell, L. C., Buchan, G., & Cunningham, J. A. (1997). Toward a stepped care approach to treating problem drinkers: The predictive utility of within treatment variables and therapist prognostic ratings. *Addiction, 92*, 1479–1489.

Brooks, A. J., & Penn, P. E. (2003). Comparing treatments for dual diagnosis: Twelve-step and self-management and recovery training. *American Journal of Drug and Alcohol Abuse, 29*, 359–383.

Brooner, R. K., Kidorf, M. S., King, V. L., Stoller, K. B., Peirce, J. M., Bigelow, G., et al. (2004). Behavioral contingencies improve counseling attendance in an adaptive treatment model. *Journal of Substance Abuse Treatment, 27*, 223–232.

Brown, T. G., Seraganian, P., Tremblay, J., & Annis, H. (2002). Process and outcome changes with relapse prevention versus 12-step aftercare programs for substance abusers. *Addiction, 97*, 677–690.

Budney, A. J., Moore, B. A., Rocha, H. L., & Higgins, S. T. (2006). Clinical trial of abstinence-based vouchers and cognitive-behavioral therapy for cannabis dependence. *Journal of Consulting and Clinical Psychology, 74*, 307–316.

Burke, B. L., Arkowitz, H., & Menchola, M. (2003). The efficacy of motivational interviewing: A meta-analysis of controlled clinical trials. *Journal of Consulting and Clinical Psychology, 71*, 843–861.

Condelli, W. S., & Hubbard, R. L. (1994). Relationship between time spent in treatment and client outcomes from therapeutic communities. *Journal of Substance Abuse Treatment, 11*, 25–33.

Connors, G. J., Carroll, K. M., DiClemente, C. C., Longabaugh, R., & Donovan, D. M. (1997). The therapeutic alliance and its relationship to alcohol treatment participation and outcome. *Journal of Consulting and Clinical Psychology, 69*, 588–598.

Copeland, J., Swift, W., Roffman, R., & Stephens, R. (2001). A randomized controlled trial of brief cognitive-behavioral interventions for cannabis use disorder. *Journal of Substance Abuse Treatment, 21*, 55–64.

Crits-Christoph, P., Siqueland, L., Blaine, J., Frank, A., Luborsky, L., Onken, L. S., et al. (1999). Psychosocial treatments for cocaine dependence: National Institute on Drug Abuse Collaborative Cocaine Treatment Study. *Archives of General Psychiatry, 56*, 493–502.

Crits-Christoph, P., Gibbons, M. B. C., Barber, J. P., Gallop, R., Beck, A. T., Mercer, D., et al. (2003). Mediators of outcome of psychosocial treatments for cocaine dependence. *Journal of Consulting and Clinical Psychology, 71*, 918–925.

Cunningham, J. A. (1999). Untreated remissions from drug use: The predominant pathway. *Addictive Behaviors, 24*, 267–270.

De Leon, G. (2000). *The therapeutic community: Theory, model, and method.* New York: Springer.

De Leon, G., Sacks, S., Staines, G., & McKendrick, K. (2000). Modified therapeutic community for homeless mentally ill chemical abusers: Treatment outcomes. *American Journal of Drug and Alcohol Abuse, 26*, 461–480.

Dennis, M. L., Scott, C. K., & Funk, R. (2003). An experimental evaluation of recovery management checkups (RMC) for people with chronic substance use disorders. *Evaluation and Program Planning, 26*, 339–352.

DeRubeis, R. J., & Crits-Christoph, P. (1998). Empirically supported individual and group psychological treatments for adult mental disorders. *Journal of Consulting and Clinical Psychology, 66*, 290–303.

Dunn, C., DeRoo, L., & Rivara, F. P. (2001). The use of brief interventions adapted from motivational interviewing across behavioral domains: A systematic review. *Addiction, 12*, 1725–1742.

Edwards, G., Orford, J., Egert, S., Guthrie, S., Hawker, A., Hensman, C., et al. (1977). Alcoholism: A controlled trial of "treatment" and "advice." *Journal of Studies on Alcohol, 38*, 1004–1031.

Eriksen, L., Bjornstad, S., & Gotestam, K. G. (1986). Social skills training in groups for alcoholics: One-year treatment outcome for groups and individuals. *Addictive Behaviors, 11,* 309–329.

Fenton, L. R., Cecero, J. J., Nich, C., Frankforter, T. L., & Carroll, K. M. (2001). Perspective is everything: The predictive validity of six working alliance instruments. *Journal of Psychotherapy Practice and Research, 10,* 262–268.

Finney, J. W. (2000). Limitations in using existing alcohol treatment trials to develop practice guidelines. *Addiction, 95,* 1491–1500.

Finney, J. W., Hahn, A. C., & Moos, R. H. (1996). The effectiveness of inpatient and outpatient treatment for alcohol abuse: The need to focus on mediators and moderators of setting effects. *Addiction, 91,* 1773–1796.

Finney, J. W., & Monahan, S. C. (1996). The cost effectiveness of treatment for alcoholism: A second approximation. *Journal of Studies on Alcohol, 57,* 229–243.

Finney, J. W., & Moos, R. H. (1996). The effectiveness of inpatient and outpatient treatment for alcohol abuse: Effect sizes, research design issues, and explanatory mechanisms [Response to commentaries]. *Addiction, 91,* 1813–1820.

Friedmann, P. D., Hendrickson, J. C., Gerstein, D. R., & Zhang, Z. (2004). The effect of matching comprehensive services to patients' needs on drug use improvement in addiction treatment. *Addiction, 99,* 962–972.

Gastfriend, D. R., Rubin, A., Sharon, E., Turner, W. M., Anton, R. F., Donovan, D. M., et al. (2003). New constructs and assessments for relapse and continued use potential in the ASAM Patient Placement Criteria. *Journal of Addictive Diseases, 22*(Suppl. 1), 95–111.

Gerstley, L., McLellan, A. T., Alterman, A. I., Woody, G. E., Luborsky, L., & Prout, M. (1989). Ability to form an alliance with the therapist: A possible marker of prognosis for clients with antisocial personality disorder. *American Journal of Psychiatry, 146,* 508–512.

Gilbert, F. S. (1988). The effect of type of aftercare follow-up on treatment outcome among alcoholics. *Journal of Studies on Alcohol, 49,* 149–159.

Greenwood, G. L., Woods, W. J., Guydish, J., & Bein, E. (2001). Relapse outcomes in randomized trial of residential and day drug abuse treatment. *Journal of Substance Abuse Treatment, 20,* 15–23.

Guydish, J., Sorensen, J. L., Chan, M., Werdegar, D., Bostrom, A., & Acampora, A. (1999). A randomized trial comparing day and residential drug abuse treatment: 18-month outcomes. *Journal of Consulting and Clinical Psychology, 67,* 428–434.

Guydish, J., Werdegard, D., Sorensen, J. L., Clark, W., & Acampora, A. (1998). Drug abuse day treatment: A randomized clinical trial comparing day and residential treatment programs. *Journal of Consulting and Clinical Psychology, 66,* 280–289.

Haaga, D., Hall, S. M., & Haas, A. (2006). Participant factors in treating substance use disorders. In L. G. Castonguay & L. E. Beutler (Eds.), *Principles of therapeutic change that work* (pp. 275–292). New York: Oxford University Press.

Hatcher, R. L., & Barends, A W. (1996). Clients' view of the alliance in psychotherapy: Exploratory factor analysis of three alliance measures. *Journal of Consulting and Clinical Psychology, 64,* 1326–1336.

Hettema, J., Steele, J., & Miller, W. R. (2005). Motivational interviewing. *Annual Review of Clinical Psychology, 1,* 91–111.

Higgins, S. T., Alessi, S. M., & Dantona, R. L. (2002). Voucher-based incentives: A substance abuse treatment innovation. *Addictive Behaviors, 27,* 887–910.

Holder, H., Longabaugh, R., Miller, W. R., & Rubonis, A. V. (1991). The cost effectiveness of treatment for alcoholism: A first approximation. *Journal of Studies on Alcohol, 52,* 517–540.

Humphreys, K., Huebsch, P. D., Finney, J. W., & Moos, R. H. (1999). A comparative evaluation of substance abuse treatment: V. Substance abuse treatment can enhance the effectiveness of self-help groups. *Alcoholism: Clinical and Experimental Research, 23,* 558–563.

Humphreys, K., & Tucker, J. (2002). Toward more responsive and effective intervention systems for alcohol-related problems. *Addiction, 97,* 126–132.

Joe, G. W., Simpson, D. D., Greener, J. M., & Rowan-Szal, G. A. (1999). Integrative modeling of client engagement and outcomes during the first 6 months of methadone treatment. *Addictive Behaviors, 22,* 649–659.

Jonson, H., Hermansson, U., Ronnberg, S., Gyllen-Hammar, C., & Forsberg, L. (1995). Comments on brief intervention of alcohol problems: A review of a review. *Addiction, 90,* 1118–1120.

Karno, M. P., & Longabaugh, R. (2004). What do we know? Process analysis and the search for a better understanding of Project MATCH's anger-by-treatment matching effect. *Journal of Studies on Alcohol, 56,* 501–512.

Karno, M. P., & Longabaugh, R. (2005a). An examination of how therapist directiveness interacts with patient anger and reactance to predict alcohol use. *Journal of Studies on Alcohol, 66,* 825–832.

Karno, M. P., & Longabaugh, R. (2005b). Less directiveness by therapists improves drinking outcomes of reactant clients in alcoholism treatment. *Journal of Consulting and Clinical Psychology, 73,* 262–267.

Lash, S. J., Burden, J. L., Monteleone, B. R., & Lehmann, L. P. (2004). Social reinforcement of substance abuse treatment aftercare participation: Impact on outcome. *Addictive Behaviors, 29,* 337–342.

Lash, S. J., Gilmore, J. D., Burden, J. L., Weaver, K. R., Blosser, S. L., & Finney, M. L. (2005). The impact of contracting and prompting substance abuse treatment entry: A pilot trial. *Addictive Behaviors, 30,* 415–422.

Lebow, J., Kelly, J., Knobloch-Fedders, L. M., & Moos, R. (2006). Relationship factors in treating substance use disorders. In L. G. Castonguay & L. E. Beutler (Eds.), *Principles of therapeutic change that work*(pp. 293–317). New York: Oxford University Press.

Longabaugh, R., Wirtz, P. W., Zweben, A., & Stout, R. L. (1998). Network support for drinking, Alcoholics Anonymous and long-term matching effects. *Addiction, 93,* 1313–1333.

Luborsky, L., Crits-Christoph, P., McLellan, A. T., Woody, G., Piper, W., Liberman, B., et al. (1986). Do therapists vary much in their success? Findings from four outcome studies. *American Journal of Orthopsychiatry, 56,* 501–512.

Lussier, J. P., Heil, S. H., Mongeon, J. A., Badger, G. J., & Higgins, S. T. (2006). A meta-analysis of voucher-based reinforcement therapy for substance use disorders. *Addiction, 101,* 192–203.

Magura, S., Staines, G., Kosanke, N., Rosenbaum, A., Foote, J., Deluca, A., et al. (2003). Predictive validity of the ASAM patient placement criteria for naturalistically matched vs. mismatched alcohol dependent patients. *American Journal on Addictions, 12,* 386–397.

Marijuana Treatment Project Research Group. (2004). Brief treatments for cannabis dependence: Findings from a randomized multisite trial. *Journal of Consulting and Clinical Psychology, 72,* 455–466.

Mattick, R. P., & Jarvis, T. (1994). In-patient setting and long duration for the treatment of alcohol dependence? Out-patient care is as good. *Drug and Alcohol Review, 13,* 127–135.

Mattson, M. E., Allen, J. P., Longabaugh, R., Nickless, C. J., Connors, G. J., & Kadden, R. M. (1994). A chronological review of empirical studies of matching alcoholic clients to treatment. *Journal of Studies on Alcohol,* Suppl. 12, 16–29.

Maude-Griffin, P. M., Hohenstein, J. M., Humfleet, G. L., Reilly, P. M., Tusel, D. J., & Hall, S. M. (1998). Superior efficacy of cognitive-behavioral therapy for urban crack cocaine abusers: Main and matching effects. *Journal of Consulting and Clinical Psychology, 66,* 832–837.

McClelland, G. H., & Judd, C. M. (1993). Statistical difficulties of detecting interactions and moderator effects. *Psychological Bulletin, 114,* 376–390.

McCrady, B. S., & Nathan, P. E. (2006). Treatment factors in treating substance use disorders. In L. G. Castonguay & L. E. Beutler (Eds.), *Principles of therapeutic change that work* (pp. 319–340). New York: Oxford University Press.

McCusker, J., Bigelow, C., Frost, R., Garfield, F., Hindin, R., Vickers-Lahti, M., et al. (1997). The effects of planned duration of residential drug abuse treatment on recovery and HIV risk behavior. *American Journal of Public Health, 87,* 1637–1644.

McCusker, J., Vickers-Lahti, M., Stoddard, A., Hindin, R., Bigelow, C., Zorn, M., et al. (1995). The effectiveness of alternative planned durations of residential drug abuse treatment. *American Journal of Public Health, 85,* 1426–1429.

McKay, J. R. (2001). Effectiveness of continuing care interventions for substance abusers: Implications for the study of long-term treatment effects. *Evaluation Review, 25,* 211–232.

McKay, J. R. (2006). Is there a case for extended interventions for alcohol and drug use disorders? *Addiction, 100,* 1594–1610.

McKay, J. R., Donovan, D. M., McLellan, T., Krupski, A., Hansten, M., Stark, K. D., et al. (2002). Evaluation of full vs. partial continuum of care in the treatment of publicly funded substance abusers in Washington State. *American Journal of Drug and Alcohol Abuse, 28,* 307–338.

McKay, J. R., Lynch, K. G., Shepard, D. S., & Pettinati, H. M. (2005). The effectiveness of telephone-based continuing care for alcohol and cocaine dependence: 24-month outcomes. *Archives of General Psychiatry, 62,* 199–207.

McKay, J. R., Lynch, K. G., Shepard, D. S., Ratichek, S., Morrison, R., Koppenhaver, J., et al. (2004). The effectiveness of telephone-based continuing care in the clinical management of alcohol and cocaine use disorders: 12-month outcomes. *Journal of Consulting and Clinical Psychology, 72,* 967–979.

McLellan, A. T., Grissom, G. R., Zanis, D., Randall, M., Brill, P., & O'Brien, C. P. (1997). Problem-service "matching" in addiction treatment: A prospective study in 4 programs. *Archives of General Psychiatry, 54,* 730–735.

McLellan, A. T., Hagan, T. A., Levine, M., Gould, F., Meyers, K., Bencivengo, M., et al. (1998). Supplementary social services improve outcomes in public addiction treatment. *Addiction, 93,* 1489–1499.

Melnick, G., De Leon, G., Thomas, G., & Kressel, D. (2001). A client-treatment matching protocol for therapeutic communities: First report. *Journal of Substance Abuse Treatment, 21,* 119–128.

Milby, J. B., Schumacher, J. E., Wallace, D., Freedman, M. J., & Vuchinich, R. E. (2005). To house or not to house: The effects of providing housing to homeless substance abusers in treatment. *American Journal of Public Health, 95,* 1259–1265.

Miller, W. R., Andrews, N. R., Wilbourne, P., & Bennett, M. E. (1998). A wealth of alternatives: Effective treatments for alcohol problems. In W. R. Miller & N. Heather (Eds.), *Treating addictive behaviors* (2nd ed., pp. 203–216). New York: Plenum Press.

Miller, W. R., & Hester, R. K. (1986). Inpatient alcoholism treatment: Who benefits? *American Psychologist, 41,* 794–805.

Miller, W. R., Meyers, R. J., Tonigan, J. S., & Grant, K. A. (2001). Community reinforcement and traditional approaches: Findings of a controlled trial. In R. J. Meyers & W. R. Miller (Eds.), *A community reinforcement approach to addiction treatment* (pp. 79–103). New York: Cambridge University Press.

Miller, W. R., & Rollnick, S. (2002). *Motivational interviewing: Preparing people for change* (2nd ed.). New York: Guildford Press.

Miller, W. R., & Sanchez, V. C. (1993). Motivating young adults for treatment and lifestyle change. In G. Howard & P. E. Nathan (Eds.), *Issues in alcohol use and misuse by young adults* (pp. 55–82). Notre Dame, IN: University of Notre Dame Press.

Miller, W. R., Walters, S. T., & Bennett, M. E. (2001). How effective is alcoholism treatment in the United States? *Journal of Studies on Alcohol, 62,* 211–220.

Miller, W. R., & Wilbourne, P. L. (2002). Mesa Grande: A methodological analysis of clinical trials of treatments for alcohol use disorders. *Addiction, 97,* 265–277.

Mokdad, A. H., Marks, J. S., Stroup, D. F., & Gerberding, J. L. (2004). Actual causes of death in the United States, 2000. *Journal of the American Medical Association, 291,* 1238–1245.

Monahan, S. C., & Finney, J. W. (1996). Explaining abstinence rates following treatment for alcohol abuse: A quantitative synthesis of patient, research design, and treatment effects. *Addiction, 91,* 787–805.

Monti, P. M., Gulliver, S. B., & Myers, M. G. (1994). Social skills training for alcoholics: Assessment and treatment. *Alcohol and Alcoholism, 29,* 627–637.

Monti, P. M., & O'Leary, T. A. (1999). Coping and social skills training for alcohol and cocaine dependence. *Psychiatric Clinics of North America, 22,* 447–470.

Monti, P. M., Rohsenow, D. J., Michalec, E., Martin, R. A., & Abrams, D. B. (1997). Brief coping skills treatment for cocaine abuse: Substance use outcomes at three months. *Addiction, 92,* 1717–1728.

Moos, R. (2006). Social contexts and substance use. In W. R. Miller & K. M. Carroll (Eds.), *Rethinking substance abuse: What the science shows and what we should do about it* (pp. 182–200). New York: Guilford Press.

Moos, R. H., Finney, J. W., & Cronkite, R. C. (1990). *Alcoholism treatment: Context, process, and outcome.* New York: Oxford University Press.

Moos, R. H., Finney, J. W., & Moos, B. (2000). Inpatient substance abuse care and the outcome of subsequent community residential and outpatient care. *Addiction, 95,* 833–846.

Moos, R. H., Finney, J. W., Ouimette, P. C., & Suchinsky, R. T. (1999). A comparative evaluation of substance abuse treatment: I. Treatment orientation, amount of care, and 1-year outcomes. *Alcoholism: Clinical and Experimental Research, 23,* 529–536.

Moos, R. H., & Moos, B. S. (1995). Stay in residential facilities and mental health care as predictors of readmission for patients with substance use disorders. *Psychiatric Services, 46,* 66–72.

Moos, R., & Moos, B. S. (2003). Long-term influence of duration and intensity of treatment on previously untreated individuals with alcohol use disorders. *Addiction, 98,* 325–337.

Morgenstern, J., Blanchard, K., Morgan, T. J., Labouvie, E., & Hayaki, J. (2001). Testing the effectiveness of cognitive behavioral treatment for substance abuse in a community setting: Within treatment and posttreatment findings. *Journal of Consulting and Clinical Psychology, 69,* 1007–1017.

Moyer, A., Finney, J. W., Elworth, J. T., & Kraemer, H. C. (2001). Can methodological features account for patient-treatment matching findings in the alcohol field? *Journal of Studies on Alcohol, 62,* 62–73.

Moyer, A., Finney, J. W., & Swearingen, C. E. (2002). Methodological characteristics and quality of alcohol treatment outcome studies, 1970–1998: An expanded evaluation. *Addiction, 97,* 253–263.

Moyer, A., Finney, J. W., Swearingen, C. E., & Vergun, P. (2002). Brief interventions for alcohol problems: A meta-analytic review of controlled investigations in treatment-seeking and non-treatment-seeking populations. *Addiction, 97,* 279–292.

Moyers, T. B., Miller, W. R., & Hendrickson, S. (2005). How does motivational interviewing work? Therapist interpersonal skill predicts client involvement within motivational interviewing sessions. *Journal of Consulting and Clinical Psychology, 73,* 590–598.

Najavits, L. M., & Weiss, R. D. (1994). Variations in therapist effectiveness in the treatment of patients with substance use disorders: An empirical review. *Addiction, 89,* 679–688.

National Institute on Drug Abuse (2005). NIDA Info-Facts: Treatment trends. Retrieved April 5, 2006, from http://www.nida.nih.gov/Infofacts/ treatment-trends.html

National Quality Forum. (2005). *Evidence-based treatment practices for substance use disorders: Workshop proceedings.* Washington, DC: National Quality Forum.

Nemes, S., Wish, E., & Messina, N. (1999). Comparing the impact of standard and abbreviated treatment in a therapeutic community: Findings from the District of Columbia Treatment Initiative Experiment. *Journal of Substance Abuse Treatment, 17,* 339–347.

Obert, J. L., McCann, M. J., Marinelli-Casey, P., Weiner, A., Minsky, S., Brethen, P., et al. (2000). The Matrix Model of outpatient stimulant abuse treatment: history and description. *Journal of Psychoactive Drugs, 32,* 157–164.

Obert, J. L., Rawson, R. A., & Miotto, K. (1997). Substance abuse treatment for "hazardous users": An early intervention. *Journal of Psychoactive Drugs, 29,* 291–298.

O'Farrell, T. J., Choquette, K. A., & Cutter, H. S. G. (1998). Couples relapse prevention sessions after behavioral marital therapy for male alcoholics: Outcomes during the three years after starting treatment. *Journal of Studies on Alcohol, 59,* 357–370.

O'Farrell, T. J., Choquette, K. A., Cutter, H. S. G., Brown, E. D., & McCourt, W. F. (1993). Behavioral marital therapy with and without additional couples relapse prevention sessions for alcoholics and their wives. *Journal of Studies on Alcohol, 54,* 652–666.

O'Farrell, T. J. & Fals-Stewart, W. (2001). Family-involved alcoholism treatment: An update. In M. Galanter (Ed.), *Recent developments in alcoholism; Vol. 15. Services research in the era of managed care* (pp. 329–356). New York: Plenum.

Ouimette, P. C., Finney, J. W., & Moos, R. H. (1997). Twelve step and cognitive-behavioral treatment for substance abuse: A comparison of treatment effectiveness. *Journal of Consulting and Clinical Psychology, 65,* 230–240.

Ouimette, P. C., Moos, R., & Finney, J. (1998). Influence of outpatient treatment and 12-step group involvement on one-year substance abuse treatment outcomes. *Journal of Studies on Alcohol, 59,* 513–522.

Petry, N. M., & Bickel, W. K. (1999). Therapeutic alliance and psychiatric severity as predictors of completion of treatment for opioid dependence. *Psychiatric Services, 50,* 219–227.

Pettinati, H. M., Meyers, K., Evans, B. D., Ruetsch, C. R., Kaplan, F. N., Jensen, J. M., et al. (1999). Inpatient alcohol treatment in a private healthcare setting: Which patients benefit and at what cost? *American Journal of the Addictions, 8,* 220–233.

Pettinati, H. M., Weiss, R. D., Dundon, W., Miller, W. R., Donovan, D., Ernst, D. B., et al. (2005). A structured approach to medical management: A psychosocial intervention to support pharmacotherapy in the treatment of alcohol dependence. *Journal of Studies on Alcohol,* Suppl. 15, S170–S179.

Polcin, D. L. (2003). Rethinking confrontation in alcohol and drug treatment: Consideration of the clinical context. *Substance Use and Misuse, 38,* 165–184.

Prendergast, M. L., Podus, D., Chang, E., & Urada, D. (2002). The effectiveness of drug abuse treatment: A meta-analysis of comparison group studies. *Drug and Alcohol Dependence, 67,* 53–72.

Prendergast, M., Podus, D., Finney, J., Greenwell, L., & Roll, J. (in press). Contingency management for treatment of substance use disorders: A meta-analysis. *Addiction.*

Project MATCH Research Group. (1997a). Matching alcoholism treatments to client heterogeneity: Project MATCH posttreatment drinking outcomes. *Journal of Studies on Alcohol, 58,* 7–29.

Project MATCH Research Group. (1997b). Project MATCH secondary a priori hypotheses. *Addiction, 92,* 1671–1698.

Project MATCH Research Group. (1998a). Matching alcoholism treatments to client heterogeneity: Project MATCH three-year drinking outcomes. *Alcoholism: Clinical and Experimental Research, 22,* 1300–1311.

Project MATCH Research Group. (1998b). Therapist effects in three treatments for alcohol problems. *Psychotherapy Research, 8,* 455–474.

Rawson, R. A., Shoptaw, S. J., Obert, J. L., McCann, M. J., Hasson, A. L., Marinelli-Casey, P. J., et al. (1995). An intensive outpatient approach for cocaine abuse treatment: The Matrix Model. *Journal of Substance Abuse Treatment, 12,* 117–127.

Raytek, H. S., McCrady, B. S., Epstein, E. E., & Hirsch, L. S. (1999). Therapeutic alliance and the retention of couples in conjoint alcoholism treatment. *Addictive Behaviors, 24,* 317–330.

Robert Wood Johnson Foundation (2001). *Substance abuse: The nation's number one health problem.* Prepared for the Robert Wood Johnson Foundation by the Schneider Institute of Health Policy, Brandeis University, Princeton, NJ. Retrieved September 15, 2006, from http://www.rwjf.org/files/publications/other/SubstanceAbuseChartbook.pdf#search=%22Schneider%20Institute%20for%20Health%20Policy%20AND%20Substance%20Abuse%22

Rohsenow, D. J., Monti, P. M., Martin, R. A., Colby, S. M., Myers, M. G., Gulliver, S. B., et al. (2004). Motivational enhancement and coping skills training for cocaine abusers: Effects on substance use outcomes. *Addiction, 99,* 862–874.

Rosenblum, A., Cleland, C., Magura, S., Mahmood, D., Kosanke, N., & Foote, J. (2005). Moderators of effects of motivational enhancements to cognitive behavioral therapy. *American Journal of Drug and Alcohol Abuse, 31,* 35–58.

Rychtarik, R. G., Connors, G. J., Wirtz, P. W., Whitney, R. B., McGillicuddy, N. B., & Fitterling, J. M. (2000). Treatment settings for persons with alcoholism: Evidence for matching clients to inpatient versus outpatient care. *Journal of Consulting and Clinical Psychology, 68,* 277–289.

Sannibale, C., Hurkett, P., Van Den Bossche, E., O'Connor, D., Zador, D., Capus, C., et al. (2003). Aftercare attendance and post-treatment functioning of severely substance dependent residential treatment clients. *Drug and Alcohol Review, 22,* 181–190.

Saxe, L., Dougherty, Esty, K., & Fine, M.(1983). *The effectiveness and costs of alcoholism treatment.* Washington, DC: Office of Technology Assessment.

Schneider, R., Mittelmeier, C., & Gadish, D. (1996). Day versus inpatient treatment for cocaine dependence: An experimental comparison. *Journal of Mental Health Administration, 23,* 234–245.

Shoptaw, S., Rawson, R. A., McCann, M. J., & Obert, J. L. (1994). The Matrix Model of outpatient stimulant abuse treatment: Evidence of efficacy. *Journal of Addictive Diseases, 13,* 129–141.

Simpson, D. D., Joe, G. W., & Brown, B. (1997). Treatment retention and follow-up outcomes in the Drug Abuse Treatment Outcome Study (DATOS). *Psychology of Addictive Behaviors, 11,* 294–307.

Simpson, D. D., Joe, G. W., Fletcher, B. W., Hubbard, R. L., & Anglin, M. D. (1999). A national evaluation of treatment outcomes for cocaine dependence. *Archives of General Psychiatry, 56,* 507–514.

Simpson, D. D., Joe, G. W., & Rowan-Szal, G. A. (1997). Drug abuse treatment retention and process effects on follow-up outcomes. *Drug and Alcohol Dependence, 47,* 227–237.

Smith, D. E., & McCrady, B. S. (1991). Cognitive impairment among alcoholics: Impact on drink refusal skill acquisition and treatment outcome. *Addictive Behaviors, 16,* 265–274.

Smith, J. E., Meyers, R. J., & Delaney, H. D. (1998). The community reinforcement approach with homeless alcohol-dependent individuals. *Journal of Consulting and Clinical Psychology, 66,* 541–548.

Smith, J. E., Meyers, R. J., & Miller, W. R. (2001). The community reinforcement approach to the treatment of substance use disorders. *American Journal of Addiction, 10*(Suppl.), 51–59.

Smith, L. A., Gates, S., & Foxcroft, D. (2006). Therapeutic communities for substance related disorder. *Cochrane Database of Systematic Reviews,* Issue 1, Art. No. CD005338. DOI:10.1002/14651858.CD005338.

Snow, M. G., Prochaska, J. O., & Rossi, J. (1994). Processes of change in Alcoholics Anonymous: Maintenance factors in long-term sobriety. *Journal of Studies on Alcohol, 55,* 362–371.

Sobell, L. C., Ellingstad, T. P., & Sobell, M. B. (2000). Natural recovery from alcohol and drug problems: Methodological review of the research with suggestions for future directions. *Addiction, 95,* 749–764.

Sobell, M. B., & Sobell, L. C. (2000). Stepped care as a heuristic approach to the treatment of alcohol problems. *Journal of Consulting and Clinical Psychology, 68,* 573–579.

Sorensen, J. L., Hall, S. M., Loeb, P., Allen, T., Glaser, E. M., & Greenberg, P. D. (1988). Dissemination of a job seekers' workshop to drug treatment programs. *Behavior Therapy, 19,* 143–155.

Sorensen, J. L., & Midkiff, E. E. (2000). Bridging the gap between research and drug abuse treatment. *Journal of Psychoactive Drugs, 32,* 379–382.

Stanton, M. D., & Shadish, W. R. (1997). Outcome, attrition and family-couples treatment for drug abuse: A meta-analysis and review of the controlled, comparative studies. *Psychological Bulletin, 122,* 170–191.

Stinson, F. S., Grant, B. F., Dawson, D. A., Ruan, W. J., Juang, B., & Saha, T. (2005). Comorbidity between *DSM-IV* alcohol and specific drug use disorders in the United States: Results from the national Epidemiologic Survey on Alcohol and Related Conditions. *Drug and Alcohol Dependence, 80,* 105–116.

Swearingen, C. E., Moyer, A, & Finney, J. W. (2003). Alcoholism treatment outcome studies, 1970–1998: An expanded look at the nature of the research. *Addictive Behaviors, 28,* 415–436.

UKATT Research Team. (2005). Effectiveness of treatment for alcohol problems: Findings of the randomized UK alcohol treatment trial (UKATT). *British Medical Journal, 331,* 541–544.

Wells, E. A., Peterson, P. L., Gainey, R. R., Howkins, J. D., & Catalano, R. F. (1994). Outpatient treatment for cocaine abuse: A controlled comparison of relapse prevention and twelve step approaches. *American Journal of Drug Abuse, 20,* 1–17.

Welte, J., Hynes, G., & Sokolow, L. (1981). Effect of length of stay in inpatient alcoholism treatment on outcome. *Journal of Studies on Alcohol, 42,* 483–499.

Wilk, A. I., Jenson, N. M., & Havighurst, T. C. (1997). Meta-analysis of randomized control trials addressing brief interventions in heavy alcohol drinkers. *Journal of General Internal Medicine, 12,* 274–283.

7

Pharmacological Treatment
of Schizophrenia

Zafar Sharif
Daniel Bradford
Scott Stroup
Jeffrey Lieberman

Schizophrenia is a chronic mental disorder with a lifetime prevalence rate of approximately 1%. The first antipsychotic drug, chlorpromazine, was introduced in 1954, followed by several similar drugs. With the later introduction of clozapine, risperidone, olanzapine, quetiapine, ziprasidone, and aripiprazole, antipsychotic drugs have come to be classified as conventional (chlorpromazine-like) or atypical (clozapine-like). Both of these broad classes of medications have been demonstrated to safely improve psychotic symptoms in the acute phase of the illness and reduce risk of relapse in the maintenance phase of treatment. The atypical antipsychotics offer hope for enhanced efficacy in the treatment of schizophrenic psychopathology with a reduced burden of extrapyramidal motor dysfunction. Because of the limited efficacy of antipsychotic medication in resolving the full range of schizophrenic psychopathology, adjunctive treatments are often used to reduce morbidity. Concomitant medications such as benzodiazepines, lithium, carbamazepine, valproic acid, antidepressants, glutamate agonists, and dopamine agonists have been used alone and in combination with antipsychotic drugs in order to improve treatment response. In this chapter, we review controlled trials of the pharmacological agents used to treat schizophrenia.

BACKGROUND

Schizophrenia is a chronic psychiatric disorder with a lifetime prevalence rate of approximately 1%. The diagnosis is dependent on the presence of specific symptoms such as delusions, hallucinations, formal thought disorder, and unusual behavior lasting for at least 1 month and the persistence in variable intensity of significant social and occupational deterioration prior, or subsequent, to the psychotic symptoms. Schizophrenic psychopathology has been characterized as divided into two, and possibly three, symptom clusters: positive symptoms comprised of delusions, hallucinations, and formal thought disorder; negative symptoms comprised of deficits in emotional and

verbal expression and in motivation; and disorganization symptoms reflected by disordered thought processes, bizarre behavior, and inappropriate affect (Liddle, Carpenter, & Crow, 1994). In addition, patients with schizophrenia frequently exhibit affective symptoms during both the psychotic phase and the residual phase of the illness. Increasing attention is being paid to cognitive symptoms of schizophrenia, which have been shown to relate more strongly to functional outcome than positive symptom severity (Green, 1996; Harvey et al., 1998). Cognitive deficits include impairments in attention, learning and secondary memory, verbal fluency, and executive functioning. Approximately 75% of patients with schizophrenia have clinically meaningful deficits in at least two cognitive domains, and 90% have deficits in at least one domain (Palmer et al., 1997). Cognitive deficits antedate the clinical onset of the illness, may worsen over time, and are strongly correlated with functional outcome (Marder & Fenton, 2004).

Treatment strategies need to both target the acute psychotic phase of the disorder and achieve maintenance of treatment effect, with reduction in relapse risk in longer term treatment. The illness course and outcome are variable among individuals, although complete symptom remission and return to premorbid status is not common. Progressive deterioration over time characterizes the course of a significant minority of patients, particularly in the first few years of the illness. The first antipsychotic drug, chlorpromazine, was introduced in 1954 and was followed by several similar drugs; with the later introduction of clozapine, risperidone, olanzapine, quetiapine, ziprasidone, and aripiprazole, antipsychotic drugs have come to be classified as conventional or typical (chlorpromazine-like) and atypical (clozapine-like). Although there is no consensus definition of atypical antipsychotic drugs, they are generally thought to produce fewer extrapyramidal side effects (EPS) and tardive dyskinesia than conventional drugs, to have greater efficacy (in refractory patients and against negative symptoms), and to induce only limited prolactin elevation. Antipsychotic medications have been clearly demonstrated to be effective and safe for both the acute and maintenance phases of treatment for schizophrenia. The efficacy of conventional antipsychotic drugs and their propensity to produce both acute and chronic side effects have been thoroughly studied. The newer atypical antipsychotic drugs hold out the promise for increased therapeutic efficacy with significantly less risk of extrapyramidal and neurocognitive adverse effects (Kinon & Lieberman, 1996). A landmark study by Kane, Honigfeld, Singer, and Meltzer (1988), which compared clozapine to chlorpromazine, demonstrated superior efficacy of clozapine in reducing symptoms in 30% of rigorously defined treatment-resistant patients. More recent studies of clozapine in treatment-refractory schizophrenia have generally confirmed this finding and provided support for its use in this population. The data supporting superiority of the other atypicals over conventional antipsychotics are less robust and vary with the atypical being evaluated. Concomitant medications such as benzodiazepines, lithium, carbamazepine, valproic acid, dopamine agonists, and glutamatergic agonists

have been used alone and in combination with antipsychotic drugs to improve treatment response, although clear demonstration of the effectiveness of these strategies is lacking. In addition, antidepressants have been used extensively to treat the depressive symptoms associated with schizophrenia.

We will begin with a review of the controlled trial literature for the typical and atypical antipsychotics, followed by a review of the various augmentation strategies that have been evaluated.

TYPICAL ANTIPSYCHOTICS

Acute and Maintenance Treatment Effects

The introduction of the prototypical conventional antipsychotic drug chlorpromazine in the 1950s, with the subsequent development of other antipsychotic agents with similar pharmacological activity, led to a revolution in the treatment of schizophrenia. These drugs are credited with providing the first effective medical management strategy for schizophrenia and constitute one of the great medical advances of the 20th century. Early doubts regarding the efficacy of these compounds led to the design of rigorous clinical trials, such as the placebo-controlled, double-blind study with thoughtful subject inclusion and exclusion criteria, random treatment assignment, and the use of standardized rating instruments to prove the value of these drugs. More than 100 placebo-controlled trials have conclusively demonstrated the effectiveness of antipsychotic drugs (Davis, Barter, & Kane, 1989). Placebo-controlled studies in which antipsychotic efficacy could not be demonstrated are generally restricted to poorly designed studies that involved doses of chlorpromazine less than 300 mg/day (D. F. Klein & Davis, 1969). In general, the studies have found that approximately 60% of subjects treated with antipsychotic drugs, compared with 20% of placebo-treated subjects, demonstrated substantial resolution of acute positive symptoms within a 6-week trial. Only 8% of medication-treated subjects showed no improvement or worsening, whereas nearly half of placebo-treated subjects did not improve or worsened (National Institute of Mental Health–Psychopharmacology Service Center Collaborative Study Group, 1964). All symptoms associated with schizophrenia improved on antipsychotic drugs, although the positive symptoms seemed to respond to a greater degree and more consistently than negative symptoms. However, despite improvement in symptoms, which is clinically important and was partly responsible for deinstitutionalization, patient functioning and social reintegration did not consistently improve with the use of typical antipsychotic drugs. This disappointing observation was made soon after the introduction of these drugs into clinical practice (Schooler, Goldberg, Boothe, & Cole, 1967). Although dozens of typical antipsychotic drugs have become available to clinicians in the United States since 1954, an extensive body of evidence has confirmed that these drugs are essentially similar in their efficacy profiles. However, an individual patient may show a better response to one particular drug than to another (Gardos, 1974).

The practice of administering large parenteral doses of high-potency antipsychotics within a 24-hour period (*rapid neuroleptization*) has not demonstrated any gains in the onset of therapeutic efficacy compared with standard doses and has largely been discontinued as a therapeutic strategy. Accumulating data suggest that the time to onset of therapeutic effect of antipsychotic drugs during the treatment of an acute episode of schizophrenia may be quite variable. Davis et al. (1989) reported that onset of effect is usually manifest within the first 1 to 3 weeks and that most gains are noted within 6 to 8 weeks. Agid, Kapur, Arenovich, and Zipursky (2003) conducted a meta-analysis of 42 double-blind comparator-controlled studies and found that antipsychotic effect was evident within the 1st week of treatment and that improvement in the first 2 weeks was greater than during any subsequent 2-week period. In a double-blind, placebo-controlled study comparing intramuscular olanzapine with intramuscular haloperidol, Kapur et al. (2005) reported that onset of specific antipsychotic effect was evident within the first 24 hours, and that improvement in psychosis was independent of change in agitation and excitement. However, some patients, including first-episode patients (Lieberman, 1993; Robinson, Woerner, Alvir, Geisler, et al., 1999), may require several months to achieve their full clinical response and symptom remission. In another study of patients with first-episode schizophrenia, Emsley, Rabinowitz, and Medori (2006) found that clinical response (greater than 20% improvement in total Positive and Negative Symptom Scale [PANSS] score) was achieved in 77% of the sample. In this group of responders, response was

achieved in 23%, 23%, 19%, and 13% of patients at weeks 1, 2, 3, and 4, respectively. However, in 11% of patients, response was evident between 4 and 8 weeks of treatment, and in 11% not until after the 8th week of treatment. These results suggest that time to antipsychotic response varies widely among patients with first-episode schizophrenia (Emsley et al., 2006); this is likely true for more chronic patients as well. When a patient fails to respond to a standard course of treatment, clinicians generally employ maneuvers such as increasing the dose, switching to another typical antipsychotic, or maintaining the initial treatment for an extended trial. Little evidence from controlled clinical trials supports the efficacy of any of these strategies (Kinon et al., 1993; Levinson et al., 1990; Rifkin, Doddi, Karajgi, Borenstein, & Wachspress, 1991; Van Putten, Marder, & Mintz, 1990; Volavka et al., 1992). There is little evidence to support the usefulness of doses beyond the range of 400 to 1,000 mg/day of chlorpromazine or its equivalent dose of other antipsychotics; extremely large doses of 2,000 mg of chlorpromazine daily or its equivalent are not generally associated with greater efficacy (Bjorndal et al., 1980; Ericksen, Hurt, & Chang, 1978; McCreadie & MacDonald, 1977; Neborsky, Janowsky, Munson, & Depry, 1981; Quitkin, Rifkin, & Klein, 1975) and can lead to a greater incidence of side effects.

Significant efforts are under way to identify factors that may be associated with antipsychotic treatment response and refractoriness. For example, a delay in the initiation of antipsychotic drug treatment following onset of psychosis in first-episode schizophrenia (Loebel et al., 1992), and in the treatment of acute exacerbations (May et al., 1976; Wyatt, 1995), may be associated with poorer clinical outcomes. Robinson, Woerner, Alvir, Geisler, et al. (1999) reported that 87% of their sample of first-episode patients with schizophrenia or schizoaffective disorder responded to treatment within 1 year, with a median response time of 9 months. They demonstrated that male gender, a history of obstetric complications, poorer attention at baseline, more severe hallucinations and delusions, and the development of EPS during antipsychotic treatment were associated with a significantly lower likelihood of response. Gunduz-Bruce et al. (2005) evaluated the relationship between duration of untreated psychosis and time to response for hallucinations and delusions in 118 patients with first-episode schizophrenia who received open-label treatment with conventional antipsychotics and were followed for up to 5 years. Time to response for delusions was significantly longer than that for hallucinations, and duration of untreated psychosis was significantly correlated with time to response for delusions but not for hallucinations. The results suggest that duration of untreated psychosis may be specifically associated with time to response for delusions (Gunduz-Bruce et al., 2005).

Numerous studies have demonstrated that continuation of antipsychotic medication beyond treatment of the acute episode is necessary to reduce the risk of psychotic relapse as evidenced by the fact that most patients will experience a clinical worsening if their treatment is discontinued (Davis, 1975; Kane & Lieberman, 1987). Controlled clinical trials of drug discontinuation demonstrate that after 1 year of maintenance treatment, 30% of patients will relapse on medication as compared with a rate of 65% in patients who have undergone placebo substitution. Even those patients who have been successfully maintained in the community for 2 to 3 years on antipsychotic drugs will demonstrate a relapse rate of 66% by 1 year after their treatment is discontinued (Hogarty, Ulrich, Mussare, & Aristigueta, 1976). First-episode patients show a slightly lower relapse rate, with 40% of patients on placebo experiencing a relapse, compared with none while on medication during the year following initial recovery (Kane, Rifkin, Quitkin, Nayak, & Ramos-Lorenzi, 1982). Robinson, Woerner, Alvir, Bilder, et al. (1999) showed that discontinuing drug therapy increased the risk of relapse almost five times in a sample of patients with first-episode schizophrenia and schizoaffective disorder. This study also showed an 82% cumulative risk of relapse for patients who had recovered from a first episode of psychosis. Those who had one relapse within 5 years had a 78% chance of having a second relapse and an 86% chance of having a third. Thus, maintenance antipsychotic therapy seems justified, even for patients recovering from their first episode of schizophrenia. The benefits of maintenance antipsychotic drug treatment, however, are tempered by the inherent risk to the patient of long-term side effects such as the development of tardive dyskinesia. Limiting antipsychotic drug exposure by introducing "drug holidays" or reducing the dose has intuitive appeal for minimizing side-effect risk. However, maintenance studies of the dose-response relationship for up to 1 year of continuous antipsychotic

drug treatment indicate that standard drug doses (fluphenazine decanoate 12.5 to 50 mg biweekly; haloperidol decanoate 50 to 200 mg monthly) provide significantly greater prophylaxis against relapse than do doses of one half to one tenth as much (Hogarty et al., 1988; Johnson, Ludlow, Street, & Taylor, 1987; Kane et al., 1983; Kane, Woerner, & Sarantakos, 1986; Kane et al., 1993; Marder et al., 1987; Schooler, Keith, Severe, & Mathews, 1993), although the lower doses may be associated with better social adjustment and fewer extrapyramidal side effects. A targeted approach that involves slowly titrating patients off maintenance medication with reintroduction of the medication rapidly during presumptive incipient relapsing has not been found to be more effective than the continuous administration of maintenance medication and is associated with risks of symptom exacerbation and relapse (Carpenter et al., 1990; Gaebel et al., 1993; Herz et al., 1991; Jolley, Hirsch, Morrison, McRink, & Wilson, 1990; Schooler et al., 1993).

ATYPICAL ANTIPSYCHOTICS

The atypical antipsychotics offer hope for enhanced efficacy in the treatment of schizophrenic psychopathology with a reduced burden of extrapyramidal motor dysfunction. The number of double-blind studies comparing the acute treatment effects of atypical antipsychotics with the effects of their typical counterparts and the number of studies comparing effects in treatment-refractory populations have grown dramatically in the past few years. Although advantages for the atypical drugs have been shown in many studies, particularly for clozapine, it remains unclear whether the newer atypical drugs have true advantages in effectiveness and side-effect profiles over typical drugs prescribed at appropriate doses. For example, the data used to support the superiority of atypical antipsychotics over conventional antipsychotics on negative symptoms are difficult to interpret because some features of EPS caused by typical antipsychotics (e.g., flat affect, bradykinesia), the so-called *secondary* negative symptoms, may be impossible to distinguish from *primary* negative symptoms of the disease (Kane et al., 2001; Remington & Kapur, 2000). Rating scales commonly used to assess outcomes in clinical trials in schizophrenia do not reliably distinguish primary from secondary negative symptoms.

Atypical agents, in the order in which they were approved by the Food and Drug Administration (FDA), include clozapine, risperidone, olanzapine, quetiapine, ziprasidone, and aripiprazole. Other atypical antipsychotics such as sertindole, zotepine, and amisulpiride, which are not available in the United States, will not be covered in this chapter. We will review the available evidence supporting the use of each drug in chronic schizophrenia, in patients with first-episode, and in patients with treatment-resistant schizophrenia. This is followed by summaries of the meta-analyses of published studies, the Clinical Antipsychotic Trials of Intervention Effectiveness (CATIE), and side-effect profiles of the atypical antipsychotics.

Clozapine

Baldessarini and Frankenburg (1991) reviewed 14 double-blind studies from 1971 through 1988 that compared the efficacy of clozapine to a conventional antipsychotic in the treatment of schizophrenic psychopathology; these studies were not exclusively of treatment-resistant populations. Overall, they reported that 9% more clozapine-treated patients improved, and mean ratings were 13% better in clozapine-treated patients than in those treated with conventional antipsychotics, though the differences were not statistically significant. Rates of EPS, however, were markedly lower in clozapine-treated patients. Wahlbeck, Cheine, and Essali (2000) reviewed 31 mostly short-term (less than 13 weeks' duration), randomized, controlled trials comparing clozapine with typical antipsychotic drugs in patients with treatment-resistant schizophrenia, as well as those with a history of prior response to antipsychotics. The review included studies with a total of 2,589 participants, most of whom were men (74%), with an average age of 38 years. Clinical improvement was seen more frequently in those taking clozapine. In the short term, patients on clozapine had fewer relapses than those on typical antipsychotic drugs, and there was a trend to a similar finding in long-term treatment. The clinical efficacy of clozapine was more pronounced in patients resistant to typical neuroleptics in terms of clinical improvement and symptom reduction. The clinical effect of clozapine, however, at least in the short term, was not reflected in measures of global functioning such as ability to leave the hospital and maintain an occupation.

When studies that included only patients with treatment-resistant schizophrenia are selected, the superiority of clozapine over typical antipsychotics is most consistently demonstrated. A pivotal study (Kane et al., 1988) of the effectiveness of clozapine in treatment-resistant schizophrenia entered 268 such patients into a double-blind comparison with chlorpromazine. Treatment resistance was defined as having failed to respond to at least three prior antipsychotics and without any period of good functioning in the past 5 years, and then not responding to a single-blind 6-week haloperidol prospective lead-in trial. At 6 weeks, 30% of the clozapine-treated group but only 4% of the chlorpromazine-treated group met the a priori response criteria of a reduction greater than 20% from baseline in the Brief Psychiatric Rating Scale (BPRS) total score plus either a posttreatment Clinical Global Impression (CGI) score of 3 (mild) or lower, or a posttreatment BPRS total score of 35 or lower. Since the initial Kane et al. study, several double-blind comparisons of clozapine and a typical antipsychotic have been conducted in patients with treatment-resistant schizophrenia (Buchanan, Breier, Kirkpatrick, Ball, & Carpenter, 1998; Hong, Chen, Chiu, & Sim, 1997; Kane et al., 2001; Kumra et al., 1996; Rosenheck et al., 1997). One open-label study with random treatment assignment and long-term follow-up has also been published (Essock, Hargreaves, Covell, & Goethe, 1996). The Kumra et al. study was a double-blind comparison of clozapine and haloperidol in treatment-refractory childhood schizophrenia. Two of the studies (Kane et al., 2001; Buchanan et al., 1998) included patients who were said to be partially responsive to typical antipsychotics. Four of the six studies found a significant difference favoring clozapine. Of note, however, the two studies that showed the most modest advantages for clozapine (Essock et al., 1996; Rosenheck et al., 1997) were the two longest trials, with durations of 2 years and 1 year, respectively. A meta-analysis of seven trials comparing clozapine to typical antipsychotic drugs in treatment-refractory schizophrenia (Chakos, Lieberman, Hoffman, Bradford, & Sheitman, 2001) showed an advantage for clozapine with regard to total psychopathology, categorical response to treatment (measure of the number of patients who met an arbitrary cutoff for response), extrapyramidal symptoms, tardive dyskinesia, and study completion rates. Studies comparing clozapine to other atypical antipsychotics in treatment-resistant schizophrenia are described in the respective sections on those drugs.

The efficacy of clozapine in the maintenance phase of treatment is supported by three open-label studies. Meltzer, Burnett, Bastani, and Ramirez (1990) reported that the rehospitalization rate among treatment-resistant schizophrenia patients after 1 year of clozapine treatment was reduced by 83% in comparison to the year prior to clozapine treatment. Miller, Perry, Cadoret, and Andreasen (1992) found that patients treated with clozapine for 2.5 years had fewer and shorter durations of hospitalization as compared with the previous 22.5 years. Brier, Buchanan, Irish, and Carpenter (1993) also reported that a year of clozapine treatment was superior to the previous year of conventional neuroleptics, with both fewer exacerbations of illness and fewer hospitalizations. An open mirror-image clinical study has found that during 1 year of treatment with risperidone, the number of days of hospitalization are reduced as compared with the preceding reference period (Addington et al., 1993).

Clozapine remains the only antipsychotic specifically approved by the FDA for treatment-resistant schizophrenia. Additionally, clozapine is approved for reduction of suicide risk in patients with schizophrenia. The controlled trial that led to this indication (Meltzer et al., 2003) included 980 patients who were at relatively high risk of suicide and were randomized to double-blind treatment with either clozapine or olanzapine and followed for up to 2 years; approximately 25% of the sample had treatment-resistant schizophrenia. Suicidal behavior was significantly less in patients treated with clozapine versus olanzapine as reflected by fewer clozapine-treated patients attempting suicide, requiring hospitalization or rescue interventions to prevent suicide, or requiring concomitant treatment with antidepressants or anxiolytics.

Unfortunately, the reported incidence rate of 1% for clozapine-induced agranulocytosis (Alvir, Lieberman, Safferman, Schwimmer, & Schaaf, 1993) has limited the extent of the drug's use in clinical practice. Clozapine has also been associated with an increased risk of myocarditis and a dose-dependent risk for seizures; other side effects that commonly occur include sedation, weight gain, hypotension, tachycardia, hypersalivation, and constipation.

In summary, the demonstrated efficacy of cloz-apine among the subgroup of refractory patients, with no acute EPS and the absence of risk for tardive dyskinesia, represents a landmark achievement in psychopharmacology. The success of clozapine provided the impetus for an enormous research effort that has resulted in the development of several other atypical antipsychotic drugs.

Risperidone

Several double-blind, controlled studies have been published that compared the efficacy of risperidone to a conventional antipsychotic. Chouinard et al. (1993), in a multicenter placebo-controlled study of 135 chronic schizophrenia patients treated with either 2, 6, 10, or 16 mg/day of risperidone, 20 mg/day of haloperidol, or placebo, found that patients treated with risperidone at 6 mg/day had greater reduction in the total PANSS and the PANSS general psychopathology subscale than patients treated with haloperidol at 20 mg/day. Haloperidol treatment resulted in a statistically significant increase in EPS compared with doses of 2, 6, and 16 mg/day of risperidone; however, 10 mg of risperidone resulted in equal amounts of EPS. Marder and Meibach (1994), in a multicenter study of 388 schizophrenia patients treated with one of four doses of risperidone (2, 6, 10, or 16 mg/day), 20 mg/day of haloperidol, or placebo, reported statistically significant differences in overall clinical improvement from 6, 10, and 16 mg/day of risperidone than from placebo, and significantly greater improvement from 6 and 16 mg/day of risperidone than from haloperidol as assessed by change in the total PANSS score. Both negative and positive symptom scores were reduced significantly more with 6 and 16 mg/day of risperidone than with placebo, but only positive symptoms were reduced significantly by haloperidol compared with placebo. There were no significant differences found in the reduction of negative symptoms when any of the four doses of risperidone were directly compared to haloperidol. Both 16 mg/day of risperidone and 20 mg/day of haloperidol resulted in significant increases in parkinsonian side effects compared with placebo; the remaining doses of risperidone did not differ from placebo in parkinsonian side-effect liability. Finally, Peuskens (1995), in a multicenter parallel-group, double-blind 8-week study of 1,362 patients with schizophrenia treated with either 1, 4, 8, 12, or 16 mg/day of risperidone or 10 mg/day of haloperidol, found no significant advantage on the PANSS and CGI assessments for any dose of risperidone compared with haloperidol. However, 1, 4, 8, and 12 mg/day of risperidone produced significantly lower incidence rates of EPS than haloperidol 10 mg/day.

Hunter, Joy, Kennedy, Gilbody, and Song (2003) conducted a review of all randomized controlled trials (RCTs) comparing risperidone to any conventional neuroleptic treatment for individuals with schizophrenia or other similar serious mental illnesses. In the short term, risperidone was more likely to produce an improvement in the PANSS when compared with haloperidol ($n = 2,368$, 9 RCTs); a similar, favorable outcome for risperidone was found in long-term studies ($n = 859$, 2 RCTs). Risperidone was also more likely to reduce relapse at 1-year follow-up, compared with haloperidol ($n = 367$, 1 RCT). Fewer participants treated with risperidone left studies before completion, for both short-term ($n = 3,066$, 16 RCTs) and long-term trials ($n = 1,270$, 4RCTs). Persons given risperidone had significantly fewer general movement disorders (including extrapyramidal side effects) than those receiving older typical antipsychotics ($n = 2,702$, 10 RCTs). Significantly fewer participants given risperidone used antiparkinsonian drugs ($n = 2,524$, 11 RCTs). Four studies ($n = 1,708$) found risperidone-treated patients were more likely to gain weight than were patients treated with typical antipsychotics. Risperidone was no more or less likely than haloperidol to cause sexual problems such as erectile dysfunction ($n = 106$, 2 RCTs).

The efficacy of risperidone compared with haloperidol in longer term treatment and relapse prevention has also been rigorously evaluated. Csernansky, Mahmoud, and Brenner (2002) conducted a long-term, double-blind, randomized trial comparing the two drugs. They found that risperidone was associated with a significantly lower risk for relapse by study end point compared with haloperidol (Kaplan-Meier estimates of relapse risk were 34% vs. 60%, respectively). Rabinowitz et al. (2001) evaluated time to readmission in a naturalistic 2-year follow-up study for patients discharged on risperidone ($n = 268$), olanzapine ($n = 313$), or conventional antipsychotics ($n = 458$). At 24 months, 67% of the risperidone-treated patients and 69% of the olanzapine-treated patients remained in the community as compared with 52% of the patients treated with conventional antipsychotics.

A recent double-blind, randomized study (Schooler et al., 2005) of risperidone and haloperidol in first-episode patients that utilized appropriate doses for both drugs (approximately 3 mg/day) found that in the acute phase of the illness, both drugs were comparable in efficacy. However, relapse rates were significantly lower in risperidone-treated patients (42% and 55%, respectively for risperidone- and haloperidol-treated patients) over a median follow-up period of 206 days. Additionally, risperidone was associated with a significantly longer median time to relapse (466 days for risperidone-treated patients vs. 205 days for haloperidol-treated patients). The advantage for risperidone in reducing relapse risk was evident even though both groups had comparable symptom improvement. Risperidone was superior to haloperidol in EPS liability but caused more prolactin elevation. Weight gain was initially greater with risperidone, but at study end point there was no difference.

The efficacy of risperidone compared with conventional antipsychotics in treatment-refractory populations has been studied to a lesser degree. Two rigorous double-blind studies have compared risperidone with typical antipsychotics in treatment-refractory populations. Wirshing et al. (1999), in an 8-week double blind comparison of risperidone and haloperidol, found clinical superiority of risperidone after 4 weeks of treatment, but this difference disappeared after 4 more weeks of treatment In a 14-week study comparing clozapine, risperidone, olanzapine, and haloperidol in a rigorously defined treatment-refractory sample of 157 inpatients, Volavka et al. (2002) showed risperidone to be superior to haloperidol for negative symptoms but not total PANSS score.

The efficacy of risperidone compared with clozapine in treatment-resistant schizophrenia has also been evaluated. In a 12-week prospective, double-blind, multicenter study, Azorin et al. (2001) compared the efficacy and safety of clozapine and risperidone in 273 patients with severe chronic schizophrenia and poor previous treatment response. The magnitude of improvement in mean BPRS and CGI scores from baseline to end of the study was significantly greater in the clozapine group than in the risperidone group. Statistically significant differences in favor of clozapine were also seen for most of the secondary efficacy measures (PANSS, Calgary Depression Scale, Psychotic Depression Scale, and Psychotic Anxiety Scale). Using less strict criteria for the definition of treatment-resistant schizophrenia, Klieser et al. (1995) and Bondolfi et al. (1998), in double-blind, randomized trials comparing risperidone with clozapine, obtained somewhat more optimistic response rates for risperidone.

Risperidone has recently become available in a long-acting injectable formulation for intramuscular administration every 2 weeks. The efficacy and safety of long-acting risperidone have been evaluated in two large clinical trials (Fleischhacker et al., 2003; Kane et al., 2003). Kane et al. (2003), in a 12-week, randomized, double-blind, placebo-controlled, multicenter trial, treated 400 patients with schizophrenia with either long-acting risperidone (25 mg, 50 mg, or 75 mg every 2 weeks) or placebo injection; they found that long-acting risperidone was significantly more effective than placebo in mean total PANSS, as well as mean positive and mean negative subscale scores. Clinical improvement (greater than 20% reduction in total PANSS score) was observed in 17% of placebo patients and in 47% and 48% of patients receiving 25 mg and 50 mg, respectively, of long-acting risperidone (Kane et al., 2003). The 75-mg dose was associated with no efficacy advantage over the lower doses and was associated with an increased rate of adverse events; it is therefore not a marketed dose. The rate of extrapyramidal symptoms was 9% in the placebo group, and 3% and 14% in the 25-mg and 50-mg long-acting risperidone groups, respectively. The recommended starting dosage for adults is 25 mg every 2 weeks, with a dose range of 25 mg, 37.5 mg, or 50 mg every 2 weeks.

In summary, the available data suggest that risperidone may be somewhat more effective than typical antipsychotics in acute and maintenance treatment; however, its utility in treatment-refractory populations has not been convincingly established, although there is some evidence it may be superior to conventional antipsychotics but not as effective as clozapine in this population. Persistent prolactin elevation remains a problem with risperidone. The advantage of lower EPS liability compared with typical antipsychotics is diminished at higher doses (more than 6 mg/day), although higher doses are usually not necessary for therapeutic effect.

Olanzapine

The FDA approved olanzapine in 1996 for the treatment of schizophrenia. Beasley et al. (1996) reported on the efficacy of olanzapine in a 6-week study of three dose ranges of olanzapine (5 ± 2.5, 10 ± 2.5,

15 ± 2.5 mg/day) compared with one dose range of haloperidol (15 ± 5 mg/day) and with placebo in 335 schizophrenia patients. The middle and higher doses of olanzapine as well as haloperidol were significantly superior to placebo in improving overall symptomatology and positive symptoms, as assessed by the BPRS. Only the low and high doses of olanzapine were superior to placebo in improving negative symptom as assessed by the Scale for the Assessment of Negative Symptoms (SANS), while the higher dose of olanzapine was superior to haloperidol. There were no statistically significant differences between olanzapine- and haloperidol-treated patients on BPRS total and CGI scores at the end point of the study. No acute dystonia was observed with olanzapine, and at the high dose of olanzapine, rates of parkinsonism and akathisia were approximately one third and one half less, respectively, than those observed in the haloperidol group. In a second study, Beasley et al. (1997) reported on a 6-week trial involving 431 patients with schizophrenia and found no significant differences between olanzapine and haloperidol with regard to reduction in positive symptoms, negative symptoms, or total psychopathology. Patients treated with olanzapine, however, had acute extrapyramidal symptoms or prolactin elevations less often than those treated with haloperidol. Tollefson et al. (1997), in a study of 1,996 patients with schizophrenia or schizoaffective disorder, found olanzapine to be superior to haloperidol for total BPRS score, and also showed statistically significant advantages for olanzapine in change in negative symptoms, extrapyramidal symptom profile, effect on prolactin levels, and categorical response rate. In a meta-analysis Duggan et al. (2005) reported that olanzapine was superior to typical antipsychotics (14 randomized controlled trials, $N = 3,344$) in total PANSS, as well as positive and negative symptom scores, and caused fewer EPS but significantly more weight gain. When compared with other atypical antipsychotics (11 RCTs, $N = 1,847$), olanzapine did not differentiate from other atypicals on efficacy outcomes, although it was associated with fewer extrapyramidal adverse events but caused greater weight gain.

The potential of olanzapine in maintaining long-term therapeutic effect compared with conventional antipsychotics has also been proved (Tran, Dellva, Tollefson, Wentley, & Beasley, 1998). The data from the extension phases of three double-blind studies comparing olanzapine with haloperidol were pooled to form one group for each drug. Olanzapine-treated subjects experienced less relapse than haloperidol-treated subjects ($p = .034$), and the Kaplan-Meier estimated 1-year risk of relapse was 19.7% with olanzapine and 28% with haloperidol. Similar advantages for olanzapine were evident in a study in patients with first-episode schizophrenia. Lieberman et al. (2003) conducted a double-blind, randomized study of olanzapine and haloperidol in first-episode patients and found that in treatment of the acute phase of the illness, both drugs were comparable in efficacy. However, at the last observation point (12 weeks), significantly more patients were still in treatment in the olanzapine arm versus the haloperidol arm (67% vs. 54%). Olanzapine was associated with significantly more weight gain than haloperidol.

Three major studies have compared olanzapine with typical antipsychotics in treatment-refractory patients. Conley et al. (1998) described a study very similar in design to the original Kane et al. (1988) study that established clozapine as a treatment for refractory schizophrenia. In this 6-week trial of 84 patients randomized to either olanzapine or chlorpromazine, no differences were found between the two drugs for positive or negative symptoms or total psychopathology. Breier et al. (1999) conducted a prospective, double-blind, 6-week study of 526 patients who were determined to be partially responsive to typical antipsychotics. In this study, olanzapine was superior to haloperidol in reducing negative and depressive symptoms, and it produced less akathisia and fewer extrapyramidal symptoms in both last observation carried forward and completer analyses, as well as greater improvement in total symptoms and positive symptoms among completers. More patients treated with olanzapine completed the study, and fewer olanzapine-treated patients left the study due to lack of efficacy. Finally, in the Volavka et al. (2002) study, olanzapine was found to be superior to haloperidol for total PANSS score, the study's primary measure of efficacy. When compared with clozapine in patients with treatment-resistant illness (Duggan et al., 2005), a meta-analysis of four randomized, controlled trials ($N = 457$) found no clear differences in efficacy between the two drugs.

On the whole, the available evidence suggests that olanzapine has some efficacy advantages over typical antipsychotics both in the acute and maintenance treatment phases of the illness and in the treatment of patients selected for prior treatment resistance to typical antipsychotics. However, substantial weight gain and metabolic disturbances have emerged as serious side effects.

Quetiapine

The FDA approved quetiapine in 1998, and its efficacy has been evaluated in several methodologically rigorous clinical trials. Two 6-week double-blind, placebo-controlled studies enrolled 109 and 286 patients, respectively (Borison, Arvanitis, & Miller, 1996; Small, Hirsch, Arvanitis, Miller, & Link, 1997); the first study used a mean dose of quetiapine of 307 mg, and the second study used both a low-dose (mean 209 mg) and a high-dose group (mean 407 mg). Evidence of a benefit for the quetiapine-treated groups over the placebo-treated groups was shown by significant reductions in BPRS total scores, CGI scores, and BPRS activation and thought disturbance subscores, and on the SANS total score. In a randomized, double-blind 6-week study (Peuskens, Link, et al., 1997) that compared the efficacy of quetiapine to chlorpromazine among 201 patients, with doses up to 750 mg for each, no significant differences were found between groups on BPRS total or factor scores, CGI, or SANS scores. Arvanitis and Miller (1997) conducted a 6-week double-blind trial that compared the efficacy of five fixed doses of quetiapine (75, 150, 300, 600, or 750 mg/day) to 12 mg/day of haloperidol and placebo in 361 schizophrenia patients. They reported that all doses of quetiapine, as well as haloperidol, were superior to placebo in reducing total and positive-symptom BPRS scores, but only 300 mg of quetiapine was superior to placebo at reducing SANS total scores. Copolov, Link, and Kowalcyk (2000), conducted a 6-week double-blind, randomized, parallel-group trial comparing quetiapine (mean dose 455 mg/day) with haloperidol (mean dose 8 mg/day) in 488 hospitalized patients. They found comparable improvements in psychopathology for the two drugs, with fewer extrapyramidal symptoms and less prolactin elevation in the quetiapine group. Quetiapine did not cause EPS at greater rates than placebo in the three placebo-controlled studies. In the direct comparison with chlorpromazine, neither medication was associated with EPS.

The data for the effectiveness of quetiapine in treatment-resistant schizophrenia are very limited. Buckley, Goldstein, and Emsley reported a post hoc analysis of a double-blind randomized trial comparing quetiapine to haloperidol in patients who had failed to improve with fluphenazine 20 mg/day in a 4-week, open-label phase. This sample of 95 patients was randomized to receive either a fixed dose of quetiapine 600 mg/day or haloperidol 20 mg/day, in a double-blind fashion, for an additional 8 weeks. Although there was a statistically significant advantage for quetiapine in the proportion of patients with a CGI Severity (CGI-S) score of 3 or lower at end point, there was no difference in response rates based on the PANSS score (greater than 20% reduction) or CGI-improvement scale (CGI-I). Similarly, Conley et al. (2005) were not able to demonstrate a significant superiority of quetiapine or risperidone over fluphenazine in a small ($N = 38$) double-blind trial lasting 12 weeks in treatment-resistant patients.

Quetiapine appears to be similarly efficacious as conventional antipsychotics and is associated with minimal EPS and prolactin elevation. Sedation and orthostasis may be problematic side effects for some patients.

Ziprasidone

The FDA approved ziprasidone in February 2001 for the treatment of schizophrenia. Several studies have shown it to be effective against positive and negative symptoms of schizophrenia with little or no weight gain, a feature that distinguishes it from many of the current antipsychotics. Approval of ziprasidone was delayed by the FDA in 1998 pending more data on QT-interval changes in cardiac rhythm that theoretically could cause a dangerous arrhythmia called *torsade de pointes*. The drug was approved after the manufacturer submitted further safety data, including the fact that more than 4,000 patients had been treated in clinical trials with ziprasidone without evidence of torsade de pointes. The FDA does not require an EKG prior to treatment, and cardiac checkups during treatment are not mandated. To date, there has been no evidence from the clinical experience with ziprasidone that it is associated with cardiac toxicity.

The efficacy of ziprasidone in treating schizophrenia has been established in six main studies: two versus placebo, one versus haloperidol, one versus risperidone, and two versus olanzapine. Keck et al. (1998) conducted a 4-week double-blind comparison of placebo and ziprasidone at 40 mg/day and 120 mg/day in 139 patients with schizophrenia and schizoaffective disorder. Ziprasidone at 120 mg/day produced statistically significant improvement in BPRS total and CGI-S scores. The drug did not cause movement disorders at a rate higher than placebo. Daniel et al. (1999) compared ziprasidone at 80 mg/day and 160 mg/day to placebo in a 6-week double-blind trial of 302 patients. They demonstrated superiority of both doses to placebo in reducing the PANSS total, BPRS total, BPRS core items, CGI-S, and PANSS negative subscale scores. Ziprasidone at 160 mg/day was also shown to significantly reduce depressive symptoms in patients with clinically significant depression at baseline. The drug was well tolerated and caused movement disorders and weight gain at rates similar to placebo. In the only published study comparing ziprasidone with a typical antipsychotic, Goff et al. (1998) found ziprasidone at 160 mg/day to be superior to placebo and comparable to haloperidol in improving BPRS total, BPRS psychosis core, and CGI-S scores. Ziprasidone had a much lower propensity to cause extrapyramidal symptoms and prolactin elevation than haloperidol. Addington, Pantelis, Dineen, Benattia, and Romano (2004) compared ziprasidone ($n = 149$) and risperidone ($n = 147$) in an 8-week randomized, double-blind trial in patients with acute exacerbation of schizophrenia or schizoaffective disorder. Both agents equally improved psychotic symptoms, and both were generally well tolerated. Simpson, Glick, Weiden, Romano, and Siu (2004) conducted a multicenter, double-blind, flexible-dose trial in which patients were randomly assigned to receive either ziprasidone ($N = 136$) or olanzapine ($N = 133$) for 6 weeks. Both antipsychotics were equally efficacious in improving symptoms and global illness severity, but olanzapine-treated patients experienced more weight gain and lipid abnormalities. Similar results were found in a 6-month extension of the above study in patients who were responders in the 6-week acute trial (Simpson et al., 2005). However, in a similar 28-week study Brier et al. (2005) found that although both drugs were efficacious, olanzapine was superior to ziprasidone in the PANSS score (total and all subscales) as well as the CGI; olanzapine was associated with significant weight gain and detrimental effect on lipid profiles.

The existing evidence on ziprasidone indicates that it is an effective antipsychotic, at least comparable to haloperidol in treating schizophrenia. It is associated with minimal weight gain and metabolic disturbances, is not sedating, and does not elevate serum prolactin. Further study and clinical experience are needed to determine if this drug has a role in treatment-refractory schizophrenia or other special populations.

Aripiprazole

Aripiprazole was approved by the FDA in 2002 and has a mode of action that is distinct from those of currently available antipsychotic drugs. In addition to 5-HT$_{2A}$ and D$_2$ receptor antagonism, aripiprazole acts as a potent partial dopamine D$_2$ receptor agonist and a partial serotonin 5-HT$_{1A}$ agonist. Partial agonist activity at the D$_2$ receptor and the 5-HT$_{1A}$ receptor may confer efficacy against negative, cognitive, and affective symptoms of schizophrenia. In Phase III comparative clinical studies, aripiprazole 15 to 30 mg/day was at least as effective as haloperidol and risperidone in short-term treatment of acute exacerbation of schizophrenia and superior to placebo. Consistent with an atypical profile, aripiprazole has a low propensity to induce EPS. It is not associated with hyperprolactinemia and has a low liability for causing weight gain. In a 4-week short-term study, in which more than 400 patients were randomized to treatment with either aripiprazole (15 or 30 mg/day), haloperidol (10 mg/day), or placebo, both active treatments produced statistically significant improvements from baseline in PANSS total, PANSS positive, and CGI-S scores compared with placebo (Kane et al., 2002). A significantly greater improvement was seen in PANSS negative subscale score with aripiprazole (15 mg) than with placebo ($p = .006$). In a second placebo-controlled trial of 4 weeks' duration that compared the efficacy of aripiprazole (20 and 30 mg/day) with risperidone (6 mg/day) and placebo in 404 patients with acute exacerbation of schizophrenia or schizoaffective disorder (Potkin et al., 2003), both doses of aripiprazole produced significant improvements in the three primary efficacy measures (PANNS total score, PANSS positive score, and CGI-S score) compared with placebo. The risperidone group also showed significantly greater improvement in all primary efficacy measures compared with the placebo group.

A 26-week placebo-controlled trial in which aripi-

prazole 15 mg/day was administered to patients with stable chronic disease found that aripiprazole was significantly more effective than placebo in preventing relapse (34% vs. 57%), and there was no difference between treatments with respect to the overall incidence of adverse events (Pigott et al., 2003). The long-term efficacy and safety of aripiprazole (30 mg/day) relative to haloperidol (10 mg/day) was investigated in two 52-week, randomized, double-blind, multicenter studies that were pooled for analysis (Kasper et al., 2003). The studies enrolled 1,294 patients with a diagnosis of chronic schizophrenia who were in acute relapse and were known to have previously responded to antipsychotic medications. Aripiprazole demonstrated long-term efficacy that was comparable or superior to that of haloperidol across all symptom measures, including significantly greater improvements for PANSS negative subscale scores and Montgomery-Asberg Depression Rating Scale (MADRS) total score. The time to discontinuation for any reason was significantly greater with aripiprazole than with haloperidol, and aripiprazole was associated with significantly lower scores than haloperidol on all extrapyramidal symptoms assessments.

These data indicate that aripiprazole is effective in short- and long-term treatment of schizophrenia with efficacy that is at least comparable to that of other available antipsychotics. It also has a favorable side-effect profile that includes limited sedation, no prolactin elevation, and minimal weight gain. Aripiprazole has not been systematically evaluated in patients with treatment-resistant schizophrenia.

Summary of Meta-Analyses of Efficacy and Tolerability of Atypical Antipsychotics

In addition to meta-analyses for individual atypical antipsychotics referenced earlier, several rigorous meta-analyses have recently been published (Davis, Chen, & Glick, 2003; Geddes, Freemantle, Harrison, & Bebbington, 2000; Leucht, Pitschel-Walz, Abraham, & Kissling, 1999; Leucht, Wahlbeck, Hamann, & Kissling, 2003) about the relative efficacy and safety/tolerability of atypical antipsychotics compared with conventional antipsychotics, and atypical antipsychotics compared with each other. In general, the studies included in these meta-analyses were conducted mostly in patients in acute exacerbation, did not include treatment-resistant patients, were of relatively short duration, and assessed limited efficacy and safety outcome measures.

The first meta-analysis by Leucht, Pitschel-Walz, Abraham, and Kissling (1999) included studies with risperidone, olanzapine, quetiapine, and sertindole. They found a very modest efficacy advantage on total symptomatology for risperidone and olanzapine compared with haloperidol, with no difference for quetiapine and sertindole. On negative symptoms both olanzapine and risperidone were superior to haloperidol, but again the effect size was very small. Sertindole was no different from haloperidol in the treatment of negative symptoms, and quetiapine in one study (Peuskens, Link, 1997) was equivalent to chlorpromazine, whereas in another (Arvanitis, Miller et al., 1997) it was statistically *inferior* to haloperidol. Compared with haloperidol, all atypicals were associated with lower anticholinergic use, although the effect was weakest for risperidone. Interestingly, in a double-blind sertindole study that used a low 4-mg/day dose of haloperidol, there was still a statistically higher use of anticholinergic medication in this group of patients compared with pooled sertindole dose groups, suggesting that even at relatively low doses, high-potency conventional antipsychotics are associated with significant EPS liability (Leucht et al., 1999). In two studies that used either a midpotency or a low-potency typical antipsychotic (perphenazine, chlorpromazine), no difference in concomitant anticholinergic use was found compared with the atypical antipsychotic. Dropout rates because of lack of efficacy were statistically lower only for olanzapine compared with haloperidol; olanzapine also demonstrated lower dropout rates because of adverse events. Quetiapine had lower dropout rates compared with haloperidol related to adverse events and did not differ in dropouts for lack of efficacy; risperidone did not show an advantage over haloperidol in dropout rates related to either lack of efficacy or adverse events. This meta-analysis therefore suggested minor efficacy advantages for olanzapine and risperidone, moderate overall tolerability advantage for quetiapine and olanzapine, and a lower EPS liability, as reflected in lower anticholinergic use, for all the atypical antipsychotics compared with haloperidol. However, in a second meta-analysis comparing atypical antipsychotics to low-potency typical antipsychotics, Leucht et al. (2003) found no advantage on EPS liability for the atypical antipsychotics (other than clozapine), although a moderate superiority in

efficacy for the atypicals as a group was documented.

The meta-analysis by Geddes et al. (2000) was even less optimistic about the superiority of atypicals over conventional drugs. They included 52 randomized trials with a total of 12,649 patients treated with risperidone, clozapine, olanzapine, quetiapine, amisulpiride, and sertindole. Overall, they found that atypical antipsychotics had slightly superior efficacy and better tolerability, and a lower risk of causing EPS. However, when they controlled for comparator dose of the typical antipsychotic and separately analyzed data for patients who received 12 mg/day of haloperidol equivalents or less, all advantages of the atypical antipsychotics except for a modest EPS advantage disappeared. Essentially the conclusion from this meta-analysis was that other than a slight superiority on EPS profile, all other differences in outcomes between atypical and typical antipsychotics could be accounted for by a higher-than-necessary dose of the comparator typical antipsychotic.

The final meta-analysis, conducted by Davis et al. (2003), included 124 randomized trials of atypical versus conventional antipsychotics, and 18 trials comparing different atypical antipsychotics. These researchers found significantly greater effect size for efficacy for clozapine (0.49), risperidone (0.25), olanzapine (0.21), and amisulpiride (0.29) compared with typical agents. The mean effect sizes for the above drugs (other than clozapine) corresponded to about a 4- to 6-point advantage on the PANSS compared with typical antipsychotics. For perspective, the difference between the atypical antipsychotics and the typical antipsychotic comparator group was about half as much further improvement over that seen with typical antipsychotic as compared with placebo. The effect size of efficacy of clozapine versus typical antipsychotics was double that of other atypicals versus typical antipsychotics. Quetiapine, sertindole, ziprasidone, aripiprazole, and remoxipride demonstrated similar efficacy as typical antipsychotics. Distinct from the results of the Geddes et al.(2000) meta-analysis, these authors did not find that the dose of the comparator typical antipsychotic had any effect on the outcome. The Davis meta-analysis did not address safety and tolerability issues.

In summary, these meta-analyses collectively suggest an EPS advantage for the atypical antipsychotics and probable superior overall symptom efficacy for clozapine, risperidone, olanzapine, and amisulpiride over typical antipsychotics, with clozapine demonstrating the most robust separation, especially in treatment-resistant populations.

Impact on Cognitive Functioning of Atypical Antipsychotics

The superiority of the atypical antipsychotics in improving cognitive function in schizophrenia relative to typical antipsychotics is not well established. Iatrogenic impairments in cognitive test performance in patients on the older drugs may result from EPS, anticholinergic effects, and sedative effects (Green & Braff, 2001; Mortimer, 1997; Velligan & Miller, 1999). The improvement reported in cognitive functioning with the atypical antipsychotics relative to conventional agents may at least in part be attributable to elimination or relative reduction of some of these deleterious effects of the typical antipsychotics. In general the atypical antipsychotics have demonstrated improvement in verbal fluency, digit symbol substitution, executive function, and fine-motor control (Green et al., 1997; Meltzer & McGurck, 1999), and a meta-analysis by Keefe, Silva, Perkins, and Lieberman (1999) found a significant overall advantage for atypical antipsychotics on cognitive test performance. However, Green et al. (2002) in a prospective 2-year study found no advantage on cognitive functioning for risperidone (mean dose 6 mg/day) compared with haloperidol (mean dose 5 mg/day) in stable outpatients with schizophrenia. Similarly, a recent double-blind, randomized 12-week trial (Keefe et al., 2004) comparing olanzapine (mean dose 9.6 mg/day) with low-dose haloperidol (4.6 mg/day) found that both drugs improved verbal fluency, motor functions, working memory, verbal memory, and vigilance to a similar degree in primary analysis. On secondary analysis, a minor advantage was noted for olanzapine, but statistical significance levels were not corrected for multiple analyses that were conducted to yield this conclusion. Keefe et al. (2006) conducted a double-blind, randomized, controlled, parallel study with neurocognition assessed at baseline and at 8, 24, and 52 weeks comparing olanzapine, risperidone, and haloperidol. A total of 414 inpatients or outpatients with schizophrenia and schizoaffective disorder were treated with olanzapine ($n =$ 159), risperidone ($n = 158$), or haloperidol ($n = 97$). At the 52-week end point, neurocognition significantly improved in each group, with no significant differences among groups. Olanzapine- and risperi-

done-treated patients significantly improved on domains of executive function, learning/memory, processing speed, attention/vigilance, verbal working memory, and motor functions. Additionally, risperidone-treated patients improved on domains of visuospatial memory. Haloperidol-treated patients improved only on domains of learning/memory. Harvey, Rabinowitz, Eerdekens, and Davidson (2005) reported on improvement in cognitive function in a long-term, double-blind study comparing risperidone with haloperidol in first-episode patients. The study was conducted in a large group of 533 patients experiencing their first episode of schizophrenia or a related psychosis; 359 patients were reexamined at the 3-month follow-up. Although both drugs improved certain aspects of cognitive function, comparison of differential effects on a composite measure of cognitive functioning found that risperidone was significantly more beneficial than haloperidol after 3 months of treatment. Thus, there appear to be modest advantages for the atypical antipsychotics on improvement in cognitive function compared with typical antipsychotics. Further research is needed to definitively address this issue.

Clinical Antipsychotic Trials of Intervention Effectiveness

Many of the studies cited thus far, or used in meta-analyses, are of short-term duration and designed primarily for regulatory approval. Comparators are typically a placebo or a single fixed-dose active agent. Results are often not generalizable because the studies lack representative patient samples, clinical settings, and treatment conditions. The Clinical Antipsychotic Trials of Intervention Effectiveness (CATIE) trial, funded by the National Institute of Mental Health, was a randomized comparison of the long-term effectiveness of olanzapine, risperidone, quetiapine, ziprasidone, and perphenazine (Stroup et al., 2003). The trial was designed to mimic clinical practice and was conducted between January 2001 and December 2004. It included approximately 1,500 patients with schizophrenia, using broad inclusion and minimal exclusion criteria from 57 community sites, public health systems, and academic settings. The primary outcome of CATIE was time to all-cause treatment discontinuation; secondary outcomes included discontinuation due to lack of efficacy, tolerability, patient decision, physician decision, psychopathology, safety, neurocognitive functioning, and cost-effectiveness. Patients in Phase 1 were initially randomly assigned to receive olanzapine (7.5 to 30 mg/day), perphenazine (8 to 32 mg/day), quetiapine (200 to 800 mg/day), or risperidone (1.5 to 6mg/day) under double-blind conditions and followed for up to 18 months or until treatment was discontinued for any reason. Ziprasidone (40 to 160 mg/day) was approved for use by the FDA after the study began and was added to the study in January 2002. Patients whose assigned treatment was discontinued could "switch" and receive other treatments in Phases 2 and 3. With the exception of additional antipsychotic agents, concomitant medications were permitted throughout the trial.

In Phase 1 of the study (Lieberman, 2005), olanzapine was found to be superior to risperidone and quetiapine in terms of the time to *all-cause* discontinuation. Olanzapine was not statistically superior to ziprasidone or to perphenazine in time to all-cause discontinuation after adjustments for multiple comparisons. The percentage of patients who discontinued their medications for any cause prior to 18 months ranged from 64% (olanzapine) to 82% (quetiapine), with an overall discontinuation rate of 74%. The time to the discontinuation of treatment for *lack of efficacy* was longer in the olanzapine group than in the perphenazine, quetiapine, risperidone, and the ziprasidone groups; however, the difference between the olanzapine and ziprasidone groups was not significant after adjustment for multiple comparisons. Patients taking olanzapine had the lowest rate of hospitalization for an exacerbation of schizophrenia (11%) versus 15 to 20% for the other agents. Patients taking olanzapine showed the highest rate of discontinuation due to side effects (18%), whereas risperidone had the lowest rate (10%). More patients discontinued perphenazine because of extrapyramidal effects (8% vs. 2 to 4% for the other agents). Quetiapine was associated with a higher rate of anticholinergic effects than any of the other agents (31% vs. 20 to 25%). There were no significant differences among the groups in the incidence of EPS, akathisia, or movement disorders as reflected by either the Simpson-Angus Extrapyramidal Signs Scale or the AIMS Global Severity Scale. There were no substantially different effects of the medications on the corrected QT interval on electrocardiography, and no patients developed torsades de pointes. There were no significant differences among the groups in the

incidence of new cataracts, in the rates of suicide attempts, or in suicidal ideation. There were few substantial differences among the groups in the rates or types of medications added during the study. Patients in the olanzapine and risperidone groups were the least likely to receive additional anxiolytic agents, and patients on perphenazine were most likely to receive anticholinergic drugs. Nine percent of patients discontinued olanzapine because of weight gain or metabolic effects versus a 1 to 4% discontinuation rate for patients taking the other four drugs. Patients in the olanzapine group gained more weight than patients in any other group, with an average weight gain of 2 lb (0.9 kg) per month, whereas patients taking perphenazine and ziprasidone showed a small weight loss per month. A larger proportion of patients (30%) in the olanzapine group gained 7% or more of their baseline body weight than patients taking any of the other agents (7 to 16%). Olanzapine was also associated with greater increases in glycosylated hemoglobin, glucose, total cholesterol, and triglycerides than the other study drugs after adjustment for the duration of treatment. Ziprasidone was the only medication associated with improvement in each of these metabolic variables. Only risperidone was associated with a substantial increase in prolactin levels. The main findings of Phase 1 were that perphenazine, a typical antipsychotic, was similar in effectiveness to risperidone, quetiapine, and ziprasidone and only modestly less effective than olanzapine, and that all drugs were associated with a high rate of discontinuation. Limitations included a dose of olanzapine that was higher than the maximum approved dose, which may have conferred an efficacy advantage to olanzapine, and the fact that patients with tardive dyskinesia (approximately 200) were not randomized to perphenazine for obvious ethical reasons. Because patients with tardive dyskinesia may be more treatment resistant, the study design may thus have favored perphenazine.

In Phase 2 of the study, subjects who had discontinued their first assigned treatment were offered entry into one of two possible treatment arms. If the drug in Phase 1 was discontinued primarily due to efficacy failure, patients were offered entry to a randomized trial that would compare open-label clozapine treatment with blinded treatment with an atypical antipsychotic not previously received in Phase 1 of the trial (McEvoy et al., 2006). Patients were randomly assigned to open-label treatment with clozapine ($n = 49$) or to blinded treatment with olanzapine ($n = 19$), quetiapine ($n = 15$), or risperidone ($n = 16$). Time until treatment discontinuation *for any reason* was the primary outcome measure and was significantly longer for clozapine (median = 10.5 months) than for quetiapine (median = 3.3 months) or risperidone (median = 2.8 months), but not for olanzapine (median = 2.7 months). Time to discontinuation because of *inadequate therapeutic effect* was significantly longer for clozapine than for olanzapine, quetiapine, or risperidone. At 3-month assessments, PANSS total scores had decreased more in patients treated with clozapine than in patients treated with quetiapine or risperidone but not olanzapine. Thus, for these patients with schizophrenia who prospectively failed to improve with an atypical antipsychotic, clozapine was more effective than switching to another newer atypical antipsychotic. These advantages for clozapine were strong enough to achieve statistical significance despite the small sample sizes (McEvoy et al., 2006) and underscore the superior therapeutic effect of this agent in treatment-resistant populations.

In the other arm of Phase 2 (Stroup et al., 2006), subjects ($N = 444$) who had discontinued the first atypical antipsychotic due to either inadequate therapeutic effect or tolerability issues in Phase 1 of the CATIE investigation were randomly reassigned to double-blind treatment with a different atypical antipsychotic (olanzapine, 7.5 to 30 mg/day [$n = 66$]; quetiapine, 200 to 800 mg/day [$n = 63$]; risperidone, 1.5 to 6.0 mg/day [$n = 69$]; or ziprasidone, 40 to 160 mg/day [$n = 135$]). The time to treatment discontinuation was longer for patients treated with risperidone (median, 7.0 months) and olanzapine (6.3 months) than with quetiapine (4.0 months) and ziprasidone (2.8 months). There were no differences in the incidence of EPS among the drugs as reflected by rating scale measures of severity or reasons for discontinuing treatment. Patients receiving olanzapine gained more weight than did patients receiving any of the other drugs, with a mean of 1.3 pounds per month. Patients receiving ziprasidone had a mean loss of 1.7 pounds per month. Those receiving risperidone and quetiapine had negligible mean changes in weight over the course of Phase 2. Olanzapine was associated with substantial increases in total cholesterol and triglycerides, whereas risperidone and ziprasidone were associated with decreases in these parameters, even after adjusting for drug exposure. Patients

receiving risperidone experienced substantial increase in prolactin levels and higher rates of adverse effects involving sexual functioning (29%) relative to the other groups (11 to 17%). Risperidone was also associated with higher rates of gynecomastia or galactorrhea (5%) relative to the other groups (less than 1%). More patients receiving quetiapine experienced orthostatic faintness (13%) relative to the other groups (4 to 7%). In summary, both risperidone and olanzapine were superior to quetiapine and ziprasidone on the primary outcome measure in this group of patients with chronic schizophrenia who had discontinued previous therapy with a different atypical antipsychotic.

Summary of Safety and Tolerability of Atypical Antipsychotics

The biggest advance in side-effect profile of atypical antipsychotics is the lower risk of acute EPS. Among the types of EPS, acute dystonia is very rare, whereas akathisia still occurs, albeit to a lesser degree, with all the newer agents. Within the group, clozapine and quetiapine have the lowest (almost absent) risk of parkinsonism, whereas risperidone and, to a lesser extent, olanzapine are associated with dose-related parkinsonism. Ziprasidone and aripiprazole can also occasionally induce EPS, although it is not clear if there is a dose relationship with these drugs. Lower rates of tardive dyskinesia have also been reported with risperidone compared with haloperidol (0.6% vs. 4.1%, respectively) in a 1-year double-blind study (Csernansky et al., 2002), and for olanzapine (Beasley et al., 1999) compared with haloperidol (0.5% vs. 7.4%, respectively). A review of 11 long-term studies of atypical antipsychotics by Correll, Leucht, and Kane (2004) supported a lower risk of tardive dyskinesia for atypicals as a group compared with typical antipsychotics.

Weight gain has emerged as a major problem with some of the atypical antipsychotics (Newcomer, 2005). Olanzapine and clozapine are most notorious in this respect, and in some patients, rapid and massive weight gain can occur. Quetiapine and risperidone are intermediate in weight gain liability, and ziprasidone and aripiprazole rarely cause significant weight gain (Newcomer, 2005). Weight gain in patients with schizophrenia is especially problematic because these patients are usually overweight at baseline, have high rates of smoking, and are usually physically inactive. This combination of risk factors along with an increased risk of glucose dysregulation and hyperlipidemia reported to varying degrees with these agents (Newcomer, 2005) can create a potentially fatal constellation of risk factors for cardiovascular disease and stroke. These adverse effects, in their entirety, may well be worse than tardive dyskinesia, which was the primary concern for the older antipsychotics (Casey et al., 2004). The diabetes risk appears to be greatest for clozapine and olanzapine, less for risperidone and quetiapine, and lowest for ziprasidone and aripiprazole (Newcomer, 2005). Risperidone causes sustained prolactin elevation, and therefore patients who previously developed prolactin-induced side effects (galactorrhea, gynecomastia, menstrual irregularities, and sexual dysfunction) on older agents should probably be tried first on one of the other atypical antipsychotics. Ziprasidone is associated with QT prolongation, although the significance of this is not clear because related adverse events have not materialized after 5 years of clinical use. Clozapine, in addition to agranulocytosis risk, is associated with significant orthostasis, tachycardia, seizures (dose-related), myocarditis, constipation (at times severe), and various other side effects, making it a challenging drug to use in clinical practice.

OTHER PHARMACOLOGICAL TREATMENTS

Because of the limited efficacy of antipsychotic medication in resolving the full range of schizophrenic psychopathology, and the frequently occurring comorbid symptoms that occur over the course of the illness (e.g., anxiety, depression, mood lability, and motor unrest), adjunctive treatments are often utilized in order to reduce morbidity. In the next section we review controlled trials of pharmacological agents that have been used to treat patients with schizophrenia. We report on the efficacy of these drugs when used either in combination with an antipsychotic drug or as a lone treatment, to treat both schizophrenic psychopathology and comorbid conditions. The classes of medication described are antianxiety/hypnotics, antidepressants, mood stabilizers, dopamine agonists, and glutamatergic agents. In addition, we briefly review the efficacy of electroconvulsive therapy as a treatment for schizophrenic psychopathology and the adjunctive use of other antipsychotics in addition to clozapine for patients who have failed an adequate clozapine trial.

The use of adjunctive pharmacological treatments in schizophrenia patients has been the subject of numerous reviews (Christison, Kirch, & Wyatt, 1991; Donaldson, Gelenberg, & Baldessarini, 1983; Johns & Thompson, 1995; Lindenmayer, 1995; Meltzer, 1992; Meltzer, Sdommers, & Luchins, 1986; Rifkin, 1993; Siris, 1993; Wolkowitz, 1993). Given our space limitations, and the large number of studies involved, where applicable, recent review articles are summarized and updated with reports of subsequently published methodologically rigorous studies.

Antianxiety Agents

Benzodiazepines have been used to treat patients with schizophrenia since the early 1960s. Wolkowitz and Pickar (1991) reported on 14 double-blind studies published from 1961 to 1982 in which benzodiazepines alone were used to treat schizophrenic psychopathology. Nine of the 14 studies, including all those since 1975, reported some positive effects; however, in almost all studies, there was variability in response, with some patients doing well while others did poorly. The authors noted that due to methodological limitations, the conclusions that may be drawn from the data are limited, though there is some evidence that benzodiazepines alone have an antipsychotic effect for at least some patients. The authors also reviewed the efficacy of benzodiazepines when used as adjunctive agents to antipsychotics. Of 16 double-blind studies published from 1966 to 1989, 11 indicated some positive results, though again, in nearly all studies some individual patients responded well and others poorly. In one of the larger studies, Csernansky et al. (1988) conducted a double-blind comparison of alprazolam, diazepam, and placebo for the treatment of negative symptoms in outpatients with schizophrenia who had been maintained on antipsychotics; they were not able to demonstrate a sustained significant benefit of benzodiazepines on negative symptoms.

Benzodiazepines have also been compared with antipsychotics and a combination of both classes of drugs in the management of acute agitation and psychosis in acutely relapsed patients over the first few hours or days. Salzman et al. (1991), in a double-blind study that compared the efficacy at 2, 24, and 48 hours of 2 mg of intramuscular lorazepam and 5 mg of intramuscular haloperidol administered to 60 psychotic inpatients (26 with schizophrenia), reported that lorazepam and haloperidol both reduced aggression, agitation, and assaultive behavior; however, at 2 hours the number of patients who showed a decrease in aggression was significantly greater with lorazepam. Barbee, Mancuso, Freed, and Todorov (1992) compared the efficacy of haloperidol with that of either alprazolam or placebo over a 72-hour period in 28 acutely psychotic schizophrenia patients and reported that both groups improved significantly, though the combination of haloperidol and alprazolam was more effective in controlling agitation than haloperidol alone, particularly in the first 48 hours, with lower doses of antipsychotic medication needed in the combination-treated group. This study suggested that benzodiazepine augmentation may be useful in limiting the quantity of antipsychotics used for the acute treatment of schizophrenia (Bodkin, 1990). Battaglia et al. (1997) conducted a prospective, randomized, double-blind, multicenter trial of 98 psychotic, agitated, and aggressive patients comparing lorazepam treatment, haloperidol treatment, and combination treatment. All three treatments were effective in achieving significant reductions in scores on the Agitated Behavior Scale after 1 hour and in a modified Brief Psychiatric Rating Scale after 2 and 3 hours. Combination treatment of lorazepam and haloperidol was found to be superior to either alone.

Carpenter, Buchanan, Kirkpatrick, and Breier (1999) endeavored to determine if diazepam could help to prevent a psychotic relapse when given for indications of disturbed sleep, increased anxiety or other dysphoric affect, agitation and irritability, increased suspiciousness, and peculiar perceptual experiences thought to be prodromal of an impending psychotic exacerbation. They conducted a double-blind, randomized clinical trial with 53 patients with schizophrenia, comparing diazepam with placebo and with fluphenazine. They found that diazepam was superior to placebo and comparable to fluphenazine in preventing a psychotic relapse.

Few studies in the literature have specifically addressed in a double-blind fashion the use of benzodiazepines to treat nonpsychotic symptoms common in people with schizophrenia. Nevertheless, there is some evidence to suggest that schizophrenia patients with anxiety, depression, hostility, irritability, and motor unrest may benefit from benzodiazepines

(Wolkowitz & Pickar, 1991). A well-designed, small, double-blind study that looked at benzodiazepine response among six anxious schizophrenia patients over 12 weeks, with multiple crossovers (Kellner, Wilson, Muldawer, & Pathak, 1975), concluded that some patients from this subgroup may experience reduced anxiety with adjunctive benzodiazepine use.

Despite the evidence for a role of benzodiazepines in the treatment of at least some schizophrenia patients, there has been little recent systematic research in this area, perhaps because of the introduction of atypical antipsychotics, the potential for dependency, and the reluctance to prescribe these agents to patients with comorbid substance abuse disorders. In addition, there are reports that benzodiazepines may result in a "disinhibiting" (Karson, Weinberger, Bigelow, & Wyatt, 1982) or worsening of psychopathology in some patients (Wolkowitz & Pickar, 1991). Nevertheless, at a minimum benzodiazepines appear to be useful adjuncts to antipsychotics in the treatment of agitation or anxiety, especially during acute psychotic relapse, as well as in managing the prodromal symptoms of an impending psychotic exacerbation.

Antidepressants

The efficacy of antidepressant medication for the treatment of schizophrenic psychopathology, used either alone or as adjuncts to antipsychotics, was first comprehensively reviewed by Siris, Van Kammen, and Docherty (1978) in an analysis of the results of double-blind, controlled studies. When antidepressants were used alone, only 1 of 14 studies demonstrated clearly positive findings; however, 2 of 12 studies that compared a combination of a tricyclic antidepressant and an antipsychotic with an antipsychotic alone found a superior response from the combination. Poor results were also observed when a combination of an monoamine oxidase inhibitor and an antipsychotic were compared with an antipsychotic alone, with only 1 of 12 studies demonstrating a clear superiority for the combination. The authors acknowledged that antidepressants do not appear indicated as a sole treatment for schizophrenia; however, they cautioned that the overwhelming preponderance of negative findings may have resulted from weaknesses in study design, in particular, inadequate antidepressant dosages. In addition, the authors recommended that future research efforts be targeted to specific depressive syndromes that afflict a significant percentage of patients over the course of their illness (McGlashan & Carpenter, 1976).

Subsequent recognition that a secondary or post-psychotic depression occurs among schizophrenia patients (Siris, 1991) led to additional research interest in adjunctive antidepressant usage, the efficacy of which was reviewed by analysis of double-blind studies (Plasky, 1991). Of six placebo-controlled studies using tricyclic antidepressants in addition to an antipsychotic, two demonstrated a significant reduction in depression. The author noted that these two studies were of patients whose acute psychosis was under control and suggested that adjunctive antidepressant treatment may be successful for the treatment of depression only when the acute psychotic episode has stabilized. Furthermore, Plasky (1991) noted that in two studies of acutely psychotic patients the antidepressants appeared to have resulted in a worsening of the psychosis, and cautioned about premature use of antidepressant medication. Hogarty et al. (1995) reported on a 12-week double-blind, placebo-controlled study of 33 depressed, stable schizophrenia patients maintained on antipsychotics. The authors found that desipramine was significantly superior to placebo in reducing depression. They, like others (Plasky, 1991), concluded that the chronic depression found in schizophrenia patients, in contrast to the acute episodic forms, is responsive to antidepressant medication.

Siris et al. (1991) studied the therapeutic efficacy of adjunctive imipramine when added to fluphenazine decanoate and benztropine among 27 well-stabilized patients with schizophrenia and schizoaffective disorder with negative symptoms who also met criteria for postpsychotic depression. The authors found that the imipramine-treated group had superior global and negative symptom ratings at 6 to 9 weeks. They explained their positive findings in this subgroup of patients as support for a syndromal overlap of postpsychotic depression and negative symptoms (Siris et al., 1988). In a later study, Siris, Pollack, Bermanzohn, and Stronger (2000) used the same protocol in a more heterogeneous sample of 72 patients with postpsychotic episodes of depression to test the generalizability of their previous finding. They again found an improvement in negative symptoms favoring the imipramine treated group, but the effect was somewhat smaller. The authors attributed the diminished effect size to differences in the sam-

ple, since the later sample was thought to be sicker than the first yet was treated with lower doses of antipsychotic. In an additional double-blind, placebo-controlled study that examined the efficacy of antidepressants as an adjunctive treatment for negative symptoms in 30 schizophrenia patients, Silver and Nassar (1992) found fluvoxamine superior to placebo. The authors noted that neither depression nor extrapyramidal symptoms improved, leading them to conclude that fluvoxamine's benefit was on "primary" negative symptoms. Silver, Barash, Aharon, Kaplan, and Poyurovsky (2000) reported on another sample of 53 patients with schizophrenia who received fluvoxamine in addition to an antipsychotic and had significantly better SANS scores than those treated with antipsychotic and placebo. Berk, Ichim, and Brook (2001) conducted a 6-week randomized, placebo-controlled trial of mirtazapine and haloperidol versus placebo and haloperidol in 30 patients with schizophrenia. At the study end, there was a 42% reduction in PANSS negative symptom scores in the mirtazapine group compared with placebo. Because there was no difference between the two groups on the Hamilton Depression Scale at the study end, the authors suggested that the improvement in negative symptoms was not simply an improvement in primary mood symptoms. Finally, Rummel, Kissling, and Leucht (2005) published a meta-analysis of seven randomized controlled trials ($N = 202$) comparing the effectiveness of the combination of antidepressants and antipsychotics with antipsychotics alone for patients with schizophrenia who had pronounced negative symptoms. Except for one study, all the included studies used typical antipsychotics. The authors found a statistically significant superiority in the outcome of reduction of negative symptoms with the combination of antipsychotics and antidepressants compared with antipsychotics alone.

The utility of adjunctive antidepressant usage in longer term treatment has been evaluated in one study. A randomized, double-blind protocol (Siris, Bermanzohn, Mason, & Shuwall, 1994) examined 24 schizophrenia or schizoaffective patients, all of whom had been successfully treated with imipramine, fluphenazine decanoate, and benztropine for 6 months, who were then either continued on imipramine or tapered off and followed for 1 year. Continued imipramine treatment prevented relapse into either depression or psychosis.

In conclusion, the available data suggest that adjunctive antidepressant treatment is warranted when a patient reports persistent symptoms of depression when not in an acute episode of his or her illness, and for those with prominent negative symptoms.

Mood Stabilizers

Lithium

Lithium salts have been used both alone and as an adjunct to antipsychotics in the treatment of schizophrenia patients (Atre-Vaidya & Taylor, 1989; Christison et al., 1991; see Table 7.1). Atre-Vaidya and Taylor (1989) reported on three studies (Carman, Bigelow, & Wyatt, 1981; Growe, Crayton, Klass, Evans, & Strizich, 1979; Small, Kellams, Milstein, & Moore, 1975) that examined lithium as an adjunct to antipsychotics for treatment-refractory patients. The three studies included 48 patients, of whom 17 had a diagnosis of schizoaffective disorder. Small et al. (1975) reported the most impressive results: 10 of 20 completers improved with adjunctive lithium treatment compared with antipsychotic alone; however, these authors were unable to discern any predictors of response. The other two studies reported more modest positive findings. Wilson (1993), in a study that compared haloperidol alone with the combination of haloperidol plus lithium in an 8-week trial with 21 treatment-resistant schizophrenia patients, reported no advantage for the combination. Terao et al. (1995), in a study of 21 treatment-resistant schizophrenia patients treated in an 8-week crossover design with lithium or placebo in addition to an antipsychotic, reported that lithium patients had significantly lower anxiety and depression scores, but there was no benefit for other symptoms. Hogarty et al. (1995), as part of a larger study, compared adjunctive lithium with placebo among 29 anxious, stable schizophrenia patients and found at 12 weeks an advantage for lithium in reducing anxiety and depression; however, this benefit was limited only to female patients. Schulz et al. (1999) studied 41 patients with diagnoses of either schizophrenia or schizoaffective disorder who had had only partial response to fluphenazine decanoate. Patients were randomized to either lithium or placebo for 8 weeks of treatment, with patients in the placebo group then able to enter an open-label treatment with lithium for 8 weeks. The double-blind study showed no significant differences in treatment response between the lithium and placebo groups. However, patients originally treated with placebo added to antipsychotic did show significant symptom reduction in the open-label adjunctive lithium phase of the study. Small, Klapper, Malloy, and Steadman (2003) conducted a controlled, double-blind, crossover trial of adjunctive lithium treatment in 10 hospitalized schizophrenia and 10 schizoaffective patients receiving clozapine maintenance therapy with partial therapeutic response. Patients with schizophrenia did not improve on the combination; schizoaffective patients demonstrated improvement on CGI, PANSS total and negative symptom scales, and the cognitive measures. Mean plasma lithium levels were relatively low (0.49 mmol/L in the schizophrenia group; 0.61 mmol/L in the schizoaffective group). Mean lithium levels did not differ between responders (0.60 mmol/L) and nonresponders (0.52 mmol/L). Two patients in the schizophrenia group developed neurological toxicity at modest lithium levels. A similar report of neurotoxicity on the combination of clozapine and lithium manifested as ataxia, coarse tremor, myoclonus, facial spasm, and increased deep tendon reflex had been previously reported (Lee & Yang, 1999).

Leucht, Kissling, and McGrath (2004) conducted a meta-analysis that included 20 controlled studies of lithium alone or as an augmentation agent in treatment of schizophrenia. They found that lithium as a sole agent was ineffective. Eleven trials evaluated lithium as an augmentation strategy, and although more patients were classified as responders on combination therapy, the advantage was not significant when patients with prominent affective symptoms were excluded from the analysis. Significantly more patients taking lithium left the trials early, suggesting poor tolerability of lithium augmentation compared with antipsychotic alone (Leucht et al., 2004).

In summary, most of the available literature suggests that in the absence of affective symptoms, augmentation of antipsychotics with lithium is not effective in the treatment of schizophrenia. However, because there have been reports of a benefit in some treatment-refractory patients, a trial of lithium should be considered if the patient has not adequately responded or was unable to tolerate an atypical agent, such as clozapine. Earlier concern about potentially toxic interactions between an antipsychotic and lithium (Cohen & Cohen, 1974) appears not to be supported by the vast majority of the published literature

TABLE 7.1 Mood Stabilizers

Author	Study Design (Double-Blind)	N Patients	Results
Atre-Vaidya & Taylor (1989) (review article)	Lithium and neuroleptic vs. neuroleptic alone	3 studies 48 patients	Positive findings reported in all 3 studies
Johnstone et al. (1988)	Study of "functional" psychoses 4 cells 1. neuroleptic 2. lithium 3. neuroleptics plus lithium 4. placebo Patients treated for 4 weeks	120 (not all schizophrenic)	No evidence that lithium is beneficial in treating psychosis
Wilson (1993)	Lithium plus haloperidol vs. haloperidol in treatment-resistant patients; 8-week trial	21	No advantage for the combination
Terao et al. (1995)	Lithium plus neuroleptic vs. neuroleptic alone; 8-week crossover design	21	No benefit for lithium on negative symptoms through anxiety and depression improved.
Hogarty et al. (1995)	Lithium plus neuroleptic vs. neuroleptic alone; 12-week trial for anxious stable patients	29	Lithium beneficial in reducing anxiety in female patients only.
Christison et al. (1991) (review article)	Carbamazepine (CBZ) and neuroleptic vs. neuroleptic alone	5 studies 251 patients	3 of 5 studies had reported some positive results. CBZ augmentation found superior to neuroleptic in patients with "violence, agression and paranoia" in the largest ($n = 162$ patients) study
Carpenter et al. (1991)	Patients withdrawn from stable neuroleptic regimen for 95 days and placed on CBZ or placebo	27	Both groups had a high rate of relapse
Linnoila et al. (1976)	Valproic acid and neuroleptic vs. neuroleptic in 2-week (each phase) crossover design	32	14 of 32 VPA treated patients had an improvement in global psychopathology
Ko et al. (1985)	Valproic acid and neuroleptic vs. neuroleptic alone in 4-week (each phase) crossover design	6	No significant differences between groups
Dose et al. (1998)	Valproate plus haloperidol vs. placebo plus haloperidol	42	No significant difference at end point. Superiority of valproate on "hostile belligerance."
Hesslinger et al. (1999)	Haloperidol vs. haloperidol plus	18	No significant difference.
Casey et al. (2003); Citrome et al. (2004)	Olanzapine or risperidone plus valproate or placebo	249	No significant difference at end point but more rapid response and significant advantage in valproate

(Rifkin, 1993). However, patients coadministered lithium and clozapine may be at higher risk of neurotoxicity.

Carbamazepine

Christison et al. (1991) reviewed five double-blind studies published through 1989, which all added either carbamazepine or placebo to a stable antipsychotic regimen (see Table 7.1). The results of these studies were mixed, with modest positive results seen in three. The study by Okuma et al. (1989) included 162 patients of whom 127 met criteria for *DSM-III* schizophrenia and 35 for schizoaffective disorder; this study was larger than the other four combined. All patients were described as treatment resistant with "excited psychotic states." Carbamazepine augmentation was found superior to an antipsychotic alone in patients with "violence, aggression, and paranoia"; however, the authors acknowledged that the overall differences between groups was small. Carpenter et al. (1991), using a different study design, compared the efficacy of carbamazepine with that of placebo after 27 patients had been withdrawn from stable antipsychotic doses and found that carbamazepine offered no advantage over placebo, with both groups having high relapse rates off antipsychotics.

Leucht, Wahlbeck, Hamann, and Kissling (2003) reviewed 10 randomized controlled trials ($N = 283$) comparing carbamazepine (as a sole or an adjunctive compound) with placebo or no intervention in participants with schizophrenia or schizoaffective disorder. Carbamazepine was not effective in preventing relapse in the only randomized, controlled trial that compared carbamazepine monotherapy with placebo. Carbamazepine tended to be less effective than perphenazine in the only trial comparing carbamazepine with an antipsychotic. Although there was a trend indicating a benefit from carbamazepine as an adjunct to antipsychotics, it did not reach statistical significance. The authors concluded that, at present, carbamazepine augmentation could not be recommended for routine use.

Overall, there is some evidence to support carbamazepine as an adjunctive agent to antipsychotics in the treatment of schizophrenia, particularly in a subpopulation of aggressive, agitated patients. Due to carbamazepine's ability to upregulate hepatic enzymes, plasma antipsychotic levels may drop with concomitant carbamazepine use, requiring antipsychotic dose adjustment.

Valproic Acid

Valproic acid (VPA) as an adjunct to antipsychotics has been the focus of a few controlled studies. Linnoila, Viukari, and Kietala (1976), in a double-blind, crossover study of 32 chronic psychiatric patients with dyskinesias, each phase lasting 14 days, found that the combination of VPA with an antipsychotic was superior to an antipsychotic alone in reducing global psychopathology in 14 of 32 patients. Ko, Korpi, Freed, Zalcman, and Bigelow (1985) compared adjunctive VPA with placebo in a 4-week study of 6 schizophrenia patients and found no significant differences between groups. Wassef et al. (2000) conducted a 21-day double-blind, randomized, placebo-

controlled study of valproic acid as add-on treatment to haloperidol in 12 hospitalized patients with acute exacerbations of chronic schizophrenia. At study end, the valproic acid group had greater improvements than the placebo group on the CGI scale, the BPRS, and the SANS.

Casey et al. (2003) investigated the use of divalproex with an antipsychotic agent in 249 patients hospitalized for acute exacerbation of schizophrenia (see Table 7.1). They conducted a 28-day multicenter, double-blind, placebo-controlled, randomized study that compared the efficacy of atypical antipsychotic monotherapy (olanzapine or risperidone) with that of combination treatment with divalproex sodium. Statistically significant treatment differences favoring combination therapy were observed as soon as Day 3 for PANSS total score and persisted through Day 21. However, the advantage was lost by Day 28. In the same study, Citrome et al. (2004) examined the specific antihostility effects of adding divalproex sodium to olanzapine or risperidone. Combination therapy had a significantly greater antihostility effect at Days 3 and 7 than monotherapy, but this advantage was not maintained beyond the 1st week of treatment. The authors concluded that divalproex sodium may be useful as an adjunctive agent in specifically reducing hostility in the 1st week of treatment among patients with schizophrenia experiencing an acute psychotic episode.

Basan, Kissling, and Leucht (2004) conducted a meta-analysis of five ($N = 379$) randomized controlled trials comparing valproate as an adjunctive compound for patients with schizophrenia or schizophrenia-like disorders. Some of the single studies showed inconsistent beneficial effects on some aspects of response, but no overall superiority of valproate augmentation at study end points was shown.

Definitive conclusions on the efficacy of VPA for the treatment of schizophrenia patients are therefore premature based on the limited data available.

Dopamine Agonists

Dopamine agonists have been associated with an exacerbation of psychotic symptoms in 40 to 60% of schizophrenia patients; however, these agents have also been used as a treatment for patients with prominent negative symptoms (Table 7.2). This strategy is consistent with the hypothesis that a hypodopaminergic state is responsible for the negative symptoms of the illness (Davidson et al, 1991). The efficacy of L-

TABLE 7.2 Dopamine Agonists

Author	Study Design (Double-Blind)	No. of Patients	Results
Gerlach & Luhdorf (1975)	L-dopa vs. placebo added to antipsychotic in 12-week (each phase) crossover design	18	Significant "activation" in some patients, though no difference in global ratings
Inanaga et al. (1975)	L-dopa plus antipsychotic vs. antipsychotic alone	104	Significantly more L-dopa-treated patients rated as "excellent" responders
Brambilla et al. (1979)	L-dopa vs. placebo in 4-week (each phase) crossover design	6	2 patients much improved
Gattaz et al. (1989)	Bromocriptine plus haloperidol vs. haloperidol alone; 3-week study	30	No significant improvement at 24 hours that dissipated by 21 days
Goldberg et al. (1991)	Dextroamphetamine administered in a single dose to haloperidol-treated patients	21	Improvement on measures of affect and cognition
Barch & Carter (2005)	Single-dose amphetamine or placebo; stable patients taking fluphenazine or haloperidol	10 patients 10 healthy controls	Improvement in certain cognitive functions
Jungerman et al. (1999)	Double-blind, placebo-controlled augmentation of antipsychotic with selegiline-stable outpatients	16	No benefit of adding selegiline
Bodkin et al. (2005)	Double-blind, placebo-controlled augmentation of antipsychotic with selegiline-stable outpatients	67	Selegiline superior to placebo for negative symptoms; no worsening of psychosis
Carpenter et al. (2000)	Double-blind, placebo-controlled augmentation of antipsychotic with mazindol-stable outpatients	39	No difference from placebo; no worsening of psychosis

dopa has been assessed in three double-blind treatment studies (Christison, 1991), two of which used it as an adjunct to antipsychotics (Gerlach & Luhdorf, 1975; Inanaga et al., 1975). Gerlach and Luhdorf (1975), in a study of 18 schizophrenia patients with prominent negative symptoms, reported significant activation in some patients, though the overall change in level of functioning was small. Inanaga et al. (1975), in a study of 104 schizophrenia inpatients with negative symptoms, reported that there were significantly more "excellent responders" among the L-dopa-treated patients, though there was no difference in the number considered "good" or "fair." Brambilla et al. (1979) studied six chronic patients with both positive and negative symptoms in a crossover design with placebo, each phase lasting 4 weeks, and found two of the patients much improved.

Gattaz, Rost, Hubner, and Bauer (1989), in a study of 30 schizophrenia patients who received either haloperidol plus bromocriptine or haloperidol alone, reported a nonsignificant improvement in overall functioning at 24 hours for the bromocriptine-treated group, though by 21 days there were no differences observed. Goldberg, Bigelow, Weinberger, Daniel, and Kleinman (1991) administered a single dose of dextroamphetamine to 21 patients with chronic schizophrenia who had been stabilized on haloperidol and found improvement on a number of variables that assessed affect and cognition. Barch and Carter (2005) had similar findings with single-dose amphetamine administration to 10 patients on stable medication regimens; the relevance of the results from these single-dose administration studies for the role of dopamine agonists in the long-term treatment of negative symptoms or cognitive deficits in schizophrenia is unclear.

Bodkin, Siris, Bermanzohn, Hennen, and Cole (2005) tested the efficacy of selegiline (a selective monoamine oxidase B inhibitor) augmentation of antipsychotic medication for negative symptoms in outpatients with schizophrenia who had negative symptoms of moderate or greater severity. They conducted a low-dose (10 mg/day), 12-week, double-blind, placebo-controlled, multicenter trial in 67 patients who did not have severe positive symptoms at baseline, did not meet criteria for coexisting major depression, and had been maintained on a stable regimen of antipsychotic medication. Negative symptoms were found to be significantly more improved in the patients who received selegiline, and there was no worsening of BPRS thought disturbance. Previously, Jungerman, Rabinowitz, and Klein (1999) had conducted a similar double-blind, placebo-controlled augmentation study of selegiline and found that both selegiline- and placebo-treated groups showed a statistically significant but clinically marginal improvement over the 8 weeks of treatment. However, the small sample size of this study ($N = 16$) limits the significance of their findings.

Carpenter et al. (2000) evaluated the efficacy of mazindol (a dopamine reuptake inhibitor) compared with placebo in a double-blind, crossover-design trial involving 39 patients with schizophrenia or schizoaffective disorder with negative symptoms. Outcome following mazindol supplementation was comparable to that with placebo supplementation. Results for deficit and nondeficit schizophrenia subjects were similar and were not affected by whether the concurrent antipsychotic drug treatment was clozapine, fluphenazine, or haloperidol, and could not be accounted for by outliers (Carpenter et al., 2000). Mazindol addition to ongoing antipsychotic therapy did not exacerbate positive symptoms.

Dopamine agonists have been the subject of too few controlled studies to allow us to draw definitive conclusions. However, the above studies suggest that they may represent an underutilized class of medication, particularly for the treatment of negative symptoms. Clinicians' hesitancy to use these agents due to concern about exacerbating psychotic symptoms may not be warranted if patients are maintained on antipsychotics (Perovich, Lieberman, Fleischhacker, & Alvir, 1989).

Glutamate Agonists

Phencyclidine (PCP) was first observed by Luby, Cohen, Rosenbaum, Gottlieb, and Kelly (1959) to produce a syndrome similar to schizophrenic psychosis with its associated emotional withdrawal, apathy, and cognitive impairment. A later study by Anis et al. (1983) demonstrating that PCP blocks the N-methyl-D-aspartic acid (NMDA) subtype of the glutamate receptors in a noncompetitive manner led to an intensified effort to understand the role of glutamate receptors in schizophrenia. Because PCP inhibits the neurotransmission of glutamate through NMDA receptors (i.e., is an NMDA antagonist), it was hypothesized that reduced glutamate activity (possibly through NMDA receptor hypofunction) caused the symptoms of schizophrenia (Javitt & Zukin, 1991). From this hypothesis it was inferred that agents that facilitate the stimulation of NMDA receptors would be therapeutic in schizophrenia similar to the way in which amphetamine's effects on dopamine supported the development of D_2 antagonists as antipsychotic agents in the context of the dopamine hypothesis of schizophrenia. In this context, four glutamate agonists have been studied to date: glycine, D-cycloserine, D-serine, and sarcosine (Table 7.3).

Seven double-blind studies have evaluated the use of glycine as a treatment adjunctive to antipsychotic medications. Potkin et al. (1992) studied the efficacy of glycine added for 6 weeks to antipsychotic treatment among inpatients with limited treatment response. This study, which used a relatively low dose of glycine of 15 g/day, found a small improvement in the glycine group ($n = 11$) versus the placebo group ($n = 8$) but no statistically significant advantages for the glycine group on the BPRS or SANS. In a similar study of 14 patients, but with a higher dose (30 g/day) of glycine, Javitt, Zylberman, Zukin, Heresco-Levy, and Lindenmayer (1994) found significant improvements in PANSS negative scores. Heresco-Levy et al. (1996) used an even higher dose of glycine (60 g/day) to augment typical antipsychotics ($n = 7$) and clozapine ($n = 4$) in patients with treatment-resistant schizophrenia. They found highly significant improvements in negative, depressive, and cognitive symptoms in the glycine group, with 73% of the patients having a 30% or better improvement in negative symptoms. Heresco-Levy et al. (1999) used an add-on, crossover design to evaluate glycine (60 g/day) in patients resistant to typical antipsychotics ($n = 15$) and clozapine ($n = 7$). The study found highly significant improvements in the glycine group for negative, depressive, and cognitive symptoms, the response being significantly correlated with low pretreatment glycine levels. Whereas the aforementioned studies used samples of patients treated with either typical antipsychotic drugs or clozapine, two studies

TABLE 7.3 Glutamate Agonists (Adapted from Abi-Saab et al., 2001)

Author	Study Design (Double Blind)	No. of Patients	Results
Potkin et al. (1992)	Low-dose glycine, placebo-controlled, add-on for 6 weeks, type of antipsychotic not reported	18	Small improvement on CGI; no significant improvement on other measures
Javitt et al. (1994)	High-dose glycine, placebo-controlled, add-on for 8 weeks, type of antipsychotic not reported	14	Significant improvement in negative scores
Heresco-Levy et al. (1996)	High-dose glycine, placebo-controlled, add-on, crossover design for 6 weeks in each phase	7 on typical antipsychotics, 4 on clozapine	Significant improvement in PANSS total and negative symptoms scores
Potkin et al. (1999)	High-dose glycine, placebo-controlled, add-on for 12 weeks	19 on clozapine	No advantages for glycine; Patients on clozapine alone had lower positive symptoms scores
Heresco-Levy et al. (1996)	High-dose glycine, placebo-controlled, add-on, crossover for 6 weeks in each phase	15 on typical antipsychotics and 7 on clozapine	Significant improvements in negative, depressive, and cognitive symptoms
Evins et al. (2000)	High-dose glycine, placebo-controlled, add-on, parallel-group for 8 weeks	30 on clozapine	No advantages for glycine
Heresco-Levy et al. (2004)	High-dose glycine, double-blind, placebo-controlled, 6-week crossover	5 on risperidone and 12 on olanzapine; history of treatment resistance on conventional antipsychotics	Significant improvements in negative, positive, and cognitive symptoms
Rosse et al. (1996)	Low-dose DCS, placebo-controlled, add-on, parallel-group for 4 weeks	13 on molindone	No advantages for DCS
Goff et al. (1999)	Medium dose DCS, placebo-controlled, add-on, crossover for 6 weeks	17 on clozapine	No advantages for DCS; worsening of negative symptoms on DCS
Goff , Hendersoin (1999)	Medium-dose DCS, placebo-controlled, add-on, parallel-group for 8 weeks	47 on typical antipsychotics	Advantage for DCS in negative symptoms
Evins et al. (2002)	2-week escalating-dose trials; 5, 15, 50, and 250 mg/day	10 on risperidone	Only 50-mg/day dose was associated with improvement in negative symptoms
Tsai et al. (1998)	DS, placebo-controlled, add-on, parallel-group for 6 weeks	25 on typical antipsychotics and 4 on risperidone	Advantages for DS in positive, negative, and cognitive symptoms
Tsai et al. (1999)	DS, placebo-controlled, add-on, parallel-group for 6 weeks	20 on clozapine	No advantages for DS

TABLE 7.3 (continued)

Author	Study Design (Double Blind)	No. of Patients	Results
Heresco-Levy et al. (2005)	DS, double-blind, placebo-controlled, 6-week crossover trial	21 on risperidone; 18 on olanzapine; history of treatment resistance on conventional antipsychotics	Significant improvement in negative, positive, cognitive, and depression symptoms
Tsai et al. (2004)	Sarcosine, 6-week double-blind, placebo-controlled trial	38 (20 on risperidone)	Significant improvement in positive, negative, cognitive
Lane et al. (2005)	Sarcosine vs. DS, 6-week randomized, double-blind, placebo-controlled trial	65 patients in acute exacerbation treated with risperidone	Sarcosine superior to both placebo and D-serine groups in PANSS total, SANS scores, PANSS depressive, and PANSS general subscales; DS group did not differ from risperidone-alone group

evaluated the effect of glycine when added to the treatment regimens of patients treated with clozapine alone. Interestingly, both studies (Evins, Fitzgerald, Wine, Rosselli, & Goff, 2000; Potkin, Jin, Bunney, Costa, & Gulasekaram, 1999) failed to show advantages for glycine when it was added to clozapine treatment. Heresco-Levy, Ermilov, Lichtenberg, Bar, and Javitt (2004) added high-dose glycine to the stable medication regimen of 5 patients on risperidone and 12 on olanzapine who had failed previous typical antipsychotic trials. In this double-blind, placebo-controlled, 6-week crossover treatment trial, high-dose adjuvant glycine treatment was associated with improvements in negative, positive, and cognitive symptoms. Despite these encouraging results, glycine is known to have poor CNS bioavailability, and the doses needed to effect clinical benefit (30 to 60 g/day) are very difficult to administer.

D-cycloserine (DCS) freely crosses the blood-brain barrier and acts as a partial agonist at the glycine regulatory site on the NMDA receptor. Because of this latter feature, DCS stimulates NMDA receptor function at low doses but inhibits endogenous glycine activity at higher doses, thus lowering NMDA receptor function. The drug is effective in treating negative symptoms in a narrow therapeutic range when added to typical antipsychotic regimens, as evidenced by Goff, Tsai, et al. (1999) in a study of 47 patients with a medium dose of DCS. Studies by Goff, Tsai, Manoach, and Coyle (1995) and Rosse, Fay-McCarthy, Kendrick, Davis, and Deutsch (1996) established that very low or very high doses of DCS either did not improve or even worsened psychotic symptoms. Consistent with the findings with glycine, Goff, Henderson, Evins, and Amico (1999) demonstrated that DCS did not improve symptoms when added to clozapine treatment. Evins, Amico, Posever, Toker, and Goff (2002) found that a 50-mg/day dose (but not 5, 15, or 250 mg/day) of DCS improved negative symptoms by about 10% when added to risperidone in 10 patients with schizophrenia. The narrow therapeutic window of DCS ultimately makes it a difficult compound to use clinically.

Another glutamate agonist candidate for the treatment of schizophrenia is D-serine (DS), which is a full NMDA agonist with greater CNS bioavailability than glycine. A study by Tsai, Yang, Chung, Lange, and Coyle (1998) evaluated the use of DS in 29 patients (25 treated with typical antipsychotics and 4 treated with risperidone) with deficit syndrome schizophrenia and found improvements in positive, negative, and cognitive symptoms. In a later add-on study of clozapine, Tsai et al. (1999) found that symptoms did not improve with adjunctive D-serine. Heresco-Levy et al. (2005) conducted a double-blind, placebo-controlled, 6-week crossover trial with

30 mg/kg/day of D-serine added to the antipsychotic medication of 39 patients with schizophrenia (21 on risperidone and 18 on olanzapine). D-serine administration resulted in significant ($p < .001$) improvements in negative, positive, cognitive, and depression symptoms as measured by the PANSS. For approximately one third of the sample, D-serine treatment resulted in significant (greater than 20%) reductions in Brief Psychiatric Rating Scale total scores. D-serine was well tolerated, and no detrimental changes in clinical laboratory parameters were noted (Heresco-Levy et al., 2005).

The glycine transporter-1 is a novel target for the pharmacotherapy to enhance N-methyl-D-aspartate function. Inhibition of the glycine transporter-1 would be expected to increase synaptic glycine levels and augment NMDA receptor function. N-methylglycine (sarcosine) is an endogenous antagonist of glycine transporter-1, which potentiates glycine's action on the N-methyl-D-aspartate glycine site. Tsai, Lane, Yang, Chong, and Lange (2004) conducted a 6-week double-blind, placebo-controlled trial of sarcosine (2 g/day), added to the stable antipsychotic regimens of 38 patients with schizophrenia (20 on risperidone). Patients who received sarcosine treatment had significant improvements in their positive, negative, cognitive, and general psychiatric symptoms. Similar therapeutic effects were observed when only the subset of risperidone-treated patients was analyzed. Sarcosine was well tolerated, and no significant side effects were noted. Lane, Chang, Liu, Chiu, and Tsa (2005) conducted a 6-week randomized, double-blind, placebo-controlled trial to determine whether D-serine (2 g/day) or sarcosine (2 g/day) had better efficacy when added to risperidone treatment in 65 patients with acute exacerbation of schizophrenia. The sarcosine group was superior to both the placebo and D-serine groups in improvement in PANSS total scores, SANS scores, PANSS depressive, and PANSS general subscales. Unlike other studies that have found a benefit for D-serine, in this study adjunctive D-serine with risperidone did not differ significantly from risperidone monotherapy in all efficacy domains.

Glycine, DCS, DS, and sarcosine all show some benefit for the treatment of negative, cognitive, and psychotic symptoms when dosed appropriately. Though dosing challenges with glycine and DCS may make them impractical for clinical use, studies with these compounds provide strong support for the role of glutamate in the pathophysiology of schizophrenia,

as well as furthering the understanding of the unique pharmacological mechanism of clozapine. DS is the most promising agent in this group based on the current findings. This line of research will hopefully lead to improved symptom reduction for patients with schizophrenia and clues leading to the development of other novel therapeutic agents.

Electroconvulsive Therapy

Electroconvulsive therapy (ECT), which was an acceptable treatment option for schizophrenia before the introduction of antipsychotic medication, has been the subject of few controlled studies. Information gathered from open trials suggests that ECT works best in schizophrenia patients in the early stages of their illness, in those with catatonic or affective symptoms, and in conjunction with an antipsychotic (Salzman, 1980). ECT is rarely used in the treatment of schizophrenia patients today except in the most refractory cases.

Three double-blind, controlled studies of schizophrenia patients maintained on antipsychotics who received either ECT or sham ECT have produced consistent results. Taylor and Fleminger et al. (1980), in a study of 20 patients (not all with schizophrenia), found that the ECT group improved much more rapidly than the sham group (antipsychotic-alone group), but the differences disappeared by 16 weeks. Brandon et al. (1985), in a study of 19 schizophrenia patients, found ECT superior at 2 and 4 weeks, but by 12 weeks there was no clear difference. Abraham and Kulhara (1987), in a study of 22 patients, found ECT augmentation beneficial in the first 8 weeks, but no difference between groups by 12 weeks. Interestingly, May et al. (1981), in a 5-year prospective study of 228 first-episode schizophrenia patients who received one of five treatments by random assignment (antipsychotics, ECT, psychotherapy, psychotherapy plus antipsychotic, or milieu), found that the outcomes in all groups were poor, but that the ECT-treated group fared best.

Chanpattana, Chakrabhand, Buppanharun, and Sackeim (2000) conducted a double-blind comparison of three different stimulus intensities (seizure threshold, two times seizure threshold, and four times seizure threshold) of bilateral ECT plus flupenthixol in the treatment of 62 patients with schizophrenia. They concluded that treatment with high-dosage bilateral ECT speeds clinical response in patients with schizophrenia. Chanpattana et al. (1999)

compared flupenthixol alone, continuation electro-convulsive therapy (ECT) alone, and combined continuation ECT and flupenthixol in a 6-month single-blind study of 58 patients with treatment-resistant schizophrenia who had met response criteria after an acute phase of treatment with bilateral ECT and flupenthixol (12 to 24 mg/day). Patients treated with the combination of bilateral ECT and flupenthixol relapsed at a rate of 40% (6/15), whereas patients in the bilateral ECT-alone and flupenthixol-alone groups relapsed at a rate of 93% (14/15). All 8 of the patients treated with the combination of the two treatments maintained therapeutic benefits at follow up of 3 to 17 months.

Tharyan and Adams (2005) reviewed 26 randomized controlled clinical trials that compared ECT with placebo (sham ECT), nonpharmacological interventions, and antipsychotics for people with schizophrenia, schizoaffective disorder, or chronic mental disorder. When ECT was compared with sham ECT, more people improved in the real ECT group (N = 392, 10 RCTs). There was no evidence that this early advantage for ECT was maintained over the medium to long term. When ECT was compared with antipsychotic drug treatments (total N = 443, 10 RCTs), results favor the medication group. Limited evidence suggested that ECT combined with antipsychotic drugs results in greater improvement in mental state (N = 40, 1 RCT) than with antipsychotic drugs alone. When continuation ECT was added to antipsychotic drugs, the combination was superior to the use of antipsychotics alone (n = 30) or continuation ECT alone (n = 30). Unilateral and bilateral ECT were equally effective in terms of global improvement (N = 78, 2 RCTs). One trial showed a significant advantage for 20 treatments over 12 treatments for numbers globally improved at the end of the ECT course (N = 43). The authors concluded that the evidence suggested that ECT, combined with treatment with antipsychotic drugs, may be considered an option for people with schizophrenia, particularly when rapid global improvement and reduction of symptoms is desired, as well as for those with schizophrenia who show limited response to medication alone.

Augmentation of Clozapine With Other Antipsychotics

Almost certainly because they are a preselected group of the most treatment-refractory individuals, a considerable proportion of patients treated with clozapine

do not respond, or respond only partially to clozapine and are left with substantial residual psychopathology. A review of data from clozapine clinical trials by Buckley, Wiggins, Sebastian, and Singer (2001) found that about half of patients with treatment-refractory symptoms do not respond to clozapine. Most augmentation strategies for antipsychotics (including clozapine) have been reviewed above. One augmentation strategy for patients who have failed an adequate clozapine trial that has been evaluated in several controlled and open trials is the use of an antipsychotic with high D_2 antagonist affinity to supplement the low D_2 occupancy of clozapine. Freudenreich and Goff (2002) reviewed the controlled (but mostly open) augmentation trials of clozapine in which another antipsychotic was added to ongoing clozapine treatment in patients who had had minimal or suboptimal response to clozapine. A total of 147 patients participated in these studies. Antipsychotics used for augmentation were chlorpromazine, sulpiride, risperidone, pimozide, and loxapine. Only two double-blind, randomized trials were available for this review: a positive trial of sulpiride/clozapine combination and a preliminary report of a negative trial of chlorpromazine/clozapine combination. Risperidone augmentation of clozapine was the most commonly reported combination, although no adequately controlled trial had been reported at the time of the review (Freudenreich & Goff, 2002). There was a suggestion that about half of the patients clearly responded to risperidone augmentation, with improvement evident within a few weeks. Subsequent to the Freudenreich and Goff (2002) review, three double-blind, placebo-controlled, randomized controlled studies of augmentation of clozapine with risperidone have been published. Josiassen et al. (2005) conducted a 12-week trial in 40 patients unresponsive or partially responsive to a steady dose of clozapine monotherapy (mean duration of treatment = 396.9 weeks) to which was added either placebo (n = 20) or up to 6 mg/day of risperidone (n = 20). From baseline to week 6 and week 12, mean BPRS total and positive symptom subscale scores were reduced significantly in both groups, but the reductions were significantly greater with clozapine/risperidone treatment. Yagcioglu et al. (2005) conducted a 6-week double-blind study of 30 patients with schizophrenia who had partial response to clozapine despite being treated for a mean of 32 months and who were randomly assigned to risperidone (n = 16), up to 6 mg/day, or placebo (n = 14). Significant improvement was noted in both groups on a variety of measures of psychopathology, but there was significantly greater improvement in the placebo-treated patients on the PANSS positive symptom subscale, which was the primary outcome measure. Honer et al. (2006), in a randomized, multicenter, double-blind study, evaluated 68 patients with schizophrenia who had a poor response to treatment with clozapine and were then randomized to receive 8 weeks of daily augmentation with 3 mg of risperidone or with placebo. Total PANSS score for the severity of symptoms decreased from baseline to 8 weeks in both the risperidone group and the placebo group, and there was no statistically significant difference in symptomatic benefit between augmentation with risperidone and placebo. The improvement associated with placebo augmentation in patients with chronic, refractory disease in the above studies is in contrast to the minimal effect of placebo alone observed in a meta-analysis (Sherwood, Thornton, & Honer, 2006) of randomized clinical trials of atypical antipsychotic drugs for acute schizophrenia over a similar treatment period (Honer et al., 2006). The authors opined that the nonspecific effects of being in a treatment trial may be greater in patients with chronic, refractory forms of schizophrenia than in those who are either having acute exacerbations or are in earlier phases of the illness. In summary, the controlled studies in aggregate do not lend support to augmentation of clozapine with other antipsychotics in patients who either have failed or have had a suboptimal response to an adequate trial of clozapine alone.

CONCLUSIONS

Pharmacological treatment has had a profoundly positive impact on the course of schizophrenia, the vast majority of patients no longer requiring chronic institutionalization. Nevertheless, schizophrenia remains a major public health concern, with patients over the course of their illness displaying varying degrees of social and vocational disability, and remaining susceptible to psychotic exacerbations even when compliant with medication. The relatively recent introduction of atypical agents has been promising, with a reduction of negative symptomatology, reduced motor side effects, and enhanced efficacy in some refractory patients. It is hoped that the future will bring novel agents that can specifically target de-

sired receptors to both enhance efficacy and further limit side effects. The difficulties in the pharmacological management of schizophrenia patients are compounded by an enhanced susceptibility to other psychiatric symptoms compared with the general population. The use of adjunctive medications to treat comorbid conditions has been examined in a limited number of methodologically rigorous studies, but targeted treatment trials with antidepressants for "postpsychotic depression," and benzodiazepines for anxiety and agitation may offer an opportunity to limit morbidity. Early identification of schizophrenia/schizophreniform disorder and aggressive treatment with antipsychotic medication to prevent the deterioration witnessed in some patients should be of the highest priority because the overall efficacy of pharmacological treatments remains limited.

REFERENCES

Abi-Saab, W. M., D'Souza, D. C., Madonick, S. H., & Krystal, J. H. (2001). Targeting the glutamate system. In A. Breier, P. V. Tran, J. M. Herrera, G. D. Tollefson, & F. P. Bymaster (Eds.), *Current issues in the psychopharmacology of schizophrenia* (pp. 304–332). Philadelphia: Lippincott Williams and Wilkins Healthcare.

Abraham, K. R., & Kulhara, P. (1987). The efficacy of electroconvulsive therapy in the treatment of schizophrenia. *British Journal of Psychiatry, 151,* 152–155.

Addington, D. E., Jones, B., Bloom, D., Chouinard, G., Remington, G., & Albright, P. (1993). Reduction of hospital days in chronic schizophrenic patients treated with risperidone: A retrospective study. *Clinical Therapeutics, 15,* 917–926.

Addington, D. E., Pantelis, C., Dineen, M., Benattia, I., & Romano, S. J. (2004). Efficacy and tolerability of ziprasidone versus risperidone in patients with acute exacerbation of schizophrenia or schizoaffective disorder: an 8-week, double-blind, multicenter trial. *Journal of Clinical Psychiatry, 65,* 1624–1633.

Agid, O., Kapur, S., Arenovich, T., & Zipursky, R. B. (2003). Delayed-onset hypothesis of antipsychotic action: A hypothesis tested and rejected. *Archives of General Psychiatry, 60,* 1228–1235.

Alvir, J. M., Lieberman, J. A., Safferman, A. Z., Schwimmer, J. L., & Schaaf, J. A. (1993). Clozapine-induced agranulocytosis: Incidence and risk factors in the United States. *New England Journal of Medicine, 329,* 162–167.

Anis, N. A., Berry, S. C., Burton, N. R., & Lodge, D. (1983). The dissociative anaesthetics, ketamine and phencyclidine, selectively reduce excitation of central mammalian neurones by N-methyl-aspartate. *British Journal of Pharmacology*, 79, 565–575.

Arvanitis, L. A., & Miller, B. G. (1997). Multiple fixed doses of "Seroquel" (quetiapine) in patients with acute exacerbation of schizophrenia: A comparison with haloperidol and placebo. The Seroquel Trial 13 Study Group. *Biological Psychiatry*, 42, 233–246.

Atre-Vaidya, N., & Taylor, M. A. (1989). Effectiveness of lithium in schizophrenia: Do we really have an answer? *Journal of Clinical Psychiatry*, 50, 170–173.

Azorin, J. M., Spiegel, R., Remington, G., Vanelle J. M. Pere J. J., Giguere M., et al. (2001). A double-blind comparative study of clozapine and risperidone in the management of severe chronic schizophrenia. *American Journal of Psychiatry*, 158, 1305–1313.

Baldessarini, R. J., & Frankenburg, F. R. (1991). Clozapine: A novel antipsychotic agent [see comments]. *New England Journal of Medicine*, 324, 746–754.

Barbee, J. G., Mancuso, D. M., Freed, C. R., & Todorov, A. A. (1992). Alprazolam as a antipsychotic adjunct in the emergency treatment of schizophrenia. *American Journal of Psychiatry*, 149, 506–510.

Barch, D. M., & Carter, C. S. (2005). Amphetamine improves cognitive function in medicated individuals with schizophrenia and in healthy volunteers. *Schizophrenia Research*, 77, 43–58

Basan, A., Kissling, W., & Leucht, S. (2004). Valproate as an adjunct to antipsychotics for schizophrenia: A systematic review of randomized trials. *Schizophrenia Research*, 70, 33–37.

Battaglia, J., Moss, S., Rush, J., Kang, J., Mendoza, R., Leedom, L., et al. (1997). Haloperidol, lorazepam, or both for psychotic agitation? A multi-center, prospective, double blind, emergency department study. *American Journal of Emergency Medicine*, 15, 335–340.

Beasley, C. M., Dellva, M. A., Tamura, R. N., Morgenstern, H., Glazer, W. M., Ferguson, K., et al. (1999). Randomized double-blind comparison of the incidence of tardive dyskinesia in patients with schizophrenia during long-term treatment with olanzapine or haloperidol. *British Journal of Psychiatry*, 174, 23–30.

Beasley, C. M., Jr., Hamilton, S. H., Crawford, A. M., Dellva, M. A., Tollefson, G. D., Tran, P. V., et al. (1997). Olanzapine versus haloperidol: Acute phase results of the international double-blind olanzapine trial. *European Neuropsychopharmacology*, 7, 125–137.

Beasley, C. M., Tollefson, G., Tran, P., Satterlee, W., Sanger, T., & Hamilton, S. . (1996). Olanzapine versus placebo and haloperidol: Acute phase results of the North American double-blind olanzapine trial. *Neuropsychopharmacology*, 14, 111–123.

Berk, M., Ichim, C., & Brook, S. (2001). Efficacy of mirtazapine addon therapy to haloperidol in the treatment of the negative symptoms of schizophrenia: A double-blind randomized placebo-controlled study. *International Clinical Psychopharmacology*, 16, 87–92.

Bjorndal, N., Bjerre, M., Gerlach, J., Kristjansen, P., Magelund, G., Oestrich, I. H., et al. (1980). High dosage haloperidol therapy in chronic schizophrenic patients: A double-blind study of clinical response, side effects, serum haloperidol, and serum prolactin. *Psychopharmacology (Berlin)*, 67, 17–23.

Bodkin, J. A. (1990). Emerging uses for high-potency benzodiazepines in psychotic disorders. *Journal of Clinical Psychiatry*, 51(5):41–46.

Bodkin, J. A., Siris, S. G., Bermanzohn, P. C., Hennen, J., & Cole, J. O. (2005). Double-blind, placebo-controlled, multicenter trial of selegiline augmentation of antipsychotic medication to treat negative symptoms in outpatients with schizophrenia. *American Journal of Psychiatry*, 162, 388–390.

Bondolfi, G., Dufour, H., Patris, M., May, J. P., Billeter, U., Eap, C. B., et al. (1998). Risperidone versus clozapine in treatment-resistant chronic schizophrenia: A randomized double-blind study. *American Journal of Psychiatry*, 155, 499–504.

Borison, R. L., Arvanitis, L. A., & Miller, B. G. (1996). ICI 204,636, an atypical antipsychotic: Efficacy and safety in a multicenter, placebo-controlled trial in patients with schizophrenia. U.S. SEROQUEL Study Group. *Journal of Clinical Psychopharmacology*, 16, 158–169.

Brambilla, F., Scarone, S., Ponzano, M., Maffei, C., Nobile, P., Rovere, C., et al. (1979). Catecholaminergic drugs in chronic schizophrenia. *Neuropsychobiology*, 5, 185–200.

Brandon, S., Cowley, P., McDonald, C., Neville, P., Palmer, R., & Wellstood-Eason, S. (1985). Leicester ECT Trial: Results in schizophrenia. *British Journal of Psychiatry*, 146, 177–183.

Breier, A., Berg, P. H., Thakore, J. H., Naber, D., Gattaz, W. F., Cavazzoni, P., et al. (2005). Olanzapine versus ziprasidone: Results of a 28-week double-blind study in patients with schizophrenia. *American Journal of Psychiatry*, 162, 1879–1887.

Breier, A., Buchanan, R. W., Irish, D., & Carpenter, W. T., Jr. (1993). Clozapine treatment of outpatients with schizophrenia: Outcome and long-term response patterns. *Hospital and Community Psychiatry, 44,* 1145–1149.

Breier, A., & Hamilton, S. H. (1999). Comparative efficacy of olanzapine and haloperidol for patients with treatment-resistant schizophrenia [see comments]. *Biological Psychiatry, 45,* 403–411.

Breier, A. F., Malhotra, A. K., Su, T.-P., Pinals, D. A., Elman, I., Adler, C. M., et al. (1999). Clozapine and risperidone in chronic schizophrenia: Effects on symptoms, parkinsonian side effects, and neuroendocrine response. *American Journal of Psychiatry, 156,* 294–298

Buchanan, R. W., Breier, A., Kirkpatrick, B., Ball, P., & Carpenter, W. T., Jr. (1998). Positive and negative symptom response to clozapine in schizophrenic patients with and without the deficit syndrome. *American Journal of Psychiatry, 155,* 751–760.

Buckley, P. F., Goldstein, J. M., & Emsley, R. A. (2004). Efficacy and tolerability of quetiapine in poorly responsive, chronic schizophrenia. *Schizophrenia Research, 66,* 143–150.

Buckley, P. F., Wiggins, L. D., Sebastian, S., & Singer, B. (2001). Treatment-refractory schizophrenia. *Current Psychiatry Reports, 3,* 393–400.

Carman, J. S., Bigelow, L. B., & Wyatt, R. J. (1981). Lithium combined with neuroleptics in chronic schizophrenic and schizoaffective patients. *Journal of Clinical Psychiatry, 42,* 124–128.

Carpenter, W. T., Jr., Breier, A., Buchanan, R. W., Kirkpatrick, B., Shepard, P., & Weiner, E. (2000). Mazindol treatment of negative symptoms. *Neuropsychopharmacology, 23,* 365–374.

Carpenter, W. T., Jr., Buchanan, R. W., Kirkpatrick, B., & Breier, A. F. (1999). Diazepam treatment of early signs of exacerbation in schizophrenia. *American Journal of Psychiatry, 156,* 299–303.

Carpenter, W. T., Jr., Hanlon, T. E., Heinrichs, D. W., Summerfelt, A. T., Kirkpatrick, B., Levine, J., et al. (1990). Continuous versus targeted medication in schizophrenic outpatients: Outcome results. *American Journal of Psychiatry, 147,* 1138–1148.

Carpenter, W. T., Kurg, R., Kirkpatrick, B., Hanlon, T. E., Summerfelt, T., Buchanan, R. W., et al. (1991). Carbamazepine maintenance treatment in outpatient schizophrenics. *Archives of General Psychiatry, 48,* 69–72.

Casey, D. E., Daniel, D. G., Wassef, A. A., Tracy, K. A., Wozniak, P., & Sommerville, K. W. (2003). Effect of divalproex combined with olanzapine or risperidone in patients with an acute exacerbation of schizophrenia. *Neuropsychopharmacology, 28,* 182–192.

Casey, D. E., Haupt, D. W., Newcomer, J. W., Henderson, D. C., Sernyak, M. J., Davidson, M., et al. (2004). Antipsychotic-induced weight gain and metabolic abnormalities: Implications for increased mortality in patients with schizophrenia. *Journal of Clinical Psychiatry, 65*(Suppl. 7), 4–18.

Chakos, M., Lieberman, J., Hoffman, E., Bradford, D., & Sheitman, B. (2001). Effectiveness of second-generation antipsychotics in patients with treatment-resistant schizophrenia: A review and meta-analysis of randomized trials. *American Journal of Psychiatry, 158,* 518–526.

Chanpattana, W., Chakrabhand, M. L., Buppanharun, W., & Sackeim, H. A. (2000). Effects of stimulus intensity on the efficacy of bilateral ECT in schizophrenia: A preliminary study. *Biological Psychiatry, 48,* 222–228.

Chanpattana, W., Chakrabhand, M. L., Sackeim, H. A., Kitaroonchai, W., Kongsakon, R., Techakasem, P., et al. (1999). Continuation ECT in treatment-resistant schizophrenia: A controlled study. *Journal of Electroconvulsive Therapy, 15,* 178–192.

Chouinard, G., Jones, B., Remington, G., Bloom, D., Addington, D., MacEwan, G. W., et al. (1993). A Canadian multicenter placebo-controlled study of fixed doses of risperidone and haloperidol in the treatment of chronic schizophrenic patients *Journal of Clinical Psychopharmacology, 13,* 25–40.

Christison, G. W., Kirch, D. G., & Wyatt, R. J. (1991). When symptoms persist: Choosing among alternative somatic treatments for schizophrenia. *Schizophrenia Bulletin, 17,* 217–245.

Citrome, L., Casey, D. E., Daniel, D. G., Wozniak, P., Kochan, L. D., & Tracy, K. A. (2004). Adjunctive divalproex and hostility among patients with schizophrenia receiving olanzapine or risperidone. *Psychiatr Services, 55,* 290–294.

Claghorn, J., Honigfeld, G., Abuzzahab, F. S., Sr., Wang, R., Steinbook, R., Tuason, V., et al. (1987). The risks and benefits of clozapine versus chlorpromazine. *Journal of Clinical Psychopharmacology, 7,* 377–384.

Cohen, W. J., & Cohen, N. H. (1974). Lithium carbonate, haloperidol and irreversible brain damage. *Journal of the American Medical Association, 230,* 1283–1287.

Conley, R. R., Kelly, D. L., Nelson, M. W., Richardson, C. M., Feldman, S., Benham, R., et al. (2005). Risperidone, quetiapine, and fluphenazine in the treatment of patients with therapy-refractory schizophrenia. *Clinical Neuropharmacology, 28,* 163–168.

Conley, R. R., Tamminga, C. A., Bartko, J. J., Richardson, C., Peszke, M., Lingle, J., et al. (1998). Olanzapine compared with chlorpromazine in treatment-resistant schizophrenia. *American Journal of Psychiatry, 155,* 914–920.

Copolov, D. L., Link, C. G., & Kowalcyk, B. (2000). A multicentre, double-blind, randomized comparison of quetiapine (ICI 204,636, "Seroquel") and haloperidol in schizophrenia *Psychological Medicine, 30,* 95–105.

Correll, C. U., Leucht, S., & Kane, J. M. (2004). Lower risk for tardive dyskinesia associated with second-generation antipsychotics: A systematic review of 1-year studies. *American Journal of Psychiatry, 161,* 414–425.

Csernansky, J. G., Mahmoud, R., & Brenner, R. (2002). A comparison of risperidone and haloperidol for the prevention of relapse in patients with schizophrenia. *New England Journal of Medicine, 346,* 16–22.

Csernansky, J. G., Riney, S. J., Lombrozo, L., Overall, J. E., & Hollister, L. E. (1988). Double-blind comparison of alprazolam, diazepam, and placebo for the treatment of negative schizophrenic symptoms. *Archives of General Psychiatry, 45,* 655–659.

Daniel, D. G., Zimbroff, D. L., Potkin, S. G., Reeves, K. R., Harrigan, E. P., Lakshminarayan, M. (1999). Ziprasidone 80mg/day and 160mg/day in the acute exacerbation of schizophrenia and schizoaffective disorder: A six-week placebo-controlled trial. *Neuropsychopharmacology, 20,* 491–505.

Davidson, M., Kahn, R. S., Knott, P., Kaminsky, R., Cooper, M., DuMont, K., et al. (1991). Effects of neuroleptic treatment on symptoms of schizophrenia and plasma homovanillic acid concentrations. *Archives of General Psychiatry, 48,* 910–913.

Davis, J. M. (1975). Overview: Maintenance therapy in psychiatry: I. Schizophrenia. *American Journal of Psychiatry, 132,* 1237–1245.

Davis, J. M., Barter, J. T., & Kane, J. M. (1989). Antipsychotic drugs. In H. I. Kaplan & B. J. Sadock (Eds.), *Comprehensive textbook of psychiatry* (5th ed., pp. 1591–1627). Baltimore: Williams and Wilkins.

Davis, J. M., Chen, N., & Glick, I. D. (2003). A meta-analysis of the efficacy of second-generation antipsychotics. *Archives of General Psychiatry, 60,* 553–564.

Donaldson, S. R., Gelenberg, A. J., & Baldessarini, R. J. (1983). The pharmacologic treatment of schizophrenia: A progress report. *Schizophrenia Bulletin, 9,* 504–527.

Dose, M., Hellweg, R., Yassouridis, A., Theison, M., & Emrich, H. M. (1988). Combined treatment of schizophrenic psychoses with haloperidol and valproate. *Pharmacopsychiatry, 31,* 122–125.

Duggan, L., Fenton, M., Rathbone, J., Dardennes, R., El-Dosoky, A., & Indran, S. (2005,). Olanzapine for schizophrenia. *Cochrane Database of Systematic Reviews,* (2):CD001359.

Emsley, R., Rabinowitz, J., & Medori, R. (2006). Time course for antipsychotic treatment response in first-episode schizophrenia. *American Journal of Psychiatry, 163,* 743–745.

Ericksen, S. E., Hurt, S. W., & Chang, S. (1978). Haloperidol dose, plasma levels, and clinical response: A double-blind study. *Psychopharmacology Bulletin, 14,* 15–16.

Essock, S. M., Hargreaves, W. A., Covell, N. H., & Goethe, J. (1996). Clozapine's effectiveness for patients in state hospitals: Results from a randomized trial. *Psychopharmacology Bulletin, 32,* 683–697.

Evins, A. E., Amico, E., Posever, T. A., Toker, R., & Goff, D. C. (2002). D-cycloserine added to risperidone in patients with primary negative symptoms of schizophrenia. *Schizophrenia Research, 56,* 19–23.

Evins, A. E., Fitzgerald, S. M., Wine, L., Rosselli, R., & Goff, D. C. (2000). Placebo-controlled trial of glycine added to clozapine in schizophrenia. *American Journal of Psychiatry, 157,* 826–828.

Fleischhacker, W. W., Eerdekens, M., Karcher, K., Remington, G., Llorca, P. M., Chrzanowski, W., et al. (2003). Treatment of schizophrenia with long-acting injectable risperidone: A 12-month open-label trial of the first long-acting second-generation antipsychotic. *Journal of Clinical Psychiatry,64,* 1250–1257.

Freudenreich, O., & Goff, D. C. (2002). Antipsychotic combination therapy in schizophrenia: A review of efficacy and risks of current combinations. *Acta Psychiatrica Scandinavica, 106,* 323–330.

Gaebel, W., Frick, U., Kopcke, W., Linden, M., Muller, P., Muller-Spahn, F., et al. (1993). Early antipsychotic intervention in schizophrenia: Are prodromal symptoms valid predictors of relapse? *British Journal of Psychiatry,* Suppl. (21):8–12.

Gardos, G. (1974). Are antipsychotic drugs interchangeable? *Journal of Nervous and Mental Disease, 159,* 343–348.

Gattaz, W. F., Rost, W., Hubner, C. K., & Bauer, K. (1989). Acute and subchronic effects of low-dose bromocriptine in haloperidol-treated schizophrenics. *Biological Psychiatry, 25,* 247–255.

Geddes, J., Freemantle, N., Harrison, P., & Bebbington, P. (2000). Atypical antipsychotics in the treatment of schizophrenia: Systematic overview and meta-regression analysis. *British Medical Journal, 321,* 1371–1376.

Gelenberg, A. J., & Doller, J. C. (1979). Clozapine versus chlorpromazine for the treatment of schizophrenia: Preliminary results from a double-blind study. *Journal of Clinical Psychiatry, 40,* 238–240.

Gerlach, J., & Luhdorf, K. (1975). The effect of L-dopa on young patients with simple schizophrenia, treated with antipsychotic drugs: A double-blind cross-over trial with madopar and placebo. *Psychopharmacologia, 44,* 105–110.

Gillies, D., Beck, A., McCloud, A., Rathbone, J., & Gillies, D. (2005). Benzodiazepines alone or in combination with antipsychotic drugs for acute psychosis. *Cochrane Database of Systematic Reviews, 4,* CD003079.

Goff, D. C., Henderson, D. C., Evins, A. E., & Amico, E. (1999). A placebo-controlled crossover trial of D-cycloserine added to clozapine in patients with schizophrenia. *Biological Psychiatry, 45,* 512–514.

Goff, D. C., Posever, T., Herz, L., Simmons, J., Kletti, N., Lapierre, K., et al. (1998). An exploratory haloperidol-controlled dose-finding study of ziprasidone in hospitalised patients with schizophrenia or schizoaffective disorder. *Journal of Clinical Psychopharmacology, 18,* 296–304.

Goff, D. C., Tsai, G., Levitt, J., Amico, E., Manoach, D., Schoenfeld, D. A., et al. (1999). A placebo-controlled trial of D-cycloserine added to conventional neuroleptics in patients with schizophrenia. *Archives of General Psychiatry, 56,* 21–27.

Goff, D. C., Tsai, G., Manoach, D. S., & Coyle, J. T. (1995). Dose-finding trial of D-cycloserine added to neuroleptics for negative symptoms in schizophrenia. *American Journal of Psychiatry, 152,* 1213–1215.

Goldberg, T. E., Bigelow, L. B., Weinberger, D. R., Daniel, D. G., & Kleinman, J. E. (1991). Cognitive and behavioral effects of the coadministration of dextroamphetamine and haloperidol in schizophrenia. *American Journal of Psychiatry, 148,* 78–84.

Green, M. F. (1996). What are the functional consequences of neurocognitive deficits in schizophrenia? *American Journal of Psychiatry, 153,* 321–330.

Green, M. F., & Braff, D. L. (2001). Translating the basic and clinical cognitive neuroscience of schizophrenia to drug development and clinical trials of antipsychotic medications. *Biological Psychiatry, 49,* 374–384.

Green, M. F., Marder, S. R., Glynn, S. M., McGurk, S. R., Wirshing, W. C., Wirshing, D. A., et al. (2002). The neurocognitive effects of low-dose haloperidol: A two-year comparison with risperidone. *Biological Psychiatry, 51,* 972–978.

Green, M. F. . Marshall, B. D., Jr., Wirshing, W. C., Ames, D., Marder, S. R., McGurk, S., et al. (1997). Does risperidone improve verbal working memory

in treatment-resistant schizophrenia? *American Journal of Psychiatry, 154,* 799–804.

Growe, G. A., Crayton, J. W., Klass, D. B., Evans, H., & Strizich, M. (1979). Lithium in chronic schizophrenia. *American Journal of Psychiatry, 136,* 454–455.

Gunduz-Bruce, H., McMeniman, M., Robinson, D. G., Woerner, M. G., Kane, J. M., & Schooler, N. R. (2005). Duration of untreated psychosis and time to treatment response for delusions and hallucinations. *American Journal of Psychiatry, 162,* 1966–1969.

Harvey, P. D., Howanitz, E., Parrella, M., White, L., Davidson, M., Mohs, R. C., et al. (1998). Symptoms, cognitive functioning, and adaptive skills in geriatric patients with lifelong schizophrenia: A comparison across treatment sites. *American Journal of Psychiatry, 155,* 1080–1086.

Harvey, P. D., Rabinowitz, J., Eerdekens, M., & Davidson, M. (2005). Treatment of cognitive impairment in early psychosis: A comparison of risperidone and haloperidol in a large long-term trial. *American Journal of Psychiatry, 162,* 1888–1895.

Heresco-Levy, U., Ermilov, M., Lichtenberg, P., Bar, G., & Javitt, D. C. (2004). High-dose glycine added to olanzapine and risperidone for the treatment of schizophrenia. *Biological Psychiatry, 55,* 165–171.

Heresco-Levy, U., Javitt, D. C., Ebstein, R., Vass, A., Lichtenberg, P., Bar, G., et al. (2005). D-serine efficacy as add-on pharmacotherapy to risperidone and olanzapine for treatment-refractory schizophrenia. *Biological Psychiatry, 57,* 577–585.

Heresco-Levy, U., Javitt, D. C., Ermilov, M., Mordel, C., Horowitz, A., & Kelly, D. (1996). Double-blind, placebo-controlled, crossover trial of glycine adjuvant therapy for treatment-resistant schizophrenia. *British Journal of Psychiatry, 169,* 610–617.

Heresco-Levy, U., Javitt, D. C., Ermilov, M., Mordel, C., Silipo, G., & Lichtenstein, M. (1999). Efficacy of high-dose glycine in the treatment of enduring negative symptoms of schizophrenia. *Archives of General Psychiatry, 56,* 29–36.

Herz, M. I., Glazer, W. M., Mostert, M. A., Sheard, M. A., Szymanski, H. V., Hafez, H., et al. (1991). Intermittent vs maintenance medication in schizophrenia: Two-year results. *Archives of General Psychiatry, 48,* 333–339.

Hesslinger, B., Normann, C., Langosch, J. M., Klose, P., Berger, M., & Walden, J. (1999). Effects of carbamazepine and valproate on haloperidol plasma levels and on psychopathologic outcome in schizophrenic patients. *Journal of Clinical Psychopharmacology, 19,* 310–315.

Hogarty, G. E., McEvoy, J. P., Munetz, M., DiBarry, A. L., Bartone, P., Cather, R., et al. (1988). Dose of fluphenazine, familial expressed emotion, and outcome in schizophrenia: Results of a two-year controlled study. *Archives of General Psychiatry, 45,* 797–805.

Hogarty, G. E., McEvoy, J. P., Ulrich, R. F., DiBarry, A. L., Bartone, P., Cooley, S., et al. (1995). Pharmacotherapy of impaired affect in recovering schizophrenic patients. *Archives of General Psychiatry, 52,* 29–41.

Hogarty, G. E., Ulrich, R. F., Mussare, F., & Aristigueta, N. (1976). Drug discontinuation among long-term, successfully maintained schizophrenic outpatients. *Diseases of the Nervous System, 37,* 494–500.

Honer, W. G., Thornton, A. E., Chen, E. Y., Chan, R. C., Wong, J. O., Bergmann, A., et al. (2006). Clozapine alone versus clozapine and risperidone with refractory schizophrenia. *New England Journal of Medicine, 354,* 472–482.

Hong, C. J., Chen, J. Y., Chiu, H. J., & Sim, C. B. (1997). A double-blind comparative study of clozapine versus chlorpromazine on Chinese patients with treatment-refractory schizophrenia. *International Clinical Psychopharmacology, 12,* 123–130.

Hunter, R. H., Joy, C. B., Kennedy, E., Gilbody, S. M., & Song, F. (2003). Risperidone versus typical antipsychotic medication for schizophrenia. *Cochrane Database of Systematic Reviews, 2,* CD000440.

Inanaga, K., Nakazawa, Y., Inoue, K., Tachibana, H., Oshima, M., & Kotorii, T. (1975). Double-blind controlled study of L-dopa therapy in schizophrenia. *Japonica, 29,* 123–143.

Javitt, D. C., & Zukin, S. R. (1991). Recent advances in the phencyclidine model of schizophrenia. *American Journal of Psychiatry, 148,* 1301–1308.

Javitt, D. C., Zylberman, I., Zukin, S. R., Heresco-Levy, U., & Lindenmayer, J. P. (1994). Amelioration of negative symptoms in schizophrenia by glycine. *American Journal of Psychiatry, 151,* 1234–1236.

Johns, C. A., & Thompson, J. W. (1995). Adjunctive treatments in schizophrenia: Pharmacotherapies and electoconvulsive therapy. *Schizophrenia Bulletin, 21,* 607–619.

Johnson, D. A., Ludlow, J. M., Street, K., & Taylor, R. D. (1987). Double-blind comparison of half-dose and standard-dose flupenthixol decanoate in the maintenance treatment of stabilised out-patients with schizophrenia. *British Journal of Psychiatry, 151,* 634–638.

Jolley, A. G., Hirsch, S. R., Morrison, E., McRink, A., & Wilson, L. (1990). Trial of brief intermittent antipsychotic prophylaxis for selected schizophrenic outpatients: clinical and social outcome at two years. *British Medical Journal, 301,* 837–842.

Josiassen, R. C., Joseph, A., Kohegyi, E., Stokes, S., Dadvand, M., Paing, W. W., et al. (2005). Clozapine augmented with risperidone in the treatment of schizophrenia: A randomized, double-blind, placebo-controlled trial. *American Journal of Psychiatry, 162,* 130–136.

Jungerman, T., Rabinowitz, D., & Klein, E. (1999). Deprenyl augmentation for treating negative symptoms of schizophrenia: A double-blind, controlled study. *Journal of Clinical Psychopharmacology, 19,* 522–525.

Kane, J. M., Carson, W. H., Saha, A. R., McQuade, R. D., Ingenito, G. G., Zimbroff, D. L., et al. (2002). Efficacy and safety of aripiprazole and haloperidol versus placebo in patients with schizophrenia and schizoaffective disorder. *Journal of Clinical Psychiatry, 63,* 763–771.

Kane, J. M., Davis, J. M., Schooler, N. R., Marder, S. R., Brauzer, B., & Casey, D. E. (1993). A one-year comparison of four dosages of haloperidol decanoate [Abstract]. *Schizophrenia Research, 9,* 239–240.

Kane, J. M., Eerdekens, M., Lindenmayer, J. P., Keith, S. J., Lesem, M., & Karcher, K. (2003). Long-acting injectable risperidone: Efficacy and safety of the first long-acting atypical antipsychotic. *American Journal of Psychiatry, 160,* 1125–1132.

Kane, J. M., Gunduz, H., & Malhotra, A. K. (2001). Second generation antipsychotics in the treatment of schizophrenia: Clozapine. In *Current issues in the psychopharmacology of schizophrenia* (pp. 209–223). Philadelphia: Lippincott Williams and Wilkins Healthcare.

Kane, J., Honigfeld, G., Singer, J., & Meltzer, H. (1988). Clozapine for the treatment-resistant schizophrenic: A double-blind comparison with chlorpromazine. *Archives of General Psychiatry, 45,* 789–796.

Kane, J. M., & Lieberman, J. M. (1987). Maintenance pharmacotherapy in schizophrenia. In H. Y. Meltzer (Ed.), *Psychopharmacology: The third generation of progress* (pp. 1103–1109). New York: Raven Press.

Kane, J. M., Marder, S. R., Schooler, N. R., Wirshing, W. C., Umbricht, D., Baker, R. W., et al. (2001). Clozapine and haloperidol in moderately refractory schizophrenia: A six-month double-blind comparison. *Archives of General Psychiatry, 58,* 965–972.

Kane, J. M., Rifkin, A., Quitkin, F., Nayak, D., & Ramos-Lorenzi, J. (1982). Fluphenazine vs placebo in patients with remitted, acute first episode schizophrenia. *Archives of General Psychiatry, 39*, 70–73.

Kane, J. M., Rifkin, A., Woerner, M., Reardon, G., Sarantakos, S., Schiebel, D., et al. (1983). Low-dose antipsychotic treatment of outpatient schizophrenics: I. Preliminary results for relapse rates. *Archives of General Psychiatry, 40*, 893–896.

Kane, J. M., Woerner, M., & Sarantakos, S. (1986). Depot antipsychotics: A comparative review of standard, intermediate, and low-dose regimens. *Journal of Clinical Psychiatry, 47*(Suppl.), 30–33.

Kapur, S., Arenovich, T., Agid, O., Zipursky, R., Lindborg, S., & Jones, B. (2005). Evidence for onset of antipsychotic effects within the first 24 hours of treatment. *American Journal of Psychiatry, 162*, 939–946.

Karson, C. N., Weinberger, D. R., Bigelow, L., & Wyatt, R. J. (1982). Clonazepam treatment of chronic schizophrenia: Negative results in a double-blind, placebo-controlled trial. *American Journal of Psychiatry, 139*, 1627–1628.

Kasper, S., Lerman, M. N., McQuade, R. D., Saha, A., Carson, W. H., Ali, M., et al. (2003). Efficacy and safety of aripiprazole vs. haloperidol for long-term maintenance treatment following acute relapse of schizophrenia. *International Journal of Neuropsychopharmacology, 6*, 325–337.

Keck, P., Jr., Buffenstein, A., Ferguson, J., Feighner, J., Jaffe, W., Harrigan, E. P., et al. (1998). Ziprasidone 40 and 120 mg/day in the acute exacerbation of schizophrenia and schizoaffective disorder: A 4-week placebo-controlled trial. *Psychopharmacology, 140*, 173–184.

Keefe, R. S., Seidman, L. J., Christensen, B. K., Hamer, R. M., Sharma, T., Sitskoorn, M. M., et al. (2004). Comparative effect of atypical and conventional antipsychotic drugs on neurocognition in first-episode psychosis: A randomized, double-blind trial of olanzapine versus low doses of haloperidol. *American Journal of Psychiatry, 161*, 985–995.

Keefe, R. S., Silva, S. G., Perkins, D. O., & Lieberman, J. A. (1999). The effects of atypical antipsychotic drugs on neurocognitive impairment in schizophrenia: A review and meta-analysis. *Schizophrenia Bulletin, 25*, 201–222.

Keefe, R. S., Young, C. A., Rock, S. L., Purdon, S. E., Gold, J. M., & Breier, A.(2006). One-year double-blind study of the neurocognitive efficacy of olanzapine, risperidone, and haloperidol in schizophrenia. *Schizophrenia Research, 81*, 1–15.

Kellner, R., Wilson, R. M., Muldawer, M. D., & Pathak, D. (1975). Anxiety in schizophrenia: The responses to chlordiazepoxide in an intensive design study. *Archives of General Psychiatry, 32*, 1246–1254.

Kinon, B. J., Kane, J. M., Johns, C., Perovich, R., Ismi, M., Koreen, A., et al. (1993). Treatment of antipsychotic-resistant schizophrenic relapse. *Psychopharmacology Bulletin, 29*, 309–314.

Kinon, B. J., & Lieberman, J. A. (1996). Mechanisms of action of atypical antipsychotic drugs: A critical analysis. *Psychopharmacology, 124*, 2–34.

Klein, D. F., & Davis, J. M. (1969). Review of the antipsychotic drug literature. In D. F. Klein & J. M. David (Eds.), *Diagnosis and drug treatment of psychiatric disorders* (pp. 52–138). Baltimore: Williams and Wilkins.

Klein, E., Bental, E., Lerer, B., & Belmaker, R. H. (1984). Carbamazepine and haloperidol v placebo and haloperidol in excited psychoses: A controlled study. *Archives of General Psychiatry, 41*, 165–170.

Klieser, E., Lehmann, E., Kinzler, E., Wurthmann, C., & Heinrich, K. (1995). Randomized, double-blind, controlled trial of risperidone versus clozapine in patients with chronic schizophrenia. *Journal of Clinical Psychopharmacology, 15*(1 Suppl. 1):45S–51S.

Ko, G. N., Korpi, E. R., Freed, W. J., Zalcman, S. J., & Bigelow, L. B. (1985). Effect of valproic acid on behavior and plasma amino acid concentrations in chronic schizophrenic patients. *Biological Psychiatry, 20*, 209–215.

Kontaxakis, V. P., Ferentinos, P. P., Havaki-Kontaxaki, B. J., & Roukas, D. K. (2005). Randomized controlled augmentation trials in clozapine-resistant schizophrenic patients: A critical review. *European Psychiatry, 20*, 409–415.

Kumra, S., Frazier, J. A., Jacobsen, L. K., McKenna, K., Gordon, C. T., Lenane, M. C., et al. (1996). Childhood-onset schizophrenia: A double-blind clozapine-haloperidol comparison. *Archives of General Psychiatry, 53*, 1090–1097.

Lane, H. Y., Chang, Y. C., Liu, Y. C., Chiu, C. C., & Tsa, G. E. (2005). Sarcosine or D-serine add-on treatment for acute exacerbation of schizophrenia: A randomized, double-blind, placebo-controlled study. *Archives of General Psychiatry, 62*, 1196–1204.

Lee, M. S., Kim, Y. K., Lee, S. K., & Suh, K. Y. (1998). A double-blind study of adjunctive sertraline in haloperidol-stabilized patients with chronic schizophrenia. *Journal of Clinical Psychopharmacology, 18*, 399–403.

Lee, S. H., & Yang, Y. Y. (1999). Reversible neurotoxicity induced by a combination of clozapine and lithium: A case report. *Chung Hua i Hsueh Tsa Chih, 62*, 184–187.

Leon, C. A. (1979). Therapeutic effects of clozapine: A 4-year follow-up of a controlled clinical trial. *Acta Psychiatrica Scandinavica, 59*, 471–480.

Leucht, S., Kissling, W., & McGrath, J. (2004). Lithium for schizophrenia revisited: A systematic review and meta-analysis of randomized controlled trials. *Journal of Clinical Psychiatry, 65,* 177–186.

Leucht, S., McGrath, J., White, P., & Kissling, W. (2002). Carbamazepine augmentation for schizophrenia: How good is the evidence? *Journal of Clinical Psychiatry, 63,* 218–224.

Leucht, S., Pitschel-Walz, G., Abraham, D., & Kissling, W. (1999). Efficacy and extrapyramidal side-effects of the new antipsychotics olanzapine, quetiapine, risperidone, and sertindole compared to conventional antipsychotics and placebo: A meta-analysis of randomized controlled trials. *Schizophrenia Research, 35,* 51–68.

Leucht, S., Wahlbeck, K., Hamann, J., & Kissling, W. (2003). New generation antipsychotics versus low-potency conventional antipsychotics: A systematic review and meta-analysis. *Lancet, 361,* 1581–1589.

Levinson, D. F., Simpson, G. M., Singh, H., Yadalam, K., Jain, A., Stephanos, M. J., et al. (1990). Fluphenazine dose, clinical response, and extrapyramidal symptoms during acute treatment [see comments]. *Archives of General Psychiatry, 47,* 761–768.

Liddle, P., Carpenter, W. T., & Crow, T. (1994). Syndromes of schizophrenia. *British Journal of Psychiatry, 165,* 721–727.

Lieberman, J. A. (1993). Prediction of outcome in first-episode schizophrenia. *Journal of Clinical Psychiatry, 54*(Suppl.), 13–17.

Lieberman, J. A., Stroup, T. S., McEvoy, J. P., Swartz, M. S., Rosenheck, R. A., Perkins, D. O., et al. (2005). Effectiveness of antipsychotic drugs in patients with chronic schizophrenia. *New England Journal of Medicine, 353,* 1209–1223.

Lieberman, J. A., Tollefson, G., Tohen, M., Green, A. I., Gur, R. E., Kahn, R., et al. (2003). Comparative efficacy and safety of atypical and conventional antipsychotic drugs in first-episode psychosis: A randomized, double-blind trial of olanzapine versus haloperidol. *American Journal of Psychiatry, 160,* 1396–1404.

Lindenmayer, J. P. (1995). New pharmacotherapeutic modalities for negative symptoms in psychosis. *Acta Psychiatrica Scandinavica, 91,* 15–19.

Linnoila, M., Viukari, M., & Kietala, O. (1976). Effect of sodium valproate on tardive dyskinesia. *British Journal of Psychiatry, 129,* 114–119.

Loebel, A. D., Lieberman, J. A., Alvir, J. M., Mayerhoff, D. I., Geisler, S. H., Szymanski, S. R. (1992). Duration of psychosis and outcome in first-episode schizophrenia. *American Journal of Psychiatry, 149,* 1183–1188.

Luby, E. D., Cohen, B. D., Rosenbaum, G., Gottlieb, J. S., & Kelly, R. (1959). Study of a new schizophreniomimetic drug: Sernyl. *American Medical Association Archives of Neurological Psychiatry, 81,* 363–369.

Marder, S. R., & Fenton, W. (2004). Measurement and Treatment Research to Improve Cognition in Schizophrenia: NIMH MATRICS initiative to support the development of agents for improving cognition in schizophrenia. *Schizophrenia Research, 72,* 5–9.

Marder, S. R., & Meibach, R. C. (1994). Risperidone in the treatment of schizophrenia. *American Journal of Psychiatry, 151,* 825–835.

Marder, S. R., Van Putten, T., Mintz, J., Lebell, M., McKenzie, J., & May, P. R. (1987). Low and conventional-dose maintenance therapy with fluphenazine decanoate: Two year outcome. *Archives of General Psychiatry, 44,* 518–521.

May, P. R., Tuma, A. H., Dixon, W. J., Yale, C., Thiele, D. A., & Kraude, W. H. (1981). Schizophrenia: A follow-up study of the results of five forms of treatment. *Archives of General Psychiatry, 38,* 776–784.

May, P. R., Tuma, A. H., Yale, C., Potepan, P., & Dixon, W. J. (1976): Schizophrenia: A follow-up study of results of treatment. *Archives of General Psychiatry, 33,* 481–486

McCreadie, R. G., & MacDonald, I. M. (1977). High dosage haloperidol in chronic schizophrenia. *British Journal of Psychiatry, 131,* 310–316.

McEvoy, J. P., Lieberman, J. A., Stroup, T. S., Davis, S. M., Meltzer, H. Y., Rosenheck, R. A., et al. (2006). Effectiveness of clozapine versus olanzapine, quetiapine, and risperidone in patients with chronic schizophrenia who did not respond to prior atypical antipsychotic treatment. *American Journal of Psychiatry, 163,* 600–610.

McGlashan, T. H., & Carpenter, W. T. (1976). Postpsychotic depression in schizophrenia. *Archives of General Psychiatry, 33,* 231–239.

Meltzer, H. Y. (1992). Treatment of the antipsychotic-nonresponsive schizophrenic patient. *Schizophrenia Bulletin, 18,* 515–541.

Meltzer, H Y., Alph, L., Green, A. I., Altamura, A. C., Anand, R., Bertoldi, A., et al. (2003). Clozapine treatment for suicidality in schizophrenia: International Suicide Prevention Trial (InterSePT). *Archives of General Psychiatry, 60,* 82–91.

Meltzer, H. Y., Burnett, S., Bastani, B., & Ramirez, L. F. (1990). Effects of six months of clozapine treatment on the quality of life of chronic schizophrenic patients. *Hospital and Community Psychiatry, 41,* 892–897.

Meltzer, H. Y., & McGurk, S. R. (1999). The effects of clozapine, risperidone, and olanzapine on cognitive function in schizophrenia. *Schizophrenia Bulletin, 25,* 233–255.

Meltzer, H. Y., Sdommers, A. A., & Luchins, D. J. (1986). The effect of antipsychotics and other psychotropic drugs on negative symptoms in schizophrenia. *Journal of Clinical Psychopharmacology, 6,* 329–338.

Miller, D. D., Perry, P. J., Cadoret, R., & Andreasen, N. C. (1992). A two and one-half year follow-up of treatment-refractory schizophrenics treated with clozapine. *Biological Psychiatry, 31*(Suppl.), 85A.

Mortimer, A. M. (1997). Cognitive function in schizophrenia: Do neuroleptics make a difference? *Pharmacology, Biochemistry and Behavior, 56,* 789–795.

Nachshoni, T., Levin, Y., Levy, A., Dritz, A., & Neumann, M. (1994). A double-blind trial of carbamazepine in negative symptom schizophrenia. *Society of Biological Psychiatry, 35,* 22–26.

National Institute of Mental Health–Psychopharmacology Service Center Collaborative Study Group. (1964). Phenothiazine treatment in acute schizophrenia. *Archives of General Psychiatry, 10,* 246–261.

Neborsky, R., Janowsky, D., Munson, E., & Depry, D. (1981). Rapid treatment of acute psychotic symptoms with high- and low-dose haloperidol: Behavioral considerations. *Archives of General Psychiatry, 38,* 195–199.

Neppe, V. M. (1983). Carbamazepine as adjunctive treatment in nonepileptic chronic inpatients with EEG temporal lobe abnormalities. *Journal of Clinical Psychiatry, 44,* 326–331.

Newcomer, J. W. (2005). Second-generation (atypical) antipsychotics and metabolic effects: a comprehensive literature review. *CNS Drugs, 19*(Suppl. 1), 1–93.

Okuma, T., Yamashita, I., Takahashi, R., Itoh, H., Otsuki S., Watanabe, S., et al. (1989). A double-blind study of adjunctive carbamazepine versus placebo on excited states of schizophrenic and schizoaffective disorders. *Acta Psychiatrica Scandinavica, 80,* 250–259.

Palmer, B. W., Heaton, R. K., Paulsen, J. S., Kuck, J., Braff, D., Harris, M. J., et al. (1997). Is it possible to be schizophrenic yet neuropsychologically normal? *Neuropsychology, 11,* 437–446.

Perovich, R. M., Lieberman J. A., Fleischhacker, W. W., & Alvir, J. (1989). The behavior toxicity of bromocriptine in patients with psychiatric illness. *Journal of Clinical Psychopharmacology, 9,* 417–422.

Peuskens, J. (1995). Risperidone in the treatment of patients with chronic schizophrenia: A multi-national, multi-centre, double-blind, parallel-group study versus haloperidol. *British Journal of Psychiatry, 166,* 712–726.

Peuskens, J., & Link, C. G. (1997). A comparison of quetiapine and chlorpromazine in the treatment of schizophrenia. *Acta Psychiatrica Scandinavica, 96,* 265–273.

Pickar, D., Owen, R. R., Litman, R E., Konicki, E., Gutierrez, R., & Rapaport, M. H. (1992). Clinical and biologic response to clozapine in patients with schizophrenia: Crossover comparison with fluphenazine. *Archives of General Psychiatry, 49,* 345–353.

Pigott, T. A., Carson, W. H., Saha, A. R., Torbeyns, A. F., Stock, E. G., Ingenito, G. G. (2003). Aripiprazole for the prevention of relapse in stabilized patients with chronic schizophrenia: A placebo-controlled 26-week study. *Journal of Clinical Psychiatry, 64,* 1048–1056.

Plasky, P. (1991). Antidepressant usage in schizophrenia. *Schizophrenia Bulletin, 17,* 649–657.

Potkin, S. G., Costa, J., Roy, S., Sramek, J., Jin, Y., & Gulasekaram, B. (1992). Glycine in the treatment of schizophrenia: Theory and preliminary results. In H. Y. Meltzer (Ed.), *Novel antipsychotic drugs.* New York: Raven Press.

Potkin, S. G., Jin, Y., Bunney, B. G., Costa, J., & Gulasekaram, B. (1999). Effect of clozapine and adjunctive high-dose glycine in treatment-resistant schizophrenia. *American Journal of Psychiatry, 156,* 145–147.

Potkin, S. G., Saha, A. R., Kujawa, M. J., Carson, W. H., Ali, M., Stock, E., et al. (2003). Aripiprazole, an antipsychotic with a novel mechanism of action, and risperidone vs placebo in patients with schizophrenia and schizoaffective disorder. *Archives of General Psychiatry, 60,* 681–690.

Quitkin, F., Rifkin, A., & Klein, D. F. (1975). Very high dosage vs standard dosage fluphenazine in schizophrenia: A double-blind study of nonchronic treatment-refractory patients. *Archives of General Psychiatry, 32,* 1276–1281.

Rabinowitz, J., Lichtenberg, P., Kaplan, Z., Mark, M., Nahon, D., & Davidson, M. (2001). Rehospitalization rates of chronically ill schizophrenic patients discharged on a regimen of risperidone, olanzapine, or conventional antipsychotics. *American Journal of Psychiatry, 158,* 266–269.

Remington, G., & Kapur, S. (2000). Atypical antipsychotics: Are some more atypical than others? *Psychopharmacology (Berlin), 148,* 3–15

Rifkin, A, (1993). Pharmacologic strategies in the treatment of schizophrenia. *Psychiatric Clinics of North America, 16,* 351–363.

Rifkin, A., Doddi, S., Karajgi, B., Borenstein, M., & Wachspress, M. (1991). Dosage of haloperidol for schizophrenia. *Archives of General Psychiatry, 48,* 166–170.

Robinson, D., Woerner, M. G., Alvir, J. M., Bilder, R., Goldman, R., Geisler, S., et al. (1999). Predictors of relapse following response from a first episode of schizophrenia or schizoaffective disorder. *Archives of General Psychiatry, 56,* 241–247.

Robinson, D. G., Woerner, M. G., Alvir, J. M., Geisler, S., Koreen, A., Sheitman, B., et al. (1999). Predictors of treatment response from a first episode of schizophrenia or schizoaffective disorder. *American Journal of Psychiatry, 156,* 544–549.

Rosenheck, R., Cramer, J., Xu, W., Thomas, J., Henderson, W., Frisman, L., et al. (1997). A comparison of clozapine and haloperidol in hospitalized patients with refractory schizophrenia. *New England Journal of Medicine, 337,* 809–815.

Rosse, R. B., Fay-McCarthy, M., Kendrick, K., Davis, R. E., & Deutsch, S. I. (1996). D-cycloserine adjuvant therapy to molindone in the treatment of schizophrenia. *Clinical Neuropharmacology, 19,* 444–450.

Rummel, C., Kissling, W., & Leucht, S. (2005). Antidepressants as add-on treatment to antipsychotics for people with schizophrenia and pronounced negative symptoms: A systematic review of randomized trials. *Schizophrenia Research, 80,* 85–97.

Salzman, C. (1980). The use of ECT in the treatment of schizophrenia. *American Journal of Psychiatry, 137,* 1032–1041.

Salzman, C., Solomon, D., Miyawaki, E., Glassman, R., Rood, L., Flowers, E., et al. (1991). Parenteral lorazepam versus parenteral haloperidol for the control of psychotic disruptive behavior. *Journal of Clinical Psychiatry, 52,* 177–180.

Schexnayder, L. W., Hirschowitz, J., Sautter, F. J., & Garver, D. L. (1995). Predictors of response to lithium in patients with psychoses. *American Journal of Psychiatry, 152,* 1511–1513.

Schooler, N. R., Goldberg, S. C., Boothe, H., & Cole, J. O. (1967). One year after discharge: Community adjustment of schizophrenic patients. *American Journal of Psychiatry, 123,* 986–995.

Schooler, N. R., Keith, S. J., Severe, J. B., & Mathews, S. M. (1993). Treatment strategies in schizophrenia: Effects of dosage reduction and family management outcome [Abstract]. *Schizophrenia Research, 9,* 260.

Schooler, N., Rabinowitz, J., Davidson, M., Emsley, R., Harvey, P. D., Kopala, L., et al. (2005). Risperidone and haloperidol in first-episode psychosis: A long-term randomized trial. *American Journal of Psychiatry, 162,* 947–953.

Schulz, S. C., Thompson, P. A., Jacobs, M., Ninan, P. T., Robinson, D., Weiden, P. J., et al. (1999). Lithium augmentation fails to reduce symptoms in poorly responsive schizophrenic outpatients. *Journal of Clinical Psychiatry, 60,* 366–372.

Sherwood, M., Thornton, A. E., & Honer, W. G. (2006). A meta-analysis of profile and time-course of symptom change in acute schizophrenia treated with atypical antipsychotics. *International Journal of Neuropsychopharmacology, 9,* 357–366.

Shopsin, B., Klein, H., Aaronsom, M., & Collora, M. (1979). Clozapine, chlorpromazine, and placebo in newly hospitalized, acutely schizophrenic patients: A controlled, double-blind comparison. *Archives of General Psychiatry, 36,* 657–664.

Silver, H., Barash, I., Aharon, N., Kaplan, A., & Poyurovsky, M. (2000). Fluvoxamine augmentation of antipsychotics improves negative symptoms in psychotic chronic schizophrenic patients: A placebo-controlled study. *International Clinical Psychopharmacology, 15,* 257–261.

Silver, H., & Nassar, A. (1992). Fluvoxamine improves negative symptoms in treated chronic schizophrenia: An add-on double-blind, placebo-controlled study. *Biological Psychiatry, 31,* 698–704.

Simpson, G. M., Glick, I. D., Weiden, P. J., Romano, S. J., & Siu, C. O. (2004). Randomized, controlled, double-blind multicenter comparison of the efficacy and tolerability of ziprasidone and olanzapine in acutely ill inpatients with schizophrenia or schizoaffective disorder. *American Journal of Psychiatry, 161,* 1837–1847.

Simpson, G. M., Weiden, P., Pigott, T., Murray, S., Siu, C O., & Romano, S. J. (2005). Six-month, blinded, multicenter continuation study of ziprasidone versus olanzapine in schizophrenia. *American Journal of Psychiatry, 162,* 1535–1538.

Siris, S. (1993). Adjunctive medication in the maintenance treatment of schizophrenia and its conceptual implications. *British Journal of Psychiatry, 163,* 66–78.

Siris, S. G. (1991). Diagnosis of secondary depression in schizophrenia: Implications for *DSM-IV. Schizophrenia Bulletin, 17,* 75–97.

Siris, S. G., Adam, F., Cohen, M., Mandeli, J., Aronson, A., & Casey, E. (1988). Postpsychotic depression and negative symptoms: An investigation of syndrome overlap. *American Journal of Psychiatry, 145,* 1532–1537.

Siris, S. G., Bermanzohn, P. C., Gonzalez, A., Mason, S. E., White, C. V., Shuwall, M. A. (1991). The use of antidepressants for negative symptoms in a subset of schizophrenic patients. *Psychopharmacology Bulletin, 27,* 331–335.

Siris, S. G., Bermanzohn, P. C., Mason, S. E., & Shuwall, M. A. (1994). Maintenance imipramine therapy for secondary depression in schizophrenia. *Archives of General Psychiatry, 51,* 109–115.

Siris, S., Pollack, S., Bermanzohn, P., & Stronger, R. (2000). Adjunctive imipramine for a broader group of post-psychotic depressions in schizophrenia. *Schizophrenia Research, 44,* 187–192.

Siris, S. G., Van Kammen, D. P., & Docherty, J. P. (1978). Use of antidepressant drugs in schizophrenia. *Archives of General Psychiatry, 35,* 1368–1377.

Small, J. G., Hirsch, S. R., Arvanitis, L. A., Miller, B. G., & Link, C. G. (1997). Quetiapine in patients with schizophrenia: A high- and low-dose double-blind comparison with placebo. Seroquel Study Group. *Archives of General Psychiatry, 54,* 549–557.

Small, J. G., Kellams, J. J., Milstein, V., & Moore, J. (1975). A placebo-controlled study of lithium combined with antipsychotics in chronic schizophrenic patients. *American Journal of Psychiatry, 132,* 1315–1317.

Small, J. G., Klapper, M. H., Malloy, F. W., & Steadman, T. M. (2003). Tolerability and efficacy of clozapine combined with lithium in schizophrenia and schizoaffective disorder. *Journal of Clinical Psychopharmacology, 23,* 223–228.

Stroup, T. S., Lieberman, J. A., McEvoy, J. P., Swartz, M. S., Davis, S. M., Rosenheck, R. A., et al. (2006). Effectiveness of olanzapine, quetiapine, risperidone, and ziprasidone in patients with chronic schizophrenia following discontinuation of a previous atypical antipsychotic. *American Journal of Psychiatry, 163,* 611–622.

Stroup, T. S., McEvoy, J. P., Swartz, M. S., Byerly, M. J., Glick, I. D., Canive, J. M., et al. (2003). The National Institute of Mental Health Clinical Antipsychotic Trials of Intervention Effectiveness (CATIE) project: Schizophrenia trial design and protocol development. *Schizophrenia Bulletin, 29,* 15–31.

Tandon, R. (2004). Quetiapine has a direct effect on the negative symptoms of schizophrenia. *Human Psychopharmacology, 19,* 559–563.

Taylor, P., & Fleminger, J. J. (1980). ECT for schizophrenia. *Lancet, 1,* 1380–1382.

Terao, T., Oga, T., Nozaki, S., Ohta, A., Ohtsubo, Y., Yamamoto, S., et al. (1995). Lithium addition to antipsychotic treatment in chronic schizophrenia: A randomized, double-blind, placebo-controlled, cross-over study. *Acta Psychiatrica Scandinavica, 92,* 220–224.

Tharyan, P., & Adams, C. E. (2005). Electroconvulsive therapy for schizophrenia. *Cochrane Database of Systematic Reviews, 2,* CD000076.

Tollefson, G. D., Beasley, C. M., Jr., Tran, P. V., Street, J. S., Krueger, J. A., Tamura, R. N., et al. (1997). Olanzapine versus haloperidol in the treatment of schizophrenia and schizoaffective and schizophreniform disorders: Results of an international collaborative trial. *American Journal of Psychiatry, 154,* 457–465.

Tran, P. V., Dellva, M. A., Tollefson, G. D., Wentley, A. L., & Beasley, C. M., Jr. (1998). Oral olanzapine versus oral haloperidol in the maintenance treatment of schizophrenia and related psychoses. *British Journal of Psychiatry, 172,* 499–505.

Tsai, G., Lane, H. Y., Yang, P., Chong, M. Y., & Lange, N. (2004). Glycine transporter I inhibitor, N-methylglycine (sarcosine), added to antipsychotics for the treatment of schizophrenia. *Biological Psychiatry, 55,* 452–456.

Tsai, G., Yang, P., Chung, L. C., Lange, N., & Coyle, J. T. (1998). D-serine added to antipsychotics for the treatment of schizophrenia. *Biological Psychiatry, 44,* 1081–1089.

Tsai, G. E., Yang, P., Chung, L. C., Tsai, I. C., Tsai, C. W., & Coyle, J. T. (1999). D-serine added to clozapine for the treatment of schizophrenia. *American Journal of Psychiatry, 156,* 1822–1825.

Van Putten, T., Marder, S. R., & Mintz, J. (1990). A controlled dose comparison of haloperidol in newly admitted schizophrenic patients. *Archives of General Psychiatry, 47,* 754–758.

Velligan, D. I., & Miller, A. L. (1999). Cognitive dysfunction in schizophrenia and its importance to outcome: The place of atypical antipsychotics in treatment. *Journal of Clinical Psychiatry, 60*(Suppl. 23), 25–28.

Volavka, J., Cooper, T., Czobor, P., Bitter, I., Meisner, M., Laska, E., et al. (1992). Haloperidol blood levels and clinical effects. *Archives of General Psychiatry, 49,* 354–361.

Volavka, J., Czobor, P., Sheitman, B., Lindenmayer, J. P., Citrome, L., McEvoy, J. P., et al. (2002). Clozapine, olanzapine, risperidone, and haloperidol in the treatment of patients with chronic schizophrenia and schizoaffective disorder. *American Journal of Psychiatry, 159,* 255–262.

Wahlbeck, K., Cheine, M., & Essali, M. A. (2000). Clozapine versus typical neuroleptic medication for schizophrenia. *Cochrane Database of Systematic Reviews, 2,* CD000059.

Wassef, A. A., Dott, S. G., Harris, A., Brown, A., O'Boyle, M., Meyer, W. J., et al. (2000). Randomized, placebo-controlled pilot study of divalproex sodium in the treatment of acute exacerbations of chronic schizophrenia. *Journal of Clinical Psychopharmacology, 20,* 357–361.

Wilson, W. H. (1993). Addition of lithium to haloperidol in non-affective, antipsychotic non-responsive schizophrenia: A double-blind, placebo controlled, parallel design clinical trial. *Psychopharmacology, 111,* 359–366.

Wirshing, D. A., Marshall, B. D., Jr., Green, M. F., Mintz, J., Marder, S. R., Wirshing, W. C. (1999). Risperidone in treatment-refractory schizophrenia. *American Journal of Psychiatry, 156,* 1374–1379.

Wolkowitz, O. M. (1993). Rational polypharmacy in schizophrenia. *Annals of Clinical Psychiatry, 5,* 79–90.

Wolkowitz, O. M., & Pickar, D. (1991). Benzodiazepines in the treatment of schizophrenia: A review and reappraisal. *American Journal of Psychiatry, 148,* 714–726.

Wyatt, R. J. (1995). Early intervention for schizophrenia: Can the course of the illness be altered? *Biological Psychiatry, 38,* 1–3.

Yagcioglu, A. E., Kivircik Akdede, B. B., Turgut, T. I., Tumuklu, M., Yazici, M. K., Alptekin, K., et al. (2005). A double-blind controlled study of adjunctive treatment with risperidone in schizophrenic patients partially responsive to clozapine: Efficacy and safety. *Journal of Clinical Psychiatry, 66,* 63–72.

8

Psychosocial Treatments
for Schizophrenia

Alex Kopelowicz
Robert Paul Liberman
Roberto Zarate

Data from hundreds of intervention research studies validate a biopsychosocial view of treatment for schizophrenia that combines pharmacotherapy with psychosocial treatments and social support. Based on the stress-vulnerability-protective factors model, these treatments work by strengthening biological, personal, and environmental factors that protect against relapse while mitigating the stressors that adversely affect the course of schizophrenia. Psychiatric treatment and rehabilitation must be integrated in a seamless approach aimed at restoring persons with schizophrenia to their best possible level of functioning and quality of life.

The Schizophrenia PORT recommendations (Lehman et al., 2004) highlight six evidence-based, psychosocial treatments for schizophrenia. *Skills training* enables persons with schizophrenia to acquire instrumental and affiliative skills to improve community functioning. Structured, educational *family interventions* lead to reduced rates of relapse and hospital admissions while decreasing family burden and improving patient-family interactions. *Supported employment* approaches increase the likelihood that persons with schizophrenia will obtain and maintain competitive employment. *Cognitive behavioral psychotherapy* has been shown to reduce the severity of symptoms, including delusions, hallucinations, negative symptoms, and depression. *Behavior modification and social learning/token economy* programs structure, support, and reinforce prosocial behaviors in persons with schizophrenia. These empirically validated, biobehavioral treatments are most efficacious when delivered in a continuous, comprehensive, and well-coordinated manner within a service delivery system such as *assertive community treatment.*

OVERVIEW OF SCHIZOPHRENIA

Diagnosis

Schizophrenia, the most disabling of the major mental disorders, requires two or more of the following: (a) delusions, (b) hallucinations, (c) disorganized speech, (d) grossly disorganized or catatonic behavior, and (e) negative symptoms. These symptoms must impair social and occupational functioning and be continuously present for at least 6 months. Because other disorders, some with known etiologies, can mimic schizophrenia, before making the diagnosis it is necessary to exclude psychoses resulting from substance abuse, medical conditions that affect the brain (e.g., tumors, Cushing's disease), pervasive developmental disorders, and mood disorders (e.g., bipolar disorder or psychotic depression). In this chapter reviewing the psychological and behavioral treatments for schizophrenia, we shall include schizoaffective disorder with schizophrenia, since the two have very similar clinical features, prognoses, and responses to treatments. Because schizophrenia spectrum disorders are almost always treated with antipsychotic drugs, an evaluation and interpretation of the literature on psychological and behavioral treatments must view the treatments as biobehavioral, that is, multidimensional therapies with pharmacological and psychosocial components.

Etiology and Course of Illness

Although there is no definitive evidence identifying one or more causal factors in the etiology of schizophrenia, most authorities would view the extraordinary heterogeneity in psychopathology, psychosocial functioning, course of illness, and treatment response in this disorder as indicating that our current ignorance of central nervous system functioning masks the likelihood of more than one etiology in what we see as the final common pathway of psychosis. There are sufficient data from family and adoptive studies to suggest that complex, multigenetic factors may account for a significant proportion of the etiology of schizophrenia and that schizotypal personality traits may be the genetically determined phenotype (Siever & Davis, 2004). Furthermore, recent findings in molecular genetic studies suggest a link between an array of specific genes and schizophrenia (Badner & Gershon, 2002; Mowry & Nancarrow, 2001; Walker, Kestler, Bollini, & Hochman, 2004). Strong evidence also supports the role of socioenvironmental factors in influencing the course of the disorder. In particular, early identification and diagnosis followed by appropriate and continuous biopsychosocial treatment have been shown to improve the long-term outcome of persons with schizophrenia (Wyatt & Henter, 2001).

The onset of schizophrenia typically occurs during late adolescence and early adulthood; childhood-onset cases represent a tiny minority. The disorder affects males and females equally, but males are disproportionately represented in treatment facilities, presumably because their illness-linked disruptive behavior and functioning become more visible and intolerable to families and society. The mean onset of the disorder is about 5 years later for females (late 20s) than for males (early 20s; Riecher-Rossler & Hafner, 2000), most likely because female hormones serve a protective function against abnormalities in neurotransmitter systems (Stevens, 2002).

The long-term course of the disorder can be divided into three groupings, although accessibility to and use of comprehensive, high-quality, and continuous treatment will increase the proportion of persons with schizophrenia who have better outcomes, regardless of the level of functioning at which they begin their treatment odyssey. One type of course is marked by one or more psychotic episodes with relatively rapid return to premorbid functioning and good prospects for recovery. The second and most common course is characterized by many years of recurrent acute psychotic relapses or exacerbations, with periods of full or partial remission and varying degrees of residual impairments in functioning. A final group of about 15% of individuals with schizophrenia fails to respond to currently available treatments and demonstrate the third form of the disorder, with prolonged and persistent psychotic symptoms with moderate to severe personal and social disabilities. The proportion of individuals with treatment-refractory schizophrenia is gradually diminishing with the advent of novel, atypical antipsychotic drugs such as clozapine.

Evidence from several countries documents that more than 50% of individuals with well-diagnosed and severe forms of schizophrenia can achieve good states of remission and psychosocial functioning 20 to 30 years after their initial periods of illness (Harding, Zubin, & Strauss, 1992). A key element in recovery requires the patient and practitioner(s) to forge an informed partnership, in which the patient is not a passive recipient of treatment but is an active participant in managing symptoms, preventing or containing relapses, and pursuing long-term social, personal, and occupational goals with abundant social support and training of skills (Kopelowicz & Liberman, 2003).

Consensus among authorities in the field supports an explanatory and heuristic model of the etiology, course, and outcome of schizophrenia that incorporates *vulnerability, stress, and protective factors* (Nuechterlein et al., 1994). Vulnerability factors (e.g., genes, aberrant development of brain neural networks and neurotransmitter systems) are relatively enduring abnormalities of individuals at risk for schizophrenia that are present before, during, and after psychotic episodes. Stressors include role expectations, daily hassles, and major life events that demand adaptive changes from the individual, challenge the individual's coping abilities, and sometimes serve as triggers for psychotic episodes (e.g., drugs of abuse, high stress in the patient's living environment, major life events, and even toxic side effects of antipsychotic medications). Personal and environmental protective factors (e.g., social skills, supportive family, judicious use of antipsychotic medication embedded in comprehensive and continuous treatment services) allow a vulnerable individual to buffer the deleterious effects of stressors superimposed on vulnerability and avoid or mitigate relapse (Ventura & Liberman, 2000).

Prevalence and Cost

Based on epidemiological studies, almost 3 million persons in the United States are afflicted with schizophrenia or schizoaffective disorder, representing 1.1% of the population (Narrow, Rae, Robins, Lee, & Regier, 2002). There are more than 300,000 acute episodes in schizophrenia patients annually in the United States, and the overall economic cost of this disorder to the nation, in terms of care and lost income, has been estimated as being more than $62 billion per year (Wu et al., 2005). An estimated 100,000 hospital beds on any given day are occupied by persons with schizophrenia (Rupp & Keith, 1993). Approximately 15% of the homeless population in the United States suffers from schizophrenia, and many of these individuals also have a substance abuse disorder (Folsom & Jeste, 2002).

The direct economic cost of this disorder (e.g., long-term care, outpatient services, acute hospital care, and prescription drugs) has been calculated at $39 billion per year (McCombs et al., 2000). In addition, indirect costs, such as the loss of income for a male diagnosed as having schizophrenia late in adolescence, have been calculated to be $1.25 million per person (Wyatt, Henter, Leary, & Taylor, 1995). Another indirect cost to society comes from the involvement of the law enforcement and correctional systems in providing crisis intervention and long-term institutionalization for persons with schizophrenia who commit criminal offenses. The lifetime prevalence of schizophrenia among prisoners in correctional facilities is 6.2% (Regier et al., 1990). In California, it costs more than $25,000 per year to maintain each of its 25,000 mentally ill prisoners with only custodial services (Lamb & Weinberger, 1998). State psychiatric hospitals can spend more than $125,000 per year on services for a person with schizophrenia (Rothbard, Kuno, Schinnar, Hadley, & Turk, 1999).

Historical Perspective and Scope of Literature

Former students of B. F. Skinner who obtained positions in psychiatric hospitals were the first to conduct empirical studies of psychological and behavioral treatments for schizophrenia in the late 1950s and early 1960s. Lindsley and colleagues published single-case, controlled studies and laboratory analogues of treatment, showing that environmental antecedents and consequences could powerfully influence psychotic behaviors (Liberman, 1976). These investigators also documented that presentation of reinforcement produced increases in desirable, adaptive behavior on which the reinforcement was contingent, and withdrawal of reinforcement produced decreases. By the mid-1960s, Ayllon and Azrin (1965) had established the first token economy, the application of reinforcement principles to an entire ward system of patients. Within 15 years, behavior modification was creatively and successfully employed to bring about reliable and sustainable improvements with mute and withdrawn psychotic patients, self-stimulating, self-injurious, and echolalic autistic children, and chronic mental patients with bizarre behaviors (Ullman & Krasner, 1975).

The original studies were carried out with "hopeless" and treatment-refractory patients who had failed to respond to antipsychotic medications. The back wards of psychiatric hospitals were hospitable to the pioneers in behavior modification of schizophrenia, where resistance was not as strong as in treatment settings where clinicians clung to more traditional, psychodynamic therapies. From 1968 to 1975, there was an exponential increase in publications devoted to the token economy and other behavior modification approaches to individuals with chronic forms of schizophrenia (Liberman, 1976). Behavioral approaches were conducive to the growing scientific norm in psychiatry, fertilized by the empiricism of psychopharmacology. Adherents of both behavior modification and psychopharmacology relied on empiricism to document the value of their interventions; in addition, for patients who did not respond optimally to psychopharmacology, behavior therapy offered both effective symptomatic and rehabilitative treatments. These were Type 3 studies (using the criteria of this book), pinpointing, measuring, and modifying specific, molecular, and aberrant behaviors and utilizing A-B or case control designs. They were heuristic, however, in stimulating further work that would become more rigorous and methodologically substantial.

In the early 1970s, the second generation of behaviorally oriented clinicians and researchers began to publish the results of their work with persons having schizophrenia (Fichter, Wallace, & Liberman, 1976; Liberman, King, & DeRisi, 1976; Liberman, Teigen, Patterson, & Baker, 1973; Paul & Lentz, 1977). These second-generation studies focused more on strengthening prosocial behaviors rather than eliminating or weakening bizarre behaviors. Some of the most disastrous effects of long-term institutionalization of persons with schizophrenia were the constriction of interpersonal behavior and withdrawal from social interaction. The "good" patient in a custodial setting was quiet and unobtrusive. Enhancing the social repertoires of such patients was vital to their becoming capable of leaving the hospital and adjusting to life in the community. Competence in carrying on conversations, asking for directions, obtaining necessities, and, in general, navigating the social pathways was a prerequisite for successful reentry and tenure in the community. The investigators who carried out the studies of the 1970s also recognized the limitations of generalization of treatment when the latter was conducted solely in hospitals without planning for the "transfer of training" into the community (Liberman, McCann, & Wallace, 1976).

Over the past 25 years, the literature on the behavioral or psychosocial treatment and rehabilitation of persons with schizophrenia has continued to expand, appearing in literally hundreds of journals devoted to psychiatry, clinical psychology, behavior therapy, and psychosocial and vocational rehabilitation, as well as journals dedicated to this disorder (e.g., *Schizophrenia Bulletin, Schizophrenia Research*). Books devoted to psychosocial treatment of schizophrenia could fill a moderate-sized library. Rather than aim for an exhaustive review of the entire literature of the past decade, which would be an undertaking well beyond the scope of this chapter, we have drawn from the most recently published Schizophrenia Patient Outcomes Research Team (PORT) recommendations (Lehman et al., 2004). These recommendations were derived from an ongoing, federally funded project designed to evaluate and improve the quality of care for persons with schizophrenia based on the principles of evidence-based medicine.

The 2004 PORT recommendations, which are based on a comprehensive review of experimental treatment outcomes literature on schizophrenia published through the end of 2002, have become a well-recognized benchmark for evaluating patterns of treatment practices and quality of care, as well as the model for the dissemination of "tool kits" designed to facilitate the provision of evidence-based treatments by community-based mental health practitioners (Drake, Goldman, et al., 2001). Moreover, the summary recommendations of PORT are congruent with the most recent Practice Guidelines for the Treatment of Schizophrenia, developed through literature reviews and expert consensus by the American Psychiatric Association (2004).

STATUS OF TREATMENTS

Introduction

The prevailing stress–vulnerability–protective factors model of schizophrenia helps the clinician to understand the etiology, course, and treatment of this chronic disorder. Stressors, such as major life events and high expressed emotion in family and residential settings, can adversely affect the course of the disorder in vulnerable individuals who lack the protection of medication, psychosocial treatment, social support, and natural coping ability (Liberman, Kopelowicz, & Silverstein, 2004). For veteran practitioners who consider only biological treatments as useful in preventing relapse and disability, this chapter and the evidence that supports the protective value of psychosocial treatments (Lehman et al., 2004) may serve as an antidote to the biological reductionism that often characterizes schizophrenia research and treatment.

On the other hand, it is essential to view treatments of schizophrenia as always occurring within a matrix that includes interventions that interact with one another at the pharmacological, behavioral, and environmental support levels. The quality, consistency, accessibility, continuity, and comprehensiveness of services will inevitably affect the outcome as measured by symptoms, relapse, social functioning, attainment of personal goals, and subjective satisfaction with life. Inadequate or excessive drug treatment attenuates the benefits of behavioral interventions; lack of available encouragement and reinforcement in one's social support system mitigates the effects of skills training and adherence to medication.

Treatments of schizophrenia also tend to be *outcome specific*; that is, pharmacotherapy predominantly improves symptoms and delays relapse, skills training has its main impact on social functioning, family interventions focus on improving the emotional climate of the home and reducing the burden and stress of the illness experienced by the patient and relative alike, and assertive community treatment reduces time in the hospital and improves stability of housing. Careful orchestration of pharmacotherapy with psychosocial treatments and community support services within the matrix of an effective means of flexibly delivering all interventions, as required by changing individual needs, can significantly improve the course and outcome of the disorder, as well as promote recovery in a substantial number of persons (Kopelowicz & Liberman, 2003).

The PORT recommendations (Lehman et al., 2004) identified six psychosocial interventions as evidence-based practices for individuals with schizophrenia. These practices are *skills training, family interventions, supported employment, cognitive behavior therapy, token economy*, and *assertive community treatment*. Two other, more recent evidence-based treatments that were not included in the PORT guidelines, *integrated dual diagnosis treatment* and *cognitive rehabilitation*, will also be discussed in this chapter. To rate the evidence that supports each of these treatments, we use a multilevel, multidimensional set of criteria. Although few studies incorporate such an approach, the field is moving toward an appreciation of the value of a comprehensive assessment of outcome, measuring changes in (a) psychopathology (symptoms, bizarre and intolerable behaviors, and relapse rates); (b) social and instrumental role functioning (deficits in activities of community living, social competence and social adjustment); (c) illness self-management (including medication adherence, avoiding drugs of abuse, identifying prodromal signs of relapse, and coping with persistent symptoms); (d) care burden (of the disorder on the family or other caregivers in daily contact with the patient); and (e) subjective quality of life in areas of

finances, medical and psychiatric care, recreational and social activities, family life, spiritual life, work or school, and overall perceived quality of life.

A multidimensional approach to the evaluation of outcome for persons with severe and disabling mental disorders is "much easier said than done" and is plagued with methodological complications. For example, multiple employment measures may be required in studying vocational rehabilitation to properly capture the degree of independent and instrumental role functioning in a job (sheltered vs. volunteer vs. transitional vs. supported vs. competitive) and the duration, mobility, salary level, and satisfaction of the consumer and employer with the job performed (Bond & Boyer, 1988).

At the same time, multiple measures offer advantages in assessing the comprehensiveness of the construct of social skills (Liberman, 1982). The efficacy of supported education or supported employment services may be reflected by changes in self-concept and subsequent vocational attainment, as well as educational accomplishments. Because schizophrenia is a lifelong disorder requiring lifelong services, it is not possible in a time-limited study to identify longitudinal outcomes that may be sequentially linked to a particular treatment. For instance, improvement in social skills at Time A may not have evident impact on the individual's social and community functioning at Time B because opportunities, encouragement, and reinforcement for using the learned skills may emerge in the person's environment only at Time C, many months or years after the study assessment has been completed.

Another challenge to the use of a multidimensional approach for measuring change brought by behavioral and psychosocial treatments is the issue of social validity. For example, because assessment measures do not typically include ethnically based response sets, differences in language, linguistic nuances, and translation of items from standardized assessments may create aberrant response patterns (Sue & Sue, 1987). Certain goals for minority clients may not be isomorphic with the rehabilitation goals of the majority population; for example, independent living status may have less relevance to clients from poverty backgrounds (who cannot afford independent housing) or from backgrounds with extended kin networks and coresidence traditions (Cook, 1995). Of course, this is not just a problem of assessment. Rehabilitation services delivered to ethnic minorities by practitioners who do not fully understand or positively relate to the client because of ethnic or cultural differences can lead to suboptimal outcomes (Sue, Fujino, Hu, Takeuchi, & Zane, 1991).

In addition to the importance of a multidimensional approach to evaluating the efficacy of treatments, it is also desirable to ensure that a particular treatment is, in fact, appropriate for the phase or stage of an individual's disorder. For example, higher doses of antipsychotic medication may be required for the acute, florid phase of illness, but lower doses usually provide a higher benefit-risk ratio for those in the maintenance or recovery phases. Similarly, although social skills training is utilitarian and of tangible benefit to persons in the reconstituting, maintenance, and recovery phases, patients in the acute psychotic stage of schizophrenia may have a diminished capacity to learn social skills — their distractibility and overarousal may, in fact, be adversely affected by the demands of a classroom-type learning environment. The multidimensional approach to treatment evaluation is depicted in Figure 8.1.

It is also necessary to place modalities of treatment — whether pharmacological or psychosocial — in the context of a system of mental health care delivery. The treatments must be coordinated, comprehensive, continuous, and integrated; therefore, a single practitioner in an office practice can treat very few persons with schizophrenia adequately. Instead, the pervasive deficits and requirements for linkage to multiple human service agencies require a team approach. The various modalities that have been documented to be efficacious in schizophrenia need to be organized, financed, and delivered by an agency or group of mental health practitioners that serves as a fixed point of responsibility. To ensure that the reader grasps the importance of an integrative approach to the treatment of schizophrenia, in which specific treatment modalities (as shown along the horizontal axis in Figure 8.1) are embedded in a service delivery system, the ratings of relatively well demarcated modalities will be followed by a section on the system of mental health delivery, focusing on models of agency-based treatment teams and case management.

Most available treatment research literature is about "efficacy," not "effectiveness." Efficacy is evaluated in highly controlled, clinical research studies conducted in specialized research settings, using highly selected subjects, supervised by academic personnel, and often working with the aid of grant support. There are precious few studies of effectiveness, where practitioners who may or may not demonstrate fidelity to the treatment parameters are carrying out the treatments under evaluation with the full range of patients in ordinary clinical service systems. Effectiveness is evaluated in mental health services research where the use of carefully diagnosed populations and inflexible treatment manuals derived from clinical research is not always possible or desirable (Fensterheim & Raw, 1996). A final stage in the validation of a modality lies in its effective dissemination from a host site or from academically engineered studies to a wide adoption by a broad range of mental health programs. Mental health services research is only in its infancy; thus, we shall be rating treatments primarily in terms of their documented efficacy, not effectiveness. When effectiveness evidence is available, we shall document it in our ratings.

Therapeutic Relationship and Supportive Therapy

Although not included as a separate entity in the PORT guidelines, the supportive qualities inherent in treatment relationships (e.g., with prescribing psychiatrist, nursing staff on an inpatient unit, case manager) are considered a necessary albeit not sufficient basis for therapeutic change (Frank & Gunderson, 1990). In the past few decades, individual and group therapies for persons with schizophrenia have evolved from being informed by psychoanalytic theories and techniques to being inseminated by more supportive, collaborative, educational, practical, and active qualities. The qualities of the therapeutic alliance that are deemed facilitative of improvement, even if the specific modality is termed "supportive therapy," are characterized by the following:

- a positive therapeutic relationship;
- a focus on reality issues, solving problems in everyday life, and practical advice;
- an active, directive, and educational role by the therapist, who uses his own life experiences and self-disclosure as a role model for the patient;
- encouragement and education of the patient and family for proper use of antipsychotic medication.

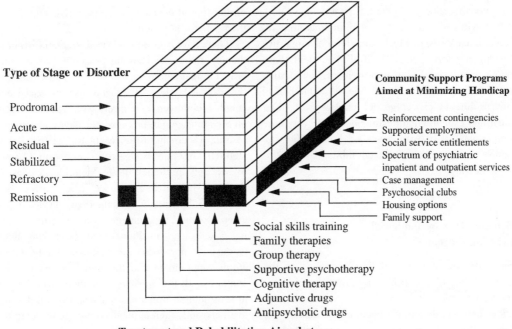

Type of Stage or Disorder

Prodromal

Acute

Residual

Stabilized

Refractory

Remission

Community Support Programs Aimed at Minimizing Handicap

Reinforcement contingencies
Supported employment
Social service entitlements
Spectrum of psychiatric
inpatient and outpatient services
Case management
Psychosocial clubs
Housing options
Family support

Social skills training
Family therapies
Group therapy
Supportive psychotherapy
Cognitive therapy
Adjunctive drugs
Antipsychotic drugs

**Treatment and Rehabilitation Aimed at
Reducing Impairments and Disabilities**

FIGURE 8.1 The complex cube of psychiatric rehabilitation reflects the three major dimensions of treatment planning and implementation. The specific modalities of assessment and intervention are displayed along the horizontal axis and keyed to the phase or stage of the individual's disorder. Whatever the array of specific treatment modalities indicated for an individual, a treatment delivery system and social support program (e.g., housing, case management, entitlements, and benefits) must be available if the treatments are to make an impact. In the graphic shown, an individual with schizophrenia that is in clinical remission is receiving maintenance antipsychotic medication, supportive psychotherapy (e.g., from his or her case manager), family intervention, and social skills training. A large number of social support services are concurrently being provided to this individual, as shown in the axis moving into the background of the figure.

Although supportive forms of individual therapy have been broadly applied by practitioners in the course of delivering pharmacotherapy or more specific psychosocial services to persons with schizophrenia, only three Type 1 studies attest to its efficacy (Penn et al., 2004). All these studies were well controlled with random assignment and comparison treatments. However, the evidence for the efficacy of supportive individual therapy was ambiguous, and in one of the studies, extraordinarily high attrition limits the generalizability of the findings. In one study, individual supportive therapy led to worse outcomes at the 6-month point, but for those who survived past the first year and continued in supportive therapy, their relapse rates and social functioning were significantly better at the 2-year follow-up point (Hogarty, Goldberg, & Schooler, 1974). In a second

study, reality-adapted supportive therapy was no better than exploratory insight-oriented therapy on most measures, but it did result in reduced rates of rehospitalization and improved role functioning (Gunderson et al., 1984). A third study found that a phase-specific individual therapy targeted to enhancing personal and social adjustment and forestalling relapse was efficacious for patients who were living with their families, but not with patients who were living alone (Hogarty et al., 1997).

Supportive group therapy is also widely used, especially with outpatients. The same principles of supportive therapy are used in these groups, which may vary in emphasis from medication education to setting realistic goals, encouraging coping efforts, and socialization. Six Type 2 empirical trials of supportive group therapy have been reported; most found this modality superior to control treatments (Malm, 1982). Moreover, the results of numerous randomized clinical trials, in which some form of supportive therapy has served as a "control" treatment, have documented significant improvements by participants in that condition. Given the inevitable bias of investigators to expect greater efficacy with their cherished experimental treatments, it is all the more impressive that so many so-called nonspecific supportive services have produced substantial benefits for their subjects.

Behavior Therapy and Social Learning Programs

Since the initial empirical demonstrations in the 1960s of the utility of behavioral principles of learning for persons with schizophrenia (Ayllon & Azrin, 1968), behavior therapy has been used to manage the full spectrum of symptoms, deficits, and disturbing behaviors found in this disorder (Brenner, Hodel, & Roder, 1990; Kazdin, 1982; Wong, Massel, Mosk, & Liberman, 1986). The majority of the hundreds of Type 3 empirical studies documenting the efficacy of reinforcement schedules, stimulus control, social modeling, shaping, and fading have used subjects longitudinally as their own controls. These simple case designs (e.g., ABAB) have featured baseline periods followed by intervention, withdrawal of intervention, and return to intervention, as well as multiple baseline designs where each of three or four subjects have differing durations on baseline conditions before receiving the intervention.

These experimental designs lack the generalizability of randomized clinical trials with groups of subjects receiving different treatments, but they do possess one methodological advantage, namely, capitalizing on and controlling for the vast interindividual differences in schizophrenia. Even when findings from large randomized controlled trials yield statistically significant differences between means, such designs are not necessarily informative for the individual patient in treatment who needs a type and "dose" of psychosocial treatment relevant to his or her personal goals, assets, deficits, and stage of disorder. Studies that use subjects as their own controls permit "fine-tuning" the intervention until it shows clear-cut effects. Such studies resonate with clinicians who apply and adjust their therapeutic interventions based

on the special characteristics and serial responses of their patients to various treatments.

There have been seven Type 1 studies of behavior therapy and social learning programs (token economy) for treatment-refractory patients participating in hospital or day hospital programs where social and tangible reinforcers were given to patients contingent on their engaging in prosocial behavior and activities (Austin, Liberman, King, & DeRisi, 1976; Baker, Hall, Hutchison, & Bridge, 1977; Fullerton, Cayner, & McLaughlin-Reidel, 1978; Menditto, Valdes, & Beck, 1994; Paul & Lentz, 1977; Schwartz & Bellack, 1975; Spiegler & Agigian, 1976). Typically, the token economy, supplemented with structured learning of self-care, recreational, and social skills, helps to organize and focus the staff-patient interactions around appropriate and functional behaviors. This contrasts with the inevitable attention given by staff in unstructured milieus to maladaptive and destructive behaviors, thereby inadvertently reinforcing the very problems that brought the patient to the hospital in the first place.

The results of these studies have uniformly shown the efficacy of the token economy; however, because the delivery of contingent social reinforcement is a key element in the token economy, component analyses should "deconstruct" the multifaceted nature of this wardwide, 24-hour-per-day treatment modality. One such study found that day hospital patients were motivated to improve their behavior by the social reinforcement accompanying the contingent tokens rather than by the tangible rewards associated with the token exchanges (Liberman, Fearn, DeRisi, Roberts, & Carmona, 1977). Generalization of improved behavior from a highly structured token economy to the more randomly programmed "real world" requires graded levels of reinforcement schedules and contingencies; hence, regressed patients who enter a token economy will require frequent reinforcement of target behaviors and the use of shaping, whereas those whose functioning has improved to the point of discharge readiness will benefit from a "credit card" level wherein they have free and continuous access to privileges and rewards as long as they meet criteria for maintaining their performance at a high level.

The most rigorous and well-controlled study of the token economy randomly assigned treatment refractory patients to a social learning program, milieu therapy, or customary, custodial care (Paul & Lentz,

1977). Patients were prepared for community life by having case managers visit the venues where the improved patients would be discharged to create opportunities and encouragement by using "natural reinforcers" and caregivers so that the patients would continue to utilize their learned skills. On all measures of outcome—symptoms, activities of daily living, social behavior, discharge, tenure in the community, and cost-effectiveness—the patients in the social learning–token economy program fared significantly better. A review of social learning and token economy programs highlighted the empirical validation these programs achieved, as well as the reasons few of these programs followed patients and staff as deinstitutionalization accelerated in the two decades after 1980 (Liberman, 2000).

Cognitive Behavior Therapy

Although cognitive behavior therapy has been well documented for efficacy in depressive and anxiety disorders, it has only recently been tested for efficacy with persons with schizophrenia. There are several different approaches to cognitive therapy, each based on the assumption that changing an individual's thoughts, attitudes, perceptions, behavior, self-efficacy, and information-processing deficits can have favorable effects on symptoms, learning skills, emotional distress, and personal functioning.

Cognitive behavior therapy tailors the therapeutic approach that Beck and colleagues developed for depression and anxiety to psychosis within the context of the vulnerability-stress model of schizophrenia (Garety, Fowler, & Kuipers, 2000). Conventional cognitive-behavior methods such as uncovering and changing irrational, automatic thoughts and negative self-appraisals using Socratic questioning are combined with interventions specific for psychosis, including helping patients to empirically challenge delusions and hallucinations and teaching patients techniques for distraction, displacement, and other ways to cope with persistent psychotic symptoms (Kingdon & Turkington, 1994).

The efficacy of cognitive behavior therapy for patients with schizophrenia has now been tested in at least six Type 1 studies and eight Type 2 studies. In each of these studies, cognitive behavior therapy was added to customary psychiatric care (i.e., antipsychotic medication plus case management) and compared with either customary care alone (Garety, Kuip-

ers, Fowler, Chamberlain, & Dunn, 1994; Kuipers et al., 1997; Turkington, Kingdon, & Turner, 2002) or an active comparison group (Durham et al., 2003; Gumley et al., 2003; Lewis et al., 2002; Rector, Seeman, & Segan, 2003; Sensky et al., 2000; Tarrier, Beckett, & Harwood, 1993; Tarrier et al., 1998). Most of these studies and several meta-analyses (Gould, Mueser, Bolton, Mays, & Goff, 2001; Pilling et al., 2002a; Zimmermann, Favrod, Trieu, & Pomini, 2005) have suggested that cognitive behavior therapy has advantages over control conditions for reducing severity of symptoms, including delusions, hallucinations, negative symptoms, and depression, with treatment gains maintained up to 18 months posttreatment. Other review articles have identified certain methodological limitations—such as strict selection criteria biased toward enrolling higher functioning, more insightful individuals—calling into question whether the findings from these studies can be generalized to the majority of individuals with schizophrenia (Tarrier & Wykes, 2004).

Structured, Educational Family Interventions

With the growing number of international demonstrations of the family emotional climate as one of the most powerful predictors of relapse in schizophrenia (Bebbington & Kuipers, 1994; Bertrando et al., 1992; Falloon, Held, Coverdale, Rocone, & Laidlaw, 1999; Jenkins & Karno, 1992; Lopez, Hipke, Polo, Jenkins, & Karno, 2004), interventions have been designed and empirically validated that aim at engaging families as active participants in the treatment and rehabilitation process, while improving their coping capacities and those of their mentally ill members. A variety of terms have been coined to describe these interventions, including *family psychoeducation, behavioral family management, behavioral family therapy, family-aided assertive community treatment,* and *multifamily therapy* (Dixon, Adams, & Luckstead, 2000).

These approaches have substantial elements in common, including structured and clear expectations for participation by family members and patient; outreach and other efforts to connect with the family and provide them with support, practical education about the nature of schizophrenia, and how to cope with it; assisting the family to effectively utilize available treatments and community resources; teaching stress management techniques; encouraging family members to pursue their own goals and well-being without becoming emotionally overinvolved with each other; and teaching the family better means of communicating and problem solving (McFarlane, 2002).

The family psychoeducation approach with the best empirical support is multiple family group therapy (MFG; McFarlane, 2002). MFG consists of three components: engagement or "joining" sessions, a Survival Skills workshop, and longer term multiple family group sessions. To engage patients and family members in the treatment enterprise, three initial "joining" sessions are conducted with each of the families separately. These sessions are also used to assess the special needs, strengths, and problems of each family unit. They take place while the patient is separately undergoing treatment of acute psychotic symptoms followed by orientation to the purposes of the multiple family group therapy in which the patient will subsequently participate.

The three joining sessions offer each family an individualized approach designed to facilitate the process of engaging in treatment. The sessions are designed to familiarize the family with the therapists who will be conducting the ongoing multiple family sessions and to educate them about the need for ongoing treatment. The sessions also help the family identify and overcome the obstacles to pursuing outpatient treatment. In most applications of psychoeducational family therapy, patients are not included in the initial sessions because their level of symptomatic and cognitive impairments would interfere with the engagement of the family and limit any learning that could take place.

The Survival Skills workshop is a 6-hour educational workshop held on a single day with all families that will be involved in the continuing MFG therapy. The workshop is primarily didactic, with open discussion of the information provided by lecture and videotape about the etiology, biology, genetics, symptoms, and treatment of serious mental illness.

Following the Survival Skills workshop, a group of between five and seven families meets twice monthly for at least 9 months and then continues monthly for 6 months or more. Depending on the needs and progress of each family and patient unit, some families can participate in family therapy for up to 2 years. All sessions are co-led by the clinicians who conducted the joining sessions and the Survival

Skills workshop. Each group session is structured in the following manner: a brief caring and sharing period followed by group discussion that includes questions and answers related to each family unit's concerns and problems. Therapists encourage the families to share their personal experiences, describe their coping strategies for dealing with family and patient problems, and provide group support for one another. The principal technique used in the ongoing family sessions is teaching coping and problem-solving skills, with families serving as the role models for one another as they describe their own experiences using these skills in their home environments. Each MFG session ends with reviews of the gains made by family members that week.

More than 20 Type 1 clinical trials have been conducted using structured, educational family interventions, all showing the superiority of adding family intervention to customary treatment (Falloon et al., 1985; Goldstein, Rodnick, Evans, May, & Steinberg, 1978; Hogarty et al., 1986; Leff, Kuipers, Berkowitz, Eberlein-Vries, & Sturgeon, 1982; Liberman, Falloon, & Aitchison, 1984; Randolph et al., 1994) and one indicating superiority of multifamily groups over single-family interventions (McFarlane et al., 1995). Further, meta-analyses have consistently shown reductions in relapse rates, improved social functioning, enhanced quality of life, better cost-effectiveness (Pilling et al., 2002a; Pitschel-Waltz, Leucht, Bauml, Kissling, & Engel, 2001) and reduced family burden (Cuijpers, 1999) for programs that provide at least 9 months of biweekly family sessions. In terms of relapse rates, these structured family interventions have been found to reduce relapse and rehospitalization rates by up to one half when compared with medication and case management alone.

Social Skills Training

Social skills training consists of learning activities that use behavioral techniques that enable persons with schizophrenia and other disabling mental disorders to acquire instrumental and affiliative skills for improved functioning in their communities (Bellack, Mueser, Gingerich, & Agresta, 2004; Liberman, DeRisi, & Mueser, 1989). Trainers draw on behavioral learning principles and techniques such as behavioral rehearsal (role playing), social modeling, abundant positive reinforcement for incremental improvements in social skills, active coaching and prompting, in vivo exercises, and homework assignments (Bellack et al., 2004). Training can be done with standardized curricula, or modules, that provide knowledge and skills that most persons with schizophrenia need for improved life functioning and management of their illness (e.g., use of antipsychotic medication, communication with mental health professionals, recognizing prodromal signs of relapse, developing a relapse prevention plan, coping with persistent psychotic symptoms, avoiding street drugs and alcohol, developing leisure skills, conversation skills). Skills training should be individualized, with goals for improving personal effectiveness derived from each person's long-term aspirations for role functioning.

Sessions are typically conducted once to three times per week, with groups of 4 to 10 patients in office, community mental health center, day hospital, or hospital settings. Skills training is facilitated by patients being reasonably well stabilized on their medications and able to follow instructions, pay attention to the training process, and tolerate sessions lasting 45 to 90 minutes. Thus, social skills training is generally conducted with patients who are living in the community where learned skills can be applied (Heinssen, Liberman, & Kopelowicz, 2000). Because of the attentional requirements of the training, this modality is not suitable for patients with persistent, high levels of thought disorder and cognitive impairment, unless specially designed for this small subgroup (Massel, Corrigan, Liberman, & Milan, 1991; Mueser, Wallace, & Liberman, 1995). Moreover, floridly and acutely symptomatic patients may require additional efforts. Three Type 1 studies have demonstrated that they too may benefit from skills training if the intervention is geared to their level of cognitive capacity and symptomatology (Kopelowicz, Wallace, & Zarate, 1998; Menditto et al., 1996; Silverstein et al., 1999).

Evidence for the efficacy of social skills training addresses the following outcome dimensions: acquisition, durability, and utilization of the skills in real life; improvements in social functioning; reductions in relapse rates and rehospitalization; and enhanced quality of life. More than 40 Type 1 or Type 2 studies and four meta-analyses (Benton & Schroeder, 1990; Corrigan, 1991; Dilk & Bond, 1996; Pilling et al., 2002b) have addressed one or more of these areas of outcome. Overall, there is excellent and well-replicated evidence for the efficacy of social skills training

in the acquisition of the skills taught, with durability extending for at least 1 year. Generalization of the skills to real life use, social functioning, reductions in relapse rates, and enhanced quality of life have been studied less frequently, but the limited data are positive, especially when training extends for 1 year or longer and the intervention includes a generalization component such as case managers and other caregivers who provide opportunities, encouragement, and reinforcement for patients to use the skills in everyday life that they learned during training (Pilling et al., 2002b).

Four Type 1 studies demonstrate that the incorporation of generalization techniques into the skills training enterprise, particularly creating opportunities in the living environment to use the skills and receive the appropriate rewards, increases the likelihood of skill transfer to everyday life settings (Glynn et al., 2002; Kopelowicz, Zarate, Gonzalez Smith, Mintz, & Liberman, 2003; Liberman, Glynn, Blair, Ross, & Marder, 2002; Liberman et al., 1998). Liberman and colleagues compared the community functioning of stable outpatients with schizophrenia after treatment with social skills training or psychosocial occupational training. Skills training was provided by paraprofessionals for 12 hours weekly over the course of 6 months, followed by 18 months of case management geared toward facilitating the use of the learned skills in the community. Patients who received skills training showed significantly greater competence in independent living skills during a 2-year follow up of everyday community functioning, suggesting that skills learned were utilized in the patients' natural environment (Liberman et al., 1998).

Another study utilized In-Vivo Amplified Skills Training (IVAST), which involves specialized case managers who routinely and frequently conduct additional training sessions in participants' environments. The sessions help them adapt their behaviors to their environments and practice that adaptation. Evaluations of IVAST have shown that participants with the extra support achieved higher levels of interpersonal problem-solving skills, significantly greater social adjustment, and better quality of life over a 2-year period than participants with the standard skills training alone (Liberman et al., 2002). A Type 3 study that used indigenous community supporters selected by the patients rather than paraprofessionals as "generalization aides" replicated the finding of improved interpersonal and community functioning 1 year after the 6-month skills training was completed (Tauber, Wallace, & Lecomte, 2000).

Still another technique found to be effective in generalizing the benefits of skills training to the home environment is to involve family members. For instance, Kopelowicz and colleagues (2003) incorporated the participation of families to facilitate learning of illness management skills by Latinos with schizophrenia. In addition to directly training patients on the requisite skills, family members were taught how to provide opportunities for their ill relatives to implement illness management behaviors, encourage their relatives to actually implement the behaviors, and reward them with positive feedback when they did so.

The effects of the intervention were evaluated in a rigorous experimental design with a total of 86 Spanish-speaking families. The results indicated that the participants learned the skills, transferred them to their living environments, and maintained their use for at least 6 months after training, the duration of the follow-up in this study. Moreover, participants in skills training had lower rates of positive and negative symptoms at the end of training and at the 6-month follow up and fewer hospitalizations during the 9 months of the study and 1 year later than the individuals receiving customary care only.

Vocational Rehabilitation

Lifelong unemployment and subsequent dependence on disability pensions have contributed to the profound stigmatization of persons with schizophrenia, poor quality of life, and burden on their families and society. Until the past decade, most efforts at vocational rehabilitation were carried out in sheltered workshops or psychosocial rehabilitation clubhouses where individuals with mental disorders had little opportunity to learn marketable skills for community employment. In addition, state-run vocational rehabilitation agencies gave short shrift to the mentally ill and frequently coordinated their services in nonfunctional and ineffective ways with mental health professionals who were responsible for all other psychiatric services. Fragmentation led to futility and nihilism by rehabilitation specialists as well as psychiatric practitioners (Cook, Lehman, et al., 2005).

Fortunately, vocational rehabilitation of individuals with schizophrenia is receiving increased atten-

tion. Legislation, including the Americans With Disabilities Act (U.S. Department of Justice, 1998) and the Work Incentives Improvement Act of 1999, as well as federal initiatives such as the President's Task Force on Employment of Adults With Disabilities, underscores the support our society has now given to employing individuals with mental and physical disabilities. Nevertheless, a review of the recent literature reveals that, in spite of recent progress, few individuals with schizophrenia receive vocational rehabilitation services (Bond, Becker, et al., 2001). Moreover, individuals with schizophrenia benefit less from vocational rehabilitation programs than do individuals with other psychiatric disorders, and they continue to experience low levels of employment and vocational functioning (Cook, Leff, et al., 2005).

A number of principles have been identified from the literature on vocational rehabilitation about what works for individuals with severe mental illness (Cook & Razzano, 2000). The first is the importance of *situational assessment* in the evaluation of vocational skills and work capacity. *Situational assessment* involves direct, longitudinal observation and rating of job performance and attitudes in actual or simulated work environments (Cook et al., 1994; Massel et al., 1990). Based on such ratings, Rogers, Anthony, Cohen, & Davies (1997) were able to accurately predict the employment status of 275 patients 6 months later. The second principle is the emphasis on *rapid placement* in gainful community employment rather than undergoing lengthy vocational training. For instance, clients who were placed in jobs immediately had higher employment rates and greater job satisfaction than did those receiving prevocational services prior to job placement (Bond, Dietzen, McGrew, & Miller, 1995).

The third principle emphasizes the importance of *ongoing, individually tailored, vocational support.* Making vocational support accessible to clients on an ongoing basis after job placement is a hallmark of the supported employment model discussed below (Wehman & Moon, 1988). A related principle is *tailoring job development and support to the client's preferences.* For example, Becker, Drake, Farabaugh, and Bond (1996) reported that 143 individuals with severe mental illness who obtained jobs in their preferred fields were twice as likely to retain their positions than were those working in nonpreferred fields.

Perhaps the overarching principle is to offer patients *competitive, supported employment* rather than sheltered or unpaid work. Supported employment is based on the following principles:

1. Vocational rehabilitation is an integral, not separate, component of psychiatric treatment. It requires that specialists in job development and placement be part of the treatment team.
2. The goal of supported employment is to place an individual in competitive employment in the community, with vocational assessment and training taking place on the job. Jobs are selected and support services are provided according to the preferences of the consumer.
3. Job coaching and supports from mental health and rehabilitation professionals, including ready access to psychiatric, pharmacological, and crisis services, are provided indefinitely—consistent with the long-term, stress-related nature of schizophrenia and other disabling disorders.

Bolstered by consistent findings from nine Type 1 or Type 2 studies, supported employment is now recognized as an evidence-based practice for persons with schizophrenia (Bond, 2004). In most of these studies, those who received integrated supported employment and psychiatric services were three times more likely to obtain a job, and at least twice as likely to be competitively employed at any point during these studies as compared with control conditions (e.g., group therapy or traditional vocational rehabilitation services). Moreover, the degree of integration between psychiatric and vocational services was directly correlated with improved employment outcomes (Bond, Becker, et al., 2001).

Although there is no evidence that engagement in supported employment leads to increased stress, exacerbation of symptoms, or other negative clinical outcomes (Bond, 2004), achieving long-term job retention has not been clearly demonstrated by supported employment (Lehman et al., 2002). A skills training approach developed to overcome obstacles to sustained employment, the Workplace Fundamentals Module, has been found to improve the job retention rate of persons with schizophrenia and other serious mental disabilities. This module includes several skill areas designed to teach patients who are participating in supported employment how to (a) anticipate stressors on the job, (b) utilize stress management techniques, (c) manage medications on the job despite stigmatizing attitudes, (d) solicit per-

formance feedback and assistance from one's supervisor or employer, and (e) start conversations and relationships with coworkers (Wallace & Tauber, 2004). Two randomized controlled trials of supported employment in conjunction with the Workplace Fundamentals Module are under way at the University of California, Los Angeles, and the Dartmouth Psychiatric Research Center among individuals with recent-onset and chronic schizophrenia, respectively.

Case Management and Treatment Teams

During the past 25 years, well-controlled research has documented the improved outcomes and lower costs associated with brief hospitalization for acute psychotic episodes and the use of community-based alternatives to hospitalization, such as partial hospitals and intensive case management built into continuous, outpatient treatment teams (Herz & Marder, 2002). For example, a mean duration of hospitalization of 11 days followed by day hospital and outpatient treatment produced better symptom outcomes than 60 days of hospitalization with outpatient follow-up. Social functioning 1 and 2 years later also was better for the patients who were hospitalized briefly and then returned to their natural social and family support networks (Herz, Endicott, & Spitzer, 1977).

Thus, patients with schizophrenia and other disabling mental disorders should be discharged when the specific indications for hospitalization are no longer present (e.g., high risk of assault, florid and disabling psychotic symptoms). In addition, clinicians should attempt to ensure that appropriate continuity of care, social and family supports, and housing are available before the patient is discharged—to avoid the "revolving door" phenomenon of hospitalization-discharge-rehospitalization and the tragic but all too common homelessness that afflicts so many thousands of the seriously mentally ill today.

Case management and the treatment teams in which it is imbedded are the "glue" that holds together and coordinates the services that patients need to succeed in the community. The modal form of case management is reactive to problems and crises that patients frequently experience in coping with daily hassles, major life events, poverty, stigma, social isolation, and medication noncompliance. With caseloads of 70 or more, it is difficult for case managers to provide any services beyond appointments with psychiatrists and crisis intervention.

At its best, when caseloads are smaller and team-work is optimal, case management can encourage patients to participate in one or more of the biopsy-chosocial services that have been described above. In addition, optimal case management provides the mechanism for assuring that patients obtain those services appropriate for their phase of illness, tailored to the individual's symptom status, psychosocial functioning, personal goals, and environmental re-sources. At a minimum, case managers monitor the actual use and quality of services they broker and co-ordinate with various agencies and practitioners to fulfill the goals of their severely mentally ill clients. In theory, but all too often not in actual practice, each case manager is a focal point of accessibility and accountability that maximizes the effectiveness and efficiency of services (Mueser, Bond, Drake, & Resnick, 1998).

Three main forms of case management have evolved, distinguished by the level of training, qual-ity, and amount of direct clinical services delivered to the client. The earliest form, the brokerage model, was established in an attempt to ensure that patients being discharged from large psychiatric hospitals would not get "lost" in the community but would be contacted and engaged by case managers and given referrals and follow-up regarding their needs for psy-chiatric medications, housing, and social security en-titlements. During this early phase, case managers tended to be paraprofessionals and did not have the skills to provide direct clinical services to their clien-tele. The brokerage model of case management has been found to be relatively ineffective in fulfilling the needs of severely mentally ill individuals. For ex-ample, one Type 3 study evaluated the effects of this brokerage model of case management with 417 se-verely mentally ill individuals who had been hospi-talized at least twice (Franklin, Solovitz, Mason, Clemons, & Miller, 1987). It found that the costs and use of services increased after case management was introduced into the mental health agency, but there was no corresponding improvement in func-tioning or reduction in the rates and duration of sub-sequent hospitalizations.

In the second generation of case management, termed *clinical case management*, the case manager has clinical training and skills, functions as a primary therapist, and can provide interventions that improve individuals' clinical states, role functioning, and en-vironmental supports. This model attempts to pro-vide comprehensive and continuous services to cli-ents and has been found to result in improvements in subjective quality of life and satisfaction with case management (Huxley & Warner, 1992). The clinical case manager, however, can easily become over-loaded with responsibilities and subject to "burnout" (Bond, Pensec, Dietzen, & McCafferty, 1991). Two Type 2 studies of clinical case management have found empirical support for its efficacy, although one study was flawed by its use of historical controls and lack of randomization (Goering, Wasylenki, Farkas, Lancee, & Ballantyne, 1988; Modrcin, Rapp, & Poertner, 1988).

The most comprehensive model of case manage-ment—the Training in Community Living program developed 25 years ago by Stein and Test and their colleagues (Stein & Santos, 1998; Stein & Test, 1985)—has been shown to be effective in 15 Type 1 studies (see Bond, Drake, et al., 2001 for a review). This model, also known as Assertive Community Treatment (ACT), organizes the service delivery sys-tem into multidisciplinary clinical treatment teams that serve as fixed points of responsibility for assisting patients in meeting all their needs from the day that they enter the program to a time extending many years into the future. Each member of the interdisci-plinary team serves case management functions, with a ratio of one staff member for every 10 to 20 clients.

Services are delivered in individuals' own envi-ronments and include direct assistance with manag-ing their illnesses (e.g., medication, 24-hour crisis availability); modifying the environment to enhance its supportiveness (e.g., facilitating entitlements, fam-ily education, development of social networks); di-rect assistance with the tasks of community living (e.g., rehabilitation services, including home visits); and supported employment, which is supervised by a vocational specialist on the ACT team. An array of comprehensive and continuous services, keyed to each individual's changing needs, is provided by the team, avoiding the frequent fragmentation and occa-sional internecine "warfare" among service providers who are contracted through brokerage to deliver dif-ferent types of services.

The effects of ACT have been favorable, with the qualification that services may need to extend for an indefinite period of time with a frequency and inten-sity that match the changing needs, interests, motivation, and priorities of the patient. The originators of ACT found that 14 months of ACT services resulted in lowered rates of hospitalization, more time in independent living, and improvements in role functioning (Stein & Test, 1980). Type 1 replications of the ACT model (Hoult, 1986; Lehman, Dixon, Kernan, & DeForge, 1997; Rosenheck & Dennis, 2001; Rosenheck, Neale, Leaf, Milstein, & Frisman, 1995) confirmed these results, particularly for lowered rates of hospitalization, improved stability of housing, and cost effectiveness, especially among persons who were high utilizers of mental health services (Mueser et al., 1998). It has been determined that, for role functioning and quality of life (e.g., friendships, employment) to improve, the ACT team must invest the time and effort of specialists on the team to teach social and vocational skills and create opportunities to use the skills in real-life situations (McFarlane et al., 2000).

From an early study of ACT that found that erosion of the gains achieved by 14 months occurred when patients were referred to customary care in the community (Test, Knoedler, & Allness, 1985), it was thought that ACT must be available indefinitely to ensure maintenance and extension of the clinical gains (Burns & Santos, 1995). However, one Type 1 study in which patients who had received ACT services for 20 months were randomly assigned to receive ACT or standard case management for 15 additional months showed very little difference between the groups at follow-up (Audini, Marks, Lawrence, Connolly, & Watts, 1994). One explanation for the discrepant results may be that those patients in ACT whose use of services is relatively low and who have made significant gains in functioning can be transferred to less intensive services without untoward effects. The results of one Type 3 study support this conclusion (Salyers, Masterson, Fekete, Picone, & Bond, 1998).

Figure 8.2 depicts the tripartite model of clinical case management in the shape of a triangle. At the base of the triangle are the basic clinical skills required to form and maintain a therapeutic alliance. The left limb of the triangle comprises a clinician's technical skills in assessment and treatment. The right limb of the triangle includes consultative, advocacy, coordinating, and liaison skills required to open up community-based resources for the client, such as housing and social service entitlements. In employing demonstrably efficacious and cost-effec-

tive methods of clinical case management or assertive community treatment, it is important for practitioners to utilize the treatment methods with fidelity to the key features of the innovative model. For example, agencies that have implemented ACT with caseloads that are significantly greater than 1 to 20 per case manager or treatment team member have not been successful in achieving good outcomes (McGrew, Bond, Dietzen, & Salyers, 1994; McHugo, Drake, Teague, & Xie, 1999).

For most of its 25-year history, ACT was successful in reducing rehospitalization and improving the satisfaction and quality of life of its charges. However, there was little evidence that ACT led to reduced symptoms or improved psychosocial functioning. It is only in the past 5 years that ACT teams have added designated and competent practitioners to supplement the supportive and crisis-oriented services of the ACT team. As ACT enhances its service delivery profile by recruiting experts in disease management, social skills training, family intervention, and vocational rehabilitation, it should yield more substantial improvements in symptoms, social functioning, and independence.

Dual Diagnosis: Substance Abuse and Mental Disorders

Although not included in the 2003 PORT recommendations for the treatment of schizophrenia, integrated dual diagnosis treatment is emerging as an evidence-based practice for clients with severe mental illness (Drake, Essock, et al., 2001). Substance abuse and schizophrenia co-occur in high proportions of urban and rural populations (Fowler, Carr, Carter, & Lewin, 1998; Mueser et al., 2000; RachBeisel, Scott, & Dixon, 1999), and this population presents special challenges to the treatment team and case manager in diagnosis, substance-specific interactions, psychosocial treatments, and psychopharmacology (Torrey et al., 2002). In most cases, substance abuse and schizophrenia are treated by totally different agencies, resulting in fragmented and often incompatible approaches. Even when continuity of care is assured by a fixed point of clinical accountability, poor treatment outcomes can ensue from overemphasizing the treatment of either disorder rather than providing a synchronous, seamless (i.e., integrated) approach that targets both abstinence from substance

FIGURE 8.2 Competencies of clinical case managers can be organized into three major domains: (a) The bottom limb of the triangle represents relationship and personal engagement skills; (b) the left limb of the triangle represents technical biobehavioral assessment and treatment skills; and (c) the right limb of the triangle represents consultation-liaison and advocacy skills.

abuse and remission of psychotic symptoms (Drake, Noordsy, & Ackerson, 1995).

In recent years, the prominence of this population has been recognized and advances have been made in improving outcome by the integration of mental health and substance abuse treatment services (Drake, Mercer-McFadden, Mueser, McHugo, & Bond, 1998). Two controlled studies have compared integrated treatment programs with nonintegrated interventions. One of the studies included random assignment but without independent assessments; the other utilized a quasi-experimental design. In these studies, integrated treatment achieved better outcomes in terms of drug abuse, hospitalization, and more stable residences (Drake, Yovetich, Bebout, Harris, & McHugo, 1997; Godley, Hoewing-Robertson, & Godley, 1994). Two studies of integrated treatment have included research controls, comparing different forms of integrated treatment. In one study of 147 dually diagnosed clients randomly assigned to three modes of treatment, those who received training with the modules of the UCLA Social and Independent Living Skills Program (Liberman et al., 1993) had greater reductions in substance abuse over 18 months than did those in 12-step or intensive case management programs (Jerrell &

Ridgely, 1995). In the other study, substance abuse services were combined with assertive community treatment or with standard case management (Drake, Mueser, Clark, & Wallach, 1996). Clients assigned to ACT had better outcomes on some measures of substance abuse and quality of life, but the groups were similar in terms of reduced hospitalization and psychiatric symptoms.

Despite this progress in integrating mental health and substance abuse treatments, dual disorders often persist for many years, and the current success rates are still clearly low. In addition, relatively little research has evaluated specific intervention modalities, although the incorporation of motivational interviewing techniques has been found to result in significantly greater improvement than routine care in patients' general functioning and the percentage of days of abstinence from drugs or alcohol over a 12-month period (Barrowclough et al., 2001).

FUTURE DIRECTIONS

Cognitive Rehabilitation

It should come as no surprise that the efficacy of psychosocial treatments, requiring as they do a functional brain capable of assimilating and retaining information and skills, is attenuated by cognitive impairments that are enduring traits in most individuals with schizophrenia (Bowie & Harvey, 2005). With the appreciation of the role of neurocognition in determining the social and vocational functioning of patients with schizophrenia (Green, Kern, & Heaton, 2004), the past decade has witnessed the growth of cognitive rehabilitation for direct training or compensation of sustained attention, speed of information processing, executive functions, verbal learning and memory, working memory, and social cognition. As this mode of treatment developed, Type 1 studies focused primarily on laboratory demonstrations of the efficacy of instructions, coaching, and contingent reinforcement on remediating discrete cognitive capacities that are impaired in schizophrenia. Thus, more than 20 randomized controlled trials demonstrated that behavioral interventions could produce significant improvements in memory, attention, and executive functions. In fact, some of the studies suggest that impairments in cognitive functioning can be normalized (Krabbendam & Aleman, 2003).

Once the successful training of specific cognitive functions was well documented in laboratory studies, the technique was translated into applied, clinical studies. For instance, there have been five Type 1 studies of the effects of computer-assisted cognitive training with evidence that the training was instrumental in improving social and vocational functioning (Fiszdon, Bryson, Wexler, & Bell, 2004; Hogarty et al., 2004; Medalia, Revheim, & Casey, 2001; Spaulding et al., 1999; Wykes et al., 2003). Cognitive remediation strategies have also been targeted directly at the deficits in social perception that have been posited to underlie social dysfunction in schizophrenia. The rationale for these interventions is that if patients are unable to correctly interpret interpersonal cues, they will have significant difficulty interacting effectively in these situations (Liberman, Mueser, & Wallach, 1986). Typically, patients are first taught to accurately perceive various parameters associated with selected social cues, such as facial affect, verbal tone, and body language. This procedure is followed by instruction in social problem solving. Using videotaped vignettes, patients learn to identify the problem, generate a number of potential solutions to the problem, and evaluate the alternative responses that might be made for successfully dealing with the particular social situation. There is only limited evidence that this method actually results in

more salutary brain functioning or social adjustment (Storzbach & Corrigan, 1996).

Until recently, methods for remediating cognitive impairments in schizophrenia have utilized rather conventional behavioral techniques, such as monetary reinforcement and instructions. These techniques have not resulted in impressive durability or generalizability of treatment; hence, new strategies for remediation are being developed and evaluated. One approach is to capitalize on the implicit or procedural learning capacity of individuals with schizophrenia. Implicit learning involves those psychomotor actions that are repetitive and overlearned and that can be employed "without thinking" or conscious awareness. Examples are riding a bicycle, catching a ball, saying nighttime prayers, or hitting a nail with a hammer. Procedural learning has been shown to be unimpaired in schizophrenia (Kern, Green, Wallace, & Goldstein, 1996).

A novel and effective means of utilizing procedural or implicit learning to compensate for deficits in verbal learning and memory in persons with schizophrenia is termed *errorless learning*. In this method, the task to be learned—whether it be social or instrumental—is broken down into its constituent components, and training is done by having the individual observe how a model selects the correct response, followed by prompts and reinforcement that promote similar correct responses in the subject. In one Type 2 study, this method has been shown to be superior to customary "trial-and-error" learning in teaching persons with schizophrenia to master entry-level tasks typical of those required in competitive employment (Kern, Liberman, Kopelowicz, Mintz, & Green, 2002). A subsequent Type 2 study demonstrated that errorless learning techniques could be effectively extended to broader, more complex functions such as social problem solving (Kern et al., 2005).

Similarly, spatial visual learning is not as impaired in schizophrenia and can be utilized to overcome obstacles posed by verbal learning; for example, pictures of a concept, event, or interpersonal skill could be used to teach a wider repertoire of skills. One such approach is Cognitive Adaptation Training, a manual-driven set of compensatory strategies designed to bypass specific neurocognitive deficits by using signs, checklists, and electronic devices to cue and sequence appropriate behaviors. Clinicians first assess the cognitive deficits of the patient and provide prostheses in the home that prompt a patient to engage in the specified behavior. For example, to remind a patient to take his or her medications at the correct time, the therapist may attach a large picture of a medication bottle to the patient's refrigerator with a magnet or may ensure that the medication bottle is kept in clear view so the patient will see it during the day. Medication containers with electronically timed alarms are also used to build and maintain daily activity schedules and to remind patients to attend treatment sessions. Two Type 2 studies have shown that these techniques significantly improve adaptive functioning, quality of life, and rates of relapse in schizophrenia patients compared with control conditions (Velligan et al., 2000; Velligan et al., 2002).

Early Intervention Strategies to Promote Recovery

Substantial evidence has accumulated pointing to the relationship between the prompt and continuous treatment of psychotic symptoms and positive outcomes (Loebel, Lieberman, Alvir, Mayerhoff, Geisler, & Szymanski, 1992; Wyatt & Henter, 1998). Taking advantage of the importance of early and continued intervention for psychosis, several investigators have mounted studies in which young persons with the early prodromal signs of schizophrenia and with the first episode of schizophrenia are identified, engaged in treatment, and provided long-term services that are consonant with the individuals' personal goals and developmental stage (Johannessen, Larsen, McGlashan, & Gavlum, 2000; McGorry & Jackson, 1999; Penn, Waldheter, Perkins, Mueser, & Lieberman, 2005). The treatments offered by these scientist-practitioners are multimodal, including group and individual therapies with supportive and cognitive-behavioral elements.

In terms of the primary prevention of schizophrenia, that is, treatment of the at-risk individual prior to the onset of a frank psychotic episode, no studies have yet been reported that extend beyond 2 years after the young persons have begun treatment. The early, prepsychosis intervention model appears to be feasible as it has been possible to recruit and engage teenagers who have distress and symptoms that are similar to the prodromes of schizophrenia relapse (i.e., social withdrawal, unusual perceptual experiences, ideas of reference, etc.). However, results to date have not been encouraging, with little differ-ence in the incidence of psychotic disorders between those who receive low-dose antipsychotic medication plus limited psychoeducational and supportive interventions and those who are simply followed (McGorry et al., 2002; Woods et al., 2003).

A larger database exists to support the value of secondary prevention, that is, pharmacological and psychosocial treatment delivered during the period immediately after a first episode of psychosis. Of extant studies of psychosocial treatment of first-episode psychosis, 16 used a single modality and 13 used multiple services (Penn et al., 2005). Ten studies employed a Type 1 design, and 19 employed a Type 2 or Type 3 design. The results of comprehensive, multielement programs are promising in reducing symptoms and rehospitalizations as well as improving functional outcomes. Among those programs using single modalities, cognitive behavior therapy has shown modest efficacy in reducing symptoms, enabling youth to accept their illness, and improving subjectively reported quality of life. Single-modality programs have shown little success in reducing relapses or rehospitalizations or in improving psychosocial functioning.

Dissemination and Adoption of Evidence-Based Practices

Empirical documentation of a treatment's efficacy rarely is sufficient to promote its dissemination and adoption by clinicians (Backer, Liberman, & Kuehnel, 1986). Even with new medications, which require only a physician's change in prescription, pharmaceutical firms use small armies of representatives to "teach" and introduce physicians how to use the new medication. The utilization of a psychosocial innovation — such as social skills training — is much more difficult to bring about because it requires extended training and supervision of staff, as well as sustained, intensive efforts to achieve regular and frequent attendance by patients.

The experiences of the past 50 years in medicine, mental health, and various industrial and commercial realms can inform those facing the challenge of disseminating and adopting evidence-based treatments. To meet this challenge, efforts to disseminate high-quality treatments and rehabilitation to ordinary hospital- or community-based clinical programs must consider the specific obstacles that impede practitioners from shifting gears to a higher level of care.

These obstacles lie in the attributes of the innovative and evidence-based treatment itself; resistance and inertia of the practitioners being asked to make changes in the way they provide services; challenges in the training of practitioners to learn new techniques and use them with fidelity; and administrative and organizational commitment, leadership, mandates, resources, and reinforcement contingencies that support the innovative services.

Transfer of evidence-based treatment technology is possible by designing dissemination methods that address these obstacles. Designing user-friendly modalities or adapting more complex evidence-based services so they can be readily comprehended and utilized by ordinary, line-level staff increases the likelihood that practitioners will find the modalities useful and will succeed in their implementation. Encouraging practitioners to "reinvent" and modify evidence-based procedures so they fit into the particular constraints and resources of their agencies also will increase the chances that they will embrace new, improved services even if the procedures are no longer exactly the ones initially studied in controlled, clinical trials. Using active and directive in-service training methods, involving line-level staff in the design of their own training, and gaining the use of patients from the adopting agency for demonstrations all combine to improve the chances that the host organization will improve their treatment skills. When trainers purveying evidence-based treatments are able to frame the ideology and goals of the novel services to those services with which staff members are familiar and identified, adoption of the new techniques is more likely to occur (Corrigan, Steiner, McCracken, Blaser, & Barr, 2001).

Consulting with the upper-level and midlevel managers of mental health organizations before conducting dissemination activities can pay handsome dividends. The administrative "soil" can be fertilized for the adoption of evidence-based practices by doing the following:

- Identifying and liaising with local advocates or "champions" for the new techniques, those who have the respect of their colleagues and possess leadership and teaching abilities.
- Persuading top management to include evidence-based practices in the mission statement of the agency and to lend their authority for mandates to staff members to learn and employ

the practices. These mandates can include the granting of authority and accountability to those practitioners who have shown an interest and competence in using evidence-based practices.

- Developing operationalized criteria for annual performance appraisals of clinicians and quality assurance indicators that include the appropriate use of the "best practices" being introduced.

Using these principles for dissemination over a 25-year period, the scientist-practitioners of the UCLA Clinical Research Center for Schizophrenia and Psychiatric Rehabilitation instigated changes in the administrative and clinical activities of 11 statewide mental health programs. In 5 of them, ranging from Hawaii to Wyoming and Texas to South Carolina, the introduction and effective use of evidence-based practices resulted in the state facilities emerging from sanctions related to charges of inadequate psychosocial rehabilitation services and depriving patients of their rights to treatment. Needless to say, an institution or state is highly motivated to improve the quality of services when failure to do so may lead to class-action suits and probationary status imposed by the U.S. Department of Justice.

An international project has been successful in promoting the use of scientifically-validated treatments by employing similar methods for their dissemination and adoption of evidence-based practices. This effort, coordinated by Ian Falloon and his colleagues and known as the Optimal Treatment Project, has promoted high-quality, comprehensive, and coordinated services in Spain, New Zealand, Australia, England, Germany, Sweden, Norway, Japan, Hungary, and Italy. The evidence-based services include early detection and intervention of schizophrenia spectrum disorders, rational pharmacotherapy, social skills training, family participation in treatment, assertive community treatment, problem-solving therapy, supported employment, stress management, and continuous goal-oriented monitoring of outcomes. These services are competency based and consumer oriented. User-friendly treatment manuals were distributed to the various sites with intensive training, ongoing supervision, and external consultation.

More than 1,000 patients have received these "optimal" services, with significant improvements in their social adjustment and quality of life and significant reductions in rehospitalization. After 2 years of using the above evidence-based practices, 34% of the participating patients had full remission of psychotic symptoms, had recovered full psychosocial functioning, and virtually eliminated illness-related, family stress. This contrasted with a recovery rate of 18% in patients and families assigned to the "best" available services in each locale. It must be noted that these salutary outcomes have come at a high financial and manpower cost to the participating mental health systems and considerable pressures, stress, and burden to the consulting and training team. It was realized early on that it was important to encourage flexibility in the use of evidence-based practices, with each international site adopting the principles and techniques in ways that were compatible with its culture, resources, patient population, and staffing (Falloon, Montero, Sungur, Mastroeni, & Malm, 2004).

SUMMARY

Given the protean symptoms, cognitive impairments, and disabilities of persons with schizophrenia, multiple psychosocial treatment modalities must be delivered to patients if their multidimensional needs are to be met. Aside from tacit acknowledgments of the concomitant use of antipsychotic medications, most research reports focus on the primary modality under study while giving short shrift to numerous other elements of what is almost always a comprehensive treatment program. The most effective treatment of schizophrenia includes a combination of the evidence-based approaches described in this chapter delivered in a continuous and integrated manner through a service delivery system that is responsive to the strengths, interests, and goals of the patient.

REFERENCES

American Psychiatric Association. (2004). Practice Guideline for the Treatment of Patients with Schizophrenia, second edition. *American Journal of Psychiatry, 161*(Suppl.), 1–56.

Audini, B., Marks, M., Lawrence, R. E., Connolly, J., & Watts, V. (1994). Home-based versus out-patient/in-patient care for people with serious mental illness: Phase II of a controlled study. *British Journal of Psychiatry, 165*, 204–210.

Austin, N. K., Liberman, R. P., King, L. W., & DeRisi, W. J. (1976). A comparative evaluation of two day hospitals: Behavior therapy vs. milieu therapy. *Journal of Nervous and Mental Disease, 163*, 253–261.

Ayllon, T., & Azrin, N. H. (1965). The measurement and reinforcement of behavior of psychotics. *Journal of the Experimental Analysis of Behavior, 8*, 357–383.

Ayllon, T., & Azrin, N. H. (1968). Reinforcer sampling: A technique for increasing the behavior of mental patients. *Journal of Applied Behavior Analysis, 1*, 13–20.

Backer, T. E., Liberman, R. P., & Kuehnel, T. G. (1986). Dissemination and adoption of innovative psychosocial interventions. *Journal of Consulting and Clinical Psychology, 54*, 111–118.

Badner, J. A., & Gershon, E. S. (2002). Meta-analysis of whole-genome linkage scans of bipolar disorder and schizophrenia. *Molecular Psychiatry, 7*, 405–411.

Baker, R., Hall. J. N., Hutchison, K., & Bridge, G. (1977). Symptom changes in chronic schizophrenic patients on a token economy: A controlled experiment. *British Journal of Psychiatry, 131*, 381–393.

Barrowclough, C., Haddock, G., Tarrier, N., Lewis, S. W., Moring, J., O'Brien, R., et al. (2001). Randomized controlled trial of motivational interviewing, cognitive behavior therapy, and family intervention for patients with comorbid schizophrenia and substance use disorders. *American Journal of Psychiatry, 158*, 1706–1713.

Bebbington, P., & Kuipers, L. (1994). The predictive utility of expressed emotion in schizophrenia: An aggregate analysis. *Psychological Medicine, 24*, 707–718.

Becker, D., Drake, R., Farabaugh, A., & Bond, G. R. (1996). Job preferences of clients with severe psychiatric disorders participating in supported employment programs. *Psychiatric Services, 47*, 1223–1226.

Bellack, A. S., Mueser, K. T., Gingerich, S., & Agresta, J. (2004). *Social skills training for schizophrenia* (2nd ed.). New York: Guilford Press.

Benton, M. K., & Schroeder, H. E. (1990). Social skills training with schizophrenics: A meta-analytic evaluation. *Journal of Consulting and Clinical Psychology, 58*, 741–747.

Bertrando, P., Beltz, J., Bressi, C., Clerici, M., Farma, T., Invernizzi, G., et al. (1992). Expressed emotion and schizophrenia in Italy: A study of an urban population. *British Journal of Psychiatry, 161*, 223–229.

Bond, G. R. (2004). Supported employment: Evidence for an evidence-based practice. *Psychiatric Rehabilitation Journal, 27,* 345–359.

Bond, G. R., Becker, D. R., Drake, R. E., Rapp, C. A., Meisler, N., Lehman, A. F., et al. (2001). Implementing supported employment as an evidence-based practice. *Psychiatric Services, 52,* 313–322.

Bond, G. R., & Boyer, S. L. (1988). Rehabilitation programs and outcomes. In J. A. Ciardello, & M. D. Bell (Eds.), *Vocational rehabilitation of persons with prolonged mental illness* (pp. 231–263). Baltimore: Johns Hopkins University Press.

Bond, G. R., Dietzen, L., McGrew, J., & Miller, L.(1995). Accelerating entry into supported employment for persons with severe psychiatric disabilities. *Rehabilitation Psychology, 40,* 75–94.

Bond, G. R., Drake, R. E., Mueser, K. T., & Latimer, E. (2001b). Assertive community treatment for people with severe mental illness: Critical ingredients and impact on clients. *Disease Management and Health Outcomes, 9,* 141–159.

Bond, G. R., Pensec, M., Dietzen, L., & McCafferty, D. (1991). Intensive case management for frequent users of psychiatric hospitals in a large city: A comparison of team and individual caseloads. *Psychosocial Rehabilitation Journal, 15,* 90–98.

Bowie, C. R., & Harvey, P. D. (2005). Cognition in schizophrenia: Impairments, determinants and functional importance. *Psychiatric Clinics of North America, 28,* 613–633.

Brenner, H., Hodel, B., & Roder, V. (1990). Integrated cognitive and behavioral interventions in treatment of schizophrenia. *Psychosocial Rehabilitation Journal, 13,* 41–43.

Burns, B. J., & Santos, A. B. (1995). Assertive community treatment: An update of randomized trials. *Psychiatric Services, 46,* 669–675.

Cook, J. A. (1995). Research on psychosocial rehabilitation services for persons with psychiatric disabilities. *Psychotherapy and Rehabilitation Research Bulletin, 4,* 3–5.

Cook, J. A., Bond, G., Hoffschmidt, S., Jonas, E., Razzano, L. A., & Weakland, R. (1994). *Situational assessment: Assessing vocational performance among persons with severe mental illness* (pp. 7–16). Chicago: Thresholds National Research and Training Center on Rehabilitation and Mental Illness.

Cook, J. A., Leff, H. S., Blyler, C. R., Gold, P. B., Goldberg, R. W., Mueser, K. T., et al. (2005). Results of a multisite randomized trial of supported employment interventions for individuals with severe mental illness. *Archives of General Psychiatry, 62,* 505–512.

Cook, J. A., Lehman, A. F., Drake, R., McFarlane, W. R., Gold, P. B., Leff, H. S., et al. (2005). Integration of psychiatric and vocational services: A multisite randomized, controlled trial of supported employment. *American Journal of Psychiatry, 162,* 1948–1956.

Cook, J. A., & Razzano, L. (2000). Vocational rehabilitation for persons with schizophrenia: Recent research and implications for practice. *Schizophrenia Bulletin, 26,* 87–103.

Corrigan, P. W. (1991). Social skills training in adult psychiatric populations: A meta-analysis. *Journal of Behavior Therapy and Experimental Psychiatry, 22,* 203–210.

Corrigan, P. W., Steiner, L., McCracken, S. G., Blaser, B., & Barr, M. (2001). Strategies for disseminating evidence-based practices to staff who treat people with serious mental illness. *Psychiatric Services, 52,* 1598–1606.

Cuijpers, P. (1999). The effects of family interventions on relatives' burden: A meta-analysis. *Journal of Mental Health, 8,* 275–285.

Dilk, M. N., & Bond, G. R. (1996). Meta-analytic evaluation of skills training research for individuals with severe mental illness. *Journal of Consulting and Clinical Psychology, 64,* 1337–1346.

Dixon, L., Adams, C., & Luckstead, A. (2000). Update on family psychoeducation for schizophrenia. *Schizophrenia Bulletin, 26,* 5–20.

Drake, R. E., Essock, S. M., Shaner, A., Carey, K. B., Minkoff, K., Kola, L., et al. (2001). Implementing dual diagnosis services for clients with severe mental illness. *Psychiatric Services, 52,* 469–476.

Drake, R. E., Goldman, H. E., Leff, H. S., Lehman, A. F., Dixon, L., Mueser, K. T, et al. (2001). Implementing evidence-based practices in routine mental health service settings. *Psychiatric Services, 52,* 179–182.

Drake, R. E., Mercer-McFadden, C., Mueser, K. T., McHugo, G. J., & Bond, G. R. (1998). Review of integrated mental health and substance abuse treatment for patients with dual disorders. *Schizophrenia Bulletin, 24,* 589–608.

Drake, R. E., Mueser, K. T., Clark, R. E., & Wallach, M. A. (1996). The course, treatment, and outcome of substance disorder in persons with severe mental illness. *American Journal of Orthopsychiatry, 66,* 42–51.

Drake, R. E., Noordsy, D. L., & Ackerson, T. (1995). Integrating mental health and substance abuse treatments for persons with chronic mental disorders. In A. F Lehman & L. B Dixon (Eds.), *Double jeopardy: Chronic mental illness and substance use disorders* (pp. 251–264). Chur, Switzerland: Harwood.

Drake, R. E., Yovetich, N., Bebout, R. R., Harris, M., & McHugo, G. J. (1997). Integrated treatment for dually diagnosed homeless adults. *Journal of Nervous and Mental Disease, 185*, 298–305.

Durham, R. C., Guthrie, M., Morton, V., Reid, D. A., Treliving, L. R., Fowler, D., et al. (2003). Tayside-Fife clinical trial of cognitive-behavioral therapy for medication-resistant psychotic symptoms. *British Journal of Psychiatry, 182*, 303–311.

Falloon, I. R. H., Boyd, J. L., McGill, C. W., Williamson, M., Razani, J., Moss, H. B., et al. (1985). Family management in the prevention of morbidity of schizophrenia. *Archives of General Psychiatry, 42*, 887–896.

Falloon, I. R. H, Held, T., Coverdale, J., Rocone, R., & Laidlaw, T. (1999). A review of long-term benefits of international studies of family interventions in schizophrenia. *Psychiatric Rehabilitation Skills, 3*, 268–290.

Falloon, I. R. H., Montero, I., Sungur, M., Mastroeni, A., & Malm, U. (2004). Implementation of evidence-based treatment for schizophrenic disorders: Two-year outcome of an international field trial of optimal treatment. *World Psychiatry, 3*, 104–109.

Fensterheim, H., & Raw, S. D. (1996). Psychotherapy research is not psychotherapy practice. *Clinical Psychological Scientist-Practitioner, 3*, 168–171.

Fichter, M., Wallace, C. J., & Liberman, R. P. (1976). Improving social interaction in a chronic psychotic using discriminated avoidance. *Journal of Applied Behavioral Analysis, 9*, 377–386.

Fiszdon, J. M., Bryson, G. J., Wexler, B. E., & Bell, M. D. (2004). Durability of cognitive remediation training in schizophrenia: Performance on two memory tasks at six-month and 12-month follow up. *Psychiatry Research, 125*, 1–7.

Folsom, D., & Jeste, D. V. (2002). Schizophrenia in homeless persons: A systematic review of the literature. *Acta Psychiatrica Scandinavica, 105*, 404–413.

Fowler, I. L., Carr, V. J., Carter, N. T., & Lewin, T. J. (1998). Patterns of current and lifetime substance use in schizophrenia. *Schizophrenia Bulletin, 24*, 443–455.

Frank, A. K., & Gunderson, J. G. (1990). The role of the therapeutic alliance in the treatment of schizophrenia: Relationship to course and outcome. *Archives of General Psychiatry, 47*, 228–236.

Franklin, J. L., Solovitz, B., Mason, M., Clemons, J. R., & Miller, G. E. (1987). An evaluation of case management. *American Journal of Public Health, 77*, 675–678.

Fullerton, D. T., Cayner, J. J., & McLaughlin-Reidel, T. (1978). Results of a token economy. *Archives of General Psychiatry, 35*, 1451–1453.

Garety, P. A., Fowler, D., & Kuipers, E. (2000). Cognitive-behavioral therapy for medication-resistant symptoms. *Schizophrenia Bulletin 26*, 73–86.

Garety, P. A., Kuipers, L., Fowler, D., Chamberlain, F., & Dunn, G. (1994). Cognitive behavioural therapy for drug-resistant psychosis. *British Journal of Medical Psychology, 67*, 259–271.

Glynn, S. M., Marder, S. R., Liberman, R. P., Blair, K., Wirshing, W. C., Wirshing, D. A., et al. (2002). Supplementing clinic-based skills training for schizophrenia with manual-based community support: Effects on social adjustment of patients with schizophrenia. *American Journal of Psychiatry, 159*, 829–837.

Godley, S. H., Hoewing-Robertson, R., & Godley, M. D. (1994). *Final MISA report.* Bloomington, IN: Lighthouse Institute.

Goering, P. N., Wasylenki, D. A., Farkas, M., Lancee, W. J., & Ballantyne, R. (1988). What difference does case management make? *Hospital and Community Psychiatry, 39*, 272–276.

Goldstein, M. J., Rodnick, E. H., Evans, J. R., May, P. R. A., & Steinberg, M. R. (1978). Drug and family therapy in the aftercare treatment of acute schizophrenia. *Archives of General Psychiatry, 35*, 169–177.

Gould, R. A., Mueser, K. T., Bolton, M. A., Mays, V. K., & Goff, D. C. (2001). Cognitive therapy for psychosis in schizophrenia: An effect size analysis. *Schizophrenia Research, 48*, 335–342.

Green, M. F., Kern, R. S., & Heaton, R. K. (2004). Longitudinal studies of cognition and functional outcome in schizophrenia: Implications for MATRICS. *Schizophrenia Research, 72*, 41–51.

Gumley, A., O'Grady, M., McNay, L., Reilly, J., Power, K., & Norrie, J. (2003). Early intervention for relapse in schizophrenia: Results of a 12-month randomized controlled trial of cognitive behavioral therapy. *Psychological Medicine, 33*, 419–431.

Gunderson, J. G., Frank, A. F., Katz, H. M., Vannicelli, M. L., Frosch, J. P., & Knapp, P. H. (1984). Effects of psychotherapy in schizophrenia: II. Comparative outcome of two forms of treatment. *Schizophrenia Bulletin, 10*, 564–598.

Harding, C. M., Zubin, J., & Strauss, J. S. (1992). Chronicity in schizophrenia revisited. *British Journal of Psychiatry, 161*, 27–37.

Heinssen, R. K., Liberman, R. P., & Kopelowicz, A. (2000). Psychosocial skills training for schizophrenia: Lessons from the laboratory. *Schizophrenia Bulletin, 26*, 21–46.

Herz, M. I., Endicott, J., & Spitzer, R. L. (1977). Brief hospitalization: A two year follow-up. *American Journal of Psychiatry, 134*, 502–507.

Herz, M. I., & Marder, S. R. (2002). *Schizophrenia: Comprehensive treatment and management*. Philadelphia: Lippincott Williams and Wilkins.

Hogarty, G. E., Anderson, C. M., Reiss, D. J., Kornblith, S. J., Greenwald, D. P., Javna, C. D., et al. (1986). Family education, social skills training and maintenance chemotherapy in aftercare treatment of schizophrenia. *Archives of General Psychiatry, 43,* 633–642.

Hogarty, G. E., Flesher, S., Ulrich, R., Carter, M., Greenwald, D., Pogue-Geile, M., et al. (2004). Cognitive enhancement therapy for schizophrenia: Effects of a two-year randomized trial on cognition and behavior. *Archives of General Psychiatry, 61,* 866–876.

Hogarty, G. E., Goldberg, S. C., & Schooler, N. (1974). Drug and sociotherapy in the aftercare of schizophrenic patients: III. Adjustment of non-relapsed patients. *Archives of General Psychiatry, 31,* 609–618.

Hogarty, G. E., Kornblith, S. J., Greenwald, D., DiBarry, A. L., Cooley, S., Ulrich, R. F., et al. (1997). Three year trials of Personal Therapy among schizophrenic patients living with or independent of family: I. Description of study and effects on relapse rates. *American Journal of Psychiatry, 154,* 1504–1513.

Hoult, J. (1986). Community care of the acutely mentally ill. *British Journal of Psychiatry, 149,* 137–144.

Huxley, P., & Warner, R. (1992). Case management, quality of life, and satisfaction with services of long-term psychiatric patients. *Hospital and Community Psychiatry, 43,* 799–802.

Jenkins, J. H., & Karno, M. (1992). The meaning of expressed emotion: Theoretical issues raised by cross-cultural research. *American Journal of Psychiatry, 149,* 9–21.

Jerrell, J. M., & Ridgely, M. S. (1995). Comparative effectiveness of three approaches to serving people with severe mental illness and substance abuse disorders. *Journal of Nervous and Mental Disease, 183,* 566–576.

Johannessen, J. O., Larsen, T. K., McGlashan, T., & Vaglum, P. (2000). Early intervention in psychosis: The TIPS project, a multi-centre study in Scandinavia. In B. Martindale & A. Bateman (Eds.), *Psychosis: Psychological approaches and their effectiveness* (pp. 210–234). London: Gaskell/Royal College of Psychiatrists.

Kazdin, A. E. (1982). The token economy: A decade later. *Journal of Applied Behavior Analysis, 15,* 431–445.

Kern, R. S., Green, M. F., Mitchell, S., Kopelowicz, A. J., Mintz, J., & Liberman, R. P. (2005). Extensions of errorless learning for social problem-solving deficits in schizophrenia. *American Journal of Psychiatry, 162,* 513–519.

Kern, R. S., Green, M. F., Wallace, C. J., & Goldstein, M. J. (1996). Verbal vs. procedural learning in chronic schizophrenic inpatients. *Cognitive Neuropsychiatry, 2,* 16–22.

Kern, R. S., Liberman, R. P., Kopelowicz, A., Mintz, J., & Green, M. F. (2002). Applications of errorless learning for improving work performance in schizophrenia. *American Journal of Psychiatry, 159,* 1921–1926.

Kingdon, D. G., & Turkington, D. (1994). *Cognitive-behavioral therapy of schizophrenia*. New York: Guilford Press.

Kopelowicz, A., & Liberman, R. P. (2003). Integrating treatment with rehabilitation for persons with major mental illnesses. *Psychiatric Services, 54,* 1491–1498.

Kopelowicz, A., Wallace, C. J., & Zarate, R. (1998). Teaching psychiatric inpatients to re-enter the community: A brief method of improving the continuity of care. *Psychiatric Services, 49,* 1313–1316.

Kopelowicz, A., Zarate, R., Gonzalez Smith, V., Mintz, J., & Liberman, R. P. (2003). Disease management in Latinos with schizophrenia: A family-assisted, skills training approach. *Schizophrenia Bulletin, 29,* 211–228.

Krabbendam, L., & Aleman, A. (2003). Cognitive rehabilitation in schizophrenia: A quantitative analysis of controlled studies. *Psychopharmacology, 169,* 376–382.

Kuipers, L., Garety, P., Fowler, D., Dunn, G., Bebbington, P., Freeman, D., et al. (1997). London–East Anglia randomized controlled trial of cognitive-behavioral therapy for psychosis: I. Effects of the treatment phase. *British Journal of Psychiatry, 171,* 319–327.

Lamb, H. R., & Weinberger, L. E. (1998). Persons with severe mental illness in jails and prisons: A review. *Psychiatric Services, 49,* 483–492.

Leff, J., Kuipers, L., Berkowitz, R., Eberlein-Vries, R., & Sturgeon, D. (1982). A controlled trial of social intervention in the families of schizophrenic patients: Two-year follow-up. *British Journal of Psychiatry, 146,* 594–600.

Lehman, A. F., Dixon, L. B., Kernan, E., & DeForge, B. (1997). A randomized trial of assertive community treatment for homeless persons with severe mental illness. *Archives of General Psychiatry, 54,* 1038–1043.

Lehman, A. F., Goldberg, R. W., Dixon, L. B., McNary, S., Postrado, L., Hackman, A., et al. (2002). Improving employment outcomes for persons with severe mental illnesses. *Archives of General Psychiatry, 59,* 165–172.

Lehman, A. F., Kreyenbuhl, J., Buchanan, R. W., Dickerson, F. B., Dixon, L. B., Goldberg, R., et al. (2004). The schizophrenia patient outcomes research team: Updated treatment recommendations 2003. *Schizophrenia Bulletin, 30,* 193–217.

Lewis, S., Tarrier, N., Haddock, G., Bentall, R., Kinderman, P., Kingdon, D., et al. (2002). Randomized controlled trial of cognitive-behavioral therapy in early schizophrenia: Acute-phase outcomes. *British Journal of Psychiatry, 181*(Suppl. 43), S91–S97.

Liberman, R. P. (1976). Behavior therapy for schizophrenia. In L. J. West & D. Flinn (Eds.), *Treatment of schizophrenia* (pp. 142–169). New York: Grune and Stratton.

Liberman, R. P. (1982). Assessment of social skills. *Schizophrenia Bulletin, 8,* 62–83.

Liberman, R P. (2000). The token economy: Images of psychiatry. *American Journal of Psychiatry, 157,* 1398.

Liberman, R. P., DeRisi, W. J., & Mueser, K. T. (1989). *Social skills training for psychiatric patients.* Elmsford, NY: Pergamon Press.

Liberman, R. P., Falloon, I. R. H., & Aitchison, R. A. (1984). Multiple family therapy for schizophrenia: A behavioral, problem-solving approach. *Psychosocial Rehabilitation Journal, 7,* 60–77.

Liberman, R. P., Fearn, C. H., DeRisi, W. J., Roberts, J., & Carmona, M. (1977). The credit incentive system: Motivating the participation of patients in a day hospital. *British Journal of Social and Clinical Psychology, 16,* 85–94.

Liberman, R. P., Glynn, S., Blair, K. E., Ross, D., & Marder, S. R. (2002). In vivo amplified skills training: Promoting generalization of independent living skills for clients with schizophrenia. *Psychiatry, 65,* 137–155.

Liberman, R. P., King, L. W., & DeRisi, W. J. (1976). Behavior analysis and therapy in community mental health. In H. Leitenberg (Ed.), *Handbook of behavior analysis and modification* (pp. 47–68). Englewood Cliffs, NJ: Prentice-Hall.

Liberman, R. P., Kopelowicz, A., & Silverstein, S. (2004). Psychiatric rehabilitation. In B. J. Sadock, & V. A. Sadock (Eds.), *Comprehensive textbook of psychiatry* (pp. 3218–3245). New York: Lippincott Williams and Wilkins.

Liberman, R. P., McCann, M. J., & Wallace, C. J. (1976). Generalization of behaviour therapy with psychotics. *British Journal of Psychiatry, 129,* 490–496.

Liberman, R. P., Mueser, K. T., & Wallace, C. J. (1986). Social skills training for schizophrenic individuals at risk for relapse. *American Journal of Psychiatry, 143,* 523–526.

Liberman, R. P., Teigen, J., Patterson, R., & Baker, V. (1973). Reducing delusional speech in chronic paranoid schizophrenics. *Journal of Applied Behavior Analysis, 6,* 57–64.

Liberman, R. P., Wallace, C.J., Blackwell, G., Eckman, T., Vaccaro, J. V., & Kuehnel, T. G. (1993). Innovations in skills training for the seriously mentally ill. *Innovations and Research, 2,* 43–60.

Liberman, R. P., Wallace, C. J., Blackwell, G., Kopelowicz, A., Vaccaro, J. V., & Mintz, J. (1998). Skills training vs. psychosocial occupational therapy for persons with persistent schizophrenia. *American Journal of Psychiatry, 155,* 1087–1091.

Loebel, A. D., Lieberman, J. A., Alvir, J. M., Mayerhoff, D. I., Geisler, S. H., & Szymanski, S. R. (1992). Duration of psychosis and outcome in first-episode schizophrenia. *American Journal of Psychiatry, 149,* 1183–1188.

Lopez, S. R., Hipke, K. N., Polo, A. J., Jenkins, J. H., & Karno, M. (2004). Ethnicity, expressed emotion, attributions, and course of schizophrenia: Family warmth matters. *Journal of Abnormal Psychology, 113,* 428–439.

Malm, U. (1982). The influence of group therapy on schizophrenia. *Acta Psychiatrica Scandinavica, 65*(Suppl.), 65–73.

Massel, H., Liberman, R., Mintz, J., Jacobs, H., Rush, T., Gianni, C., et al. (1990). Evaluating the capacity to work in the mentally ill. *Psychiatry, 53,* 31–43.

Massel, H. K., Corrigan, P. W., Liberman, R. P., & Milan, M. (1991). Conversation skills training in thought-disordered schizophrenics through attention focusing. *Psychiatry Research, 38,* 51–61.

McCombs, J. S., Nichol, M. B., Johnstone, B. M., Stimmel, G. L., Shi, J., & Smith, R. S. (2000). Antipsychotic drug use patterns and the cost of treating schizophrenia. *Psychiatric Services, 51,* 525–527.

McFarlane, W. R. (2002). *Multifamily groups in the treatment of severe psychiatric disorders.* New York: Guilford Press.

McFarlane, W. R., Dushay, R. A., Deakins, S. M., Statsny, P., Lukens, E. P., Toran, J., et al. (2000). Employment outcomes in family-aided assertive community treatment. *American Journal of Orthopsychiatry, 70,* 203–214.

McFarlane, W. R., Lukens, E., Link, B., Dushay, R., Deakins, S., Newmark, M., et al. (1995). Multiple-family groups and psychoeducation in the treatment of schizophrenia. *Archives of General Psychiatry, 52,* 679–687.

McGorry, P. D., Jackson, H. J. (1999). *The recognition and management of early psychosis: A preventive approach.* New York: Cambridge University Press.

McGorry, P. D., Yung, A. R., Phillips, L. J., Yuen, H. P., Francey, S., Cosgrave, E. M., et al. (2002). Randomized controlled trial of interventions designed to reduce the risk of progression to first-episode psychosis in a clinical sample with sub-threshold symptoms. *Archives of General Psychiatry, 59,* 921–928.

McGrew, J., Bond, G., Dietzen, L., & Salyers, M. (1994). Measuring the fidelity of implementation of a mental health program model. *Journal of Consulting and Clinical Psychology, 62,* 670–678.

McHugo, G. J., Drake, R. E., Teague, G. B., & Xie, H. (1999). Fidelity to assertive community treatment and client outcomes in the New Hampshire Dual Disorders Study. *Psychiatric Services, 50,* 818–824.

Medalia, A., Revheim, N., & Casey, M. (2001). The remediation of problem-solving skills in schizophrenia. *Schizophrenia Bulletin, 27,* 259–267.

Menditto, A. A., Beck, N. C., Stuve, P., Fisher, J. A., Stacy, M., Logue, M. B., et al. (1996). Effectiveness of clozapine and a social learning program for severely disabled psychiatric inpatients. *Psychiatric Services, 47,* 46–51.

Menditto, A. A., Valdes, L. A., & Beck, N. C. (1994). Implementing a comprehensive social-learning program within the forensic psychiatric service of Fulton State Hospital. In P. W. Corrigan & R. P. Liberman (Eds.), *Behavior therapy in psychiatric hospitals* (pp. 61–78). New York: Springer.

Modrcin, M., Rapp, C. A., & Poertner, J. (1988). The evaluation of case management services with the chronically mentally ill. *Evaluation and Program Planning, 11,* 307–314.

Mowry, B. J., & Nancarrow, D. J. (2001). Molecular genetics of schizophrenia. *Clinical and Experimental Pharmacology and Physiology, 28,* 66–69.

Mueser, K. T., Bond, G. R., Drake, R. E., & Resnick, S. G. (1998). Models of community care for severe mental illness: A review of research on case management. *Schizophrenia Bulletin, 24,* 37–74.

Mueser, K. T., Wallace, C. J., & Liberman, R. P. (1995). New developments in social skills training. *Behaviour Change, 12,* 31–40.

Mueser, K. T., Yarnold, P. R., Rosenberg, S. D., Swett, C., Miles, K. M., & Hill, D. (2000). Substance use disorder in hospitalized severely mentally ill psychiatric patients: Prevalence, correlates, and subgroups. *Schizophrenia Bulletin, 26,* 179–192.

Narrow, W. E., Rae, D. S., Robins, L. N., Lee, N., & Regier, D. A. (2002). Revised prevalence based estimates of mental disorders in the United States: Using a clinical significance criterion to reconcile 2 surveys' estimates. *Archives of General Psychiatry, 59,* 115–123.

Nuechterlein, K. H., Dawson, M. E., Ventura, J., Gitlin, M., Subotnik, K. L., Snyder, K. S., et al. (1994). The vulnerability/stress model of schizophrenic relapse. *Acta Psychiatrica Scandinavica, 89,* 58–64.

Paul, G. L., & Lentz, R. J. (1977). *Psychosocial treatment of chronic mental patients: Milieu versus social-learning programs.* Cambridge, MA: Harvard University Press.

Penn, D. L., Mueser, K. T., Tarrier, N., Gloege, A., Cather, C., Serrano, D., et al. (2004). Supportive therapy for schizophrenia: Possible mechanisms and implications for adjunctive psychosocial treatments. *Schizophrenia Bulletin, 30,* 101–112.

Penn, D. L., Waldheter, E. J., Perkins, D. O., Mueser, K. T., & Lieberman, J. A. (2005). Psychosocial treatment for first-episode psychosis: A research update. *American Journal of Psychiatry, 162,* 2220–2232.

Pilling, S., Bebbington, D., Kuipers, E., Garety, P., Geddes, J., Orbach, G., et al. (2002a). Psychological treatments in schizophrenia: I. Meta-analysis of family intervention and cognitive behavioral therapy. *Psychological Medicine, 32,* 763–782.

Pilling, S., Bebbington, P., Kuipers, E., Garety, P., Geddes, J., Orbach, G., et al. (2002b). Psychological treatments in schizophrenia: II. Meta-analyses of randomized controlled trials of social skills training and cognitive remediation. *Psychological Medicine, 32,* 783–791.

Pitschel-Waltz, G., Leucht, S., Bauml, J., Kissling, W., & Engel, R. R. (2001). The effect of family interventions on relapse and rehospitalization in schizophrenia: A meta-analysis. *Schizophrenia Bulletin, 27,* 73–92.

RachBeisel, J., Scott, J., & Dixon, L. (1999). Co-occurring severe mental illness and substance use disorders: A review of recent research. *Psychiatric Services, 50,* 1427–1434.

Randolph, E., Eth, S., Glynn, S., Paz, G., Van Vort, W., Shaner, A., et al. (1994). Efficacy of behavioral family management in reducing relapse in veteran schizophrenics. *British Journal of Psychiatry, 164,* 501–506.

Rector, N. A., Seeman, M. V., & Segan, Z. V. (2003). Cognitive therapy for schizophrenia: A preliminary randomized controlled trial. *Schizophrenia Research, 63,* 1–11.

Regier, D. A., Farmer, M. E., Rae, D. S., Locke, B. Z., Keith, S. J., Judd, L. L., et al. (1990). Comorbidity of mental disorders with alcohol and other drug abuse. *Journal of American Medical Association*, 264, 2511–2518.

Riecher-Rossler, A., & Hafner, H. (2000). Gender aspects in schizophrenia: Bridging the border between social and biological psychiatry. *Acta Psychiatrica Scandinavica,102*(Suppl.), 58–62.

Rogers, E. S., Anthony, W. A., Cohen, M., & Davies, R. (1997). Prediction of vocational outcome based on clinical and demographic indicators among vocationally ready clients. *Community Mental Health Journal, 33*, 99–112.

Rosenheck, R., & Dennis, D. (2001). Time-limited assertive community treatment for homeless persons with severe mental illness. *Archives of General Psychiatry, 58*, 1073–1080.

Rosenheck, R., Neale, M., Leaf, P., Milstein, R., & Frisman, L. (1995). Multisite experimental cost study of intensive psychiatric community care. *Schizophrenia Bulletin, 21*, 129–140.

Rothbard, A. B., Kuno, E., Schinnar, A. P., Hadley, T. R., & Turk, R. (1999). Service utilization and cost of community care for discharged state hospital patients: A 3-year follow-up study. *American Journal of Psychiatry, 156*, 920–927.

Rupp, A., & Keith, S. (1993). The costs of schizophrenia. *Psychiatric Clinics of North America, 16*, 413–423.

Salyers, M. P., Masterson, T. W., Fekete, D. M., Picone, J. J., & Bond, G. R. (1998). Transferring clients from intensive case management: Impact on client functioning. *American Journal of Orthopsychiatry, 68*, 233–245.

Schwartz, J., & Bellack, A. S. (1975). A comparison of a token economy with standard inpatient treatment. *Journal of Consulting and Clinical Psychology, 43*, 107–108.

Sensky, T., Turkington, D., Kingdon, D. G., Scott, J., Siddle, R., O'Carroll, M., et al. (2000). A randomized controlled trial of cognitive-behavioral therapy for persistent symptoms in schizophrenia resistant to medication. *Archives of General Psychiatry, 57*, 165–173.

Siever, L. J., & Davis, K. L. (2004). The pathophysiology of schizophrenia disorders: Perspectives from the spectrum. *American Journal of Psychiatry, 161*, 398–413.

Silverstein, S., Valone, C., Jewell, T., Corry, R., Ngheim, K., Saytes, M., et al. (1999). Integrating shaping and skills training techniques in the treatment of chronic refractory individuals with schizophrenia. *Psychiatric Rehabilitation Skills, 3*, 41–58.

Spaulding, W. D., Fleming, S. K., Reed, D., Sullivan, M., Storzbach, D., & Lam, M. (1999). Cognitive

functioning in schizophrenia: Implications for psychiatric rehabilitation. *Schizophrenia Bulletin, 25*, 275–289.

Spiegler, M. D., & Agigian, H. (1976). *An Educational-Behavioral-Social Systems Model for rehabilitating psychiatric patients.* New York: Brunner/Mazel.

Stein, L. I., & Santos, A. (1998). *Assertive community treatment of persons with severe mental illness.* New York: Norton.

Stein, L. I., & Test, M. A. (1980). Alternative to mental hospital treatment: I. Conceptual model, treatment program, and clinical evaluation. *Archives of General Psychiatry, 37*, 392–397.

Stein, L. I., & Test, M. A. (Eds.) (1985). *The Training in Community Living model: A decade of experience.* San Francisco: Jossey-Bass.

Stevens, J. R. (2002). Schizophrenia: Reproductive hormones and the brain. *American Journal of Psychiatry, 159*, 713–719.

Storzbach, D. M., & Corrigan, P. W. (1996). Cognitive rehabilitation for schizophrenia. In P. W. Corrigan, & S. C. Yudofsky (Eds.), *Cognitive rehabilitation for neuropsychiatric disorders* (pp. 311–327). Washington, DC: American Psychiatric Press.

Sue, S., Fujino, D. C., Hu, L., Takeuchi, D., & Zane, N. (1991). Community mental health services for ethnic minority groups: A test of the cultural responsiveness hypothesis. *Journal of Consulting and Clinical Psychology, 59*, 533–540.

Sue, S., & Sue, D. (1987). Cultural factors in the clinical assessment of Asian Americans. *Journal of Consulting and Clinical Psychology, 55*, 479–487.

Tarrier, N., Beckett, R., & Harwood, S. (1993). A trial of two cognitive-behavioral methods of treating drug-resistant residual psychotic symptoms in schizophrenia. *British Journal of Psychiatry, 162*, 524–532.

Tarrier, N., & Wykes, T. (2004). Is there evidence that cognitive behavior therapy is an effective treatment for schizophrenia? A cautious or cautionary tale? *Behaviour Research and Therapy, 42*, 1377–1401.

Tarrier, N., Yusupoff, L., Kinney, C., McCarthy, E., Gledhill, A., Haddock, G., et al. (1998). Randomised controlled trial of intensive cognitive behaviour therapy for patients with chronic schizophrenia. *British Medical Journal, 317*, 303–307.

Tauber, R., Wallace, C. J., & Lecomte, T. (2000). Enlisting indigenous community supporters in skills training programs for persons with severe mental illness. *Psychiatric Services, 51*, 1428–1432.

Test, M. A., Knoedler, W. H., & Allness, D. J. (1985). The long-term treatment of schizophrenics in a community support program. In L. I. Stein, M. A.

Test (Eds.), *The Training in Community Living model: A decade of experience* (pp. 17–27). San Francisco: Jossey-Bass.

Torrey, W. C., Drake, R. E., Cohen, M., Fox, L. B., Lynde, D., Gorman, P., et al. (2002). The challenge of implementing and sustaining integrated dual disorders treatment programs. *Community Mental Health Journal, 38,* 507–521.

Turkington, D., Kingdon, D., & Turner, T. (2002). Effectiveness of a brief cognitive-behavioral therapy intervention in the treatment of schizophrenia. *British Journal of Psychiatry, 180,* 523–527.

Ullman, L. P., & Krasner, L. (1975). *A psychological approach to abnormal behavior* (2nd ed.). Englewood Cliffs, NJ: Prentice-Hall.

U.S. Department of Justice. (1998). *Enforcing the ADA: A status report from the Department of Justice, July–September.* Washington, DC: U.S. Department of Justice, Civil Rights Division.

Velligan, D. I., Bow-Thomas, C. C., Huntzinger, C., Ritch, J., Ledbetter, N., Prihoda, T .J., et al. (2000). Randomized controlled trial of the use of compensatory strategies to enhance adaptive functioning in outpatients with schizophrenia. *American Journal of Psychiatry, 157,* 1317–1323.

Velligan, D. I., Prihoda, T. J., Ritch, J. L., Maples, N., Bow-Thomas, C. C., & Dassori, A. (2002). A randomized single-blind pilot study of compensatory strategies in schizophrenic outpatients. *Schizophrenia Bulletin, 28,* 283–292.

Ventura, J., & Liberman, R. P. (2000). Psychotic disorders. In G. Fink (Ed.), *Encyclopedia of Stress* (pp. 316–325). San Diego: Academic Press.

Walker, E., Kestler, L., Bollini, A., & Hochman, K. M. (2004). Schizophrenia: Etiology and course. *Annual Review of Psychology, 55,* 401–430.

Wallace, C. J., & Tauber, R. (2004). Supplementing supported employment with workplace skills training. *Psychiatric Services, 55,* 513–515.

Wehman, P. H., & Moon, M. S. (1988). *Vocational rehabilitation and supported employment.* Baltimore: Paul H. Brookes.

Wong, S. E., Massel, H. K., Mosk, M. D., & Liberman, R. P. (1986). Behavioral approaches to the treatment of schizophrenia. In G. D. Burrows, T. R. Norman, & G. Rubinstein (Eds.), *Handbook of studies on schizophrenia* (pp. 79–100). Amsterdam: Elsevier Science.

Woods, S. W., Breier, A., Zipursky, R. B., Perkins, D. O., Addington, J., Miller, T. J., et al. (2003). Randomized trial of olanzapine versus placebo in the symptomatic acute treatment of the schizophrenic prodrome. *Biological Psychiatry, 54,* 453–464.

Wu, E. Q., Birnbaum, H. G., Shi, L., Ball, D. E., Kessler, R. C., Moulis, M., et al. (2005). The economic burden of schizophrenia in the United States in 2002. *Journal of Clinical Psychiatry, 66,* 1122–1129.

Wyatt, R. J., & Henter, I. D. (1998). The effects of early and sustained intervention on the long-term morbidity of schizophrenia. *Journal of Psychiatric Research, 32,* 169–177.

Wyatt, R. J., & Henter, I. (2001). Rationale for the study of early intervention. *Schizophrenia Research, 51,* 69–76.

Wyatt, R. J., Henter, I., Leary, M., & Taylor, E. (1995). An economic evaluation of schizophrenia—1991. *Social Psychiatry and Psychiatric Epidemiology, 30,* 196–205.

Wykes, T., Reeder, C., Williams, C., Corner, J., Rice, C., & Everitt, B. (2003). Are the effects of cognitive remediation therapy durable? Results from an exploratory trial in schizophrenia. *Schizophrenia Research, 61,* 163–174.

Zimmermann, G., Favrod, J., Trieu, V. H., & Pomini, V. (2005). The effect of cognitive behavioral treatment on the positive symptoms of schizophrenia spectrum disorders: A meta-analysis. *Schizophrenia Research, 77,* 1–9.

9

Pharmacological Treatments
for Unipolar Depression

Charles B. Nemeroff
Alan F. Schatzberg

The treatment of unipolar major depression with antidepressant medication is well established on the basis of scores of randomized placebo-controlled trials involving thousands of patients. Tricyclic antidepressants (TCAs) were the first to be studied extensively; meta-analyses of placebo-controlled trials show them to be consistently and significantly more efficacious than a placebo. Because of a narrow safety margin and significant drug-induced adverse side effect problems, TCAs have now largely been replaced as the first-line treatment of depression by selective serotonin reuptake inhibitors (SSRIs) — fluoxetine, sertraline, paroxetine, citalopram, and escitalopram; serotonin norepinephrine reuptake inhibitors (SNRIs) — venlafaxine and duloxetine; as well as other compounds, including, for example, bupropion and mirtazapine. Each of these agents has been shown to be superior to a placebo and as effective as comparator TCAs or SSRIs in controlled trials. Clinical trials consistently show them to be better tolerated than TCAs, and they clearly have a wider margin of safety. However, there is a controversy concerning whether TCAs are more effective than SSRIs for the treatment of the most severely ill depressed patients. Monoamine oxidase inhibitors (MAOIs), while also more effective than placebo, have generally been reserved for treatment-refractory patients; however, a recently released transdermally delivered selegiline may be used in less refractory patients. It is now generally recognized that patients with recurrent major depression benefit from continued antidepressant treatment, and there is evidence that TCAs, SSRIs, SNRIs, and so forth are all effective for the long-term management of recurrent major depression. An important issue in evaluating the antidepressant literature is to distinguish between response rated as a reduction in the level of symptoms on a rating scale and response rated as true remission from illness.

The efficacy of antidepressant medications has been well established in myriad controlled clinical trials, and in general the response of patients with unipolar depression is comparable to the success rates of treatment of major medical disorders such as coronary artery disease (by angioplasty), hypertension, and diabetes. Meta-analyses of the vast database of double-blind, placebo-controlled clinical trials have revealed a highly statistically significant effect of all of the currently available antidepressants approved by the Food and Drug Administration (FDA) for the management of acute unipolar depression. No other mental illness has received this much scrutiny. Because the FDA submission usually involves comparison to both a placebo and an already approved antidepressant, such as a tricyclic, large numbers of patients, literally thousands, have been involved in these trials.

The antidepressants currently available in the United States are usually classified by their purported neurochemical mechanism of action (e.g., see Table

9.1). Not only have all of the listed antidepressants been demonstrated to be effective in treating major depression, but no single antidepressant has ever been conclusively demonstrated to be more effective than any other antidepressant (Nemeroff, 1994). However, there is some controversy (see below) regarding whether certain antidepressants such as venlafaxine, duloxetine, mirtazapine, and tricyclic antidepressants (TCAs) might be more effective than the others, particularly for severe or treatment-refractory depression. One of the important issues to discuss in this chapter is, of course, the definition of response in an antidepressant drug trial. A 50% decline in a dimensional measure of depression severity such as the Hamilton Depression Rating Scale (HAM-D) or the Montgomery-Asberg Depression Rating Scale (MADRS) is the generally accepted definition of a responder. However, many patients with severe depression (HAM-D scores, for example, greater than 28) can exhibit a 50% improvement in depression severity and therefore can be considered responders but may have considerable residual depressive symptoms (e.g., a HAM-D score of 13). Thus, patients included as responders may, in fact, be partial responders and clearly not euthymic. More stringent definitions of response include HAM-D scores of less than 7 or some other measure of euthymia. Use of the more stringent definitions of response may reveal differences in antidepressant efficacy.

Another poorly understood issue is the response of depressed patients to a placebo, which can occur at surprisingly high rates, in clinical trials comparing a placebo and an antidepressant. This is no trivial issue because novel antidepressants must be shown to be statistically superior to a placebo and as efficacious as an already approved antidepressant, usually a TCA, in order to receive FDA approval. This subject has previously been discussed in considerable detail (Schatzberg & Kraemer, 2000), but the primary point to be made to the reader who is not familiar with clinical psychopharmacology trials in depression is that placebo treatment is not identical to no treatment. Patients taking part in clinical trials spend considerable periods of time with the staff (research nurses, research assistants), as well as with the trial physicians. The quantity of time spent by patients in clinical trials far exceeds the time spent by a patient treated by a mental health professional in a "standard" fee-for-service setting and certainly is greater than the time spent by those in managed-care settings. The contact with the research team, frequently lasting 3 to 6 hours per visit, clearly has effects on the patient's clinical state. Because of the availability of treatments, both psychotherapeutic and psychopharmacological, with documented efficacy, "no treatment," theoretically an appropriate comparison to a novel antidepressant, would not be approved by institutional review boards reviewing such an experimental design. This is a reasonable stance in view of the morbidity and mortality (secondary to suicide and increased risk of cardiovascular and cerebrovascular disease) in untreated depressed patients. Alternative approaches to evaluating meaningfulness of clinical effects have been reviewed in detail elsewhere (Schatzberg & Kraemer, 2000; Kraemer & Kupfer, 2006).

TABLE 9.1 Tricyclic and Tetracyclic Agents: Pharmacological Effects

	Reuptake Blockade		Receptor Blockade		
Drug	NE	5-HT	ACh	H_1	α_1
Imipramine	+	+	++	+	++
Desipramine	+++	0	+	0	+
Amitriptyline	±	++	++++	++++	+++
Nortriptyline	++	±	++	+	+
Doxepin	++	+	++	+++	++
Trimipramine	+	0	++	+++	++
Protriptyline	++	0	+++	+	+
Clomipramine	+	+++	++	+	++
Maprotiline	++	0	+	++	+
Amoxapine	++	0	0	±	++

Note: Based on Potter, Manji, and Rudorfer (1998). Reprinted with permission.

NE = norepinephrine; 5HT = serotonin; ACh = acetylcholine; H_1 = histamine-1; α_1 = alpha-1; + = mild effect; ++++ = marked effect.

Another issue that has received considerable attention is the rapidity of response to antidepressants. It is generally acknowledged that antidepressants require 3 to 5 weeks before their therapeutic response is clinically evident, likely due to neurochemical effects on receptor regulation and/or gene expression. In psychopharmacological research, antidepressants that work more rapidly are the "Holy Grail."

This is a very complex issue, and space constraints preclude a comprehensive discussion of this controversial topic. However, it is important to note that the so-called lag time in antidepressant drug response in clinical trials is, of course, a mean of patients who respond relatively quickly, patients who respond after a few weeks, and patients who are nonresponders. In addition, the definition of response (given above) obviously has a major impact here; few patients show complete euthymia after 1 week. It has often been stated that if patients do not respond to antidepressants after 4 to 6 weeks, they should be treated for an additional 4 to 6 weeks. However, several studies (Boyer & Feighner, 1994; Nierenberg et al., 1995) have revealed that if the patient has not responded to paroxetine by 3 weeks of treatment or fluoxetine by 4 weeks of treatment, there is little likelihood that additional treatment, at that dose, will be successful.

Unfortunately, a generation of studies attempting to identify biological markers that predict treatment response to one or another antidepressant failed to provide valid predictors of either response or nonresponse to any antidepressant drug class. However, pharmacogenetics and brain imaging offer considerable potential for predicting response (Murphy, Kremer, Rodrigues, & Schatzberg, 2003a, 2003b; Murphy, Hollander, Rodrigues, Kremer, & Schatzberg, 2004). The short form of the serotonin transporter promoter may predict poor response to a selective serotonin reuptake inhibitor (SSRI) or intolerance to such therapy (Murphy et al., 2004). Functionally, the use of positron emission tomography (PET) to label neurotransmitter transporters and receptors in vivo may provide for the first time the ability to determine whether a given patient shows, for example, a deficit in serotonin transporter binding, which might predict response to one of the SSRIs.

Other critical areas that the reader might wish to consider are issues of age, gender, and comorbid medical disorders. For many years, there was a dearth of studies of antidepressant use in children and adolescents, and what was available did little to convince one of the antidepressants' efficacy. There was still widespread belief among clinicians that antidepressants are effective in this age-group, but few controlled studies had demonstrated such efficacy (see DeVane & Sallee, 1996, and Fisher & Fisher, 1996, for a review). Evidence for the efficacy of fluoxetine (Emslie et al., 1997), paroxetine (Keller et al., 2001), and citalopram (Wagner et al., 2004) in children and adolescents is now available. Clearly, further studies are needed in this important area. Similarly, there are many failed reports of efficacy of various classes of antidepressants in the elderly (Roose & Schatzberg, 2005; Schatzberg & Roose, 2006). This group has been plagued with high placebo response rates, although here too there are some positive trials with second-generation agents.

The exclusion of women of childbearing potential from clinical trials because of fears of potential teratogenic effects of antidepressants has resulted in an embarrassing lack of knowledge of pharmacokinetics and clinical efficacy in the population that has the highest prevalence rate of unipolar depression. Further studies with a focus on antidepressant-gonadal-steroid interactions are advisable.

Finally, and of paramount importance, is the documentation of antidepressant efficacy and tolerability in patients with comorbid medical disorders. Prevalence rates of unipolar depression in patients with medical disorders such as cancer, diabetes, myocardial infarction, Parkinson's disease, multiple sclerosis, and Alzheimer's disease are remarkably high (25 to 50%), and for many years relatively few controlled treatment trials had been conducted in these populations (see Boswell, Anfinson, & Nemeroff, 1997, for a review). However, such studies are now even more vitally important to conduct because there is increasing evidence that depression is associated with an increased risk of death after myocardial infarction (Frasure-Smith, Lesperance, & Talajic, 1993, 1995) and stroke. Similarly, depression has been suggested to have a profound negative impact on patients with cancer (McDaniel, Musselman, Porter, Reed, & Nemeroff, 1995). In the past few years, several controlled trials of SSRIs in medically ill patients with depression have been conducted. Virtually all of them, including those that examined patients with depression and comorbid stroke, cancer, Parkinson's disease, chronic obstructive pulmonary disease, multiple sclerosis, or diabetes, have clearly documented efficacy of the antidepressant.

However, because the majority of patients with medical disorders are also prescribed a variety of other medications, it is of paramount importance to prescribe antidepressant medications that are safe and, in particular, have no untoward drug-drug interactions with other prescribed medications. This is not a trivial issue because most antidepressants are bound to plasma proteins and therefore can displace other commonly prescribed drugs, such as coumadin, from their protein-binding site, increasing plasma coumadin concentrations and increasing bleeding times with potentially adverse consequences. Moreover, in recent years it has become evident that many antidepressants inhibit the activity of certain hepatic cytochrome P_{450} isoenzymes, which are responsible for metabolizing a wide variety of other commonly prescribed medications. Such drug-drug interactions, if not acknowledged, could lead to increases in plasma concentrations of drugs such as astemizole, a commonly prescribed antihistamine, that at high levels can exert toxic effects on the heart. These data have been comprehensively reviewed (DeVane, 1994; Ereshefsky, 1996; Nemeroff, DeVane, & Pollack, 1996). Of note, however, is that for nontricyclic agents, slow drug metabolism seems to be a less pressing and potentially less dangerous issue (Murphy et al., 2003b).

A final area of crucial importance is maintenance treatment of depression and assessment of its efficacy compared with placebo treatment. For many years, it was generally recommended that, after a single episode of depression, patients should be treated for 6 months. If a patient has suffered more than one episode of depression, if the first episode was particularly severe (e.g., with a serious suicide attempt) or particularly difficult to treat, or if the patient has a very strong family history, long-term treatment should be considered. All of the reported studies that have evaluated treatment with antidepressants for 1 year or longer compared with a placebo have found highly significant beneficial effects of antidepressant treatment. Such studies have included TCAs, SSRIs, venlafaxine, and so forth. These data have been reviewed extensively (Blacker, 1996; Hirschfeld & Schatzberg, 1994; Thase & Sullivan, 1995).

A final point should be made about the use of more than one medication to treat depression. For many years, the prevailing opinion in psychiatry has been that monotherapy for depression is highly desirable and, conversely, that polypharmacy is to be avoided. This is certainly not the case in other branches of medicine, in which polypharmacy is virtually the rule. Failure of a single agent to provide adequate control of hypertension, diabetes, or a neoplasm invariably leads to the use of two or three pharmacological agents. If the goal is to return the patient to complete euthymia, combination therapy of more than one psychotropic agent, as well as combination psychopharmacology and psychotherapy, may be necessary. Indeed, some combinations—for example, addition of antipsychotics—may rapidly convert nonresponders to responders (Shelton et al., 2001).

TRICYCLIC ANTIDEPRESSANTS

Tricyclic antidepressants were for many years the treatments of choice for major depression. They were originally introduced into the United States in the 1960s. In this country, seven TCAs are approved for treatment of major depression, and one additional compound—clomipramine—is approved for obsessive compulsive disorder (OCD) but is viewed throughout the world as an efficacious antidepressant. Two other compounds (maprotiline and amoxapine) have four-ringed structures and are variants of the tricyclic class. Amoxapine is related to the antipsychotic agent loxapine. There is a large amount of literature demonstrating efficacy of the TCAs (Potter, Manji, & Rudorfer, 1998). In the United States, some of the original randomized clinical trials (RCTs) in psychiatry included imipramine or amitriptyline and showed these agents to be effective in what we now term *major depression*. Efficacy of the TCAs has been revisited in SSRI comparator trials, and the TCAs still appear to be more effective than a placebo and to be of comparable efficacy to the SSRIs. Janicak, Davis, Preskorn, & Ayd (1993) performed meta-analyses of the TCA RCTs literature and reported these antidepressants to be overwhelmingly more effective than a placebo. For example, 50 studies that had compared imipramine with a placebo reported an aggregate response rate to the TCA of 68%, compared with a 40% response rate to the placebo, a difference significant at the $p < 10^{-40}$ level.

Imipramine was used in a comparator treatment against cognitive behavior therapy in the National Institute of Mental Health (NIMH) collaborative treatment study of outpatients with major depression. That study suggested that more severely depressed patients responded better to the TCA than they did to the psychosocial treatment (Elkin et al., 1989), although other studies did not bear this out (Hollon et al., 1992).

Some investigators have argued that the TCAs are more effective than the SSRIs in the treatment of more severely depressed or melancholic inpatients in that they are more likely to induce remission within 4 to 6 weeks. In a study by the Danish University Antidepressant Group (Danish University Antidepressant Group [DUAG], 1990), clomipramine produced significantly higher rates of remission than did paroxetine. In another report on inpatients by this group (DUAG, 1986), clomipramine was also significantly more effective than citalopram. More recently, Roose, Glassman, Attia, and Woodring (1994) reported that nortriptyline was more effective than fluoxetine in hospitalized cardiac patients with melancholia. Other studies have not borne out such differences (see below), although the perception of superior efficacy continues among some investigators.

The tricyclic antidepressants alone are less effective in major depression with psychotic features (delusional depression) or in those with so-called atypical features. In the former, TCA monotherapy has been found to be effective in only 35% of patients, in contrast to a 65% response rate in their nondelusional counterparts, a difference that is highly statistically significant (Chan et al., 1987). In delusional depressives, TCAs in combination with antipsychotics have been reported to be significantly more effective than TCAs alone (Schatzberg & Rothschild, 1992). For such patients, clinical practice now calls for combining TCAs or other antidepressants with antipsychotic agents. The presence of atypical features (hypersomnia, hyperphagia, prominent anxiety, reverse diurnal mood variation) predicts poorer responses to imipramine than to monoamine oxidase inhibitors (MAOIs) according to some RCTs (see below).

The TCAs as a class are potent inhibitors of the reuptake of norepinephrine into presynaptic neurons; they exert fewer effects on serotonin reuptake (see Table 9.1). The one major exception is clomipramine, which is a potent serotonin reuptake blocker with a demethylated metabolite that is a potent norepinephrine reuptake blocker. Norepinephrine reuptake blocking effects probably account for some patients' becoming activated (increased anxiety or agitation) on these agents. Generally, such effects are

dose related and can be minimized by conservative dosing. Over time, TCAs are frequently anxiolytic in their effects.

The TCAs all have some affinity for muscarinic cholinergic receptors as antagonists (see Table 9.1) and produce dry mouth, blurred vision, constipation, urinary hesitancy, memory disturbance, and tachycardia. Agents within the class vary in the degree to which they produce these side effects, with the so-called secondary tricyclics, which represent demethylated metabolites of parent tertiary TCAs, exerting more limited anticholinergic effects than their parents. Examples are nortriptyline (the metabolite of amitriptyline) and desipramine (the metabolite of imipramine).

The TCAs are also antihistaminic, with amitriptyline and doxepin being most potent at this site (see Table 9.1) and being most likely to produce sedation and weight gain. These agents also block alpha$_1$-adrenergic receptors and produce orthostatic hypotension. Here, too, these side effects are mainly dose related and can be minimized by using lower doses of drugs, particularly when initiating treatment. Some patients may, however, not be able to tolerate even the most minimal doses of these agents.

Because of their alpha$_1$-adrenergic and anticholinergic effects, the TCAs are potentially cardiotoxic in overdose and have relatively narrow safety margins (low therapeutic index). They can result in death when taken in overdose and are the number one cause of overdose death among prescription drugs in the United States. Generally, clinicians initiating treatment with a TCA begin at low doses (e.g., 50 mg of amitriptyline, imipramine, or desipramine or 25 mg of nortriptyline) to avoid side effects as much as possible and to maximize compliance. Over 7 to 10 days, doses are increased gradually to 150 mg per day of amitriptyline, imipramine, or desipramine or to 75 mg per day of nortriptyline. After 2 weeks of these doses, further gradual dosage increments can be undertaken to achieve the maximum recommended doses. Therapeutic dosage ranges are summarized in Table 9.2.

There is a relatively rich literature on the relationship of TCA plasma levels to clinical response. Generally, such relationships were demonstrated in studies of more severely depressed patients. Glassman, Perel, Shostak, Kantor, and Fleiss (1977) reported a so-called sigmoidal relationship between imipramine plasma concentrations and clinical response, with

TABLE 9.2 Typical Therapeutic Dosage Ranges of Tricyclic and Tetracyclic Antidepressant Drugs (Adult Patients)

Drug		Therapeutic Dose Range (mg/day)
Generic Name	Trade Name*	
Imipramine	Tofranil	150–300
Desipramine	Norpramin	150–300
Amitriptyline	Elavil	150–300
Nortriptyline	Pamelor, Aventyl	50–150
Doxepin	Sinequan	150–300
Trimipramine	Surmontil	150–200
Clomipramine	Anafranil	75–200
Maprotiline	Ludiomil	75–200
Amoxapine	Asendin	200–400

*Original trade names—all are now generic.

maximum response rates observed at plasma levels greater than or equal to 200 ng/ml of imipramine plus desipramine. A relationship between imipramine plasma level and clinical response has not been observed for milder depressives. For nortriptyline, a so-called therapeutic window has been described, with nortriptyline blood levels less than approximately 50 ng/ml and greater than 150 ng/ml being associated with poorer response than is seen at levels between 50 and 150 ng/ml (Asberg, Cronholm, Sjoqvist, & Tuck, 1971). Virtually identical data are available for protriptyline. Similarly, amitriptyline is also thought to have a therapeutic window of approximately 95 to 200 ng/ml (amitriptyline and nortriptyline). Some have argued that desipramine also has a therapeutic window, but data here are more limited.

Maintenance therapy with the TCAs has been the focus of two major studies. In one, Prien et al. (1984) reported relatively low efficacy for maintenance imipramine therapy; however, in that study patients were often maintained at relatively low doses. This reflected the common practice of the day. In the more recent study of Frank et al. (1990), imipramine was clearly demonstrated to be more effective than a placebo in 3-year maintenance therapy of recurrent unipolar depression (20% recurrence on imipramine vs. approximately 90% on the placebo). This study maintained patients at the doses to which they had responded. Moreover, lower dose versus full-dose maintenance strategies were tested in a subset of subjects (Frank et al., 1993). Full doses were significantly more effective than half doses (30% recurrence vs. 70% recurrence, respectively). Thus, main-

tenance therapy with TCAs appears to require continuing patients on the doses effective during acute treatment. This has now become standard practice.

MONOAMINE OXIDASE INHIBITORS

The development of the MAOIs is one of the most interesting chapters in the history of psychopharmacology. When tuberculosis was ravaging civilizations and patients infected with the tubercular bacillus were admitted to sanitoriums for long-term care, new antitubercular drugs were tested for efficacy in these settings. One such antitubercular drug, iproniazid, was noted to produce mood elevation in many patients. This led to the development of the three MAOIs in the United States: phenelzine, tranylcypromine, and isocarboxazid. These are all irreversible, nonselective MAOIs (i.e., inhibit both A and B isoforms) and, compared with newer antidepressants (see below), have a less favorable side-effect profile. MAO A metabolizes NE and 5-HT in brain and important aminergic compounds (e.g., tyramine) in gut. MAO A inhibition in gut necessitates patients being placed on dietary restrictions. Although reversible MAOIs with a more favorable side-effect profile have been developed (e.g., moclobemide), they are not available for clinical use in the United States.

Recently, a transdermal formulation of selegiline has been approved in the United States for treating major depression. At low doses, oral selegiline is an MAO B inhibitor, and at these doses, it does not require dietary restrictions. Inhibition of MAO A activity in brain appears key for achieving antidepressant response. When delivered transdermally, selegiline appears to exert MAO A and B inhibition in brain but not to inhibit MAO A in gut. This then appears to obviate the need for dietary restrictions, particularly at the lowest dose (i.e., 6 mg/day).

The MAOIs are believed to produce their therapeutic effects by preventing the degradation of monoamines, particularly serotonin, norepinephrine, and dopamine (DA), all posited to be reduced in availability in patients with unipolar depression. All of the available MAOIs have been shown to be effective in the treatment of unipolar depression and, in particular, atypical depression characterized by hypersomnia and hyperphagia (Krishnan, 2004). Table 9.3 lists the currently available MAOIs and their usual dose ranges. In addition to unipolar depression, MAOIs also appear effective, like SSRIs and certain TCAs, in the treatment of panic disorder. They are also effective in the treatment of bipolar depression. Some disadvantages of oral MAOIs include the necessity of dosing multiple times per day, associated with considerably poorer compliance when compared with once-a-day dosing, and the necessity of dietary constraints.

Certain foods that contain high concentrations of tyramine, an endogenous amine, such as aged meats and cheeses, chocolate, and Chianti wine, as well as over-the-counter cold medications (e.g., pseudoephedrine), are absolute contraindications in patients prescribed oral MAOIs because of the so-called cheese reaction, characterized by severe hypertension and possible medical sequelae such as stroke. Symptoms of this syndrome include severe headache, flushing, palpitations, and nausea. As described, this is less of an issue with transdermal selegiline.

Although now not practical, the proper manner to prescribe nonhydrazine MAOIs phenelzine and isocarboxazid was to first measure baseline platelet MAO activity, begin treatment with a phenelzine or isocarboxazid, and to repeat the platelet MAO activity measurement after 3 to 4 weeks of treatment. The best treatment responses are associated with 80 to 90% inhibition of platelet MAO activity. Because patients vary widely as to their MAO activity, it is impossible to predict the ideal dose of a MAOI for any given patient. Percentage of MAO inhibition does not appear to correlate with response to tranylcypromine.

In addition to the drug-drug and drug-food interactions noted above, MAOIs have a number of other untoward side effects, including orthostatic hypotension, sexual dysfunction, dizziness, insomnia, tachycardia, palpitations, and edema.

The MAOIs have not been generally considered first-line treatments for depression because of their unfavorable side-effect profile, dietary restrictions, need for dosing multiple times per day, and the general unavailability of platelet MAO activity measurements. They did appear to be more effective than the TCAs and perhaps the SSRIs for patients with so-called atypical depression characterized by leaden paralysis, lack of reactivity, hypersomnia, and so forth.

SELECTIVE SEROTONIN REUPTAKE INHIBITORS

Since their introduction in 1988, the selective serotonin reuptake inhibitors have become first-line treatments (Rush & the Depression Guideline Panel of the Agency for Health Care Policy and Research, 1994) for most patients with major depression (Table

TABLE 9.3 Monoamine Oxidase Inhibitors

Drug		Dose Range (mg/day)
Generic Name	Trade Name	
Phenelzine	Nardil	45–90
Tranylcypromine	Parnate	10–30
Isocarboxizid	Marplan	10–30
Selegine*	Emsam*	6–12*

*Transdermal delivery.

9.4). The first of these agents was fluoxetine. Five others have been released in the U.S. market: sertraline, paroxetine, fluvoxamine, citalopram, and escitalopram. Of these, fluvoxamine is approved for use in the United States only for OCD, but it is used as an antidepressant in many other countries. In this chapter, we emphasize the SSRIs approved for use in major depression in this country. These agents work primarily by blocking the reuptake of serotonin into presynaptic neurons. They have virtually no effect to date on blocking norepinephrine reuptake (except paroxetine at high doses), and they also do not interfere with various ligands binding to muscarinic cholinergic, alpha$_1$-adrenergic, or histamine H$_1$ receptors. Thus, they produce little — if any — dry mouth, constipation, or urinary hesitance (anticholinergic effects), orthostatic hypotension (alpha$_1$-adrenergic blockade), or sedation and weight gain (H$_1$ blockade). Paroxetine is an exception in that it has weak anticholinergic and norepinephrine reuptake blockade potential and does produce some dry mouth, albeit less than is seen with the TCAs. It is also mildly sedating in some patients.

The side effects associated with increased serotonin availability and commonly seen with the SSRIs include nausea, diarrhea, insomnia, nervousness, and sexual dysfunction. The first four of these are commonly dose dependent, so that more conservative dosing frequently prevents their occurrence. Sexual dysfunction is less clearly dose related and can be seen even at low doses. The initial trials failed to report high rates of sexual dysfunction (e.g., delayed ejaculation in men and anorgasmia in women) with SSRI therapy. These side effects have become apparent with wider spread long-term use. It is probable that many depressed patients are not aware of or are not bothered by sexual dysfunction in the initial weeks of treatment but do become troubled by this annoying side effect over time as they resume their normal activities. In the initial trials of fluoxetine, sexual dysfunction was noted in some 4% of subjects. Currently, estimates are that at least 30 to 40% of patients on SSRIs experience it.

Because these drugs have limited anticholinergic and noradrenergic effects, they are not cardiotoxic and are thus safe in overdoses. This represented a major step forward in treatment over the TCAs, which have a narrow safety margin (discussed above in the TCA section).

The SSRIs can be coadministered with the TCAs, but this needs to be done cautiously because, as a class, these agents generally inhibit P$_{450}$ isoenzymes in the liver that metabolize TCAs and result in higher blood levels and increased side effects (DeVane, 1994; Nemeroff et al., 1996). Citalopram has little effect on P$_{450}$ systems. The coprescription of SSRIs with MAOIs is contraindicated because of a risk of the serotonergic syndrome — characterized by myoclonic jerks, hyperpyrexia, and coma. The efficacy of the SSRIs has been clearly demonstrated in numerous RCTs; these data have been reviewed elsewhere (Nemeroff, 1994). Published data are most extensive for fluoxetine, sertraline, and paroxetine, with these drugs having been studied in several thousand patients.

In the eight RCTs published before the release of fluoxetine that formed the basis of the FDA submission, fluoxetine was significantly more effective than the placebo in the four placebo-controlled studies and was generally comparable to TCA in the six comparison trials (Schatzberg, 1995a). In the majority of studies, the dropout rate was lower (often sig-

TABLE 9.4 Typical Antidepressant Therapeutic Dosage Ranges of Selective Serotonin Reuptake Inhibitors (Adult Patients)

Drug		Therapeutic Dose Range (mg/day)
Generic Name	Trade Name	
Fluoxetine	Prozac	20–80
Paroxetine	Paxil	20–50
Sertraline	Zoloft	50–200
Citalopram	Celexa	20–40
Fluvoxamine	Fluvoxamine	100–300
Escitalopram	Lexapro	10–20

nificantly) for fluoxetine than for the TCA or placebo. Subsequent to the FDA submission, thousands of papers have appeared in the archival literature. Studies have continued to show significantly greater efficacy for fluoxetine over the placebo in patients of all age-groups with major depression. Two recent RCTs of fluoxetine in children and adolescents with major depression has found the drug to be significantly more effective than the placebo in that age-group (Emslie et al., 1997). More than 25 million patients have been treated with fluoxetine since its introduction.

Efficacy studies of paroxetine have also been reviewed in detail by our group and others (DeBattista & Schatzberg, 1995, Herr & Nemeroff, 2004). We reviewed nearly 30 RCTs of paroxetine for major depression. Paroxetine was significantly more effective than the placebo in 8 of 11 comparison studies. Paroxetine was comparable in efficacy to the TCA in all but 5 studies, which found either the TCA or paroxetine to be more effective. Overall, dropout rates for paroxetine due to adverse events were lower in patients on paroxetine than on TCAs. An early inpatient study in Denmark reported greater efficacy with clomipramine than paroxetine, and this study has been cited in the debate on SSRI efficacy in more severely depressed patients. However, this study used a relatively low dose of paroxetine (30 mg/day).

Sertraline efficacy data have been reviewed in detail elsewhere by Janicak et al. (1993); Mendels (1995), and Shim and Yonkers (2004). Sertraline has been reported to be more effective than a placebo in two large-scale clinical trials ($N = 545$) and to be of comparable efficacy to standard TCAs in two studies ($N = 320$). Sertraline has also been reported to be effective in the treatment of postpartum depression (Stowe, Casarella, Landry, & Nemeroff, 1995). Citalopram was introduced into the U.S. market in 1998, as was escitalopram in 2002. The enantiomer appears to be at least as effective as the parent, with potentially fewer side effects. However, both are highly effective agents (e.g., Feighner & Overo, 1999; Mendels Kiev, & Fabre, 1999; Roseboom & Kalin, 2004). Some have argued that alterations in the basic pharmacology, including greater effects on transporter and reuptake sites and fewer P_{450} effects, result in stronger efficacy and better tolerability for the S enantiomer, although this is still debated.

As indicated earlier, there has been an ongoing debate regarding whether the SSRIs, particularly fluoxetine, are as effective as the TCAs and more recently the dual uptake blockers in the treatment of patients with major depression, particularly the generally medically ill. These data have been reviewed in detail elsewhere (Anderson, 1998; Schatzberg, 1996; Thase, Entsuah, & Rudolph, 2001). Although there are occasional reports in the literature that an SSRI was less effective in these subjects, the overall data from RCTs originally did not bear out this conclusion. In one study, we compared desipramine and fluoxetine in a group of moderately to severely depressed patients (Bowden et al., 1993). The two drugs were of comparable efficacy; however, fluoxetine had a far more benign side-effect profile. In a small-scale study of more severely depressed inpatients, Clerc, Ruimy, and Verdeau-Palles (1994) reported that venlafaxine (a mixed uptake blocker) was significantly more effective at 4 to 6 weeks than fluoxetine. Subsequently, Thase, Entsuah, and Rudolph (2001) reported on a pooled analysis of eight studies comparing venlafaxine with SSRIs and reported significantly greater response with venlafaxine. Further analyses that included a larger pool of studies pointed to the superiority of venlafaxine over fluoxetine but not over other SSRIs, particularly paroxetine (Nemeroff et al., 2003). Thus, the debate is likely to continue for some time, although to date the data overall do not support the impression of lower efficacy.

Because fluoxetine was reported in the early trials to be "activating," some clinicians and investigators advised against using it in depressed patients with prominent anxiety. Analyses of the comparative clinical trials have revealed that the drug is as effective in anxious depressives as it is in major depressives without anxiety (Schatzberg, 1995b; Tollefson, Holman, & Sayler, 1994). Some patients may, however, require starting at a lower dose (e.g., 10 mg/day of fluoxetine). Significant SSRI efficacy in purely anxious patients (e.g., panic disorder) has been revealed in RCTs as well. Thus, the SSRIs (including fluoxetine) appear effective in both depressed and anxious patients or in those who demonstrate mixed symptoms. SSRIs are effective in the treatment of bipolar depression and less likely to cause a switch into mania than TCAS or MAIOs (Nemeroff et al., 2001).

All SSRIs have been reported to be significantly more effective than a placebo in preventing relapse or recurrence for up to 1 year of treatment. For example, of patients treated with fluoxetine for 1 year,

26% experienced a relapse or recurrence, in contrast to 57% on a placebo (Montgomery et al., 1988). Similarly, 14% of patients treated with paroxetine relapsed or recurred versus 30% on a placebo (Montgomery & Dunbar, 1993). The sertraline relapse rate over 44 weeks of continuation treatment was 13%, in contrast to 46% for a placebo (Doogan & Caillard, 1992). Similarly, citalopram was significantly more effective than placebo in preventing relapse (Montgomery, Rasmussen, & Tanghoj, 1993). There are similar data for the newer SSRIs. These data are all remarkably similar and point to the efficacy of the SSRIs during continuation and maintenance treatment. Of note is that, in these longer term studies, new side effects of the SSRIs have not emerged. Thus, the relative safety of this class of agents appears to be maintained after long-term treatment.

All the SSRIs that are marketed as antidepressants have half-lives of about 24 hours and can be given in a once-a-day dose. The long half-life of norfluoxetine (7 to 14 days), an active metabolite of fluoxetine, suggested that the drug can be given one or two times a week. Indeed, once-weekly fluoxetine has now been approved for the treatment of depression by the FDA. Such data are not available for paroxetine, citalopram, or sertraline. Paroxetine has no active metabolites and is unlikely to be effective when prescribed on a weekly or twice-weekly basis. Sertraline's demethylated metabolite has a half-life (3 days) that is much shorter than that of norfluoxetine and is formed in relatively lower concentrations. This drug is also not a likely candidate for less frequent prescription.

Therapeutic antidepressant dosage ranges for the SSRIs are summarized in Table 9.4. The standard starting dose for fluoxetine, paroxetine, and citalopram is 20 mg/day; for sertraline, it is 50 mg/day. For most patients, 20 mg/day of fluoxetine is the therapeutic dose, with 40 mg/day the next most common dose. Some patients require higher doses (e.g., 60 to 100 mg/day) to respond, whereas others derive benefit from 10 mg/day. In double-blind studies, 20 mg/day and 40 mg/day appeared to be the most effective doses, but a 5-mg/day dose also was more effective than a placebo. (For review of dosage issues, see Schatzberg, 1995a.) Paroxetine is generally effective at doses of 20 to 30 mg/day, with a maximum recommended dose in major depression of 50 mg/day. The usual starting dose is 20 mg/day. Sertraline may be effective at 50 mg/day, but many studies report average doses of 100 to 150 mg/day. The starting dose is typically 50 mg/day. The recommended maximum dose is 200 mg/day. For citalopram, the recommended starting dose is 20 mg/day, aiming for therapeutic doses of approximately 40 mg/day; for the S enantiomer, starting dose is 10 mg/day, with recommended daily dose being 10 to 20 mg./day. In elderly patients or for those with prominent anxiety or agitation, the recommended starting doses for SSRIs are 50% lower. Citalopram is effective at 20 to 40 mg/day, the 40-mg/day dose being used commonly by psychiatrists. To date, there are no available data that correlate antidepressant responses to SSRI plasma levels.

VENLAFAXINE (EFFEXOR)

Venlafaxine (Effexor) is a dual serotonin/norepinephrine (5HT/NE) reuptake inhibitor approved for the treatment of depression; its pharmacological and clinical properties have been reviewed elsewhere (Andrews, Ninan, & Nemeroff, 1996. Thase & Sloan, 2004). Because there is evidence that reduced availability of both NE and 5HT occurs in patients with depression and, moreover, because of evidence that both NE and 5HT reuptake blockade are associated with therapeutic efficacy in depression, an uptake blocker of both monoamines was considered of interest, especially if such a drug lacked the adverse side-effect profile of the TCAs. Venlafaxine is indeed such an agent at its higher dose range and can be conceptualized as a TCA without the anticholinergic, antiadrenergic, and antihistaminergic effects of the TCAs. It therefore should have all of the efficacy and none of the unfavorable side effects of the TCAs.

There is indeed evidence that this is the case. Unlike TCAs, venlafaxine produces no orthostatic hypotension, is not particularly lethal in most overdoses, and produces no dry mouth, constipation, blurry vision, or sedation. Its side-effect profile resembles exactly what one would predict from its postulated mechanism of action, namely, the combination of the SSRIs' side effects (nausea, headache, sexual dysfunction, and insomnia) and the NE reuptake blockers' side effects (hypertension, tachycardia, and sweating). The original preparation was associated with considerable nausea. This has been obviated with the introduction of an extended release formulation (XR). The starting dose is 75 mg/day. Although

75 mg is often an effective dose in many patients, others require doses up to 225 mg per day or even higher (Table 9.5). Another major advantage of venlafaxine is its lack of inhibition of any of the cytochrome P$_{450}$ hepatic isoenzymes responsible for drug-drug interactions with certain of the SSRIs (see the introductory section of this chapter). This allows for the combination of venlafaxine with TCAs and other medications in nonresponsive patients without concerns about increases in TCA plasma levels and associated toxicity.

In contradistinction to the apparently less optimal side-effect profile of venlafaxine compared with the SSRIs is its reputation for superb efficacy in the treatment of unipolar depression, particularly in treatment-refractory patients. There is little doubt among most psychopharmacologists that venlafaxine is successful in treating a sizable proportion of patients who have failed trials with other antidepressants, including SSRIs; this has been reported in an open study (Nierenberg, Feighner, Rudolph, Cole, & Sullivan, 1994). In the last edition, we noted that we had treated approximately 25 patients who failed trials with other antidepressants and electroconvulsive therapy (ECT) who were venlafaxine responders. Less clear is whether venlafaxine acts more rapidly than other antidepressants, an active avenue of investigation. Because of its short half-life, venlafaxine attains steady-state plasma levels very rapidly compared with other antidepressants.

In addition to its acknowledged efficacy in treatment-refractory depression is the evidence that venlafaxine is more effective than the SSRIs in severe depression (frequently defined as the melancholic subtype or the endogenous subtype) or in hospitalized depressed patients. Two early double-blind controlled studies have evaluated the efficacy of venlafaxine for severe depression. In one (Guelfi, White, Hackett, Guichoux, & Magni, 1995), venlafaxine was shown to be effective for severe depression when compared with a placebo; most impressive was the lack of any effect of the placebo in this population. In a second study (Clerc et al., 1994), fluoxetine and venlafaxine were compared in depressed inpatients; both drugs were effective, but venlafaxine was more effective than fluoxetine, and the antidepressant effect had a more rapid onset of action. As noted earlier, Thase, Entsuah, and Rudolph (2001) conducted a pooled analysis of approximately 2,000 patients showing that venlafaxine is more effective than placebo or SSRI, largely fluoxetine, in attaining remission in patients with major depression. Subsequently, Nemeroff et al. (2003) reviewed about 25 additional studies and reported venlafaxine appears to be more effective than fluoxetine in major depression. It did not appear to be more effective than other SSRIs, particularly paroxetine.

DULOXETINE

Duloxetine is similar in structure to fluoxetine but, unlike the latter, has both potent norepinephrine and serotonin reuptake blocking effects. The drug, which was introduced in the United States in 2004, is approved for major depression, as well as for diabetic neuropathic pain. It is being actively studied for fibromyalgia.

TABLE 9.5 Atypical Antidepressants

Drug		Dose Range (mg/day)
Generic Name	Trade Name	
Trazadone	Desyrel	300–600
Nefazadone*	Serzone*	400–600
Bupropion	Wellbutrin XL**	150–300**
Venlafaxine XR	Effexor XR	75–225
Mirtazapine	Remeron	30–45
Duloxetine	Cymbalta	60–120

*Serzone trade named product not currently available. Generic nefazaone is available.

**Also available as Wellbutrin and Wellbutrin SR with upper dose limitations of 450 mg and 400 mg/day, respectively.

As discussed under venlafaxine, there has been a perception that dual uptake blockers may be more effective than are pure serotonergic agents, although, again, this is still in some debate. As a dual uptake inhibitor, duloxetine appears to enhance filtering of pain signals and to decrease the chronic physical pain often seen in depression. This may account for perceived enhanced efficacy. The drug has been reported to be significantly more effective than placebo at 60 mg/day (Detke, Lu, Goldstein, McNamara, & Demitrack, 2002; Goldstein, Mallinckrodt, Lu, & Demitrack, 2002).

The drug's side effect profile is similar to those of SSRIs, with nausea being perhaps the most common adverse event, occurring in as many as 40% of subjects started at 60 mg/day. Generally, 30 mg/day is used to start drug-naive patients to lessen the frequency and severity of nausea. Therapeutic dose is generally 60 to 120 mg/day.

BUPROPION (WELLBUTRIN)

Bupropion (Wellbutrin) is an amino ketone that has little effect on 5HT, NE, or DA reuptake but has been demonstrated to be effective for major depression. How it exerts its therapeutic effects via an effect on DA systems remains unclear, but it may be due to the action of an active metabolite.

Like that of the other antidepressants, the efficacy of bupropion in the treatment of major depression is comparable to that of TCAs, as well as of fluoxetine and trazodone. Because of its short half-life, bupropion was originally administered twice per day; for that reason, as well as because of a propensity for high doses of the drug to produce seizures, a slow-release form of the drug was developed, studied in clinical trials, and then released. This preparation has the advantage of once-a-day dosing and a risk of seizures no greater than that observed with other antidepressants.

Bupropion has certain advantages when compared with TCAs, including a lack of orthostatic hypertension, few cardiovascular effects, and no anticholinergic effects. Bupropion produces no sedation or cognitive impairment and, most important, in contrast to the SSRIs, produces no sexual dysfunction. In contrast to the TCAs, which are well known to produce weight gain, treatment with bupropion results in weight loss in many patients, which in certain clinical circumstances can be problematic.

Bupropion was also shown in two small studies to be effective in the treatment of bipolar depression, with little propensity to cause a switch into mania, though this was not confirmed in a subsequent study. Whether bupropion is effective in the treatment of refractory depression remains unknown.

TRAZODONE (DESYREL)

Trazodone was the first antidepressant introduced in the United States that was not lethal when taken in overdose. A triazolopyridine derivative, it is structurally unrelated to the tricyclics but is related to nefazodone (discussed in the next section). Trazodone is believed to act as an antidepressant primarily by virtue of its effects as a serotonin type 2 ($5HT_2$) receptor antagonist. Trazodone has a short half-life of 3 to 9 hours, but it can be administered once per day. In addition to antagonism of the $5HT_2$ receptor, trazodone is also known to be a weak inhibitor of serotonin reuptake, far less potent than any of the marketed SSRIs. Several trials revealed that trazodone is as effective as TCAs and fluoxetine in the treatment of major depression, though many clinicians have the impression that it is not effective in moderate to severe depression.

The major side effects include sedation, which can often limit the drug's clinical usefulness, though frequently trazodone was combined with SSRIs to reverse SSRI-induced insomnia. Trazodone clearly has fewer anticholinergic side effects than TCAs, but its primary drawback, particularly in the elderly, is orthostatic hypotension, thought to be due to alpha$_1$-adrenergic receptor blockade. Another potentially serious adverse side effect of trazodone is the fact that a small percentage of men develop priapism after trazodone use, and in a small percentage of those individuals, surgical intervention is necessary. It is also important to point out that trazodone has been associated with arrhythmias in patients with preexisting cardiac disease.

In terms of dosing, trazodone is usually begun at a dose of 100 to 150 mg/day and is increased to doses of 400 to 600 mg/day. Although such doses can be administered once per day, they are often administered in divided doses, particularly when the dose exceeds 300 mg/day.

NEFAZODONE (SERZONE)

The antidepressant nefazodone, structurally related to trazodone, is a potent $5HT_2$ antagonist, as well as an inhibitor of both 5HT and NE reuptake (Owens, Ieni, Knight, Winders, & Nemeroff, 1995; Taylor et al., 1995). It is an effective antidepressant and has the advantages of producing no sexual dysfunction, a major advantage compared with the SSRIs, and also preserves normal sleep architecture. Like the SSRIs, nefazodone has also been shown to be effective in reducing the anxiety associated with major depression as assessed with the Covi scale.

One disadvantage of this drug was the necessity for twice-daily dosing due to its short half-life and the necessity to titrate the dose. Although the manufacturer recommends a dose of 100 mg twice per day as the starting dose, many clinicians recommended a starting dose of 50 mg twice a day due to the sedation commonly observed with this drug. Nefazodone had to be administered in a dose range of 300 to 600 mg/day to achieve maximal efficacy. The greatest disadvantage was the emergence of severe liver toxicity and need for transplantation seen in 1/250,000 exposures. This resulted in the manufacturer ceasing production, although a generic form is still available.

In a landmark study, Keller and colleagues (2000) reported that nefazodone combined with cognitive-behavior therapy (CBT) is very effective in the treatment of patients with chronic depression and more effective than either treatment given alone.

Nefazadone is an inhibitor of P_{450}-3A4, and caution should be used when using benzodiazepines such as alprazolam, triazolam, or midazolam in combination with nefazadone because these drugs are also metabolized by the enzyme. When they are co-administered with nefazodone, marked elevations of plasma concentrations can occur.

MIRTAZAPINE (REMERON)

Mirtazapine (Remeron) is a novel antidepressant that is one of the newest entries into the antidepressant market in the United States. This tetracyclic is believed to act primarily as an alpha$_2$-antagonist at auto- and heteroreceptors and is also a 5HT2A and $5HT_3$ receptor antagonist. Its net effect is the increase of 5HT and NE neurotransmission (de Boer, 1996).

Its major advantages include a single daily dose, the lack of sexual dysfunction, and safety in overdose and sedating properties, which is particularly helpful in depressed patients with profound insomnia as often seen in the elderly patient. Its major side effects include marked daytime somnolence, to which patients eventually become tolerant, as well as increased appetite, weight gain, and dizziness. Of 2,796 patients in clinical trials, 2 developed agranulocytosis and 1 developed severe neutropenia. Wide-scale use postrelease has not revealed an increased risk of this reaction. The drug has become commonly used in geriatric patients, where sedation is a potential benefit and in whom weight gain is less common (Schatzberg, Kremer, & Rodrigues, 2002). Its efficacy has been reported to be faster and slightly greater than that of the SSRIs in several studies (Benkert, Szegedi, & Kohnen, 2000; Schatzberg et al., 2001), and the drug has been shown to be effective in SSRI nonresponders (Thase, Kremer, & Rodrigues, 2001).

DISCUSSION

For all classes of antidepressants available in the United States, efficacy has been demonstrated in RCTs. The differences among these classes of agents revolve primarily around their side effects and safety. The first-generation TCAs and MAOIs are less well tolerated and are more dangerous in overdose than are the newer agents. For this reason alone, the SSRIs and other newer agents represent important steps forward in the treatment of major depression. Moreover, the TCAs are largely noradrenergic in their reuptake blocking effects, exerting little effect on serotonin reuptake (clomipramine is a notable exception). The difference in monoamine reuptake blockade most likely accounts for a wider range of efficacy for the SSRIs (e.g., panic, OCD, bulimia, premenstrual syndrome), as well as for their demonstrated effects in milder forms of depression, such as dysthymia.

Although the various classes enjoy efficacy for major depression, a number of issues about their relative efficacy for specific subgroups or subtypes of depression remain in debate. For example, as indicated earlier, some argue that the TCAs are more efficacious antidepressants and are more likely to induce remission in melancholic depressives than the SSRIs. These data and the venlafaxine and mirtazapine findings suggest the need in treating severely ill patients to have drugs that exert potent noradrenergic effects. Another issue is whether the MAOIs (and perhaps the SSRIs) are more effective in atypical depressives than are the TCAs. These areas require further prospective study.

The relatively high placebo response rates in outpatient studies are of concern in some studies, with both known and investigational antidepressants failing to separate from the placebo. Research and clinical experience suggest more severely ill patients show less in the way of placebo response, but they also show less in the way of drug response. Thus, just including more severely ill patients is not a panacea. As indicated in the introduction, we need to clarify what placebo treatment in a study actually represents and what it should include. Certainly, a great deal of supportive hand-holding and patient contact do not reflect a no-treatment condition but instead constitute powerful interventions. This area requires further study so that we can design better protocols to test drug efficacy.

Of related importance is that the Food and Drug Administration may approve a drug that has been shown to separate from the placebo in two studies, but that also has several so-called failed trials in which efficacy was not demonstrated. The result can be to cloud a new agent in some doubt and to undercut confidence in the drug. Thus, there is also a need to think through how much and in what types of patients efficacy should be required before approval. Although many issues remain regarding the range of efficacy for antidepressants, these drugs are certainly effective in patients with major depression, and their prescription and use have had a tremendous impact on the lives of many depressed patients.

ACKNOWLEDGMENTS

In the past three years, Charles B. Nemeroff and Alan F. Schatzberg have consulted to GSK, Lilly, Pfizer, Jannsen, BMS, Forest Laboratories, Wyeth, and Somerset. Nemeroff has also consulted with Solvay. Schatzberg has equity in Pfizer and is a named inventor on pharmacogenetic intellectual property licensed to Pathways Diagnostics.

The authors are supported, in part, by National Institute of Mental Health Grants NIH MH-58922, MH-39415, and MH-42088 (CBN), and by NIH MH50604 and MH 47573(AFS).

REFERENCES

Anderson, I. M. (1998). SSRI's versus tricyclic antidepressants in depressed inpatients: A meta-analysis of efficacy and tolerability. *Depression and Anxiety,* 7(Suppl.), 1–17.

Andrews, J. M., Ninan, P. T., & Nemeroff, C. B. (1996). Venlafaxine: A novel antidepressant that has a dual mechanism of action. *Depression, 4,* 48–56.

Asberg, M., Cronholm, B., Sjoqvist, F., & Tuck, D. (1971). Relationship between plasma level and therapeutic effect of nortriptyline. *British Medical Journal, 3,* 331–334.

Benkert, O., Szegedi, A., & Kohnen, R. (2000). Mirtazapine compared with paroxetine in major depression. *Journal of Clinical Psychiatry, 61,* 656–663.

Blacker, D. (1996). Maintenance treatment of major depression: A review of the literature. *Harvard Review of Psychiatry, 4,* 1–9.

Boswell, E. G., Anfinson, T. J., & Nemeroff, C. B. (1997). Depression associated with endocrine disorders. In M. Robertson & C. Katona (Eds.), *Depression and physical illness* (pp. 255–292). Sussex, England: Wiley.

Bowden, C. L., Schatzberg, A. F., Rosenbaum, A., Contreras, S. A., Samson, J. A., Dessain, E., et al. (1993). Fluoxetine and desipramine in major depressive disorder. *Journal of Clinical Psychopharmacology, 13,* 305–311.

Boyer, W. F., & Feighner, J. P. (1994). Clinical significance of early non-response in depressed patients. *Depression, 2,* 32–35.

Chan, C. H., Janicak, P. G., Davis, J. M., Altman, E., Andriukaitis, S., & Hedeker, D. (1987). Response of psychotic and nonpsychotic depressed patients to tricyclic antidepressants. *Journal of Clinical Psychiatry, 48,* 197–200.

Clerc, G. E., Ruimy, P., Verdeau-Palles, J. (1994). A double-blind comparison of venlafaxine and fluoxetine in patients hospitalized for major depression and melancholia. *International Clinical Psychopharmacology, 9,* 139–143.

Danish University Antidepressant Group. (1986). Citalopram: Clinical effect profile in comparison with clomipramine: A controlled multicenter study. *Psychopharmacology, 90,* 131–138.

Danish University Antidepressant Group. (1990). Paroxetine: A selective serotonin reuptake inhibitor showing better tolerance, but weaker antidepressant effect than clomipramine in a controlled multicenter study. *Journal of Affective Disorders,* 18, 289–299.

DeBattista, C., & Schatzberg, A. F. (1995). Paroxetine. In H. I. Kaplan & B. J. Sadock (Eds.), *Comprehensive textbook of psychiatry* (Vol. 2, 6th ed., pp. 2063–2069). Baltimore: Williams and Wilkins.

de Boer, T. (1996). The pharmacologic profile of mirtazapine. *Journal of Clinical Psychiatry,* 57(Suppl. 4), 19–25.

Detke, M. J., Lu Y., Goldstein, D. J., McNamara, R. K., Demitrack, M. A. (2002). Duloxetine 60 mg. once daily dosing versus placebo in the acute treatment of major depression. *Journal of Psychiatric Research,* 36, 383–390.

DeVane, C. L., & Sallee, F. R. (1996). Serotonin selective reuptake inhibitors in child and adolescent psychopharmacology: A review of published experience. *Journal of Clinical Psychiatry,* 57, 55–65.

DeVane, L. (1994). Pharmacokinetics of the newer antidepressants: Clinical relevance. *American Journal of Medicine,* 97(Suppl. 6A), 13–22.

Doogan, D. P., & Caillard, V. (1992). Sertraline in the prevention of depression. *British Journal of Psychiatry,* 160, 217–222.

Elkin, I., Sheat, T., Watkins, J., et al. (1989). NIMH Treatment of Depression Collaborative Research Program: 1. General effectiveness of treatments. *Archives of General Psychiatry,* 46, 971–982.

Emslie, G. J., Rush, A. J., & Weinberg, W. A., Kowatch, R. A., Hughes, C. W., Carmody, T., et al. (1997). A double-blind, randomized, placebo-controlled trial of fluoxetine in children and adolescents with depression. *Archives of General Psychiatry,* 54, 1031–1037.

Ereshefsky, L. (1996). Drug interactions of antidepressants. *Psychiatric Annals,* 26, 342–350.

Feighner, J., & Overo, K. (1999). Multicenter, placebo-controlled, fixed-dose study of citalopram in moderate-to-severe depression. *Journal of Clinical Psychiatry,* 60, 1–7.

Fisher, R. L., & Fisher, S. (1996). Antidepressants for children: Is scientific support necessary? *Journal of Nervous and Mental Disease,* 184, 99–108.

Frank, E., Kupfer, D. J., Perel, J. M., Cornes, C., Jarrett, D. B., Mallinger, A. G., et al. (1990). Three-year outcomes for maintenance therapies in recurrent depression. *Archives of General Psychiatry,* 47, 1093–1099.

Frank, E., Kupfer, D. J., Perel, J. M., Cornes, C., Mallinger, A. G., Thase, M. E., et al. (1993). Comparison of full-dose versus half-dose pharmacotherapy in the maintenance treatment of recurrent depression. *Journal of Affective Disorders,* 27, 139–145.

Frasure-Smith, N., Lesperance, F., & Talajic, M. (1993). Depression following myocardial infarction: Impact on 6 month survival. *Journal of the American Medical Association,* 270, 1819–1861.

Frasure-Smith, N., Lesperance, F., & Talajic, M. (1995). Depression and 18 month prognosis after myocardial infarction. *Circulation,* 91, 999–1005.

Glassman, A. H., Perel, J. M., Shostak, M., Kantor, S. J., & Fleiss, J. L. (1977). Clinical implications of imipramine plasma levels for depressive illness. *Archives of General Psychiatry,* 34, 197–204.

Goldstein, D. J., Mallinckrodt, C., Lu, Y., & Demitrack, M. A. (2002). Duloxetine in the treatment of major depressive disorder: A double-blind placebo-controlled trial. *Journal of Clinical Psychiatry,* 63, 225–231.

Guelfi, J. D., White, C., Hackett, D., Guichoux, J. Y., & Magni, G. (1995). Effectiveness of venlafaxine in patients hospitalized for major depression and melancholia. *Journal of Clinical Psychiatry,* 56, 450–458.

Herr, K. D., & Nemeroff, C. B. (2004). Paroxetine. In A. F. Schatzberg & C. B. Nemeroff (Eds.), *Textbook of psychopharmacology* (3rd ed., pp. 251–281). Washington, DC: American Psychiatric Press.

Hirschfeld, R. M., & Schatzberg, A. F. (1994). Long-term management of depression. *American Journal of Medicine,* 97(Suppl. 6A), 33–38.

Hollon, S. D., DeRubeis, R., Evans, M. D., Wiemer, M. J., Garvey, M. J., Grove, W. M., et al. (1992). Cognitive therapy and pharmacotherapy for depression: Singly and in combination. *Archives of General Psychiatry,* 49, 774–781.

Janicak, P. G., Davis, J. M., Preskorn, S. H., & Ayd, F. J. (1993). *Principles and practice of psychopharmacology.* Baltimore: Williams and Wilkins.

Keller, M. B., McCullogh, J. P., & Klein, D. N., Arnow, B., Dunner, D. L, Gelenberg, A. J., et al. (2000). A comparison of nefazodone, cognitive behavioral analysis system of psychotherapy, and their combination for treatment of chronic depression. *New England Journal of Medicine,* 342, 1462–1470.

Keller, M. B., Ryan, N. D., Strober, M., Klein, R. G., Kutcher, Sp. P., Birmaher, B., et al. (2001). Efficacy of paroxetine in the treatment of adolescent major depression: A randomized, controlled trial. *Journal of the American Academy of Child and Adolescent Psychiatry,* 40, 762–772.

Kraemer, H. C., & Kupfer, D. J. (2006). Size of treatment effects and their importance to clinical research and practice. *Biological Psychiatry,* 59, 990–996.

Krishnan, K. R. R. (2004). Monoamine oxidase inhibitors. In A. F. Schatzberg & C. B. Nemeroff (Eds.), *Textbook of psychopharmacology* (3rd ed., pp. 303–314). Washington, DC: American Psychiatric Association Press.

McDaniel, J. S., Musselman, D. L., Porter, M. R., Reed, D. A., & Nemeroff, C. B. (1995). Depression in patients with cancer: Diagnosis, biology and treatment. *Archives of General Psychiatry, 52*, 89–99.

Mendels, J. (1995). Sertraline. In H. I. Kaplan & B. J. Sadock (Eds.), *Comprehensive textbook of psychiatry* (Vol. 2, 6th ed., pp. 2069–2073). Baltimore: Williams and Wilkins.

Mendels, J., Kiev, A., & Fabre, L. (1999). Double-blind comparison of citalopram and placebo in depressed patients with melancholia. *Depression and Anxiety, 9*, 54–60.

Montgomery, S. A., Dufour, H., Brion, S., Gailledreaux, J., Laqueille, X., Ferrey, G., et al. (1988). The prophylactic efficacy of fluoxetine in unipolar depression. *British Journal of Psychiatry, 153*(Suppl. 3), 69–76.

Montgomery, S. A., & Dunbar, G. (1993). Paroxetine is better than placebo in relapse prevention and the prophylaxis of recurrent depression. *International Journal of Clinical Psychopharmacology, 8*, 189–195.

Montgomery, S. A., Rasmussen, J. G. C., & Tanghoj, P. (1993). A 24-week study of 20 mg citalopram, 40 mg citalopram, and placebo in the prevention of relapse of major depression. *International Journal of Clinical Psychopharmacology, 8*, 181–188.

Murphy, G. M., Jr., Hollander, S. B., Rodrigues, H. E., Kremer, C., & Schatzberg, A. F. (2004). Effects of the serotonin transporter gene promoter polymorphism on mirtazapine and paroxetine efficacy and adverse events in geriatric major depression. *Archives of General Psychiatry, 61*, 1163–1169.

Murphy, G. M., Kremer, C, Rodrigues, H, & Schatzberg, A. F. (2003a). Mitrazapine versus Paroxetine Study Group. The apolipoprotein E epsilon4 allele and antidepressant efficacy in cognitively intact elderly depressed patients. *Biological Psychiatry, 7*, 665–673.

Murphy, G. M., Jr., Kremer, C., Rodrigues, H. E., & Schatzberg, A. F. (2003b). Pharmacogenetics of antidepressant medication intolerance. *American Journal of Psychiatry, 10*, 1830–1835,

Nemeroff, C. B. (1994). Evolutionary trends in the pharmacotherapeutic management of depression. *Journal of Clinical Psychiatry, 55*, 3–15.

Nemeroff, C. B., DeVane, C. L., & Pollack, B. G. (1996). Newer antidepressants and the cytochrome P450 system. *American Journal of Psychiatry, 153*, 311–320.

Nemeroff, C. B., Evans, D. L., & Gyulai, L., Sachs, G. S., Bowden, C. L., Gergel, I. P., et al. (2001). Double-blind, placebo-controlled comparison of imipramine and paroxetine in the treatment of bipolar depression. *American Journal of Psychiatry, 158*, 906–912.

Nemeroff, C. B., Willard, L., Entsuah, E., et al. (2003). Venlafaxine and SSRI's. New Research Abstracts, 156th Annual Meeting of the American Psychiatric Association. San Francisco, CA.

Nierenberg, A. A., Feighner, J. P., Rudolph, R., Cole, J. O., & Sullivan, J. (1994). Venlafaxine for treatment-resistant depression. *Journal of Clinical Psychopharmacology, 14*, 419–423.

Nierenberg, A. A., McLean, N. E., Alpert, J. E., Worthington, J. J., Rosenbaum, J. F., & Fava, M. (1995). Early nonresponse to fluoxetine as a predictor of poor 8-week outcome. *American Journal of Psychiatry, 152*, 1500–1503.

Owens, M. J., Ieni, J. R., Knight, D. L., Winders, K., & Nemeroff, C. B. (1995). The serotonergic antidepressant nefazodone inhibits the serotonin transporter: In vivo and ex vivo studies. *Life Sciences, 57*, 373–380.

Potter, W. Z., Manji, A. K., & Rudorfer, M. V. (1998). Tricyclics and tetracyclics. In A. F. Schatzberg & C. B. Nemeroff (Eds.), *Textbook of psychopharmacology* (2nd ed., pp. 199–218). Washington, DC: American Psychiatric Press.

Prien, R. F., Kupfer, D. J., Mansky, P. A., Small, J. G., Tuason, V. B., Voss, C. B., et al. (1984). Drug therapy in the prevention of recurrences in unipolar and bipolar affective disorders: A report of the NIMH Collaborative Study Group comparing lithium carbonate, imipramine, and a lithium carbonate–imipramine combination. *Archives of General Psychiatry, 41*, 1096–1104.

Roose, S. P., Glassman, A. H., Attia, E., & Woodring, S. (1994). Comparative efficacy of selective serotonin reuptake inhibitors and tricyclics in the treatment of melancholia. *American Journal of Psychiatry, 151*, 1735–1739.

Roose, S. P., & Schatzberg, A. F. (2005). The efficacy of antidepressants in the treatment of late-life depression. *Journal of Clinical Psychopharmacology, 25*(4 Suppl. 1), S1–S7.

Roseboom, P. H., & Kalin, N. H. (2004). Citalopram and S-citalopram. In A. F. Schatzberg & C. B. Nemeroff (Eds.), *Textbook of psychopharmacology* (pp. 291–302). Washington, DC: American Psychiatric Press.

Rush, J. A., & the Depression Guideline Panel of the Agency for Health Care Policy and Research. (1994). Synopsis of the clinical practice guidelines for diagnosis and treatment of depression in primary care. *Archives of Family Medicine, 3*, 85–92.

Schatzberg, A. F. (1995a). Fluoxetine. In H. I. Kaplan & R. J. Sadock (Eds.), *Comprehensive textbook of psychiatry* (Vol. 2, 6th ed., pp. 2056–2063). Baltimore: Williams and Wilkins.

Schatzberg, A. F. (1995b). Fluoxetine in the treatment of comorbid anxiety and depression [Monograph]. *Journal of Clinical Psychiatry, 13*(2), 2–12.

Schatzberg, A. F. (1996). Treatment of severe depression with the selective serotonin reuptake inhibitors. *Depression, 4*, 182–189.

Schatzberg, A. F., Cole, J. D., & DeBattista, C. (2005). Manual of clinical psychopharmacology (5th ed.) Washington, DC: American Psychiatric Press.

Schatzberg, A. F., & Kraemer, H. C. (2000). Use of placebo control groups in evaluating efficacy of treatment of unipolar major depression. *Biological Psychiatry, 47*, 736–744.

Schatzberg, A., Kremer, C., Rodrigues, H., Bari, M., Baumel, B., Blake, L., et al. (2001). Mirtazapine versus paroxetine in elderly depressed patients. *Abstracts, 41st Annual NCDEU Meeting*, Poster I-62.

Schatzberg, A. F., Kremer, C., & Rodrigues, H. E. (2002). Double-blind randomized comparison of mirtazapine and paroxetine in elderly depressed patients. *American Journal of Geriatric Psychiatry, 10*, 541–550.

Schatzberg, A. F., & Roose, S.A. (2006). A double-blind, placebo-controlled study of venlafaxine and fluoxetine in geriatric outpatients with major depression. *American Journal of Geriatric Psychiatry, 14*, 361–370.

Schatzberg, A. F., & Rothschild, A. J. (1992). Psychotic (delusional) major depression: Should it be included as a distinct syndrome in *DSM-IV? American Journal of Psychiatry, 149*, 733–745.

Shelton, R. C., Tollefson, G. D, Tohen, M., Stahl, S., Gannon, K. S., Jacobs, T. G., et al. (2001). A novel augmentation strategy for treating resistant major depression. *American Journal of Psychiatry, 158*, 131–134.

Shim, J., & Yonkers, K. A. (2004). Sertraline. In A. F. Schatzberg & C. B. Nemeroff (Eds.), *Textbook of psychopharmacology* (3rd ed., pp. 247–257). Washington, DC: American Psychiatric Press.

Stowe, Z. N., Casarella, J., Landry, J., & Nemeroff, C. B. (1995). Sertraline in the treatment of women with post-partum major depression. *Depression, 3*, 49–55.

Taylor, D. P., Carter, R. B., Eison, A. S., Mullins, U. L., Smith, H. L., Torrente, J. R., et al. (1995). Pharmacology and neurochemistry of nefazodone, a novel antidepressant drug. *Journal of Clinical Psychiatry, 6*(Suppl.), 3–11.

Thase, M. E., Entsuah, A. R., & Rudolph, R. L. (2001). Remission rates during treatment with venlafaxine or selective serotonin reuptake inhibitors. *British Journal of Psychiatry, 178*, 234–241.

Thase, M. E., Kremer, C., & Rodrigues, H. (2001). Mirtazapine versus sertraline after SSRI non-response. *Abstracts, 41st Annual NCDEU Meeting*, Poster II-1.

Thase, M. E., & Sloan, D. M. E. (2004). Venlafaxine. In A. F. Schatzberg & C. B. Nemeroff (Eds.), *Textbook of psychopharmacology* (3rd ed., pp. 349–360). Washington, DC: American Psychiatric Press.

Thase, M. E., & Sullivan, L. R. (1995). Relapse and recurrence of depression: A practical approach for prevention. *CNS Drugs, 4*, 261–277.

Tollefson, G. D., Holman, S. L., & Sayler, M. E. (1994). Fluoxetine, placebo, and tricyclic antidepressants in major depression with and without anxious features. *Journal of Clinical Psychiatry, 55*, 50–59.

Wagner, K. D., Robb A. S., Findling R. L., Jim, J., Gutierrez, M. M., & Heydorn, W. E. (2004). A randomized placebo-controlled trial of citalopram for the treatment of major depression in children and adolescents. *American Journal of Psychiatry, 161*, 1079–1083.

10

Psychosocial Treatments for Major Depressive Disorder

W. Edward Craighead

Erin S. Sheets

Alisha L. Brosse

Stephen S. Ilardi

Behavior therapy (BT), cognitive-behavior therapy (CBT), and interpersonal psychotherapy (IPT) have each been shown by at least two Type 1 or Type 2 randomized controlled trials, as well as by four meta-analytic reports of the literature, to be effective psychosocial interventions for patients meeting criteria for major depressive disorder (MDD). All three psychosocial treatments have yielded substantial reductions in scores on the two major depression rating scales (the Beck Depression Inventory and the Hamilton Rating Scale for Depression), significant decreases in percentage of patients meeting the criteria for MDD at posttreatment, and substantial maintenance of effects well after treatment has ended. The data for outcomes of psychosocial and pharmacological interventions for major depressive episodes suggest that the two treatment modes are equally efficacious. At least one major study lends strong support for the superior effectiveness of combined psychosocial and pharmacological treatments with severe and chronic depression. Additional recently published data suggest that psychosocial interventions may be as effective as antidepressant medications in the treatment of severely depressed patients.

Major depressive disorder (MDD) is one of the most commonly diagnosed psychiatric disorders among adults, with U.S. lifetime prevalence rates of approximately 17%, with 20 to 25% for women and 9 to 12% for men; point prevalence rates are approximately 6% and 3% for women and men, respectively (American Psychiatric Association [APA], 1994; Kessler et al., 2005).

These prevalence rates and gender differences are relatively constant across the *adult* life span. In addition, the prevalence of MDD has been increasing in recent birth cohorts (Fergusson, Horwood, Ridder, & Beautrais, 2005; Lewinsohn, Hops, Roberts, Seeley, & Andrews, 1993; Weissman et al., 1996), which suggests that the lifetime prevalence will be higher for current younger cohorts. The age of first episode of MDD has been decreasing (Burke, Burke, Regier, & Rae, 1990; Lewinsohn, Clarke, Seeley, & Rohde, 1994), so that the peak years for first onset are presently between 15 and 29 years of age (Burke et al., 1990; Fergusson et al., 2005; Hankin et al., 1998). Thus, MDD is a major health problem for which it is important to develop better treatments.

Depression engenders not only extraordinary personal and family suffering but also significant societal burdens, such as an increased use of social and medical services (Johnson, Weissman, & Klerman, 1992). There are also enormous financial costs for treatment and for lost productivity due to absenteeism from work (Greenberg, Stiglin, Finkelstein, & Berndt, 1993; Wells et al., 1989). In fact, when considered among all diseases, MDD is the world's fourth leading cause of disability-adjusted life years (Murray & Lopez, 1997).

In order to receive a diagnosis of *major depressive disorder*, a person must experience marked distress or a decrease in level of functioning. In addition, the 2 weeks before examination must be characterized by the almost daily occurrence of a dysphoric mood (sad, empty, or tearful) or a loss of interest or pleasure in almost all activities (APA, 1994). The individual must also experience at least four (only three if both dysphoric mood and loss of interest or pleasure are present) of the following seven symptoms (with the second through sixth occurring nearly every day):

1. Significant weight loss (while not trying to lose weight), significant weight gain, or a change in appetite
2. Insomnia or hypersomnia
3. Psychomotor agitation or retardation
4. Fatigue or loss of energy
5. Feelings of worthlessness or excessive or inappropriate guilt
6. Decreased concentration or indecisiveness
7. Recurrent thoughts of death or suicidal ideation, plan, or attempt

Substantial advances have been made over the past three decades in the successful treatment of depression. Treatments of choice now include not only somatic interventions (antidepressant medications and electroconvulsive treatment) but also a number of psychosocial interventions—behavior therapy (BT; including marital therapy), cognitive-behavior therapy (CBT), and interpersonal psychotherapy (IPT). This chapter reviews the evidence regarding the efficacy of these specific psychosocial treatments (including their combinations with somatic treatments), discusses the possible mechanisms of change in these therapies, and addresses numerous issues regarding the appropriate use of psychosocial treatments. This review includes only those studies that obtained information for diagnosis via a structured interview such as the Structured Clinical Interview for *DSM* (*SCID*; First, Spitzer, Gibbon, & Williams, 1995; Spitzer, Williams, Gibbon, & First, 1992) and employed a formal, defined diagnostic system such as the Research Diagnostic Criteria (Spitzer, Endicott, & Robins, 1978) or the *DSM-IV*. Further, to be included, an investigation must have employed cutoff scores on standard depression severity measures, such as clinical rating scales or self-report measures, as a criterion for admission to the study. In other words, by virtue of the severity, frequency, and duration of their observed symptoms, the participants in these studies are comparable in severity to those who might seek and receive outpatient treatment by a mental health professional for an MDD. Within this book, these studies would all be considered Type 1 studies. Based on the preceding criteria, only behavior therapy, cognitive-behavior therapy, and interpersonal psychotherapy that have been studied in at least two comparative Type 1 outcome trials for outpatients between the ages of 18 and 65 years have been included in this review.

BEHAVIOR THERAPY

Description

The first behavioral treatment program of significance was developed by Lewinsohn, who built on previous behavioral formulations of depression (Ferster, 1973; Skinner, 1953; see Lewinsohn & Gotlib, 1995, for a summary of Lewinsohn's contributions). Although numerous flavors of behavior therapy have been developed for treatment of MDD, they all have in common the assumption that MDD is related to a decrease of behaviors that produce positive reinforcement. As such, behavior therapies for depression have focused largely on monitoring and increasing positive daily activities, improving social and communication skills, increasing adaptive behaviors such as positive and negative assertion, increasing response-contingent positive reinforcement for adaptive behaviors, and decreasing negative life experiences.

Empirical Evidence

In a randomized clinical trial (RCT), Lewinsohn and his group demonstrated that, relative to various control groups, behavior therapy (BT) increased pleasant experiences and reduced aversive experiences, which produced concomitant decreases in depression severity (see Lewinsohn & Gotlib, 1995). This work was extended by Bellack, Hersen, and Himmelhoch (1981, 1983) and Hersen, Bellack, Himmelhoch, and Thase (1984), who demonstrated that BT was as effective as the antidepressant amitriptyline (AMI) in reducing depression over a 12-week treatment period; these effects were maintained over a 6-month follow-up period with six to eight booster sessions.

Consistent with Rehm's (1977) suggestions, McLean and Hakstian (1979) added problem-solving and self-control procedures to the behavior therapy treatment package, and they conducted a 10-week clinical trial comparing this expanded behavioral treatment package to relaxation therapy, insight-oriented psychotherapy, and amitriptyline. The behavior therapy program was equal or superior to the other treatment conditions. (Although questions have been raised regarding the adequacy of the medication dosage, the results for amitriptyline were generally comparable to those obtained in other antidepressant medication studies.) These results were maintained at a 27-month follow-up, at which time the behavior therapy subjects were more socially active and productive than were participants in all the other treatment conditions (McLean & Hakstian, 1990).

Rehm's self-control therapy (1977) has been found to be superior to nonspecific psychosocial treatments and no-treatment controls (Rehm, 1990), but it has not been compared with standard antidepressant treatment. It is worth noting that the apparently essential ingredient (and perhaps the most important contribution) of this self-control therapy is the *self-monitoring* of thoughts and behaviors (Rehm, 1990), a component that is included in most other empirically supported psychosocial depression treatment protocols.

Three recent Type 1 evaluations of BT have been reported. Jacobson and his colleagues (1996) tested the hypothesized theory of change in Beck's cognitive therapy for depression by comparing the full CBT package to its component parts—"behavioral activation" (BA) and "behavioral activation plus modification of automatic dysfunctional thoughts" (AT). The BA treatment was similar to the behavioral interventions previously reviewed and included techniques such as monitoring daily activities, assessment of pleasure and mastery of activities, assignment of increasingly difficult activities, imaging of behaviors to be performed, discussion of specific problems and identification of behavioral solutions to those problems, and interventions to ameliorate social skills deficits. The primary finding of this study was that BA, AT, and the full CBT package were equally effective, both immediately after the 20-session treatment trial and at 6-month follow-up. Furthermore, BA performed equally well over a 2-year follow-up period, with patients across the three treatments hav-

ing equivalent rates of relapse, time to relapse, and number of well weeks (Gortner, Gollan, Dobson, & Jacobson, 1998).

In a follow-up replication study of Jacobson's CBT component analysis, Dimidjian and colleagues (2006) compared an expanded model of behavioral activation, cognitive therapy, the antidepressant paroxetine, and pill placebo in a 16-week MDD treatment trial. In addition to the BA techniques employed in Jacobson and colleagues' trial, the expanded BA model emphasized the importance of avoidance and withdrawal, particularly from interpersonal situations and daily routines. The model also examined the function of ruminative thinking, rather than thought content, and stressed shifting attention from rumination toward direct experience. The study aimed to examine the efficacy of BA relative to cognitive therapy and antidepressant medication in a placebo-controlled trial. An additional aim was to test the psychosocial treatments as alternatives to paroxetine for the subset of participants who met criteria for moderate to severe depression. Dimidjian and colleagues randomly assigned 241 individuals to the four treatment conditions. Contrary to a primary hypothesis, the investigators found that, among the more severely depressed patients, behavioral activation and paroxetine were comparably effective treatments, while each treatment significantly outperformed cognitive therapy (CT). Participants in the BA and paroxetine groups also displayed equivalent *weekly* improvement, as measured by both self-report and clinical ratings, and superior improvement relative to the cognitive therapy group. Furthermore, a significantly greater percentage of participants randomized to expanded BA reached remission when compared with individuals in either the paroxetine or the CT condition. As Dimidjian and colleagues note, these findings challenge current treatment recommendations, which state that moderate to severe depression necessitates medication. Behavioral activation interventions expanded to include an emphasis on avoidance behaviors and the function of rumination may provide an equally efficacious treatment alternative for severely depressed patients who prefer not to take antidepressant medications.

Keller and colleagues (2000) randomly assigned 681 adults with chronic major depression (MDD of at least 2 years' duration, current MDD superimposed on a preexisting dysthymic disorder, or recurrent MDD with incomplete remission between episodes and a total duration of continuous illness of at least 2 years) to 12 weeks of treatment with either the cognitive-behavioral analysis system of psychotherapy (CBASP),[1] the antidepressant nefazodone, or the combination of CBASP and nefazodone. The CBASP approach (McCullough, 2000) focuses on the consequences of patient's behavior and the use of social problem solving to address interpersonal difficulties. The overall rate of response was equivalent in the CBASP and nefazodone groups, though patients receiving nefazodone had a more rapid reduction in symptoms during the first 4 weeks of treatment. Immediately following treatment, the combination of CBASP and nefazodone was superior to either treatment on its own. Results at the end of the 16-week continuation phase (for participants who reached remission or a partial response during acute treatment) support the superiority of combined treatment (Kocsis et al., 2003). A greater proportion of participants who received CBASP and nefazodone, compared with the monotherapy conditions, maintained full or partial remission status through the continuation phase. Findings from the same multiphase investigation suggest that CBASP may also be an effective maintenance treatment intended to prevent the recurrence of major depression (D. N. Klein et al., 2004).

A recent follow-up (Nemeroff et al., 2003) to the Keller et al. (2000) study has provided most interesting results regarding the relative contributions of psychotherapy and pharmacotherapy among depressed patients who suffered an early life traumatic event (e.g., sexual abuse, loss of a parent). Nemeroff and colleagues reanalyzed data for the 681 patients in the CBASP depression treatment study. These analyses indicated that among those chronically depressed patients who had suffered from early childhood trauma (such as loss of parents at an early age, physical abuse, sexual abuse), psychotherapy (CBASP) was superior to nefazadone alone. Further, the combination of the antidepressant with CBASP resulted in only minimally greater effectiveness than CBASP alone. Although in need of replication with studies in which patients are randomly assigned based on early life abuse, this study strongly suggests that an individual, disorder-specific psychotherapy should be the first line of treatment for depressed patients who have suffered from early life trauma. It is also important that future studies investigate what the underlying neurobiological pathway of effective CBASP is

and how it compares to the mechanisms of change in CBT for major depression (see Goldapple et al., 2004).

Behavior Marital Therapy

Another development in behavioral approaches to the treatment of depression has been the employment of behavior marital therapy (BMT) with individuals who are suffering concurrently from MDD and marital distress. Both O'Leary and colleagues' and Jacobson and colleagues' standard BMT (Beach, Sandeen, & O'Leary, 1990; Jacobson, Dobson, Fruzetti, Schmaling, & Salusky, 1991; O'Leary & Beach, 1990) have been demonstrated to be equal to individual CBT for the alleviation of depression among individuals with both MDD and marital discord. BMT was found to have the added advantage of being superior to individual CBT in the reduction of marital discord, a finding that argues for the use of BMT with depressed patients who are also experiencing marital discord. None of these studies, however, employed appropriate follow-up procedures to test prophylactic effects of BMT versus individual CBT following successful treatment. However, given that "marital disputes" is the most frequently discussed topic among depressed patients in maintenance therapy (Weissman & Klerman, 1973) and that marital friction is an enduring problem among formerly depressed patients even when they are asymptomatic (Bothwell & Weissman, 1977), it seems likely that successful BMT will reduce the rate of relapse among successfully treated MDD patients in discordant marriages. Unfortunately, BMT has not been evaluated with adequate numbers of *severely* depressed patients in discordant marriages to know if these findings will be applicable to such patients or whether the presence of severe depression will necessitate alternative or adjunctive treatments.

Conclusion

Consistent findings support the efficacy of BT for depression. For several years the findings for BT had been overshadowed by outcome studies that focused on cognitive-behavior therapy and interpersonal psychotherapy as psychosocial interventions for an MDD. However, given the applicability of BT to depressed patients of all age-groups (see Lewinsohn & Gotlib, 1995) and the relative efficacy, efficiency, and endurance of behavioral interventions, as well as the recent results for BA, CBASP, and BMT, it seems that this was an unwarranted and premature turn of events. From a historical perspective, it appears to have been due primarily to the sociology of science and to no small extent to the exclusion of behavior therapy from the well-publicized National Institute of Mental Health (NIMH) clinical trial (Elkin, Parloff, Hadley, & Autry, 1985), rather than to the relative scientific merit and empirical outcomes of the then-available comparative treatment studies.

COGNITIVE-BEHAVIOR THERAPY

Description

The most extensively evaluated psychosocial treatment for MDD is Beck's cognitive-behavior therapy (CBT; Beck, Rush, Shaw, & Emery, 1979), alternatively referred to simply as cognitive therapy (CT). Cognitive-behavior therapy is a short-term (16 to 20 sessions over a period of 12 to 16 weeks), directive therapy designed to change the depressed patient's negative view of the self, world, and future. The therapy begins with the presentation of the rationale, which is designed to inform the client of the therapy model and the process of therapeutic change. Subsequent early CBT sessions consist of the implementation of strategies designed to increase active behavioral performance. The purpose of such an increase is to allow the monitoring of behaviors and their associated thoughts and feelings; behavioral changes are not posited to be directly responsible for the desired changes in depression. During the third week, expanded self-monitoring techniques are introduced to demonstrate the relationship between thoughts and feelings; patients are taught to evaluate their thoughts for logical errors, which include arbitrary inference, selective abstraction, overgeneralization, magnification and minimalization, personalization, and dichotomous thinking (Beck, 1976). In the middle of therapy (around session 8 or 9), the concept of *schema*, or beliefs underlying negative and positive thoughts, is introduced, and therapy begins to focus on changing those negative schemas that are posited to have been activated, thus precipitating the MDD. Toward the end of therapy (sessions 14 through 16), the focus shifts to termination and the use of cognitive strategies to prevent relapse or a future recurrence of depression.

Empirical Evidence

A number of studies have compared the effectiveness of CBT with several tricyclic antidepressant medications (Elkin et al., 1989; Hollon et al., 1992; Rush, Beck, Kovacs, & Hollon, 1977; Simons, Murphy, Levine, & Wetzel, 1986).[2] With the possible exception of the NIMH Treatment of Depression Collaborative Research Program (TDCRP; Elkin et al., 1989), the essential finding in all these studies is that CBT is equally effective as tricyclic antidepressant medication in alleviating MDD among outpatients[3] (see Tables 10.1 and 10.2). Similarly, CBT was as effective as a monoamine oxidase inhibitor (phenelzine), and more effective than pill placebo, in the treatment of atypical depression (Jarrett et al., 1999). CBT was also equally effective as antidepressant medication when study physicians were free to prescribe the antidepressant of their choice (and free to switch medications during the treatment trial), provided they prescribed at or above established therapeutic doses (Blackburn & Moore, 1997).

Typically, 50 to 70% of MDD patients who complete a course of CBT no longer meet criteria for MDD at posttreatment, with pre-post changes from the high 20s to single digits for the Beck Depression Inventory (BDI) scores and changes from the high teens/low 20s to single digits for the Hamilton Rating Scale for Depression (HRSD) scores (see Tables 10.1 and 10.2). Furthermore, among the samples studied, CBT appeared to confer some enduring prophylactic effects inasmuch as only 20 to 30% of those successfully treated relapsed during the first year following treatment. Indeed, 16 weeks of CBT produced a 1-year follow-up success rate that equals or slightly exceeds that achieved by a full year of antidepressant treatment (Evans et al., 1992), and CBT's maintenance effects are clearly superior to short-term (16 weeks) antidepressant treatment (16 weeks is not the recommended treatment period, but it is, unfortunately, longer than the actual average length of completed medication treatment in clinical practice; Bull et al., 2002; Nemeroff, 2003; Olfson, Marcus, Tedeschi, & Wan, 2006).

Because the TDCRP study (Elkin et al., 1989) has received so much attention, including its significant role in the development of guidelines (not

TABLE 10.1 Hamilton Rating Scale for Depression Scores and Percentages "Recovered" for Major Random Clinical Trials Reviewed in This Chapter

Study	CBT									IPT			BT			BMT	
	1	2	3	4	5	9	10[a]	11	13	6[c]	3	7	5	8	12	9	10[b]
N	15	19	37	16	44	12	20	36	24	17	47	25	47	42	216	12	8
Pre	21.2	18.5	19.2	24.8	18.6	—	20.0	18.36	19.2	17.3	18.9	22.2	17.3	—	26.4	—	23.4
Post	5.8	6.4	7.6	8.8	6.8	—	4.5	10.25	10.7	10.2	6.9	7.0	6.5	—	15.1	—	7.2
Percentage recovered	—	63[g]	51[h]	50[h]	—	—	—	58[e], 44[h]	33[h]	—	55[h]	64[i]	—	—	33[f]	—	—

Study	Medications											BT Plus Medications	Placebo Plus CM	
	1	2	3	4	5	6	7	8	11	12	13	12	3	11
N	14	16	37	32[b]	—	20	14	49	36	220	43	226	34	36
Pre	22.4	19.7	19.2	24.0	—	16.8	25.5	—	16.75	26.8	20.4	27.4	19.1	17.42
Post	9.3	7.0	7.0	8.4	—	10.0	8.2	—	8.64	14.7	12.3	9.7	8.8	14.44
Percentage recovered	—	50[g]	57[h]	53[h]	—	—	43[i]	—	58[e], 42[h]	29[f]	24[h]	48[f]	29[h]	28[e], 19[h]

Source: List of studies: 1. Rush et al. (1977); 2. Murphy et al. (1984); 3. Elkin et al. (1989); 4. Hollon et al. (1992); 5. Jacobson et al. (1996); 6. DiMascio et al. (1979); 7. Bellack et al. (1981); 8. McLean & Hakstian (1979); 9. O'Leary & Beach (1990); 10. Jacobson et al. (1991); 11. Jarrett et al. (1999); 12. Keller et al. (2000); 13. Blackburn & Moore (1997).

BDI = Beck Depression Inventory; BMT = behavior marital therapy; BT = behavior therapy; CBT = cognitive-behavior therapy; HRSD = Hamilton Rating Scale of Depression; IPT = interpersonal psychotherapy.

[a] Data are only for completers who met criteria for MDD and either presence or absence of marital discord.

[b] Data are only for completers who met criteria for comorbid MDD and marital discord; BMT was less effective for MDD and no marital discord.

[c] Data are available only for all patients who entered and completed at least 1 week of treatment.

[d] N = 31 for Post.

[e] HRSD ≤ 9.

[f] HRSD ≤ 8.

[g] HRSD ≤ 7.

[h] HRSD ≤ 6.

[i] HRSD and BDI ≤ 10.

TABLE 10.2 Beck Depression Inventory Scores and Percentages "Recovered" for Major Random Clinical Trials Reviewed in This Chapter

Measure	CBT									IPT			BT		BMT	
Study	1	2	3	4	5	9	10[a]	11	13	6	7	3	8	5	9	10[b]
N	18	19	37	16	44	12	20	36	24	17	25	47	42[c]	48	12	8
Pre	30.3	29.7	26.8	30.4	28.9	26	26.3	25.83	27.3	—	27.1	25.5	26.8	29.3	22	26.4
Post	5.9	9.5	10.2	7.9	9.7	6	6.5	11.72	19.0	—	7.4	7.7	9.7	8.5	5	7.0
Percentage recovered	83[d]	53[d]	65[e]	62[e]	57[g]	—	80[e]	53[e]	—	—	64[f]	70[e]	50[g]	50[g]	—	88[e]

Measure	Medications									Placebo +CM		
Study	1	2	3	4	5	6	7	8	11	11	3	13
N	14	16	36	32	—	17	14	49[c]	36	36	35	43
Pre	30.8	29.3	27.1	31.1	—	—	29.6	27.2	24.86	26.19	28.1	29.2
Post	13.0	8.9	6.5	10.5	—	—	12.8	14.2	9.67	18.94	11.0	21.5
Percentage recovered	36[d]	56[d]	69[e]	56[e]	—	—	43[f]	25[g]	69[e]	28[e]	51[e]	—

Source: List of studies: 1. Rush et al. (1977); 2. Murphy et al. (1984); 3. Elkin et al. (1989); 4. Hollon et al. (1992); 5. Jacobson et al. (1996); 6. DiMascio et al. (1979); 7. Bellack et al. (1981); 8. McLean & Hakstian (1979); 9. O'Leary & Beach (1990); 10. Jacobson & Beach (1991); 11. Jarrett et al. (1999); 12. Keller et al. (2000); 13. Blackburn & Moore (1997).

BDI = Beck Depression Inventory; BMT = behavior marital therapy; BT = behavior therapy; CBT = cognitive-behavior therapy; HRSD = Hamilton Rating Scale of Depression; IPT = interpersonal psychotherapy.

[a] Data are only for completers who met criteria for MDD and either presence or absence of marital discord.

[b] Data are only for completers who met criteria for comorbid MDD and marital discord; BMT was less effective for MDD and no marital discord.

[c] Data are available only for all patients who entered treatment.

[d] BDI ≤ 10.

[e] BDI ≤ 9.

[f] BDI and HRSD ≤ 10.

[g] BDI ≤ 7.

standards) for treatment of outpatients suffering from an MDD (Agency for Health Care Policy and Research [AHCPR], 1993; American Psychiatric Association, 1993), it is worthy of special note. This study included 250 outpatients who were randomly assigned to one of four 16-week treatment conditions: CBT, IPT, imipramine hydrochloride plus clinical management (IMP-CM), or pill placebo plus clinical management (PLA-CM). Both the IMP-CM and the PLA-CM conditions included a "clinical management" component (20 minutes per week talking with an experienced psychiatrist), whose additive effects simply are not known.

The results of the TDCRP for those patients who *completed treatment* generally support the equality of the three presumed active treatments in ameliorating depression at posttreatment (as measured by a Hamilton Depression Rating Scale score of 6 or less; CBT, 51%; IPT, 55%; and IMP-CM, 57%); however, only IPT and IMP-CM produced significantly greater reductions in depression than PLA-CM (29%) over the course of treatment, and only then for a few of the outcome measures (Elkin et al., 1989). Even these acute treatment effects were not maintained at the 18-month follow-up: Because the percentages of patients remaining nondepressed and not receiving treatment for depression were quite low (CBT 30%, IPT 26%, IMP plus CM 19%, and PLA plus CM 20%), none of the active treatments was superior to the PLA-CM condition at the 18-month follow-up (Shea, Elkin, et al., 1992). These follow-up outcomes indicate that all treatments in this study had considerably weaker effects than had typically been reported in other long-term follow-up studies of these same psychotherapies. Of course, as D. F. Klein (1996) has noted, such short-term treatment (16 weeks) with antidepressant medication would not be expected to produce sustained effectiveness.

Based on the original report of the TDCRP data at conferences and in print, it has been noted (Craighead, Evans, & Robins, 1992; Hollon, Shelton, & Loosen, 1991), and sustained by reanalyses of the original data tape (Jacobson & Hollon, 1996a), that the lack of unequivocal findings (coupled with the uniqueness of some of the exploratory findings) assures that any interpretation of the TDCRP data is likely to be controversial. One of the major problems described in the original report of the TDCRP was "consistently significant treatment-by-site interactions for the more severely depressed and functionally im-

paired patients" (Elkin, Gibbons, Shea, & Shaw, 1989, p. 980). Even though this conclusion has been somewhat attenuated with the use of more sophisticated reanalysis of the data (Elkin et al., 1995; Elkin, Gibbons, Shea, & Shaw, 1996), the general pattern for a treatment-by-site-by-severity interaction is still acknowledged, and the authors conclude: "In regard to the general efficacy of CBT in the treatment of severely depressed (and functionally impaired) outpatients . . . we believe . . . that the answer is not yet in" (Elkin et al., 1996, p. 101).

In their reanalysis of the TDCRP data on this issue, Jacobson and Hollon (1996a) underscore the importance of this site-by-treatment-by-severity interaction. They present data illustrating that at one site CBT did as well as IMP-CM and better than PLA-CM with severely depressed patients (probably not coincidentally, this was also the site at which CBT was rated as having been done the best; see Elkin et al., 1996). At a second site, the data favored either IPT or IMP-CM over both CBT and PLA-CM, with the last two groups not significantly different from one another. At the third site, there were not enough subjects to warrant a comparison. In fact, it is ironic that so much has been made of the findings among the severely depressed patients, since even across three sites there were 15 or fewer severely depressed patients per condition, and "severity" was not taken into account in the random assignment procedure except for the minimal cutoff criterion of 14 on the HRSD.

The essential point here is that the findings regarding the appropriateness of CBT alone for severely depressed patients are inconclusive from the TDCRP data. Finally, although little has been made of it, there was also a treatment by marital status confound (compounded by differential treatment effects for single and married patients), making interpretation of the data even more difficult (see Jarrett, Eaves, Grannemann, & Rush, 1991; Sotsky et al., 1991).

In response to the findings of the TDCRP, DeRubeis and colleagues (2005) conducted a placebo-controlled trial comparing the efficacy of CT and the antidepressant paroxetine (with lithium or desipramine augmentation, if necessary) for adults with moderate to severe depression. A total of 240 individuals were randomly assigned to a 16-week trial of ADM, 16 weeks of CT, or 8 weeks of pill placebo. At 8 weeks, participants in the antidepressant medication (ADM) condition displayed significant improvement compared with the pill placebo condition; there was a nonsignificant trend of greater improvement due to CT compared with pill placebo. At 16 weeks, 58% of patients treated with CT and 58% of patients treated with ADM met response criteria. Additionally, 40% of the CT condition and 46% of the ADM condition were in remission at the end of acute treatment. Due to a significant site by treatment interaction, the findings indicate that with more experienced therapists, CT is as effective as antidepressant medications in treating moderate to severe major depression.

In a companion, continuation study, Hollon and colleagues (2005) examined the efficacy of CT and ADM treatment in preventing depressive relapse among the 104 responders of the CT/ADM study. Participants who responded to ADM during the initial 16-week trial were randomly assigned to continuation ADM treatment or withdrawal onto pill placebo. Participants who responded to CT during the acute phase of treatment were asked to refrain from enrolling in additional treatment for depression during the yearlong continuation phase. These participants were allowed up to three booster sessions, at least 1 month apart, during the continuation period. In this investigation, acute treatment with CT significantly reduced the risk for relapse by 70% compared with the placebo withdrawal group. There was a nonsignificant trend for continuation ADM reducing risk for relapse by approximately 50%. Participants who completed CT were no more likely to relapse during the 12-month continuation phase than were participants who continued ADM treatment. Overall, these findings indicate substantial, enduring effects of CT that rival pharmacological treatment for severely depressed patients.

Another line of investigation includes studies that have provided a full course of slightly varying forms of CBT following successful treatment of MDD with another type of intervention (e.g., medications). For example, Fava, Grandi, Zielezny, Rafanelli, and Canestrari (1996) compared their form of CBT, "well being therapy," with "clinical management" (CM) following a course of successful treatment (though patients still had residual symptoms of depression) with ADM. All patients were withdrawn from ADM prior to the maintenance phase. As has been typical of short-term treatment with ADM, the 4-year relapse rate following termination of medica-

tions was 70%. In contrast, the relapse rate was 35% for the participants who received the additional 10 sessions of Fava's intervention. The difference had dissipated by the 6-year follow-up (75% clinical management vs. 50% CBT) and was no longer statistically significant (Fava, Rafanelli, Grandi, Canestrari, & Morphy, 1998).

In a second study, Paykel and colleagues (1999) studied patients who had responded (but had residual symptoms) to acute treatment with antidepressant medications (ADM). In contrast to the Fava et al. (1996) study, all patients were maintained on therapeutic doses of ADM during the maintenance phase. Patients were randomized to receive either 20 weeks of CBT or CM with ADM. At the end of the 20-week maintenance treatment phase, relatively few participants had achieved full remission, but those who received CBT were at a significant advantage (25% vs. 13% in CM). Furthermore, across the entire study period (maintenance phase and 1-year follow-up), the combination of continued ADM with maintenance CBT resulted in a lower rate of relapse (29%) than did continued CM with ADM (47%).

Two studies (Teasdale et al., 2000; Ma & Teasdale, 2004) evaluated mindfulness-based cognitive therapy (MBCT) for the prevention of relapse/recurrence of MDD after discontinuation of ADM. MBCT is an eight-session group intervention based on the combination of a mindfulness-based stress reduction program (Kabat-Zinn, 1990) and components of CBT for depression. Teasdale's notion is that the critical variables to change in cognitive therapy are styles of "thinking about thinking" rather than the content of irrational thinking. Thus, MBCT targets thought processes, helping participants become more aware of and relate differently to their cognitive experiences (Segal, Williams, & Teasdale, 2002). MBCT has been evaluated in two studies; in both, participants were recently recovered from an episode of MDD, had been treated with an ADM, and were not currently engaged in treatment (including medication) at the time of recruitment. Compared with treatment as usual, MBCT substantially reduced the risk of relapse by approximately 50% in participants with three or more previous episodes of MDD. MBCT had no positive impact on patients with later onset and two or fewer episodes of MDD; there were, however, too few participants of this latter group of depressed patients to draw any conclusions (e.g., only four completers in one study).

Conclusion

Given the substantial number of studies supporting the efficacy of CBT with patients diagnosed with an MDD, it is concluded that CBT is a viable treatment of choice for patients with an MDD.[4] Data to date indicate that CBT confers resistance to relapse to MDD whether it is presented as the primary treatment or given as a supplement following successful treatment via some other intervention. Given the widely varying outcomes across studies and the apparent differential competence with which the therapy was delivered across sites in a multisite study, it is particularly important that therapists delivering CBT be well trained before they undertake the therapy with patients.

INTERPERSONAL PSYCHOTHERAPY

Description

Interpersonal psychotherapy was originally developed as a time-limited (12 to 16 weeks), weekly intervention for unipolar, nonpsychotic depression (Klerman, Weissman, Rounsaville, & Chevron, 1984). The IPT model is derived in large part from Sullivan's interpersonal theory (1953) and the psychobiological theory of Meyer (1957), with its emphasis on the reciprocal relationship between biological and psychosocial facets of psychopathology. Although the IPT model "makes no assumptions about the causes of depression" (Klerman & Weissman, 1993, p. 6), it does suggest that the patient's interpersonal relations may play a significant role in both the onset and the maintenance of MDD. Accordingly, IPT focuses on the identification and amelioration of the patient's difficulties in interpersonal functioning associated with the current MDD; the primary problem areas targeted include unresolved grief, interpersonal disputes, role transitions, and interpersonal deficits (e.g., social isolation).

Empirical Evidence

As shown in Tables 10.1 and 10.2, there have been only two reported RCTs of IPT for the acute treatment of MDD in middle-aged adults. Both of these studies included long-term follow-up assessments designed to evaluate the prophylactic effects of acute

IPT treatment. In addition, there have been two separate controlled studies of "maintenance" IPT following remission of the MDD.

The first RCT of IPT for the acute treatment of MDD was conducted by the treatment's originators, Weissman and Klerman and their colleagues (DiMascio et al., 1979; Weissman et al., 1979). They randomly assigned 81 patients to treatment with 16 weeks of IPT, amitriptyline (AMI), combined IPT and AMI, or a "nonscheduled" (i.e., therapy on request, up to one session per month) supportive psychotherapy control. All three treatments were superior to the nonscheduled control condition, and the combination of IPT and AMI was slightly more effective than either condition alone (this last finding was only marginally significant, with $p < .10$).

The second and most frequently cited RCT of IPT is the previously summarized NIMH multisite clinical trial, the TDCRP (Elkin et al., 1989). As noted, the principal significant finding concerned the clinical rating of depression as measured by the Hamilton Rating Scale for Depression (HRSD). All groups began with a pretreatment mean of about 19 and, using the criterion of a posttest HRSD score of 6 or less, both IPT (55%) and IMI-CM (57%) had a significantly greater proportion of patients who achieved the recovery criterion than was observed in the PLA-CM condition (29%). In a secondary data analysis (Elkin et al., 1995), IPT and IMI-CM were also found to be of comparable efficacy among the subset of patients who were severely depressed (defined as a pretreatment HRSD score of 20 or greater). However, as previously highlighted, the presence in this investigation of either a strong trend or a significant treatment-by-site-by-severity interaction (depending on the analysis) precludes the drawing of definitive conclusions from this finding (Elkin et al., 1996; Jacobson & Hollon, 1996b).

After the completion of treatment, patients in both the Weissman et al. (Weissman, Klerman, Prusoff, Sholomskas, & Padian, 1981) and the TDCRP (Elkin et al., 1989) studies were evaluated longitudinally for several months in a naturalistic follow-up design as a means of examining possible prophylactic effects achieved with the acute therapeutic interventions. In the first study, no prophylactic effect was associated with IPT versus AMI based on a 12-month follow-up (Weissman et al, 1981); however, the authors reported significantly greater adaptive social functioning among IPT patients. The TDCRP study also found no relative prophylactic effects for IPT. Among patients who recovered during acute treatment, the percentages of patients who remained well during the 18 months of follow-up were as follows: IPT (26%), CBT (30%), IMI-CM (19%), and PLA-CM (20%; Shea, Elkin et al., 1992). Primarily because of the small number of subjects and corresponding lack of statistical power, none of these differences was statistically significant; therefore, none of the acute treatment differences was maintained over the follow-up, and none of the treatments was superior even to PLA-CM.

The IPT protocol has also been employed as an ongoing maintenance therapy following recovery from an MDD. Klerman, DiMascio, Weissman, Prusoff, and Paykel (1974) found a nearly equivalent prophylactic benefit associated with weekly maintenance IPT or AMI over an 8-month follow-up period, with relapse rates of only 17% and 12%, respectively. Among a group of chronic and treatment-resistant depressed patients, Frank and her colleagues (1990) reported a significant decrease in relapse probability associated with monthly IPT maintenance sessions over a 36-month follow-up period. For this sample, however, there was a substantially larger prophylactic benefit associated with maintenance IMI, with a 36-month relapse rate of only 18% in the IMI group compared with 46% in the IPT group.

Conclusion

The data regarding IPT as a treatment alone and in combination with antidepressants for MDD are very favorable. IPT appears to be an efficacious intervention for the acute treatment of MDD.

PATIENT CHARACTERISTICS THAT MODERATE TREATMENT RESPONSE

Although each of the empirically supported interventions reviewed herein (CBT, IPT, BT) has been shown to be efficacious for a majority of depressed individuals, treatment response is highly variable from patient to patient, and a growing body of evidence documents the existence of patient characteristics that moderate treatment response. Following is a brief summary of relevant findings.

The amelioration of dysfunctional cognitive phenomena is the sine qua non of CBT. Accordingly, one might expect the subset of depressed patients with high pretreatment levels of dysfunctional, depressotypic cognitions to be especially likely to benefit from CBT. But the very opposite appears to be the case; that is, patients who score *low* on pretreatment measures of depressotypic cognition tend to experience the most favorable responses in CBT (Hamilton & Dobson, 2002; Rector, Bagby, Segal, Joffe, & Levitt, 2000; Rude & Rehm, 1991; Simons, Gordon, Monroe, & Thase, 1995). Furthermore, MDD patients who report low levels of depressotypic cognitions appear to respond preferentially to CBT in comparison with either IPT or pill placebo (Sotsky et al., 1991), a finding consistent with the hypothesis that effective therapies capitalize on patients' preexisting strengths rather than compensate for their presenting weaknesses (Cronbach & Snow, 1977). Other patient characteristics associated with favorable outcomes in CBT include low pretreatment depression severity (Elkin et al., 1995; Organista, Munoz, & Gonzalez, 1994; Persons, Bostrom, & Bertagbolli, 1999), absence of chronic depression (Hamilton & Dobson, 2002; Howland, 1991); low social relationship dysfunction (Sotsky et al., 1991), high learned resourcefulness (Simons, Lustman, Wetzel, & Murphy, 1985; see also Burns, Rude, Simons, Bates, & Thase, 1994), experience of intact marriage (i.e., nonsingle/nondivorced marital status; Jarrett et al., 1991; Sotsky et al., 1991), absence of co-occurring social phobia (DeRubeis et al., 2005), left-hemispheric verbal processing advantage (Bruder et al, 1997), and normal REM latency during sleep EEG (Simons et al., 1995). Because CBT, in comparison with selective serotonin reuptake inhibitor (SSRI) pharmacotherapy, is associated with reduced cortical activity in medial frontal and cingulate pathways involved in the phenomenon of depressive rumination (Goldapple et al., 2004), CBT may also prove to be especially efficacious with highly ruminative patients.

Although Axis II personality disorder comorbidity has frequently been observed to predict poor response to various antidepressant interventions (Ilardi & Craighead, 1994/1995; Shea, Widiger & Klein, 1992), there does not appear to be a robust association between personality pathology and unfavorable outcome in CBT (Hardy et al., 1995; Kuyken, Kurzer, DeRubeis, Beck, & Brown, 2001; Shea et al., 1990;

Simons & Thase, 1990). In fact, in the TDCRP, co-morbid Axis II pathology was predictive of poor treatment response in every treatment modality except CBT (Shea et al., 1990). If replicated, this finding would suggest CBT is a treatment of choice (alone or in combination with antidepressants) for the large subset of MDD patients with comorbid personality disorders. Intriguingly in this respect, CBASP (arguably a form of CBT; see note 1) has been found to be superior to antidepressant medication (nefazodone) in the treatment of depressed patients with a history of childhood trauma (Nemeroff et al., 2003) — itself a potential developmental precursor of Axis II pathology.

In keeping with the aforementioned *capitalization hypothesis* (Cronbach & Snow, 1977), the TDCRP found that patients with particularly *low* levels of social dysfunction responded more favorably to IPT than to other treatment interventions (Sotsky et al., 1991). Among variables linked to an unfavorable IPT response are Axis II comorbidity (Pilkonis & Frank, 1988; Shea et al., 1990), higher pretreatment depression severity (Hollon et al., 2005), trait neuroticism (Frank, Kupfer, Jacob, & Jarrett, 1987), cognitive dysfunction (Blatt, Quinlan, Pilkonis, & Shea, 1995; Sotsky et al., 1991), and a lifetime history of panic-agoraphobic spectrum symptoms (Frank et al., 2000). Especially high relapse-proneness following a favorable acute response to IPT has been observed among elderly (older than 70) depressed patients (Reynolds et al., 1999).

Although sorely needed, there has been very little research on patient characteristics that moderate treatment response to BT for MDD. In one of the few relevant investigations, patients who endorsed "existential" reasons for their depression (i.e., attributed the depression to their feeling that life was meaningless) were found to respond less favorably to BT than to CBT (Addis & Jacobson, 1996). Conversely, however, evidence from a recent randomized controlled trial suggests that BT may be superior to CBT overall in the treatment of more severely depressed patients (Dimidjian et al., 2006).

CONCLUSIONS AND FUTURE RESEARCH DIRECTIONS

Although additional research regarding the effectiveness of psychosocial interventions for MDD is still needed, adequate published data exist to permit the conclusion that three forms of psychotherapy — BT, CBT, and IPT — are efficacious interventions for depressed outpatients. This conclusion is consistent with major meta-analytic reports of psychosocial treatments for MDD (Dobson, 1989; Nietzel, Russell, Hemmings, & Gretter, 1987; Robinson, Berman, & Neimeyer, 1990). Addtionally, recent research indicates that BT and CBT interventions may be as effective as antidepressant medications in the treatment of *severely* depressed patients. Initial reports on this topic were mixed (e.g., Elkin et al., 1995; Hollon et al., 1992; Schulberg, Pilkonis, & Houck, 1998). However, a mega-analysis (DeRubeis, Gelfand, Tang, & Simons, 1999) suggests no treatment differences for CBT versus medications or their combination for severely depressed patients. The two large, placebo-controlled investigations (DeRubeis et al., 2005; Dimidjian, 2006) reviewed above provide preliminary evidence that psychosocial interventions alone can be as effective as antidepressant medications in treating moderately to severely depressed patients.

Despite the established efficacy of the above-reviewed psychotherapeutic interventions, it now seems clear that about one third of MDD patients in research studies will not respond favorably to the first treatment they receive, whether it be a somatic or a psychosocial intervention, and only one third of MDD patients will remit with short-term treatment. Except for the fairly consistent finding that patients with comorbid MDD and Axis II disorders tend to fare somewhat differentially to various treatments but relatively poorly in all treatments (especially during posttreatment follow-up periods), there is a dearth of research identifying salient clinical and demographic features that characterize the one third of patients who are refractory to their first psychosocial treatment. Furthermore, we know very little about whether this subset of initially refractory patients may respond favorably to a second treatment, although reported crossover studies suggest that many individuals who fail on one antidepressant will experience treatment gains when switched to a different medication (see Nemeroff & Schatzberg, 1998). Psychotherapy researchers have only recently begun to employ such complex crossover designs in treatment studies for MDD, so at present there is little empirical data to guide clinicians providing psychotherapy for patients who have failed to improve following an initial psychosocial intervention. It is extremely timely and significant that we identify psychosocial and neurobiological markers of treatment responders and remitters.

Treatment outcome research with long-term follow-up has increasingly pointed to high recurrence rates and to the need for continued intervention beyond acute treatment (Mueller et al., 1999). Some (e.g., Andrews, 2001) have even gone so far as to argue that MDD needs to be managed like a chronic disease. Numerous clinical research efforts are under way to improve the sustainability of acute treatment gains. These approaches include a tapered schedule of psychotherapeutic "booster sessions" in the months following acute treatment (e.g., Frank et al., 1990; Jarrett et al., 1998) and prophylactic programs for recovered patients designed specifically to prevent the recurrence of the disorder (Craighead, 2000; Fava, Rafanelli, Grandi, Canestrari, & Morphy, 1998).

It is also essential that placebo-controlled trials with severely depressed patients continue in order to clarify the prophylactic effects (vis-à-vis relapse and recurrence) of BT, CBT, and IPT in comparison with antidepressant medications. Not only is it important to determine the relative efficacy of these treatments with respect to short-term outcome; it is equally significant—from both clinical and public health standpoints—to know how they fare on a comparative basis in the long term. It will also be important to determine the relative short-term and long-term financial costs, including those that occur in the context of relapse and recurrence of MDD, associated with these psychosocial versus pharmacological treatment conditions. Preliminary evidence suggests that maintenance IPT for highly recurrent MDD was less effective at preventing recurrence than was ADM; on the other hand, various forms of CBT have been shown to be more efficacious then treatment as usual whether CBT was added to maintenance ADM or given to unmedicated patients.

Finally, it is suggested that future research attention be devoted to planning, developing, and evaluating treatments that simultaneously affect MDD and comorbid disorders (e.g., marital discord, Axis II personality disorders, substance abuse, physical illness). This approach has been successfully employed, for example, in the study of comorbid MDD and marital discord (Jacobson et al., 1991), and preliminary data support the efficacy of behavioral marital therapy for the subgroup of MDD patients who are also in discordant marriages. Such an approach to treatment outcome research appears likely to have a large payoff—perhaps greater than that afforded by the identification and targeting of MDD subtypes based solely on variations in presenting depressive symptomatology—and may prove especially promising with respect to the prevention of MDD recurrence in comorbid populations.

NOTES

1. Though it might be argued that CBASP is a form of CBT, we have included this study in the BT section. Though there is some focus on cognitive factors associated with depression, this focus is in service of helping the person achieve a behavioral goal; the primary emphasis of treatment is on problem solving and change of interpersonal behavior. "This approach draws on many behavioral, cognitive, and interpersonal techniques used in other forms of psychotherapy. It teaches patients to focus on the consequences of their behavior and to use a social problem-solving algorithm to address interpersonal difficulties. It is more structured and directive than interpersonal psychotherapy and differs from cognitive therapy by focusing primarily on interpersonal interactions (including those with therapists). In this type of psychotherapy, patients learn how their cognitive and behavioral patterns produce and perpetuate their interpersonal problems and learn how to remedy maladaptive patterns of interpersonal behavior" (Keller et al., 2000, p. 1463).

2. Additional comparative outcome trials of CBT have been conducted in other countries with different diagnostic systems; the most notable of these studies are those by Blackburn, Bishop, Glen, Whalley, and Christie (1981); Blackburn, Eunson, and Bishop (1986); Teasdale, Fennell, Hibbert, and Amies (1984).

3. It must be remembered that MDD patients who are suffering from psychotic features or are imminently suicidal have been excluded from all these evaluation studies comparing the effectiveness of antidepressant medications and psychosocial treatments.

4. Although space limitations preclude discussion, two topics warrant brief mention: treatment of the elderly and treatment in inpatient settings. Several studies by Thompson and colleagues (Thompson & Gallagher, 1984; Thompson, Gallagher, & Breckenridge, 1987) and one by Steuer and colleagues (1984) have demonstrated that CBT is as effective as antidepressant medication for the treatment of depression among the elderly. Thompson and colleagues (1987) also found that short-term psychodynamic psychotherapy was equally as effective as CBT and antidepressant medications for depres-

sion among the elderly. There is modest evidence that the presence of Axis II personality disorders predicts poor outcome among these patients (Thompson, Gallagher, & Czirr, 1988). In a study of IPT (a shortened version), Sloane, Staples, and Schneider (1985) compared the efficacy of 6 weeks of treatment with either IPT or nortriptyline in a small sample (N = 43) of elderly depressed patients. By the end of treatment, there was a nonsignificant trend for a superior response to IPT; however, this trend was largely due to patients' poor tolerance of medication side effects, and a corresponding high rate of attrition, in the nortriptyline group. Although this study is frequently cited to support the relative effectiveness of IPT, the absence of details on dependent measures and data analytic techniques severely limits the contribution of this investigation.

There are several systematic studies of CBT with MDD inpatients. In a stringent test of the intervention, Thase and his colleagues (e.g., Thase, 1994; Thase, Bowler, & Harden, 1991) treated unmedicated MDD inpatients for up to 4 weeks with daily CBT. Although a large percentage of these patients responded well to CBT, the outcome was poorer for those inpatients whose HRSD scale scores were 25 or higher or who had hypercortisolemia. The other studies (Bowers, 1990; Miller, Norman, Keitner, Bishop, & Dow, 1989) have combined CBT with antidepressant medications, and this combination seems to reduce relapse among such patients if booster sessions of CBT are maintained following hospital discharge.

REFERENCES

Addis, M. E., & Jacobson, N. S. (1996). Reasons for depression and the process and outcome of cognitive-behavioral psychotherapies. *Journal of Consulting and Clinical Psychology, 64,* 1417–1424.

Agency for Health Care Policy and Research (AHCPR), U.S. Department of Human Services. (1993). New federal guidelines seek to help primary care providers recognize and treat depression. *Hospital and Community Psychiatry, 44,* 598.

American Psychiatric Association. (1993). Practice guidelines for major depressive disorder in adults. *American Journal of Psychiatry, 150*(Suppl. 4), 1–26.

American Psychiatric Association. (1994). *Diagnostic and statistical manual of mental disorders* (4th ed.). Washington, DC: Author.

Andrews, G. (2001). Should depression be managed as a chronic disease. *British Medical Journal, 322,* 419–421.

Beach, S. R. H., Sandeen, E. E., & O'Leary, K. D. (1990). *Depression in marriage: A model for etiology and treatment.* New York: Guilford Press.

Beck, A. T. (1976). *Cognitive therapy and the emotional disorders.* New York: International Universities Press.

Beck, A.T., Rush, A. J., Shaw, B. F., & Emery, G. (1979). *Cognitive therapy of depression: A treatment manual.* New York: Guilford Press.

Bellack, A. S., Hersen, M., & Himmelhoch, J. (1981). Social skills training compared with pharmacotherapy and psychotherapy in the treatment of unipolar depression. *American Journal of Psychiatry, 138,* 1562–1566.

Bellack, A. S., Hersen, M., & Himmelhoch, J. (1983). A comparison of social skills training, pharmacotherapy and psychotherapy for depression. *Behaviour Research and Therapy, 21,* 101–107.

Blackburn, I. M., Bishop, S., Glen, A. I. M., Whalley, L. J., & Christie, J. E. (1981). The efficacy of cognitive therapy in depression: A treatment trial using cognitive therapy and pharmacotherapy, each alone and in combination. *British Journal of Psychiatry, 139,* 181–189.

Blackburn, I. M., Eunson, K. M., & Bishop, S. (1986). A two-year naturalistic follow-up of depressed patients treated with cognitive therapy, pharmacotherapy and a combination of both. *Journal of Affective Disorders, 10,* 67–75.

Blackburn, I. M. & Moore, R. G. (1997). Controlled acute and follow-up trial of cognitive therapy and pharmacotherapy in out-patients with recurrent depression. *British Journal of Psychiatry, 171,* 328–334.

Blatt, S. J., Quinlan, D. M., Pilkonis, P. A., & Shea, M. T. (1995). Impact of perfectionism and need for approval on the brief treatment of depression: The National Institute of Mental Health Treatment of Depression Collaborative Research Program revisited. *Journal of Consulting and Clinical Psychology, 63,* 125–132.

Bothwell, S., & Weissman, M. M. (1977). Social impairments four years after an acute depressive episode. *American Journal of Orthopsychiatry, 47,* 231–237.

Bowers, W. A. (1990). Treatment of depressed in-patients: Cognitive therapy plus medication, relaxation plus medication, and medication alone. *British Journal of Psychiatry, 156,* 73–78.

Bruder, G. E., Leite, P., Stewart, J. W., Mercier, M. A., Agosti, V., Donovan, S., et al. (1997). Outcome of cognitive-behavioral therapy for depression: Relation to hemispheric dominance in verbal processing. *Journal of Abnormal Psychology, 106,* 138–144.

Bull, S. A., Hu, X. H., Hunkeler, E. M., Lee, J. Y., Ming, E. E., Markson, L. E., et al. (2002). Discontinuation of use and switching of antidepressants:

Influence of patient-physician communication. *Journal of the American Medical Association, 288,* 1403–1409.

Burke, K. C., Burke, J. D., Regier, P. A., & Rae, P. S. (1990). Age at onset of selected mental disorders in five community populations. *Archives of General Psychiatry, 47,* 511–518.

Burns, D. D., Rude, S., Simons, A. D., Bates, M. A., & Thase, M. E. (1994). Does learned resourcefulness predict the response to cognitive behavioral therapy for depression? *Cognitive Therapy and Research, 18,* 277–291.

Craighead, W. E. (2000, August). *Recurrence of major depression: Prevalence, prediction, and prevention.* Paper presented at the meetings of the American Psychological Association, Washington, DC.

Craighead, W. E., Evans, D. D., & Robins, C. J. (1992). Unipolar depression. In S. M. Turner, K. S. Calhoun, & H. E. Adams (Eds.), *Handbook of clinical behavior therapy* (2nd ed., pp. 99–116). New York: Wiley.

Cronbach, L. J., & Snow, R. E. (1977). *Aptitudes and instructional methods.* New York: Irvington.

DeRubeis, R. J., Gelfand, L. A., Tang, T. Z., & Simons, A. D. (1999). Medications versus cognitive behavior therapy for severely depressed outpatients: Meta-analysis of four randomized comparisons. *American Journal of Psychiatry, 156,* 1007–1013.

DeRubeis, R. J., Hollon, S. D., Amsterdam, J. D., Shelton, R. C., Young, P. R., Salomon, R. M., et al. (2005). Cognitive therapy vs. medications in the treatment of moderate to severe depression. *Archives of General Psychiatry, 62,* 409–416.

DiMascio, A., Weissman, M. M., Prusoff, B. A., Neu, C., Zwilling, M., & Klerman, G. L. (1979). Differential symptom reduction by drugs and psychotherapy in acute depression. *Archives of General Psychiatry, 36,* 1450–1456.

Dimidjian, S., Hollon, S. D., Dobson, K. S., Schmaling, D. B., Kohlenberg, R. J., Addis, M. E., et al. (2006). Randomized trial of behavioral activation, cognitive therapy, and antidepressant medication in the acute treatment of adults with major depression. *Journal of Consulting and Clinical Psychology, 74,* 658–670.

Dobson, K. S. (1989). A meta-analysis of the efficacy of cognitive therapy for depression. *Journal of Consulting and Clinical Psychology, 57,* 414–419.

Elkin, I., Gibbons, R. D., Shea, M. T., & Shaw, B. F. (1996). Science is not a trial (but it can sometimes be a tribulation). *Journal of Consulting and Clinical Psychology, 64,* 92–103.

Elkin, I., Gibbons, R. D., Shea, M. T., Sotsky, S. M., Watkins, J. T., Pilkonis, P. A., et al. (1995). Initial severity and differential treatment outcome in the National Institute of Mental Health Treatment of Depression Collaborative Research Program. *Journal of Consulting and Clinical Psychology, 63,* 841–847.

Elkin, I., Parloff, M. B., Hadley, S. W., & Autry, J. H. (1985). NIMH Treatment of Depression Collaborative Research Program: Background and research plan. *Archives of General Psychiatry, 42,* 305–316.

Elkin, I., Shea, M. T., Watkins, J. T., Imber, S. D., Sotsky, S. M., Collins, J. F., et al. (1989). National Institute of Mental Health Treatment of Depression Collaborative Research Program: General effectiveness of treatments. *Archives of General Psychiatry, 46,* 971–982.

Evans, M. D., Hollon, S. D., DeRubeis, R. J., Piasecki, J. M., Grove, W. M., Garvey, M. J., et al. (1992). Differential relapse following cognitive therapy and pharmacotherapy for depression. *Archives of General Psychiatry, 49,* 802–808.

Fava, G. A., Grandi, S., Zielezny, M., Rafanelli, C., & Canestrari, R. (1996). Four-year outcome for cognitive behavioral treatment of residual symptoms in major depression. *American Journal of Psychiatry, 153,* 945–947.

Fava, G. A., Rafanelli, C., Grandi, S., Canestrari, R., & Morphy, M. A. (1998). Six-year outcome for cognitive behavioral treatment of residual symptoms in major depression. *American Journal of Psychiatry, 155,* 1443–1445.

Fergusson, D. M., Horwood, L. J., Ridder, E. M., & Beautrais, A. L. (2005). Subthreshold depression in adolescence and mental health outcomes in adulthood. *Archives of General Psychiatry, 62,* 66–72.

Ferster, C. B. (1973). A functional analysis of depression. *American Psychologist, 28,* 857–870.

First, M. B., Spitzer, R. L., Gibbon, M., Williams, J. B. W. (1995). *Structured clinical interview for DSM-IV Axis I disorders-patient edition.* SCID-I/P, version 2.0.

Frank, E., Kupfer, D. J., Jacob, M., & Jarrett, D. (1987). Personality features and response to acute treatment in recurrent depression. *Journal of Personality Disorders, 1,* 14–26.

Frank, E., Kupfer, D. J., Perel, T. M., Comes, C. L., Jarrett, D. J., Mallinger, A., et al. (1990). Three-year outcomes for maintenance therapies in recurrent depression. *Archives of General Psychiatry, 47,* 1093–1099.

Frank, E., Shear, M. K., Rucci, P., Cyranowski, J. M., Endicott, J., Fagiolini, A., et al. (2000). Influence of panic-agoraphobic spectrum symptoms on treatment response in patients with recurrent major depression. *American Journal of Psychiatry, 157,* 1101–1107.

Goldapple, K., Segal, Z., Garson, C., Lau, M., Bieling, P., Kennedy, S., et al. (2004). Modification of cortical-limbic pathways in major depression. *Archives of General Psychiatry, 61,* 34–41.

Gortner, E. T., Gollan, J. K., Dobson, K. S., & Jacobson, N. S. (1998). Cognitive-behavioral treatment for depression: Relapse prevention. *Journal of Consulting and Clinical Psychology, 66,* 377–384.

Greenberg, P. E., Stiglin, L. E., Finkelstein, S. N., & Berndt, E. R. (1993). The economic burden of depression in 1990. *Journal of Clinical Psychiatry, 54,* 405–418.

Hamilton, K. E., & Dobson, K. S. (2002). Cognitive therapy of depression: Pretreatment patient predictors of outcome. *Clinical Psychology Review, 22,* 875–894.

Hankin, B. L., Abramson, L. Y., Moffitt, I. E., Silva, P.A., McGee, R., & Angell, K. E. (1998). Development of depression from preadolescence to young adulthood: Emerging gender differences in a 10-year longitudinal study. *Journal of Abnormal Psychology, 107,* 128–140.

Hardy, G. E., Barkham, M., Shapiro, D. A., Stiles, W. B., Rees, A., & Reynolds, S. (1995). Impact of Cluster C personality disorders on outcomes of contrasting brief psychotherapies for depression. *Journal of Consulting and Clinical Psychology, 63,* 997–1004.

Hersen, M., Bellack, A. S., Himmelhoch, J. M., & Thase, M. E. (1984). Effects of social skill training, amitriptyline, and psychotherapy in unipolar depressed women. *Behavior Therapy, 15,* 21–40.

Hollon, S. D., DeRubeis, R. J., Evans, M. D., Wiemer, M. J., Garvey, M. J., Grove, W. M., et al. (1992). Cognitive therapy and pharmacotherapy for depression: Singly and in combination. *Archives of General Psychiatry, 49,* 774–781.

Hollon, S. D., DeRubeis, R. J., Shelton, R. C., Amsterdam, J. D., Salomon, R. M., O'Reardon, J. P., et al. (2005). Prevention of relapse following cognitive therapy vs. medications in moderate to severe depression. *Archives of General Psychiatry, 62,* 417–422.

Hollon, S. D., Shelton, R. C., & Loosen, P. T. (1991). Cognitive therapy and pharmacotherapy for depression. *Journal of Consulting and Clinical Psychology, 59,* 88–99.

Howland, R. H. (1991). Pharmacotherapy for dysthymia: A review. *Journal of Clinical Psychopharmacology, 11,* 83–92.

Ilardi, S. S., & Craighead, W. E. (1994/1995). Personality pathology and response to somatic treatments

for major depression: A critical review. *Depression, 2,* 200–217.

Jacobson, N. S., Dobson, K. S., Fruzetti, A. E., Schmaling, K. B., & Salusky, S. (1991). Marital therapy as a treatment for depression. *Journal of Consulting and Clinical Psychology, 59,* 547–557.

Jacobson, N. S., Dobson, K. S., Truax, P. A., Addis, M. E., Koerner, K., Gollan, J. K., et al. (1996). A component analysis of cognitive-behavioral treatment for depression. *Journal of Consulting and Clinical Psychology, 64,* 295–304.

Jacobson, N. S., & Hollon, S. D. (1996a). Cognitive-behavior therapy versus pharmacotherapy: Now that the jury's returned its verdict, it's time to present the rest of the evidence. *Journal of Consulting and Clinical Psychology, 64,* 74–80.

Jacobson, N. S., & Hollon, S. D. (1996b). Prospects for future comparisons between drugs and psychotherapy: Lessons from the CBT-versus-pharmacotherapy exchange. *Journal of Consulting and Clinical Psychology, 64,* 104–108.

Jarrett, R. B., Basco, M. R., Risser, R., Ramanan, J., Marwill, M., Kraft, D., et al. (1998). Is there a role for continuation phase cognitive therapy for depressed outpatients? *Journal of Consulting and Clinical Psychology, 66,* 1036–1040.

Jarrett, R. B., Eaves, G. G., Grannemann, B. D., & Rush, A. J. (1991). Clinical, cognitive, and demographic predictors of response to cognitive therapy for depression: A preliminary report. *Psychiatry Research, 37,* 245–260.

Jarrett, R. B., Schaffer, M., McIntire, D., Witt-Browder, A., Kraft, D., & Risser, R. C. (1999). Treatment of atypical depression with cognitive therapy or phenelzine: A double-blind, placebo-controlled trial. *Archives of General Psychiatry, 56,* 431–437.

Johnson, J., Weissman, M. M., & Klerman, G. L. (1992). Service utilization and social morbidity associated with depressive symptoms in the community. *Journal of the American Medical Association, 267,* 1478–1483.

Kabat-Zinn, J. (1990). *Full catastrophe living: The program of the Stress Reduction Clinic at the University of Massachusetts Medical Center.* New York: Delta.

Keller, M. B., McCullough, J. P., Klein, D. N., Arnow, B., Dunner, D. L., Gelenberg, A. J., et al. (2000). A comparison of nefazodone, the cognitive behavioral-analysis system of psychotherapy, and their combination for the treatment of chronic depression. *New England Journal of Medicine, 342,* 1462–1470.

Kessler, R. C., Berglund, P., Demler, O., Jin, R., Merikangas, K. R., & Walters, E. E. (2005). Lifetime prevalence and age-of-onset distributions of *DSM-IV* disorders in the National Comorbidity Survey Replication. *Archives of General Psychiatry, 62,* 593–602.

Klein, D. F. (1996). Preventing hung juries about therapy studies. *Journal of Consulting and Clinical Psychology, 64,* 80–87.

Klein, D. N., Santiago, N. J., Vivian, D., Arnow, B., Blalock, J. A., Dunner, D. L., et al. (2004). Cognitive-behavioral analysis system of psychotherapy as a maintainence treatment for chronic depression. *Journal of Consulting and Clinical Psychology, 72,* 681–688.

Klerman, G. L., DiMascio, A., Weissman, M., Prusoff, B., & Paykel, E. S. (1974). Treatment of depression by drugs and psychotherapy. *American Journal of Psychiatry, 131,* 186–190.

Klerman, G. L., & Weissman, M. M. (1993). Interpersonal psychotherapy for depression: Background and concepts. In G. L. Klerman & M. M. Weissman (Eds.), *New applications of interpersonal psychotherapy* (pp. 3–26). Washington, DC: American Psychiatric Press.

Klerman, G. L., Weissman, M. M., Rounsaville, B. J., & Chevron, E. S. (1984). *Interpersonal psychotherapy of depression.* New York: Basic Books.

Kocsis, J. H., Rush, A. J., Markowitz, J. C., Borian, F. E., Dunner, D. L., Koran, L. M., et al. (2003). Continuation treatment of chronic depression: A comparison of nefazodone, cognitive-behavioral analysis system of psychotherapy, and their combination. *Psychopharmacology Bulletin, 37,* 73–87.

Kuyken, W., Kurzer, N., DeRubeis, R. J., Beck, A. T., & Brown, G. K. (2001). Response to cognitive therapy in depression: The role of maladaptive beliefs and personality disorders. *Journal of Consulting and Clinical Psychology, 69,* 560–566.

Lewinsohn, P. M., Clarke, G. N., Seeley, J. R., & Rohde, P. (1994). Major depression in community adolescents: Age at onset, episode duration, and time to recurrence. *Journal of the American Academy of Child and Adolescent Psychiatry, 33,* 809–818.

Lewinsohn, P. M., & Gotlib, I. H. (1995). Behavioral theory and treatment of depression. In E. E. Becker & W. R. Leber (Eds.), *Handbook of depression* (pp. 352–375). New York: Guilford Press.

Lewinsohn, P. M., Hops, H., Roberts, R. E., Seeley, J. R., & Andrews, J. A. (1993). Adolescent psychopathology: I. Prevalence and incidence of depression and other *DSM-III-R* disorders in high school students. *Journal of Abnormal Psychology, 102,* 133–144.

Ma, S. H., & Teasdale, J. D. (2004). Mindfulness-based cognitive therapy for depression: Replication and exploration of differential relapse prevention effects. *Journal of Consulting and Clinical Psychology, 72,* 31–40.

McCullough, J. P. (2000). *Treatment of chronic depression: Cognitive behavioral analysis system of psychotherapy.* New York: Guilford Press.

McLean, P. D., & Hakstian, A. R. (1979). Clinical depression: Comparative efficacy of outpatient treatments. *Journal of Consulting and Clinical Psychology, 47,* 818–836.

McLean, P. D., & Hakstian, A. R. (1990). Relative endurance of unipolar depression treatment effects: Longitudinal follow-up. *Journal of Consulting and Clinical Psychology, 58,* 482–488.

Meyer, A. (1957). *Psychobiology: A science of man.* Springfield, IL: Charles C. Thomas.

Miller, I. W., Norman, W. H., Keitner, G. I., Bishop, S. B., & Dow, M. G. (1989). Cognitive-behavioral treatment of depressed inpatients. *Behavior Therapy, 20,* 25–47.

Mueller, T. I., Leon, A. C., Keller, M. B., Solomon, D. A., Endicott, J., Coryell, W., et al. (1999). Recurrence after recovery from major depressive disorder during 15 years of observational follow-up. *American Journal of Psychiatry, 156,* 1000–1006.

Murphy, G. E., Simons, A. D., Wetzel, R. D., & Lustman, P. J. (1984). Cognitive therapy and pharmacotherapy: Singly and together in the treatment of depression. *Archives of General Psychiatry, 41,* 33–41.

Murray, J. L., & Lopez, A. D. (1997). Global mortality, disability, and the contribution of risk factors: Global Burden of Disease Study. *Lancet, 349,* 1436–1442.

Nemeroff, C. B. (2003). Improving antidepressant adherence. *Journal of Clinical Psychiatry, 64*(Suppl. 18), 25–30.

Nemeroff, C. B., Heim, C. M., Thase, M. E., Klein, D. N., Rush, A. J., Schatzberg, A. F., et al. (2003). Differential responses to psychotherapy versus pharmacotherapy in patients with chronic forms of major depression and childhood trauma. *Proceedings of the National Academy of Sciences, 100,* 14293–14296.

Nemeroff, C. B., & Schatzberg, A. F. (1998). Pharmacological treatment of unipolar depression. In P. E. Nathan & J. M. Gorman (Eds.), *A guide to treatments that work* (pp. 212–225). New York: Oxford University Press.

Nietzel, M. T., Russell, R. L., Hemmings, K. A., & Gretter, M. L. (1987). Clinical significance of psychotherapy for unipolar depression: A meta-analytic approach to social comparison. *Journal of Consulting and Clinical Psychology, 55*, 156–161.

O'Leary, K. D., & Beach, S. R. H. (1990). Marital therapy: A viable treatment for depression and marital discord. *American Journal of Psychiatry, 147*, 183–186.

Olfson, M., Marcus, S. C., Tedeschi, M., & Wan, G. J. (2006). Continuity of antidepressant treatment for adults with depression in the United States. *American Journal of Psychiatry, 163*, 101–108.

Organista, K. C., Munoz, R. F., & Gonzalez, G. (1994). Cognitive-behavioral therapy for depression in low-income and minority medical outpatients: Description of a program and exploratory analyses. *Cognitive Therapy and Research, 18*, 241–259.

Paykel, E. S., Scott, J., Teasdale, J. D., Johnson, A. L., Garland, A., Moore, R. et al. (1999). Prevention of relapse in residual depression by cognitive therapy. *Archives of General Psychiatry, 56*, 829–835.

Persons, J. B., Bostrom, A., & Bertagbolli, A. (1999). Results of randomized controlled trials of cognitive therapy for depression generalize to private practice. *Cognitive Therapy and Research, 2*, 535–548.

Pilkonis, P. A., & Frank, E. (1988). Personality pathology in recurrent depression: Nature, prevalence, and relationship to treatment response. *American Journal of Psychiatry, 145*, 435–441.

Rector, N. A., Bagby, R. M., Segal, Z. V., Joffe, R. T., & Levitt, A. (2000). Self-criticism and dependency in depressed patients treated with cognitive therapy or pharmacotherapy. *Cognitive Therapy and Research, 24*, 571–584.

Rehm, L. P. (1977). A self-control model of depression. *Behavior Therapy, 8*, 787–804.

Rehm, L. P. (1990). Cognitive and behavioral theories. In B. B. Wolman & G. Stricker (Eds.), *Depressive disorders: Facts, theories, and treatment methods* (pp. 64–91). New York: Wiley.

Reynolds, C. F., III, Frank, E., Dew, M. A., Houck, P. R., Miller, M., Mazumdar, S., et al. (1999). Treatment of 70+-year-olds with recurrent major depression: Excellent short-term but brittle long-term response. *American Journal of Geriatric Psychiatry, 7*, 64–69.

Robinson, L. A., Berman, J. S., & Neimeyer, R. A. (1990). Psychotherapy for the treatment of depression: A comprehensive review of controlled outcome research. *Psychological Bulletin, 108*, 30–49.

Rude, S. S., & Rehm, L. P. (1991). Response to treatments for depression: The role of initial status on targeted cognitive and behavioral skills. *Clinical Psychology Review, 11*, 493–514.

Rush, A. J., Beck, A. T., Kovacs, M., & Hollon, S. D. (1977). Comparative efficacy of cognitive therapy in the treatment of depressed outpatients. *Cognitive Therapy and Research, 1*, 17–36.

Schulberg, H. C., Pilkonis, P. A., & Houck, P. (1998). The severity of major depression and choice of treatment in primary care practice. *Journal of Consulting and Clinical Psychology, 66*, 932–938.

Segal, Z. V., Williams, J. M. G., & Teasdale, J. D. (2002). *Mindfulness-based cognitive therapy for depression: A new approach to preventing relapse.* New York: Guilford Press.

Shea, M. T., Elkin, I., Imber, S. D., Sotsky, S. M., Watkins, J. T., Collins, J. F., et al. (1992). Course of depressive symptoms over follow-up: Findings from the National Institute of Mental Health Treatment of Depression Collaborative Research Program. *Archives of General Psychiatry, 49*, 782–787.

Shea, M. T., Pilkonis, P. A., Beckham, E., Collins, J. F., Elkin, I., Sotsky, S. M., et al. (1990). Personality disorders and treatment outcome in the NIMH Treatment of Depression Collaborative Research Program. *American Journal of Psychiatry, 147*, 711–718.

Shea, M. T., Widiger, T. A., & Klein, M. H. (1992). Comorbidity of personality disorders and depression: Implications for treatment. *Journal of Consulting and Clinical Psychology, 60*, 857–868.

Simons, A. D., Gordon, J. S., Monroe, S. M., & Thase, M. E. (1995). Toward an integration of psychologic, social, and biologic factors in depression: Effects on outcome and course of cognitive therapy. *Journal of Consulting and Clinical Psychology, 63*, 369–377.

Simons, A. D., Lustman, P. J., Wetzel, R. D., & Murphy, G. E. (1985). Predicting response to cognitive therapy of depression: The role of learned resourcefulness. *Cognitive Therapy and Research, 9*, 79–89.

Simons, A. D., Murphy, G. E., Levine, J. L., & Wetzel, R. D. (1986). Cognitive therapy and pharmacotherapy for depression. *Archives of General Psychiatry, 43*, 43–48.

Simons, A. D., & Thase, M. E. (1990). Mood disorders. In M. E. Thase, B. A. Edelstein, & M. Hersen (Eds.), *Handbook of outpatient treatment of adults: Nonpsychotic mental disorders* (pp. 91–138). New York: Plenum Press.

Skinner, B. F. (1953). *Science and human behavior.* New York: Free Press.

Sloane, R. B., Staples, F. R., & Schneider, L. S. (1985). Interpersonal therapy versus nortriptyline for depression in the elderly. In G. Burrows, T. R. Norman, & L. Dermerstein (Eds.), *Clinical and pharmacological studies in psychiatric disorders* (pp. 344–346). London: John Libbey.

Sotsky, S. M., Glass, D. R., Shea, M. T., Pilkonis, P. A., Collins, J. F., Elkin, I., et al. (1991). Patient predictors of response to psychotherapy and pharmacotherapy: Findings in the NIMH Treatment of Depression Collaborative Research Program. *American Journal of Psychiatry*, 148, 997–1008.

Spitzer, R. L., Endicott, J., & Robins, E. (1978). Research diagnostic criteria: Rationale and reliability. *Archives of General Psychiatry*, 35, 773–782.

Spitzer, R. L., Williams, J. B. W., Gibbon, M., & First, M. (1992). The structured clinical interview for *DSM-III-R* (SCID): I. History, rationale, and description. *Archives of General Psychiatry*, 49, 624–636.

Steuer, J. L, Mintz, J., Harnmen, C. L., Hill, M. A., Jarvik, L. F., McCarley, T., et al. (1984). Cognitive-behavioral and psychodynamic group psychotherapy in treatment of geriatric depression. *Journal of Consulting and Clinical Psychology*, 52, 180–189.

Sullivan, H. S. (1953). *The interpersonal theory of psychiatry*. New York: Norton.

Teasdale, J. D., Fennell, M. J., Hibbert, G. A., & Amies, P. L. (1984). Cognitive therapy for major depressive disorder in primary care. *British Journal of Psychiatry*, 144, 400–406.

Teasdale, J. D., Segal, Z. C., Williams, J. M. G., Ridgeway, V. A., Soulsby, J. M., & Lau, M. A. (2000). Prevention of relapse/recurrence in major depression by mindfulness-based cognitive therapy. *Journal of Consulting and Clinical Psychology*, 68, 615–623.

Thase, M. E. (1994). Cognitive behavior therapy of severe unipolar depression. In L. Grauhaus & J. F. Greden (Eds.), *Severe depressive disorders* (pp. 269–296). Washington, DC: American Psychiatric Press.

Thase, M. E., Bowler, K., & Harden, T. (1991). Cognitive behavior therapy of endogenous depression: II. Preliminary findings in 16 unmedicated inpatients. *Behavior Therapy*, 22, 469–477.

Thompson, L. W., & Gallagher, D. (1984). Efficacy of psychotherapy in the treatment of late-life depression. *Advances in Behaviour Research and Therapy*, 6, 127–139.

Thompson, L. W., Gallagher, D., & Breckenridge, J. S. (1987). Comparative effectiveness of psychotherapies for depressed elders. *Journal of Consulting and Clinical Psychology*, 55, 385–390.

Thompson, L. W., Gallagher, D., & Czirr, R. (1988). Personality disorder and outcome in the treatment of late-life depression. *Journal of Geriatric Psychiatry*, 21, 133–146.

Weissman, M. M., Bland, R. C., Canino, G. J., Faravelli, C., Greenwald, S., Hwu, H., et al. (1996). Cross-national epidemiology of major depression and bipolar disorder. *Journal of the American Medical Association*, 276, 293–299.

Weissman, M. M., & Klerman, G. L. (1973). Psychotherapy with depressed women: An empirical study of content themes and reflection. *British Journal of Psychiatry*, 123, 55–61.

Weissman, M. M., Klerman, G. L., Prusoff, B. A., Sholomskas, D., & Padian, N. (1981). Depressed outpatients: Results 1 year after treatment with drugs and/or interpersonal psychotherapy. *Archives of General Psychiatry*, 38, 51–55.

Weissman, M. M., Prusoff, B. A., DiMascio, A., Neu, C., Goklaney, M., & Klerman, G. L. (1979). The efficacy of drugs and psychotherapy in the treatment of acute depressive episodes. *American Journal of Psychiatry*, 136, 555–558.

Wells, K. B., Stewart, A., Hays, R. D., Burnam, A., Rogers W., Daniels, M., et al. (1989). The functioning and well-being of depressed patients: Results from the medical outcomes study. *Journal of the American Medical Association*, 262, 914–919.

Wilson, P. H., Goldin, J. C., & Charbonneau-Powis, M. (1983). Comparative efficacy of behavioral and cognitive treatments of depression. *Cognitive Therapy and Research*, 7, 111–124.

11

Psychosocial Treatments
for Bipolar Disorder

David J. Miklowitz
W. Edward Craighead

Whereas pharmacological interventions remain the primary treatment for bipolar disorder, adjunctive psychosocial interventions have the potential to increase adherence to medication regimens, decrease hospitalizations and relapses, improve quality of life, and enhance mechanisms for coping with stress. Controlled studies have established that individual, family, and group psychoeducation, designed to provide information to bipolar patients and their families about the disorder, its pharmacological treatment, and the treatments' side effects, leads to lower rates of recurrence and greater adherence to pharmacological treatment among bipolar patients. Type 1 and 2 studies have evaluated cognitive behavioral therapy (CBT) as an ancillary treatment. These studies indicate that CBT is associated with better medication adherence and significantly fewer recurrences and/or rehospitalizations. One Type 1 study has evaluated the effectiveness of IPSRT (interpersonal and social rhythm therapy) for bipolar disorder. IPSRT demonstrated its greatest symptomatic effects during a maintenance treatment period, especially if bipolar patients had been successful in stabilizing their daily and nightly routines during an acute treatment period. Finally, four Type 1 studies in adult and pediatric patients have shown that marital/family therapy may be effectively combined with pharmacotherapy to reduce recurrences and improve medication adherence and family functioning.

Up to 4% of the adult population in the United States experiences bipolar disorder (Kessler, Berglund, Demler, Jin, & Walters, 2005). For more than 90% of those patients, the disorder is characterized by a recurrent course of mood fluctuation over the lifetime (American Psychiatric Association, 2000). Several studies indicate that a substantial proportion (up to 75%) experience lengthy periods of intermorbid residual symptoms despite pharmacotherapy (e.g., Gitlin, Swendsen, Heller, & Hammen, 1995; Harrow, Goldberg, Grossman, & Meltzer, 1990; Keller et al., 1986). Bipolar disorder is the sixth-leading cause of disability among the physical and psychiatric disorders (Murray & Lopez, 1996).

Bipolar disorder has a strong impact on patients' work and social functioning. Approximately one of every three patients shows deficits in work functioning 2 years after hospitalization (Coryell, Andreasen, Endicott, & Keller, 1987), only 20% work at expected levels of employment during the 6 months after an episode (Dion, Tohen, Anthony, & Waternaux, 1988), and more than 50% show declines in occupational functioning over the 5 years following an episode (Coryell et al., 1993; Goldberg, Harrow, & Grossman, 1995). The effects of manic episodes can be observed 5 years later on social, occupational, and family functioning (Coryell et al., 1993). The risk of suicide in bipolar patients is between 15 and

20%, about 15 times that for the normal population (APA, 2000; Isometsae, 1993; Harris & Barraclough, 1997). Unfortunately, despite recent advances in the treatment of this debilitating disorder, it is estimated that fewer than one third of bipolar patients receive treatment—a lower percentage than for any other major psychiatric disorder (Goodwin & Jamison, 1990).

A common etiological explanation for bipolar disorder maintains that it results from biological dysregulations (with a major genetic component) that are either activated or maintained by psychosocial stressors such as negative family environments or stressful life events (e.g., Craighead & Miklowitz, 2000; Miklowitz & Johnson, 2006). Because of the biological dysregulations associated with bipolar disorder, pharmacological treatments are the primary line of intervention. Although lithium carbonate has dramatically improved both acute and prophylactic treatment, anticonvulsant agents and the atypical antipsychotics are being increasingly used as first-line agents (Goldberg, 2004; McElroy & Keck, 2000). With one or more of these medications, the majority of patients can now experience some level of mood stabilization with continued use.

Ironically, although patients can now benefit more from psychosocial interventions due to the mood stabilization available through pharmacotherapy, adjunctive psychosocial treatments are utilized less frequently than they were before the introduction of lithium (Zaretsky & Segal, 1994/1995). However, the 1994 NIMH Task Force concluded, "Pharmacotherapy alone does not meet the needs of many bipolar patients" (Prien & Rush, 1996, pp. 217). Because biological treatments have been so extensively studied, the 1989 NIMH consensus conference on bipolar disorders concluded the use of adjunctive psychosocial treatments was the area in need of the greatest development in treatment studies (Potter & Prien, 1989). Progress has been made during the past 15 years, but it remains true that the clinical research literature evaluating the effectiveness of psychosocial interventions as adjuncts to medications is small.

Within the context of pharmacological interventions as the primary treatment for bipolar disorder, psychosocial interventions have been designed to increase adherence to medication regimens, decrease hospitalizations and relapses, and improve the patients' quality of life. The major components of a multifaceted psychosocial treatment program include psychoeducation with special attention to medication adherence and symptom management, individual cognitive-behavioral or interpersonal therapy, and marital or family therapy. In this chapter we review the empirical outcome data for each of these treatment components.

PSYCHOEDUCATION

Bipolar patients frequently express resentment at how little information they receive about their disorder or their medications (Goodwin & Jamison, 1990). The few studies that do exist show a positive effect of psychoeducation for both patients and their families. The primary focus of psychoeducation is the provision of information regarding the multifaceted nature of the disorder and its successful treatment.

The issue of medication adherence is a particularly salient aspect of the education and treatment of bipolar disorder. Despite the high risk of relapse due to nonadherence, up to 59% of patients on long-term lithium maintenance do not adhere or only partially adhere to their prescribed medications (Strakowski et al., 1998). Because of their more limited side-effects profile, it has been presumed that adherence to the anticonvulsants is better, but the data provide only limited support for this presumption (Lenzi, Lazzerini, Placidi, Cassano, & Akiskal, 1989; Weiss et al., 1998). Nonadherence comes with high costs: In a naturalistic, 18-month prospective study of 37 adolescents whose bipolar disorder had been stabilized with lithium carbonate during inpatient hospitalization, the relapse rate among patients who discontinued medication was 92.3%, compared with 37.5% for patients who continued lithium prophylaxis without interruption (Strober, Morrell, Lampert, & Burroughs, 1990). Further, sudden discontinuation of lithium is a strong predictor of illness recurrence (Suppes, Baldessarini, Faedda, Tondo, & Tohen, 1993). Therefore, enhancing medication adherence is one of the most important goals of ancillary psychosocial treatments.

Early Psychoeducational Studies

Seltzer, Roncari, and Garfinkel (1980) evaluated the effects of psychoeducation on medication adherence among 67 psychiatric patients (44 schizophrenic, 16 bipolar, and 7 unipolar affective) who were treated with neuroleptic, lithium, or tricyclic antidepressant drugs. Within each diagnostic group, patients were divided into nonrandomized control and experimental groups (Type 3 trial). Patients in the experimental group were given a series of nine lectures about the nature of their disorder and its pharmacological management. "Educated" patients tended to adhere better to medication regimes at the outpatient follow-up 5 months later and were less fearful of medication side effects and addiction. Medication adherence was negatively related to fear of side effects and positively related to education and the resulting knowledge about the disorder and its treatment.

In a Type 2 trial, Peet and Harvey (1991) evaluated a minimal psychoeducational intervention — a 12-minute videotape lecture with written handouts containing factual information about lithium. Of consecutive patients attending a lithium clinic, 60 were randomly assigned to one of two groups: one group ($N = 30$) received the educational program immediately, and the other group of 30 served as a wait-list control group that received the program 6 weeks later. After the wait-list control group had received the educational program, the preintervention and postintervention data were analyzed for all 60 patients. The educational program resulted in significant increases in patient knowledge about lithium; for example, their knowledge increased from a baseline comparable to the knowledge of social workers to a level similar to that of community psychiatric nurses. Patients' attitudes toward lithium also became more favorable after education. For all 60 patients medication adherence improved, as measured by either self-reported tablet omissions or plasma lithium levels (Harvey & Peet, 1991). Thus, it appears that even a very minimal psychoeducational component can improve both patient attitudes and medication adherence. Unfortunately, this study did not include a long-term follow-up, so it is not possible to determine whether these gains were maintained over time, or whether this intervention led to lower relapse rates following symptom remission.

One Type 3 study (van Gent & Zwart, 1991) examined the effects of educating the partners of bipolar patients. The subjects in this study were 26 manic bipolar patients and their partners: 14 partners attended psychoeducation sessions without the partners being present, and the partners of the 12 remaining patients served as controls. At postintervention and at a 6-month follow-up, partners who attended psychoeducational sessions demonstrated a greater knowledge of the disorder, medications, social support, and coping strategies. However, patients' medication adherence did not change over the 12-month follow-up, compared with either the pre-intervention values or the control group values.

It is possible that patient education leads only to changes in medication adherence; however, there may be additional effects of the enhanced social support gained from education of the patient's family or spouse, such as lower rates of relapse or improved quality of life. More recent psychoeducation studies have examined these issues.

Later Psychoeducational Studies

Later psychoeducational studies have focused on manual-based interventions, more tightly controlled experimental designs, and longer periods of follow-up. In a Type 1 trial, Perry, Tarrier, Morriss, McCarthy, and Limb (1999) compared patients who received medication management with patients who received medication management and a 7- to 12-session psychoeducational intervention ($N = 69$). The psychoeducation consisted of sessions to teach patients to recognize emergent symptoms of bipolar disorder when they occurred and to seek appropriate medical/preventative interventions. During an 18-month follow-up period, manic relapses were significantly delayed among bipolar patients in the psychoeducation versus the medication-only group; no differences were found in survival times prior to depressive relapses. Psychoeducation also had a stronger impact on social and occupational functioning than did medication management. There were no differences between the groups in medication adherence.

A group in Barcelona, Spain (Colom et al., 2003) developed a group psychoeducational intervention. In a Type 1 randomized trial ($N = 120$), one group of patients received psychopharmacology and 21 weekly sessions of group psychoeducation, and another received psychopharmacology and 21 unstructured, nondidactic group support sessions. The experimental group psychoeducation focused on illness management (e.g., relapse prevention planning) and decreasing the stigma of mental illness. Patients had been in remission for at least 6 months prior to entering the trial. At the end of 2 years, the rate of relapse in group psychoeducation was 67%, and in the unstructured groups, 92%. Patients in the experimental group also had higher and more stable lithium levels (Colom et al., 2005). The rate of dropout in the structured psychoeducation groups was somewhat higher (27%) than in the unstructured groups (12%).

Finally, a Type 1 study by Simon, Ludman, Unutzer, Bauer, Operskalski, and Rutter (2005) examined group psychoeducation within the context of a multicomponent care-management intervention. Patients (N = 441) had all been treated within a managed care network within the prior year. They were randomly assigned to pharmacotherapy alone or a care-management program consisting of pharmacotherapy, telephone-based monitoring, care planning within an interdisciplinary team, and group psychoeducation. The group psychoeducation model focused on individual life goal setting (Bauer & McBride, 1996). Over a two-year follow-up, patients in the program had lower mania scores and spent less time hypomanic or manic than those in the control group (Simon, Ludman, Bauer, Unutzer, & Operskalski, 2006). The intervention did not differentially affect depressive symptoms.

INDIVIDUAL PSYCHOTHERAPY INTERVENTIONS

Interpersonal and Social Rhythm Therapy

Interpersonal psychotherapy (IPT; Weissman, Markowitz, & Klerman, 2000) is an individual therapy that was originally developed as a treatment for major depressive disorder. This present-focused, short-term therapy assumes a biopsychosocial origin of depressive disorders. IPT typically focuses on one of four problem areas: grief over loss, interpersonal disputes (persistent conflicts with significant others), role transitions (changes in a person's occupational or social/family situations), and interpersonal skill deficits. IPT has been found to be effective in alleviating depressive symptoms in a major clinical trial (Elkin et al., 1989; Elkin et al., 1995) and a 3-year maintenance trial of recurrent depressive disorders (Frank et al., 1990).

Based on modifications of IPT, interpersonal and social rhythm therapy (IPSRT), developed by Frank and her colleagues (Frank, Swartz, & Kupfer, 2000), is an adjunctive individual therapy for bipolar disorder. IPSRT is based on the social rhythm stability hypothesis (Ehlers, Frank, & Kupfer, 1988). The pri-

mary modification to IPT is that IPSRT encourages patients to recognize the impact of interpersonal events on their social and circadian rhythms. There are two goals for IPSRT: (a) to help patients to understand and renegotiate the social context associated with mood disorder symptoms; and (b) to encourage patients to recognize the impact of interpersonal events on their social and circadian rhythms, and to regularize these rhythms in order to gain control over their mood cycling.

In IPSRT patients are given the Social Rhythm Metric (Monk, Kupfer, Frank, & Ritenour, 1991), a daily self-report device on which they record their sleep/wake times, levels of social stimulation, timing of daily routines (eating, exercise, work, etc), and daily mood. By reviewing data from this assessment device, patients gradually see how changes in their mood states can occur as a function of variable daily routines, sleep/wake cycles, and patterns of interpersonal stimulation, and reciprocally how these factors are affected by their moods. In time, patients become motivated to regulate their rhythms and find balances among these factors as a means of stabilizing their moods.

Much like IPT, IPSRT utilizes clarifying and interpretative interventions to help patients resolve current interpersonal problems (e.g., ongoing disputes with coworkers) and explore ways to prevent these problems from emerging in the future. The objective is to bring about an optimal balance in the patient's daily patterns of social activities, social stimulation, and sleep and wake cycles, a balance that is presumed to help stabilize mood states. A clinician may explore a bipolar patient's grief over lost hopes, aspirations, and a sense of a healthy self, and then encourage the patient to set realistic goals in the context of having a long-term, biologically based mood disorder. Like other psychosocial therapies, IPSRT includes education about bipolar disorder and strategies for improving drug adherence (Frank, Kupfer, Ehlers, & Monk, 1994).

The University of Pittsburgh Medical Center conducted a controlled Type 1 trial of IPSRT in conjunction with lithium and other mood stabilizers (Frank et al., 1997; Frank et al., 2005). Patients were assigned to IPSRT or to a comparison individual therapy, intensive clinical management. Sessions of intensive clinical management were of comparable frequency to IPSRT but consisted of 20-minute sessions (vs. 45 minutes for IPSRT) with a psychotherapist who focused on symptom management and medication adherence. Randomization occurred at two time points—during a preliminary, postepisode acute treatment phase, and again during a long-term preventative phase. IPSRT or intensive clinical management sessions were held weekly during the preliminary phase (until the patient had stabilized) and biweekly and then monthly during maintenance prevention, for up to 2 years.

There were no differences between the IPSRT and intensive clinical management treatment strategies on time to stabilization of the acute episode. (Frank et al., 1997). However, patients assigned to IPSRT in the acute phase survived longer without a mood disorder recurrence in the maintenance treatment phase than those in intensive clinical management, even if they were not assigned to IPSRT in the maintenance phase. Patients in IPSRT also showed greater stabilization of their daily routines and sleep/wake cycles during the acute phase than patients in intensive clinical management, and the ability to stabilize routines during the acute phase was associated with a lower likelihood of recurrence during the maintenance phase. Thus, consistency of a patient's routines may protect against recurrences of bipolar disorder (Frank et al., 2005).

A Type 3 trial of IPSRT in conjunction with family-focused treatment revealed positive benefits of the combined model over treatment as usual (Miklowitz, Richards, et al., 2003). Patients (N = 30) who received an average of 30 individual IPSRT and family psychoeducational sessions (with parents or spouses) had longer survival times prior to depressive relapse and greater stabilization of depressive symptoms over 1 year than patients (N = 70) who received pharmacotherapy, two sessions of family psychoeducation, and crisis intervention as needed. This was, however, an open trial with a historical comparison group.

Cognitive-Behavior Therapy

During the past decade there has been increased interest in the study of individual CBT in conjunction with mood-stabilizing medications for the treatment of bipolar disorder. The primary assumption of CBT is that mood swings are in part a function of negative thinking patterns (both self-statements and core dysfunctional schemata) that can be alleviated by a combination of behavioral activation and cognitive

restructuring strategies to increase the patient's engagement with the environment.

In the first controlled Type 2 study of individual therapy as an ancillary psychosocial treatment for bipolar disorder, one half of 28 newly admitted lithium-treated outpatients were randomly assigned to receive only lithium, while the other 14 received lithium and an additional preventive compliance intervention based on principles of CBT (Cochran, 1984). The therapeutic program was designed to alter specific cognitions and behaviors hypothesized to interfere with medication adherence. The intervention consisted of six weekly individual 1-hour therapy sessions. At both posttreatment and 6-month follow-up, patients who received the intervention had significantly better medication adherence. Also, over the 6-month follow-up period, the intervention group had significantly fewer hospitalizations (2 vs. 8). Although the groups did not differ significantly in total number of relapses (9 vs. 14), patients in the intervention group had significantly fewer mood disorder episodes (5 episodes experienced by 3 intervention patients vs. 11 episodes experienced by eight standard-treatment patients) judged to be precipitated by medication nonadherence.

A large-scale (N = 103) Type 1 randomized study (Lam et al., 2003; Lam, Hayward, Watkins, Wright, & Sham, 2005) compared a 6-month CBT (average of 14 sessions plus 2 booster sessions) with pharmacotherapy versus a control group (usual care and pharmacotherapy). Patients had been in remission for at least 6 months but were considered relapse prone because they had had at least three episodes in the past 5 years. The results suggested a short-term advantage for CBT: at 1 year, the relapse rate in the CBT condition was 44% and in the control condition, 75%. Patients in CBT also had higher social functioning and were better able to cope with manic prodromes. In an 18-month follow-up after the initial 1-year study, patients in CBT and usual care did not differ in relapse rates. However, CBT continued to be associated with better self-reported mood and fewer days spent in episodes.

Interestingly, the effects of CBT were stronger on depression than on mania (Lam et al., 2005). Family interventions have also been found to have stronger effects on depression than on mania symptoms (Miklowitz, George, Richards, Simoneau, & Suddath, 2003), whereas purely psychoeducational interventions—notably those oriented around symptom management—have stronger effects on mania than on depression (Perry et al., 1999; Simon et al., 2005). Possibly, the prodromal symptoms of manic episodes are easier to identify than those of depressive episodes, and interventions aimed specifically at recognition of early symptoms would be expected to have a stronger preventative impact on manic recurrences. Lam and associates recommend that CBT techniques may need to be reformulated to address the specific cognitive distortions and styles associated with hypomania or grandiosity (dynamism, persuasiveness, and productiveness).

The largest Type 1 CBT trial to date was conducted in the United Kingdom (Scott et al., 2006). Patients ($N = 253$) were recruited in five different sites in a variety of clinical states. Patients were randomly assigned to CBT plus medications (22 sessions) or treatment as usual and medications. No differences emerged between CBT and treatment as usual on time to recurrence. However, there was a treatment by prior episodes interaction: CBT was associated with longer survival times prior to recurrences in patients with fewer than 12 prior episodes, whereas treatment as usual was associated with longer survival among patients with 12 or more prior episodes. These results may suggest that CBT is more appropriate early in the course of bipolar illness, or perhaps among patients who are less severely recurrent.

The mechanisms of action of CBT treatments—whether they have a direct impact on patients' cognitive styles, core dysfunctional beliefs, or behavioral activation, or whether they increase the patients' knowledge of bipolar disorder and use of illness management strategies (e.g., medication adherence, seeking emergency interventions prior to relapses)—have not been examined. Given the results of these previous studies and the allegiance to the CBT model among many community clinicians, further empirical studies are clearly warranted.

MARITAL AND FAMILY INTERVENTIONS

The cycling of bipolar disorder affects and is affected by the family context (Miklowitz, Goldstein, Nuechterlein, Snyder, & Mintz, 1988). Just as the patient needs to understand the disorder and its treatment, the parents and/or spouse needs to learn skills to cope with the disorder's effects on interpersonal interactions and relationships.

Current successful approaches to family or marital treatment are psychoeducational, meaning that the clinician views the dysfunction of the couple or family as largely due to a lack of knowledge, coping strategies, and interpersonal skills necessary for dealing with the disorder. Psychoeducational family and marital interventions include teaching the patient and close relatives (typically the spouse or parents) about the symptoms, course, and treatment of bipolar disorder and emphasizing strategies for relapse prevention. Psychoeducational marital and family interventions are most successfully administered concurrently with pharmacotherapy (typically mood-stabilizing medications, with or without adjunctive agents).

Marital and Family Difficulties

The marital interactions of bipolar patients are often problematic, both during patients' episodes and during well intervals. In a study of marital interaction patterns (McKnight, Nelson-Gray, & Gullick, 1989), bipolar patients' interactions with spouses during manic episodes were highly active (including interruptions and conversational dominance by the manic partner). When these patients were in remission, there was a reduction in negative interactions, but this reduction was not replaced by positive interactions (such as generating positive solutions to problems). These findings indicate a need for problem-solving and communication training for couples and families in which a member suffers from bipolar disorder.

Stressful family environments are predictive of the course of bipolar disorder. Specifically, if an episodic bipolar patient returns to a "high expressed emotion" (high-EE) family, in which one or both key relatives (parents or spouse) show critical, hostile, or emotionally overinvolved attitudes, the patient has up to a five times greater risk of relapse in the next 9 to 12 months than a patient who returns to a "low-EE" family (that is, a less critical and normally involved family; Miklowitz, Goldstein, Nuechterlein, Snyder, & Mintz, 1988; Miklowitz et al., 2000; O'Connell, Mayo, Flatow, Cuthbertson, & O'Brien, 1991; Priebe, Wildgrube, & Müller-Oerlinghausen,

1989). Two studies further suggest that negative pa-tient-relative verbal interactional patterns predict poor symptomatic and social functioning in 1-year community follow-ups (Miklowitz et al., 1988; O'Con-nell, Mayo, Flatow, Cuthbertson, & O'Brien, 1991). Thus, the family environment plays a strong prognos-tic role in mood disorders (see also the meta-analysis of Butzlaff & Hooley, 1998).

On the positive side, bipolar patients with high levels of social and emotional support from their friends and families recover more quickly from a bi-polar episode than patients with low levels of such support (Johnson, Winett, Meyer, Greenhouse, & Miller, 1999). Thus, family and marital interventions that maximize the protective effects of the family context are potentially powerful adjuncts to pharma-cotherapy in relapse prevention.

The Cornell and Brown University Studies

Several investigations have examined whether family or marital interventions, as adjunctive to pharmaco-therapy, lead to improved outcomes of bipolar disor-der. A group at the Cornell University Medical Col-lege (Clarkin et al., 1990; Clarkin, Hass, & Glick, 1988; Glick, Clarkin, Haas, Spencer, & Chen, 1991; Haas et al., 1988; Spencer et al., 1988) developed and tested an inpatient family intervention (IFI) for families of hospitalized psychiatric (including bipo-lar) patients. The IFI is a brief (average of nine weekly or twice-weekly sessions) therapy involving both patients and key relatives. It focuses on helping participants cope with the hospitalization and make plans for a positive postdischarge adjustment. Similar to an outpatient, crisis-oriented family program de-veloped by Goldstein and his colleagues (Goldstein, Rodnick, Evans, May, & Steinberg, 1978) for pa-tients with schizophrenia, IFI encourages patients and family members to (a) accept that the disorder is real and probably chronic, and that medical and psychosocial treatments will be necessary after hospi-tal discharge; (b) identify stressors both within and outside of the family (e.g., aversive family interaction patterns or stressful events) that may precipitate epi-sodes of psychiatric disorder; and (c) learn ways to modify these family patterns and cope with future stressors (Glick et al., 1991).

In a Type 1 controlled clinical trial (N=186) in-volving hospitalized patients with major affective,

schizophrenic, and other Axis I disorders, IFI was combined with standard hospital treatment (includ-ing pharmacotherapy) and compared with hospital treatment alone. At hospital discharge, the treatment effects were mostly evident in female patients with affective (including bipolar) disorders. However, the treatment effects were broader at the 6-month and 18-month posthospital follow-ups: female patients with major affective and schizophrenic disorders ex-hibited better global and symptomatic functioning if they had received IFI than if they had received the comparison treatment. Finally, among female pa-tients from the affective disorder and schizophrenic groups, family treatment was associated with im-provements at 6 and 18 months in family attitudes, including feelings of rejection held by family mem-bers toward the patient and perceptions of family burden (Clarkin et al., 1990; Glick et al., 1991; Spencer et al., 1988).

Of the 50 affective disorder patients, 21 met crite-ria for bipolar disorder (Clarkin et al., 1990). When the treatment effects for bipolar patients were graphed separately by gender, treatment effects were seen only among the 14 female bipolar patients; thus, the sample size is too small to allow firm con-clusions about the treatment's effects on bipolar pa-tients. Furthermore, the obtained effect seems to have been due largely to the poor showing for stan-dardized treatment among the female bipolar pa-tients rather than a strong improvement among the female bipolar patients in IFI. Perhaps due to lack of statistical power, the effect of treatment on global functioning for bipolar patients alone was only mar-ginally significant at 6 months, and it was nonsig-nificant at 18 months. For role functioning (e.g., work performance), the effect of treatment was not significant at 6 months, but it was significant at 18 months. In short, while inpatient family intervention may be a useful adjunctive therapy for hospitalized bipolar patients, the results from this study are equiv-ocal.

Clarkin, Carpenter, Hull, Wilner, and Glick (1998) conducted a Type 2 study of 33 married bipo-lar patients randomized to standard medications only or to standard medications plus a marital interven-tion. The marital intervention was 25 sessions over 11 months and focused on improving spousal com-munication and attitudes, educating the couple about the disorder, and enhancing adherence to drug treatments. No effects were obtained for the marital intervention on symptomatic adjustment or recurrences during the 11-month treatment period. Patients in the marital intervention group, however, showed greater improvements in global functioning than those in the standard medication group. Medication adherence was, on average, higher in the family group throughout the 11-month period.

In a Type 1 trial, Miller, Solomon, Ryan, and Keitner (2004) at Brown University Medical Center assigned 92 bipolar patients who were either manic or depressed to one of three treatment conditions: (a) standard treatment, consisting of medication plus active clinical management by a psychiatrist; (b) standard treatment plus family therapy (six to eight sessions over 4 months of treatment, and follow-up "booster sessions"); and (c) standard treatment plus multifamily groups, in which four to six families met together in 1½-hour sessions over 6 weeks, followed by "reunion meetings" over the next 6 months. The family treatments were oriented toward education about the disorder and problem solving. The investigators attempted to build on their earlier finding that, over a 5-year follow-up, the odds of rehospitalization were twice as high among bipolar patients whose families were "dysfunctional" (as judged by observer-rated and self-report instruments) during a baseline manic episode than among patients whose families were nondysfunctional at baseline.

Results indicated that the two family-treated groups did not differ from the standard care group in time to recover or proportion recovered. Thus, family intervention did not hasten the stabilization that would be expected from pharmacotherapy alone. The study, however, did not examine prophylaxis against recurrences.

Family-Focused Treatment: The Colorado and UCLA Studies

Miklowitz and Goldstein (1990, 1997) developed a 9-month, family-focused treatment (FFT) for bipolar adults who have been recently hospitalized or are being treated on an outpatient basis for a recent acute episode. FFT is delivered in 21 sessions titrated over 9 months (12 weekly, 6 biweekly, and 3 monthly). The model is similar to Falloon, Boyd, and McGill's (1984) behavioral family management for schizo-phrenic disorders, but it is adapted to the needs of bipolar patients and their families.

The treatment model comprises three modules. In the first module, psychoeducation, patients and relatives are given information about how to cope with bipolar disorder. This includes didactic material about the symptoms, diagnosis, causes, and prognosis of the disorder; vulnerability and stress interactions, and risk and protective factors. It also includes a relapse prevention drill, in which participants identify the patient's prodromal signs of mania or depression and the family develops plans for how to intervene should these appear (e.g., arranging an emergency medical visit or hospitalization). Later modules of FFT (communication enhancement training and problem-solving skills training) involve teaching the patients and family members the skills for dealing with disorder-related conflicts; this is accomplished through the use of role playing and behavioral rehearsal assignments.

FFT was first investigated in a Type 3 pilot study of nine bipolar I patients and their families (Miklowitz & Goldstein, 1990). These patients were compared with 23 historical controls who did not receive FFT but were maintained on comparable, aggressively delivered pharmacotherapy. Relapse rates over the 9 months of treatment or follow-up were 11% (1/9) in FFT versus 61% (14/23) of the historical controls.

Miklowitz, George, Richards, and colleagues (2003) at the University of Colorado reported the results of a Type 1 clinical trial of FFT. Bipolar I patients (N=101) were randomized to FFT (9 months, 21 sessions) or a brief psychoeducation comparison condition called crisis management (CM), consisting of two sessions of family education followed by 9 months of crisis intervention, delivered on an as-needed basis. All patients received standard pharmacotherapy from community psychiatrists. Survival analyses indicated that patients in FFT and pharmacotherapy had higher 2-year survival rates without relapsing (52%) and longer survival times during the 2-year study than patients in CM plus pharmacotherapy (17%). Patients in FFT stabilized more completely over 2 years in terms of depressive symptoms and, to a lesser but still significant extent, manic symptoms. Moreover, patients in FFT had higher rates of medication adherence over the 2-year study. Improvements in medication adherence mediated the effects of FFT on manic, but not depressive, symptoms.

Within the Colorado trial, Simoneau, Miklowitz, Richards, Saleem, and George (1999) examined whether FFT leads to improvements in the quality of family communication and problem-solving skills. Simoneau et al. coded videotapes and transcripts of problem-solving interactions from a subset of families assessed prior to and following the 9-month FFT or CM protocols (N=44). No differential effects were found for treatments in reducing the frequency of negative communication behaviors (i.e., criticisms, disagreements, negative nonverbal behaviors) among patients and family members. Within the FFT group, however, positive communication behaviors among patients and relatives increased from the pre- to the posttreatment period. When the family was not treated (CM), positive communication decreased slightly over the pre- to posttreatment period. Moreover, treatment-associated increases in positive interactional behaviors (particularly patients' nonverbal behaviors) predicted greater improvement over the study year in patients' mood disorder — notably depressive — symptoms. Thus, FFT may achieve its effects in part through increasing the protective influences of the family environment.

The Colorado study compared FFT to a brief psychoeducational comparison group that was not matched on amount of therapist attention. In a subsequent randomized Type 1 trial, Rea et al. (2003) of the University of California, Los Angeles, compared 9 months of clinic-based FFT to an individually focused therapy. Bipolar patients began the study during a hospitalized manic episode (N = 53) and were maintained on mood-stabilizing medications. Patients in individually focused therapy received regular sessions of education, support, and problem solving, with a duration and pacing of sessions that was identical to FFT (21 weekly, biweekly, and monthly sessions). Patients in the FFT group had longer delays prior to relapsing, but only when the full 2- to 3-year study period was considered. Patients who received FFT also had a lower risk of rehospitalization (12%) than patients in individual therapy (60%) during a 1- to 2-year posttreatment interval. No group differences were observed in the first year, suggesting that for some patients and families, the effects of FFT may not be "absorbed" until the full course of treatment is complete.

Of particular significance for health care cost containment is that patients in FFT were less likely to be hospitalized when they did relapse than were the individually treated patients. Thus, FFT appears to have assisted patients and families in avoiding a hospitalization when a relapse occurred.

Application of Family Interventions to Pediatric-Onset Bipolar Disorder

There has been recent interest in applying the principles of family psychoeducational therapy to pediatric-onset bipolar disorder. The early-onset form of the disorder is characterized by chronicity of symptoms, rapid cycling, a preponderance of mixed episodes, slow recoveries from acute episodes, and significant psychosocial impairment (Pavuluri, Birmaher, & Naylor, 2005). It may be particularly important to intervene with child- and adolescent-onset bipolar disorder because the human brain is most malleable at these ages (Giedd, 2004; Spear, 2000). The modification of dysfunctional neurological pathways — via psychosocial interventions, psychopharmacology, or both — may reduce the severity, frequency, and life disruptions of future manic and/or depressive episodes.

Fristad, Gavazzi, and Mackinaw-Koons (2003) have published the only Type 1 randomized trial of a family intervention for school-aged bipolar patients (N = 35). Their multifamily group model is conducted in eight 90-minute sessions involving parents and children. It involves a combination of education, communication training, problem solving, and a "tool kit" for emotional self-management. Relative to parents on the waiting list, parents who participated in the multi-family groups demonstrated a greater understanding of mood disorder, more positively toned family interactions, more adaptive beliefs about treatment, and an increased use of appropriate services for their children over a 6-month study period. Children in the groups also reported more positive support from their parents.

In a Type 3 open trial, Miklowitz, George, Axelson, Kim, Birmaher, Schneck, and colleagues (2004; Miklowitz, Biuckians, & Richards, in press) examined a 21-session version of FFT involving 20 bipolar teens (mean age, 15 years). All patients received pharmacotherapy and entered FFT following an acute period of illness. Over 2 years, significant improvements were observed in observer-rated depression scores (Cohen's $d = 0.87$), mania scores ($d = 1.19$), total mood symptom scores ($d = 1.05$), and parent-rated Child Behavior Checklist total problem behavior scores ($d = 0.99$).

In another Type 3 open trial, Pavuluri et al. (2004) examined a 12-session treatment (the "Rainbow model") consisting of FFT sessions, individual cognitive-behavioral therapy sessions, and pharmacotherapy. Among 34 school-aged bipolar children, reductions were observed in mania, aggression, psychosis, depression, and global-functioning scores from pre- to posttreatment.

In summary, family interventions are promising adjuncts to pharmacotherapy in stabilizing the course of adult and early-onset bipolar disorder. Their mechanisms of action — whether they modify levels of expressed emotion, family interactional behavior, medication adherence, ability to recognize and cope with prodromal symptoms, knowledge of the illness, or social support, and, in turn, whether such improvements map differently on to changes in manic or depressive symptoms — remain to be clarified in future trials.

CONCLUSIONS

There are now more randomized trials of psychosocial treatments for bipolar disorder than was true in earlier editions of this volume. Those studies that are complete suggest an advantage for patients receiving psychosocial intervention and medication in the domains of time to recurrence, symptom stabilization, and medication compliance. There remains a pressing need for more controlled research regarding specific psychosocial interventions as adjunctive treatments for this serious disorder, particularly with psychosocial functioning as an outcome variable.

A key unanswered question concerns the stages of the disorder at which psychotherapy will be most effective with bipolar patients. Should psychotherapy begin during an acute illness episode and continue throughout the stabilization and maintenance phases? Alternatively, will patients who are first stabilized pharmacologically be more receptive to psychosocial treatments? Some of the treatment models reviewed here are initiated when patients have been remitted for some time (CBT, group psychoeduca-

tion), whereas others treat patients who are stabilizing from an acute manic or depressive episode (FFT, IPSRT). Future research should attempt to identify whether certain psychosocial interventions are more or less effective when patients are symptomatic versus remitted.

The disorder subtypes that will benefit most from various forms of individual, family, or group therapy need to be identified. Must bipolar patients have a certain level of cognitive and psychosocial functioning before they will benefit from psychosocial interventions? Does this level vary according to whether the treatment is more behavioral, cognitive, or insight oriented? It is also possible that bipolar I versus bipolar II patients, rapid-cycling patients, or patients with and without psychotic features will require different types, or at least different frequencies of psychosocial sessions. Relevant here are recent findings from the Systematic Treatment Enhancement Program for Bipolar Disorder, which found in a naturalistic study that bipolar patients who were more severely depressed and functionally impaired benefited most from intensive adjunctive psychotherapy, whereas patients who were less severely ill and impaired benefited most from less frequent contacts (i.e., maintenance check-ins; Miklowitz, Otto, et al., 2006).

Finally, the application of psychosocial interventions during the earliest phases of the disorder (e.g., cases in which the onset has occurred in childhood or adolescence, or in which genetically at-risk children are in the subsyndromal, pre-onset phases) deserves much more attention. Early intervention may change the long-term trajectory of the illness, which in turn should result in better functional outcomes, lower rates of suicide, and lower personal and societal costs.

Answering the above questions requires controlled Type 1 clinical trials of specific, manualized treatments, including documentation of treatment integrity (adherence to treatment protocols and competence of the therapy delivered). Such studies will require careful selection and assessment of the domains of outcome that different psychosocial interventions presumably influence (e.g., symptoms, social-occupational functioning, medication adherence, sleep/wake cycle regularity, cognitive styles, and family functioning). The successful investigation of these questions may broaden prevailing views of the treatment of bipolar disorder beyond purely pharmacological approaches to integrative models that provide more powerful protection against recurrences of the disorder.

REFERENCES

American Psychiatric Association. (2000). *Diagnostic and statistical manual of mental disorders* (4th ed., Text Revision). Washington, DC: Author.

Baastrup, P. C., & Schou, M. (1967). Lithium as a prophylactic agent. *Archives of General Psychiatry, 16,* 162–172.

Bauer, M. S., & McBride, L. (1996). *Structured group psychotherapy for bipolar disorder: The life goals program.* New York: Springer.

Butzlaff, R. L., & Hooley, J. M. (1998). Expressed emotion and psychiatric relapse: A meta-analysis. *Archives of General Psychiatry, 55,* 547–552.

Callahan, A. M., & Bauer, M. S. (1999). Psychosocial interventions for bipolar disorder. *Psychiatric Clinics of North America, 22,* 675–688.

Clarkin, J. F., Carpenter, D., Hull, J., Wilner, P., & Glick, I. (1998). Effects of psychoeducational intervention for married patients with bipolar disorder and their spouses. *Psychiatric Services, 49,* 531–533.

Clarkin, J. F., Glick, I. D., Haas, G. L., Spencer, J. H., Lewis, A. B., Peyser, J., et al. (1990). A randomized clinical trial of inpatient family intervention: V. Results for affective disorders. *Journal of Affective Disorders, 18,* 17–28. 46.

Clarkin, J. F., Haas, G. L., & Glick, I. D. (Eds.). (1988). *Affective disorders and the family: Assessment and treatment.* New York: Guilford Press.

Cochran, S. D. (1984). Preventing medical noncompliance in the outpatient treatment of bipolar affective disorders. *Journal of Consulting and Clinical Psychology, 52,* 873–878.

Colom, F., Vieta, E., Martinez-Aran, A., Reinares, M., Goikolea, J. M., Benabarre, A., et al. (2003). A randomized trial on the efficacy of group psychoeducation in the prophylaxis of recurrences in bipolar patients whose disease is in remission. *Archives of General Psychiatry, 60,* 402–407.

Colom, F., Vieta, E., Sanchez-Moreno, J., Martinez-Aran, A., Reinares, M., Goikolea, J., et al. (2005). Stabilizing the stabilizer: Group psychoeducation enhances the stability of serum lithium levels. *Bipolar Disorders, 7*(Suppl. 5), 32–36.

Coryell, W., Andreasen, N. C., Endicott, J., & Keller, M. (1987). The significance of past mania or hypomania in the course and outcome of major depression. *American Journal of Psychiatry, 144,* 309–315.

Coryell, W., Scheftner, W., Keller, M., Endicott, J., Maser, J., & Klerman, G. L. (1993). The enduring psychosocial consequences of mania and depression. *American Journal of Psychiatry, 150,* 720–727.

Craighead, W. E., & Miklowitz, D. J. (2000). Psychosocial interventions for bipolar disorder. *Journal of Clinical Psychiatry, 61,* 58–64.

Dion, G. L., Tohen, M., Anthony, W. A., & Waternaux, C. S. (1988). Symptoms and functioning of patients with bipolar disorder six months after hospitalization. *Hospital and Community Psychiatry, 39,* 652–657.

Ehlers, C. L., Frank, E., & Kupfer, D. J. (1988). Social zeitgebers and biological rhythms: A unified approach to understanding the etiology of depression. *Archives of General Psychiatry, 45,* 948–952.

Elkin, I., Gibbons, R. D., Shea, M. T., Sotsky, S. M., Watkins, J. T., Pilkonis, P. A., et al. (1995). Initial severity and differential treatment outcome in the National Institute of Mental Health Treatment of Depression Collaborative Research Program. *Journal of Consulting and Clinical Psychology, 63,* 841–847.

Elkin, I., Shea, M. T., Watkins, J. T., Imber, S. D., Sotsky, S. M., Collins, J. F., et al. (1989). National Institute of Mental Health Treatment of Depression Collaborative Research Program: General effectiveness of treatments. *Archives of General Psychiatry, 46,* 971–982.

Falloon, I. R. H., Boyd, J. L., & McGill, C. W. (1984). *Family care of schizophrenia: A problem-solving approach to the treatment of mental illness.* New York: Guilford Press.

Frank, E., Hlastala, S., Ritenour, A., Houck, P., Tu, X. M., Monk, T. H., et al. (1997). Inducing lifestyle regularity in recovering bipolar disorder patients: Results from the maintenance therapies in bipolar disorder protocol. *Biological Psychiatry, 41,* 1165–1173.

Frank, E., Kupfer, D. J., Ehlers, C. L., & Monk, T. H. (1994). Interpersonal and social rhythm therapy for bipolar disorder: Integrating interpersonal and behavioral approaches. *Behavior Therapist, 17,* 143.

Frank, E., Kupfer, D. J., Perel, J. M., Cornes, C. L., Jarrett, D. J., Mallinger, A., et al. (1990). Three-year outcomes for maintenance therapies in recurrent depression. *Archives of General Psychiatry, 47,* 1093–1099.

Frank, E., Kupfer, D. J., Thase, M. E., Mallinger, A. G., Swartz, H. A., Fagiolini, A. M., et al. (2005). Two-year outcomes for interpersonal and social rhythm therapy in individuals with bipolar I disorder. *Archives of General Psychiatry, 62,* 996–1004.

Frank, E., Swartz, H. A., & Kupfer, D. J. (2000). Interpersonal and Social Rhythm Therapy: Managing the chaos of bipolar disorder. *Biological Psychiatry, 48,* 593–604.

Fristad, M. A., Gavazzi, S. M., & Mackinaw-Koons, B. (2003). Family psychoeducation: An adjunctive intervention for children with bipolar disorder. *Biological Psychiatry, 53,* 1000–1009.

Fristad, M. A., Goldberg-Arnold, J. S., & Gavazzi, S. M. (2002). Multifamily psychoeducation groups (MFPG) for families of children with bipolar disorder. *Bipolar Disorders, 4,* 254–262.

Giedd, J. N. (2004). Structural magnetic resonance imaging of the adolescent brain. *Annals of the New York Academy of Sciences, 1021,* 77–85.

Gitlin, M. J., Swendsen, J., Heller, T. L., & Hammen, C. (1995). Relapse and impairment in bipolar disorder. *American Journal of Psychiatry, 152,* 1635–1640.

Glick, I. D., Clarkin, J. F., Haas, G. L., Spencer, J. H., & Chen, C. L. (1991). A randomized clinical trial of inpatient family intervention: VI. Mediating variables and outcome. *Family Process, 30,* 85–99.

Goldberg, J. F. (2004). The changing landscape of psychopharmacology. In S. L. Johnson & R. L. Leahy (Eds.), *Psychological treatment of bipolar disorder* (pp. 109–138). New York: Guilford Press.

Goldberg, J. F., Harrow, M. & Grossman, L. S. (1995). Course and outcome in bipolar affective disorder: A longitudinal follow-up study. *American Journal of Psychiatry, 152,* 379–385.

Goldstein, M. J., Rodnick, E. H., Evans, J. R., May, P. R. A., & Steinberg, M. R. (1978). Drug and family therapy in the aftercare of acute schizophrenics. *Archives of General Psychiatry, 35,* 1169–1177.

Goodwin, F. K., & Jamison, K. R. (1990). *Manic-depressive illness.* New York: Oxford University Press.

Haas, G. L., Glick, I. D., Clarkin, J. F., Spencer, J. H., Lewis, A. B., Peyser, J., et al. (1988). Inpatient family intervention: A randomized clinical trial: II. Results at hospital discharge. *Archives of General Psychiatry, 45,* 217–224.

Harris, E. C., & Barraclough, B. (1997). Suicide as an outcome for mental disorders: A meta-analysis. *British Journal of Psychiatry, 170,* 205–208.

Harrow, M., Goldberg, J. F., Grossman, L. S., & Meltzer, H. Y. (1990). Outcome in manic disorders: A naturalistic follow-up study. *Archives of General Psychiatry, 47,* 665–671.

Harvey, N. S., & Peet, M. (1991). Lithium maintenance: II. Effects of personality and attitude on health information acquisition and compliance. *British Journal of Psychiatry, 158,* 200–204.

Isometsae, E. T. (1993). Course, outcome, and suicide risk in bipolar disorder: A review. *Psychiatrica Fennica, 24,* 113–124.

Johnson, S. L., Winett, C. A., Meyer, B., Greenhouse, W. J., & Miller, I. (1999). Social support and the course of bipolar disorder. *Journal of Abnormal Psychology, 108,* 558–566.

Keller, M. B., Lavori, P. W., Coryell, W., Andreasen, N. C., Endicott, J., Clayton, P. J., et al. (1986). Differential outcome of pure manic, mixed/cycling, and pure depressive episodes in patients with bipolar illness. *Journal of the American Medical Association, 255,* 3138–3142.

Kessler, R. C., Berglund, P., Demler, O., Jin, R., & Walters, E. E. (2005). Lifetime prevalence and age-of-onset distributions of *DSM-IV* disorders in the National Comorbidity Survey replication. *Archives of General Psychiatry, 62,* 593–602.

Klerman, G. L., Weissman, M. M., Rounsaville, B. J., & Chevron, E. S. (1984). *Interpersonal psychotherapy of depression.* New York: Basic Books.

Lam, D. H., Hayward, P., Watkins, E. R., Wright, K., & Sham, P. (2005). Relapse prevention in patients with bipolar disorder: Cognitive therapy outcome after 2 years. *American Journal of Psychiatry, 162,* 324–329.

Lam, D. H., Watkins, E. R., Hayward, P., Bright, J., Wright, K., Kerr, N., et al. (2003). A randomized controlled study of cognitive therapy of relapse prevention for bipolar affective disorder: Outcome of the first year. *Archives of General Psychiatry, 60,* 145–152.

Lenzi, A., Lazzerini, F., Placidi, G. F., Cassano, G. B., & Akiskal, H. S. (1989). Predictors of compliance with lithium and carbamazepine regimens in the long-term treatment of recurrent mood and related psychotic disorders. *Pharmacopsychiatry, 22,* 34–37.

McElroy, S. L., & Keck, P. E. (2000). Pharmacologic agents for the treatment of acute bipolar mania. *Biological Psychiatry, 48,* 539–557.

McKnight, D. L., Nelson-Gray, R. O., & Gullick, E. (1989). Interactional patterns of bipolar patients and their spouses. *Journal of Psychopathology and Behavioral Assessment, 11,* 269–289.

Miklowitz, D. J., Biuckians, A., & Richards, J. A. (in press). Early-onset bipolar disorder: A family treatment perspective. *Development and Psychopathology.*

Miklowitz, D. J., George, E. L., Axelson, D. A., Kim, E. Y., Birmaher, B., Schneck, C., et al. (2004). Family-focused treatment for adolescents with bipolar disorder. *Journal of Affective Disorders*, 82(Suppl. 1), 113–128.

Miklowitz, D. J., George, E. L., Richards, J. A., Simoneau, T. L., & Suddath, R. L. (2003). A randomized study of family-focused psychoeducation and pharmacotherapy in the outpatient management of bipolar disorder. *Archives of General Psychiatry, 60*, 904–912.

Miklowitz, D. J., & Goldstein, M. J. (1990). Behavioral family treatment for patients with bipolar affective disorder. *Behavior Modification, 14*, 457–489.

Miklowitz, D. J., & Goldstein, M. J. (1997). *Bipolar disorder: A family-focused treatment approach.* New York: Guilford Press.

Miklowitz, D. J., Goldstein, M. J., Nuechterlein, K. H., Snyder, K. S., & Mintz, J. (1988). Family factors and the course of bipolar affective disorder. *Archives of General Psychiatry, 45*, 225–231.

Miklowitz, D. J., & Johnson, S. L. (2006). The psychopathology and treatment of bipolar disorder. *Annual Review of Clinical Psychology, 2*, 199–235.

Miklowitz, D. J., Otto, M. W., Wisniewski, S. R., Araga, M., Frank, E., Reilly-Harrington, N., et al. (2006). Psychotherapy, symptom outcomes, and role functioning over one year among patients with bipolar disorder. *Psychiatric Services, 57*, 959–965.

Miklowitz, D. J., Richards, J. A., George, E. L., Suddath, R. L., Frank, E., Powell, K., et al. (2003). Integrated family and individual therapy for bipolar disorder: Results of a treatment development study. *Journal of Clinical Psychiatry, 64*, 182–191.

Miklowitz, D. J., Simoneau, T. L., George, E. A., Richards, J. A., Kalbag, A., Sachs-Ericsson, N., et al. (2000). Family-focused treatment of bipolar disorder: 1-year effects of a psychoeducational program in conjunction with pharmacotherapy. *Biological Psychiatry, 48*, 582–592.

Miller, I. W., Solomon, D. A., Ryan, C. E., & Keitner, G. I. (2004). Does adjunctive family therapy enhance recovery from bipolar I mood episodes? *Journal of Affective Disorders, 82*, 431–436.

Monk, T. H., Kupfer, D. J., Frank, E., & Ritenour, A. M. (1991). The Social Rhythm Metric (SRM): Measuring daily social rhythms over 12 weeks. *Psychiatry Research, 36*, 195–207.

Murray, C. J. L., & Lopez, A. D. (1996). *The global burden of disease: A comprehensive assessment of mortality and disability from diseases, injuries, and risk factors in 1990 and projected to 2020.* Cambridge, MA: Harvard University Press.

O'Connell, R. A., Mayo, J. A., Flatow, L., Cuthbertson, B., & O'Brien, B. E. (1991). Outcome of bipolar disorder on long-term treatment with lithium. *British Journal of Psychiatry, 159*, 123–129.

Pavuluri, M. N., Birmaher, B., & Naylor, M. W. (2005). Pediatric bipolar disorder: A review of the past 10 years. *Journal of the American Academy of Child and Adolescent Psychiatry, 44*, 846–871.

Pavuluri, M. N., Graczyk, P. A., Henry, D. B., Carbray, J. A., Heidenreich, J., & Miklowitz, D. J. (2004). Child- and family-focused cognitive behavioral therapy for pediatric bipolar disorder: Development and preliminary results. *Journal of the American Academy of Child and Adolescent Psychiatry, 43*, 528–537.

Peet, M., & Harvey, N. S. (1991). Lithium maintenance: I. A standard education programme for patients. *British Journal of Psychiatry, 158*, 197–200.

Perry, A., Tarrier, N., Morriss, R., McCarthy, E. & Limb, K. (1999). Randomised controlled trial of efficacy of teaching patients with bipolar disorder to identify early symptoms of relapse and obtain treatment. *British Medical Journal, 16*, 149–153.

Post, R. M. (1993). Issues in the long-term management of bipolar affective illness. *Psychiatric Annals, 23*, 86–93.

Potter, W. Z., & Prien, R. F. (1989). *Report on the NIMH Workshop on the Treatment of Bipolar Disorder.* Unpublished manuscript available from R. F. Prien, NIMH, Parklawn Building, 5600 Fisher's Lane, Rockville, MD 20857.

Priebe, S., Wildgrube, C., & Müller-Oerlinghausen, B. (1989). Lithium prophylaxis and expressed emotion. *British Journal of Psychiatry, 154*, 396–399.

Prien, R. F., & Rush, A. J. (1996). National Institute of Mental Health workshop report on the treatment of bipolar disorder. *Biological Psychiatry, 40*, 215–220.

Rea, M. M., Tompson, M., Miklowitz, D. J., Goldstein, M. J., Hwang, S., & Mintz, J. (2003). Family focused treatment vs. individual treatment for bipolar disorder: Results of a randomized clinical trial. *Journal of Consulting and Clinical Psychology, 71*, 482–492.

Robins, L. N., Helzer, J. E., Weissman, M. M., Orvaschel, H., Gruenberg, E., Burke, J. D., et al. (1984). Lifetime prevalence of specific psychiatric disorders in three sites. *Archives of General Psychiatry, 41*, 949–958.

Scott, J., Paykel, E., Morriss, R., Bentall, R., Kinderman, P., Johnson, T., et al. (2006). Cognitive behaviour therapy for severe and recurrent bipolar disorders: A randomised controlled trial. *British Journal of Psychiatry, 188*, 313–320.

Seltzer, A., Roncari, I., & Garfinkel, P. E. (1980). Effect of patient education on medication compliance. *Canadian Journal of Psychiatry, 25*, 638–645.

Shakir, S. A., Volkmar, F. R., Bacon, S., & Pfefferbaum, A. (1979). Group psychotherapy as an adjunct to lithium maintenance. *American Journal of Psychiatry, 136,* 455–456.

Simon G.E., Ludman, E. J., Bauer, M. S., Unutzer, J., & Operskalski, B. (2006). Long-term effectiveness and cost of a systematic care program for bipolar disorder. Archives of General Psychiatry 2006, *63,* 500–508.

Simon, G. E., Ludman, E. J., Unutzer, J., Bauer, M. S., Operskalski, B., & Rutter, C. (2005). Randomized trial of a population-based care program for people with bipolar disorder. *Psychological Medicine, 35,* 13–24.

Simoneau, T. L., Miklowitz, D. J., Richards, J. A., Saleem, R., & George, E. L. (1999). Bipolar disorder and family communication: Effects of a psychoeducational treatment program. *Journal of Abnormal Psychology, 108,* 588–597.

Spear, L. P. (2000). The adolescent brain and age-related behavioral manifestations. *Neuroscience and Biobehavioral Reviews, 24,* 417–463.

Spencer, J. H., Glick, I. D., Haas, G. L., Clarkin, J. F., Lewis, A. B., Peyser, J., et al. (1988). A randomized clinical trial of inpatient family intervention: III. Effects at 6-month and 18-month follow-ups. *American Journal of Psychiatry, 145,* 1115–1121.

Strakowski, S. M., Keck, P. E., McElroy, S. L., West, S. A., Sax, K. W., Hawkins, J. M., et al. (1998). Twelve-month outcome after a first hospitalization for affective psychosis. *Archives of General Psychiatry, 55,* 49–55.

Strober, M., Morrell, W., Lampert, C., & Burroughs, J. (1990). Relapse following discontinuation of lithium maintenance therapy in adolescents with bipo-lar I illness: A naturalistic study. *American Journal of Psychiatry, 147,* 457–461.

Suppes, T., Baldessarini, R. J., Faedda, G. L., Tondo, L., & Tohen, M. (1993). Discontinuation of maintenance treatment in bipolar disorder: Risks and implications. *Harvard Review of Psychiatry, 1,* 131–144.

Targum, S. D., Dibble, E. D., Davenport, Y. B., & Gershon, E. S. (1981). The Family Attitudes Questionnaire: Patients' and spouses' views of bipolar illness. *Archives of General Psychiatry, 38,* 562–568.

van Gent, E. M., & Zwart, F. M. (1991). Psychoeducation of partners of bipolar-manic patients. *Journal of Affective Disorders, 21,* 15–18.

Volkmar, F. R., Bacon, S., Shakir, S. A., & Pfefferbaum, A. (1981). Group therapy in the management of manic-depressive illness. *American Journal of Psychotherapy, 35,* 226–234.

Weiss, R. D., Greenfield, S. F., Najavits, L. M., Soto, J. A., Wyner, D., Tohen, M., et al. (1998). Medication compliance among patients with bipolar disorder and substance use disorder. *Journal of Clinical Psychiatry, 59,* 172–174.

Weissman, M. M., Markowitz, J., & Klerman, G. L. (2000). *Comprehensive guide to interpersonal psychotherapy.* New York: Basic Books.

Weissman, M. M., & Myers, J. K. (1978). Affective disorders in a US urban community: The use of Research Diagnostic Criteria in an epidemiological survey. *Archives of General Psychiatry, 35,* 1304–1311.

Yalom, I. D. (1975). *The theory and practice of group psychotherapy.* New York: Basic Books.

Zaretsky, A. E., & Segal, Z. V. (1994/1995). Psychosocial interventions in bipolar disorder. *Depression, 2,* 179–188.

12

Pharmacological Treatments
for Bipolar Disorder

Paul E. Keck Jr.

Susan L. McElroy

The vast majority of clinical trials in patients with bipolar disorders have been conducted in groups with bipolar I illness, although a few trials have recently emerged specifically in patients with bipolar II disorder. The pharmacological management of bipolar disorder involves the treatment of acute manic, hypomanic, mixed, and depressive episodes, as well as the prevention of further episodes and subsyndromal symptoms. Lithium, divalproex, carbamazepine, risperidone, olanzapine, quetiapine, ziprasidone, and aripiprazole have demonstrated efficacy in the treatment of acute mania in randomized, controlled (Type 1) trials. Although the pharmacological treatment of acute bipolar depression remains understudied, data from randomized, controlled trials indicate that lithium, olanzapine, olanzapine-fluoxetine, quetiapine, lamotrigine, tricyclics, MAOIs, fluoxetine, and pramipexole have efficacy in this phase of the illness. The optimal duration of antidepressant treatment, in combination with mood stabilizers, is still unknown. Lithium, lamotrigine, olanzapine, and aripiprazole have been shown to have efficacy in relapse prevention. Less extensive data suggest that divalproex and carbamazepine are also efficacious as preventative treatments.

Bipolar disorder is a common, severe, and recurrent psychiatric illness. In the United States, the 12-month prevalence rate of bipolar I and II disorders is estimated at 2.6% (Kessler, Chiu, Demler, Merikangas, & Walters, 2005). In 1990, bipolar disorder was the sixth-leading cause of disability worldwide and was projected to remain so in the first two decades of this century (Murray & Lopez, 1996). Bipolar disorder is characterized by disturbances in mood, cognition, and behavior and is often associated with psychotic symptoms (McElroy, Keck, & Strakowski, 1996). Untreated bipolar disorder carries substantial risks of morbidity and mortality (Mitchell, Slade, & Andrews, 2004). Morbidity is not simply limited to mood episodes themselves. For example, full recovery of functioning often lags behind remission of symptoms by many months (Dion, Tohen, Anthony, & Waternaux, 1988; Keck et al., 1998). In addition, recurrent mood episodes may lead to progressive deterioration in functioning between episodes, and the number of episodes, in turn, may adversely affect subsequent treatment response and prognosis (Prien & Gelenberg, 1989; Swann, Bowden, Calabrese, Dilsaver, & Morris, 1999). Thus, morbidity due to the illness is not limited to acute mood episodes but may linger and lead to prolonged deficits in social and vocational functioning (Calabrese et al., 2003; Fagiolini et al., 2005). Bipolar disorder can also be a lethal illness. Suicide attempts are made by at least 25% of patients (Hopkins & Gelenberg, 1994).

Bipolar disorder is a highly heritable illness (Gershon, 1989). Concordance rates between monozygotic twins for bipolar disorder range from 65 to 75% compared with concordance rates for dizygotic twins of approximately 14% (Gurling, 1995). In family studies, the lifetime prevalence rates of mood disorders among first-degree relatives of bipolar probands are elevated compared with prevalence rates for these disorders in first-degree relatives of people without psychiatric illness (Gurling, 1995).

The *Diagnostic and Statistic Manual of Mental Disorders* (American Psychiatric Association [APA], 2000) delineates four types of bipolar disorders: bipolar I disorder, bipolar II disorder, cyclothymic disorder, and bipolar disorder not otherwise specified. The *DSM-IV-TR* criteria for manic, hypomanic, depressive, and mixed episodes are summarized in Table 12.1. The criteria for bipolar I disorder require the presence of at least one manic or mixed episode; the manic or mixed episode is not better accounted for by schizoaffective disorder; is not superimposed on schizophrenia, schizophreniform disorder, delusional disorder, or psychotic disorder not otherwise specified; and is not due to a general medical condition or a substance-induced disorder. The criteria for bipolar II disorder require the presence of one or more major depressive episodes and at least one hypomanic episode, but without the occurrence of a manic or mixed episode. The criteria for cyclothymic disorder require, for at least 2 years (in children and adolescents for at least 1 year), the presence of numerous periods of hypomanic and depressive symptoms during the 2-year period; the person has not been without hypomanic or depressive symptoms for more than 2 months at a time; and no major depressive, manic, or mixed episode has been present during the first 2 years of the disturbance. The category of bipolar disorder not otherwise specified includes disorders with bipolar features that do not meet criteria for any specific bipolar disorder. For example, patients with major depressive episodes and periods of hypomania lasting less than 4 days would fall into this category. Recent studies suggest that the duration criterion for hypomania of four days is arbitrary and longer than many patients with bipolar II disorder experience hypomanic symptoms (Benazzi & Akiskal, 2003).

The vast majority of psychopharmacological treatment research has focused on patients with bipolar I disorder. Thus, this chapter will review, primarily, the treatment of bipolar I disorder. The few studies that included patients with bipolar II disorder will be noted as such. Since the pharmacological treatment of bipolar I disorder involves the acute treatment of manic, mixed, and depressive episodes, as well as maintenance treatment to prevent cycling, recurrent mood episodes, and subsyndromal symptoms, we review below studies of both acute and long-term treatment. Finally, because studies of the pharmacological treatment of bipolar disorder vary in design, we will make careful distinction between conclusions based on randomized, controlled trials and open trials, case series, and case reports.

PSYCHOPHARMACOLOGICAL TREATMENT FOR ACUTE MANIC AND MIXED EPISODES

Lithium

In 1970, lithium was the first drug approved by the U.S. Food and Drug Administration (FDA) for the treatment of "manic episodes of manic-depressive illness" (Goodwin & Jamison, 1990). Six controlled studies demonstrated that lithium was superior to placebo for the treatment of acute mania (Bowden et al., 1994, 2005; Goodwin, Murphy, & Bunney, 1969; Maggs, 1963; Schou, Juel-Nielson, Stromgren, & Voldby, 1954; Stokes, Shamoian, Stoll, & Patton, 1971). Early lithium trials had several methodological limitations that were addressed in more recent studies. For example, only two studies (Bowden et al., 1994, 2005) utilized a parallel design, whereas the earliest four studies were crossover trials of varying duration (Goodwin et al., 1969; Maggs, 1963; Schou et al., 1954; Stokes et al., 1971). Two studies used nonrandom assignment to lithium or placebo (Goodwin et al., 1969; Stokes et al., 1971), and the diagnostic criteria used to define bipolar disorder in the early lithium studies (Goodwin et al., 1969; Maggs, 1963; Schou et al., 1954; Stokes et al., 1971) were not necessarily comparable to those of the *Diagnostic and Statistical Manual of Mental Disorders* (APA, 1987) or *DSM-IV-TR* (APA, 2000).

In the first placebo-controlled, crossover study, Schou et al. (1954) reported a definite response in 12 (40%) and a probable response in 15 (50%) of 30 patients with typical bipolar disorder based on a global impression of improvement. In the first study to use formal rating scales and to analyze data statistically, 28 patients with mania were randomized to

TABLE 12.1 Summary of *DSM-IV* Criteria for Mood Episodes Occurring in Bipolar Disorders

1. Manic Episode
   A. A distinctive period of abnormally and persistently elevated, expansive, or irritable mood, lasting at least 1 week (or any duration if hospitalization is necessary).
   B. During the period of mood disturbance, three (or more) of the following symptoms have persisted (four if the mood is only irritable) and have been present to a significant degree:
      i. Inflated self-esteem or grandiosity
      ii. Decreased need for sleep
      iii. More talkative than usual or pressure to keep talking
      iv. Flight of ideas or subjective experience of racing thoughts
      v. Distractibility
      vi. Increase in goal-directed activity or psychomotor agitation
      vii. Excessive involvement in pleasurable activities that have a high potential for painful consequences
   C. The symptoms do not meet criteria for a mixed episode.
   D. The mood disturbance is sufficiently severe to cause marked impairment in occupational functioning or in usual social activities or relationships with others, or to necessitate hospitalization to prevent harm to self or others, or there are psychotic features.
   E. The symptoms are not due to the direct physiological effects of a substance or general medical condition.
2. Major Depressive Episode
   A. Five (or more) of the following symptoms present during the same 2-week period and represent a change from previous functioning; at least one of the symptoms is either (1) depressed mood or (2) loss of interest or pleasure.
      i. Depressed mood most of the day, nearly every day, as indicated by either subjective report or observation by others (note: in children and adolescents, can be irritable mood)
      ii. Markedly diminished interest or pleasure in all, or almost all, activities most of the day, nearly every day
      iii. Significant weight loss when not dieting or weight gain, or decrease or increase in appetite nearly every day (note: in children, consider failure to make expected weight gains)
      iv. Insomnia or hypersomnia nearly every day
      v. Psychomotor agitation or retardation nearly every day
      vi. Fatigue or loss of energy nearly every day
      vii. Feelings of worthlessness or excessive or inappropriate guilt nearly every day
      viii. Diminished ability to think or concentrate, or indecisiveness, nearly every day
      ix. Recurrent thoughts of death, suicidal ideation, or a suicide attempt or a specific plan
   B. The symptoms do not meet criteria for a mixed episode.
   C. The symptoms cause clinically significant distress or impairment in social, occupational, or other important areas of functioning.
   D. The symptoms are not due to the direct physiological effects of a substance or a general medical condition.
   E. The symptoms are not better accounted for by bereavement.
3. Mixed Episode
   A. The criteria are met both for a manic episode and for a major depressive episode nearly every day for at least 1 week.
   B. The mood disturbance is sufficiently severe to cause marked impairment in occupational functioning or in usual social activities or relationships with others, or to necessitate hospitalization to prevent harm to self or others, or there are psychotic features.
   C. The symptoms are not due to the direct physiological effects of a substance or a general medical condition.
4. Hypomanic Episode
   A. A distinct period of persistently elevated, expansive, or irritable mood, lasting throughout at least 4 days, that is clearly different from the usual nondepressed mood.
   B. During the period of mood disturbance, three (or more) of the following symptoms have persisted (four if the mood is only irritable) and have been present to a significant degree:
      i. Inflated self-esteem or grandiosity
      ii. Decreased need for sleep
      iii. More talkative than usual or pressure to keep talking
      iv. Flight of ideas or subjective experience of racing thoughts
      v. Distractibility
      vi. Increase in goal-directed activity or psychomotor agitation
      vii. Excessive involvement in pleasurable activities that have a high potential for painful consequences
   C. The episode is associated with an unequivocal change in functioning that is uncharacteristic of the person when not symptomatic.
   D. The disturbance in mood and the change in functioning are observable by others.
   E. The episode is not severe enough to cause marked impairment in social or occupational functioning, or to necessitate hospitalization, and there are no psychotic features.
   F. The symptoms are not due to the direct physiological effects of a substance or a general medical condition.

Source: American Psychiatric Association, *DSM-IV-TR*, 2000, pp. 168–172.

three consecutive 14-day periods of lithium-rest-placebo or placebo-rest-lithium (Maggs, 1963). Results were based only on the 18 study completers. In this group, lithium was superior to placebo during the 2nd week of treatment.

In the first study conducted in the United States, Goodwin et al. (1969) compared the longitudinal efficacy of lithium with placebo in 12 patients with mania; 8 (67%) displayed a complete response and 1 (8%) a partial response to lithium. In the fourth study, Stokes et al. (1971) used a crossover design with alternating 7- to 10-day trial periods on lithium or placebo. These brief trial periods may have limited the opportunity for patients to display a more substantial lithium response, while the equally brief placebo period may have been confounded by residual lithium effects. With these caveats, Stokes et al. (1971) reported a 75% response rate (partial or full) with lithium, compared with 40% on placebo.

Two more recent studies utilized lithium as an active comparator in placebo-controlled, parallel-group trials of divalproex (Bowden et al., 1994) and quetiapine (Bowden et al, 2005), respectively. In both trials the mean improvement in lithium-treated patients at study end point was superior to placebo and comparable to the investigational agent. Response rates among active treatment groups were also comparable after 3 weeks (divalproex 48%; lithium 49%, Bowden et al., 1994; quetiapine 53%, lithium 53%, Bowden et al., 2005). Significant differences in improvement in manic symptoms were evident in patients receiving lithium or divalproex compared with placebo at day 10 (Bowden et al., 1994), and in patients receiving lithium or quetiapine compared with placebo at day 7 (Bowden et al., 2005). Several post hoc analyses have attempted to identify predictors of acute lithium response. Clinical features associated with favorable lithium response include family history of lithium response (P. Grof et al., 2002), pure mania with minimal concurrent depressive symptoms (Swann et al., 1997), and relatively few lifetime mood episodes (Swann et al., 1999).

Lithium has been compared with first-generation (neuroleptic) antipsychotic agents in nine controlled trials in the treatment of acute bipolar mania (Garfinkel, Stancer, & Persad, 1980; Johnson, Gershon, Burdock, Floyd, & Hekiman, 1971; Johnson, Gershon, & Hekiman, 1968; Platman, 1970; Prien, Caffey, & Klett, 1972; Segal, Berk, & Brook, 1998; Shopsin, Gershon, Thompson, & Collins, 1975; Spring, Schweid, Gray, Steinberg, & Horwitz, 1970; Taka-

hashi, Sakuma, Itoh, Itoh, & Kurihara, 1975). Interpretation of the results of some of these studies is difficult due to the inclusion of manic patients with schizoaffective disorder; the lack of standardized rating scales for mania; lack of utilization of last observation carried forward (LOCF) or comparable analyses; and the possibility of a Type II error (failure to find a significant difference between treatments because of insufficient sample size; Johnson, Gershon, & Hekiman, 1968; Johnson et al., 1971; Platman, 1970; Segal et al., 1998; Shopsin et al., 1975). Two studies also titrated lithium to serum concentrations to the low end of the therapeutic range (Shopsin et al., 1975; Takahashi et al., 1975).

In summary, data from the controlled trials reviewed above indicate that lithium is superior in efficacy to placebo, with an onset of action within 7 to 10 days with gradual titration, and usually requires a 2- to 4-week trial at therapeutic levels to reach maximum effect. These data also suggest that lithium is superior to first-generation antipsychotics for amelioration of mood symptoms and exerts improvement in psychosis in tandem with improvement in the overall manic syndrome (Prien et al., 1972). On the other hand, first-generation antipsychotics had a more rapid onset of action and were more effective initially in agitated patients (Prien et al., 1972).

Typical (First-Generation) Antipsychotics

Prior to the introduction of lithium, antipsychotic medications were one of the few available classes of medications for the treatment of acute mania and as maintenance treatment for patients with bipolar disorder (Baldessarini, 1985). However, the emergence of lithium, valproate, carbamazepine, and atypical or second-generation antispsychotics has limited the role of typical antipsychotics to the acute treatment of psychotic mania or psychotic depression in conjunction with thymoleptic agents. There is one double-blind, placebo-controlled trial of a typical antipsychotic, chlorpromazine, in the treatment of bipolar mania (Klein, 1967). Not surprisingly, chlorpromazine (1,200 mg/day) was superior to imipramine (300 mg/day) or placebo in a 7-week trial involving only 13 patients rated globally for improvement. Most other studies examining typical antipsychotics in the treatment of acute mania have included these agents as active comparators in trials of lithium, valproate, carbamazepine, or atypical antipsychotics reviewed elsewhere in this chapter.

Valproate

Valproate and its divalproex formulation have been shown to be effective in the treatment of acute mania in nine controlled trials (Bowden et al., 1994; Brennan, Sandyk, & Borsook, 1984; Emrich, Von Zerssen, & Kissling, 1981; Freeman, Clothier, Pazzaglaia, Lesem, & Swann, 1992; Hirschfeld, Allen, McEvoy, Keck, & Russell, 1999; Pope, McElroy, Keck, & Hudson, 1991; Post, Berretini, Uhde, & Kellner, 1984; Tohen, Baker, et al., 2002; Zajecka et al., 2002). These nine studies include comparisons of valproate with placebo in crossover trials (Brennan et al., 1984; Emrich et al., 1981; Post et al., 1984), with placebo in a parallel-group trial in treatment-refractory patients (Pope et al., 1991), with lithium in two parallel-group trials (Freeman et al., 1992; Hirschfeld et al., 1999), with placebo and lithium in a parallel-group trial (Bowden et al., 1994), and with olanzapine in two parallel-group trials (Tohen, Baker, et al., 2002; Zajecka et al., 2002).

In the most rigorous placebo-controlled trials, response rates to valproate ranged from 48% (Bowden et al., 1994) to 53% (Pope et al., 1991). The onset of antimanic response was evident by day 7 in each trial, despite gradual titration from baseline. Both lithium comparison trials were underpowered to detect a potential difference in efficacy between the two agents (Freeman et al., 1992; Hirschfeld et al., 1999). Nevertheless, Freeman et al. (1992) reported that patients with mixed mania were more likely to respond to valproate than to lithium. This observation is consistent with a post hoc analysis of findings from the Bowden et al. (1994) study reported by Swann et al. (1997). Hirschfeld et al. (1999), and Hirschfeld, Baker, Wozniak, Tracy, & Sommerville (2003) specifically addressed the tolerability of divalproex oral loading (30 mg/kg/day for 2 days, then 20 mg/kg/day) and observed no significant differences in adverse events among patients randomized to divalproex loading, divalproex gradual titration, or lithium gradual titration. These findings confirmed earlier observations from open trials suggesting that divalproex oral loading was well tolerated (Keck, McElroy, Tugrul, & Bennett, 1993; McElroy, Keck, Tugrul, & Bennett, 1993; McElroy, Keck, Stanton, et al., 1996).

Divalproex was compared with olanzapine in two head-to-head trials (Tohen, Baker, et al., 2002; Zajecka et al., 2002). Tohen, Baker, et al. (2002) found a significantly greater mean reduction in manic symptoms in patients treated with olanzapine compared with divalproex at 3 weeks. In contrast, Zajecka et al. (2002) did not find significant differences in efficacy between the two agents at 3 weeks. Both studies found overall better tolerability in patients receiving divalproex compared with olanzapine. These studies differed in the starting dose of each agent and in sample size. Tohen, Baker, et al. (2002) compared olanzapine 15 mg/day as a starting dose with divalproex gradual titration in a study adequately powered to yield significant differences in efficacy. Zajecka et al. (2002) compared divalproex loading with olanzapine 10 mg/day as a starting dose in a study not adequately powered to yield potentially significant differences in efficacy. Taken together, the results of these two trials suggest that olanzapine may have a slight edge over divalproex in short-term efficacy in acute mania, but divalproex may have a slight edge in tolerability.

McElroy et al. (1996) compared divalproex loading with haloperidol in an open randomized trial specifically in patients with psychotic mania. There were no significant differences in mean improvement in manic or psychotic symptoms between the two treatment groups. The improvement in psychosis observed with divalproex was consistent with findings in other studies (Bowden et al., 1994; Pope et al., 1991), and with improvement in manic psychosis with lithium in earlier studies.

Valproate has been studied as treatment adjunctive to first-generation antipsychotics in the treatment of acute bipolar mania (Muller-Oerlinghausen, Retzow, Henn, Giedke, & Walden, 1999). In this multicenter, double-blind, parallel-group, 3-week trial, 136 patients receiving first-generation antipsychotics were randomized to valproate or placebo. By study end point, significantly more valproate-treated patients displayed a decrease in the need for concomitant antipsychotic medications. In summary, data from the controlled trials reviewed above indicate that valproate has a broad spectrum of efficacy in acute manic and mixed episodes, with or without psychosis, and appears to be comparable to lithium in overall antimanic efficacy.

Carbamazepine

Although a number of double-blind controlled trials provided preliminary evidence of carbamazepine's efficacy in the treatment of acute mania (Keck, McElroy, & Nemeroff, 1992), these findings were substantiated only recently in the first large, multicenter, randomized, placebo-controlled, parallel-group trials conducted (Weisler et al., 2004; Weisler et al., 2005). In the first such trial, Weisler et al. (2004) randomized 204 inpatients hospitalized for a manic or mixed episode to an extended-release formulation of carbamazepine or placebo over 3 weeks. The carbamazepine-treated patients displayed significantly greater mean improvement in manic symptoms compared with patients receiving placebo by day 14. In addition, significantly more patients in the carbamazepine group were responders (42%) compared with the placebo group (22%). In a subgroup analysis, there was no significant difference in mean reduction of manic symptoms in patients with mixed episodes who received carbamazepine compared with placebo, due in part to a high placebo response in this subgroup.

Weisler et al. (2005) conducted a second, similar trial in which 239 bipolar inpatients with manic or mixed episodes were randomized to extended-release carbamazepine or placebo for up to 3 weeks. In this trial, patients in the carbamazepine group displayed a significantly greater mean reduction in manic symptoms compared with patients receiving placebo beginning at the time of the first rating following baseline, at day 7. At study end point, 61% of patients receiving carbamazepine were responders compared with 29% receiving placebo (LOCF, day 21).

Unlike the first trial (Weisler et al., 2004), response rates were significantly greater in both manic and mixed patients receiving carbamazepine compared with placebo. Aside from the subgroup analyses in these two trials, there are no consistent data regarding clinical predictors of acute response to carbamazepine.

Carbamazepine has been compared with lithium (Lerer, Moore, Meyendorff, Cho, & Gershon, 1987; Small, 1990) and chlorpromazine (Grossi, Sacchetti, & Vita, 1984; Okuma et al., 1979) in head-to-head trials. These studies, although individually limited by sample sizes likely too small to detect significant differences in efficacy, nevertheless found generally comparable antimanic activity among patients receiving carbamazepine, lithium, or chlorpromazine.

Risperidone

The efficacy of risperidone in the treatment of acute bipolar manic and mixed episodes has been established as monotherapy in a two randomized, placebo-controlled trials (Hirschfeld et al., 2004; Khanna et al.,

2005); as adjunctive therapy with lithium or divalproex in one placebo-controlled trial (Sachs, Grossman, Ghaemi, Okamato, & Bowden, 2002) and one open-label trial (Vieta et al., 2002); and in comparison trials with olanzapine, haloperidol, and lithium (Brown, Ahmed, & Schuh, 2004; Segal et al., 1998; Smulevich et al., 2005). Risperidone was not superior to placebo in combination with lithium, carbamazepine, or divalproex in one trial (Yatham, Grossman, Augustyns, Vieta, & Ravindran, 2003). However, since this study included patients receiving carbamazepine, it is possible that there may have been significant reductions in plasma risperidone concentrations in these patients, undermining risperidone's efficacy. Hirschfeld et al. (2004) observed a significant mean reduction in manic symptoms by day 3 of the 3-week trial. In addition, risperidone exerted comparable efficacy in patients with manic and mixed episodes and with or without psychotic symptoms. Risperidone treatment was associated with low rates of extrapyramidal side effects when administered at average doses of less than 4 mg/day (Hirschfeld et al, 2004; Sachs et al., 2002; Yatham et al., 2003) but not when administered at average doses of 6 mg/day (Khanna et al., 2005; Segal et al., 1998).

Olanzapine

In monotherapy trials, olanzapine was superior to placebo (Tohen et al., 1999; Tohen, Goldberg, et al., 2000) and divalproex (Tohen, Baker, et al., 2002), and comparable to lithium (Berk, Ichim, & Brook, 1999), divalproex (Zajecka et al., 2002), haloperidol (Tohen, Goldberg, et al., 2003), and risperidone (Brown et al., 2004) in mean improvement in manic symptoms in randomized, controlled trials ranging from 3 to 6 weeks. Olanzapine-treated patients displayed significantly greater improvement in manic symptoms compared with patients receiving placebo by day 7 in one trial (Tohen et al., 2000), and day 21 in another (Tohen et al., 1999). The addition of olanzapine was also superior to placebo in patients who had partially responded to lithium or divalproex monotherapy for at least 2 weeks (Tohen, Chengappa, et al., 2002). There were no significant differences among patients with manic or mixed, rapid or nonrapid cycling, psychotic or nonpsychotic symptoms in studies in which sample sizes allowed post hoc comparisons (Baldessarini, Tondo, & Hennen, 2003). Initial starting doses of 15 mg/day appeared to exert more rapid antimanic efficacy compared with

10 mg/day (Tohen et al., 1999; Tohen et al., 2000). In addition, one study found significant improvement in agitation within 1 day in patients receiving olanzapine 20 to 40 mg/day compared with 10 mg/day augmented by benzodiazepine use (Baker, Kinon, Maguire, Liu, & Hill, 2003). These results are consistent with a study of the intramuscular (IM) formulation of olanzapine, in which patients receiving olanzapine 10 mg IM displayed significant reductions in manic agitation within 2 hours of administration compared with patients receiving IM placebo (Meehan et al., 2001).

Quetiapine

Quetiapine was superior to placebo in two monotherapy 12-week trials (Bowden et al., 2005; McIntyre, Brecher, Paulsson, Huizar, & Mullen, 2005), in three studies in combination with lithium or divalproex (DelBello, Schwiers, & Rosenberg, 2002; Sachs et al., 2004; Yatham et al., 2004), and comparable to divalproex in one head-to-head comparison in adolescents (DelBello et al., 2005). The two placebo-controlled monotherapy trials also included active comparators of lithium (Bowden et al., 2005) or haloperidol (McIntyre et al., 2005). In these trials, there was no significant difference in efficacy between patients receiving quetiapine and either lithium or haloperidol, although the studies were not powered to detect such a difference if one existed. Significant differences in efficacy in favor of quetiapine over placebo were evident by day 4 in the two monotherapy trials, and patients receiving quetiapine displayed cumulative improvement in manic symptoms at 3 and 12 weeks (Vieta, Mullen, Brecher, Paulsson, & Jones, 2005). The mean model dose of quetiapine associated with antimanic efficacy in most studies was approximately 600 mg/day (Vieta et al., 2005). Many of these trials excluded patients with mixed episodes (Bowden et al., 2005; McIntyre et al., 2005; Sachs et al., 2004; Yatham et al., 2004), so a comparative analysis of response between manic and mixed patients could not be conducted. There were no significant differences in response rates to quetiapine in patients with or without psychotic symptoms (Vieta et al., 2005).

Ziprasidone

In two 3-week, placebo-controlled, monotherapy trials, ziprasidone (mean dose 120 to 130 mg/day) pro-

duced significant reductions in manic symptoms by day 2 of treatment (Keck, Versaini, et al., 2003; Potkin, Keck, Segal, Ice, & English, 2005). Ziprasidone-treated patients also had significantly higher response rates compared with patients receiving placebo. Ziprasidone was equally effective in patients with manic and mixed episodes and with and without psychotic symptoms. A third acute treatment monotherapy trial compared ziprasidone and haloperidol treatment with placebo up to 12 weeks (Ramey, Giller, English, & Ice, 2005). Ziprasidone-treated patients again displayed significantly greater improvement at day 2 and day 21 compared with patients receiving placebo. There were no significant differences in efficacy between the ziprasidone (mean dose 121 mg/day) and haloperidol (mean dose 16 mg/day) groups at week 3 or week 12.

Ziprasidone was not superior to placebo as an adjunctive treatment with lithium in a study designed to prove superior onset of action by day 14 (Weisler, Dunn, & English, 2003). However, patients receiving ziprasidone in combination with lithium had significantly greater improvement in manic symptoms by day 4 compared with patients receiving placebo in combination with lithium.

Aripiprazole

Aripiprazole was superior to placebo in two 3-week randomized, controlled trials in patients with manic and mixed episodes (Bourin, 2003; Keck, Marcus, et al., 2003) and comparable in efficacy to haloperidol in a 12-week, adequately powered comparison trial (Vieta et al., 2003). Both placebo-controlled trials initiated aripiprazole at 30 mg/day with good tolerability, and patients displayed significantly greater improvement in manic symptoms compared with placebo by day 4 of both trials. The aripiprazole groups also had significantly higher response rates compared with the placebo groups. The mean dose of aripiprazole in the haloperidol comparison was 23 mg/day. There were no significant differences in response to aripiprazole among patients with manic and mixed episodes, and with or without psychotic symptoms.

Other Agents

In randomized, controlled trials in patients with acute bipolar mania, several agents have failed to demonstrate significant antimanic activity to date. These agents include gabapentin (Pande, Crockatt,

Janney, Werth, & Tsaroucha, 2000; Frye et al., 2000), topiramate (McElroy & Keck, 2004), and verapamil (Janicak, Sharma, Pandey, & Davis, 1998; Walton, Berk, & Brook, 1996). In addition, several agents—lamotrigine, oxcarbazepine, tiagabine, and levetiracetam—have been studied in randomized, controlled trials that have yielded mixed or insufficient evidence of antimanic efficacy thus far.

Three controlled studies have evaluated lamotrigine in bipolar patients with acute mania (Anand, Oren, & Berman, 1999; Frye et al., 2000; Ichim, Berk, & Brook, 2000). Frye et al. (2000) did not find significant differences in response rates for manic symptoms among lamotrigine, gabapentin, and placebo in a series of 6-week crossover trials in 28 patients with treatment-refractory rapid-cycling bipolar disorder. However, manic symptoms were quite low at baseline, raising the possibility that meaningful differences among the three treatment groups might not have been detected. In the second study, Anand et al. (1999) randomized 16 outpatients with mania, hypomania, or mixed episodes who were refractory to or intolerant of lithium and who had a young mania rating scale (YMRS) score of greater than 12 to lamotrigine ($N = 8$) or placebo ($N = 8$) for 8 weeks. Lamotrigine or placebo was either added to ongoing lithium treatment in inadequately responsive patients or administered as monotherapy to lithium-intolerant patients. There were no significant differences between lamotrigine- and placebo-treated patients in mean reduction of manic symptoms or in responder rates. However, response rates were elevated in both groups: lamotrigine, 63%, and placebo, 50%. Its small sample size and high placebo response rate limit interpretation of this trial. In the third controlled trial, 30 hospitalized patients with acute bipolar mania were randomized to lithium or lamotrigine for up to 4 weeks (IchimBerk, & Brook, 2000). Both treatment groups improved significantly in measures of manic symptoms, but with no significant difference between groups. The small sample size, low lithium levels (mean 0.7 mEq/L), and absence of a placebo group limited this trial.

Oxcarbazepine, the 10-keto analog of carbamazepine, has been studied in two controlled trials as monotherapy for patients with acute bipolar mania (Emrich, Dose, & VonZerssen, 1985; Muller & Stoll, 1984). In the first trial, 20 patients were randomized to receive oxcarbazepine or haloperidol. Although both treatment groups displayed a mean reduction in manic symptoms of 55%, it is difficult to interpret this study because of its small size, the use of chlorpromazine as an as-needed adjunctive medication, and the absence of a placebo control group. In the second study, a placebo-controlled crossover trial, four of six patients exhibited a greater than 50% reduction in symptoms with oxcarbazepine (Emrich et al., 1985). One recent retrospective chart review found comparable reduction in manic symptoms in patients treated with oxcarbazepine and valproate (Raja & Azzoni, 2003). Despite these meager data regarding the efficacy of oxcarbazepine in the treatment of manic symptoms, oxcarbazepine has been included in the revised American Psychiatric Association guidelines for the treatment of bipolar disorder (Hirschfeld et al., 2002) and the Texas implementation of medication algorithms for the treatment of bipolar I disorder (Suppes et al., 2005) based on unproven assumptions that its efficacy should parallel that of carbamazepine.

There are no published randomized, controlled trials of tiagabine or levetiracetam in the treatment of bipolar mania. In open-label pilot trials, tiagabine did not appear to exert antimanic efficacy (Grunze et al., 1999; Suppes et al., 2002). In contrast, open-label pilot studies (Bersani 2004; Braunig & Kruger, 2003; Grunze, Langosch, Born, Schaub, & Walden, 2003; Post et al., 2005) suggest that levetiracetam may be beneficial in the treatment of manic symptoms, although these preliminary impressions require confirmation in randomized, controlled trials.

Akhondzadeh, Mohajari, Reza, & Amini (2003) conducted a randomized, placebo-controlled trial of the 5-HT_2 antagonist ritanserin as adjunctive treatment with lithium and haloperidol in 45 treatment-naive patients with acute bipolar mania. Patients receiving adjunctive ritanserin had significantly better improvement in manic symptoms and had lower rates of extrapyramidal side effects compared with patients receiving adjunctive placebo. These intriguing findings require replication.

PSYCHOPHARMACOLOGICAL TREATMENTS FOR ACUTE BIPOLAR DEPRESSION

Lithium and Antidepressants

After years of being understudied, the pharmacological treatment of bipolar depression has received renewed attention in a number of recent Type 1 randomized, controlled trials (Keck, McElroy, & Nelson, 2003). The majority of controlled trials to date assessed the efficacy of lithium in comparison to placebo or tricyclic antidepressants (Baron, Gershon, Rudy, Jonas, & Buchshaum, 1975; Donnelly, Goodwin, Waldman, & Murphy, 1978; Fieve, Platman, & Plutchnik, 1968; Goodwin et al., 1969; Goodwin, Murphy, Dunner, & Bunney, 1972; Greenspan, Schildkraut, Gordon, Levy, & Durrell, 1979; Keck, Welge, Strakowski, Arnold, & McElroy, 2000; Mendels, 1976; Nemeroff et al., 2001; Noyes, Dempsey, Blum, & Cavenaugh, 1974; Stokes et al., 1971). All but one (Nemeroff et al., 2001) placebo-controlled trials utilized crossover designs with short time intervals, ranging from 1 to 28 days of lithium or placebo exposure. These short intervals limit the interpretation of the study results because of the potential confounding effects of lingering lithium activity during the placebo period and because optimal lithium response may have required a longer trial (Zornberg & Pope, 1993). Abrupt discontinuation of lithium may have contributed to a more rapid rate of episode recurrence than that attributable to the natural course of the illness (Suppes, Baldessarini, Faedda, & Tohen, 1991). Moreover, these studies did not exclusively enroll patients with bipolar depression, and they did not report switch rates into hypomania, mania, or mixed states. Primary outcome measures were also often not specified at the outset of these trials (Muzina & Calabrese, 2003). With these limitations in mind, pooled results from five crossover studies that provided sufficient data to assess degree of response revealed that 29 (36%) of 80 patients with acute bipolar depression displayed an unequivocal response to lithium; 63 (79%) patients had at least partial improvement (Zornberg & Pope, 1993).

Two controlled studies assessed the efficacy of lithium against tricyclic antidepressant monotherapy (Donnelly et al., 1978; Watanabe, Ishino, & Otsuki, 1975). Neither trial found significant differences in efficacy between patients receiving lithium or imipramine. A number of other controlled studies examined the efficacy of tricyclics in comparison to other classes of antidepressant agents (Altshuler et al., 1995; Ashberg-Wistedt, 1982; Baumhackl et al., 1989; Cohn, Collins, Ashbrook, & Wernicke, 1980; Himmelhoch, Thase, Mallinger, & Houck, 1991; Kessel & Holt, 1975; Levine et al., 1995; Nemeroff et al., 2001; Sachs et al., 1994; Silverstone, 2001). The

most recent trial comparing imipramine, paroxetine, or placebo added to lithium for breakthrough bipolar depressive episodes did not find a significant difference in acute efficacy among the three groups (Nemeroff et al., 2001). A post hoc analysis revealed that patients with lithium levels of less than 0.8 mEql/L displayed significantly greater improvement in depressive symptoms when randomized to paroxetine compared with placebo. However, in patients with lithium levels greater than 0.8 mEq/L, there were no significant differences in mean reduction of depressive symptoms. Two previous controlled trials comparing serotonin reuptake inhibitor (SRI) antidepressants with tricyclics had significant methodological limitations (Ashberg-Wistedt, 1982; Cohn et al., 1980). In the first study, a double-blind, randomized comparison of fluoxetine and imipramine with placebo, only 64 (72%) of 89 patients remained in the trial after 3 weeks, and only 44 (49%) completed the 6-week study because of side effects or lack of efficacy (Cohn et al., 1980). Furthermore, 7 (16%) subjects completing the study received lithium, but the remainder did not. If treatment dropouts were counted as treatment failures, the response rates in this study were not significantly different for fluoxetine (60%) and imipramine (40%). Both were superior to placebo. The second SRI comparison trial involved only 4 patients in a 4-week crossover trial of zimelidine and desipramine, with no conclusive findings due to the small sample size (Ashberg-Wistedt, 1982).

Two studies compared tricyclics with reversible monoamine oxidase inhibitors (MAOIs Baumhackl et al., 1989; Silverstone, 2001) and one with an irreversible MAOI (Himmelhoch et al., 1991). In the most methodologically rigorous of these studies, tranylcypromine had significantly greater efficacy than imipramine in 56 patients (bipolar I, $N = 24$; bipolar II, $N = 32$) treated for 4 weeks without lithium or another mood stabilizer (Himmelhoch et al., 1991). Of 26 tranylcypromine-treated patients, 21 (81%) displayed a significant antidepressant response compared with 10 (48%) of 21 imipramine-treated patients. Response rates did not differ between bipolar I and bipolar II patients. Silverstone (2001) compared the reversible MOA-A inhibitor moclobemide with imipramine, either as monotherapy or added to ongoing mood stabilizers, in an 8-week trial of 156 patients (75% outpatients) with bipolar I depression. In the moclobemide group, 46% of patients were receiving lithium (two in combination with carbamazepine). In the imipramine group, 49% were receiving lithium (five in combination with carbamazepine and one with valproate). Both treatment groups had significant mean reductions in depressive symptoms from baseline, but without a significant difference in efficacy between groups. More patients switched into mania in the imipramine group (11%) than in the moclobemide group (4%), and they switched earlier in treatment, although these differences were not significant. The authors did not report whether switches occurred less commonly among patients receiving mood stabilizers. Baumhackl et al. (1989), in an earlier, smaller ($N = 32$), 4-week, monotherapy comparison trial between moclobemide and imipramine, similarly failed to find a significant difference in efficacy between the two agents.

A number of other small pilot trials of antidepressants, usually in combination with mood stabilizers, have been conducted in patients with bipolar depression. Young et al. (2000) compared the efficacy of adjunctive paroxetine with a second mood stabilizer (lithium or divalproex) in a 6-week trial in 27 outpatients with breakthrough bipolar depressive episodes (type I, $N = 11$; type II, $N = 16$) despite treatment with therapeutic doses of lithium or divalproex for at least 3 months. In the combination mood stabilizer group, patients receiving lithium were randomized to divalproex and vice versa. Both adjunctive treatment groups displayed significant reductions in depressive symptoms, but without significant differences in efficacy between groups. Because of the small sample size and the limited duration of the trial, no conclusions could be reached about the relative efficacy of the different strategies.

Kessel and Holt (1975) compared maprotiline and imipramine in 14 patients for 6 weeks, with no significant differences in response rates. Sachs et al. (1994) compared desipramine with bupropion in 19 patients with bipolar I depression and found that although both agents produced comparable response rates, patients treated with desipramine (50%) were significantly more likely to switch into hypomania or mania than patients receiving bupropion (10%).

Two preliminary placebo-controlled, randomized adjunctive trials assessed the efficacy and safety of the dopamine D_2/D_3 receptor agonist pramipexole in the treatment of bipolar I and bipolar II depressed patients (Goldberg, Burdick, & Endick, 2004; Zarate et al., 2004). Goldberg et al. (2004) randomized 22 patients (bipolar I, $N = 15$; bipolar II, $N = 7$) to pram-

ipexole (mean maximum dose, 1.7 mg/day) or placebo added to existing mood stabilizers for 6 weeks. Eight (67%) patients receiving pramipexole and two (20%) patients receiving placebo had more than a 50% reduction in depressive symptoms at study end point. Pramipexole-treated patients also had greater improvement in mean percentage reduction of depressive symptoms from baseline compared with patients receiving placebo. One patient in the pramipexole group experienced hypomanic symptoms, compared with none in the placebo group. Zarate et al. (2004) conducted a 6-week trial of similar design except that only patients with bipolar II disorder were included ($N = 21$). The response rate (greater than 50% improvement in depressive symptoms from baseline) was significantly higher in the pramipexole group (60%) compared with the placebo group (9%). One patient on pramipexole and two on placebo experienced hypomanic symptoms. These intriguing findings suggest that pramipexole may have efficacy as an adjunctive treatment for bipolar depression and are consistent with open-label reports in patients with bipolar (Perugi, Ruffolo, Frare, & Toni, et al., 2001; Sporn, Ghaemi, Sambur, & Rankin, 2000) and unipolar depression (Sporn et al., 2000; Lattanzi et al., 2002).

Antidepressant-induced mood switching or cycle acceleration is an important risk of antidepressant treatment in patients with bipolar depression. Reported switch rates among patients with bipolar depression treated with antidepressants have ranged widely, from 4 to 70% (Sachs, Koslow, & Ghaemi, 2000). These disparate estimates reflect differences in data collected from naturalistic compared with controlled trials, whether or not patients were receiving concomitant mood stabilizers, the duration of study, and the specific type of antidepressant and mood stabilizer combinations. A number of recent studies have attempted to clarify the switch rates and the degree to which mood stabilizers reduce this risk in patients with bipolar depression. Bottlender et al. (2001) reviewed the medical records of 158 patients with bipolar I depression to determine the incidence of mania and hypomania in relation to treatment. The overall switch rate was 25%. Among those patients who experienced a mood switch, 80% were receiving tricyclic antidepressants, a significantly higher proportion than those not switching who were receiving tricyclics (51%). Overall switch rates were 34% for patients receiving tricyclic agents, 12% for those receiving SRIs, 8% with MAOIs, and 14% for other agents. The protective effect of a mood stabilizer was most apparent for patients receiving tricyclics, in whom twice as many switched when not receiving a concomitant mood stabilizer. These findings are consistent with earlier studies suggesting that coadministration of lithium reduced the risk of antidepressant-associated switching by approximately 50% (Boerlin, Gitlin, Zoellner, & Hammen, 1998; Henry, Sorbara, Lacoste, Gindre, & Leboyer, 2001; Prien et al., 1984; Rouillon, Lejoyeaux, & Filteau, 1992).

Post and colleagues (Post et al., 2001; Post et al., 2004) analyzed switch data from the Stanley Foundation Bipolar Network trial comparing adjunctive sertraline, bupropion, or venlafaxine with mood stabilizers in patients with bipolar depression. Thirteen (14%) of 95 patients experienced a mood switch during the 10-week acute treatment trial: 7% into hypomania and 6% into mania. During the subsequent maintenance trial up to 1 year, 33% switched: 20% into hypomania and 13% into mania (Post et al., 2001). The switch rate with venlafaxine was slightly but significantly higher than with the other two agents (Post et al., 2004). This finding is consistent with an earlier report by Vieta, Martinez-Aran, et al. (2002), who also found a higher switch rate in patients receiving adjunctive venlafaxine compared with paroxetine in an open-label comparison trial. Because of the lack of placebo control groups in these studies, it is difficult to compare these rates with those associated with spontaneous rates from the illness, but the switch rates into mania were lower than anticipated.

In a meta-analysis of the rate of treatment-emergent switch into mania, with data derived from clinical trials comparing SRIs (fluoxetine, fluvoxamine, paroxetine, and sertraline), tricyclics, or placebo in 415 patients with bipolar depression, Peet (1994) reported that manic switch occurred significantly more commonly with tricyclics (11%) than with SRIs (4%) or placebo (4%).

Lamotrigine

Two published randomized, placebo-controlled trials examined the efficacy of lamotrigine in the treatment of acute bipolar depression (Calabrese et al., 1999; Frye et al., 2000). Calabrese et al. (1999) randomized 195 patients with bipolar I depression to lamotrigine monotherapy 50 mg/day, 200 mg/day, or placebo. Both lamotrigine doses were superior to pla-

cebo. Although the difference between the two doses was not significant, there was a trend toward a modest advantage for the higher dose group, an advantage that may have become more apparent with a longer trial given the gradual titration required.

Switch rates were not significantly different among the three groups: placebo, 5%; lamotrigine 50 mg/day, 3%; and lamotrigine 200 mg/day, 8%. Frye et al. (2000), in a crossover trial previously described, reported that patients displayed significantly greater improvement in depressive symptoms while receiving lamotrigine (mean dose 274 mg/day) compared with placebo. The design of this trial did not allow for the examination of possible differences in switch rates. Taken together, the results of these two trials suggest that monotherapy with lamotrigine at 50 to 275 mg/day was efficacious in the treatment of bipolar depression.

Atypical Antipsychotics

Atypical antipsychotics have been investigated in the treatment of acute bipolar depression based on predictions of antidepressant activity based on their pharmacological properties, as well as evidence of improvement in depressive symptoms in clinical trials in patients with psychotic disorders (Keck & Licht, 2000). Three controlled trials examined the efficacy of combination olanzapine and fluoxetine (Amsterdam & Shults, 2005; Brown et al., 2006; Tohen, Vieta, et al., 2003). Tohen, Vieta, et al. (2003) compared olanzapine (mean dose 9 mg/day), the combination of olanzapine (mean dose 7 mg/day) and fluoxetine (mean dose 38 mg/day), and placebo in an 8-week trial in 833 patients with bipolar I depression. Both active treatment groups displayed significantly greater improvement in depressive symptoms than the placebo group, beginning at week 1. In addition, the olanzapine-fluoxetine group displayed significantly greater improvement in depressive symptoms compared with the olanzapine group at weeks 4, 6, and 8. There were no significant differences in switch rates: olanzapine, 6%; olanzapine-fluoxetine, 6%; placebo, 7%. The response to olanzapine-fluoxetine in this study was also consistent with the marked antidepressant response reported by Shelton et al. (2001) for patients with treatment-refractory nonpsychotic major depressive disorder.

Amsterdam and Shults (2005) compared switch rates among patients with bipolar I ($N = 32$) and bipolar II ($N = 2$) depression randomized to fluoxetine (10 to 30 mg/day), olanzapine (5 to 20 mg/day), or olanzapine (5 to 15 mg/day) and fluoxetine (10 to 40 mg/day) for up to 8 weeks. They found comparable efficacy among all three treatment groups, and induction of mania over the time of the trial. These investigators also reported low switch rates in open-label monotherapy trials of venlafaxine (Amsterdam & Garcia-Espana, 2000) and fluoxetine (Amsterdam, Shults, Brunswick, & Hundert, 2004) in depressed patients with bipolar II and bipolar disorder NOS. Brown et al. (2006) conducted a 7-week, head-to-head comparison of olanzapine-fluoxetine with lamotrigine (titrated to 200 mg/day) in 205 depressed patients with bipolar I disorder. Patients receiving olanzapine-fluoxetine had significantly greater improvement than lamotrigine-treated patients across the 7-week treatment period. The lamotrigine group may have had a greater response with a longer trial given the need for gradual lamotrigine titration. There were no significant differences in switch rates between the olanzapine-fluoxetine (4%) and lamotrigine (5%) groups.

Shelton & Stahl (2004) randomized 30 patients with bipolar I ($N = 21$) or bipolar II ($N = 9$) depression despite treatment with a stable and therapeutic dose of a mood stabilizer to adjunctive treatment with paroxetine, risperidone, or the combination over 12 weeks. All three groups displayed significant reductions in depressive symptoms from baseline to end point without significant differences among groups. One patient in the paroxetine group developed hypomanic symptoms during the trial. The results of this trial are limited by the small sample size, heterogeneity in mood stabilizer treatment, and significant difference in mean maximum paroxetine dose between the paroxetine group (35 mg/day) and the paroxetine-risperidone group (22 mg/day). The lower paroxetine dose in the combination group may have been due to inhibition of paroxetine metabolism by risperidone.

Calabrese et al. (2005) examined the efficacy of quetiapine 300 mg/day, 600 mg/day, or placebo in an 8-week trial involving 542 outpatients with bipolar I ($N = 360$) or bipolar II ($N = 182$) depression. Both quetiapine groups had significantly greater improvement in depressive symptoms compared with the placebo group from week 1 onward. Responder rates (proportion of patients with greater than 50% improvement in depressive symptoms from baseline to endpoint) were also significantly higher in the quetiapine 300 mg/day (58%) and 600 mg/day (58%) groups compared with placebo (36%). Treatment-emergent mania rates were similar for the quetiapine (3%) and placebo (4%) groups. Patients with bipolar I depression had greater improvement with quetiapine compared with bipolar II patients. There were no significant differences in efficacy between the two quetiapine dosage groups, but the 300 mg/day group had better overall tolerability.

Carbamazepine

Three small controlled studies evaluated the efficacy of carbamazepine in the treatment of patients with unipolar and bipolar depression (Kramlinger & Post, 1989; Post, Uhde, & Roy-Byrne, 1986; Small, 1990). In the first of these studies, a placebo-controlled crossover trial (median 45 days per treatment interval), Post et al. (1986) reported marked improvement in 12 (34%) of 35 patients (24 bipolar, 11 unipolar) with treatment-resistant depression. A trend toward greater improvement in patients with bipolar than unipolar depression was observed, and the switch to placebo was associated with deterioration in carbamazepine responders. In the second study, Small (1990) compared the response of 28 patients (4 bipolar, 24 unipolar) with treatment-resistant depression in a 4-week trial of lithium, carbamazepine, or their combination. All patients were then treated with both agents for an additional 4 weeks. Of patients receiving carbamazepine or the combination, 32% displayed moderate or marked improvement compared with 13% of lithium-treated patients. These results are consistent with those of Post et al. (1986), although the cohort studied by Small had significantly fewer bipolar patients. Finally, Kramlinger and Post (1989) evaluated the antidepressant effect of lithium versus placebo augmentation of carbamazepine and found that six (46%) of 13 patients who had not responded to carbamazepine alone responded to lithium augmentation.

Valproate

The antidepressant activity of divalproex has been examined in two small placebo-controlled trials in patients with bipolar depression (Davis, Bartolucci, & Petty, 2005; Sachs, Collins, & Altshuler, 2001). In a multisite study, Sachs et al. (2001) randomized 45 patients with bipolar disorder, type I, type II, and NOS, to divalproex (mean serum concentration, 62 mcg/mL) or placebo and found higher response rates in the divalproex group (43%) compared with the placebo group (27%). However, these differences were not significant, and there was no significant difference in mean reduction of depressive symptoms from baseline to end point between the two groups. The divalproex group had significantly greater improvement in depressive symptoms at weeks 2, 4, and 5 only. Davis et al. (2005) conducted a single-site, 8-week study of similar design involving 25 outpatients with bipolar I depression, but with a higher mean valproic acid concentration (81 mcg/mL). In this latter study, patients receiving divalproex had significantly greater reductions in depressive and anxiety symptoms than patients receiving placebo. These positive results require confirmation in a larger trial.

Other Agents

Two placebo-controlled trials evaluated the efficacy of formulations of omega-3 fatty acids in the treatment of bipolar depression (Keck et al., 2006; Stoll et al., 1999). Stoll et al. (1999) reported significant improvement in depressive symptoms in patients who received a combination of EPA/DHA adjunctively or as monotherapy for 4 months compared with placebo. In contrast, Keck et al. (2006) did not find significant efficacy for EPA 6 g/day compared with placebo used adjunctively with ongoing mood stabilizers. In a study comparing inositol with placebo in patients with both bipolar and unipolar depression, Levine et al. (1995) found inositol superior to placebo in the overall group, but the number of patients with bipolar depression was too small ($N = 6$) to detect meaningful treatment effects.

Zarate et al. (2005) reported preliminary evidence that the glutamate-modulating agent, riluzole, was effective in improving depressive symptoms from baseline to end point when added to mood stabilizers in an open-label trial in 14 patients with bipolar I and II disorder. There were no switches into hypomania or mania. These results were consistent with similar open-label findings reported in patients with treatment-resistant major depressive disorder (Zarate, Payne, Quiroz, et al., 2004).

Nahas, Kozel, Li, Anderson, & George (2003) compared daily left prefrontal repetitive transcranial magnetic stimulation (rTMS) for 2 weeks with sham rTMS in 23 depressed patients with bipolar I ($N = 12$) or bipolar II ($N = 9$) disorder. No manic switches were observed, but there were also no significant differences in responder rates between the two groups. A trend in favor of mean improvement in depressive symptoms in the active rTMS group may have been significant with a larger sample size.

MAINTENANCE PSYCHOPHARMACOLOGICAL TREATMENT

Lithium

During the late 1960s and 1970s, 10 double-blind, placebo-controlled studies involving 514 patients with bipolar disorder demonstrated that lithium was superior to placebo in preventing recurrent affective episodes (Hopkins & Gelenberg, 1994). The average relapse rate over 1 year was 34% for lithium-treated patients compared with 81% for those receiving placebo. These data also revealed that lithium exerted greater efficacy in preventing mania than in preventing depressive episodes. Of these 10 studies, 4 were discontinuation trials (Keck, Welge, Strakowski, et al., 2000; Keck, Welge, & McElroy, 2000; Maj, 2000). Because abrupt discontinuation of lithium appears to precipitate relapse (Baldessarini et al., 1996), this design may have artificially elevated the recurrence rate in patients receiving placebo. Geddes, Burgess, Hawton, Jamison, & Goodwin (2004) conducted a systematic review and meta-analysis of randomized controlled trials comparing lithium and placebo in the long-term treatment of bipolar disorders as part of the Cochrane Collaboration. They identified five randomized controlled trials involving 770 patients. Lithium was more effective than placebo in preventing all relapses (random effects relative risk = 0.65, 95% CI = 0.50 to 0.84) and manic relapses (relative risk = 0.62, 95% CI 0.40 to 0.95). However, the protective effect of lithium on depressive relapses was smaller and less substantial (relative risk = 0.72, 95% CI 0.49 to 1.07). Subsequent naturalistic treatment studies of patients maintained on lithium for more than 1 year indicate that a substantial number of patients do not respond adequately to lithium prophylaxis and that complete prevention of mood episode recurrence is a relatively rare outcome (Baldessarini, Tondo, & Hennen, 2002; Maj, 2000).

Analyses of suicide risk in patients treated with lithium suggest that lithium may exert a specific long-term preventative effect on suicide (Baldessarini, Tondo, & Hennen, 2003). This risk reduction appears to exceed that predicted by the effects of no treatment and of treatment with divalproex (Goodwin et al., 2003; Tondo, Hennen, & Baldessarini, 2001). Nevertheless, this apparent benefit has not been definitively established in a large, prospective treatment trial controlling for a number of potential confounding effects.

Identification of clinical predictors of response to lithium prophylaxis has been an important area of inquiry over the past several decades. Predictors of favorable response to lithium prophylaxis include a family history of bipolar disorder (Mander, 1986; Mendlewicz, Fieve, & Stallone, 1973; Prien, Caffey, & Klett, 1974), family history of lithium response (P. Grof et al., 2002), and an illness course characterized by a mania-depression-euthymia episode sequence (Faedda, Baldessarini, Tohen, Strakowski, & Waternaux, 1991; E. Grof et al., 1987; Haag et al., 1986; Koukopoulos et al., 1980). Conversely, predictors of poor maintenance efficacy include rapid cycling (Dunner, Fleiss, & Fieve, 1976), multiple prior episodes (Swann et al., 1999), co-occurring anxiety or alcohol or substance use disorder (Himmelhoch, Neil, & May, 1980; Feske et al., 2000), and familial negative affective style (Miklowitz, Goldstein, Neuechterlein, Snyder, & Mintz, 1988; Miklowitz, et al., 2000). With other choices for maintenance treatment becoming available, assessment for these predictors is becoming increasingly important (Keck & Licht, 2000).

In patients successfully treated with lithium prophylaxis, the risks of discontinuing lithium appear to be substantial. For example, in a meta-analysis by Suppes et al. (1991) of 14 studies involving a total of 257 bipolar patients who discontinued lithium, the risk of recurrence was approximately 28 times higher per month without medication than with medication. More than 50% of patients who discontinued successful maintenance treatment experienced a relapse (more often of mania than of depression) within 6 months. Other studies found that the risk of recurrence is significantly lower if lithium is discontinued gradually (Baldessarini et al., 1996).

The optimal lithium serum concentration is also directly relevant to successful lithium prophylaxis. Gelenberg et al. (1989) found that the risk of relapse was 2.6 times higher in bipolar patients randomized to low (0.4 to 0.6 mol/L) serum concentrations than those with standard (0.8 to 1.0 mol/L) levels. However, patients treated with standard concentrations experienced significantly more side effects. In a second analysis of data from this study, Keller et al. (1992) found that patients randomly assigned to the lower range of lithium levels were more likely to experience subsyndromal symptoms, and that their symptoms were more likely to worsen at any time than were the symptoms of patients in the standard-level group. Furthermore, the first occurrence of subsyndromal symptoms increased the risk of full-episode relapse fourfold. Perlis et al. (2002) also reanalyzed data from the original study and found that patients who had a drop in lithium levels, either due to random assignment to the lower level group or during the trial, were most likely to relapse, and that this was the most powerful predictor of relapse. Finally, in a review of all studies examining maintenance treatment with lithium and lithium serum levels, Hopkins and Gelenberg (2000) concluded that therapeutic response is correlated with lithium concentration within the range of 0.6 to 1.2 mol/L, as are side effects. Taken together, these studies suggest that lithium should be optimally titrated to the highest level within the therapeutic range consistent with adequate tolerability and that eradication of subsyndromal symptoms, not just prevention of full affective episodes, is an important treatment goal.

Lamotrigine

Lamotrigine was the second medication, after lithium, to receive approval for the long-term treatment of bipolar disorder by the U.S. FDA. This indication was based on the results of two 18-month, placebo-controlled lithium comparison studies in which patients entered the trials following stabilization of an acute hypomanic or manic (Bowden et al., 2003) or depressive (Calabrese, Bowden, et al., 2003) episode, respectively. These designs were chosen because of data suggesting that prior mood episode predicts subsequent episode polarity in relapse (MacQueen et al., 2002; Calabrese et al., 2004). In the study by Bowden et al. (2003), patients were randomized to lamotrigine (100 to 400 mg/day), lithium (0.8 to 1.1 mEq/L), or placebo as double-blind maintenance treatment for up to 18 months following an 8- to 16-week open-label phase during which treatment with lamotrigine was initiated and other psychotropics were discontinued. Of 349 patients who entered the open-label phase, 175 met stabilization criteria and entered the randomization phase. Both lamotrigine and lithium were superior to placebo in prolonging the time to intervention for any mood episode. Lamotrigine, but not lithium, was superior to placebo in prolonging time to a depressive episode, whereas lithium, but not lamotrigine, was superior to placebo in prolonging time to a manic, hypomanic, or mixed episode. The second study (Calabrese et al., 2003) was of similar design, except that there were three fixed dosage lamotrigine groups (50, 200, or 400 mg/day). The findings of this study were entirely consistent with the results of the Bowden et al. (2003) trial and with an earlier 1-year open-label continuation study (McElroy, Zarate, et al., 2004).

Lamotrigine was compared with placebo in the only published randomized, controlled parallel-group trial conducted specifically in patients with rapid-cycling bipolar I and II disorders (Calabrese et al., 2000). There was no significant difference in efficacy between lamotrigine and placebo in time to additional pharmacotherapy for emerging symptoms, the primary outcome measure in this 6-month trial involving 324 patients. However, significantly more patients remained stable on lamotrigine (41%) compared with placebo (26%) at the end of 6 months. Although not statistically significant, there was a trend toward better response in patients with bipolar II compared with bipolar I disorder.

Olanzapine

Olanzapine has also received an indication for relapse prevention in patients with bipolar disorder. Three randomized, controlled trials evaluated the efficacy of olanzapine monotherapy in the long-term prevention of mood episodes in patients with bipolar disorder (Tohen, Ketter, et al., 2003; Tohen et al., 2005; Tohen et al., 2006). The first long-term study was a 47-week maintenance of effect comparison with divalproex in patients who had initially responded to either agent for acute mania (Tohen, Ketter, et al., 2003). The median times to manic relapse were 270 days for the olanzapine group and 74 days for the divalproex group. These differences were not significant. There were also no significant differences in relapse rates between the olanzapine (45%) and divalproex (52%) groups. The second long-term trial

was a relapse prevention study comparing olanzapine with lithium in 543 patients with bipolar I disorder who were initially stabilized on the combination of the two agents following a manic or mixed episode for 6 to 12 weeks (Tohen et al., 2005). Of the initial 543 patients, 431 met symptomatic remission criteria and were randomized to olanzapine (5 to 20 mg/day) or lithium (0.6 to 1.2 mEq/L) for up to 1 year. Significantly more olanzapine-treated patients (47%) completed the trial than lithium-treated (33%) patients. Although there were no significant differences in overall relapse rates into a mood episode between the olanzapine (30%) and lithium (39%) groups, patients receiving olanzapine had significantly lower manic relapses (14%) compared with patients receiving lithium (28%). Relapse rates into depression were similar for the olanzapine (16%) and lithium (15%) groups. Tohen et al. (2006) also conducted a 48-week placebo-controlled trial of olanzapine monotherapy in relapse prevention of bipolar I disorder. Patients who met criteria for symptomatic remission from a manic or mixed episode at two consecutive weekly visits following 6 to 12 weeks of open-label treatment with olanzapine (5 to 20 mg/day) were randomized to olanzapine (N = 225) or placebo (N = 136) for up to 48 weeks. Patients receiving olanzapine had a significantly longer time to symptomatic relapse (median 174 days) compared with patients receiving placebo (median 22 days). Time to symptomatic recurrence of manic, mixed, and depressive episodes was also significantly longer in the olanzapine group. The overall relapse rates for olanzapine-treated patients were significantly lower (47%) compared with patients receiving placebo (80%). The findings from these trials indicate that olanzapine has efficacy in relapse prevention in patients with bipolar I disorder and suggest that it may be superior to lithium in prevention of manic recurrence.

Aripiprazole

The efficacy of aripiprazole in relapse prevention in recently (less than 3 months) manic patients with bipolar I disorder was examined in one 6-month, placebo-controlled trial (Keck et al., 2006). A total of 633 patients enrolled in the trial; 567 entered the stabilization phase and received aripiprazole 15 or 30 mg/day, of whom 206 (37%) completed. A total of 161 patients entered the 6-month randomization phase after meeting stabilization criteria, which included symptomatic remission for at least 6 weeks on aripiprazole monotherapy. Aripiprazole was superior to placebo in delaying time to relapse into any mood episode and in percentage relapses (aripiprazole, 25%; placebo, 43%). Within mood episodes, aripiprazole was superior to placebo primarily in the prevention of manic or mixed episodes, probably due to enrollment of patients recently manic or mixed.

Carbamazepine

Nine controlled studies have assessed the efficacy of carbamazepine for the maintenance treatment of patients with bipolar disorder (Bellaire, Demish, & Stoll, 1988; Coxhead, Silverstone, & Cookson, 1992; Denicoff et al., 1997; Greil et al., 1997; Hartong et al., 2003; Lusznat, Murphy, & Nunn, 1988; Okuma et al., 1981; Placidi et al., 1986; Watkins, Callendar, & Thomas, 1987). However, the efficacy of carbamazepine in the prevention of mood episodes has been controversial (Murphy, Gannon, & McGennis, 1989; Dardennes, Even, Bange, & Heim, 1995). This controversy stems in part from the heterogeneity in design, sample size, liberal use of rescue medications, and other factors affecting trial outcomes among the controlled maintenance studies, and the availability of only one placebo-controlled maintenance trial (Okuma et al., 1981). Interpretation of this latter study is further limited by the use of rescue medications other than lithium or carbamazepine to treat breakthrough symptoms. The use of these adjunctive medications limits the degree to which relapse rates can be directly attributable to carbamazepine or placebo in this study.

Hartong et al. (2003) conducted one of the most rigorous trials of carbamazepine prophylaxis in treatment-naive patients with bipolar I disorder. Patients ($N = 94$) with at least two prior mood episodes in the previous 3 years were randomly assigned to lithium or carbamazepine using a double-dummy parallel-group design beginning with an index episode of hypomania, mania, or depression and followed for up to 2 years. No adjunctive thymoleptic medications were allowed. Fewer patients receiving lithium (27%) developed a mood episode compared with patients receiving carbamazepine (42%). Most relapses in the lithium group occurred within the first 3 months of the trial, whereas the relapse rate in the carbamazepine group was approximately 40% per year. How-

ever, slightly more patients treated with lithium (36%) than carbamazepine (26%) dropped out of the study, yielding 36% of lithium-treated patients completing 2 years with no episodes compared with 32% on carbamazepine.

Valproate

A 1-year randomized, double-blind, placebo-controlled, lithium-comparator trial of divalproex by Bowden et al. (2000) did not find a significant difference in time to any mood episode among the three groups. A post hoc survival analysis that included both time to any mood episode and time to early discontinuation for any reason as treatment failure events found that patients in the divalproex group had significantly longer time in study compared with the lithium group (Bowden, 2003). The more substantial benefits in relapse prevention for divalproex and lithium were for mania rather than depression (Bowden, 2003). In contrast, time to depression was longer and need for rescue intervention with antidepressants significantly less in the divalproex group compared with the lithium and placebo groups (Gyulai et al., 2003).

Revicki et al. (2005) conducted an open-label 1-year study of the clinical effectiveness (efficacy and tolerability) of divalproex compared with lithium in 201 patients with bipolar I disorder randomized to either drug initially for the treatment of an acute manic or mixed episode requiring hospitalization. Divalproex-treated patients (12%) were less likely to discontinue study medications for lack of efficacy or adverse events compared with lithium-treated patients (23%). No other significant differences in clinical outcome measures were evident between the two groups.

Combination Therapy

The efficacy of mood stabilizer combinations compared with mood stabilizer monotherapy is a remarkably understudied aspect of the long-term treatment of bipolar disorders. Only two such prospective randomized trials exist: a 1-year pilot trial comparing the combination of lithium and divalproex with lithium and placebo (Solomon et al., 1997), and a large 18-month trial comparing the combination of olanzapine with lithium or divalproex versus placebo with lithium or divalproex (Tohen et al., 2004). Solomon et al. (1997) found lower relapse rates in patients receiving divalproex and lithium (N = 5) compared with patients receiving placebo and lithium (N = 7), but higher rates of side effects in the combination treatment group. Tohen et al. (2004) reported significantly lower relapse rates in patients receiving combination olanzapine with lithium or divalproex compared with placebo plus lithium or divalproex. The greatest protective effect in the combination group was in the prevention of manic relapse. Again, not surprisingly, side effects, in particular weight gain, were more common in the combination group. The results of this study need to be considered in light of the original cohort selection, which was based on patients who were partial nonresponders to monotherapy with lithium or divalproex after 2 weeks of treatment for manic or mixed symptoms (Tohen, Chengappa, et al., 2002).

Three large naturalistic studies found the combination of lithium and carbamazepine superior to lithium monotherapy in bipolar disorder relapse prevention, although these studies were enriched for carbamazepine responders, and the side effect burden was not unexpectedly greater in the combination therapy groups (Baethge et al., 2005; Bocchetta, Chillotti, Severino, Ardau, & Del Zompo,1997; Denicoff et al., 1997).

Two studies addressed the impact of antipsychotic discontinuation on relapse in patients initially treated with the combination of an antipsychotic (usually a first-generation agent) and antimanic mood stabilizer for acute mania (Saksa, Baker, & Woods, 2004; Zarate & Tohen, 2004). Zarate and Tohen (2004) randomized 37 patients receiving perphenazine in combination with lithium, carbamazepine, or valproate to remain on perphenazine or switch to placebo for 6 months immediately after remission of an acute manic episode for which they received both agents. Patients who continued on the combination of perphenazine and mood stabilizer were significantly more likely to have a shorter time to depressive relapse, to discontinue the study, and to have increased rates of dysphoria, depressive symptoms, and extrapyramidal symptoms. The study by Saksa et al. (2004) was limited by a high dropout rate, but two of five patients randomized to discontinue adjunctive antipsychotic therapy relapsed into psychotic and manic recurrence, respectively, within 1 month of antipsychotic taper.

CO-OCCURRING PSYCHIATRIC DISORDERS

Patients with bipolar disorders have among the highest rates of psychiatric comorbidity of all primary psychiatric illnesses (McElroy et al., 2001). The presence of co-occurring psychiatric disorders can affect treatment selection. Unfortunately, very few studies have specifically addressed the long-term treatment of patients with bipolar disorder and psychiatric comorbidity. Frankenburg and Zanarini (2002) conducted a 6-month placebo-controlled trial of divalproex in 30 female patients with bipolar II disorder and co-occurring borderline personality disorder. Divalproex was superior to placebo in reducing measures of interpersonal sensitivity, anger, hostility, and aggression. Salloum et al. (2005) conducted a 24-week, double-blind, placebo-controlled trial of adjunctive divalproex or placebo in 59 patients with bipolar I disorder and co-occurring alcohol dependence receiving lithium and psychosocial treatment. Patients receiving divalproex had a significantly lower proportion of heavy drinking days and a trend toward fewer drinks per heavy drinking days compared with patients receiving placebo. Higher serum valproic acid concentrations correlated with better alcohol use outcomes. There were no significant differences between the two groups in mood symptom improvement.

FUTURE RESEARCH AND CONCLUSIONS

There have been substantial advances in the pharmacological treatment of bipolar disorder in the last decade. Well-done, randomized, controlled trials have established the efficacy of lithium, divalproex, carbamazepine, chlorpromazine, haloperidol, risperidone, olanzapine, quetiapine, ziprasidone, and aripiprazole in the treatment of acute mania. Research into neglected but important aspects of the management of bipolar disorder — the treatment of acute bipolar depression and the long-term prevention of relapse — has finally gained momentum. Four agents have U.S. FDA indications for relapse prevention of bipolar I disorder: lithium, lamotrigine, olanzapine, and aripiprazole. Studies of the efficacy of quetiapine and ziprasidone in the long-term treatment of bipolar disorder are under way. Although only one formulation, the combination of olanzapine and fluoxetine, has an indication for acute bipolar depression, evidence is beginning to emerge that some agents, most notably quetiapine and lamotrigine, may also be efficacious in this pole of the illness without increasing the risk of hypomanic or manic switch. Recent studies have also shed light on the lack of efficacy of some agents thought to have potential in the treatment of bipolar disorder, for example, gabapentin and topiramate. The thymoleptic properties of levetiracetam, oxcarbazepine, and zonisamide require careful delineation in randomized, controlled trials.

Important therapeutic questions remain unanswered. For example, the optimal duration of antidepressant treatment in combination with antimanic mood stabilizers, balanced against the risk of switch induction, is unclear from the available research. Very little data exist regarding the efficacy and effectiveness of long-term treatment of bipolar disorder with combinations of mood-stabilizing agents, even though this is common practice. Entirely novel treatment approaches such as vagal nerve stimulation and rapid transcranial magnetic stimulation have not been adequately explored in patients with bipolar disorder.

REFERENCES

The following coding system, with codes provided at the end of each reference entry, indicates the nature of the supporting evidence from each citation:

1. Randomized, prospective, clinical trial. A study must include comparison groups with random assignment, blinded assessments, clear presentation of inclusion and exclusion criteria, state-of-the-art diagnostic methods, adequate sample size to provide statistical power, and clearly described statistical methods.

2. Clinical trial. A study in which an intervention is made but some aspect of the Type 1 study criteria is missing.

3. Clinical study. A study that has clear methodological limitations. These studies include open treatment studies designed to obtain pilot data, naturalistic studies, and case control studies.

4. A review with secondary data analysis (e.g., meta-analysis or comparably designed trials).

5. A review without secondary data analysis designed to convey an impression of the available literature.

6. A textbook, reference manual, case reports, small case series, and opinion papers.

Akhondzadeh, S., Mohajari, H., Reza, H. M., & Amini, H. (2003). Ritanserin as an adjunct to lithium and haloperidol for the treatment of medication-naïve patients with acute mania: A double blind and placebo controlled trial. BMC Psychiatry, 3, 76–79. (1)

Altshuler, L. L., Post, R. M., Leverich, G. S., Mikalanskas, K., Rosoff, A., & Ackerman, L. (1995). Antidepressant-induced mania and cycle acceleration: A controversy revisited. American Journal of Psychiatry, 152, 1130–1138. (3)

American Psychiatric Association. (1987). Diagnostic and statistical manual of mental disorders (3rd ed., Revised). Washington, DC: Author. (6)

American Psychiatric Association. (2000). Diagnostic and statistical manual of mental disorders (4th ed., Text revision). Washington, DC: Author. (6)

Amsterdam, J. D., & Garcia-Espana, F. (2000). Venlafaxine monotherapy in women with bipolar II and unipolar depression. Journal of Affective Disorders, 59, 225–229. (3)

Amsterdam, J. D., & Shults, J. (2005). Comparison of fluoxetine, olanzapine, and combined fluoxetine plus olanzapine initial therapy of bipolar type I and type II major depression — lack of manic induction. Journal of Affective Disorders, 87, 121–130. (2)

Amsterdam, J. D., Shults, J., Brunswick, D. J., & Hundert, M. (2004) Short-term fluoxetine monotherapy for bipolar type II or bipolar NOS major depression-low manic switch rate. Bipolar Disorders, 6, 75–81. (3)

Anand, A., Oren, D. A., Berman, R. M. (1999, June). Lamotrigine treatment of lithium failure in outpatient mania: A double-blind, placebo-controlled trial. Abstracts of the Third International Conference on Bipolar Disorder. Pittsburgh, PA. (2)

Ashberg-Wistedt, A. (1982). Comparison between zimelidine and desipramine in endogenous depression. Acta Psychiatrica Scandinavica, 66, 129–138. (2)

Baethge, C., Baldessarini, R. J., Mathiske-Schmidt, K., Hennen, J., Berghofer, A., Muller-Oerlinghausen, B., et al. (2005). Long-term combination therapy versus monotherapy with lithium and carbamazepine in 46 bipolar I patients. Journal of Clinical Psychiatry, 66, 174–182. (3)

Baker, R. W., Kinon, B. J., Maguire, G. A., Liu, H., & Hill, A. L. (2003). Effectiveness of rapid initial dose escalation of up to forty milligrams per day of oral olanzapine in acute agitation. Journal of Clinical Psychopharmacology, 23, 132–137. (2)

Baldessarini, R. J. (1985), *Chemotherapy in psychiatry.* Cambridge, MA: Harvard University Press. (6)

Baldessarini, R. J., Hennen, J., Wilson, M., Calabrese, J., Chengappa, R., Keck, P. E., Jr., et al. (2003). Olanzapine versus placebo in acute mania: Treatment responses in subgroups. *Journal of Clinical Psychopharmacology, 23,* 370–376. (4)

Baldessarini, R. J., Tondo, L., Faedda, G. L., Suppes, T. R., Floris, G., & Rudas, N. (1996). Effects of the rate of discontinuing lithium maintenance treatment in bipolar disorders. *Journal of Clinical Psychiatry, 57,* 441–448. (3)

Baldessarini, R. J., Tondo, L., & Hennen, J. (2002). Is lithium still worth using? An update of selected recent research. *Harvard Review of Psychiatry, 10,* 59–75. (4)

Baldessarini, R. J., Tondo, L., & Hennen, J. (2003). Lithium treatment and suicide risk in major affective disorders: Update and new findings. *Journal of Clinical Psychiatry, 64*(Suppl. 50), 44–52. (4)

Baron, M., Gershon, E. S., Rudy, V., Jonas, W. Z., & Buchsbaum, M. (1975). Lithium carbonate response in depression. *Archives of General Psychiatry, 32,* 1107–1111. (2)

Baumhackl, U., Biziere, K., Fischback, G., Geretsegger, C., Hebenstreit, G., Radmayr, E. et al. (1989). Efficacy and tolerability of moclobemide compared with imipramine in depressive disorder (*DSM-III*): An Austrian double-blind, multicentre study. *British Journal of Psychiatry, 155*(Suppl.), 78–83. (2)

Bellaire, W., Demish, K., & Stoll, K. D. (1988). Carbamazepine versus lithium prophylaxis of recurrent affective episodes. *Psychopharmacology, 96*(Suppl.), 287. (2)

Benazzi, F., & Akiskal, H. S. (2003). Redefining the evaluation of bipolar II: Beyond the strict SCID-CV guidelines for hypomania. *Journal of Affective Disorders, 73,* 33–38. (3)

Berk, M., Ichim, L., & Brook, S. (1999). Olanzapine compared to lithium in mania: A double-blind randomized controlled trial. *International Clinical Psychopharmacology, 14,* 339–343. (2)

Bersani, G. (2004). Levetiracetam in bipolar spectrum disorders: First evidence of efficacy in an open, add-on study. *Human Psychopharmacology, 19,* 355–366. (3)

Bocchetta, A., Chillotti, C., Severino, G., Ardau, R., & Del Zompo, M. (1997). Carbamazepine augmentation in lithium-refractory bipolar patients: A prospective study on long-term prophylactic effectiveness. *Journal of Clinical Psychopharmacology, 17,* 92–96. (3)

Boerlin, H. L., Gitlin, M. J., Zoellner, L. A., & Hammen, C. L. (1998). Bipolar depression and antidepressant-induced mania: A naturalistic study. *Journal of Clinical Psychiatry, 59,* 374–379. (3)

Bottlender, R., Rudolf, D., Strauss, A., & Moller, H. J. (2001). Mood-stabilizers reduce the risk of developing antidepressant-induced maniform states in acute treatment of bipolar I depressed patients. *Journal of Affective Disorders, 63,* 79–83. (3)

Bourin, M., Auby, P., Marcus, R. N., et al. (2003, May). Aripiprazole versus haloperidol for maintained treatment effect of acute mania. *New research abstracts of the American Psychiatric Association Annual Meeting,* San Francisco, CA. (1)

Bowden, C. L. (2003). Acute and maintenance treatment with mood stabilizers. *International Journal of Neuropsychopharmacology, 6,* 269–275. (4)

Bowden, C. L., Brugger, A. M., Swann, A. C., Calabrese, J. R., Janicak, P. G., Petty, F., et al. (1994). Efficacy of divalproex sodium vs. placebo in the treatment of mania. *Journal of the American Medical Association, 271,* 918–924. (1)

Bowden, C. L., Calabrese, J. R., McElroy, S. L., Gyulai, L., Wassef, A., Petty, F. et al. (2000). A randomized, placebo- controlled 12-month trial of divalproex and lithium in treatment of outpatients with bipolar I disorder. *Archives of General Psychiatry, 57,* 481–489. (1)

Bowden, C. L., Calabrese, J. R., Sachs, G. S., Yatham, L. N., Asghar, S. A., Hompland, M., et al. (2003). A placebo-controlled 18-month trial of lamotrigine and lithium maintenance treatment in recently manic or hypomanic patients with bipolar I disorder. *Archives of General Psychiatry, 60,* 392–400. (1)

Bowden, C. L., Grunze, H., Mullen, J., Brecher, M., Paulsson, B., Jones, M., et al. (2005). A randomized, double-blind, placebo-controlled efficacy and safety study of quetiapine or lithium as monotherapy for mania in bipolar disorder. *Journal of Clinical Psychiatry, 66,* 111–121. (1)

Bowden, C. L., Myers, J. E., Grossman, F., & Xie, Y. (2004). Risperidone in combination with mood stabilizers: A 10-week continuation phase study in bipolar I disorder. *Journal of Clinical Psychiatry, 60,* 392–400. (3)

Braunig, P., & Kruger, S. (2003). Levetiracetam in the treatment of rapid cycling bipolar disorder. *Journal of Psychopharmacology, 17,* 239–241. (3)

Brennan, M. J. W., Sandyk, R., & Borsook, D. (1984). Use of sodium valproate in the management of affective disorders: Basic and clinical aspects. In H. M. Emrich, T. Okuma, & A. A. Muller (Eds.), *Anticonvulsants in affective disorders.* Amsterdam: Excerpta Medica. (2)

Brown, E. B., Ahmed, S., & Schuh, L. M. (2004). Olanzapine versus risperidone treatment of bipolar I disorder. *New research abstracts of the American Psychiatric Association Annual Meeting.* New York, NY: NR 783. (1)

Calabrese, J. R., Bowden, C. L., Sachs, G., Ascher, J. A., Monaghan, E., & Rudd, G. D. (1999). A double-blind placebo-controlled study of lamotrigine monotherapy in outpatients with bipolar I depression. *Journal of Clinical Psychiatry, 60,* 79–88. (1)

Calabrese, J. R., Bowden, C. L., Sachs, G., Yaltham, L. N., Behnke, K., Mehtonen, O. P., et al. (2003). A placebo-controlled, 18-month trial of lamotrigine and lithium maintenance treatment in recently depressed patients with bipolar I disorder. *Journal of Clinical Psychiatry, 64,* 1013–1024. (1)

Calabrese, J. R., Hirschfeld, R. M. A., Reed, M., Davies, M. A., Frye, M. A., Keck, P. E., Jr., et al. (2003). Impact of bipolar disorder on a U.S. community sample. *Journal of Clinical Psychiatry, 64,* 425–432. (3)

Calabrese, J. R., Keck, P. E., Jr., Macfadden, W., Minkwitz, M., Ketter, T. A., Weisler, R. H., et al. (2005). A randomized, double- blind, placebo-controlled trial of quetiapine in the treatment of bipolar I or II depression. *American Journal of Psychiatry, 162,* 1351–1360. (1)

Calabrese, J. R., Suppes, T., Bowden, C. L., Sachs, G. S., Swann, A. C., McElroy, S. L., et al. (2000). A double-blind, placebo-controlled, prophylaxis study of lamotrigine in rapid-cycling bipolar disorder. *Journal of Clinical Psychiatry, 61,* 841–850. (1)

Calabrese, J. R., Vieta, E., El-Mallakh, R., Findling, R. L., Youngstrom, E. A., Elhaj, O., et al. (2004). Mood state at study entry as predictor of the polarity of relapse in bipolar disorder. *Biological Psychiatry, 56,* 957–963. (4)

Cohn, J., Collins, G., Ashbrook, E., & Wernicke, J. F. (1980). A comparison of fluoxetine, imipramine and placebo in patients with bipolar depressive disorder. *International Clinical Psychopharmacology, 3,* 313–322. (2)

Coxhead, N., Silverstone, T., & Cookson, J. (1992). Carbamazepine versus lithium in the prophylaxis of bipolar affective disorder. *Acta Psychiatrica Scandinavica, 85,* 114–118. (2)

Dardennes, R., Even, C., Bange, F., & Heim, A. (1995). Comparison of carbamazepine and lithium in the prophylaxis of bipolar affective disorders: A meta-analysis. *British Journal of Psychiatry, 166,* 375–381. (4)

Davis, L. L., Bartolucci, A., & Petty, F. (2005). Divalproex in the treatment of bipolar depression: A placebo-controlled study. *Journal of Affective Disorders, 85,* 259–266. (2)

DelBello, M. P., Kowatch, R., Adler, C. M., Stanford, K. E., Welge, J. A. & Barzman, D. H. (2006). A double-blind randomized pilot study comparing quetiapine and divalproex for adolescent mania. *Journal of the American Academy Child Adolescent Psychiatry, 45,* 305–313. (2)

DelBello, M. P., Schwiers, M. L., & Rosenberg, H. L. (2002). A double-blind, randomized, placebo-controlled study of quetiapine as adjunctive treatment for adolescent mania. *Journal of the American Academy of Child and Adolescent Psychiatry, 41,* 1216–1223. (1)

Denicoff, K. D., Smith-Jackson, E. E., Disney, E. R., Ali, S. O., Leverich, G. S., & Post, R. M. (1997). Comparative prophylactic efficacy of lithium, carbamazepine and the combination in bipolar disorder. *Journal of Clinical Psychiatry, 58,* 470–478. (2)

Dion, G. L., Tohen, M., Anthony, W. A., & Waternaux, C. S. (1988). Symptoms and functioning of patients with bipolar disorder six months after hospitalization. *Journal of Hospital and Community Psychiatry, 39,* 652–657. (3)

Donnelly, E. F., Goodwin, F. K., Waldman, I. N., & Murphy, D. L. (1978). Prediction of antidepressant responses to lithium. *American Journal of Psychiatry, 135,* 552–556. (2)

Dunner, D. L., Fleiss, J. L., & Fieve, R. R. (1976). Lithium carbonate prophylaxis failure. *British Journal of Psychiatry, 129,* 40–44. (4)

Emrich, H. M., Dose, M., & Von Zerssen, D. (1985). The use of sodium valproate, carbamazepine, and oxcarbazepine in patients with affective disorders. *Journal of Affective Disorders, 8,* 243–250. (3)

Emrich, H. M., Von Zerssen, D., & Kissling, W. (1981). On a possible role of GABA in mania: Therapeutic efficacy of sodium valproate. In E. Costa, G. Dicharia, & G. L. Gessa (Eds.), *GABA and benzodiazepine receptors* (pp. 620–632). New York: Raven Press. (2)

Faedda, G. L., Baldessarini, R. J., Tohen, M., Strakowski, S. M., & Waternaux, C. (1991). Episode sequence in bipolar disorder and response to lithium treatment. *American Journal of Psychiatry, 148,* 1237–1239. (4)

Fagiolini, A., Kupfer, D. J., Masalehdan, A., Scott, J. A., Houck, P. R., & Frank, E. (2005). Functional impairment in the remission phase of bipolar disorder. *Bipolar Disorders, 7,* 281–285. (3)

Feske, U., Frank, E., Mallinger, A. G., Houck, P. R., Fagiolini, A., Shear, M. K., et al. (2000). Anxiety as a correlate of response to the acute treatment of bipolar I disorder. *American Journal of Psychiatry*, 157, 956–962. (4)

Fieve, R. R., Platman, S. R., & Plutchnik, R. R. (1968). The use of lithium in affective disorders: Acute endogenous depression. *American Journal of Psychiatry*, 149, 79–83. (2)

Frankenburg, F. R., & Zanarini, M. C. (2002). Divalproex sodium treatment of women with borderline personality disorder and bipolar II disorder: A double-blind placebo-controlled pilot study. *Journal of Clinical Psychiatry*, 63, 442–446. (1)

Freeman, T. W., Clothier, J. L., Pazzaglia, P., Lesem, M. D., & Swann, A. C. (1992). A double-blind comparison of valproic acid and lithium in the treatment of acute mania. *American Journal of Psychiatry*, 149, 247–250. (2)

Frye, M. A., Ketter, T. A., Kimbrell, T. A., Dunn, R. T., Speer, A. M., Osuch, E. A., et al. (2000). A placebo-controlled study of lamotrigine and gabapentin monotherapy in refractory mood disorders. *Journal of Clinical Psychopharmacology*, 20, 607–614. (1)

Garfinkel, P. E., Stancer, H. C., & Persad, E. (1980). A comparison of haloperidol, lithium carbonate, and their combination in the treatment of acute mania. *Journal of Affective Disorders*, 2, 279–288. (2)

Geddes. J. R., Burgess, S., Hawton, K., Jamison, K., & Goodwin, G. M. (2004). Long-term lithium therapy for bipolar disorder: Systematic review and meta-analysis of randomized controlled trials. *American Journal of Psychiatry*, 161, 217–222. (4)

Gelenberg, A. J., Kane, J. M., Keller, M. B., Lavori, P., Rosenbaum, J. F., Cole, K., et al. (1989). Comparison of standard and low serum levels of lithium for maintenance treatment of bipolar disorder. *New England Journal of Medicine*, 321, 1489–1493. (1)

Gershon, E. (1989). Recent developments in genetics of manic-depressive illness. *Journal of Clinical Psychiatry*, 50(Suppl.), 4–7. (6)

Goldberg, J. F., Burdick, K. E., & Endick, C. J. (2004). Preliminary randomized, double-blind, placebo-controlled trial of pramipexole added to mood stabilizers for treatment-resistant bipolar depression. *American Journal of Psychiatry*, 161, 564–566. (1)

Goodwin, F. K., Fireman, B., Simon, G. E., Hunkeler, E. M., Lee, J., & Revicki, D. (2003). Suicide risk in bipolar disorder during treatment with lithium and divalproex. *Journal of the American Medical Association*, 290, 1467–1473. (3)

Goodwin, F. K., & Jamison, K. R. (1990). *Manic-depressive illness*. New York: Oxford University Press. (6)

Goodwin, F. K., Murphy, D. L., & Bunney, W. E., Jr. (1969). Lithium carbonate treatment in depression and mania: A longitudinal double-blind study. *Archives of General Psychiatry*, 21, 486–496. (2)

Goodwin, F. K., Murphy, D. L., Dunner, D. L., & Bunney, W. E., Jr. (1972). Lithium response in unipolar versus bipolar depression. *American Journal of Psychiatry*, 129, 76–79. (2)

Greenspan, K., Schildkraut, J. J., Gordon, E. K., Levy, B., & Durell, J. (1979). Catecholamine metabolism in affective disorders. *Journal of Psychiatry Research*, 7, 171–182. (2)

Greil, W., Ludwig-Mayerhofer, W., Erazo, N. Schochlin, C., Schmidt, S., Engel, R. R., et al. (1997). Lithium versus carbamazepine in the maintenance treatment of bipolar disorders: A randomized study. *Journal of Affective Disorders*, 43, 151–161. (2)

Grof, E., Haag, M., Grof, P., & Haag, H. (1987). Lithium response and the sequence of episode polarities: Preliminary report on a Hamilton sample. *Progress in Neuropsychopharmacology and Biological Psychiatry*, 11, 199–203. (3)

Grof, P., Duffy, A., Cavazzoni, P., Grof, E., Garnham, J., MacDougall, M., et al. (2002). Is response to lithium a familial trait? *Journal of Clinical Psychiatry*, 63, 942–947. (4)

Grossi, E., Sacchetti, E., & Vita, A. (1984). Carbamazepine vs. chlorpromazine in mania: A double-blind trial. In H. M. Emrich, T. Okuma, & A. A. Muller (Eds.), *Anticonvulsants in affective disorders* (pp. 121–131). Amsterdam: Excerpta Medica. (2)

Grunze, H., Erfurth, A., Marcuse, A., Amann, B., Normann, C., & Walden, J. (1999). Tiagabine appears not to be efficacious in the treatment of acute mania. *Journal of Clinical Psychiatry*, 60, 759–762. (3)

Grunze, H., Langosch, J., Born, C., Schaub, G., & Walden, J. (2003). Levetiracetam in the treatment of acute mania: An open add-on study with on-off-on design. *Journal of Clinical Psychiatry*, 64, 781–784. (3)

Gurling, H. (1995). Linkage findings in bipolar disorder. *Nature Genetics*, 10, 8–9. (4)

Gyulai, L., Bowden, C. L., McElroy, S. L., Calabrese, J. R., Petty, F., Swann, A. C., et al. (2003). Maintenance efficacy of divalproex in the prevention of bipolar depression. *Neuropsychopharmacology*, 28, 1374–1382. (3).

Haag, M., Heidorm, A., Haag, H., & Greil, W. (1986). Response to stabilizing lithium therapy and sequence of affective polarity. *Pharmacopsychiatry*, 19, 278–279. (3)

Hartong, E. G., Moleman, P., Hoogduin, C. A., Broekman, T. G., Nolen, W. A., & LitCar Group. (2003). Prophylactic efficacy of lithium versus carbamazepine in treatment-naïve bipolar patients. *Journal of Clinical Psychiatry, 64,* 144–151. (2)

Henry, C., Sorbara, F., Lacoste, J, Gindre, C., & Leboyer, M. (2001). Antidepressant-induced mania in bipolar patients: Identification of risk factors. *Journal of Clinical Psychiatry, 62,* 249–255. (3)

Himmelhoch, J. M., Neil, J. F., & May, S. J. (1980). Age, dementia, dyskinesias, and lithium response. *American Journal of Psychiatry, 137,* 941–945. (3)

Himmelhoch, J. M., Thase, M. E., Mallinger, A. G., & Houck, P. (1991). Tranylcypromine versus imipramine in anergic bipolar depression. *American Journal of Psychiatry, 148,* 910–915. (1)

Hirschfeld, R. M. A., Allen, M. H., McEvoy, J., Keck, P. E., Jr., & Russell, J. M. (1999). Safety and tolerability of oral loading of divalproex in acutely manic bipolar patients. *Journal of Clinical Psychiatry, 60,* 815–818. (2)

Hirschfeld, R. M. A., Baker, J. D., Wozniak, P., Tracy, K., & Sommerville, K. W. (2003). The safety and efficacy of oral-loaded divalproex versus standard-titration divalproex, lithium, olanzapine, and placebo in the treatment of acute mania associated with bipolar disorder. *Journal of Clinical Psychiatry, 64,* 841–846. (4)

Hirschfeld, R. M. A., Bowden, C. L., Gitlin, M. J., Thase, M., Keck, P. E., Jr., Perlis, R., et al. (2002). Practice guideline for the treatment of patients with bipolar disorder (revised). *American Journal of Psychiatry, 159*(Suppl.), 1–50. (6)

Hirschfeld, R. M. A., Keck, P. E., Jr., Kramer, M., Karcher, K., Canuso, C., & Eerdekens, M., et al. (2004). Rapid antimanic effect of risperidone monotherapy: A 3-week multicenter, double-blind, placebo-controlled trial. *American Journal of Psychiatry, 161,* 1057–1065. (1)

Hopkins, H. S. & Gelenberg, A. J. (1994). Treatment of bipolar disorder: How far have we come? *Psychopharmacology Bulletin, 30,* 27–37. (5)

Hopkins, H. S., & Gelenberg, A. J. (2000). Serum lithium levels and the outcome of maintenance therapy of bipolar disorder. *Bipolar Disorders, 2,* 174–179. (4)

Ichim, L., Berk, M., & Brook, S. (2000). Lamotrigine compared with lithium in mania: A double-blind, placebo-controlled trial. *Journal of Affective Disorders, 12,* 5–10. (2)

Janicak, P., Sharma, R., Pandey, G., & Davis, J. M. (1998). Verapamil for the treatment of acute mania: A double-blind, placebo-controlled trial. *American Journal of Psychiatry, 155,* 972–973. (1)

Johnson, G., Gershon, S., Burdock, E., Floyd, A., & Hekiman, L. (1971). Comparative effects of lithium and chlorpromazine in the treatment of acute manic states. *British Journal of Psychiatry, 155,* 267–276. (2)

Johnson, G., Gershon, S., & Hekiman, L. J. (1968). Controlled evaluation of lithium and chlorpromazine in the treatment of manic states: An interim report. *Comprehensive Psychiatry, 9,* 563–573. (2)

Keck, P. E., Jr., Calabrese, J. R., McQuade, R. D., Carson, W. H., Carlson, B. X., Rolli, L. M., et al. (2006). A randomized, double-blind, placebo-controlled, 26-week trial of aripiprazole in recently manic patients with bipolar I disorder. *Journal of Clinical Psychiatry, 67,* 626–637. (1)

Keck, P. E., Jr., & Licht, R. (2000). Antipsychotic medications in the treatment of mood disorders. In P. F. Buckley & J. L. Waddington (Eds.), *Schizophrenia and mood disorders: The new drug therapies in clinical practice* (pp. 199–211). Boston: Butterworth-Heinemann. (5)

Keck, P. E., Jr., Marcus, R., Tourkodimitris, S., Ali, M., Liebeskind, A., Saha, A., et al. (2003). A placebo-controlled, double-blind study of the efficacy and safety of aripiprazole in patients with acute bipolar mania. *American Journal of Psychiatry, 160,* 1651–1658. (1)

Keck, P. E., Jr., McElroy, S. L., & Nelson, E. B. (2003). Advances in the pharmacological treatment of bipolar depression. *Biological Psychiatry, 53,* 671–679. (4)

Keck, P. E., Jr., McElroy, S. L., & Nemeroff, C. B. (1992). Anticonvulsants in the treatment of bipolar disorder. *Journal of Neuropsychiatry and Clinical Neuroscience, 4,* 595–605. (5)

Keck, P. E., Jr., McElroy, S. L., Strakowski, S. M., West, S. A., Sax, K. W., Hawkins, J. M., et al. (1998). Twelve-month outcome of bipolar patients following hospitalization for a manic or mixed episode. *American Journal of Psychiatry, 155,* 646–652. (3)

Keck, P. E., Jr., McElroy, S. L., Tugrul, K. C., & Bennett, J. A. (1993). Valproate oral loading in the treatment of acute mania. *Journal of Clinical Psychiatry, 54,* 305–308. (3).

Keck, P. E., Jr., Mintz, J., McElroy, S. L., Freeman, M. P., Suppes, T., Frye, M. A., et al. (2006). Randomized, placebo-controlled trials of eicosapentanoic acid (EPA) in bipolar depression and rapid cycling bipolar disorder. *Biological Psychiatry, 36,* 1117–1119. (1)

Keck, P. E., Jr., Versiani, M., Potkin, S., West, S. A., Giller, E., Ice K., et al. (2003). Ziprasidone in the treatment of acute bipolar mania: A three-week, placebo-controlled, double-blind, randomized trial. *American Journal of Psychiatry, 160,* 741–748. (1)

Keck, P. E, Jr., Welge, J. A., & McElroy, S. L., Arnold, L. M., & Strakowski, S. M. (2000). Placebo effect in randomized, placebo-controlled maintenance studies of patients with bipolar disorder. *Biological Psychiatry, 47*, 756–759. (4)

Keck, P. E., Jr., Welge, J. A., Strakowski, S. M., Arnold, L. M., & McElroy, S. L. (2000). Placebo effect in randomized, controlled studies of acute bipolar mania and depression. *Biological Psychiatry, 47*, 748–755. (4)

Keller, M. B., Lavori, P. W., Kane, J. M., Gelenberg, A. J., Rosenbaum, J. F., Walzer, E. A., et al. (1992). Subsyndromal symptoms in bipolar disorder: A comparison of standard and low serum levels of lithium. *Archives of General Psychiatry, 49*, 371–376. (4)

Kessel, A., & Holt, F. (1975). A controlled study of tetra-cyclic antidepressant maprotiline (Ludiomil). *Medical Journal of Australia, 1*, 773–776. (2)

Kessler, R. C., Chiu, W. T., Demler, O., Merikangas, K. R., & Walters, E. E. (2005). Prevalence, severity, and comorbidity of 12-month DSM-IV disorders in the National Comorbidity Survey replication. *Archives of General Psychiatry, 62*, 617–627. (3)

Khanna, S., Vieta, E., Lyons, B., Grossman, F., Eerdekens, M., & Kramer, M. (2005). Risperidone in the treatment of acute bipolar mania: A double-blind, placebo-controlled trial of 290 patients. *British Journal of Psychiatry, 187*, 229–234. (1)

Klein, D. F. (1967). Importance of psychiatric diagnosis in prediction of clinical drug effects. *Archives of General Psychiatry, 16*, 118–126. (2)

Koukopoulos, A., Reginaldi, D., & Laddomada, P. (1980). Course of the manic-depressive cycle and changes caused by treatment. *Pharmakopsychiatrie Neuropsychopharmakologie, 13*, 156–167. (3)

Kramlinger, K. G., & Post, R. M. (1989). The addition of lithium to carbamazepine. *Archives of General Psychiatry, 46*, 794–800. (3)

Lattanzi, L., Dell'Osso, L., Cassano, P., Pini, S., Rucci, P., Houck, P. R., et al. (2002). Pramipexole in treatment-resistant depression: A 16-week naturalistic study. *Bipolar Disorders, 4*, 307–314. (3)

Lerer, B., Moore, N., Meyendorff, E., Cho, S. R., & Gershon, E. (1987). Carbamazepine versus lithium in mania: A double-blind study. *Journal of Clinical Psychiatry, 48*, 89–93. (2)

Levine, J., Barak, Y., Gonzalves, M., Szor, H., Elizur, A., Kotman, O., et al. (1995). Double-blind, controlled trial of inositol treatment of depression. *American Journal of Psychiatry, 152*, 792–794. (2)

Lusznat, R. M., Murphy, D. P., & Nunn, C. M. H. (1988). Carbamazepine versus lithium in the treatment and prophylaxis of mania. *British Journal of Psychiatry, 109*, 56–65. (2)

MacQueen, G. M., Young, L. T., Marriott, M., Robb, J., Begin, H., & Young, L. T. (2002). Previous mood state predicts response and switch rates in patients with bipolar depression. *Acta Psychiatrica Scandinavica, 105*, 414–418. (4)

Maggs, R. (1963). Treatment of manic illness with lithium carbonate. *British Journal of Psychiatry, 109*, 56–65. (2)

Maj, M. (2000). The impact of lithium prophylaxis on the course of bipolar disorder: A review of the research evidence. *Bipolar Disorders, 2*, 93–101. (4)

Maj, M., Pirozzi, R., & Kemali, D. (1991). Long-term outcome of lithium prophylaxis in bipolar patients. *Archives of General Psychiatry, 48*, 772. (3)

Mander, A. J. (1986). Clinical prediction of outcome and lithium response in bipolar affective disorder. *Journal of Affective Disorders, 11*, 35–41. (3)

McElroy, S. L., Altshuler, L. L., Suppes, T., Keck, P. E., Jr., Frye, M. A., Denicoff, K. D., et al. (2001). Axis I psychiatric comorbidity and its relationship to historical illness variables in 288 outpatients with bipolar disorder. *American Journal of Psychiatry, 158*, 420–426. (3)

McElroy, S. L., & Keck, P. E., Jr. (2004) Topiramate. In A. F. Schatzberg & C. B. Nemeroff (Eds.), *Textbook of psychopharmacology* (3rd ed., pp. 627–638). Washington, DC: American Psychiatric Publishing. (5)

McElroy, S. L., Keck, P. E., Jr., Stanton, S. P., Tugrul, K. C., Bennett, J. A., & Strakowski, S. M. (1996). A randomized comparison of divalproex oral loading versus haloperidol in the initial treatment of acute psychotic mania. *Journal of Clinical Psychiatry, 59*, 142–146. (2)

McElroy, S. L., Keck, P. E., Jr., & Strakowski, S. M. (1996). Mania, psychosis, and antipsychotics. *Journal of Clinical Psychiatry, 57*, 14–26. (5)

McElroy, S. L., Keck, P. E., Jr., Tugrul, K. C., & Bennett, J. A. (1993). Valproate as a loading treatment in acute mania. *Neuropsychobiology, 27*, 146–149. (3)

McElroy, S. L., Zarate, C. A., Cookson, J., Suppes, T., Huffman, R. F., Greene, P., et al. (2004). A 52-week, open-label continuation study of lamotrigine in the treatment of bipolar depression. *Journal of Clinical Psychiatry, 65*, 204–210. (3)

McIntyre, R. S., Brecher, M., Paulsson, B., Huizar, K., & Mullen, J. (2005). Quetiapine or haloperidol as monotherapy for bipolar mania: A 12-week, double-blind, randomized, parallel-group, placebo-controlled trial. *European Neuropsychopharmacology, 15*, 573–585. (1)

Meehan, K., Zhang, F., David, S., Tohen, M., Janicak, P., Small, J., et al. (2001). A double-blind, randomized comparison of the efficacy and safety of intra-muscular injections of olanzapine, lorazepam, or placebo in treating acutely agitated patients diagnosed with bipolar mania. *Journal of Clinical Psychopharmacology, 21,* 389–397. (1)

Mendels, J. (1976). Lithium in the treatment of depression. *American Journal of Psychiatry, 134,* 373–378. (2)

Mendlewicz, J., Fieve, R. R., & Stallone, F. (1973). Relationship between effectiveness of lithium therapy and family history. *American Journal of Psychiatry, 130,* 1011–1013. (3)

Miklowitz, D. J., Goldstein, M. J., Neuechterlein, K. H., Snyder, K. S., & Mintz, J. (1988). Family factors and the course of affective disorder. *Archives of General Psychiatry, 45,* 225–231. (4)

Miklowitz, D. J., Simoneau, T. L., George, E. L, Richards, J. A., Kalbag, A., Sachs-Ericsson, N., et al. (2000). Family-focused treatment of bipolar disorder: One-year effects of a psychoeducational program in conjunction with pharmacotherapy. *Biological Psychiatry, 48,* 582–592. (2)

Mitchell, P. B., Slade, T., & Andrews, G. (2004). Twelve-month prevalence and disability of DSM-IV bipolar disorder in an Australian general population survey. *Psychological Medicine, 34,* 777–785. (3)

Muller, A. A., & Stoll, K. D. (1984). Carbamazepine and oxcarbazepine in the treatment of manic syndromes: Studies in Germany. In H. M. Emrich, T. Okuma, & A. A. Muller (Eds.), *Anticonvulsants in affective disorders* (pp. 148–154). Amsterdam: Excerpta Medica. (2)

Muller-Oerlinghausen, B., Retzow, A., Henn, F. A., Giedke, H., & Walden, J. (1999). The European Valproate Mania Study Group: Valproate as an adjunct medication for the treatment of acute mania: A prospective, randomized, double-blind, placebo-controlled trial. *Journal of Clinical Psychopharmacology, 20,* 195–203. (1)

Murphy, D. J., Gannon, M. A., & McGennis, A. (1989). Carbamazepine in bipolar affective disorder. *Lancet, 2,* 1151–1152. (4)

Murray, C. J. L., & Lopez, A. D. (1996). *The global burden of disease: Summary.* Cambridge, MA: Harvard School of Public Health. (6)

Muzina, D. J., & Calabrese, J. R. (2003). Recent placebo-controlled acute trials in bipolar depression: Focus on methodology. *International Journal of Neuropsychopharmacology, 6,* 285–291. (4)

Nahas, Z., Kozel, F. A., Li, X., Anderson, B., & George, M. S. (2003). Left prefrontal transcranial magnetic resonance stimulation (TMS) treatment of depression in bipolar affective disorder: A pilot study of acute safety and efficacy. *Bipolar Disorders, 5,* 40–47. (2)

Nemeroff, C. B., Evans, D. L., Gyulai, L., Sachs, G. S., Bowden, C. L., Gergel, I. P., et al. (2001). Double-blind, placebo-controlled comparison of imipramine and paroxetine in the treatment of bipolar depression. *American Journal of Psychiatry, 158,* 906–912. (1)

Noyes, R., Dempsey, G. M., Blum, A., & Cavanaugh, G. L. (1974). Lithium treatment of depression. *Comprehensive Psychiatry, 15,* 187–193. (2)

Okuma, T., Inanga, K., Otsuki, S., Sarai, K., Takahashi, R., Hazama, H., et al. (1979). Comparison of the antimanic efficacy of carbamazepine and chlorpromazine. *Psychopharmacology, 66,* 211–217. (2)

Okuma, T., Inanga, K., Otsuki, S., Sarai, K., Takahashi, R., Hazama, H., et al. (1981). A preliminary study on the efficacy of carbamazepine prophylaxis of manic depressive illness. *Psychopharmacology, 73,* 95–96. (2)

Pande, A. C., Crockatt, J. G., Janney, C. A., Werth, G. L., & Tsaroucha, G. (2000). Gabapentin in bipolar disorder: A placebo-controlled trial of adjunctive therapy. *Bipolar Disorders, 2,* 249–255. (1)

Peet, M. (1994). Induction of mania with selective serotonin reuptake inhibitors and tricyclic antidepressants. *British Journal of Psychiatry, 164,* 549–550. (4)

Perlis, R. H., Sachs, G. S., Lafer, B., Otto, M., Faraone, S. V., Kane, J. M., et al. (2002). Effect of abrupt change from standard to low serum levels of lithium: A re-analysis of double-blind lithium maintenance data. *American Journal of Psychiatry, 159,* 1155–1159. (4)

Perugi, G., Ruffolo, G., Frare, F., & Toni, C. (2001). Adjunctive dopamine agonists in treatment-resistant bipolar II depression: An open case series. *Pharmacopsychiatry, 34,* 137–141. (3)

Placidi, G. F., Lenzi, A., Lazzerini, F., Cassano, G. B., & Akisal, H. S. (1986). The comparative efficacy and safety of carbamazepine versus lithium: A randomized, double-blind 3-year trial. *Journal of Clinical Psychiatry, 47,* 490–494. (2)

Platman, S. R. (1970). A comparison of lithium carbonate and chlorpromazine in mania. *American Journal of Psychiatry, 127,* 351–353. (2)

Pope, H. G., Jr., McElroy, S. L., Keck, P. E., Jr., & Hudson, J. I. (1991). Valproate in the treatment of acute mania: A placebo-controlled study. *Archives of General Psychiatry, 48,* 62–68. (1)

Post, R. M., Altshuler, L. L., Frye, M. A., Suppes, T., McElroy, S. L., Keck, P. E., Jr., et al. (2005). Preliminary observations on the effectiveness of levetiracetam in the open adjunctive treatment of refractory bipolar disorder. *Journal of Clinical Psychiatry, 66,* 370–374. (3)

Post, R. M, Altshuler, L. L., Frye, M. A., Suppes, T., Rush, A. J., Keck, P. E., Jr., et al. (2001). Rate of switch in bipolar patients prospectively treated with second-generation antidepressants as augmentation to mood stabilizers. *Bipolar Disorders, 3,* 259–265.

Post, R. M., Altshuler, L. L., Leverich, G. S., Suppes, T., McElroy, S. C., Keck, P. E., Jr., et al. (2004, September). Switch rate on velafaxine compared with bupropion and sertaline. *European Stanley Conference on Bipolar Disorder,* Aarhus, Denmark. (4)

Post, R. M., Berretini, W., Uhde, T. W., & Kellner, C. (1984). Selective response to the anticonvulsant carbamazepine in manic depressive illness: A case study. *Journal of Clinical Psychopharmacology, 4,* 178–185. (2)

Post, R. M., Uhde, T. W., & Roy-Byrne, P. P. (1986). Antidepressant effects of carbamazepine. *American Journal of Psychiatry, 43,* 29–34. (2)

Potkin, S., Keck, P. E., Jr., Segal, S., Ice, K., & English, P. (2005). Ziprasidone in acute bipolar mania: A 21-day randomized, double-blind, placebo-controlled replication trial. *Journal of Clinical Psychopharmacology, 25,* 818–820. (1)

Prien, R. F., Caffey, E. M., Jr., & Klett, C. J. (1972). Comparison of lithium carbonate and chlorpromazine in the treatment of mania: Report of the Veterans Administration and National Institute of Mental Health Collaborative Study Group. *Archives of General Psychiatry, 26,* 146–153. (1)

Prien, R. F., Caffey, E. M., Jr., & Klett, C. J. (1974). Factors associated with treatment success in lithium carbonate prophylaxis. *Archives of General Psychiatry, 31,* 189–192. (3)

Prien, R. F., & Gelenberg, A. J. (1989). Alternatives to lithium for preventative treatment of bipolar disorder. *American Journal of Psychiatry, 146,* 840–848. (5)

Prien, R. F., Kupfer, D. J., Mansky, P. A., Small, J. G., Tuason, V. B., Voss, C. B., et al. (1984). Drug therapy in the prevention of recurrences in unipolar and bipolar affective disorders: Report of the NIMH Collaborative Study Group comparing lithium carbonate, imipramine, and a lithium carbonate-imipramine combination. *Archives of General Psychiatry, 41,* 1096–1104. (1)

Raja, M., & Azzoni, A. (2003). Oxcarbazepine vs. valproate in the treatment of mood and schizoaffective disorders. *International Journal of Neuropsychopharmacology, 6,* 409–414. (3)

Ramey, T. S., Giller, E. L., English, P., & Ice, K. (2005, June). Ziprasidone efficacy and safety in acute bipolar mania: 12-week study. *Abstracts of the 6th International Conference on Bipolar Disorders,* Pittsburgh, PA. (1)

Revicki, D. A., Hirschfeld, R. M. A., Ahearn, E. P., Weisler, R. H., Palmer, C., Keck, P. E., Jr., et al. (2005). Effectiveness and medical costs of divalproex versus lithium in the treatment of bipolar disorder: Results of a naturalistic clinical trial. *Journal of Affective Disorders, 86,* 183–193. (2)

Rouillon, F., Lejoyeaux, M., & Filteau, M. J. (1992). Unwanted effects of long-term treatment. In S. A. Montgomery & F. Rouillon (Eds.), *Long-term treatment of depression* (pp. 84–88). New York: Wiley. (5)

Sachs, G. S., Chengappa, K. N. R., Suppes, T., Mullen, J. A., Brecher, M., Devine, N. A., et al. (2004). Quetiapine with lithium or divalproex for the treatment of bipolar mania: A randomized, double-blind, placebo-controlled study. *Bipolar Disorders, 6,* 213–223. (1)

Sachs, G. S., Collins, M. A., & Altshuler, L. L. (2001, December). Divalproex sodium versus placebo for the treatment of bipolar depression. *Abstracts of the 40th Annual Meeting of the American College of Neuropsychopharmacology.* San Juan, Puerto Rico. (2)

Sachs, G. S., Grossman, F., Ghaemi, S. N., Okamoto, A., & Bowden, C. L. (2002). Combination mood stabilizer with risperidone or haloperidol for treatment of acute mania: A double-blind, placebo-controlled comparison of efficacy and safety. *American Journal of Psychiatry, 159,* 1146–1154. (1)

Sachs, G. S., Koslow, C. L., & Ghaemi, S. N. (2000). The treatment of bipolar depression. *Bipolar Disorders, 2,* 256–260. (4)

Sachs, G. S., Lafer, B., Stoll, A., Banov, M., Thibault, A. B., Tohen, M., et al. (1994). A double-blind trial of bupropion versus desipramine for bipolar depression. *Journal of Clinical Psychiatry, 55,* 391–393. (2)

Saksa, J., Baker, C. B., & Woods, S. W. (2004). Mood-stabilizer-maintained, remitted bipolar patients: Taper and discontinuation of adjunctive antipsychotic medication. *General Hospital Psychiatry, 26,* 233–236. (2)

Salloum, I. M., Cornelius, J. R., Daley, D. C., Kirisei, L., Himmelhoch, J. M., Thase, M. E., et al. (2005). Efficacy of valproate maintenance in patients with bipolar disorder and alcoholism: A double-blind placebo-controlled study. *Archives of General Psychiatry, 62,* 37–45. (1)

Schou, M., Juel-Nielson, N., Stromgren, E., & Voldby, H. (1954). The treatment of manic psychoses by administration of lithium salts. *Journal of Neurology, Neurosurgery, and Psychiatry, 17,* 250–260. (2)

Segal, J., Berk, M., & Brook, S. (1998). Risperidone compared with both lithium and haloperidol in mania: A double-blind randomized controlled trial. *Journal of Clinical Neuropharmacology, 21*, 176–180. (2)

Shelton, R. C., & Stahl, S. M. (2004). Risperidone and paroxetine given singly and in combination for bipolar depression. *Journal of Clinical Psychiatry, 65*, 1715-1719. (2)

Shelton, R. C., Tollefson, G. D., Tohen, M., Stahl, S., Gannon, K. S., Jacobs, T. G., et al. (2001). A novel augmentation strategy for treating resistant major depression. *American Journal of Psychiatry, 158*, 131–134. (1)

Shopsin, B., Gershon, S., Thompson, H., & Collins, P. (1975). Psychoactive drugs in mania: A controlled comparison of lithium carbonate, chlorpromazine, and haloperidol. *Archives of General Psychiatry, 32*, 34–42. (2)

Silverstone, T. (for the Moclobemide Study Group). (2001). Moclobemide vs. imipramine in bipolar depression: A multicenter double blind clinical trial. *Acta Psychiatrica Scandinavica, 104*, 104–109. (2)

Small, J. G. (1990). Anticonvulsants in affective disorders. *Psychopharmacology Bulletin, 26*, 25–36. (2)

Smulevich, A. B., Khanna, S., Eerdekens, M., Karcher, K., Kramer, M., & Grossman, F. (2005). Acute and continuation risperidone monotherapy in bipolar mania: A 3-week placebo-controlled trial followed by a 9-week double-blind trial of risperidone and haloperidol. *European Neuropsychopharmacology, 15*, 75–84. (2)

Solomon, D. A., Ryan, C. E., Keitner, G. I., Miller, I. W., Shea, M. T., Kazim, A., et al. (1997). A pilot study of lithium carbonate plus divalproex sodium for the continuation and maintenance treatment of patients with bipolar I disorder. *Journal of Clinical Psychiatry, 58*, 95–99. (2)

Sporn, J., Ghaemi, S. N., Sambur, M. R., & Rankin, R. A. (2000). Pramipexole augmentation in the treatment of unipolar and bipolar depression: A retrospective chart review. *Annals of Clinical Psychiatry, 12*, 137–140. (3)

Spring, G., Schweid, D., Gray, C., Steinberg, J., & Horwitz, M. (1970). A double-blind comparison of lithium and chlorpromazine in the treatment of manic states. *American Journal of Psychiatry, 126*, 10–13. (2)

Stokes, P. E., Shamoian, C. A., Stoll, P. M., & Patton, M. J. (1971). Efficacy of lithium as acute treatment of manic-depressive illness. *Lancet, 1*, 1319–1325. (2)

Stoll, A., Severus, W. E., Freeman, M. P., Reuter, S., Zboyan, H. A., Diamond, E., et al. (1999). Omega 3 fatty acids in bipolar disorder: A preliminary double-blind, placebo-controlled trial. *Archives of General Psychiatry, 56*, 407–412. (2)

Suppes, T., Baldessarini, R. J., Faedda, G. L., & Tohen, M. (1991). Risk of recurrence following discontinuation of lithium in bipolar disorder. *Archives of General Psychiatry, 48*, 1082–1088. (4)

Suppes, T., Chisholm, K. A., Dhavale, D., Frye, M. A., Altshuler, L. L., McElroy, S. L., et al. (2002). Tiagabine in treatment refractory bipolar disorder: A clinical case series. *Bipolar Disorders, 4*, 283–289. (3)

Suppes, T., Dennehy, E. B., Hirschfeld, R. M. A., Altshuler, L. L., Bowden, C. L., Calabrese, J. R., et al. (2005). The Texas implementation of medications algorithms: Update to the algorithms for treatment of bipolar I disorder. *Journal of Clinical Psychiatry, 66*, 870–886. (5)

Swann, A. C., Bowden, C. L., Calabrese, J. R., Dilsaver, S. C., & Morris, D. D. (1999). Differential effects of number of previous episodes of affective disorder in response to lithium or divalproex in acute mania. *American Journal of Psychiatry, 156*, 1264–1266. (4)

Swann, A. C., Bowden, C. L., Morris, D., Calabrese, J. R., Petty, F., Small, J., et al. (1997). Depression during mania: Treatment response to lithium or divalproex. *Archives of General Psychiatry, 54*, 37–42. (4)

Takahashi, R., Sakuma, A., Itoh, K., Itoh, H., & Kurihara, M. (1975). Comparison of the efficacy of lithium carbonate and chlorpromazine in mania: Report of the collaborative study group of treatment in Japan. *Archives of General Psychiatry, 32*, 1310–1318. (2)

Tohen, M., Baker, R. W., Altshuler, L. L., Zarate, C. A., Jr., Suppes, T., Ketter, J. A., et al. (2002). Olanzapine versus divalproex in the treatment of acute mania. *American Journal of Psychiatry, 159*, 1011–1017. (1)

Tohen, M., Calabrese, J. R., Sachs, G. S., Banov, M. B., Detke, H. C., Risser, R., et al. (2006). A randomized, placebo-controlled trial of olanzapine as maintenance therapy in patients with bipolar I disorder responding to acute olanzapine treatment. *American Journal of Psychiatry, 163*, 247–256. (1)

Tohen, M., Chengappa, K. N. R., Suppes, T., Zarate, C. A., Calabrese, J. R., & Bowden, C. L. (2002). Efficacy of olanzapine in the treatment of mania in patients partially responsive to lithium or valproate. *Archives of General Psychiatry, 59*, 62–69. (1)

Tohen, M., Chengappa, K. N. R., Suppes, T., Baker, R. W., Zarate, C. A., Bowden, C. L., et al. (2004). Relapse prevention in bipolar I disorder: 18-month comparison of olanzapine plus mood stabilizer v. mood stabilizer alone. *British Journal of Psychiatry, 184,* 337–345. (1)

Tohen, M., Goldberg, J. F., Gonzalez-Pinto, A., Azorin, J. M., Azorin, A. M., & Vieta, E. (2003). A 12-week, double-blind comparison of olanzapine vs. haloperidol in the treatment of acute mania. *Archives of General Psychiatry, 60,* 1218–1226. (1)

Tohen, M., Greil, W., Calabrese, J. R., Sachs, G. S., Yatham, L. N., Oerlinghausen, B., et al. (2005). Olanzapine versus lithium in the maintenance treatment of bipolar disorder: A 12-month, randomized, double-blind, controlled clinical trial. *American Journal of Psychiatry, 162,* 1281–1290. (1)

Tohen, M., Jacobs, T. G., Grundy, S. L., McElroy, S. L., Banov, M. C., Janicak, P. G., et al. (2000). Efficacy of olanzapine in acute bipolar mania: A double-blind, placebo-controlled study. *Archives of General Psychiatry, 57,* 841–849. (1)

Tohen, M., Ketter, T. A., Zarate, C. A., Suppes, T., Frye, M., Altshuler, L., et al. (2003). Olanzapine versus divalproex sodium for the treatment of acute mania and maintenance of remission: A 47-week study. *American Journal of Psychiatry, 160,* 1263–1271. (2)

Tohen, M., Sanger, T. M., McElroy, S. L., Tollefson, G. D., Chengappa, K. N., Daniel, D. G., et al. (1999). Olanzapine versus placebo in the treatment of acute mania. *American Journal of Psychiatry, 156,* 702–709. (1)

Tohen, M., Vieta, E., Calabrese, J., Ketter, T. A., Sachs, G. S., Bowden, C. L., et al. (2003). Efficacy of olanzapine and olanzapine-fluoxetine combination in the treatment of bipolar I depression. *Archives of General Psychiatry, 60,* 1079–1088. (1)

Tondo, L., Hennen, J., & Baldessarini, R. J. (2001). Lower suicide risk with long-term lithium treatment in major affective illness: A meta-analysis. *Acta Psychiatrica Scandinavica, 104,* 163–172. (4)

Vieta, E., Bourin, M., Sanchez, R., Marcus, R., Stock, E., McQuade, R., et al. (2005). Effectiveness of aripiprazole v. haloperidol in acute bipolar mania: double-blind, randomized, comparative 12-week trial. *British Journal of Psychiatry, 187,* 235–242. (1)

Vieta, E., Brugue, E., Goikolea, J. M., Sanchez-Moreno, J., Reinares, M., Comes, M., et al. (2004). Acute and continuation risperidone monotherapy in mania. *Human Psychopharmacology, 19,* 41–45. (3)

Vieta, E., Herraiz, M., Parramon, G., Goikolea, J. M., Fernandez, A., & Benabarre, A. (2002). Risperidone in the treatment of mania: Efficacy and safety results from a large, multicentre, open study in Spain. *Journal of Affective Disorders, 72,* 15–19. (2)

Vieta, E., Martinez-Aran, A., Goikolea, J. M., Torrent, C., Colom, F., Benabarre, A., et al. (2002). A randomized trial comparing paroxetine and venlafaxine in the treatment of bipolar depressed patients taking mood stabilizers. *Journal of Clinical Psychiatry, 63,* 508–512. (2)

Vieta, E., Mullen, J., Brecher, M., Paulsson, B., & Jones, M. (2005). Quetiapine monotherapy for mania associated with bipolar disorder: Combined analysis of two international, double-blind, randomized, controlled studies. *Current Medical Research and Opinion, 21,* 923–934. (4)

Walton, S., Berk, M., & Brook, S. (1996). Superiority of lithium over verapamil in mania: A randomized, controlled, single-blind trial. *Journal of Clinical Psychiatry, 57,* 543–546. (2)

Watanabe, S., Ishino, H., & Otsuki, S. (1975). Double-blind comparison of lithium and imipramine in treatment of depression. *Archives of General Psychiatry, 32,* 659-668. (2)

Watkins, S. E., Callendar, K., & Thomas, D. R. (1987). The effect of carbamazepine and lithium on remission from affective illness. *British Journal of Psychiatry, 150,* 180–182. (2)

Weisler, R. H., Dunn, J., & English, P. (2003, September). Ziprasidone in adjunctive treatment of acute bipolar mania: A randomized, double-blind placebo-controlled trial. *Abstracts of the 16th Annual Meeting of the European College of Neuropsychopharmacology,* Prague, Czech Republic. (2)

Weisler, R. H., Kalali, A. H., Ketter, T. A., & SPD417 Study Group. (2004). A multicenter, randomized, double-blind, placebo-controlled trial of extended-release carbamazepine capsules as monotherapy for bipolar disorder patients with manic or mixed episodes. *Journal of Clinical Psychiatry, 65,* 478–484. (1)

Weisler, R. H., Keck, P. E., Jr., Swann, A. C., Culter, A. J., Ketter, T. A., Kalali, A. H., et al. (2005). Extended-release carbamazepine capsules as monotherapy for acute mania in bipolar disorder: A multicenter, randomized, double-blind, placebo-controlled trial. *Journal of Clinical Psychiatry, 66,* 323–330. (1)

Yatham, L. N., Grossman, F., Augustyns, I., Vieta, E., & Ravindran, A. (2003). Mood stabilizers plus risperidone or placebo in the treatment of acute mania: International, double-blind, randomized, controlled trial. *British Journal of Psychiatry, 182,* 141–147. (1)

Yatham, L. N., Paulsson, B., Mullen, J., & Vagaro, A. M. (2004). Quetiapine versus placebo in combination with lithium or divalproex for the treatment of bipolar mania. *Journal of Clinical Psychopharmacology, 24,* 599–606. (1)

Young, L. T., Joffe, R. T., Robb, J. C., MacQueen, G. M., Marriott, M., Patelis-Siotis, I., et al. (2000). Double-blind comparison of addition of a second mood stabilizer versus an antidepressant to an initial mood stabilizer for treatment of patients with bipolar depression. *American Journal of Psychiatry, 157,* 124–126. (2)

Zajecka, J. M., Weisler, R., Sachs, G., Swann, A. C., Wozniak, P., Sommerville, K. W. (2002). A comparison of the efficacy, safety, and tolerability of divalproex sodium and olanzapine in the treatment of bipolar disorder. *Journal of Clinical Psychiatry, 63,* 1148–1155. (2)

Zarate, C. A., Jr., Payne, J. L., Quiroz, J., Sporn, J., Denicoff, K. D., Luckenbaugh, D. A., et al. (2004). An open-label trial of riluzole in patients with treatment-resistant major depression. *American Journal of Psychiatry, 161,* 171–174. (3)

Zarate, C. A., Jr., Payne, J. L., Singh, J., Quiroz, J., Luckenbaugh, D. A., Denicoff, K. D., et al. (2004). Pramipexole for bipolar II depression: A placebo-controlled proof of concept study. *Biological Psychiatry, 56,* 54–60. (2)

Zarate, C. A., Jr., Quiroz, J. A., Singh, J. B., Denicoff, K. D., DeJesus, G., Luckenbaugh, D. A., et al. (2005). An open-label trial of the glutamate-modulating agent riluzole in combination with lithium for the treatment of bipolar depression. *Biological Psychiatry, 57,* 430–432. (3)

Zarate, C. A., Jr., & Tohen, M. (2004). Double-blind comparison of the continued use of antipsychotic treatment versus its discontinuation in remitted manic patients. *American Journal of Psychiatry, 161,* 169–171. (2)

Zornberg, G. L., & Pope, H. G., Jr. (1993). Treatment of depression in bipolar disorder: New directions for research. *Journal of Clinical Psychopharmacology, 13,* 397–408. (4)

13

Psychological Treatments for Panic Disorders, Phobias, and Generalized Anxiety Disorder

David H. Barlow

Laura B. Allen

Shawnee L. Basden

A substantial number of excellent studies, largely Type 1, have established the clinical efficacy of situational in vivo exposure for patients with panic disorder with moderate to severe agoraphobia. A substantial number of Type 1 studies have established the efficacy of cognitive-behavioral treatments for persons with panic disorder with no more than mild agoraphobia; these treatments focus on cognitive therapy, exposure to interoceptive sensations similar to physiological panic sensations, and breathing retraining. One large clinical trial (Type 1) has been reported that explores the efficacy of separate and combined psychological and pharmacological treatment of panic disorder. Recently, two large effectiveness trials (Type 1) have established successful dissemination of the cognitive-behavioral treatment. The treatment of choice for specific phobias is exposure-based procedures, particularly in vivo exposure; this consensus reflects a very large number of Type 1 studies of these procedures with patients with specific phobias. The most common treatment approaches to social phobia include social skills training (SST), relaxation techniques, exposure-based methods, and multicomponent cognitive-behavioral treatments, with the latter, as well as exposure-based procedures, attaining the highest level of treatment efficacy in Type 1 studies. In early studies, different treatment conditions for patients with generalized anxiety disorder (GAD) did not lead to differential improvement rates, although most studies showed that active treatments were superior to nondirective approaches and uniformly superior to no treatment. Recently, however, a few studies have suggested that the most successful psychological treatments for GAD combine relaxation exercises and cognitive therapy with the goal of bringing the worry process itself under the patient's control.

The development of empirically supported psychological treatments has been, perhaps, most evident in the appearance of effective new treatments for anxiety disorders, particularly during the last decade. Prior to 1970, anxiety disorders were a highly prevalent but ill-defined group of problems subsumed under the general headings of "anxiety neuroses" or "phobic neuroses." Treatment of neurosis was most often carried out in the context of long-term psychotherapy, with little or no evidence available on the efficacy of this approach (Barlow, 1988; Hayes, Barlow, & Nelson-Gray, 1999). During the late 1960s and into the 1970s, clinical trials began to establish the efficacy of exposure-based treatments for phobic disorders, specifically agoraphobia and specific phobias. In addition, early experimental analyses began to appear suggesting the efficacy of specific psychological treatments for obsessive-compulsive disorder (e.g., Mills, Agras, Barlow, & Mills, 1973; Rachman & Hodgson, 1980).

The successful delineation of specific anxiety disorders with the appearance of the third edition of the *Diagnostic and Statistical Manual of Mental Disorders (DSM-III)* in 1980 (American Psychiatric Association [APA], 1980) led to the development of more structured and targeted psychological and drug treatments. From the period 1985 through 1995, effective and empirically supported psychological treatments were developed for panic disorder with no more than mild agoraphobia, generalized anxiety disorder, and social phobia, as well as post-traumatic stress disorder (Barlow, 1996; Barlow & Lehman, 1996). In addition, substantial improvements were made in the treatment of panic disorder with agoraphobia and certain varieties of specific phobia as our knowledge of the psychopathology and pathophysiology of these conditions deepened. From 1995 through 2005, additional evidence accumulated on the efficacy and effectiveness of these procedures, particularly from major clinical trials, including those evaluating the separate and combined effects of these approaches and pharmacological treatments.

In this chapter, we review systematically the current status of the evidence regarding efficacious empirically supported treatments for panic disorder with and without agoraphobia, specific phobia, social phobia, and generalized anxiety disorder. This is followed by a brief concluding section on future directions in treatment development and research for these disorders.

Empirical studies are evaluated according to a template created by the American Psychological Association to guide the development of practice guidelines (APA, 2002; American Psychological Association Task Force on Psychological Intervention Guidelines, 1995). This template evaluates studies along two axes, one that examines the treatments' efficacy (internal validity) and a second that examines the clinical utility (effectiveness or external validity) of the treatments being researched. This template is depicted in Table 13.1. The studies held to the most rigorous research standards are classified as Type 1 studies, whereas those that fall short of this standard of excellence are classified as Type 2 studies. Research studies conducted with more substantial methodological limitations are classified as Type 3 through Type 6 studies.

PANIC DISORDER WITH AGORAPHOBIA

Though panic attacks have been discussed in the literature over the centuries (e.g., Freud 1895/1961), they were largely ignored by the diagnostic system until the last few decades. The diagnoses of panic disorder and of agoraphobia with panic attacks were not included in the diagnostic system until the publication of *DSM-III* in 1980 (APA, 1980). The most recent version of this diagnostic system, the fourth edition, text revision, (*DSM-IV-TR;* APA, 2000), includes the related diagnoses of panic disorder without agoraphobia (PD), panic disorder with agoraphobia (PDA), and agoraphobia without history of panic disorder.

Individuals diagnosed with panic disorder report experiencing recurrent unexpected panic attacks that consist of physical symptoms such as racing heart, shortness of breath, dizziness, sweating, and trembling or shaking. Moreover, they experience continued anxiety focused on experiencing future panic attacks and worry about consequences of the panic attacks or changes in their behavior due to the panic attacks. It is the additional anxiety about the attacks, combined with catastrophic cognitions in the face of panic, that distinguishes individuals with panic disorder from nonclinical panickers (Craske & Barlow, 2001). In addition, those with agoraphobia avoid situations that trigger panic attacks, and for which escape would be difficult in the event of a panic attack, such as crowded shopping malls, restaurants, or movie theaters. Finally, individuals are diagnosed with agoraphobia without history of panic disorder when they experience agoraphobic avoidance due to anxiety focused on specific somatic symptoms, some of which may be defining symptoms of a panic attack yet have never met criteria for a full, unexpected panic attack. It should be noted that, clinically, patients presenting with agoraphobia without history of panic disorder can be treated with protocols intended for patients with panic disorder with agoraphobia, and they will usually benefit from such treatment (Craske & Barlow, 2001).

Reports on the prevalence of panic disorder, panic disorder with agoraphobia, and agoraphobia without history of panic disorder vary somewhat. The National Comorbidity Survey (NCS), conducted in the United States, cited a lifetime prevalence for

TABLE 13.1 Overview of Template for Constructing Psychological Intervention Guidelines

Efficacy (Internal Validity)	*Clinical Utility or Effectiveness (External Validity)*

1. Better than alternative therapy
2. Better than nonspecific therapy (RCTs)
3. Better than no therapy (RCTs)
4. Quantified clinical observations
5. Strongly positive clinical consensus
6. Mixed clinical consensus
7. Strongly negative clinical consensus
8. Contradictory evidence
 	
Note: Confidence in treatment efficacy is based on both (a) the absolute and relative efficacy of the treatment and (b) the quality of the studies on which the judgment is made, as well as their replicability. Confidence in efficacy increases from item 8 (lowest) to item 1 (highest).
	1. Feasibility
	  a. Patient acceptability (cost, pain, duration, side effects, etc.)
	  b. Patient choice in face of relatively equal efficacy
	  c. Probability of compliance
	  d. Ease of disseminability (e.g., number of practitioners with competence, requirements for training, opportunities for training, need for costly technologies or additional support personnel)
	
	2. Generalizability
	  a. Patient characteristics: cultural background issues, gender issues, developmental issues, other relevant patient characteristics
	  b. Therapist characteristics
	  c. Issues of robustness when applied in practice settings with different time frames and the like
	  d. Contextual factors regarding setting in which treatment is delivered
	
	3. Costs and benefits
	  a. Costs of delivering intervention to individual and society
	  b. Costs of withholding effective intervention from individual and society
	
	Note: Confidence in clinical utility as reflected on these dimensions should be based on systematic and objective methods and strategies for assessing these characteristics of treatment as they are applied in actual practice. In some cases, randomized clinical trials will exist. More often, data will be in the form of quantified clinical observations (clinical replication series) or other strategies such as health economic calculations.

RCT = randomized clinical trial.

Source: From American Psychological Association Task Force on Psychological Intervention Guidelines (1995). Used with permission.

panic disorder with or without agoraphobia at 3.5% of the population (Kessler et al., 1994). This same report noted the lifetime prevalence of agoraphobia without history of panic disorder to be 5.3% of the population. Differences between these figures and earlier epidemiological reports may be due to different geographic areas sampled, different age ranges surveyed, and the utilization of different research methods. Kessler et al. (1994) utilized a more advanced methodology than previous surveys had; consequently, the results of the NCS are considered to be more credible than other epidemiological data currently available. In a replication of the NCS, the NCS-R, Kessler, Berglund, Demler, Jin, and Walters (2005) utilized the updated *DSM-IV* rather than the *DSM-III-R* to assign psychological disorders. As a result, changes in prevalence rated may reflect a change in diagnostic criteria rather than actual changes in the community. The NCS-R noted the prevalence of panic disorder with or without agoraphobia at 4.7% of the population, and the prevalence of agoraphobia without a history of panic at 1.4% of the population. These rates reflect an increase in the prevalence rated for PDA/PD and a dramatic decrease in the rates of agoraphobia without panic.

Finally, it seems that many more women than men experience these disorders. A meta-analysis found that fully three fourths of the participants in research studies on the treatment of the panic disorders are women (Gould, Otto, & Pollack, 1995). In addition, the NCS found the lifetime prevalences of panic dis-order and agoraphobia without history of panic disor-der for women to be at least twice those listed for men (5.0% and 7.0% vs. 2.0% and 3.5%, respectively; Kessler et al., 1994). These findings replicate the sex ratio in earlier reports (e.g., Myers et al., 1984; Thorpe & Burns, 1983). Sex differences in the preva-lence of panic disorder and agoraphobia were not re-ported in the NCS-R. The most common explana-tion for this marked difference in prevalence among men and women involves cultural factors. In most cultures around the world, it is more acceptable for women to report fear and to avoid various situations due to this fear. Men, however, are expected to mini-mize their fears and overcome avoidant tendencies regardless of the cost. Many men seem to turn to alcohol to self-medicate their anxiety and panic (Bar-low, 1988, 2002; Kushner, Abrams, & Borchardt, 2000).

Most individuals with panic disorder can clearly recall life stressors that occurred around the time they experienced the onset of their panic attacks. One study noted that 72% of patients with panic dis-order reported life stress existing when their panic attacks began (Craske, Miller, Rotunda, & Barlow, 1990). Moreover, patients with panic disorder often experience other Axis I disorders concurrent with their panic disorder (Brown, Campbell, Lehman, Grisham, & Mancill, 2001; Sanderson, Di Nardo, Rapee, & Barlow, 1990), and studies have noted that between 25 and 75% of patients with panic disorder meet criteria for an Axis II personality disorder, most often avoidant or dependent personality disorders (Chambless & Renneberg, 1988; Reich, Noyes, & Troughton, 1987).

Our own model of etiology, referred to as the "tri-ple vulnerabilities model" (Barlow, 2002), posits a nonspecific biological predisposition to experience stress or emotionality and possibly a separate herita-bility for a low threshold to experience panic attacks (the first vulnerability). Specifically, this generalized biological predisposition, combined with early devel-opment of a sense of uncontrollability over poten-tially threatening life events (a generalized psycho-logical predisposition; the second vulnerability), creates a diathesis. The later experience of life stress then triggers an unexpected panic attack, and in those with first and second vulnerabilities (the diathesis), and a specific psychological vulnerability to focus anxiety on "dangerous" somatic symptoms (the third

vulnerability), anxiety becomes focused on the next possible panic attack, and panic disorder subsequently develops. Agoraphobia may then follow as a compli-cation of panic disorder in a large proportion of these individuals, mostly women (Barlow, 1988, 2000, 2002; Barlow, Chorpita, & Turovsky, 1996).

In this section, we first review the development and evaluation of early treatments for agoraphobia (in vivo exposure), and then provide a description of the development and evaluation of psychological treatments targeting PDA and PD. More cost-effec-tive treatments are reviewed, as well as translational research (effectiveness studies). Finally, combination treatments are discussed, as well as future directions in treatment development and assessment for this disorder.

Treatment of Agoraphobia (Situational In Vivo Exposure)

There has been a long-standing controversy regard-ing the nature of the relationship between PD and agoraphobia, and there has been some debate among clinicians about whether agoraphobia without a his-tory of panic (AWOPD) actually exists (Barlow, 2000). The DSM-III considered agoraphobia to be a separate phobic disorder (APA, 1980); with the publi-cation of the DSM-III-R (APA, 1987), however, ago-raphobia was viewed as diagnostically secondary to PD. This change was primarily the result of findings that suggested that, in clinical samples, agoraphobia typically developed as a result of the experience of panic attacks or limited symptoms attacks (Craske & Barlow, 1988; Turner, Williams, Beidel, & Mezzich, 1986). Accordingly, the development of treatments specifically designed to address agoraphobia occurred primarily in the 1960s and 1970s.

One of these initial treatments was systematic de-sensitization. This procedure involved imaginal ex-posure to feared situations coupled with muscle re-laxation. Systematic desensitization was used at that time, since it was believed that actual exposure to feared situations (situational in vivo exposure) might be too intense and would have deleterious effects. Studies conducted to examine the efficacy of system-atic desensitization consistently found this approach to be largely ineffective (Gelder & Marks, 1966; Marks, 1971). During this same era, researchers be-gan to treat patients with agoraphobia successfully by conducting graduated in vivo exposure exercises

(Agras, Leitenberg, & Barlow, 1968). In this procedure, patients, under the supervision of a clinician, were expected to engage in exposure practices by which they systematically ventured away from safe places and into the situations they had been avoiding.

During the next several years, situational in vivo exposure continued to be evaluated and was found to be more effective than no treatment or attentional control procedures (Barlow, 1988, 2002; Jansson & Öst, 1982; Mavissakalian & Barlow, 1981). Situational in vivo exposure treatment routinely begins with the patient creating a hierarchy of feared situations or activities that have been consistently avoided. Examples of such items include driving out of a safety zone (which may be either several blocks or several miles from the home), shopping in a crowded mall alone, and going out to dinner in a restaurant or seeing a movie in a theater. Patients are then encouraged to repeatedly enter and remain in these feared situations, utilizing therapeutic coping procedures learned during sessions, until their anxiety diminishes. Although patients with more severe agoraphobia may require the presence of their therapist during the initial exposures, most patients are able to conduct these exercises either alone or with a friend or family member who acts as a supportive coach (Barlow, 1988, 2002).

Throughout the past few decades, researchers have examined the clinical efficacy of situational in vivo exposure utilizing the highest methodological standards. Nearly all these studies fall into the top two categories of the internal validity axis (Axis 1) of the APA template; moreover, the vast majority also can be characterized as Type 1 studies according to the classification system of this volume. These studies have consistently shown evidence of the efficacy of situational in vivo exposure; the current consensus among researchers is that situational in vivo exposure is a highly effective treatment for many patients with panic disorder with agoraphobia.

Several reviews and meta-analyses conducted in the 1980s found that 60 to 75% of patients who completed situational in vivo exposure treatments show evidence of clinical improvement (Barlow, 1988, 2002; Jacobson, Wilson, & Tupper, 1988; Jansson & Öst, 1982; Munby & Johnston, 1980; Trull, Nietzel, & Main, 1988). Yet relatively few of these patients were "cured" or completely symptom free at the conclusion of their exposure treatment. However, clinical gains that were achieved from this approach were maintained at long-term follow-up. For example, Jansson, Jerremalm, and Öst (1986) reported maintenance of gains and some continued improvement at a 15-month follow-up. Burns, Thorpe, and Cavallaro (1986) also noted continuation of gains up to 8 years following treatment, albeit punctuated by brief setbacks.

Fava, Zielezny, Savron, and Grandi (1995) have also published long-term follow-up results of their research on exposure-based treatments for agoraphobia conducted in Bologna, Italy. This study falls into the Type 2 category due to the lack of a comparison group in the study design. However, since the efficacy of situational in vivo exposure has been proved extensively in the past, many researchers currently studying situational in vivo exposure do not view a comparison treatment group as a necessary treatment component in this type of research. Fava and his colleagues (1995) treated more than 90 patients with 12 sessions of self-paced, graduated, exposure-based treatment. These 30-minute sessions were administered biweekly over a 6-month period. At the end of treatment, 87% of the patients were panic free and considered to be much improved on the global clinical measures. These patients were then followed for up to 7 years after treatment, with 67% still in remission at that point in time.

Using survival analysis to estimate the probability that the patients would remain in remission after they successfully completed exposure treatment, results indicated that 96% of the patients remained in remission throughout the first 2 years after treatment. In addition, 77% of the patients remained in remission throughout the first 5 years after treatment, and 67% for the first 7 years after the completion of exposure treatment. Study results indicated that residual agoraphobia and the presence of a personality disorder were the most significant predictors of relapse for the patients in the study.

Strategies to Improve the Effectiveness of Exposure-Based Procedures

Researchers have tried a number of strategies to improve the effectiveness of situational, in vivo, exposure-based treatments. For example, a number of studies attempted to determine whether adding relaxation training to situational in vivo exposure would improve the clinical efficacy of the situational in vivo exposure. In most of these studies, the combined treatments were no more effective than situational in vivo exposure alone (Michelson, Mavissakalian, & Marchione, 1988; Öst, Hellström, & Westling, 1989; Öst, Jerremalm, & Jansson, 1984). In addition, researchers have attempted to improve the efficacy of situational in vivo exposure by adding cognitive therapy components such as paradoxical intention or Beck and Emery's (1985) cognitive therapy to exposure protocols. Again, the combined treatments were most often found to be no more effective than situational in vivo exposure alone (Emmelkamp, Brilman, Kuiper, & Mersch, 1986; Emmelkamp & Mersch, 1982; Michelson et al., 1988; Öst et al., 1989; Williams & Rappaport, 1983). Finally, three controlled studies examining the effectiveness of situational in vivo exposure and breathing retraining found the combined treatment to be no more effective than situational in vivo exposure alone and may in fact detract from optimal treatment outcomes (Bonn, Readhead, & Timmons, 1984; Craske, Rowe, Lewin, & Noriega-Dimitri, 1997; De Ruiter, Rijken, Garssen, & Kraaimaat, 1989; Schmidt et al., 2000). However, when considering the use of any of these added elements to traditional in vivo exposure, one must consider the potential for that element to act as a "safety aid." From the perspective of exposure-extinction paradigms, which serve as the theoretical basis of in vivo–based exposure treatments, these control strategies (relaxation training and breathing retraining) may retard the extinction process by reducing actual exposure to the anxiety-provoking elements of the stimulus.

Michelson, Marchione, and Greenwald (1989) reported results from a study comparing the effectiveness of three different treatment conditions — graded situational in vivo exposure alone, graded situational in vivo exposure plus cognitive therapy, and graded situational in vivo exposure plus relaxation training. This Type 1 study is one of the few of that era reporting differential efficacy among conditions. The researchers found the treatment condition consisting of situational in vivo exposure and cognitive therapy to be the most effective of the three conditions. At posttreatment assessment, 86% of the patients receiving situational in vivo exposure plus cognitive therapy achieved high end-state functioning as compared with 73% of the situational in vivo exposure plus relaxation training group and 65% of the situational in vivo exposure alone group. In addition, follow-up comparisons continued to underscore the effectiveness of the combined situational in vivo exposure plus cognitive therapy treatment condition. Of the situational in vivo exposure plus cognitive therapy patients, 87% were considered to have achieved high end-state functioning at the 1-year follow-up assessment, whereas 65% of the situational in vivo exposure alone patients and 47% of the situational in vivo exposure plus relaxation training patients had achieved this same clinical status.

Many researchers have manipulated the pace of situational in vivo exposure treatment to show evidence of maximum therapeutic gains. Massed and intensive exposure sessions have been repeatedly compared with spaced and graduated exposure sessions. Barlow (1988, 2002) discussed several advantages to spaced and graduated situational in vivo exposure. Advantages include lower attrition rates, as well as lower relapse rates (Hafner & Marks, 1976; Jansson & Öst, 1982). In addition, gradual changes in agoraphobic avoidance are believed to be less stressful to the interpersonal system of the patient (Barlow, 1988, 2002).

Yet the empirical literature does not entirely support this perspective, since other studies have not found spaced and graduated situational in vivo exposures to hold such distinct advantages. For example, Chambless (1990) treated patients with agoraphobia and patients with specific phobias with either spaced exposures (conducted weekly) or massed exposures (conducted daily). The two conditions were found to be equally effective at both the posttreatment and 6-month follow-up assessments. Moreover, no differential dropout rates between the two conditions were found.

Perhaps the most striking finding regarding the effectiveness of massed, ungraded situational in vivo exposure was reported from a study conducted in Germany. Feigenbaum (1988) treated a large number of severely agoraphobic persons with intensive, massed situational in vivo exposure. This innovative treatment consisted of massed exposures conducted throughout 4 to 10 days, during which individuals were expected to experience the situations they feared for several hours every day. Often, treatment began with therapist-assisted exposure exercises that were then followed by self-directed exposure. These patients were expected to engage in exposures such as using public transportation in a metropolitan area, taking an overnight train to a foreign city, and riding a cable car high above the Alps during the course of their intensive treatment. The progress of these patients was compared to the progress of patients who experienced more graded exposure exercises, gradually working up their hierarchy of feared situations.

Although the two conditions proved to be equally effective at both the posttreatment assessment and the 8-month follow-up assessment, massed, ungraded, situational in vivo exposure proved to be superior at the 5-year follow-up assessment point. These results were later replicated with a much larger sample size (Feigenbaum, 1988). Feigenbaum and his colleagues treated more than 120 patients, and more than 75% were found to be symptom free at the 5-year follow-up assessment.

Researchers have also focused their attention during treatment on the interpersonal support systems of persons with agoraphobia as a means of further improving treatment outcome. Because panic disorder with agoraphobia, at its more severe levels, produces a great deal of dependency, researchers theorized that the incorporation of spouses or partners in treatment might facilitate the treatment process. Barlow, O'Brien, and Last (1984) found that spousal involvement significantly improved treatment effectiveness for a number of women with agoraphobia. In their study, two groups of women were offered identical exposure-based treatments, but the women in one group were asked to have their spouses accompany them to treatment sessions. While the patients in both groups showed evidence of clinical improvements, a significantly greater percentage of patients in the spouse-accompanied group were treatment responders at the posttreatment assessment (86% vs. 43%, respectively). In addition, follow-up results of these same patients determined that the gap in treatment efficacy between the two groups increased during the 1st and 2nd years after treatment (Cerny, Barlow, Craske, & Himadi, 1987).

Finally, Arnow, Taylor, Agras, and Telch (1985) examined the effectiveness of communication skills training with spouses or partners by adding it to a situational in vivo exposure protocol. The combined communication skills training and situational in vivo exposure treatment was found to show evidence of greater clinical improvement at both the posttreatment and the 8-month follow-up assessment. In contrast, Cobb, Mathews, Childs-Clarke, and Blowers (1984) found no additional benefit from including spouses in their treatment protocol, although procedural differences in the treatment administration might account for this finding (see Cerny et al., 1987).

Briefer Cost-Effective Modifications to Exposure-Based Procedures

Researchers have also studied the effectiveness of more self-directed treatment protocols for agoraphobic avoidance. These studies explore questions raised on the second axis of the APA template mentioned above; they examine the clinical utility or external validity of these treatments. For example, Ghosh and Marks (1987) conducted a study that explored the effectiveness of a 10-week self-directed exposure treatment administered in three different conditions (therapist instructed, computer instructed, and book instructed). They enlisted a select group of patients to enter this study; patients with severe personality disorders or severe depression were not eligible for the protocol treatment. Patients in all three treatment conditions received the same initial introduction to treatment, which consisted of a review of the self-directed exposure program explained by a trained clinician.

After the initial assessment, patients in the book-instructed condition (bibliotherapy) received no additional clinical appointments during the 10-week course of treatment, though they were contacted on three occasions to determine if they were engaged in the self-directed treatment program. In contrast, the patients in the computer-instructed condition had weekly 30-minute computer sessions. These were preceded by a brief 10-minute appointment with a clinician who merely assessed the patient's mental status. The patients in the therapist-instructed condition had weekly sessions with their psychiatrist that lasted on average 40 minutes per session.

Ghosh and Marks (1987) found that patients in all three treatment conditions were significantly improved after the 10-week treatment. They found no differences among the three treatment conditions, suggesting that self-directed bibliotherapy can be both a clinically effective and a cost-effective treatment for agoraphobic avoidance, at least in the cases treated in this study. In contrast, Holden, O'Brien, Barlow, Stetson, and Infantino (1983) found bibliotherapy ineffective with patients with more severe levels of agoraphobia; these patients required the intervention of a therapist.

Swinson, Fergus, Cox, and Wickwire (1995) studied the efficacy of telephone-administered self-exposure instructions. This research explored the viability of a more cost-effective administration of situational in vivo exposure. They examined whether self-directed exposure would be an effective treatment modality for patients unable to attend more-traditional therapy sessions conducted in person. Most of the patients enrolled in the study (over 70%) suffered from moderate or severe levels of agoraphobic avoidance. In addition, the patients had suffered from panic disorder and agoraphobia for a mean duration of approximately 13 years. The patients were offered a 10-week course of treatment that included eight telephone sessions with the therapist; the results were compared with those of patients in a wait-list control group. The telephone-administered exposure instructions were found to be effective in reducing the agoraphobic avoidance at posttreatment in comparison to the wait-list control group; moreover, the 3- and 6-month follow-up assessments showed evidence of continued treatment gains. Finally, the clinical improvements were comparable to gains made by patients treated in the more-traditional venue of individual face-to-face treatment sessions.

Treatment of Panic

Psychological treatments focusing on the unexpected and uncued panic attacks experienced by individuals with panic disorder were developed relatively recently. Since publication of DSM-III (APA, 1980), several psychological treatments aimed at targeting panic attacks directly have been developed, and numerous research trials have been conducted to test their efficacy. The majority of these are cognitive-behavioral treatments, and they share many commonalities. They focus on education about the nature of anxiety and panic, cognitive therapy, and some form of exposure and coping skills acquisition. Typically, different aspects of treatment are emphasized in the various protocols. A selection of the more widely utilized treatments is reviewed here. The studies reviewed in this discussion are categorized as Type 1 research, since they were all conducted utilizing the highest methodological standards.

Panic Control Treatment

In the mid-1980s, Barlow and Craske (2000, in press) developed a psychological treatment protocol for panic attacks now known as the *panic control treatment* (PCT). This treatment focuses on exposing the patient to interoceptive sensations similar to physiological panic sensations. In addition to these systematized exposures, PCT includes a cognitive restructuring component directed at misconceptions about anxiety and panic, as well as "automatic" cognitions that focus on the overestimations of threat and danger associated with panic attacks. Finally, breathing retraining is incorporated into PCT; it serves to correct tendencies to hyperventilate in some panic patients and also provides a meditational calming exercise that can be effectively utilized by most patients, although more recent versions of the treatment discourage the use of breathing retraining because there is a significant likelihood for these skills to be misused as a way to avoid the full experience of anxiety (as discussed earlier in the chapter). Panic control training has been extensively studied throughout the past several years, with good results.

In the first controlled study of PCT (Barlow, Craske, Cerny, & Klosko, 1989), three treatment conditions (PCT alone, relaxation alone, and PCT combined with relaxation) were compared with a wait-list control condition. The relaxation component consisted of progressive muscle relaxation training along with instructions to apply this relaxation when in anxiety-provoking situations. At posttreatment, all three treatment conditions proved to be more effective than the wait-list control condition. Of the patients, 60% in the relaxation condition and 87% in the PCT alone and PCT combined with relaxation conditions achieved panic-free status by the conclusion of the 15-week treatment.

Craske, Brown, and Barlow (1991) reported on a 2-year follow-up of this study. These follow-up data revealed that 81% of the patients in the PCT alone condition were panic free 2 years after acute treatment, compared with only 43% of the patients in the PCT combined with relaxation condition and 36% of the patients in the relaxation alone condition. One possibility is that the patients in the PCT combined with relaxation condition were not able to show evidence of greater therapeutic gains due to the abbreviated nature of the two treatments in this condition; that is, neither the PCT nor relaxation therapy was presented as thoroughly in the combined treatment condition as compared with the two other treatment conditions, since only 1 hour per week was allotted to each condition.

In another study, Klosko, Barlow, Tassinari, and Cerny (1990) compared the efficacy of PCT and alprazolam to a drug placebo condition and a wait-list control condition. In this study, posttreatment assessment results showed that 87% of the patients in the PCT condition had achieved panic-free status, compared with 50% of the patients in the alprazolam condition, 36% of the patients in the placebo drug condition, and 33% of the patients in the wait-list control condition. The PCT was found to be significantly more effective than the other three conditions (Barlow & Brown, 1995).

Schmidt et al. (2000) conducted a controlled outcome study designed to assess the necessity of breathing retraining in the context of PCT. Seventy-seven patients with panic disorder were randomly assigned to receive PCT with or without breathing retraining or to a delayed treatment control. The findings were consistent with treatment equivalence, with 38% of the PCT group meeting the recovery criteria for high end-state functioning, compared with 21% of the PCT and breathing retraining group and 0% of the wait-list group. Moreover, by the 12-month follow-up, 57% of the PCT group met the recovery criteria, compared with 37% of the combined group. This one study suggests that, although breathing retraining appears not to affect initial posttreatment outcome, it may yield a poorer long-term outcome.

In yet another study, Telch et al. (1993) found PCT to be effective when administered in a group treatment format. Patients were given 8 weeks of group PCT, and their progress was compared with that of patients in a wait-list control condition. At the conclusion of treatment, 85% of the patients who had received PCT had achieved panic-free status as compared with 30% of the patients in the wait-list control condition. In addition, when a more stringent composite outcome measure (considering panic attack frequency, as well as levels of general anxiety and avoidance behavior) was utilized, 63% of the patients in the PCT condition were considered improved compared with 9% of the patients in the wait-list control condition. At the 6-month follow-up, 79% of the patients who had received PCT had remained panic free, and 63% were still considered to be clinically improved according to the composite outcome measure.

One criticism of the majority of research examining the efficacy of PCT is that most treatment trials target participants displaying minimal to moderate levels of agoraphobia, and little is known about the effect of PCT on agoraphobia specifically. In an attempt to target agoraphobia more specifically in the context of panic treatment, Craske, De Cola, Sachs, and Pontillo (2003) conducted a treatment outcome study to examine whether PCT with an additional in vivo exposure component would be more effective in treating patients with PDA than traditional PCT alone. Results indicated that the two treatment conditions were equally efficacious, suggesting the additional component added no benefits above and beyond the relatively robust treatment outcome effect of PCT alone.

In a large multisite study that compared single and combined effects of cognitive-behavioral treatment and imipramine for patients with panic disorder with no more than limited agoraphobia, patients were randomly assigned to receive either imipramine only, cognitive-behavioral therapy only (PCT), placebo only, PCT plus imipramine, or PCT plus placebo (Barlow, Gorman, Shear, & Woods, 2000). In this study patients were treated weekly for 3 months. They were then seen in a maintenance condition monthly for six additional months (except for nonresponders to the drug-only condition), and then followed-up for 6 months after treatment discontinuation. The results indicated that all the treatment groups were significantly superior to placebo after the acute and maintenance phases of treatment, with some evidence that among those who responded, the drug produced a better quality of response (e.g., less depression). However, PCT plus imipramine was generally not superior to PCT plus placebo immediately following treatment, although there was some advantage for the combined treatment after 6 months of maintenance. But 6 months after the termination of treatment, significantly more patients in the imipramine-alone group or the PCT plus imipramine group relapsed compared with groups receiving PCT without imipramine (PCT alone and PCT plus placebo). This study suggests that PCT produces a more durable response than medication. Further investigation is needed of the long-term effects of adding medications to cognitive-behavioral therapy, and of the most effective ways to combine medications with cognitive-behavioral therapy in order to offset potential relapse.

The third edition of a comprehensive PCT treatment manual for panic disorder titled *Mastery of Your Anxiety and Panic* (MAP-3; Barlow & Craske,

2000; Craske, Barlow, & Meadows, 2000) presents clinicians with a step-by-step guide to conducting the various aspects of PCT therapy. A fourth edition of this manual is currently available (Barlow & Craske, 2007).

Cognitive Therapy

In a controlled trial of more-traditional cognitive therapy, Beck, Sokol, Clark, Berchick, and Wright (1992) compared the efficacy of 12 weeks of cognitive therapy with 8 weeks of brief supportive therapy. After 8 weeks of treatment, 71% of the patients who received cognitive therapy were panic free as compared with 25% of the patients who received supportive therapy. Moreover, at posttreatment 94% of the patients in the cognitive therapy condition were panic free, and at the 1-year follow-up assessment, 87% of these patients continued to be panic free.

Clark and his colleagues also developed a psychological treatment for panic disorder consisting of a unique variation of cognitive therapy (Clark, 1989; Salkovskis & Clark, 1991). This treatment also attempts to change patients' appraisals of bodily sensations and is similar to the PCT discussed above. However, Clark's approach places a greater emphasis on the cognitive therapy component of the treatment protocol.

Clark et al. (1994) conducted a randomized controlled trial comparing the effectiveness of three active treatments (cognitive therapy, applied relaxation [AR], and imipramine) to a wait-list control condition. Patients randomly assigned to one of the three active treatment conditions met weekly with a clinician throughout the first 3 months of the study; furthermore, they continued to meet with their therapist for a monthly booster session throughout the 3 months following the acute treatment phase of the study. Posttreatment results conducted after 6 months showed that all three active treatments were significantly more effective than the wait-list control condition. In fact, the cognitive therapy treatment was superior to the wait-list control condition on all panic and anxiety treatment outcome measures; the AR condition and the imipramine treatment condition were superior to the wait-list control condition on just over half and fewer than half of the treatment outcome measures, respectively.

At posttreatment, 75% of the patients in the cognitive therapy condition were panic free compared with 70% of the patients in the imipramine condition and 40% of the patients in the AR condition. Moreover, the 9-month follow-up results that followed the discontinuation of the imipramine treatment showed that the patients in the cognitive therapy condition largely maintained their treatment gains. Of the patients who received cognitive therapy, 85% remained panic free, while 60% of the patients who received imipramine and 47% of the patients who were treated with AR were panic free.

Also, during the time between the posttreatment and 9-month follow-up, 40% of the patients in the imipramine treatment condition had sought further treatment compared with 25% of the patients in the AR condition and 5% of the patients in the cognitive therapy condition. At the final assessment point, the cognitive therapy condition was found to be significantly more effective than either the AR or the imipramine condition.

Alternative Treatments

A study conducted by Öst and Westling (1995) reports positive results with AR treatment. In this study, patients were randomly assigned to 12 sessions of either an AR treatment or cognitive therapy treatment. Results showed that both treatments were equally effective. At posttreatment, 65% of the patients in the AR condition and 74% of patients in the cognitive therapy condition were panic free. At the 1-year follow-up, 82% of the patients who had received AR treatment and 89% of the patients who had received cognitive therapy treatment were panic free. It is interesting to note that, for the patients treated in this study, no relapses occurred during the 1-year post-acute treatment; in fact, many of the patients who had been experiencing panic attacks at the posttreatment assessment had achieved panic-free status by the 1-year follow-up. Thus, AR was a bit less effective than results from studies conducted by Clark et al. (1994) or Barlow et al. (1989), and this approach has not been systematically replicated or otherwise pursued.

In 1994, Shear, Pilkonis, Cloitre, and Leon developed a new approach called *emotion-focused therapy* (EFT) that focuses on interpersonal triggers for panic attacks rather than interoceptive cues. Attrition was high in this first study, but preliminary results from this study were promising. In a further evaluation by Shear, Houck, Greeno, and Masters (2001), patients were randomly assigned to either EFT, CBT, imipramine, or placebo. Treatment included approximately 3 months of weekly visits and six monthly maintenance sessions. This study found that EFT was less effective than either CBT or imipramine for symptoms of panic disorder. In addition, EFT results at postacute and postmaintenance were similar to placebo. At follow-up, EFT patients fared better than those receiving placebo, but still less well than those treated with CBT or imipramine.

There is increasing evidence to suggest that aerobic exercise alone may lead to reductions in anxiety and mood disorders in general (for a review, see Salmon, 2001). Although studies are currently under way to examine the efficacy of aerobic exercise specifically, studies have already shown that aerobic exercise has a significant effect on anxiety sensitivity, a known precursor of panic attacks and panic disorder (Broman-Fulks, Berman, Rabian, & Webster, 2004). Additionally, research has shown that successful traditional cognitive-behavioral treatment for panic disorder also results in decreased levels of anxiety sensitivity (Telch et al., 1993). Research suggests that aerobic exercise may be a more intense form of interoceptive exposure and thus may decrease anxiety associated with bodily sensations similar to the mechanism associated with the interoceptive component of panic control treatment. This approach requires further research, and indeed studies are currently under way in this area.

Brief Cost-Effective Treatments

Several studies have explored the effectiveness of cognitive-behavioral treatment for panic disorder when it is administered in a more cost-effective manner, such as with limited therapist contact. These studies explore the questions raised on the second axis of the APA template, the clinical utility or external validity of these treatments. Cote, Gauthier, Laberge, Cormier, and Plamondon (1994) conducted a study in which patients were randomly assigned to receive cognitive-behavioral treatment with either a standard amount of therapist contact (weekly hourlong sessions) or reduced therapist contact (twice-monthly hourlong sessions with twice-monthly 10-minute telephone contacts). Results of this study demonstrated that both treatment modalities were equally effective; more than 73% of the patients in both groups were both panic free and clinically improved

at the 6-month follow-up assessment. It should be noted that therapist time in the reduced therapist contact condition was still considerable, amounting to approximately 10 hours of contact, as compared with approximately 20 hours of contact in the standard condition. Lidren et al. (1994) examined the effectiveness of self-directed treatment utilizing a manual (bibliotherapy) compared with cognitive-behavioral therapy administered in a group therapy setting. Patients in both conditions were treated for 8 weeks and compared with patients in a wait-list control condition. Patients in both of the active treatment conditions showed evidence of significant clinical improvement at posttreatment assessments, while the patients in the wait-list control condition did not. Moreover, patients in the bibliotherapy and group therapy conditions maintained their treatment gains at the 3- and 6-month follow-up assessments. In addition, an attrition rate of zero was reported for this study, pointing to the desirability of these interventions for patients suffering from panic attacks.

In an attempt to increase the cost-effectiveness of CBT for panic, a number of researchers have attempted to shorten the traditional treatment duration, which is typically 12 to 15 weeks. This often involves more intense sessions that occur over shorter time duration. Craske, Maidenberg, and Bystritsky (1995) compared the effectiveness of a four-session PCT protocol to a four-session nondirective supportive therapy protocol. The brief PCT was found to be significantly more effective than the nondirective supportive therapy on a number of measures. Clark et al. (1999) randomly assigned 43 panic disorder patients to either standard cognitive therapy consisting of up to 12 one-hour sessions in the first 3 months or brief cognitive therapy where patients attended five sessions in addition to using between-session self-study modules. Both treatments produced significantly better results than a wait-list control group. Deacon and Abramowitz (2006) examined the effectiveness of a brief (2-day), intensive cognitive-behavioral therapy for PD. They found that 6 out of 10 patients were panic free after treatment and continued to report nonclinical levels of panic symptomatology at 1-month follow-up. In addition, studies are currently under way at our center in Boston to examine whether memory-enhancing medications and cognitive rehabilitation used in conjunction with cognitive-behavioral treatments may allow for shorter and less intense treatment durations. Clinicians have also attempted to decrease the treatment duration of cognitive treatments.

With the advance of technology, researchers have attempted to utilize the popularity of the Internet to increase both treatment dissemination and time and cost-effectiveness. Carlbring et al. (2005) randomly assigned 49 patients diagnosed with PD/PDA to either a 10-module CBT based self-help program on the Internet or to 10 weekly sessions of CBT. They found the Internet-administered self-help plus minimal therapist contact via e-mail to be as effective as traditional individual CBT. These results were maintained at 1-year follow-up. Klein, Richards, and Austin (2006) randomly assigned 55 patients with panic disorder to Internet-based CBT with therapist e-mail contact, therapist-assisted CBT manual with therapist telephone contact, or information control. They found that both CBT treatment groups were effective in reducing panic symptomatology, panic-related cognition, and negative affect. In addition, they found that these treatments were effective in decreasing general practitioner visits associated with panic symptomatology and improving overall physical health ratings. Interestingly, the Internet treatment was found to be more effective than the CBT manual/telephone contact on all outcome measures. These results suggest that the Internet may be an interesting, cost-effective, and efficacious way of delivering CBT. However, more studies are needed to examine whether Internet-based treatments are effective in treating panic disorder associated with more severe levels of agoraphobia and with diagnostic comorbidity.

Current Status

Table 13.2 summarizes the results of studies of psychological treatment for panic disorder through 2005. Nearly all these studies are classified as Type 1; the study by Öst, Westling, and Hellström (1993) falls into the Type 2 category due to an absence of comparison groups. Most studies demonstrate the effectiveness of PCT or similar cognitive-behavioral approaches for patients with panic disorder with no more than mild agoraphobia (compared with either no treatment or credible psychotherapeutic alternatives).

Table 13.3 summarizes the results of a comprehensive meta-analysis of treatment outcome for panic disorder with all levels of agoraphobic avoidance (Gould et al., 1995). Included in the meta-analysis

were 43 controlled studies. As can be seen in the table, the cognitive-behavioral treatments yielded the greatest effect size and the smallest rates of patient attrition when compared with either pharmacological treatment or treatments that combined both psychological and pharmacological treatments. Moreover, the subset of cognitive-behavioral treatments that utilized interoceptive exposure yielded an even greater effect size, although most of these studies included patients with no more than mild agoraphobic avoidance.

Translational Research (Effectiveness Studies)

Now several large Type 1 effectiveness studies have appeared evaluating the clinical utility of CBT procedures delivered under naturalistic conditions in primary care settings. Addis, Hatgis, Bourne, and Mansfield (2004) compared the efficacy of PCT to treatment as usual in a managed care setting. This study was unique in that few studies have attempted to examine the efficacy of PCT in traditional treatment settings rather than laboratory settings. In this study, 80 patients who were enrolled in a managed care health plan and were diagnosed with panic disorder with or without agoraphobia were randomly assigned either to PCT treatment delivered by a recently trained PCT therapist or to treatment as usual (TAU). In this case, TAU involved whatever treatment orientation the therapist felt was appropriate for each individual client. Using a number of treatment outcome variables, the researchers found that although both groups showed a significant decrease in panic symptomatology from pre- to posttreatment, among the treatment completers, an average of 49% of those in the PCT and 18.8% of those in the treatment as usual conditions achieved significant change from pre- to posttreatment.

Follow-up data at 1 and 2 years following acute treatment with the same sample revealed that those who received PCT during acute treatment evidenced lower levels of panic severity and phobic avoidance and a greater likelihood of achieving and maintaining clinically significant change. An interesting finding was that benzodiazepine use during the follow-up period was associated with greater panic severity for individuals who received PCT at acute treatment. There was no relationship between benzodiazepine use during follow-up and panic severity in the TAU

TABLE 13.2 Clinical Trials of Cognitive-Behavioral Treatments for Panic Disorder: Intent-to-Treat Analysis

Study	Length of Follow-Up (Months)	Treatment (N)	% Panic Free	Significant Comparison (% Panic Free) Other Treatments (Yes/No)	Wait List (Yes/No)
Craske et al. (1991)[a]	24	PCT (N = 15)	81	Yes: AR = 36% Yes: PCT & AR = 43%	
Klosko et al. (1990)	PT	PCT (N = 15)	87	No: AL = 50% Yes: PL = 36%	Yes: 33%
Newman et al. (1990)	12	CTM (N = 24) CTNM (N = 19)	87 87	— —	
Cote et al. (1994)	12	CBTM (N = 13) CBTNM (N = 8)	92 100	— —	
Beck et al. (1992)	PT	CT (N = 17)	94	Yes: ST = 25%[b]	
Black et al. (1993)	PT	CT (N = 25)	32	Yes: FL = 68% No: PL = 20%	
Magraf and Schneider (1991)	4 weeks	CT (N = 22)	91		
Öst et al. (1993)	12	CT (N = 19)	89[c]	No: AR = 74%[c]	Yes: 5%
Telch et al. (1993)	PT	PCT (N = 34)	85		Yes: 30%
Clark et al. (1994)	12	CT (N = 17)	76[c]	Yes: AR = 43%[c] Yes: IMI = 49%[c]	
Shear et al. (1994)	6	CBT (N = 23)	45	No: NPT = 45%	
Craske et al. (1995)	PT	CBT (N = 16)	53	Yes: NPT = 8%	
Barlow et al. (2000)	12	CBT (N = 77) CBT + PL (N = 63) CBT + IMI (N = 65)	31.9 41 26	Yes: PL = 13 Yes: IMI = 19.7	
Öst et al. (2004)	PT	E (N = 25) CBT (N = 26)	67 79	— —	
Addis et al. (2004)	PT	PCT (N = 13)	43	Yes: TAU = 19%	
Roy-Byrne et al. (2005)	12	PCT + MED[d] (N = 119)	63	YES: TAU = 38%	

Source: Reprinted and adapted with permission from Barlow and Lehman (1996), © 1996 American Medical Association. All rights reserved.

Al = alprazolam; AR = applied relaxation; CBT = cognitive behavioral therapy; CBTM = cognitive-behavioral therapy and medication; CBTNM = cognitive-behavioral therapy without medication; CT = cognitive therapy; CTM = cognitive therapy and medication; CTNM = cognitive therapy without medication; E = exposure in vivo; FL = fluvoxamine; IMI = imipramine; NPT = nonprescriptive treatment; PL = pill placebo; PCT = exposure and cognitive restructuring; PT = posttreatment; ST = supportive therapy; TAU = treatment as usual; MED = medication.

[a]Follow-up study of Barlow et al. (1989).

[b]At 8 weeks, which was the end of supportive therapy. At this time, 71% of CT patients were panic free.

[c]Percentage of patients panic free at follow-up who had received no additional treatment during the follow-up period.

[d]Algorithm-based pharmacotherapy provided by primary care physician with guidance from a psychiatrist.

group. This result echoes findings from other combination treatment outcome studies that suggest a negative result from combining CBT and benzodiazepines. The study suggests that this negative effect may continue even after treatment has ended, although the authors warn that when drug and CBT treatments were combined in this study, there was no clear and consistent practice (medication use was not under the control of study personnel).

In a more recent study, Roy-Byrne et al. (2005) identified and treated 232 primary care patients meeting *DSM-IV* criteria for panic disorder across six primary care clinics that were ethnically and socioeconomically diverse. Patients were randomized to receive

TABLE 13.3 Meta-Analysis of 43 Controlled Studies of Treatment of Panic Disorder with Agoraphobia

	Cognitive-Behavioral Therapy	Cognitive Therapy and Interoceptive Exposure	Pharmacological Treatment	Combination Treatment
Effect size	.68	.88	.47	.56
Dropouts	5.6%		19.8%	22%

Source: Data from Gould et al. (1995).

either treatment as usual or CBT that consisted of six sessions of panic control treatment modified for the primary care setting delivered over the course of 12 weeks. Up to six follow-up telephone contacts were permitted during the subsequent 9 months. Patients also received a copy of a manual for patients, *Mastery of Your Anxiety and Panic: Client Workbook for Agoraphobia* (Barlow & Craske, 2000) modified for primary care settings. Pharmacotherapy provided by the primary care physician, with guidance from a psychiatrist, was provided to both groups, with no differences in the utilization of drugs across the groups. Nevertheless, panic control treatment resulted in sustained and gradually increasing improvement relative to treatment as usual on panic disorder symptomatology, overall mental health functioning, and disability scales. It is noteworthy that the CBT was delivered by midlevel behavioral health specialists with little or no CBT experience prior to training for this study.

In a second study, Rollman et al. (2005) identified 191 patients with either panic disorder, generalized anxiety disorder, or both across four primary care practice settings. Patients were randomly assigned to a telephone-based care intervention in which they could choose any combination of the following treatments: the *MAP-3* client workbook (Barlow & Craske, 2000), the *Mastery of Your Anxiety and Worry* workbook for GAD (Craske, Barlow, & O'Leary, 1992), a guideline-based trial of anxiolytic pharmacotherapy, or referral to a community mental health specialist. In the second condition, patients identified with the appropriate diagnoses were flagged, and information on the diagnostic work-up was sent to the primary care physician, who then engaged in treatment as usual.

In fact, 80% of the patients chose the anxiety self-management workbooks, whereas the proportion of patients taking medication or requiring a referral to

a mental health specialist did not differ by treatment assignment. Interestingly, the treatment was delivered by nonbehavioral health specialists with little or no formal training in mental health. The extent of the intervention by these therapists was to telephone the patients at regular intervals to promote adherence and refer patients to specific relevant sections in the workbooks. They would also review their lesson plans during the follow-up telephone contacts to confirm that patients understood the text and performed the relevant exercises. Intervention patients had a median of seven telephone contacts with their care manager, with 79% having three or more contacts.

Results indicated that the intervention patients reported reduced anxiety and depressive symptoms, improved quality of life, and more hours worked and fewer days absent from work than usual care patients; these results were maintained at a 12-month follow-up. Results were somewhat better for those patients with panic disorder or comorbid panic disorder and GAD than those with GAD alone.

Psychological Treatments in Combination With Pharmacotherapy

Research on the effectiveness of combined psychological and pharmacological treatment conducted during the last decade, and prior to Barlow et al. (2000), focused primarily on combining pharmacotherapy with exposure-based treatments for patients with moderate to severe levels of agoraphobia. Studies that compared the effectiveness of tricyclic antidepressants such as imipramine and exposure-based procedures with exposure alone have, for the most part, shown evidence of superior posttreatment results for the combined treatment (Mavissakalian, 1996; Mavissakalian & Perel, 1985; Telch, Agras, Taylor, Roth, & Gallen, 1985). However, these results generally were not maintained at follow-up assessments due to the high incidence of relapse experienced by patients in the combined treatment condition after imipramine discontinuation had occurred (e.g., Mavissakalian & Michelson, 1986). The Barlow et al. (2000) clinical trial of panic disorder with no more than mild agoraphobia showed equivalence of monotherapies, no marked advantage of combining treatments, and more durability of CBT. The Clark et al. (1994) study also showed equivalence of monotherapies and greater durability of CBT. It did not test combination treatments. Overall, there is a good deal of room for improvement in the efficacy of these approaches, and results from all studies underscore the need to study effective maintenance strategies for this chronic condition. Marks et al. (1993) also found that a combined treatment consisting of alprazolam, a high-potency benzodiazepine, and exposure therapy was similar in its effectiveness to either alprazolam or exposure therapy administered alone. While this result was found at the posttreatment evaluation, the effectiveness of the combined treatment did not remain at the 6-month follow-up assessment, much as in Barlow et al. (2000). Those patients who received the combination treatment experienced a high relapse rate after the discontinuation of the alprazolam; thus, overall gains were reduced below the point of those receiving exposure alone. Of more concern are reports that high-potency benzodiazepines may interfere with and detract from CBT treatment gains (Brown & Barlow, 1995; Otto, Pollack, & Sabatino, 1996).

Psychological treatments, including modifications of PCT, have also been utilized to help patients discontinue benzodiazepines. For example, Otto et al. (1993) conducted a study in which patients using alprazolam experienced either a slow taper of the drug or a slow taper in conjunction with 10 weeks of PCT. Results indicated that more than 75% of the patients in the combined PCT-taper condition were able to discontinue their alprazolam usage, while only 25% of the slow taper alone condition were able to do so.

Spiegel, Bruce, Gregg, and Nuzzarello (1994) conducted a similar study. Patients were discontinued very gradually and flexibly from alprazolam. One treatment condition included 12 weekly sessions of individual PCT during the taper, while the other treatment condition involved routine supportive medical management. Nearly all patients were able to discontinue their medication usage (80% of the patients in the taper plus supportive medical

management condition and 90% of the patients in the taper plus PCT condition). At the 6-month follow-up, fully half of the patients in the taper plus supportive medical management condition had relapsed and begun using alprazolam again, whereas no patients in the taper plus PCT condition had done so. Results from a 3-year follow-up revealed that 33% of the patients in the PCT condition had experienced a relapse between 6 and 18 months after their treatment was discontinued. Moreover, 70% of the patients in the supportive medical management condition had experienced a relapse and required additional treatment during the 3-year follow-up period (Spiegel et al., 1994). These data suggest that an innovative combination treatment in which high-potency benzodiazepines are administered initially to those who need immediate relief or otherwise desire medication treatment, followed by psychological treatment such as PCT, may be quite effective for patients with panic disorder. It is possible that the future of combined treatment lies in these sequential strategies, as opposed to simultaneous administration of drug and psychological treatment.

Along these lines, clinical investigators have begun to examine the effectiveness of psychological treatments for patients who were previous nonresponders to pharmacological treatment. For example, Pollack, Otto, Kaspi, Hammerness, and Rosenbaum (1994) found that 12 weeks of group cognitive-behavioral therapy helped patients who had shown evidence of an incomplete response to previous pharmacotherapy. While these patients had not shown evidence of improvement while using medication, they experienced significant improvement in global functioning, as well as panic attack frequency, after the 12-week cognitive-behavioral treatment. These results suggest that there might be a select group of patients with panic disorder who may not benefit from medication treatment, but then are able to show evidence of improvement when effective psychological treatments are administered. Reversing the sequence for those who initially fail with cognitive-behavioral treatments by subsequently administering an effective pharmacological treatment might produce similar results.

We know that even those individuals doing well at follow-ups of a year or more with cognitive-behavioral approaches often experience "setbacks" or other exacerbations of symptoms that occasionally progress to a full relapse (e.g., Burns et al., 1986). Often, these episodes are associated with emergent life stress or other difficulties (Brown, Antony, & Barlow, 1995). Thus, a finding that 75% of all patients treated responded to treatment at posttreatment, and 65% at a 2-year follow-up, may mask the fact that a number of these patients may have experienced significant setbacks in the months between the assessments. In view of the chronicity of panic disorder with agoraphobia, there is a need to investigate strategies to prevent exacerbations of symptoms, as well as full relapse. Based on preliminary studies demonstrating the possible value of maintenance strategies (e.g., Jansson et al., 1986; Öst, 1989), researchers at our center and elsewhere attempted to develop more comprehensive and effective maintenance strategies for the purpose of preventing exacerbations or full relapse. These efforts resulted in a large multicenter study examining long-term strategies for the maintenance of positive treatment results for panic disorder. In this study, all patients received PCT as the first line of treatment. Those who evidenced treatment gains after receiving PCT were then assigned to a maintenance condition, in which they received 6 monthly sessions of PCT. Patients who did not respond to the initial phase of PCT were randomly assigned to receive either additional CBT sessions or a trial of paroxetine. The goal of this study was to better understand the utility of maintenance sessions for those who respond to PCT, as well as to examine the effectiveness of pharmacotherapy versus additional CBT for CBT nonresponders. Results from this study are expected to be reported shortly.

Future Directions

It is clear that although cognitive-behavioral approaches to treating anxiety are highly efficacious and becoming more widely accepted, there still exist substantial problems, especially when considering the problem of treatment dissemination, the problem of treatment resistance, and the problem of maintaining treatment gains over time (or treatment relapse). As a result, researchers in anxiety disorders have begun to develop unified treatments that afford better treatment dissemination, new combination treatments to address treatment-resistant individuals, and specific maintenance programs for those individuals who have a successful treatment experience.

Some of the criticisms of CBT approaches are the reliance of the treatments on manuals and on clini-cians who are skilled in delivering the manualized interventions. The development of these often complex treatments has resulted in problems with treatment dissemination and an increased demand for adequately trained professionals. A better understanding of the nature of anxiety disorders and the underlying commonalities among anxiety disorders has led to the possibility of harvesting a set of therapeutic procedures that may delineate a unified intervention for emotional disorders (Barlow, Allen, & Choate, 2004; Campbell-Sills & Barlow, in press). Briefly, the major components of the unified treatment developed by Barlow and colleagues involve altering antecedent cognitive reappraisals, preventing emotional avoidance, and facilitating action tendencies not associated with the emotion that is dysregulated. Understandably, some of the components in this treatment are identical to those commonly employed in CBT treatments for panic (e.g., interoceptive and situational exposure). Studies are currently under way at our center in Boston to examine the efficiency and effectiveness of this treatment. The unified treatment approach will be reviewed further in the conclusion to this chapter.

Recent advances in translation research as discussed earlier in this chapter provide a solid framework for understanding the limitations of combination treatments for anxiety disorders. For instance, researchers have consistently found that while traditional combination treatments provide minimal advantage over CBT alone, there appears to be a detrimental effect of receiving CBT in the context of pharmacotherapy for the maintenance of treatment gains over time; during follow-up periods, those in combination conditions tend to have greater relapse rates and higher reported levels of anxiety than individuals treated with CBT alone during acute treatment (Barlow et al., 2000; Marks et al., 1993; Otto, Smits, & Reese, 2005). Thus the combination of antidepressant treatment and cognitive-behavioral therapy for anxiety disorders has yielded somewhat disappointing results. However, with the increasing attention being given to translational approaches, new strategies for pharmacotherapy to increase treatment response to exposure-based cognitive-behavior therapy have surfaced and may constitute the future direction of combination treatments. The drugs do not specifically work to decrease anxiety per se but work to increase executive functioning (memory, decision making, complex reasoning), which may lead to better treatment outcomes in a more indirect manner.

One such drug is D-cycloserine (DCS), an antibiotic medication originally developed to treat tuberculosis, and a partial N-methyl-D-aspartate (NMDA) agonist that has been shown to facilitate the extinction of learned fear in laboratory animals. With clear and consistent results across many fear-based extinction studies in animals, it is likely that this drug holds the potential to be beneficial to exposure-based cognitive-behavioral therapies. Researchers have found some support for the use of the drug to augment CBT in social anxiety (Hofmann et al., 2006), and studies are currently under way at our site to examine the usefulness of DCS for augmenting CBT in panic disorder.

SPECIFIC PHOBIA

The *DSM-IV-TR* diagnosis of specific phobia replaces the diagnosis of simple phobia listed in *DSM-III-R* (APA, 1987). In *DSM-IV-TR*, a specific phobia is defined as a marked and persistent fear cued by the presence or anticipation of an object or situation. The fear must be considered to be excessive or unreasonable and must be associated with functional impairment or subjective distress. In addition, the specific phobia must not be better accounted for by another *DSM-IV-TR* disorder (APA, 1994).

Five subtypes of specific phobias are included in *DSM-IV-TR*: animal, natural-environmental, blood-injection-injury, situational, and other. The "other" type serves as a catch-all category for specific phobias such as choking or vomiting that do not readily fall into any of the first four subtypes. These subtypes were devised by the *DSM-IV* Anxiety Disorders Work Group as more information was gained about the heterogeneity among the specific phobias along a variety of dimensions (APA, 1996). These dimensions include age of onset, gender composition, patterns of comorbidity, and type of physiological reaction to the phobic situation, as well as other important variables such as natural course and type of treatment indicated. For example, the mean age of onset for animal, blood, storm, and water phobias tends to be in early childhood, whereas the mean age of onset for situational height phobia is in adolescence (Antony & Barlow, 2002; Craske & Sipsas,

1992; Curtis, Hill, & Lewis, 1990; Marks & Gelder, 1966; Öst, 1987).

The *DSM-IV-TR* diagnosis of specific phobia, when considered overall, is highly prevalent (Antony & Barlow, 1996). Yet when specific phobias are given as primary diagnoses, the clinician is not likely to observe an additional clinical diagnosis. In other words, principal diagnoses of specific phobias tend to have lower rates of comorbidity than principal diagnoses of most other Axis I disorders (Moras, Di Nardo, Brown, & Barlow, 1994). In a study conducted based on data from the NCS study (Kessler et al., 1994), Curtis, Magee, Eaton, Wittchen, and Kessler (1998) found that of the 915 individuals with a lifetime history of a specific phobia, only 24.4% had a single phobia. The remaining cases had two (26.4%), three (23.5%), four (10.4%), or more than four (17.3%) phobias.

According to the original NCS, approximately 11% of the population experience a specific phobia during his or her lifetime, as compared with the estimated 12.5% in a recently published replication of the original NCS (Kessler et al., 1994; Kessler et al., 2005). Gender differences are marked, with a lifetime prevalence for women noted to be 15.7% of the population compared with 6.7% for men. Interestingly, this gender difference in prevalence is most pronounced for the animal type of specific phobia and least apparent for height, flying, and blood-injury-injection phobias (Antony & Barlow, 2002).

Treatments for Specific Phobias

A consensus has developed that the treatment of choice for specific phobias is exposure-based procedures, particularly in vivo exposure. Exposure has been shown to be effective for a wide spectrum of specific phobias. Although imaginal exposure has been shown to produce fear reduction (Baker, Cohen, & Saunders, 1973) and should be used if situational in vivo exposure treatment is not feasible, in vivo exposure is generally accepted as the most powerful treatment for specific phobias (APA, 1994; Antony & Barlow, 2002; Barlow, 1988, 2002; Marks, 1987).

In vivo exposure treatment often appears deceptively simple, yet there are many facets to the procedure (Antony & Barlow, 2002). Therapists usually initiate exposure treatment with a few office visits. During these initial sessions, the therapist gathers more specific information about the patient's feelings, thoughts, and behaviors concerning the phobic object or situation. The patient is informed that systematic, repeated in vivo exposure will allow the patient to become desensitized to the phobic object or situation. The clinician also lets patients know that all in vivo exposures will be predictable and under their control, and he or she teaches patients a variety of adaptive coping strategies to utilize throughout treatment. Finally, the clinician and patient create a hierarchy of feared situations concerning the phobic object or situation and formulate a treatment plan consisting of in vivo exposure practices.

Extensive literature exists demonstrating the effectiveness of in vivo exposure treatments for specific phobias. Over the past few decades, in vivo exposure has been successfully utilized to treat most types of specific phobia (Antony & Barlow, 2002). For example, clinical investigators have demonstrated the effectiveness of in vivo exposure to treat phobias of animals (e.g., Muris, Mayer, & Merckelbach, 1998; Öst, 1989; Öst, Ferebee, & Furmark, 1997; Öst, Salkovskis, & Hellström, 1991), heights (e.g., Bourque & Ladouceur, 1980), and flying (Beckham, Vrana, May, Gustafson, & Smith, 1990; Howard, Murphy, & Clarke, 1983; Öst, Brandberg, & Alm, 1997; Solyom, Shugar, Bryntwick & Solyom, 1973). In addition, in vivo exposure has been utilized to treat fear of dentists (Jerremalm, Jansson, & Öst, 1986b; Liddell, Di Fazio, Blackwood, & Ackerman, 1994), as well as choking phobia (McNally, 1986, 1994), with good results. In addition, blood-injury-injection phobias also have been successfully treated with in vivo exposure, although these phobias and their treatments are unique and are described below (Öst, 1989; Öst & Sterner, 1987).

Though exposure-based treatments for specific phobias are considered to be fairly straightforward, they are composed of many factors that may have an impact on the clinical results of treatment. These factors include the duration and temporal spacing of exposure sessions, the level of therapist involvement, and the incorporation of additional treatment components into exposure sessions. The following discussion reviews the available empirical evidence regarding these factors.

In general, it appears that massed exposure sessions result in the most robust clinical improvement (Marks, 1987). In fact, in as little as one session of therapist-guided exposure, 90% of persons with animal or injection phobias were found to be much improved or completely recovered (Öst, 1989). Öst treated more than 20 patients with a specific phobia for a particular animal or injections with in vivo exposure and therapist modeling. He completed each of these sessions in less than 3 hours, with a mean session length of approximately 2 hours. Of the patients, 90% showed evidence of immediate clinical improvement, and their clinically significant improvement was retained at follow-up assessments conducted up to 4 years posttreatment. Rowe and Craske (1998) examined the benefits of an expanding-spaced exposure schedule versus massed exposure. In this model, sessions begin close together and gradually spread out as treatment progresses. They found that massed exposure led to significantly more fear reduction in a group of spider phobics. However, they also found that an expanding-spaced schedule was less likely than a massed schedule to be associated with a return of fear following treatment.

The degree of therapist involvement in exposure treatment is also considered to be an important component of the treatment. Though relatively few studies have directly examined the influence of the therapist's presence, most empirical findings point to the importance of therapist involvement during exposure treatment. For example, Öst et al. (1991) found that whereas 71% of persons with spider phobia improved with therapist-assisted exposure treatment, only 6% of persons who engaged in self-directed exposures evidenced clinical improvement. In a follow-up study, Hellström and Öst (1995) found that the manner in which self-help treatment is disseminated affects the outcome for individuals with spider phobias. In this study, five different treatments were compared: (a) a single session of therapist-assisted exposure, (b) a spider phobia–specific manual used in the home, (c) a spider phobia–specific manual used in the clinic, (d) a nonspecific manual used in the home, and (e) a nonspecific manual used in the clinic. The percentages of individuals who were significantly improved were 80%, 10%, 63%, 9%, and 10%, respectively. These findings suggest that self-help manuals can be beneficial to individuals when they are used in a clinic setting.

In addition, O'Brien and Kelley (1980) found that patients who engaged in therapist-directed exposure sessions for snake phobia showed significantly greater improvement than patients who engaged in self-directed exposure sessions. Finally, although Bourque and Ladouceur (1980) found no differences in treatment outcome when they varied the degree of therapist involvement in the exposure sessions, their results might be due to the methodological limitations of their study. In their study design, even the patients in the self-directed exposure condition were presented with the exposure rationale by their therapist prior to engaging in the self-directed exposure. Moreover, they received verbal reinforcement from their therapist immediately after they completed their self-directed exposures.

Other empirical studies have shown that certain types of specific phobias require adaptation of exposure-based procedures that incorporate additional treatment components. For example, individuals with blood-injury-injection phobia tend to have a physiological reaction that can often inspire a fainting response. This physiological reaction, known as a *vasovagal syncope*, consists of an immediate increase in both heart rate and blood pressure when the person encounters the phobic stimulus, followed by a significant decrease in both heart rate and blood pressure. It is this decrease in both heart rate and blood pressure that so often induces fainting in these individuals (Page, 1994). A physical strategy that prevents the fainting response has been developed and added to exposure treatment. This coping strategy, known as *applied tension*, serves to temporarily sustain the patient's blood pressure and heart rate at an increased level, thereby eliminating the possibility of fainting.

The applied tension technique consists of completely tensing all the large muscle groups of the body (arms, torso, and legs) for 15 seconds and subsequently releasing the tensing for a similar time period. Patients are expected to begin the applied tension technique before the injection procedure is begun (completing at least five cycles), and they are to continue the applied tension technique both during and after the injection procedure to maintain an adequate blood pressure and heart rate. This applied tension technique has been empirically validated as an additional component of exposure treatment (Öst & Sterner, 1987). In addition, Hellström, Fellenius, and Öst (1996) showed that a single session of applied tension along with a maintenance program of self-exposure is as effective as a five-session course of the same treatment.

Several treatment manuals for the specific phobias exist. The program developed and manualized at our center presents general information regarding the nature and treatment of specific phobias, as well as detailed treatment information for several of the most common specific phobias; it has been updated recently (Antony, Craske, & Barlow, 2006). In addition, the treatments presented in this manual incorporate additional treatment strategies to be utilized in conjunction with in vivo exposure treatments. For example, cognitive strategies used to combat cognitive distortions and anxious thought patterns and interoceptive exposure utilized to desensitize patients to the physical sensations they associate with the phobic object or situation are included as additional treatment components.

Future Directions

Though a great deal of treatment outcome research exists for specific phobias, much remains to be learned. For example, researchers have only just begun to examine differences among the specific phobia subtypes. Little is known about different characteristics of the five subtypes, and additional information in this area could improve treatments for specific phobias. Just as patients with blood-injury-injection phobias benefit from the utilization of applied tension coupled with exposure therapy, many patients with other specific phobia subtypes might respond more robustly to exposure treatments tailored specifically to their phobic object or situation. For example, studies have shown that, compared with nonphobic controls, individuals with height phobias report an inflated probability of the possibility of serious injury resulting from falling from a ladder (Menzies and Clarke, 1995).

It is interesting to note, based on preliminary evidence, that while a therapist's guidance seems necessary for patients with specific phobias to show evidence of improvement, self-directed bibliotherapy seems effective in treating panic disorder with agoraphobia (e.g., Ghosh & Marks, 1987). If subsequent research supports this finding, factors that might be relevant include differences in the disorders, as well as the differing natures of exposure treatments appropriate for each of them. For example, patients with specific phobias may need a therapist's assistance to come into initial contact with the phobic object. Also, due to the unique nature of many specific phobias, patients may need the therapist's guidance to create a diversity of in vivo exposure experiences of adequate duration and difficulty. In contrast, patients with panic disorder and agoraphobia often fear having panic attacks in many common situations; they rarely believe that there is something inherently dangerous about the situation itself. With the assistance of a manual, motivated patients suffering from panic disorder with agoraphobia may be able to create their own fear and avoidance hierarchy of common situations and conduct effective self-directed in vivo exposures. Of course, these hypotheses are merely speculative at this time, given the limited empirical evidence regarding the effectiveness of self-directed exposure treatment for patients with either specific phobias or panic disorder with agoraphobia.

Moreover, in this era of managed care, when cost effectiveness is considered to be of utmost importance, further research should be conducted to determine which of the many specific phobias can be treated in just one therapist-assisted in vivo exposure session. Though information has been gained regarding such intensive treatments for patients with certain animal and injection phobias, as well as blood phobias (Hellström, Fellenius, & Öst, 1996; Öst, 1989), it has yet to be determined if other common specific phobias (e.g., height) and, in particular, situational phobias such as flying or claustrophobia would respond as well to such a treatment modality.

Öst (1989) has suggested that specific phobias such as phobias of heights, elevators, and darkness might respond very well to therapist-assisted, one-session exposure treatment. However, Öst speculates that flying phobia might require additional therapist-assisted sessions to incorporate substantial patient education regarding the flying process. In addition, Öst wonders whether or not claustrophobia would respond well to a one-session treatment, since usually it is not circumscribed but instead encompasses many different situations. Since situational phobias are thought to be on a continuum with panic disorder with agoraphobia, there is reason to suspect the applicability of single-session treatments. Some studies are currently under way to examine the possible effectiveness of therapist-assisted, single-session exposure treatment, but this is an area of research that could benefit from even further attention.

In the past few years, clinicians have begun to take advantage of technological advances for the treatment of specific phobias. For example, a number of investigators have begun to use virtual reality to expose patients to simulated situations such as

heights (Rothbaum et al., 1995), flying (Rothbaum, Hodges, & Smith, 1999), and spiders (Carlin, Hoffman, & Weghorst, 1997). Although a large number of studies examining the effectiveness of virtual reality exposure (VRE) treatments have been conducted utilizing case study methodology involving one or two patients, few studies have involved treatment comparison groups and/or control groups and an adequately large sample size. In the literature to date, these controlled trials have predominantly been conducted with patients experiencing a fear of flying and a fear of spiders. Rothbaum, Hodges, Smith, Lee, and Price (2000) conducted a controlled study of VRE treatment for fear of flying. Forty-five patients were randomly assigned to receive either VRE treatment, standard exposure treatment (SE), or wait list (WL). The results indicated that VRE and SE were both superior to WL, with no differences between VRE and SE. VRE and SE were shown to be effective by decreases in symptoms as measured by standardized questionnaires, by the number of participants to actually fly on a real airplane following treatment, on anxiety ratings during the flight, on self-ratings of improvement, and on patient satisfaction with treatment. The gains observed in treatment were maintained at a 6-month follow-up. By 6 months posttreatment, 93% of VRE participants and 93% of SE participants had flown. Similar studies examining the efficacy of VRE treatment for fear of flying have consistently found VRE treatment to be more effective at decreasing fear and avoidance of flying when compared with attention-placebo group treatment (Maltby, Kirsch, Mayers, & Allen, 2002), cognitive treatment, and wait-list control (Mühlberger, Weideman & Pauli, 2003). In an interesting version of VRE treatment, Garcia-Palacios, Hoffman, Carlin, Furness, and Botella (2002) randomly assigned 23 patients with a fear of spiders to either wait-list control or VRE treatment with tactile stimulation. In this study, tactile stimulation consisted of patients feeling a "hairy" fabric similar to the sensation of feeling a spider while watching a virtual spider. They found VRE treatment with tactile stimulation to be more effective than wait-list control on all outcome measures, including self-report and behavioral tests.

Although VRE treatments clearly appear to hold some promise as a valuable form of treatment for specific phobias, an important consideration is whether VRE treatments can generalize to naturalistic settings. One concern is the often substantial number of dropouts that are found in VRE treatment outcome studies (Krijn, Emmelkamp, Olafsson, & Biemond, 2004). Research suggests that the major contributing factor to dropout rates in these studies is the degree to which the patient feels "present" in the experience; this involves feeling that one is in the present world rather than in the virtual world. Krijn et al. (2004) found that reported level of "presence" during VRE treatments was highly correlated with treatment dropout, with lower degrees of "presence" associated with higher dropout rates. In addition, other patient factors such as degree of absorption and hypnotizability may mediate the effectiveness of VRE treatments (Wiederhold & Wiederhold, 2000). As our understanding of the nature of anxiety and technological innovations advances, it is clear that VRE will continue to offer interesting, and perhaps more effective, treatment options for the treatment of specific phobias.

SOCIAL PHOBIA

Social phobia has recently been estimated as the most prevalent of all anxiety disorders, with a lifetime prevalence of 12.1% (Kessler et al., 2005). Moreover, social phobia is the fourth most prevalent of all mental disorders, exceeded only by major depressive disorder, alcohol abuse, and specific phobia. This finding is truly remarkable, especially since social phobia was not included as a separate diagnostic category until DSM-III (APA, 1980).

According to DSM-IV-TR (APA, 2000), individuals with social phobia fear a number of social and performance situations because of concerns that they will act in a way that will be humiliating or embarrassing or that they will visibly manifest anxiety symptoms (e.g., sweating, shaking, or blushing). For patients with social phobia, the fear and avoidance of people typically result in several areas of impairment, including occupational, academic, and social functioning (cf. Hope & Heimberg, 1993). The median age of onset of social phobia is estimated to be 13 years, with 95% of patients reporting onset before age 35 (Kessler et al., 2005). Moreover, according to Brown, Campbell, and colleagues (2001), 72% of 186 individuals with a principal diagnosis of social phobia also experienced lifetime major comorbid Axis I disorders such as major depressive disorder

(44%), dysthymia (17%), alcohol abuse (15%), generalized anxiety disorder (14%), drug abuse (11%), obsessive-compulsive disorder (10%), and specific phobia (10%). There is also evidence that from 22.1% to 70% of individuals with social phobia also meet criteria for avoidant personality disorder (cf. Hope & Heimberg, 1993).

Little is known about the etiology of social phobia, but numerous studies have examined possible factors, including behavioral inhibition, genetics, biological mechanisms, developmental factors, conditioning, and cognitive models (Herbert, 1995). Barlow (1988; Barlow, Chorpita, & Turovsky, 1996; Hofmann & Barlow, 2002), invoking the "triple vulnerability" theory once again, hypothesizes that one must be biologically vulnerable to anxious apprehension to develop social phobia, and also evidence both general and specific psychological vulnerabilities. Focusing on biological vulnerabilities, there is good evidence that genetics plays a role in social phobia. After interviewing 2,163 female twins, Kendler, Neale, Kessler, Heath, and Eaves (1992) reported that probandwise concordance for social phobia was greater in monozygotic (24.4%) than dizygotic (15.3%) twin pairs. In another study examining the contribution of genetics in social phobia, first-degree relatives of social phobia probands ($n = 83$) had a significantly increased risk (16% vs. 5%, relative risk = 3.12) for social phobia, as compared with first-degree relatives of never mentally ill controls ($n = 231$; Fyer, Mannuzza, Chapman, Liebowitz, & Klein, 1993). This biological vulnerability may express itself in exaggerated reactivity to social evaluation situations. That is, for reasons of evolutionary significance, we are biologically vulnerable to the effects of anger, criticism, and other means of social disapproval. Alternatively, the vulnerability could be a more nonspecific diathesis to experience anxiety generally.

As in all anxiety disorders, a generalized psychological vulnerability also exists in which individuals learn that important, personally salient events in their lives, particularly challenging or threatening events, are unpredictable and uncontrollable. In addition, research suggests that at least some patients with social phobia are predisposed to focus anxious apprehension about events involving social evaluation (the specific psychological vulnerability). Social anxiety in social evaluative situations involving performance forms the basis from which a false alarm (panic attack) develops in specific social situations.

Of course, in some cases, individuals may have direct experience with a traumatic form of social rejection or humiliation, resulting in a true alarm. Another pathway to the acquisition of social phobia occurs when socially anxious individuals occasionally experience some performance deficits, even without an encounter with an alarm. Subsequent anxious apprehension in the future may lead to additional performance deficits, which sets off the vicious cycle of anxious apprehension (Hofmann & Barlow, 2002). Although the pathways of acquisition may vary, they all have biological vulnerability, general and specific psychological vulnerabilities, and stress/trauma in common.

Treatment of Social Phobia

Research on cognitive-behavioral treatments for social phobia has substantially increased in recent years. The most common approaches include social skills training (SST), relaxation techniques, exposure-based methods, and multicomponent cognitive-behavioral treatments (Heimberg & Juster, 1995; Rodebaugh, Holaway, & Heimberg, 2004; Turk, Heimberg, & Hope, 2001). In this section, as above, empirical studies are evaluated according to the template created by the American Psychological Association to guide the development of practice guidelines described above (APA, 2002; American Psychological Association Task Force on Psychological Intervention Guidelines, 1995 [see Table 1]; Barlow & Barlow, 1995). Effective treatments in this section are organized into one of the following three categories of increasing confidence in treatment efficacy: (a) better than no therapy (randomized clinical trials [RCTs]), (b) better than nonspecific therapy (RCTs), and (c) better than alternative therapy (RCTs). All studies individually reviewed are Type 1 unless otherwise noted.

Social Skills Training

The rationale for social skills training (SST) is based on the concept that people with social phobias are deficient in verbal and nonverbal social skills. Heimberg and Juster (1995) point out that, although social skills deficits are inferred from poor social behavior, the term is often confused with performance deficits. They also conclude that, although nine studies have used SST as a treatment condition, with

some resulting in significant improvement, all but one failed to include appropriate control groups. Therefore, it is not possible to conclude that training in social skills was the component that led to positive outcomes (Heimberg & Juster, 1995). Similarly, Donahue, Van Hasselt, and Hersen (1994) conclude that the heterogeneity of the samples and the paucity of controlled comparisons do not permit definitive conclusions on SST efficacy. Due to the recognized cognitive contributions in the maintenance of social phobia, as well as the fact that most individuals with social phobia have adequate social skills, therapy in recent years has targeted cognitive and behavioral interventions for the treatment of social phobia. Therefore, SST has been investigated less in recent years (Mersch, 1995).

Referring to the aforementioned template of treatment efficacy, we cannot definitively state at this time that SST is superior to even a wait-list control because of methodological limitations. This conclusion gains credence given that the only controlled study of SST completed two decades ago found that 15 weeks of SST did not result in better clinical outcomes than a wait-list control group (Marzillier, Lambert, & Kelley, 1976).

Although SST by itself does not appear to be efficacious, there is some indication that combined SST and exposure appears to hold some promise (Turner, Beidel, Cooley, Woody, & Messer, 1994). In this pilot study of a comprehensive multicomponent treatment (which was a Type 3 study), 13 patients with severe (generalized) social phobia demonstrated significant improvements posttreatment. The authors report that 84% of those completing treatment (four dropped out) showed moderate to high end-state functioning, although pretreatment status could not be calculated because there were no pretreatment Clinical Global Impression (CGI) ratings. Moreover, there was no control group. Recently, another investigation compared the efficacy of cognitive-behavioral group therapy (CBGT) with and without SST (Herbert, Gaudiano, & Rheingold, 2005). The authors found significant improvement in social phobia symptoms for both groups, although the combined group produced the largest effect sizes. These preliminary findings suggest the importance of controlled clinical trials for this combined treatment. Furthermore, additional dismantling studies need to be conducted to explore whether the SST component itself leads to additional improvement above and beyond the gains made from the other components. Obviously, targeting SST specifically to the patients with clearly assessed social skill deficits should produce the most substantial effects.

Relaxation Treatments

The effectiveness of relaxation training and other strategies targeting arousal reduction for social phobia has not yet been adequately evaluated (Heimberg & Juster, 1995; Turk, Heimberg, & Hope, 2001). Two groups of investigators have concluded that progressive muscle relaxation alone is not an effective treatment (Al-Kubaisy et al., 1992; Alström, Nordlund, Persson, Harding, & Ljungqvist, 1984). There has been some indication by Öst, Jerremalm, and Johansson (1981) and Jerremalm, Jansson, and Öst (1986a) that applied relaxation (AR), including application training in which relaxation skills are used during anxiety-producing role-plays, is an effective treatment for social phobia (cf. Heimberg & Juster, 1995). In the three controlled clinical trials conducted in this area (Alström et al., 1984; Jerremalm et al., 1986a; Öst et al., 1981), AR was inferior to self-instruction training, exposure, and supportive counseling and was no better than SST (Donahue et al., 1994). At this time, there is no strong body of literature to support relaxation procedures alone as an effective treatment for social phobia.

Exposure and Cognitive Therapy

There is a growing body of literature in support of multifaceted treatment for social phobia based on exposure to feared social situations and cognitive therapy (Barlow & Lehman, 1996). Social phobia is partially maintained by the avoidance of anxiety-producing situations and the negative reinforcement that occurs as a result (Donahue et al., 1994). Barlow (1988; Hofmann & Barlow, 2002) views some form of exposure as a central part of any psychological treatment for social phobia; many others would agree. The essential part of exposure is to have a patient repeatedly confront the situation they fear until their anxiety response habituates. The exposures can be conducted in vivo, with the stimulus encountered in the natural environment, or through imaginal exercises. Many treatment programs involve simulated social interactions in which the therapist (and confederates, if necessary) role-plays the anxiety-produc-

ing social situation. The cognitive component of treatment addresses the role of fear of negative evaluation by identifying and modifying maladaptive cognitions that occur in these situations (Donahue et al., 1994). Although many current treatments for social phobia are conducted in a group format (to facilitate exposure), there is also evidence that individual treatment protocols are as, if not more, effective (Stangier, Heidenreich, Peitz, Lauterbach, & Clark, 2003).

In an early study examining combination treatments, Butler, Cullington, Munby, Amies, and Gelder (1984) randomly assigned 45 socially phobic outpatients to one of the three following conditions: in vivo exposure plus anxiety management (AM), in vivo plus a nonspecific filler, and wait-list. The AM program consisted of distraction, relaxation, and rational self-talk. At posttreatment, both active treatment groups were superior to the wait-list controls. However, at 6-month follow-up, patients who received the combination treatment were more improved than the in vivo exposure alone group.

Mattick and Peters (1988) concluded that cognitive restructuring exercises may enhance the effects of exposure therapy for people with social phobia. In their study, 26 patients were randomly assigned to guided exposure, while 25 patients received guided exposure and cognitive restructuring. There were improvements in both groups at follow-up, but patients in the combined condition fared better at the 3-month follow-up.

In a subsequent study, Mattick, Peters, and Clarke (1989) randomly assigned 43 patients with social phobia to guided exposure alone, cognitive restructuring alone, guided exposure and cognitive restructuring, or a wait-list. All active treatment conditions were significantly better than the wait-list on a behavioral avoidance test (BAT), as well as self-report measures of negative evaluation and irrational beliefs. Patients in the combined condition evidenced the most improvement on the BAT. The authors conclude that exposure therapy combined with cognitive restructuring was the most effective intervention overall.

Heimberg et al. (1990) compared a treatment package called cognitive-behavioral group treatment (CBGT), consisting primarily of in-session exposure exercises, cognitive restructuring, and homework exercises to a credible placebo condition. This placebo condition, called educational supportive group therapy (ES), was a nondirective supportive group treatment that also consisted of psychoeducation about social phobia. Both groups improved significantly at posttreatment, but CBGT patients were more improved on some key measures at both posttreatment and 6-month follow-up. Moreover, a 5-year follow-up on a portion of the patients from the original study indicated that individuals who received CBGT were more likely to be improved and to maintain their gains relative to the ES group (Heimberg, Salzman, Halt, & Blendell, 1993). This investigation provides further support for combination treatments involving both exposure and cognitive restructuring.

More recently, Hofmann and colleagues compared the efficacy of cognitive-behavioral group therapy (CBGT), exposure group therapy (EGT), and a wait-list control group (WL) for individuals with social phobia (Hofmann, 2004; Hofmann, Moscovitch, Kim, & Taylor, 2004). Ninety participants (30 per group) received 12 weekly sessions of group treatment. The CBGT treatment protocol was developed by Heimberg (1991), and the EGT treatment protocol consisted of repeated in-session in vivo exposures to social situations (including video feedback, didactic training, and weekly homework assignments) and was conducted without explicit cognitive restructuring procedures (Hofmann, 1999). Wait-list participants were randomly assigned to receive either CBGT or EGT after the waiting period; however, their treatment data were not included in the results. All participants were asked to complete a follow-up assessment 6 months after treatment termination.

At posttreatment, the two active treatment groups were both significantly better than the wait-list control group, according to two self-report measures of social anxiety and a behavioral stress test, although CBGT and EGT did not differ from each other. However, at a 6-month follow-up, individuals who received CBGT reported significantly less social anxiety, suggesting that the addition of cognitive restructuring to an exposure-based treatment protocol may aid in maintaining treatment gains.

To date, only a few studies have compared effective pharmacotherapy treatments to effective psychological treatments. In the first published study of this nature, 65 patients with social phobia were assigned randomly to one of the four following conditions: cognitive-behavioral group treatment, alprazolam with instructions for self-directed exposure (EXP), phenelzine with EXP, or placebo with EXP (Gelernter et al., 1991). All treatments, including the combination

of a placebo plus self-exposure instructions, were associated with substantial improvements in severe and chronic social phobia, although the results failed to demonstrate definitively the superiority of one treatment over another.

Turner, Beidel, and Jacob (1994) assigned 72 patients with social phobia randomly to receive behavior therapy (flooding), atenolol, or a placebo. On composite and improvement indices, the behavior therapy patients were significantly more improved and demonstrated superior end-state functioning. However, although beta blockers such as atenolol may minimize the somatic symptoms associated with social phobia, such as trembling (Barlow, 1988), these drugs seem incapable of reducing other difficulties associated with this disorder (Turner, Beidel, & Jacob, 1994). Other research has suggested that atenolol is not the most effective drug treatment for social phobia (Heimberg & Juster, 1995).

An important multisite (the State University of New York at Albany, Center for Stress and Anxiety Disorders, and the New York State Psychiatric Institute) collaborative project directed by Richard Heimberg and Michael Liebowitz randomly assigned 133 individuals with social phobia to one of the following four treatment conditions: CBGT, phenelzine, a psychological placebo (ES), and a pill placebo (Heimberg et al., 1998). Results indicated the following:

1. CBGT and phenelzine were equally effective after 12 weeks of treatment, with approximately 60% of patients completing treatment in each group showing substantial improvement. Both were superior to ES and pill placebo, which produced improvement rates of approximately 27% and 33%, respectively.
2. After 12 weeks, phenelzine was more effective than CBGT on some self-report measures.

Following the acute phase of the study, responders to this trial entered a 6-month maintenance phase followed by a 6-month treatment-free phase (Liebowitz et al., 1999). Of the 31 patients who completed acute treatment with phenelzine, 20 were classified as responders and were, therefore, eligible to enter the maintenance phase. Similarly, 21 of the 36 patients who received CBGT during the acute phase were classified as responders, eligible to enter the maintenance phase of the study. Of these patients, 6 in the phenelzine group and 7 in the CBGT group declined participation in maintenance. Following the 6-month maintenance phase, no differences were detected between the phenelzine patients (three relapsed, one dropped out) and CBGT patients (two relapsed, one dropped out). At this point, those patients classified as responders in the phenelzine group (10/14) and the CGBT group (11/14) were eligible to enter a 6-month treatment free-phase. Following this treatment-free phase, again, there was no difference found in the dropout rates between the two groups, with each group having only one. Although the relapse rate in the phenelzine group (3/14) was higher than in the CBGT group (0/14) at the end of the treatment-free phase, the difference did not reach statistical significance due to the small sample size.

Recent data have also suggested the advantage of monotherapy over combination therapy. Clark and colleagues compared cognitive therapy (CT), fluoxetine combined with self-exposure (FLU plus SE), and placebo combined with self-exposure (PLA plus SE) in patients with generalized social phobia (Clark et al., 2003). The cognitive therapy was based on the model for maintenance of social phobia developed by Clark and Wells (1995) and included several specific components: (a) developing a personal model of social phobia for each patient that is consistent with the general model presented; (b) safety behaviors and self-focused attention experiments; (c) shifting focus of attention to the social situation; (d) video feedback; (e) behavioral experiments; (f) identifying problematic anticipatory and postevent processing; and (g) challenging dysfunctional assumptions. At posttreatment (16 weeks), results indicated that patients in the CT condition were superior to patients in the FLU plus SE and PLA plus SE conditions (which did not differ from each other) on all measures of social phobia. Following the posttreatment assessment, individuals in the PLA plus SE condition were withdrawn from the study, and the remaining patients entered a 3-month booster phase where up to three additional treatment sessions were administered. In addition, patients in the FLU plus SE condition maintained the full dose of fluoxetine. Following the booster session, the CT condition was superior to FLU plus SE on the composite measure of social phobia, as well as four of the individual measures of social phobia. These findings were maintained at 12-month follow-up, suggesting both the superiority and the durability of CT, as compared with FLU plus

SE. In addition, the effect sizes for the CT condition were double those reported by Heimberg and colleagues (Heimberg et al., 1998).

Another recent large-scale, multisite RCT compared five treatment conditions for 295 participants diagnosed with social phobia: fluoxetine (FLU), comprehensive cognitive-behavioral group therapy (CCBT, a modification of CBGT that includes a social skills training component), pill placebo (PBO), and their combination (FLU/CCBT and PBO/CCBT; Davidson et al., 2004). Although participants in the FLU condition were significantly improved after 4 weeks (as compared with all other treatment conditions), by the end of 14 weeks there were no significant differences between the four active treatments on measures of social phobia symptoms, and all active treatments were better than PBO. In addition, response rates did not differ between FLU, CCBT, FLU/CCBT, and PBO/CCBT (all significantly better than PBO), which suggests that combination treatments do not confer a significant advantage over monotherapy. However, the authors did note that many patients across all the treatment conditions were still symptomatic following treatment, which may suggest longer term pharmacological treatment and modification of cognitive-behavioral treatment protocols to improve efficacy (Davidson et al., 2004).

Based on the empirical research, we can conclude that combined exposure and cognitive therapy treatments are superior to wait-list, nonspecific therapy, and, in some cases, alternative therapies.

Psychological Intervention Guidelines

If we return to the psychological intervention guidelines template mentioned above, exposure-based procedures are the only treatment for social phobia that attain the highest level of treatment efficacy, "better than alternative therapy." Heimberg and Juster (1995) and Turk, Heimberg, and Hope (2001) maintain that every study with this approach demonstrates significant reductions in social phobia, compared with various control groups. Moreover, there is some evidence to support the idea that combining exposure with cognitive restructuring is even more effective that exposure alone (Butler et al., 1984; Hofmann et al., 2004; Mattick & Peters, 1988; Mattick et al., 1989).

Table 13.4 (Barlow & Lehman, 1996) indicates that combining exposure and cognitive therapy is

TABLE 13.4 Controlled Trials of Psychosocial Treatments for Social Phobia

Study	Length of Follow-Up (Months)	Treatment (N)	Percentage Clinical Improvement of Completers (If Available)	Significant Comparison (Percentage Clinical Improvement)	
				Other Treatments (Yes/No)	Wait List (Yes/No)
Butler et al. (1984)	6	AMT & E (N = 15)		Yes: E	Yes
Mattick and Peters (1988)	3	E & CR (N = 11)	86	Yes: E = 52%	Yes
Mattick et al. (1989)	3	E & CR (N = 25)		Yes: E	Yes
Heimberg et al. (1990)	6	CBGT (N = 20)	81	Yes: ES = 47%	
Heimberg et al. (1993)[a]	54–75	CBGT (N = 10)		Yes: ES (most)	
Hope et al. (1990)	6	CBGT (N = 13)		No: E	Yes
Gelernter et al. (1991)	2	CBGT (N = 20)		No: PH, AL, PL	
Lucas and Telch (1993)	PT	CBGT (N = 18) CBTI	61 50	Yes: ES = 24%	
Heimberg et al. (1998)	PT	CBGT (N = 28)	75	No: PH = 77% Yes: PL = 41% Yes: ES = 35%	
Liebowitz et al. (1999)[b]	6–12	CBGT (N = 14)		Yes: ES = 27% No: PH	
Haug et al. (2003)	6–12	E + PL (N = 93)		No: E + ST No: ST No: PL	
Clark et al. (2003)	12	CT (N = 20)		Yes: FL + SE Yes: PL + SE	
Davidson et al. (2004)		CBGT (N = 60)	65	No: GBGT + FL = 67% No: CBGT + PL = 59% No: FL = 64% Yes: PL = 39%	
Hofmann (2004)	6	CBGT (N = 30)		No: EGT Yes: WL	

Source: Reprinted and adapted with permission from Barlow and Lehman (1996), © 1996 American Medical Association. All rights reserved.

AL = alprazolam; AMT = anxiety management therapy; CBGT = cognitive-behavioral group treatment; CBTI = cognitive-behavioral treatment—individual; CR = cognitive restructuring; E = exposure; EGT = exposure group therapy; ES = educational supportive group psychotherapy (placebo treatment); FL = fluoxetine; PL = pill placebo; PH = phenelzine; PT = posttreatment; SE = self-exposure; ST = sertraline; WL = wait-list control.

[a]Follow-up study of Heimberg et al. (1990).

[b]Follow-up study of Heimberg et al. (1998).

more effective than exposure alone or educational supportive group psychotherapy in all but one case. In this study (Hope, Heimberg, & Bruch, 1990), CBGT and exposure alone were equally effective, and both were superior to wait-list control. Two studies that included medication did not demonstrate the superiority of combined treatments over drug treatments. Gelernter et al. (1991) found that all treatments (CBGT, alprazolam and exposure, phenelzine and exposure, placebo and exposure) were associated with substantial improvements, although the superiority of one treatment over another was not definitively demonstrated. Heimberg et al. (1998) found that CBGT and phenelzine treatments were equally effective and superior to a placebo and educational supportive treatments. Finally, Davidson et al. (2004) found that cognitive-behavioral group therapy produced similar results when administered as a monotherapy or when given in combination with fluoxe-tine or placebo.

Looking at other treatment approaches, at this time we cannot definitively state that social skills training or relaxation is better than no therapy. This is partially due to the methodological limitations of these studies. However, AR, which includes expo-sure, appears promising.

Future Directions

Clearly, more research needs to be done to evaluate the effectiveness of certain treatments compared with wait-list controls, nonspecific treatment, and alterna-tive therapies. Given the favorable outcomes of the combined cognitive and exposure treatments, it is imperative that we, as researchers, disseminate this treatment to clinicians for widespread use. Barlow and Lehman (1996) conclude that few attempts have been made to make these treatments more "user friendly" and present them for use by clinicians. To date, little work has been done to evaluate specific treatments beyond their original settings. One of the challenges for treatment outcome studies is the dis-semination of the results to practicing clinicians. Al-though previous studies have been criticized for the exclusion of "messy" patients, it appears as though there have been greater attempts to expand the gen-eralizability of research findings (Barlow, 2004). For example, the exclusion criteria in the study by Hof-mann (2004) were limited to only (a) prior nonre-sponse to adequately delivered study treatment; (b) current diagnosis of substance abuse or dependence; (c) current active suicidal potential; and (d) current diagnosis of bipolar disorder, schizophrenia, or other psychotic disorder. Clark et al. (2003) also identified minimal exclusion criteria. In addition, one study on the generalizability of cognitive-behavioral group treatment for social phobia compared clients in a highly controlled efficacy study with those who re-fused random assignment (and the possibility of a drug condition) or were excluded (Juster, Heimberg, & Engelberg, 1995). Although the refusers and ex-cluded clients differed systematically from the in-cluded clients on a number of variables, such as de-gree of social support and socioeconomic status, all patients showed evidence of comparable clinical gain from the treatment under evaluation. We must continue to create and evaluate effective treatments for social phobia while simultaneously disseminating

them to practitioners and evaluating their effective-ness "in the field." Along these lines, recent evidence suggests that group treatment for social phobia can be conducted in an intensive format over a period of 1 to 2 weeks, as opposed to several months, with pa-tients continuing to improve up to 1 year after treat-ment (Mörtberg, Berglund, & Sundin, 2005). Virtual reality is also a possible avenue for increasing dissem-ination of treatments, with some preliminary evi-dence suggesting that it can be as effective as stan-dard group therapy (Klinger et al., 2005). Short-term, intensive treatments or virtual reality treatments would facilitate dissemination by reducing costs and therapist involvement, thus allowing efficacious treat-ments to be more readily available to clinicians and patients.

GENERALIZED ANXIETY DISORDER

The diagnostic criteria for generalized anxiety disor-der (GAD) have undergone substantial modification over the past two decades (Brown, O'Leary, & Bar-low, 2001). In the past, the diagnostic category of GAD, first formulated in 1980 (APA, 1980), resulted in enormous confusion (Barlow, 1988, 2002; Barlow & Wincze, 1998). This was partly due to its residual status, which meant that the diagnosis of GAD could not be assigned if a person met criteria for any other mental disorder (Brown et al., 2001). This conven-tion was based on the notion that generalized anxiety was an integral part of many disorders and therefore could not be easily separated from the general clini-cal presentation. In DSM-III-R (APA, 1987), for the first time key defining features (e.g., excessive worry and persistent somatic concerns) were presented that elevated GAD beyond a strictly residual category (Brown et al., 2001). These criteria were further de-lineated and sharpened by DSM-IV and DSM-IV-TR (APA, 1994, 2000), as the number of associated physical symptoms associated with worry were re-duced and the lack of control over worry was high-lighted as a diagnostic feature. Recent estimates sug-gest the lifetime prevalence of GAD to be 5.7% according to DSM-IV criteria (Kessler et al., 2005).

As a result of changes in the diagnostic criteria and new data on prevalence, research on important characteristics of GAD, as well as empirical treat-ment outcome studies, have increased in the past de-cade. However, given that GAD may be the "basic" anxiety disorder in the sense that generalized anxiety is a consistent component of other anxiety disorders with the possible exception of specific phobia, treatments for GAD have still received surprisingly little attention (Barlow, 1988, 2002; Brown et al., 2001; Rapee, 1991).

Our model (Barlow, 1988, 2000, 2002) of the etiology of GAD suggests that biological and psychological vulnerabilities line up to create a diathesis for chronic anxiety. Stress-related negative life events trigger neurobiological reactions such as increased corticotropin-releasing factor, chronic activation of the hypothalamic-pituitary adrenocorticol axis, and the sense that events are proceeding in an uncontrollable and unpredictable way. The focus of attention is shifted from the task at hand to a maladaptive self-evaluative mode, which further increases arousal. This results in increased vigilance and the narrowing of attention to the threat or challenge. This arousal-driven cognitive process continues to escalate in a negative feedback loop, resulting occasionally in performance disruption, attempts to cope, including situational avoidance, if possible, and/or a maladaptive worry process that seems to serve as a method of avoiding core negative affect (Barlow, 2000, 2002; Borkovec, 1994; Craske, 1999).

Treatment of Generalized Anxiety Disorder

Until recently, clinical outcome studies have demonstrated only modest treatment gains in GAD symptomatology. These minimal treatment gains have been hypothesized to result from, among other things, high rates of comorbidity found in patients with GAD. In fact, studies have found GAD to be the most frequently assigned additional diagnosis for patients who meet criteria for another anxiety or mood disorder (cf. Brown, Campbell, et al., 2001). The modest treatment gains seen in patients with GAD in early studies may also have resulted from the fact that GAD tends to be chronic, with patients often recalling a lifelong history of the disorder (Brown et al., 2001).

In general, different treatment conditions have not led to differential improvement rates. Given the vagueness of earlier criteria, initial studies on the treatment of GAD utilized nonspecific treatment approaches such as relaxation or biofeedback, in contrast to specific treatment components directed at key features of other anxiety disorders, such as panic dis-

order. With the successive refinements of GAD criteria in *DSM-IV* and *DSM-IV-TR*, researchers now have more information regarding the key features to target in treatment. It has only been in the last decade that more rigorous controlled trials of treatment for GAD have been conducted, utilizing more specific treatment techniques, aimed at targeting the key features of the disorder, such as cognitive therapy, behavior therapy, and combinations of several treatment components.

To properly evaluate the question of treatment choice, one must consider both the efficacy of the treatment and the clinical utility of that technique. In this section, as above, the treatment techniques reviewed focus on treatment efficacy. However, because there are fewer treatment outcome studies for GAD (relative to other disorders), they are organized in three categories of increasing confidence in treatment efficacy: (a) better than no therapy (randomized clinical trials [RCTs]), (b) better than nonspecific therapy (RCTs), and (c) better than alternative therapy (RCTs).

Better Than No Therapy

In an early Type 2 investigation, five patients meeting *DSM-III* (APA, 1980) criteria for GAD received a treatment package consisting of electromyographic (EMG) biofeedback, relaxation, and cognitive treatment; they were compared with four GAD patients assigned to a wait-list (Barlow et al., 1984). Those receiving active treatment had 18 sessions over a 14-week period. Compared with controls, the patients receiving the active treatment demonstrated a generalized improvement at posttreatment and 3-month follow-up on a variety of measures, including physiological reactivity, self-report questionnaires, and clinician ratings.

Another early controlled clinical trial for the treatment of GAD was conducted to investigate the efficacy of anxiety management (AM), a multicomponent treatment package in the form of a self-help booklet that was utilized in conjunction with therapist-conducted treatment sessions (Butler, Cullington, Hibbert, Klimes, & Gelder, 1987). In this study, 45 patients meeting research diagnostic criteria (RDC) for GAD were randomly assigned to either the AM ($n = 22$) or the wait-list (WL) ($n = 23$) condition.

The treatment components included psychoeducation about anxiety, relaxation, distraction, cognitive restructuring, and exposure through graded practice. In addition, patients were encouraged to identify their strong points and engage in rewarding and pleasurable activities. Patients could stop treatment after a minimum of four sessions if they were no longer experiencing the symptoms of anxiety, their anxiety ratings were stable for 2 weeks, and their therapist agreed that the patient could control his or her symptoms. The average length of treatment was 8.7 sessions.

Patients were actively involved in their treatment by establishing goals and creating homework assignments, as well as scheduling more pleasurable activities and noting areas in their life in which things were going well. Some of the exercises were first practiced with the therapist in session and in addition at home. Furthermore, patients were encouraged to reduce their medication intake. During booster sessions at the end of treatment, the treatment components were reviewed, as well as relapse prevention strategies.

At the end of treatment, the patients receiving AM had improved significantly, as compared with the wait-list controls, on every measure, including the State-Trait Anxiety Inventory, the Hamilton rating scales for anxiety and depression, and problem ratings of severity and interference. In addition, these gains were maintained or improved at 6-month follow-up. Although these results are extremely encouraging, it should be noted that patients were excluded if they had suffered from anxiety for 2 years or more, thus eliminating the patients with more chronic levels of anxiety.

Other studies have added a "placebo" therapy condition to examine whether improvements are caused by specific anxiety treatment techniques or merely general therapy effects. Referring to our template of increasing treatment efficacy, we would have greater confidence in the efficacy of a certain treatment if it was shown to be superior to a nonspecific or placebo therapy. Two investigations that used both wait-list controls and a nondirective treatment condition were unable to demonstrate differential effectiveness between the active therapies and the nondirective treatments, although all treatments were superior to wait-list control groups (Blowers, Cobb, & Mathews, 1987; White & Keenan, 1992).

In one such investigation (Blowers et al., 1987), 66 patients meeting DSM-III criteria for GAD were assigned to one of three groups: anxiety management

training (AMT), nondirective counseling (NDC), or wait-list (WL) control. All patients were assessed pretreatment, posttreatment, and at 6-month follow-up. The AMT package involved relaxation exercises and a cognitive component based on an abbreviated version of Beck and Emery's cognitive therapy (1985). Patients in the NDC condition were offered the rationale that they could be helped by understanding and becoming aware of their thoughts and feelings and would find the symptoms of anxiety to be less distressing as a result. There were few significant differences in the active treatment conditions, but both were superior to the wait-list controls according to self-report measures and clinician ratings.

Other researchers have also encountered the finding that different active treatments have not led to differential efficacy (Barlow, Rapee, & Brown, 1992; Borkovec & Mathews, 1988; Durham & Turvey, 1987). In a study conducted in our center (Barlow et al., 1992), 65 patients meeting DSM-III-R criteria as established by the DSM-III-R-compatible Anxiety Disorders Interview Schedule-Revised (ADIS-R; Di Nardo & Barlow, 1988) were randomized to one of four treatment groups: applied progressive muscle relaxation (REL), cognitive restructuring (COG), a combination of relaxation and cognitive restructuring (COM), or a wait-list (WL). All patients in the active treatment conditions received 15 hourlong sessions conducted by senior doctoral students and staff psychologists. Treated patients were significantly better compared with those in the wait-list control group. However, as stated above, differential efficacy was not found among active treatment components. Moreover, differential dropout rates were encountered among the active treatments (8% in the COM group to 38% in the REL group).

The two additional studies mentioned above also did not find a difference among treatment conditions, although they did not assign a wait-list control group. Durham and Turvey (1987) randomly assigned 41 patients to either behavior therapy or Beck's cognitive therapy and found that there were no significant differences posttreatment. At 6-month follow-up, however, there was a trend for those receiving cognitive therapy to continue to improve or maintain their gains more frequently than those patients receiving behavior therapy. In another investigation, Borkovec and Mathews (1988) randomly assigned 30 patients to one of three groups: progressive muscle relaxation (PMR) with nondirective therapy, PMR with coping desensitization, or PMR with cognitive therapy. All patients had significant improvement, but they did not differ from each other.

More recently, two separate studies have been conducted comparing a new cognitive-behavioral treatment for GAD compared with a wait-list control group (Dugas et al., 2003; Ladouceur et al., 2000). Based on recent research suggesting the role of intolerance of uncertainty in GAD, the authors utilized a treatment protocol that specifically targets worry (e.g., components are aimed to target four aspects of GAD: intolerance of uncertainty, erroneous beliefs about worry, poor problem orientation, and cognitive avoidance). In the first trial using an individual treatment protocol, 26 patients were included (14 received immediate treatment, 12 were assigned to a delayed treatment wait-list control), and results indicated that patients in the treatment condition were significantly improved, as compared with the wait-list control (Ladouceur et al., 2000). Furthermore, the treatment led to significant changes on outcome measures, which were maintained at a 1-year follow-up. Additionally, 20 of the 26 patients (77%) no longer met criteria for GAD following treatment. In the second trial, which included treatment components of awareness training (i.e., learning to be aware of worries) and cognitive exposure (i.e., each patient would record a "worst fear" on an audiotape and listen to the recording daily, until the scenario no longer provoked anxiety), 52 GAD patients received 14 sessions of group therapy for their symptoms (Dugas et al., 2003). Of these, 25 received immediate treatment, and 27 were assigned to a delayed treatment control condition. At posttreatment, treated patients demonstrated significant improvement on all measures, as compared with wait-list patients, and results were maintained through 24-month follow-up. The authors suggest that group cognitive-behavioral treatment may be a viable and less costly option for individuals with GAD (Dugas et al., 2003).

Better Than Nonspecific Therapy

Several controlled clinical trials have found that a certain type of treatment is better than nondirective treatment (Borkovec & Costello, 1993; Borkovec et al., 1987). In the earlier study (Borkovec et al., 1987), 30 patients who met DSM-III criteria according to the Anxiety Disorders Interview Schedule (ADIS; Di Nardo, O'Brien, Barlow, Waddell, & Blanchard,

1983) were randomly assigned to one of two groups: progressive muscle relaxation (PMR) with cognitive therapy (CT) or PMR with nondirective therapy (ND). Overall, all patients improved substantially at the end of treatment and also at the 6-to 12-month follow-up, as shown by clinician ratings, self-report questionnaires, and daily self-monitoring. However, the PMR and CT group was superior to the PMR and ND group on all but one posttreatment outcome measure. In addition, patients receiving cognitive therapy attributed more of their improvement to the cognitive component of treatment than patients receiving nondirective therapy did to the general psychotherapy they received. The authors conclude that cognitive therapy contains an active ingredient above and beyond the nonspecific psychotherapy treatment factors.

Better Than Alternative Therapy

A final group of studies has been conducted that compares at least two efficacious psychotherapy treatments to each other. According to the template, demonstrated efficacy in this category results in the highest level of confidence in a given treatment. Although most investigations of this type have not resulted in significant differences emerging among active treatments (Barlow et al., 1992; Blowers et al., 1987; Borkovec & Mathews, 1988; Durham & Turvey, 1987; White & Keenan, 1992), a few empirical studies have demonstrated the superiority of one active treatment over another (Butler, Fennell, Robson, & Gelder, 1991; Durham et al., 1994).

In an empirical investigation, 57 patients meeting DSM-III-R criteria for GAD were randomly assigned to one of three treatment groups: cognitive-behavioral treatment (CBT), behavior therapy (BT), or a wait list control group (Butler et al., 1991). In this controlled clinical trial, independent assessments were conducted pretreatment, posttreatment, at 6-month follow-up, and at 18-month follow-up. Treatment lasted for up to 12 sessions; patients could stop treatment after four sessions if they no longer experienced significant symptoms of anxiety, their anxiety ratings were stable for at least 2 weeks, and their therapist agreed with the patient that the patient could control anxiety symptoms effectively.

The BT package consisted of progressive muscle relaxation, reducing avoidance through graduated exposure, and building confidence by reinitiating pleasurable activities. The rationale for BT was that anxiety is maintained by avoidance of anxiety-producing situations, the person's reaction to the symptoms, and loss of confidence. The CBT package consisted of cognitive therapy as described by Beck and Emery (1985), as well as behavioral assignments. The rationale of CBT treatment was that anxiety is maintained by anxious thoughts and lack of self-confidence, which can be controlled by recognizing anxious thoughts, seeking helpful alternatives, and taking action to test these alternatives.

Results showed a superiority of CBT over BT, as demonstrated through measures of anxiety, depression, and cognition. However, the patients in the BT group improved significantly on all but one measure of anxiety and maintained their gains 6 months later. The authors (Butler et al., 1991) note that theirs is one of the few studies in which CBT is shown to be superior to BT, and they offer several possible explanations:

1. BT could not adequately address additional problems such as depression or social anxiety.
2. Cognitive techniques can be effectively applied to treatment reservations and low motivation.
3. CBT deals with worry, as well as somatic symptoms.
4. This study employed unusually rigorous methods of double-checking the integrity of treatment to reduce error variance and overlap between CBT and BT.

In the second study mentioned in the "Better Than Nonspecific Therapy" section above, Borkovec and Costello (1993) compared the efficacy of CBT, AR, and ND in a sample of 55 patients who met DSM-III-R criteria for GAD. For this study, patients in the ND condition were told that the goals of treatment were to enhance self-understanding and to discover things they could do differently to affect how they feel. All three treatments were equal in length and were reported to be highly credible to the patients. The AR and CBT treatment conditions did not differ significantly from each other but were both superior to ND at posttreatment. However, during a 1-year follow-up, 57.9% of patients receiving CBT met a high end-state functioning criterion (meaning they were close to "cured"), which was significantly better than the 33.3% of patients receiving AR who met this criterion and the 22.2% of patients receiving

ND therapy who met this criterion. In addition, significantly fewer patients receiving CBT or AR requested additional treatment (15.8% and 16.7%, respectively) as compared with ND (61.1%).

In another controlled clinical trial, 110 patients who met DSM-III-R criteria for GAD were randomly assigned to receive one of the following treatments over a 6-month period: 16 to 20 sessions of cognitive therapy, 8 to 10 sessions of cognitive therapy, 16 to 20 sessions of psychodynamic psychotherapy, 8 to 10 sessions of psychodynamic psychotherapy, or 8 to 10 sessions of behaviorally based anxiety management training (Durham et al., 1994). Experienced therapists conducted the cognitive therapy and psychodynamic therapy sessions, and the anxiety management sessions were conducted by registrars in psychiatry after a brief period of training.

Although all treatments resulted in substantial improvements, cognitive therapy was significantly more effective than analytic therapy, with about 50% of cognitive therapy patients "considerably" better at follow-up. There was no significant effect for level of contact. Although the authors make the point that significant improvements in symptoms can be made after only brief therapist training, it remains unclear whether there is a significant advantage for the experienced therapist because experienced and inexperienced therapists were conducting different types of treatment. Because therapist experience differed according to treatment type, this is considered to be a Type 2 study.

More recently, Arntz (2003) compared two treatments, cognitive therapy (CT), based on treatment approaches by Beck and Emery (1985) and Butler et al. (1991), and applied relaxation (AR), based on the protocol developed by Öst (1987) in a randomized clinical trial with 45 patients. After a 3- to 6-month wait period and a brief introduction session with the therapist, all patients received either 12 weekly individual sessions of CT (with the inclusion of behavioral experiments to test erroneous cognitions) or AR (which included graduated exposures to feared situations during the final weeks of treatment).

Both treatments resulted in significant improvement for patients, and recovery rates and rates of clinically significant changes were similar for both CT and AR. Although not statistically significant, it appeared as though AR demonstrated its effects 1 month after treatment, while the effects of CT caught up at the 6-month follow-up assessment.

Additional research has also suggested that a comprehensive CBT package is not necessarily more efficacious than the individual protocol components. Borkovec, Newman, Pincus, and Lytle (2002) compared three treatments for GAD: (a) applied relaxation training combined with self-control desensitization (SCD), (b) cognitive therapy (CT), and (c) their combination (CBT). Contrary to expectations, there were no significant differences among the three groups on self-report or clinician-rated measures, suggesting that SCD and CT are not necessarily more efficacious when used in combination.

Cognitive-behavioral therapy has also been shown to be superior to benzodiazepine medication in several controlled clinical trials (Lindsay, Gamsu, McLaughlin, Hood, & Espie, 1987; Power et al., 1990; Power, Jerrom, Simpson, Mitchell, & Swanson, 1989). In one study (Power et al., 1990), 101 patients meeting *DSM-III* criteria for GAD were randomly assigned to one of the following 10-week treatment conditions: CBT, diazepam (DZ), placebo, CBT plus DZ, or CBT plus placebo. Posttreatment and 6-month follow-up measures indicated a superiority of all CBT treatments, especially CBT alone and the CBT/DZ combination. For more information on psychopharmacological treatments of GAD, please refer to chapter 14.

Future Directions

The more we learn about the nature of GAD, the more we should be able to improve our psychotherapeutic treatments. Additional dismantling studies should assist in determining the specific mechanisms of action in successful therapy. At this time, the most successful psychological treatments combine relaxation exercises and cognitive therapy with the goal of bringing the worry process itself under the patient's control (Barlow & Lehman, 1996). The results of studies comparing cognitive therapy or cognitive-behavioral therapy to other treatments or a wait list are summarized in Table 13.5 (Barlow & Lehman, 1996). Although one of the clinical trials (Butler et al., 1987) eliminated people who reported having anxiety for more than 2 years, the essence of GAD is that it seems to be characterological, with most people reporting that they have been worriers all of their lives. Thus, it is imperative that we study this population as Butler et al. (1991) did in a later project.

Until recently, most studies have not demonstrated differential rates of efficacy for active treatment techniques. However most studies have shown that active treatments are superior to nondirective approaches and uniformly superior to no treatment. Although more research in this area is still warranted, we have made substantial progress in the past decade. On the horizon is a unique treatment approach for GAD that draws from traditional components of cognitive-behavioral therapy, including psychoeducation, monitoring, and relaxation exercises, as well as strategies from other therapies such as Hayes, Strosahl, and Wilson's (1999) Acceptance and Commitment Therapy (ACT), Linehan's Dialectical Behavior Therapy (DBT; Linehan, 1993), and Segal and colleagues' Mindfulness-Based Cognitive Therapy (MBCT; Segal, Williams, & Teasdale, 2002). The new treatment, acceptance-based behavior therapy for GAD, encourages acceptance and awareness of worry, rather than thought challenging, and mindful action as an alternative to the habitual inaction that often results from the worry associated with GAD (Orsillo, Roemer, & Barlow, 2003). An initial investigation of this treatment in a group format suggested that an acceptance-based approach may be helpful for patients with GAD (Orsillo et al., 2003). A more recent adaptation of the protocol, now in individual format, was used in an open trial for 16 patients with a principal diagnosis of GAD. Results indicated that patients showed significant improvements in GAD symptoms, as well as improved quality of life (Roemer & Orsillo, in press). Although further research is clearly warranted, these initial findings may indicate the utility of acceptance-based approaches for treating GAD.

In addition, as mentioned previously, Dugas and colleagues (Dugas et al., 2003; Ladouceur et al., 2000) have continued developing a treatment protocol specifically targeting what are believed to be essential aspects of GAD (e.g., positive beliefs about worry and intolerance of uncertainty). Initial investigations in both individual and group format suggest that this treatment protocol may also provide a more comprehensive and effective treatment for patients with chronic anxiety and worry. Wells (1995) has highlighted the importance of the metacognitive processes involved in worry. Although this treatment protocol has not yet been empirically evaluated, it also has potential for expanding our knowledge of and treatment for GAD.

TABLE 13.5 Controlled Trials of Cognitive-Behavioral Treatments

Study	Length of Follow-Up (Months)	Treatment (N)	Percentage Clinical Improvement of Completers (If Available)	Significant Comparison (Percentage Clinical Improvement)	
				Other Treatments (Yes/No)	Wait List (Yes/No)
Barlow, Cohen et al. (1984)	6	CBT (N = 5)			Yes
Blowers et al. (1987)	6	CBT (N = 20)		Yes: ND (some measures)	Yes
Borkovec et al. (1987)	6–12	CT + PR (N = 16)		Yes: ND + PR (some measures)	
Butler et al. (1987)	6	CBT (N = 22)	58.5		Yes (0%)
Borkovec and Mathews (1988)	12	CT + PR (N = 6)		No: SCD + PR	No: N + PR
Power et al. (1989)	PT	CBT (N = 10)		Yes: PL (one central measure) No: DZ (one central measure)	
Power et al. (1990)	PT	CBT (N = 21)	61.9	No: CBT + DZ = 69.8% No: CBT + PL = 55.6% Yes: DZ = 30.3% Yes: PL = 17.5%	
Butler et al. (1991)	6	CBT (N = 18)	42	Yes: BT = 5%	Yes
Barlow et al. (1992)	6	CBT (N = 29)	55		Yes
White and Keenan (1992)	6	CBT (N = 26)		No: BT, CT	Yes Yes
Borkovec and Costello (1993)	12	CBT (N = 18)	57.9	Yes: ND = 26.7% Yes: AR = 37.5%	
Durham et al. (1994)[a]	6	CT (N = 40)	>60	Yes: AP < 31% Yes: AMT < 37%	
Ladouceur et al. (2000)	6–12	CBT (N = 14)	54		Yes
Borkovec et al. (2002)	6–24	CT (N = 23)	52	No: CBT = 38% No: AR + SCD = 48%	
Arntz (2003)	6	CT (N = 25)	50	No: AR = 46%	
Dugas et al. (2003)	6–24	CBT-G (N = 25)	62		Yes
Rollman et al. (2005)[b]	12	I (N = 116)		Yes: UC	

Source: Reprinted and adapted with permission from Barlow and Lehman (1996), © 1996 American Medical Association. Adapted from Borkovec and Whisman (1996). All rights reserved.

AMT = anxiety management training; AP = analytic psychotherapy; APL = attention placebo; AR = applied relaxation; BT = behavior therapy; CBT = cognitive-behavioral therapy; CBT-G = cognitive-behavioral therapy–group format; CT = cognitive therapy; DZ = diazepam; FU = follow-up; I = intervention (either self-management workbook, trial of pharmacotherapy, or referral to mental health care provider); ND = nondirective therapy; PL = pill placebo; PR = progressive relaxation; PT = posttreatment; SCD = self-control desensitization; UC = usual care.

[a]Intent-to-treat.

[b]Study comparison included patients with diagnosis of GAD, although it was not designated whether GAD was assigned as principal.

If efficacious treatments can be found for the most resistant and chronically anxious patients, then treatments should also benefit those who are on the less severe end of the anxiety continuum. Perhaps as much as 30 to 40% of the population may experience anxiety severe enough to warrant some clinical intervention (cf. Barlow, 1988, 2002). In one survey, 33% of over 6,000 patients completing an up-to-date screening instrument in the offices of 75 physicians in a large health maintenance organization reported elevated symptoms of anxiety and/or anxiety disorders (Fifer et al., 1994).

Additional surveys also suggest that people with anxiety difficulties are prevalent in primary care settings (Barlow, Lerner, & Esler, 1996; Rollman et al., 2005). Rollman et al. (2005) compared the effectiveness of a telephone-based managed care intervention with treatment as usual for patients diagnosed with either panic disorder or generalized anxiety disorder. Patients were randomly assigned to one of the two interventions and assessed at baseline, 2-, 4-, 8-, and 12-month follow-up. Of 191 patients, 90% were given a diagnosis of GAD (although it was not designated whether GAD was assigned as the principal diagnosis in these cases) and were offered one of three intervention options: (a) a workbook designed to assist with self-management of anxiety with follow-up contact from a care manager (Craske, Barlow, & O'Leary, 1992), (b) a trial of pharmacotherapy, or (c) a referral to a community mental health care provider. Of note, the vast majority of patients (80%) chose the self-management workbook. At 12-month follow-up, although the intervention was less successful in reducing anxiety symptoms for patients with GAD only, the patients included in the full cohort (including patients with GAD alone and patients with GAD and panic disorder) who received an intervention showed significant improvement in anxiety symptoms, as compared with those who received usual care. These data suggest that treatment in a primary care setting is not only feasible and acceptable to patients but also successful in reducing symptoms that may lead to reductions in health care costs. In an era of rising costs of health care, developing brief, cost-effective, and perhaps self-directed treatments with proven efficacy for the treatment of anxiety in primary care offices will be an important step, particularly since individuals with anxious symptoms, even if not fully syndromal, are impaired and at risk for the development of more severe disorders (Barlow & Lehman, 1996; Barlow, Lerner, & Esler, 1996).

CONCLUSIONS

We have reviewed the development of effective psychological treatments for a variety of anxiety disorders, but it is fair to say that we have only reached the first plateau of the development of these procedures. Although we now have treatments that are clearly more effective than credible alternative psychological interventions for most disorders, we are only beginning to explore the effectiveness of these procedures outside of research trials. In addition to questions about the generality of effectiveness across patients, settings, and therapists of differing skills and abilities, questions have also been raised about the feasibility of these treatments, as well as their cost-effectiveness. Many of these issues are outlined succinctly in the template for psychological intervention guidelines referred to above (APA, 2002; American Psychological Association Task Force on Psychological Intervention Guidelines, 1995), which provides a road map for future research. Some research along these lines is beginning to appear, suggesting, in an encouraging way, that many of these procedures are just as effective or more effective when applied in a variety of practice settings as they are in the clinical research settings in which they were developed (Barlow, 1996; Barlow & Barlow, 1995).

Equally important will be improving efforts to disseminate these treatments to the variety of practice settings in which they should prove useful, many of them primary care settings, in order to meet the demands of many patients with these disorders desiring brief effective treatments. Evidence indicates that effective psychological treatments are only recently available and much less readily available than pharmacological treatments in most settings (Barlow, 1996; Barlow, Levitt, & Bufka, 1999). Thus, it is not enough simply to develop these treatments and report on their effectiveness. Rather, it is the responsibility of those involved in treatment development to make these treatments as user friendly as possible and to evaluate alternative methods of training and dissemination that would ensure that these approaches reach the greatest number of people who need them.

REFERENCES

Addis, M. E., Hatgis, C., Bourne, L., & Mansfield, A. (2004). Effectiveness of cognitive-behavioral treatment for panic disorder versus treatment as usual in a managed care setting. *Journal of Consulting and Clinical Psychology, 72*, 625–635.

Agras, W. S., Leitenberg, H., & Barlow, D. H. (1968). Social reinforcement in the modification of agoraphobia. *Archives of General Psychiatry, 19*, 423–427.

Al-Kubaisy, T., Marks, I. M., Lagsdail, S., Marks, M. P., Lovell, K., Sungur, M., et al. (1992). Role of exposure homework in phobia reduction: A controlled study. *Behavior Therapy, 23*, 599–621.

Alström, J. E., Nordlund, C. L., Persson, G., Harding, M., & Ljungqvist, C. (1984). Effects of four treatment methods on social phobic patients not suitable for insight-oriented psychotherapy. *Acta Psychiatrica Scandinavica, 70*, 97–110.

American Psychiatric Association. (1980). *Diagnostic and statistical manual of mental disorders* (3rd ed.). Washington, DC: Author.

American Psychiatric Association. (1987). *Diagnostic and statistical manual of mental disorders* (3rd ed., rev.). Washington, DC: Author.

American Psychiatric Association. (1994). *Diagnostic and statistical manual of mental disorders* (4th ed.). Washington, DC: Author.

American Psychiatric Association. (1996). *DSM-IV sourcebook* (Vol. 2). Washington, DC: Author.

American Psychiatric Association. (2000). *Diagnostic and statistical manual of mental disorders* (4th ed., Text revision). Washington, DC: Author.

American Psychological Association. (2002). Criteria for evaluating treatment guidelines. *American Psychologist, 57*, 1052–1059.

American Psychological Association Task Force on Psychological Intervention Guidelines. (1995, February). *Template for developing guidelines: Interventions for mental disorders and psychosocial aspects of physical disorders.* Washington, DC: American Psychological Association.

Antony, M. M., & Barlow, D. H. (1996). Social and specific phobias. In D. H. Taylor & A. Tasman (Eds.), *Psychiatry.* Philadelphia: Saunders.

Antony, M. M., & Barlow, D. H. (2002). Specific phobias. In D. H. Barlow, *Anxiety and its disorders: The nature and treatment of anxiety and panic* (2nd ed.; pp. 380–417). New York: Guilford Press.

Antony, M. M., Craske, M. G., & Barlow, D. H. (2006). *Mastery of your specific phobia.* San Antonio, TX: Graywind Publications/Psychological Corporation.

Arnow, B. A., Taylor, C. B., Agras, W. S., & Telch, M. J. (1985). Enhancing agoraphobia treatment outcome by changing couple communication patterns. *Behavior Therapy, 16*, 452–467.

Arntz, A. (2003). Cognitive therapy versus applied relaxation as treatment of generalized anxiety disorder. *Behaviour Research and Therapy, 41*, 633–646.

Baker, B. L., Cohen, D. C., & Saunders, J. T. (1973). Self-directed desensitization for acrophobia. *Behaviour Research and Therapy, 11*, 79–89.

Barlow, D. H. (1988). *Anxiety and its disorders: The nature and treatment of anxiety and panic.* New York: Guilford Press.

Barlow, D. H. (1996). The effectiveness of psychotherapy: Science and policy. *Clinical Psychology: Science and Practice, 3*, 236–240.

Barlow, D. H. (2000). Unraveling the mysteries of anxiety and its disorders from the perspective of emotion theory. *American Psychologist, 55*, 1247–1263.

Barlow, D. H. (2002). *Anxiety and its disorders: The nature and treatment of anxiety and panic* (2nd ed.). New York: Guilford Press.

Barlow, D. H. (2004). Psychological treatments. *American Psychologist, 59*, 869–878.

Barlow, D. H., Allen, L. B., & Choate, M. L. (2004). Towards a unified treatment for emotional disorders. *Behavior Therapy, 35*, 205–230.

Barlow, D. H., & Barlow, D. G. (1995). Practice guidelines and empirically validated psychosocial treatments: Ships passing in the night? *Behavioral Health-Care Tomorrow, May–June*, 25–29, 76.

Barlow, D. H., & Brown, T. A. (1995). Correction to Klosko et al. (1990). *Journal of Consulting and Clinical Psychology, 63*, 830.

Barlow, D. H., Chorpita, B. F., & Turovsky, J. (1996). Fear, panic, anxiety, and disorders of emotion. In D. A. Hope (Ed.), *Nebraska Symposium on Motivation: Perspectives on anxiety, panic, and fear* (Vol. 43, pp. 251–328). Lincoln: University of Nebraska Press.

Barlow, D. H., Cohen, A. S., Waddell, M. T., Vermilyca, B.B., Kloska, J. S., Blanchard, E. B., et al. (1984). Panic and generalized anxiety disorders: Nature and treatment. *Behavior Therapy, 15*, 431–449.

Barlow, D. H., & Craske, M. G. (2000) *Mastery of your anxiety and panic (MAP-3): Client workbook for anxiety and panic* (3rd ed.). San Antonio, TX: Graywind Publications/Psychological Corporation.

Barlow, D. H., & Craske, M. G. (2007). *Mastery of your anxiety and panic, workbook.* (4th ed.). New York: Oxford University Press.

Barlow, D. H., Craske, M. G., Cerny, J. A., & Klosko, J. S. (1989). Behavioral treatment of panic disorder. *Behavior Therapy, 20,* 261–282.

Barlow, D. H., Gorman. J. M., Shear, M. K., & Woods, S. W. (2000). Cognitive-behavioral therapy, imipramine, or their combination for panic disorder: A randomized control trial. *Journal of the American Medical Association, 283,* 2529–2536.

Barlow, D. H., & Lehman, C. (1996). Advances in the psychosocial treatment of anxiety disorders: Implications for national health care. *Archives of General Psychiatry, 53,* 727–735.

Barlow, D. H., Lerner, J. A., & Esler, J. K. L. (1996). Behavioral health care in primary care settings: Recognition and treatment of anxiety disorders. In R. J. Resnick & R. H. Rozeosky (Eds.), *Health psychology through the life span: Practice and research opportunities* (pp. 133–148). Washington, DC: American Psychological Association Press.

Barlow, D. H., Levitt, J. T., & Bufka, L. F. (1999). The dissemination of empirically supported treatments: A view to the future. *Behaviour Research and Therapy, 37*(Suppl. 1), S147–S162.

Barlow, D. H., O'Brien, G. T., & Last, C. G. (1984). Couples treatment of agoraphobia. *Behavior Therapy, 15,* 41–58.

Barlow, D. H., Rapee, R. M., & Brown, T. A. (1992). Behavioral treatment of generalized anxiety disorder. *Behavior Therapy, 23,* 551–570.

Barlow, D. H., & Wincze, J. (1998). *DSM-IV and beyond: What is generalized anxiety disorder? Acta Psychiatric Scandinavia, 98,* 23–29.

Beck, A. T., & Emery, C. (1985). *Anxiety disorders and phobias: A cognitive perspective.* New York: Basic Books.

Beck, A. T., Sokol, L., Clark, D. A., Berchick, R., & Wright, F. (1992). A crossover study of focused cognitive therapy for panic disorder. *American Journal of Psychiatry, 149,* 778–783.

Beckham, J. C., Vrana, S. R., May, J. G., Gustafson, D. J., & Smith, G. R. (1990). Emotional processing and fear measurement synchrony as indicators of treatment outcome in fear of flying. *Journal of Behavior Therapy and Experimental Psychiatry, 21,* 153–162.

Black, D. W., Wesner, R., Bowers, W., & Gabel, J. (1993). A comparison of fluvoxamine, cognitive therapy, and placebo in the treatment of panic disorder. *Archives of General Psychiatry, 50,* 44–50.

Blowers, C., Cobb, J., & Mathews, A. (1987). Generalised anxiety: A controlled treatment study. *Behavior Research and Therapy, 25,* 493–502.

Bonn, J. A., Readhead, C. P. A., & Timmons, B. H. (1984). Enhanced adaptive behavioral response in agoraphobic patients pretreated with breathing retraining. *Lancet, 2,* 665–669.

Borkovec, T. D. (1994). The nature, functions, and origins of worry. In G. C. L. Davey & F. Tallis (Eds.), *Worrying: Perspectives on theory, assessment and treatment* (pp. 5–33). Cichester, England: Wiley.

Borkovec, T. D., & Costello, E. (1993). Efficacy of applied relaxation and cognitive-behavioral therapy in the treatment of generalized anxiety disorder. *Journal of Consulting and Clinical Psychology, 61,* 611–619.

Borkovec, T. D., & Mathews, A. M. (1988). Treatment of nonphobic anxiety disorders: A comparison of nondirective, cognitive, and coping desensitization therapy. *Journal of Consulting and Clinical Psychology, 56,* 877–884.

Borkovec, T. D., Mathews, A. M., Chambers, A., Ebrahimi, S., Lytle, R., & Nelson, R. (1987). The effects of relaxation training with cognitive or nondirective therapy and the role of relaxation-induced anxiety in the treatment of generalized anxiety. *Journal of Consulting and Clinical Psychology, 55,* 883–933.

Borkovec, T. D., Newman, M. G., Pincus, A. L., & Lytle, R. (2002). A component analysis of cognitive-behavioral therapy for generalized anxiety and the role of interpersonal problems. *Journal of Consulting and Clinical Psychology, 70,* 288–298.

Borkovec, T. D., & Whisman, M. A. (1996). Psychosocial treatment for generalized anxiety disorder. In M. Mavissakalian & R. Prien (Eds.), *Long-term treatments of anxiety disorders* (pp. 171–199). Washington, DC: American Psychiatric Press.

Bourque, P., & Ladouceur, R. (1980). An investigation of various performance-based treatments with acrophobics. *Behaviour Research and Therapy, 18,* 161–170.

Broman-Fulks, J. J., Berman, M. E., Rabian, B. A., & Webster, M. J. (2004). Effects of aerobic exercise on anxiety sensitivity. *Behaviour Research and Therapy, 42,* 125–136.

Brown, T. A., Antony, M. M., & Barlow, D. H. (1995). Diagnostic comorbidity in panic disorder: Effect on treatment outcome and course of comorbid diagnoses following treatment. *Journal of Consulting and Clinical Psychology, 63,* 408–418.

Brown, T. A., & Barlow, D. H. (1995). Long-term outcome in cognitive-behavioral treatment of panic disorder: Clinical predictors and alternative strategies for assessment. *Journal of Consulting and Clinical Psychology, 63,* 754–765.

Brown, T. A., Campbell, L. A., Lehman, C. L., Grisham, J. R., & Mancill, R. B. (2001). Current and lifetime comorbidity of the *DSM-IV* anxiety and mood disorders in a large clinical sample. *Journal of Abnormal Psychology*, 110, 585–599.

Brown, T. A., O'Leary, T. A., & Barlow, D. H. (2001). Generalized anxiety disorder. In D. H. Barlow (Ed.), *Clinical handbook of psychological disorders: A step-by-step treatment manual* (pp. 154–208). New York: Guilford Press.

Burns, L. E., Thorpe, C. L., & Cavallaro, L. A. (1986). Agoraphobia 8 years after behavioral treatment: A follow-up study with interview, self-report, and behavioral data. *Behavioral Therapy*, 17, 580–591.

Butler, G., Cullington, A., Hibbert, G., Klimes, I., & Gelder, M. (1987).Anxiety management for persistent generalised anxiety. *British Journal of Psychiatry*, 151, 535–542.

Butler, G., Cullington, A., Munby, M., Amies, P., & Gelder, M. (1984). Exposure and anxiety management in the treatment of social phobia. *Journal of Consulting and Clinical Psychology*, 52, 642–650.

Butler, G., Fennell, M., Robson, P., & Gelder, M. (1991). Comparison of behavior therapy and cognitive behavior therapy in the treatment of generalized anxiety disorder. *Journal of Consulting and Clinical Psychology*, 59, 167–175.

Campbell-Sills, L., & Barlow, D.H. (in press). Incorporating emotion regulation into conceptualization and treatment of anxiety and mood disorders. In J. J. Gross (Ed.), *Handbook of emotion regulation*. New York: Guilford Press.

Carlbring, P., Nilsson-Ihrfelt, E., Waara, J., Kollenstam, C., Buhrman, M., Kaldo, V., et al. (2005). Treatment of panic disorder: Live therapy vs. self-help via the Internet. *Behaviour Research and Therapy*, 43, 1321–1333.

Carlin, A. S., Hoffman, H. G., & Weghorst, S. (1997). Virtual reality and tactile augmentation in the treatment of spider phobia: A case report. *Behaviour Research and Therapy*, 35, 153–158.

Cerny, J. A., Barlow, D. H., Craske, M. G., & Himadi, W. G. (1987). Couples treatment of agoraphobia: A two-year follow-up. *Behavior Therapy*, 18, 401–415.

Chambless, D. L. (1990). Spacing of exposure sessions in treatment of agoraphobia and simple phobia. *Behavior Therapy*, 21, 217–229.

Chambless, D. L., & Renneberg, B. (1988, September). *Personality disorders of agoraphobics*. Paper presented at the World Congress of Behavior Therapy, Edinburgh, Scotland.

Clark, D. M. (1989). Anxiety states: Panic and generalized anxiety. In K. Hawton, P. Salkovskis, J. Kirk, & D. M. Clark. (Eds.), *Cognitive behaviour therapy for psychiatric problems: A practical guide* (pp. 52–96). New York: Oxford University Press.

Clark, D. M., Ehlers, A., McManus, F., Hackmann, A., Fennell, M., Campbell, H., et al. (2003). Cognitive therapy versus fluoxetine in generalized social phobia: A randomized, placebo-controlled trial. *Journal of Consulting and Clinical Psychology*, 71, 1058–1067.

Clark, D. M., Salkovskis, P. M., Hackmann, A., Middleton, H., Anastasiades, P., & Gelder, M. (1994). A comparison of cognitive therapy, applied relaxation, and imipramine in the treatment of panic disorder. *British Journal of Psychiatry*, 164, 759–769.

Clark, D. M., Salkovskis, P. M., Hackmann, A., Wells, A., Ludgate, J., & Gelder, M. (1999). Brief cognitive therapy for panic disorder: A randomized control trial. *Journal of Consulting and Clinical Psychology*, 67, 583–589.

Clark, D. M., & Wells, A. (1995). A cognitive model of social phobia. In R. Heimberg, M. Liebowitz, D. A. Hope, & F. R. Schneier (Eds.), *Social phobia: Diagnosis, assessment, and treatment* (pp. 69–93). New York: Guilford Press.

Cobb, J. P., Mathews, A. M., Childs-Clarke, A., & Blowers, C. M. (1984). The spouse as co-therapist in the treatment of agoraphobia. *British Journal of Psychiatry*, 144, 282–287.

Cote, C., Gauthier, J. G., Laberge, B., Cormier, H. J., & Plamondon, J. (1994). Reduced therapist contact in the cognitive behavioral treatment of panic disorder. *Behavior Therapy*, 25, 123–145.

Craske, M. G. (1999). *Anxiety disorders: Psychological approaches to theory and treatment*. Boulder, CO: Westview Press.

Craske, M. G., & Barlow, D. H. (1988). A review of the relationship between panic and avoidance. *Clinical Psychology Review*, 8, 667–685.

Craske, M. G., & Barlow, D. H. (2001). Panic disorder and agoraphobia. In D. H. Barlow (Ed.), *Clinical handbook of psychological disorders* (3rd ed., pp. 1–59). New York: Guilford Press.

Craske, M. G., Barlow, D. H., & Meadows, E. (2000). *Mastery of your anxiety and panic: Therapist guide for anxiety, panic, and agoraphobia (MAP-3)*. San Antonio, TX: Graywind Publications/Psychological Corporation.

Craske, M. G., Barlow, D. H., & O'Leary, T. (1992). *Mastery of your anxiety and worry*. San Antonio, TX: Graywind Publications/Psychological Corporation.

Craske, M. G., Brown, T. A., & Barlow, D. H. (1991). Behavioral treatment of panic disorder: A two-year follow-up. *Behavior Therapy*, 22, 289–304.

Craske, M. G., De Cola, J. P., Sachs, A. D., & Pontillo, D. C. (2003). Panic control treatment for agoraphobia. *Journal of Anxiety Disorders, 17,* 321–333.

Craske, M. G., Maidenberg, E., & Bystritsky, A. (1995). Brief cognitive-behavioral versus nondirective therapy for panic disorder. *Journal of Behavior Therapy and Experimental Psychiatry, 26,* 113–120.

Craske, M. G., Miller, P. P., Rotunda, R., & Barlow, D. H. (1990). A descriptive report of features of initial unexpected panic attacks in minimal and extensive avoiders. *Behaviour Research and Therapy, 28,* 395–400.

Craske, M. G., Rowe, M., Lewin, M., & Noriega-Dimitri, R. (1997). Breathing retraining versus interoceptive exposure within cognitive-behavioral treatment for panic disorder with agoraphobia. *British Journal of Clinical Psychology, 36,* 85–99.

Craske, M. G., & Sipsas, A. (1992). Animal phobias versus claustrophobias: Exteroceptive versus interoceptive cues. *Behaviour Research and Therapy, 30,* 569–581.

Curtis, G. C., Hill, E. M., & Lewis, J. A. (1990). *Heterogeneity of DSM-III-R simple phobia and the simple phobia/agoraphobia boundary: Evidence from the ECA study.* Report to the DSM-IV Anxiety Disorders Work Group. Ann Arbor: University of Michigan.

Curtis, G. C., Magee, W. J., Eaton, W. W., Wittchen, H. U., & Kessler, R. C. (1998). Specific fears and phobias: Epidemiology and classification. *British Journal of Psychiatry, 173,* 212–217.

Davidson, J. R. T., Foa, E. B., Huppert, J. D., Keefe, F. J., Franklin, M. E., Compton, J. S., et al. (2004). Fluoxetine, comprehensive cognitive behavioral therapy, and placebo in generalized social phobia. *Archives of General Psychiatry, 61,* 1005–1013.

Deacon, B., & Abramowitz, J. (2006). A pilot study of two-day cognitive-behavioral therapy for panic disorder. *Behaviour Research and Therapy, 44,* 807–817.

De Ruiter, C., Rijken, H., Garssen, B., & Kraaimaat, F. (1989). Breathing retraining, exposure, and a combination of both in the treatment of panic disorder with agoraphobia. *Behaviour Research and Therapy, 27,* 663–672.

Di Nardo, P. A., & Barlow, D. H. (1988). *Anxiety Disorders Interview Schedule-Revised* (ADIS-R). Albany, NY: Graywind Publications/Psychological Corporation.

Di Nardo, P. A., O'Brien, C. T., Barlow, D. H., Waddell, M. T., & Blanchard, E. (1983). Reliability of *DSM-III* anxiety disorder categories using a new structured interview. *Archives of General Psychiatry, 40,* 1070–1078.

Donahue, B. C., Van Hasselt, V. B., & Hersen, M. (1994). Behavioral assessment and treatment of social phobia. *Behavior Modification, 18,* 262–288.

Dugas, M. J., Ladouceur, R., Léger, E., Freeston, M. H., Langlois, F., Provencher, M. D., et al. (2003). Group cognitive-behavioral therapy for generalized anxiety disorder: Treatment outcome and long-term follow-up. *Journal of Consulting and Clinical Psychology, 71,* 821–825.

Durham, R. C., Murphy, T., Allan, T., Richard, K., Treliving, L. R., & Fenton, G. W. (1994). Cognitive therapy, analytic psychotherapy and anxiety management training for generalized anxiety disorder. *British Journal of Psychiatry, 165,* 315–323.

Durham, R. C., & Turvey, A. A. (1987). Cognitive therapy versus behavior therapy in the treatment of chronic general anxiety. *Behavior Research and Therapy, 25,* 229–234.

Emmelkamp, P. M., Brilman, E., Kuiper, H., & Mersch, P. P. (1986). The treatment of agoraphobia: A comparison of self-instructional training, rational emotive therapy, and exposure in vivo. *Behavior Modification, 10,* 37–53.

Emmelkamp, P. M. G., & Mersch, P. P. (1982). Cognition and exposure in viva in the treatment of agoraphobia: Short-term and delayed effects. *Cognitive Therapy and Research, 6,* 77–90.

Fava, G. A., Zielezny, M., Savron, G., & Grandi, S. (1995). Long-term effects of behavioural treatment for panic disorder with agoraphobia. *British Journal of Psychiatry, 166,* 87–92.

Feigenbaum, W. (1988). Long-term efficacy of ungraded versus graded massed exposure in agoraphobics. In I. Hand & H. Wittchen (Eds.), *Panic and phobias: Treatments and variables affecting course and outcome* (pp. 83–88). Berlin: Springer-Verlag.

Fifer, S. K., Mathias, S. D., Patrick, D. L., Majonson, P. D., Lubeck, D. P., & Buesching, D. P. (1994). Untreated anxiety among adult primary care patients in a health maintenance organization. *Archives of General Psychiatry, 51,* 740–750.

Freud, S. (1961). On the grounds for detaching a particular syndrome from neurasthenia under the description of anxiety neurosis. In J. Strachey (Ed. & Trans.), *The standard edition of the complete psychological works of Sigmund Freud* (Vol. 3, pp. 85–116). London: Hogarth Press. (Original work published 1895)

Fyer, A. J., Mannuzza, S., Chapman, T. F., Liebowitz, M. R., & Klein, D. F. (1993). A direct interview family study of social phobia. *Archives of General Psychiatry, 50,* 286–293.

Garcia-Palacios, A., Hoffman, H., Carlin, A., Furness, T. A., III, & Botella, C. (2002). Virtual reality in the treatment of spider phobia: A controlled study. *Behaviour Research and Therapy, 40,* 983–993.

Gelder, M. G., & Marks, I. M. (1966). Severe agoraphobia: A controlled prospective trial of behavioral therapy. *British Journal of Psychiatry, 112,* 309–319.

Gelernter, C. S., Uhde, T. W., Cimbolic, P., Arnkoff, C. B., Vittone, B. J., Tancer, M. E., et al. (1991). Cognitive-behavioral and pharmacological treatments for social phobia: A controlled study. *Archives of General Psychiatry, 48,* 938–945.

Ghosh, A., & Marks, I. M. (1987). Self-treatment of agoraphobia by exposure. *Behavior Therapy, 18,* 3–16.

Gould, R. A., Otto, M. W., & Pollack, M. H. (1995). A meta-analysis of treatment outcome for panic disorder. *Clinical Psychology Review, 15,* 819–844.

Hafner, J., & Marks, I. M. (1976). Exposure *in vivo* of agoraphobics: Contributions of diazepam, group exposure, and anxiety evocation. *Psychological Medicine, 6,* 71–88.

Haug, T. T., Blomhoff, S., Hellstrøm, K., Holme, I., Humble, M., Madsbu, H. P., et al. (2003). Exposure therapy and sertraline in social phobia: 1-year follow-up of a randomised controlled trial. *British Journal of Psychiatry, 182,* 312–318.

Hayes, S. C., Barlow, D. H., & Nelson-Gray, R. O. (1999). *The scientist practitioner: Research and accountability in the age of managed care* (2nd ed.). Boston: Allyn and Bacon.

Hayes, S. C., Strosahl, K. D., & Wilson, K. G. (1999). *Acceptance and commitment therapy: An experiential approach to behavior change.* New York: Guilford Press.

Heimberg, R. G. (1991). *Cognitive behavioral treatment of social phobia in a group setting: A treatment manual.* Unpublished treatment manual, Center for Stress and Anxiety Disorders, State University of New York at Albany.

Heimberg, R. G., Dodge, C. S., Hope, D. A., Kennedy, C. R., Zallo, L., & Becker, R. E. (1990). Cognitive-behavioral group treatment for social phobia: Comparison to a credible placebo control. *Cognitive Therapy and Research, 14,* 1–23.

Heimberg, R. G., & Juster, H. P. (1995). Cognitive-behavioral treatments: Literature review. In R. C. Heimberg, M. R. Liebowitz, D. A. Hope, & F. R. Schneier (Eds.), *Social phobia: Diagnosis, assessment, and treatment* (pp. 261–309). New York: Guilford Press.

Heimberg, R. G., Liebowitz, M. R., Hope, D. A., Schneier, F. R., Holt, C. S., Welkowitz, L. A., et al. (1998). Cognitive-behavioral group therapy versus phenelzine therapy for social phobia: 12-week outcome. *Archives of General Psychiatry, 55,* 1133–1141.

Heimberg, R. G., Salzman, D. G., Halt, C. S., & Blendell, K. A. (1993). Cognitive-behavioral group treatment for social phobia: Effectiveness at five-year follow-up. *Cognitive Therapy and Research, 17,* 325–339.

Hellström, K., Fellenius, J., & Öst, L.-G. (1996). One versus five sessions of applied tension in the treatment of blood phobia. *Behaviour Research and Therapy, 34,* 101–112.

Hellström, K., & Öst, L.-G. (1995). One-session therapist directed exposure vs. two forms of manual directed self-exposure in the treatment of spider phobia. *Behavior Research and Therapy, 33,* 959–965.

Herbert, J. D. (1995). An overview of the current status of social phobia. *Applied and Preventive Psychology, 4,* 39–51.

Herbert, J. D., Gaudiano, B. A., & Rheingold, A. A. (2005). Social skills training augments the effectiveness of group cognitive behavioral therapy for social anxiety disorder. *Behavior Therapy, 36,* 125–138.

Hofmann, S. G. (1999). *Behavior group therapy for social phobia.* Unpublished treatment manual, Boston University, Boston, MA.

Hofmann, S. G. (2004). Cognitive mediation of treatment change in social phobia. *Journal of Consulting and Clinical Psychology, 72,* 392–399.

Hofmann, S. G., & Barlow, D. H. (2002). Social phobia (social anxiety disorder). In D. H. Barlow, *Anxiety and its disorders: The nature and treatment of anxiety and panic* (2nd ed., pp. 454–476). New York: Guilford Press.

Hofmann, S. G., Meuret, A. E., Jasper, S., Simon, N. M., Pollack, M. H., Eisenmenger, K., et al. (2006). Augmentation of exposure therapy with D-cycloserine for social anxiety disorder. *Archives of General Psychiatry, 63,* 298–303.

Hofmann, S. G., Moscovitch, D. A., Kim, H-J., & Taylor, A. N. (2004). Changes in self-perception during treatment of social phobia. *Journal of Consulting and Clinical Psychology, 72,* 588–596.

Holden, A. E., O'Brien, G. T., Barlow, D. H., Stetson, D., & Infantino, A. (1983). Self-help manual for agoraphobia: A preliminary report of effectiveness. *Behavior Therapy, 14,* 545–556.

Hope, D. A., & Heimberg, R. G. (1993). Social phobia and social anxiety. In D. H. Barlow (Ed.), *Clinical handbook of psychological disorders* (2nd ed., pp. 99–136). New York: Guilford Press.

Hope, D. A., Heimberg, R. G., & Bruch, M. A. (1990, March). *The importance of cognitive intervention in behavioral group therapy for social phobia.* Paper presented at the 10th National Conference on

Phobias and Related Anxiety Disorders, Bethesda, MD.

Howard, W. A., Murphy, S. M., & Clarke, J. C. (1983). The nature and treatment of fear of flying: A controlled investigation. *Behavior Therapy*, *14*, 557–567.

Jacobson, N. S., Wilson, L., & Tupper, C. (1988). The clinical significance of treatment gains resulting from exposure-based interventions for agoraphobia: A reanalysis of outcome data. *Behavior Therapy*, *19*, 539–554.

Jansson, L., Jerremalm, A., & Öst, L.-G. (1986). Follow-up of agoraphobic patients treated with exposure in vivo or applied relaxation. *British Journal of Psychiatry*, *149*, 486–490.

Jansson, L., & Öst, L.-G. (1982). Behavioral treatments for agoraphobia: An evaluative review. *Clinical Psychology Review*, *2*, 311–336.

Jerremalm, A., Jansson, L., & Öst, L.-G. (1986a). Cognitive and physiological reactivity and the effects of different behavioral methods in the treatment of social phobia. *Behaviour Research and Therapy*, *24*, 171–180.

Jerremalm, A., Jansson, L., & Öst, L.-G. (1986b). Individual response patterns and the effects of different behavioral methods in the treatment of dental phobia. *Behaviour Research and Therapy*, *24*, 587–596.

Juster, H. R., Heimberg, R. C., & Engelberg, B. (1995). Self selection and sample selection in a treatment study of social phobia. *Behaviour Research and Therapy*, *33*, 321–324.

Kendler, K. S., Neale, M. C., Kessler, R. C., Heath, A. C., & Eaves, L. J. (1992). The genetic epidemiology of phobias in women: The interrelationship of agoraphobia, social phobia, situational phobia, and simple phobia. *Archives of General Psychiatry*, *49*, 273–281.

Kessler, R. C., Berglund, P., Demler, O., Jin, R., & Walters, E. E. (2005). Lifetime prevalence and age-of-onset distributions of DSM-IV disorders in the national comorbidity survey replication. *Archives of General Psychiatry*, *62*, 593–602.

Kessler, R. C., McGonagle, K. A., Zhao, S., Nelson, C. B., Hughes, M., Eshleman, S., et al. (1994). Lifetime and 12-month prevalence of DSM III-R psychiatric disorders in the United States: Results from the national comorbidity survey. *Archives of General Psychiatry*, *51*, 8–19.

Klein, B., Richards, J. C., & Austin, D. W. (2006). Efficacy of Internet therapy for panic disorder. *Journal of Behavior Therapy and Experimental Psychiatry*, *37*, 213–238.

Klinger, E., Bouchard, S., Légeron, P., Roy, S., Lauer F., Chemin, I., et al. (2005). Virtual reality therapy versus cognitive behavior therapy for social phobia: A preliminary controlled study. *Cyberpsychology and Behavior*, *8*, 76–88.

Klosko, J. S., Barlow, D. H., Tassinari, R., & Cerny, J. A. (1990). A comparison of alprazolam and behavior therapy in treatment of panic disorder. *Journal of Consulting and Clinical Psychology*, *58*, 77–84.

Krijn, M., Emmelkamp, P. M. G., Biemond, R., de Wilde de Ligney, C., Schuemie, M. J., & van der Mast, C. A. P. G. (2004). Treatment of acrophobia in virtual reality: The role of immersion and presence. *Behaviour Research and Therapy*, *42*, 229–239.

Krijn, M., Emmelkamp, P. M. G., Olafsson, R. P., & Biemond, R. (2004). Virtual reality exposure of anxiety disorders: A review. *Clinical Psychology Review*, *24*, 259–281.

Kushner, M. G., Abrams, K., & Borchardt, C. (2000). The relationship between anxiety disorders and alcohol use disorders: A review of major perspectives and findings. *Clinical Psychology Review*, *20*, 149–171.

Ladouceur, R., Dugas, M. J., Freeston, M. H., Léger, E., Gagnon, F., & Thibodeau, N. (2000). Efficacy of a cognitive-behavioral treatment for generalized anxiety disorder: Evaluation in a controlled clinical trial. *Journal of Consulting and Clinical Psychology*, *68*, 957–964.

Liddell, A., Di Fazio, L., Blackwood, J., & Ackerman, C. (1994). Long-term follow-up of treated dental phobics. *Behaviour Research and Therapy*, *32*, 605–610.

Lidren, D. M., Watkins, P. L., Gould, R. A., Clum, G. A., Asterino, M., & Tullach, H. L. (1994). A comparison of bibliotherapy and group therapy in the treatment of panic disorder. *Journal of Consulting and Clinical Psychology*, *62*, 865–869.

Liebowitz, M. R., Heimberg, R. G., Schneier, F. R., Hope, D. A., Davies, S., Holt, C. S., et al. (1999). Cognitive-behavioral group therapy versus phenelzine in social phobia: Long-term outcome. *Depression and Anxiety*, *10*, 89–98.

Lindsay, W. R., Gamsu, C. V., McLaughlin, F., Hood, E., & Espie, C. A. (1987). A controlled trial of treatment for generalized anxiety. *British Journal of Clinical Psychology*, *26*, 3–15.

Linehan, M. M. (1993). *Cognitive-behavioral treatment of borderline personality disorder*. New York: Guilford Press.

Lucas, R. A., & Telch, M. J. (1993, November). *Group versus individual treatment of social phobia*. Paper presented at the annual meeting of the Association for Advancement of Behavior Therapy, Atlanta, GA.

Maltby, N., Kirsch, I., Mayers, M., & Allen, G. J. (2002). Virtual reality exposure therapy for the treatment of fear of flying: A controlled investigation. *Journal of Consulting and Clinical Psychology, 70,* 1112–1118.

Margraf, J., & Schneider, S. (1991, November). *Outcome and active ingredients of cognitive-behavioral treatment of social phobia.* Paper presented at the annual meeting of the Association for Advancement of Behavior Therapy, Atlanta, GA.

Marks, I. M. (1971). Phobic disorders four years after treatment: A prospective follow-up. *British Journal of Psychiatry, 129,* 362–371.

Marks, I. M. (1987). *Fears, phobias, and rituals.* New York: Oxford University Press.

Marks, I. M., & Gelder, M. G. (1966). Different ages of onset in varieties of phobia. *American Journal of Psychiatry, 123,* 218–221.

Marks, I. M., Swinson, R. P., Basaglu, M., Kuch, K., Nashirvani, H., O'Sullivan, G., et al. (1993). Alprazolam and exposure alone and combined in panic disorder with agoraphobia: A controlled study in London and Toronto. *British Journal of Psychiatry, 162,* 776–787.

Marzillier, J. S., Lambert, C., & Kelley, J. (1976). A controlled evaluation of systematic desensitization and social skills training for socially inadequate psychiatric patients. *Behaviour Research and Therapy, 14,* 225–238.

Mattick, R. P., & Peters, L. (1988). Treatment of severe social phobia: Effects of guided exposure with and without cognitive restructuring. *Journal of Consulting and Clinical Psychology, 56,* 251–260.

Mattick, R. P., Peters, L., & Clarke, J. C. (1989). Exposure and cognitive restructuring for social phobia: A controlled study. *Behavior Therapy, 20,* 3–23.

Mavissakalian, M. R. (1996). Antidepressant medications for panic disorder. In M. Mavissakalian & R. Prien (Eds.), *Anxiety disorders: Psychological and pharmacological treatments* (pp. 265–284). Washington, DC: American Psychiatric Press.

Mavissakalian, M., & Barlow, D. H. (Eds.). (1981). *Phobia: Psychological and pharmacological treatment.* New York: Guilford Press.

Mavissakalian, M., & Michelson, L. (1986). Two-year follow-up of exposure and imipramine treatment of agoraphobia. *American Journal of Psychiatry, 143,* 1106–1112.

Mavissakalian, M., & Perel, J. (1985). Imipramine in the treatment of agoraphobia: Dose-response relationships. *American Journal of Psychiatry, 142,* 1032–1036.

McNally, R. J. (1986). Behavioral treatment of choking phobia. *Journal of Behavior Therapy and Experimental Psychiatry, 17,* 185–188.

McNally, R. J. (1994). Choking phobia: A review of the literature. *Comprehensive Psychiatry, 35,* 83–89.

Menzies, R. G. & Clarke, J. C. (1995). Danger expectancies and insight in acrophobia. *Behaviour Research and Therapy, 33,* 215–221.

Mersch, P. P. A. (1995). The treatment of social phobia: The differential effectiveness of exposure *in vivo* and an integration of exposure *in vivo,* rational emotive therapy and social skills training. *Behaviour Research and Therapy, 33,* 259–269.

Michelson, L., Marchione, K., & Greenwald, M. (1989, November). *Cognitive-behavioral treatments of agoraphobia.* Paper presented at the annual meeting of the Association for the Advancement of Behavior Therapy, Washington, DC.

Michelson, L., Mavissakalian, M., & Marchione, K. (1988). Cognitive, behavioral, and psychophysiological treatments of agoraphobia: A comparative outcome investigation. *Behavior Therapy, 19,* 97–120.

Mills, H. L., Agras, W. S., Barlow, D. H., & Mills, J. R. (1973). Compulsive rituals treated by response prevention. *Archives of General Psychiatry, 28,* 524–529.

Moras, K., Di Nardo, P. A., Brown, T. A., & Barlow, D. H. (1994). *Comorbidity, functional impairment, and depression among the* DSM-III-R *anxiety disorders.* Unpublished manuscript.

Mörtberg, E., Berglund, G., & Sundin, Ö. (2005) Intensive cognitive behavioural group treatment for social phobia: A pilot study. *Cognitive Behaviour Therapy, 34,* 41–49.

Mühlberger, A., Weidemann, G., & Pauli, P. (2003). Efficacy of a one-session virtual reality exposure treatment for fear of flying. *Psychotherapy Research, 13,* 323–336.

Munby, J., & Johnston, D. W. (1980). Agoraphobia: The long-term follow-up of behavioral treatment. *British Journal of Psychiatry, 137,* 418–427.

Muris, P., Mayer, B., & Merckelbach, H. (1998). Trait anxiety as a predictor of behavior therapy outcome in spider phobia. *Behavioral and Cognitive Psychotherapy, 26,* 87–91.

Myers, J. K., Weissman, M. M., Tisebler, G. L., Holzer, C. E., III, Leaf, P. J., Orvasehel, H., et al. (1984). Six-month prevalence of psychiatric disorders in three communities. *Archives of General Psychiatry, 41,* 959–967.

Newman, C. F., Beck, J. S., & Beck, A. T. (1990, November). *Efficacy of cognitive therapy in reducing panic attacks and medication.* Paper presented at the annual meeting of the Association for Advancement of Behavior Therapy, San Francisco.

O'Brien, T. P., & Kelley, J. E. (1980). A comparison of self-directed and therapist-directed practice for fear reduction. *Behaviour Research and Therapy, 18,* 573–579.

Orsillo, S. M., Roemer, L., & Barlow, D. H. (2003). Integrating acceptance and mindfulness into existing cognitive-behavioral treatment for GAD: A case study. *Cognitive and Behavioral Practice, 10,* 222–230.

Öst, L.-G. (1987). Age of onset of different phobias. *Journal of Abnormal Psychology, 96,* 223–229.

Öst, L.-G. (1989). One-session treatment for specific phobias. *Behaviour Research and Therapy, 27,* 1–7.

Öst, L.-G., Brandberg, M., & Alm, T. (1997). One versus five session of exposure in the treatment of flying phobia. *Behaviour Research and Therapy, 35,* 987–996.

Öst, L.-G., Ferebee, I., & Furmark, T. (1997). One session group therapy of spider phobia: Direct versus indirect treatments. *Behaviour Research and Therapy, 35,* 721–732.

Öst, L.-G., Hellström, K., & Westling, B. E. (1989, November). *Applied relaxation, exposure in vivo, and cognitive methods in the treatment of agoraphobia.* Paper presented at the annual meeting of the Association for the Advancement of Behavior Therapy, Washington, DC.

Öst, L.-G., Jerremalm, A., & Jansson, L. (1984). Individual response patterns and the effects of different behavioral methods in the treatment of agoraphobia. *Behaviour Research and Therapy, 22,* 697–707.

Öst, L.-G., Jerremalm, A., & Johansson, J. (1981). Individual response patterns and the effects of different behavioral methods in the treatment of social phobia. *Behaviour Research and Therapy, 19,* 1–16.

Öst, L.-G., Salkovskis, P. M., & Hellström, K. (1991). One-session therapist directed exposure versus self-exposure in the treatment of spider phobia. *Behavior Therapy, 22,* 407–422.

Öst, L.-G., & Sterner, U. (1987). Applied tension: A specific behavioral method for treatment of blood phobia. *Behaviour Research and Therapy, 25,* 25–29.

Öst, L.-G., Thulin, U., & Ramnerö, J. (2004). Cognitive behavior therapy vs *in vivo* in the treatment of panic disorder with agoraphobia. *Behaviour Research and Therapy, 42,* 1105–1127.

Öst, L.-G., & Westling, B. E. (1995). Applied relaxation versus cognitive behavior therapy in the treatment of panic disorder. *Behaviour Research and Therapy, 33,* 145–158.

Öst, L.-G., Westling, B. E., & Hellström, K. (1993). Applied relaxation, exposure *in vivo* and cognitive methods in the treatment of panic disorder with

agoraphobia. *Behaviour Research and Therapy, 31,* 383–395.

Otto, M. W., Pollack, M. H., & Sabatino, S. A. (1996). Maintenance of remission following cognitive behavior therapy for panic disorder: Possible deleterious effects of concurrent medication treatment. *Behavior Therapy, 27,* 473–482.

Otto, M. W., Pollack, M. H., Sachs, G. S., Teiter, S. R., Meltzer-Brody, S., & Rosenbaum, J. F. (1993). Discontinuation of benzodiazepine treatment: Efficacy of cognitive-behavioral therapy for patients with panic disorder. *American Journal of Psychiatry, 150,* 1485–1490.

Otto, M. W., Smits, J. A. J., & Reese, H. E. (2005). Combination psychotherapy and pharmacotherapy for mood and anxiety disorders in adults: Review and analysis. *Clinical Psychology: Science and Practice, 12,* 72–86.

Page, A. C. (1994). Blood-injury phobia. *Clinical Psychology Review, 14,* 443–461.

Pollack, M. H., Otto, M. W., Kaspi, S. P., Hammerness, P. G., & Rosenbaum, J. F. (1994). Cognitive behavior therapy for treatment-refractory panic disorder. *Journal of Clinical Psychiatry, 55,* 200–205.

Power, K. G., Jerrom, D. W. A., Simpson, R. J., Mitchell, M. J., & Swanson, V. (1989). A controlled comparison of cognitive-behaviour therapy, diazepam, and placebo in the management of generalized anxiety. *Behavioural Psychotherapy, 17,* 1–14.

Power, K. G., Simpson, R. J., Swanson, V., Wallace, L. A., Feistner, A. T. C., & Sharp, D. (1990). A controlled comparison of cognitive-behaviour therapy, diazepam, and placebo, alone and in combination, for the treatment of generalised anxiety disorder. *Journal of Anxiety Disorders, 4,* 267–292.

Rachman, S. J., & Hodgson, R. J. (1980). *Obsessions and compulsions.* Englewood Cliffs, NJ: Prentice-Hall.

Rapee, R. M. (1991). Generalized anxiety disorder: A review of clinical features and theoretical concepts. *Clinical Psychology Review, 11,* 419–440.

Reich, J., Noyes, R., & Troughton, E. (1987). Dependent personality disorder associated with phobic avoidance in patients with panic disorder. *American Journal of Psychiatry, 144,* 323–326.

Rodebaugh, T. L., Holaway, R. M., & Heimberg, R. G. (2004). The treatment of social anxiety disorder. *Clinical Psychology Review, 24,* 883–908.

Roemer, L., & Orsillo, S. M. (in press). An open trial of an acceptance-based behavior therapy for generalized anxiety disorder. *Behavior Therapy.*

Rollman, B. L., Belnap, B. H., Mazumdar, S., Houck, P. R., Zhu, F., Gardner, W., et al. (2005). A randomized trial to improve the quality of treatment for panic and generalized anxiety disorders in primary care. *Archives of General Psychiatry, 62,* 1332–1341.

Rothbaum, B. O., Hodges, L. F., Kooper, R., Opdyke, D., Williford, J. S., & North, M. (1995). Effectiveness of computer-generated (virtual reality) graded exposure in the treatment of acrophobia. *American Journal of Psychiatry, 152,* 626–628.

Rothbaum, B. O., Hodges, L. F., & Smith S. (1999). Virtual reality exposure therapy abbreviated treatment manual: Fear of flying application. *Cognitive and Behavioral Practice, 6,* 234–244.

Rothbaum, B. O., Hodges, L., Smith, S., Lee, J. H., & Price, L. (2000). A controlled study of Virtual Reality Exposure Therapy for the fear of flying. *Journal of Consulting and Clinical Psychology, 68,* 1020–1026.

Rowe, M. K., & Craske, M. G. (1998). Effect of an expanding-spaced vs. massed exposure schedule on fear reduction and return of fear. *Behavior Research and Therapy, 36,* 701–717.

Roy-Byrne, P. P., Craske, M. G., Stein, M. B., Sullivan, G., Bystritsky, A., Katon, W., et al. (2005). A randomized effectiveness trial of cognitive-behavioral therapy and medication for primary care panic disorder. *Archives of General Psychiatry, 62,* 290–298.

Salkovskis, P. M., & Clark, D. M. (1991). Cognitive therapy for panic disorder. *Journal of Cognitive Psychotherapy, 5,* 215–226.

Salmon, P. (2001). Effects of physical exercise on anxiety, depression, and sensitivity to stress: A unifying theory. *Clinical Psychology Review, 21,* 33–61.

Sanderson, W. S., Di Nardo, P. A., Rapee, R. M., & Barlow, D. H. (1990). Syndrome comorbidity in patients diagnosed with a *DSM-III-R* anxiety disorder. *Journal of Abnormal Psychology, 99,* 308–312.

Schmidt, N. B., Woolaway-Bickel, K., Trakowski, J., Santiago, H., Storey, J., Koselka, M., et al. (2000). Dismantling cognitive-behavioral treatment for panic disorder: Questioning the utility of breathing retraining. *Journal of Consulting and Clinical Psychology, 68,* 417–424.

Segal, Z. V., Williams, J. M. G., & Teasdale, J. D. (2002). *Mindfulness-based cognitive therapy for depression: A new approach to preventing relapse.* New York: Guilford Press.

Shear, M. K., Houck, P., Greeno, C., & Masters, B. S. (2001). Emotion-focused psychotherapy for patients with panic disorder. *American Journal of Psychiatry, 158,* 1993–1998.

Shear, M. K., Pilkonis, P. A., Cloitre, M., & Leon, A. C. (1994). Cognitive behavioral treatment compared with nonprescriptive treatment of panic disorder. *Archives of General Psychiatry, 51,* 395–401.

Solyom, L., Shugar, R., Bryntwick, S., & Solyom, C. (1973). Treatment of fear of flying. *American Journal of Psychiatry, 130,* 423–427.

Spiegel, D. A., Bruce, T. J., Gregg, S. F., & Nuzzarello, A. (1994). Does cognitive behavior therapy assist slow-taper alprazolam discontinuation in panic disorder? *American Journal of Psychiatry, 151,* 876–881.

Stangier, U., Heidenreich, T., Peitz, M., Lauterbach, W., & Clark, D. M. (2003). Cognitive therapy for social phobia: Individual versus group treatment. *Behaviour Research and Therapy, 41,* 991–1007.

Swinson, R. P., Fergus, K. D., Cox, B. J., & Wickwire, K. (1995). Efficacy of telephone-administered behavioral therapy for panic disorder with agoraphobia. *Behaviour Research and Therapy, 33,* 465–469.

Telch, M. J., Agras, W. S., Taylor, C. B., Roth, W. T., & Gallen, C. (1985). Combined pharmacological and behavioral treatment for agoraphobia. *Behaviour Research and Therapy, 23,* 325–335.

Telch, M. J., Lucas, J. A., Schmidt, N. B., Hanna, H. H., Jaimcz, T. S., & Lucas, R. A. (1993). Group cognitive-behavioral treatment of panic disorder. *Behaviour Research and Therapy, 31,* 279–287.

Thorpe, C. L., & Burns, L. E. (1983). *The agoraphobic syndrome.* New York: Wiley.

Trull, T. J., Nietzel, M. T., & Main, A. (1988). The use of meta-analysis to assess the clinical significance of behavior therapy for agoraphobia. *Behavior Therapy, 19,* 527–538.

Turk, C. L., Heimberg, R. G., & Hope, D. A. (2001). Social anxiety disorder. In D. H. Barlow (Ed.), *Clinical handbook of psychological disorders: A step-by-step treatment manual* (3rd ed., pp. 114–153). New York: Guilford Press.

Turner, S. M., Beidel, D. C., Cooley, M. R., Woody, S. R., & Messer, S. C. (1994). A multicomponent behavioral treatment for social phobia: Social Effectiveness Therapy. *Behaviour Research and Therapy, 32,* 381–390.

Turner, S. M., Beidel, D. C., & Jacob, R. G. (1994). Social phobia: A comparison of behavior therapy and atenolol. *Journal of Consulting and Clinical Psychology, 62,* 350–358.

Turner, S. M., Williams, S. L., Beidel, D. C., & Mezzich, J. E. (1986). Panic disorder and agoraphobia with panic attacks: Covariation along the dimensions of panic and agoraphobic fear. *Journal of Abnormal Psychology, 95,* 384–388.

Wells, A. (1995). The metacognitive model of GAD: Assessment of meta-worry and relationship with *DSM-IV* generalized anxiety disorder. *Cognitive Therapy and Research, 29,* 107–121.

White, J., & Keenan, M. (1992). Stress control: A controlled comparative investigation of large group therapy for generalized anxiety disorder. *Behavioral Psychotherapy, 20,* 97–114.

Wiederhold, B. K., & Wiederhold, M. D. (2000). Lessons learned from 600 virtual reality sessions. *Cyberpsychology and Behavior, 3,* 393–400.

Williams, S. L., & Rappaport, A. (1983). Cognitive treatment in the natural environment for agoraphobics. *Behavior Therapy, 14,* 299–313.

14

Pharmacological Treatments for Panic Disorder, Generalized Anxiety Disorder, Specific Phobia, and Social Anxiety Disorder

Peter P. Roy-Byrne

Deborah S. Cowley

Selective serotonin reuptake inhibitors (SSRIs) are now considered by most experts to be the first-line pharmacological treatment for panic disorder based on their low rate of side effects, lack of dietary restrictions, and absence of tolerance and withdrawal symptoms. Similarly, SSRIs are an attractive first-line treatment for social anxiety disorder. The pharmacological treatments of choice for generalized anxiety disorder are buspirone and antidepressants, including SSRIs and venlafaxine. Both buspirone and antidepressants provide a promising alternative to benzodiazepines. Benzodiazepines, although effective for all these disorders, carry with them the risk of physiological dependence and withdrawal symptoms and ineffectiveness for comorbid depression. Their greatest utility at present seems to be as an initial or adjunctive medication for patients with disabling symptoms requiring rapid relief and for those unable to tolerate other medications. Chronic treatment with benzodiazepines is generally safe and effective but should probably be reserved for patients who are nonresponsive or intolerant to other agents. Controlled trials are necessary to determine whether patients with specific phobias respond to pharmacological agents, particularly serotonin reuptake inhibitors.

Eighteen Type 1 placebo-controlled trials have conclusively shown the efficacy of the selective serotonin reuptake inhibitors (SSRIs) paroxetine (3 studies), sertraline (3 studies), fluvoxamine (7 studies), fluoxetine (2 studies), citalopram (2 studies), and escitalopram (1 study) for panic disorder. Sixteen placebo-controlled studies, 11 for imipramine and 5 for clomipramine, have shown that the tricyclic antidepressants are effective for treating panic disorder. Other heterocyclics are less well studied, although 1 placebo-controlled trial has shown efficacy for desipramine. The benzodiazepines alprazolam and clonazepam have been shown effective for panic disorder in 8 and 4 Type 1 placebo-controlled studies, respectively. There are also controlled data indicating the efficacy of other benzodiazepines, including lorazepam and diazepam. Numerous Type 1 double-blind, controlled trials have examined the efficacy of benzodiazepines for the treatment of generalized anxiety disorder. Benzodiazepines have been found superior to a placebo in most recent studies, and all benzodiazepines appear equally effective. Buspirone, pharmacologically unrelated to benzodiazepines, has been shown in several double-blind studies to be comparable to benzodiazepines in the treatment of generalized anxiety disorder. Placebo-controlled trials have also shown efficacy in generalized anxiety disorder for antidepressants, including tricyclics (3 studies), extended-release venlafaxine (4 studies), paroxetine (3 studies), escitalopram (3 studies), and sertraline (one study). The phobic disorders include specific and social phobias, but no pharmacological intervention has been shown to be effective for specific phobia. Twenty placebo-controlled trials suggest that the SSRIs fluvoxamine (4 studies), sertraline (4 studies), paroxetine (8 studies), escitalopram (2 studies), fluoxetine (1 study), and citalopram (1 study) are effective for social phobia (social anxiety disorder). Five placebo-controlled trials have demonstrated the efficacy of venlafaxine. In addition, double-blind, randomized trials have supported the efficacy of the monoamine oxidase inhibitors phenelzine (4 studies), meclobamide (4 studies), and broforamine (3 studies) in the treatment of social anxiety disorder. Two controlled trials found efficacy in social phobia for the benzodiazepines clonazepam and alprazolam.

Panic attacks, "generalized" or free-floating anxiety, and context-dependent fears (phobias) are the modern syndromes previously known as "neurotic anxiety" and thought at that time (before publication of the third edition of the *Diagnostic and Statistical Manual of Mental Disorders*; American Psychiatric Association [APA], 1980) to be poorly responsive to pharmacotherapy. However, since the early 1980s, beginning with the introduction of *DSM-III*, we have seen a growing appreciation of the important role of pharmacotherapy in the treatment of these syndromes and an accumulating body of evidence documenting the efficacy of specific classes of medication for specific anxiety disorders (APA, 1980). This chapter reviews the clinical characteristics and pharmacotherapy of the three major anxiety disorders: panic disorder (with or without agoraphobia), generalized anxiety disorder, and phobic disorders (principally social phobia). Selected literature will largely focus on the most rigorously designed studies. Other levels of evidence will be cited only to address key clinical issues not yet studied in randomized controlled trials.

PANIC DISORDER

Panic attacks are sudden, unexpected bursts of extreme anxiety accompanied by at least four physical or cognitive symptoms that include palpitations; chest discomfort; shortness of breath; dizziness; sweating; numbness or tingling; hot or cold flashes; abdominal discomfort; nausea or diarrhea; depersonalization or derealization; and fear of dying, going crazy, or losing control. Panic disorder is characterized by the presence of recurrent spontaneous (i.e.,

unexpected) panic attacks followed by a month of persistent anxiety about having attacks, concern about the implications of attacks (often marked by hypochondriacal preoccupations), or avoidance of situations that the individual feels will bring on attacks (agoraphobia). Although as many as one third to one half of the population will experience a panic attack in their lifetime, only about 1 in 10 of these people will develop the recurrent attacks and accompanying chronic anxiety, bodily/illness preoccupation, or phobic avoidance that characterize panic disorder (Norton, Cox, & Malan, 1992).

Panic disorder is a chronic illness with prevalences in the general population of 1.5% (1 month; Eaton, Kessler, Wittchen, & Magee, 1994), 2.3 to 2.7% (12 month; Kessler, Chiu, Demler, Merikangas, & Walters, 2005), and 3.5 to 4.7% (lifetime; Kessler, Berglund, et al., 2005). Twice as many women as men are affected, with peak age of onset typically in the late teens and early 20s (Eaton et al., 1994). Although there is an increased rate of the disorder in family members, greater concordance in monozygotic versus dizygotic twins, and a body of evidence suggesting that multiple genes of small effect likely mediate vulnerability to panic attacks, the results of genetic linkage and association studies thus far have been negative (Roy-Byrne, Craske, & Stein, 2006). Since the late 1980s, pathophysiological theories have focused on dysregulation of brain stem respiratory control centers and nearby noradrenergic and serotonergic nuclei that project to subcortical and limbic sites known to modulate emotion and its autonomic nervous system components (Papp, Coplan, & Gorman, 1992). More recently, theories have focused on the pivotal role of the amygdala, with brain stem abnormalities seen as a possible downstream effect (Roy-Byrne & Cowley, 1998), consistent with recent neuroimaging studies showing structural, functional, receptor, and neurotransmitter abnormalities in amygdala-related subcortical and frontal lobe circuits (Roy-Byrne et al., in press). In addition, stressful life events occur at an increased rate around the time of panic onset (Roy-Byrne, Geraci, & Uhde, 1986) and both interoceptive conditioning and an increased tendency to amplify body sensations, and an anxious experience via catastrophic and other cognitive distortions (Barlow, 2002; Bouton, Mineka, & Barlow, 2001) constitute psychological factors that maintain panic. Hence, the disorder is likely to involve a heritable biological vulnerability and a series of stressful triggers modulated perhaps by a cognitive style that may have both innate and learned origins.

Despite demonstration of the antipanic efficacy of imipramine in the early 1960s, subsequent studies showing the efficacy of benzodiazepines and behavioral treatment in the 1980s, and the more recent demonstration of SSRI antipanic efficacy, evidence-based treatment for panic disorder has been poorly integrated into clinical practice. The surprisingly high utilization rate of nonspecific psychotherapy and ineffective medication regimens observed in the 1980s (Taylor et al., 1989) has been improved on only modestly in both psychiatric (Goisman, Warshaw, & Keller, 1999; Yonkers et al., 1996), and primary care settings (Roy-Byrne et al., 2002), with rates of adequate medication (30 to 50%) and cognitive-behavioral treatment (CBT; 10 to 30%) still quite low in these respective settings.

The mainstays of pharmacological treatment of panic disorder have been, in order of historic and chronological development, tricyclic antidepressants and monoamine oxidase inhibitors (MAOIs) in the 1960s and 1970s, high-potency benzodiazepines in the 1980s, and, more recently, in the 1990s, selective serotonin reuptake inhibitors. Currently, two benzodiazepines (alprazolam and clonazepam) and three SSRIs (paroxetine, fluoxetine, and sertraline) have Food and Drug Administration (FDA) approval for panic. However, other SSRIs and heterocyclic and MAOI antidepressants are also effective, highlighting the fact that there is, in general, poor concordance between established efficacy and approved indication for panic, as well as other anxiety, disorders. This review of antipanic treatments includes agoraphobia under the rubric of panic disorder, since virtually all clinical medication trials have included patients with panic disorder complicated by phobic avoidance. In fact, because there is no evidence that agoraphobia exists in the absence of a history of panic attacks in clinical settings, the fourth edition of the *Diagnostic and Statistic Manual of Mental Disorders* (*DSM-IV*; APA, 1994) precludes the diagnosis of agoraphobia in the absence of a history of panic attacks).

Selective Serotonin Reuptake Inhibitors

Extensive evidence now supports the efficacy of SSRIs in the treatment of panic disorder. These newer, more tolerable agents have largely replaced benzodiazepines as first-line medication for panic in the judgment of numerous experts (Papp et al., 1997; Uhlenhuth, Balter, Ban, & Yang, 1998). Currently, three of the six available selective SSRIs (paroxetine, sertraline, and fluoxetine) are approved by the FDA for treatment of panic. Type 1, double-blind, placebo-controlled studies, using both flexible and fixed doses, support the short-term (8 to 12 weeks) antipanic efficacy of paroxetine (Ballenger, Wheadon, Steiner, Bushnell, & Gergel, 1998; Lecrubier, Bakker, Dunbar, & Judge, 1997; Oehrberg et al., 1995), sertraline (Londborg et al., 1998; Pohl, Wolkow, & Clary, 1998; Pollack, Otto, Worthington, Manfro, & Wolkow, 1998), and fluoxetine (Michelson et al., 2001; Michelson et al., 1998) The sertraline studies were unique in also documenting improvements in quality of life, in addition to panic-related symptoms. For fluoxetine, an open case series has also documented efficacy for up to 26 months with once-weekly dosing with 10 to 60 mg of this long-half-life compound (Emmanuel, Ware, Brawman-Mintzer, Ballenger, & Lydiard, 1999). Seven double-blind, placebo-controlled studies have shown efficacy for the now infrequently prescribed and marketed SSRI fluvoxamine (Asnis et al., 2001; Black, Wesner, Bowers, & Gabel, 1993; de Beurs, van Balkom, Lange, Koele, & van Dyck, 1995; Den Boer & Westenberg, 1988; Hoehn-Saric, McLeod, & Hipsley, 1993; Nair et al., 1996; Sandmann et al., 1998). Finally, two double-blind, placebo-controlled trials have demonstrated antipanic efficacy for citalopram (Leinonen et al., 2000; Wade, Lepola, Koponen, Pedersen, & Pedersen, 1997), and one trial has shown efficacy for the S-isomer of citalopram, escitalopram (Stahl, Gergel, & Li, 2003). These SSRI studies have shown effects on panic frequency, generalized anxiety, disability, and phobic avoidance, although not all studies measured all of these components.

Continued efficacy over the long term has been demonstrated in placebo-controlled discontinuation designs following acute placebo-controlled trials, for paroxetine over 36 weeks following a 12-week trial (Lecrubier et al., 1997), for sertraline over 28 weeks following a 1-year-long open-label extension after a 10-week acute trial (Rapaport et al., 2001), for fluoxetine over 24 weeks following a 10-week trial (Michelson et al., 1999), and for citalopram over 52 weeks following an 8-week trial (Lepola et al., 1998). In most of these trials, improvement in patients already improved after the acute trial continued to grow over the longer term.

Studies have shown that doses of 40 mg paroxetine, 100 to 200 mg sertraline, 10 to 20 mg fluoxetine, 100 to 200 mg fluvoxamine, and 20 to 30 mg of citalopram have been optimally effective. Although no consistent dose-response effects have been shown across class, studies have suggested higher doses may be beneficial for paroxetine (Ballenger, Wheadon, et al., 1998) and fluoxetine (Michelson et al., 2001), and perhaps counterproductive for sertraline at the 200-mg dose (Londborg et al., 1998). Early overstimulation has been especially noted with fluoxetine in open reports (Schneier et al., 1990), prompting recommendations for low (5 mg) starting doses, although recent trials began at 10 mg with less problem (Michelson et al., 2001). Such effects have been infrequently noted with the other SSRIs (2 of 80 sertraline patients [Pohl et al., 1998] and two of 67 paroxetine patients [Ballenger, 1999] started at the low end of those dose ranges). Furthermore, the side effect burden with this class of medication has been much less severe, with higher percentages of patients completing treatment (82%) than in studies of tricyclics (69%; Bakker, van Balkom, & Spinhoven, 2002). However, abrupt withdrawal of SSRIs has been associated with a withdrawal syndrome marked by irritability, nausea, dizziness, and headache in the case of both fluvoxamine (Black, Wesner, & Gabel, 1993) and paroxetine (Oehrberg et al., 1995), probably due to their relatively shorter half-life compared with fluoxetine and sertraline, although similar but milder symptoms have been observed with sertraline discontinuation (Rapaport et al., 2001). The common practice of switching patients to the longer acting fluoxetine before discontinuation has not been tested in a controlled trial.

The time course of effect has been shown to be delayed, as it is with tricyclics and MAO inhibitor antidepressants. In the various studies, superiority to placebo has emerged, depending on the effect and study, as early as 2 weeks (Pollack et al., 1998) and as late as 4 weeks (Ballenger, Wheadon et al., 1998), with some patients responding later, at 9 to 12 weeks (Michelson et al., 2001; Oehrberg et al., 1995), in studies supplying response rates over time. Early improvement does seem to predict more complete response, that is, remission, at the end of the acute trial (Pollack et al., 2002). One interesting meta-analysis showed a greater effect size for serotonergic antidepressants than for both tricyclics and benzodiazepines (Boyer, 1995), with the effect reduced but still

maintained when only studies using high-dose imipramine or alprazolam were compared. However, other meta-analyses have failed to show a clear efficacy advantage of antidepressants over benzodiazepines (Den Boer, 1998), or one for SSRIs over tricyclic antidepressants (Bakker et al., 2002), although three studies using direct comparisons have shown SSRI superiority to noradrenergic heterocyclics (fluvoxamine vs. maprotiline [Den Boer & Westenberg, 1990]; zimelidine vs. imipramine [Evans, Kenardy, Schneider, & Hoey, 1986]; and clomipramine vs. desipramine [Sasson et al., 1999]). These findings suggest, but do not conclusively demonstrate, that serotonergic antidepressants may have an advantage as antipanic agents.

Tricyclic (Heterocyclic) Antidepressants

Extensive evidence supports the efficacy of tricyclic antidepressants (TCAs), including the predominantly serotonergic TCA clomipramine, in panic disorder. The initial demonstration of reduction in panic attacks, but more variable and sometimes less robust effects on anticipatory anxiety and phobic avoidance, with imipramine compared with a placebo has been replicated many times since the late 1970s (D. F. Klein, 1964). Designs have varied in duration (6 weeks to 9 months), dosage (i.e., whether minimally effective doses of 150 mg have been used), breadth of symptoms measured (panic, phobia, disability), sample size, proportion of sample with comorbid phobia and depression, and use of additional behavioral therapies. Sixteen placebo-controlled trials have conclusively shown that TCAs are superior to a placebo for reduction of panic attacks and associated anxious and phobic symptomatology, 11 for imipramine (D. H. Barlow, Gorman, Shear, & Woods, 2000; "Drug Treatment of Panic Disorder" 1992; Mavissakalian & Michelson, 1986; Mavissakalian & Perel, 1995; Nair et al., 1996; Schweizer, Rickels, Weiss, & Zavodnick, 1993; Sheehan, Ballenger, & Jacobsen, 1980; Taylor et al., 1990; Uhlenhuth, Matuzas, Glass, & Easton, 1989; Zitrin, Klein, & Woerner, 1978; Zitrin, Klein, Woerner, & Ross, 1983) and 5 for the nonselective serotonin-reuptake inhibitor clomipramine (Broocks et al., 1998; Caillard, Rouillon, Viel, & Markabi, 1999; Fahy, O'Rourke, Brophy, Schazmann, & Sciascia, 1992; Johnston, Troyer, & Whitsett, 1988; Modigh, Westberg, & Eriksson, 1992). One study actually showed clomipramine superiority to imipramine at 12 weeks (Modigh et al., 1992), although the side effect profile of this drug is far more burdensome now that newer, more tolerable SSRIs are available. For imipramine, use of higher doses was more likely to show beneficial effects, and some studies also showed a clear dose-response relationship, with daily doses of 1.5 mg/kg or greater yielding beneficial effects. More recent data have suggested that therapeutic plasma levels are lower for phobia than for panic, explaining the occasionally observed dissociation between effects on these two different measures and further documenting the need for approximately 1.5 to 2.0 mg/kg of imipramine for phobia and 2.0 to 2.5 mg/kg for panic (Mavissakalian & Perel, 1995). Studies suggesting that lower doses of clomipramine (e.g., 75 mg) could also be effective did not include comparisons with higher doses as in the above imipramine studies.

Time course of effect can only be estimated from reported mean values, which are the average of numerous, somewhat variable, individual time course profiles. Nonetheless, most studies do not show drug placebo response differences until week 4, with maximal responses continuing for many measures to the trial's end (usually week 8). One of the earlier studies actually showed significant continuing improvement in phobic avoidance between weeks 14 and 26, reinforcing Klein's original hypothesis that panic improves before phobia (Zitrin et al., 1983). Experts reviewing open trial data maintain that peak effects on panic, phobia, and anxiety measures may be delayed until 10 to 12 weeks in many patients consistent with effects for SSRIs (Lydiard & Ballenger, 1987; Oehrberg et al., 1995). In general, antipanic effects of TCAs may, in some patients, take as long as, if not longer than, traditionally reported antidepressant effects.

Many studies show that TCAs are less well tolerated than, for example, benzodiazepines, with many patients dropping out of clinical trials both early (30% in the large Cross National Study; more than 50% in some smaller studies) and late (e.g., 20% during maintenance treatment) in a recent study (Barlow et al., 2000). One direct comparison showed that imipramine was more poorly tolerated than the SSRI fluvoxamine (Bakish et al., 1996). Although these trials do not provide clear indications of the reasons, open studies suggest that the most common reason for early discontinuation is overstimulation/jitteri-

ness, and for later discontinuation it is weight gain (Noyes, Garvey, Cook, & Samuelson, 1989). Low initial doses, slower titration, and use of adjunctive benzodiazepines or beta blockers may attenuate early overstimulation. Elevated heart rate and blood pressure with imipramine may be a problem in older patients or those with cardiac conditions (Taylor et al., 1990).

Few other heterocyclic agents have been studied. Desipramine was superior to a placebo for anxiety and phobia but not for panic attack frequency reduction at a mean dose of 177 mg/day in the only study of this agent performed (Lydiard et al., 1993). Based on SSRI class effects, as well as open trials of these other tricyclic agents, it is likely that other TCAs are also effective. Nortriptyline's lower rate of postural hypotension and anticholinergic effects than imipramine may improve tolerability in some patients. Of other antidepressants in this class, lesser efficacy is suggested for trazodone (than for imipramine and alprazolam) and maprotiline (than for fluvoxamine; Charney et al., 1986; Den Boer & Westenberg, 1988). Unfortunately, these two studies were not placebo controlled.

Benzodiazepines

The availability of high-potency benzodiazepines with the introduction of alprazolam in the mid-1980s reversed a prior tendency to view this class of medications as ineffective for panic disorder. Eight placebo-controlled, double-blind trials have found alprazolam to be superior to placebo in the treatment of panic attacks, with 55 to 75% of patients free of attacks at the end point of the study (Ballenger et al., 1988; Chouinard, Annable, Fontaine, & Solyom, 1982; "Drug Treatment of Panic Disorder," 1992; Lydiard et al., 1992; Munjack et al., 1989; Schweizer, Rickels, et al., 1993; Sheehan, Raj, Harnett-Sheehan, Soto, & Knapp, 1993; Uhlenhuth et al., 1989). Completer analyses showed less striking and sometimes only nonsignificant differences because of the high placebo dropout rate. Alprazolam showed similar robust effects on phobic avoidance (six of seven studies), disability (five of five studies), anticipatory anxiety (three of three studies), and generalized anxiety (seven of eight studies). Although daily mean doses of 5 to 6 mg were used in these studies, two studies of lower, 2-mg fixed doses (Lydiard et al., 1992; Uhlenhuth et al., 1989) also showed superiority to a placebo, although panic-free rates were lower than those seen with higher doses (25 to 50% vs. 55 to 75%). An extended-release formulation of alprazolam, given once or twice daily, has been shown to be comparably effective to the immediate-release compound (Schweizer, Patterson, Rickels, & Rosenthal, 1993).

The time course of effect with alprazolam is much more rapid than with antidepressants. In general, superiority to a placebo was evident in the first week or two of treatment. While some experts suggest a superiority of these agents for phobia and anticipatory anxiety, panic attacks still appear to improve before phobia with this class of medication as well (Lydiard & Ballenger, 1987). While patients with significant primary major depression were excluded in most trials, patients meeting criteria for major depression judged secondary to panic disorder were included in some studies (mean Hamilton Depression Rating Scale [HAM-D] around 15) and in general fared as well as those without a major depression diagnosis (Ballenger et al., 1988).

The tolerability of alprazolam was in general superior to that of imipramine, with greater retention in studies looking at head-to-head comparisons ("Drug Treatment of Panic Disorder," 1992; Schweizer, Rickels, et al., 1993; Uhlenhuth et al., 1989). Unfortunately, there are no head-to-head studies with SSRIs. The most common adverse effects of alprazolam were sedation or drowsiness, reported in 38 to 75% of patients, and memory impairment, reported in up to 15% of patients. The frequent lack of patient awareness of memory effects suggests caution prescribing these agents in older patients or those needing to perform complex cognitive tasks.

Four placebo-controlled trials have also supported the efficacy of clonazepam for panic disorder and demonstrated a similar rapid time course, spectrum of anxiolytic action, and side effect profile, with 1 mg being the minimal effective dose (Beauclair, Fontaine, Annable, Holobow, & Chouinard, 1994; Moroz & Rosenbaum, 1999; Rosenbaum, Moroz, & Bowden, 1997; Tesar et al., 1991). One study demonstrated antipanic efficacy for diazepam, and head-to-head comparisons with alprazolam in other non-placebo-controlled studies have shown uniform equivalence with lorazepam (Charney & Woods, 1989; Dunner, Ishiki, Avery, Wilson, & Hyde, 1986; Schweizer, Fox, Case, & Rickels, 1988). One double-blind discontinuation study has documented longer term efficacy of alprazolam over the course of a year (Dager et al., 1992), and numerous other open naturalistic follow-ups, without a placebo comparison, suggest longer term efficacy for this and other benzodiazepines.

The main public health concern regarding benzodiazepines has focused on their abuse potential, even though panic patients on long-term treatment do not escalate their doses over time (in fact, their doses go down) and abuse of these drugs does not occur in patients without comorbid alcohol or substance abuse (Garvey & Tollefson, 1986; Nagy, Krystal, Woods, & Charney, 1989). There is also no evidence of tolerance to the therapeutic effects of benzodiazepines in the several long-term studies that have been done. However, virtually all studies show that discontinuation of alprazolam in panic disorder patients is associated with withdrawal symptoms, recurrent panic attacks, and failure to complete the taper in 25 to 50% of patients after as little as 6 to 8 weeks of treatment (Pecknold, Swinson, Kuch, & Lewis, 1988; Roy-Byrne, Dager, Cowley, Vitaliano, & Dunner, 1989). The use of a fairly rapid taper (several weeks) in all these studies fails to mirror the current clinical practice of a long, gradual taper, shown to reduce the incidence of withdrawal in one series to 7% (Pecknold, 1990). A more recent study with clonazepam used a longer (though still too rapid) 7-week taper and found symptomatic worsening but no deterioration beyond the original baseline symptom level (i.e., "rebound anxiety"), in contrast to the rebound anxiety noted in all alprazolam studies in at least a portion (approximately 20%) of patients (Moroz & Rosenbaum, 1999). Direct comparisons of alprazolam with imipramine indicate greater taper difficulty and symptom recrudescence over the short term (1 month; A. J. Fyer, Liebowitz, & Gorman, 1989; Rickels, Schweizer, Weiss, & Zavodnick, 1993). However, studies showing that relapse rates after imipramine discontinuation gradually increase over 6 months suggest that this difference in short-term (1-month) relapse rates may merely reflect the mirror image of the time course in initial response (i.e., alprazolam more rapid, 1 to 2 weeks, and imipramine more slowly, 1 to 3 months) ("Drug Treatment of Panic Disorder," 1992; Mavissakalian & Perel, 1992). This suggests that much withdrawal may in fact be symptom reemergence/relapse, although this relapse is perhaps fueled by bona fide withdrawal reactions.

Monoamine Oxidase Inhibitors

In six double-blind, placebo-controlled studies, classic mixed MAO inhibitors (phenelzine, $N = 5$; iproniazid, $N = 1$) have been shown to be superior to a placebo for overall syndrome improvement (panic, anxiety, and phobia; Lipsedge et al., 1973; Mountjoy, Roth, Garside, & Leitch, 1977; Sheehan et al., 1980; C. Solyom, Solyom, LaPierre, Pecknold, & Morton, 1981; L. Solyom et al., 1973; Tyrer, Candy, & Kelly, 1973). Unfortunately, in these older, pre-*DSM-III* studies, patients were not selected to meet diagnostic criteria for panic, there were no separate measures of panic frequency obtained, and measures of phobic avoidance or anxiety employed were different from those used in later panic studies. Of the studies, three of the six employed adjunctive exposure treatment or supportive psychotherapy, and one employed adjunctive diazepam. All these studies employed relatively low doses (usually 45 mg phenelzine). Although higher doses are now recommended by most experts, there are no data to support this. The one study comparing phenelzine to imipramine suggested that phenelzine was superior for phobic avoidance, providing the only empirical evidence to support the impression of many clinicians that this class of medications may have special efficacy for treatment of resistant patients (Sheehan et al., 1980). A number of active drug comparisons, but without placebo, have shown that the selective MAO-A inhibitors brofaromine and meclobamide were equivalent to standard SSRIs (fluvoxamine, fluoxetine, and clomipramine), although the only placebo-controlled study failed to show efficacy for meclobamide (Kruger & Dahl, 1999; Loerch et al., 1999; van Vliet, Den Boer, Westenberg, & Slaap, 1996).

The time course of MAOI effect is more difficult to estimate precisely from these older studies. Delayed effects are suggested by superior effects at 8 weeks compared with 4 weeks. Of the two studies that lasted 12 weeks, one showed greater efficacy at 12 weeks than at 6 weeks (Sheehan et al., 1980). In general, the time course of effect is likely to be comparable to that seen for other antidepressants.

These medications are well tolerated in the short term due to the absence of early overstimulation effects. However, weight gain, insomnia with paradoxical daytime sedation, sexual dysfunction, and the need to follow a special low-monoamine diet limit their acceptability for some patients. A recent placebo-controlled study showed that the selective and reversible MAO inhibitor brofaromine, which does not require a diet, is effective for panic, with a 70% response rate, confirming both open trials and a blind comparative trial showing equivalence to clomipramine (Bakish, Saxena, Bowen, & D'Souza, 1993; Garcia-Borreguero et al., 1992; van Vliet, Westenberg, & Den Boer, 1993).

Other Antidepressants

Of other "newer" antidepressants, only venlafaxine (mean dose 166 mg) has been proved effective in uncomplicated panic disorder in two placebo-controlled trials (Bradweijn, Stein, Salinas, Emlien, & Whitaker, 2005; Pollack, Worthington, et al., 1996). Nefazodone has been shown to be effective in depression, accompanied by panic attacks, only in a subanalysis of one controlled depression trial (Zajecka, 1996). Finally, mirtazapine has been reported to be effective in open case series (Carpenter, Leon, Yasmin, & Price, 1999). Whether any of these agents would be more useful than the SSRIs is unknown, although the dual neurotransmitter effects of venlafaxine and mirtazapine might be an advantage.

Other Agents

Although treatment-resistant panic disorder occurs, it is relatively uncommon when adequate doses of the above medication classes have been tried, especially in conjunction with skilled cognitive-behavioral therapy. Moreover, treatment resistance is much less common than persistent panic disorder due to treatment delivery failure (i.e., failure to access, receive, or adhere to appropriate treatment). Few additional classes of medication are effective. Anticonvulsants have been frequently reported effective in open trials, but only gabapentin (Pande et al., 2000), in a secondary analysis focusing on high-severity panic, and valproate, in a small crossover study (Lum, Fontaine, Elie, & Ontiveros, 1990), have been shown effective in placebo-controlled designs. In contrast, carbamazepine has been shown to be ineffective in a placebo-controlled design (Uhde, Stein, & Post,

1988). One small placebo-controlled trial showed that the calcium channel blocker verapamil was an effective antipanic agent (E. Klein & Uhde, 1988), although curiously no other open reports have followed up on this preliminary finding. Another placebo-controlled study documented the efficacy of inositol, a precursor of a key second messenger for signal transduction in certain C-protein-linked receptors (Benjamin et al., 1995). In placebo-controlled studies, clonidine has not been found to be effective (Uhde et al., 1989), nor has propranolol (Munjack et al., 1989), bupropion (Sheehan, Davidson, Manschreck, & Van Wyck Fleet, 1983), or buspirone (Sheehan, Raj, Sheehan, & Soto, 1990).

Combined augmentation treatment using multiple agents has been infrequently studied. Early addition of a benzodiazepine to an antidepressant, with withdrawal after 4 to 6 weeks to speed initial response, has been shown to be effective for clonazepam added to sertraline (Goddard et al., 2001) and for alprazolam added to imipramine (Woods et al., 1992). Subsequent discontinuation of the benzodiazepine worsened symptoms in the alprazolam study, probably because of the short half-life of the drug and consequent more severe withdrawal. Strategies of switching medications, either within or between classes, or augmenting with other medications have not been examined, with the exception of a single study demonstrating that the beta blocker and serotonin 1A receptor antagonist pindolol, when added to fluoxetine in nonresponsive patients, is superior to placebo (Hirschmann et al., 2000). Despite this intriguing study, this strategy is not widely used in clinical practice.

Predictors of Response

Studies have generally found that more severely ill patients, whether defined by longer duration of illness (Basoglu et al., 1994), greater symptom severity (Pollack et al., 1994), comorbid depression (Rosenberg, Beech, Mellergard, & Ottosson, 1991), comorbid agoraphobia (Woodman & Noyes, 1994), or comorbid personality disorder (Black, Wesner, Gabel, Bowers, & Monahan, 1994), respond less well to medication, although not all reports have replicated every result every time. This is consistent with the results of naturalistic outcome studies (Roy-Byrne & Cowley, 1995), suggesting that these factors are associated with poorer long-term outcome.

Duration of Treatment/Chronic Treatment

As previously noted, all classes of agents described have been shown to retain their effectiveness over 8 to 12 months (Dager et al., 1992; Lecrubier & Judge, 1997; Michelson et al., 1999; Schweizer, Rickels et al., 1993). However, questions remain about the optimal duration of treatment following remission of panic attacks. Suggestions that long-term benzodiazepine treatment, for anxious patients in general, is associated with cognitive deterioration have not been borne out by studies showing similar memory function in anxious patients off long-term benzodiazepines (Lucki, Rickels, & Geller, 1986).

Current consensus recommendations for treatment duration are 1 to 2 years, based on limited controlled data (Ballenger et al., 1998; Work Group on Panic Disorder, 1998). Many naturalistic studies have shown relapse rates between 30% and 90% following medication discontinuation after 6 to 12 months of treatment (reviewed in Roy-Byrne & Cowley, 1995). Relapse in these studies appears strongly related to illness characteristics, specifically Axis I (depression and phobic avoidance) and Axis II comorbidity.

Eight studies have examined relapse in treatment responders using placebo-controlled discontinuation designs. Relapse rates were 45% and 65% with imipramine and clomipramine discontinuation after 10 weeks of single-blind placebo substitution (Gentil et al., 1993). Double-blind randomized studies have shown rates of 38% and 30% within 3 months of placebo substitution of imipramine (Mavissakalian & Perel, 1992) and paroxetine (Burnham, Steiner, Gergel, 1995), 37% within a year of imipramine discontinuation (Mavissakalian & Perel, 1999), only 8% within 6 months of placebo substitution of fluoxetine, and 24% after 6 months of placebo substitution of sertraline (Rapaport et al., 2001). Because the comparative drug relapse rates in all these studies varied from 5 to 15%, and because different definitions of relapse were used, a precise estimate is difficult. Nonetheless, all these studies suggest that relapse risk is likely 25 to 50% for patients with panic treated acutely (3 to 12 months), and it is likely that, based on naturalistic studies, relapse rates would grow over time.

Combined Treatment

A number of studies have shown that medication is superior to a placebo when both are added to some form of cognitive-behavioral therapy in panic disorder. This includes studies with SSRIs (De Beurs et al., 1995; Oehrberg et al., 1995), as well as imipramine (Mavissakalian & Michelson, 1986; Zitrin, Klein, & Woerner, 1980). Although this suggests combined treatment might be preferable, recent studies have suggested that, over the longer term, CBT effectiveness may be reduced in patients who have received it in the context of medication, once that medication is discontinued, whether it is imipramine (Barlow et al., 2000) or a benzodiazepine (Marks et al., 1993). Such findings suggest that learning new coping strategies on medication may not be as enduring once that medication is discontinued.

GENERALIZED ANXIETY DISORDER

Generalized anxiety disorder (GAD) is characterized by excessive worry about a number of different areas. The worry is difficult to control, occurs most of the time for at least 6 months, and is accompanied by significant distress or functional impairment, as well as by at least three of the following six symptoms: restlessness or feeling on edge, easy fatigability, concentration difficulties, irritability, muscle tension, and sleep disturbance. Since its original definition in 1980, GAD has been a problematic diagnosis with changing diagnostic criteria, poor interrater reliability (Di Nardo, Moras, Barlow, Rapee, & Brown, 1993), and high rates of psychiatric comorbidity (Brawman-Mintzer et al., 1993; Breslau & Davis, 1985). Up to 90% of patients with GAD have a lifetime history and 60% a current history of at least one other Axis I disorder, the most common being social anxiety disorder, specific phobias, depression, dysthymia, panic disorder, and substance abuse or dependence (Brawman-Mintzer et al., 1993). However, it is evident that there exists a group of patients with primary or isolated, severe, generalized anxiety associated with significant functional impairment (Kessler, DuPont, Berglund, & Wittchen, 1999).

Generalized anxiety disorder usually begins in the teens or early adulthood and is twice as common in women as in men. In the National Comorbidity Survey, GAD had a 12-month prevalence of 3.1% and a lifetime prevalence of 5.7% in the general adult population of the United States (Kessler, Berglund et al., 2005; Kessler, Chiu et al., 2005). However, individuals in this survey with episodes lasting 1 to 5 months, as opposed to 6 months or more, show similar degrees of impairment and comorbidity (Kessler, Brandenburg, et al., 2005), and those meeting all criteria except for excessive worry, although having a milder presentation, show substantial impairment, comorbidity, and rates of treatment seeking (Ruscio et al., 2005), suggesting that there is a larger percentage of the population with clinically significant generalized anxiety than these prevalence figures would indicate.

The pathophysiology of GAD is unclear. Early psychophysiological studies suggested that GAD was characterized by decreased "autonomic flexibility," with diminished autonomic responsivity and delayed recovery after a variety of laboratory stressors (Cowley & Roy-Bryne, 1991; Thayer, Friedman, Borkovec, Johnsen, & Molina, 2000). More recent studies have implicated alterations in gamma-aminobutyric acid (GABA)-benzodiazepine receptor function; in serotonergic, noradrenergic, glutaminergic systems; and in corticotropin releasing factor (CRF) in the pathophysiology of GAD, whereas neuroimaging studies have shown increased cortical and decreased basal ganglia activity in these patients (Nutt, 2001). GAD shows significant familial aggregation, with a meta-analysis of family and twin studies yielding an overall heritability of 0.32 (Hettema, Neale, & Kendler, 2001). Stressful life events, especially involving loss and danger, predispose to the onset of GAD (Kendler, Hettema, Butera, Gardner, & Prescott, 2003).

Historically, generalized anxiety has been treated with barbiturates, methaqualone, or, since the 1960s and 1970s, benzodiazepines. Since the early 1990s, alternative medication treatments, including buspirone and antidepressants, have been used for GAD. In addition, effective cognitive-behavioral therapy approaches specific for GAD have now been developed.

Benzodiazepines

Numerous double-blind, controlled trials have examined the efficacy of benzodiazepines in the treatment of generalized anxiety. For example, in 1978, Solomon and Hart reviewed 78 double-blind studies, concluding that benzodiazepines had not been shown to be superior to a placebo in the treatment of "neurotic anxiety" (Solomon & Hart, 1978).

In 1988, Barlow reviewed eight double-blind 2- to 6-week trials performed between 1978 and 1983 and, using the Hamilton Anxiety Rating Scale as the outcome measure, found 22 to 62% reductions in score in benzodiazepine-treated patients with generalized anxiety versus 18 to 48% decreases in placebo groups (Barlow, 1988). He concluded that the effects of benzodiazepines were marginal. However, dropout rates were substantially higher in placebo groups in five of six studies supplying this information, perhaps reflecting lack of efficacy. Two studies performed in the early 1980s suggested that patients with *DSM-III* GAD seen in primary care settings responded equally well to diazepam and a placebo after the first week or two of treatment (Catalan, Gath, Edmonds, & Ennis, 1984; Shapiro, Struening, Shapiro, & Milcarek, 1982). However, diazepam was superior to a placebo for those with the most severe anxiety (Shapiro et al., 1982).

More recently, with diagnostic criteria for GAD requiring both persistent, hard-to-control worrying and a 6-month duration, benzodiazepines have been found superior to a placebo in acute (4- to 6-week) double-blind treatment of GAD in most (Borison, Albrecht, & Diamond, 1990; Boyer & Feighner, 1993; Cutler et al., 1993; Enkelmann, 1991; Laakmann et al., 1998; Rickels, Downing, Schweizer, & Hassman, 1993; Rickels, Schweizer, Csanalosi, Case, & Chung, 1988; Rickels, Schweizer, DeMartinis, Mandos, & Mercer, 1997) but not all (Pecknold et al., 1989; Ross & Matas, 1987) studies. All benzodiazepines appear equally effective (Shader & Greenblatt, 1993). About two thirds of patients experience moderate to marked improvement of anxiety symptoms (usually assessed using Hamilton anxiety and Clinical Global Impression [CGI] ratings) with these medications, with therapeutic effects evident rapidly, within the first 1 to 2 weeks. Doses are lower by approximately half than those used in treating panic disorder (usually the equivalent of 10 to 25 mg/day of diazepam). Benzodiazepines appear particularly effective for somatic anxiety symptoms (Rickels et al., 1982). Patients with minor depressive symptoms respond more poorly to most of these agents (Rickels et al., 1993), with the possible exception of alprazolam, and both high-and low-anxiety volunteers given lorazepam demonstrated increases in negative emotions and decreases in positive emotions (Garcia et al., 2000).

Side effects of benzodiazepines in GAD are similar to those in panic disorder and include sedation, psychomotor impairment, anterograde amnesia (Lucki et al., 1986), and tolerance, although GAD patients may be less vulnerable than panic patients to withdrawal symptoms (E. Klein, Colin, Stolk, & Lenox, 1994). Of note, as with panic, dose escalation is rare in GAD patients without a history of substance abuse. For example, no dosage increases were observed in 119 anxious patients taking benzodiazepines for an average of 8 years (Rickels, Case, Schweizer, Swenson, & Fridman, 1986).

Azapirones

Buspirone, an azapirone anxiolytic and 5HT-1A receptor partial agonist, has been shown in several double-blind studies to be comparable to benzodiazepines, including diazepam, lorazepam, clorazepate, oxazepam, and alprazolam, for the acute treatment of GAD, yielding 30 to 50% reductions in Hamilton anxiety scale scores in 2- to 6-week trials (Ansseau, Papart, Gerard, von Frenckell, & Franck, 1990; Cohn, Bowden, Fisher, & Rodos, 1986; Enkelmann, 1991; Feighner, Merideth, & Hendrickson, 1982; Laakmann et al., 1998; Murphy, Owen, & Tyrer, 1989; Petracca et al., 1990; Rickels, Fox, Greenblatt, Sandler, & Schless, 1988; Rickels et al., 1982; Strand et al., 1990). Other azapirones, including ipsapirone and gepirone, have also proved effective in placebo-controlled, double-blind trials but are not available in the United States (Borison et al., 1990; Boyer & Feighner, 1993; Cutler et al., 1993; Rickels et al., 1997).

In comparison with benzodiazepines, buspirone has a delayed (2- to 4-week) onset of action, may affect psychic anxiety symptoms to a greater extent than physical symptoms, and has the advantage of being nonsedating and without evidence of tolerance or withdrawal symptoms (Feighner & Cohn, 1989; Rickels et al., 1982). Common side effects of buspirone include nausea, dizziness, and headaches. Average therapeutic doses are 20 to 45 mg/day, although doses of up to 60 mg/day may be necessary. Buspirone displays antidepressant effects in patients with comorbid depression, usually at higher doses of 45 to 60 mg/day (Gammans et al., 1992).

In general, patients on chronic benzodiazepine treatment do not respond well when switched to buspirone (DeMartinis, Rynn, Rickels, & Mandos, 2000; Lader & Olajide, 1987). For example, in a reanalysis of treatment results in 735 patients with

GAD treated with buspirone, a benzodiazepine, or a placebo, clinical improvement was similar with buspirone versus benzodiazepine treatment in those patients with no prior history of benzodiazepine treatment and in those whose benzodiazepine treatment had ended a month or more prior to the study. In those with recent benzodiazepine treatment (within the past month), there was greater attrition with buspirone treatment due to lack of efficacy and less clinical improvement than with benzodiazepine treatment (DeMartinis et al., 2000). A double-blind study of 44 GAD patients switched to buspirone versus a placebo after 5 weeks of lorazepam treatment, with lorazepam tapered during the first 2 weeks of buspirone versus placebo treatment, was more promising and showed that buspirone was superior to a placebo and comparable to lorazepam in anxiolytic effects (Delle Chiaie et al., 1995). There was no evidence of benzodiazepine withdrawal symptoms. However, the duration of lorazepam treatment was quite short. In a study examining imipramine versus buspirone versus placebo for treatment of 107 patients with GAD who had used benzodiazepines for an average of 8.5 years, the success rate of the 4- to 6-week benzodiazepine taper was significantly higher with imipramine (82.6%) than with buspirone (67.9%) or placebo (37.5%; Rickels, DeMartinis, et al., 2000).

Antidepressants

When panic disorder and GAD initially were described as distinct anxiety disorders, panic disorder was postulated to differ from GAD in responding to antidepressant treatment. However, since the mid-1980s, a number of antidepressants, including venlafaxine, imipramine, trazodone, paroxetine, escitalopram, and sertraline, have been shown in double-blind trials to be effective in treating GAD (Davidson, DuPont, Hedges, & Haskins, 1999; Gelenberg, Lydiard. et al., 2000; Haskins, Rudolph, Pallay, & Derivan, 1998; Hoehn-Saric, McLeod, & Zimmerli, 1988; Kahn et al., 1986; Rickels et al., 1993; Rickels, Pollack, Sheehan, & Haskins, 2000; Rocca, Fonzo, Scotta, Zanalda, & Ravizza, 1997). Venlafaxine, paroxetine, and escitalopram are now approved by the Food and Drug Administration for treatment of this disorder. Citalopram has been shown effective for late-life anxiety disorders (primarily GAD) in a single double-blind trial (Lenze et al., 2005) and was promising in an open trial in 13 adults with GAD (Varia & Rauscher, 2002). In addition, case series and open trials support the use of clomipramine (Wingerson, Nguyen, & Roy-Byrne, 1992), mirtazapine (Goodnick, Puig, DeVane, & Freund, 1999; Gambi et al., 2005), and nefazodone (Hedges, Reimherr, Strong, Halls, & Rust, 1996) in patients diagnosed with GAD, and trials in patients with depression and co-morbid anxiety suggest that fluoxetine (Versiani et al., 1999), fluvoxamine (Houck, 1998), and amitryptiline (Versiani et al., 1999) hold promise as treatments for generalized anxiety.

In an early double-blind trial, Kahn et al. (1986) reported the surprising result that imipramine performed better than chlordiazepoxide in the treatment of nondepressed outpatients retrospectively diagnosed as having GAD (Kahn et al., 1986). Following up on this, Hoehn-Saric et al. (1988), in a study of nondepressed patients with GAD, found that imipramine was comparable to alprazolam after the first 2 weeks of treatment (Hoehn-Saric et al., 1988). Imipramine was more effective in reducing psychic anxiety symptoms such as obsessionality, dysphoria, negative anticipatory thinking, and interpersonal sensitivity; alprazolam was superior in alleviating cardiovascular and autonomic symptoms.

Rickels et al. (Rickels et al., 1993) compared imipramine (mean dose 143 mg/day), trazodone (mean dose 255 mg/day), diazepam (mean dose 26 mg/day), and a placebo in 230 patients with GAD treated for 8 weeks. Although all active treatments were superior to the placebo, diazepam yielded the most improvement in anxiety ratings for the first 2 weeks, and imipramine was the most effective treatment thereafter, with 73% of patients moderately or markedly improved compared with 69% on trazodone, 66% on diazepam, and 47% on the placebo. Once more, antidepressants reduced psychic anxiety symptoms to a greater extent than did diazepam. Patients on antidepressants also reported more side effects.

Rocca et al. (1997) compared paroxetine, imipramine, and 2'-chlordesmethyl-diazepam in 81 patients with GAD (Rocca et al., 1997). All three treatment conditions resulted in significant clinical improvement in about two thirds of patients. As in prior studies, the benzodiazepine resulted in more rapid improvement, but the antidepressants resulted in more improvement by the 4th week. In addition, paroxetine and imipramine were most effective for psychic anxiety symptoms, whereas 2'-chlordesmethyl-diazepam was superior for somatic symptoms.

A number of controlled studies have now demonstrated the efficacy of SSRIs, and the combined serotonin and norepinephrine reuptake inhibitor venlafaxine, in the treatment of GAD. Promising observations in double-blind trials that venlafaxine was more effective than placebo in treating symptoms of anxiety in depressed outpatients (Feighner, Entsuah, & McPherson, 1998; Khan, Upton, Rudolph, Entsuah, & Leventer, 1998) then led to four Type 1 double-blind, placebo-controlled trials, which established the efficacy of this agent in nondepressed patients with generalized anxiety disorder (Davidson et al., 1999; Gelenberg, Lydiard, et al., 2000; Haskins et al., 1998; Rickels, Pollack, et al., 2000). Venlafaxine XR, in doses of 75 to 225 mg/day, yielded significantly greater decreases in anxiety than placebo within the first 2 to 3 weeks of treatment. Davidson et al. (1999) found that venlafaxine XR (75 or 150 mg/day) was more effective than buspirone (30 mg/day) throughout their 8-week study (Davidson et al., 1999), and Gelenberg, Lydiard, et al. (2000) showed persistent treatment gains over 28 weeks of treatment, with response rates (defined as a 40% decreases in Hamilton Anxiety score or CGI of 1 or 2) at weeks 6 to 28 of 69% with venlafaxine XR 75 to 225 mg/day compared with 42 to 46% in the placebo group (Gelenberg, Lydiard, et al., 2000). Patients treated in venlafaxine efficacy studies showed decreases in both psychic and somatic anxiety symptoms, although, consistent with prior antidepressant trials, effects on psychic anxiety were more pronounced (Meoni, Hackett, & Lader, 2004).

Recent 8- to 12-week trials have demonstrated efficacy of paroxetine 20 to 50 mg/day (Pollack et al., 2001; Rickels, DeMartinis, et al., 2000), sertraline 50 to 150 mg/day (Allgulander, Dahl, et al., 2004; Ball, Kuhn, Wall, Shekhar, & Goddard, 2005), and escitalopram 10 to 20 mg/day (Davidson, Bose, Korotzer, & Zheng, 2004; Goodman, Bose, & Wang, 2005), with response rates of 50 to 70% compared with 30 to 40% on placebo. Paroxetine significantly reduced the Hamilton Anxiety (HAM-A) anxious mood item compared with placebo as early as week 1, produced greater reductions in disability than placebo, and was equally effective at 20 and 40 mg/day doses (Pollack et al., 2001; Rickels et al., 2003). Escitalopram, in pooled results from three double-blind, placebo-controlled trials, differed significantly from placebo in total HAM-A score and in psychic anxiety by week 1 at a dose of 10 mg/day (Goodman et al., 2005) and was associated with improved quality of life (D. J. Stein, Andersen, & Goodman, 2005). Sertraline treatment significantly decreased both psychic and somatic anxiety scores, although its effect on psychic anxiety was more pronounced (Dahl et al., 2005). A controlled 8-week study directly comparing paroxetine and sertraline demonstrated similar efficacy and tolerability for both agents (Ball et al., 2005), whereas a 24-week comparison of escitalopram and paroxetine demonstrated similar reductions in HAM-A scores, but a significantly higher rate of discontinuation due to adverse events with paroxetine (22.6%) versus escitalopram (6.6%; Bielski, Bose, & Chang, 2005).

Other antidepressants show promise as treatments for GAD. For example, an open, 12-week trial of mirtazapine 30 mg/day in 44 outpatients with GAD yielded a response (defined, as in most of the SSRI trials described above, as a 50% or greater decrease in HAM-A score and a CGI improvement score of 1 or 2) in 79.5% of patients (Gambi et al., 2005). Citalopram 10 to 60 mg/day (mean dose 33 mg/day) resulted in improvement in all 13 GAD patients treated in an open trial, with 11 considered responders (Varia & Rauscher, 2002). In a controlled trial of 34 anxious patients over the age of 60, most of whom had GAD, patients treated with citalopram had a 65% response rate at 8 weeks, compared with a 24% response rate with placebo (Lenze et al., 2005).

Thus, a growing body of literature supports the use of antidepressants in GAD. Given their tolerability, efficacy for comorbid depression, and lack of risk of tolerance and dependence, the SSRIs and venlafaxine provide promising first-line treatments for this condition.

Other Medications

About one third of patients with GAD remain symptomatic despite treatment. Thus, studies have attempted to find pharmacological treatments with novel mechanisms of action, anxioselective GABA receptor agonists without risks of tolerance and withdrawal, and augmentation strategies to improve our ability to help treatment-resistant patients.

Studies performed prior to 1980 showed no efficacy of beta blockers for the treatment of generalized anxiety (Hayes & Schulz, 1987). One more recent double-blind, placebo-controlled trial was more promising (Meibach, Mullane, & Binstok, 1987). This 3-week, multicenter study of propranolol (average maximum dose 189 mg/day) versus chlordiazepoxide (average dose 50 mg/day) versus a placebo in 417 outpatients with "anxiety sufficiently severe to warrant treatment with an anxiolytic agent" showed the superiority of both active drugs but fewer side effects with propranolol than with chlordiazepoxide. Surprisingly, propranolol was particularly effective in reducing psychic symptoms of anxiety. Open trials of betaxolol, a long-acting beta blocker that enters the central nervous system, in 18 inpatients and 13 outpatients with anxiety disorders (including 16 inpatients and 11 outpatients with GAD) showed marked improvement in anxiety ratings in most patients (Swartz, 1998). Nevertheless, most experts continue to feel that beta blockers are not an effective primary treatment for GAD and should be reserved for use as an adjunct, particularly in patients with prominent autonomic symptoms.

A multicenter, double-blind, 4-week trial of hydroxyzine (50 mg/day) versus a placebo in 133 GAD patients displayed significantly greater reductions in anxiety in the hydroxyzine group, although side effects were more common than in the placebo group (Ferreri, Hantouche, & Billardon, 1994). Similarly, both hydroxyzine (50 mg/day) and buspirone (20 mg/day) were superior to placebo in a double-blind, multicenter, 4-week trial in a total of 244 patients with generalized anxiety disorder (Lader & Scotto, 1998). A 12-week study comparing hydroxyzine (50 mg/day), bromazepam (6 mg/day), and placebo in 334 patients with GAD demonstrated significantly higher response and remission rates with both active drugs than with placebo (Losier, McGrath, & Klein, 1996).

Pregabalin, an inhibitor of excitatory neurotransmitter release, has been studied in two double-blind, placebo-controlled trials. In the first, patients with GAD were treated for 4 weeks with alprazolam 1.5 mg/day, placebo, or one of three doses of pregabalin (300, 450, or 600 mg/day). Both alprazolam and pregabalin were superior to placebo in decreasing psychic and somatic anxiety symptoms, and the 300 mg/day pregabalin dose was superior to both placebo and

alprazolam at treatment end point (Rickels et al., 2005). Pregabalin was well tolerated, with discontinuation rates due to adverse events being 3% for pregabalin 300 mg/day, 8% for the 450-mg/day dose, 15% for the 600-mg/day dose, 14% for alprazolam, and 10% for placebo. The most common side effects of pregabalin were somnolence, dizziness, and dry mouth. Another 6-week study showed superiority of pregabalin (200, 400, or 450 mg/day) to placebo starting at week 1 with either BID or TID dosing (Pohl, Feltner, Fieve, & Pande, 2005).

Of 18 patients in an 8-week open trial of riluzole, an antiglutaminergic agent, 15 completed the trial, 12 responded, and 8 remitted (Mathew et al., 2005). Tiagabine, a GABA reuptake inhibitor, was well tolerated and had comparable anxiolytic effects to paroxetine in a 10-week open-label trial (Rosenthal, 2003), whereas ocinaplon, an anxioselective GABA receptor ligand, produced greater reductions in anxiety than placebo in a 2-week trial (Lippa et al., 2005).

Deramciclane, a camphor derivative and 5-HT2A/2C receptor antagonist, was superior to placebo in an 8-week trial, especially in reducing psychic anxiety symptoms, and was well tolerated, with the most common adverse event being headache (Naukkarinen et al., 2005). Opipramol, a tricyclic compound and D2-, 5-HT2-, and H1-antagonist with high affinity for sigma receptors, was superior to placebo and equivalent to alprazolam in a 4-week controlled trial of 307 patients with GAD (Moller, Volz, Reimann, & Stoll, 2001).

Kava kava, an extract of the plant *Piper methysticum*, used in the South Pacific to induce relaxation and sleep, has been shown to be effective for generalized anxiety (Pittler & Ernst, 2000). However, concerns about hepatotoxicity with kava kava have limited the clinical use of this agent. Passionflower (*Passiflora incarnate*) was equal in effectiveness to oxazepam in one 4-week trial (Akhondzadeh et al., 2001).

Atypical antipsychotics have been tested in placebo-controlled trials as adjunctive or augmentation treatments for GAD. Olanzapine (mean dose 8.7 mg/day) versus placebo augmentation for nonresponders to fluoxetine 20 mg/day yielded a greater proportion of responders and a trend toward more remitters in a small sample of 26 patients, but was associated with significant weight gain (Pollack, Simon, et al., 2006). In 40 patients continuing to experience GAD symptoms despite 4 weeks of anxiolytic treatment, the addition of risperidone 0.5 to 1.5 mg/day versus placebo in a double-blind, 5-week study led to significantly greater reductions in total and psychic anxiety scores (Brawman-Mintzer, Knapp, & Nietert, 2005).

Duration of Treatment/Chronic Treatment

Although there is extensive literature regarding acute treatment of generalized anxiety, there is less information available regarding long-term efficacy or the optimal duration of treatment.

Few studies have examined results of benzodiazepine treatment beyond the first 6 weeks. Cutler et al. (1993) found lorazepam more effective than a placebo after 6 weeks, but not after 8 weeks, of treatment, primarily due to continued improvement in the placebo group (Cutler et al., 1993). Both alprazolam and lorazepam remained superior to a placebo after 16 weeks in another study (Cohn & Wilcox, 1984). In a study of 101 GAD patients treated with cognitive-behavioral treatment, a placebo, or diazepam for 10 weeks, the greatest improvement was seen in patients receiving a combination of CBT and diazepam, and diazepam alone was more effective than a placebo alone (Power, Simpson, Swanson, & Wallace, 1990). Rickels, Fox, et al. (1988) showed the continued efficacy of clorazepate over a 6-month trial, with no tolerance to anxiolytic effects, but there was no placebo comparison.

Thus, benzodiazepines seem to have continued anxiolytic effects for up to 6 months, but the paucity of studies leaves us without a clear answer to the question of whether benzodiazepines are superior to a placebo after the initial phase of treatment. Buspirone has shown continued efficacy over a treatment period of 3 to 6 months (Feighner, 1987; Murphy et al., 1989; Rickels, Schweizer, et al., 1988). Long-term treatment with antidepressants has been examined in 6-month trials of venlafaxine and paroxetine, a 24- to 76-week trial of escitalopram, and a 6-month comparison of escitalopram and paroxetine (Gelenberg, Delgado, & Nurnberg, 2000; Stocchi et al., 2003; Allgulander, Florea, & Huusom, 2005; Bielski et al., 2005). All these studies support the ongoing efficacy of antidepressants for GAD with longer term treatment. Two (Allgulander et al., 2005; Stocchi et al., 2003) specifically address the issue of relapse using placebo-controlled discontinuation trials. In a 6-

month study of 566 patients with GAD who had responded to 8 weeks of paroxetine, those randomized to long-term placebo treatment were significantly more likely to relapse than those maintained on active medication (39.9% vs. 10.9%), and those on paroxetine were twice as likely to achieve remission (Stocchi et al., 2003). A similar study of 375 responders to acute treatment with escitalopram randomized to double-blind continuation treatment with escitalopram versus placebo showed a 56% relapse rate in patients on placebo versus 19% in those on escitalopram; the rate of discontinuation due to adverse events was similar in the two groups (7% with escitalopram vs. 8% with placebo; Allgulander et al., 2005). These studies not only demonstrate ongoing efficacy of antidepressants for GAD but also suggest that relapse rates are significant if medication is discontinued within 6 months after the acute treatment phase.

Two other studies have addressed the issue of optimal duration of treatment. Rickels, Case, Downing, and Winokur (1983) found that 50% of patients treated with diazepam for 6 weeks had relapsed 3 months later, and 63% had relapsed after 1 year. In another trial performed by the same group (Rickels, Schweizer, et al., 1988), 45 patients with GAD who responded to 6 months of treatment with clorazepate or buspirone were then followed up 6 and 40 months after the end of the study. At 6 months, 55% of clorazepate-treated patients and 38% of those treated with buspirone reported moderate to marked anxiety. At 40 months, 34 patients were contacted, and 57% of clorazepate-treated versus 25% of buspirone-treated subjects reported moderate to severe anxiety. These data suggest that for many people, GAD is a chronic illness requiring treatment for longer than 6 months. The apparently better outcome with initial buspirone treatment is interesting but may be attributable to the higher dropout rate in the buspirone group during the initial treatment period, with only the most treatment-responsive patients remaining in the study.

Combined Treatment

Cognitive-behavioral treatment has been proved to be an effective treatment for GAD. Given the substantial rate of nonresponse in medication trials, combining psychotherapy and pharmacotherapy seems a promising strategy. Very few studies have examined combined treatment, however. A 10-week trial of diazepam, CBT, and combined treatment showed the greatest improvement in the diazepam plus CBT group, although similar proportions of patients from each group were taking psychotropic medications at 6-month follow-up (Power et al., 1990). In a study by Lader and Bond (1998), 60 patients with GAD were randomized to buspirone plus anxiety management, buspirone and nondirective therapy, placebo and anxiety management, or placebo and nondirective therapy. All treatment groups improved, with no significant differences between groups.

SPECIFIC PHOBIA

Specific (formerly simple) phobias are fears and avoidance of discrete objects or situations such as spiders and heights. Specific phobias are common, with 12-month and lifetime prevalences of 8.7% and 12.5%, respectively (Kessler, Berglund, et al., 2005; Kessler, Chiu, et al., 2005). The treatment of choice for specific phobias is behavior therapy, specifically, systematic desensitization. Recently, successful treatment of specific phobia with fluoxetine has been reported in two patients with major depression and comorbid fear of flying (Abene & Hamilton, 1998). A small double-blind, placebo-controlled 4-week pilot study examining the efficacy of paroxetine up to 20 mg/day versus placebo for specific phobias showed significant superiority of paroxetine in reducing phobia scores on the Fear Questionnaire and Hamilton Anxiety scores (Benjamin, Ben-Zion, Karbofsky, & Dannon, 2000). The presence of comorbid depression in the first example, and the fact that "flying phobia" is a heterogeneous condition with some cases possibly related to underlying panic and more widespread phobias make these two reports questionable.

While, in general, pharmacological treatments have not proved effective for specific phobias, there is increasing interest in understanding how they may interact with the associative learning processes underlying desensitization. There is controlled evidence indicating that use of benzodiazepines may reduce therapeutic effects of exposure treatment (Wilhelm & Roth, 1997) and intriguing pilot data that d-cycloserine, an NMDA antagonist, facilitates extinction of height phobia (Ressler et al., 2004). This latter study treated acrophobia with two virtual reality sessions and found that administration of the drug versus placebo before each session resulted in greater long-lasting improvement 1 week and 3 months later, measured both in the virtual reality chamber and in self-reports of subsequent reductions in height fear and increased exposure to heights on one's own.

SOCIAL ANXIETY DISORDER

Social anxiety disorder (previously social phobia) is defined as a fear of social or performance situations in which the person fears scrutiny and negative evaluation by others, humiliation, and embarrassment. Feared social situations are avoided or endured with distress, and social anxiety causes significant functional impairment. Social anxiety disorder has been subdivided into a "specific" form limited to one or a few situations (the most common of which is public speaking) and a "generalized" form involving fear and avoidance of multiple social situations. Some authors have argued that generalized social anxiety disorder is indistinguishable from avoidant personality disorder (Widiger, 1992).

Social anxiety disorder is common. The National Comorbidity Replication Survey found a 12-month prevalence of social anxiety disorder of 6.8% and a lifetime prevalence of 12.1% (Kessler, Berglund, et al., 2005; Kessler, Chiu, et al., 2005). Social anxiety disorder has an early age of onset, with a peak in childhood and the teenage years (Schneier, Johnson, Hornig, Liebowitz, & Weissman, 1992), is more common in women than in men (Bourdon et al., 1988), and is associated with significant disability, with 22% of those with uncomplicated social anxiety disorder receiving public assistance and more than 50% of social phobics reporting at least moderate functional impairment due to social anxiety (Schneier et al., 1994). In up to 70% of cases, social anxiety disorder is accompanied by, and commonly precedes, other significant comorbid psychiatric disorders, such as depression, other anxiety disorders, and alcohol abuse and dependence (Schneier et al., 1992).

The neurobiological mechanisms of social anxiety disorder are as yet poorly understood. Animal models of subordination stress and attachment, as well as challenge testing in humans, suggest possible alterations in serotonergic, dopaminergic, noradrenergic, opioid, and oxytocin function; imaging studies have implicated basal ganglia structures, the amygdala, and cortical regions (Mathew, Coplan, & Gorman, 2001). Behavioral inhibition, with autonomic arousal in response to novelty, increased salivary cortisol, and high norepinephrine activity starting in infancy, and shyness and introversion as a toddler, is strongly associated with later social anxiety disorder, suggesting an underlying inborn vulnerability in many individuals (Rosenbaum et al., 1991). In addition, family and twin studies suggest that social anxiety disorder is familial and has a modest heritable component (M. R. Fyer, Frances, Sullivan, Hurt, & Clarkin, 1988; Kendler, Neale, Kessler, Heath, & Eaves, 1992).

Since the mid-1980s, behavioral and cognitive-behavioral techniques have been proved effective in the treatment of social anxiety disorder (Otto, 1999), and a number of double-blind, placebo-controlled studies have examined the efficacy of psychopharmacological treatments (Muller, Koen, Seedat, & Stein, 2005). Liebowitz et al. published the first open and then controlled trials of medication treatment for patients with social anxiety disorder (Liebowitz, Fyer, Gorman, Campeas, & Levin, 1986; Liebowitz et al., 1992). These trials used the beta blocker atenolol, based on prior reports of the utility of beta blockers in treating performance anxiety; and the MAO inhibitor phenelzine, based on the efficacy of this medication in treating mixed agoraphobia and social anxiety disorder and its success in treating atypical depression, which shares with social anxiety disorder the prominent symptom of interpersonal sensitivity. Since these early trials, controlled studies have examined the efficacy of both reversible and irreversible MAO inhibitors, benzodiazepines, serotonin reuptake inhibitors, venlafaxine, gabapentin, and beta blockers.

Several meta-analyses have found moderate to large effect sizes for all these medication classes in the acute treatment of social anxiety disorder (Black et al., 2004). Currently, the SSRIs and venlafaxine are considered the first-line pharmacological treatments, based on their established efficacy for both social anxiety disorder and common comorbid conditions, in addition to their tolerability, safety, and lack of dietary restrictions or risk of tolerance and withdrawal. Interestingly, though, and as in generalized anxiety disorder, the most commonly prescribed psychotropic medications for social anxiety disorder in clinical practice remain benzodiazepines (Vasile, Bruce, Goisman, Pagano, & Keller, 2005).

Serotonin Reuptake Inhibitors

There are now 22 published double-blind, placebo-controlled trials of serotonin reuptake inhibitors for acute treatment of generalized social anxiety disorder (Allgulander, 1999; Baldwin, Bobes, Stein, Scharwachter, & Faure, 1999; Blomhoff et al., 2001; Katzelnick et al., 1995; D. J. Stein et al., 1999; M. B. Stein, Fyer, Davidson, Pollack, & Wiita, 1999; M. B. Stein et al., 1998; van Vliet, Den Boer, & Westenberg, 1994), with 20 of these trials demonstrating superiority of drug versus placebo. Paroxetine and sertraline are approved by the FDA for the treatment of social anxiety disorder, and fluvoxamine and escitalopram have also been proved effective in double-blind trials. Citalopram was superior to placebo in a small, 4-week controlled study comparing citalopram, a neurokinin-1 receptor antagonist, and placebo (Furmark et al., 2005). The efficacy of fluoxetine has been examined in three double-blind studies (Kobak, Greist, Jefferson, & Katzelnick, 2002) . In one of these, fluoxetine failed to separate from placebo over 14 weeks, but the placebo rate was high (Kobak et al., 2002). In another comparison of cognitive therapy, fluoxetine plus self-exposure, and placebo plus self-exposure for 16 weeks, cognitive therapy was superior to both of the other groups, which did not differ significantly from each other (D. M. Clark et al., 2003). In a third, 14-week trial studying fluoxetine, cognitive-behavioral group therapy, and combined treatment, all active treatments yielded significantly higher response rates than placebo at end point and did not differ from each other (Davidson, Foa, et al., 2004). Response rates were 50.9% for fluoxetine and 31.7% for placebo, providing some support for efficacy of fluoxetine in social anxiety disorder. Fluoxetine has also been reported to relieve symptoms of social anxiety emerging during clozapine treatment in one small open trial (Pallanti, Quercioli, Rossi, & Pazzagli, 1999).

Paroxetine has demonstrated efficacy for social anxiety disorder at doses of 20 to 50 mg/day, with significant decreases in Liebowitz Social Anxiety Scale (LSAS) scores as early as week 2, significant reductions in social avoidance and social disability, and overall response rates of 55 to 66% versus 24 to 36% for placebo-treated patients after 11 to 12 weeks (Allgulander, 1999; Allgulander, Dahl, et al., 2004; Baldwin et al., 1999; Lepola, Bergtholdt, St. Lambert, Davy, & Ruggiero, 2004; Liebowitz, Gelenberg,

& Munjack, 2005; Liebowitz et al., 2002; D. J. Stein et al., 1999; L. I. Stein & Santos, 1998). Of note, although some patients responded early, an analysis of three paroxetine trials demonstrated that 46 of 166 patients who were nonresponders at week 8 (27.7%) were responders at week 12, arguing for at least 12-week treatment trials in many patients (D. J. Stein, Stein, Pitts, Kumar, & Hunter, 2002).

Sertraline trials for 10 to 24 weeks have shown superiority to placebo at doses of 50 to 200 mg/day (Blomhoff et al., 2001; Katzelnick et al., 1995; Liebowitz et al., 2003; van Ameringen et al., 2001). Four 12-week trials of fluvoxamine, at 100 to 300 mg/day of the regular or controlled release formulation, have demonstrated superiority of drug over placebo (Davidson, Foa, et al., 2004; D. J. Stein et al., 1999; van Vliet et al., 1994; Westenberg, Stein, Yang, Li, & Barbato, 2004). Finally, in two 12-week studies, escitalopram at 5 to 20 mg/day produced significant reductions in social anxiety scores and disability (Kasper, Stein, Loft, & Nil, 2005; Lader, Stender, Burger, & Nil, 2004). Response rates with these agents were comparable to those seen with paroxetine and, when reported, ranged from 40 to 55% for the SSRI and 7 to 30% for placebo.

These studies clearly establish that paroxetine, fluvoxamine, sertraline, escitalopram, and probably other serotonergic antidepressants are effective in the treatment of social anxiety disorder.

Venlafaxine

Four 12-week, double-blind, placebo-controlled trials of extended-release venlafaxine (venlafaxine ER) 75 to 225 mg/day have demonstrated efficacy of this agent for generalized social anxiety disorder, with response rates of 44 to 69% for venlafaxine and 30 to 36% for placebo (Allgulander, Mangano, et al., 2004; Liebowitz et al., 2005; Rickels, Mangano, & Khan, 2004). Venlafaxine treatment, versus placebo, was associated with significantly greater decreases in social anxiety and social and work disability, with reductions in social anxiety occurring as early as week 1 or 2 in one study (Liebowitz et al., 2005). Two of these four studies used paroxetine as an active comparator and showed similar efficacy and rates of adverse events with these two medications (Allgulander, Mangano, et al., 2004; Liebowitz et al., 2005).

Monoamine Oxidase Inhibitors

In 1986, Liebowitz et al. reported that 7 of 11 patients with *DSM-III* social phobia showed a "marked" response to phenelzine, and the other 4 had "moderate" improvement (Liebowitz et al., 1986). Since then, four double-blind, randomized trials have supported the efficacy of phenelzine for social anxiety disorder (Gelernter et al., 1991; Heimberg et al., 1998; Liebowitz et al., 1992; Versiani et al., 1992). Liebowitz et al. treated 74 patients with social anxiety disorder with phenelzine (mean dose, 75.7 mg/day), atenolol (mean dose, 97.6 mg/day), or a placebo. By week 8, "response" rates (much or very much improved as assessed by an independent rater) were 64% for phenelzine, 30% for atenolol, and 23% for the placebo (Liebowitz et al., 1992).

Gelernter et al., in a study of 65 social phobics (most with specific social phobia) given phenelzine, alprazolam, a placebo, or group cognitive-behavioral therapy, found that all groups improved, perhaps because all patients were encouraged to expose themselves to feared situations (Gelernter et al., 1991). Nevertheless, patients taking phenelzine were more likely than those in the other groups to display functional improvement and to fall below the mean score for the general population on the social phobia subscale of the Fear Questionnaire at the end of 12 weeks. Versiani et al. completed a double-blind trial of phenelzine, the reversible MAO inhibitor moclobemide, and placebo (Versiani et al., 1992). After 8 weeks, phenelzine and moclobemide were both significantly more effective than the placebo, and these gains were maintained for a further 8 weeks. Responders were then maintained on active medication or changed to a placebo. Those switched to the placebo demonstrated significant increases in symptomatology that persisted for at least 5 weeks, a finding suggesting a high rate of relapse. Finally, Heimberg et al. compared 12 weeks of phenelzine, pill placebo, cognitive-behavioral group treatment (CBGT), and an educational supportive group in 133 patients with social anxiety disorder (Heimberg et al., 1998). Both CBGT and phenelzine were superior to the control conditions, although response for phenelzine was more marked than for CBGT response at 6 weeks.

Thus, double-blind trials support the efficacy of phenelzine in the treatment of social anxiety disorder. Interestingly, isolated case reports suggest that phenelzine may also be effective in the treatment of conditions related to social anxiety disorder, such as elective mutism (Golwyn & Weinstock, 1990) and social anxiety secondary to physical disfigurement (Oberlander, Schneier, & Liebowitz, 1994). Other irreversible MAO inhibitors have not been studied in double-blind trials. However, an open trial of tranyl-cypromine yielded 20 "marked responders" among 29 subjects (Versiani, Mundim, Nardi, & Liebowitz, 1988).

Irreversible MAO inhibitors such as phenelzine have significant side effects, most notably hyperten-sive crisis, insomnia, weight gain, and sexual dys-function. Reversible MAO inhibitors, such as moclo-bemide and brofaramine, bind reversibly, are selective for the A isoenzyme of monoamine oxidase, and have fewer side effects, including a much lower rate of hypertensive crisis. The efficacy of reversible MAO inhibitors in social phobia has been demonstrated in four double-blind, placebo-controlled trials of moclo-bemide ("The International Multicenter Clinical Trial Group," 1997; Noyes et al., 1997; Schneier et al., 1998; Versiani et al., 1992) and three of brofara-mine (Fahlen, Nilsson, Borg, Humble, & Pauli, 1995; Lott et al., 1997; van Vliet et al., 1993), and an open trial suggests that moclobemide is similar in efficacy to the SSRI citalopram (Atmaca, Kuloglu, Tezcan, & Unal, 2002). Unfortunately, despite the promise of the reversible MAO inhibitors moclobe-mide and brofaromine for social anxiety disorder, these medications are unavailable in the United States. Of note, selegiline, which is a reversible MAO inhibitor in low doses, has been reported to be effective for social anxiety disorder (Simpson, Schneier, Marshall, et al., 1998).

Beta Blockers

Despite an early, promising open study of atenolol for social phobia (Gorman, Liebowitz, Fyer, Cam-peas, & Klein, 1985) and several studies demonstrat-ing the efficacy of single doses of beta blockers for treating performance anxiety in nonclinical groups such as musicians and public speakers (Jefferson, 1995), beta blockers have not proved effective in double-blind trials with patients with social anxiety disorder. For example, in the comparison of phenel-zine, atenolol, and placebo by Liebowitz et al. (1992) mentioned above, atenolol was not significantly more effective than a placebo.

Behavior therapy, primarily flooding, was superior to both a placebo and atenolol in one study (Turner, Beidel, & Jacob, 1994), and propranolol showed no advantage over a placebo in a study in which subjects also received social skills training (Falloon, Lloyd, & Harpin, 1981). Pindolol 5 mg TID was studied as a possible augmentation of paroxetine for generalized social anxiety disorder in a 4-week double-blind trial but was no more effective than placebo (M. B. Stein, Sareen, Hami, & Chao, 2001).

Beta blockers, for example, propranolol 10 to 40 mg taken as needed, 45 to 60 minutes before a per-formance, have been shown to reduce autonomic symptoms such as tremor, sweating, and tachycardia in individuals with performance anxiety who do not necessarily meet criteria for social anxiety disorder (reviewed in Muller et al., 2005).

Benzodiazepines

In open trials, both alprazolam, at doses of 3 to 8 mg/day, and clonazepam, 1 to 6 mg/day, have been effective in the treatment of social anxiety disorder (Davidson, Tupler, & Potts, 1994). The only double-blind, placebo-controlled trial of alprazolam was that of Gelernter et al. (1991). Although alprazolam (mean dose 4.2 mg/day) was not superior to a pla-cebo, this study was complicated by the inclusion of self-directed exposure in all treatment groups. Clo-nazepam, at an average dose of 2.4 mg/day, decreased social anxiety, interpersonal sensitivity, phobic avoid-ance, and disability in a 10-week double-blind study of 75 patients with social anxiety disorder (Davidson et al., 1993). Response rates were 78.3% for clonaze-pam and 20% for a placebo. Clonazepam was similar in efficacy to cognitive-behavioral group therapy in a 12-week trial (Otto et al., 2000). Clonazepam has also been studied as an adjunctive treatment in a ran-domized, double-blind, 10-week trial of clonazepam 1 to 3 mg/day versus placebo combined with open label paroxetine 20 to 40 mg/day (Seedat & Stein, 2004). At 10 weeks, the paroxetine plus clonazepam group had a 79% response rate, compared with a 43% response rate for paroxetine plus placebo, al-though given the small sample size (19 completers), this difference was significant only at a trend level ($p < .06$).

Use of benzodiazepines for social anxiety disorder is complicated both by their side effects and by the high rate of comorbid alcohol abuse or dependence

(Schneier et al., 1992), which may put patients at an increased risk for benzodiazepine abuse and dependence.

Other Medications

Surprisingly, there have been no controlled trials of tricyclic antidepressants for patients with social anxiety disorder. Although isolated case reports suggest that they may be effective (Benca, Matuzas, & Al-Sadir, 1986), and a large sample of 765 patients with agoraphobia or social phobia responded well to open-label clomipramine (Beaumont, 1977), other anecdotal evidence has been cited suggesting that tricyclics are inferior to MAO inhibitors (Liebowitz et al., 1986; Versiani et al., 1988), and an open trial of imipramine (Simpson, Schneier, Campeas, et al., 1998) indicated both lack of efficacy and a high dropout rate due to side effects. Open trials of buspirone appeared promising, particularly when doses exceeded 45 mg/day (Munjack, Brun, & Baltazar, 1991; Schneier et al., 1993). However, two double-blind trials using buspirone showed no significant improvement with doses averaging 32 mg/day in musicians seeking treatment for performance anxiety (D. B. Clark & Agras, 1991) and no difference between buspirone 30 mg/day and placebo in 30 patients with social anxiety disorder (van Vliet, Den Boer, Westenberg, & Pian, 1997). However, an open trial suggests that buspirone may be an effective augmentation agent in partial responders to SSRIs (van Ameringen, Mancini, & Wilson, 1996).

A randomized, double-blind, placebo-controlled 14-week trial using flexible doses of gabapentin (900 to 3,600 mg/day in three divided doses; mean dose 2,100 mg/day) in 69 patients with social anxiety disorder yielded response rates (CGI of 1 or 2) of 32% with gabapentin versus 14% with placebo (Pande et al., 1999). Side effects of gabapentin included dizziness, dry mouth, somnolence, nausea, flatulence, and decreased libido. Based on these results, three other anticonvulsants have been studied in social anxiety disorder. Pregabalin 600 mg/day, but not 150 mg/day, was superior to placebo in a double-blind 10-week trial in 94 patients with social anxiety disorder, with the most frequent side effects being somnolence and dizziness (Pande et al., 2004). In 16 patients treated with levetiracetam versus placebo, the effect size for Liebowitz Social Anxiety Scale scores was 0.50 after 7 weeks (Zhang, Connor, & Davidson,

2005). Finally, a 16-week open trial of flexibly dosed topiramate (maximum dose 400 mg/day) in 23 patients with social anxiety disorder resulted in rates of remission and response of 26% and 48%, respectively (van Ameringen, Mancini, Pipe, Oakman, & Bennett, 2004).

Successful treatment of social anxiety disorder with bupropion (Emmanuel, Lydiard, & Ballenger, 1991), clonidine (Goldstein, 1987), and the dopamine agonist pergolide (Villarreal, Johnson, Rubey, Lydiard, & Ballanger, 2000) has been reported. Case reports have also shown that nefazodone (van Ameringen, Mancini, & Oakman, 1999; Worthington, Zucker, Fones, Otto, & Pollack, 1998), mirtazapine (Van Veen, van Vliet, & Westenberg, 2002), and reboxetine (Atmaca, Tezcan, & Kuloglu, 2003) are useful in the treatment of social anxiety disorder. Atypical antipsychotics may hold promise as novel treatments for social anxiety disorder (Barnett, Kramer, Casat, Connor, & Davidson, 2002; Schutters, van Megen, & Westenberg, 2005). For example, olanzapine 5 to 20 mg/day was superior to placebo in a small, double-blind, 8-week trial, with the most common side effects being drowsiness and dry mouth (Barnett et al., 2002).

Duration of Treatment/Chronic Treatment

Social anxiety disorder is frequently a chronic illness requiring long-term treatment (Reich, Goldenberg, Vasile, Goisman, & Keller, 1994). Although data regarding long-term treatment and the optimal duration of treatment are limited, a number of studies are beginning to examine these issues.

Several studies have found continued efficacy of serotonin reuptake inhibitors, venlafaxine, clonazepam, phenelzine, and selective MAO inhibitors with treatment for 5 months or more. For example, sertraline was well tolerated and effective in a 20-week controlled trial (van Ameringen et al., 2001), escitalopram was well tolerated and produced further improvement versus placebo between 12 and 24 weeks of treatment at 5 to 20 mg/day (Lader et al., 2004), fluvoxamine controlled release (CR) 100 to 300 mg/day continued to yield gains in symptomatic improvement and reduction of disability between 12 and 24 weeks of treatment (D. J. Stein, Westenberg, Yang, Li, & Barbato, 2003), and venlafaxine XR at a low dose (75 mg/day) or a high dose (150 to 225 mg/day) was effective throughout a 28-week trial, with no significant differences in outcome between the low- and high-dose groups (M. B. Stein, Pollack, Bystritsky, Kelsey, & Mangano, 2005). In 26 patients with social anxiety disorder treated with clonazepam for an average of 11.3 months (range, 1 to 29 months), clonazepam was well tolerated, 20 patients were able to reduce their dose, and 5 discontinued their medication (Davidson, Ford, Smith, & Potts, 1991). A trial comparing a placebo and brofaromine followed responders for 9 months (Fahlen et al., 1995). Those on brofaromine showed further symptomatic improvement over this period.

A number of longer term trials have examined the issue of optimal treatment duration, by studying relapse rates with discontinuation of medication at various time points. Connor et al. assigned patients who had responded to 6 months of clonazepam treatment to continued treatment or to a gradual taper (0.25 mg every 2 weeks) with double-blind placebo substitution, for 5 months. Relapse rates were 0% in the continued treatment and 21% in the taper group (Connor et al., 1998). However, currently this taper would probably be performed more gradually. In the 9-month brofaromine trial, 6 of 10 placebo-treated patients relapsed, versus none of 22 maintained on brofaromine (Fahlen et al., 1995, Rosenbaum et al., 1991).

Versiani, Amrein, & Montgomery (1997) reported that, of 59 patients who responded to moclobemide and were continued on treatment for 2 years, 88% deteriorated when the medication was then discontinued. Reinstitution of moclobemide restored the therapeutic response. After another 2 years, medication was discontinued, and up to 6 to 24 months later, 63% of patients had no or mild symptoms. Alcohol abuse was the strongest predictor of negative treatment outcome. In a later follow-up study of patients originally treated acutely with phenelzine or cognitive-behavioral group therapy (Heimberg et al., 1998; Liebowitz et al., 1999), patients responding to phenelzine or CBGT were maintained on treatment for 6 months and then followed for a 6-month treatment-free phase. Most patients maintained their gains during the maintenance phase, but relapse rates were higher in phenelzine-treated patients than in the CBGT group once treatment was discontinued.

Four studies have examined relapse rates in patients with social anxiety disorder who responded to acute treatment with an SSRI and then entered a double-blind phase in which they were maintained on active medication or switched to placebo (Montgomery, Nil, Durr-Pal, Loft, & Boulenger, 2005; D. J. Stein, Versiani, Hair, & Kumar, 2002; M. B. Stein et al., 1996; Walker et al., 2000). Sixteen paroxetine responders after 11 weeks were randomized to an additional 12 weeks of paroxetine versus placebo in the first of these studies (M. B. Stein et al., 1996). One of eight patients on paroxetine relapsed, compared with five of eight on placebo. Fifty sertraline responders after a 20-week trial were switched to double-blind sertraline versus placebo for an additional 24 weeks and had a relapse rate of 4% on continued sertraline versus 36% on placebo (Walker et al., 2000). Of 323 patients responding to acute treatment with paroxetine, significantly fewer patients relapsed when maintained on 24 weeks of active medication than when switched to placebo (14% vs. 39%; D. J. Stein, Versiani, et al., 2002). Finally, 371 responders to escitalopram showed a 2.8 times greater risk of relapse when treated with placebo versus medication for another 24 weeks (Montgomery et al., 2005). Overall, the rate of withdrawal from this study, excluding relapses, was 13.2% for escitalopram and 8.3% for placebo.

Overall, these data suggest that many patients with social anxiety disorder benefit from continued treatment beyond the acute phase of clinical trials. The optimal duration of treatment remains unclear but appears to be longer than 6 months after acute treatment for a substantial number of people. The World Federation of Societies of Biological Psychiatry and the International Consensus Group on Depression and Anxiety recommend that patients with social anxiety disorder remain on effective treatment at therapeutic dosages for at least 1 year (Ballenger et al., 1998; Bandelow, Zohar, Hollander, Kasper, & Moller, 2002).

Combined Treatment

Cognitive-behavior therapy yields large effect sizes in the treatment of social anxiety disorder (Butler, Chapman, Forman, & Beck, 2006). Two major studies have examined combining CBT with pharmacotherapy to boost response rates. Blomhoff et al. (2001) randomized 387 patients with generalized social anxiety disorder in a primary care setting to sertraline, placebo, sertraline plus exposure therapy, or placebo plus exposure therapy for 24 weeks. Exposure therapy was provided by primary care physicians. Response rates for both sertraline groups were significantly higher than that of the placebo group, and there was a trend for enhanced efficacy in the sertraline plus placebo group. Another study by Davidson et al. (Davidson, Foa, et al., 2004) compared 14 weeks of fluoxetine, comprehensive cognitive-behavioral group therapy, group CBT plus fluoxetine, group CBT plus placebo, and placebo in 295 patients with generalized social anxiety disorder. All active treatments were superior to placebo, but similar to each other, with no advantage seen with combined treatment (response rate 54.2% vs. 51.7% with CCBT and 50.9% with fluoxetine). Clearly, further studies of combined treatment are needed.

SUMMARY

Since the early 1980s, a number of pharmacological treatments have been shown effective for panic disorder, generalized anxiety disorder, and social anxiety disorder. SSRIs are now considered by most experts to be the first-line pharmacological treatment for panic disorder based on their low rate of side effects; lack of dietary restrictions, and absence of tolerance and withdrawal symptoms. Similarly, SSRIs are an attractive first-line treatment for social anxiety disorder. The pharmacological treatments of choice for GAD are buspirone and antidepressants, including SSRIs and venlafaxine. Both buspirone and antidepressants provide a promising alternative to benzodiazepines. Benzodiazepines, although effective for all these disorders, carry with them the risk of physiological dependence and withdrawal symptoms and ineffectiveness for comorbid depression. Their greatest utility at present seems to be as an initial or adjunctive medication for patients with disabling symptoms requiring rapid relief and for those unable to tolerate other medications. Chronic treatment with benzodiazepines is generally safe and effective but should probably be reserved for patients who are nonresponsive or intolerant to other agents. Controlled trials are necessary to determine whether patients with specific phobias respond to pharmacological agents, particularly serotonin reuptake inhibitors.

Overall, little is known regarding the optimal duration of treatment or long-term outcome of the conditions discussed in this chapter. However, all four disorders begin early in life, often in childhood or adolescence, and follow a chronic or waxing and waning course in many people. Thus, further study of treatment of anxiety disorders in children and of long-term management of panic disorder, GAD, specific phobia, and social anxiety disorder is very important. The major challenges in acute treatment of all of these disorders are to determine the most effective and also cost-effective initial combination of pharmacological and nonpharmacological treatments and to develop new anxiolytic agents with a rapid onset of action but without the risks of tolerance and withdrawal. For existing agents, particular subtypes of these disorders or types of comorbidity may respond better to some agents than to others, and studies of combination treatments may enhance efficacy, especially in patients unresponsive to or only minimally improved with single agents. Development of novel anxiolytic agents, such as corticotropin-releasing hormone (CRH) antagonists, glutamate receptor agonists and antagonists, and anxioselective benzodiazepine-GABA receptor ligands, will also provide new avenues of treatment that may be safer and more effective, although improving delivery of existing treatments will continue to be a major focus of efforts to improve mental health in the larger population.

REFERENCES

Abene, M. V., & Hamilton, J. D. (1998). Resolution of fear of flying with fluoxetine treatment. *Journal of Anxiety Disorders, 12,* 599–603.

Akhondzadeh, S., Naghavi, H. R., Vazirian, M., Shayeganpour, A., Rashidi, H., & Khani, M. (2001). Passionflower in the treatment of generalized anxiety: A pilot double-blind randomized controlled trial with oxazepam. *Journal of Clinical Pharmacy and Therapeutics, 26,* 363–367.

Allgulander, C. (1999). Paroxetine in social anxiety disorder: A randomized placebo-controlled study. *Acta Psychiatrica Scandinavica, 100,* 193–198.

Allgulander, C., Dahl, A. A., Austin, C., Morris, P. L., Sogaard, J. A., Fayyad, R., et al. (2004). Efficacy of sertraline in a 12-week trial for generalized anxiety disorder. *American Journal of Psychiatry, 161,* 1642–1649.

Allgulander, C., Florea, I., & Huusom, A. K. (2005). Prevention of relapse in generalized anxiety disorder by escitalopram treatment. *International Journal of Neuropsychopharmacology, 9,* 1–11.

Allgulander, C., Mangano, R., Zhang, J., Dahl, A. A., Lepola, U., Sjodin, I., et al. (2004). Efficacy of venlafaxine ER in patients with social anxiety disorder: A double-blind, placebo-controlled, parallel-group comparison with paroxetine. *Human Psychopharmacology, 19,* 387–396.

American Psychiatric Association. (1980). *Diagnostic and statistical manual of mental disorders* (3rd ed.). Washington, DC: Author.

American Psychiatric Association. (1994). *Diagnostic and statistical manual of mental disorders* (4th ed.). Washington, DC: Author.

Ansseau, M., Papart, P., Gerard, M. A., von Frenckell, R., & Franck, G. (1990). Controlled comparison of buspirone and oxazepam in generalized anxiety. *Neuropsychobiology, 24,* 74–78.

Asnis, G. M., Hameedi, F. A., Goddard, A. W., Potkin, S. G., Black, D., Jameel, M., et al. (2001). Fluvoxamine in the treatment of panic disorder: A multicenter, double-blind, placebo-controlled study in outpatients. *Psychiatry Research, 103,* 1–14.

Atmaca, M., Kuloglu, M., Tezcan, E., & Unal, A. (2002). Efficacy of citalopram and moclobemide in patients with social phobia: Some preliminary findings. *Human Psychopharmacology, 17,* 401–405.

Atmaca, M., Tezcan, E., & Kuloglu, M. (2003). An open clinical trial of reboxetine in the treatment of social phobia. *Journal of Clinical Psychopharmacology, 23,* 417–419.

Bakish, D., Hooper, C. L., Filteau, M. J., Charbonneau, Y., Fraser, G., West, D. L., et al. (1996). A double-blind placebo-controlled trial comparing fluvoxamine and imipramine in the treatment of panic disorder with or without agoraphobia. *Psychopharmacology Bulletin, 32,* 135–141.

Bakish, D., Saxena, B. M., Bowen, R., & D'Souza, J. (1993). Reversible monoamine oxidase-A inhibitors in panic disorder. *Clinical Neuropharmacology, 16*(Suppl. 2), S77–S82.

Bakker, A., Van Balkom, A. J., & Spinhoven, P. (2002). SSRIs v. TCAs in the treatment of panic disorder: A meta-analysis. *Acta Psychiatrica Scandinavica, 106,* 163–167.

Baldwin, D., Bobes, J., Stein, D. J., Scharwachter, I., & Faure, M. (1999). Paroxetine in social phobia/social anxiety disorder: Randomized, double-blind, placebo-controlled study. Paroxetine Study Group. *British Journal of Psychiatry, 175,* 120–126.

Ball, S. G., Kuhn, A., Wall, D., Shekhar, A., & Goddard, A. W. (2005). Selective serotonin reuptake inhibitor treatment for generalized anxiety disorder: A double-blind, prospective comparison between paroxetine and sertraline. *Journal of Clinical Psychiatry, 66,* 94–99.

Ballenger, J. C. (1999). Clinical guidelines for establishing remission in patients with depression and anxiety. *Journal of Clinical Psychiatry, 60*(Suppl. 22), 29–34.

Ballenger, J. C., Burrows, G. D., DuPont, R. L., Lesser, I. M., Noyes, R., Peckhold, J. C., et al. (1988). Alprazolam in panic disorder and agoraphobia: Results from a multicenter trial: I. Efficacy in short-term treatment. *Archives of General Psychiatry, 45,* 413–422.

Ballenger, J. C., Davidson, J. R., Lecrubier, Y., Nutt, D. J., Baldwin, D. S., Den Boer, J. A., et al. (1998). Consensus statement on panic disorder from the International Consensus Group on Depression and Anxiety. *Journal of Clinical Psychiatry, 59*(Suppl. 8), 47–54.

Ballenger, J. C., Davidson, J. R., Lecrubier, Y., Nutt, D. J., Bobes, J., Beidel, D. C., et al. (1998). Consensus statement on social anxiety disorder from the International Consensus Group on Depression and Anxiety. *Journal of Clinical Psychiatry, 59*(Suppl. 17), 54–60.

Ballenger, J. C., Wheadon, D. E., Steiner, M., Bushnell, W., & Gergel, I. P. (1998). Double-blind, fixed-dose, placebo-controlled study of paroxetine in the treatment of panic disorder. *American Journal of Psychiatry, 155,* 36–42.

Bandelow, B., Zohar, J., Hollander, E., Kasper, S., & Moller, H. J. (2002). World Federation of Societies of Biological Psychiatry (WFSBP) guidelines for the pharmacological treatment of anxiety, obsessive-compulsive and posttraumatic stress disorders. *World Journal of Biological Psychiatry, 3,* 171–199.

Barlow, D. H. (1988). *Anxiety and its disorders: The nature and treatment of anxiety and panic.* New York: Guilford Press.

Barlow, D. H. (2002). *Anxiety and its disorders: The nature and treatment of anxiety and panic* (2nd ed.). New York: Guilford Press.

Barlow, D. H., Gorman, J. M., Shear, M. K., & Woods, S. W. (2000). Cognitive-behavioral therapy, imipramine, or their combination for panic disorder: A randomized controlled trial. *Journal of the American Medical Association, 283,* 2529–2536.

Barnett, S. D., Kramer, M. L., Casat, C. D., Connor, K. M., & Davidson, J. R. (2002). Efficacy of olanzapine in social anxiety disorder: A pilot study. *Journal of Psychopharmacology, 16,* 365–368.

Basoglu, M., Marks, I. M., Swinson, R. P., Noshirvani, H., O'Sullivan, G., & Kuch, K. (1994). Pre-treatment predictors of treatment outcome in panic disorder and agoraphobia related with alprazolam and exposure. *Journal of Affective Disorders, 30,* 123–132.

Beauclair, L., Fontaine, R., Annable, L., Holobow, N., & Chouinard, G. (1994). Clonazepam in the treatment of panic disorder: A double-blind, placebo-controlled trial investigating the correlation between clonazepam concentrations in plasma and clinical response. *Journal of Clinical Psychopharmacology, 14,* 111–118.

Beaumont, G. (1977). A large open multicentre trial of clomipramine (Anafranil) in the management of phobic disorders. *Journal of International Medical Research, 5*(Suppl. 5), 116–123.

Benca, R., Matuzas, W., & Al-Sadir, J. (1986). Social phobia, MVP, and response to imipramine. *Journal of Clinical Psychopharmacology, 6,* 50–51.

Benjamin, J., Ben-Zion, I. Z., Karbofsky, E., & Dannon, P. (2000). Double-blind placebo-controlled pilot study of paroxetine for specific phobia. *Psychopharmacology (Berlin), 149,* 194–196.

Benjamin, J., Levine, J., Fux, M., Aviv, A., Levy, D., & Belmaker, R. H. (1995). Double-blind, placebo-controlled, crossover trial of inositol treatment for panic disorder. *American Journal of Psychiatry, 152,* 1084–1086.

Bielski, R. J., Bose, A., & Chang, C. C. (2005). A double-blind comparison of escitalopram and paroxetine in the long-term treatment of generalized anxiety disorder. *Annals of Clinical Psychiatry, 17,* 65–69.

Black, D. W., Carney, C. P., Peloso, P. M., Woolson, R. F., Schwartz, D. A., Voelker, M. D., et al. (2004). Gulf War veterans with anxiety: Prevalence, comorbidity, and risk factors. *Epidemiology, 15,* 135–142.

Black, D. W., Wesner, R., Bowers, W., & Gabel, J. (1993). A comparison of fluvoxamine, cognitive therapy, and placebo in the treatment of panic disorder. *Archives of General Psychiatry, 50,* 44–50.

Black, D. W., Wesner, R., & Gabel, J. (1993). The abrupt discontinuation of fluvoxamine in patients with panic disorder. *Journal of Clinical Psychiatry, 54,* 146–149.

Black, D. W., Wesner, R. B., Gabel, J., Bowers, W., & Monahan, P. (1994). Predictors of short-term treatment response in 66 patients with panic disorder. *Journal of Affective Disorders, 30,* 233–241.

Blomhoff, S., Haug, T. T., Hellstrom, K., Holme, I., Humble, M., Madsbu, H. P., et al. (2001). Randomised controlled general practice trial of sertraline, exposure therapy and combined treatment in generalised social phobia. *British Journal of Psychiatry, 179,* 23–30.

Borison, R. L., Albrecht, J. W., & Diamond, B. I. (1990). Efficacy and safety of a putative anxiolytic agent: Ipsapirone. *Psychopharmacology Bulletin, 26*(2), 207–210.

Bourdon, K. H., Boyd, J. H., Rae, D. S., Burns, B. J., Thompson, J. W., & Locke, B. Z. (1988). Gender differences in phobias: Results of the ECA community survey. *Journal of Anxiety Disorders, 2,* 227–241.

Bouton, M. E., Mineka, S., & Barlow, D. H. (2001). A modern learning theory perspective on the etiology of panic disorder. *Psychological Review, 108,* 4–32.

Boyer, W. (1995). Serotonin uptake inhibitors are superior to imipramine and alprazolamin alleviating panic attacks: A meta-analysis. *International Clinical Psychopharmacology, 10,* 45–49.

Boyer, W. F., & Feighner, J. P. (1993). A placebo-controlled double-blind multicenter trial of two doses of ipsapirone versus diazepam in generalized anxiety disorder. *International Clinical Psychopharmacology, 8,* 173–176.

Bradweijn, J., Stein, A. A., Salinas, E., Emlien, G., & Whitaker, T. (2005). Venlafaxine extended-release capsules in panic disorder. *British Journal of Psychiatry, 187,* 352–359.

Brawman-Mintzer, O., Knapp, R. G., & Nietert, P. J. (2005). Adjunctive risperidone in generalized anxiety disorder: A double-blind, placebo-controlled study. *Journal of Clinical Psychiatry, 66,* 1321–1325.

Brawman-Mintzer, O., Lydiard, R. B., Emmanuel, N., Payeur, R., Johnson, M., Roberts, J., et al. (1993). Psychiatric comorbidity in patients with generalized anxiety disorder. *American Journal of Psychiatry, 150,* 1216–1218.

Breslau, N., & Davis, G. C. (1985). *DSM-III* generalized anxiety disorder: An empirical investigation of more stringent criteria. *Psychiatry Research, 15,* 231–238.

Broocks, A., Bandelow, B., Pekrun, G., George, A., Meyer, T., Bartmann, U., et al. (1998). Comparison of aerobic exercise, clomipramine, and placebo in the treatment of panic disorder. *American Journal of Psychiatry, 155,* 603–609.

Burnham, D. B., Steiner, M. X., Gergel, I. P. (1995). Paroxetine long-term efficacy in panic disorder and prevention of relapse: A double-blind study. In *American College of Neuropsychopharmacology Annual Meeting: Abstracts of Panels and Posters* (pp. 201). Nashville, TN: American College of Neuropsychopharmacology.

Butler, A. C., Chapman, J. E., Forman, E. M., & Beck, A. T. (2006). The empirical status of cognitive-behavioral therapy: A review of meta-analyses. *Clinical Psychological Review, 26,* 17–31.

Caillard, V., Rouillon, F., Viel, J. F., & Markabi, S. (1999). Comparative effects of low and high doses of clomipramine and placebo in panic disorder: A double-blind controlled study. French University Antidepressant Group. *Acta Psychiatrica Scandinavica, 99,* 51–58.

Carpenter, L. L., Leon, Z., Yasmin, S., & Price, L. H. (1999). Clinical experience with mirtazapine in the treatment of panic disorder. *Annals of Clinical Psychiatry, 11,* 81–86.

Catalan, J., Gath, D., Edmonds, G., & Ennis, J. (1984). The effects of non-prescribing of anxiolytics in general practice: I. Controlled evaluation of psychiatric and social outcome. *British Journal of Psychiatry, 144,* 593–602.

Charney, D. S., & Woods, S. W. (1989). Benzodiazepine treatment of panic disorder: A comparison of alprazolam and lorazepam. *Journal of Clinical Psychiatry, 50,* 418–423.

Charney, D. S., Woods, S. W., Goodman, W. K., Rifkin, B., Kinch, M., Aiken, B., et al. (1986). Drug treatment of panic disorder: The comparative efficacy of imipramine, alprazolam, and trazodone. *Journal of Clinical Psychiatry, 47,* 580–586.

Chouinard, G., Annable, L., Fontaine, R., & Solyom, L. (1982). Alprazolam in the treatment of generalized anxiety and panic disorders: A double-blind placebo-controlled study. *Psychopharmacology (Berlin), 77,* 229–233.

Clark, D. B., & Agras, W. S. (1991). The assessment and treatment of performance anxiety in musicians. *American Journal of Psychiatry, 148,* 598–605.

Clark, D. M., Ehlers, A., McManus, F., Hackmann, A., Fennell, M., Campbell, H., et al. (2003). Cognitive therapy versus fluoxetine in generalized social phobia: A randomized placebo-controlled trial. *Journal of Consulting and Clinical Psychology, 71,* 1058–1067.

Cohn, J. B., Bowden, C. L., Fisher, J. G., & Rodos, J. J. (1986). Double-blind comparison of buspirone and clorazepate in anxious outpatients. *American Journal of Medicine, 80,* 10–16.

Cohn, J. B., & Wilcox, C. S. (1984). Long-term comparison of alprazolam, lorazepam and placebo in patients with an anxiety disorder. *Pharmacotherapy, 4,* 93–98.

Connor, K. M., Davidson, J. R., Potts, N. L., Tupler, L. A., Miner, C. M., Malik, M. L., et al. (1998). Discontinuation of clonazepam in the treatment of social phobia. *Journal of Clinical Psychopharmacology, 18,* 373–378.

Cowley, D. S., & Roy-Bryne, P. P. (1991). The biology of generalized anxiety disorder and chronic anxiety. In R. M. Rapee & D. H. Barlow (Eds.), *Chronic anxiety* (pp. 52–75). New York: Guilford Press.

Cutler, N. R., Sramek, J. J., Keppel Hesselink, J. M., Krol, A., Roeschen, J., Rickels, K., et al. (1993). A double-blind, placebo-controlled study comparing the efficacy and safety of ipsapirone versus lorazepam in patients with generalized anxiety disorder: A prospective multicenter trial. *Journal of Clinical Psychopharmacology, 13,* 429–437.

Dager, S., Roy-Byrne, P., Hendrickson, H., Cowley, D., Avery, D., Hall, K., et al. (1992). Long-term outcome of panic states during double blind treatment and after withdrawal of alprazolam and placebo. *Annals of Clinical Psychiatry, 4,* 251–258.

Dahl, A. A., Ravindran, A., Allgulander, C., Kutcher, S. P., Austin, C., & Burt, T. (2005). Sertraline in generalized anxiety disorder: Efficacy in treating the psychic and somatic anxiety factors. *Acta Psychiatrica Scandinavica, 111,* 429–435.

Davidson, J. R., Bose, A., Korotzer, A., & Zheng, H. (2004). Escitalopram in the treatment of generalized anxiety disorder: Double-blind, placebo controlled, flexible-dose study. *Depression and Anxiety, 19,* 234–240.

Davidson, J. R., DuPont, R. L., Hedges, D., & Haskins, J. T. (1999). Efficacy, safety, and tolerability of venlafaxine extended release and buspirone in outpatients with generalized anxiety disorder. *Journal of Clinical Psychiatry, 60,* 528–535.

Davidson, J. R., Foa, E. B., Huppert, J. D., Keefe, F. J., Franklin, M. E., Compton, J. S., et al. (2004). Fluoxetine, comprehensive cognitive behavioral therapy, and placebo in generalized social phobia. *Archives of General Psychiatry, 61,* 1005–1013.

Davidson, J. R., Ford, S. M., Smith, R. D., & Potts, N. L. (1991). Long-term treatment of social phobia with clonazepam. *Journal of Clinical Psychiatry, 52*(Suppl.), 16–20.

Davidson, J. R., Potts, N., Richichi, E., Krishnan, R., Ford, S. M., Smith, R., et al. (1993). Treatment of social phobia with clonazepam and placebo. *Journal of Clinical Psychopharmacology, 13,* 423–428.

Davidson, J. R., Tupler, L. A., & Potts, N. L. (1994). Treatment of social phobia with benzodiazepines. *Journal of Clinical Psychiatry, 55*(Suppl.), 28–32.

de Beurs, E., van Balkom, A. J., Lange, A., Koele, P., & van Dyck, R. (1995). Treatment of panic disorder with agoraphobia: Comparison of fluvoxamine, placebo, and psychological panic management combined with exposure and of exposure in vivo alone. *American Journal of Psychiatry, 152,* 683–691.

Delle Chiaie, R., Pancheri, P., Casacchia, M., Stratta, P., Kotzalidis, G. D., & Zibellini, M. (1995). Assessment of the efficacy of buspirone in patients affected by generalized anxiety disorder, shifting to buspirone from prior treatment with lorazepam: A placebo-controlled, double-blind study. *Journal of Clinical Psychopharmacology, 15*, 12–19.

DeMartinis, N., Rynn, M., Rickels, K., & Mandos, L. (2000). Prior benzodiazepine use and buspirone response in the treatment of generalized anxiety disorder. *Journal of Clinical Psychiatry, 61*, 91–94.

Den Boer, J. A. (1998). Pharmacotherapy of panic disorder: Differential efficacy from a clinical viewpoint. *Journal of Clinical Psychiatry, 59*(Suppl. 8), 30–36; Discussion 37–38.

Den Boer, J. A., & Westenberg, H. G. (1988). Effect of a serotonin and noradrenaline uptake inhibitor in panic disorder: A double-blind comparative study with fluvoxamine and maprotiline. *International Clinical Psychopharmacology, 3*, 59–74.

Den Boer, J. A., & Westenberg, H. G. (1990). Serotonin function in panic disorder: A double blind placebo controlled study with fluvoxamine and ritanserin. *Psychopharmacology (Berlin), 102*, 85–94.

Di Nardo, P., Moras, K., Barlow, D. H., Rapee, R. M., & Brown, T. A. (1993). Reliability of *DSM-III-R* anxiety disorder categories. Using the Anxiety Disorders Interview Schedule-Revised (ADIS-R). *Archives of General Psychiatry, 50*, 251–256.

Drug Treatment of Panic Disorder. Comparative efficacy of alprazolam, imipramine, and placebo. Cross-National Collaborative Panic Study, Second Phase Investigators. (1992). *British Journal of Psychiatry, 160*, 191–202; Discussion 202–195.

Dunner, D. L., Ishiki, D., Avery, D. H., Wilson, L. G., & Hyde, T. S. (1986). Effect of alprazolam and diazepam on anxiety and panic attacks in panic disorder: A controlled study. *Journal of Clinical Psychiatry, 47*, 458–460.

Eaton, W. W., Kessler, R. C., Wittchen, H. U., & Magee, W. J. (1994). Panic and panic disorder in the United States. *American Journal of Psychiatry, 151*, 413–420.

Emmanuel, N. P., Lydiard, R. B., & Ballenger, J. C. (1991). Treatment of social phobia with bupropion. *Journal of Clinical Psychopharmacology, 11*, 276–277.

Emmanuel, N. P., Ware, M. R., Brawman-Mintzer, O., Ballenger, J. C., & Lydiard, R. B. (1999). Once-weekly dosing of fluoxetine in the maintenance of remission in panic disorder. *Journal of Clinical Psychiatry, 60*, 299–301.

Enkelmann, R. (1991). Alprazolam versus buspirone in the treatment of outpatients with generalized anxiety disorder. *Psychopharmacology (Berlin), 105*, 428–432.

Evans, L., Kenardy, J., Schneider, P., & Hoey, H. (1986). Effect of a selective serotonin uptake inhibitor in agoraphobia with panic attacks: A double-blind comparison of zimeldine, imipramine and placebo. *Acta Psychiatrica Scandinavica, 73*, 49–53.

Fahlen, T., Nilsson, H. L., Borg, K., Humble, M., & Pauli, U. (1995). Social phobia: The clinical efficacy and tolerability of the monoamine oxidase-A and serotonin uptake inhibitor brofaromine. A double-blind placebo-controlled study. *Acta Psychiatrica Scandinavica, 92*, 351–358.

Fahy, T. J., O'Rourke, D., Brophy, J., Schazmann, W., & Sciascia, S. (1992). The Galway Study of Panic Disorder: I. Clomipramine and lofepramine in *DSM-III-R* panic disorder: A placebo controlled trial. *Journal of Affective Disorders, 25*, 63–75.

Falloon, I. R., Lloyd, G. G., & Harpin, R. E. (1981). The treatment of social phobia: Real-life rehearsal with nonprofessional therapists. *Journal of Nervous and Mental Disease, 169*, 180–184.

Feighner, J. P. (1987). Buspirone in the long-term treatment of generalized anxiety disorder. *Journal of Clinical Psychiatry, 48*(Suppl.), 3–6.

Feighner, J. P., & Cohn, J. B. (1989). Analysis of individual symptoms in generalized anxiety: A pooled, multistudy, double-blind evaluation of buspirone. *Neuropsychobiology, 21*, 124–130.

Feighner, J. P., Entsuah, A. R., & McPherson, M. K. (1998). Efficacy of once-daily venlafaxine extended release (XR) for symptoms of anxiety in depressed outpatients. *Journal of Affective Disorders, 47*, 55–62.

Feighner, J. P., Merideth, C. H., & Hendrickson, G. A. (1982). A double-blind comparison of buspirone and diazepam in outpatients with generalized anxiety disorder. *Journal of Clinical Psychiatry, 43*, 103–108.

Ferreri, M., Hantouche, E. G., & Billardon, M. (1994). Value of hydroxyzine in generalized anxiety disorder: Controlled double-blind study versus placebo. *Encephale, 20*, 785–791.

Furmark, T., Appel, L., Michelgard, A., Wahlstedt, K., Ahs, F., Zancan, S., et al. (2005). Cerebral blood flow changes after treatment of social phobia with the neurokinin-1 antagonist Gr205171, citalopram, or placebo. *Biological Psychiatry, 58*, 132–142.

Fyer, A. J., Liebowitz, M. R., & Gorman, J. M. (1989, December). *Comparative discontinuation of alprazolam and imipramine in panic patients.* Paper presented at the 27th annual meeting of the American College of Neuropsychopharmacology, San Juan, Puerto Rico.

Fyer, M. R., Frances, A. J., Sullivan, T., Hurt, S. W., & Clarkin, J. (1988). Comorbidity of borderline personality disorder. *Archives of General Psychiatry*, 45, 348–352.

Gambi, F., De Berardis, D., Campanella, D., Carano, A., Sepede, G., Salini, G., et al. (2005). Mirtazapine treatment of generalized anxiety disorder: A fixed dose, open label study. *Journal of Psychopharmacology*, 19, 483–487.

Gammans, R. E., Stringfellow, J. C., Hvizdos, A. J., Seidehamel, R. J., Cohn, J. B., Wilcox, C. S., et al. (1992). Use of buspirone in patients with generalized anxiety disorder and coexisting depressive symptoms: A meta-analysis of eight randomized, controlled studies. *Neuropsychobiology*, 25, 193–201.

Garcia, C., Micallef, J., Dubreuil, D., Philippot, P., Jouve, E., & Blin, O. (2000). Effects of lorazepam on emotional reactivity, performance, and vigilance in subjects with high or low anxiety. *Journal of Clinical Psychopharmacology*, 20, 226–233.

Garcia-Borreguero, D., Lauer, C. J., Ozdaglar, A., Wiedemann, K., Holsboer, F., & Krieg, J. C. (1992). Brofaromine in panic disorder: A pilot study with a new reversible inhibitor of monoamine oxidase-A. *Pharmacopsychiatry*, 25, 261–264.

Garvey, M. J., & Tollefson, G. D. (1986). Prevalence of misuse of prescribed benzodiazepines in patients with primary anxiety disorder or major depression. *American Journal of Psychiatry*, 143, 1601–1603.

Gelenberg, A. J., Delgado, P., & Nurnberg, H. G. (2000). Sexual side effects of antidepressant drugs. *Current Psychiatry Reports*, 2, 223–227.

Gelenberg, A. J., Lydiard, R. B., Rudolph, R. L., Aguiar, L., Haskins, J. T., & Salinas, E. (2000). Efficacy of venlafaxine extended-release capsules in nondepressed outpatients with generalized anxiety disorder: A 6-month randomized controlled trial. *Journal of the American Medical Association*, 283, 3082–3088.

Gelernter, C. S., Uhde, T. W., Cimbolic, P., Arnkoff, D. B., Vittone, B. J., Tancer, M. E., et al. (1991). Cognitive-behavioral and pharmacological treatments of social phobia: A controlled study. *Archives of General Psychiatry*, 48, 938–945.

Gentil, V., Lotufo-Neto, F., Andrade, L., Cordas, T., Bernik, M., Ramos, R., et al. (1993). Clomipramine, a better reference drug for panic/agoraphobia: 1. Effectiveness comparison with imipramine. *Journal of Psychopharmacology*, 7, 316–324.

Goddard, A. W., Brouette, T., Almai, A., Jetty, P., Woods, S. W., & Charney, D. (2001). Early coadministration of clonazepam with sertraline for panic disorder. *Archives of General Psychiatry*, 58, 681–686.

Goisman, R. M., Warshaw, M. G., & Keller, M. B. (1999). Psychosocial treatment prescriptions for generalized anxiety disorder, panic disorder, and social phobia, 1991–1996. *American Journal of Psychiatry*, 156, 1819–1821.

Goldstein, S. (1987). Treatment of social phobia with clonidine. *Biological Psychiatry*, 22, 369–372.

Golwyn, D. H., & Weinstock, R. C. (1990). Phenelzine treatment of elective mutism: A case report. *Journal of Clinical Psychiatry*, 51, 384–385.

Goodman, W. K., Bose, A., & Wang, Q. (2005). Treatment of generalized anxiety disorder with escitalopram: Pooled results from double-blind, placebo-controlled trials. *Journal of Affective Disorders*, 87, 161–167.

Goodnick, P. J., Puig, A., DeVane, C. L., & Freund, B. V. (1999). Mirtazapine in major depression with comorbid generalized anxiety disorder. *Journal of Clinical Psychiatry*, 60, 446–448.

Gorman, J. M., Liebowitz, M. R., Fyer, A. J., Campeas, R., & Klein, D. F. (1985). Treatment of social phobia with atenolol. *Journal of Clinical Psychopharmacology*, 5, 298–301.

Haskins, J. T., Rudolph, R., Pallay, A., & Derivan, A. T. (1998). Double-blind placebo-controlled study of once daily venlafaxine XR in outpatients with generalized anxiety disorder. *European Neuropsychopharmacology*, 8(Suppl. 1), S257.

Hayes, P. E., & Schulz, S. C. (1987). Beta-blockers in anxiety disorders. *Journal of Affective Disorders*, 13, 119–130.

Hedges, D. W., Reimherr, F. W., Strong, R. E., Halls, C. H., & Rust, C. (1996). An open trial of nefazodone in adult patients with generalized anxiety disorder. *Psychopharmacology Bulletin*, 32, 671–676.

Heimberg, R. G., Liebowitz, M. R., Hope, D. A., Schneier, F. R., Holt, C. S., Welkowitz, L. A., et al. (1998). Cognitive behavioral group therapy vs phenelzine therapy for social phobia: 12-week outcome. *Archives of General Psychiatry*, 55, 1133–1141.

Hettema, J. M., Neale, M. C., & Kendler, K. S. (2001). A review and meta-analysis of the genetic epidemiology of anxiety disorders. *American Journal of Psychiatry*, 158, 1568–1578.

Hirschmann, S., Dannon, P. N., Iancu, I., Dolberg, O. T., Zohar, J., & Grunhaus, L. (2000). Pindolol augmentation in patients with treatment-resistant panic disorder: A double-blind, placebo-controlled trial. *Journal of Clinical Psychopharmacology*, 20, 556–559.

Hoehn-Saric, R., McLeod, D. R., & Hipsley, P. A. (1993). Effect of fluvoxamine on panic disorder. *Journal of Clinical Psychopharmacology, 13,* 321–326.

Hoehn-Saric, R., McLeod, D. R., & Zimmerli, W. D. (1988). Differential effects of alprazolam and imipramine in generalized anxiety disorder: Somatic versus psychic symptoms. *Journal of Clinical Psychiatry, 49,* 293–301.

Houck, C. (1998). An open-label pilot study of fluvoxamine for mixed anxiety-depression. *Psychopharmacology Bulletin, 34,* 225–227.

The International Multicenter Clinical Trial Group on Moclobemide in Social Phobia. (1997). Moclobemide in social phobia: A double-blind, placebo-controlled clinical study. *European Archives of Psychiatry and Clinical Neuroscience, 247,* 71–80.

Jefferson, J. W. (1995). Social phobia: A pharmacologic treatment overview. *Journal of Clinical Psychiatry, 56*(Suppl. 5), 18–24.

Johnston, D. G., Troyer, I. E., & Whitsett, S. F. (1988). Clomipramine treatment of agoraphobic women: An eight-week controlled trial. *Archives of General Psychiatry, 45,* 453–459.

Kahn, R. J., McNair, D. M., Lipman, R. S., Covi, L., Rickels, K., Downing, R., et al. (1986). Imipramine and chlordiazepoxide in depressive and anxiety disorders: II. Efficacy in anxious outpatients. *Archives of General Psychiatry, 43,* 79–85.

Kasper, S., Stein, D. J., Loft, H., & Nil, R. (2005). Escitalopram in the treatment of social anxiety disorder: Randomised, placebo-controlled, flexible-dosage study. *British Journal of Psychiatry, 186,* 222–226.

Katzelnick, D. J., Kobak, K. A., Greist, J. H., Jefferson, J. W., Mantle, J. M., & Serlin, R. C. (1995). Sertraline for social phobia: A double-blind, placebo-controlled crossover study. *American Journal of Psychiatry, 152,* 1368–1371.

Kendler, K. S., Hettema, J. M., Butera, F., Gardner, C. O., & Prescott, C. A. (2003). Life event dimensions of loss, humiliation, entrapment, and danger in the prediction of onsets of major depression and generalized anxiety. *Archives of General Psychiatry, 60,* 789–796.

Kendler, K. S., Neale, M. C., Kessler, R. C., Heath, A. C., & Eaves, L. J. (1992). The genetic epidemiology of phobias in women: The interrelationship of agoraphobia, social phobia, situational phobia, and simple phobia. *Archives of General Psychiatry, 49,* 273–281.

Kessler, R. C., Berglund, P., Demler, O., Jin, R., Merikangas, K. R., & Walters, E. E. (2005). Lifetime prevalence and age-of-onset distributions of *DSM-IV* disorders in the National Comorbidity Survey Replication. *Archives of General Psychiatry, 62,* 593–602.

Kessler, R. C., Brandenburg, N., Lane, M., Roy-Byrne, P., Stang, P. D., Stein, D. J., et al. (2005). Rethinking the duration requirement for generalized anxiety disorder: Evidence from the National Comorbidity Survey Replication. *Psychological Medicine, 35,* 1073–1082.

Kessler, R. C., Chiu, W. T., Demler, O., Merikangas, K. R., & Walters, E. E. (2005). Prevalence, severity, and comorbidity of 12-month *DSM-IV* disorders in the National Comorbidity Survey Replication. *Archives of General Psychiatry, 62,* 617–627.

Kessler, R. C., DuPont, R. L., Berglund, P., & Wittchen, H. U. (1999). Impairment in pure and comorbid generalized anxiety disorder and major depression at 12 months in two national surveys. *American Journal of Psychiatry, 156,* 1915–1923.

Khan, A., Upton, G. V., Rudolph, R. L., Entsuah, R., & Leventer, S. M. (1998). The use of venlafaxine in the treatment of major depression and major depression associated with anxiety: A dose-response study. Venlafaxine Investigator Study Group. *Journal of Clinical Psychopharmacology, 18,* 19–25.

Klein, D. F. (1964). Delineation of two drug-responsive anxiety syndromes. *Psychopharmacologia, 17,* 397–408.

Klein, E., Colin, V., Stolk, J., & Lenox, R. H. (1994). Alprazolam withdrawal in patients with panic disorder and generalized anxiety disorder: Vulnerability and effect of carbamazepine. *American Journal of Psychiatry, 151,* 1760–1766.

Klein, E., & Uhde, T. W. (1988). Controlled study of verapamil for treatment of panic disorder. *American Journal of Psychiatry, 145,* 431–434.

Kobak, K. A., Greist, J. H., Jefferson, J. W., & Katzelnick, D. J. (2002). Fluoxetine in social phobia: A double-blind, placebo-controlled pilot study. *Journal of Clinical Psychopharmacology, 22,* 257–262.

Kruger, M. B., & Dahl, A. A. (1999). The efficacy and safety of moclobemide compared to clomipramine in the treatment of panic disorder. *European Archives of Psychiatry and Clinical Neuroscience, 249*(Suppl. 1), S19–S24.

Laakmann, G., Schule, C., Lorkowski, G., Baghai, T., Kuhn, K., & Ehrentraut, S. (1998). Buspirone and lorazepam in the treatment of generalized anxiety disorder in outpatients. *Psychopharmacology (Berlin), 136,* 357–366.

Lader, M., & Bond, A. J. (1998). Interaction of pharmacological and psychological treatments of anxiety. *British Journal of Psychiatry, 34* (Suppl.), 42–48.

Lader, M., & Olajide, D. (1987). A comparison of buspirone and placebo in relieving benzodiazepine withdrawal symptoms. *Journal of Clinical Psychopharmacology, 7*, 11–15.

Lader, M., & Scotto, J. C. (1998). A multicentre double-blind comparison of hydroxyzine, buspirone and placebo in patients with generalized anxiety disorder. *Psychopharmacology (Berlin), 139*, 402–406.

Lader, M., Stender, K., Burger, V., & Nil, R. (2004). Efficacy and tolerability of escitalopram in 12- and 24-week treatment of social anxiety disorder: Randomised, double-blind, placebo-controlled, fixed-dose study. *Depression and Anxiety, 19*, 241–248.

Lecrubier, Y., Bakker, A., Dunbar, G., & Judge, R. (1997). A comparison of paroxetine, clomipramine and placebo in the treatment of panic disorder: Collaborative Paroxetine Panic Study investigators. *Acta Psychiatrica Scandinavica, 95*, 145–152.

Lecrubier, Y., & Judge, R. (1997). Long-term evaluation of paroxetine, clomipramine and placebo in panic disorder: Collaborative Paroxetine Panic Study Investigators. *Acta Psychiatrica Scandinavica, 95*, 153–160.

Leinonen, E., Lepola, U., Koponen, H., Turtonen, J., Wade, A., & Lehto, H. (2000). Citalopram controls phobic symptoms in patients with panic disorder: Randomized controlled trial. *Journal of Psychiatry and Neuroscience, 25*, 25–32.

Lenze, E. J., Mulsant, B. H., Shear, M. K., Dew, M. A., Miller, M. D., Pollock, B. G., et al. (2005). Efficacy and tolerability of citalopram in the treatment of late-life anxiety disorders: Results from an 8-week randomized, placebo-controlled trial. *American Journal of Psychiatry, 162*, 146–150.

Lepola, U., Bergtholdt, B., St Lambert, J., Davy, K. L., & Ruggiero, L. (2004). Controlled-release paroxetine in the treatment of patients with social anxiety disorder. *Journal of Clinical Psychiatry, 65*, 222–229.

Lepola, U. M., Wade, A. G., Leinonen, E. V., Koponen, H. J., Frazer, J., Sjodin, I., et al. (1998). A controlled, prospective, 1-year trial of citalopram in the treatment of panic disorder. *Journal of Clinical Psychiatry, 59*, 528–534.

Liebowitz, M. R., DeMartinis, N. A., Weihs, K., Londborg, P. D., Smith, W. T., Chung, H., et al. (2003). Efficacy of sertraline in severe generalized social anxiety disorder: Results of a double-blind, placebo-controlled study. *Journal of Clinical Psychiatry, 64*, 785–792.

Liebowitz, M. R., Fyer, A. J., Gorman, J. M., Campeas, R., & Levin, A. (1986). Phenelzine in social phobia. *Journal of Clinical Psychopharmacology, 6*, 93–98.

Liebowitz, M. R., Gelenberg, A. J., & Munjack, D. (2005). Venlafaxine extended release vs placebo and paroxetine in social anxiety disorder. *Archives of General Psychiatry, 62*, 190–198.

Liebowitz, M. R., Heimberg, R. G., Schneier, F. R., Hope, D. A., Davies, S., Holt, C. S., et al. (1999). Cognitive-behavioral group therapy versus phenelzine in social phobia: Long-term outcome. *Depression and Anxiety, 10*, 89–98.

Liebowitz, M. R., Schneier, F., Campeas, R., Hollander, E., Hatterer, J., Fyer, A., et al. (1992). Phenelzine vs atenolol in social phobia: A placebo-controlled comparison. *Archives of General Psychiatry, 49*, 290–300.

Liebowitz, M. R., Stein, M. B., Tancer, M., Carpenter, D., Oakes, R., & Pitts, C. D. (2002). A randomized, double-blind, fixed-dose comparison of paroxetine and placebo in the treatment of generalized social anxiety disorder. *Journal of Clinical Psychiatry, 63*, 66–74.

Lippa, A., Czobor, P., Stark, J., Beer, B., Kostakis, E., Gravielle, M., et al. (2005). Selective anxiolysis produced by ocinaplon, a GABA(a) receptor modulator. *Proceedings of the National Academy of Sciences of the United States of America, 102*, 7380–7385.

Lipsedge, M. S., Hajioff, J., Huggins, P., Napier, L., Pearce, J., Pike, D. J., et al. (1973). The management of severe agoraphobia: A comparison of iproniazid and systematic desensitization. *Psychopharmacologia, 32*, 67–80.

Loerch, B., Graf-Morgenstern, M., Hautzinger, M., Schlegel, S., Hain, C., Sandmann, J., et al. (1999). Randomised placebo-controlled trial of moclobemide, cognitive-behavioural therapy and their combination in panic disorder with agoraphobia. *British Journal of Psychiatry, 174*, 205–212.

Londborg, P. D., Wolkow, R., Smith, W. T., Duboff, E., England, D., Ferguson, J., et al. (1998). Sertraline in the treatment of panic disorder: A multisite, double-blind, placebo-controlled, fixed-dose investigation. *British Journal of Psychiatry, 173*, 54–60.

Losier, B. J., McGrath, P. J., & Klein, R. M. (1996). Error patterns on the continuous performance test in non-medicated and medicated samples of children with and without ADHD: A meta-analytic review. *Journal of Child Psychology and Psychiatry and Allied Disciplines., 37*, 971–987.

Lott, M., Greist, J. H., Jefferson, J. W., Kobak, K. A., Katzelnick, D. J., Katz, R. J., et al. (1997). Brofaromine for social phobia: A multicenter, placebo-controlled, double-blind study. *Journal of Clinical Psychopharmacology, 17*, 255–260.

Lucki, I., Rickels, K., & Geller, A. M. (1986). Chronic use of benzodiazepines and psychomotor and cognitive test performance. *Psychopharmacology (Berlin)*, 88(4), 426–433.

Lum, M., Fontaine, R., Elie, R., & Ontiveros, A. (1990). Divalproex sodium's antipanic effect in panic disorder: A placebo-controlled study. *Biological Psychiatry*, 27, 164a–165a.

Lydiard, R. B., & Ballenger, J. C. (1987). Antidepressants in panic disorder and agoraphobia. *Journal of Affective Disorders*, 13, 153–168.

Lydiard, R. B., Lesser, I. M., Ballenger, J. C., Rubin, R. T., Laraia, M., & DuPont, R. (1992). A fixed-dose study of alprazolam 2 mg, alprazolam 6 mg, and placebo in panic disorder. *Journal of Clinical Psychopharmacology*, 12, 96–103.

Lydiard, R. B., Morton, W. A., Emmanuel, N. P., Zealberg, J. J., Laraia, M. T., Stuart, G. W., et al. (1993). Preliminary report: Placebo-controlled, double-blind study of the clinical and metabolic effects of desipramine in panic disorder. *Psychopharmacology Bulletin*, 29, 183–188.

Marks, I. M., Swinson, R. P., Basoglu, M., Kuch, K., Noshirvani, H., O'Sullivan, G., et al. (1993). Alprazolam and exposure alone and combined in panic disorder with agoraphobia: A controlled study in London and Toronto. *British Journal of Psychiatry*, 162, 776–787.

Mathew, S. J., Amiel, J. M., Coplan, J. D., Fitterling, H. A., Sackeim, H. A., & Gorman, J. M. (2005). Open-label trial of riluzole in generalized anxiety disorder. *American Journal of Psychiatry*, 162, 2379–2381.

Mathew, S. J., Coplan, J. D., & Gorman, J. M. (2001). Neurobiological mechanisms of social anxiety disorder. *American Journal of Psychiatry*, 158, 1558–1567.

Mavissakalian, M., & Michelson, L. (1986). Agoraphobia: Relative and combined effectiveness of therapist-assisted in vivo exposure and imipramine. *Journal of Clinical Psychiatry*, 47, 117–122.

Mavissakalian, M., & Perel, J. M. (1992). Protective effects of imipramine maintenance treatment in panic disorder with agoraphobia. *American Journal of Psychiatry*, 149, 1053–1057.

Mavissakalian, M. R., & Perel, J. M. (1995). Imipramine treatment of panic disorder with agoraphobia: Dose ranging and plasma level response relationships. *American Journal of Psychiatry*, 152, 673–682.

Mavissakalian, M. R., & Perel, J. M. (1999). Long-term maintenance and discontinuation of imipramine therapy in panic disorder with agoraphobia. *Archives of General Psychiatry*, 56, 821–827.

Meibach, R. C., Mullane, J. F., & Binstok, C. (1987). A placebo-controlled multicenter trial of propranolol and chlordiazepoxide in the treatment of anxiety. *Current Therapeutic Research*, 41, 65–76.

Meoni, P., Hackett, D., & Lader, M. (2004). Pooled analysis of venlafaxine XR efficacy on somatic and psychic symptoms of anxiety in patients with generalized anxiety disorder. *Depression and Anxiety*, 19, 127–132.

Michelson, D., Allgulander, C., Dantendorfer, K., Knezevic, A., Maierhofer, D., Micev, V., et al. (2001). Efficacy of usual antidepressant dosing regimens of fluoxetine in panic disorder: Randomised, placebo-controlled trial. *British Journal of Psychiatry*, 179, 514–518.

Michelson, D., Lydiard, R. B., Pollack, M. H., Tamura, R. N., Hoog, S. L., Tepner, R., et al. (1998). Outcome assessment and clinical improvement in panic disorder: Evidence from a randomized controlled trial of fluoxetine and placebo. The Fluoxetine Panic Disorder Study Group. *American Journal of Psychiatry*, 155, 1570–1577.

Michelson, D., Pollack, M., Lydiard, R. B., Tamura, R., Tepner, R., & Tollefson, G. (1999). Continuing treatment of panic disorder after acute response: Randomised, placebo-controlled trial with fluoxetine. The Fluoxetine Panic Disorder Study Group. *British Journal of Psychiatry*, 174, 213–218.

Modigh, K., Westberg, P., & Eriksson, E. (1992). Superiority of clomipramine over imipramine in the treatment of panic disorder: A placebo-controlled trial. *Journal of Clinical Psychopharmacology*, 12, 251–261.

Moller, H. J., Volz, H. P., Reimann, I. W., & Stoll, K. D. (2001). Opipramol for the treatment of generalized anxiety disorder: A placebo-controlled trial including an alprazolam-treated group. *Journal of Clinical Psychopharmacology*, 21, 59–65.

Montgomery, S. A., Nil, R., Durr-Pal, N., Loft, H., & Boulenger, J. P. (2005). A 24-week randomized, double-blind, placebo-controlled study of escitalopram for the prevention of generalized social anxiety disorder. *Journal of Clinical Psychiatry*, 66, 1270–1278.

Moroz, G., & Rosenbaum, J. F. (1999). Efficacy, safety, and gradual discontinuation of clonazepam in panic disorder: A placebo-controlled, multicenter study using optimized dosages. *Journal of Clinical Psychiatry*, 60, 604–612.

Mountjoy, C. Q., Roth, M., Garside, R. F., & Leitch, I. M. (1977). A clinical trial of phenelzine in anxiety depressive and phobic neuroses. *British Journal of Psychiatry*, 131, 486–492.

Muller, J. E., Koen, L., Seedat, S., & Stein, D. J. (2005). Social anxiety disorder: Current treatment recommendations. CNS Drugs, 19, 377–391.

Munjack, D., Brun, J., & Baltazar, P. (1991). A pilot study of buspirone in the treatment of social phobia. Journal of Anxiety Disorders, 5, 87–88.

Munjack, D. J., Crocker, B., Cabe, D., Brown, R., Usigli, R., Zulueta, A., et al. (1989). Alprazolam, propranolol, and placebo in the treatment of panic disorder and agoraphobia with panic attacks. Journal of Clinical Psychopharmacology, 9, 22–27.

Murphy, S. M., Owen, R., & Tyrer, P. (1989). Comparative assessment of efficacy and withdrawal symptoms after 6 and 12 weeks' treatment with diazepam or buspirone. British Journal of Psychiatry, 154, 529–534.

Nagy, L. M., Krystal, J. H., Woods, S. W., & Charney, D. S. (1989). Clinical and medication outcome after short-term alprazolam and behavioral group treatment in panic disorder: 2.5 year naturalistic follow-up study. Archives of General Psychiatry, 46, 993–999.

Nair, N. P., Bakish, D., Saxena, B., Amin, M., Schwartz, G., & West, T. E. (1996). Comparison of fluvoxamine, imipramine, and placebo in the treatment of outpatients with panic disorder. Anxiety, 2, 192–198.

Naukkarinen, H., Raassina, R., Penttinen, J., Ahokas, A., Jokinen, R., Koponen, H., et al. (2005). Deramciclane in the treatment of generalized anxiety disorder: A placebo-controlled, double-blind, dose-finding study. European Neuropsychopharmacology, 15, 617–623.

Norton, C. R., Cox, B. J., & Malan, J. (1992). Nonclinical panickers: A critical review. Clinical Psychology Review, 12, 121–139.

Noyes, R., Jr., Garvey, M. J., Cook, B. L., & Samuelson, L. (1989). Problems with tricyclic antidepressant use in patients with panic disorder or agoraphobia: Results of a naturalistic follow-up study. Journal of Clinical Psychiatry, 50, 163–169.

Noyes, R., Jr., Moroz, G., Davidson, J. R., Liebowitz, M. R., Davidson, A., Siegel, J., et al. (1997). Moclobemide in social phobia: A controlled dose-response trial. Journal of Clinical Psychopharmacology, 17, 247–254.

Nutt, D. J. (2001). Neurobiological mechanisms in generalized anxiety disorder. Journal of Clinical Psychiatry, 62(Suppl. 11), 22–27; Discussion 28.

Oberlander, E. L., Schneier, F. R., & Liebowitz, M. R. (1994). Physical disability and social phobia. Journal of Clinical Psychopharmacology, 14, 136–143.

Oehrberg, S., Christiansen, P. E., Behnke, K., Borup, A. L., Severin, B., Soegaard, J., et al. (1995). Paroxetine in the treatment of panic disorder: A randomised, double-blind, placebo-controlled study. British Journal of Psychiatry, 167, 374–379.

Otto, M. W. (1999). Cognitive-behavioral therapy for social anxiety disorder: Model, methods, and outcome. Journal of Clinical Psychiatry, 60(Suppl. 9), 14–19.

Otto, M. W., Pollack, M. H., Gould, R. A., Worthington, J. J., III, Mcardle, E. T., & Rosenbaum, J. F. (2000). A comparison of the efficacy of clonazepam and cognitive-behavioral group therapy for the treatment of social phobia. Journal of Anxiety Disorders, 14, 345–358.

Pallanti, S., Quercioli, L., Rossi, A., & Pazzagli, A. (1999). The emergence of social phobia during clozapine treatment and its response to fluoxetine augmentation. Journal of Clinical Psychiatry, 60, 819–823.

Pande, A. C., Davidson, J. R., Jefferson, J. W., Janney, C. A., Katzelnick, D. J., Weisler, R. H., et al. (1999). Treatment of social phobia with gabapentin: A placebo-controlled study. Journal of Clinical Psychopharmacology, 19, 341–348.

Pande, A. C., Feltner, D. E., Jefferson, J. W., Davidson, J. R., Pollack, M., Stein, M. B., et al. (2004). Efficacy of the novel anxiolytic pregabalin in social anxiety disorder: A placebo-controlled, multicenter study. Journal of Clinical Psychopharmacology, 24, 141–149.

Pande, A. C., Pollack, M. H., Crockatt, J., Greiner, M., Chouinard, G., Lydiard, R. B., et al. (2000). Placebo-controlled study of gabapentin treatment of panic disorder. Journal of Clinical Psychopharmacology, 20, 467–471.

Papp, L., Coplan, J., & Gorman, J. (1992). Neurobiology of anxiety. In A. Tasman & M. B. Riba (Eds.), Review of Psychiatry (Vol. 11, pp. 307–322). Washington, DC: American Psychiatric Press.

Papp, L. A., Schneier, F. R., Fyer, A. J., Leibowitz, M. R., Gorman, J. M., Coplan, J. D., et al. (1997). Clomipramine treatment of panic disorder: Pros and cons. Journal of Clinical Psychiatry, 58, 423–425.

Pecknold, J. (1990, June 19 22). Discontinuation studies: Short-term and long-term. Paper presented at the conference Panic and Anxiety: A Decade of Progress, Geneva, Switzerland.

Pecknold, J. C., Matas, M., Howarth, B. G., Ross, C., Swinson, R., Vezeau, C., et al. (1989). Evaluation of buspirone as an antianxiety agent: Buspirone and diazepam versus placebo. Canadian Journal of Psychiatry, 34, 766–771.

Pecknold, J. C., Swinson, R. P., Kuch, K., & Lewis, C. P. (1988). Alprazolam in panic disorder and agoraphobia: Results from a multicenter trial: III. Discontinuation effects. *Archives of General Psychiatry, 45,* 429–436.

Petracca, A., Nisita, C., McNair, D., Melis, G., Guerani, G., & Cassano, G. B. (1990). Treatment of generalized anxiety disorder: Preliminary clinical experience with buspirone. *Journal of Clinical Psychiatry, 51*(Suppl.), 31–39.

Pittler, M. H., & Ernst, E. (2000). Efficacy of kava extract for treating anxiety: Systematic review and meta-analysis. *Journal of Clinical Psychopharmacology, 20,* 84–89.

Pohl, R. B., Feltner, D. E., Fieve, R. R., & Pande, A. C. (2005). Efficacy of pregabalin in the treatment of generalized anxiety disorder: Double-blind, placebo-controlled comparison of bid versus tid dosing. *Journal of Clinical Psychopharmacology, 25,* 151–158.

Pohl, R. B., Wolkow, R. M., & Clary, C. M. (1998). Sertraline in the treatment of panic disorder: A double-blind multicenter trial. *American Journal of Psychiatry, 155,* 1189–1195.

Pollack, M. H., Otto, M. W., Sachs, G. S., Leon, A., Shear, M. K., Deltito, J. A., et al. (1994). Anxiety psychopathology predictive of outcome in patients with panic disorder and depression treated with imipramine, alprazolam and placebo. *Journal of Affective Disorders, 30,* 273–281.

Pollack, M. H., Otto, M. W., Worthington, J. J., Manfro, G. G., & Wolkow, R. (1998). Sertraline in the treatment of panic disorder: A flexible-dose multicenter trial. *Archives of General Psychiatry, 55,* 1010–1016.

Pollack, M. H., Rapaport, M. H., Fayyad, R., Otto, M. W., Nierenberg, A. A., & Clary, C. M. (2002). Early improvement predicts endpoint remission status in sertraline and placebo treatments of panic disorder. *Journal of Psychiatric Research, 36,* 229–236.

Pollack, M. H., Simon, N. M., Zalta, A. K., Worthington, J. J., Hoge, E. A., Mick, E., et al. (2006). Olanzapine augmentation of fluoxetine for refractory generalized anxiety disorder: A placebo controlled study. *Biological Psychiatry, 3,* 211–215.

Pollack, M. H., Worthington, J. J., III, Otto, M. W., Maki, K. M., Smoller, J. W., Manfro, G. G., et al. (1996). Venlafaxine for panic disorder: Results from a double-blind, placebo-controlled study. *Psychopharmacology Bulletin, 32,* 667–670.

Pollack, M. H., Zaninelli, R., Goddard, A., McCafferty, J. P., Bellew, K. M., Burnham, D. B., et al. (2001). Paroxetine in the treatment of generalized anxiety disorder: Results of a placebo-controlled, flexible-

dosage trial. *Journal of Clinical Psychiatry, 62,* 350–357.

Power, K. G., Simpson, R. J., Swanson, V., & Wallace, L. A. (1990). Controlled comparison of pharmacological and psychological treatment of generalized anxiety disorder in primary care. *British Journal of General Practice, 40,* 289–294.

Rapaport, M. H., Wolkow, R., Rubin, A., Hackett, E., Pollack, M., & Ota, K. Y. (2001). Sertraline treatment of panic disorder: Results of a long-term study. *Acta Psychiatrica Scandinavica, 104,* 289–298.

Reich, J., Goldenberg, I., Vasile, R., Goisman, R., & Keller, M. (1994). A prospective follow-along study of the course of social phobia. *Psychiatry Research, 54,* 249–258.

Ressler, K. J., Rothbaum, B. O., Tannenbaum, L., Anderson, P., Graap, K., Zimand, E., et al. (2004). Cognitive enhancers as adjuncts to psychotherapy: Use of D-cycloserine in phobic individuals to facilitate extinction of fear. *Archives of General Psychiatry, 61,* 1136–1144.

Rickels, K., Case, W. G., Downing, R. W., & Winokur, A. (1983). Long-term diazepam therapy and clinical outcome. *Journal of the American Medical Association, 250,* 767–771.

Rickels, K., Case, W. G., Schweizer, E., Swenson, C., & Fridman, R. B. (1986). Low-dose dependence in chronic benzodiazepine users: A preliminary report on 119 patients. *Psychopharmacology Bulletin, 22,* 407–415.

Rickels, K., DeMartinis, N., Garcia-Espana, F., Greenblatt, D. J., Mandos, L. A., & Rynn, M. (2000). Imipramine and buspirone in treatment of patients with generalized anxiety disorder who are discontinuing long-term benzodiazepine therapy. *American Journal of Psychiatry, 157,* 1973–1979.

Rickels, K., Downing, R., Schweizer, E., & Hassman, H. (1993). Antidepressants for the treatment of generalized anxiety disorder: A placebo-controlled comparison of imipramine, trazodone, and diazepam. *Archives of General Psychiatry, 50,* 884–895.

Rickels, K., Fox, I. L., Greenblatt, D. J., Sandler, K. R., & Schless, A. (1988). Clorazepate and lorazepam: Clinical improvement and rebound anxiety. *American Journal of Psychiatry, 145,* 312–317.

Rickels, K., Mangano, R., & Khan, A. (2004). A double-blind, placebo-controlled study of a flexible dose of venlafaxine ER in adult outpatients with generalized social anxiety disorder. *Journal of Clinical Psychopharmacology, 24,* 488–496.

Rickels, K., Pollack, M. H., Feltner, D. E., Lydiard, R. B., Zimbroff, D. L., Bielski, R. J., et al. (2005). Pregabalin for treatment of generalized anxiety disorder: A 4-week, multicenter, double-blind, placebo-controlled trial of pregabalin and alprazolam. *Archives of General Psychiatry, 62,* 1022–1030.

Rickels, K., Pollack, M. H., Sheehan, D. V., & Haskins, J. T. (2000). Efficacy of extended-release venlafaxine in nondepressed outpatients with generalized anxiety disorder. *American Journal of Psychiatry, 157,* 968–974.

Rickels, K., Schweizer, E., Csanalosi, I., Case, W. G., & Chung, H. (1988). Long-term treatment of anxiety and risk of withdrawal: Prospective comparison of clorazepate and buspirone. *Archives of General Psychiatry, 45,* 444–450.

Rickels, K., Schweizer, E., DeMartinis, N., Mandos, L., & Mercer, C. (1997). Gepirone and diazepam in generalized anxiety disorder: A placebo-controlled trial. *Journal of Clinical Psychopharmacology, 17,* 272–277.

Rickels, K., Schweizer, E., Weiss, S., & Zavodnick, S. (1993). Maintenance drug treatment for panic disorder: II. Short- and long-term outcome after drug taper. *Archives of General Psychiatry, 50,* 61–68.

Rickels, K., Weisman, K., Norstad, N., Singer, M., Stoltz, D., Brown, A., et al. (1982). Buspirone and diazepam in anxiety: A controlled study. *Journal of Clinical Psychiatry, 43,* 81–86.

Rickels, K., Zaninelli, R., McCafferty, J., Bellew, K., Iyengar, M., & Sheehan, D. (2003). Paroxetine treatment of generalized anxiety disorder: A double-blind, placebo-controlled study. *American Journal of Psychiatry, 160,* 749–756.

Rocca, P., Fonzo, V., Scotta, M., Zanalda, E., & Ravizza, L. (1997). Paroxetine efficacy in the treatment of generalized anxiety disorder. *Acta Psychiatrica Scandinavica, 95,* 444–450.

Rosenbaum, J. F., Biederman, J., Hirshfeld, D. R., Bolduc, E. A., Faraone, S. V., Kagan, J., et al. (1991). Further evidence of an association between behavioral inhibition and anxiety disorders: Results from a family study of children from a non-clinical sample. *Journal of Psychiatric Research, 25,* 49–65.

Rosenbaum, J. F., Moroz, G., & Bowden, C. L. (1997). Clonazepam in the treatment of panic disorder with or without agoraphobia: A dose-response study of efficacy, safety, and discontinuance. Clonazepam Panic Disorder Dose-Response Study Group. *Journal of Clinical Psychopharmacology, 17,* 390–400.

Rosenberg, R., Beech, P., Mellergard, M., & Ottosson, J. O. (1991). Alprazolam, imipramine and placebo treatment of panic disorder: Predicting therapeutic response. *Acta Psychiatrica Scandinavica, 365* (Suppl.), 45–52.

Rosenthal, M. (2003). Tiagabine for the treatment of generalized anxiety disorder: A randomized, open-label, clinical trial with paroxetine as a positive control. *Journal of Clinical Psychiatry, 64,* 1245–1249.

Ross, C. A., & Matas, M. (1987). A clinical trial of buspirone and diazepam in the treatment of generalized anxiety disorder. *Canadian Journal of Psychiatry, 32,* 351–355.

Roy-Byrne, P. P., & Cowley, D. S. (1995). Course and outcome in panic disorder: A review of recent follow-up studies. *Anxiety, 1,* 151–160.

Roy-Byrne, P. P., & Cowley, D. S. (1998). Search for pathophysiology of panic disorder. *Lancet, 352,* 1646–1647.

Roy-Byrne, P. P., Craske, M., & Stein, M. (2006). Panic disorder. *Lancet, 368,* 1023–1032.

Roy-Byrne, P. P., Dager, S. R., Cowley, D. S., Vitaliano, P., & Dunner, D. L. (1989). Relapse and rebound following discontinuation of benzodiazepine treatment of panic attacks: Alprazolam versus diazepam. *American Journal of Psychiatry, 146,* 860–865.

Roy-Byrne, P. P., Geraci, M., & Uhde, T. W. (1986). Life events and the onset of panic disorder. *American Journal of Psychiatry, 143,* 1424–1427.

Roy-Byrne, P. P., Russo, J., Dugdale, D. C., Lessler, D., Cowley, D., & Katon, W. (2002). Undertreatment of panic disorder in primary care: Role of patient and physician characteristics. *Journal of the American Board of Family Practice, 15,* 443–450.

Ruscio, A. M., Lane, M., Roy-Byrne, P., Stang, P. E., Stein, D. J., Wittchen, H. U., et al. (2005). Should excessive worry be required for a diagnosis of generalized anxiety disorder? Results from the US National Comorbidity Survey replication. *Psychological Medicine, 35,* 1761–1772.

Sandmann, J., Lorch, B., Bandelow, B., Hartter, S., Winter, P., Hiemke, C., et al. (1998). Fluvoxamine or placebo in the treatment of panic disorder and relationship to blood concentrations of fluvoxamine. *Pharmacopsychiatry, 31,* 117–121.

Sasson, Y., Iancu, I., Fux, M., Taub, M., Dannon, P. N., & Zohar, J. (1999). A double-blind crossover comparison of clomipramine and desipramine in the treatment of panic disorder. *European Neuropsychopharmacology, 9,* 191–196.

Schneier, F. R., Goetz, D., Campeas, R., Fallon, B., Marshall, R., & Liebowitz, M. R. (1998). Placebo-controlled trial of moclobemide in social phobia. *British Journal of Psychiatry, 172,* 70–77.

Schneier, F. R., Heckelman, L. R., Garfinkel, R., Campeas, R., Fallon, B. A., Gitow, A., et al. (1994).

Functional impairment in social phobia. *Journal of Clinical Psychiatry, 55,* 322–331.

Schneier, F. R., Johnson, J., Hornig, C. D., Liebowitz, M. R., & Weissman, M. M. (1992). Social phobia: Comorbidity and morbidity in an epidemiologic sample. *Archives of General Psychiatry, 49,* 282–288.

Schneier, F. R., Liebowitz, M. R., Davies, S. O., Fairbanks, J., Hollander, E., Campeas, R., et al. (1990). Fluoxetine in panic disorder. *Journal of Clinical Psychopharmacology, 10,* 119–121.

Schneier, F. R., Saoud, J. B., Campeas, R., Fallon, B. A., Hollander, E., Coplan, J., et al. (1993). Buspirone in social phobia. *Journal of Clinical Psychopharmacology, 13,* 251–256.

Schutters, S. I., van Megen, H. J., & Westenberg, H. G. (2005). Efficacy of quetiapine in generalized social anxiety disorder: Results from an open-label study. *Journal of Clinical Psychiatry, 66,* 540–542.

Schweizer, E., Fox, I., Case, G., & Rickels, K. (1988). Lorazepam vs. alprazolam in the treatment of panic disorder. *Psychopharmacology Bulletin, 24,* 224–227.

Schweizer, E., Patterson, W., Rickels, K., & Rosenthal, M. (1993). Double-blind, placebo-controlled study of a once-a-day, sustained-release preparation of alprazolam for the treatment of panic disorder. *American Journal of Psychiatry, 150,* 1210–1215.

Schweizer, E., Rickels, K., Weiss, S., & Zavodnick, S. (1993). Maintenance drug treatment of panic disorder: I. Results of a prospective, placebo-controlled comparison of alprazolam and imipramine. *Archives of General Psychiatry, 50,* 51–60.

Seedat, S., & Stein, M. B. (2004). Double-blind, placebo-controlled assessment of combined clonazepam with paroxetine compared with paroxetine monotherapy for generalized social anxiety disorder. *Journal of Clinical Psychiatry, 65,* 244–248.

Shader, R. I., & Greenblatt, D. J. (1993). Use of benzodiazepines in anxiety disorders. *New England Journal of Medicine, 328,* 1398–1405.

Shapiro, A. K., Struening, E. L., Shapiro, E., & Milcarek, B. I. (1982). Diazepam: How much better than placebo? *Journal of Psychiatric Research, 17,* 51–73.

Sheehan, D. V., Ballenger, J., & Jacobsen, G. (1980). Treatment of endogenous anxiety with phobic, hysterical, and hypochondriacal symptoms. *Archives of General Psychiatry, 37,* 51–59.

Sheehan, D. V., Davidson, J., Manschreck, T., & Van Wyck Fleet, J. (1983). Lack of efficacy of a new antidepressant (bupropion) in the treatment of panic disorder with phobias. *Journal of Clinical Psychopharmacology, 3,* 28–31.

Sheehan, D. V., Raj, A. B., Harnett-Sheehan, K., Soto, S., & Knapp, E. (1993). The relative efficacy of high-dose buspirone and alprazolam in the treatment of panic disorder: A double-blind placebo-controlled study. *Acta Psychiatrica Scandinavica, 88,* 1–11.

Sheehan, D. V., Raj, A. B., Sheehan, K. H., & Soto, S. (1990). Is buspirone effective for panic disorder? *Journal of Clinical Psychopharmacology, 10,* 3–11.

Simpson, H. B., Schneier, F. R., Campeas, R. B., Marshall, R. D., Fallon, B. A., Davies, S., et al. (1998). Imipramine in the treatment of social phobia. *Journal of Clinical Psychopharmacology, 18,* 132–135.

Simpson, H. B., Schneier, F. R., Marshall, R. D., Campeas, R. B., Vermes, D., Silvestre, J., et al. (1998). Low-dose selegiline (L-deprenyl) in social phobia. *Depression and Anxiety, 7,* 126–129.

Solomon, K., & Hart, R. (1978). Pitfalls and prospects in clinical research on antianxiety drugs: Benzodiazepines and placebo a research review. *Journal of Clinical Psychiatry, 39,* 823–831.

Solyom, C., Solyom, L., LaPierre, Y., Pecknold, J., & Morton, L. (1981). Phenelzine and exposure in the treatment of phobias. *Biological Psychiatry, 16,* 239–247.

Solyom, L., Heseltine, G. F., McClure, D. J., Solyom, C., Ledwidge, B., & Steinberg, G. (1973). Behaviour therapy versus drug therapy in the treatment of phobic neurosis. *Canadian Psychiatric Association Journal, 18,* 25–32.

Stahl, S. M., Gergel, I., & Li, D. (2003). Escitalopram in the treatment of panic disorder: A randomized, double-blind, placebo-controlled trial. *Journal of Clinical Psychiatry, 64,* 1322–1327.

Stein, D. J., Andersen, H. F., & Goodman, W. K. (2005). Escitalopram for the treatment of GAD: Efficacy across different subgroups and outcomes. *Annals of Clinical Psychiatry, 17,* 71–75.

Stein, D. J., Berk, M., Els, C., Emsley, R. A., Gittelson, L., Wilson, D., et al. (1999). A double-blind placebo-controlled trial of paroxetine in the management of social phobia (social anxiety disorder) in South Africa. *South African Medical Journal, 89,* 402–406.

Stein, D. J., Stein, M. B., Pitts, C. D., Kumar, R., & Hunter, B. (2002). Predictors of response to pharmacotherapy in social anxiety disorder: An analysis of 3 placebo-controlled paroxetine trials. *Journal of Clinical Psychiatry, 63,* 152–155.

Stein, D. J., Versiani, M., Hair, T., & Kumar, R. (2002). Efficacy of paroxetine for relapse prevention in social anxiety disorder: A 24-week study. *Archives of General Psychiatry, 59,* 1111–1118.

Stein, D. J., Westenberg, H. G., Yang, H., Li, D., & Barbato, L. M. (2003). Fluvoxamine CR in the long-term treatment of social anxiety disorder: The 12- to 24-week extension phase of a multicentre, randomized, placebo-controlled trial. *International Journal of Neuropsychopharmacology, 6,* 317–323.

Stein, L. I., & Santos, A. B. (1998). *Assertive community treatment of persons with severe mental illness.* New York: Norton.

Stein, M. B., Chartier, M. J., Hazen, A. L., Kroft, C. D., Chale, R. A., Cote, D., et al. (1996). Paroxetine in the treatment of generalized social phobia: Open-label treatment and double-blind placebo-controlled discontinuation. *Journal of Clinical Psychopharmacology, 16,* 218–222.

Stein, M. B., Fyer, A. J., Davidson, J. R., Pollack, M. H., & Wiita, B. (1999). Fluvoxamine treatment of social phobia (social anxiety disorder): A double-blind, placebo-controlled study. *American Journal of Psychiatry, 156,* 756–760.

Stein, M. B., Liebowitz, M. R., Lydiard, R. B., Pitts, C. D., Bushnell, W., & Gergel, I. (1998). Paroxetine treatment of generalized social phobia (social anxiety disorder): A randomized controlled trial. *Journal of the American Medical Association, 280,* 708–713.

Stein, M. B., Pollack, M. H., Bystritsky, A., Kelsey, J. E., & Mangano, R. M. (2005). Efficacy of low and higher dose extended-release venlafaxine in generalized social anxiety disorder: A 6-month randomized controlled trial. *Psychopharmacology (Berlin), 177,* 280–288.

Stein, M. B., Sareen, J., Hami, S., & Chao, J. (2001). Pindolol potentiation of paroxetine for generalized social phobia: A double-blind, placebo-controlled, crossover study. *American Journal of Psychiatry, 158,* 1725–1727.

Stocchi, F., Nordera, G., Jokinen, R. H., Lepola, U. M., Hewett, K., Bryson, H., et al. (2003). Efficacy and tolerability of paroxetine for the long-term treatment of generalized anxiety disorder. *Journal of Clinical Psychiatry, 64,* 250–258.

Strand, M., Hetta, J., Rosen, A., Sorensen, S., Malmstrom, R., Fabian, C., et al. (1990). A double-blind, controlled trial in primary care patients with generalized anxiety: A comparison between buspirone and oxazepam. *Journal of Clinical Psychiatry, 51*(Suppl.), 40–45.

Swartz, C. M. (1998). Betaxolol in anxiety disorders. *Annals of Clinical Psychiatry, 10,* 9–14.

Taylor, C. B., Hayward, C., King, R., Ehlers, A., Margraf, J., Maddock, R., et al. (1990). Cardiovascular and symptomatic reduction effects of alprazolam and imipramine in patients with panic disorder: Results of a double-blind, placebo-controlled trial. *Journal of Clinical Psychopharmacology, 10,* 112–118.

Taylor, C. B., King, R., Margraf, J., Ehlers, A., Telch, M., Roth, W. T., et al. (1989). Use of medication and in vivo exposure in volunteers for panic disorder research. *American Journal of Psychiatry, 146,* 1423–1426.

Tesar, G. E., Rosenbaum, J. F., Pollack, M. H., Otto, M. W., Sachs, G. S., Herman, J. B., et al. (1991). Double-blind, placebo-controlled comparison of clonazepam and alprazolam for panic disorder. *Journal of Clinical Psychiatry, 52,* 69–76.

Thayer, J. F., Friedman, B. H., Borkovec, T. D., Johnsen, B. H., & Molina, S. (2000). Phasic heart period reactions to cued threat and nonthreat stimuli in generalized anxiety disorder. *Psychophysiology, 37,* 361–368.

Turner, S. M., Beidel, D. C., & Jacob, R. G. (1994). Social phobia: A comparison of behavior therapy and atenolol. *Journal of Consulting and Clinical Psychology, 62,* 350–358.

Tyrer, P., Candy, J., & Kelly, D. (1973). A study of the clinical effects of phenelzine and placebo in the treatment of phobic anxiety. *Psychopharmacologia, 32,* 237–254.

Uhde, T. W., Stein, M. B., & Post, R. M. (1988). Lack of efficacy of carbamazepine in the treatment of panic disorder. *American Journal of Psychiatry, 145,* 1104–1109.

Uhde, T. W., Stein, M. B., Vittone, B. J., Siever, L. J., Boulenger, J. P., Klein, E., et al. (1989). Behavioral and physiologic effects of short-term and long-term administration of clonidine in panic disorder. *Archives of General Psychiatry, 46,* 170–177.

Uhlenhuth, E. H., Balter, M. B., Ban, T. A., & Yang, K. (1998). International study of expert judgement on therapeutic use of benzodiazepines and other psychotherapeutic medications: V. Treatment strategies in panic disorder, 1992–1997. *Journal of Clinical Psychopharmacology, 18*(6 Suppl. 2), 27s–31s.

Uhlenhuth, E. H., Matuzas, W., Glass, R. M., & Easton, C. (1989). Response of panic disorder to fixed doses of alprazolam or imipramine. *Journal of Affective Disorders, 17,* 261–270.

van Ameringen, M. A., Lane, R. M., Walker, J. R., Bowen, R. C., Chokka, P. R., Goldner, E. M., et al. (2001). Sertraline treatment of generalized social phobia: A 20-week, double-blind, placebo-controlled study. *American Journal of Psychiatry, 158,* 275–281.

van Ameringen, M., Mancini, C., & Oakman, J. M. (1999). Nefazodone in social phobia. *Journal of Clinical Psychiatry, 60,* 96–100.

van Ameringen, M., Mancini, C., Pipe, B., Oakman, J., & Bennett, M. (2004). An open trial of topiramate in the treatment of generalized social phobia. *Journal of Clinical Psychiatry, 65,* 1674–1678.

van Ameringen, M., Mancini, C., & Wilson, C. (1996). Buspirone augmentation of selective serotonin reuptake inhibitors (SSRIs) in social phobia. *Journal of Affective Disorders, 39,* 115–121.

van Veen, J. F., van Vliet, I. M., & Westenberg, H. G. (2002). Mirtazapine in social anxiety disorder: A pilot study. *International Clinical Psychopharmacology, 17,* 315–317.

van Vliet, I. M., Den Boer, J. A., & Westenberg, H. G. (1994). Psychopharmacological treatment of social phobia: A double-blind placebo-controlled study with fluvoxamine. *Psychopharmacology (Berlin), 115,* 128–134.

van Vliet, I. M., Den Boer, J. A., Westenberg, H. G., & Pian, K. L. (1997). Clinical effects of buspirone in social phobia: A double-blind placebo-controlled study. *Journal of Clinical Psychiatry, 58,* 164–168.

van Vliet, I. M., Den Boer, J. A., Westenberg, H. G., & Slaap, B. R. (1996). A double-blind comparative study of brofaromine and fluvoxamine in outpatients with panic disorder. *Journal of Clinical Psychopharmacology, 16,* 299–306.

van Vliet, I. M., Westenberg, H. G., & Den Boer, J. A. (1993). MAO inhibitors in panic disorder: Clinical effects of treatment with brofaromine. A double-blind placebo-controlled study. *Psychopharmacology (Berlin), 112,* 483–489.

Varia, I., & Rauscher, F. (2002). Treatment of generalized anxiety disorder with citalopram. *International Clinical Psychopharmacology, 17,* 103–107.

Vasile, R. G., Bruce, S. E., Goisman, R. M., Pagano, M., & Keller, M. B. (2005). Results of a naturalistic longitudinal study of benzodiazepine and SSRI use in the treatment of generalized anxiety disorder and social phobia. *Depression and Anxiety, 22,* 59–67.

Versiani, M., Amrein, R., & Montgomery, S. A. (1997). Social phobia: Long-term treatment outcome and prediction of response a moclobemide study. *International Clinical Psychopharmacology, 12,* 239–254.

Versiani, M., Mundim, F. D., Nardi, A. E., & Liebowitz, M. R. (1988). Tranylcypromine in social phobia. *Journal of Clinical Psychopharmacology, 8,* 279–283.

Versiani, M., Nardi, A. E., Mundim, F. D., Alves, A. B., Liebowitz, M. R., & Amrein, R. (1992). Pharmacotherapy of social phobia: A controlled study with moclobemide and phenelzine. *British Journal of Psychiatry, 161,* 353–360.

Versiani, M., Ontiveros, A., Mazzotti, G., Ospina, J., Davila, J., Mata, S., et al. (1999). Fluoxetine versus amitriptyline in the treatment of major depression with associated anxiety (anxious depression): A double-blind comparison. *International Clinical Psychopharmacology, 14,* 321–327.

Villarreal, G., Johnson, M. R., Rubey, R., Lydiard, R. B., & Ballanger, J. C. (2000). Treatment of social phobia with the dopamine agonist pergolide. *Depression and Anxiety, 11,* 45–47.

Wade, A. G., Lepola, U., Koponen, H. J., Pedersen, V., & Pedersen, T. (1997). The effect of citalopram in panic disorder. *British Journal of Psychiatry, 170,* 549–553.

Walker, J. R., van Ameringen, M. A., Swinson, R., Bowen, R. C., Chokka, P. R., Goldner, E., et al. (2000). Prevention of relapse in generalized social phobia: Results of a 24-week study in responders to 20 weeks of sertraline treatment. *Journal of Clinical Psychopharmacology, 20,* 636–644.

Westenberg, H. G., Stein, D. J., Yang, H., Li, D., & Barbato, L. M. (2004). A double-blind placebo-controlled study of controlled release fluvoxamine for the treatment of generalized social anxiety disorder. *Journal of Clinical Psychopharmacology, 24,* 49–55.

Widiger, T. A. (1992). Generalized social phobia versus avoidant personality disorder: A commentary on three studies. *Journal of Abnormal Psychology, 101,* 340–343.

Wilhelm, F. H., & Roth, W. T. (1997). Acute and delayed effects of alprazolam on flight phobics during exposure. *Behaviour Research and Therapy, 35,* 831–841.

Wingerson, D., Nguyen, C., & Roy-Byrne, P. P. (1992). Clomipramine treatment for generalized anxiety disorder. *Journal of Clinical Psychopharmacology, 12,* 214–215.

Woodman, C. L., & Noyes, R., Jr. (1994). Panic disorder: Treatment with valproate. *Journal of Clinical Psychiatry, 55,* 134–136.

Woods, S. W., Nagy, L. M., Koleszar, A. S., Krystal, J. H., Heninger, G. R., & Charney, D. S. (1992). Controlled trial of alprazolam supplementation during imipramine treatment of panic disorder. *Journal of Clinical Psychopharmacology, 12,* 32–38.

Work Group on Panic Disorder, American Psychiatric Association. (1998). Practice guideline for the treatment of patients with panic disorder. *American Journal of Psychiatry, 155*(Suppl. 5), 1–34.

Worthington, J. J., III, Zucker, B. G., Fones, C. S., Otto, M. W., & Pollack, M. H. (1998). Nefazodone for social phobia: A clinical case series. *Depression and Anxiety, 8,* 131–133.

Yonkers, K. A., Ellison, J. M., Shera, D. M., Pratt, L. A., Cole, J. O., Fierman, E., et al. (1996). Description of antipanic therapy in a prospective longitudinal study. *Journal of Clinical Psychopharmacology, 16*, 223–232.

Zajecka, J. M. (1996). The effect of nefazodone on co-morbid anxiety symptoms associated with depression: Experience in family practice and psychiatric outpatient settings. *Journal of Clinical Psychiatry, 57*(Suppl. 2), 10–14.

Zhang, W., Connor, K. M., & Davidson, J. R. (2005). Levetiracetam in social phobia: A placebo-controlled pilot study. *Journal of Psychopharmacology, 19*, 551–553.

Zitrin, C. M., Klein, D. F., & Woerner, M. G. (1978). Behavior therapy, supportive psychotherapy, imipramine, and phobias. *Archives of General Psychiatry, 35*, 307–316.

Zitrin, C. M., Klein, D. F., & Woerner, M. G. (1980). Treatment of agoraphobia with group exposure in vivo and imipramine. *Archives of General Psychiatry, 37*, 63–72.

Zitrin, C. M., Klein, D. F., Woerner, M. G., & Ross, D. C. (1983). Treatment of phobias: I. Comparison of imipramine hydrochloride and placebo. *Archives of General Psychiatry, 40*, 125–138.

15

Cognitive Behavioral Treatment of Obsessive-Compulsive Disorder

Martin E. Franklin

Edna B. Foa

Cognitive behavioral therapy (CBT) involving exposure and ritual prevention (EX/RP) is a well-established treatment for obsessive-compulsive disorder (OCD) in adults. Support for its efficacy is derived from many Type 1 and Type 2 studies; more recently the literature on more cognitively based treatments for OCD has provided further empirical support for this approach as well. Combined treatment studies examining EX/RP plus serotonin reuptake inhibitors or clomipramine have provided some advantages for the combined regimen over the monotherapies, but equivocal findings have emerged as well. In recent years there has been increased attention paid to the treatment of pediatric OCD using CBT, and now there are several Type 1 studies documenting the efficacy of this approach for youth with OCD. Further research is needed to examine predictors of outcome and to examine the effectiveness of CBT for OCD in a variety of clinical settings.

The symptoms that characterize what we now call *obsessive-compulsive disorder* (OCD) have been recognized for centuries in many cultures (for a review, see Pitman, 1994). However, it was only in the last three decades that effective psychosocial and pharmacological therapies for OCD were developed and studied. In this chapter we will briefly discuss diagnostic and theoretical issues, then review the literature about available treatments. We have focused primarily on the outcome of cognitive behavioral treatment (CBT) by exposure and ritual prevention (originally referred to as "response prevention"; EX/RP) because most experts consider it to be the treatment of choice for OCD (March, Frances, Carpenter, & Kahn, 1997). Notably, three studies with adults that have examined the effectiveness of EX/RP outside the context of controlled research (Type 1) trials suggest that its benefits are not limited to the highly selected patient samples that often characterize randomized controlled trials (RCTs; Franklin, Abramowitz, Kozak, Levitt, & Foa, 2000; Rothbaum

& Shahar, 2000; Warren & Thomas, 2001). Given the substantial new developments in CBT outcome research in pediatric OCD, we will include a review of that literature as well.

DEFINITION OF OCD

According to the most recent version of the *Diagnostic and Statistical Manual of Mental Disorders* (American Psychiatric Association [APA], 2000), OCD is characterized by recurrent obsessions and/or compulsions that interfere considerably with daily functioning. Obsessions are "persistent ideas, thoughts, impulses, or images that are experienced as intrusive and inappropriate and cause marked anxiety or distress" (p. 418). Compulsions are "repetitive behaviors . . . or mental acts . . . the goal of which is to prevent or reduce anxiety or distress" (p. 418).

There are several points to highlight regarding the current definition of OCD. First, the emphasis on the functional relationship between obsessions and compulsions, that is, compulsions are performed in order to decrease distress associated with obsessions (Foa & Tillmanns, 1980), became more prominent in the *DSM-IV-TR* definition of OCD because of strong empirical support for this view. Second, in the *DSM-IV-TR* field study on OCD, 90% of participants reported that their compulsions aim to either prevent harm associated with their obsessions or reduce obsessional distress; only 10% perceived their compulsions as unrelated to obsessions (Foa et al., 1995). Accordingly, *obsessions* are defined as thoughts, images, or impulses that cause marked anxiety or distress, and *compulsions* are defined as overt (behavioral) or covert (mental) actions that are performed in an attempt to reduce the distress brought on by obsessions or according to rigid rules.

Data from that field study also indicated that the vast majority (more than 90%) of obsessive-compulsives manifest both obsessions and behavioral rituals. When mental rituals are included, only 2% of the sample reported obsessions only (Foa et al., 1995). Behavioral rituals are equivalent to mental rituals (such as silently repeating prayers) in their functional relationship to obsessions: Both serve to reduce obsessional distress, prevent feared harm, or restore safety. Thus, the previously prevailing view that obsessions are mental events and compulsions are behavioral events is not valid: Although all obsessions are indeed mental events, compulsions may be either behavioral or mental.

It has been argued that a continuum of "insight" or "strength of belief" more accurately represents the clinical picture of OCD than the previously prevailing view that *all* obsessive-compulsives recognize the senselessness of their obsessions and compulsions (Kozak & Foa, 1994), which led to the inclusion of a subtype of OCD known as OCD "with poor insight." Poor insight has been found to be a poor prognostic indicator for treatment response (e.g., Foa, Abramowitz, Franklin, & Kozak, 1999), so its assessment prior to initiating treatment is of considerable importance.

PREVALENCE AND COURSE

Once thought to be a rare disorder, OCD is estimated to occur in about 2.5% of the adult population in the United States (Karno, Golding, Sorenson, & Burnam, 1988); epidemiological studies with children and adolescents suggest similar lifetime prevalence rates in these samples (e.g., Flament et al., 1988; Valleni-Basile et al., 1994). Slightly more than half of the adults suffering from OCD are female (Rasmussen & Tsuang, 1986), whereas a 2:1 male-to-female ratio has been observed in several pediatric clinical samples (e.g., Hanna, 1995; Swedo, Rapoport, Leonard, Lenane, & Cheslow, 1989). Age of onset typically ranges from early adolescence to young adulthood, with earlier onset in males; modal onset is at age 13–15 in males and 20 to 24 in females (Rasmussen & Eisen, 1990). However, cases of OCD have been documented in children as young as age 2 (Rapoport, Swedo, & Leonard, 1992). Development of the disorder is usually gradual, but more acute onset has been reported in some cases. A subset of pediatric patients suffer from a similar clinical course of illness now referred to as Pediatric Autoimmune Neuropsychiatric Disorders Associated with Strep (PANDAS), in which patients experience dramatic onset of OCD and/or tic symptoms following strep infection (Swedo et al., 1998). Notably, these exacerbations in PANDAS are often followed by periods of relative symptom quiescence, until such time that the child is reinfected. Although chronic waxing and waning of symptoms is typical of OCD, episodic and deteriorating courses have been observed in about 10% of patients (Rasmussen & Eisen, 1989). OCD is frequently associated with impairments in general functioning, such as disruption of gainful employment (Leon, Portera, & Weissman, 1995), and with marital and other interpersonal relationship difficulties (Emmelkamp, de Haan, & Hoogduin, 1990; Riggs, Hiss, & Foa, 1992). Adolescents identified as having OCD (Flament et al., 1988) reported in a subsequent follow-up study that they had withdrawn socially to prevent contamination and to conserve energy for obsessive-compulsive behaviors (Flament et al., 1990).

ETIOLOGY AND MAINTENANCE OF OCD

Several theoretical accounts of the etiology and maintenance of OCD have been published. Mowrer's (1939, 1960) two-stage theory for the acquisition and maintenance of fear and avoidance behavior was invoked by Dollard and Miller (1950) to explain

OCD. Accordingly, a neutral event comes to elicit fear after being experienced along with an event that by its nature causes distress. Distress can be conditioned to mental events (e.g., thoughts), as well as to physical events (e.g., floors, bathrooms). Once fear is acquired, escape or avoidance patterns (i.e., compulsions) develop to reduce fear and are maintained by the negative reinforcement of fear reduction. While Mowrer's theory does not adequately account for fear acquisition (Rachman & Wilson, 1980), it is consistent with observations about the maintenance of compulsive rituals: Obsessions give rise to anxiety/distress, and compulsions reduce it (e.g., Roper & Rachman, 1976; Roper, Rachman, & Hodgson, 1973).

Cognitive theorists such as Salkovskis (1985) have offered a thorough cognitive analysis of OCD. Specifically, Salkovskis proposed that five assumptions are specifically characteristic of OCD: (a) Thinking of an action is analogous to its performance; (b) failing to prevent (or failing to try to prevent) harm to self or others is morally equivalent to causing the harm; (c) responsibility for harm is not diminished by extenuating circumstances; (d) failing to ritualize in response to an idea about harm constitutes an intention to harm; and (e) one should exercise control over one's thoughts (Salkovskis, 1985, p. 579). An interesting implication of this theory is that whereas the obsessive intrusions may be seen by the patient as unacceptable, the mental and overt rituals that they prompt will be acceptable. Foa and Kozak (1985) hypothesized that individuals with OCD often conclude that a situation is dangerous based on the absence of evidence for safety, and fail to make inductive leaps about safety from information about the absence of danger. For example, in order to feel safe, an OCD sufferer requires a guarantee that the toilet seat is safe before sitting on it, whereas a person without OCD would sit on the toilet seat unless there was something particular about it indicating danger, such as visible brown spots on the seat. Consequently, rituals that are performed to reduce the likelihood of harm can never really provide safety and must be repeated.

The prevailing biological account of OCD hypothesizes that abnormal serotonin metabolism is expressed in OCD symptoms. The efficacy of serotonin reuptake inhibitors (SRIs) for OCD as compared to nonserotonergic compounds and to pill placebo (PBO) has provided empirical support for this hypothesis (Zohar & Insel, 1987). Significant correla-

tions between clomipramine (CMI) plasma levels and improvement in OCD have led researchers to suggest that serotonin function mediates obsessive-compulsive symptoms, thus lending further support to the serotonin hypothesis (e.g., Insel, Mueller, Alterman, Linnoila, & Murphy, 1985). However, studies that directly investigated serotonin functioning in obsessive compulsives are inconclusive; for example, serotonin platelet uptake studies have failed to differentiate obsessive compulsives from controls (Insel et al., 1985; Weizman et al., 1986). Also inconsistent with the serotonin hypothesis is the finding that clomipramine, a nonselective serotonergic medication, appears to produce greater OCD symptom reduction than selective serotonin reuptake inhibitors such as fluoxetine, fluvoxamine, and sertraline (Greist, Jefferson, Kobak, Katzelnick, & Serlin, 1995). With respect to other biological theories, research being conducted at the National Institute of Mental Health on PANDAS may shed light on the role of basal ganglia dysfunction in certain neuropsychiatric conditions including OCD (Swedo et al., 1998). Some have even proposed that childhood-onset OCD represents a phenomenologically and etiologically distinct subtype of the disorder, bearing a close genetic relationship to tic disorders and possibly sharing a common or similar pathogenesis (Eichstedt & Arnold, 2001).

EARLY TREATMENTS FOR OCD

Until the middle of the 1960s, OCD was considered to be refractory to treatment: neither psychodynamic psychotherapy nor a wide variety of pharmacotherapies had proved successful in ameliorating OCD symptoms. Early case reports employing exposure procedures (e.g., systematic desensitization, paradoxical intention, imaginal flooding, satiation) also yielded generally unimpressive results, as did several operant conditioning procedures aimed at blocking or punishing obsessions and compulsions (e.g., thought stopping, aversion therapy, covert sensitization). A shift in thinking about OCD treatment occurred when Meyer (1966) reported on two patients treated successfully with a behavioral program that included prolonged exposure to obsessional cues and strict prevention of rituals (EX/RP). This treatment program was subsequently found to be very successful in 10 of 15 cases and partly effective in the remainder; after 5 years, only 2 of 15 patients in this open clinical trial had relapsed (Meyer & Levy, 1973; Meyer, Levy, & Schnurer, 1974). Another shift occurred with the finding that the tricyclic clomipramine (Anafranil) was effective in reducing OCD symptoms (e.g., Fernandez-Cordoba & Lopez-Ibor Alino, 1967). Subsequent research efforts were aimed at developing these treatments further and determining their relative efficacy.

REVIEW OF OCD TREATMENT OUTCOME LITERATURE

In the three decades following these initial reports, the efficacy of two treatments has been clearly established: cognitive behavioral therapy by EX/RP and pharmacotherapy with serotonin reuptake inhibitors. We will discuss results from controlled studies of EX/RP for adults employing a set of criteria that we label the "gold standard" for treatment outcome studies; we will also review the studies meeting these same standards conducted thus far on the treatment of children and adolescents with OCD.

"Gold Standard" (Type 1) OCD Treatment Outcome Studies

The following study selection criteria were used: (a) The sample comprised OCD patients, (b) there was at least one comparison group, and (c) there were at least 8 patients per experimental cell. The validity of each study's results will be evaluated by considering the set of criteria that defines our "ideal" treatment outcome study. These include (a) clearly defined inclusion/exclusion criteria; (b) reliable and valid diagnostic methods; (c) random assignment to treatment condition; (d) blind assessments by trained assessors using reliable and valid outcome measures; (d) manualized treatments; (f) measures of treatment adherence; (g) adequate sample size for statistical power; (h) appropriate statistical analyses; and (i) exposure and ritual prevention that meets acceptable clinical practice standards as suggested by expert consensus (see Kozak & Foa, 1996). Adequate planned systematic exposure was defined as involving confrontation of obsession-evoking stimuli of sufficient duration (typically 90 minutes or longer), frequency (15 to 20 sessions), and spacing (initially at least once per week but often more frequently). Adequate ritual prevention should occur immediately after exposure and in-

clude patients' voluntary compliance with instructions to refrain from ritualizing and procedures to help the patient achieve the greatest reduction in rituals possible. Exposure and ritual prevention should also be exercised between sessions.

We will review these studies by topic in order to provide a sense of which issues in OCD treatment outcome have already been addressed adequately, as well as acknowledgment of those areas that need to be addressed.

The Separate Effects of Exposure In Vivo, Imaginal Exposure, and Ritual Prevention

In early studies of the efficacy of EX/RP for OCD (e.g., Foa & Goldstein, 1978; Meyer et al., 1974), exposure and ritual prevention were implemented concurrently, thus making it impossible to determine the contribution of each procedure alone to outcome. To address this issue, Foa, Steketee, Grayson, Turner, and Latimer (1984) assigned patients with washing rituals to either treatment by exposure only, ritual prevention only, or their combination. Each treatment was conducted intensively (15 daily 2-hour sessions conducted over 3 weeks) and followed by a home visit. Blind assessors evaluated patients' symptoms at pretreatment, posttreatment, and follow-up; patients also completed self-report measures at each assessment. All treatments were effective, and gains were maintained at follow-up ($M = 12$ months, range 3 to 24 months). The combined treatment was superior to the single-component treatments on almost every symptom measure at both posttreatment and follow-up. In comparing the single-component treatments to one another, EX patients had lower ratings of anxiety than RP patients upon confrontation with feared contaminants in a posttreatment exposure test, and RP patients reported greater decreases in urge to ritualize than did EX patients, suggesting that the two components affect OC symptoms differently.

Patients were allocated to groups by a serial assignment procedure to balance for level of depression, gender, and therapist. In studies with small samples (cell sizes ranged from 9 to 12), this procedure is advantageous to random assignment because it ensures across-group equality on outcome-related factors. Inclusion/exclusion criteria were clearly described, and blind assessors rated patients' symptoms using reliable and valid outcome measures. Treatments were described in detail, although they were not manualized and treatment integrity was not assessed. Statistical analyses were generally appropriate, although setting a more conservative alpha level or correcting for the large number of tests may have been advisable.

In the Foa and Goldstein (1978) open clinical trial, EX/RP was accompanied by imaginal exposure (I/EX). To examine the additive effect of imaginal exposure, patients with checking rituals were treated with either 10 two-hour sessions of EX/RP delivered over 2 weeks or 10 sessions of EX/RP plus I/EX (Foa, Steketee, Turner, & Fischer, 1980). Sessions were 2 hours long and consisted of either 90-minute I/EX and 30-minute in vivo EX or 2 hours of in vivo EX only. No posttreatment group differences were detected on six OC symptom outcome measures. However, group differences did emerge at follow-up (M follow-up = 11 months, range 3 months to 2.5 years): On four out of six measures, the group receiving I/EX was less symptomatic compared with pretreatment. Thus, imaginal exposure seems to contribute to maintenance of treatment gains. The results of this study underscore the importance of obtaining follow-up data; in the absence of these data, the effects of I/EX would not have been detected.

The Foa et al. (1980) study specified inclusion/exclusion criteria, treatments were described clearly and implemented in accordance with accepted clinical practice standards, blind assessors rated symptom severity, and statistical analyses were conducted appropriately. Although the design met some of our "gold standard" criteria, several methodological problems should be noted. Patients were assigned to condition according to order of applying for treatment rather than at random, diagnostic methods were not described, measures of treatment adherence were not included, and sample size (15) was marginal.

To further examine whether the addition of I/EX to EX/RP enhances treatment efficacy, de Araujo, Ito, Marks, and Deale (1995) replicated the Foa et al. (1980) design, but the treatment program and the patient population differed across the two studies. Patients in this study had a range of rituals, and treatment included a mean of nine weekly 90-minute sessions of either in vivo EX or 30-minute I/EX and 60 minutes in vivo EX. At posttreatment, both groups evidenced reductions on measures of OC symptoms, including the Yale-Brown Obsessive Compulsive Scale (Y-BOCS), as well as on measures of depression and disability. No group differences were found either at posttreatment or at 6-month follow-up, suggesting no augmentive effect for imaginal exposure.

The de Araujo et al. (1995) study had several strengths, including utilization of random assignment to condition, blind assessors, clearly stated inclusion/exclusion criteria, adequate sample size for completer data ($n = 23$ per cell), appropriate outcome measures (Y-BOCS), Hamilton Depression (HAM-D), and clearly described treatments. However, assessor training was not described, diagnostic methods were not explicated ("patients who met DSM-III-R criteria for OCD . . ."), and treatment adherence was not measured. Moreover, because in the Foa et al. (1980) study the effects of imaginal exposure were not detected until an average of 11 months posttreatment, the length of follow-up (6 months) in the de Araujo et al. (1995) study may have been insufficient to detect such effects. Also, the treatment procedure and patient samples of the two studies differed in important ways that were likely to produce different results. Specifically, treatment was conducted daily in the Foa et al. study, sessions were of 2 hours; duration, and imaginal exposure was 90 minutes long; in the de Araujo et al. study, treatment was conducted weekly, sessions were 90 minutes in duration, and imaginal exposure was conducted over 30 minutes only. These procedural differences are troublesome because they reflect a general tendency in treatment research, namely, researchers who intend to examine the replicability of a previous result do not always adhere to the procedure of the treatment they choose to examine, and therefore resultant differences in outcome are uninterpretable.

EX/RP Versus Anxiety Management Training

One very small early study had suggested the superiority of EX/RP over relaxation using a crossover design (Marks, Hodgson, & Rachman, 1975), but the question of whether nonspecific factors explain the observed symptom reductions in EX/RP treatment studies was addressed more recently by Lindsay, Crino, and Andrews (1997). Eighteen patients were randomly assigned to intensive (daily) regimens of either EX/RP or anxiety management training (AMT). Results on therapist-rated Y-BOCS and several self-report OCD inventories indicated that EX/RP was clearly superior to AMT, even though both groups rated their therapists as highly supportive and understanding. This study adds further evidence to the efficacy of EX/RP and suggests that supportive and understanding therapists offering face-valid treatments with a comprehensive rationale do not result in reduced OCD symptoms in the absence of EX/RP (Lindsay et al., 1997).

Lindsay et al.'s study met several of the gold standard criteria for EX/RP outcome studies, including clearly described inclusion/exclusion and therapist ratings of OCD symptoms using the Y-BOCS, a reliable and valid outcome measure. Both treatments were manualized, although treatment integrity was not assessed. Statistical analyses were appropriate, including Bonferroni correction for multiple tests to limit Type I error. As noted by the authors, limitations include the small sample size, the failure to assess credibility of the control group, and the fact that random assignment did not equalize gender ratios. Additionally, the absence of independent evaluators to conduct symptom ratings (ratings were conducted by therapists instead) does allow for the possibility that rater bias may have affected outcome.

Individual Versus Group EX/RP

Efficacy of group and individual behavior therapy was examined in a study by Fals-Stewart, Marks, and Schafer (1993). OCD patients were randomly assigned to receive EX/RP conducted individually, group EX/RP treatment, or a psychosocial placebo (relaxation). Each of the active treatments was 2 weeks long, with sessions held twice weekly, and included daily exposure homework assignments. Results indicated significant reductions in OC symptoms at posttreatment only in the two active treatments. Moreover, no differences between individual and group EX/RP were detected at posttreatment or at 6-month follow-up, although profile analysis of Y-BOCS scores collected throughout treatment indicated a faster reduction in symptoms for patients receiving individual treatment. These results offer evidence for the efficacy of group treatment, considered by the authors to be especially important in light of efficiency and practicality of treatment delivery afforded by group approaches.

Fals-Stewart et al.'s (1993) study had several strengths. Diagnostic interviews were conducted by trained social workers, and outcome measures were acceptable (e.g., Y-BOCS). Sample size was more than sufficient (30 to 32 per cell), and there were only 4 dropouts from treatment following randomization. Statistical analyses were appropriate, and therapy was provided by trained social workers experienced with OCD treatment. Difficulties interpreting the study's results arise, however, from the inclusion/exclusion criteria and from the specific form of EX/RP used. Patients were excluded from the study if they were diagnosed with *any* personality disorder or with comorbid major depression with a Beck Depression Inventory (BDI) greater than 22. This exclusion criterion, together with the relatively low pretreatment Y-BOCS scores (range 19 to 22) and the fact that none of the 93 patients had ever received previous treatment for OCD, renders the sample atypical. This limits the generalizability of findings that group and individual treatments are equally effective. Notably, a pediatric OCD study described below also found that individual and group treatments were both highly efficacious and did not differ from one another (Barrett, Healy-Farrell, & March, 2004), lending additional empirical support to the contention that group treatments can be helpful in treating OCD.

Family Involvement Versus Standard Treatment

Influenced by findings that efficacy of exposure therapy for panic disorder with agoraphobia is enhanced by partner assistance, Emmelkamp et al. (1990) examined whether such assistance would also enhance the efficacy of EX/RP for OCD. Patients who were married or living with a romantic partner were randomly assigned to receive EX/RP either with or without partner involvement in treatment. Each treatment lasted 5 weeks and consisted of eight 45- to 60-minute sessions with the therapist; exposures were not practiced in session. Patients and partners rated their symptoms at four assessment periods; independent evaluators rated patients only before and after treatment. Results indicated that OCD severity was significantly reduced immediately after treatment for both groups. No group differences were detected, and initial marital distress did not predict outcome. It is important to note that, similar to the results from Emmelkamp and his colleagues described earlier, while the mean pre-post symptom reduction reached statistical significance, the modest reduction may not reflect clinically significant improvement.

In the Emmelkamp et al. (1990) study, eligible patients (those with partners) were randomly assigned to treatment. Blind assessors were used, but only at two assessment periods, and training on the measures was not discussed. Inclusion/exclusion criteria were clearly described, although diagnostic methods were not. Sample size (50) was more than adequate, and there were very few treatment dropouts. Statistical analyses were conducted appropriately, although in the tabular presentation of results the group condition was collapsed. Description of treatments did not include sufficient details regarding how ritual prevention was discussed with patients, and treatment adherence data were not provided. As with previously discussed studies, no therapist-assisted exposure was included, and between-sessions exposure homework was assigned only twice per week. These diluted procedures seem to have produced only modest symptom reductions.

Mehta (1990) also examined the adjunctive role of family involvement in EX/RP treatment in a study conducted in India. In order to adapt the treatment to serve the large numbers of young unmarried people seeking OCD treatment and the "joint family system" prevalent in India, a family-based rather than spouse-based treatment approach was utilized. Patients ($n = 30$) previously nonresponsive to pharmacotherapy were randomly assigned to receive treatment by systematic desensitization and EX/RP either with or without family assistance. Sessions in both conditions were held twice per week for 12 weeks; response prevention was "gradual . . . to reduce the frequency of the target behaviors until they reached a desired level." In the family condition, a designated family member (parent, spouse, or adult child) assisted with homework assignments, supervised relaxation therapy, participated in response prevention, and was instructed to be supportive when patients became depressed and anxious. On the only measure of OCD symptoms, the Maudsley Obsessive Compulsive Inventory (MOCI), a greater improvement was found for the family-based intervention at post-treatment and 6-month follow-up.

In Mehta's (1990) study, patients were randomly assigned to treatment, and sample size was satisfactory. However, OC symptoms were assessed exclusively by self-report (MOCI), introducing a possible bias. Inclusion/exclusion criteria and diagnostic methods were not specified in sufficient detail. Although the number of treatment sessions was sufficient, treatment descriptions were sketchy (e.g., degree to which relaxation training was emphasized), and no treatment adherence data were provided. The statistical analyses consisted of between-subjects t-tests at each assessment occasion; a mixed-design ANOVA would have been more appropriate. Despite its shortcomings, the study does provide interesting information about the efficacy of EX/RP treatment within the context of a culture where family relationships are thought to be especially important. All three of the RCTs that have examined CBT for pediatric OCD have also included the families in treatment at least to some extent (Barrett et al., 2004; de Haan, Hoogduin, Buitelaar, & Keijsers, 1998; Pediatric OCD Treatment Study Team, 2004; Piacentini, Jacobs, & Bergman, 2005), but the amount and type of family contact that would be optimal have yet to be established.

Cognitive Therapies

Cognitive therapies have emerged from the cognitive models of OCD, and the efficacy of several of these protocols has now been established. Small outcome studies by Emmelkamp and colleagues provided the initial empirical foundation for cognitive therapies (Emmelkamp & Beens, 1991; Emmelkamp, van der Helm, van Zanten, & Plochg, 1980; Emmelkamp, Visser, & Hoekstra, 1988); these were followed by positive studies demonstrating the efficacy of cognitively oriented therapies for particular subtypes of OCD, one focused on treatment of washers (Jones & Menzies, 1998) and the other on primary obsessionals (Freeston, Ladouceur, Gagnon, & Thibodeau, 1997). Direct comparison studies are now available in which the efficacy of OCD-specific cognitive therapy (CT) is directly compared with that of exposure and response prevention. In a randomized study that did not include a control condition, Whittal, Thordarson, and McLean (in press) found that EX/RP and CT were comparable at posttreatment and at 3-month follow-up; within-subjects effect sizes obtained from this study suggested that both conditions yielded symptom reductions that were comparable with those obtained in other studies that have examined CT and EX/RP (Cottraux et al., 2001; Freeston et al., 1997; McLean et al., 2001; van Balkom et al., 1998). Thus, the data suggest that CT, which in most of the protocols tested has included at least some form of exposure (i.e., behavioral experiments), holds considerable promise in the treatment of OCD in adults.

In order to examine the combined efficacy of cognitive and behavioral therapies delivered with and without concomitant SRI pharmacotherapy, van Balkom et al. (1998) conducted the largest of the CT studies. In it, they randomly assigned patients to (a) cognitive therapy for weeks 1 through 16; (b) EX/RP for weeks 1 through 16; (c) fluvoxamine for weeks 1 through 16 plus cognitive therapy in weeks 9 through 16; (d) fluvoxamine for weeks 1 through 16 plus EX/RP in weeks 9 through 16; and (e) wait-list for weeks 1 to 8. Notably, behavioral experiments (exposures) were not introduced into the cognitive treatment until after session 6 (week 8). Conversely, in the first six EX/RP sessions, care was taken by the therapist to specifically avoid any discussion of disastrous consequences. The authors regarded this procedure as measuring the effects of "purer" versions of cognitive therapy and EX/RP. Cognitive therapy focused primarily on themes of danger overestimation and inflated personal responsibility. EX/RP included self-exposure, with patients determining the speed at which they worked through the fear hierarchy. Sessions in both treatment conditions lasted for 45 minutes. Results indicated that all active treatments were superior to wait-list at week 8. Additionally, after 8 weeks of cognitive therapy without behavioral experiments and EX/RP without discussion of disastrous consequences, Y-BOCS reductions of 15% and 25% were observed for cognitive therapy and EX/RP, respectively. At posttreatment, patients in all active treatments improved significantly on almost all measures, including the Y-BOCS and Beck Depression Inventory (BDI; Beck, Ward, Mendelson, Mock, & Erbaugh, 1961). However, inspection of the mean reduction in Y-BOCS scores for the EX/RP condition suggested that outcome at posttreatment (46% Y-BOCS reduction for CT; 32% for EX/RP) was inferior to that achieved in other studies (e.g., Foa, Kozak, Steketee, & McCarthy, 1992). It should be noted that the mean posttreatment score in the EX/RP group of 17.1 would be considered sufficiently severe to meet initial severity criteria for many OCD treatment studies. The authors indicate that the lack of observed differences between the combined conditions and the monotherapies suggests that clinicians should start with either cognitive therapy or EX/RP alone rather than with combination treatments.

Random assignment to treatments, reliable and valid diagnostic procedures, clear inclusion and exclusion criteria, use of treatment manuals, attention to treatment adherence, adequate sample size, and sophisticated statistical analyses all constitute strengths of van Balkom et al.'s (1998) report. In particular, the authors use state-of-the-art reliable change indices to examine the clinical relevance of their data. However, several methodological shortcomings should be noted. No mention is made of assessor blindness or training, nor are data on treatment adherence provided. Most important, as noted above, the EX/RP version employed in this study was inadequate. First, the length of session was relatively short (45 minutes), and sessions were held once per week instead of the more frequent schedule recommended. Second, it is unclear how much homework patients were asked to complete between sessions, how long their homework exposures were, and to what extent patients complied with homework assignments. Third, discussion of negative consequences in the first six sessions is an important component of EX/RP, and banning such discussion constitutes further dilution of this treatment and its rationale (see Foa & Kozak, 1996). As would be expected, the results of this truncated treatment were at best modest, with a mean 32% reduction of OCD symptoms after 16 weeks of treatment.

EX/RP Versus Pharmacotherapy With Serotonin Reuptake Inhibitors

In order to glean information from only those studies that meet accepted methodological standards in the field, we restricted our review of the EX/RP versus pharmacotherapy studies to those in which: (a) patients had an established diagnosis of OCD; (b) the design included at least two treatment groups, one of which received SRI or CBT monotherapy (with or without PBO) and the other of which received combined treatment; (c) adequate methodology was employed (see above description of gold standard studies). The six Type 1 studies that met these requirements are discussed below.

Marks, Stern, Mawson, Cobb, and McDonald (1980) conducted the first study that directly compared EX/RP to medication and also allowed for an examination of the efficacy of combined treatment. Using a complex experimental design, 40 patients were randomly assigned to receive initial treatment with either CMI or placebo (PBO) for 4 weeks, followed by 6 weeks of inpatient psychological treatment (daily 45 minute sessions). During the first 3 weeks of this second phase, 10 patients from each medication condition received EX/RP, and the other 10 received relaxation. At week 7, the relaxation groups were switched to EX/RP, and the other patients continued to receive EX/RP. Thus, a direct comparison of CMI plus EX/RP, EX/RP plus PBO, and CMI plus relaxation could be made only at week 7. At the end of the 6-week psychosocial treatment period (week 10), patients were discharged from the hospital but remained on medication until week 36, when a drug taper period commenced. Patients were followed for 1 year following drug discontinuation. Results suggested that, compared with PBO, CMI produced significant improvements in mood and rituals only in those patients who were initially depressed. Compared with relaxation at week 7, EX/RP was associated with greater reductions in rituals but not in mood. Combined treatment did achieve a slight additive effect at week 7 that was no longer evident at follow-up, but the design of this study precluded unequivocal evaluation of the durability of these gains.

Marks et al. (1988) followed up this study with an RCT in which 49 obsessive-compulsive patients were randomized to one of four treatment conditions, three of which included CMI for approximately 6 months and one, PBO. One of the CMI groups received antiexposure instructions for 23 weeks; antiexposure consisted of instructing patients to avoid feared situations or stimuli. The second CMI group had self-controlled exposure for 23 weeks, and the third group received self-controlled exposure for 8 weeks followed by therapist-aided exposure from week 8 until week 23; the PBO group also received self-controlled exposure for 8 weeks followed by therapist-aided exposure until week 23. Most important for our purposes here, CMI plus EX/RP yielded superior outcome at week 8 compared with EX/RP plus PBO on measures of rituals, depression, and social adjustment. At week 23, however, CMI plus EX/RP did not separate from EX/RP plus PBO. Thus, a small but transitory advantage was found for combined treatment over EX/RP monotherapy.

Increasing interest in selective SRIs (SSRIs) and awareness of CMI's unfavorable side effect profile and cardiotoxicity risks prompted comparison of the SSRIs versus combined treatment. Cottraux et al.

(1990) compared the efficacy of fluvoxamine (FLV), EX/RP, and combined treatment. Patients were assigned to one of three conditions: FLV with antiexposure instructions, FLV plus EX/RP, and pill placebo (PBO) with EX/RP. Treatment continued for 24 weeks, after which EX/RP was stopped and medication was tapered over 4 weeks. EX/RP treatment was provided in weekly sessions and consisted of two distinct treatment phases: self-controlled exposure between sessions and imaginal exposure during sessions for the first 8 weeks, followed by 16 weeks of therapist-guided EX/RP. At posttreatment (week 24), reduction in assessor-rated duration of rituals per day was comparable for FLV plus antiexposure versus FLV plus EX/RP, and both were superior to PBO plus EX/RP. FLV plus EX/RP did produce slightly greater improvement in depression at posttreatment than did PBO plus EX/RP, but this difference was no longer evident at follow-up. The means suggest an advantage for combined treatment at the week 24 assessment, but the differences on OCD measures failed to reach statistical significance; insufficient statistical power is invoked as a possible explanation for why the null hypothesis was not rejected. Interestingly, the FLV plus antiexposure group complied minimally with therapy instructions: most reported doing exposure on their own, thus invalidating the comparison between exposure and antiexposure with FLV.

Interest in dismantling the effects of CT from EX/RP and in evaluating combined treatment prompted van Balkom et al. (1998) to design an RCT in which 117 OCD patients were randomized to: (a) CT, (b) EX/RP, (c) FLV plus CT, (d) FLV plus EX/RP, and (e) wait-list. CT and EX/RP were conducted over 16- to 45-minute sessions (6 in the first 8 weeks, followed by 10 in the remaining weeks). In the two combined treatments, FLV was administered alone for 8 weeks, after which medication was stabilized and 10 sessions of CT or EX/RP were added for an additional 8 weeks. The wait-list condition was conducted over 8 weeks. Results indicated that, at midtreatment ($n = 100$), all four active treatments were superior to wait-list, with no significant differences among them. At posttreatment ($n = 86$), the active treatments again failed to separate from one another, suggesting that the addition of FLV did not enhance efficacy of CT or EX/RP, at least as administered in this study.

Hohagen et al. (1998) examined the relative efficacy of combined treatment versus EX/RP plus PBO.

Fifty-eight patients were randomly assigned to one of the two conditions, and EX/RP in both conditions involved a 3-week assessment period followed by a 4-week regimen of thrice-weekly EX/RP. Analyses were conducted on a subset of patients ($n = 49$), with nine outliers dropped in order to equate the two groups on baseline OCD symptom severity. Results indicated that both groups improved significantly and comparably on compulsions, but that the patients who received EX/RP plus FLV were significantly better at posttreatment on obsessions than those who received EX/RP plus PBO. Subanalyses indicated that patients who suffered from secondary depression also fared better if they were receiving EX/RP plus FLV.

Recently, Foa et al. (2005) compared CMI, intensive EX/RP, and their combination (EX/RP plus CMI) with PBO. The EX/RP protocol included an intensive phase (15 two-hour sessions conducted over 3 weeks) followed by weekly sessions delivered over 8 weeks. Results indicated that all active treatments were superior to PBO and that EX/RP was superior to CMI; with respect to the issue of combined treatment versus the monotherapies, results indicated that while EX/RP plus CMI was superior to CMI, EX/RP plus CMI did not differ significantly from EX/RP alone. The design adopted in this study may not have been optimal for identifying an additive effect because the intensive portion of the EX/RP program was completed before the effects of CMI could be realized.

With respect to the hypothesis that combined treatment is superior to EX/RP monotherapy, two studies failed to detect any additive effect on OCD symptoms (Foa et al., 2005; van Balkom et al., 1998), two found a small but transitory advantage (Marks et al., 1980; 1988), one found a difference on measures of depression and a trend on measures of OCD favoring combined treatment at posttreatment that were no longer evident at follow-up (Cottraux et al., 1990), and one (Hohagen et al., 1998) found an advantage for combined treatment over EX/RP alone on obsessions but not on compulsions. Of the two studies that allowed for a clear comparison of combined treatment versus SRI monotherapy, one found an advantage for combined treatment (Foa et al., 2005) and one did not (Cottraux et al., 1990). Collectively, the data may be summarized as being *suggestive* of an advantage for combined treatment, but the picture is by no means clear, nor is the broad statement of its superiority supported. Notably, the two largest of these studies (Foa et al., 2005; van Balkom et al., 1998) did not detect any advantage for combined treatment over EX/RP alone. It is important to note that methodological and procedural differences across these studies, including on variables found to influence outcome in meta-analytic studies such as EX/RP session frequency (e.g., Abramowitz, 1996), may account for differences across studies (for a more detailed discussion of this issue, see Foa, Franklin, & Moser, 2002).

Taken together, the most methodologically sound studies that have directly compared EX/RP monotherapy with combined treatment suggest collectively that although EX/RP is certainly not impeded by SRI pharmacotherapy, there does not appear to be a strong enhancement over EX/RP alone. However, because the designs tested thus far have generally involved simultaneous start of SRI and EX/RP, we do not know whether the addition of EX/RP after SRI treatment had already been initiated would show a superiority of combined treatment. Two reasonable avenues of pursuit in further examining the utility of combined treatment approaches would be (a) to determine whether allowing more opportunity for a response to SRIs at an adequate dose and duration by premedicating patients prior to EX/RP will afford a better test of the relative efficacy of combined treatment over the monotherapies as an initial treatment response; and (b) to examine the utility of combined approaches in a different pool of OCD patients, such as those who have failed to respond adequately to either of the monotherapies alone.

CBT for Pediatric OCD

Age-downward extension of CBT programs for EX/RP began with case series and open clinical trials conducted in the 1980s and 1990s, but only in the past few years have RCT findings been published. Collectively the RCT findings converged with results achieved in the pediatric open trials and with the extensive literature on adult OCD in suggesting that CBT is also efficacious for children and adolescents with OCD (for a recent meta-analysis, see Abramowitz, Whiteside, & Deacon, 2005). Four controlled CBT trials for pediatric OCD have been completed to date (Barrett et al., 2004; de Haan et al., 1998; Pediatric OCD Treatment Study Team, 2004; Piacentini et al., 2005). Below we summarize results from these RCTs.

In the first published study, de Haan et al. (1998) randomly assigned 22 children (mean age 13.7 years, 50% female) to 12 weeks of clomipramine (CMI; mean dose = 2.5 mg/kg) or CBT (EX/RP plus cognitive restructuring). CBT was conducted twice weekly, and the total length of the study was 10 weeks. Both CBT and CMI led to significant improvement; however, even with the relatively small cell sizes, EX/RP was significantly more efficacious than CMI with respect to reduction in symptom severity as measured by the CY-BOCS. A notable limitation of the design of this study was the absence of a no-treatment control group, which limits the extent to which observed treatment effects for both conditions can be specifically attributed to the interventions themselves rather than to the passage of time or nonspecific factors such at psychoeducation, attention, and so forth.

Barrett et al. (2004) compared individual cognitive-behavioral family-based therapy (CBFT, $n = 24$), group CBFT (GCBFT, $n = 29$), and wait-list control (WL, $n = 24$) in 77 OCD youngsters aged 7 to 17 years. Both active treatments consisted of a 14-week manualized protocol that included both parent and sibling components. Participants in the WL group were assessed at baseline and 4 to 6 weeks later. Both active treatments demonstrated significant improvement as compared with the WL group. At posttreatment, 88% of CBFT, 76% of GCBFT, and 0% of WL youngsters no longer met criteria for OCD according to parental report on the Anxiety Disorders Interview Schedule (ADIS). Notably, CBFT showed 65% reduction on the CY-BOCS according to child-only reports as compared with 61% for GCBFT and no change for WL. Observed gains were largely maintained over a 6-month follow-up. Of interest, there were no treatment-related gains on any of the family measures despite the considerable involvement of family in the active interventions. Although unlikely, the shorter duration (4 to 6 weeks) of the WL condition in this study leaves open the possibility that nonspecific effects would have been evident had the WL run the full 14-week course.

In a recently completed randomized controlled trial at UCLA, Piacentini et al. (2005) compared individual CBT (EX/RP plus cognitive therapy) supplemented with a weekly manualized family intervention (F/EX/RP, $n = 49$) to a psychosocial comparison condition, relaxation training/psychoeducation ($n = 22$). Participants ranged in age from 8 to 17 years.

The family intervention was designed to (a) reduce level of conflict and feelings of anger, blame, and guilt; (b) facilitate disengagement from the child's OCD symptoms; (c) rebuild normal (OCD-free) family interaction patterns; and (d) foster an environment conducive to maintaining treatment gains. Both treatments consisted of 14 manualized sessions delivered over 12 weeks. Responders in both conditions were reassessed at 1-month and 6-month follow-ups. Initial results from this study indicate that F/EX/RP was superior to RT in terms of clinician-rated response rate (clinical global improvement score of much or very much improved), but differences on primary continuous outcome measures (e.g., CY-BOCS), although favoring F/EX/RP, did not reach statistical significance. The lack of significant differences on the continuous outcomes is somewhat surprising given that relaxation training has not been shown effective for adult OCD (Fals-Stewart et al., 1993). However, these findings are consistent with results from Silverman et al. (1999) and Last, Hansen, and Franco (1998), both of whom found CBT and a psychosocial comparison condition (psychoeducation/support) equally effective for non-OCD child anxiety disorders.

The Pediatric OCD Treatment Study (POTS) is the largest controlled child OCD trial to date (Pediatric OCD Treatment Study Team, 2004). This multicenter trial of 112 youngsters (aged 7 to 17, with 28 in each treatment group) with OCD compared CBT (i.e., EX/RP), the SSRI medication sertraline (SER), and their combination (COMB) to pill placebo (PBO). Treatment was provided according to detailed manuals of 14 sessions conducted over a 12-week period (Stage I). Stage I responders advanced to an additional 4 weeks of open treatment followed by discontinuation of all active treatment and follow-up evaluations at weeks 16, 20, 24, and 28 (Stage II; Franklin, Foa, & March, 2003). Using an intent-to-treat analytic strategy, all three active treatments significantly outperformed pill placebo. In addition, COMB proved superior to both CBT and SER, which did not differ from one another. However, an examination of "excellent responders," those with a posttreatment score of less than 10 on the CY-BOCS, revealed a significant advantage for the CBT conditions. COMB was associated with a 54% excellent response rate compared with 39% for CBT but only 21% for SER and 3% for PBO. Notably, a significant site by treatment interaction was identified such that CBT alone at Penn was superior to CBT at Duke, with the reverse being true for SER alone. These latter results suggest that in some cases and other certain circumstances, CBT alone may be as effective as combined treatment.

FUTURE DIRECTIONS

Although a great deal is already known about the efficacy of EX/RP and pharmacotherapy for OCD, several issues await further research. Several studies have indicated that OCD patients who respond to SRIs are likely to relapse when the medication is withdrawn, suggesting the need for long-term administration of this treatment. Despite this drawback of psychopharmacology, a substantial number of OCD patients prefer this treatment over EX/RP because they find the latter too frightening. Perhaps the optimal treatment for most patients should involve medication at the start followed by EX/RP implemented after medication has lessened the OCD symptoms and thereby increases the acceptability of EX/RP. In a study now completed at Penn and Columbia (E. B. Foa and M. R. Liebowitz, principal investigators) patients who evidenced partial response to an SRI were randomized to either EX/RP or stress management training (SMT) to examine the augmentative effects of these two cognitive behavioral approaches. Other augmentation strategies have also been evaluated, such as pharmacotherapy with an atypical neuroleptic (McDougal, Epperson, Pelton, Wasylink, & Price, 2000); these alternatives are important to consider with patients who have substantial residual symptoms following SRI pharmacotherapy yet will not accept or do not have access to EX/RP. Psychosurgical alternatives may also hold promise for treatment-refractory patients with severe symptoms and related impairment (Pallanti, Hollander, & Goodman, 2004), although critical long-term follow-up data have yet to be collected regarding the durability of such approaches.

As is apparent from the above review, many variants of EX/RP programs have been utilized in outcome studies, but the effects of the different parameters on treatment outcome have not been studied systematically. Studies comparing intensive versus weekly EX/RP protocols both consisting of treatment components believed to be important (e.g., imaginal and in vivo exposure, strict ritual prevention, thera-

pist-assisted exposure) will help determine the degree to which outcome is compromised simply by decreasing frequency of sessions. Results of a comparison of twice-weekly EX/RP treatment to findings from an otherwise identical intensive (daily) EX/RP regimen suggest superior outcome for the intensive treatment at posttreatment but not at 3-month follow-up (Abramowitz, Foa, & Franklin, 2003), which suggests the possibility that twice-weekly EX/RP may indeed be a viable alternative to intensive treatment. We also need more studies comparing therapist-aided exposure versus self-exposure before advocating reduction of therapist contact. Early investigations did address some of these issues, but their methodologies were flawed and the number of patients too small to arrive at firm conclusions.

Researchers have already identified several factors that are associated with poor outcome of EX/RP and medication (e.g., presence of schizotypal personality disorder; Minichiello, Baer, & Jenike, 1987). More recent studies have also suggested that severe overvalued ideation (Foa et al., 1999) and severe depression (Abramowitz et al., 2000) may also attenuate outcome somewhat. These patient characteristics must therefore be evaluated and taken into account by EX/RP therapists. Further, given that psychiatric comorbidity appears to be the rule, studies are needed to examine the best way to treat these OCD patients. Several alternative strategies may be used, such as treating the comorbid condition, then addressing OCD, but the evidence base for the treatment of OCD patients with substantial psychiatric comorbidity remains weak.

Despite overwhelming evidence for its efficacy, EX/RP's availability for adults and children continues to be limited. The paucity of therapists trained in its use may be a function at least in part of OCD's relatively low prevalence because it may be difficult to develop expertise in this form of treatment if OCD patients are encountered only occasionally in one's general practice clinic. Effectiveness studies that include extensive training of "frontline" clinicians followed by access to expert supervision may help overcome this shortage of trained treatment providers. Notably, Valderhaug, Gotestam, Larsson, and Piacentini (2004) have already conducted such a study in pediatric OCD in which EX/RP delivered by supervised counselors in rural Norway yielded substantial and lasting reductions in OCD symptom severity. The dissemination of less intensive treatment regimens may also help to increase the use of EX/RP, as intensive therapy may be rejected on practical grounds by clinicians and patients alike. Instead of such widespread dissemination efforts, another alternative to make EX/RP more available would be to support the development of regional centers of expertise that would function as many cancer treatment centers currently do: working actively with referral sources to solicit and accept cases, providing training opportunities for those who wish to specialize, and attempting to ensure that excellent clinical care is available for patients and their families within a reasonable distance from home. It is likely that endeavors such as these will be attempted in the next decade because it is unfortunately the case that EX/RP remains largely an "ivory tower" treatment that is not easily accessed by many of those who might benefit from it most.

ACKNOWLEDGMENT

This chapter was supported by NIMH grants MH45404 and MH55126.

REFERENCES

Abramowitz, J. S. (1996). Variants of exposure and response prevention in the treatment of obsessive-compulsive disorder: A meta-analysis. *Behavior Therapy, 27*, 583–600.

Abramowitz, J. S, Foa, E. B., & Franklin, M. E. (2003). Exposure and ritual prevention for obsessive-compulsive disorder: Effects of intensive versus twice-weekly sessions. *Journal of Consulting and Clinical Psychology, 71*, 394–398.

Abramowitz, J. S., Franklin, M. E., Street, G. P., Kozak, M. J., & Foa, E. B. (2000). The effects of pre-treatment depression on cognitive-behavioral treatment outcome in OCD clinic outpatients. *Behavior Therapy, 31*, 517–528.

Abramowitz, J. S., Whiteside, S. P., & Deacon, B. J. (2005). The effectiveness of treatment for pediatric obsessive-compulsive disorder: A meta-analysis. *Behavior Therapy, 36*, 55–63.

American Psychiatric Association. (2000). *Diagnostic and statistical manual of mental disorders* (4th ed., Text revision). Washington, DC: Author.

Barrett, P., Healy-Farrell, L., & March, J. S. (2004). Cognitive-behavioral family treatment of childhood obsessive-compulsive disorder: A controlled trial. *Journal of the American Academy of Child and Adolescent Psychiatry, 43*, 46–62.

Beck, A. T., Ward, C. H., Mendelson, M., Mock, J., & Erbaugh, J. (1961). An inventory for measuring depression. *Archives of General Psychiatry, 4*, 561–571.

Cottraux, J., Mollard, E., Bouvard, M., Marks, I., Sluys, M., Nury, A. M., et al. (1990). A controlled study of fluvoxamine and exposure in obsessive-compulsive disorder. *International Clinical Psychopharmacology, 5*, 17–30.

Cottraux, J., Note, I., Yao, S. N., Lafont, S., Note, B., Mollard, E., et al. (2001). A randomized controlled trial of cognitive therapy versus intensive behavior therapy in obsessive compulsive disorder. *Psychotherapy and Psychosomatics, 70*, 288–297.

de Araujo, L. A., Ito, L. M., Marks, I. M., & Deale, A. (1995). Does imagined exposure to the consequences of not ritualising enhance live exposure for OCD? A controlled study. I. Main outcome. *British Journal of Psychiatry, 167*, 65–70.

de Haan, E., Hoogduin, K. A. L., Buitelaar, J. K., & Keijsers, G. P. J. (1998). Behavior therapy versus clomipramine for the treatment of obsessive-compulsive disorder in children and adolescents. *Journal of the American Academy of Child and Adolescent Psychiatry, 37*, 1022–1029.

Dollard, J., & Miller, N. E. (1950). *Personality and psychotherapy: An analysis in terms of learning, thinking and culture.* New York: McGraw-Hill.

Eichstedt, J. A., & Arnold, S. L. (2001). Childhood-onset obsessive-compulsive disorder: A tic-related subtype of OCD? *Clinical Psychology Review, 21*, 137–158.

Emmelkamp, P. M. G., & Beens, H. (1991). Cognitive therapy with obsessive-compulsive disorder: A comparative evaluation. *Behaviour Research and Therapy, 29*, 293–300.

Emmelkamp, P. M. G., de Haan, E., & Hoogduin, C. A. L. (1990). Marital adjustment and obsessive-compulsive disorder. *British Journal of Psychiatry, 156*, 55–60.

Emmelkamp, P. M. G., van der Helm, M., van Zanten, B. L., & Plochg, I. (1980). Treatment of obsessive-compulsive patients: The contribution of self-instructional training to the effectiveness of exposure. *Behaviour Research and Therapy, 18*, 61–66.

Emmelkamp, P. M. G., Visser, S., & Hoekstra, R. J. (1988). Cognitive therapy vs. exposure *in vivo* in the treatment of obsessive-compulsives. *Cognitive Therapy and Research, 12*, 103–114.

Fals-Stewart, W., Marks, A. P., & Schafer, J. (1993). A comparison of behavioral group therapy and individual behavior therapy in treating obsessive-compulsive disorder. *Journal of Nervous and Mental Disease, 181,* 189–193.

Fernandez-Cordoba, E., & Lopez-Ibor Alino, J. (1967). Monochlorimipramine in mental patients resisting other forms of treatment. *Actas Luso-Espanolas de Neurologia y Psiquitria, 26,* 119–147.

Flament, M. F., Koby, E., Rapoport, J. L., Berg, C. J., Zahn, T., Cox, C., Denckla, M., et al. (1990). Childhood obsessive-compulsive disorder: A prospective follow-up study. *Journal of Child Psychology and Psychiatry and Allied Disciplines, 31,* 363–380.

Flament, M. F., Whitaker, A., Rapoport, J. L., Davies, M., Zaremba, C., Kalikow, K., et al. (1988). Obsessive compulsive disorder in adolescence: An epidemiological study. *Journal of the American Academy of Child and Adolescent Psychiatry, 27,* 764–771.

Foa, E. B., Abramowitz, J. S., Franklin, M. E., & Kozak, M. J. (1999). Feared consequences, fixity of belief, and treatment outcome in OCD. *Behavior Therapy, 30,* 717–724.

Foa, E. B., Franklin, M. E., & Moser, J. (2002). Context in the clinic: How well do CBT and medications work in combination? *Biological Psychiatry, 51,* 989–997.

Foa, E. B., & Goldstein, A. (1978). Continuous exposure and complete response prevention in the treatment of obsessive-compulsive neurosis. *Behavior Therapy, 9,* 821–829.

Foa, E. B., & Kozak, M. J. (1985). Treatment of anxiety disorders: Implications for psychopathology. In A. H. Tuma & J. D. Maser (Eds.), *Anxiety and the anxiety disorders* (pp. 421–452). Hillsdale, NY: Erlbaum.

Foa, E. B., & Kozak, M. J. (1996). Psychological treatment for obsessive-compulsive disorder. In M. R. Mavissakalian & R. F. Prien (Eds.), *Long-term treatments of anxiety disorders* (pp. 285–309). Washington, DC: American Psychiatric Press.

Foa, E. B., Kozak, M. J., Goodman, W. K., Hollander, E., Jenike, M., & Rasmussen, S. (1995). *DSM-IV* field trial: Obsessive-compulsive disorder. *American Journal of Psychiatry, 152,* 90–94.

Foa, E. B., Kozak, M. J., Steketee, G. S., & McCarthy, P. R. (1992). Treatment of depressive and obsessive-compulsive symptoms in OCD by imipramine and behavior therapy. *British Journal of Clinical Psychology, 31,* 279–292.

Foa, E. B., Liebowitz, M. R., Kozak, M. J., Davies, S. O., Campeas, R., Franklin, M. E., et al. (2005). Treatment of obsessive compulsive disorder by exposure and ritual prevention, clomipramine, and their combination: A randomized, placebo-controlled trial. *American Journal of Psychiatry, 162,* 151–161.

Foa, E. B., Steketee, G., Grayson, J. B., Turner, R. M., & Latimer, P. (1984). Deliberate exposure and blocking of obsessive-compulsive rituals: Immediate and long-term effects. *Behavior Therapy, 15,* 450–472.

Foa, E. B., Steketee, G., Turner, R. M., & Fischer, S. C. (1980). Effects of imaginal exposure to feared disasters in obsessive-compulsive checkers. *Behaviour Research and Therapy, 18,* 449–455.

Foa, E. B., & Tillmanns, A. (1980). The treatment of obsessive-compulsive neurosis. In A. Goldstein & E. B. Foa (Eds.), *Handbook of behavioral interventions: A clinical guide* (pp. 416–500). New York: Wiley.

Franklin, M. E., Abramowitz, J. S., Kozak, M. J., Levitt, J., & Foa, E. B. (2000). Effectiveness of exposure and ritual prevention for obsessive compulsive disorder: Randomized compared with non-randomized samples. *Journal of Consulting and Clinical Psychology, 68,* 594–602.

Franklin, M. E., Foa, E. B., & March, J. S. (2003). The Pediatric OCD Treatment Study (POTS): Rationale, design and methods. *Journal of Child and Adolescent Psychopharmacology, 13*(Suppl. 1), 39–52.

Freeston, M.H., Ladouceur, R., Gagnon, F., & Thibodeau, N. (1997). Cognitive-behavioral treatment of obsessive thoughts: A controlled study. *Journal of Consulting and Clinical Psychology, 65,* 405–413.

Greist, J. H., Jefferson, J. W., Kobak, K. A., Katzelnick, D. J., & Serlin, R. C. (1995). Efficacy and tolerability of serotonin transport inhibitors in obsessive-compulsive disorder: A meta-analysis. *Archives of General Psychiatry, 52,* 53–60.

Hanna, G. L. (1995). Demographic and clinical features of obsessive-compulsive disorder in children and adolescents. *Journal of the American Academy of Child and Adolescent Psychiatry, 34,* 19–27.

Hohagen, F., Winkelman, G., Rasche-Rauchale, H., Hand, I., Konig, A., Munchau, N., et al. (1998). Combination of behaviour therapy with fluvoxamine in comparison with behaviour therapy and placebo: Results of a multicentre study. *British Journal of Psychiatry, 173,* 71–78.

Insel, T. R., Mueller, E. A., Alterman, I., Linnoila, M., & Murphy, D. L. (1985). Obsessive-compulsive disorder and serotonin: Is there a connection? *Biological Psychiatry, 20,* 1174–1188.

Jones, M. K., & Menzies, R. G. (1998). Danger ideation reduction therapy for obsessive-compulsive washers: A controlled trial. *Behaviour Research and Therapy, 36,* 959–970.

Karno, M., Golding, J. M., Sorenson, S. B., & Burnam, M. A. (1988). The epidemiology of obsessive-compulsive disorder in five US communities. *Archives of General Psychiatry, 45,* 1094–1099.

Kozak, M. J., & Foa, E. B. (1994). Obsessions, overvalued ideas, and delusions in obsessive-compulsive disorder. *Behaviour Research and Therapy, 32,* 343–353.

Kozak, M. J., & Foa, E. B. (1996). Obsessive compulsive disorder. In V. B. V. Hasselt & M. Hersen (Eds.), *Sourcebook of psychological treatment manuals for adult disorders* (pp. 65–122). New York: Plenum Press.

Last, C. G., Hansen, C., & Franco, N. (1998). Cognitive-behavioral treatment of school phobia. *Journal of the American Academy of Child and Adolescent Psychiatry, 37,* 404–411.

Leon, A. C., Portera, L., & Weissman, M. M. (1995). The social costs of anxiety disorders. *British Journal of Psychiatry, 166*(Suppl. 27), 19–22.

Lindsay, M., Crino, R., & Andrews, G. (1997). Controlled trial of exposure and response prevention in obsessive-compulsive disorder. *British Journal of Psychiatry, 171,* 135–139.

March, J. S., Frances, A., Carpenter, D., & Kahn, D. (1997). The Expert Consensus Guideline Series: Treatment of obsessive compulsive disorder. *Journal of Clinical Psychiatry, 58*(Suppl. 4), 1–72.

Marks, I., Hodgson, R., & Rachman, S. (1975). Treatment of chronic obsessive-compulsive neurosis by *in vivo* exposure. *British Journal of Psychiatry, 127,* 349–364.

Marks, I. M., Lelliott, P. T., Basoglu, M., Noshirvani, H., Monteiro, W., Cohen, D., et al. (1988). Clomipramine, self-exposure and therapist-aided exposure for obsessive-compulsive rituals. *British Journal of Psychiatry, 152,* 522–534.

Marks, I. M., Stern, R. S., Mawson, D., Cobb, J., & McDonald, R. (1980). Clomipramine and exposure for obsessive-compulsive rituals — I. *British Journal of Psychiatry, 136,* 1–25.

McDougal, C. J., Epperson, C. N., Pelton, G. H., Wasylink, S., & Price, L. H. (2000). A double-blind, placebo-controlled study of risperidone addition in serotonin reuptake inhibitor-refractory obsessive-compulsive disorder. *Archives of General Psychiatry, 57,* 794–801.

McLean, P. L., Whittal, M. L., Thordarson, D. S., Taylor, S., Sochting, I, Koch, W. J., et al. (2001). Cognitive versus behavior therapy in the group treatment of obsessive-compulsive disorder. *Journal of Consulting and Clinical Psychology, 69,* 205–214.

Mehta, M. (1990). A comparative study of family-based and patient-based behavioural management in obsessive-compulsive disorder. *British Journal of Psychiatry, 157,* 133–135.

Meyer, V. (1966). Modification of expectations in cases with obsessional rituals. *Behaviour Research and Therapy, 4,* 273–280.

Meyer, V., & Levy, R. (1973). Modification of behavior in obsessive-compulsive disorders. In H. E. Adams & P. Unikel (Eds.), *Issues and trends in behavior therapy* (pp. 77–136). Springfield, IL: Charles C. Thomas.

Meyer, V., Levy, R., & Schnurer, A. (1974). The behavioural treatment of obsessive-compulsive disorders. In H. R. Beech (Ed.), *Obsessional states* (pp. 233–258). London: Methuen.

Minichiello, W. E., Baer, L., & Jenike, M. A. (1987). Schizotypal personality disorder: A poor prognostic indicator for behavior therapy in the treatment of obsessive-compulsive disorder. *Journal of Anxiety Disorders, 1,* 273–276.

Mowrer, O. H. (1939). A stimulus-response analysis of anxiety and its role as a reinforcing agent. *Psychological Review, 46,* 553–565.

Mowrer, O. H. (1960). *Learning theory and behavior.* New York: Wiley.

Pallanti, S., Hollander, E., & Goodman, W. K. (2004). A qualitative analysis of nonresponse: Management of treatment-refractory obsessive-compulsive disorder. *Journal of Clinical Psychiatry, 65*(Suppl. 114), 6–10.

Pediatric OCD Treatment Study Team. (2004). Cognitive-behavioral therapy, sertraline, and their combination for children and adolescents with obsessive-compulsive disorder: The Pediatric OCD Treatment Study (POTS) randomized controlled trial. *Journal of the American Medical Association, 292,* 1969–1976.

Piacentini, J. C., Jacobs, C., & Bergman, R. L. (2005). *Cognitive behavior therapy for childhood OCD: Efficacy and predictors of treatment response.* Manuscript submitted for publication.

Pitman, R. (1994). Obsessive compulsive disorder in Western history. In E. Hollander, J. Zohar, D. Marazziti, & B. Olivier (Eds.), *Current insights in obsessive compulsive disorder* (pp. 3–10). New York: Wiley.

Rachman, S. J., & Wilson, G. T. (1980). *The effects of psychological therapy.* Oxford, UK: Pergamon Press.

Rapoport, J. L., Swedo, S. E., & Leonard, H. L. (1992). Childhood obsessive compulsive disorder. 144th Annual Meeting of the American Psychiatric Association: Obsessive compulsive disorder: Integrating theory and practice (1991, New Orleans, Louisiana). *Journal of Clinical Psychiatry, 53*(Suppl.), 11–16.

Rasmussen, S. A., & Eisen, J. L. (1989). Clinical features and phenomenology of obsessive compulsive disorder. *Psychiatric Annals, 19*, 67–73.

Rasmussen, S. A., & Eisen, J. L. (1990). Epidemiology of obsessive compulsive disorder. *Journal of Clinical Psychiatry, 51*(2, Suppl.), 10–13.

Rasmussen, S. A., & Tsuang, M. T. (1986). Clinical characteristics and family history in *DSM-III* obsessive-compulsive disorder. *American Journal of Psychiatry, 143*, 317–322.

Riggs, D. S., Hiss, H., & Foa, E. B. (1992). Marital distress and the treatment of obsessive compulsive disorder. *Behavior Therapy, 23*, 585–597.

Roper, G., & Rachman, S. (1976). Obsessional-compulsive checking: Experimental replication and development. *Behaviour Research and Therapy, 14*, 25–32.

Roper, G., Rachman, S., & Hodgson, R. (1973). An experiment of obsessional checking. *Behaviour Research and Therapy, 11*, 271–277.

Rothbaum B. O., & Shahar, F. (2000). Behavioral treatment of obsessive-compulsive disorder in a naturalistic setting. *Cognitive and Behavioral Practice, 7*, 262–270.

Salkovskis, P. M. (1985). Obsessional compulsive problems: A cognitive behavioral analysis. *Behaviour Research and Therapy, 23*, 571–583.

Silverman, W. K., Kurtines, W. M., Ginsburg, G. S., Weems, C. F., Rabian, B., & Serafini, L. T. (1999). Contingency management, self-control, and education support in the treatment of childhood phobic disorders: A randomized clinical trial. *Journal of Consulting and Clinical Psychology, 67*, 675–687.

Swedo, S. E., Leonard, H. L., Garvey, M., Mittleman, B., Allen, A. J., Perlmutter, S., et al. (1998). Pediatric autoimmune neuropsychiatric disorders associated with streptococcal infections: Clinical description of the first 50 cases. *American Journal of Psychiatry, 155*, 264–271.

Swedo, S. E., Rapoport, J. L., Leonard, H. L., Lenane, M., & Cheslow, D. (1989). Obsessive-compulsive disorder in children and adolescents: Clinical phenomenology of 70 consecutive cases. *Archives of General Psychiatry, 46*, 335–341.

Valderhaug, R., Gotestam, K. G., Larsson, B., & Piacentini, J. C. (2004, May). *An open clinical trial of cognitive behaviour therapy for childhood obsessive-compulsive disorder in regular outpatient clinics.* Paper presented at the SOGN Centre Conference on Pediatric Anxiety Disorders in Children and Adolescents, Oslo, Norway.

Valleni-Basile, L. A., Garrison, C. Z., Jackson, K. L., Waller, J. L., McKeown, R. E., Addy, C. L., et al. (1994). Frequency of obsessive-compulsive disorder in a community sample of young adolescents. *Journal of the American Academy of Child and Adolescent Psychiatry, 33*, 782–791.

van Balkom, A. J. L. M., de Haan, E., van Oppen, P., Spinhoven, P., Hoogduin, K. A. L., & van Dyk, R. (1998). Cognitive and behavioral therapies alone versus in combination with fluvoxamine in the treatment of obsessive-compulsive disorder. *Journal of Nervous and Mental Disease, 186*, 492–499.

Warren, R., & Thomas, J. C. (2001). Cognitive-behavior therapy of obsessive-compulsive disorder in private practice: An effectiveness study. *Journal of Anxiety Disorders, 15*, 277–285.

Weizman, A., Carmi, M., Hermesh, H., Shahar, A., Apter, A., Tyano, S., et al. (1986). High-affinity imipramine binding and serotonin uptake in platelets of eight adolescent and ten adult obsessive-compulsive patients. *American Journal of Psychiatry, 143*, 335–339.

Whittal, M. L., Thordarson, D. S., McLean, P. D. (in press). Treatment of obsessive-compulsive disorder: Cognitive behavior therapy vs. exposure and response prevention. *Behaviour Research and Therapy.*

Zohar, J., & Insel, T. R. (1987). Drug treatment of obsessive-compulsive disorder. *Journal of Affective Disorders, 13*, 193–202.

16

Pharmacological Treatments
for Obsessive-Compulsive Disorder

Darin D. Dougherty
Scott L. Rauch
Michael A. Jenike

There is overwhelming evidence of the most rigorous type supporting the efficacy of serotonin reuptake inhibitors (SRIs) in the treatment of obsessive-compulsive disorder (OCD). Along with SRIs, behavior therapy must be considered a viable first-line therapy. The best available data suggest that behavior therapy, and perhaps cognitive therapy, is at least as effective as medication in some instances, and may be superior with respect to risks, costs, and enduring benefits. A variety of second-line medication treatments for OCD have been studied in a controlled or systematic fashion. Augmentation of SRIs with clonazepam or buspirone, and with high-potency neuroleptics in cases of a comorbid tic disorder are all provisionally recommended based on the marginal available data. Other augmentation strategies find very limited support at present.

DIAGNOSTIC CRITERIA AND CLINICAL CHARACTERISTICS

Obsessive-compulsive disorder (OCD) is a common condition, with lifetime prevalence estimates of approximately 2 to 3% in the United States and up to 5.5% worldwide (Angst, 1994; Karno, Golding, Sorenson, & Burnam, 1988; Rasmussen & Eisen, 1994). The hallmark signs and symptoms of OCD, which is classified among the anxiety disorders, include intrusive unwanted thoughts (i.e., obsessions) and repetitive behaviors (i.e., compulsions; American Psychiatric Association [APA], 1994). Classic obsessions include violent, religious, or sexual themes, as well as preoccupations with contamination, pathological doubting or uncertainty, concerns with symmetry, and a general sense that something bad will happen if a particular ritual is not performed in precisely the right manner. Classic compulsions include washing, cleaning, counting, checking, repeating, and arranging behaviors. For most, the disease manifests itself as

multiple obsessions and multiple compulsions (Rasmussen & Eisen, 1994). Experiencing occasional unwanted thoughts, performing repetitive or ritualistic behaviors, and having transient feelings of anxiety are all part of normal human experience. However, in order to meet the criteria for OCD, the symptoms must be sufficiently intense or frequent to cause marked distress or impair functioning. In fact, people with OCD are often severely impaired by the symptoms of their disease. Unlike psychosis, OCD is characterized by intact insight; because people with OCD recognize that their thoughts and behaviors are extreme or nonsensical, they are often embarrassed or ashamed of their condition and frightened that they may be "going crazy." In severe cases of OCD, insight can become tenuous as obsessions progress to overvalued ideas, prompting the special diagnostic designation of "OCD with poor insight" (APA 1994).

The differential diagnosis of OCD includes other psychiatric disorders that are characterized by repetitive thoughts or behaviors. For instance, the obsessions of OCD are to be distinguished from the ruminations of major depression, the racing thoughts of mania, the psychotic thoughts of schizophrenia, and the preoccupation with food and body image associated with eating disorders. Likewise, the compulsions of OCD are to be distinguished from the tics of Tourette's syndrome (TS), the ritualized self-injurious behaviors of borderline personality disorder, the rhythmic movements that can present in autism or mental retardation, and the stereotypes of complex partial seizures. By definition, the diagnosis of OCD should not be made if the symptoms can be attributed to another disorder or are the consequence of substance use (APA, 1994).

Although the current diagnostic scheme classifies OCD as an anxiety disorder, a variety of disorders from other categories within *Diagnostic and Statistical Manual of Mental Disorders* (APA, 1994) are also characterized by repetitive symptoms (Hollander., 1993, Hollander et al., 1996; McElroy, Phillips, & Keck, 1994). The term *obsessive-compulsive spectrum disorders* (OCSDs) has been coined to reflect the notion that a family of similar disorders may exist that share some common phenomenological, etiological, and perhaps pathophysiological characteristics. Such OCSDs include TS (characterized by intrusive sensations and urges, as well as a drive to perform motor and vocal tics), trichotillomania (characterized by compulsive hair pulling), and body dysmorphic disorder (characterized by a preoccupation with certain aspects of one's own appearance). It remains to be seen whether the concept of OCSDs will prove clinically useful or neurobiologically valid, as well as which disorders can be meaningfully grouped together and by what criteria. Comorbidity with OCD is common; in addition to other OCSDs, frequently coexisting conditions include major affective disorders, other anxiety disorders, and substance use disorders (Karno et al., 1988; Rasmussen & Eisen, 1994).

ETIOLOGY AND NEUROBIOLOGY

Although the cause of OCD remains unknown, family-genetic studies suggest that there may be multiple etiological subtypes (e.g., Pauls & Leckman 1986; Pauls, Alsobrook, Goodman, Rasmussen, & Leckman, 1995). Specifically, family-genetic studies indicate that in some cases OCD seems to arise sporadically,

whereas in others there exists an apparent familial relationship suggestive of an autosomal dominant mode of inheritance with incomplete penetrance. In several twin studies summarized by Rasmussen and Tsuang (1986), concordance rates ranged from 53 to 87% for monozygotic twins and from 22 to 47% for dizygotic twins depending on the sample and the diagnostic criteria. In cohorts where a familial relationship is present, in some cases the affected members present with only OCD, whereas in other pedigrees the affected individuals have OCD or a tic disorder or both. The apparent phenomenological and familial overlap between OCD and TS extends to neurobiology as well. Again, although the pathophysiology of these disorders is incompletely understood, for both OCD and TS, contemporary neurobiological models implicate dysfunction in one or another of several segregated corticostriatal pathways (Baxter et al., 1990; Insel, 1992; Rapoport & Wise, 1988; Rauch & Jenike, 1993; Rauch, Whalen, Dougherty, & Jenike, 1998). OCD seems to involve subtle structural abnormalities in the caudate nucleus, as well as functional dysregulation of neural circuits comprising orbitofrontal cortex, cingulate cortex, and the caudate. Similarly, TS seems to involve subtle structural abnormalities in the putamen. In this way, OCD can be conceptualized as a disease involving cognitive and paralimbic corticostriatal networks, whereas TS involves a sensorimotor corticostriatal network (see Rauch et al., 1998, for review). Recent research suggests that autoimmune processes, precipitated in some cases by beta-hemolytic streptococcal infection, may cause damage to striatal neurons in occasional sporadic childhood-onset cases of OCD and TS (Allen, Leonard, & Swedo, 1995; Swedo 1994; Swedo, Leonard, & Kiessling, 1994; Swedo et al., 1998). Neurochemically, serotonergic systems have been implicated in OCD (Rauch et al., 1998), whereas dopaminergic systems have been implicated in TS (e.g., Mallison et al., 1995). This reflects the neurochemistry of the projections to the relevant striatal territories and also parallels what has been observed regarding the effective pharmacotherapy for these disorders in terms of monotherapies (see Rauch et al., 1998). Of note, however, some recent imaging studies have also implicated the dopaminergic system in OCD (see Denys, Zohar, & Westenberg, 2004; Denys, van der Wee, Janssen, De Geus, & Westenberg, 2004), which resonates with emerging evidence supporting augmentation therapy with dopaminergic antagonist medications for OCD (e.g., McDougle, Epperson, Pelton, Wasylink, & Price, 2000; Denys, de Geus, van Megen, & Westenberg, 2004).

OCD: A HISTORICAL PERSPECTIVE

Descriptions of probable OCD date back to the 15th century, and up through the 1700s the malady was conceptualized in religious or supernatural terms (Hunter & Macalpine, 1982; Pitman, 1994). Treatments such as exorcism notwithstanding, clinical reports and attempts to medically or scientifically characterize OCD did not emerge until the late 1800s, when neurologists including Georges Gilles de la Tourette (1885) described OCD symptoms in the context of movement disorders. In the early 1900s, other clinicians contributed eloquent phenomenological descriptions of obsessive-compulsive symptoms (Janet, 1903; Meige & Feindel, 1907), but little progress was made toward effective treatment of OCD. Freud's case of the Rat man (1909/1924) introduced the application of psychodynamic principles in attempts to both understand and relieve what he termed *obsessional neurosis.*

It was not until 1967 that the tricyclic antidepressant clomipramine, the first available serotonergic reuptake inhibitor (SRI), emerged as an effective treatment for OCD (Fernandez & Lopez-Ibor, 1967). Contemporaneously, behavioral therapy for OCD was emerging as a viable treatment modality and the object of formal study (Rachman, Hodgson, & Marks, 1971). Interestingly, it was also in the 1960s that Ballantine and colleagues first began their pioneering efforts to systematically study the safety and efficacy of anterior cingulotomy, a neurosurgical treatment for severe treatment-refractory OCD and other psychiatric illnesses (Ballantine, Bouckoms, Thomas, & Giriunas, 1987).

The subsequent quarter century has seen great development in the assessment and treatment of OCD. Several educational and self-help books written for lay audiences (e.g., Baer, 1991; Rapoport, 1989), articles appearing in the general medical literature (Jenike, 1989), and the birth of an advocacy group (OC Foundation, Inc., 676 State St., New Haven, CT 06511; 203–315–9190; http://www.ocfoundation.org) all contributed to a growing awareness of OCD. Whereas it had still been believed that OCD was a relatively

rare disorder (approximately 0.1% lifetime prevalence), publication of the Epidemiological Catchment Area study results (Karno et al., 1988) surprised much of the psychiatric and public health community by suggesting that OCD had a lifetime prevalence of 2.6%, ranking it as the fourth most common psychiatric illness in the United States. In 1989, a collaborative group of investigators from Yale University and Brown University published studies reporting on the validation of a scale for quantifying the severity of OCD symptoms (Goodman, Price, Rasmussen, Mazure, Fleischmann et al., 1989, Goodman, Price, Rasmussen, Mazure, Delgado et al. 1989). The Yale-Brown Obsessive Compulsive Scale (YBOCS) has since become the gold standard measure for many of the clinical trials that followed. During this same era the pharmaceutical industry produced a new class of compounds known as *selective serotonergic reuptake inhibitors* (SSRIs) that, like clomipramine (CMI), acted via blockade of serotonergic reuptake sites. Unlike CMI, however, these new SSRIs had much lower affinities for adrenergic and cholinergic receptors, presumably conferring upon them a more favorable side-effect profile. Investigators in psychopharmacology proceeded to systematically study these new agents, as well as other novel compounds, while their psychotherapist counterparts conducted investigations of cognitive and behavioral treatments. During the 1990s alone, there were more than 1,500 reports about drug treatments and OCD published in medical sources. Moreover, neuroscience advances have brought us closer to understanding the etiology and pathophysiology of OCD and related disorders.

CONTEMPORARY TREATMENT FOR OCD

Numerous reviews have been written in the last few years regarding treatment recommendations for OCD (e.g., Dominguez & Mestre, 1994; Dougherty, Rauch, & Jenike, 2004; Goodman, McDougle, & Price, 1992; Jenike 1993a, 1993b; Jenike, 1998; Jenike & Rauch, 1994; Montgomery 1994; Rauch & Jenike, 1994; see Table 16.1). There is broad agreement among experts in the field that first-line treatments for OCD include SRIs (CMI or SSRIs) and/or behavior therapy. When these first-line interventions fail, second-line pharmacological approaches include augmentation of SRIs with additional medications or

TABLE 16.1 Sample Treatment Recommendations for OCD

Treatment	Dosage	Time Course
First Line		
Behavior therapy		
Exposure and response prevention		At least 20 hours
Medication: Serial SRI trials (consider at least two SSRI trials and one of CMI)		
CMI	150–250 mg/day	12 weeks
Fluoxetine	40–80 mg/day	12 weeks
Sertraline	50–200 mg/day	12 weeks
Fluvoxamine	200–300 mg/day	12 weeks
Paroxetine	40–60 mg/day	12 weeks
Citalopram	40–60 mg/day	12 weeks
Escitalopram	20–30 mg/day	12 weeks
Second Line		
Modifications to behavior therapy		
Consider inpatient sessions; home visits or other in situ sessions; or cognitive therapy		
Medication: SRI augmentation		
Clonazepam	0.5–5 mg/day	4 weeks
Buspirone	15–60 mg/day	8 weeks
Neuroleptics		
Pimozide	1–3 mg/day	4 weeks
Haloperidol	0.5–10 mg/day	4 weeks
Risperidone	0.5–6 mg/day	4 weeks
Olanzapine	2.5–15 mg/day	4 weeks
Medication: Alternative monotherapies		
Clonazepam	0.5–5 mg/day	4 weeks
Buspirone	30–60 mg/day	6 weeks
Phenelzine	60–90 mg/day	10 weeks
Third Line		
Consider neurosurgery (only if OCD is long-standing, severe, debilitating, and unresponsive to an exhaustive array of other treatments)		

trials of alternative medications as monotherapies in place of SRIs. Third-line treatments may include experimental treatments such as unproven augmentation therapies or intravenous CMI if available (Fallon et al.; 1992, Fallon et al. 1998; Koran, Sallee, & Pallanti, 1997; Warneke, 1989). Finally, other non-pharmacological treatments, including neurosurgery and electroconvulsive therapy (ECT), have remained more controversial and are reserved for particular clinical situations or as treatments of last resort. In the following section, the scientific evidentiary basis for these various treatment recommendations is reviewed. Although the focus in this chapter is on psychopharmacology, the authors wish to explicitly emphasize that most experts view behavior therapy as a critical and effective first-line treatment for OCD, and that this brand of treatment is all too often overlooked or unavailable.

Measures of Symptom Severity and Treatment Response

Before reviewing the extensive database on clinical trials in OCD, it is worth considering the instruments available for measuring severity of symptoms and clinical improvement. The tools for quantifying the dependent variables in these studies as well as the thresholds that are adopted to operationalize "treatment response" profoundly impact the results and interpretations of clinical research.

As noted above, the gold standard instrument for quantifying OCD symptom severity is the YBOCS (Goodman, Price, Rasmussen, Mazure, Fleischmann, et al., 1989, Goodman, Price, Rasmussen, Mazure, Delgado et al. 1989), a rater-administered scale scored from 0 to 40, with high values reflecting more severe symptoms. The YBOCS comprises 10 elements, 5 elements about obsessions and 5 about compulsions (i.e., frequency/time consumed, interference, distress, resistance, and control over symptoms). Each element is rated from 0 to 4. Alternative contemporary rater-administered instruments include unidimensional global scales (Pato, Eisen, & Pato, 1994). The National Institute of Mental Health Global Obsessive Compulsive Scale (NIMH-GOCS; Insel et al., 1983) is a 15-point scale that has been shown to correlate with the YBOCS, although the descriptive anchor points of the NIMH-GOCS tend to emphasize elements of interference and resistance. Clinical Global Improvement (CGI; see Pato et al., 1994) scales represent another type of unidimensional rater-administered instruments that are commonly used in clinical trials, such as the 7-point CGI with anchor points including, 1 = very much improved, 4 = no change, and 7 = very much worse. The rater-administered CGI has also been shown to correlate well with the YBOCS and NIMH-GOCS; modified versions of the CGI can be self-administered by patients. Other self-administered instruments include the Leyton Obsessional Inventory (LOI; Cooper 1970) and the Maudsley Obsessive Compulsive Inventory (MOCI; Rachman & Hodgson, 1980). As inventories, both consist of symptom-related and/or trait-related questions with binary response options (i.e., yes/no or true/false). Self-ratings can be particularly problematic in OCD, which, together with the fact that these scales are limited to specific symptom sets, make them suboptimal for characterizing symptom severity or gauging clinical improvement in treatment trials (see Kim, Dysken, & Kuskowski, 1990; Pato et al., 1994).

Typically, for studies that report a percentage of responders, criteria for response might include decrease in YBOCS of at least 25% or 35%, and/or a CGI of 1 or 2. Therefore, it is important to appreciate that a substantial proportion of "responders" in these studies remain symptomatic and meaningfully affected by their residual illness.

First-Line Pharmacotherapy: SRIs

Currently, the SRIs are the first-line treatment for OCD (Dougherty & Rauch, 1997). There is overwhelming evidence from multiple randomized, double-blind, placebo-controlled studies supporting the efficacy of SRIs in the treatment of OCD (Table

16.2). Specifically, in adults, well-designed and well-controlled trials have demonstrated the relative efficacy of CMI versus placebo, as well as the relative efficacy of SSRIs, including fluoxetine, sertraline, paroxetine, and fluvoxamine versus placebo. Moreover, SRIs have been shown to be significantly more effective than non-SRI tricyclic antidepressants (TCAs) in placebo-controlled as well as non-placebo-controlled studies (Table 16.3). In the only randomized, double-blind, placebo-controlled study involving non-SRI TCAs, nortriptyline was not shown to be significantly more effective than placebo (Thoren, Asberg, Cronholm, Jornestedt, & Traskman, 1980; Table 16.2), supporting the view that non-SRI TCAs are not an effective monotherapy for OCD.

Despite a wide range of observed SRI response rates, large-scale studies have generally yielded approximately 40 to 60% responders, with mean improvement in the active treatment group of approximately 20 to 40% (see Greist, Jefferson, Kobak, Chouinard, et al., 1995). In terms of the relative efficacy among SRIs, a large-scale meta-analysis of multicenter trials of SRIs was performed by Greist, Jefferson, Kobak, Katzelnick, and colleagues (1995) in which CMI ($n = 520$), fluoxetine ($n = 355$), sertraline ($n = 325$), and fluvoxamine ($n = 320$) were all shown to be significantly superior to placebo. This meta-analysis further indicated that CMI might have superior efficacy over SSRIs. Although the meta-analysis of Greist et al. had many strengths, including that all studies used comparable parameters and were conducted at essentially the same centers, the results should be interpreted with caution. Since there was a serial progression in the availability of these agents and in the performance of these trials, CMI was studied on an SRI-naive population, whereas each successive agent was undoubtedly tried on a cohort comprising a larger subpopulation of patients with histories of past SRI unresponsiveness. Consequently, each successive trial might well have been conducted on a more treatment-resistant population, biasing the efficacy in favor of agents studied in earlier years (i.e., CMI). In fact, a growing number of studies (see Table 16.3) and a recent comprehensive literature review (Pigott & Seay, 1999) suggest that the SRIs all have comparable efficacy. However, despite these group data, any single individual may respond very well to one or two agents of the SRI medications and not the others. Thus, serial

TABLE 16.2 Placebo-Controlled Trials of SRI Therapy for Obsessive-Compulsive Disorder (Adults)

Treatment Conditions	N	Comments	Study
CMI vs. placebo	20	CMI significantly superior to placebo	Karabanow (1977)
CMI vs. placebo crossover	14	CMI significantly superior to placebo	Montgomery (1980)
CMI vs. nortriptyline vs. placebo	24	CMI, but not nortriptyline, superior to placebo	Thoren et al. (1980)
CMI vs. placebo	12	CMI significantly superior to placebo	Mavissakalian et al. (1985)
CMI vs. placebo	27	CMI significantly superior to placebo	Jenike et al. (1989)*
CMI vs. placebo	32	73% improved on CMI; 6% improved on placebo	Greist et al. (1990)*
CMI vs. placebo	239	38% average decrease in symptoms with CMI 3% average decrease in symptoms with placebo	CMI collaborative group (1991)
CMI vs. placebo	281	44% average decrease in symptoms with CMI 5% average decrease in symptoms with placebo	CMI collaborative group (1991)
CMI vs. placebo	36	CMI significantly superior to placebo	Foa et al. (2005)
CMI vs. venlafaxine	47/26	50% CMI responders; 36% venlafaxine responders; no statistically significant difference	Albert et al. (2002)
CMI vs. fluvoxamine	227	Both effective with no statistically significant difference	Mundo et al. (2001)
CMI vs. fluvoxamine	65/68	Both effective with no statistically significant difference	Mundo et al. (2000)
Sertraline vs. placebo	325	Sertraline significantly superior to placebo	Greist et al. (1995)
Sertraline vs. placebo	167	Sertraline significantly superior to placebo	Kronig et al. (1999)
Sertraline vs. fluoxetine	77/73	Equivalent improvement on Y-BOCS; higher proportion of remission with sertraline	Bergeron et al. (2002)
Sertraline vs. desipramine	166	Sertraline significantly superior to desipramine	Hoehn-Saric et al. (2000)
Fluvoxamine vs. placebo	16	Fluvoxamine significantly superior to placebo	Perse et al. (1987)
Fluvoxamine vs. placebo	42	Fluvoxamine significantly superior to placebo	Goodman et al. (1989)
Fluvoxamine vs. placebo	38	Fluvoxamine significantly superior to placebo	Jenike, Hyman, et al. (1990)
Fluvoxamine vs. placebo	320	Fluvoxamine significantly superior to placebo	Rasmussen et al. (in press)
Fluvoxamine vs. placebo	160	Fluvoxamine significantly superior to placebo	Goodman et al. (1996)
Fluvoxamine vs. BT vs. placebo	31	BT superior to fluvoxamine, which was superior to placebo	Nakatani et al. (2005)
Fluvoxamine CR vs. placebo	127/126	Fluvoxamine CR significantly superior to placebo	Hollander, Koran, et al. (2003)
Fluoxetine vs. placebo	355	Fluoxetine (20, 40, 60 mg) significantly superior to placebo	Tollefson, Rampey, et al. (1994)

TABLE 16.2 (continued)

Treatment Conditions	N	Comments	Study
Fluoxetine vs. placebo	217	Fluoxetine (40, 60 mg) significantly superior to placebo; 20-mg effects equal to placebo	Montgomery et al. (1993)
Paroxetine vs. placebo	348	Paroxetine (40, 60 mg) significantly superior to placebo; 20-mg effects equal to placebo	Wheadon et al. (1993)
Paroxetine vs. venlafaxine	75/75	Equally efficacious	Denys et al. (2003)

trials of each agent may be required to determine which drug is best.

Data regarding duration of treatment, optimal dose, and side effects are also plentiful, but difficult to interpret with confidence because studies were often not designed to specifically answer these questions. The collective wisdom, purportedly supported by the data from the multicenter trials as well as anecdotal clinical experience, has been that response to SRIs is typically delayed such that an adequate trial of an SRI requires at least 10 weeks' duration. Indeed, a meaningful proportion of responders continue to emerge past the 8-week mark in these studies, as well as in anecdotal clinical experience. Ex-

TABLE 16.3 Non-Placebo-Controlled Trials of Drug Therapy for OCD (Adults)

Treatment Conditions	N	Comments	Study
CMI vs. amitriptyline	20	CMI significantly superior to amitriptyline	Ananth et al. (1981)
CMI vs. amitriptyline	39	95% improved on CMI 56% improved on amitriptyline	Zhao (1991)
CMI vs. clorgyline	13	CMI effective; clorgyline ineffective	Insel et al. (1983)
CMI vs. clorgyline	12	CMI superior to clorgyline	Zahn et al. (1984)
CMI vs. doxepin	32	78% markedly improved on CMI 36% markedly improved on doxepin	Cui (1986)
CMI vs. fluvoxamine	6	Comparable efficacy	Den Boer et al. (1987)
CMI vs. fluvoxamine	66	Comparable efficacy	Freeman et al. (1994)
CMI vs. fluvoxamine	79	Comparable efficacy	Koran et al. (1996)
CMI vs. fluvoxamine	26	Comparable efficacy	Milanfranchi et al. (1997)
CMI vs. fluvoxamine	133	Comparable efficacy	Mundo et al. (2000)
CMI vs. fluoxetine	11	Comparable efficacy	Pigott et al. (1990)
CMI vs. fluoxetine	55	Comparable efficacy	Lopez-Ibor et al. (1996)
CMI vs. imipramine	16	CMI superior to imipramine	Volavka et al. (1985)
CMI vs. imipramine crossover	12	CMI superior to imipramine	Lei (1986)
CMI vs. paroxetine	406	Comparable efficacy	Zohar et al. (1996)
Fluvoxamine vs. paroxetine vs. citalopram	30	Comparable efficacy	Mundo, Bianchi, et al. (1997)
Citalopram	29	76% improved in 24-week open-label trial	Koponen et al. (1997)
Citalopram	18	14 of 18 showed reduced Y-BOCS score in open-label trial	Marazziti et al. (2001)
Venlafaxine	39	69% improved in open-label trial	Hollander et al. (2003)

Source: Adapted from Jenike 1998.

perts also suggest that optimal doses of SRIs for OCD may exceed those typically used for major depression (e.g., Montgomery et al., 1993), although the dose-comparison studies of OCD have not always shown significant dose-dependent responses across the OCD study population (e.g., Greist, Chouinard, et al., 1995). As for side effects, although the meta-analysis of Greist, Jefferson, Kobak, Katzelnick et al. (1995) did not find any significant difference between medication groups regarding dropout rates due to side effects, this is a relatively insensitive measure of side-effect profile. Also, the aforementioned cohort effects apply for side effects as well; subjects participating in the early CMI trials may have viewed that agent as the only available course of treatment, whereas subjects in later SSRI trials may have been aware of the wider variety of available treatments, making them less willing to endure nuisance side effects. Clearly, as with other TCAs, the risks and side effects mediated by anticholinergic and antiadrenergic mechanisms (e.g., constipation, cardiac conduction disturbances, orthostatic hypotension) are more commonly associated with CMI than with SSRIs. Furthermore, CMI is believed to pose a significant risk with regard to lowering seizure threshold. All SRIs can pose risks (e.g., serotonergic syndrome) and produce a variety of side effects (e.g., nausea, sleep disturbances, sexual disturbances) attributable to their primary mechanism of action via serotonergic reuptake blockade (Grimsley & Jann, 1992). There is no substantive evidence that any SRI is significantly superior or inferior to any other with regard to serotonergically mediated side effects.

Though many clinicians use SRIs as a long-term treatment for OCD, few controlled studies of long-term pharmacotherapy of OCD have been conducted. While most open studies have demonstrated high relapse rates of OCD symptoms within weeks of discontinuation (Thoren et al., 1980; Pato, Zohar-Kaduch, Zohar, & Murphy, 1988), one open-label study of SRI discontinuation found that only 23% of patients relapsed within 1 year (Fontaine & Chouinard, 1989). One randomized, double-blind study incorporating substitution of desipramine for clomipramine in a crossover design found that 89% of patients in the substituted group encountered relapse during a 2-month period (Leonard et al., 1991). More recently, three placebo-controlled relapse prevention studies have been conducted. One study assigned responders to fluoxetine to either continued treatment with fluoxetine ($n = 36$) or placebo ($n = 35$) and found 1-year relapse rates of 17.5% and 38%, respectively (Romano, Goodman, Tamura, & Gonzales, 2001). Another study assigned responders to sertraline to either continued treatment with sertraline or placebo and found relapse rates of 21% versus 59%, respectively (Koran, Hackett, Rubin, Wolkow, & Robinson, 2002). Finally, one study found that paroxetine responders assigned to continued treatment with paroxetine or placebo exhibited relapse rates of 38% versus 59%, respectively (Hollander, Allen et al., 2003). Some investigators have proposed using lower doses of SRIs for OCD maintenance treatment based on open-label trials (Pato, Hill, & Murphy, 1990; Ravizza, Barzega, Bellino, Bogetto, & Maina, 1996), and two controlled studies have demonstrated the efficacy of this approach (Mundo, Bareggi, Pirola, Bellodi, & Smeraldi et al., 1997; Tollefson, Birkett, Koran, & Genduso, 1994). Thus, the data suggest that discontinuation of SRIs in patients with OCD results in a high relapse rate, though there is still some debate regarding maintenance dosages of SRIs.

In addition to the above data regarding pharmacotherapy for OCD in adults, there are analogous studies in children and adolescents documenting the efficacy of CMI over non-SRI TCAs as well as placebo (see Table 16.4). There are a growing number of placebo-controlled studies of SSRIs for OCD in children, which likewise support the efficacy of SRIs in treating OCD in children. A recent meta-analysis suggests that clomipramine may be superior to the SSRIs in treating pediatric OCD (Geller et al., 2003).

Second-Line Pharmacotherapy: SRI Augmentation and Alternative Monotherapies

For patients who do not derive satisfactory reduction of symptoms with SRI therapy, second-line pharmacological treatments include SRI augmentation and alternative monotherapies. It is important to appreciate that only a minority of patients with OCD do not respond favorably to SRIs and that this relatively treatment resistant group may be quite heterogeneous, including with respect to underlying pathophysiology. Therefore, specific subsequent treatments may be very effective for some subset of this popula-

TABLE 16.4 Controlled Trials of SRI Therapy for OCD (Children and Adolescents)

Treatment Conditions	N	Comments	Study
CMI vs. desipramine vs. placebo	8 adolescents	No significant differences crossover	Rapoport et al. (1980)
CMI vs. placebo cross-over	14 children	CMI superior to placebo	Flament et al. (1985a, 1985b)
CMI vs. desipramine	48	CMI superior to desipramine; 64% of patients relapsed when desipramine substituted for CMI	Leonard et al. (1988)
CMI substituted with desipramine in half of subjects	26	89% receiving desipramine relapsed 18% remaining on CMI relapsed	Leonard et al. (1991)
CMI vs. placebo	61	37% average decrease with CMI 8% average decrease with placebo	DeVeaugh-Geiss et al. (1992)
Fluoxetine vs. placebo	14 children	Fluoxetine superior to placebo	Riddle et al. (1992)
Sertraline vs. placebo	187	Sertraline superior to placebo	March et al. (1998)
Fluoxetine vs. placebo	43	Fluoxetine superior to placebo	Liebowitz et al. (2002)
Fluoxetine vs. placebo	103	Fluoxetine superior to placebo	Geller at al. (2001)
Sertraline, BT, combination of sertraline and BT, or placebo	112	Combined > BT = sertraline > placebo	POTS Team (2004)
Fluvoxamine vs. placebo	120	Fluvoxamine superior to placebo	Riddle et al. (2001)

Source: Adapted from Jenike 1998.

CMI = clomipramine.

tion while having only modest mean efficacy for the overall cohort. Consequently, some second-line treatment trials have focused on the number or proportion of patients who meet responder criteria rather than the mean decrease in symptom severity over the entire study population. Moreover, in some instances, attention has been focused on the clinical characteristics that might distinguish responders from nonresponders.

Augmentation of SRIs

Numerous agents have been tried as augmentors in combination with SRIs for patients who were unresponsive or only partially responsive to SRIs alone (see Dougherty et al., 2004; Jenike, 1998; McDougle & Goodman, 1997). However, few controlled trials of such strategies have been conducted (see Table 16.5). Despite numerous case reports suggesting that lithium might be an effective augmentor in combi-

nation with various SRIs, the only two controlled trials of lithium, added to fluvoxamine (McDougle et al., 1991) and CMI (Pigott et al., 1991), respectively, speak against the efficacy of these combinations.

Similarly, the encouraging results from case series and uncontrolled trials of buspirone augmentation (see Dougherty et al., 2004; Jenike, 1998; McDougle & Goodman, 1997) were followed by only marginal success in controlled trials. In Pigott, L'Heueux, Hill, and colleagues' 1992 study of buspirone plus CMI, despite a 29% responder rate, there was not significant improvement over the entire cohort with respect to OCD symptoms, and 3 of 14 subjects suffered an exacerbation of more than 25% on measures of depression, for unclear reasons. In Grady and colleagues' (1993) double-blind crossover study of buspirone augmentation of fluoxetine, only 1 of 14 subjects showed improvement, which may have reflected the brief duration of treatment (only 4 weeks

TABLE 16.5 SRI Augmentation Therapies for OCD: Controlled Trials

Augmenting Agent	SRI	N	Trial	Results	Study
Lithium	Fluvoxamine	30	2- or 4-week double-blind placebo-controlled	Very little improvement	McDougle et al. (1991)
Lithium	CMI	9	Double-blind crossover (with T3)	None	Pigott et al. (1991)
L-triiodo-thyronine (T3)	CMI	9	Double-blind crossover (with lithium)	None	Pigott et al. (1999)
Buspirone	CMI	14	2-week placebo, then 10-weeks buspirone	4/14 (29%) improved an additional 25% on buspirone; 3/14 (21%) worsened >25% on depression scores	Pigott et al. (1992a)
Buspirone	Fluoxetine	14	Double-blind crossover with placebo; 4 weeks per treatment condition	1/14 (7%) improved significantly more with buspirone	Grady et al. (1993)
Haloperidol	Fluvoxamine	34	Double-blind placebo-controlled, with 17 per group; 4-week trial; after failing fluvoxamine alone	11/17 (65%) responded to haloperidol; 0/17 to placebo; 8/8 with tics responded to haloperidol	McDougle et al. (1994)
Clonazepam	CMI or fluoxetine	16	Placebo-controlled, crossover; 4-week trial; after 20-week stable dose on CMI or fluoxetine	Significant improvement in OCD on one of three measures for clonazepam vs. placebo; significant improvement in global anxiety as well	Pigott et al. (1992c) (see Rauch & Jenike, 1994)
Clonazepam	Sertraline	37	Placebo-controlled,	No significant difference	Crockett et al. (2004)
Risperidone	SRI	36	Double-blind, placebo-controlled; 6-week trial after 12 weeks on SRI	50% responders; significant ($p < .001$) reduction in Y-BOCS	McDougle et al. (2000)
Risperidone	SRI	16	Double-blind, placebo-controlled; 8-week trial after at least 12 weeks on SRI	40% responders	Hollander et al. (2003)
Risperidone	SRI	16	Double-blind, placebo-controlled; 2-week crossover trial with haloperidol	Both risperidone and haloperidol superior to placebo	Li et al. (2005)
Olanzapine	Fluoxetine	44	Placebo controlled; 6-week trial after 8 weeks on fluoxetine	No significant difference	Shapira et al. (2004)
Olanzapine	SRI	26	Double-blind, placebo-controlled; 6-week trial	Significant improvement of Y-BOCS	Bystritsky et al. (2004)
Quetiapine	SRI	40	Double-blind, placebo-controlled; 8-week trial	Quetiapine superior to placebo	Denys et al. (2004)
Quetiapine	SRI	42	Double-blind, placebo-controlled; 6-week trial	No significant difference between quetiapine and placebo	Carey et al. (2005)
Quetiapine	SRI	27	Single-blind, placebo-controlled; 8-week trial	9/14 in active group had 60% or greater decrease in Y-BOCS score; no improvement with placebo	Atmaca et al. (2002)

in each phase). Finally, McDougle, Goodman, Leckman, Holzer, and colleagues (1993) found greater improvement with placebo than with buspirone in a double-blind, placebo-controlled study of buspirone augmentation of fluvoxamine for 6 weeks.

Contrary to a small case series reporting unimpressive results (Jenike, 1998), the use of clonazepam as an augmentor with CMI or fluoxetine has been studied in a placebo-controlled fashion, with some studies suggesting significant antiobsessional efficacy as well as a nonspecific decrease in anxiety measures (Pigott, L'Heueux, Rubenstein, Hill, & Murphy, 1992; see Rauch & Jenike, 1994) and another study finding no significant difference when compared with placebo (Crockett, Churchill, & Davidson, 2004).

The most impressive augmentation data document the benefits of adding low doses of dopamine antagonists (both conventional and atypical neuroleptics) to SRI pharmacotherapy in patients with treatment-refractory OCD (McDougle et al., 1990; McDougle et al., 1994; McDougle et al., 2000). Some data (McDougle, Goodman, Leckman, Barr, et al., 1993) initially suggested that OCD patients with comorbid tics may be less responsive to SRI monotherapy than OCD patients without tics. More recent studies have demonstrated the efficacy of SRI augmentation with neuroleptics in OCD patients with and without comorbid tics (McDougle et al., 2000). Although initial studies demonstrated the efficacy of SRI augmentation with conventional neuroleptics, more recent uncontrolled studies of augmentation with atypical neuroleptics have yielded encouraging preliminary results with risperidone (Jacobsen, 1995; McDougle, Epperson et al., 1995; Pfanner et al., 2000; Ravizza , Barzega, Bellino, Bogetto, & Maina, 1996b; Saxena, Wang, Bystritsky, & Baxter, 1996; Thomsen, 2004), olanzapine (Bogetto, Bellino, Vaschetto, & Ziero, 2000; D'Amico et al., 2003; Francobandiera, 2001; Koran, Ringold, & Elliott, 2000; Marazziti et al., 2005), and quetiapine (Bogan, Koran, Choung, Vapnik, & Bystritsky, 2005; Denys, van Megen, & Westenberg, 2002; Misri & Millis, 2004; Mohr, Vythilingum, Emsley, & Stein, 2002). In addition, three controlled trials of risperidone augmentation of an SRI (Hollander , Baldini, Rossi, Sood, & Pallanti, 2003; Li et al., 2005; McDougle et al., 2000) demonstrated efficacy. Of two controlled trials of olanzapine augmentation, one study (Bystritsky et al., 2004) yielded positive results

but the other (Shapira et al., 2004) did not. Finally, two controlled studies (Atmaca, Kuloglu, Tezcan, & Gecici, 2002; Denys, de Geus, et al., 2004) of quetiapine augmentation yielded positive results but another (Carey et al., 2005) did not.

Pertinent negative findings include those from a controlled crossover trial of L-triiodothyronine added to CMI, which did not yield significant antiobsessional benefits (Pigott et al., 1991).

Numerous other agents have been tried in combination with SRIs, including clonidine, tryptophan, fenfluramine, pindolol, riluzole, trazodone, and nortriptyline, as well as other antidepressants (see Dougherty et al., 2004; Jenike, 1998; McDougle & Goodman, 1997, for reviews). The small number of subjects, lack of sufficient controls, and mixed results preclude drawing even preliminary conclusions regarding the potential efficacy of such strategies. If an augmenting agent is indicated for treatment of some comorbid condition (e.g., lithium for bipolar disorder, trazodone for insomnia, or clonidine for TS), and no strong contraindication is present, then a trial of the agent in combination with an SRI is easily rationalized. Anecdotally, these strategies have appeared to be of tremendous benefit in some isolated cases. No studies have sought to establish the optimal dosage or duration of treatment for any of these augmentation strategies. Therefore, current guidelines reflect the parameters used in the reported successful trials, as well as anecdotal experience with OCD and other psychiatric disorders.

Alternative Monotherapies

For patients who fail to derive satisfactory response from trials of SRIs alone as well as augmentation strategies, the next recommended step is to consider alternative monotherapies in place of SRIs. In addition to uncontrolled data, positive controlled studies lend some support for trials of clonazepam, monoamine oxidase inhibitors (MAOIs), and buspirone (see Table 16.6).

In the case of clonazepam, one placebo-controlled study (Hewlett, Vinogradov, & Agras, 1992) supports its efficacy in OCD, and another placebo-controlled study failed to demonstrate efficacy in OCD (Hollander, Kaplan, & Stahl, 2003). If clonazepam is used as a monotherapy for OCD, recommendations regarding dosage (i.e., 0.5 to 5 mg/day) and duration (i.e., 4 weeks or longer) have no controlled empirical

TABLE 16.6 Alternative Medications as Monotherapies for OCD: Controlled Trials

Treatment Conditions	N	Comments	Study
Clorgyline vs. CMI	13	Clorgyline ineffective; CMI effective	Insel et al. (1983)
Clorgyline vs. CMI	12	Clorgyline inferior to CMI	Zahn et al. (1984)
Phenelzine vs. CMI	30	Both effective and comparable	Vallejo et al. (1992)
Clonazepam vs. CMI vs. Clonidine vs. active placebo crossover	25	35% average decrease with clonazepam; Clonazepam comparable to CMI and superior to active placebo	Hewlett et al. (1992)
Clonazepam vs. placebo	27	No significant difference	Hollander et al. (2003)
Buspirone vs. CMI crossover	20	Both effective and comparable, >20% improvement in >55% in both groups	Pato et al. (1991)
Fluoxetine vs. phenelzine vs. placebo	64	Fluoxetine group improved significantly more than Phenelzine or placebo groups	Jenike et al. (1997)
Trazodone vs. placebo	21	No significant difference	Pigott et al. (1992b)

basis and are simply extrapolated from clinical experience with benzodiazepines for other anxiety disorders, and these few reports in OCD.

Non-placebo-controlled studies involving the MAOI clorgyline speak against its efficacy in OCD, showing no significant decrease in OCD severity (Insel et al., 1983) and inferior efficacy in comparison to SRIs (Insel et al., 1983; Zahn, Insel, & Murphy, 1984). In contrast, small case series suggested beneficial results from the MAOI phenelzine in patients with comorbid OCD and panic disorder (Jenike, Surman, Cassem, Zusky, & Anderson, 1983). A non-placebo-controlled study of phenelzine versus CMI suggested significant clinical improvement in both groups and no significant difference in efficacy between the two agents (Vallejo et al., 1992). The results of Vallejo and colleagues must be interpreted with caution, however, since the study was underpowered to identify a difference between CMI and phenelzine, and suboptimal clinical measures of improvement were employed. In fact, a subsequent placebo-controlled trial of phenelzine and fluoxetine demonstrated that patients treated with fluoxetine improved significantly more than those in the placebo or phenelzine groups (Jenike et al., 1997). This study did note that a subgroup of patients with symmetry obsessions did respond to phenelzine, however. Therefore, the efficacy of phenelzine as a monotherapy for OCD should be regarded as provisional. Specific recommendations regarding dosage (i.e., phenelzine 60 to 90 mg/day) have little empirical basis, reflecting extrapolation from clinical practice with MAOIs for

major depression and panic disorder; duration of trials (i.e., 4 weeks or longer) mirrors that of SRIs for OCD. In addition to the usual low-tyramine diet and other precautions typically indicated in the context of an MAOI trial, it is critical to be cautious regarding the transition from serotonergic medications to an MAOI due to the risks of dangerous interactions, including serotonergic crisis. Current guidelines are based primarily on the half-life of the agents involved rather than direct empirical data related to adverse events per se. Conservative recommendations are washout periods of at least 2 weeks when transitioning from CMI or a short-half-life SSRI to an MAOI, at least 5 weeks when transitioning from fluoxetine to an MAOI, and at least 2 weeks when transitioning from phenelzine to an SRI.

Although one open trial of buspirone did not yield significant antiobsessional benefit (Jenike & Baer, 1988), a controlled trial of buspirone versus CMI suggested that both were comparably effective (Pato, Pigott, Hill, Grover, Bernstein, & Murphy, 1991). The relatively short duration of the trial, the modest power for detecting a difference between treatments, and the absence of a placebo group mitigate against drawing firm conclusions from Pato and colleagues' study. Still, given the excellent tolerability of buspirone, other circumstantial evidence of possible efficacy as an augmentor, and its general efficacy as an anxiolytic, the clinical use of buspirone as an alternative monotherapy for cases of treatment-resistant OCD seems justified pending further information. Specific recommendations regarding dosage (i.e., up to 60 mg/day) and duration of trials (i.e., 6 weeks or longer) have little empirical basis, simply reflecting the protocol adopted in the study by Pato and colleagues.

Some preliminary findings worthy of mention include case reports and small trials of positive results with memantine (Poyurovsky, Weizman, Weizman, & Koran, 2005), tramadol (Goldsmith, Shapira, & Keck, 1999), gabapentin (Cora-Locatelli, Greenberg, Martin, & Murphy, 1998), and glutamate-modulating drugs (Pittenger, Krystal, & Coric, 2006), as well as a controlled trial suggesting that oral morphine may be effective for treating refractory OCD (Koran et al., 2005). Other pertinent negative findings are also worthy of mention. In contrast to promising results with risperidone as an augmentor, an open trial of the atypical antipsychotic clozapine suggests inefficacy as an antiobsessional monotherapy (McDougle, Barr, et al., 1995). Although one case report suggested antiobsessional benefit in a patient with OCD (Young, Bostic, & McDonald, 1994), and another described a marked reduction in OC symptoms for a patient with schizophrenia (LaPorta, 1994), several case reports suggest that clozapine can actually precipitate OC symptoms in patients with psychotic disorders (see McDougle, Barr, et al., 1995, for review). Controlled trials have failed to demonstrate the efficacy of trazodone (Pigott, L'Heureux, Rubenstein, Bernstein, et al., 1992), clonidine (Hewlett, Vinogradov, & Agras, 1992), and diphenhydramine (Hewlett et al., 1992) as monotherapies for OCD.

Nonpharmacological Therapies

Behavior Therapy

It is extremely challenging to design and conduct a controlled study of psychotherapy. Among other issues, the optimal analog to placebo treatment in medication trials is unclear. Perhaps consequently, much of the clinical research to date regarding behavior therapy for OCD has focused on determining salient elements of the therapy rather than comparing behavior therapy to other treatments or placebo (see Baer & Minichiello, 1990, 1998). The gold standard mode of behavior therapy for OCD is exposure and response prevention. This entails the patient actually being exposed to provocative stimuli (e.g., touching a "contaminated" object) and refraining from carrying out his or her usual compulsions (e.g.,

refraining from hand washing) — that is response prevention. It appears that in vivo exposure and response prevention represent the salient elements of effective behavior therapy regardless of setting, supervision, or addition of cognitive techniques (Emmelkamp & de Lange, 1983; Emmelkamp & Kraanen, 1977; Emmelkamp, Van Der Helm, Van Zanten, & Ploch, 1980).

One challenge or limitation of exposure and response prevention therapy relates to generalizability of results, since gains are often specific to the symptoms explicitly addressed and sometimes limited to the settings in which the therapies are practiced (Rachman et al., 1971; Rachman et al., 1979; Rachman & Hodgson, 1980). Although it is commonly believed that behavior therapy is more effective for compulsive rituals than for obsessive thoughts, only one (Foa & Goldstein, 1978) of four behavior therapy studies (Foa & Goldstein, 1978; Foa, Steketee, & Milby, 1980; Foa, Steketee, Grayson, Turner & Latimer, 1984; Solyom & Sookman, 1977) addressing this issue found a significantly greater improvement in compulsions versus obsessions. In all four studies, significant gains were made in both obsessions and compulsions. However, patients with pure obsessions (e.g., intrusive thoughts of sex or violence without accompanying compulsions) tended to fare worse than patients with obsessions and compulsions (e.g., contamination with cleaning or doubting with checking; Rachman & Hodgson, 1980).

There are numerous partially controlled trials of exposure and response prevention behavior therapy that have consistently shown impressive antiobsessional efficacy (Boulougouris, 1977; Fals-Stewart, Marks, & Schafer, 1993; Foa et al., 1984; Lindsay, Crino, & Andrews, 1997; Marks, Hodgson, & Rachman, 1975; Rachman, Marks, & Hodgson, 1971, 1973). Dropout rates for these studies averaged approximately 20% (Rachman & Hodgson, 1980). Still, follow-up studies suggested that treatment gains were maintained for up to 1 to 5 years after discontinuation of active treatment, although these results were confounded by occasional "booster" sessions (Marks et al., 1975; Marks, 1981; Mawson, Marks, & Ramm, 1982). The study of Boulougouris (1977) stands as a notable exception in that patients who were treated with 11 sessions of behavior therapy maintained their gains over a 2- to 5-year follow-up period in the absence of any intercurrent therapy sessions. Furthermore, a meta-analysis (Christensen, Hadzi-Pavlovic,

Andrews, & Mattick, 1987; Quality Assurance Project, 1985) based on data from 38 studies between 1961 and 1984 found comparable effect sizes for CMI (1.7) and behavior therapy (1.8) at the end of treatment; the benefits from exposure and response prevention persisted at a mean 80-week follow-up (effect size = 1.7), whereas no such follow-up data were available for CMI. In contrast, psychosurgery resulted in an effect size of 1.4 and dropped to 1.0 at the 60-week follow-up. In a separate study, Pato and colleagues (1988) showed that almost 90% of patients who received CMI therapy for OCD relapsed after discontinuation of the medication. Thus, pending well-controlled head-to-head studies, based on partially controlled data and the limited method of meta-analysis, the implication is that in comparison with CMI or psychosurgery, behavior therapy may produce the highest mean effect size and the most enduring gains following discontinuation of active treatment.

Only a small number of studies directly comparing behavior therapy versus medication have been reported. Rachman and colleagues (1979) found behavior therapy to significantly outperform CMI, as well as no significant incremental benefit from the two treatments in combination. This study is limited, however, in that the CMI condition entailed relatively low doses (mean, 164 mg/day; maximum, 225 mg/day), as well as inadequate duration of CMI treatment (6 weeks). In another head-to-head comparison of behavior therapy and CMI, medication was found to be more effective for reducing obsessional doubt, whereas behavior therapy was more effective for reducing compulsive rituals (Solyom & Sookman, 1977). In practice, medication and behavior therapy are routinely used in concert, and experts in the field have long recommended this as an optimal treatment approach (e.g., Baer & Minichiello, 1998; Rauch & Jenike, 1994). Numerous studies (Honagen et al., 1998, Marks, Stern, Mawson, Cobb, & McDonald, 1980; Marks et al., 1988; O'Connor, 1999) have demonstrated that the combination of behavioral therapy and medication is more effective than either treatment alone, whereas two studies (Foa et al., 2005; van Balkom et al., 1998) found that the addition of SRIs to patients being treated with either cognitive therapy or exposure and response prevention was not superior to either cognitive therapy or exposure and response prevention used in patients not taking medication.

Beyond exposure and response prevention, limited trials of alternative behavioral methods have supported the use of imaginal flooding for checkers (Steketee, Foa, & Grayson, 1982) and "thought stopping" for patients with pure obsessions (Rimm & Masters, 1974). Moreover, cognitive therapy can also be effective for OCD (see Abramowitz, Taylor, & McKay, 2005). Finally, although controlled data are not currently available regarding cognitive-behavior therapy for OCD in children and adolescents, preliminary findings of open trials and case reports suggest that, with age-appropriate modifications to the regimen, results can be comparable to those in adults (Franklin et al., 1998; March, Mulle, & Herbel, 1994; March, 1995; Scahill, Vitulano, Brenner, Lynch, & King, 1996).

Neurosurgery

Despite a large body of uncontrolled data reporting antiobsessional benefits from a variety of neurosurgical procedures (see Cosgrove & Rauch, 1995; Jenike, Rauch, Baer, & Rasmussen, 1998; Mindus et al., 1994, for reviews), thus far, ethical factors and technical limitations have precluded the performance of sham-controlled studies to definitively establish the efficacy of these strategies. Neurosurgical treatment of OCD is reserved for patients with severe and debilitating illness who have failed an exhaustive array of other available treatment options and who provide informed consent or assent. Currently, the most commonly employed neurosurgical treatments for OCD include anterior cingulotomy, anterior capsulotomy, subcaudate tractotomy, and limbic leukotomy. In recent prospective trials of cingulotomy and capsulotomy, approximately 45% of patients experienced symptom reduction of at least 35% (Dougherty et al., 2002; Mindus et al., 1994). Studies directly comparing the relative efficacy and safety among the different neurosurgical approaches are also lacking. Adverse effects, in the context of contemporary techniques, include seizure and transient headache. Perhaps surprisingly, discernible adverse effects on cognition or personality are rare (see Corkin 1980; Jenike et al., 1998; Mindus et al., 1994). With the advent of innovative surgical devices that allow functional neurosurgery without craniotomy (e.g., by gamma knife), the performance of ethical double-blind sham-controlled trials of neurosurgery for OCD is now feasible. One such study, testing the efficacy of anterior capsulotomy, is currently being conducted by a collaborative research team involving investigators from Brown University and Massachusetts General Hospital. Deep brain stimulation (DBS), which utilizes surgically implanted electrodes that may be turned on and off to stimulate or inhibit activity in surrounding brain tissue, has been used for the treatment of neurological diseases such as Parkinson's disease and intractable pain (Devinsky, Beric, & Dogali, 1994). Initial investigations of the efficacy of DBS for the treatment of OCD have been encouraging (Gabriels, Cosyns, Nuttin, Demeulemeester, & Gybels, 2003). More definitive data are sorely needed to determine the efficacy of neurosurgical treatments.

Electroconvulsive Therapy

There are no controlled data regarding the efficacy of electroconvulsive therapy for OCD. Given the high comorbidity of major affective illness in OCD, and the well-established efficacy of ECT for major depression, it is not surprising that some patients with OCD have reportedly shown clinical improvement with ECT. Several limited case series and anecdotal reports suggest that ECT may be useful in some circumstances, and such intervention would seem prudent in cases where ECT is indicated based on the presence of comorbid severe affective illness (see Jenike & Rauch, 1994). Controlled data are needed, however, before meaningful conclusions can be drawn regarding the specific antiobsessional efficacy of ECT for OCD. In this regard, important considerations include the effects of ECT on patients with OCD in the absence of major depressive disorder, the careful clinical distinction between genuine OCD versus ruminations or intrusive thoughts due to a different diagnosis, and the use of clinical instruments to tease apart antidepressant effects versus antiobsessional effects versus global improvement. Currently available data do not provide compelling support for the use of ECT in OCD without comorbid ECT-responsive conditions.

NEW HORIZONS AND FUTURE TREATMENTS FOR OBSESSIVE-COMPULSIVE DISORDER

Future OCD treatment research can be divided into two categories: (a) initiatives to assess and optimize the use of currently available treatments, and (b) initiatives to develop new treatments. As documented by the above review, there is much work to be done in establishing the efficacy of various treatments, following up on preliminary data with well-controlled prospective trials. Moreover, optimal doses and durations for various treatments need to be determined empirically and in a scientifically rigorous fashion. Clinical subtyping or characterization based on symptom dimensions may uncover important predictors of treatment response (Ackerman, Greenland, Bystritsky, Morgenstern, & Katz, 1994; Mataix-Cols, Rauch, Manzo, Jenike, & Baer, 1999; Mataix-Cols, Marks, Greist, Kobak, & Baer, 2002; Ravizza, Barzega, Bellino, Bogetto, & Maina, 1995), informing patients and clinicians which treatments should be tried first or avoided in particular cases. Public policy issues regarding treatment access loom large for mental health care delivery in the United States. Education of health care consumers, as well as policy makers and clinicians, will be critical to high-quality care in the years ahead. Primary care physicians must be informed about OCD, and trends in training must be established to ensure an adequate supply of therapists with expertise in behavioral methods. Technological innovations, such as telepsychiatry, may help to provide specialized assessment and treatment to remote regions and ultimately reduce the costs of care (Baer 1991; Baer et al., 1995).

Truly novel treatments for OCD may emerge from advances in our understanding of its pathophysiology or serendipitously. As new compounds become available that interact with the serotonergic and dopaminergic systems via specific receptor subtypes (e.g., 5HT1D, 5HT1A, or 5HT3; Swerdlow, 1995), it is likely that several will be antiobsessional candidates. Beyond monoaminergic systems, agents that modulate neuropeptidergic transmission may represent the next wave of psychopharmacological agents to be tested in OCD and related disorders. For instance, we have proposed that, based on the neurochemistry of corticostriatal pathways, substance P antagonists might serve as potent antiobsessionals (Rauch et al., 1998). Such compounds are already available within the pharmaceutical industry but currently are being studied only for other indications. The hypothalamic neuropeptide oxytocin is also the subject of intensive study because of its purported role in species-specific grooming behaviors (Leckman et al., 1994). Beyond neuropharmacology, research regarding autoimmune-mediated causes of OCD have prompted investigation of plasmaphoresis to clear autoantibodies plus prophylactic antibiotic treatment to prevent subsequent infections and further damage (Swedo, 1994; Swedo et al., 1994; Allen et al., 1995). Also, transcranial magnetic stimulation (TMS), which has shown promise as an alternative treatment for major depression, has been shown to be efficacious in the treatment of OCD in one preliminary study (Greenberg et al., 1997). Finally, recent neuroimaging studies have documented consistent brain activity changes following successful treatment with either SRIs or behavior therapy (Baxter et al., 1992; Schwartz, Stoessel, Baxter, Martin, & Phelps, 1996). Such findings underscore the potential power of neuroimaging methods in searching for predictors of treatment responsiveness.

is now considerable clinical experience with neurosurgery for severe, debilitating, treatment-refractory OCD. The apparent modest success rates with neurosurgery and its relative safety based on open trials would seem to pose a reasonable option for a small number of cases. Still, controlled data on neurosurgery are sorely needed. The future of OCD treatment will hopefully entail rigorous research to more clearly establish the efficacy and safety of preexisting treatment options, as well as a refined sense of which patients might respond preferentially to which interventions, at what dose, and after how long. Furthermore, we can look forward to emerging novel treatment strategies that might include modified cognitive-behavior therapies; new compounds acting via serotonergic, dopaminergic, or neuropeptidergic systems; and interventions that counteract autoimmune processes.

SUMMARY

In conclusion, the past 30 years have seen tremendous advances in the treatment and understanding of OCD, with a recent acceleration of progress. It is now appreciated that OCD is a common disorder, and effective treatments including medication, behavior therapy, and neurosurgery have emerged. There is overwhelming evidence of the most rigorous type supporting the efficacy of SRIs in the treatment of OCD. Along with SRIs, behavior therapy must be considered a viable first-line therapy. The best available data suggest that behavior therapy, and perhaps cognitive therapy, are at least as effective as medication in some instances and may be superior with respect to risks, costs, and enduring benefits. A variety of second-line medication treatments for OCD have been studied in a controlled or systematic fashion. Augmentation of SRIs with clonazepam or buspirone and augmentation with high-potency neuroleptics in cases of a comorbid tic disorder are all provisionally recommended based on the marginal available data. Other augmentation strategies find very limited support at present. Alternative monotherapies, including buspirone, clonazepam, and phenelzine, have all been the subject of positive controlled or partially controlled studies. However, the quality of these data make recommendations for these strategies tentative as well, pending additional information. Beyond second-line treatments, the current database is inadequate for making difficult treatment decisions. There

ACKNOWLEDGMENT

Drs. Rauch and Jenike are supported in part by the David Judah Research Fund.

REFERENCES

Abramowitz, J. S., Taylor, S., & McKay, D. (2005). Potentials and limitations of cognitive treatments for obsessive-compulsive disorder. *Cognitive Behavior Therapy, 34,* 140–147.

Ackerman, D. L., Greenland. S., Bystritsky, A., Morgenstern, H., & Katz, R. J. (1994). Predictors of treatment response in obsessive-compulsive disorder: Multivariate analyses from a multicenter trial of clomipramine. *Journal of Clinical Psychopharmacology, 14,* 247–254.

Albert, U., Aguglia, E., Maina, G., & Bogetto, F. (2002). Venlafaxine versus clomipramine in the treatment of obsessive-compulsive disorder: A preliminary single-blind, 12-week, controlled study. *Journal of Clinical Psychiatry, 63,* 1004–1009.

Allen, A. J., Leonard, H. L., & Swedo, S. E. (1995). Case study: A new infection-triggered, autoimmune subtype of pediatric OCD and Tourette's syndrome. *Journal of the American Academy of Child and Adolescent Psychiatry, 34,* 307–311.

American Psychiatric Association. (1994). *Diagnostic and statistical manual of mental disorders* (4th ed.). Washington, DC: Author.

Ananth, J., Pecknold, J. C., van den Steen, N., & Engelsmann, F. (1981). Double-blind comparative study of clomipramine and amitriptyline in obsessive neurosis. *Progress in Neuro-psychopharmacology, 5,* 257–262.

Angst, J. (1994). The epidemiology of obsessive compulsive disorder. In E. Hollander, J. Zohar, D. Marazziti, & B. Olivier (Eds.), *Current insights in obsessive compulsive disorder* (pp. 93–104). Chichester, England: Wiley.

Atmaca, M., Kuloglu, M., Tezcan, E., & Gecici, O. (2002). Quetiapine augmentation in patients with treatment resistant obsessive-compulsive disorder: A single-blind, placebo-controlled study. *International Clinical Psychopharmacology, 17,* 115–119.

Baer, L. (1991). *Getting control.* Boston: Little, Brown.

Baer, L., Cukor, P., Jenike, M. A., Leahy, L., O'Laughlin, J., & Coyle, J. T. (1995). Pilot study of telemedicine for patients with obsessive-compulsive disorder. *American Journal of Psychiatry, 152,* 1383–1385.

Baer, L., & Minichiello, W. E. (1990). Behavioral treatment for obsessive-compulsive disorder. In R. Noyes Jr., M. Roth, & G. D. Burrows (Eds.), *Handbook of anxiety: Vol. 4. The treatment of anxiety* (pp. 363–387). Amsterdam: Elsevier Science Publishers.

Baer, L., & Minichiello, W. E. (1998). Behavior therapy for obsessive-compulsive disorder. In M. A. Jenike, L. Baer, & W. E. Minichiello (Eds.), *Obsessive-compulsive disorders: Practical management* (3rd ed., pp. 337–367). Boston: Mosby–Year Book.

Baer, L., Minichiello, W. E., Jenike, M. A., & Holland, A. (1989). Use of a portable computer program to assist behavioral treatment in a case of obsessive compulsive disorder. *Journal of Behavior Therapy & Experimental Psychiatry, 19,* 237–240.

Ballantine, H. T., Bouckoms, A. J., Thomas, E. L., & Giriunas, I. E. (1987). Treatment of psychiatric illness by stereotactic cingulotomy. *Biological Psychiatry, 22,* 807–819.

Baxter, L. R., Jr., Schwartz, J. M., Bergman, K. S., Szuba, M.P., Guze, B.H., Mazziotta, J.C., Alazraki, A., et al. (1992). Caudate glucose metabolic rate changes with both drug and behavior therapy for obsessive-compulsive disorder. *Archives of General Psychiatry, 49,* 681–689.

Baxter, L. R., Schwartz, J. M., Guze, B. H., Bergman, K., & Szuba, M.P. (1990). Neuroimaging in obsessive-compulsive disorder: Seeking the mediating neuroanatomy. In M. A. Jenike, L. Baer, & W. E. Minichiello (Eds.), *Obsessive compulsive disorder: Theory and management* (2nd ed., pp. 167–188). Chicago: Year Book Medical Publishers.

Bergeron, R., Ravindran, A. V., Chaput, Y. Goldner, E., Swinson, R., van Ameringen, M.A., Austin, C., et al. (2002). Sertraline and fluoxetine treatment of obsessive-compulsive disorder: Results of a double-blind, 6-month treatment study. *Journal of Clinical Psychopharmacology, 22,* 148–154.

Bisserbe, J. C., Wiseman, R. L., Goldberg, M. S., and the Franco-Belgian OCD Study Group. (1995). A double-blind comparison of sertraline and clomipramine in outpatients with obsessive-compulsive disorder [Abstract]. *American Psychiatric Association, New Research, 173.*

Bogan, A. M., Koran, L. M., Choung, H. W., Vapnik, T., & Bystritsky, A.(2005). Quetiapine augmentation in obsessive-compulsive disorder resistant to serotonin reuptake inhibitors: An open-label study. *Journal of Clinical Psychiatry, 66,* 73–79.

Bogetto, F., Bellino, S., Vaschetto, P., & Ziero, S. (2000). Olanzapine augmentation of fluvoxamine-refractory obsessive-compulsive disorder (OCD): A 12-week open trial. *Psychiatry Research 96,* 91–98.

Boulougouris, J. C. (1977). Variables affecting the behavior modification of obsessive-compulsive patients treated by flooding. In J. C. Boulougouris & A. D. Rabavilas (Eds.), *The treatment of phobic and obsessive compulsive disorders* (pp. 73–84). Oxford: Pergamon Press.

Bystritsky, A., Ackerman, S. L., Rosen, R. M., Vapnik, T., Borbis, E., Maidment, K.M., et al.(2004). Augmentation of serotonin reuptake inhibitors in refractory obsessive-compulsive disorder using adjunctive olanzapine: A placebo-controlled trial. *Journal of Clinical Psychiatry, 65,* 565–568.

Carey, P. D., Vythilingum, B., Seedat, S., Muller, J. E., van Ameringen, M., & Stein, D.J. (2005). Quetiapine augmentation of SRIs in treatment refractory obsessive-compulsive disorder: A double-blind, randomised, placebo-controlled study. *BioMed Central Psychiatry, 5,* 5.

Chouinard, G., Goodman, W., Greist, J., Jenike, M., Rasmussen, S., White, K., Hackett, E., et al. (1990). Results of a double-blind placebo controlled trial using a new serotonin uptake inhibitor, sertraline, in obsessive-compulsive disorder. *Psychopharmacology Bulletin, 26,* 279–284.

Christensen, H., Hadzi-Pavlovic, D., Andrews, G., & Mattick, R. (1987). Behavior therapy and tricyclic medication in the treatment of obsessive-compulsive disorder: A quantitative review. *Journal of Consulting and Clinical Psychology, 55,* 701–711.

Clomipramine Collaborative Group. (1991). Clomipramine in the treatment of patients with obsessive-compulsive disorder. *Archives of General Psychiatry, 48,* 730–738.

Connor, K. M., Payne, V. M., Gadde, K. M., Zang, W., & Davidson, J.R. (2005). The use of aripiprazole in obsessive-compulsive disorder: Preliminary observations in 8 patients. *Journal of Clinical Psychiatry, 66,* 49–51.

Cooper, J. (1970). The Leyton obsessional inventory. *Psychiatric Medicine, 1,* 48.

Cora-Locatelli, G., Greenberg, B. D., Martin, J., & Murphy, D. L. (1998). Gabapentin augmentation for fluoxetine-treated patients with obsessive-compulsive disorder. *Journal of Clinical Psychiatry, 59,* 480–481.

Corkin, S. (1980). A prospective study of cingulotomy. In E. S. Valenstein (Ed.), *The psychosurgery debate* (pp. 164–204). San Francisco: Freeman.

Cosgrove, G. R., & Rauch, S. L. (1995). Psychosurgery. *Neurosurgical Clinics of North America, 6,* 167–176.

Crockett, B. A., Churchill, E., & Davidson, J. R. (2004). A double-blind combination study of clonazepam with sertraline in obsessive-compulsive disorder. *Annals of Clinical Psychiatry, 16,* 127–132.

Cui, Y. E. (1986). A double-blind trial of clomipramine and doxepin in obsessive-compulsive disorder. *Chung Hua Shen Ching Shen Ko Tsa Chih, 19,* 279–281.

D'Amico, G., Cedro, C., Muscatello, M. R., Pandolfo, G., DiRosa, A.E., Zoccali, R., et al. (2003). Olanzapine augmentation of paroxetine-refractory obsessive-compulsive disorder. *Progress in Neuropsychopharmacology and Biological Psychiatry, 27,* 619–623.

Dannon, P. N., Sasson, Y., Hirschmann, S., Iancu, I., Grunhaus, L. J., & Zohar, J. (2000). Pindolol augmentation in treatment-resistant obsessive compulsive disorder: A double-blind placebo controlled trial. *European Neuropsychopharmacology, 10,* 165–169.

Den Boer, J. A., Westenberg, H. G. M., Kamerbeek, W. D. J., Verhoeven, W. M., & Kahn, R. S. (1987). Effect of serotonin uptake inhibitors in anxiety disorders: A double-blind comparison of clomipramine and fluvoxamine. *International Clinical Psychopharmacology, 2,* 21–32.

Denys, D., de Geus, F., van Megen, H. J., & Westenberg, H. G. (2004). A double-blind, placebo-controlled trial of quetiapine addition in patients with obsessive-compulsive disorder refractory to serotonin reuptake inhibitors. *Journal of Clinical Psychiatry, 65,* 1040–1048.

Denys, D., van der Wee, N., Janssen, J., De Geus, F., & Westenberg, H. G. (2004). Low level of dopaminergic D2 receptor binding in obsessive-compulsive disorder. *Biological Psychiatry, 55,* 1041–1045.

Denys, D., van der Wee, N., van Megen, H. J., & Westenberg, H. G. (2003). A double- blind comparison of venlafaxine and paroxetine in obsessive-compulsive disorder. *Journal of Clinical Psychopharmacology, 23,* 568–575.

Denys, D., van Megen, H., & Westenberg, H. (2002). Quetiapine addition to serotonin reuptake inhibitor treatment in patients with treatment-refractory obsessive-compulsive disorder: An open-label study. *Journal of Clinical Psychiatry, 63,* 700–703.

Denys, D., Zohar, J., & Westenberg, H. G. (2004). The role of dopamine in obsessive-compulsive disorder: Preclinical and clinical evidence. *Journal of Clinical Psychiatry, 65*(Suppl. 14), 11–17.

DeVeaugh-Geiss, J., Moroz, G., & Biederman, J., Cantwell, D., Fontaine, R., Greist, J., et al. (1992). Clomipramine hydrochloride in childhood and adolescent obsessive-compulsive disorder: A multicenter trial. *Journal of the American Academy of Child and Adolescent Psychiatry, 31,* 45–49.

Devinsky, O., Beric, A., & Dogali, M. (Eds.). (1994). *Electrical and magnetic stimulation of the brain and spinal cord.* New York: Raven Press.

Dominguez, R. A., & Mestre, S. M. (1994). Management of treatment-refractory obsessive compulsive disorder patients. *Journal of Clinical Psychiatry, 55*(Suppl. 10), 86–92.

Dougherty, D. D., Baer, L., Cosgrove, G. R., Cassem, E. H., Price, B. H., Neirenberg, A. A., et al. (2002). Prospective long-term follow-up of 44 patients who received cingulotomy for treatment-refractory obsessive-compulsive disorder. *American Journal of Psychiatry, 159,* 269–275.

Dougherty, D. D., & Rauch, S. L. (1997). Serotonin-reuptake inhibitors in the treatment of OCD. In E. Hollander & D. J. Stein (Eds.), *Obsessive-compulsive disorders: Diagnosis — etiology — treatment* (pp. 145–160). New York: Marcel Dekker.

Dougherty, D. D., Rauch, S. L., & Jenike, M. A. (2004). Pharmacotherapy for obsessive-compulsive disorder. *Journal of Clinical Psychology, 60,* 1195–1202.

Emmelkamp, P. M G., & de Lange, I. (1983). Spouse involvement in the treatment of obsessive-compulsive patients. *Behaviour Research and Therapy, 21,* 341–346.

Emmelkamp, P. M. G., & Kraanen, J. (1977). Therapist-controlled exposure in vivo versus self-controlled exposure in vivo: A comparison with obsessive-compulsive patients. *Behaviour Research and Therapy, 15,* 491–495.

Emmelkamp, P. M. G., Van Der Helm, M., Van Zanten, B. L., & Plochg, I. Treatment of obsessive-compulsive patients: The contribution of self-instructional training to the effectiveness of exposure. *Behaviour Research and Therapy, 18*, 61–66.

Fallon, B. A., Campeas, R., Schneier, F. R., Marshall, R. . Davies, S., Goetz, D., et al. (1992). Open trial of intravenous clomipramine in five treatment refractory patients with obsessive compulsive disorder. *Journal of Neuropsychiatry, 4*, 70–75.

Fallon, B. A., Liebowitz, M. R., Campeas, R., Schneier, F. R., Marshall, R., Davies, S., et al. (1998). Intravenous clomipramine for obsessive-compulsive disorder refractory to oral clomipramine: A placebo-controlled study. *Archives of General Psychiatry, 55*, 918–924.

Fals-Stewart, W., Marks, A. P., & Schafer, J. (1993). A comparison of behavioral group therapy and individual behavior therapy in treating obsessive-compulsive disorder. *Journal of Nervous and Mental Disease, 181*, 189–193.

Fernandez, C. E., & Lopez-Ibor, A J. (1967). Monochlorimipramine in the treatment of psychiatric patients resistant to other therapies. *Actas Luso Espanolas de Neurologia, Psiquiatria y Ciencias Afines, 26*, 119.

Flament, M. F., Rapoport, J. L., Berg, C. J., Sceery, W., Kilts, C., Mellstrom, B., et al. (1985). Clomipramine treatment of childhood obsessive-compulsive disorder. *Archives of General Psychiatry, 42*, 977–983.

Flament, M. F., Rapoport, J. L., & Kilts, C. . (1985). A controlled trial of clomipramine in childhood obsessive-compulsive disorder. *Psychopharmacology Bulletin, 21*, 150–151.

Foa, E. B., & Goldstein, A. (1978). Continuous exposure and complete response prevention in the treatment of obsessive-compulsive neurosis. *Behavior Therapy, 9*, 821–829.

Foa, E. B., Liebowitz, M. R., Kozak, M. J., Davies, S., Campeas, R., Franklin, M. E., et al. (2005). Randomized, placebo-controlled trial of exposure and ritual prevention, clomipramine, and their combination in the treatment of obsessive-compulsive disorder. *American Journal of Psychiatry, 162*, 151–161.

Foa, E. B., Steketee, G., Grayson, J. B., Turner, R. M., & Latimer, P. (1984). Deliberate exposure and blocking of obsessive-compulsive rituals: Immediate and long term effects. *Behavior Therapy, 15*, 450–472.

Foa, E. B., Steketee, G., & Milby, J. B. (1980). Differential effects of exposure and response prevention in obsessive-compulsive washers. *Journal of Clinical and Consulting Psychology, 48*, 71–79.

Fontaine, R., & Chouinard, G. (1989). Fluoxetine in the long-term maintenance treatment of obsessive-compulsive disorder. *Psychiatric Annals, 19*, 88–91.

Francobandiera, G. (2001). Olanzapine augmentation of serotonin uptake inhibitors in obsessive-compulsive disorder: An open study. *Canadian Journal of Psychiatry, 46*, 356–358.

Franklin, M. E., Kozak, M. J., Cashman, L. A., Coles, M. E., Rheingold A. A., & Foa, E. B. (1998). Cognitive-behavioral treatment of pediatric obsessive-compulsive disorder: An open clinical trial. *Journal of the American Academy of Child and Adolescent Psychiatry, 37*, 412–419.

Freeman, C. P. L., Trimble, M. R., Deakin, J. F. W., Stokes, T. M., & Ashford, J. J. (1994). Fluvoxamine versus clomipramine in the treatment of obsessive compulsive disorder: A multicenter, randomized, double-blind, parallel group comparison. *Journal of Clinical Psychiatry, 55*, 301–305.

Freud S. (1924). Notes upon a case of obsessional neurosis. In *Collected papers* (Vol. 2, pp. 122–132). London: Hogarth Press. (Original work published 1909)

Gabriels, L., Cosyns, P., Nuttin, B., Demeulemeester, H., & Gybels, J. (2003). Deep brain stimulation for treatment-refractory obsessive-compulsive disorder: Psychopathological and neuropsychological outcome in three cases. *Acta Psychiatrica Scandinavica, 107*, 241–243.

Geller, D. A., Biederman, J., Stewart, S. E., Mullin, B., Martin, A., Spencer, T., et al. (2003). Which SSRI? A meta-analysis of pharmacotherapy trials in pediatric obsessive-compulsive disorder. *American Journal of Psychiatry, 160*, 1919–1928.

Geller, D. A., Hoog, S. L., Heiligenstein, J. H., Ricardi, R. K., Tamura, R., Kluszynski, S., et al. (2001). Fluoxetine treatment for obsessive-compulsive disorder in children and adolescents: A placebo-controlled clinical trial. *Journal of the American Academy of Child and Adolescent Psychiatry, 40*, 773–779.

Gilles de la Tourette, G. (1985). Étude sur une affection nerveuse caracterisée par de l'incoordination motrice accompagnée d'écholalie et de coprolalie. *Archives of Neurology, 9*, 19–42, 158–200.

Goldsmith, T. B., Shapira, N. A., &Keck, P. E., Jr. (1999). Rapid remission of OCD with tramadol hydrochloride. *American Journal of Psychiatry, 156*, 660–661.

Goodman, W. K., Kozak, M. J., Liebowitz, M., & White, K. L. (1996). Treatment of obsessive-compulsive disorder with fluvoxamine: A multicentre, double-blind, placebo-controlled trial. *International Clinical Psychopharmacology, 11*, 21–29.

Goodman, W. K., McDougle, C. J., & Price, L. H. (1992). Pharmacotherapy of obsessive compulsive disorder. *Journal of Clinical Psychiatry*, *53*(Suppl.), 29–37.

Goodman, W. K., Price, L. H., Delgado, P. L., Palumbo, J., Krystal, J. H., Nagy, L. M., et al. (1990). Specificity of serotonin reuptake inhibitors in the treatment of obsessive compulsive disorder. *Archives of General Psychiatry*, *47*, 577–585.

Goodman, W. K., Price, L. H., Rasmussen, S. A., Delgado, P. L., Heninger, G. R., & Charney, D. S. (1989). Efficacy of fluvoxamine in obsessive-compulsive disorder: A double-blind comparison with placebo. *Archives of General Psychiatry*, *46*, 36–44.

Goodman, W. K., Price, L. H., Rasmussen, S. A., Mazure, C., Fleischmann, R. L., Hill, C. L, et al. (1989). The Yale-Brown Obsessive Compulsive Scale (Y-BOCS), part I: Development, use, and reliability. *Archives of General Psychiatry*, *46*, 1006–1011.

Goodman, W. K., Price, L. H., Rasmussen, S. A., Mazure, C., Delgado, P., Heninger, G. R., et al. (1989). The Yale-Brown Obsessive Compulsive Scale (Y-BOCS), part II: Validity. *Archives of General Psychiatry*, *46*, 1012–1016.

Grady, T. A., Pigott, T. A., L'Heureux, F., Hill, J. L., Bernstein, S. E., & Murphy, D. L. (1993). A double-blind study of adjuvant buspirone hydrochloride in fluoxetine treated patients with obsessive compulsive disorder. *American Journal of Psychiatry*, *150*, 819–821.

Greenberg, B. D., George, M. S., Dearing, J., Benjamin, J., Schaepfer, T. E., Altemus, M., et al. (1997). Effect of prefrontal repetitive transcranial magnetic stimulation (rTMS) in obsessive compulsive disorder: A preliminary study. *American Journal of Psychiatry*, *154*, 867–869.

Greist, J. H., Chouinard, G., DuBoff, E., Halaris, A., Kim, S.W., Koran, L., et al. (1995). Double-blind comparison of three doses of sertraline and placebo in the treatment of outpatients with obsessive compulsive disorder. *Archives of General Psychiatry*, *52*, 289–295.

Greist, J. H., Jefferson, J. W., Kobak, K. A., Chouinard, G., Duboff, E., Halaris, A., et al. (1995). A 1 year double-blind placebo-controlled fixed dose study of sertraline in the treatment of obsessive-compulsive disorder. *International Clinical Psychopharmacology*, *10*, 57–65.

Greist, J. H., Jefferson, J. W., Kobak, K. A., Katzelnick, D. J., & Serlin, R. C. (1995). Efficacy and tolerability of serotonin transport inhibitors in obsessive-compulsive disorder: A meta-analysis. *Archives of General Psychiatry*, *52*, 53–60.

Greist, J. H., Jefferson, J. W., Rosenfeld, R., Gutzmann, L. D., March, J. S., & Barklage, N. E. (1990). Clomipramine and obsessive-compulsive disorder: A placebo-controlled double-blind study of 32 patients. *Journal of Clinical Psychiatry*, *51*, 292–297.

Grimsley, S. R., & Jann, M. W. (1992). Paroxetine, sertraline, and fluvoxamine: New selective serotonin reuptake inhibitors. *Clinical Pharmacy*, *11*, 930–957.

Hewlett, W. A. (1993). The use of benzodiazepines in obsessive compulsive disorder and Tourette's syndrome. *Psychiatric Annals*, *23*, 309–316.

Hewlett, W., Vinogradov, S., & Agras, W. (1992). Clomipramine, clonazepam, and clonidine treatment of obsessive compulsive disorder. *Journal of Clinical Psychopharmacology*, *12*, 420–430.

Hoehn-Saric, R., Ninan, P., Black, D. W., Stahl, S., Greist, J. H., Lydiard, B., et al. (2000). Multicenter double-blind comparison of sertraline and desipramine for concurrent obsessive-compulsive disorder and major depressive disorders. *Archives of General Psychiatry*, *57*, 76–82.

Hollander, E. (1993). Obsessive-compulsive spectrum disorders. *Psychiatric Annals*, *23*, 355–407.

Hollander, E., Allen, A., Steiner, M., Wheadon, D. E., Oakes, R., Burnham, D. B., et al. (2003). Acute and long-term treatment and prevention of relapse of obsessive-compulsive disorder with paroxetine. *Journal of Clinical Psychiatry*, *64*, 1113–1121.

Hollander, E., Baldini Rossi, N., Sood, E., & Pallanti, S. (2003). Risperidone augmentation in treatment-resistant obsessive-compulsive disorder: A double-blind, placebo-controlled study. *The International Journal of Neuropsychopharmacology 6*, 397–401.

Hollander, E., Friedberg, J., Wasserman, S., Allan, A., Birnbaum, M., & Koran, L. M.(2003). Venlafaxine in treatment-resistant obsessive-compulsive disorder. *Journal of Clinical Psychiatry*, *64*, 546–550.

Hollander, E., Kaplan, A., & Stahl, S. M. (2003). A double-blind, placebo-controlled trial of clonazepam in obsessive-compulsive disorder. *The World Journal of Biological Psychiatry*, *4*, 30–34.

Hollander, E., Koran, L. M., Goodman, W. K., Greist, J. H., Ninan, P. T., Yang, H., et al. (2003). A double-blind, placebo-controlled study of the efficacy and safety of controlled-release fluvoxamine in patients with obsessive-compulsive disorder. *Journal of Clinical Psychiatry*, *64*, 640–647.

Hollander, E., Kwon, J. H., Stein, D. J., Broatch, J., Rowland, C. T., & Himelein, C. A. (1996). Obsessive-compulsive and spectrum disorders: Overview and quality of life issues. *Journal of Clinical Psychiatry*, *57*(Suppl. 8), 3–6.

Honagen, F., Winkelman, G., Rasche-Rauchle, H., Hand, I. Konig, A., Munchau, N., et al. (1998). Combination of behaviour therapy with fluvoxamine in comparison with behaviour therapy and placebo. *British Journal of Psychiatry, 173*(Suppl. 35), 71–78.

Hunter, R., & Macalpine, I. (1982). *Three hundred years of psychiatry 1535–1860: A history presented in selected English texts.* Hartsdale, NY: Carlisle.

Insel, T. R. (1992). Toward a neuroanatomy of obsessive-compulsive disorder. *Archives of General Psychiatry, 49,* 739–744.

Insel, T. R., Murphy, D. L., Cohen, R. M., Alterman, I., Kilts, C. & Linnoila, M (1983). Obsessive-compulsive disorder: A double-blind trial of clomipramine and clorgyline. *Archives of General Psychiatry, 40,* 605–612.

Jacobsen, F. M. (1995). Risperidone in the treatment of severe affective illness and obsessive-compulsive disorder. *Journal of Clinical Psychiatry, 56,* 423–429.

Janet, P. (1903). *Les obsessions et al psychasthenie* (Vol. 1). Paris: Alcan.

Jenike, M. A. (1989). Obsessive compulsive and related disorders: A hidden epidemic. *New England Journal of Medicine, 321,* 539–541.

Jenike, M. A. (1990). Drug treatments of obsessive-compulsive disorders. In M. A. Jenike, L. Baer, & W. E. Minichiello (Eds.), *Obsessive compulsive disorders: Theory and management* (2nd ed., pp. 249–282). Chicago: Year Book Medical Publishing.

Jenike, M. A. (1993a). Augmentation strategies for treatment-resistant obsessive-compulsive disorder. *Harvard Review of Psychiatry, 1,* 17–26.

Jenike, M. A. (1993b). Obsessive-compulsive disorder: Efficacy of specific treatments as assessed by controlled trials. *Psychopharmacology Bulletin, 29,* 487–499.

Jenike, M. A. (1998). Drug treatment of obsessive-compulsive disorders. In M. A. Jenike, L. Baer, & W. E. Minichiello (Eds.), *Obsessive-compulsive disorders: Practical management* (3rd ed., pp. 469–532). Boston: Mosby–Year Book.

Jenike, M. A. (2004). Obsessive compulsive disorder. *New England Journal of Medicine, 350,* 259–265.

Jenike, M. A., & Baer, L. (1988). Buspirone in obsessive-compulsive disorder: An open trial. *American Journal of Psychiatry, 145,* 1285–1286.

Jenike, M. A., Baer, L., Minichiello, W. E., Rauch, S. L., & Buttolph, M. L. (1997). Placebo-controlled trial of fluoxetine and phenelzine for obsessive-compulsive disorder. *American Journal of Psychiatry, 154,* 1261–1264.

Jenike, M. A., Baer, L., Summergrad, P., Weilburg, J. B., Holland, A., & Seymour, R. (1989). Obsessive-compulsive disorder: A double-blind, placebo-controlled trial of clomipramine in 27 patients. *American Journal of Psychiatry, 146,* 1328–1330.

Jenike, M. A., Baer, L., Summergrad, P., Minichiello, W. E., Holland, A., & Seymour, R. (1990). Sertraline in obsessive-compulsive disorder: A double-blind comparison with placebo. *American Journal of Psychiatry, 147,* 923, 928.

Jenike, M. A., Hyman, S. E., Baer, L. ., Holland, A., Minichiello, W. E., Buttolph, L., et al. (1990). A controlled trial of fluvoxamine for obsessive-compulsive disorder: Implications for a serotonergic theory. *American Journal of Psychiatry, 147,* 1209–1215.

Jenike, M. A., & Rauch, S. L. (1994). Managing the patient with treatment resistant obsessive compulsive disorder: Current strategies. *Journal of Clinical Psychiatry, 55*(3, Suppl.):11–17.

Jenike, M. A., & Rauch, S. L. (1995). Electroconvulsive therapy for obsessive-compulsive disorder: Drs. Jenike and Rauch reply. *Journal of Clinical Psychiatry, 56,* 81–82.

Jenike, M. A., Rauch, S. L., Baer, L., & Rasmussen, S. A. (1998). Neurosurgical treatments of obsessive-compulsive disorder. In M. A. Jenike, L. Baer, & W. E. Minichiello (Eds.), *Obsessive-compulsive disorders: Practical management* (3rd ed., pp. 592–610). Boston: Mosby–Year Book.

Jenike, M. A., Surman, O. S., Cassem, N. H., Zusky, P., & Anderson, W. H. (1983). Monoamine oxidase inhibitors in obsessive-compulsive disorder. *Journal of Clinical Psychiatry, 44,* 131–132.

Karabanow, O. (1977). Double-blind controlled study in phobias and obsessions. *Journal of International Medical Research, 5*(Suppl. 5), 42–48.

Karno, M., Golding, J. M., Sorenson, S. B., & Burnam, A. (1988). The epidemiology of obsessive-compulsive disorder in five US communities. *Archives of General Psychiatry, 45,* 1094–1099.

Kim, S., Dysken, M., & Kuskowski, M., (1990). The Yale-Brown obsessive compulsive scale: A reliability and validity study. *Psychiatric Research, 34,* 94–106.

Koponen, H., Lepola, U., Leinonen, E., Jokinen, R., Penttinen, J., & Turtonen, J. (1997). Citalopram in the treatment of obsessive-compulsive disorder: An open pilot study. *Acta Psychiatrica Scandinavica, 96,* 343–346.

Koran, L. M., Aboujaoude, E., Bullock, K. D., Franz, B., Gamel, N., & Elliott, M. (2005). Double-blind treatment with oral morphine in treatment-resistant obsessive-compulsive disorder. *Journal of Clinical Psychiatry, 66,* 353–359.

Koran, L. M., Hackett, E., Rubin, A., Wolkow, R., & Robinson, D. (2002). Efficacy of sertraline in the long-term treatment of obsessive-compulsive disorder. *American Journal of Psychiatry, 159,* 88–95.

Koran, L. M., McElroy, S. L., Davidson, J. R. T., Rasmussen, S. A., Hollander, E., & Jenike, M. A. (1996). Fluvoxamine versus clomipramine for obsessive-compulsive disorder: A double-blind comparison. *Journal of Clinical Psychopharmacology, 16,* 121–129.

Koran, L. M., Ringold, A. L., & Elliott, M A. (2000). Olanzapine augmentation for treatment-resistant obsessive-compulsive disorder. *Journal of Clinical Psychiatry, 61,* 514–517.

Koran, L. M., Sallee, F. R., & Pallanti, S. (1997). Rapid benefit of intravenous pulse loading of clomipramine in obsessive-compulsive disorder. *American Journal of Psychiatry, 154,* 396–401.

Kozak, M. J., Foa, E. B., & Steketee, G. (1988). Process and outcome of exposure treatment with obsessive-compulsives: Psychophysiological indicators of emotional processing. *Behavior Therapy, 19,* 157–169.

Kronig, M. H., Apter, J., Asnis, G., Bystritsky, A., Curtis, G., Ferguson, J., et al. (1999). Placebo-controlled, multicenter study of sertraline treatment for obsessive-compulsive disorder. *Journal of Clinical Psychopharmacology, 19,* 172–176.

LaPorta, L. D. (1994). More on obsessive-compulsive symptoms and clozapine [Letter]. *Journal of Clinical Psychiatry, 55,* 312.

Leckman, J. F., Goodman, W. K., North, W. G., Chappell, P. B., Price, L. H., Pauls, D. L., et al. (1994). The role of central oxytocin in obsessive-compulsive disorder and related normal behavior. *Psychoneuroendocrinology, 19,* 723–749.

Lei, B. S. (1986). A cross-over treatment of obsessive compulsive neurosis with imipramine and clomipramine. *Chung Hua Shen Ching Shen Ko Tsa Chih, 19,* 275–278.

Leonard, H. L., Swedo, S. E., Lenane, M. C., Rettew, D. C., Cheslow, D. L., Hamburger, S. D., et al. (1991). A double-blind desipramine substitution during long-term clomipramine treatment in children and adolescents with obsessive-compulsive disorder. *Archives of General Psychiatry, 48,* 922–927.

Leonard, H. L., Swedo, S., Rapoport, J. L., Koby, E. V., Lenane, M. C., Cheslow, D. L., et al. (1988). Treatment of childhood obsessive-compulsive disorder with clomipramine and desmethylimiparmine: A double-blind crossover comparison. *Psychopharmacology Bulletin, 24,* 93–95.

Li, X., May, R. S., Tolbert, L. C., Jackson, W.T., Flournoy, J.M., & Baxter, L.R. (2005). Risperidone and haloperidol augmentation of serotonin reuptake inhibitors in refractory obsessive-compulsive disorder: A crossover study. *Journal of Clinical Psychiatry, 66,* 736–743.

Liebowitz, M. R., Turner, S. M., Piacentini, J., Beidel, D. C., Clarvit, S. R., Davies, S. O., et al. (2002). Fluoxetine in children and adolescents with OCD: A placebo-controlled trial. *Journal of the American Academy of Child and Adolescent Psychiatry, 41,* 1431–1438.

Lindsay, M., Crino, R., & Andrews, G. (1997). Controlled trial of exposure and response prevention in obsessive-compulsive disorder. *British Journal of Psychiatry, 171,* 135–139.

Lopez-Ibor, J. J., Jr., Saiz, J., Cottraux, J., Vinas, R., Bourgeois, M., Hernandez, M., et al. (1996). Double-blind comparison of fluoxetine versus clomipramine in the treatment of obsessive compulsive disorder. *European Neuropsychopharmacology, 6,* 111–118.

Mallison, R. T., McDougle, C. J., van Dyck, C. H., Scahill, L., Baldwin, R. M., Seibyl, J. P., et al. (1995). I-123-CIT SPECT imaging of striatal dopamine transporter binding in Tourette's disorder. *American Journal of Psychiatry, 152,* 1359–1361.

Marazziti, D., Dell'Osso, L., Gemignani, A., Ciapparelli, A., Presta, S., Nasso, E. D., et al. (2001). Citalopram in refractory obsessive-compulsive disorder: An open study. *International Clinical Psychopharmacology, 16,* 215–219.

Marazziti, D., Pfanner, C., Dell'Osso, B., Ciapparelli, A., Presta, S., Corretti, G., et al. (2005). Augmentation strategy with olanzapine in resistant obsessive compulsive disorder: An Italian long-term open-label study. *Journal of Psychopharmacology, 19,* 392–394.

March, J. S. (1995). Cognitive-behavioral psychotherapy for children and adolescents with OCD: A review and recommendations for treatment. *Journal of the American Academy of Child and Adolescent Psychiatry, 34,* 7–18.

March, J. S., Biederman, J., Wolkow, R., Safferman, A., Mardekian, J., Cook, E. H., et al. (1998). Sertraline in children and adolescents with obsessive-compulsive disorder: A multicenter randomized controlled trial. *Journal of the American Medical Association, 280,* 1752– 1756.

March, J. S., Mulle, K., & Herbel, B. (1994). Behavioral psychotherapy for children and adolescents with obsessive-compulsive disorder: An open trial of a new protocol-driven treatment package. *Journal of* the American Academy of Child and Adolescent Psychiatry, 33, 333–341.

Marks, I. M. (1981). Review of behavioral psychotherapy: I. Obsessive-compulsive disorders. American Journal of Psychiatry, 138, 584–592.

Marks, I. M., Hodgson, R., & Rachman, S. (1975). Treatment of chronic obsessive-compulsive neurosis by in-vivo exposure: A two-year follow-up and issues in treatment. British Journal of Psychiatry, 127, 349–364.

Marks, I. M., Lelliott, P., Basoglu, M., Noshirvani, H., Monteiro, W., & Cohen, D., et al. (1988). Clomipramine, self-exposure and therapist-aided exposure for obsessive-compulsive rituals. British Journal of Psychiatry, 152, 522–534.

Marks, I. M., Stern, R. S., Mawson, D., Cobb, J., & McDonald, R. . (1980). Clomipramine and exposure for obsessive-compulsive rituals. British Journal of Psychiatry, 136, 1–25.

Mataix-Cols, D., Marks, I. M., Greist, J. H., Kobak, K. A., & Baer, L. (2002). Obsessive-compulsive symptom dimensions as predictors of compliance with and response to behaviour therapy: Results from a controlled trial. Psychotherapy and Psychosomatics, 71, 255–262.

Mataix-Cols, D., Rauch, S. L., Manzo, P. A., Jenike, M. A., & Baer, L. (1999). Use of factor-analyzed symptom dimensions to predict outcome with serotonin reuptake inhibitors and placebo in the treatment of obsessive-compulsive disorder. American Journal of Psychiatry, 156, 1409–1416.

Mavissakalian, M., Turner, S. M., Michelson, L., & Jacob, R. (1985). Tricyclic antidepressants in obsessive-compulsive disorder: Antiobsessional or antidepressant agents? American Journal of Psychiatry, 142, 572–576.

Mawson, D., Marks, I. M., & Ramm, L. (1982). Clomipramine and exposure for chronic obsessive-compulsive rituals: III. Two year follow-up and further findings. British Journal of Psychiatry, 140, 11–18.

McDougle, C. J., Goodman, W. K., Leckman, J. F., Barr, L. C., Heninger, G. R., & Price, L. H. (1993. The efficacy of fluvoxamine in obsessive-compulsive disorder: Effects of comorbid chronic tic disorder. Journal of Clinical Psychopharmacology, 13, 354–358.

McDougle, C. J., Goodman, W. K., Leckman, J. F., Holzer, J. C., Barr, L. C., McCance-Katz, E., et al. (1993). Limited therapeutic effect of addition of buspirone in fluvoxamine-refractory obsessive-compulsive disorder. American Journal of Psychiatry, 150, 647–649.

McDougle, C. J., Barr, L. C., Goodman, W. K., Pelton G. H., Aronson, S. C., Anand, A., et al. (1995). Lack of efficacy of clozapine monotherapy in refractory obsessive-compulsive disorder. American Journal of Psychiatry, 152, 1812–1814.

McDougle, C. J., Epperson, C. N., Pelton, G. H., Wasylink, S., & Price, L. H. (2000). A double-blind, placebo-controlled study of risperidone addition in serotonin reuptake inhibitor-refractory obsessive-compulsive disorder. Archives of General Psychiatry, 57, 794–801.

McDougle, C. J., Fleischmann, R. L., Epperson, C. N., Wasylink, S., Leckman, J. F., & Price, L. H. (1995). Risperidone addition in fluvoxamine-refractory obsessive-compulsive disorder: Three cases. Journal of Clinical Psychiatry, 56, 526–528.

McDougle, C. J., & Goodman, W. K. (1997). Combination pharmacological treatment strategies. In E. Hollander, & D. J. Stein (Eds.), Obsessive-compulsive disorders: Diagnosis — etiology — treatment (pp. 203–223). New York: Marcel Dekker.

McDougle, C. J., Goodman, W. K., Leckman, J. F., Lee, N. C., Heninger, G. R., & Price, L. H. (1994). Haloperidol addition in fluvoxamine-refractory obsessive-compulsive disorder: A double-blind, placebo-controlled study in patients with and without tics. Archives of General Psychiatry, 51, 302–308.

McDougle, C. J., Goodman, W. K., Price, L. H., Delgado, P. L., Krystal, J. H., Charney, D. S., et al. (1990). Neuroleptic addition in fluvoxamine refractory obsessive compulsive disorder. American Journal of Psychiatry, 147, 652–654.

McDougle, C. J., Price, L. H., Goodman, W. K., Charney, D. S., & Heninger, G. R. (1991). A controlled trial of lithium augmentation in fluvoxamine-refractory obsessive compulsive disorder: Lack of efficacy. Journal of Clinical Psychopharmacology, 11, 175–184.

McElroy, S. L., Phillips, K. A., & Keck, P. E. (1994). Obsessive compulsive spectrum disorder. Journal of Clinical Psychiatry, 55(Suppl.), 15–32.

Meige, H., & Feindel, E. (1907). Tics and their treatment (Trans. S. A. K. Wilson). New York: William Wood.

Milanfranchi, A., Ravagli, S., Lensi, P., Marazziti, D., & Cassano, G. B. (1997). A double-blind study of fluvoxamine and clomipramine in the treatment of obsessive-compulsive disorder. International Clinical Psychopharmacology, 12, 131–136.

Mindus, P., Rauch, S. L., Nyman, H., Baer, L., Edman, G., & Jenike, M. A. (1994). Capsulotomy and cingulotomy as treatments for malignant obsessive compulsive disorder: An update. In E. Hollander, J. Zohar, D Marazziti, & B. Olivier (Eds.), Current *insights in obsessive compulsive disorder* (pp. 245–276). Chichester, England: Wiley.

Misri, S., & Millis, L. (2004). Obsessive-compulsive disorder in the postpartum: Open-label trial of quetiapine augmentation. *Journal of Clinical Psychopharmacology, 24,* 624–627.

Mohr, N., Vythilingum, B., Emsley, R. A., & Stein, D. J. (2002). Quetiapine augmentation of serotonin reuptake inhibitors in obsessive-compulsive disorder. *International Clinical Psychopharmacology, 17,* 37–40.

Montgomery, S. A. (1980). Clomipramine in obsessional neurosis: A placebo-controlled trial. *Pharmaceutical Medicine, 1,* 189–192.

Montgomery, S. A. (1994). Pharmacological treatment of obsessive compulsive disorder. In E. Hollander, J. Zohar, D. Marazziti, & B. Olivier (Eds.), *Current insights in obsessive compulsive disorder* (pp. 215–225). Chichester, England: Wiley.

Montgomery, S. A., Kasper, S., Stein, D. J., Bang Hedegaard, K., & Lemming, O. M. (2001). Citalopram 20 mg, 40 mg and 60 mg are all effective and well tolerated compared with placebo in obsessive compulsive disorder. *International Clinical Psychopharmacology, 16,* 75–86.

Montgomery, S. A., McIntyre, A., Osterheider, M., Sarteschi, P., Zitterl, W., Zohar, J., et al. (1993). A double-blind placebo-controlled study of fluoxetine in patients with *DSM-III-R* obsessive-compulsive disorder. *European Neuropsychopharmacology, 3,* 143–152.

Mundo, E., Bareggi, S. R., Pirola, R., Bellodi, L., & Smeraldi, E. (1997). Long-term pharmacotherapy of obsessive-compulsive disorder: A double-blind controlled study. *Journal of Clinical Psychopharmacology, 17,* 4–10.

Mundo, E., Bianchi, L., & Bellodi, L. (1997). Efficacy of fluvoxamine, paroxetine, and citalopram in the treatment of obsessive-compulsive disorder: A single-blind study. *Journal of Clinical Psychopharmacology, 17,* 267–271.

Mundo, E., Maina, G., & Uslenghi, C. (2000). Multicentre, double-blind, comparison of fluvoxamine and clomipramine in the treatment of obsessive-compulsive disorder. *International Clinical Psychopharmacology, 15,* 69–76.

Mundo, E., Rouillon, F., Figuera, M. L., & Stigler, M. (2001). Fluvoxamine in obsessive-compulsive disorder: Similar efficacy but superior tolerability in comparison with clomipramine. *Human Psychopharmacology, 16,* 461–468.

Nakatani, E., Nakagawa, A., Nakao, T., Yoshizato, C., Nabeyama, M., Kudo, A., et al. (2005). A randomized controlled trial of Japanese patients with ob-

sessive-compulsive disorder: Effectiveness of behavioral therapy and fluvoxamine. *Psychotherapy and Psychosomatics, 74,* 269–276.

O'Connor, K., Todorov, C., Robillard, S., Borgeat, F., & Brault, M. (1999). Cognitive-behaviour therapy and medication in the treatment of obsessive-compulsive disorder: A controlled study. *Canadian Journal of Psychiatry, 44,* 64–71.

Pallanti, S., Quercioli, L., Paiva, R. S., & Koran, L. M. (1999). Citalopram for treatment-resistant obsessive-compulsive disorder. *European Psychiatry, 14.* 101–106.

Pato, M. T., Eisen, J. L., & Pato, C. N. (1994). Rating scales for obsessive compulsive disorder. In E. Hollander, J. Zohar, D. Marazziti, & B. Olivier (Eds.), *Current insights in obsessive compulsive disorder* (pp. 77–92). Chichester, England: Wiley.

Pato, M. T., Hill, J. L., & Murphy, D. L. (1990). A clomipramine dosage reduction study in the course of long-term treatment of obsessive-compulsive patients. *Psychopharmacology Bulletin, 26,* 211–214.

Pato, M. T., Pigott, T. A., Hill, J. L., Grover, G. N., Bernstein, S., & Murphy, D. L. (1991). Controlled comparison of buspirone and clomipramine in obsessive-compulsive disorder. *American Journal of Psychiatry, 148,* 127–129.

Pato, M. T., Zohar-Kaduch, R., Zohar, J., & Muphy, D.L. (1988). Return of symptoms after discontinuation of clomipramine in patients with obsessive compulsive disorder. *American Journal of Psychiatry, 145,* 1521–1525.

Pauls, D. L., Alsobrook, J. P., Goodman, W., Rasmussen, S., & Leckman, J. F. (1995). A family study of obsessive-compulsive disorder. *American Journal of Psychiatry, 152,* 76–84.

Pauls, D. L., & Leckman, J. F. (1986). The inheritance of Gilles de la Tourette's syndrome and associated behaviors: Evidence for autosomal dominant transmission. *New England Journal of Medicine, 315,* 993–997.

Pediatric OCD Treatment Study (POTS) Team. (2004). Cognitive-behavior therapy, sertraline, and their combination for children and adolescents with obsessive-compulsive disorder: The Pediatric OCD Treatment Study (POTS) randomized controlled trial. *Journal of the American Medical Association, 292,* 1969–1976.

Perse, T. L., Greist, J. H., Jefferson, J. W., Rosenfeld, R., & Dar, R. (1987). Fluvoxamine treatment of obsessive-compulsive disorder. *American Journal of Psychiatry, 144,* 1543–1548.

Pfanner, C., Marazziti, D., Dell'Osso, L., Presta, S., Gemignani, A., Milanfranchi, A., et al. (2000). Risperidone augmentation in refractory obsessive-compulsive disorder: An open-label study. *International Clinical Psychopharmacology, 15,* 297–301.

Pigott, T. A., L'Heueux, F., Hill, J. L., Bihari, K., Bernstien, S. E., & Murphy, D. L. (1982). A double-blind study of adjuvant buspirone hydrochloride in clomipramine-treated patients. *Journal of Clinical Psychopharmacology, 12,* 11–18.

Pigott, T. A., L'Heueux, F., Rubenstein, C. S., Bernstein, S. E., Hill, J. L., & Murphy, D. L. (1992). A double-blind, placebo controlled study of trazodone in patients with obsessive-compulsive disorder. *Journal of Clinical Psychopharmacology, 12,* 156–162.

Pigott, T. A., L'Heueux, F., Rubenstein, C. S., Hill, J. L., & Murphy, D. L. (1992, May). *A controlled trial of clonazepam augmentation in OCD patients treated with clomipramine or fluoxetine.* Paper presented at the American Psychiatry Association Annual Meeting, Washington, DC.

Pigott, T. A., Pato, M. T., Bernstein, S. E., Grover, G. N., Hill, J. L., Tolliver, T. J., et al. (1990). Controlled comparisons of clomipramine and fluoxetine in the treatment of obsessive-compulsive disorder. *Archives of General Psychiatry, 47,* 926–932.

Pigott, T. A., Pato, M. T., L'Heueux, F., Hill, J. L., Grover, G. N., Bernstein, S. E., et al. (1991). A controlled comparison of adjuvant lithium carbonate or thyroid hormone in clomipramine-treated patients with obsessive compulsive disorder. *Journal of Clinical Psychopharmacology, 11,* 242–248.

Pigott, T. A., & Seay, S. M. (1999). A review of the efficacy of selective serotonin reuptake inhibitors in obsessive-compulsive disorders. *Journal of Clinical Psychiatry, 60,* 101–106.

Pitman, R. K. (1994). Obsessive compulsive disorder in western history. In E. Hollander, J. Zohar, D. Marazziti, & B. Olivier (Eds.), *Current insights in obsessive compulsive disorder* (pp. 3–10). Chichester, England: Wiley.

Pittenger, C., Krystal, J. H., & Coric, V. (2006). Glutamate-modulating drugs as novel pharmacotherapeutic agents in the treatment of obsessive-compulsive disorder. *NeuroRx: The Journal of the American Society for Experimental Neurotherapeutics, 3,* 69–81.

Poyurovsky, M., Weizman, R., Weizman, A., & Koran, L. (2005). Memantine for treatment-resistant OCD. *American Journal of Psychiatry, 162,* 2191–2192.

Quality Assurance Project. (1985). Treatment outlines for the management of obsessive-compulsive disorders. *Australian and New Zealand Journal of Psychiatry, 19,* 240–253.

Rachman, S., Cobb, J., Grey, S., McDonald, B., Mawson, D., Sartory, G., et al. (1979). The behavioural treatment of obsessional-compulsive disorders, with and without clomipramine. *Behaviour Research and Therapy, 17,* 467–478.

Rachman, S. J., & Hodgson, R. J. (1980). *Obsessions and compulsions.* Englewood Cliffs, NJ: Prentice-Hall.

Rachman, S., Hodgson, R., & Marks, I. M. (1971). The treatment of chronic obsessive-compulsive neurosis. *Behaviour Research and Therapy, 9,* 237–247.

Rachman, S., Marks, I. M., & Hodgson, R. (1973). The treatment of obsessive-compulsive neurotics by modeling and flooding in vivo. *Behaviour Research and Therapy, 11,* 463–471.

Rapoport, J., Elkins, R., & Mikkelsen, E. (1980). Clinical controlled trial of clomipramine in adolescents with obsessive-compulsive disorder. *Psychopharmacology Bulletin, 16,* 61–63.

Rapoport, J. L., & Wise, S. P. (1988). Obsessive-compulsive disorder: Evidence for basal ganglia dysfunction. *Psychopharmacology Bulletin, 24,* 380–384.

Rapoport, J. L. (1980). *The boy who couldn't stop washing.* New York: Dutton.

Rasmussen, S. A., & Eisen, J. L. (1994). The epidemiology and differential diagnosis of obsessive compulsive disorder. *Journal of Clinical Psychiatry, 55*(Suppl.), 5–14.

Rasmussen, S. A., Goodman, W. K., Greist, J. H., Jenike, M. A., Kozak, M. J., Liebowitz, M., et al. (in press). Fluvoxamine in the treatment of obsessive compulsive disorder: A multi- center, double-blind placebo-controlled study in outpatients. *American Journal of Psychiatry.*

Rasmussen, S. A., & Tsuang, M. T. (1986). Clinical characteristics and family history in DSM-III obsessive-compulsive disorder. *American Journal of Psychiatry, 143,* 317–322.

Rauch, S. L., Baer, L., & Jenike, M. A. (1996). Management of treatment resistant obsessive compulsive disorder: Practical considerations and strategies. In M. H. Pollack, M. W. Otto, & J. F. Rosenbaum (Eds.), *Challenges in psychiatric treatment: Pharmacologic and psychosocial perspectives* (pp. 201–218). New York: Guilford Press.

Rauch, S. L., & Jenike, M. A. (1993). Neurobiological models of obsessive-compulsive disorder. *Psychosomatics, 34,* 20–32.

Rauch, S. L., & Jenike, M. A. (1994). Management of treatment resistant obsessive-compulsive disorder: Concepts and strategies. In B. Berend, E. Hollander, D. Marazitti, & J. Zohar (Eds.), *Current insights in obsessive-compulsive disorder* (pp. 227–244). Chichester, England: Wiley.

Rauch, S. L., Whalen, P. J., Dougherty, D., & Jenike, M. A. (1998). Neurobiologic models of obsessive-compulsive disorder. In M. A. Jenike, L. Baer, & W. E. Minichiello (Eds.), *Obsessive-compulsive disorders: Practical management* (3rd ed., pp. 222–253). Boston: Mosby–Year Book.

Ravizza, L., Barzega, G., Bellino, S., Bogetto, F., & Maina, G. (1995). Predictors of drug treatment response in obsessive-compulsive disorder. *Journal of Clinical Psychiatry, 56*, 368–373.

Ravizza, L., Barzega, G., Bellino, S., Bogetto, F., & Maina, G. (1996a). Drug treatment of obsessive-compulsive disorder (OCD): Long-term trial with clomipramine and selective serotonin reuptake inhibitors (SSRIs). *Psychopharmacology Bulletin, 32*, 167–173.

Ravizza, L., Barzega, G., Bellino, S., Bogetto, F., & Maina, G. (1996b). Therapeutic effect and safety of adjunctive risperidone in refractory obsessive-compulsive disorder. *Psychopharmacology Bulletin, 32*, 677–682.

Remington, G., & Adams, M. (1994). Risperidone and obsessive-compulsive symptoms. *Journal of Clinical Psychopharmacology, 14*, 358–359.

Riddle, M. A., Reeve, E. A., Yaryura-Tobias, J. A., Yang, H. M., Claghorn, J. L., Gaffney, G., et al. (2001). Fluvoxamine for children and adolescents with obsessive-compulsive disorder: A randomized, controlled, multicenter trial. *Journal of the American Academy of Child and Adolescent Psychiatry, 40*, 222–229.

Riddle, M. A., Scahill, L., King, R. A., Hardin, M. T., Anderson, G. M., Org, S. I., et al. (1992). Fluoxetine in the treatment of obsessive-compulsive disorder in children and adolescents. *Journal of the American Academy of Child and Adolescent Psychiatry, 31*, 575.

Rimm, D. C., & Masters, J. C. (1974). *Behavior therapy: Techniques and empirical findings.* New York: Academic Press.

Romano, S., Goodman, W., Tamura, R., & Gonzales, J. (2001). Long-term treatment of obsessive-compulsive disorder after an acute response: A comparison of fluoxetine versus placebo. *Journal of Clinical Psychopharmacology, 21*, 46–52.

Saxena, S., Wang, D., Bystritsky, A., & Baxter, L. R., Jr. (1996). Risperidone augmentation of SRI treatment for refractory obsessive-compulsive disorder. *Journal of Clinical Psychiatry, 57*, 303–306.

Scahill, L., Vitulano, L. A., Brenner, E. M., Lynch, K. A., & King, R. A. (1996). Behavioral therapy in children and adolescents with obsessive-compulsive disorder: A pilot study. *Journal of Child and Adolescent Psychopharmacology, 6*, 191–202.

Schwartz, J. M., Stoessel, P. W., Baxter, L. R., Martin, K. M., & Phelps, M. E. (1996). Systematic changes in cerebral glucose metabolic rate after successful behavior modification. *Archives of General Psychiatry, 53*, 109–113.

Shapira, N. A., Ward, H. E., Mandoki, M., Murphy, T. K., Yang, M. C., Blier, P., et al. (2004). A double-blind, placebo-controlled trial of olanzapine addition in fluoxetine-refractory obsessive-compulsive disorder. *Biological Psychiatry, 55*, 553–555.

Solyom, L., & Sookman, D. (1977). A comparison of clomipramine hydrochloride (Anafranil) and behaviour therapy in the treatment of obsessive neurosis. *Journal of International Medical Research, 5*(Suppl. 5), 49–106.

Steketee, G., Foa, E., & Grayson, J. B. (1982). Recent advances in the behavioral treatment of obsessive-compulsives. *Archives of General Psychiatry, 39*, 1365–1371.

Swedo, S. E. (1994). Sydenham's chorea: A model for childhood autoimmune neuropsychiatric disorders. *Journal of the American Medical Association, 272*, 1788–1791.

Swedo, S. E., Leonard, H. L., Garvey, M., Mittleman, B., Allen, A. J., Perlmutter, S., et al. (1998). Pediatric autoimmune neuropsychiatric disorders associated with streptococcal infections: Clinical description of the first 50 cases. *American Journal of Psychiatry, 155*, 264–271.

Swedo, S. E., Leonard, H. L., & Kiessling, L. S. (1994). Speculations on antineuronal antibody-mediated neuropsychiatric disorders of childhood. *Pediatrics, 93*, 323–326.

Swerdlow, N. R. (1995). Serotonin, obsessive-compulsive disorder and the basal ganglia. *International Review of Psychiatry, 7*, 115–129.

Thomsen, P. H. (2004). Risperidone augmentation in the treatment of severe adolescent OCD in SSRI-refractory cases: A case-series. *Annals of Clinical Psychiatry, 16*, 201–207.

Thoren, P., Åsberg, M., Cronholm, B., Jornestedt, L., & Traskman, L. (1980). Clomipramine treatment of obsessive compulsive disorder: I. A controlled clinical trial. *Archives of General Psychiatry, 37*, 1281–1285.

Tollefson, G. D., Birkett, M., Koran, L., & Genduso, L. (1994). Continuation treatment of OCD: Double-blind and open-label experience with fluoxetine. *Journal of Clinical Psychiatry, 55*(10, Suppl.), 69–76.

Tollefson, G. D., Rampey, A. H., Jr., Potvin, J. H., Jenike, M. A., Rush, A. J., Dominguez, R. A., et al. (1994). A multicenter investigation of fixed-dose fluoxetine in the treatment of obsessive-compulsive disorder. *Archives of General Psychiatry, 51,* 559–567.

Vallejo, J., Olivares, J., Marcos, T., Bulbena, A., & Menchon, J. (1992). Clomipramine versus phenelzine in obsessive-compulsive disorder: A controlled trial. *British Journal of Psychiatry, 161,* 665–670.

van Balkom, A. J., de Haan, E., van Oppen, P., Spinhoven, P., Hoogduin, K. A., & van Dyck, R. (1998). Cognitive and behavioral therapies alone versus in combination with fluvoxamine in the treatment of obsessive-compulsive disorder. *Journal of Nervous Mental Disorders, 186,* 492–499.

Volavka, J., Neziroglu, F., & Yaryura-Tobias, J. A. (1985). Clomipramine and imipramine in obsessive-compulsive disorder. *Psychiatry Research, 14,* 83–91.

Warneke, L. B. (1989). The use of intravenous clomipramine therapy in obsessive compulsive disorder. *Canadian Journal of Psychiatry, 34,* 853–859.

Wheadon, D. E., Bushnell, W. D., & Steiner, M. (1993, December). *A fixed dose comparison of 20, 40, or 60 mg of paroxetine to placebo in the treatment of OCD.* Paper presented at the annual meeting of the American College of Neuropsychopharmacology, Honolulu, HI.

Young, C. R., Bostic, J. Q., & McDonald, C. L. (1994). Clozapine and refractory obsessive compulsive disorder: A case report [Letter]. *Journal of Clinical Psychopharmacology, 14,* 209–211.

Zahn, T. P., Insel, T. R., &Murphy, D. L. (1984). Psychophysiological changes during pharmacological treatment of patients with obsessive-compulsive disorder. *British Journal of Psychiatry, 145,* 39–44.

Zhao, J. P. (1991). A controlled study of clomipramine and amitriptyline for treating obsessive-compulsive disorder. *Chung Hua Shen Ching Shen Ko Tsa Chih, 24,* 68–70.

Zohar, J., & Judge, R., (1996). Paroxetine versus clomipramine in the treatment of obsessive-compulsive disorder. *British Journal of Psychiatry, 169,* 468–474.

17

Pharmacological Treatment
of Posttraumatic Stress Disorder

Julia A. Golier

Juliana Legge

Rachel Yehuda

There have been rapid advances made in the pharmacological treatment of chronic posttraumatic stress disorder (PTSD) in the last decade. Based on numerous controlled clinical trials, antidepressants are the first-line pharmacological treatment for this disorder. Multiple studies suggest the selective serotonin reuptake inhibitors (fluoxetine, sertraline, and paroxetine) are efficacious in reducing PTSD-specific symptoms and improving global outcome; tricyclic antidepressants (imipramine) and monoamine oxidase inhibitors (phenelzine) have also been found to be efficacious. For those who are resistant or refractory to antidepressant treatment, prazosin is emerging as a beneficial adjunctive agent in treating PTSD-related sleep disturbances and nightmares, and atypical antipsychotics (risperidone, olanzapine) appear to be efficacious against a broad range of symptoms, though their potential for causing metabolic side effects may limit their use. Controlled clinical trials are needed to assess whether anticonvulsants, cortisol, and sympatholytics are efficacious, and how and when pharmacotherapy can supplement or enhance psychotherapy outcomes. The pace of advances in recent years suggests that the promise of even more effective pharmacological treatments for PTSD is likely to be realized in the coming years.

BRIEF DESCRIPTION OF PTSD
AS CURRENTLY DEFINED IN *DSM-IV*

The diagnosis of posttraumatic stress disorder (PTSD) first appeared in the third edition of the *Diagnostic and Statistical Manual of Mental Disorders* (American Psychiatric Association [APA], 1980), with the intention of describing the characteristic symptoms that occur in individuals following exposure to extremely traumatic events. Although classified as an anxiety disorder, PTSD also has features of mood, dissociative, and personality disorders and, in its most severe forms, psychotic disorders.

DIAGNOSTIC CRITERIA

The first diagnostic criterion (Criterion A) for PTSD is that a person must experience or witness an event that involves "actual or threatened physical harm" to the self or others, and have an immediate subjective response to this experience that involves "intense fear, helplessness or horror" (APA, 1994).

The symptoms of PTSD are then classified into three discrete clusters that constitute diagnostic Criteria B through D. Intrusive symptoms (Criterion B) include (a) having recurrent and unwanted recollections of the event; (b) having distressing dreams of the event; and (c) acting and feeling as if the event were reoccurring (e.g., dissociative flashback). Additionally, (d) psychological and (e) physiological distress following exposure to symbolic representations of the event may also occur. Avoidant symptoms (Criterion C) reflect both behaviors indicative of actively avoiding reminders of the trauma and symptoms of generalized emotional numbing. The former include (a) efforts to avoid thoughts, feelings, or talk of the trauma; (b) efforts to avoid reminders of the trauma; and (c) inability to recall important aspects of the trauma (e.g., psychogenic amnesia). The latter symptoms are (d) markedly diminished interest in normally significant activities; (e) feelings of detachment or estrangement from others; (f) restricted range of affect; and (g) sense of a foreshortened future. Hyperarousal symptoms (Criterion D) include: (a) difficulty falling or staying asleep; (b) irritability or angry outbursts; (c) difficulties with concentration; (d) hypervigilance; and (e) exaggerated startle response. Meeting diagnostic criteria for PTSD requires the concurrent presence of one intrusive symptom, three avoidant symptoms, and two hyperarousal symptoms.

In addition to the above criteria, symptoms must be present for at least 1 month (Criterion E) and must be accompanied by clinically significant impairment in social, occupational, or other areas of functioning (Criterion F). If symptoms last for more than 3 months following the traumatic event, the diagnosis of chronic PTSD is given. The diagnosis of delayed-onset PTSD is given if symptoms begin at least 6 months after the traumatic event. PTSD may be diagnosed in any person who meets the above diagnostic criteria, regardless of other preexisting or concurrent psychopathology.

PREVALENCE

Epidemiological studies have demonstrated that PTSD is a common psychiatric condition, with an estimated lifetime prevalence of between 1 and 14% in the U.S. general population (Breslaum Davis, Andreski, & Peterson, 1991; Davidson, Hughes, Blazer, & George, 1991; Helzer, Robins, & McEvoy, 1987; Kessler, Sonnega, Bromet, Hughes, & Nelson, 1995; Shore, Vollmer, & Tatum, 1989). The high frequency of PTSD primarily reflects the extraordinarily high prevalence of interpersonal violence in

this society. More than 50% of adults in the United States have experienced a traumatic event based on the *DSM-IV* criteria (Kessler et al., 1995). Estimates of the prevalence of PTSD among those exposed to Criterion A stressors range from 3 to 58% (APA, 1994). This wide range reflects the fact that some types of traumatic events are more likely to result in PTSD than others. Among those who have experienced torture, such as concentration camp survivors and prisoners of war, the prevalence of PTSD can be quite high, with estimates of 50 to 75% in such samples (Goldstein, van Kammen, Shelly, Miller, & Kammen, 1987; Kluznick, Speed, Van Valenburg, & Magraw, 1986). Among war veterans, estimates of lifetime PTSD are about 30%. However, in individuals who have been exposed to natural disasters such as earthquakes, volcanic eruptions, and bush fires, the prevalence of lifetime PTSD is lower, with estimates ranging from 3.5 to 16% (McFarlane, 1992; Shore, Tatum, & Vollmer, 1986; Shore et al., 1989). Estimates of the prevalence of PTSD in trauma survivors may also vary depending on the amount of time that has elapsed between the traumatic event and assessment of PTSD. The few studies that have examined the longitudinal course of PTSD prospectively demonstrated that frequency of PTSD following a specific traumatic event declines with time (Kessler et al., 1995; McFarlane, 1989; Rothbaum, Foa, Riggs, Murdock, & Walsh, 1992), with symptoms for the majority of trauma survivors resolving within 2 to 3 years. However, for the minority of individuals who remain symptomatic, the symptoms of PTSD may intensify over time, as does the risk of developing secondary and chronic comorbid mood or anxiety disorder, substance abuse, and memory impairment (Freedy, Shaw, & Jarrell, 1992; Green, Lindy, Grace, & Leonard, 1992; Kulka et al., 1990; North, Smith, & Spitznagel, 1994; Golier et al., 2002).

ETIOLOGY

By definition, exposure to a traumatic event is a necessary requirement for the development of PTSD. However, only a minority of persons exposed to even the most severe traumas develops PTSD. Therefore, there are other risk factors that influence the development or persistence of symptoms following trauma exposure. These include the severity of the trauma (Foy, Sipprelle, Rueger, & Carroll, 1984; March,

1993; Yehuda, Southwick, & Giller, 1992); past history of stress, abuse, or trauma (Bremner, Southwick, Johnson, Yehuda, & Charney, 1993; Zaidi & Foy, 1994); history of behavioral or psychological problems (Helzer et al., 1987); premorbid psychopathology (McFarlane et al., 1989); genetic factors (True et al., 1993); family history of psychopathology (Davidson, Swartz, Storck, Krishnan, & Hammett, 1985); and lower IQ (Macklin et al., 1998) as well as subsequent exposure to reactivating environmental events (Goldstein et al., 1987; Kluznick et al., 1986; McFarlane, 1990; Schnurr, Friedman, & Rosenberg, 1993; Solomon & Preager, 1992; 1994; True et al., 1993; Yehuda et al., 1995). Women are also at increased risk for developing PTSD, likely as a result of a greater exposure to assault (Breslau et al., 2002). An awareness of the risk factors can have significant implications for the treatment of this chronic, heterogeneous, and multifaceted disorder, since the associated psychopathology may not simply be a direct response to a traumatic event.

BRIEF OVERVIEW OF PSYCHOTHERAPY IN PTSD

When first described in the *DSM-III*, PTSD was conceptualized as defining normative symptoms that occur following exposure to extremely stressful events. Because of the emphasis on both the environmental etiology of PTSD and the psychological nature of the response, earliest formulations of treatment were psychosocial in nature. Psychodynamic theories emphasized that PTSD occurred when normal coping mechanisms were overwhelmed, and avoidance interfered with the processing of the trauma (Horowitz, 1974; Schwartz, 1990). These theories postulated that the symptoms of PTSD would be relieved when the individual could integrate the traumatic event into his or her life narrative and self-concept. The chosen vehicle for achieving this integration was psychodynamic psychotherapy. The aim of psychotherapy for trauma survivors was to modify the maladaptive defenses and coping strategies used in the aftermath of the trauma by helping the patient fully process the traumatic experience, with all its implications, and emerge from the experience intact and capable of continuing to engage with others and in the world.

Behavioral theorists explained PTSD as a conditioned fear response and postulated that effective treatments involved reexposing individuals to aspects of the traumatic event through psychoeducation and systematic desensitization or the more extreme technique of "flooding" (Keane, Fairbank, Caddell, & Zimering, 1989). Theoretically, symptoms could be relieved by applying learning principals and monitoring the response to traumatic reminders until patients became desensitized to these stimuli (Cooper & Clum, 1989; Keane et al., 1989). More recent treatments have combined behavioral and cognitive principles (Foa, Steketee, & Olasov Rothbaum, 1989; Foa, Olasov, Rothbaum, Riggs, & Murdock, 1991; Kilpatrick, Veronen, & Resick, 1982). These treatments make use of behavioral principles such as extinction and habituation and/or incorporate anxiety-reducing techniques, such as relaxation training (Kilpatrick et al., 1982). An important goal of these treatments is to help the patients modify their misperceptions about the trauma (such as that they could have anticipated, avoided, or mitigated the event or its impact), as well as addressing the maladaptive behavioral responses.

Based on the empirical literature, psychotherapies that utilize cognitive-behavioral techniques coupled with psychoeducation are among the most effective treatments for chronic PTSD (Foa, 2000; Solomon & Johnson, 2002). Among these are prolonged exposure therapy (Foa et al., 1989), cognitive-processing therapy (Resick & Schnicke 1992), and eye-movement desensitization reprocessing (Shapiro, 1996). Other psychotherapies that have been show to be effective include imagery rehearsal training (Forbes et al., 2003; Krakow et al., 2001) and virtual reality therapy (Rothbaum et al., 1999). Many of these are very effective treatments for PTSD and are reviewed elsewhere in this volume (see chapter 15).

PHARMACOTHERAPY IN ADULTS WITH PTSD

Rationale for the Use of Pharmacotherapy in PTSD

An early view of the role of pharmacotherapy in the treatment of PTSD suggested that medications should be considered primarily as adjunctive to psychotherapy by modulating anxiety and depression to facilitate therapy. Antidepressants and anxiolytics were also considered to be indicated owing to the high rates of comorbid mood and anxiety disorders in PTSD. However, as research in the biological underpinnings of PTSD progressed, it became evident that there were alterations in the catecholaminergic and serotonergic systems and in the hypothalamic-pituitary-adrenal (HPA) axis in PTSD that were distinct from the alterations seen in other psychiatric disorders (e.g., Charney, Deutch, Krystal, Southwick, & Davis, 1993; Yehuda, Giller, & Mason, 1993). This provided for a rational approach to pharmacotherapy in PTSD that might reduce symptoms by acting on neurotransmitter systems implicated by these alterations. Increasing appreciation of the prevalence, severity, and chronicity of PTSD together with the availability of novel psychotropic agents on the market have also fueled the advances made in the pharmacological treatment of this disorder and supported the notion that medication can be a primary treatment for core symptoms of PTSD (Davidson, 1992; Friedman, 1988).

Assessment of the Efficacy of Pharmacotherapy in PTSD

Table 17.1 summarizes the open-label and controlled pharmacological trials in the acute-phase treatment of chronic PTSD. The medications studied include antidepressants, antipsychotics, benzodiazepines, hypnotic agents, anticonvulsants and mood stabilizers, and sympatholytics as well as other medications that are emerging as potential treatments (e.g., cortisol).

The medications are listed by category, and for each drug the studies are ranked according to their type (Type 1 though Type 4). To facilitate comparisons among the studies, the table includes information regarding the sample size and gender distribution, treatment population, the percent change in total PTSD symptoms from baseline to treatment end point, and the scales used to measure it. Additionally, the rate of treatment response is provided, as well as information regarding whether there were beneficial effects on specific symptoms (intrusive, avoidant, or hyperarousal symptoms, depression, or sleep).

The earliest studies used measures of depression or anxiety as primary outcome measures (e.g., the Hamilton Rating Scale for Depression (HAM-D; Hamilton, 1960) before validated scales for PTSD were available. Others have relied on self-report instruments of PTSD symptoms such as the Impact of Events Scale (Horowitz, Wilner, & Alvarez, 1979) and the Mississippi Scale for PTSD (Keane, Caddell, & Taylor, 1988). Over time, studies have increasingly relied on validated clinician-rated instruments such as the Clinician Administered PTSD Scale (CAPS; Blake et al., 1990), the Treatment of PTSD scale (TOP-8; Davidson & Colket, 1997), and Structured Interview for PTSD (SIP; Davidson, Malik, & Travers, 1997). For more global measures of outcome, the Clinical Global Impression-Severity (CGI-S) and Clinical Global Impression-Improvement (CGI-I) scale (Guy, 1976) are used. Responder status in PTSD studies is often defined as subjects having been "much improved" or "very much improved" on the CGI. Other definitions of responder status are based on categorical levels of symptom improvement (most often defined as a 30% reduction in PTSD symptom severity), which are used alone or in combination with the CGI-I score. Less often, remission rates are reported, which is defined as the patient no longer meets criteria for the diagnosis or has a CAPS score of 20 or lower, which is indicative of only mild symptoms.

This table summarizes "acute phase" treatment of PTSD, referring to the initiation of a course of treatment. It does not refer to acute PTSD; for the majority of studies, the illness had been present for years to decades prior to the treatment trial, which often was not the first treatment trial. Details of the duration of illness, time since trauma exposure, and extent of treatment history could not be provided for each study but are mentioned for some of the most influential studies or when such information was particularly germane (e.g., studies of PTSD resistant to selective serotonin reuptake inhibitors [SSRIs]). The extent of psychiatric comorbidity is also not explicitly summarized in the table, but for virtually every study there were high rates of comorbid disorders. Major depression was almost always the most common comorbid condition. Generalized anxiety disorder, dysthymia, social phobia, panic disorder, agoraphobia, and a lifetime history of alcohol or substance abuse/dependence were also common comorbid conditions. Primary psychotic disorders and active substance abuse were almost always exclusionary.

The trials were most typically completed on relatively stabilized outpatients. Thus for many studies, there were likely earlier clinical interventions related to establishing stability, assessing safety and dangerousness, engaging the trauma survivor in treatment, forming a therapeutic alliance, and treating active substance abuse that may have preceded the initiation of the treatment trials but are not specifically addressed in the studies under review.

Acute Phase Treatment in PTSD

Monoamine Oxidase Inhibitors

Monoamine oxidase inhibitors (MAOIs) were among the first medications to be systematically studied in the treatment of PTSD. An open trial of phenelzine published in 1981 noted dramatic reduction in traumatic dreams, flashbacks, and violent outbursts in five veterans with traumatic war neurosis (Hogben & Cornfield, 1981). Subsequent studies supported this pattern of reduction in intrusive symptoms in open trials in U.S. combat veterans with PTSD (Davidson, Walker, & Kilts, 1987; Milanes et al., 1984). To date there have been two controlled trials of phenelzine. In a randomized, double-blind, crossover trial of 13 patients with PTSD of mixed trauma type, 4 weeks of phenelzine was not efficacious (Shestatzky, Greenberg, & Lerer, 1988). In an 8-week double-blind, placebo-controlled trial, veterans were randomized to phenelzine (60 to 75 mg/day), imipramine (200 to 300 mg/day), or placebo. Active medication was associated with significant decreases in PTSD symptoms as measured by the impact of events scale (IES), particularly intrusive symptoms. The magnitude of effect was largest in the phenelzine-treated group, which experienced 68% global improvement, compared with 45% improvement with imipramine and 28% improvement in the placebo group. Improvement was evident in the absence of a medication effect on anxiety or depression. Thus, this was one of the first studies to demonstrate that medications can improve PTSD symptoms independent of their antidepressant efficacy.

A disadvantage with the use of MAOIs is the necessity for diet restrictions and the risk of hypertensive crisis from tyramine-containing foods and other medications. This drawback to MAOIs has been obviated with the development of reversible inhibitors of monoamineoxidase-A that do not interact with normal dietary quantities of tyramine and have a more favorable side-effect profile. Among these are moclobemide and brofaromine. In a 12-week open-label study of moclobemide in 20 patients with

PTSD, significant improvement was evident in total PTSD symptoms, depression, anxiety, and overall functioning. The effect sizes were quite large, and 55% of the subjects no longer met criteria for PTSD, by far the highest remission rate reported in a medication trial in PTSD. In contrast, a controlled trial of brofaromine was negative. In a large ($N = 118$) multicenter, double-blind, parallel trial, the maximum improvement in total CAPS scores over 12 weeks was 33% in the brofaromine group and 31% in the placebo group. Of note, moclobemide is not available in the United States, and brofaromine was withdrawn from the market in 1994. Together, the data do not provide uniform support for the use of MAOIs as a class of drug in PTSD, but they do support the use of phenelzine and moclobemide in particular in the treatment of chronic PTSD.

Tricyclic and Tetracyclic Antidepressants

Prior to the introduction of SSRIs, tricyclic antidepressants were the most-studied class of medications in PTSD. In addition to multiple positive retrospective reviews and case reports (Birkhimer, DeVane, & Muniz, 1985; Blake, 1986; Bleich, Siegel, Garb, & Lerer, 1986; Burstein et al., 1988; Falcon et al., 1985; Shen & Park, 1983; Turchan, Holmes, & Wasserman, 1992), there have been three randomized clinical trials of tricyclic antidepressants, one trial each for imipramine (Kosten, Frank, Dan, McDougle, & Giller, 1991), desipramine (Reist et al., 1989), and amitriptyline (Davidson et al., 1990).

A 4-week, double-blind, crossover study of desipramine (200 mg/day) versus placebo was conducted with 18 U.S. veterans. Desipramine treatment was associated with significant improvement in depression, but IES scores were virtually unchanged after desipramine or placebo (Reist et al., 1989). Given that it subsequently became clear that 8 weeks is the minimum duration of a treatment trial in PTSD and that there are other methodological limitations (absence of clinician-rated PTSD scales, small sample size), this negative controlled study should be considered preliminary. In the previously mentioned trial of phenelzine and imipramine (Kosten et al., 1991), 8 weeks of imipramine (200 to 300 mg/day) was superior to placebo in combat veterans with PTSD, with reduction in overall PTSD symptoms and intrusive symptoms. An 8-week trial of amitriptyline (150 to 300 mg/day) was conducted in veterans from World

TABLE 17.1 Pharmacological Treatment Trials in Chronic PTSD

Drug Type	Study Type	First Author (year)	Drug	Duration	Subjects	Mean Age (yrs)	Population
MAOIs	1	Baker (1995)	Brofaromine	12 weeks	118 (88.7% men)	45	Mixed trauma, primarily combat related
	1	Kosten (1991)	Phenelzine	8 weeks	37 (100% men)	39	Combat veterans
	2	Shestatzky (1988)	Phenelzine	4 weeks	13 (not specified)	39	Mixed trauma, primarily combat related
	3	Neal (1997)	Moclobemide	12 weeks	20 (85% men)	31	Civilians and veterans, mixed trauma, primarily motor vehicle accidents
	3	Lerer (1987)	Phenelzine	4 weeks	22 (100% men)	28	Combat veterans
Tricyclic or tetracyclic	1	Davidson, Kudler (1990)	Amitriptyline	8 weeks	40 (100% men)	NR	Combat veterans
	1	Kosten (1991)	Imipramine	8 weeks	41 (100% men)	39	Combat veterans
	2	Reist (1989)	Desipramine	4 weeks	18 (100% men)	NR	Combat veterans
	2	Davidson (2003)	Mirtazapine	8 weeks	29 (81% women)	48	Civilians and veterans, mixed trauma
	3	Chung (2004)	Mirtazapine	6 weeks	51 (100% men)	59	Combat veterans
	3	Kim (2005)	Mirtazapine		12 (75% men)	34	Korean veterans
	3	Bahk (2002)	Mirtazapine	24 weeks	15 (66.7% men)	36	NR
	3	Connor, Davidson et al. (1999)	Mirtazapine	8 weeks	6 (88.4% women)	41	Mixed civilian trauma, primarily vehicle accidents
SSRIs	1	Connor, Davidson et al. (1999)	Fluoxetine	12 weeks	53 (93% women)	36	Mixed civilian trauma, primarily sexual abuse
	1	Martenyi (2002)	Fluoxetine	12 weeks	301 (81% men)	38	Mixed trauma, 48% combat exposure
	1	van der Kolk (1994)	Fluoxetine	5 weeks	64 (66% men)	41	Mixed trauma, primarily combat or assault
	2	Hertzberg (2000)	Fluoxetine	12 weeks	12 (100% men)	46	Combat veterans
	3	Nagy (1993)	Fluoxetine	10 weeks	27 (100% men)	45	Combat veterans
	3	McDougle (1991)	Fluoxetine	10 weeks	20 (100% men)	41	Combat veterans

PTSD SX Scale	% Improvement Total PTSD Sx		Response Rates		Efficacy on Subscales and Comorbid Symptoms				
	Drug	PBO	Drug	PBO	Int.	Avoid.	Hyp.	Dep	Sleep
CAPS	33.2%	30.9%	33.0%	31.0%	No	No	No	NR	NR
IES	44.4%	5.1%*	68.0%	28.0%*	Yes	Yes	NR	No	NR
PTSD	5.0%	6.2%	NR	NR	No	No	No	No	NR
IES	48.6%*		61.0%		Yes	Yes	NR	Yes	Yes
DSM-III	14.7%		18.2%		Yes	No	Yes	No	Yes
SIP	32.1%	20.4%	50.0%	16.6%*	No	Yes	NR	Yes	NR
IES	24.9%	5.1%*	65.0%	28.0%*	Yes	No	NR	No	NR
IES	2.5%	.9%	NR	NR	No	No	NR	Yes	NR
SIP	42.8%	22.0%	64.7%	20.0%*	NR	NR	NR	No	NR
CAPS	43.4%*		96.0%		Yes	Yes	Yes	Yes	NR
SIP	52.8%*		NR		NR	NR	NR	Yes	NR
SIP	46.2%*		NR		NR	NR	NR	Yes	NR
SIP	37.1%*		33.0%		NR	NR	NR	NR	NR
DUKE	79.7%	34.4%*	85.0%	62.0%‡	NR	NR	NR	NR	NR
CAPS	43.0%	20.7%*	59.9%	43.8%*	Yes	No	Yes	Yes	NR
CAPS			NR		No	Yes	Yes	Yes	NR
SIP	2.1%	2.3%	17.0%	33.3%	No	No	No	NR	NR
CAPS	34.0%*		37.0%		Yes	Yes	Yes	Yes	Yes
	NR		65.0%		NR	NR	NR	NR	NR

(continued)

TABLE 17.1 (continued)

Drug Type	Study Type	First Author (year)	Drug	Duration	Subjects	Mean Age (yrs)	Population
	3	Burdon (1991)	Fluoxetine Amitrptyline	4+ weeks	150 (100% men)	NR	Veterans
	3	Brady (2000)	Sertraline	12 months	187 (73% women)	40	Mixed civilian trauma, primarily physical or sexual assault
	1	Davidson (2001)	Sertraline	12 weeks	208 (78% women)	38	Mixed civilian trauma, primarily physical or sexual assault
	1	Zohar (2002)	Sertraline	12 weeks	42 (95% men)	41	Military veterans, primarily combat
	1	Brady (1995)	Sertraline	10 weeks	9 (67% men)	35	Mixed civilian trauma, comorbid ETOH dependence
	1	Marshall (2001)	Paroxetine	12 weeks	563 (~66% women)	42	Mixed civilian trauma
	1	Tucker (2001)	Paroxetine	12 weeks	323 (65.8% women)	42	Mixed trauma types, primarily assault, also combat
	3	Marshall (1998)	Paroxetine	12 weeks	17 (76% women)	38	Mixed civilian trauma, primarily sexual abuse
	3	Davidson (1998)	Fluvoxamine	8 weeks	15 (53% women)	41	Mixed civilian trauma, primarily traumatic bereavement and childhood sexual abuse
	3	Marmar (1996)	Fluvoxamine	10 weeks	11 (100% men)	50	Combat veterans
		Tucker (2000)	Fluvoxamine	10 weeks	17 (76% female)	39	Mixed civilian trauma, primarily sexual abuse
	3	Escalona (2002)	Fluvoxamine	14 weeks	15 (100% men)	47	Combat veterans
	3	Neylan (2001)	Fluvoxamine	10 weeks	21 (100% men)	60	Combat veterans
Other Antidepressants	1	Davis (2004)	Nefazadone	12 weeks	42 (98% men)	54	Predominantly combat veterans
	3	Davidson (1998)	Nefazadone	12 weeks	17 (76% women)	46	Private practice, mixed trauma
	3	Davis (2000)	Nefazadone	8 weeks	36 (97% men)	49	Combat veterans
	3	Garfield (2001)	Nefazadone	9 weeks	19 (100% men)	50	Combat veterans
	3	Hertzberg (1998)	Nefazadone	12 weeks	10 (100% men)	46	Combat veterans
	3	Neylan (2003)	Nefazadone	12 weeks	10 (100% men)	54	Combat veterans

PTSD SX Scale	% Improvement Total PTSD Sx		Response Rates		Efficacy on Subscales and Comorbid Symptoms				
	Drug	PBO	Drug	PBO	Int.	Avoid.	Hyp.	Dep	Sleep
	NR		NR		NR	NR	Yes	Yes	Yes
CAPS	43.3%	30.9%*	53.0%	32.0%*	No	Yes	Yes	Yes	NR
CAPS	44.6%	36.2%*	60.0%	38.0%*	No	Yes	No	No	No
CAPS	20.5%	14.5%	41.0%	20.0%	No	No	No	No	NR
IES	61.0%*		NR		Yes	Yes	Yes	Yes	NR
CAPS	53.0% (20mg) 51.0% (40mg)	34.0%*	62.0% (20mg) 54.0% (40mg)	37.0%*	Yes	Yes	Yes	Yes	NR
CAPS	47.8%	33.7%*	58.8%	38.0%*	Yes	Yes	Yes	NR	NR
IES	48.0%*		NR		No	Yes	Yes	Yes	NR
IES	47.4%*		64.2%		Yes	Yes	Yes	NR	NR
IES	42.3%*		NR		Yes	Yes	Yes	Yes	NR
CAPS	72.3%*		NR		NR	Yes	Yes	Yes	Yes
CAPS	36.2%*		NR		Yes	Yes	No	No	No
IES	32.1%*		NR		Yes	Yes	Yes	Yes	Yes
CAPS	23.6%	16.2%*	46.0%	42.0%	No	No	Yes	Yes	NR
SIP	46.1%*		43.8%		Yes	Yes	Yes	NR	Yes
CAPS	28.1%*		NR		Yes	Yes	Yes	Yes	NR
CAPS	27.0%*		NR		No	No	No	No	NR
CAPS	31.0%*		100.0%		Yes	Yes	Yes	Yes	Yes
CAPS	18.1%*		NR		No	No	Yes	Yes	NR

(*continued*)

TABLE 17.1 (continued)

Drug Type	Study Type	First Author (year)	Drug	Duration	Subjects	Mean Age (yrs)	Population
	3	Zisook (2000)	Nefazadone	12 weeks	19 (100% men)	NR	Combat veterans, treatment refractory
	3	Canive (1988)	Buproprion	6 weeks	17 (100% men)	51	Combat veterans
	2	Kaplan (1996)	Inositol	4 weeks	17 (62% men)	40	Mixed trauma, civilians and veterans, primarily accidents
	3	Hertzberg (1995)	Trazodone	8–12 weeks	6 (100% men)	46	Combat veterans
	3	Warner (2001)	Trazodone (adjunctive)	8 weeks	74 (100% men)	50	Inpatient combat veterans
Antipsychotics	1	Hamner (2003)	Risperidone (adjunctive)	5 weeks	40 (100% men)	51	Vietnam combat veterans with psychotic symptoms
	1	Bartzokis (2005)	Risperidone (adjunctive)	16 weeks	65 (100% men)	52	Combat veterans medication resistant primarily medicated
	3	David (2004)	Risperidone (adjunctive)	12 weeks	17 (100% men)	54	Vietnam veterans, treatment resistant on stable medication
	3	Kozaric-Kovacic (2005)	Risperidone (monotherapy)	6 weeks	27 (100% men)	37	Croatian war veterans, treatment resistant with psychotic symptoms
	2	Butterfield (2001)	Olanzapine (monotherapy)	10 weeks	15 (93% women)	43	Women's veterans clinic, rape survivors, physical abuse/assault
	3	Pivac (2004)	Olanzapine	6 weeks	28 (100% men)	37	Hospitalized Croation combat veterans
	3	Petty (2001)	Olanzapine (monotherapy)	8 weeks	30 (100% men)	50	Combat veterans
	3	Ahearn (2006)	Quetiapine (adjunctive)	8 weeks	15 (53.3% men)	49	Veterans, mixed trauma, primarily sexual abuse or combat exposure
	3	Hamner (2003)	Quetiapine (adjunctive)	6 weeks	20 (95% men)	53	Veterans, primarily combat trauma
	3	Pivac (2004)	Fluphenazine	6 weeks	27 (100% men)	38	Hospitalized Croation combat veterans
Benzodiazepine	2	Braun (1990)	Alprazolam	NR	10 (100% men)	38	Civilians and veterans, primarily combat exposure
	3	Cates (2004)	Clonazepam	2 weeks	6 (100% men)	NR	Combat veterans
Anticonvulsant/ Mood Stabilizer	2	Hertzberg (1999)	Lamotrigine	12 weeks	15 (64% men)	45	Civilians and veterans, mixed trauma, primarily military related

PTSD SX Scale	% Improvement Total PTSD Sx		Response Rates		Efficacy on Subscales and Comorbid Symptoms				
	Drug	PBO	Drug	PBO	Int.	Avoid.	Hyp.	Dep	Sleep
CAPS	31.0%*		NR		No	No	NR	No	NR
CAPS	9.6%‡		NR		No	No	Yes	Yes	NR
IES	10.6%	−1.1%	NR		No	No	NR	No	NR
CAPS	14.6%		67.0%		No stats	No stats	No stats	No stats	NR
	NR		NR		NR	NR	NR	NR	NR
CAPS	10.0%	11.3%	NR		No	No	No	NR	NR
CAPS	13.7%	5.0%*	41.0%	4.0%*	No	No	Yes	No	NR
CAPS	12.8%*		47.0%		Yes	No	Yes	No	NR
CAPS	62.0%*		NR		Yes	Yes	Yes	Yes	NR
SIP	51.6%	63.9%	60.0%	60.0%	No	No	No	No	NR
	NR		NR		Yes	Yes	Yes	NR	NR
CAPS	29.6%*		NR		Yes	Yes	Yes	Yes	NR
CAPS	42.0%*		60.0%		Yes	Yes	Yes	No	Yes
CAPS	24.8%*		58.0%		Yes	Yes	Yes	Yes	Yes
	NR				Yes	Yes	Yes	NR	NR
PTSD	13.9%	4.0%	NR		No	No	NR	No	NR
	NR		NR		NR	NR	NR	NR	NR
	NR		50.0%	25.0%	Yes	No	No	NR	NR

(continued)

TABLE 17.1 (continued)

Drug Type	Study Type	First Author (year)	Drug	Duration	Subjects	Mean Age (yrs)	Population
	3	Wolf (1988)	Carbamazepine	NR	10 (100% men)	37	Inpatient combat veterans
	3	Lipper (1986)	Carbamazepine	5 weeks	10 (100% men)	38	Veterans, primarily combat veterans
	3	Clark (1999)	Divalproex	8 weeks	16 (100% men)	48	Combat veterans
	3	Bremner (2004)	Phenytoin	12 weeks	9 (55% women)	NR	Mixed trauma
	3	Taylor (2003)	Tiagabine	8 weeks	7 (100% women)	40	Private practice
	3	Berlant (2004)	Topiramate (adjunctive)	4 weeks	33 (85% female)	46	Private practice, primarily sexual or physical assault
	4	Berlant (2002)	Topiramate (adjunctive)	1–119 weeks	35 (74% women)	41	Mixed trauma, primarily assault
	3	Fesler (1991)	Valproate	8+ weeks	14 (100% men)	43	Combat veterans
	4	Hamner (2001)	Gabapentin (adjunctive)	4–144 weeks	30 (100% men)	51	Vietnam combat veterans
Sympatholytic	3	Connor (2005)	Tiagabine	12 weeks	26 (73% women)	41	Mixed civilian trauma, primarily physical or sexual assault
	3	Kinzie (1994)	Clonidine	2 weeks	4 (100% men)	NR	Cambodian refugees
	3	Kinzie (1989)	Clonidine, imipramine	12+ months	9 (66.7% women)	54	Cambodian refugees primarily
	2	Raskind (2003)	Prazosin	20 weeks	10 (100% men)	53	Combat veterans
	3	Raskind (2002)	Prazosin	8 weeks	59 (100% men)	59	Combat veterans
	3	Peskind (2003)	Prazosin	8 weeks	9 (100% men)	76	8 combat veterans, 1 Holocaust survivor
	3	Taylor (2002)	Prazosin	6 weeks	5 (80% women)	48	Mixed civilian trauma
Other	2	Heresco-Levy (2002)	D-cycloserine	4 weeks	11 (82% men)	43	Mixed civilian trauma

PTSD SX Scale	% Improvement Total PTSD Sx		Response Rates		Efficacy on Subscales and Comorbid Symptoms				
	Drug	PBO	Drug	PBO	Int.	Avoid.	Hyp.	Dep	Sleep
	NR		NR		NR	NR	NR	NR	NR
PTSD	36.0%*				Yes	No	No	Yes	Yes
CAPS	17.7%*		NR		Yes	No	Yes	Yes	NR
CAPS	41.5%*		NR		Yes	Yes	Yes	No	Yes
PCL	34.1%*		86.0%		Yes	Yes	Yes	NR	Yes
PCL	49.0%*		70%		Yes	Yes	Yes	NR	Decreased nightmares
PCL	35.0%*		NR		Yes	NR	NR	NR	Decreased nightmares
	NR		NR		No	Yes	Yes	NR	Yes
	NR		73.0%		Yes	NR	NR	NR	Decreased nightmares
SIP	53.9%*		NR		NR	NR	NR	Yes	Yes
	NR		NR		NR	NR	NR	No	NR
	NR		66.7%		NR	No	NR	Yes	Yes
CAPS	27.6%	−3.5%*	NR		Yes	Yes	Yes	NR	Yes
	NR		27.1%		NR	NR	NR	NR	Decreased nightmares
	NR		89.0%		NR	NR	NR	NR	Decreased insomnia and nightmares
CAPS	35.7%		NR		NR	NR	NR	NR	Decreased insomnia and nightmares
CAPS	−7.0%	−11.0%	NR		No	No	No	No	NR

(continued)

TABLE 17.1 (continued)

Drug Type	Study Type	First Author (year)	Drug	Duration	Subjects	Mean Age (yrs)	Population
	3	Drake (2003)	Baclofen	8 weeks	14 (100% men)	50	Combat veterans
	3	Lubin (2002)	Naltrexone	2 weeks	8 (75% men)	36	Civilians and veterans, mixed trauma, 50% battle trauma
	2	Aerni (2003)	Cortisol	4 weeks	48 (67% men)	48	Mixed trauma types

Type 1 studies are randomized, placebo-controlled, double blind studies with adequate sample size and proficient study design Type 2 studies also involve a comparison group, but do not meet all the standards of Type 1 (e.g. small sample size, no randomization). Type 3 studies are open-label treatment or case control studies. Type 4 studies are case series or secondary data analysis.
*refers to significant differences; ‡ trend-level differences.
Regarding statistical significance. In Type 1 and 2 studies, significant differences in percent improvement in PTSD total symptoms and in response rates refer to group differences between the medication and placebo group. For Type 3 studies, significant symptom improvement refers to changes from baseline to endpoint in the treatment group.
CAPS = Clinician Administered PTSD Scale
SIP = Structured Interview for PTSD
PCL = PTSD Checklist

War II, the Korea War, or the Vietnam War with PTSD who were also receiving supportive psychotherapy (Davidson et al., 1990). Among study completers there were significant reductions in measures of anxiety and depression but no significant effect on the IES. There was a significant difference in some measures of clinical response (e.g., 50% of the amitriptyline group had a final CGI of less than 2 as compared with 16.6% of the placebo group), but not those dependent on PTSD symptom reduction (27.2% of the amitriptyline group had a greater than 50% drop in PTSD symptom score as compared with 16.6% of the placebo group). Thus, amitriptyline appears to improve clinical outcomes in PTSD, but the effect is not mediated primarily by reduction in PTSD-specific symptoms.

Several small, open-label studies have suggested that the tetracyclic antidepressant mirtazapine may be efficacious in PTSD. In six outpatients with both PTSD and major depression treated for 8 weeks, 33% showed clinical response on the CGI-I scale (Connor, Davidson, Weisler, & Ahearn, 1998). In another, 15 patients were treated with a flexible dose of mirtazapine with significant reductions in PTSD symptoms (Bahk et al., 2002). One double-blind, placebo-controlled trial has been reported (Davidson et al., 2003). Twenty-nine patients with chronic PTSD secondary to a variety of trauma types were randomized

to a fixed-dose of mirtazapine (45 mg/day) for 8 weeks. The results were positive for some but not all primary outcome measures. Significantly higher response rates were found for mirtazapine than for placebo based on the global improvement measure of the Short PTSD Rating Interview (65% vs. 22%); however, there were not significant group differences in reduction of total symptoms on this same measure. Mirtazapine was associated with greater symptom improvement in some secondary measures (Structured Interview for PTSD, Hospital Anxiety Scale) but not others (Davidson Trauma Scale, Hospital Depression Scale).

Selective Serotonin Reuptake Inhibitors

The largest Type 1 studies of pharmacotherapy in PTSD have examined the efficacy of selective serotonin reuptake inhibitors (SSRIs), including fluoxetine, sertraline, and paroxetine. The first controlled trial of fluoxetine in PTSD was conducted at two different sites, an outpatient trauma clinic and a Veterans Administration (VA) outpatient clinic (van der Kolk, 1994). Sixty-four subjects, nearly half of whom were combat veterans, were randomized to 5 weeks of double-blind treatment with placebo or fluoxetine. For the sample as a whole, fluoxetine was superior to placebo in reducing overall PTSD symptoms. Im-

PTSD SX Scale	% Improvement Total PTSD Sx		Response Rates		Efficacy on Subscales and Comorbid Symptoms				
	Drug	PBO	Drug	PBO	Int.	Avoid.	Hyp.	Dep	Sleep
CAPS	23.4%*		81.8%		No	Yes	Yes	Yes	NR
RPI	4.2%		NR		No	No	No	Yes	NR
CAPS	38.0%*		NR		Yes	Possibly	No	NR	NR

IES = Impact of Events Scale
PTSD = Posttraumatic Stress Disorder
DSM-III = *Diagnostic and Statistical Manual of Mental Disorders, Third Edition*
Duke = Duke Global Rating Scale for PTSD
RPI = Revised PTSD Inventory
Int. = Intrusive subscale for PTSD
Avoid. = Avoidance subscale for PTSD
Hyp. = Hyperarousal subscale for PTSD
Dep. = Depression
NR. = Not Reported

provement was also noted in numbing and hyperarousal symptoms but not avoidance and intrusive symptoms. The subsample from the trauma clinic had notably greater improvement than the veteran sample. In the veteran subsample, fluoxetine did not have a statistically significant effect on PTSD symptoms, but it did have a significant effect on depressive symptoms.

Numerous open-label studies had suggested fluoxetine is efficacious in combat-related PTSD (Burdon, Sutker, Foulks, Crane, & Thompson, 1991; Dow & Kline, 1997; McDougle, Southwick, Charney, & James, 1991; Nagy, Morgan, Southwick, & Charney, 1993; Shay, 1992), but a subsequent small, double-blind trial appeared to confirm the lack of efficacy in combat-related PTSD reported in the van der Kolk study. Twelve male Vietnam veterans from an outpatient VA PTSD clinic were randomized to receive fluoxetine (10 to 60 mg/day; mean 48 mg/day) or placebo for 12 weeks (Hertzberg, Feldman, Beckham, Kudler, & Davidson, 2000). The response rate in the fluoxetine group was 17% as compared with 33% in the placebo group, and there were no significant fluoxetine-related differences in PTSD symptom severity measures.

Subsequent studies in civilian PTSD found fluoxetine efficacious. In a predominantly female (91%) and Caucasian (93%) sample of subjects with chronic PTSD, primarily secondary to sexual or physical assault, 12 weeks of fluoxetine was associated with significantly greater reduction in total PTSD symptom severity, evident as early as 2 weeks (Connor, Sutherland, Tupler, Malik, & Davidson, 1999). The response rate in the fluoxetine group was not significantly higher than in the placebo group (85% vs. 62%), but the fluoxetine-treated group had higher end-state functioning. Another placebo-controlled trial in civilian PTSD similarly found fluoxetine improved quality of life (Malik et al., 1999).

It was unclear whether the discrepancies in the outcome of fluoxetine treatment in civilian versus combat-PTSD reflected differences in responsiveness based on trauma type or on other factors relevant to many chronic VA patients such as chronicity of illness, very high rates of comorbid psychiatric illness and substance abuse, or compensation-seeking. To address this question, a large ($N = 301$), double-blind, placebo-controlled trial of fluoxetine was conducted in a sample of PTSD subjects who were predominantly male (81%) and Caucasian (91%); 48% had experienced a combat-related trauma. Unlike the previous fluoxetine studies, it was not performed by the U.S. Department of Veterans Affairs but rather at sites in Belgium, Croatia, Israel, South Africa, and Yugoslavia (Martenyi, Brown, Zhang, Prakash, & Koke 2002) in subjects who had been exposed to combat, or were victims of or witnesses to war, or had witnessed another person's death. In this 12-week, flexible dose (20 to 60 mg/day) study, the response rate in the fluoxetine group (defined as 50% or greater decrease in TOP-8 total score and a CGI-I score of much or very much improved) was 59.9%, significantly higher than the rate of 43.8% in the placebo group. The fluoxetine-treated group also had significantly greater reduction in total PTSD symptom severity, and in particular in intrusive and hyperarousal symptoms, depression, and anxiety.

In the subgroup analysis, statistically greater improvements compared with placebo were apparent in White subjects compared with non-White subjects, in those with combat-related PTSD compared with those with other traumas, in those with multiple traumas as compared with those with a single trauma, and in those without dissociative symptoms. The most robust effect sizes were for those without dissociative symptoms (1.20) and for those with combat-related trauma (0.78). There was a statistically significant treatment effect for men ($N = 245$) but not for women ($N = 56$); however, the effect sizes in women and men (0.53 vs. 0.35, respectively) were similar. Thus, these results suggest that neither combat exposure nor male gender is associated with poor response to fluoxetine in veterans, and that combat-related PTSD may be more responsive to fluoxetine when treated earlier.

Sertraline is one of two medications approved by the Food and Drug Administration (FDA) specifically for PTSD. Open-label studies suggested that sertraline was effective in the treatment of PTSD in survivors of rape (Rothbaum, Ninan, & Thomas, 1996) and in subjects with comorbid PTSD and alcohol dependence in whom there was a reduction of both PTSD symptom and alcohol use (Brady, Sonne, & Roberts, 1995). There have been two large, multicenter, double-blind, placebo-controlled trials of sertraline in the acute phase treatment of chronic PTSD. The first was a 12-week trial of a flexible dose of sertraline (50 to 200 mg) versus placebo in outpatients with a *DSM-III* diagnosis of moderate to severe PTSD (Brady et al., 2000). A total of 187 subjects were randomized. The majority were women (73%) who had physical or sexual assault as the index trauma (61.5%). Eighty-eight percent were Caucasian, and 9% were African American. The mean age of sertraline-treated patients was 40.2 years, the mean duration of illness 13.1 years, and mean time from

traumatic event 19.9 years. The prevalence of major depression was 36%, other anxiety disorders 18%, a history of alcohol abuse/dependence 22%, and a history of substance abuse/dependence 14% in the sertraline-treated group; the sertraline and placebo groups did not differ on demographic and clinical characteristics or rates of discontinuation. Of the common side effects, insomnia was significantly greater in the sertraline than the placebo group (16.0% vs. 4.3%).

Treatment with sertraline (mean dose 133.3 ± 59.2 mg/day) yielded significantly greater efficacy than placebo (based on last-observation-carried-forward analysis) on three of four a priori outcome measures: baseline–to–end point change in total CAPS scores, CGI-S, and CGI-I. There was a trend toward significant reductions on the IES scale. There was a significantly greater response rate in the sertraline than the placebo group (53% vs. 32%; defined as a greater than 30% reduction from baseline in CAPS total severity score and CGI-I score). Additionally, sertraline was associated with significantly greater improvement in depression and on multiple measures of social and occupational functioning. Sertraline did not improve reexperiencing symptoms, a core feature of the disorder, as measured on either the CAPS or the IES.

A subsequent 12-week, multicenter, controlled trial of a flexible dose (50 to 200 mg) of sertraline was conducted in a sample that was demographically and clinically similar to that in the aforementioned study (Davidson, Rothbaum, van der Kolk, Sikes, & Farfel, 2001). Treatment with sertraline was associated with a higher response rate than placebo (60% vs. 38%) and significantly greater improvement in total CAPS score, the CGI-S, and the CGI-I. As in the study by Brady et al. (2002) sertraline was not associated with improvement in reexperiencing symptoms; additionally, there was no improvement in hyperarousal symptoms, anxiety, or depression or on the Pittsburgh Sleep Quality Index (PSQI), a self-rated scale that assesses sleep quality and disturbances (Buysse, Reynolds, Monk, Berman, & Kupfer, 1989).

There was a significant clinical response to sertraline in both studies and, as subsequently reported, a significantly higher rate of remission than placebo (23% vs. 14%; Davidson, 2004). However, it is of interest that sertraline was not associated with improvement in reexperiencing symptoms and inconsistently associated with reductions in hyperarousal or depressive symptoms. This raises the question of which changes in symptoms account for the clinical improvement. A pooled analysis found that the most robust effects of sertraline were on the symptoms of emotional numbing (anhedonia, foreshortened future, emotional detachment, emotional numbing), anger, and hypervigilance (Davidson, Landerman, Farfel, & Clary, 2002). The least impacted symptoms were in the reexperiencing cluster; no significant effects were found for traumatic nightmares or physical distress at reminders, and only weak effects were observed for intrusive memories, flashbacks, avoiding feelings, insomnia, and startle. Sustained sertraline-related reductions in anger were evident by the first week of treatment and partly but not fully explained the subsequent treatment effects on the remaining symptoms. Thus, sertraline-related effects were most evident for psychologically mediated symptoms (e.g., anger, emotional distress, anhedonia) and least evident for somatically mediated symptoms (e.g., nightmares, insomnia, exaggerated startle, physiological distress; Davidson, Landerman, Farfel, & Clary, 2002).

An important limitation of these two sertraline studies is that a significant majority of the subjects were women, and separate analyses of efficacy were not done in men and women (although the absence of a gender-by-treatment interaction on the CAPS change scores was noted for the second study [Davidson et al., 2001]), leaving unanswered the question of whether sertraline is as efficacious in men with PTSD. Additionally, it is not clear whether sertraline is effective in combat-related PTSD. To our knowledge, there have been no controlled studies of sertraline in U.S. combat veterans. Zohar et al. (2002) studied Israeli military veterans with PTSD (N = 42), most of whom were middle-aged men. The index traumas were combat-related violence (N = 32), motor vehicle accidents (N = 8) and captivity (N = 2), and the mean duration of illness was 7.1 (7.8) years in those randomized to sertraline and 7.6 (8.3) years in those randomized to placebo. Subjects were randomly assigned to double-blind treatment with sertraline (flexible dose 50 to 200 mg) or placebo. Based on the intent-to-treat analysis, there were no significant differences in the change in mean CAPS, CGI-S, or CGI-I scores, and the rates of response using the same criteria as the previous sertraline studies were not significantly higher in the sertraline- than the placebo-treated group (41% vs. 20%). The small sample size does not appear to fully explain the absence of significant differences. This group of study subjects had higher baseline CAPS scores than in most studies of civilian PTSD, a lower response rate, and a smaller percentage improvement in symptoms, suggesting that sertraline may be less efficacious in male combat veterans than in other traumatized groups with PTSD.

Paroxetine is the second medication to have received FDA approval for PTSD. A 12-week open-label trial of paroxetine in non-combat-related PTSD suggested it was efficacious in treating all three symptom clusters in PTSD, as well as anxiety, depressive, and dissociative symptoms (Marshall et al., 1998). Two subsequent 12-week, double-blind, placebo-controlled trials have confirmed this. The first was a fixed-dose (20 mg/day and 40 mg/day of paroxetine) study (Marshall, Beebe, Oldham, & Zaninelli, 2001). A total of 563 patients (approximately twice as many women as men) were randomized, and 355 completed this study. The most common type of trauma was physical or sexual assault (48 to 54%), and combat veterans constituted 5 to 8% of the sample. The average age was 41.8 years, and the average time elapsed since the index trauma was 15.7 years. Approximately 45% of participants met criteria for comorbid major depression, 28 to 32% met criteria for generalized anxiety disorder (GAD), 14 to 17% for panic disorder, and 9 to 12% for dysthymia.

Based on an intent-to-treat analysis, improvement was significantly greater for the paroxetine groups compared with the placebo groups on all primary efficacy measures, including the CAPS total severity score and each of the three symptom cluster scores. Response rates, based on the CGI-I, were significantly greater in the paroxetine-treated groups (54% in the 40-mg/day group, 62% in the 20-mg/day group) than in the placebo group (37%), but a dose-response relationship was not evident. There was also evidence of functional improvement in the paroxetine-treated groups based on the Sheehan Disability Scale in the areas of work, social life, and family life. Both men and women showed significant drug-versus-placebo differences in total scores on the CAPs.

In another trial, 307 outpatients with a *DSM-IV* diagnosis of PTSD were randomized to either placebo or a flexible dose (20 to 50 mg/day) of paroxetine (Tucker et al., 2001). The subject characteristics were similar to those in the aforementioned paroxetine trial. Compared with the placebo group, the paroxetine-treated group (mean dose 27.6 [6.72] mg/

day) showed significantly greater reduction in total severity of PTSD symptoms, in each of the PTSD symptom cluster scores, and in depressive symptoms, and showed greater functional improvement. Paroxetine was associated with higher rates of response (based on the CGI-I) and remission (CAPS total score of less than 20), and 58.8% of paroxetine-treated subjects responded and 29.4% remitted, as compared with 38.0% and 16.5%, respectively, of the placebo-treated subjects. In men and women, paroxetine treatment was associated with statistically significantly greater change in symptoms, and equal proportions of men and women achieved responder status.

Multiple open-label studies with fluvoxamine have been reported (Davidson, Weisler, Malik, & Tupler, 1998; Escalona, Canive, Calais, & Davidson, 2002; Marmar et al., 1996; Neylan et al., 2001; Tucker et al., 2000). Included are studies of civilian and combat-related trauma. In each study significant improvement in symptoms from baseline, ranging from 32 to 72%, was reported. Improvement in reexperiencing and avoidance was found in all studies, and all but one (Escalona et al., 2002) reported improvement in hyperarousal.

Two studies have examined the effect of fluvoxamine on sleep in greater detail. In combat veterans, improvement was evident in all domains of subjective sleep quality, and especially in combat-related dreams (Neylan et al., 2001). In a study of civilian PTSD, the mean number of hours slept increased from 4.5 to 6.8 hours per night, and there was a significant decrease in sleep difficulties and trauma-related dreams (Tucker et al., 2000). Controlled trials are warranted to examine whether fluvoxamine does indeed have efficacy for all PTSD symptom clusters and whether there are beneficial effects on sleep and nightmares, which have not been evident with other SSRIs.

Other Antidepressants

Nefazodone is a unique antidepressant that acts as a presynaptic serotonin reuptake inhibitor and a postsynaptic 5-hydroxytryptamine 2A receptor antagonist. It has been of particular interest in PTSD because it has been shown to improve objective measures of sleep quality in depressed subjects (Rush et al., 1998). To date there have been five open-label studies in veterans; in all, treatment was associated with significant improvement in clinician-rated total PTSD symptoms, as well as in the three individual classes of symptoms (Davis, Nugent, Murray, Kramer, & Petty, 2000; Garfield, Fichtner, Leveroni, & Mahableshwarkar, 2001; Hertzberg, Feldman, Beckham, Moore, & Davidson, 1998; Neylan et al., 2003; Zisook et al., 2000). A similar pattern of improvement was observed in a sample of private practice patients (Davidson, Weisler, Malik, & Connor, 1998). Based on ambulatory polysomnography, improvement in objective measures of sleep quality were observed with nefazodone treatment in Vietnam combat veterans. The improvements included increases in total sleep time and sleep maintenance and in delta sleep (Neylan et al., 2003), with corresponding improvements in subjective sleep quality (reductions in nightmares and improved scores on the PSQI.

The results of a 12-week placebo-controlled, double-blind study in combat veterans were less encouraging. Although the nefazodone group showed greater improvement in global PTSD symptoms and depression, response rates in the nefazodone group did not differ from those in the placebo group at study end point (46% vs. 40%; Davis et al., 2004). Safety concerns limit the use of nefazodone as a first-line agent. It has a "black-box" warning regarding an increased (but rare) risk of liver failure that has resulted in deaths and transplantation. Accordingly, it has been taken off the market in some countries.

Beneficial effects of venlafaxine have been noted in a case report (Hamner & Frueh, 1998) and case series (Smajkic et al., 2001). To date there is a single trial open-label trial of bupropion in combat veterans with PTSD (Canive, Clark, Calais, Qualls, & Tuason, 1998). Of the 14 study completers, 10 were classified as treatment responders. There was significant improvement in depressive symptoms, but not in PTSD symptoms, except for hyperarousal symptoms.

Antipsychotics

There are scant case reports on the use of first-generation antipsychotics in PTSD (chlorpromazine: Leber, Malek, D'Agostino, & Adelman, 1999; thioridazine: Dillard, Bendfeldt, & Jernigan, 1993) and one open-label study suggesting levomepromazine improves sleep in inpatients with PTSD (Aukst-Margetic, Margetic, Tosic, & Bilic-Prcic, 2004). Given the general impression that they are not effective against core PTSD symptoms and owing to the risk of tardive dyskinesia, their use has not been advocated in PTSD. In the last 5 years there have been a number of trials suggesting atypical antipsychotics are effective in chronic PTSD, including risperidone, olanzapine, and quetiapine.

A primary rationale for testing the efficacy of these drugs is that many patients with PTSD do not respond to first-line psychopharmacological treatments or have residual distressing symptoms and functional impairment. Accordingly, trials of atypical antipsychotics have been conducted primarily in combat veterans, treatment-resistant patients, and those with co-occurring psychotic symptoms. Assessment of outcome included changes in psychotic symptoms, based on scales typically used for schizophrenia, such as the Positive and Negative Symptoms of Schizophrenia Scale (PANSS; Kay, Fiszbein, & Opler, 1987) and the Brief Psychiatric Rating Scale (BPRS; Overall & Gorham, 1962). The Abnormal Involuntary Movement Scale (AIMS) for the measurement of tardive dyskinesia (Guy, 1976), the Barnes Akathisia Scale (Barnes, 1989), and the Simpson-Angus Scale (SAS) for the measurement of extrapyramidal symptoms (Simpson & Angus, 1970) were among the measures assessing side effects.

To date there have been one open-label (David, De Faria, Lapeyra, & Mellman, 2004) and three double-blind placebo-controlled trials (Bartzokis, Lu, Turner, Mintz, & Saunders, 2005; Hamner, et al., 2003; Kozaric-Kovacic, Pivac, Muck-Seler, & Rothbaum, 2005) of risperidone in combat-related PTSD. In the open-label study, 12 weeks of adjunctive treatment with risperidone (1 to 3 mg/day) in treatment-resistant veterans was associated with significant reduction in total CAPs score and total PANSS score (as well as PANSS measures of general psychopathology, positive symptoms, and negative symptoms) and CGI-S. With respect to safety concerns, one subject gained 25 lb, the extrapyramidal symptoms rating scale showed a nonsignificant increase from baseline, and fasting glucose levels showed a trend-level increase from baseline). A 6-week trial of risperidone (2 to 4 mg/day) as monotherapy was conducted in treatment-resistant combat veterans in which subjects with Axis I comorbidity or a family history of psychosis were specifically excluded (Kozaric-Kovacic et al., 2005). There was a significant decrease in PANSS total and subscale scores, in total PTSD symptoms (and in each of the three symptom clusters), and in the CGI-S. Of note, 12% of participants gained

weight during the trial, and 42% developed extrapyramidal side effects. A 16-week, double-blind, placebo-controlled trial of adjunctive risperidone in combat PTSD was conducted in 65 veterans (Bartzokis et al., 2005). Risperidone was associated with significant decreases in total CAPS score and the psychotic subscale of the PANSS. Response rates were significantly higher in the risperidone-treated group than in the placebo-treated group (41% vs. 4%). Risperidone treatment was not associated with changes in the BAS, AIMS, or SAS, adjusted for baseline scores, or with changes in weight, heart rate, or blood pressure. A randomized, double-blind, 5-week trial of adjunctive risperidone (1 to 6 mg/day, mean 2.5 mg/day) was conducted in combat-related PTSD with psychotic features in the absence of a primary psychotic disorder (Hamner et al., 2003). Examples of psychotic symptoms were auditory or visual hallucinations referable to the precipitating trauma or nonspecific symptoms such as whispering voices or paranoia. The risperidone group had significantly greater reductions on the PANSS (on total and global psychopathology score), but notably not on the positive symptom score or on total CAPS scores. One patient developed akathisia, but there were no treatment-associated changes on the BAS, AIMS, or SAS.

One small, double-blind, placebo-controlled study of adjunctive risperidone (0.5 to 8 mg/day) was conducted in women with moderate to severe PTSD related to childhood abuse (Reich, Winternitz, Hennen, Watts, & Stanculescu, 2004). Risperidone treatment was associated with significant symptom improvement in total PTSD symptoms, including the reexperiencing and hyperarousal subscales. Risperidone was associated with an increase in prolactin without any obvious sequelae and no difference in weight gain.

Olanzapine has been studied as monotherapy (Petty et al., 2001) and as an adjunctive agent (Stein, Kline, & Matloff, 2002) in combat-related PTSD. In the first study, following medication discontinuation, 48 veterans were treated with open-label olanzapine (5 to 20 mg/day) for 8 weeks. There was a significant reduction in total CAPS score and in each of the subscales, in the BPRS, and on measures of anxiety and depression. There were no significant changes in safety measures (BAS, AIMS, and SAS). Notably, among completers, the mean weight gain was 3.5 ± 3.1 kg. In an 8-week double-blind, placebo-controlled trial of adjunctive olanzapine (10 to 20 mg/day) in

SSRI-resistant combat veterans with PTSD (Stein et al., 2002), olanzapine treatment was associated with significantly greater reductions in total PTSD symptoms, depressive symptoms, and sleep quality. The response rates in the olanzapine- and placebo-treated groups (30% vs. 11%) were not significantly different. Weight gain, however, was significantly greater in the olanzapine than the placebo group (+13.2 lb vs. −3.0 lb). A double-blind, placebo-controlled trial of olanzapine monotherapy (5 to 20 mg/day) was conducted in female veterans with PTSD, primarily stemming from sexual assault/harassment in the military (Butterfield et al., 2001). Both the placebo group and the olanzapine group had significant decrease in symptoms. The response rate was 60% in both groups, and there were no significant group differences in changes in PTSD symptoms, in functional outcomes, or in the AIMS or BAS. However, the olanzapine-treated group had significantly greater weight grain than the placebo group (11.5 ± 4.43 lb vs. 0.9 ± 0.06 lb).

To date there have not been any controlled trials of quetiapine, but there is preliminary evidence suggesting it may be efficacious in chronic PTSD. In a case series of five medication-resistant PTSD subjects, all showed dramatic improvement in flashbacks with quetiapine (Filteau, Leblanc, & Bouchard, 2003). In a 6-week open-label study in combat veterans, adjunctive quetiapine (25 to 300 mg/day; Hamner, Deitsch, Brodrick, Ulmer, & Lorberbaum, 2003) was associated with a broad spectrum of improvement, including significant reductions in total PTSD symptom severity (and in each of the three symptom clusters), PANSS composite and positive symptom score, and the HAM-D. Fifty-eight percent of subjects met criteria for response based on the CGI. No significant changes were observed for weight or blood pressures or in the AIMS, BAS, and SAS scales. Analysis of the sleep data from this study revealed significant improvement with quetiapine on multiple measures of the PSQI, most notably sleep duration, which increased from 4.0 ± 1.0 to 6.0 ± 1.8 hours per night, and sleep quality (Robert et al., 2005).

In another open-label study, quetiapine (100 to 400 mg/day) was added to the regimen of 15 PTSD patients on stable doses of SSRIs. There was a significant reduction in total CAPS score (and in each of the subscales), as well as on multiple secondary measures including the PSQI and HAM-D. Fifty-three percent of patients had a clinical response, and one went into remission (Ahearn, Mussey, Johnson, Krohn, & Krahn, 2006). No adverse events, move-ment-related disorders, or weight gain were noted. Positive case reports of the effect of clozapine (Hamner, 1996) and ziprasidone (Siddiqui, Marcil, Bhatia, Ramaswamy, & Petty, 2005) on combat-related PTSD have also been published.

In summary, the available evidence from studies of 6 to 16 weeks' duration suggests that there is a role for atypical antipsychotics as adjunctive medications for treatment-refractory PTSD and PTSD with psychotic symptoms. Their apparent efficacy against a broad array of PTSD-specific and associated symptoms makes them an attractive option. However, side effects were evident, and weight gain was especially marked and consistently observed with olanzapine even in these short-term studies. Given the link between atypical antipsychotic agents and the metabolic syndrome, the risks of treatment with atypical antipsychotics in PTSD need to be carefully balanced against the potential benefits, and careful monitoring is warranted.

Although the literature on antipsychotics in PTSD is in its earliest stages, the use of these medications is widespread. In an observational study of veterans receiving care at a VA hospital, 9% of the 831 inpatients and 10% of the 554 outpatients with PTSD were being treated with neuroleptics. Those treated with neuroleptics had more psychiatric and social impairment, but outcomes at 1-year follow-up were not different between those treated with and without neuroleptics (Sernyak, Kosten, Fontana, & Rosenheck, 2001). In a nonveteran community clinic, 17% of those with PTSD alone and 34% of those with PTSD and major depressive disorder (MDD) were being treated with atypical antipsychotics. Given their widespread use, continued study is needed to examine which groups or subgroups may benefit from treatment with atypical antipsychotics, how long they should be treated, and how the risks can be managed and minimized.

Benzodiazepines

Benzodiazepines have generally not been recommended as a treatment for PTSD owing to concerns related to efficacy, the potential for abuse and dependence, and the potential for severe symptom exacerbation with discontinuation (Risse et al., 1990). However, they have been little studied. In a double-blind, crossover trial of 10 PTSD patients of mixed trauma type, 5 weeks of alprazolam treatment was compared with 5 weeks of placebo treatment. Alprazolam was associated with significant decreases in the Hamilton anxiety scale, but no differences were observed on clinician-rated or self-rated PTSD scales (Braun, Greenberg, Dasberg, & Lerer, 1990). A randomized, single-blind, placebo-controlled crossover study of clonazepam for sleep was conducted in a small number ($N = 6$) of combat veterans. Marginal efficacy was found for clonazepam, with mild to moderate improvements in difficulty falling or staying asleep, no change in the frequency or intensity of nightmares, and little improvement in the quality of sleep (Cates, Bishop, Davis, Lowe, & Woolley, 2004).

The paucity of studies of benzodiazepines in chronic PTSD is striking in light of the frequency with which these drugs are prescribed in clinical practice. A follow-up of 370 veterans after a brief hospitalization for PTSD showed that 45% of those without substance abuse histories and 26% of those with substance abuse histories were treated with benzodiazepines (Kosten, Fontana, Sernyak, & Rosenheck, 2000). There was no evidence that benzodiazepine had an adverse effect on 1-year outcomes. Nor was there evidence that they were associated with improvement in anxiety symptoms or functioning. However, benzodiazepine use was significantly associated with lower health care utilization (Kosten et al., 2000). Understanding the mechanisms that mediate this effect is important because PTSD is associated with significant medical morbidity and very high rates of health care utilization.

This prescribing pattern is not unique to the VA. Based on a review of Medicaid records, in a community-based sample in New Hampshire, 41% of patients with PTSD alone were prescribed benzodiazepines or other hypnotics, and 54% of patients with both MDD and PTSD were treated with benzodiazepines or related hypnotics. Given this vast discrepancy between treatment guidelines and actual clinical practice, large-scale, double-blind studies are needed to evaluate whether benzodiazepines are effective, deleterious, or neither in chronic PTSD. A broader range of outcomes may be needed to capture whether there is some other aspect of mental health (e.g., sense of well-being, decreased somatization) that might explain their widespread use and their apparent impact on reducing health care utilization.

Mood Stabilizers and Anticonvulsants

There has been interest in the use of anticonvulsants and mood stabilizers in the treatment of PTSD on clinical grounds, since PTSD can be associated with affective instability (Golier, Yehuda, Schmeidler, & Siever, 2001), irritability, and violence, symptoms for which mood stabilizers have been found to be effective in other psychiatric disorders. On a theoretical basis, it has been hypothesized that kindling perpetuates PTSD-related symptoms (Post, Weiss, Smith, Li, & McCann, 1997). Following trauma exposure, sensitization may occur such that limbic structures subsequently respond to less intense trauma-related stimuli. This phenomenon is thought to explain the recurrence of reexperiencing symptoms and increased levels of distress and physiological signs with traumatic reminders (Post et al., 1997). Raising the neuronal threshold for arousal in limbic areas could relieve the behavioral and neurobiological sensitization of trauma survivors (Keck, McElroy, & Friedman, 1992). This notion has prompted interest in the use of mood stabilizers in this disorder, including those that act on gamma-aminobutyric acid (GABA)-A (valproate) and GABA-B (carbamazepine) receptors resulting in neuronal hyperpolarization and stabilization.

Beneficial effects of carbamazepine or its analog oxcarbazepine have been noted in case reports (Berigan, 2002; Ford, 1996; Malek-Ahmadi & Hanretta, 2004) and in a case series in which Vietnam War veterans were noted to have improved impulse control and fewer angry outbursts (Wolf, Alavi, & Mosnaim, 1988). In an open-label trial, 10 combat veteran inpatients with PTSD were treated with carbamazepine at doses ranging from 600 to 1,000 mg/day (Lipper et al., 1986), with significant reductions in total PTSD symptoms and on the BPRS, as well as reductions in somatization, hostility, psychoticism, and confusion-bewilderment on self-rating scales. Seven of the 10 showed clinical response based on the CGI-I.

Valproate has been studied in two open-label studies of combat veterans with PTSD. In the first, improvement in hyperarousal, sleep, and avoidant symptoms was noted in a group of 16 combat veterans treated with 750 to 1,750 mg/day of valproate over a period of several months (Fesler, 1991). In another, following 8 weeks of adjunctive valproate (1,000 to 2,500 mg/day; mean 1,356 mg) there were significant decreases in total CAPS scores (including intrusive and hyperarousal symptoms), depression, and anxiety, and 11 of 13 subjects showed a clinical response (Clark, Canive, Calais, Qualls, & Tuason, 1999).

Several reports suggest that gabapentin, a GABA analog approved by the FDA for the treatment of partial complex seizures and neuropathic pain, may be efficacious, especially for intrusive symptoms. In one case report, it significantly reduced flashbacks in a woman with PTSD and MDD (Malek-Ahmadi, 2003); in another, it reduced nightmares in a man with treatment-resistant PTSD following an electrical injury (Brannon, Labbate, & Huber, 2000). In a retrospective review of Vietnam veterans with chronic PTSD, 73% of subjects were rated as moderately to much improved with addition of gabapentin, with improvement in insomnia and nightmares (Hamner, Brodrick, & Labbate, 2001).

Topiramate is a novel antiepileptic with a broad spectrum of pharmacological properties. In addition to its antikindling properties, its use in PTSD is supported by preclinical data showing it reduces acoustic startle in animals (Khan & Liberzon, 2004) and enhances the sensitivity of the glucocorticoid receptor in PTSD patients in vitro (Yehuda et al., 2004). In addition to positive case reports (Berlant, 2001), a retrospective review found that it decreased nightmares in 79% and flashbacks in 86% of patients with civilian PTSD (Berlant & van Kammen, 2002). In a prospective open-label study of 33 PTSD patients in private practice, topiramate was used, primarily as an adjunctive agent, over 4 weeks at a median dose of 50 mg/day. Despite the short duration of treatment, significant reductions were observed in total PTSD symptoms (and in each symptom cluster) based on the self-reported PTSD Checklist. Seventy-seven percent responded, as evidenced by a 30% or greater reduction in PTSD symptoms. With respect to intrusive symptoms, 79% ceased having reexperiencing symptoms, with a mean time to full cessation of just 15 days. These encouraging results suggest that topiramate may have a rapid rate of response in PTSD.

Tiagabine is a selective GABA reuptake inhibitor that increases extracellular GABA levels. In addition to a positive case report (Berigan, 2002) and case series (Taylor, 2003), an open-label study of tiagibine (mean dose 12.5 ± 4.0 mg/day) was completed in patients with chronic PTSD (Connor, Davidson, Weisler, Zhang, & Abraham, 2006). Among completers there was significant improvement in PTSD symptom severity, anxiety, depression, sleep quality, and level of functioning. However, during a 12-week double-blind, placebo-controlled continuation phase, relapse rates did not differ between the two groups.

Phenytoin is an anticonvulsant that blocks the cellular responses to glutamate. Interest in phenytoin in the treatment of PTSD was prompted by observations that the deleterious effects of stress on memory performance and the hippocampus in animals are blocked by phenytoin (Hui, Guang-Yu, Chong-Tao, Quan, & Xiao-Hu, 2005; Watanabe, Gould, Cameron, Daniels, & McEwen, 1992). To the extent that PTSD symptoms or the associated neuropsychological impairments and neuroanatomic alterations (Bremner et al., 1997; Gurvits et al., 1996) are mediated by similar effects of stress on humans, phenytoin could theoretically attenuate this process (Bremner et al., 2005). In an open-label study of phenytoin as monotherapy, 9 of 12 patients completed the study. Among completers there was a 41.5% reduction in total CAPs score and a significant reduction in all three PTSD symptom clusters, in the absence of significant reduction in anxiety or depression. Social and occupational functioning also improved.

Scant information is available about the efficacy of lithium carbonate in the treatment of PTSD. Van der Kolk (1983) performed an open trial of lithium carbonate (therapeutic dose: 300 to 1,500 mg/day) in 14 treatment-refractory combat veterans. Eight of them improved, with noted improvement in hyperarousal. Kitchner and Greenstein (1985) reported similarly beneficial results in an open trial with 5 combat veterans.

Multiple anticonvulsants and mood stabilizers with different mechanisms of action have been tested in PTSD. Preliminary data suggest they may be effective for core PTSD symptoms, and there is evidence in particular that valproate, gabapentin, and topiramate may be especially effective in treating reexperiencing symptoms, which are often resistant to SSRIs. As promising as the data have been, no one agent has been studied extensively, and no Type 1 trials have been conducted for any of these agents.

Sympatholytic Agents

Interest in the potential use of antiadrenergic drugs in PTSD dates back to some of the earliest scientific observations regarding the pathophysiology of this illness. Beginning with Kardiner's (1941) seminal depiction of "physioneurosis" in combat veterans, there has been evidence of increased sympathetic nervous system activation in PTSD. Abundant lines of evidence support this view, including evidence of elevated levels of catecholamines (Kosten, Mason, Giller, Ostroff, & Harkness, 1987), enhanced autonomic responses to loud tones (Orr, Lasko, Shalev, & Pitman, 1995), and increased alpha-2 receptor sensitivity (Southwick et al., 1999).

The possibility that sympatholytic antihypertensives could be effective against chronic PTSD was investigated as early as 1984. Kolb, Burris, and Griffiths (1984) studied propranolol, a nonselective beta-adrenergic receptor blocker, in 12 Vietnam combat veterans. At doses of 120 to 160 mg/day there was improvement in explosiveness, nightmares, intrusive recollections, startle response, hyperalertness, and impaired sleep, as well as in self-esteem and psychosocial function. Propranolol was also noted in a case report to reduce the reemergence of PTSD symptoms following retraumatization (Taylor & Cahill, 2002).

Kolb et al. (1984) also reported that clonidine, an alpha-2 receptor agonist, alleviated flashbacks and hyperarousal in combat veterans. Clonidine is of particular interest, since subsequent studies have demonstrated that the alpha-2 receptor antagonist yohimbine exacerbates PTSD symptoms in the laboratory and in naturalistic settings (Southwick et al., 1997; Southwick et al., 1999). In a pilot study, Kinzie, Sack, and Riley (1994) added clonidine to the treatment of nine Cambodian refugees with PTSD who did not improve with imipramine and followed them for 12 to 19 months. In this descriptive study the researchers noted that six of the patients had improvement in PTSD symptoms (two no longer met criteria for the disorder), six had improvement in sleep, six had improvement in depression, and seven had improvement in nightmares.

Prazosin, a centrally active adrenergic-1 antagonist, has been more extensively studied. Following up on a clinical observation, an initial case series using this sympatholytic antihypertensive in combat PTSD showed that at low doses at bedtime, prazosin improved severe and chronic combat-related nightmares (Raskind et al., 2000). In a small open-label trial in civilian PTSD, 6 weeks of prazosin was also associated with clinical improvement and reduction in nightmares (Taylor & Raskind, 2002). In a retrospective review of 58 male Vietnam and Gulf War veterans with treatment-refractory PTSD, those treated with at least 8 weeks of prazosin (mean dose of 9.6 ± 0.9 mg/day) showed a significant decrease in distressing dreams (Raskind et al., 2002). In the only

published study of PTSD treatment in the elderly, prazosin reduced nightmares in elderly combat veterans and a Holocaust survivor (Peskind, Bonner, Hoff, & Raskind, 2003).

Treatment with prazosin was subsequently evaluated in a double-blind, placebo-controlled, crossover trial in 10 Vietnam War combat veterans with chronic PTSD and severe nightmares. For most subjects it was an adjunctive agent. Not only was improvement in sleep difficulty and recurrent distressing dreams noted, but there were significant reductions in the PTSD total score and each of the three subscales Futhermore, prazosin treatment was associated with greater clinical global improvement than placebo (Raskind et al., 2003).

Prazosin is emerging as an effective treatment for the intractable sleep problems and nightmares associated with PTSD and may be useful for a broader range of PTSD symptoms as well. Despite the compelling scientific rationale for the use of sympatholytic agents, to date, there have been no randomized, double-blind, placebo-controlled trials of other sympathotyic agents such as clonidine, propranolol, or guanfacine in adults with chronic PTSD. They are needed to examine whether direct modulation of the noradrenergic system in PTSD is associated with a clinically meaningful treatment response.

Sedatives and Hypnotics

Disrupted sleep, which can be characterized by difficulties initiating and maintaining sleep, distressing nightmares, and phobic avoidance secondary to nightmares, is often a chronic and distressing symptom in PTSD. Sleep quality and quantity have rarely been measured in Type 1 and Type 2 studies in PTSD, but improvement in sleep has been noted in open-label studies with fluoxetine, fluvoxamine, nefazodone, tiagabine, and quetiapine. Because monotherapy is rarely sufficient to improve sleep, sedative/hypnotics are frequently prescribed; however, little empirical data are available to guide decision making regarding their use.

Trazodone is a triazolopyridine antidepressant with sedative effects that has been evaluated in two uncontrolled trials. The larger of the two is a survey of the adjunctive use of trazodone in combat veteran inpatients ($N = 74$; Warner, Dorn, & Peabody, 2001). Nineteen percent discontinued trazodone, with the most common side effects being daytime sedation and priapism (the latter occurred in 12% of subjects). Seventy-two percent of the patients who continued trazodone (mean dose 212 mg/day) found it decreased nightmares, 92% found it aided sleep onset, and 78% reported improvement in sleep maintenance.

Zolpidem tartrate, zaleplon, and eszopiclone are nonbenzodiazepine hypnotics specifically indicated for insomnia; eszopiclone is unique in being the only hypnotic that has been approved for long-term use. To date, there have not been any studies of these agents in PTSD, although a clinical report notes success in treating insomnia in chronic PTSD with zolpidem, without adverse effects, for as long as 20 months (Dieperink & Drogemuller, 1999).

Other Agents

D-cycloserine is a broad-spectrum antibiotic and antitubercular drug and a selective partial agonist at the glycine site on the N-methyl-D-aspartic acid (NMDA) receptor. In a double-blind, placebo-controlled, crossover study in 11 patients with PTSD, symptom improvement with D-cycloserine (25 mg bid) was not significantly better than with placebo (Heresco-Levy et al., 2002).

Buspirone has been reported as effective in a case study describing three combat veterans (Wells et al., 1991). Buspirone (range 35 to 60 mg) reduced associative symptoms of anxiety and depression, as well as insomnia and flashbacks.

There are two clinical reports in which the serotonin antagonist cyproheptadine was used successfully for the treatment of traumatic nightmares (Brophy, 1991; Harsch, 1986) in the range of 4 to 28 mg/day.

Summary of the Results of Acute Phase Treatment Trials of Chronic PTSD

In summary, this review of the existing literature shows that, based on Type 1 and Type 2 studies, phenelzine, imipramine, sertraline, fluoxetine, and paroxetine monotherapy have all been shown to be effective in the treatment of PTSD, as compared with placebo, based on both improvements in total PTSD symptom severity and higher response rates. Amitriptyline and mirtazapine are both superior to placebo with respect to clinical response but not total PTSD symptom reductions; nefazodone was superior

to placebo with respect to symptom improvement but not rate of response. (Among these agents, there have also been negative controlled trials of phenelzine in civilian PTSD and sertraline and fluoxetine in combat veterans.) Other negative controlled trials have been reported for brofaromine, olanzapine (as monotherapy), desipramine, inositol, and alprazolam. The results from the brofaromine study appear to be conclusive. Results for the other four agents are not definitive, given the small sample sizes (10 to 18 subjects) and, for the latter three agents, the short trial duration of 5 weeks or less.

Risperidone, olanzapine, and prazosin appear to be effective adjunctive treatments in treatment-resistant or refractory patients. All were associated with significant reductions in total PTSD symptoms; risperidone was also associated with significantly higher response rates than placebo. Reduction in PTSD-related psychotic symptoms was noted with the atypical antipsychotics and with distressing nightmares with prazosin. However, the risk-benefit ratio of the atypical antipsychotics needs to be carefully weighed in PTSD because both extrapyramidal side effects and metabolic side effects were noted even during these short-term trials.

Very few of the controlled trials in PTSD specifically assessed sleep quality or quantity. The only agent that has clearly been shown to improve sleep in PTSD is prazosin (Raskind et al., 2003). In contrast, sertraline was shown not to have beneficial effects on sleep quality in civilian PTSD and additionally was associated with a significantly greater occurrence of insomnia as a side effect (Davidson et al., 2001).

In the absence of head-to-head comparisons, it is difficult to ascertain whether a particular medication or class of medications is more effective than another for a certain set of symptoms or subtype of PTSD. However, some trends have emerged. Among the SSRIs, paroxetine consistently showed efficacy against all three PTSD symptom clusters. In contrast, sertraline is not effective in reducing reexperiencing symptoms and was associated with decreased hyperarousal and decreased depressive symptoms in only one of the three controlled trials. For fluoxetine the pattern of efficacy for the individual symptom clusters were not consistent across studies. Anticonvulsants and sympatholytics show promise as add-on medications for the reduction of reexperiencing and hyperarousal symptoms, but controlled trials are needed to determine their efficacy.

Maintenance Treatment and Relapse Prevention

The clinician now has available a number of pharmacological treatments that work in PTSD. However, partial response is a more typical outcome than complete remission. Thus the question arises as to whether efficacy is maintained and long-term treatment indicated. Only in the last few years have data become available that can begin to answer these questions.

The largest study of continuation treatment in PTSD was conducted with sertraline. Subjects who completed the double-blind sertraline studies were eligible to continue in the open-label continuation phase lasting 24 weeks (Londborg et al., 2001). Subjects remained blinded to the acute-phase treatment during the continuation phase; 92% of responders maintained their response during the continuation phase. Importantly, 54% of those who did not achieve responder status during the acute phase achieved it during the continuation phase. High baseline symptom severity was the only significant predictor of longer time to response. Comorbidity, childhood trauma, depression, and the number of traumas, among other demographic variables, were not predictors of a delayed response. Thus, these data suggest that the efficacy of sertraline treatment is maintained and that, for the most severely ill PTSD patients, several months of treatment may be needed to achieve clinical improvement.

The final phase of this series of studies of sertraline was designed to examine whether maintenance therapy protects PTSD patients from relapse or deterioration (Davidson et al., 2001). Included in the Type 1 double-blind, placebo-controlled discontinuation study were PTSD patients who had showed consistent evidence of response during the end of the continuation phase. Maintenance treatment was continued for 28 weeks. Sertraline demonstrated a significant advantage over placebo in prevention of relapse (5.3% vs. 26.1%) and acute exacerbation of PTSD symptoms (15.8% vs. 52.2%). The sample was predominantly female, but the prophylactic benefit of sertraline was evident in both men and women.

There have been two controlled studies of maintenance treatment of PTSD with fluoxetine. The first was a follow-up to the study of chronic PTSD patients, most of whom were male combat veterans. Patients who responded to acute treatment were randomized to continue in a 24-week double-blind maintenance phase on either fluoxetine (N = 69) or placebo (N = 62; Martenyi, Brown, Zhang, Koke, & Prakash, 2002). Response was stringently defined as a 50% decrease in the Treatment Outcome PTSD score (TOP-8), a CGI-S score of 2 or lower, and not meeting the criteria for PTSD. Among those who responded to fluoxetine in the acute-phase study, the completion rate in the continuation phase was higher in subjects randomized to fluoxetine than to placebo (83% vs. 66%), but based on the primary outcome of time to relapse, fluoxetine was superior to placebo in relapse prevention.

Interestingly, subjects in both groups showed further reduction in symptoms with continuation treatment, although the effect varied by trauma type. For patients with non-combat-related PTSD, placebo was associated with some improvement, but for patients with combat-related PTSD, placebo was associated with a worsening of symptoms. In a subsequent discontinuation study, PTSD subjects were randomly assigned to double-blind treatment with either fluoxetine or placebo, after having shown at least minimal response to open-label fluoxetine treatment for 6 months (up to 60 mg/day). There were a significantly higher number of relapses in the placebo group (50%) than in the fluoxetine group (22%), and a significantly earlier time to relapse in the placebo group. However, differences in relapse rates were not noted based on self-report instruments. Thus, the results from clinician and self-report data are not entirely consistent, but the results of the two studies suggest that continued therapy with fluoxetine appears to prevent relapse as compared with placebo when categorical criteria of relapse are used based on clinician assessments.

Open-label continuation studies also provide preliminary evidence for the benefits of maintenance treatment with other antidepressants. Multiyear follow-up was obtained in an open-label trial of nefazodone in combat-related PTSD at doses of 400 to 600 mg/day (Hertzberg, Feldman, Beckham, Moore, & Davidson, 2002). Of the 10 patients who responded at the end of the 12-week trial, 7 remained "much improved," 2 were "minimally improved," and 1 was worse, suggesting that efficacy was maintained for the majority of patients over several years. In a small, open-label study of mirtazapine in PTSD, gains made during the initial 8-week trial were maintained over the 6 months of treatment, and there was an increase in the number of responders over time (Kim, Pae, Chae, Jun, & Bahk, 2005). Taken together, these studies suggest treatment gains in PTSD are maintained or enhanced during maintenance treatment with antidepressants, and antidepressants are indicated in the long-term management of this chronic disorder, as they are in other affective and anxiety disorders.

Secondary Prevention of PTSD

Although stress and trauma are implicated as risk factors for many Axis I and II disorders, PTSD is the only one that by definition is manifest in direct response to a traumatic event. Thus, the immediate aftermath of a traumatic event represents a potential window of opportunity for early intervention to prevent the development of the full disorder. Concerns about terrorism and the effects of a number of recent natural and man-made disasters have brought the question of how to intervene clinically after a trauma into sharper focus. Educational, psychotherapeutic, and pharmacological approaches are all possible interventions that can be applied to trauma survivors at greatest risk for developing PTSD. Preliminary medication trials for the secondary prevention of PTSD have been conducted for cortisol, beta blockers, and benzodiazepines.

Activation of the HPA axis in response to stress leads to the release of cortisol from the adrenal gland, which, through negative feedback inhibition, ultimately serves to constrain the stress response. There is ample evidence of HPA axis dysregulation in chronic PTSD, including elevations in corticotrophin releasing factor (Baker et al., 2005; Bremner, Licinio, et al., 1997), which is a potent stimulator of the stress response. However, PTSD is not typically associated with elevated cortisol levels. Rather, it is often, but not always, associated with lower 24-hour cortisol levels (reviewed in Yehuda, 2002). It has been suggested that these HPA axis alterations contribute to over-activation of the HPA axis and sympathetic nervous system following stress (Yehuda, 2002). Whether HPA axis alterations are evident at the time of

trauma is not known, but several prospective studies suggest that lower posttraumatic cortisol levels in the acute aftermath of trauma predict the subsequent development of PTSD (McFarlane, Atchison, & Yehuda, 1997; Resnick, Yehuda, Pitman, & Foy, 1995), whereas cortisol levels at 1 week do not (Bonne et al., 2003).

These findings raise the question of whether manipulation of the HPA axis at the time of traumatization can prevent the development of PTSD. Compelling data from studies of intensive care unit (ICU) patients suggest it can. Patients treated in the ICU provide an opportunity to study the relationship between trauma, glucocorticoids, and the subsequent development of trauma-related psychopathology, since such patients often receive exogenously administered catecholamines and glucocorticoids and have high rates of PTSD resulting from life-threatening illness and its treatment (Schelling et al., 1999). In an initial retrospective case-control comparison of septic shock patients treated in an ICU, those who had received stress doses of hydrocortisone had a lower incidence of PTSD than those who had not (5 of 27 vs. 16 of 27); they also had higher scores of emotional well-being (Schelling et al., 1999). A similar result was found in a prospective, randomized, double-blind study of the hemodynamic effects of hydrocortisone on septic shock. Development of PTSD in the group treated with stress doses of hydrocortisone (1 of 9) was significantly lower than in the placebo group (7 of 11; Schelling et al., 2001). The effect did not appear to be mediated through memory consolidation, since there were not significant group differences in the recall of categories of traumatic memories from the ICU (Schelling et al., 2001).

This series of studies provides an interesting demonstration that direct administration of cortisol in the peritraumatic period prevents the development of PTSD secondary to life-threatening illness. Although this is a unique population and the doses of steroids used were high, the results may be more broadly applicable. In a small double-blind, crossover study of low doses of cortisol in patients with civilian PTSD, cortisol treatment effectively reduced PTSD symptoms, especially reexperiencing symptoms (Aerni et al., 2004). Owing to the beneficial effects of hydrocortisone observed in these controlled studies, studies of the efficacy and safety of short-term cortisol treatment for the secondary and tertiary prevention of PTSD are warranted.

The use of beta blockers in the secondary prevention of PTSD has also been explored. There is considerable evidence of overactivation of the sympathetic nervous system in PTSD and in those who are at high risk for developing PTSD after a trauma (Shalev et al., 1998; Southwick, Bremner, et al., 1999). Epinephrine strengthens memory consolidation, and it has been hypothesized that excessive release of epinephrine at the time of a traumatic event results in an exceptionally strong emotional memory and conditioned fear response that is ultimately manifested in the symptoms of PTSD (Pitman, 1989). Propranolol, which crosses the blood-brain barrier, eliminates this memory-consolidating effect in humans (Cahill, Prins, Weber, & McGaugh, 1994) and thus is considered a candidate for the prevention of PTSD.

To examine this hypothesis, traumatized persons at increased risk of PTSD (as reflected by a heart rate greater than 80 beats per minute at emergency room admission), were randomly assigned to a 10-day course of double-blind treatment with propranolol (=18) versus placebo (=23), 40 mg four times daily (Pitman et al., 2002). The first dose was given within hours of the event. At 1 month, the mean CAPs scores in the two groups did not differ. There was, however, one outlier with very high levels of PTSD symptoms in the propranolol group. This outlier may have obscured group differences, since the distribution of PTSD severity scores was significantly different in the two groups (Pitman et al., 2002). However, the rate of PTSD in the placebo completers was not statistically different than in the propranolol completers at 1 month (30% vs. 18%) or 3 months (13% vs. 11%).

A nonrandomized open-label study of propranolol in trauma victims was subsequently performed (Vaiva et al., 2003). Trauma survivors with tachycardia were offered treatment with propranolol 40 mg, three times a day for 7 days, and were assessed 2 months later. There was not a significant difference in the rates of PTSD in those who refused propranolol versus those who received the medication (3/8 vs. 1/11); however, PTSD symptom severity as measured by the TOP-8 was significantly lower in the propranolol than the no-propranolol group.

Thus, neither preliminary study shows that propranolol protects against the development of a diagnosis of PTSD, but it may reduce the severity of PTSD symptoms in the months following trauma. Larger controlled trials are needed to definitively answer this question, since the ability to prevent the development of PTSD has important ramifications for public health.

Finally, three studies have examined the effect of benzodiazepines in recent trauma survivors. The use of benzodiazepines in the aftermath of trauma is rooted in the idea that they reduce arousal, inhibit memory consolidation, and have antipanic properties (Gelpin et al., 1996). In a study of consecutive emergency room admissions, trauma survivors who reported excessive distress within the first week after a traumatic event were treated at the discretion of the research psychiatrist with either clonazepam or alprazolam and interviewed at successive points after the traumatic event (Gelpin et al., 1996). Their posttraumatic symptoms were compared with those of a control group drawn from an ongoing study and matched by gender and PTSD symptoms at 1 week. The benzodiazepine-treated group did not differ from the comparison group in PTSD or depressive symptoms at multiple assessments over 6 months. Thus, within the limits of a case-control design, this study does not suggest a beneficial effect of benzodiazepines on the course of PTSD. Rather, the development of PTSD was higher in the benzodiazepine-treated group. Considering the nonrandom assignment to treatment group, it cannot be concluded that benzodiazepines facilitated the development of PTSD.

In a pilot evaluation of temazepam in four subjects with acute symptoms following trauma, temazepam was administered for 5 nights, tapered for 2 nights, and then discontinued. At 1 week, sleep had been improved and PTSD symptom severity lessened (Mellman, Byers, & Augenstein, 1998). In a subsequent randomized, placebo-controlled trial, 22 trauma survivors manifesting early symptoms of PTSD were randomly assigned to placebo for 7 nights or temazepam, beginning on average of 14 days after the trauma. There was no improvement in sleep parameters in the temazepam group beyond its period of use (Mellman, Byers, Augenstein,1998). However, 55% of the subjects in the temazepam group and 27% of subjects in the placebo group had PTSD at final assessment. None of these studies provides definitive or even suggestive evidence that short-term use of benzodiazepines in the acute treatment of trauma is beneficial. The higher rate of PTSD development in the benzodiazepine-treated group in both the case-control and the randomized trial suggests that such treatment may in fact be deleterious. Yet a clear recommendation cannot be made on the basis of these results. Larger studies are needed to determine whether the seemingly innocuous act of prescribing a benzodiazepine in the short term to an acutely distressed trauma survivor might indeed be helpful or ultimately have adverse effects on the natural course of posttraumatic recovery.

FUTURE DIRECTIONS

The numerous Type 1 and Type 2 studies in PTSD completed in recent years support the view that pharmacotherapy can be a primary treatment for chronic PTSD. Available evidence from such studies suggests that multiple antidepressants from different classes are effective first-line agents in the acute phase and maintenance treatment of PTSD. Some atypical antipsychotics and prazosin are also effective adjunctive treatments for a broad range of symptoms in treatment-refractory PTSD.

Despite the substantial gains made, much more needs to be done to expand the pharmacological options available to treat these chronically ill individuals. The response rates for the antidepressants in the positive Type 1 studies ranged from 41 to 65%. Rates of clinical remission were rarely reported but were noted to be 23% after 3 months of treatment with sertraline (Davidson, 2004). Thus a substantial proportion, sometimes even the majority of subjects enrolled, did not show a clinically meaningful response with sustained acute treatment. Furthermore, most of those who showed a clinical response had residual symptoms and/or continued to meet criteria for the disorder. Thus, additional studies are needed to determine ways to maximize the efficacy of existing treatments whether through determination of optimal dosing and duration of treatment or by combining different agents. Much more information is needed on predictors of response to different agents to facilitate treatment matching for this heterogeneous disorder. Future studies also need to address the clinical needs of subjects not included in these studies, including geriatric patients, PTSD patients with active substance abuse, and patients with severe mental illness in whom PTSD may be a secondary but distressing condition.

Finally, almost all the agents shown to be effective in PTSD were developed and marketed for other illnesses and have secondarily been demonstrated to be useful in the treatment of PTSD. To profit from the advances made in the psychobiology of PTSD, it is important to conduct rigorous trials of medications whose use is supported by a strong theoretical basis from either preclinical or human biological studies. The anticonvulsants, cortisol, and sympatholytics all fall into this category; looking forward, corticotrophin releasing hormone receptor antagonists, when available, may also be of use in PTSD (Holsboer, 1999).

There is a dearth of empirical evidence on how or when to combine pharmacological treatment and psychotherapy. It is unclear when or whether the combination is superior to either treatment alone or whether one treatment modality can treat residual symptoms following a course of treatment with the other modality. Especially exciting is the possibility that pharmacological agents can be used for the short term to enhance outcomes in psychotherapy. One such controversial study is examining whether MDMA (ecstasy) in a controlled setting can facilitate psychotherapy in treatment-refractory PTSD (Doblin, 2002). Another possibility is the use of D-cycloserine, a partial agonist at the NMDA receptor that has been shown to improve extinction of fear in animal studies (Walker, Ressler, Lu, & Davis, 2002). To date, d-cycloserine has been shown to improve outcomes in acrophobics undergoing behavioral exposure therapy and could prove to be a useful adjunct to exposure-based psychotherapy in PTSD (Ressler et al., 2004). Fortunately, the pace of advances of treatment in PTSD over the last 5 to 10 years suggests that the promise of more effective treatments for this disorder is likely to be realized in the coming years.

REFERENCES

Aerni, A., Traber, R., Hock, C., Roozendaal, B., Schelling, G., Papassotiropoulos, A., et al. (2004). Low-dose cortisol for symptoms of posttraumatic stress disorder. *American Journal of Psychiatry, 161,* 1488–1490.

Ahearn, E. P., Mussey, M., Johnson, C., Krohn, A., & Krahn, D. (2006). Quetiapine as an adjunctive treatment for post-traumatic stress disorder: An 8-week open-label study. *International Clinical Psychopharmacology, 21,* 29–33.

American Psychiatric Association. (1980). *Diagnostic and statistical manual of mental disorders* (3rd ed.). Washington, DC: Author.

American Psychiatric Association. (1994). *Diagnostic and statistical manual of mental disorders* (4th ed.). Washington, DC: Author.

Aukst-Margetic, B., Margetic, B., Tosic, G., & Bilic-Prcic, A. (2004). Levomepromazine helps to reduce sleep problems in patients with PTSD. *European Psychiatry, 19*, 235–236.

Bahk, W. M., Pae, C. U., Tsoh, J., Chae, J. H., Jun, T. Y., Chul-Lee, et al. (2002). Effects of mirtazapine in patients with post-traumatic stress disorder in Korea: A pilot study. *Human Psychopharmacology, 17*, 341–344.

Baker, D.G., Diamond, B.I., Gillette, G., Hamner, M., Katzelnick, D., Keller, T., et al. (1995). A double-blind, randomized, placebo-controlled, multi-center study of brofaromine in the treatment of post-traumatic stress disorder. *Psychopharmacology (Berlin), 4* , 386–389.

Baker, D .G., Ekhator, N. N., Kasckow, J. W., Dashevsky, B., Horn, P. S., Bednarik, L., et al. (2005). Higher levels of basal serial CSF cortisol in combat veterans with posttraumatic stress disorder. *American Journal of Psychiatry, 162*, 992–994.

Barnes, T. R. (1989). A rating scale for drug-induced akathisia. *British Journal of Psychiatry, 154*, 672–676.

Bartzokis, G., Lu, P. H, Turner, J., Mintz, J., & Saunders, C. S. (2005). Adjunctive risperidone in the treatment of chronic combat-related posttraumatic stress disorder. *Biological Psychiatry, 57*, 474–479.

Berigan, T. (2002). Oxcarbazepine treatment of post-traumatic stress disorder. *Canadian Journal of Psychiatry, 47*, 973–974.

Berlant, J. L. (2001). Topiramate in posttraumatic stress disorder: Preliminary clinical observations. *Journal of Clinical Psychiatry, 17*, 60–63.

Berlant, J. L., & van Kammen, D. P. (2002). Open-label topiramate as primary or adjunctive therapy in chronic civilian posttraumatic stress disorder: A preliminary report. *Journal of Clinical Psychiatry, 63*, 15–20.

Berlant, J. L. (2004). Prospective open-label study of add-on and monotherapy topiramate in civilians with chronic nonhallucinatory posttraumatic stress disorder. *BioMed Central Psychiatry, 18*, 4–24.

Birkhimer, L. J., DeVane, C. L., & Muniz, C. E. (1985). Posttraumatic stress disorder: Characteristics and pharmacological response in the veteran population. *Comprehensive Psychiatry, 26*, 304–310.

Blake, D. D. (1986). Treatment of acute posttraumatic stress disorder with tricyclic antidepressants. *Southern Medical Journal, 79*, 201–204.

Blake, D. D., Weathers, F. W., Nagy, L. M., Kaloupek, D. G., Gusman, F. D., Charney, D. S., et al. (1990). A clinician rating scale for assessing current and lifetime PTSD: CAPS-1. *Behavior Therapist, 13*, 187–188.

Bleich, A., Siegel, B., Garb, R., & Lerer, B. (1986). Post-traumatic stress disorder following combat exposure: Clinical features and psychopharmacological treatment. *British Journal of Psychiatry, 149*, 365–369.

Bonne, O., Brandes, D., Segman, R., Pitman, R. K., Yehuda, R., & Shalev, A. Y. (2003). Prospective evaluation of plasma cortisol in recent trauma survivors with posttraumatic stress disorder. *Psychiatry Research, 119*, 171–175.

Brady, K., Pearlstein, T., Asnis, G. M., Baker, D., Rothbaum, B., Sikes, C. R., et al. (2002). Efficacy and safety of sertraline treatment of posttraumatic stress disorder: A randomized controlled trial. *Journal of the American Medical Association, 283*, 837–844.

Brady, K. T., Sonne, S. C., & Roberts, J. M. (1995). Sertraline treatment of comorbid posttraumatic stress disorder and alcohol dependence. *Journal of Clinical Psychiatry, 56*, 502–505.

Brannon, N., Labbate, L., & Huber, M. (2000). Gabapentin treatment for posttraumatic stress disorder. *Canadian Journal of Psychiatry, 45*, 84.

Braun, P., Greenberg, D., Dasberg, H., & Lerer, B. (1990). Core symptoms of posttraumatic stress disorder unimproved by alprazolam treatment. *Journal of Clinical Psychiatry, 51*, 236–238.

Bremner, J. D., Licinio, J., Darnell, A., Krystal, J. H., Owens, M. J., Southwick, S. M., et al. (1997). Elevated CSF corticotropin-releasing factor concentrations in posttraumatic stress disorder. *American Journal of Psychiatry, 154*, 624–629.

Bremner, J. D., Mletzko, T., Welter, S., Quinn, S., Williams, C., Brummer, M., et al. (2005). Effects of phenytoin on memory, cognition and brain structure in post-traumatic stress disorder: A pilot study. *Journal of Psychopharmacology, 19*, 159–165.

Bremner, J. D., Mletzko, T., Welter, S., Siddiq, S., Reed, L., Williams, C., et al. (2004). Treatment of posttraumatic stress disorder with phenytoin: An open-label pilot study. *Journal of Clinical Psychiatry, 65*, 1559–1564.

Bremner, J. D., Randall, P., Vermetten, E., Staib, L., Bronen, R. A., Mazure, C., et al. (1997). Magnetic resonance imaging–based measurement of hippocampal volume in posttraumatic stress disorder related to childhood physical and sexual abuse: A preliminary report. *Biological Psychiatry, 41*, 23–32.

Bremner, J. D., Southwick, S. M., Johnson, D. R., Yehuda, R., & Charney, D. S. (1993). Childhood physical abuse and combat-related posttraumatic stress disorder in Vietnam veterans. *American Journal of Psychiatry, 150,* 235–239.

Breslau, N. (2002). Gender differences in trauma and posttraumatic stress disorder. *Journal of Gender-Specific Medicine 5,* 34–40.

Breslau, N., Davis, G. C., Andreski, P., & Peterson, E. (1991). Traumatic events and post-traumatic stress disorder in an urban population of young adults. *Archives of General Psychiatry, 48,* 216–220.

Brophy, M. H. (1991). Cyproheptadine for combat nightmares in post-traumatic stress disorder and dream anxiety disorder. *Military Medicine, 156,* 100–101.

Burdon, A. P., Sutker, P. B., Foulks, E. F., Crane, M. U., & Thompson, K. E. (1991). Pilot program of treatment for PTSD [Letter]. *American Journal of Psychiatry, 148,* 1269–1270.

Burstein, A., Ciccone, P. E., Greenstein, R. A., Daniels, N., Olsen, K., Mazarek, A., et al. (1988). Chronic Vietnam PTSD and acute civilian PTSD: A comparison of treatment experiences. *General Hospital Psychiatry, 10,* 245–249.

Butterfield, M. I., Becker, M. E., Connor, K. M., Sutherland, S., Churchill, L. E., & Davidson, J. R. (2001). Olanzapine in the treatment of post-traumatic stress disorder: A pilot study. *International Clinical Psychopharmacology, 16,* 197–203.

Buysse, D. J., Reynolds, C. F., III, Monk, T. H., Berman, S. R., & Kupfer, D. J. (1989). The Pittsburgh Sleep Quality Index: A new instrument for psychiatric practice and research. *Psychiatry Research, 28,* 193–213.

Cahill, L., Prins, B., Weber, M., & McGaugh, J. L. (1994). Beta-adrenergic activation and memory for emotional events. *Nature, 371,* 702–704.

Canive, J. M., Clark, R. D., Calais, L. A., Qualls, C., & Tuason, V. B. (1998). Bupropion treatment in veterans with posttraumatic stress disorder: An open study. *Journal of Clinical Psychopharmacology, 18,* 379–383.

Cates, M. E., Bishop, M. H., Davis, L. L., Lowe, J. S., & Woolley, T. W. (2004). Clonazepam for treatment of sleep disturbances associated with combat-related posttraumatic stress disorder. *Annals of Pharmacotherapy, 38,* 1395–1399.

Charney, D. S., Deutch, A. Y., Krystal, J. H., Southwick, S. M., & Davis, M. (1993). Psychobiologic mechanisms of posttraumatic stress disorder. *Archives of General Psychiatry, 50,* 295–305.

Chung, M. Y., Min, K. H., Jun, Y. J., Kim, S. S., Kim, W. C., & Jun, E. M. (2004). Efficacy and tolerabil-ity of mirtazapine and sertraline in Korean veterans with posttraumatic stress disorder: a randomized open label trial. *Human Psychopharmacology, 7,* 489–494.

Clark, R. D., Canive, J. M., Calais, L. A., Qualls, C. R., & Tuason, V. B. (1999). Divalproex in posttraumatic stress disorder: An open-label clinical trial. *Journal of Traumatic Stress, 12,* 395–401.

Connor, K. M., Davidson, J. R., Weisler, R. H., & Ahearn, E. (1999). A pilot study of mirtazapine in post-traumatic stress disorder. *International Clinical Psychopharmacology, 14,* 29–31.

Connor, K. M., Davidson, J. R., Weisler, R. H., Zhang, W., & Abraham, K. (2006). Tiagabine for posttraumatic stress disorder: Effects of open-label and double-blind discontinuation treatment. *Psychopharmacology (Berlin), 184,* 21–25.

Connor, K. M., Sutherland, S. M., Tupler, L. A., Malik, M. L., & Davidson, J. R. (1999). Fluoxetine in post-traumatic stress disorder: Randomised, double-blind study. *British Journal of Psychiatry, 175,* 17–22.

Cooper, N. A., & Clum, B. A. (1989). Imaginal flooding as a supplementary treatment for PTSD in combat veterans: A controlled study. *Behavioral Therapy, 20,* 381–391.

David, D., De Faria, L., Lapeyra, O., & Mellman, T. A. (2004). Adjunctive risperidone treatment in combat veterans with chronic PTSD. *Journal of Clinical Psychopharmacology, 24,* 556–559.

Davidson, J., Roth, S., & Newman, E. (1991). Fluoxetine in post-traumatic stress disorder. *Journal of Traumatic Stress, 4,* 419–423.

Davidson, J., & Smith, R. (1990). Traumatic experiences in psychiatric outpatients. *Journal of Traumatic Stress, 3,* 459–475.

Davidson, J., Swartz, M., Storck, M., Krishnan, R. R., & Hammett, E. (1985). A diagnostic and family study of posttraumatic stress disorder. *American Journal of Psychiatry, 142,* 90–93.

Davidson, J., Walker, J. I., & Kilts, C. (1987). A pilot study of phenelzine in the treatment of post-traumatic stress disorder. *British Journal of Psychiatry, 150,* 252–255.

Davidson, J. R (1992). Drug therapy of post-traumatic stress disorder. *British Journal of Psychiatry, 160,* 309–314.

Davidson, J. R. (2004). Remission in post-traumatic stress disorder (PTSD): Effects of sertraline as assessed by the Davidson Trauma Scale, Clinical Global Impressions and the Clinician-Administered PTSD scale. *International Clinical Psychopharmacology, 19,* 85–87.

Davidson, J. R., & Colket, J. T. (1997). The eight-item treatment-outcome post-traumatic stress disorder scale: A brief measure to assess treatment outcome in post-traumatic stress disorder. *International Clinical Psychopharmacology, 12*, 41–45.

Davidson, J. R., Hughes, D., Blazer, D. G., & George, L. K. (1991). Post-traumatic stress disorder in the community: An epidemiological study. *Psychological Medicine, 21*, 713–721.

Davidson, J. R., Kudler, H., Smith, R., Mahorney, S. L., Lipper, S., Hammett, E., et al. (1990). Treatment of posttraumatic stress disorder with amitriptyline and placebo. *Archives of General Psychiatry, 47*, 259–266

Davidson, J. R., Landerman L. R., Farfel, G. M., & Clary, C. M. (2002). Characterizing the effects of sertraline in post-traumatic stress disorder. *Psychological Medicine, 32*, 661–670.

Davidson, J. R., Malik, M. A., & Travers, J. (1997). Structured interview for PTSD (SIP): Psychometric validation for *DSM-IV* criteria. *Depression and Anxiety, 5*, 127–129.

Davidson, J. R., Rothbaum, B. O., van der Kolk, B. A., Sikes, C. R., & Farfel, G. M. (2001). Multicenter, double-blind comparison of sertraline and placebo in the treatment of posttraumatic stress disorder. *Archives of General Psychiatry, 58*, 485–492.

Davidson, J. R., Tharwani, H. M., & Connor, K. M. (2002). Davidson Trauma Scale (DTS): Normative scores in the general population and effect sizes in placebo-controlled SSRI trials. *Depression and Anxiety, 15*, 75–78.

Davidson, J. R., Weisler, R. H., Butterfield, M. I., Casat, C. D., Connor, K. M., Barnett, S., et al. (2003). Mirtazapine vs. placebo in posttraumatic stress disorder: A pilot trial. *Biological Psychiatry, 53*, 188–191.

Davidson, J. R., Weisler, R. H., Malik, M. L., & Connor, K. M. (1998). Treatment of posttraumatic stress disorder with nefazodone. *International Clinical Psychopharmacology, 13*, 111–113.

Davidson, J. R., Weisler, R. H., Malik, M., & Tupler, L. A. (1998). Fluvoxamine in civilians with posttraumatic stress disorder. *Journal of Clinical Psychopharmacology, 18*, 93–95.

Davis, L. L., Jewell, M. E., Ambrose, S., Farley, J., English, B., Bartolucci, A., et al. (2004). A placebo-controlled study of nefazodone for the treatment of chronic posttraumatic stress disorder: A preliminary study. *Journal of Clinical Psychopharmacology, 24*, 291–297.

Davis, L. L., Nugent, A. L., Murray, J., Kramer, G. L., & Petty, F. (2000). Nefazodone treatment for chronic posttraumatic stress disorder: An open trial. *Journal of Clinical Psychopharmacology, 20*, 159–164.

Dieperink, M. E., & Drogemuller, L. (1999). Zolpidem for insomnia related to PTSD. *Psychiatic Services. 50*, 421.

Dillard, M. L., Bendfeldt, F., & Jernigan, P. (1993). Use of thioridazine in post-traumatic stress disorder. *Southern Medical Journal, 86*, 1276–1278.

Doblin, R. (2002). A clinical plan for MDMA (ecstasy) in the treatment of posttraumatic stress disorder (PTSD): Partnering with the FDA. *Journal of Psychoactive Drugs, 34*, 185–194.

Dow, B., & Kline, N. (1997). Antidepressant treatment of posttraumatic stress disorder and major depression in veterans. *Annals of Clinical Psychiatry, 9*, 1–5.

Drake, R. G., Davis, L. L., Cates, M. E., Jewell, M. E., Ambrose, S. M., & Lowe, J. S. (2003). Baclofen treatment for chronic posttraumatic stress disorder. *Annals of Pharmacotherapy, 37*, 1177–1181.

Escalona, R., Canive, J. M., Calais, L. A., & Davidson, J. R. (2002). Fluvoxamine treatment in veterans with combat-related post-traumatic stress disorder. *Depression and Anxiety, 15*, 29–33.

Falcon, S., Ryan, C., Chamberlain, K., & Curtis, G. (1985). Tricyclics: Possible treatment for posttraumatic stress disorder. *Journal of Clinical Psychiatry, 46*, 385–388.

Fesler, F. A. (1991). Valproate in combat-related posttraumatic stress disorder. *Journal of Clinical Psychiatry, 52*, 361–364.

Filteau, M. J., Leblanc, J., & Bouchard, R. H. (2003). Quetiapine reduces flashbacks in chronic posttraumatic stress disorder. *Canadian Journal of Psychiatry, 48*, 282–283.

Foa, E. B. (2000). Psychosocial treatment of posttraumatic stress disorder. *Journal of Clinical Psychiatry, 5*, 43–48.

Foa, E. B., Olasov Rothbaum, B., Riggs, D. S., & Murdock, T. B. (1991). Treatment of posttraumatic stress disorder in rape victims: A comparison between cognitive-behavioral procedures and counseling. *Journal of Consulting and Clinical Psychology, 59*, 714–723.

Foa, E. B., Steketee, G., & Olasov Rothbaum, B. (1989). Behavioral/cognitive conceptualizations of post-traumatic stress disorder. *Behavioral Therapy, 20*, 155–176.

Forbes, D., Phelps, A. J., McHugh, A. F., Debenham, P., Hopwood, M., & Creamer, M. (2003). Imagery rehearsal in the treatment of posttraumatic nightmares in Australian veterans with chronic combat-related PTSD: 12-month follow-up data. *Journal of Traumatic Stress, 16*, 509–513.

Ford, N. (1996). The use of anticonvulsants in posttraumatic stress disorder: Case study and overview. *Journal of Traumatic Stress, 9*, 857–863.

Foy, D. W., Sipprelle, R. C., Rueger, D. B., & Carroll, E. M. (1984). Etiology of posttraumatic stress disorder in Vietnam veterans. *Journal of Consulting and Clinical Psychology, 40,* 1323–1328.

Freedy, J. R., Shaw, D. L., & Jarrell, M. P. (1992). Towards an understanding of the psychological impact of natural disaster: An application of the conservation resources stress model. *Journal of Traumatic Stress, 5,* 441–454.

Friedman, M. J. (1988). Toward rational pharmacotherapy for posttraumatic stress disorder: An interim report. *American Journal of Psychiatry, 145,* 281–285.

Garfield, D. A., Fichtner, C. G., Leveroni, C., & Mahableshwarkar, A. (2001). Open trial of nefazodone for combat veterans with posttraumatic stress disorder. *Journal of Traumatic Stress, 14,* 453–460.

Gelpin, E., Bonne, O., Peri, T., Brandes, D., & Shalev, A. Y. (1996). Treatment of recent trauma survivors with benzodiazepines: A prospective study. *Journal of Clinical Psychiatry, 57,* 390–394.

Goldstein, G., van Kammen, W., Shelly, C., Miller, D. J., & van Kammen, D. P. (1987). Survivors of imprisonment in the Pacific theater during World War II. *American Journal of Psychiatry, 144,* 1210–1213.

Golier, J. A., Yehuda, R., Lupien, S. J., Harvey, P. D., Grossman, R., & Elkin, A. (2002). Memory performance in Holocaust survivors with posttraumatic stress disorder. *American Journal of Psychiatry, 159,* 1682–1688.

Golier, J. A., Yehuda, R., Schmeidler, J., & Siever, L. J. (2001). Variability and severity of depression and anxiety in post traumatic stress disorder and major depressive disorder. *Depression and Anxiety, 13,* 97–100.

Green, B. L., Lindy, J. D., Grace, M. C., & Leonard, A. C. (1992). Chronic posttraumatic stress disorder and diagnostic comorbidity in a disaster sample. *Journal of Nervous and Mental Disease, 180,* 760–766.

Gurvits, T. V., Shenton, M. E., Hokama, H., Ohta, H., Lasko, N. B., Gilbertson, M. W., et al. (1996). Magnetic resonance imaging study of hippocampal volume in chronic, combat-related posttraumatic stress disorder. *Biological Psychiatry, 40,* 1091–1099.

Guy, W. (1976). *ECDEU assessment manual for psychopharmacology* (Rev. ed.). Washington, DC: U.S. Department of Health, Education, and Welfare.

Hamilton, M. (1960). A rating scale for depression. *Journal of Neurology, Neurosurgery, andPsychiatry, 23,* 56–62.

Hamner, M. B. (1996). Clozapine treatment for a veteran with comorbid psychosis and PTSD. *American Journal of Psychiatry, 153,* 841.

Hamner, M. B., Brodrick, P. S., & Labbate, L. A. (2001). Gabapentin in PTSD: A retrospective, clinical series of adjunctive therapy. *Annals of Clinical Psychiatry, 13,* 141–146.

Hamner, M. B., Deitsch, S. E., Brodrick, P. S., Ulmer, H. G., & Lorberbaum, J. P. (2003). Quetiapine treatment in patients with posttraumatic stress disorder: An open trial of adjunctive therapy. *Journal of Clinical Psychopharmacology, 23,* 15–20.

Hamner, M. B., Faldowski, R. A., Ulmer, H. G., Frueh, B. C., Huber, M. G., & Arana, G. W. (2003). Adjunctive risperidone treatment in post-traumatic stress disorder: A preliminary controlled trial of effects on comorbid psychotic symptoms. *International Clinical Psychopharmacology, 18,* 1–8.

Hamner, M. B., & Frueh, B. C. (1998). Response to venlafaxine in a previously antidepressant treatment-resistant combat veteran with post-traumatic stress disorder. *International Clinical Psychopharmacology, 13,* 233–234.

Harsch, H. H. (1986). Cyproheptadine for recurrent nightmares. *American Journal of Psychiatry, 143,* 1491–1492.

Helzer, J. E., Robins, L. N., & McEvo, L. (1987). Posttraumatic stress disorder in the general population: Findings from the Epidemiological Catchment Area Survey. *New England Journal of Medicine, 317,* 1630–1634.

Heresco-Levy, U., Kremer, I., Javitt, D. C., Goichman, R., Reshef, A., Blanaru, M., et al. (2002). Pilot-controlled trial of D-cycloserine for the treatment of post-traumatic stress disorder. *International Journal of Neuropsychopharmacology, 5,* 301–307.

Hertzberg, M. A., Butterfield, M. I., Feldman, M. E., Beckham, J. C., Sutherland, S. M., Connor, K. M., et al. (1999). A preliminary study of lamotrigine for the treatment of posttraumatic stress disorder. *Biological Psychiatry, 45,* 1226–1229.

Hertzberg, M. A., Feldman, M. E., Beckham, J. C., & Davidson, J. R. (1996). Trial of trazodone for post-traumatic stress disorder using a multiple baseline group design. *Journal of Clinical Psychopharmacology, 16,* 294–298.

Hertzberg, M. A., Feldman, M. E., Beckham, J. C., Kudler, H. S., & Davidson, J. R. (2000). Lack of efficacy for fluoxetine in PTSD: A placebo controlled trial in combat veterans. *Annals of Clinical Psychiatry, 12,* 101–105.

Hertzberg, M. A., Feldman, M. E., Beckham, J. C., Moore, S. D., & Davidson, J. R. (1998). Open trial of nefazodone for combat-related posttraumatic stress disorder. *Journal of Clinical Psychiatry, 59,* 460–464.

Hertzberg, M. A., Feldman, M. E., Beckham, J. C., Moore, S. D., & Davidson, J. R. (2002). Three- to four-year follow-up to an open trial of nefazodone for combat-related posttraumatic stress disorder. *Annals of Clinical Psychiatry, 14*, 215–221.

Hogben, G. L., & Cornfield, R. B. (1981). Treatment of traumatic war neurosis with phenelzine. *Archives of General Psychiatry, 38*, 440–445.

Holsboer, F. (1989). The rationale for corticotropin-releasing hormone receptor (CRH-R) antagonists to treat depression and anxiety. *Journal of Psychiatric Research, 33*, 181–214.

Horowitz, M. (1974). Stress response syndromes, character style, and dynamic psychotherapy. *Archives of General Psychiatry, 31*, 768–781.

Horowitz, M. (1986). *Stress response syndromes* (2nd ed.). Northvale, NJ: Jason Aronson.

Horowitz, M., Wilner, N., & Alvarez, W. (1979). Impact of Event Scale: A measure of subjective stress. *Psychosomatic Medicine, 412*, 209–218.

Hui, Z., Guang-Yu, M., Chong-Tao, X., Quan, Y., & Xiao-Hu, X. (2005). Phenytoin reverses the chronic stress-induced impairment of memory consolidation for water maze training and depression of LTP in rat hippocampal CA1 region, but does not affect motor activity. *Brain Research. Cognitive Brain Research, 24*, 380–385.

Kaplan, Z., Amir, M., Swartz, M., & Levine, J. (1996). Inositol treatment of post-traumatic stress disorder. *Anxiety, 1*, 51–52.

Kardiner, A. (1941). *The traumatic neurosis of war.* New York: Paul Hoeber.

Kay, S. R., Fiszbein, S., & Opler, L. A. (1987). The positive and negative syndrome scale for schizophrenia. *Schizophrenia Bulletin, 13*, 261–276.

Keane, T. M., Caddell, J. M., & Taylor, K. L. (1988). Mississippi Scale for Combat-Related Posttraumatic Stress Disorder: Three studies in reliability and validity. *Journal of Consulting and Clinical Psychology, 56*, 85–90.

Keane, T. M., Fairbank, J. A., Caddell, J. M., & Zimering, R. T. (1989). Implosive (flooding) therapy reduces symptoms of PTSD in Vietnam combat veterans. *Behavioral Therapy, 20*, 245–260.

Keck, P. E., McElroy, S. L., & Friedman, L. M. (1992). Valproate and carbamazepine in the treatment of panic and posttraumatic stress disorders, withdrawal states, and behavioral dyscontrol syndromes. *Journal of Clinical Psychopharmacology, 12*(Suppl.), 36S–41S.

Kessler, R. C., Sonnega, A., Bromet, E., Hughes, M., & Nelson, C. B. (1995). Posttraumatic stress disorder in the National Comorbidity Survey. *Archives of General Psychiatry, 52*, 1048–1060.

Khan, S., & Liberzon, I. (2004). Topiramate attenuates exaggerated acoustic startle in an animal model of PTSD. *Psychopharmacology (Berlin), 172*, 225–229.

Kilpatrick, D. G., Veronen, L. J., & Resick, P. A. (1982). Psychological sequelae to rape: Assessment and treatment strategies. In D. M. Dolays & R. L. Meredith Eds.), *Behavioral medicine: Assessment and treatment strategies* (pp. 473–497). New York: Plenum Press.

Kim, W., Pae, C. U., Chae, J. H., Jun, T. Y., & Bahk, W. M. (2005). The effectiveness of mirtazapine in the treatment of post-traumatic stress disorder: A 24-week continuation therapy. *Psychiatry and Clinical Neurosciences. 59*, 743–7.

Kinzie, J. D., & Leung, P. (1989). Clonidine in Cambodian patients with posttraumatic stress disorder. *Journal of Nervous and Mental Disease, 177*, 546–550.

Kinzie, J. D., Sack, R. L., & Riley, C. M. (1994). The polysomnographic effects of clonidine on sleep disorders in posttraumatic stress disorder: A pilot study with Cambodian patients. *Journal of Nervous and Mental Disease, 182*, 585–587.

Kitchner, I., & Greenstein, R. (1985). Low-dose lithium carbonate in the treatment of posttraumatic stress disorder: Brief communication. *Military Medicine, 150*, 378–381.

Kluznick, J. C., Speed, N., Van Valenburg, C., & Magraw, R. (1986). Forty-year follow-up of United States prisoners of war. *American Journal of Psychiatry, 143*, 1443–1446.

Kolb, L. C., Burris, B. C., & Griffiths, S. (1984). Propranolol and clonidine in the treatment of post-traumatic stress disorders of war. In B. van der Kolk (Ed.), *Post-traumatic stress disorder: Psychological and biological sequellae* (pp. 98–105). Washington, DC: American Psychiatric Press.

Kosten, T. R., Fontana, A., Sernyak, M. J., & Rosenheck, R. (2000). Benzodiazepine use in posttraumatic stress disorder among veterans with substance abuse. *Journal of Nervous and Mental Disease, 188*, 454–459.

Kosten, T. R., Frank, J. B., Dan, E., McDougle, C. J., & Giller, E. L. (1991). Pharmacotherapy for post-traumatic stress disorder using phenelzine or imipramine. *Journal of Nervous and Mental Disease, 179*, 366–370.

Kosten, T. R., Mason, J. W., Giller, E. L., Ostroff, R. B., & Harkness, L.. (1987). Sustained urinary norepinephrine and epinephrine elevation in post-traumatic stress disorder. *Psychoneuroendocrinology, 12*, 13–20.

Kozaric-Kovacic, D., Pivac, N., Muck-Seler, D., & Rothbaum, B. O. (2005). Risperidone in psychotic combat-related posttraumatic stress disorder: An open trial. *Journal of Clinical Psychiatry, 66,* 922–927.

Krakow, B., Hollifield, M., Johnston, L., Koss, M., Schrader, R., Warner, T. D., et al. (2001). Imagery rehearsal therapy for chronic nightmares in sexual assault survivors with posttraumatic stress disorder: A randomized controlled trial. *Journal of the American Medical Association, 286,* 537–545.

Kulka, R. A., Schlenger, W. E., Fairbank, J. A., Hough, R. L., Jordan, B. K., Marmar, C. R., et al. (1990). *Trauma and the Vietnam War generation: Report of findings from the National Vietnam Veterans Readjustment Study.* New York: Brunner/Mazel.

Leber, K., Malek, A., D'Agostino, A., & Adelman, H. M. (1999). A veteran with acute mental changes years after combat. *Hospital Practice (Minneapolis), 34,* 21–22.

Lerer, B., Bleich, A., Kotler, M., Garb, R., Hertzberg, M., & Levin, B. (1987). Posttraumatic stress disorder in Israeli combat veterans. Effect of phenelzine treatment. *Archives of General Psychiatry, 11,* 976–981.

Lipper, S., Davidson, J. R. T., Grady, T. A., Edinger, J. D., Hammett, E. B., Mahorney, S. L., et al. (1986). Preliminary study of carbamazepine in post-traumatic stress disorder. *Psychosomatics, 27,* 849–854.

Londborg, P. D., Hegel, M. T., Goldstein, S., Goldstein, D., Himmelhoch, J. M., Maddock, R., et al. (2001). Sertraline treatment of posttraumatic stress disorder: Results of 24 weeks of open-label continuation treatment. *Journal of Clinical Psychiatry, 62,* 325–331.

Lubin, G., Weizman, A., Shmushkevitz, M., & Valevski, A. (2002). Short-term treatment of post-traumatic stress disorder with naltrexone: An open-label preliminary study. *Human Psychopharmacology, 17,* 181–185.

Macklin, M. L., Metzger, L. J., Litz, B. T., McNally, R. J., Lasko, N. B., Orr. S. P., et al. (1998). Lower precombat intelligence is a risk factor for posttraumatic stress disorder. *Journal of Consulting and Clinical Psychology, 66,* 323–326.

Malek-Ahmadi, P. (2003). Gabapentin and posttraumatic stress disorder. *Annals of Pharmacotherapy, 37,* 664–666.

Malek-Ahmadi, P., & Hanretta, A. T. (2004). Possible reduction in posttraumatic stress disorder symptoms with oxcarbazepine in a patient with bipolar disorder. *Annals of Pharmacotherapy, 38,* 1852–1854.

Malik, M. L., Connor, K. M., Sutherland, S. M., Smith, R. D., Davison, R. M., & Davidson, J. R. (1999). Quality of life and posttraumatic stress disorder: A pilot study assessing changes in SF-36 scores before and after treatment in a placebo-controlled trial of fluoxetine. *Journal of Traumatic Stress, 12,* 387–393.

March, J. S. (1993). What constitutes a stressor: The "Criterion A" issue. In J. R. T. Davidson & E. B. Foa (Eds.), *Posttraumatic stress disorder, DSM-IV and beyond* (pp. 147–172). Washington, DC: American Psychiatric Press.

Marmar, C. R., Schoenfeld, F., Weiss, D. S., Metzler, T., Zatzick, D., Wu, R., et al. (1996). Open trial of fluvoxamine treatment for combat-related posttraumatic stress disorder. *Journal of Clinical Psychiatry, 57,* 66–70.

Marshall, R. D., Beebe, K. L., Oldham, M., & Zaninelli, R. (2001). Efficacy and safety of paroxetine treatment for chronic PTSD: A fixed-dose, placebo-controlled study. *American Journal of Psychiatry, 158,* 1982–1988.

Marshall, R. D., Schneier, F. R., Fallon, B. A., Knight, C. B., Abbate, L. A., Goetz, D., et al. (1998). An open trial of paroxetine in patients with noncombat-related, chronic posttraumatic stress disorder. *Journal of Clinical Psychopharmacology, 18,* 10–18.

Martenyi, F., Brown, E. B., Zhang, H., Koke, S. C., & Prakash, A. (2002). Fluoxetine v. placebo in prevention of relapse in post-traumatic stress disorder. *British Journal of Psychiatry, 181,* 315–320.

Martenyi, F., Brown, E. B., Zhang, H., Prakash, A., & Koke, S. C. (2002). Fluoxetine versus placebo in posttraumatic stress disorder. *Journal of Clinical Psychiatry, 63,* 199–206.

McDougle, C. J., Southwick, S. M., Charney, D. S., & St. James, R. L. (1991). An open trial of fluoxetine in the treatment of posttraumatic stress disorder [Letter]. *Journal of Clinical Psychopharmacology, 11,* 325–327.

McFarlane, A. C. (1989). The aetiology of post-traumatic morbidity: Predisposing, precipitating, and perpetuating factors. *British Journal of Psychiatry, 154,* 221–228.

McFarlane, A. C. (1990). Vulnerability to posttraumatic stress disorder. In M. E. Wolf & A. D. Mosnaim (Eds.), *Posttraumatic stress disorder: Etiology, phenomenology and treatment* (pp. 2–20). Washington, DC: American Psychiatric Press.

McFarlane, A. C. (1992). Multiple diagnoses in posttraumatic stress disorder in the victims of a natural disaster. *Journal of Nervous and Mental Disease, 180,* 498–504.

McFarlane, A. C., Atchison, M., & Yehuda, R. (1997). The acute stress response following motor vehicle accidents and its relation to PTSD. *Annals of the New York Academy of Sciences, 821,* 437–441.

Mellman, T. A., Byers, P. M., & Augenstein, J. S. (1998). Pilot evaluation of hypnotic medication during acute traumatic stress response. *Journal of Traumatic Stress, 11,* 563–569.

Mellman, T. A., Kumar, A., Kulick-Bell, R., Kumar, M., & Nolan, B. (1995). Nocturnal/daytime urine noradrenergic measures and sleep in combat-related PTSD. *Biological Psychiatry, 38,* 174–179.

Milanes, F. J., Mack, C. N., Dennison, J., & Slater, V. L. (1984, June). Phenelzine treatment of post-Vietnam stress syndrome. *VA Practitioner,* 40–49.

Nagy, L. M., Morgan, C. A., III, Southwick, S. M., & Charney, D. S. (1993). Open prospective trial of fluoxetine for posttraumatic stress disorder. *Journal of Clinical Psychopharmacology, 13,* 107–113

Neal, L. A., Shapland, W., Fox, C. (1997) An open trial of moclobemide in the treatment of post-traumatic stress disorder. *International Clinical Psychopharmacology, 4,* 231–237.

Neylan, T. C., Lenoci, M., Maglione, M. L., Rosenlicht, N. Z., Leykin, Y., Metzler, T. J., et al. (2003). The effect of nefazodone on subjective and objective sleep quality in posttraumatic stress disorder. *Journal of Clinical Psychiatry, 64,* 445–450.

Neylan, T. C., Metzler, T. J., Schoenfeld, F. B., Weiss, D. S., Lenoci, M., Best, S. R., et al. (2001). Fluvoxamine and sleep disturbances in posttraumatic stress disorder. *Journal of Traumatic Stress, 14,* 461–467.

North, C. S., Smith, E. M., & Spitznagel, E. L. (1994). Posttraumatic stress disorder in survivors of a mass shooting. *American Journal of Psychiatry, 151,* 82–88.

Orr, S. P., Lasko, N. B., Shalev, A. Y., & Pitman, R. K. (1995). Physiologic responses to loud tones in Vietnam veterans with posttraumatic stress disorder. *Journal of Abnormal Psychology, 104,* 75–82.

Overall, J. E., & Gorham, D. R. (1962). The brief psychiatric rating scale. *Psychological Reports, 10,* 799–812.

Peskind, E. R., Bonner, L. T., Hoff, D. J., & Raskind, M. A. (2003). Prazosin reduces trauma-related nightmares in older men with chronic posttraumatic stress disorder. *Journal of Geriatric Psychiatry and Neurology, 16,* 165–171.

Petty, F., Brannan, S., Casada, J., Davis, L. L., Gajewski, V., Kramer, G. L., et al. (2001). Olanzapine treatment for post-traumatic stress disorder: An open-label study. *International Clinical Psychopharmacology, 16,* 331–337.

Pitman, R. K. (1989). Post-traumatic stress disorder, hormones, and memory. *Biological Psychiatry, 26,* 221–223.

Pitman, R. K., Sanders, K. M., Zusman, R. M., Healy, A. R., Cheema, F., Lasko, N. B., et al. (2002). Pilot study of secondary prevention of posttraumatic stress disorder with propranolol. *Biological Psychiatry, 51,* 189–192.

Post, R. M., Weiss, S. R., Smith, M., Li, H., & McCann, U. (1997). Kindling versus quenching: Implications for the evolution and treatment of posttraumatic stress disorder. *Annals of the New York Academy of Sciences, 821,* 285–295.

Raskind, M. A., Dobie, D. J., Kanter, E. D., Petrie, E. C., Thompson, C. E., & Peskind, E. R. (2000). The alpha-1-adrenergic antagonist prazosin ameliorates combat trauma nightmares in veterans with posttraumatic stress disorder: A report of 4 cases. *Journal of Clinical Psychiatry, 61,* 129–133.

Raskind, M. A., Peskind, E. R., Kanter, E. D., Petrie, E. C., Radant, A., Thompson, C. E., et al. (2003). Reduction of nightmares and other PTSD symptoms in combat veterans by prazosin: A placebo-controlled study. *American Journal of Psychiatry, 160,* 371–373.

Raskind, M. A., Thompson, C., Petrie, E. C., Dobie, D. J., Rein, R. J., Hoff, D. J., et al. (2002). Prazosin reduces nightmares in combat veterans with posttraumatic stress disorder. *Journal of Clinical Psychiatry, 63,* 565–568.

Reich, D. B., Winternitz, S., Hennen, J., Watts, T., & Stanculescu, C. (2004). A preliminary study of risperidone in the treatment of posttraumatic stress disorder related to childhood abuse in women. *Journal of Clinical Psychiatry, 65,* 1601–1606.

Reist, C., Kauffman, C. D., Haier, R. J., Sangdahl, C., DeMet, E. M., Chicz-DeMet, A., et al. (1989). A controlled trial of desipramine in 18 men with posttraumatic stress disorder. *American Journal of Psychiatry, 146,* 513–516.

Resick, P. A., & Schnicke, M. K. (1992). Cognitive processing therapy for sexual assault victims. *Journal of Consulting and Clinical Psychology, 60,* 748–756.

Resnick, H. S., Kilpatrick, D. G., Best, C. L., & Kramer, T. L. (1992). Vulnerability-stress factors in development of posttraumatic stress disorder. *Journal of Nervous and Mental Disease, 180,* 424–430.

Resnick, H. S., Yehuda, R., Pitman, R. K., & Foy, D. W. (1995). Effect of previous trauma on acute plasma cortisol level following rape. *American Journal of Psychiatry, 152,* 1675–1677.

Ressler, K. J., Rothbaum, B. O., Tannenbaum, L., Anderson, P., Graap, K., Zimand, E., et al. (2004). Cognitive enhancers as adjuncts to psychotherapy:

Use of D-cycloserine in phobic individuals to facilitate extinction of fear. *Archives of General Psychiatry, 61,* 1136–1144.

Risse, S. C., Whitters, A., Burke, J., Chen, S., Scurfield, R. M., & Raskind, M. A. (1990). Severe withdrawal symptoms after discontinuation of alprazolam in eight patients with combat-induced posttraumatic stress disorder. *Journal of Clinical Psychiatry, 51,* 206–209.

Robert, S., Hamner, M. B., Kose, S., Ulmer, H. G., Deitsch, S. E., & Lorberbaum, J. P. (2005). Quetiapine improves sleep disturbances in combat veterans with PTSD: Sleep data from a prospective, open-label study. *Journal of Clinical Psychopharmacology, 25,* 387–388.

Rothbaum, B. O., Foa, E. B., Riggs, D. S., Murdock, T., & Walsh, W. (1992). A prospective examination of post-traumatic stress disorder in rape victims. *Journal of Traumatic Stress 55,* 455–475.

Rothbaum, B. O., Hodges, L., Alarcon, R., Ready, D., Shahar, F., Graap, K., et al. (1999). Virtual reality exposure therapy for PTSD Vietnam veterans: A case study. *Journal of Traumatic Stress, 12,* 263–271.

Rothbaum, B. O., Ninan, P. T., & Thomas, L. (1996). Sertraline in the treatment of rape victims with posttraumatic stress disorder. *Journal of Traumatic Stress, 9,* 865–871.

Rush, A. J., Armitage, R., Gillin, J. C., Yonkers, K. A., Winokur, A., Moldofsky, H., et al. (1998). Comparative effects of nefazodone and fluoxetine on sleep in outpatients with major depressive disorder. *Biological Psychiatry, 44,* 3–14.

Schelling, G., Briegel, J., Roozendaal, B., Stoll, C., Rothenhausler, H. B., & Kapfhammer, H. P. (2001). The effect of stress doses of hydrocortisone during septic shock on posttraumatic stress disorder in survivors. *Biological Psychiatry, 50,* 978–985.

Schelling, G., Stoll, C., Kapfhammer, H. P., Rothenhausler, H. B., Krauseneck, T., Durst, K., et al. (1999). The effect of stress doses of hydrocortisone during septic shock on posttraumatic stress disorder and health-related quality of life in survivors. *Critical Care Medicine, 27,* 2678–2683.

Schnurr, P. P., Friedman, M. J., & Rosenberg, S. D. (1993). Premilitary MMPI scores as predictors of combat-related PTSD symptoms. *American Journal of Psychiatry, 150,* 479–483.

Schwartz, L. S. (1990). A biopsychosocial treatment approach to post-traumatic stress disorder. *Journal of Traumatic Stress, 3,* 221–238.

Sernyak, M. J., Kosten, T. R., Fontana, A., & Rosenheck, R. (2001). Neuroleptic use in the treatment of post-traumatic stress disorder. *Psychiatric Quarterly, 72,* 197–213.

Shalev, A. Y., Sahar, T., Freedman, S., Peri, T., Glick, N., Brandes, D., et al. (1998). A prospective study of heart rate response following trauma and the subsequent development of posttraumatic stress disorder. *Archives of General Psychiatry, 55,* 553–559.

Shapiro, F. (1996). Eye movement desensitization and reprocessing (EMDR): Evaluation of controlled PTSD research. *Journal of Behavior Therapy and Experimental Psychiatry, 27,* 209–218.

Shay, J. (1992). Fluoxetine reduces explosiveness and elevates mood of Vietnam combat vets with PTSD. *Journal of Traumatic Stress, 5,* 97–101.

Shen, W. W., & Park, S. (1983). The use of monoamine oxidase inhibitors in the treatment of traumatic war neurosis: Case report. *Military Medicine, 148,* 430–431.

Shestatzky, M., Greenberg, D., & Lerer, B. (1988). A controlled trial of phenelzine in posttraumatic stress disorder. *Psychiatry Research, 24,* 149–155.

Shore, J. H., Tatum, E. L., & Vollmer, W. M. (1986). Psychiatric reactions to disaster: The Mount St. Helens experience. *American Journal of Psychiatry, 143,* 590–595.

Shore, J. H., Vollmer, W. M., & Tatum, E. L. (1989). Community patterns of post traumatic stress disorders. *Journal of Nervous and Mental Disease, 77,* 681–685.

Siddiqui, Z., Marcil, W. A., Bhatia, S. C., Ramaswamy, S., & Petty, F. (2005). Ziprasidone therapy for post-traumatic stress disorder. *Journal of Psychiatry and Neuroscience, 30,* 430–431.

Simpson, G. M., & Angus, J. W. (1970). A rating scale for extrapyramidal side effects. *Acta Psychiatrica Scandinavica. Supplementum, 212,* 11–19.

Smajkic, A., Weine, S., Djuric-Bijedic, Z., Boskailo, E., Lewis, J., & Pavkovic, I. (2001). Sertraline, paroxetine, and venlafaxine in refugee posttraumatic stress disorder with depression symptoms. *Journal of Traumatic Stress, 14,* 445–452.

Solomon, S., Gerrity, E. T., & Muff, A. M. (1992). Efficacy of treatments for posttraumatic stress disorder. *Journal of the American Medical Association, 268,* 633–638.

Solomon, S. D., & Johnson, D. M. (2002). Psychosocial treatment of posttraumatic stress disorder: A practice-friendly review of outcome research. *Journal of Clinical Psychology, 58,* 947–959.

Solomon, Z., & Preager, E. (1992). Elderly Israeli Holocaust survivors during the Persian Gulf War: A study of psychological distress. *American Journal of Psychiatry, 149,* 1707–1710.

Southwick, S. M., Bremner, J. D., Rasmusson, A., Morgan, C. A., III, Arnsten, A., & Charney, D. S. (1999). Role of norepinephrine in the pathophysiology and treatment of posttraumatic stress disorder. *Biological Psychiatry, 46,* 1192–1204.

Southwick, S. M., Krystal, J. H., Bremner, J. D., Morgan, C. A., III, Nicolaou, A. L., Nagy, L. M., et al. (1997). Noradrenergic and serotonergic function in posttraumatic stress disorder. *Archives of General Psychiatry, 54,* 749–758.

Southwick, S. M., Morgan, C. A., III, Charney, D. S., & High, J. R. (1999). Yohimbine use in a natural setting: Effects on posttraumatic stress disorder. *Biological Psychiatry, 46,* 442–444.

Stein, M. B., Kline, N. A., & Matloff, J. L. (2002). Adjunctive olanzapine for SSRI-resistant combat-related PTSD: A double-blind, placebo-controlled study. *American Journal of Psychiatry, 159,* 1777–1779.

Taylor, F., & Cahill, L. (2002). Propranolol for reemergent posttraumatic stress disorder following an event of retraumatization: A case study. *Journal of Traumatic Stress, 15,* 433–437.

Taylor, F., & Raskind, M. A. (2002). The alpha-1-adrenergic antagonist prazosin improves sleep and nightmares in civilian trauma posttraumatic stress disorder. *Journal of Clinical Psychopharmacology, 22,* 82–85.

Taylor, F. B. (2003). Tiagabine for posttraumatic stress disorder: A case series of 7 women. *Journal of Clinical Psychiatry, 64,* 1421–1425.

True, W. R., Rice, J., Eisen, S., Heath, A. C., Goldberg, J., Lyons, M., et al. (1993). A twin study of genetic and environmental contributions to liablity for posttraumatic stress symptoms. *Archives of General Psychiatry, 50,* 257–264.

Tucker, P., Smith, K. L., Marx, B., Jones, D., Miranda, R., & Lensgraf, J. (2000). Fluvoxamine reduces physiologic reactivity to trauma scripts in posttraumatic stress disorder. *Journal of Clinical Psychopharmacology, 20,* 367–372.

Tucker, P., Zaninelli, R., Yehuda, R., Ruggiero, L., Dillingham, K., & Pitts, C. D. (2001). Paroxetine in the treatment of chronic posttraumatic stress disorder: Results of a placebo-controlled, flexible-dosage trial. *Journal of Clinical Psychiatry, 62,* 860–868.

Turchan, S. J., Holmes, V. F., & Wasserman, C. S. (1992). Do tricyclic antidepressants have a protective effect in post-traumatic stress disorder? *New York State Journal of Medicine, 92,* 400–402.

Vaiva, G., Ducrocq, F., Jezequel, K., Averland, B., Lestavel, P., Brunet, A., et al. (2003). Immediate treatment with propranolol decreases posttraumatic

stress disorder two months after trauma. *Biological Psychiatry, 54,* 947–949.

van der Kolk, B. A. (1983). Psychopharmacological issues in posttraumatic stress disorder. *Hospital and Community Psychiatry, 34,* 683–691.

van der Kolk, B. A. (1987). The drug treatment of post-traumatic stress disorder. *Journal of Affective Disorders, 13,* 203–213.

van der Kolk, B. A., Dreyfuss, D., Michaels, M., Shera, D., Berkowitz, R., Fisler, R., et al. (1994). Fluoxetine in posttraumatic stress disorder. *Journal of Clinical Psychiatry, 55,* 517–522.

Walker, D. L., Ressler, K. J., Lu, K. T., & Davis, M. (2002). Facilitation of conditioned fear extinction by systemic administration or intra-amygdala infusions of D-cycloserine as assessed with fear-potentiated startle in rats. *Journal of Neuroscience, 22,* 2343–2351.

Warner, M. D., Dorn, M. R., & Peabody, C. A. (2001). Survey on the usefulness of trazodone in patients with PTSD with insomnia or nightmares. *Pharmacopsychiatry, 34,* 128–131.

Watanabe, Y., Gould, E., Cameron, H. A., Daniels, D. C., & McEwen, B. S. (1992). Phenytoin prevents stress- and corticosterone-induced atrophy of CA3 pyramidal neurons. *Hippocampus, 2,* 31–35.

Wells, G. B., Chu, C., Johnson, R., Nasdahl, C., Ayubi, M. A., Sewell, E., et al. (1991). Buspirone in the treatment of post-traumatic stress disorder and dream anxiety disorder. *Military Medicine, 11,* 340–343.

Wolf, M. E., Alavi, A., & Mosnaim, A. D. (1988). Post-traumatic stress disorder in Vietnam veterans clinical and EEG findings: Possible therapeutic effects of carbamazepine. *Biological Psychiatry, 23,* 642–644.

Yehuda, R. (2002). Current status of cortisol findings in post-traumatic stress disorder. *Psychiatric Clinics of North America, 25,* 341–368.

Yehuda, R., Giller, E. L., & Mason, J. W. (1993). Psychoneuroendocrine assessment of posttraumatic stress disorder: Current progress and new direction. *Progress in Neuro-Psychopharmacology and Biological Psychiatry, 17,* 541–550.

Yehuda, R., Kahana, B., Schmeidler, J., Southwick, S. M., Wilson, S., & Giller, E. L. (1995). Impact of cumulative lifetime trauma and recent stress on current posttraumatic stress disorder symptoms in Holocaust survivors. *American Journal of Psychiatry, 152,* 1815–1818.

Yehuda, R., & McFarlane, A. C. (1995). Conflict between current knowledge about posttraumatic stress disorder and its original conceptual basis. *American Journal of Psychiatry, 152,* 1705–1713.

Yehuda, R., Southwick, S. M., & Giller, E. L. (1992). Exposure to atrocities and severity of chronic post-traumatic stress disorder in Vietnam combat veterans. *American Journal of Psychiatry, 149,* 333–336.

Yehuda, R., Yang, R. K., Golier, J. A., Tischler, L., Liong, B., & Decker, K. (2004). Effect of topiramate on glucocorticoid receptor mediated action. *Neuropsychopharmacology, 29,* 433–439.

Zaidi, L. Y., & Foy, D. W. (1994). Childhood abuse and combat-related PTSD. *Journal of Traumatic Stress, 7,* 33–42.

Zisook, S., Chentsova-Dutton, Y. E., Smith-Vaniz, A., Kline, N. A., Ellenor, G. L., Kodsi. A. B., et al. (2000). Nefazodone in patients with treatment-refractory posttraumatic stress disorder. *Journal of Clinical Psychiatry, 61,* 203–208.

Zohar, J., Amital, D., Miodownik, C., Kotler, M., Bleich, A., Lane, R. M., et al. (2002). Double-blind placebo-controlled pilot study of sertraline in military veterans with posttraumatic stress disorder. *Journal of Clinical Psychopharmacology, 22,* 190–195.

18

Psychosocial Treatments for Posttraumatic Stress Disorder

Lisa M. Najavits

The study of psychosocial treatments for posttraumatic stress disorder (PTSD) has improved dramatically in the past decade, with greater rigor, expansion of sampling, and diverse treatment models. At this point it is clear that PTSD treatments work better than treatment as usual; average effect sizes are in the moderate to high range; a variety of treatments are established as effective, with no one treatment having superiority; and both present-focused and past-focused models work (neither outperforms the other). Areas of future direction include the need to better understand therapist training, treatment dissemination, patient access to care; optimal treatment delivery, and mechanisms of action. Methodological issues are also discussed.

Awareness of posttraumatic stress disorder (PTSD) has increased markedly since the diagnosis originally appeared in the third edition of the *Diagnostic and Statistical Manual of Mental Disorders* (American Psychiatric Association, 1980). First conceived as a disorder primarily suffered by soldiers in wartime, it has since been understood as a disorder arising from a wide variety of traumas, including natural disaster (such as hurricane or tornado), child physical and sexual abuse, domestic violence, life-threatening illness, accidents, and terrorist attacks. A majority of people experience one or more traumas during their lifetime, with rates at 61% for men and 51% for women (Kessler, Sonnega, Bromet, Hughes, & Nelson, 1995). Yet, remarkably, most people who experience a trauma do not go on to develop PTSD. For the approximately 20 to 30% of people who do develop PTSD after exposure to trauma (Adshead, 2000), their symptoms cluster into three categories: (a) *re-experiencing* (e.g., intrusive thoughts, nightmares, and flashbacks), (b) *avoidance* (e.g., not wanting to talk about the trauma, detached feelings, and re-

stricted emotion), and (c) *arousal* (sleep problems, anger, and exaggerated startle response). Persistence of these symptoms for more than 1 month and marked decline in functioning are also required for the diagnosis. The 12-month prevalence rate of PTSD in the U.S. population is estimated at 3.5% (Kessler, Chiu, Demler, Merinkangas, & Walters, 2005).

A majority of people with PTSD have additional mental health disorders, including mood disorders, substance use disorders, other anxiety disorders, and personality disorders (Kessler, Sonnega, et al., 1995). The subjective experience of PTSD has been described as a devastating loss that "shatters assumptions" about oneself, other people, the future, and the world (Janoff-Bulman, 1992), and that affects one's sense of safety, trust, power, esteem, and intimacy (McCann & Pearlman, 1990). A broad literature on PTSD now exists within the professional field and also in literature (e.g., Frankl, 1963; Morrison, 1987; Wiesel, 1960) and film (*Once Were Warriors, Monster, This Boy's Life, Schindler's List, Saving Private Ryan*).

Historically, description of trauma occurred in ancient literature (the *Iliad*) and at various historical points largely in relation to combat, with terms such as *soldier's heart* during the American Civil War, *shell shock* during World War I, and other terms such as *combat neurosis* and *war hysteria* (Weisaeth, 2002). In 1895, Freud and Breuer proposed that trauma could lead to mental disorder, an idea radical for its time (Veterans Health Administration, 2004). After the Vietnam War, the formal diagnosis of PTSD was established in the *DSM-III*. The decades since then have seen enormous growth in the study of PTSD, including its epidemiology, assessment, neurobiological substrates, and the development and testing of new treatments for it.

This chapter offers a summary of effective psychosocial treatments for PTSD, with emphasis on their scientific validation. The chapter is organized into three sections: key principles, description and empirical validation of treatments, and future directions. The chapter only addresses treatments specifically designed for PTSD, although, interestingly, some generic treatments may help improve PTSD symptoms (e.g., Hien, Cohen, Miele, Litt, & Capstick, 2004; Levine, Eckhardt, & Targ, 2005). Also, it focuses solely on samples with PTSD; this means that it is beyond the scope of this chapter to address interventions to prevent the development of PTSD (e.g., "crisis intervention," "prevention research," or "critical incident stress debriefing"), or samples with subthreshold PTSD or trauma only. Studies of children and adolescents are not reviewed here because this literature is very limited; at this point it largely uses adult models adapted for those ages and obtains results comparable to adult studies; see Carr (2004), Taylor and Chemtob (2004), and Cohen, Berliner, and March (2000) for reviews. Treatments are included only if they are designed to treat PTSD per se rather than one specific symptom (e.g., imagery rehearsal therapy for nightmares; Krakow et al., 2001; or anger management; Chemtob, Novaco, Hamda, & Gross, 1997). Treatment modalities without a sufficient empirical base for PTSD specifically are also not reviewed; these include group therapies (for a review, see Foy et al., 2000), inpatient treatment (Courtois & Bloom, 2000), psychosocial rehabilitation (Penk & Flannery, 2000), creative therapies (Johnson, 2000), marital and family therapy (Riggs, 2000), and dialectical behavior therapy (Wagner &

Linehan, 2006). Finally, the focus in this chapter is on results at the end of treatment rather than at follow-up because internal validity of studies is generally strongest from pre- to posttreatment. Case reports are not reviewed due to space limitations.

A Note on Methodology

The studies reviewed are classified into Types 1 through 5 in keeping with the intent of this book. However, it is noteworthy that almost no PTSD treatment studies at this point meet all of the "gold standard" criteria for a methodologically sound trial (Harvey, Bryant, & Tarrier, 2003; Ironson, Freund, Strauss, & Williams, 2002), which is true for most treatment outcome trials in mental health more generally. For example, most studies do not report power analysis; and some have only partially blind evaluators. Moreover, a Type 2 study may have strengths lacking in a Type 1 study. And, many methodology issues are not addressed by the Type 1–5 classification (e.g., adherence rating; therapist training; evaluator training; rates of comorbid diagnoses in the sample; length of follow-up; adequacy of treatment dose; impact of external, uncontrolled treatments; and therapist effects). Thus, Types 1 through 5 are meant as broad guidelines only that await further refinement and validation.

KEY PRINCIPLES

Across the wide range of studies now available, several principles can be stated.

1. *PTSD treatments work (and better than treatment as usual).* A relatively large number of studies show consistent evidence that treatments specifically designed for PTSD do indeed work. This is the conclusion drawn by every major review (Types 4 and 5) on psychosocial treatments for PTSD (Adshead 2000; Bisson & Andrew, 2005; Bradley, Greene, Russ, Dutra & Westen, 2005; Butler, Chapman, Forman, & Beck, 2006; Deacon & Abramowitz, 2004; Foa, Keane, & Friedman. 2000; Harvey, et al.. 2003; Resick, Monson, & Gutner, in press; Sherman 1998; van Etten & Taylor 1998; Solomon & Johnson, 2002) and professional practice guidelines such as the International Society for Traumatic Stress Studies (Foa, et al., 2000); the Royal College of Psychiatrists and the

British Psychological Society (2005), and Veterans Health Administration (2004).

The degree of improvement is in the moderate to high range (Bradley, et al., 2005; Solomon & Johnson, 2002). For example, according to a major meta-analysis (Type 4 study) by Bradley, et al. (2005), 67% of patients who complete PTSD treatment no longer meet criteria for the disorder ("completer analysis"), and 56% of patients who enroll in PTSD treatment no longer meet criteria for the disorder ("intent-to-treat analysis"). Effect sizes, which measure the degree of change, are reported to average 1.43 from pre- to posttreatment, 1.11 when comparing PTSD treatment versus wait-list control conditions, and .83 when comparing PTSD treatment versus supportive therapy control condition. Consistent with these findings, another recent meta-analysis (Type 4 study) reports an average effect size of 1.49 across PTSD treatment studies (Royal College of Psychiatrists and the British Psychological Society, 2005).

2. *A variety of treatments are effective, thus allowing therapists and patients to choose based on their preferences.* A major advance has been the empirical validation of various models of PTSD treatment. Thus, there is no one right way, but many. It is now possible to select effective treatments (and possibly to combine them) based on the therapist's training, the treatment context, and patient presentation or preference.

3. *PTSD treatments fall into two broad categories: past-focused and present-focused (or their combination).* Past-focused models ask the patient to tell the story of the trauma in full detail, to process the memories and emotions of the event. Present-focused models teach the patient coping skills to improve functioning (e.g., assertiveness training, relaxation, grounding, cognitive restructuring). Examples of past-focused models include eye movement desensitization and reprocessing (EMDR) and exposure therapy. Examples of present-focused models include stress inoculation training and anxiety management.

4. *Overall, effective treatments do not differ significantly from each other.* For example, present- and past-focused models both work, and neither outperforms the other. This is often a surprise to therapists and patients, who may assume that telling the story of the past trauma is essential for recovery. Similarly, within any category, treatments do not differ significantly from each other. For example, among past-

focused treatments, EMDR and exposure therapy both work, and neither outperforms the other (Bradley, et al., 2005; Royal College of Psychiatrists and the British Psychological Society, 2005).

5. *Combining effective treatments is intuitively appealing, but research indicates that it is not needed.* Various studies have compared combinations of effective treatments (e.g., exposure therapy plus stress inoculation training), but the combined treatment consistently shows no greater efficacy then each treatment alone (Bryant, Moulds, Guthrie, Dang, & Nixon., 2003; Foa, et al., 2005; Foa, et al.. 1999; Foa, Rothbaum, Riggs, & Murdock, 1991; Glynn, et al., 1999; Paunovic & Ost. 2001).

6. *The empirical base has improved dramatically over the past decade.* The field has evolved in the number of studies, the array of researchers and patient populations, and the "technology" of studies (most studies now used accurate PTSD diagnoses, decent statistical methods, etc.).

7. *Despite the advances of the past decade, notable treatment obstacles remain.* Most PTSD patients never receive treatment (Kessler, Demler, et al., 2005). Also, most therapists do not use PTSD-specific treatments (Becker, Zayfert, & Anderson, 2004; Zayfert &Becker, 2000), and may lack knowledge about the disorder (Davidson, 2001; Munro, Freeman, & Law, 2004; Najavits & Kanukollu, 2005). Dropout rates from treatment remain a persistent issue (Zayfert, et al., 2005).

8. *In addition to treatments that have some empirical basis, the PTSD field has various untested treatments and some that are suspect.* Some treatments are simply not yet tested (e.g., creative therapies); others appear to hold promise by having been evaluated in case studies or uncontrolled pilot trials. A few models, even some that are widely used, do not appear to have a clear basis either theoretically or empirically (Devilly, 2005).

9. *Additional research is essential.* Areas of particular need include how to improve training and dissemination of effective treatments; greater understanding of why some treatments are adopted more often than others; higher sample sizes; broadening of populations (e.g., children and adolescents); better understanding of the interaction between patient/therapist variables and treatment models; longer follow-up; effectiveness studies; optimal timing of treatment; comorbidity; increased consensus on optimal

outcome methodology and adequate reporting of such; greater attention to external/uncontrolled treatments; access to care; and further study of promising models.

DESCRIPTION AND EMPIRICAL VALIDATION OF TREATMENTS

In this section, specific models of PTSD treatment and their empirical validation will be described. Models are classified into *past-* or *present-focused* or a combination (Najavits, Shaw, & Weiss, 1996), per point 3 above.

Past-Focused Treatments

The following treatments share a common strategy of asking the patient to describe the past trauma vividly, in all its detail. As the patient describes the trauma, he or she may be overwhelmed by intense emotions such as rage, sadness, panic, and fear. The patient is encouraged to experience these emotions and memories fully, after which (by the end of the session) the goal is to return to a calmer state. The patient essentially "works through" or "processes" the trauma. The patient is asked to repeat the trauma narrative as many times as needed until it no longer holds strong emotional power. The patient faces the overwhelming memories and emotions that have been pushed out of consciousness (the avoidance cluster of PTSD symptoms). Watching a patient do this emotional work is similar to watching someone grieve a loss (such as at a funeral), and appears to recreate the inherent human ability to mourn and to come through stronger in the end. The therapist guides the patient to focus on "hot spots" that may be particularly painful (such as the words that the rapist said at the time of the assault, the look on the face of the child as it died, or the smell of smoke at the fire). The patient may be asked to notice all senses (smell, sight, sound, touch, hearing) and to speak in the present tense, so as to increase the vividness of the memories. If the patient experienced multiple traumas, there may be an attempt to fully process the most upsetting trauma, and to move to others if needed.

Such treatment interventions go by many different names, including eye movement desensitization and reprocessing, exposure therapy (and variants such as prolonged exposure, in vivo exposure, imaginal exposure, direct therapeutic exposure, virtual reality exposure, narrative exposure, flooding, systematic desensitization, cognitive processing therapy, trauma-processing therapy, trauma-focused therapy, mourning, grief work, and "telling your story"). Among the many versions of such treatments, several have accumulated a compelling body of empirical validation. Overall, such treatments represent an elegant and powerful method that often achieves results in quite short time frames (particularly for single-incident trauma). However, such methods may also be contraindicated under some circumstances because the intense emotion that is evoked may be too disturbing for some patients who are currently unstable, such as those in violent domestic relationships, the homeless, and active substance abusers who may be prone to relapse (Keane, 1995; Najavits, 2002; Solomon & Johnson, 2002).

Some past-focused models include a focus on instilling new beliefs about the trauma for patients who may hold negative assumptions that impede recovery. These may include excessive self-blame for the trauma, concluding that the world is unsafe, or distrusting all members of the opposite sex, for example.

Eye Movement Desensitization and Reprocessing

Eye movement desensitization and reprocessing (Shapiro 1995) is the most widely adopted treatment among past-focused, empirically validated PTSD models. It follows a highly structured protocol in which the patient is asked to name the key image, belief, feeling, and body sensation associated with the trauma memory. With these in mind, the patient now tracks the therapist's raised fingers moving back and forth horizontally across the patient's visual field (called *eye movements*). The patient may experience the process as being able to view the trauma with more perspective or understanding (e.g., being able to view a child abuse scene from the perspective of adult). Using the same eye movement procedure, the therapist next works to reinforce a positive belief about the event (e.g., from "It was my fault" to "I was just a child and did my best to survive"). The patient is allowed to follow the associative memory network, one memory leading into another, until the related memories are fully processed. There is no homework for the patient in EMDR. The number of sessions may range from a few to many, depending on the complexity of the patient. Some therapists use tapping or lights instead of eye movements; the essential element is believed to be bilateral stimulation.

EMDR is now established as a premier treatment with sufficient Type 1 studies by a variety of investigators (for reviews, see, for example, Bradley et al., 2005; Butler et al., 2006; Chemtob, Tolin, van der Kolk, & Pitman, 2000a; Chemtob, Tolin, van der Kolk, & Pitman, 2000b; van Etten & Taylor, 1998). It is listed as an effective treatment by various recent consensus practice guidelines on PTSD, including the Royal College of Psychiatrists and the British Psychological Society (2005), the Veterans Health Administration (2004), and the International Society for Traumatic Stress Studies (Chemtob et al., 2000a, 2000b).

EMDR was a highly controversial treatment for many years, for various reasons, including its rapid adoption worldwide by therapists in advance of its full empirical validation, and a perceived lack of clarity on its theoretical premise. It has been established as effective only for PTSD but has been applied to a much wider range of conditions. Some suggest that it is simply a version of exposure therapy, and that the eye movement procedure is not essential (Deacon & Abramowitz, 2004). The exact mechanism of action in EMDR remains unclear (which is also true of most, if not all, PTSD treatments at this point).

There are a variety of Type 1 studies of EMDR (such as Marcus, Marquis, & Sakai, 1997; Carlson, Chemtob, Rusnak, Hedlund, & Muraoka, 1998; Power et al., 2002; Rothbaum, 1997; Rothbaum, Astin, & Marsteller, 2005; Taylor et al., 2003). Overall, EMDR does as well as the treatment to which it is most often compared, exposure therapy (Rothbaum et al., 2005), or the combination of exposure therapy plus cognitive therapy (Power et al., 2002); and outperforms biofeedback/relaxation (Carlson et al., 1998). Some studies show differences, but they go in both directions (e.g., a study in which EMDR evidenced "a slight advantage" over exposure therapy plus cognitive therapy (Power et al., 2002); and, conversely, a study in which exposure outperformed EMDR (Taylor et al., 2003). Recent meta-analyses conclude that EMDR and exposure therapy evidence no difference in outcome and/or duration of

treatment (Bradley, et al., 2005; Royal College of Psychiatrists and the British Psychological Society, 2005). In Type 1 studies, EMDR has also outperformed control conditions such as wait-list (Power et al., 2002; Rothbaum, 1997; Rothbaum et al., 2005) and routine clinical care (Carlson et al., 1998; Marcus et al., 1997), although in one study it did not outperform a relaxation control (Taylor et al., 2003).

Quite a few Type 2 studies of EMDR have also been conducted. The majority show better outcomes for EMDR when compared with control conditions (Chemtob, Nakashima, & Carlson, 2002; Devilly, Spence, & Rapee, 1998; Scheck, Schaeffer, & Gillette, 1998; Wilson, Becker, & Tinker, 1995). Moreover, in studies comparing it with active treatment, EMDR outperformed exposure therapy in one study (Ironson et al., 2002) and showed a slight advantage over exposure therapy plus stress inoculation training in another (Lee, Gavriel, Drummond, Richards, & Greenwald, 2002). Some studies are exceptions, however, with EMDR significantly less positive than an active treatment or combination of treatments (Devilly & Spence, 1999), and not significantly different than a control (Jensen, 1994). One Type 2 study (Devilly, et al., 1998) compared EMDR with and without eye movements as the efficacy of the eye movements per se remains unclear; no differences were found between the two conditions (both showed positive outcomes compared with a control condition of psychiatric support). Additional Type 2 studies (as well as Type 3) are listed in reviews (such as Bradley et al., 2005; Chemtob et al., 2000a, 2000b; Harvey et al., 2003).

EMDR has been studied in diverse populations, including female sexual assault victims (Rothbaum, 1997; Rothbaum et al., 2005), military veterans (Carlson et al., 1998; Devilly et al., 1998; Jensen, 1994), university clinic patients (Ironson et al., 2002), children who survived a hurricane (Chemtob et al., 2002), health maintenance organization patients (Marcus et al., 1997), primary care patients (Power et al., 2002), and general PTSD samples (Devilly & Spence, 1999; Lee et al., 2002; Taylor et al., 2003; Wilson et al., 1995). The length of treatment has varied among studies, from just a few sessions to longer protocols.

Issues discussed in the literature include the need for better understanding of EMDR's mechanism of action (e.g., are the eye movements necessary?) and the need for validation of EMDR for other disorders if it continues to be used for such.

Exposure Therapy

Exposure therapy has been considered a gold standard treatment for PTSD because it was the first past-focused model to achieve empirical validation. As described by Foa and Rothbaum (1998), it starts with several sessions of preparation of the patient (e.g., assessment, education about exposure). After that it can include both imaginal exposure (literally, having the patient "imagine," i.e., remember, the trauma) and in vivo exposure (having the patient confront current reminders of the trauma, such as rereading newspaper articles about it, going back to the location where it occurred if that is safe to do, or touching the clothing that was worn at the time of the trauma). Breathing retraining is also recommended. There is a strong focus on exposure homework, including writing and/or audiotaping a narrative of the trauma for exposure between sessions. It can be completed in as few as 9 sessions, with a prolonged version of 20 sessions or more recommended for complex cases. One version developed for disasters is a single session (Basoglu, Salcioglu, Livanou, Kalender, & Acar, 2005). It can also be combined with cognitive therapy or stress inoculation training (Foa & Rothbaum, 1998).

Exposure therapy is established as a premier treatment with sufficient Type 1 studies by a variety of investigators (for reviews, see, for example, Bradley et al., 2005; Butler et al., 2006; Davidson & Parker, 2001; Foa, 2000; Rothbaum, Meadows, Resick, & Foy, 2000a; Rothbaum, Meadows, Resick, & Foy, 2000b). It is listed as an effective treatment by various recent consensus practice guidelines on PTSD, including the Royal College of Psychiatrists and the British Psychological Society (2005), the Veterans Health Administration (2004), and the International Society for Traumatic Stress Studies (Rothbaum et al., 2000a, 2000b).

There are numerous Type 1 studies of exposure therapy (e.g., Basoglu et al., 2005; Boudewyns & Hyer, 1990; Bryant et al., 2003; Fecteau & Nicki, 1999; Foa et al., 2005; Foa et al., 1991; Gersons, Carlier, Lamberts, & van der Kolk, 2000; Marks, Lovell, Noshirvani, Livanou, & Thrasher, 1998; Neuner, Schauer, Klaschik, Karunakara, & Elbert, 2004; Power et al., 2002; Rothbaum et al., 2005; Tar-

rier et al., 1999; Taylor et al., 2003). Head-to-head comparisons with other PTSD models show, overall, no significant differences between exposure therapy and EMDR (Rothbaum et al., 2005), cognitive therapy (Marks et al., 1998; Tarrier et al., 1999), stress inoculation training (Foa et al., 1999), and cognitive processing therapy (Resick, Nishith, Weaver, Astin, & Feuer, 2002). Exceptions are a study in which exposure therapy outperformed both EMDR and relaxation (Taylor et al., 2003) and, conversely, a study in which EMDR showed "a slight advantage" over exposure therapy (Power et al., 2002). In one study, stress inoculation training outperformed exposure therapy (Foa et al., 1991).

Exposure therapy has also outperformed control conditions such as relaxation (Marks et al., 1998), standard counseling (Boudewyns & Hyer, 1990), supportive counseling (Bryant et al., 2003; Neuner et al., 2004), and wait-list (Basoglu et al., 2005; Fecteau & Nicki, 1999; Foa et al., 2005; Gersons et al., 2000; Glynn et al., 1999; Power et al., 2002). In a Type 1 study of military veterans, however, a group version of exposure (combined with some additional cognitive and skills interventions) showed no significant difference from the control condition (nonspecific present-focused therapy; Schnurr et al., 2003). Exposure therapy showed only a few differences from a wait-list control in one study of rape victims (Foa et al., 1991).

Interestingly, several studies have addressed whether pure exposure is sufficient by itself or whether adding cognitive therapy (cognitive restructuring and/or coping skills) improves outcomes. Several Type 1 studies indicate that the addition of cognitive therapy did not improve outcomes over and above pure exposure in various samples (Bryant et al., 2003; Foa et al., 1999; Foa et al., 2005; Foa et al. 1991); the same held true for a Type 2 study with refugees (Paunovic & Ost, 2001). Similarly, a Type 1 study that combined exposure plus behavioral family therapy found no improvement over exposure therapy alone (Glynn et al., 1999). Thus, other models that combine exposure therapy and cognitive therapy such as brief eclectic psychotherapy (Gersons, Carlier, et al., 2000), skills training in affective and interpersonal regulation/prolonged exposure (Cloitre, Koenen, Cohen, & Han, 2002), trauma treatment protocol (Devilly & Spence, 1999), and untitled combinations (Lee et al., 2002; McDonagh et al. 2005; Power et al., 2002) await similar testing to evaluate whether the combination outperforms exposure therapy and/or cognitive therapy alone.

Exposure therapy has been studied in diverse ways. For example, it has been studied with rape victims (Foa et al., 1999; Foa et al., 2005; Foa et al., 1991; Resick et al., 2002; Rothbaum et al., 2005), war veterans (Boudewyns & Hyer, 1990; Glynn et al., 1999; Schnurr et al., 2003), refugees (Neuner et al., 2004), police officers (Gersons et al., 2000), primary care patients (Power et al., 2002), motor vehicle accident survivors (Fecteau & Nicki, 1999), university clinic patients (Ironson et al., 2002), earthquake survivors (Basoglu et al., 2005), and general or chronic PTSD samples (Bryant et al., 2003; Lee et al., 2002; Marks et al., 1998; Power et al., 2002; Tarrier et al., 1999; Taylor et al., 2003). It has also been studied with both cognitive-behavioral training (CBT) experts and novices (Foa et al., 2005), showing no significant difference between them.

Various studies fit the categories of Types 2 through 5 but are not reviewed here because there are already so many Type 1 studies. Moreover, the Type 2 studies are mostly comparisons with EMDR that do not substantively change the conclusion drawn by most reviewers at this point, which is that the two treatments both work and do not show any consistent pattern of significant difference between them (see above). For more comprehensive reviews of exposure therapy, see, for example, Bradley et al. (2005); Davidson and Parker (2001); Foa (2000); Rothbaum et al. (2000a; 2000b); and van Etten and Taylor (1988).

Issues that have been discussed in the literature include exploration of why therapists may be hesitant to adopt exposure therapy (Becker et al., 2004; Feeny, Hembree, & Zoellner, 2003; Zayfert & Becker, 2000), debate about its dropout rate (Zayfert et al., 2005), and discussion of whether exposure therapy may be best suited for patients with classic PTSD symptoms rather than those who have prominent guilt, shame, or numbing (Solomon & Johnson, 2002).

Cognitive Processing Therapy

Cognitive processing therapy (CPT) was originally developed for female rape victims (Resick & Schnicke, 1992) and has been expanded to military veterans (Monson et al., in press), child sexual abuse survivors (Chard, 2005) and incarcerated adolescents (Ahrens

& Rexford, 2002). In this model, the patient writes trauma narratives as homework outside of the therapy session. In addition, there is a strong focus on cognitive restructuring to address both overly generalized beliefs ("the world is unsafe") and overly constricted beliefs ("it's all my fault"). The therapy also draws on McCann and Pearlman's (1990) trauma themes of safety, trust, power, esteem, and intimacy (Solomon & Johnson, 2002).

Three Type 1 studies evidence positive effects for CPT. It has outperformed a minimal attention control (Resick, et al., 2002) and wait-list (Ahrens & Rexford, 2002; Chard, 2005; Monson et al., in press) and has done as well as exposure therapy (the only difference was that CPT was more helpful for guilt symptoms; Resick et al., 2002). An earlier Type 2 study (Resick & Schnicke, 1992) on rape victims evidenced positive outcomes compared with wait-list.

Other Past-Focused Models

Systematic desensitization takes a gradual approach by having the patient create a list of stressful memories or reminders of the trauma and rating them from most to least disturbing. The patient is then guided to tolerate the least stressful trauma reminder, and after success in that, moves sequentially through each of the more disturbing ones. Often the patient is taught relaxation or other anxiety management tools for tolerating the trauma reminder. Type 2 studies provide evidence that systematic desensitization outperformed wait-list (Bowen & Lambert, 1986; Brom, Kleber, & Defares, 1989; Frank et al., 1988). Also, a combination of systematic desensitization plus biofeedback outperformed a no-treatment control (Peniston, 1986). However, systematic desensitization was studied primarily in the 1980s and no longer appears to draw research interest.

Flooding might be considered the opposite of systematic desensitization. In flooding, the patient is confronted with the most disturbing trauma reminders and required to tolerate them until extinction of upsetting emotion occurs. Rather than gradual or paced exposure to traumatic memory, the patient is "flooded" to produce rapid therapeutic gain. Flooding has similarities to exposure therapy but involves having the therapist present the patient with a detailed description of a traumatic scene (based on information gathered prior to the flooding session), rather than the patient telling the narrative of the event. Type 2 studies evidence flooding's superiority to a control condition (Cooper & Clum, 1989; Keane, Fairbank, Caddell, & Zimering, 1989). As with systematic desensitization, flooding appears to have lost favor with researchers, superseded by other past-focused treatments (e.g., EMDR, exposure).

Virtual reality therapy is a version of exposure therapy that makes use of advanced graphics, sound effects, and computer technology to immerse the patient in a realistic, visually rich "virtual environment." For example, one model designed for military veterans has the patient don headgear to view "a virtual Huey helicopter flying over a virtual Vietnam, and a clearing surrounded by jungle" (Rothbaum, Hodges, et al., 2001). As the patient moves, the scene appears to move, too, via body-tracking devices. A Type 3 study evidenced positive results for Vietnam veterans (Rothbaum, Hodges, Ready, Graap, & Alarcon, 2001). Applications to the World Trade Center and to the Iraq war have also been described (Difede & Hoffman, 2002; Rizzo et al., 2005). Such technology-intensive models are likely to increase in the future and may include Internet-based and telemedicine approaches.

Psychodynamic therapy encompasses a variety of approaches that may have, for example, goals of insight, resolving intrapsychic conflicts about the trauma, processing to address "information overload," exploration of the relationship with the therapist, and abreaction (expressing feelings about the trauma; Horowitz, 1976; Krupnick, 2002). Although psychodynamic therapy is widely used by therapists for all types of mental disorders, it has been little studied for the treatment of PTSD. One Type 2 study evaluated short-term psychodynamic therapy versus hypnosis, trauma desensitization, and wait-list control. All three active treatments outperformed the control (Brom et al., 1989). Finally, one Type 1 study evaluated a mixed model (brief eclectic psychotherapy, combining exposure therapy and psychodynamic therapy), and found it to outperform a wait-list control (Gersons et al., 2000). For a more detailed review, see Kudler et al. (2000).

Hypnosis is another model that is used in clinical practice, but as yet is rarely studied empirically (Cardena, 2000; Solomon & Johnson, 2002). Typically, hypnosis involves induction of an altered state of consciousness to help the patient process painful material; specific protocols vary greatly. The only study thus far on hypnosis for PTSD is the Type 2 study named in the paragraph above (Brom et al., 1989), which found positive results compared with a wait-list control. Hypnosis has also been studied for acute stress disorder (e.g., Bryant et al., 2006) but that is beyond the scope of this chapter. It is noteworthy that an American Psychological Association task force concluded that hypnosis should *not* be used for the purpose of recovering trauma memories (i.e., to access memories that are not yet conscious).

Finally, it is worth noting that although past-focused treatments have shown strong benefit, at least one model appeared to have precipitated substantial deterioration in patients. As reported by Solomon & Johnson (2002), a 4-week residential program was provided to Lebanese war veterans in which they were given intensive exposure to military cues, including "living in tents, wearing uniforms, weapons, artillery, and hand to hand combat training" (p. 950). Results showed significant decline among the treated veterans compared with an untreated control condition.

Present-Focused Treatments

Present-focused PTSD treatments help patients attain improved coping skills to function in day-to-day life. A variety of cognitive, behavioral, and interpersonal methods are typically used. These may include cognitive restructuring to help the patient acquire more adaptive thinking, developing a schedule of productive activities, learning to relate better to others (e.g., social skills training), relaxation exercises, grounding (sensory focus to distract from upsetting emotions), and education about PTSD.

Such treatments go by a variety of names, including CBT, stress inoculation training, cognitive therapy, seeking safety, dialectical behavior therapy, and psychoeducation. At this point, the strongest evidence (Type 1 studies) and widest adoption accrue to cognitive therapy, stress inoculation training, and seeking safety.

Cognitive Therapy

In cognitive therapy for PTSD, the goal is to help patients become aware of their maladaptive beliefs and modify them to become more adaptive. This may include, for example, correcting excessively negative assumptions about the trauma (e.g., self-blame); exploring the connection between beliefs, feelings, and behavior; and identifying inaccurate appraisal of threats in the current environment. Examples of models include those by Ehlers, Clark, Hackmann, McManus, & Fennell (2005), Foy (1992), Tarrier et al. (1999), and others. A cognitive component is also part of many of the past-focused models reviewed above, as well as many of the combination models reviewed below. At this point, the broader term *cognitive-behavioral therapy* is applied to a very wide array of models for PTSD; indeed virtually all the treatments covered in this chapter could be labeled cognitive behavioral (as in the review by Bisson and Andrew, 2005). In this chapter, *cognitive therapy* refers to models that do not include a past-focused component.

Several studies of cognitive therapy for PTSD have been conducted. Overall, they indicate positive results (Ehlers et al., 2003; Marks et al., 1998; Tarrier et al., 1999;); see also the review by Butler et al. (2006). Type 1 studies show positive outcomes for cognitive therapy (Ehlers et al., 2003; Marks et al. 1998; Tarrier et al., 1999;). In comparison with other models, it outperformed a self-help booklet (Ehlers et al., 2003) and did as well as exposure therapy (Tarrier et al., 1999). It outperformed control conditions such as assessment-only (Ehlers et al., 2003) and relaxation (Marks et al., 1998). In a Type 2 study, cognitive therapy outperformed wait-list (Ehlers et al., 2005). Cognitive therapy has been studied in samples such as motor vehicle accident survivors (Ehlers et al., 2003), and PTSD patients (Ehlers et al., 2005; Tarrier et al., 1999).

As noted earlier, combining cognitive therapy with exposure therapy has been evaluated in three Type 1 studies, finding no benefit for using both treatments together. In sum, both treatments work, and the combination does not outperform each treatment separately (Foa et al., 1999; Foa et al., 2005; Foa et al., 1991).

Stress Inoculation Training

Stress inoculation training for PTSD helps the patient manage anxiety and cope better. It can include breathing exercises, relaxation, psychoeducation, thought stopping, cognitive restructuring, role playing, and guided self-dialogue (Foa et al., 1991).

Stress inoculation training has been evaluated in several Type 1 studies (Foa et al., 1999; Foa et al., 1991). When compared with other models, it did as well as exposure therapy in one study (Foa et al., 1999) and, in another study, it outperformed exposure therapy and supportive counseling (Foa et al., 1991). Stress inoculation training has outperformed control conditions such as wait-list (Foa et al., 1999; Foa et al., 1991). It has been combined with exposure therapy in some studies (Devilly & Spence, 1999; Lee et al., 2002).

It is important to note that the thought-stopping technique may actually have negative impact on patients and should probably be deleted from stress inoculation training (Harvey et al., 2003).

Seeking Safety

This model (Najavits, 2002) was designed to treat comorbid PTSD and substance use disorder in women and men. It focuses on the theme of safety, with 25 cognitive, behavioral, and interpersonal skills to address both disorders at the same time (integrated therapy), from the start of treatment (first-stage therapy). Skills include, for example, grounding, honesty, compassion, integrating the split self, and setting boundaries in relationships. It emphasizes flexibility, with skills addressed in any order the therapist chooses, and variable treatment length and pacing. At this point, it is the most empirically studied and widely adopted model for that dual diagnosis.

Seeking safety has been found comparable to a "gold standard" treatment (relapse prevention) among low-income urban women in a Type 1 study (Hien et al., 2004), with both conditions outperforming a nonrandomized community care control. In another Type 1 study, seeking safety outperformed treatment as usual in an adolescent sample (Najavits, Gallop, & Weiss, in press). In a multisite Type 2 study on homeless women veterans seeking safety outperformed treatment as usual (Desai & Rosenheck, 2006). Type 3 studies include positive results on samples of women in prison (Zlotnick, Najavits, & Rohsenow, 2003), men (Najavits, Schmitz, Gotthard, & Weiss, 2005), outpatient women (Najavits, Weiss, Shaw, & Muenz, 1998), and women veterans (Weller, 2005). Other reports include feasibility studies with positive results among men and/or women veterans (Cook, Walser, Kane, Ruzek, & Woody, 2006), women in community mental health (Holdcraft & Comtois, 2002), and a multisite study of women in community programs (Morrissey et al., 2005).

Other Present-Focused Models

Several additional present-focused models each have been evaluated in a single study thus far. A Type 2 study of *anxiety management group* showed that it was superior to wait-list (Zlotnick et al., 1997). Three other models each have one Type 3 study: *interpersonal psychotherapy for PTSD* (Bleiberg & Markowitz, 2005); *cognitive behavioral couples treatment* (e.g., Jacobson, Dobson, Fruzetti, Schmaling, & Salusky, 1991) adapted for PTSD (Monson, Schnurr, Stevens, & Guthrie, 2004; see also, Sweany, 1987, as described in Riggs, 2000); and *cognitive-behavioral therapy for PTSD and severe mental illness*, such as bipolar disorder and schizophrenia (Mueser, Rosenberg, Jankowski, Hamblen, & Descamps, 2004).

Past- and Present-Focused Treatments

In this section the use of past- and present-focused treatments will be reviewed. There are two basic approaches: first, the combination of past- and present-focused treatments in an attempt to create a stronger model of therapy; and second, the comparison of past- versus present-focused treatments to determine whether one is more effective than the other.

Combinations of Past- and Present-Focused Treatments

There is an intuitive appeal to combining the best of past- and present-focused interventions. Various models attempt to do this, and at this point there are a handful of studies evaluating whether the combination is more helpful than either alone. Surprisingly, the combination is not more effective than either one alone (see the summary of this issue in the section on exposure therapy above, and also the Type 4 review by Bisson & Andrew, 2005). Examples of models that have at least one Type 1 study include the following:

Cognitive trauma therapy for battered women. This model includes exploration of trauma history, exposure, PTSD education, stress management, assertiveness, and cognitive restructuring. In both a Type 1 and a Type 2 study, it outperformed a delayed treatment control in a sample of battered women who had left the abusive partner for at least 1 month (Kubany, Hill, & Owens, 2003; Kubany et al., 2004).

Skills training in affective and interpersonal regulation-prolonged exposure. This model combines eight sessions derived from cognitive-behavioral therapy and dialectical behavior therapy, followed by eight sessions of exposure therapy modified for child abuse survivors. A Type 1 trial found positive results compared with a wait-list control (Cloitre, Chase Stovall-McClough, Miranda, & Chemtob, 2004).

Cognitive-behavioral therapy. As noted earlier, the term *cognitive-behavioral therapy* (or *trauma-focused cognitive-behavioral therapy*) has been used in several studies to denote the combination of a past-focused model (usually exposure therapy) plus cognitive therapy and/or stress inoculation training (as each is defined in the section above). In Type 1 studies, such CBTs performed almost as well as EMDR (Power et al., 2002) with primary care patients (and both treatments outperformed wait-list); outperformed supportive counseling with PTSD patients (Bryant et al., 2003); outperformed wait-list for Cambodian refugees (Hinton et al., 2005); and was equal to problem-solving therapy for women with PTSD from child abuse (McDonagh et al., 2005; and both treatments outperformed wait-list). Examples of Type 2 studies include one that found CBT superior to supportive therapy and wait-list for motor vehicle accident survivors (Blanchard et al., 2003), one that found CBT superior to EMDR (Devilly & Spence, 1999), and one that found CBT worse then EMDR (Lee et al., 2002).

Dual diagnosis models. Two models designed for co-occurring PTSD and substance use disorder combine a present- and past-focused approach: *cocaine dependence PTSD therapy* (Back, Dansky, et al., 2001) and *substance dependence PTSD therapy* (Triffleman, Carroll, & Kellogg, 1999). Both take the strategy of melding existing substance abuse treatment strategies (e.g., relapse prevention) with existing PTSD treatment strategies (e.g., exposure therapy) and have shown promising results in Type 3 pilot studies (Brady, Dansky, Back, Foa, & Caroll, 2001; Triffleman, 2000).

Comparison of Past- Versus Present-Focused Treatments

Available data indicate no difference between past- and present-focused treatments (e.g., Bisson & Andrew, 2005; Bradley et al., 2005; Marks et al., 1998; McDonagh et al., 2005; Schnurr et al., 2003). This may come as a surprise, since there is a long-standing clinical literature positing that both are essential for successful PTSD recovery (Herman, 1992). Or, some patients and/or their therapists believe that the "real work" in PTSD treatment is past focused, with present-focused work merely an adjunctive method. In fact, it now appears that both present- and past-focused PTSD treatments are effective, neither outperforms the other, and both are superior, overall, to control conditions (e.g., wait-list, treatment as usual). Thus, patient preferences and therapist training should become the ultimate determinant of which model to choose from among those that have been empirically validated.

FUTURE DIRECTIONS

Like the proverbial glass that is both half full and half empty, PTSD treatment outcome research can be viewed in terms of its major advances over the past several years, or from the framework of all that still needs to be studied. It is humbling to recognize the work that remains.

Improvement in Methodology

The technology of studying psychosocial treatments is much improved compared with 20 years ago. Indeed, the meta-analysis by Bradley and colleagues (2005) found that treatment effect size was positively associated with year of publication, indicating that more recent studies showed more robust effects. However, close inspection of research reports shows a level of methodological variability that is sometimes at odds with the simple "bottom-line message" conveyed in the abstracts. The majority of studies do not sufficiently report key issues that would be helpful for understanding their results. In the current climate, results of PTSD treatment outcome research may determine what treatments and programs are funded or discontinued (Scurfield & Wilson, 2003); thus, adequate methodology has real-world implications for patients, therapists, and programs.

Two excellent methods for evaluating the quality of clinical trials are provided in the Consolidated Standards of Reporting Trials statement (2004) and by Moncrief (see Bisson & Andrew, 2005). Insistence on one or both of these consistently by journal edi-

tors and funding agencies could have a dramatic and rapid impact.

The Moncrief scale, for example,

consideres 23 different methodological criteria and assigns scores to them on a 0–2 scale giving a maximum possible total of 46. The criteria included in the scale are objectives and specification of main outcomes a priori, sample size, follow up duration, power calculation, method of allocation, allocation concealment, clear description of treatment and adjunctive treatment, blinding of subjects, representative sample recruitment, use of diagnostic criteria, exclusion criteria and number of exclusions and refusals, description of sample demographics, blinding of assessor, assessment of compliance with treatments, details of side-effects, record of number and reasons for withdrawal by group, outcome measures described clearly or use of validated instruments, information on comparability and adjustment for differences in analysis, inclusion of withdrawals in analysis, presentation of results with inclusion of data for reanalysis of main outcomes, appropriate statistical analysis, conclusions justified and declaration of interests. (Bisson & Andrew, 2005, p. 4)

In addition to these could be added the need to report the rate of comorbid Axis I and Axis II diagnoses (given that most PTSD patients have one or more co-occurring disorders); therapist effects; adherence rating; therapist selection and training; method for assigning patients to therapists; use of a treatment manual; analysis of both completer and intent-to-treat samples; and whether patients were paid at attendance of treatment sessions. It has also been suggested that, at this point, it is "unwise to design any further studies with any form of controls other than genuine therapies with committed therapists, preferably treatments as practiced in the community, working with samples of patients resembling those seen in the community" (Bradley et al., 2005, p. 226). Finally, given the wide range of life problems and psychopathology of PTSD patients, there is a need to broaden assessment rather then just evaluating change in PTSD symptoms (Solomon & Johnson, 2002).

Broadening of Samples

Recent studies use rigorous selection of PTSD patients (rather than simply a history of trauma) and validated diagnostic tools. Also, a broader array of patient populations has been studied in terms of sociodemographic characteristics and trauma type. However, continued expansion in sampling is needed. There are still relatively few studies of children or adolescents, geriatric patients, patients with comorbid disorders, and patients with "complex" PTSD. Approximately 30% of potential patients are excluded from PTSD treatment studies, a rate lower than in other areas of mental health treatment outcome research, but nonetheless high (Bradley et al., 2005).

Studies of Dissemination

We know that treatments work, but we know little about how to train clinicians in them and how to disseminate them. Such questions may represent the next generation of clinical trials. Some treatments have been critiqued for having been adopted too early by frontline clinicians in advance of full empirical validation (e.g., EMDR), and others for not being adopted sufficiently despite a strong evidence base for them (e.g., exposure therapy). Why some treatments attain a "tipping point" (Gladwell, 2000) of popularity while others do not remains little understood. Moreover, clinical trials largely cherry-pick therapists and exclude those who do not perform well, an option not available in frontline treatment programs. Thus, there is a need for more effectiveness studies (i.e., evaluating how treatments fare in real-world implementation) and a need to better understand issues such as patient and therapist preferences for treatment (Tarrier, Liversidge, & Gregg, 2006), use of technology for enhancing treatment, and public health challenges such as how patients can access PTSD treatment in their communities.

Delivery of Treatments

Another key area is more refined study of how to deliver treatments. This might include how and when they should be combined (e.g., with pharmacotherapy or other psychosocial treatments), how long to deliver them, when to determine that a treatment is not working for particular patients, outcome differences based on modality and/or pacing of treatment, whether particular therapist characteristics are necessary for effective delivery, and greater understanding of what aspects of treatments are essential.

REFERENCES

Adshead, G. (2000). Psychological therapies for post-traumatic stress disorder. *British Journal of Psychiatry, 17,* 144–148.

Ahrens, J., & Rexford, L. (2002). Cognitive processing therapy for incarcerated adolescents with PTSD. *Journal of Aggression, Maltreatment and Trauma, 6,* 201–216.

American Psychiatric Association. (1980). *Diagnostic and statistical manual of mental disorders* (3rd ed.). Washington, DC: Author.

Back, S., Dansky, B., Carroll, K., Foa, E., & Brady, K. (2001). Exposure therapy in the treatment of PTSD among cocaine-dependent individuals: Description of procedures. *Journal of Substance Abuse Treatment, 21,* 35–45.

Basoglu, M., Salcioglu, E., Livanou, M., Kalender, D., & Acar, G. (2005). Single-session behavioral treatment of earthquake-related posttraumatic stress disorder: A randomized waiting list controlled trial. *Journal of Traumatic Stress, 18,* 1–11.

Becker, C. B., Zayfert, C., & Anderson, E. (2004). A survey of psychologists' attitudes towards and utilization of exposure therapy for PTSD. *Behaviour Research and Therapy, 42,* 277–92.

Bisson, J., & Andrew, M. (2005). Psychological treatment of post-traumatic stress disorder (PTSD). *Cochrane Database of Systematic Review, 2,* 1–60.

Blanchard, E. B., Hickling, E. J., Devinei, T., Veazey, C. H., Galovski, T. E., Mundy, E. A., et al. (2003). A controlled evaluation of cognitive behavioral therapy for posttraumatic stress in motor vehicle accident survivors. *Behaviour Research and Therapy, 41,* 79–96.

Bleiberg, K. L., & Markowitz, J. C. (2005). A pilot study of interpersonal psychotherapy for posttraumatic stress disorder. *American Journal of Psychiatry, 162,* 181–183.

Boudewyns, P. A., Hyer, L. (1990). Physiological response to combat memories and preliminary treatment outcome in Vietnam veteran PTSD patients treated with direct therapeutic exposure. *Behavior Therapy, 21,* 63–87.

Bowen, G. R., & Lambert, J. A. (1986). Systematic desensitization therapy with post-traumatic stress disorder cases. In Figley, C. R. (Ed.), *Trauma and its wake. Vol. II: Traumatic stress theory, research, and intervention* (pp. 264–279). New York: Brunner/ Mazel.

Bradley, R., Greene, J., Russ, E., Dutra, L., & Westen, D. (2005). A multidimensional meta-analysis of psychotherapy for PTSD. *American Journal of Psychiatry, 162,* 214–227.

Brady, K., Dansky, B., Back, S., Foa, E., & Caroll, K. (2001). Exposure therapy in the treatment of PTSD among cocaine-dependent individuals: Preliminary findings. *Journal of Substance Abuse Treatment, 21,* 47–54.

Brom, D., Kleber, R. J., & Defares, P. B. (1989). Brief psychotherapy for PTSD. *Journal of Consulting and Clinical Psychology, 57,* 607–612.

Bryant, R. A., Moulds, M. L., Guthrie, R. M., Dang, S. T., & Nixon, R. D. V. (2003). Imaginal exposure alone and imaginal exposure with cognitive restructuring in treatment of posttraumatic stress disorder. *Journal of Consulting and Clinical Psychology, 71,* 706–712.

Bryant, R. A., Moulds, M. L., Nixon, R. D., Mastrodomenico, J., Felmingham, K., & Hopwood, S. (2006). Hypnotherapy and cognitive behaviour therapy of acute stress disorder: A 3-year follow-up. *Behavior Research and Therapy, 44,* 1331–1335.

Butler, A. C., Chapman, J. E., Forman, E. M., & Beck, A. T. (2006). The empirical status of cognitive-behavioral therapy: A review of meta-analyses. *Clinical Psychology Review, 26,* 17–31.

Cardena, E. (2000). Hypnosis in the treatment of trauma: A promising, but not fully supported, efficacious intervention. *International Journal of Clinical Experiments, 48,* 225–238.

Carlson, J. G., Chemtob, C. M., Rusnak, K., Hedlund, N. L., & Muraoka, M. Y. (1998). Eye movement desensitization and reprocessing (EDMR) treatment for combat-related posttraumatic stress disorder. *Journal of Traumatic Stress, 11,* 3–24.

Carr, A. (2004). Interventions for post-traumatic stress disorder in children and adolescents. *Pediatric Rehabilitation, 7,* 231–244.

Chard, K. M. (2005). An evaluation of cognitive therapy for the treatment of posttraumatic stress disorder related to childhood sexual abuse. *Journal of Consulting and Clinical Psychology, 73,* 965–971.

Chemtob, C., Novaco, R., Hamada, R., & Gross, D. (1997). Cognitive-behavioral treatment for severe anger in posttraumatic stress disorder. *Journal of Consulting and Clinical Psychology, 65,* 184–189.

Chemtob, C., Tolin, D., van der Kolk, B., & Pitman, R. (2000a). Eye movement desensitization and reprocessing [literature review]. In E. B. Foa, T. M. Keane, & M. J. Friedman (Eds.), *Effective treatments for PTSD: Practice guidelines from the International Society for Traumatic Stress Studies* (pp. 139–154). New York: Guilford Press.

Chemtob, C., Tolin, D., van der Kolk, B., & Pitman, R. (2000b). Eye movement desensitization and reprocessing [treatment guidelines]. In E. B. Foa, T. M. Keane, & M. J. Friedman (Eds.), *Effective treatments for PTSD: Practice guidelines from the International Society for Traumatic Stress Studies* (pp. 333–335). New York: Guilford Press.

Chemtob, C. M., Nakashima, J., & Carlson, J. G. (2002). Brief treatment for elementary school children with disaster-related posttraumatic stress disorder: A field study. *Journal of Clinical Psychology, 58,* 99–112.

Cloitre, M., Chase Stovall-McClough, K., Miranda, R., & Chemtob, C. M. (2004). Therapeutic alliance, negative mood regulation, and treatment outcome in child abuse-related posttraumatic stress disorder. *Journal of Consulting and Clinical Psychology, 72,* 411–416.

Cloitre, M., Koenen, K. C., Cohen, L. R., & Han, H. (2002). Skills training in affective and interpersonal regulation followed by exposure: A phase-based treatment for PTSD related to childhood abuse." *Journal of Consulting and Clinical Psychology, 70,* 1067–1074.

Cohen, J. A., Berliner, L., & March, J. S. (2000). Treatment of children and adolescents. In E. B. Foa, T. M. Keane, & M. J. Friedman (Eds.), *Effective treatments for PTSD* (pp. 106–138). New York: Guilford Press.

Consolidated Standards of Reporting Trials. (2004). Retrieved February 18, 2004, from http://www.consort-statement.org/statement/revisedstatement.htm

Cook, J. M., Walser, R. D., Kane, V., Ruzek, J. I., & Woody, G. (2006). Dissemination and feasibility of a cognitive-behavioral treatment for substance use disorders and posttraumatic stress disorder in the Veterans Administration. *Journal of Psychoactive Drugs, 38,* 89–92.

Cooper, N. A., & Clum. G. A. (1989). Imaginal flooding as a supplementary treatment for PTSD in combat veterans: A controlled study. *Behavior Therapy, 20,* 381–391.

Courtois, C. A., & Bloom, S. L. (2000). Inpatient treatment. In E. B. Foa, T. M. Keane, & M. J. Friedman (Eds.), *Effective treatments for PTSD* (pp. 199–223). New York: Guilford Press.

Davidson, J. R. T. (2001). Recognition and treatment of posttraumatic stress disorder. *Journal of the American Medical Association, 286,* 584–588.

Davidson, P. R., & Parker, C. H. (2001). Eye movement desensitization and reprocessing (EMDR): A meta-analysis. *Journal of Consulting and Clinical Psychology, 69,*305–316.

Deacon, B. J., Abramowitz, J. S. (2004). Cognitive and behavioral treatments for anxiety disorders: A review of meta-analytic findings. *Journal of Clinical Psychology, 60,* 429–441.

Desai, R., & Rosenheck. R. (2006). *Effectiveness of treatment for homeless female veterans with psychiatric and/or substance abuse disorders: Impact of "Seeking Safety" and residential treatment on one-year clinical outcomes*. West Haven, CT: VA Connecticut Health Care System.

Devilly, G. J. (2005). Power Therapies and possible threats to the science of psychology and psychiatry. *Australian and New Zealand Journal of Psychiatry*, 39, 437–245.

Devilly, G. J., & Spence, S. H. (1999). The relative efficacy and treatment distress of EMDR and a cognitive-behavior trauma treatment protocol in the amelioration of posttraumatic stress disorder. *Journal of Anxiety Disorders*, 13, 131–157.

Devilly, G., Spence, S., & Rapee, R. (1998). Statistical and reliable change with eye movement desensitization and reprocessing: Treating trauma within a veteran population. *Behavior Therapy*, 29,435–455.

Difede, J., & Hoffman, H. G. (2002). Virtual reality exposure therapy for World Trade Center post-traumatic stress disorder: A case report. *Cyberpsychology and Behavior*, 5, 529–535.

Ehlers, A., Clark, D. M., Hackmann, A., McManus, F., & Fennell, M. (2005). Cognitive therapy for posttraumatic stress disorder: Development and evaluation. *Behavior Research and Therapy*, 43, 413–431.

Ehlers, A., Clark, D. M., Hackmann, A., McManus, F., Fennell, M., Herbert, C., et al. (2003). A randomized controlled trial of cognitive therapy, a self-help booklet, and repeated assessments as early interventions for posttraumatic stress disorder. *Archives of General Psychiatry*, 60, 1024–1032.

Fecteau, G., & Nicki, R. (1999). Cognitive behavioural treatment of post traumatic stress disorder after motor vehicle accident. *Behavioural and Cognitive Psychotherapy*, 27,201–214.

Feeny, N. C., Hembree, E. A., & Zoellner, L. A. (2003). Myths regarding exposure therapy for PTSD. *Cognitive Behavioral Practice*, 10, 85–90.

Foa, E. B. (2000). Psychosocial treatment of posttraumatic stress disorder. *Journal of Clinical Psychiatry*, 61(Suppl. 5), 43–48; discussion 49–51.

Foa, E. B., Dancu, C. V., Hembree, E. A., Jaycox, L. H., Meadows, E. A., & Street, G. P. (1999). A comparison of exposure therapy, stress inoculation training, and their combination for reducing posttraumatic stress disorder in female assault victims. *Journal of Consulting and Clinical Psychology*, 67, 194–200.

Foa, E. B., Hembree, E. A., Cahill, S. P., Rauch, S. A., Riggs, D. S., Feeny, N. C., et al. (2005). Randomized trial of prolonged exposure for posttraumatic stress disorder with and without cognitive restructuring: Outcome at academic and community clinics. *Journal of Consulting and Clinical Psychology*, 73, 953–964.

Foa, E. B., Keane, T. M., & Friedman, M. J. (Eds.). (2000). *Effective treatments for PTSD: Practice guidelines from the International Society for Traumatic Stress Studies*. New York: Guilford Press.

Foa, E. B., & Rothbaum, B. O. (1998). *Treating the trauma of rape: Cognitive-behavioral therapy for PTSD*. New York: Guilford Press.

Foa, E. B., Rothbaum, B. O., Riggs, D. S., & Murdock, T. B. (1991). Treatment of posttraumatic stress disorder in rape victims: A comparison between cognitive-behavioral procedures and counseling. *Journal of Consulting and Clinical Psychology*, 59, 715–723.

Foy, D. W. (1992). *Treating PTSD: Cognitive-behavioral strategies*. New York: Guilford Press.

Foy, D. W., S. M. Glynn, Schnurr, P. P., Jankowski, M. K., Wattenberg, M. S., Weiss, D. S., et al. (2000). Group therapy. In E. B. Foa, T. M. Keane, & M. J. Friedman (Eds.), *Effective treatments for PTSD* (pp. 155–175). New York: Guilford Press.

Frank, E., Anderson, B., Stewart, B. D., Dancu, C., Hughes, C., & West, D. (1988). Efficacy of cognitive behavior therapy and systematic desensitization in the treatment of rape trauma. *Behavior Therapy*, 19, 403–420.

Frankl, V. E. (1963). *Man's search for meaning*. New York: Pocket Books.

Gersons, B. P., Carlier, I. V., Lamberts, R. D., van der Kolk, B. A. (2000). Randomized clinical trial of brief eclectic psychotherapy for police officers with posttraumatic stress disorder. *Journal of Traumatic Stress*, 13, 333–347.

Gladwell, M. (2000). *The tipping point: How little things can make a big difference*. New York: Little, Brown.

Glynn, S. M., Eth, S., Randolph, E. T., Foy, D. W., Urbaitis, M., Boxer, L.,et al. (1999). A test of behavioral family therapy to augment exposure for combat-related posttraumatic stress disorder. *Journal of Consulting and Clinical Psychology*, 67, 243–251.

Harvey, A. G., Bryant, R. A., & Tarrier, N. (2003). Cognitive behaviour therapy for posttraumatic stress disorder. *Clinical Psychology Review*, 23, 501–522.

Herman, J. L. (1992). *Trauma and recovery*. New York: Basic Books.

Hien, D. A., Cohen, L. R., Miele, G. M., Litt, L. C., & Capstick, C. (2004). Promising treatments for women with comorbid PTSD and substance use disorders. *American Journal of Psychiatry*, 161, 1426–1432.

Hinton, D. E., Chhean, D., Pich, V., Safren, S. A., Hofmann, S. G., & Pollack, M. H. (2005). A randomized controlled trial of cognitive-behavior therapy for Cambodian refugees with treatment-resistant PTSD and panic attacks: A cross-over design. *Journal of Traumatic Stress, 18*, 617–629.

Holdcraft, L. C., & Comtois, K. A. (2002). Description of and preliminary data from a women's dual diagnosis community mental health program. *Canadian Journal of Community Mental Health, 21*, 91–109.

Horowitz, M. J. (1976). *Stress-response syndromes.* Northvale, NJ: Aronson.

Ironson, G., Freund, B., Strauss, J. L., & Williams, J. (2002). Comparison of two treatments for traumatic stress: A community-based study of EMDR and prolonged exposure. *Journal of Clinical Psychology, 58*, 113–128.

Jacobson, N. S., Dobson, K., Fruzetti, A. E., Schmaling, K. B., & Salusky, S. (1991). Marital therapy as a treatment for depression. *Journal of Consulting and Clinical Psychology, 59*, 547–557.

Janoff-Bulman, R. (1992). *Shattered assumptions: Towards a new psychology of trauma.* New York: Free Press.

Jensen, J. A. (1994). An investigation of eye movement desensitization and reprocessing (EMD/R) as a treatment for posttraumatic stress disorder (PTSD) symptoms of Vietnam combat veterans. *Behavior Therapy, 25*, 311–325.

Johnson, D. R. (2000). Creative therapies. In E. B. Foa, T. M. Keane, & M. J. Friedman (Eds.), *Effective treatments for PTSD* (pp. 302–316). New York: Guilford Press .

Keane, T. M. (1995). The role of exposure therapy in the psychological treatment of PTSD. *Clinical Quarterly, 5*, 3–6.

Keane, T. M., Fairbank, J. A., Caddell, J. M., & Zimering, R. T. (1989). Implosive (flooding) therapy reduces symptoms of PTSD in Vietnam combat veterans. *Behavior Therapy, 20*, 245–260.

Kessler, R. C., Chiu, W. T., Demler, O. Merinkangas, K. R., & Walters, E. E. (2005). Prevalence, severity, and comorbidity of 12-month *DSM-IV* disorders in the National Comorbidity Survey Replication. *Archives of General Psychiatry, 62*, 617–627.

Kessler, R. C., Demler, O., Frank, R. G., Olfson, M., Pincus, H. A., Walters, E. E., et al. (2005). Prevalence and treatment of mental disorders, 1990 to 2003. *New England Journal of Medicine, 352*, 2515–2523.

Kessler, R. C., Sonnega, A., Bromet, E., Hughes, M., & Nelson, C. B. (1995). Posttraumatic stress disorder in the National Comorbidity Survey. *Archives of General Psychiatry, 52*, 1048–1060.

Krakow, B., Hollifield, M., Johnston, L., Koss, M., Schrader, R., Warner, T. D., et al. (2001). Imagery rehearsal therapy for chronic nightmares in sexual assault survivors with posttraumatic stress disorder: A randomized controlled trial. *Journal of the American Medical Association, 286*, 537–545.

Krupnick, J. L. (2002). Brief psychodynamic treatment of PTSD. *Journal of Clinical Psychology, 58*, 919–932.

Kubany, E. S., Hill, E. E., & Owens, J. A. (2003). Cognitive trauma therapy for battered women with PTSD: Preliminary findings. *Journal of Traumatic Stress, 16*, 81–91.

Kubany, E. S., Hill, E. E., Owens, J. A., Iannce-Spencer, C., McCaig, M. A., Tremayne, K. J., et al. (2004). Cognitive trauma therapy for battered women with PTSD (CTT-BW). *Journal of Consulting and Clinical Psychology, 72*, 3–18.

Kudler, H. S., Blank, A. S., et al. (2000). Psychodynamic therapy. In E. B. Foa, T. M. Keane, & M. J. Friedman (Eds.), *Effective treatments for PTSD* (pp. 176–198). New York: Guilford Press.

Lee, C., Gavriel, H., Drummond, P., Richards, J., & Greenwald, R. (2002). Treatment of PTSD: Stress inoculation training with prolonged exposure compared to EMDR. *Journal of Clinical Psychology, 58*, 1071–1089.

Levine, E. G., Eckhardt, J., & Targ, E. (2005). Change in post-traumatic stress symptoms following psychosocial treatment for breast cancer. *Psycho-oncology, 14*, 618–635.

Marcus, S. V., Marquis, M., & Sakai, C. (1997). Controlled study of PTSD using EMDR in an HMO setting. *Psychotherapy, 34*, 307–315.

Marks, I., Lovell, K., Noshirvani, H., Livanou, M., & Thrasher, S. (1998). Treatment of posttraumatic stress disorder by exposure and/or cognitive restructuring: A controlled study. *Archives of General Psychiatry, 55*, 317–325.

McCann, I. L., & Pearlman, L. A. (1990). *Psychological trauma and the adult survivor: Theory, therapy, and transformation.* New York: Brunner/Mazel.

McDonagh, A., Friedman, M., McHugo, G., Ford, J., Sengupta, A., Mueser, K., et al. (2005). Randomized trial of cognitive-behavioral therapy for chronic posttraumatic stress disorder in adult female survivors of childhood sexual abuse. *Journal of Consulting and Clinical Psychology, 73*, 515–524.

Monson, C. M., Schnurr, P. P., Resick, P. A., Friedman, M. J., Yinong, Y.-X., & Stevens, S. P. (in press). A randomized controlled trial of cognitive processing therapy for veterans with military-related posttraumatic stress disorder. *Journal of Consulting and Clinical Psychology.*

Monson, C. M., Schnurr, P. P., Stevens, S. P., & Guthrie, K. A. (2004). Cognitive-behavioral couples' treatment for posttraumatic stress disorder: Initial findings. *Journal of Traumatic Stress, 17,* 341–344.

Morrison, T. (1987). *Beloved.* New York: Knopf.

Morrissey, J. P., Jackson, E. W., Ellis, A. R., Amaro, H., Brown, V. B., Najavits, L. M., et al. (2005). 12-month outcomes of trauma-informed interventions for women with co-occurring disorders. *Psychiatric Services, 56,* 1213–1222.

Mueser, K. T., Rosenberg, S. D., Jankowski, M. K., Hamblen, J. L., & Descamps, M. (2004). A cognitive-behavioral treatment program for posttraumatic stress disorder in persons with severe mental illness. *American Journal of Psychiatric Rehabilitation, 7,* 107–146.

Munro, C. G., Freeman, C. P., & Law, R. (2004). General practitioners' knowledge of post-traumatic stress disorder: A controlled study. *British Journal of General Practice, 54,* 843–877.

Najavits, L., Shaw, S., & Weiss, R. (1996, June). *Outcome of a new psychotherapy for women with posttraumatic stress disorder and substance dependence.* Annual meeting of the College of Physicians on Drug Dependence, San Juan, Puerto Rico.

Najavits, L. M. (2002). *Seeking Safety: A treatment manual for PTSD and substance abuse.* New York: Guilford Press.

Najavits, L. M., Gallop, R. J., & Weiss, R. D. (in press). Seeking Safety therapy for adolescent girls with PTSD and substance use disorder: A randomized controlled trial. *Journal of Behavioral Health Services and Research.*

Najavits, L. M., & Kanukollu, S. (2005). It can be learned, but can it be taught? Results from a statewide training initiative on PTSD and substance abuse. *Journal of Dual Diagnosis, 1,* 41–52.

Najavits, L. M., Schmitz, M., Gotthard, S., & Weiss, R. D. (2005). Seeking Safety plus exposure therapy: An outcome study on dual diagnosis men. *Journal of Psychoactive Drugs, 37,* 425–435.

Najavits, L. M., Weiss, R. D., Shaw, S. R., & Muenz, L. R. (1998). "Seeking Safety": Outcome of a new cognitive-behavioral psychotherapy for women with posttraumatic stress disorder and substance dependence. *Journal of Traumatic Stress, 11,* 437–456.

Neuner, F., Schauer, M., Klaschik, C., Karunakara, U., & Elbert, T. (2004). A comparison of narrative exposure therapy, supportive counseling, and psychoeducation for treating posttraumatic stress disorder in an African refugee settlement. *Journal of Consulting and Clinical Psychology, 72,* 579–587.

Paunovic, N., & Ost, L.-G. (2001). Cognitive-behavior therapy versus exposure therapy in the treatment of PTSD in refugees. *Behaviour Research and Therapy, 39,* 1183–1197.

Peniston, E. G. (1986). EMG biofeedback-assisted desensitization treatment for Vietnam combat veterans post-traumatic stress disorder. *Clinical Biofeedback and Health, 9,* 35–41.

Penk, W., & Flannery, R. B., Jr. (2000). Psychosocial rehabilitation. In E. B. Foa, T. M. Keane, & M. J. Friedman (Eds.), *Effective treatments for PTSD* (pp. 224–246). New York: Guilford Press.

Power, K., McGoldrick, T., Brown, K., Buchanan, R., Sharp, D., & Swanson, V. (2002). A controlled comparison of eye movement desensitization and reprocessing versus exposure plus cognitive restructuring versus wait list in the treatment of post-traumatic stress disorder. *Clinical Psychology and Psychotherapy, 9,* 299–318.

Resick, P. A., Monson, C. M., & Gutner, C. (in press). Psychosocial treatments for PTSD. In M. J. Friedman, T. M. Keane, & P. A. Resick (Eds.), *PTSD: Science and practice—a comprehensive handbook.* New York: Guilford Press.

Resick, P. A., Nishith, P., Weaver, T. L., Astin, M. C., & Feuer, C. A. (2002). A comparison of cognitive-processing therapy with prolonged exposure and a waiting condition for the treatment of chronic posttraumatic stress disorder in female rape victims. *Journal of Consulting and Clinical Psychology, 70,* 867–879.

Resick, P. A., & Schnicke, M. K. (1992). Cognitive processing therapy for sexual assault victims. *Journal of Consulting and Clinical Psychology, 60,* 748–756.

Riggs, D. S. (2000). Marital and family therapy. In E. B. Foa, T. M. Keane, & M. J. Friedman (Eds.), *Effective treatments for PTSD* (pp. 280–301). New York: Guilford Press..

Rizzo, A., Pair, J., McNerney, P. J., Eastlund, E., Manson, B., Gratch, J., et al. (2005). Development of a VR therapy application for Iraq war military personnel with PTSD. *Study of Health and Technology Information, 111,* 407–413.

Rothbaum, B., Meadows, E., Resick, P., & Foy, D. (2000a). Cognitive-behavioral therapy [literature review]. In E. B. Foa, T. M. Keane, & M. J. Friedman.(Eds.), *Effective treatments for PTSD: Practice guidelines from the International Society for Traumatic Stress Studies* (pp. 60–83). New York: Guilford Press.

Rothbaum, B., Meadows, E., Resick, P., & Foy, D. (2000b). Cognitive-behavioral therapy [treatment guidelines]. In E. B. Foa, T. M. Keane, & M. J. Friedman.(Eds.), *Effective treatments for PTSD: Practice guidelines from the International Society for Traumatic Stress Studies* (pp. 320–325). New York: Guilford Press.

Rothbaum, B. O. (1997). A controlled study of eye movement desensitization and reprocessing in the treatment of posttraumatic stress disordered sexual assault victims. *Bulletin of the Menninger Clinic, 61,* 317–334.

Rothbaum, B. O., Astin, M. C., & Marsteller, F. (2005). Prolonged exposure versus eye movement desensitization and reprocessing (EMDR) for PTSD rape victims. *Journal of Traumatic Stress, 18,* 607–616.

Rothbaum, B. O., Hodges, L. F., Ready, D., Graap, K., & Alarcon, R. D. (2001). Virtual reality exposure therapy for Vietnam veterans with posttraumatic stress disorder. *Journal of Clinical Psychology, 62,* 617–622.

Royal College of Psychiatrists & the British Psychological Society. (2005). National Clinical Practice Guideline on PTSD. Cited in Butler, A. C., Chapman, J. E., Forman, E. M., & Beck, A. T. (2006). The empirical status of cognitive-behavioral therapy: A review of meta-analyses. *Clinical Psychology Review, 26,* 17–31.

Scheck, M. M., Schaeffer, J. A., & Gillette, C. (1998). Brief psychological intervention with traumatized young women: The efficacy of eye movement desensitization and reprocessing. *Journal of Traumatic Stress, 11,* 25–44.

Schnurr, P. P., Friedman, M. J., Foy, D. W., Shea, M. T., Hsieh, F. Y., Lavori, P. W., et al. (2003). Randomized trial of trauma-focused group therapy for posttraumatic stress disorder: Results from a Department of Veterans Affairs Cooperative Study. *Archives of General Psychiatry, 60,* 481–489.

Scurfield, R. M., & Wilson, J. P. (2003). Ask not for whom the bell tolls: Controversy in post-traumatic stress disorder treatment outcome findings for war veterans. *Trauma Violence Abuse, 4,* 112–126.

Shapiro, F. (1995). *Eye movement desensitization and reprocessing: Basic principles, protocols, and procedures.* New York: Guilford Press.

Sherman, J. J. (1998). Effects of psychotherapeutic treatments for PTSD: A meta-analysis of controlled clinical trials. *Journal of Traumatic Stress, 1,* 413–435.

Solomon, S. D., & Johnson, D. M. (2002). Psychosocial treatment of posttraumatic stress disorder: A practice-friendly review of outcome research. *Journal of Clinical Psychology, 58,* 947–959.

Tarrier, N., Liversidge, T., & Gregg, L. (2006). The acceptability and preference for the psychological treatment of PTSD. *Behavior Research and Therapy, 44,* 1643–1656.

Tarrier, N., Pilgrim, H., Sommerfield, C., Faragher, B., Reynolds, M., Graham, E., et al. (1999). A randomized trial of cognitive therapy and imaginal exposure in the treatment of chronic posttraumatic stress disorder. *Journal of Consulting and Clinical Psychology, 67,* 13–18.

Taylor, S., Thordarson, D. S., Maxfield, L., Fedoroff, I. C., Lovell, K., & Ogrodniczuk, J. (2003). Comparative efficacy, speed, and adverse effects of three PTSD treatments: Exposure therapy, EMDR, and relaxation training. *Journal of Consulting and Clinical Psychology, 71,* 330–338.

Taylor, T. L., & Chemtob, C. M. (2004). Efficacy of treatment for child and adolescent traumatic stress. *Archives of Pediatric and Adolescent Medicine, 158,* 786–791.

Triffleman, E. (2000). Gender differences in a controlled pilot study of psychosocial treatments in substance dependent patients with post-traumatic stress disorder: Design considerations and outcomes. *Alcoholism Treatment Quarterly, 18,* 113–126.

Triffleman, E., Carroll, K., Kellogg, S. (1999). Substance dependence posttraumatic stress disorder therapy: An integrated cognitive-behavioral approach. *Journal of Substance Abuse Treatment, 17,* 3–14.

van Etten, M. L., & Taylor, S. (1998). Comparative efficacy of treatments for PTSD: A meta-analysis. *Clinical Psychology and Psychotherapy, 5,* 126–145.

Veterans Health Administration, VA/DoD Clinical Practice Guideline Working Group. (2004). *Management of Post-Traumatic Stress.* Office of Quality and Performance publication 10Q-CPG/PTSD-04. Washington, DC: Veterans Health Administration, Department of Veterans Affairs and Health Affairs, Department of Defense.

Wagner, A. W., & Linehan. M. M. (2006). Applications of dialectical behavior therapy to posttraumatic stress disorder and related problems. In V. M. Follette & J. I. Ruzek.(Eds.), *Cognitive-behavioral therapies for trauma* (pp. 117–145). New York: Guilford Press.

Weisaeth, L. (2002). The European history of psychotraumatology. *Journal of Traumatic Stress, 15,* 443–452.

Weller, L. A. (2005). Group therapy to treat substance use and traumatic symptoms in female veterans. *Federal Practitioner, 22,* 27–38.

Wiesel, E. (1960). *Night.* New York: Hill and Wang.

Wilson, S. A., Becker, L. A., & Tinker, R. H. (1995). Eye movement desensitization and reprocessing (EMDR) treatment for psychologically traumatized individuals. *Journal of Consulting and Clinical Psychology, 63,* 928–937.

Zayfert, C., & Becker, C. B. (2000). Implementation of empirically supported treatment for PTSD: Obstacles and innovations. *Behavior Therapist, 23,* 161–168.

Zayfert, C., DeViva, J. C., Becker, C. B., Pike, J. L., Gillock, K. L., Hayes, S. A. (2005). Exposure utilization and completion of cognitive behavioral therapy for PTSD in a "real-world" clinical practice. *Journal of Traumatic Stress, 1,* 637–645.

Zlotnick, C., Najavits, L. M., & Rohsenow, D. J. (2003). A cognitive-behavioral treatment for incarcerated women with substance use disorder and posttraumatic stress disorder: Findings from a pilot study. *Journal of Substance Abuse Treatment, 25,* 99–105.

Zlotnick, C., Shea, T. M., Rosen, K. Simpson, E., Mulrenin, K., Begin, A., et al. (1997). An affect-management group for women with posttraumatic stress disorder and histories of childhood sexual abuse. *Journal of Traumatic Stress, 10,* 425–436.

19

Psychotherapy and Pharmacotherapy for Sexual Dysfunctions

Emmanuelle Duterte

Taylor Segraves

Stanley Althof

Well-controlled (Type 1 and Type 2) investigations have demonstrated the efficacy of psychological interventions for erectile dysfunctions. However, when the oral agent sildenafil was approved by the Food and Drug Administration in 1998, its introduction was nothing short of dramatic. Sildenafil is a phosphodiesterase Type 5 inhibitor (PDE 5) that enhances the man's ability to achieve a natural erection given adequate psychic and physical stimulation. Unlike other interventions, such as self-injection, transurethral, or vacuum therapy, sildenafil does not induce erection irrespective of the man's degree of arousal. Although myths abound, sildenafil does not improve libido, promote spontaneous erections, or increase the size of the penis. The efficacy of sildenafil has been demonstrated in Type 1 multiple double-blind, placebo-controlled, multi-center studies. A large number of placebo-controlled, double-blind studies have demonstrated that fluoxetine, sertraline, clomipramine, and paroxetine can be used to delay ejaculatory latency in men with rapid ejaculation. Since the early 1970s, an array of individual, conjoint, and group therapy approaches employing behavioral strategies such as stop-start or squeeze techniques have evolved as the psychological treatments of choice for rapid ejaculation, although the impressive initial posttreatment success rates, ranging from 60 to 95%, are not necessarily sustainable; three years after treatment, success rates dwindle to 25%.

Historically, conceptualization of the etiology and treatment of sexual disorders was primarily psychological. Over the past three decades, this approach has gradually evolved into a psychobiological paradigm. The introduction of effective pharmacological therapies for both erectile disorders and rapid ejaculation has shifted many physicians from a psychobiological model to a narrower biological model. There is considerable evidence that current pharmacological therapies for male disorders are frequently successful in reversing sexual dysfunction. There is less evidence concerning the long-term efficacy of such interventions for subjective sense of sexual satisfaction and couple interaction. There is mounting evidence that high doses of testosterone increase libido in postmenopausal women. The indications for such intervention and long-term safety of this intervention are unclear. Current treatments of sexual disorders by pharmacological and psychotherapeutic methods are reviewed for hypoactive sexual desire disorder, erectile dysfunction, premature ejaculation, female orgasm disorder, male orgasm disorder, dyspareunia, vaginismus, and substance-induced sexual dysfunction. Controlled studies of psychological interventions using rigorous research requirements are limited. In the next decade, there is a pressing need for the development of biological therapies of proven efficacy for female disorders and definition of the indications for biological therapy alone, psychotherapy alone, and combined therapy. The cost-effectiveness and long-term efficacy of these approaches need to be defined.

HISTORICAL OVERVIEW OF THERAPY FOR SEXUAL PROBLEMS

Historically, the treatment of sexual dysfunctions can be divided into five eras: the psychoanalytic, the early behavioral, the Masters and Johnson, the neo–Masters and Johnson, and the current psychobiological. Prior to 1970, psychoanalytic concepts guided clinicians in their understanding and treatment of sexual problems. Sexual symptomatology was linked to discrete, unresolved, unconscious conflicts that occurred during specific developmental periods. Sexual symptoms were traced to designated constellations of conflict occurring in early childhood (Meyer, 1976). Psychoanalytic notions were heterosexist and male centered, as was clearly evident in the construction of the controversial concept of penis envy and the psychological interpretation given to the classification of orgasm as either clitoral or vaginal.

In a classical analysis, patients were seen three to five times weekly over the course of several years. Freud's revolutionary method employed free association, dream analysis, interpretation of unconscious motives, and the recapitulation of significant emotional attachments through the transference. Because of the focus on individual intrapsychic dynamics, couples treatment was rarely undertaken. The analytic literature was replete with elegant, richly detailed descriptions of individual case histories and analysis. By contemporary standards, these often fascinating reports qualify only as untested case formulations.

In the late 1950s, behavioral therapists described promising results from treating sexual disorders by utilization of symptom-oriented direct treatment approaches (Brady, 1966; Cooper, 1969; Haslam, 1965; Lazarus, 1963; Wolpe, 1958). These interventions were loosely modeled on classical conditioning paradigms and assumed that the dysfunction was a learned (conditioned) anxiety response. The guiding principle of behavior therapy (LoPicollo & LoPicollo, 1978; Marks, 1981; Obler, 1973) was to extinguish the anxiety or performance demands that interfered with normal sexual function. The most common be-

havioral technique, systematic desensitization, paired relaxation with a series of carefully designed, hierarchical, anxiety-provoking sexual situations, in vivo or by imagery. Like psychoanalysis, behavior therapy concentrated on individual psychotherapy and tended to ignore the dynamics of relationships. These studies, while more rigorously documented than the analytic reports, failed to dampen the prevailing enthusiasm for the treatment of sexual problems by analytic techniques.

In 1970, Masters and Johnson published their results of a study of 790 cases employing a quasi-residential blend of daily individual and couples psychotherapy. The ingredients of their treatment model consisted of physical examination, history taking, education, prescription of behavioral tasks, and counseling for intrapsychic or interpersonal issues that interfered with natural sexual function. Their treatment was based on three fundamental postulates: (a) a sequential four-stage progression of physiological and subjective arousal in both genders; (b) the primacy of psychogenic factors, particularly learning deficits and performance anxiety in the etiology and maintenance of sexual dysfunctions; and (c) the amenability of most sexual disorders to a brief problem-focused treatment approach (Rosen & Leiblum, 1995).

Masters and Johnson's most important contribution was the emphasis given to the deleterious effects of performance anxiety and their prescription of sensate focus exercises to alleviate this troubling state. Performance anxiety, the fear of future sexual failure based on a previous failure, is a universal experience that appears in all sexual dysfunctions, including those of organic etiology. Masters and Johnson provided clear descriptions of their treatment method and reported initial and 5-year post treatment "failure rates" for lifelong and acquired arousal, orgasm, and pain disorders. Their work revolutionized the treatment of sexual problems and generated great enthusiasm among clinicians for their novel short-term, directive treatment methods.

By present-day standards, Masters and Johnson's outcome data can be criticized on multiple grounds, for not (a) utilizing standardized, valid, and reliable assessment measures; (b) specifying the basis for classifying cases as successes or failures; (c) employing control, waiting-list, or placebo groups; and (d) blinding the investigators to the experimental conditions. In addition, it was questionable whether their results applied to typical patient populations because they studied affluent, well-educated, and highly motivated patients. These vital concerns linger because later researchers have been unable to replicate the magnitude of the positive outcomes achieved by Masters and Johnson (Heiman & LoPiccolo, 1983; Rosen & Beck, 1988; Wright, Perreault, & Mathieu, 1977; Zilbergeld & Evans, 1980). Nonetheless, their reports revolutionized the treatment of sexual problems and generated great enthusiasm among clinicians for their treatment method.

The neo–Masters and Johnson era was heralded by the publication of Helen Singer Kaplan's widely acclaimed book *The New Sex Therapy* (1974). As a discipline, sex therapy had come of age. Kaplan integrated modifications of Masters and Johnson's treatment methods with behavioral and analytic interventions. She treated couples by addressing both partners' intrapsychic and interpersonal contributions to the initiation and maintenance of the dysfunction. She distinguished between recent and remote etiological causation, recommending direct treatment approaches for the former while reserving traditional psychodynamic methods for the latter. The more commonly seen recent etiological causes were relationship deterioration, performance anxiety, widowhood, health concerns, and aging. Examples of remote influences included pre-Oedipal separation-individuation conflicts, unresolved Oedipal struggles, paraphiliac scripts, gender identity conflicts, and adolescent masturbatory guilt. Kaplan's prolific writings did not include outcome statistics on the follow-up of her suggested treatment interventions.

Treatments for sexual dysfunction proliferated and evolved into blends of psychodynamic, behavioral, and cognitive therapies utilizing individual, couples, and group formats (Althof, 1989; Gagnon, Rosen, & Leiblum, 1982; Leiblum, Rosen, & Pierce, 1976; Levine, 1992b; McCarthy & McCarthy, 1984; Rosen & Leiblum, 1989; Scharf, 1985; Zilbergeld, 1992). As the field matured, clinical investigators began to develop more sophisticated methodologies that included control groups, placebo treatments, randomization of experimental conditions, and standardized, valid, and reliable questionnaires. However, the majority of these research reports lacked long-term follow-up.

The middle 1980s ushered in the current psychobiological era. This epoch is distinguished by the medicalization (Tiefer, 1995) of treatment approaches, primarily for male sexual dysfunction. Sophisticated studies with adequate long-term follow-up describing the efficacy and psychological impact of oral agents, intracavernosal injection, vacuum tumescence therapy, and treatment of rapid ejaculation by serotonin reuptake inhibitors began to appear in the literature (Althof, 1995a, 1995b; Althof et al., 1995; Assalian, 1988; Barada & McKimmy, 1994; Goldstein et al., 1998; Segraves, Saran, Segraves, & Maguire, 1993). These studies turned the tide toward the blending of medical and psychological treatments for male sexual dysfunction.

In March 1998, sildenafil citrate received approval by the Food and Drug Administration (FDA) for the treatment of erectile dysfunction (Goldstein et al., 1998). Since its release, countless prescriptions have been written, making it one of the most prescribed medications in the United States. Subsequently, vardenafil and tadalafil were also approved as phosphodiesterase Type 5 inhibitors for the treatment of erectile dysfunction (Wylie & MacInnes, 2005). The phosphodiesterase Type 5 inhibitors transformed the treatment and research landscape. Because the oral erectogenic agents were safe and easily tolerated, the established principle of etiology guiding treatment became less meaningful. Prior to the introduction of these treatments, men diagnosed with psychogenic erectile dysfunction were treated by mental health professionals, and those with organic dysfunction were seen primarily by urologists. After the introduction of the oral erectogenic drugs, much of the care of such patients shifted to primary care physicians. These therapies altered the traditional role of the mental health professional, which had been to (a) assess the etiology of erectile dysfunction, (b) offer psychotherapy to men or couples with primarily psychological dysfunction, and/or (c) treat the conspicuous psychological sequelae of organic conditions (Althof & Seftel, 1995; Levine, 1992b). Once these new pharmacological interventions became available, the clinician's role was expanded to include identification and attenuation of the resistances to medical treatments for erectile dysfunction.

Since 1999, the medicalization of sexual dysfunction has begun to likewise influence the treatments for female sexual dysfunction. There have been studies of sildenafil for female sexual arousal disorder, testosterone patches to enhance sexual desire, and the introduction of clitoral erection devices, gels, and homeopathic remedies as well (Berman, Shuker, &

Goldstein, 1999). Although there was minimal evidence supporting a role for sildenafil in treating sexual arousal disorders (Laan, Everaerd, & Both, 2005), numerous studies found that exogenous testosterone increased libido in women with a decrease in libido after bilateral oophorectomy (Buster et al., 2005; Basson et al., 2004; Shifren et al., 2000; Utian, Braunstein, Buster, Lucas, & Simon, 2004).

NOSOLOGY

Knowledge concerning the treatment of sexual dysfunctions and interest in this area of psychobiology have grown significantly in the last 20 to 30 years. The recent emergence of this field can be appreciated by realizing that the first two editions of the *Diagnostic and Statistical Manual of Mental Disorders* published by the American Psychiatric Association (APA) — *DSM-I* (1952) and *DSM-II* (1968) — did not contain diagnostic terms for the sexual dysfunctions. The third edition, *DSM-III* (APA, 1980), provided a radical departure from the previous diagnostic manuals by including a section on sexual dysfunctions. These diagnoses and their criteria sets were based on the concept of a normal sexual response cycle for men and women (Schmidt, 1995) and were strongly influenced by the works of Masters and Johnson (1966) and Helen Singer Kaplan (1974). Changes in nomenclature for the psychosexual dysfunctions in the different versions of the *Diagnostic and Statistical Manual* are listed in Table 19.1.

The current nomenclature, *DSM-IV*, was officially adopted by the American Psychiatric Association in 1994. Sexual dysfunctions listed in *DSM-IV* include hypoactive sexual desire disorder, sexual aversion disorder, female sexual arousal disorder, male erectile disorder, female orgasmic disorder, male orgasmic disorder, premature ejaculation, dyspareunia, and vaginismus. Two new diagnostic entities were included in *DSM-IV*: sexual dysfunction due to a general medical condition and substance-induced sexual dysfunction. The *DSM-IV* criteria sets do not specify a minimum duration or frequency of a disorder before it reaches diagnostic criteria. Instead, diagnosis is contingent on the disorder's causing marked distress or interpersonal difficulty and depends to a large degree on clinical judgment. The diagnostic entities in *DSM-IV* are listed in Table

TABLE 19.1 Modifications in Sexual Disorders Nomenclature in the *Diagnostic and Statistical Manuals* of the American Psychiatric Association

1. *DSM-I* was published in 1952 and did not contain diagnostic terms for the psychosexual dysfunctions.
2. *DSM-II* was published in 1968. The only diagnostic entity pertaining to psychosexual disorders was *psychophysiological genitourinary disorders*, which referred to disorders of micturation, menstruation, and sexual function.
3. *DSM-III* was published in 1980. It included diagnoses for the psychosexual disorders. The term *homosexuality* was deleted, and the term *ego dystonic homosexuality* was added as a diagnostic entity. The term *inhibited sexual excitement* referred to both male erectile disorder and female arousal disorder.
4. *DSM-III-R* was published in 1987. The term *sexual aversion disorder* was added. The term *ego dystonic homosexuality* was deleted. The use of the term *inhibited* in diagnostic entities was deleted. The term *inhibited sexual excitement* was changed to *male erectile disorder* and *female arousal disorder*.
5. *DSM-IV* was published in 1994. Subjective criteria were dropped from definitions of *male erectile disorder* and *female arousal disorder*. The terms *sexual disorder secondary to a general medical condition* and *substance-induced sexual disorder* were added.

DSM = Diagnostic and Statistical Manual of Mental Disorders.

19.2 and the changes from *DSM-III-R* are listed in Table 19.3.

Although the diagnoses in *DSM-IV* are based primarily on disturbances in discrete phases of the sexual response cycle, there is some evidence that there is considerable overlap of diagnoses (Segraves & Segraves, 1990). For example, many individuals with hypoactive sexual disorder also meet diagnostic criteria for arousal and orgasm disorders. In one pharmaceutical study, diagnostic evaluations were available for 906 subjects, 532 females and 374 males. Approximately 40% of patients diagnosed as having hypoactive sexual desire disorder also met diagnostic criteria for arousal or orgasm disorders. In the same study, only 2% of women had a solitary diagnosis of female arousal disorder. Most patients diagnosed with a female arousal disorder also met criteria for hypoactive sexual desire disorders as well as anorgasmia. This frequent overlap among diagnostic categories needs to be kept in mind when one reviews treatment outcome research because little of this research details secondary as well as primary diagnosis. Similarly, in the clinical situation, it is often unclear which condition is primary. For example, if a patient presents for treatment with complaints of anorgasmia, as well as decreased libido, and it is unclear which problem came first, the choice of primary diagnosis may reflect the clinician's theoretical bias as much as it reflects the presented symptomatology.

The *DSM-IV* diagnostic system has been criticized extensively by clinicians (Basson et al., 2004; Laan et al., 2005). Two separate multidisciplinary in-

TABLE 19.2 *DSM-IV* Psychosexual Disorders

1. *Hypoactive sexual desire disorder:* Persistent or recurrent deficiency in or absence of sexual fantasies and desire for sexual activity.
2. *Sexual aversion disorder:* Persistent or recurrent extreme aversion to, and avoidance of, all or almost all sexual contact with a partner.
3. *Female sexual arousal disorder.* Persistent or recurrent inability to attain, or to maintain until completion of the sexual activity, an adequate lubrication and swelling response of sexual excitement.
4. *Male erectile disorder:* Persistent or recurrent inability to obtain, or to maintain until completion of the sexual activity, an adequate erection.
5. *Female orgasmic disorder:* Persistent or recurrent delay in or absence of orgasm following a normal sexual excitement phase. This diagnosis is based on the clinician's judgment that the woman's orgasmic capacity is less than would be reasonable for her age, her sexual experience, and the adequacy of sexual stimulation.
6. *Male orgasmic disorder:* Persistent or recurrent delay in or absence of orgasm following a normal excitement phase during sexual activity, with the clinician taking into account the person's age and judging the sexual stimulation to be adequate in focus, intensity, and duration.
7. *Premature ejaculation:* Persistent or recurrent ejaculation with minimal sexual stimulation before, on, or shortly after penetration and before the person wishes it.
8. *Dyspareunia:* Recurrent or persistent genital pain associated with sexual intercourse not due exclusively to vaginismus or lack of lubrication.
9. *Vaginismus:* Recurrent or persistent involuntary spasm of the musculature of the outer third of the vagina that interferes with intercourse.
10. *Sexual dysfunction due to general medical condition:* Clinically significant sexual dysfunction that results in marked distress or interpersonal difficulty; the sexual dysfunction is fully explained by the physiological effect of a general medical condition.
11. *Substance-induced sexual dysfunction:* Clinically significant sexual dysfunction that is fully explained either by substance intoxication or by medication use.

Subtypes: Lifelong versus acquired; generalized versus situational; due to psychological factors versus combined factors.

TABLE 19.3 Changes in *DSM-IV* From *DSM-III*

1. Requirement that each of the dysfunctions cause marked distress or interpersonal difficulty.
2. Female sexual arousal disorder: Requires that the diagnosis be made solely on lack of physiological arousal.
3. Male erectile disorder: Requires that the diagnosis be made solely on lack of physiological arousal.
4. Female orgasmic disorder: Name has been changed from *inhibited sexual orgasm.*
5. Male orgasmic disorder: Name has been changed from *inhibited male orgasm.*
6. *Sexual dysfunction due to general medical condition* is a new entry.
7. *Substance-induced sexual dysfunction* is a new entry.

ternational consensus panels have recommended modifications of this system (Basson, Berman, et al., 2000; Basson, Leiblum, Brott, & Derogatis, 2000; Basson, MacInnes, et al., 2000) 2000b, 2000c; Basson, 2003). The proposed new system combines organic and psychogenic etiologies into one classification system. It also distinguishes between disorders of subjective and physiological arousal and suggests that the criterion set for hypoactive sexual desire be modified to include lack of responsive desire. To date, these recommendations have not been adopted into any officially sanctioned diagnostic system.

EPIDEMIOLOGY

The largest study of the prevalence of sexual disorders in the United States was conducted by Laumann, Paik, and Rosen (1999) and is known as the National Health Social Life Survey. This survey was a probability sample of U.S. adults, aged 18 to 59. The sample consisted of 2,968 adults. All were interviewed face-to-face with a structured interview. Sexual dysfunction was more prevalent among women than men. Among males, the most common problems were difficulty with orgasm (8.3%), lack of interest (15.8%), rapid ejaculation (28.8%), and erectile difficulties (9.8%). Erectile difficulties were positively correlated with age. Women complained of painful coitus (14.4%), lack of interest (33.4%), inability to reach orgasm (24.1%), and difficulty with lubrication (18.8%). Feldman et al. (1994) studied the epidemiology of erectile dysfunction and its medical and psychosocial correlates in a random sample of men aged 40 to 70 who lived in cities and towns near Boston. A self-administered sexual question-naire was utilized. Approximately half of the population reported at least occasional problems with erections. The prevalence of erectile problems was highly correlated with age. Only 5% of men aged 40 reported total erectile failure as compared with 15% of men aged 70. Other variables associated with erectile failure were depressive symptoms, cigarette smoking, heart disease, and hypertension. A prospective study of the same sample found that the incidence of impotence was related to various cardiovascular risk factors, as well as a submissive personality (Araujo, Johannes, Derby, & McKinlay, 2000; Johannes et al., 2000).

Pinnock, Stapleton, and Marshall (1999) used a mailed questionnaire to study the prevalence of erectile problems in a probability sample of men over 40 in South Australia. Erectile dysfunction was correlated with age: only 3% of men aged 40 to 49 reported erections insufficient for coitus, compared with 64% of men aged 70 to 79. Various cardiovascular risk factors were associated with the presence of erectile dysfunction. Similar studies of the prevalence of erectile dysfunction have occurred in Thailand, Malaysia, Japan, and Italy (Parazzini et al., 2000; Shirai, Marui, Hayashi, Ishii, & Abe, 1999). In these studies, increasing age and cardiovascular risk factors were associated with erectile dysfunction. Hawton, Gath, and Day (1994) studied a community sample of middle-aged women in the Oxford area in the United Kingdom. A semistructured interview was utilized. Questions concerned sexual frequency and orgasm frequency. Marital adjustment was the main predictor of sexual activity and satisfaction. In this sample, 17% of participants stated that they experienced orgasm on all coital opportunities; 16% said they never experienced orgasm; 29% said that they experienced orgasm more than 50% of the time; 2% said that they never enjoyed coitus, whereas 41% said that they always enjoyed coitus. Dunn, Croft, and Hackett (1999) sent an anonymous postal questionnaire to a stratified random sample of the adult general population in the United Kingdom. More women than men had sexual problems. The most common sexual problems in women were vaginal dryness and infrequent orgasm.

A global study of the prevalence of sexual disorders was performed on 27,500 subjects from 29 countries (Laumann et al., 2005). In women the most common difficulties were lack of interest (26 to 43%), inability to reach orgasm (18 to 41%), and difficulty with lubrication (31%). In men, the most common difficulties were rapid ejaculation (24%) and erectile problems (17%). Most difficulties were more prevalent in East Asia and Southeast Asia than in other parts of the world. The significance of regional differences in prevalence is difficult to determine because different response rates and inquiry techniques were employed in different countries. In spite of the high prevalence of sexual problems, it is interesting that less than 18% of subjects requested help with their difficulty, and only 9% reported being asked about sexual problems by their physicians (Moreira et al., 2005).

Some sexual dysfunctions may be associated with other Axis I disorders. For example, mood disorder may be associated with an increased prevalence of hypoactive sexual desire disorder and male erectile dysfunction (Kennedy, Dickens, Eisfeld, & Bagby, 1999; Thase et al., 1999). Euthymic patients with a current diagnosis of hypoactive sexual desire have an increased lifetime prevalence of mood disorder (Schreiner-Engel & Schiavi, 1986). There are also reports of decreased libido being more common in patients with schizophrenia (Aizenberg, Zemishlany, Dorfman-Etrog, & Weizmen, 1995), anorexia nervosa (Raboch & Faltus, 1991), and anxiety disorders (Minnen & Kampman, 2000). However, most cases of sexual dysfunction do not have a clear relationship to another Axis I disorder. There also is minimal evidence of a relationship between sexual dysfunction and personality disorder or even specific personality traits (Segraves, 1989). Most clinicians assume that the immediate causes of sexual dysfunction involve anxiety about performance, a cycle of demand and negative expectancies, and self-defeating cognitions (Segraves, 1989).

WHAT CONSTITUTES A SUCCESSFUL OUTCOME FOR SEXUAL THERAPY?

Psychotherapy outcome studies are notoriously difficult to design and conduct. The challenge facing researchers is not only to design methodologically sound studies but also to design studies that demonstrate regard for the complexity of the human condition. Thus, outcomes conceived solely in terms of women's facility in achieving coital orgasm, men's prowess at delaying ejaculation, the buckling force of an erection, the blood flow through the vagina, or the frequency with which partners bring their bodies to one another employ far too narrow and mechanistic criteria for success. Sexuality outcome studies need to assess the complex interplay among biological, emotional, psychological, and relational components of individuals' and couples' lives. Thus, it is not solely how many orgasms individuals achieve but the degree of satisfaction, passion, and sense of psychological and relational well-being of two individuals.

There is also disagreement on what constitutes success even when the solely mechanistic criteria are employed. For instance, in treating female anorgasmia, what defines success — simply achieving orgasm once, achieving orgasm from manual or oral stimulation on some arbitrary percentage basis, achieving coital orgasm with or without clitoral stimulation on some arbitrary percentage basis, or another criterion? And what constitutes success in treating erectile dysfunction — the ability to consummate intercourse or the degree of penile rigidity?

The disagreements regarding success are further complicated by the primacy conferred on intercourse as the essential determinant of success. Is intercourse to be considered the sine qua non of outcome variables or simply one alternative sexual behavior in which couples may choose to engage? To date, this controversial issue has not been scientifically resolved, and success is defined through the eyes of the researcher.

METHODOLOGICAL PROBLEMS
IN SEX THERAPY OUTCOME STUDIES

Spence (1991) criticizes the methodologies of sex therapy outcome studies because they (a) employ small sample sizes; (b) do not use experimental control groups (waiting-list, no-treatment, attention placebo controls); (c) lack random allocation to conditions; (d) fail to offer clear-cut definitions of diagnostic criteria to permit replication; (e) generally do not include assessments of long-term outcome; and (f) do not adequately describe the therapy method utilized.

Although anxiety is theoretically regarded as causing sexual dysfunction, scientific investigations supporting this important concept are sorely lacking. One exception is that some studies have reported an association between anxiety disorders and the occurrence of rapid ejaculation (Corona et al., 2004; Figueira, Possidente, Marques, & Hayes, 2001). A number of studies have identified the role of cognitive distraction in sexual problems (Beck, Barlow, Sakheim, & Abrahamson, 1987; Cranston-Cuebas & Barlow, 1990; Palace & Gorzalka, 1992). Rosen and Leiblum (1995) suggested that the role of anxiety in sexual dysfunction needs to be reconceptualized. It appears that it is not anxiety per se that is responsible for initiating or maintaining sexual difficulties. In most cases, it is the alternations in perceptual and attentional processes that occur in sexually dysfunctional male and female patients.

The few studies that report long-term follow-ups have suffered from serious problems of sample attrition. Thus, the generalizations from these important studies are open to question regarding whether the results mirror the sample as a whole.

Other problems with sex therapy studies involve the contamination of study populations. This is most apparent in the early reports on erectile disorder, in which men suffering from organic etiologies were incorrectly diagnosed as suffering from psychogenic erectile dysfunction. In the Masters and Johnson era, knowledge regarding the pathophysiology of erectile function was lacking, as were more accurate diagnostic tests. Men who were not likely to benefit from a psychological intervention were inappropriately included in the population under study, and the outcome statistics were biased — in a negative direction.

Finally, the evolution of psychiatry's diagnostic nomenclature was inconsistent regarding the categorization of and the criteria for sexual dysfunctions throughout the successive publications *DSM-I* through *DSM-IV*. This is most obvious in reviewing disorders of desire. Prior to *DSM-III* in 1980, desire disorders were diagnosed as either arousal or orgasmic dysfunctions. Thus, the early studies on arousal and orgasm disorders included individuals who today would be considered incorrectly diagnosed. Unfortunately, this diagnostic inconsistency hampers researchers' attempts to replicate the results of earlier studies.

PSYCHOLOGICAL TREATMENT
OF SEXUAL DYSFUNCTIONS:
GENERAL FORMULATIONS

Masters and Johnson's innovative format of employing mixed-sex cotherapy teams working with couples in a quasi-residential, daily combination of individual and conjoint treatment was an expensive, therapist-intensive, impractical model to reproduce. Their treatment model was evaluated to ascertain if similar results could be achieved with a more conservative, conventional outpatient treatment approach. Investigators examined the impact of a single therapist versus a mixed-sex cotherapy team and weekly versus daily treatment sessions. The results indicated that couples did as well when treated on a weekly basis and by a single therapist (Clement & Schmidt 1983; Crowe, Gillan, & Golombok, 1981; Hawton, 1995; Heiman & LoPiccolo, 1983). Two studies examined whether matching the gender of the therapist with the gender of the symptom bearer would result in improved outcome: No differences were found (Crowe et al., 1981; LoPiccolo, Heiman, Hogan, & Roberts, 1985).

Hawton (1995) cautioned that not all patients with sexual complaints are suitable candidates for sex therapy. He compiled five factors associated with positive sex therapy outcome:

1. The quality of the couple's general relationship, especially the female partner's pretreatment assessment of the relationship (Hawton & Catalan, 1986);
2. The motivation of the partners, particularly the male partner, for treatment (Hawton & Fagg, 1991; Whitehead & Mathews, 1986);
3. Absence of serious psychiatric disorder in either partner;
4. Physical attraction between the partners;
5. Early compliance with the treatment program homework assignments.

Researchers have also examined the efficacy of individual versus group treatment formats. Group formats are advantageous because they are less costly in terms of therapist time, provide patients with the knowledge that they are not alone in their suffering, offer peer support, and allow patients to learn from the experiences of others. In addition, competition within the group motivates patients to change behaviors and desensitized patients to discussions of their private sexual lives (Spence, 1991). Conversely, group treatment is difficult to organize and institute because it requires the bringing together of several peoples' schedules and the fortuitous circumstance of several appropriate patients presenting with similar complaints at the same time. Group treatment also reduces the amount of time and attention any one patient can receive, increases patients' anxiety about confidentiality, and does not allow patients to proceed at either an accelerated or a delayed pace.

Spence (1991) reported that individual treatment was slightly more advantageous than group therapy for women with primary and secondary anorgasmia. Minimal differences between group and individual therapy have been reported in the treatment of premature ejaculation (Perelman, 1976), anorgasmia (Ersner-Hershfield & Kopel, 1979), and sexual anxiety (Nemetz, Craig, & Reith, 1978). Regardless of the efficacy of groups, it seems that the vast majority of patients are seen in individual or couples therapy.

Long-term follow-up studies demonstrated the positive sustained effect of therapy on individuals' and couples' subjective sense of sexual satisfaction and self-acceptance (DeAmicus, Goldberg, LoPicollo, Friedman, & Davies, 1985). These studies also documented improved marital adjustment, both immediately after termination and over the course of follow-up. Most important, these findings also hold for patients who reported little change in sexual symptomatology after treatment or who evidenced symptom relapse during treatment or follow-up. This may be interpreted to mean that individuals' attitudes toward their sexual lives and the quality of couples' relationships tend to be enhanced through the process of therapy and that this change tends to be sustained over time.

OUTCOME OF TREATMENTS FOR SPECIFIC SEXUAL DYSFUNCTIONS

Sexual Desire Disorders

Psychological Intervention

There is minimal information concerning the efficacy of psychological treatment for male hypoactive sexual desire disorder (Maurice, 2005). Most of the available information concerns the treatment of hypoactive sexual desire disorder in women (Basson, 2005). When emotional intimacy is lacking, couples are usually referred for couple counseling before sex therapy (Basson, 2003). Of women with disorders of sexual desire, 50 to 70% appear to achieve modest gains immediately following cognitive-behavioral psychotherapy (Hurlbert, 1993; McCabe, 2001; Trudel et al., 2001). However, several studies found a marked deterioration in function at 3-year follow-up (DeAmicus et al., 1985; Hawton, 1995). Half the individuals who reported success after treatment did not maintain heightened desire 3 years later. Paradoxically, couples reported improved and sustained levels of sexual satisfaction despite the regression in levels of sexual desire.

Pharmacotherapy

There is no pharmacotherapy with established efficacy for primary hypoactive sexual desire disorder. There is substantial evidence establishing that a certain minimal level of androgen is a necessary biological component of sexual desire (Davidson, Kwan, & Greenleaf, 1982), and the use of antiandrogenic drugs such as cyproterone acetate has been demonstrated to diminish libido (Kellet, 1993). However, a relationship between individual endogenous androgen production within the normal range and sexual interest has not been demonstrated, and numerous studies have failed to demonstrate a beneficial effect of exogenous androgen in eugonadal men with erectile problems and diminished sexual desire (Segraves, 1988b). In a well-controlled study, O'Carroll, Segraves, and Bancroft (1984) reported that exogenous androgen administration increased the frequency of sexual thoughts but had no effect on sexual activity in eugonadal men. It is possible that androgen administration has a subtle influence on libido in eugonadal men. There is no evidence to date that this effect is clinically significant.

Abnormally low endogenous androgen levels have been proposed as one etiology for hypoactive sexual desire disorder in females (Davis, 1999; Hoegler & Guzick, 1999). There is suggestive evidence of a relationship between endogenous androgen levels in females and libido (Bancroft, Sherwin, Alexander, Davidson, & Walker, 1991; Persky, Lief, & Strauss, 1978). However, not all investigations have replicated this finding (Davis, Davison, Donath, & Bell, 2005; Dennerstein, Dudley, Hopper, & Burger, 1997; Gayler et al., 1999). Numerous clinicians have reported success in case studies and clinical series using androgen therapy in women complaining of low libido (Davis, 1998; Rabo, 2000; Sarrel, 1999; Sarrel, Dobay, & Witta, 1998; Warnock, Bundren, & Morris, 1999). Numerous placebo-controlled studies have found that testosterone

therapy increases libido in surgically menopausal women (Gelfand, 1999; Sherwin & Gelfand, 1984, 1985, 1987; Sherwin, Gelfand, & Bender, 1985; Shifren et al., 2000; Utian et al., 2004; Bolour & Braunstein, 2005). The doses employed in these studies increased serum testosterone levels to the upper limits of normal or slightly above the normal range. There is also some evidence that testosterone improves libido in women experiencing decreased libido after natural menopause (Jolly, Kroll, & Schifren, 2004). Evidence for the use of androgens in premenopausal women experiencing low libido is not established (Basson, 1999). Supraphysiological levels of androgens clearly increase libido (Shifren et al., 2000; Tuiten et al., 2000). Whether physiological doses of androgen have a meaningful effect on libido exceeding that of placebo remains to be established (Guzick & Hoeger, 2000). Controlled trials do not indicate that over-the counter food supplements containing dihydroepiandrosterone are effective in the treatment of hypoactive sexual desire disorder (Barnhart et al., 1999). A recent single-blind study found that bupropion increased various indices of libido in women with hypoactive sexual desire disorder (Segraves et al., 2001); however, the positive effect on libido was not confirmed in a double-blind trial (Segraves, Clayton, & Croft, 2004).

Female Arousal Disorders

Female arousal disorders are typically diagnosed in women who also report desire and orgasmic difficulties. A recent laboratory study conducted by Palace (1995) evaluated the effects of heightened autonomic arousal feedback and genital and subjective responses in a large sample of dysfunctional women. She noted that general autonomic arousal (produced by exposure to a dangerous situation) significantly increased both physiological and subjective sexual arousal. These fascinating findings require further study regarding how heightened autonomic arousal can be achieved in a real-life sexual setting and whether the gains associated with this form of arousal are sustainable over time. Another laboratory placebo-controlled study of arousal measured by vaginal photoplethysmography found that ephedrine sulfate increased vaginal pulse amplitude response but not subjective sexual arousal to erotic films (Meston & Heiman, 1998). The significance of this study for clinical practice is unclear. In a single-blind study of six postmenopausal women with arousal problems, Rosen, Phillips, Gendrano, and Ferguson (1999) found that 40 mg of phentolamine increased measures of arousal on both vaginal photoplethysmography measures and self-reported sensation of vaginal lubrication and pleasurable vaginal sensations. There is minimal evidence of a beneficial effect of phosphodiesterase Type 5 inhibitors in women complaining of problems with sexual arousal. One large multinational double-blind, placebo-controlled study found no evidence of efficacy (Basson, 2001). Regardless of hormone status, sildenafil was ineffective in reversing sexual dysfunction. In laboratory studies, sildenafil does increase the vasocongestive response to sexual stimulation, but this is not associated with increased sexual pleasure (Laan et al., 2002). One double-blind study found some evidence of a positive effect of sildenafil in a small group of postmenopausal women on hormone replacement complaining of difficulty with sexual arousal but not having difficulty with libido (Berman, Berman, Toler, Gill, & Haughie, 2003).

A fairly extensive research literature suggests that a relation may exist between libido and androgen levels in women (Segraves, 2002). A recent multisite, double-blind study of androgen-estrogen therapy delivered transdermally in postmenopausal women found that high-dosage testosterone increased both subjective and objective measures of libido. Tibilone, which is seeking regulatory approval in the United States for the treatment of menopausal symptoms, has been shown to enhance sexual activity similar to androgen (Segraves, 2003a). One randomized, double-blind, crossover study of tibilone in postmenopausal women found that it was associated with significant increases in sexual desire and vaginal lubrication. A number of studies suggest that topical vaginal estrogens may significantly reduce vaginal dryness, increase genital arousal, and reduce dyspareunia (Grazziotin, 2004). Current available evidence indicates that sexual hormones may have a significant effect on all parameters of women's sexual function.

A Type 1 randomized, double-blind, placebo-controlled, multiple-site study done by Segraves et al. (2004) studied the use of bupropion sustained release for the treatment of hypoactive sexual desire disorder in premenopausal women. The outcome observed in this study is that bupropion has a positive effect on various aspects of sexual function in women diagnosed with hypoactive sexual disorder. It is probable

that its modest effect on dopamine reuptake may be responsible for its prosexual effects.

A clitoral vacuum erection device has been recently approved by the FDA. This small, battery-powered device is designed to enhance blood flow to the clitoris. There are no large-scale studies in clinical populations demonstrating a benefit of using this device.

Studies of women with hypoactive sexual desire disorder (HSDD) have reported modest gains with behavior therapy, with deterioration of these gains at 3-year follow-up (Segraves, 2003a). Since a solitary complaint of female arousal disorder is rare in premenopausal women, there is minimal evidence regarding psychotherapy for this condition.

Erectile Dysfunction

Psychological Intervention

Men with lifelong and acquired erectile dysfunctions achieved significant gains both initially and over the long term following participation in sex psychotherapy (Masters & Johnson, 1970). Men with acquired disorders tended to fare better than those with lifelong problems. Masters and Johnson reported initial failure rates of 41% for primary impotence and 26% for secondary impotence. Long-term failure rates were 41% and 31% for primary and secondary dysfunctions, respectively.

Other well-controlled investigations (DeAmicus, 1985; Hawton, Catalan, & Fagg, 1992; Heiman & LoPicolo, 1983; Kilmann et al., 1987; Reynolds, 1991) have demonstrated the efficacy of psychological interventions for erectile dysfunctions, although none of these later studies have achieved the impressive results of Masters and Johnson's original study. In an excellent review of studies of treatment for erectile dysfunction, Mohr and Beuder (1990) wrote: "The *component parts* of these treatments typically include behavioral, cognitive, systemic and interpersonal communications interventions. Averaging across studies, it appears that approximately two-thirds of the men suffering from erectile failure will be satisfied with their improvement at follow-up ranging from six weeks to six years" (p. 123). These studies utilized either a couples or a group format. The duration of couples therapy ranged between 4 and 20 weekly meetings. Group therapies met weekly for 10 to 20 meetings. All forms of intervention except biofeedback were equally effective in producing sustained change. There are few controlled reports on individual therapy for men, except for the report by Reynolds (1991), who highlighted the difficulties of treating men without partners.

All studies with long-term follow-up noted a tendency for men to suffer relapses. The most discouraging report came from Levine and Agle (1978), who treated 16 couples in a Masters and Johnson format. Posttherapy, 11 of the 16 men noted improvement in erectile function. At the 3-year follow-up, only one couple was able to sustain its gains. Hawton et al. (1992) suggested that positive treatment outcome is associated with better pretreatment communication and general sexual adjustment, especially the female partner's interest in and enjoyment of sex, the absence of a psychiatric history in the woman, and the couple's willingness to complete homework. In writing about the problem of relapse in treating all forms of sexual dysfunction, Hawton et al. (1986) reported that recurrence of or continuing difficulty with the presenting sexual problem was commonly being reported by 75% of couples; this caused little to no concern for 34% of them. Patients indicated that they discussed the difficulty with the partner, practiced the techniques learned during therapy, accepted that difficulties were likely to recur, and read books about sexuality.

Pharmacotherapy

Clearly, the most acceptable pharmacotherapy for erectile dysfunction is an oral medication. Indeed, when the oral agent sildenafil was approved by the FDA in 1998, its introduction was nothing short of dramatic. Sildenafil is a phosphodiesterase Type 5 inhibitor (PDE 5; Goldstein et al., 1998). The drug enhances the man's ability to achieve a natural erection given adequate psychic and physical stimulation. Unlike other interventions, such as self-injection, transurethral, or vacuum therapy, sildenafil does not induce erection irrespective of the man's degree of arousal. Although myths abound, sildenafil does not improve libido, promote spontaneous erections, or increase the size of the penis. The efficacy of sildenafil has been demonstrated in Type 1 multiple double-blind, placebo-controlled, multicenter studies employing outcome measures such as penile plethysmography to measure erectile response to an erotic film and a validated 15-item self-report ques-

tionnaire known as the International Index of Erectile Function (IIEF; Osterloh, Eardley, Carson, & Padma-Nathan, 1999). In these studies, there was a significant difference between all doses of sildenafil and placebo in the ability to obtain erections sufficient for penetration and the ability to maintain them after penetration. Increasing doses of sildenafil were associated with increased erectile function. Scientifically sound studies have been conducted in men with hypertension, including those currently receiving medications for their disease, and it has also been shown to be helpful to men with Type 1 and Type 2 diabetes, spinal cord injury, postradical prostatectomy, and depression. Depending on the etiology of the dysfunction, sildenafil efficacy ranges between 40% and 80%. The most common side effects include headache and facial flushing, seen in 10 to 20% of men; dyspepsia, seen in 5% of men; and red/blue color vision changes or blurry vision, seen in 3% of men. The headache and facial flushing may be explained by the vasodilatory effects of sildenafil on the cerebral circulation. The dyspepsia is due to the small overlap in sildenafil activity with Type 4 phosphodiesterase found at the gastroesophageal sphincter, leaving the gastroesophageal sphincter open. The visual issues are due to the slight overlap with Type 6 phosphodiesterase, which exists in the eye (retina). The drug comes in three strengths, 25, 50, and 100 mg; most men (more than 60%) use the 100-mg dose.

Absolute contraindications to sildenafil use are the concomitant use of nitrate drugs. Caution has been advised in patients with retinitis pigmentosa, preexisting hypotension, and multiple antihypertensive agents (American College of Cardiology and American Heart Association Consensus Group, 1999; Tomlinson, 1999). The significance of cardiac deaths is difficult to evaluate because the majority of men taking sildenafil have cardiovascular risk factors. A small number of cases of priapism have been reported on sildenafil. The primary action of sildenafil is peripheral. The drug inhibits the inactivation of cyclic guanosine monophosphate, an intracellular second messenger, by phosphodiesterase Type 5. During sexual stimulation, nitric oxide release activates gaunylate cyclase, which results in the production of cyclic guanosine monophosphate (GMP). Cyclic GMP induces calcium efflux, smooth muscle relaxation, and thus penile engorgement. Sildenafil is taken as needed, reaches maximum plasma levels

1 hour after oral dosing, and has a terminal half-life of 3 to 5 hours. To date, there is minimal information about the psychological effect of restoration of potency in men with psychogenic impotence. One 12-week study has shown that men with subsyndromal depression have an improvement in mood after the restoration of erectile function (Rosen, Seidman, Menza, Roose, & Shabsign, 1999). From this study, one cannot determine if the mood elevation is sustained. One clinician reported two cases in which the restoration of erectile function appeared to precipitate severe marital discord (Wise, 1999). Since most sildenafil prescriptions are written by physicians without training in evaluation of couple interaction, it is important to know if the case report of marital discord after restoration of erectile function is an isolated finding.

Other phosphodiesterase Type 5 inhibitors include vardenafil and tadalafil (Wylie & MacInnes, 2005). All of the PDE 5 inhibitors appear to have similar efficacy and a similar side-effect profile. The primary difference between these compounds appears to be that tadalafil has a longer duration of action. There is some evidence that combination brief counseling and pharmacotherapy are more effective in the treatment of erectile dysfunction than the use of oral erectogenic agents alone (Perelman, 2005).

Researchers from Cologne, Germany, prospectively studied the effect of long-term sildenafil therapy. Preliminary data suggest that chronic phosphodiesterase Type 5 (PDE-5) inhibitor therapy may induce both structural and physiological changes in the penis. This may reverse or even cure men suffering from organic erectile dysfunction, and this novel concept potentially opens a new area of study in reference to PDE 5 inhibitor mechanisms (Padma-Nathan et al., 2003; Sommer, Engelmann, & the German Men's Health Study Group, 2005).

Tadalafil is available in 10-mg and 20-mg tablets and should be taken orally 30 minutes to 1 hour before sexual activity. Erection has been reported to occur 15 to 30 minutes after ingestion of the tablet and can last as long as 36 hours for one dose, facilitating spontaneity. No more than one tablet should be taken in a single 24-hour period. Tadalafil is rapidly absorbed following oral administration, primarily metabolized in the liver. Mean half-life is 17.5 hours. Vardenafil is available in 2.5-mg, 5-mg, 10-mg, and 20-mg tablets. Recommended starting dose for most men is 10 mg taken orally approximately 1 hour be-

fore sexual activity. Erection occurs 30 to 60 minutes after ingestion of the tablet and usually lasts approximately 4–5 hours. Maximum dosing frequency is once daily. Vardenafil is metabolized for the most part in the liver. It has an elimination half-life of 4 to 5 hours.

Prior to sildenafil the only other oral agent for erectile dysfunction was yohimbine, a natural herb of an African tree bark. Yohimbine is an alpha-2 adrenergic antagonist (Morales, Surridge, & Marshall, 1987). Double-blind studies have shown that it has modest efficacy, mainly in men with psychogenic erectile problems (Reid et al., 1987; Riley, Goodman, Kellet, & Orr, 1989; Sondra, Mazo, Segraves, & Chanceler, 1990; Susset et al., 1989). There are few objective, placebo-controlled studies that validate the efficacy of yohimbine.

Other pharmacotherapies for erectile dysfunction include transurethral systems (MUSE) and intracorporeal injection therapy. Both these methods employ different delivery systems to introduce vasoactive substances into the corpora cavernosa of the penis. Of the two approaches, intracavernosal injection therapy has a higher success rate in producing firm erections. The parameters of such therapy, dose regimes, and side effects are well established. The efficacy for psychogenic as well as organic erectile problems appears well established (Althof et al., 1991). There is much less research concerning the psychological benefits of this form of therapy. The three most common agents used to induce erections are papaverine hydrochloride, phentolamine, and prostaglandin E1. Although they are frequently combined, each agent can be used singly (Althof & Seftel, 1995). As one might expect, there have also been a number of reports and studies employing the triple therapy of papaverine, phentolamine, and prostaglandin El, referred to as tri-mix (Barada & McKimmy, 1994). Triple therapy appears to have superior results over the use of papaverine phentolamine combination therapy for some conditions, such as severe arteriogenic disease (McMahon, 1991). Triple therapy has also been used in patients with psychogenic impotence (Bennett, Carpenter, & Barada, 1991). Papaverine and papaverine-phentolamine injection therapy have the disadvantages of delayed corporeal fibrosis, variable efficacy, systemic reactions, and the risk of prolonged erections (Levine et al., 1989).

Prostaglandin E1 has the advantages of having a reliable dose-response curve, less risk for prolonged erection, fewer systemic side effects, and less delayed corporeal fibrosis. It has the major disadvantage of pain at the injection site. With all agents, a proper dose is established, and the patient is instructed in self-administration and given a "home kit."

Probably the best study of intracavernosal therapy for psychogenic male erectile disorder was conducted by the Althof group (Althof, 1989; Turner et al., 1989). In one of their studies, 15 men with psychogenic impotence (4 lifelong, 11 acquired; average age, 49; average duration of impotence, 12 years) were compared with 74 men with organic impotence and 42 men with impotence of mixed etiology. All patients completed an extensive psychometric battery that included the Case Western Reserve University Sexual Functioning Questionnaire, the Dyadic Adjustment Scale, the Beck Depression Inventory, the Spielberger State Trait Anxiety Inventory, the Personal Evaluation Inventory, and a 40-item self-report scale. All patients were started on the same papaverine phentolamine self-injection program and assessed at baseline and 1, 3, and 6 months. At the 6-month follow-up, the men with psychogenic impotence who were still participating in the self-injection program reported an average use of four times monthly and satisfactory erections after injection on 94% of the occasions. There was no evidence of psychological deterioration, no evidence of symptom substitution, and some evidence of improvement in anxiety measures. Unfortunately, only 6 of the 15 patients with psychogenic impotence completed the trial. However, the three groups did not differ in dropout rates, with all groups experiencing approximately a 60% dropout rate. The three major factors accounting for dropout were the idea of self-injection, worry about side effects, and concern about artificiality. The available evidence does not suggest a harmful psychosocial effect of intracavernosal therapy on psychogenic erectile problems. However, these conclusions have to be tempered by the extremely small sample that completed treatment.

Transurethral therapy came into being through the development of an innovative drug delivery system that allowed medication to be applied directly to the urethral mucosa. The primary advantage of this treatment method is that it obviates the need to inject the penis to create an erection. Through vascular channels, medication placed on the urethral mucosa is transferred to the corpus cavernosum, and the result is an erection. MUSE is an acronym for medicated urethral system for erection, which deposits a semisolid pellet of prostaglandin E1 directly on the urethral mucosa. This proprietary drug delivery system consists of a polypropylene applicator with a hollow stem 3.2 cm long and 3.5 mm in diameter. Prostaglandin E1 in one of four predetermined dose levels (125, 250, 500, or 1,000 ìg) is contained within the tip of the applicator. Prior to using the MUSE, patients are instructed to void so that residual urine provides a natural lubricant for the slow and gentle insertion of the stem into the urethra. A button on the crown of the applicator is depressed, depositing the pellet approximately 3 cm into the urethra. The applicator is then withdrawn. An erectile response is evident within 10 minutes and lasts for 30 to 60 minutes. In double-blind, placebo-controlled studies, Padma-Nathan, Hellstrom, and Kaiser (1997) reported that 43% of patients had intercourse on at least one occasion. Lewis (1998) described that, by use of an external constriction device, the Actis ring, the number of patients able to achieve intercourse improved to approximately 60%. Although this device is effective in producing a Grade 3 or 4 erection in spinal cord–injured men with residual upper motor neuronal function, with erectile dysfunction, Bodner, Haas, Krueger, and Seftel (1999) found that erection created by MUSE was less acceptable to the 15 patients tested than the erection created by intracavernosal injection therapy. The most common side effects are penile pain, 32%; urethral burning, 12%; minor urethral bleeding/spotting, 5%; and flu symptoms, 4%. Priapism and cavernosal fibrosis were evident in less than 0.1% of participants. Vaginal burning or itching was noted by 5.8% of the female partners, and it is recommended that a condom barrier be employed if the female partner is pregnant. Other experimental approaches include the use of transdermal nitroglycerin and/or transdermal nitroglycerin-minoxidil to induce erections (Baert, 1989; Cavallini, 1991; Owen et al., 1995). There are not enough data available on these new methods to judge their general applicability or efficacy.

Another approach to the pharmacotherapy of erectile dysfunction has been the use of dopaminergic agents. Earlier double-blind studies suggested that levodopa has efficacy in the treatment of erectile dysfunction (Benkert, Cronhach, & Kockott, 1982; Pierini & Nusimovich, 1981). Considerable attention is currently being given to the evaluation of apomorphine for the treatment of erectile problems. Lal and coworkers at the Montreal General Hospital observed that men being treated for alcoholism with aversive conditioning utilizing apomorphine reported spontaneous erections (Lal et al., 1987, 1991). Other clinicians have noted that patients being treated for Parkinson's disease with apomorphine reported spontaneous erections (O'Sullivan & Hughes, 1998). Three separate double-blind trials have established that subcutaneous apomorphine is effective in eliciting erections approximately 20 minutes after administration (Danjou, Alexander, Warat, Combiez, & Perch, 1988; Lal, Ackman, Thavundayil, Kieley, and Etienne, 1984; Segraves, Bari, Segraves, & Spirnak, 1991). It has been hypothesized that apomorphine acts at the level of the paraventricular nucleus of the brain (Chen, Chan, & Chang, 1999). Early data suggest a significant improvement in erectile activity over placebo (Heaton, Morales, Adams, Johnston, & el-Rashidy, 1999; Mulhall & Goldstein, 1999). The main side effect appears to be nausea, which is counteracted with an oral antiemetic. The clinical utility of both subcutaneous and sublingual apomorphine has been limited by its propensity to cause nausea. Apomorphine has less efficacy than the PDE 5 inhibitors and is not available in the U.S. market (Gontero et al., 2005; Perimenis et al., 2004; Eardley, Wright, MacDonagh, Hole, & Edwards, 2004).

Phentolamine is a mixed alpha 1 and 2 antagonist. Alpha 1 adrenoceptor stimulation mediates corpora cavernosal vasoconstriction. Postjunctional alpha-2 receptors may also subserve a part of cavernosal muscle contraction. More than 700 patients with erectile dysfunction have been studied in double-blind, placebo-controlled trials studying the efficacy of oral phentolamine. In these trials the placebo response was approximately 20%, whereas phentolamine was effective in 30 to 40% of patients. The major side effects were rhinitis, headache, and dizziness (Wyllie & Anderson, 1999). Most of these studies are unpublished. Phentolamine has much less efficacy than sildenafil (Ugarte & Hurtado-Coll, 2002) and is not available on the U.S. market.

Several double-blind, placebo-controlled studies have found that naltrexone, an opiate receptor antagonist, increases the frequency of early-morning erections (Brennemann, Stitz, van Ahlen, Brensing, & Klingmuller, 1993; van Ahlen, Piechota, Kias, Brennemann, & Klingmuller, 1995). Unfortunately, two out of the three studies found that naltrexone increased early-morning erections without improving erectile function in partner sexual activities. It may

have some utility in increasing libido in men (Sathre, Komisarul, Ladas, & Godbole, 2001).

A variety of other substances are being evaluated as possible oral erectogenic agents (Gonzalez-Cadavid & Rajfer, 1999). It appears imperative that more mental health professionals become involved in investigating which forms of therapy are best suited to which types of patients and the cost-effectiveness of different approaches. From a clinical perspective, one would suspect that certain patients with erectile difficulties might benefit from cognitive-behavioral treatment combined with pharmacotherapy. This remains clinical speculation, and there is no evidence concerning the indicators for combined therapy as opposed to behavior therapy alone or pharmacotherapy alone

With the advent of new vector systems for gene therapy, this novel therapeutic approach for the treatment of ED may become a reality. The use of a genetic approach to restore neuronal signaling in injured nerves of the neurovascular bundle in patients' postradical prostatectomy represents an attractive form of therapy for this subset of patients with ED.

Vacuum Tumescence Devices

An alternative strategy for the man who is resistant to trying or has not benefited from psychotherapy and who finds the concept of self-injection of a substance into the penis somewhat aversive is the use of the external vacuum erection device. The vacuum device is placed over the penis, and a negative pressure facilitates blood flow into the penis, producing an erection. A tension ring (rubber band) is slipped from the base of the vacuum erection device to the base of the penis, maintaining the erection. Different studies utilizing diverse patient populations have reported that between 70 and 100% of men will achieve erections using this device (Althof & Seftel, 1995; Turner, Althof, & Levine, 1992). Dropout rates are around 20%. Side effects are minimal, and there is no evidence of significant negative psychological effects from employing this device. With the introduction of effective oral erectogenic agents, the use of mechanical aids has decreased.

Premature Ejaculation

Psychosocial Treatments

Since the early 1970s, an array of individual, conjoint, and group therapy approaches employing behavioral strategies such as stop-start (Masters & Johnson, 1970) or squeeze techniques (Semans, 1956) have evolved as the psychological treatments of choice for rapid ejaculation (Levine, 1992a). It is now known that the impressive initial posttreatment success rates, ranging from 60 to 95% (Hawton & Catalan, 1986; Hawton, Catalan, Martin, & Fagg, 1986; Masters & Johnson, 1966), are not necessarily sustainable. Three years after treatment, success rates dwindled to 25% (Bancroft & Coles, 1976; DeAmicus et al., 1985; Hawton et al., 1986).

Men have resorted to wearing multiple condoms, applying desensitization ointment to the penis, repeatedly masturbating prior to intercourse, not allowing partners to stimulate them, or distracting themselves by performing complex mathematical computations while making love to overcome rapid ejaculation. These tactics, however creative, curtail the pleasures of lovemaking and are generally unsuccessful.

The prevailing opinions regarding the etiology of rapid ejaculation have typically assumed that the dysfunction was either psychological or learned, depending on the theorist's assumptions about how the mind operates. Clinicians surmised that the lowered ejaculatory threshold stemmed from anxiety regarding unresolved fears of the vagina, hostility toward women, interpersonal conflicts with a particular partner, or conditioning patterned on early hurried sexual experiences with prostitutes or hasty lovemaking in the backseat of a car. Once established, performance anxiety was thought to maintain the rapid ejaculatory pattern. Strassberg, Kelly, Carroll, and Kirchzer (1987) and Godpodinoff (1989) independently speculated that a subgroup of rapid ejaculators may have a neurophysiological vulnerability and that this biological vulnerability explains some failures of psychological treatments. There is still little evidence to support this most interesting notion. Carufel and Trudel (in press) have recently described a psychotherapeutic technique that consists of teaching the male to recognize various levels of sexual excitement and then learn ways to maintain arousal at high levels yet below the ejaculatory threshold. Early evidence suggests that this approach may be as effective as the start-stop technique and more effective than a waiting list control group.

Pharmacological Treatments

A large number of placebo-controlled, double-blind studies have demonstrated that fluoxetine, sertraline, clomipramine, and paroxetine can be used to delay ejaculatory latency in men with rapid ejaculation. Consistent findings have been obtained using a variety of outcome measures, including patient estimate of time between penetration and ejaculation, partner estimate, and patient or partner report of stopwatch readings. It appears that ejaculatory delay occurs only during active drug treatment and that sustained pharmacotherapy is necessary for most men to maintain a slower pattern of ejaculation. Chronic treatment with 20 to 40 mg paroxetine (Waldinger, Hengeveld, & Zwindman, 1994, 1997), 25 to 50 mg clomipramine (Althof et al., 1995; Kim & Seo, 1998), 50 to 200 mg sertraline (Biri et al., 1998; Kim & Seo, 1998; McMahon, 1998a, 1998b; Mendels, Cameram, & Sikes, 1995), and 20 mg fluoxetine (Haensel, Klem, Hop, & Slo, 1998; Kara et al., 1996) has been shown to increase ejaculatory control in men with rapid ejaculation.

Because some patients prefer not to take medication continuously for an episodic activity, some investigators have investigated the efficacy of various drugs taken as needed. Segraves, Saran, Segraves, and Meguire (1993) reported on a double-blind, placebo-controlled study of 25 to 50 mg of clomipramine taken 6 hours prior to anticipated sexual activity. At the beginning of the study, all patients had ejaculatory latencies of less than 60 seconds after penetration. On 25 mg and 50 mg of clomipramine, this latency increased to an average of 6.1 minutes and 8.4 minutes, respectively. In a similar study, Strassberg, de Gouveia Brazao, Rowland, Tan, & Slob (1999) found that 25 mg of clomipramine taken 4 to 6 hours prior to coitus increased ejaculatory latency from less than 1 minute to an average of 3.5 minutes. Two investigators have examined the efficacy of chronic pretreatment followed by intermittent dosing as needed. Kim and Paick (1999) reported that 2 weeks of 50 mg of daily sertraline followed by 50 to 100 mg taken at the day of anticipated coitus at 5:00 p.m. resulted in significant improvement. Patients increased ejaculatory latency from an average of 23 seconds to 4 to 5 minutes of chronic and intermittent dosing. From the study design, it is impossible to determine if the chronic pretreatment was necessary for the as-needed treatment to be effective. An interesting study by McMahon and Touma (1999) examined the role of chronic pretreatment for on-demand therapy and the relative efficacy of on-demand versus daily treatment with 20 mg paroxetine. Pretreatment ejaculatory latency was approximately 24 seconds. With chronic treatment of 20 mg paroxetine daily, the average ejaculatory latency increased to 4.5 minutes. Successful patients in this group were then switched to an on-demand dosing schedule of 20 mg paroxetine taken 3 to 4 hours prior to coitus. Thirty-two percent of the previously successful patients stated that they lost ejaculatory control upon switching to an on-demand schedule. Another group of men was started on an on-demand dosing regime of 20 mg paroxetine 3 to 4 hours prior to coitus. This group reported an increase of ejaculatory latency to 1.5 minutes, which was less than the average latency of 3.9 minutes in the group switched from chronic to on-demand dosing. The available data suggest that clomipramine can be started as an on-demand drug, whereas paroxetine and sertraline might be more effective if on-demand use was preceded by chronic dosing.

Two different investigations have compared the relative efficacy of various serotonergic antidepressants on ejaculatory control in men with rapid ejaculation. Waldinger, Hengeveld, Zwindman, and Olivier (1998) investigated the relative efficacy of 20 mg paroxetine, 20 mg fluoxetine, and 50 mg sertraline and 100 mg fluvoxamine on ejaculatory delay. In this 6-week trial, paroxetine was the most effective, followed by fluoxetine and then sertraline. Fluvoxamine was not significantly different from placebo. Kim and Seo (1998) studied the effects of 4 weeks of daily therapy with fluoxetine, sertraline, or clomipramine. Clomipramine was the most effective, followed by sertraline. Fluoxetine was not statistically different from placebo. A number of investigators have investigated whether men with rapid ejaculation can be distinguished from men with good ejaculatory control on various measures, including sensory thresholds and somatosensory evoked potentials (Paick, Jeong, & Park, 1998; Xin, Choi, Rha, & Choi, 1997; Yilmaz, Tatlisen, Turan, Arman, & Ekmekcioglu, 1999). Findings to date have not been consistent. Dapoxetine, a serotonin reuptake inhibitor, is being investigated as a treatment for rapid ejaculation. To date, there is no evidence as to whether it will offer any advantages over existing compounds.

Topical anesthetic creams and sprays have also been found to be effective in delaying ejaculation. Prilocaine-lidocaine formulations have been demonstrated to be effective (Atikeler, Cecil, & Senol, 2002; Basuto & Galindo, 2004; Berkovitch, Keresteci, & Koren, 1995; Henry & Morales, 2003). Another approach is the use of SS-cream, a topical agent made from the extracts of nine natural products. It is applied to the glans penis 1 hour before sexual intercourse (Xin, Choi, & Lee, 2000). In placebo-controlled, double-blind studies, this compound significantly improved ejaculation latency and sexual satisfaction (Choi, Jung, & Moon, 2000; Xin et al., 2000). SS-cream increases the penile sensory threshold in a dose-dependent manner and has side effects that include mild local burning and mild pain.

There have been case reports that sildenafil may help in the treatment of rapid ejaculation (Chen, Mabjeesh, & Matzkin, 2003; Salonia, Maga, & Columbo, 2002). However, a recent controlled study did not find evidence of efficacy of sildenafil in the treatment of premature ejaculation (McMahon et al., 2005).

A study by Kim et al. in 2004 found that the use of hyaluronic acid gel for glans penis augmentation was safe and effective in reducing the sensitivity of the glans penis and is a promising treatment for hypersensitivity of the glans penis in premature ejaculation.

Female Orgasmic Disorder

Spence (1991) offers a cogent summary of the dilemmas to be considered in assessing the efficacy of psychological therapy for women with orgasmic disorders. The primary issue remains unresolved: is success predicated solely on coital orgasm, or orgasm through any means, or by a subjective rating of increased satisfaction within the sexual relationship? Adding to the confusion is the media's constant reinforcement of unrealistic expectations from sexual encounters. Both men and women are led to believe that all women can easily and regularly achieve intense multiple orgasms from intercourse alone.

Several studies (Kuriansky & Sharpe, 1981; Kuriansky, Sharpe, & O'Connor, 1982; Riley & Riley, 1978; Spence, 1991) have documented the success of masturbatory training programs in facilitating orgasm in women who have never achieved orgasm. Initial success rates range between 70% and 90%, with women being treated individually, in couples, or groups, or exposed to either videotapes or written material concerning masturbatory training programs. Kuriansky and Sharpe (1981) reported that 15% of their subjects were not able to sustain orgasmic achievement at a 2-year follow-up.

Whatever the success in achieving orgasm via masturbatory training, it begins to diminish as the woman moves from self-induced orgasm to partner-induced orgasm through manual or oral stimulation or intercourse-induced orgasm without manual stimulation. Immediately posttherapy, Kuriansky reported 89% of women achieved orgasm by themselves, 21% within the "context of a partner encounter," and 16% with intercourse alone. Heiman and LoPiccolo (1983) reported a two- to threefold (35 to 40% success rate) increase in coital orgasm at a 3-month follow-up. See Table 19.4 for a summary of psychotherapy outcome studies.

The long-term results for female orgasmic dysfunction differ in two significant directions from treatments of other sexual disorders. First, over time, women demonstrate an increased capacity to achieve orgasm in partner-related as well as coital encounters. Within 2 years, women achieved greater facility in achieving orgasm within the context of a partner encounter (47%) and via intercourse (26%). In addition, those women who dropped out of a treatment program also reported improved orgasmic functioning 2 years after beginning therapy. Second, the prognosis appears more positive for women with lifelong orgasmic dysfunction than for women who acquire the dysfunction after a period of normal function. These fascinating findings can be explained by (a) practice, (b) reinforcement by success, (c) decreased inhibition, and (d) increased harmony with the body and willingness to generate pleasurable internal sensations that culminate in orgasm. The worse outcome for an acquired dysfunction occurs when the problem is posited to result from psychological causes (relationship deterioration).

A case report by Ashton in 2004 cites Vardenafil as being effective in reversing selective serotonin receptor inhibitor–induced anorgasmia in a woman with no other sexual complaints.

Male Orgasmic Disorder

Male orgasmic disorder or delayed or absent ejaculation is found in only 3 to 8% of men (Hawton, 1982; Masters & Johnson, 1970; Spector & Carey, 1990). There are no large-scale, long-term controlled outcome studies of men in whom this is considered a purely psychogenic condition. There are two antithetical points of view for understanding this dysfunction: an inhibition model and a desire-deficit model. Treatment efforts are guided by the assumptions underlying these contrary models. When seen through the lens of the inhibition mode, behaviorists assume that the man is not receiving sufficient stimulation to reach the orgasmic threshold. Dynamic clinicians who adhere to the inhibition model assume that the symptom is a conscious or unconscious expression of the man's aggression (i.e., withholding or depriving his partner of something the partner desires). Treatment efforts therefore aim to increase excitement through prolonged, intense, rough stimulation or by interpreting the man's aggressive impulses. Masters and Johnson (1970) reported a failure rate of 17.6% using a combination of sensate focus, vigorous noncoital penile stimulation, and modifications in intercourse technique. Schnellen (1968) reported that 81% of men who prior to treatment were anorgasmic were successful in reaching orgasm through vibrator stimulation.

Apfelbaum (1989) presented an alternative model, suggesting that delayed ejaculation is a desire disorder disguised as a performance disorder. He criticized those employing the inhibition model, stating that intense stimulation is a demanding coercive strategy that heightens performance anxiety. His treatment efforts were aimed at having the man acknowledge his lack of both desire to have intercourse and arousal during intercourse.

TABLE 19.4 Psychotherapy Outcome Studies of Female Orgasmic Disorder

Study	Type	Outcome	Follow-up
Masters & Johnson (1970)	3	Failure rate 16.6–22.8%	Failure rate 17.6%
Kuriansky et al. (1982)	3	95% success	84% sustained
Heiman & Lo Piccolo (1983)	3	15–40% success	Sustained
DeAmicus et al. (1985)	3	64–76% success	Sustained
Kilmann et al. (1986)	3	25% improved	Sustained

Dyspareunia and Vaginismus

Dyspareunia, or painful coitus, is a common sexual complaint among women, accounting for 10 to 15% of female respondents in community-based surveys (Rosen & Leiblum, 1995). Physical factors (hymeneal scarring, infection, sexually transmitted diseases, estrogen deficiency, pelvic inflammatory disease, and vulvar vestibulitis) frequently underlie this condition (Pukall, Payne, Kao, Khalife, & Binik, 2005); however, even if the etiology is physical, there is likely to be a conditioned psychological response that may require psychological intervention (Sarrel & Sarrel, 1989; Schover, Youngs, & Canata, 1992). In addition, psychosocial factors alone, such as relationship discord and prior sexual abuse, have been cited as etiological agents (Binik et al., 1995; Rosen & Leiblum, 1989, 1995).

Vaginismus, or the persistent and recurrent involuntary spasm of the musculature of the outer third of the vagina, has been characterized as a psychosomatic disorder, a phobia, a conditioned response, or a conversion reaction (Schultz & Van de Wiel, 2005). A number of etiological factors, such as specific trauma(s), interpersonal and intrapsychic conflict, penetration anxiety, and multiple organic pathologies, cause this dysfunction. Approximately 10 to 30% of the male partners of these women report erectile or ejaculatory dysfunctions (Levine, 1988, 1992a).

Vaginismus is typically treated through a combination of (a) banning intercourse, (b) in vivo graduated self-insertion of dilators of increasing size, (c) systematic densensitization, (d) Kegel exercises, and (e) interpretation of resistance and psychodynamic fears. Masters and Johnson (1970) reported a 100% success rate in their treatment of 29 women. Spence (1991) suggested that more treatment sessions are required when women (a) have experienced the dysfunction over extended periods of time, (b) have undergone surgery, (c) have thoughts of anatomical abnormality, and (d) have a negative attitude toward their genitals. The need for treatment sessions was related to a strong desire for pregnancy, presence of an assertive husband, and sexual knowledge on the woman's part.

Substance-Induced Sexual Dysfunction

The diagnostic entity of substance-induced sexual disorders (i.e., sexual disorders associated with drug intoxication and associated with the use of prescribed medication) was introduced in *DSM-IV*. A variety of chemical agents have been associated with sexual dysfunction. Most of the reports concern substances of abuse, antihypertensive agents, and psychiatric drugs (Segraves & Balon, 2004). Sexual dysfunction has long been assumed to be related to chronic alcohol abuse. In particular, it has been assumed that chronic alcohol abuse in males is associated with erectile dysfunction (Miller & Gold, 1988; Schiavi, 1990). Although less evidence is available concerning the effects of chronic alcohol abuse in females, most clinicians assume that chronic alcohol abuse may also be detrimental to female sexual function (Rosen, 1991). There is considerable evidence that chronic alcohol abuse has deleterious effects on hypothalamic-pituitary and testicular function (Schiavi, Stimmel, Mandeli, & White, 1995). Chronic alcohol abuse is associated with damage to the central nervous system, as manifested by dementia and Wernicke-Korsakoff syndrome. Peripheral polyneuropathy is also associated with myelin and axon degeneration as a common neurological complication of chronic alcoholism. Thus, there are several mechanisms by which chronic alcohol abuse could cause sexual dysfunction.

In reality, the controlled evidence linking chronic alcohol abuse to sexual dysfunction is limited and concerns only male alcoholics. Much of the available evidence contains numerous methodological flaws. The major studies to date have either been retrospective (Lemere & Smith, 1973), lacked control groups, or had other methodological flaws, such as including patients on disulfiram treatment (Jensen, 1974) or other pharmacological agents associated with sexual dysfunction (Whalley, 1978). Studies utilizing nocturnal penile tumescence as a measure of erectile function have reported decreased erectile capacity in patients with chronic alcoholism. These studies have methodological flaws, such as studying the patient shortly after detoxification (Snyder & Karacan, 1981). Because disulfiram treatment has been shown to decrease erectile capacity (Tan, Johnson, Lambie, Vijayasenah, & Whitside, 1984), it is important that studies clearly indicate whether or not patients have received this treatment

Schiavi et al. (1995) investigated sexual function and nocturnal penile tumescence and conducted various laboratory tests, including those of testosterone, luteinizing hormone, prolactin, and liver enzymes, in 20 healthy alcoholics with at least a 10-year history of problem drinking who had been abstinent for 2 months and were in a stable sexual relationship as compared with an age-matched nonalcoholic control group. Surprisingly, they found no significant differences between the two groups in sexual function, nocturnal penile tumescence, or hormone levels. These data suggest that a history of alcoholism in the absence of significant hepatic or gonadal failure and in a period of sobriety may be compatible with normal sexual function. It should be noted that this population might represent a particular subgroup of patients with chronic alcoholism in that they were disease free and capable of maintaining a stable sexual relationship.

Evidence concerning the effects of narcotics on sexual function has been uniform and convincing. The evidence consists of anecdotal reports, surveys, and clinical studies. All the studies are uniform in finding diminished libido while the person is on narcotics (Abel, 1985). Retrospective studies suggest that normal libido returns during drug-free periods (Segraves, Madsen, Carver, & Davis, 1985). Cocaine and amphetamine use has been reported to cause increased libido and spontaneous erections (Abel, 1985). However, there is evidence that chronic abuse of these agents may lead to decreased libido and other sexual dysfunctions (Siegel, 1982). It is unclear whether sexuality returns to the baseline during abstinence from these agents.

A number of clinical series and case reports establish the likelihood of a high frequency of sexual disorders, including decreased libido, erectile dysfunction, and anorgasmia while individuals are on many antihypertensive agents (e.g., spironolactone, chlorthalidone, alpha methyldopa, reserpine, guanethidine, prapranolol, clonidine, verapamil, and infidipine; Rosen & Leiblum, 1995; Segraves, 1988a; Segraves et al., 1985), Unfortunately, most of these reports do not include control groups or utilize appropriate measures of sexual function.

In one of the few properly controlled studies in this area of inquiry, Rosen and Kostis (1991) compared sexual function in men randomly assigned to propranolol or a placebo for 3 months. Propranolol therapy led to a significant decrease in the frequency of full erections. Among antihypertensive drugs, alpha blockers such as prazosin and labetalol appear to have the lowest incidence of drug-induced sexual dysfunction, although these agents may be associated with ejaculatory inhibition (Foreman & Doherty, 1993).

Psychiatric drugs have also been reported to cause sexual problems. This is true of almost all classes of psychiatric drugs (Segraves, 2003b). Most of the evidence concerning the action of these drugs comes from clinical reports, and only a handful of controlled studies have been performed. Benzodiazepines have been frequently reported to cause delay in orgasm. This has been reported with chlordiazepoxide, lorazepam, diazepam, and alprazolam (Segraves, 1995a, 1995b). A double-blind controlled study by Riley and Riley (1988) demonstrated a dose-response relationship between diazepam dose and orgasmic delay. There have been reports of association of antipsychotic agents such as thioridazine, chlorpromazine, trifluoroperazine, and haloperidol with either decreased libido or erectile problems. Ejaculatory problems have been reported with thioridazine, chlorpromazine, chlorprothixine, mesoridazine, perphenazine, trifluoroperazine, and risperidone. The one double-blind, controlled study in this area of inquiry utilized minimal drug dosages and is thus of little value for this review (Tennett, Bancroft, & Cass, 1972). Aizenberg, Shiloh, Zamishlany, & Weizman (1996) reported that the addition of low-dose imipramine would offset sexual dysfunction induced by thioridazine. This report has not been replicated by other clinicians. Antipsychotic-induced sexual dysfunction has been reported to correlate with prolactin elevation. There has been interest in whether the newer prolactin-sparing antipsychotics would have a lower incidence of sexual dysfunction. At this point, the evidence is inconclusive, partly because of the high prevalence of sexual problems in patients with untreated schizophrenia (Aizenberg et al., 1995; Montejo et al., 1998) and partly because of methodological problems in assessment. Most reports are in agreement that risperidone causes more sexual dysfunction than olanzapine (Tran et al., 1997) and that the sexual problems with risperidone appear dose related (Marder & Meibach, 1994). The evidence concerning the relative incidence of sexual side effects on prolactin-sparing and traditional antipsychotics is in conflict (Hummer et al.; 1999; Montejo et al., 1998). There have been case reports of antipsychotic-induced sexual dysfunction being reversed by sildenafil (Salerian et al., 2000; Segraves, 1999).

Most of the antidepressants available in the United States have been reported to cause sexual dysfunction, with the possible exceptions of bupropion, mintazapine, and nefazodone (Segraves, 1995a, 1995b). This phenomenon has been confirmed in double-blind studies of many of the antidepressants (Feiger, Shrivastava, Wisselink, & Wilcox, 1996; Harrison et al., 1985; Kowalski, Stanley, & Dennerstein, 1985; Monteiro, Noshivani, Marks, & Lelliott, 1987; Segraves et al., 2000). A variety of interventions have been suggested for antidepressant-induced sexual dysfunction. These include drug holidays, changing time of dose, lowering dose, waiting for tolerance to develop, and the use of antidotes. Numerous antidotes have been reported in case reports. These include the addition of bupropion, mirtazapine, nefazodone, yohimbine, cyprohepatadine, amphetamine, and many others (Rosen, Seidman, et al., 1999). The only antidotes proven effective in double-blind trials are sildenafil (Hargreave, 1998) and buspirone (Landen, Eriksson, Agren, & Fahlen, 1999). In a controlled study of clomipramine in patients with obsessive-compulsive disorder, Monteiro et al (1987) reported that this drug significantly interfered with orgasm in all subjects who took a dose in excess of 100 mg. Many subjects experienced total anorgasmia.

FUTURE DEVELOPMENTS

The release of sildenafil has contributed to an explosion of research concerning the pharmacological treatment of human sexual disorders. A beneficial result of the search for a treatment for female sexual dysfunction has been the appreciation of the role of biological factors in female sexuality. Desire disorders are the most common female sexual complaint. This has contributed to a search for compounds that affect sexuality by acting on the central nervous system. This work will undoubtedly contribute to a better understanding of the neurophysiological substrates of human libido. Research documenting how these interventions might be optimally employed in differing psychosocial contexts will be a natural outcome of finding new pharmacological interventions for sexual difficulties. Normal sexual function involves a complicated interactive sequencing of biological, social, relational, and individual psychological events, and effective interventions will require an appreciation of the potential complexity of these different interactive influences. This appreciation is not evident in many contemporary clinical trials.

Some specific areas of advance appear almost certain to occur in the near future. More effective pharmacological treatments for sexual disorders will result in refinement of our diagnostic assessment. Pharmacotherapeutic advances will undoubtedly highlight the need for a greater understanding of the interaction of biological and psychosocial influences on sexual behavior. This understanding will undoubtedly lead to integrative biological psychosocial therapies and delineation of when therapies should be combined or used in isolation.

REFERENCES

Abel, L. (1985). *Psychoactive drugs and sex.* New York: Plenum Press.

Ackerman, M., & Carey, M. (1995). Psychology's role in the assessment of erectile dysfunction: Historical precedents, current knowledge, and methods. *Journal of Consulting and Clinical Psychology, 63,* 862–876.

Aizenberg, D., Shiloh, R., Zemishlany, Z., & Weizman, A. (1996). Low-dose imipramine for thioridazine-induced male orgasmic disorder. *Journal of Sex and Marital Therapy, 22,* 225–229.

Aizenberg, D., Zemishlany, Z., Dorfman-Etrog, P., & Weizman, A. (1995). Sexual dysfunction in male schizophrenic patients. *Journal of Clinical Psychiatry, 56,* 137–144.

Althof, S. (1989). Psychogenic impotence: Treatment of men and couples. In R. C. Rosen & S. R. Leiblum (Eds.), *Principles and practice of sex therapy: Update for the 1990s* (pp. 237–268). New York: Guilford Press.

Althof, S. E. (1995a). Pharmacological treatment for rapid ejaculation: Preliminary strategies, concerns and questions. *Sex and Marital Therapy, 10,* 247–251.

Althof, S. E. (1995b). Pharmacological treatment of rapid ejaculation. *Psychiatric Clinics of North America,8,* 85–94.

Althof, S., Levine, S., Corry, P., Risen, C., Stern, E., & Kurit, D. (1995). Clomipramine as a treatment for rapid ejaculation: A double-blind crossover trial of 15 couples. *Journal of Clinical Psychiatry, 56,* 402–407.

Althof, S., & Seftel, A. D. (1995). The evaluation and treatment of erectile dysfunction. *Psychiatric Clinics of North America, 18,* 171–192.

Althof, S., Turner, L., Levine, S., Kursh, E., Bodner, D., & Resnick, M. (1989). Why do so many people drop out from autoinjection therapy for impotence? *Journal of Sex and Marital Therapy*, 15, 121–129.

Althof, S., Turner, L., Levine, S., Risen, C., Bodner, D., Kursh, E., et al. (1991). Long-term use of intracavernous therapy in the treatment of erectile dysfunction. *Journal of Sex and Marital Therapy*, 17, 101–112.

American College of Cardiology and American Heart Association Consensus Group. (1999). Use of sildenafil (Viagra) in patients with cardiovascular disease. *Circulation*, 99, 168–177.

American Psychiatric Association. (1952). *Diagnostic and statistical manual of mental disorders*. Washington, DC: Author.

American Psychiatric Association. (1968). *Diagnostic and statistical manual of mental disorders* (2nd ed.). Washington, DC: Author.

American Psychiatric Association. (1980). *Diagnostic and statistical manual of mental disorders* (3rd ed.). Washington, DC: Author.

American Psychiatric Association. (1987). *Diagnostic and statistical manual of mental disorders* (3rd ed., rev.). Washington, DC: Author.

American Psychiatric Association. (1994). *Diagnostic and statistical manual of mental disorders* (4th ed.). Washington, DC: Author.

Apfelbaum, B. (1989). Retarded ejaculation: A much misunderstood syndrome. In R. C. Rosen & S. R. Leiblum (Eds.), *Principles and practice of sex therapy: Update for the 1990s* (pp. 168–206). New York: Guilford Press.

Araujo, A. B., Johannes, C. B., Derby, C. A., & McKinlay, J. B. (2000). Relation between psychosocial risk factors and incident erectile problems: Prospective results from the Massachusetts Male Aging Study. *American Journal of Epidemiology*, 152, 533–541.

Ashton, A. K. (2004). Vardenafil reversal of female anorgasmia. *American Journal of Psychiatry*, 161, 2133.

Assalian, P. (1988). Clomipramine in the treatment of premature ejaculation. *Journal of Sex Research*, 24, 231–235.

Atikeler, M., Cecil, I., & Senol, F. (2002). Optimal use of prilocaine-lidocaine cream in premature ejaculation. *Andrologia*, 34, 356–359.

Baert, H. C. (1989). Transcutaneous nitroglycerin therapy in the treatment of impotence. *Urology International*, 44, 309–312.

Bancroft, J., & Coles, L. (1976). Three years experience in a sexual problem clinic. *British Medical Journal*, 1, 1575–1577.

Bancroft, J. J., Sherwin, B. B., Alexander, G., Davidson, D. W., & Walker, A. (1991). Oral contraceptives and the sexuality of young women. *Archives of Sexual Behavior*, 20, 121–136.

Barada, J. H., & McKimmy, R. M. (1994). *Diagnosis and management of erectile dysfunction*. Philadelphia: Saunders.

Barnhart, K. T., Freeman, E., Grisso, J. A., Rader, D. J., Sammel, M., Kapoor, S., et al. (1999). The effect of dihydroepiandrosterone supplementation to symptomatic perimenopausal women on serum endocrine profiles, lipid profiles, and health-related quality of life. *Journal of Clinical Endocrinology and Metabolism*, 84, 3896–3902.

Basson, R. (1999). Androgen replacement for women. *Canadian Family Physician*, 45, 2100–2107.

Basson, R. . (2001). Female sexual response: The role of drugs in the management of female sexual dysfunction. *Obstetrics and Gynecology*, 98, 350–353.

Basson, R. (2003). Women's difficulties with low sexual desire and sexual avoidance. In S. Levine, C. Risen, & S. Althof (Eds.), *Handbook of clinical sexuality for mental health professionals* (pp. 111–130). New York: Brunner-Routledge.

Basson, R. (2005). Female hypoactive sexual desire disorder. In R. Balon & R. Segraves (Eds.), *Handbook of sexual dysfunction* (pp. 43–66). Boca Raton, FL: Taylor and Francis

Basson, R., Berman, I., Burnet, A., Derogatis, L., Ferguson, D., Fourcrou, J., et al. (2000). Report of the international consensus development conference on female sexual dysfunction: Definitions and classifications. *Journal of Urology*, 163, 888–893.

Basson, R., Leiblum, S., Brott, L., & Derogatis, L. (2000). Definitions of women's sexual dysfunction reconsidered: Advocating expansion and revision. *Journal of Psychosomatic Obstetrics and Gynecology*, 24, 221–234.

Basson, R., MacInnes, R., Smith, M. D., Hodgson, G., Spain, T., & Koppiker, N. (2000). Efficacy and safety of sildenafil in estrogenized women with sexual dysfunction associated with female sexual arousal disorder. *Obstetrics and Gynecology*, 95 (Suppl. 1), S-54.

Basson, R., Schultz, W., Binik, Y., Brotto, L., Eschenbach, E., Laan, E., et al. (2004). Women's sexual desire and arousal disorders and sexual pain. In T. Lue, Basson, R. R. Rosen, F. Guiliano, S. Khoury, & F. Montorsi (Eds.), *Sexual medicine: Sexual dysfunctions in men and women* (pp. 851–974). Plymouth, UK: Health Publications.

Basuto, W., & Galindo, C. (2004). Topical anaesthetic use for treating premature ejaculation: A double-blind randomized placebo-controlled study. *British Journal of Urology*, 93, 1018–1021.

Beck, J., Barlow, D., Sakheim, D. K., & Abrahamson, D. J. (1987). Shock threat and sexual arousal: The role of selective attention thought content and affective states. *Psychopharmacology, 24,* 165–172.

Benkert, O., Cronhach, G., & Kockott, G. (1982). Effect of L-dopa on sexually impotent patients. *Psychopharmacology, 23,* 91–95.

Bennett, H., Carpenter, J., & Barada, J. (1991). Improved vasoactive drug combination for pharmacological erection program. *Journal of Urology, 1,* 1564–1568.

Berkovich, M., Keresteci, A., & Koren, G. (1995). Efficacy of prilocaine-lidocaine cream in the treatment of premature ejaculation. *Journal of Urology, 154,* 1360–1361.

Berman, J., Berman, L., Toler, S., Gill, J., & Haughie, S. (2003). Efficacy and tolerability of sildenafil citrate in women with sexual arousal disorder. *Journal of Urology, 170,* 2333–2338.

Berman, J. R., Shuker, J. M., & Goldstein, I. (1999). Female sexual dysfunction. In C. C. Carson, R. S. Kirby, & I. Goldstein (Eds.), *Textbook of erectile dysfunction* (pp. 627–638). Oxford, UK: ISIS.

Binik, Y., Meana, U., Khalife, S., Bergener, S., Cohen, D., & Howe, D. (1995, March). *Painful intercourse: A controlled study.* Paper presented at the annual meeting of the Society for Sex Therapy and Research, New York.

Biri, H., Isen, K., Sinik, Z., Onaran, M., Kupeli, B., & Bozkiri, I. (1998). Sertraline in the treatment of premature ejaculation. *International Journal of Nephrology, 30,* 611–616.

Bodner, D. R., Haas, C. A. Krueger, B., & Seftel, A. D. (1999). Intraurethral alprostadil for treatment of erectile dysfunction in patients with spinal cord injury. *Urology, 53,* 199–202.

Bolour, S., & Braunstein, G. (2005). Testosterone therapy in women: A review. *International Journal of Impotence Research, 17,* 399–408.

Brady, J. P. (1966). Brevital-relaxation treatment of frigidity. *Behaviour Research and Therapy, 4,* 171–177.

Brennemann, W., Stitz, B., van Ahlen, H., Brensing, K., & Klingmuller, D. (1993). Treatment of idiopathic erectile dysfunction in men with the opiate antagonist naltrexone: A double blind study. *Journal of Andrology, 14,* 407–410.

Buster, J., Kingsberg, S., Aguirre, Q., Brown, C., Breaux, J., Buch, A., et al. (2005). Testosterone patch for low sexual desire in surgically menopausal women: A randomized trial. *Obstetrics and Gynecology, 105,* 944–952.

Carufel, F., & Trudel, G. (in press). Effects of a new functional-sexological treatment for premature ejaculation. *Journal of Sex and Marital Therapy.*

Cavallini, C. (1991). Minoxidil versus nitroglycerin: A prospective double blind controlled trial in transcutaneous erection facilitation for organic impotence. *Journal of Urology, 146,* 50–53.

Chen, J., Mabjeesh, N., & Matzkin, E. (2003). Efficacy of sildenafil as adjuvant therapy to selective serotonin reuptake inhibitor in alleviating early ejaculation. *Urology, 61,* 197–203.

Chen, K., Chan, J., & Chang, L. (1999). Dopaminergic neurotransmission at the paraventricular nucleus of hypothalamus in central regulation of penile erection in the rat. *Journal of Urology, 162,* 237–242.

Choi, H. K., Jung, G. W., & Moon, K. H. (2000). Clinical study of SS-cream in patients with lifelong premature ejaculation. *Urology, 55,* 257–261.

Clement, F., & Schmidt, C. (1983). The outcome of couple therapy for sexual dysfunctions using three different formats. *Journal of Sex and Marital Therapy, 9,* 67–81.

Cooper, A. J. (1969). Factors in male sexual inadequacy: A review. *Journal of Nervous Disease, 149,* 337–359.

Corona, G., Petrone, L., Mannucci, E., Jannini, E. A., Mansari, A., Giommmi, R., et al. (2004). Psychobiological correlates of rapid ejaculation in patients attending an andrologic unit for sexual dysfunctions. *European Urology, 46,* 615–622.

Cranston-Cuebas, M. A., & Barlow, D. H. (1990). Cognitive and affective contributions to sexual functioning. *Annual Review of Sex Research, 1,* 119–161.

Crowe, M. J., Gillan, P., & Golombok, S. (1981). Form and content in the conjoint treatment of sexual dysfunction: A controlled study. *Behavior Research and Therapy, 19,* 47–54.

Danjou, P., Alexander, L., Warat, D., Combiez, L., & Perch, A. J. (1988). Assessment of erectogenic properties of apomorphine and yohimbine in man. *Journal of Clinical Pharmacology, 26,* 733–739.

Davidson, J. M., Kwan, M., & Greenleaf, W. (1982). Hormonal replacement and sexuality in men. *Clinics in Endocrinology and Metabolism, 11,* 599–623.

Davis, S. R. (1998). The clinical use of androgens in female sexual disorders. *Journal of Sex and Marital Therapy, 24,* 153–163.

Davis, S. R. (1999). The therapeutic use of androgens in women. *Journal of Steroid Biochemistry and Molecular Biology, 69,* 171–184.

Davis, S., Davison, S., Donath, S., & Bell, R. (2005). Circulating androgen levels and self-reported sexual function in women. *Journal of the American Medical Association, 294,* 91–96.

DeAmicus, L. L., Goldberg, D. C., LoPicollo, J., Friedman, J., & Davies, L. (1985). Clinical follow-up of couples treated for sexual dysfunction. *Archives of Sexual Behavior, 14,* 467–489.

Dennerstein, L., Dudley, E. C., Hopper, J. L. & Burger, H. (1997). Sexuality, hormones and the menopause. *Maturitas, 26,* 83–93.

Dunn, K. M., Croft, P. R., & Hackett, G. I. (1999). Association of sexual problems with social, psychological, and physical problems in men and women: A cross sectional population survey. *Journal of Epidemiology and Community Health, 53,* 144–148.

Eardley, I., Wright, P., MacDonagh, R., Hole, J., & Edwards, A. (2004). An open-label randomized flexible dose crossover study to assess the comparative efficacy and safety of sildenafil citrate and apomorphine hydrochloride in men with erectile dysfunction. *British Journal of Urology, 93,* 1271–1275.

Ersner-Hershfield, R. R., & Kopel, S. (1979). Group treatment of preorgasmic women: Evaluation of partner involvement and spacing of sessions. *Journal of Consulting and Clinical Psychology, 47,* 750–759.

Feiger, A., Kiev, A., Shrivastava, R. K, Wisselink, P. G., & Wilcox, G. S. (1996). Nefazodone versus sertraline in outpatients with major depression: Focus on efficacy, tolerability, and effects on sexual dysfunction. *Journal of Clinical Psychiatry, 57*(Suppl.), 1–11.

Feldman, H. A., Goldstein, F., Hatzichristau, D. G., Krane, R. T., Segraves, M. D., & McKunlav, J. B. (1994). Impotence and its medical and psychosocial correlates: Results of the Massachusetts Male Aging Study. *Journal of Urology, 151,* 54–61.

Figueira, I., Possidente, E., Marques, C., & Hayes, K. (2001). Sexual dysfunction: A neglected complication of panic disorder and social phobia. *Archives of Sexual Behavior, 30,* 369–377.

Foreman, M., & Doherty, P. (1993). Experimental approaches for the development of pharmacological therapies for erectile dysfunction. In A. J. Riley, M. Peet, & C. Wilson (Eds.), *Sexual pharmacology* (pp. 97–113). Oxford, UK: Clarendon Press.

Gagnon, J., Rosen, R., & Leiblum, S. (1982). Cognitive and social aspects of sexual dysfunction: Sexual scripts in sex therapy. *Journal of Sex and Marital Therapy, 8,* 44–56.

Gayler, K. T., Conaglen, H. M., Hare, A., & Conaglen, J. V. (1999). The effect of gynecological surgery on sexual desire. *Journal of Sex and Marital Therapy, 25,* 81–88.

Gelfand, M. M. (1999). The role of androgens in surgical menopause. *American Journal of Obstetrics and Gynecology, 180,* 325–327.

Godpodinoff, J. L. (1989). Premature ejaculation: Clinical subgroups and etiology. *Journal of Sex and Marital Therapy, 15,* 130–134.

Goldstein, I., Lue, T., Padma-Nathan, H., Rosen, R., Steers, W., Wicker, P., et al. (1998). Oral sildenafil in the treatment of erectile dysfunction. *New England Journal of Medicine, 338,* 1397–1404.

Gontero, P., D'Antonio, R., Pretti, G., Fontana, F., Kocjancic, E, Allochis, G., et al. (2005). Clinical efficacy of apomorphine SL in erectile dysfunction of diabetic men. *International Journal of Impotence Research, 17,* 80–85.

Gonzalez-Cadavid, N. F., & Rajfer, J. (1999). Future therapeutic alternatives in the treatment of erectile dysfunction. In C. C. Carson, R. S. Kirby, & I. Goldstein (Eds.), *Textbook of erectile dysfunction* (pp. 355–364). Oxford, UK: ISIS.

Grazziotin, A. (2004, October). *Is there enough evidence for the pharmacologic treatment of female sexual dysfunction? New research in female sexual dysfunction.* CME Female Sexual Dysfunction at the 11th World Congress of the International Society for Sexual and Impotence Research, Buenos Aires, Argentina.

Guzick, D. S., & Hoeger, K. (2000). Sex, hormones, and hysterectomies. *New England Journal of Medicine, 343,* 730–731.

Haensel, S. M., Klem, T. M., Hop, W. C., & Slo, A. K. (1998). Fluoxetine and premature ejaculation. *Journal of Clinical Psychopharmacology, 18,* 72–77.

Hargreave, T. B. (1998). *Efficacy of sildenafil in the treatment of erectile dysfunction in patients with depression.* Glasgow, Scotland: CINP.

Harrison, W., Stewart, J., Ehrhardt, A., Rabkin, J., McGrath, P., Liebowitz, M., et al. (1985). A controlled study of the effects of antidepressants on sexual function. *Psychopharmacology Bulletin, 21,* 85–88.

Haslam, M. (1965). The treatment of psychogenic dyspareunia by reciprocal inhibition. *British Journal of Psychiatry, 111,* 280–287.

Hawton, K. (1982). The behavioral treatment of sexual dysfunction. *British Journal of Psychiatry, 140,* 94–101.

Hawton, K. (1995). Treatment of sexual dysfunctions by sex therapy and other approaches. *British Journal of Psychiatry, 161,* 307–314.

Hawton, K., & Catalan, J. (1986). Prognostic factors in sex therapy. *Behaviour Research and Therapy, 24,* 377–385.

Hawton, K., Catalan, J., & Fagg, J. (1992). Sex therapy for erectile dysfunction: Characteristics of couples, treatment outcome, and prognostic factors. *Archives of Sexual Behavior, 71,* 161–175.

Hawton, K., Catalan, J., Martin, P., & Fagg, J. (1986). Long-term outcome of sex therapy. *Behaviour Research and Therapy, 24*, 665–675.

Hawton, K., & Fagg, J, (1991). Low sexual desire and sex therapy: Results and prognostic factors. *Behaviour Research and Therapy, 29*, 217–224.

Hawton, K., Gath, D., & Day, A. (1994). Sexual function in a community sample of middle-aged women with partners: Effect of age, marital, socioeconomic, psychiatric, gynecological and menopausal factors. *Archives of Sexual Behavior, 23*, 375–395.

Heaton, J. P., Morales, A., Adams, M. A, Johnston, D., & el-Rashidy, R. (1999). Recovery of erectile function by oral administration of apomorphine. *Urology, 45*, 200–206.

Heiman, J., & LoPicolo, J. (1983). Clinical outcome of sex therapy. *Archives of General Psychiatry, 40*, 443–449.

Henry, R., & Morales, A. (2003). Topical lidocaine-prilocaine spray for the treatment of premature ejaculation: A proof of concept study. *International Journal of Impotence Research, 15*, 277–281.

Hoegler, K. M. & Guzick, D. S. (1999). Androgens in menopause. *Clinical Obstetrics and Gynecology, 42*, 883–894.

Hummer, M., Kemmler, G., Kurz, M., Kurzthaler, I., Oberhauser, H., & Fleischacher, W. W. (1999). Sexual disturbance during clozapine and haloperidol treatment for schizophrenia. *American Journal of Psychiatry, 156*, 631–633.

Hurlbert, D. F. (1993). A comparative study using orgasm consistency training in the treatment of women reporting hypoactive sexual desire. *Journal of Sexual and Marital Therapy, 19*, 41–55.

Jensen, S. B. (1974). Sexual function and dysfunction in younger married alcoholics. *Acta Psychiatrica Scandinavica, 59*, 543–549.

Johannes, C. B., Araujo, A B., Feldman, H. A., Derby, C. A., Kleinman, K. P., & McKinlay, J. B. (2000). Incidence of erectile dysfunction in men 40 to 69 years old: Longitudinal results from the Massachusetts Male Aging Study. *Journal of Urology, 163*, 460–463.

Jolly, E., Kroll, R., & Schifren, J. (2004, October). *Improved sexual function in naturally menopausal women using testosterone patch.* Paper presented at the annual meeting of the International Society Study Women's Sexual Health, Atlanta, Georgia.

Kaplan, H. S. (1974). *The new sex therapy: Active treatment of sexual dysfunctions.* New York: Brunner/Mazel.

Kara, H., Aydin, S., Yucel, M., Agargun, M. Y., Odabas, O., & Yilmaz, Y. (1996). The efficacy of fluoxetine in the treatment of premature ejaculation. *Journal of Urology, 156*, 1631–1632.

Kellet, J. (1993). The nature of human sexual desire and its modification by drugs. In J. Riley, M. Peet, & C. Wilson (Eds.), *Sexual pharmacology* (pp. 100–145). Oxford, UK: Clarendon Press.

Kennedy, S. H., Dickens, S. E., Eisfeld, B. S., & Bagby, R. M. (1999). Sexual dysfunction before antidepressant therapy in major depression. *Journal of Affective Disease, 56*, 201–208.

Kilmann, P. R., Milan, R. J., Boland, J. P., Nankin, H., Davidson, E., West, M. O., et al. (1987). Group treatment of secondary erectile dysfunction. *Journal of Sex and Marital Therapy, 13*, 168–182.

Kilmann, P. R., Mills, K., Caid, C., Davidson, E., Bella, B., Milan, R., et al. (1986). Treatment of secondary orgasmic dysfunction: An outcome study. *Archives of Sexual Behavior, 15*, 211–229.

Kim, S. C., & Seo, K. K. (1998). Efficacy and safety of fluoxetine, sertraline and clomipramine in patients with premature ejaculation. *Journal of Urology, 159*, 425–427.

Kim, S. W., & Paick, J. S. (1999). Short-term analysis of the effects of as needed use of sertraline for the treatment of premature ejaculation. *Urology, 54*, 544–547.

Kongkanand, A. (2000). Prevalence of erectile dysfunction in Thailand. *Thai Erectile Dysfunction Epidemiological Study Group, 23*(Suppl. 2), 77–80.

Kowalski, G., Stanley, R. D. & Dennerstein, L. (1985). The sexual side effects of antidepressant medication: A double blind comparison of two antidepressants in a non-psychiatric population. *British Journal of Psychiatry, 147*, 413–418.

Kuriansky, J. B., & Sharpe, L. (1981). Clinical and research implications of the evaluation of women's group therapy for anorgasmia: A review. *Journal of Sex and Marital Therapy, 7*, 268–277.

Kuriansky, J. B., Sharpe, L., & O'Connor, D. (1982). Treatment of anorgasmia: Long-term effectiveness of a short-term behavioral group therapy. *Journal of Sex and Marital Therapy, 8*, 29–43.

Laan, E., Everaerd, W., & Both, S. (2005). Female sexual arousal disorder. In R. Balon & R. Segraves (Eds.), *Handbook of sexual dysfunction* (pp. 123–154). Boca Raton, FL: Taylor and Francis.

Laan, E., Van Lunsen, R., Everaerd, W., Riley, A., Scott, E., & Boolell, M. (2002). The enhancement of vaginal vasocongestion in healthy premenopausal women. *Journal of Women's Health and Gender-Based Medicine, 11*, 357–365.

Lal, S., Ackman, D., Thavundayil, J. X., Kieley, M. E., & Etienne, P. C. (1984). Effect of apomorphine, a dopamine receptor agonist, on penile tumescence to normal subjects. *Progress in Neuropsychopharmacology, 8,* 695–699.

Lal, S., Kiely, M. E., Thavundyil, J. X., Stewart, J. D., Assalian, P., & Ackman, C. F. (1991). Effect of bromocriptine in patients with apomorphine-responsive erectile impotence: An open study. *Journal of Psychiatry and Neuroscience, 16,* 262–266.

Lal, S., Laryea, E., Thawndayil, J., Nir, N. P., Negrete, J., Ackman, D., et al. (1987). Apomorphine-induced penile tumescence in impotent patients: Preliminary findings. *Progress in Neuropsychopharmacology and Biological Psychiatry, 143,* 819–820.

Landen, M., Eriksson, F., Agren, H., & Fahlen, T. (1999). Effect of buspirone on sexual dysfunction in depressed men treated with selective serotonin reuptake inhibitors. *Journal of Clinical Psychopharmacology, 19,* 266–271.

Laumann, E., Nicolosi, A., Glasser, P., Paik, A., Gingell, C., Moreira, E., et al. (2005). Sexual problems among men and women aged 40 to 80 years: Prevalence and correlates identified in the Global Study of Sexual Attitudes and Behavior. *International Journal of Impotence Research, 17,* 39–57.

Laumann, E. O., Paik, A., & Rosen, R. (1999). Sexual dysfunction in the United States: Prevalence and predictors. *Journal of the American Medical Association, 281,* 537–544.

Lazarus, A. A. (1963). The treatment of chronic frigidity by systematic desensitization. *Journal of Nervous and Mental Disease, 136,* 272–278.

Leiblum, S., Pervin, L. A., & Campbell, H. C. (1983).The treatment of vaginismus. In S. R. Leiblum & R. Rosen (Eds.), *Principles and practice of sex therapy* (pp.167–194). New York: Guilford Press.

Leiblum, S. R. & Rosen, R. (Eds.). (1989). *Principles and practice of sex therapy: Update for the 1990s.* New York: Guilford Press.

Leiblum, S. R., Rosen, R., & Pierce, D. (1976). Group treatment format: Mixed sexual dysfunctions. *Archives of Sexual Behavior, 5,* 313–321.

Lemere, F., & Smith, J. (1973). Alcohol-induced sexual impotence. *American Journal of Psychiatry, 150,* 212–213.

Levine, S. B. (1988). *Sex is not simple.* Columbus: Ohio Psychology.

Levine, S. B. (1992a). Intrapsychic and interpersonal aspects of impotence: Psychogenic erectile dysfunction. In R. C. Rosen & S. R. Leiblum (Eds.), *Erectile disorders: Assessment and treatment* (pp. 198–225). New York: Guilford Press.

Levine, S. B. (1992b). *Sexual life: A clinician's guide.* New York: Plenum Press.

Levine, S. B., & Agle, D. (1978). The effectiveness of sex therapy for chronic secondary psychological impotence. *Journal of Sex and Marital Therapy, 4,* 235–258.

Levine, S. B., Althof, S., Turner, L., Risen, C., Bodner, D., Kursh, E. G., et al. (1989). Side effects of self-administration of intracavernosal papaverine and phentolamine for the treatment of impotence. *Journal of Urology, 141,* 54–57.

Lewis, R. W. (1998). Tranurethral alprostadil with MUSE vs intracavernosus alprostadil: A comparative study in 103 patients with erectile dysfunction. *International Journal of Impotence Research, 10,* 61–62.

LoPiccolo, J., Heiman, J., Hogan, D., & Roberts, C. (1985). Effectiveness of single therapists versus cotherapy teams in sex therapy. *Journal of Consulting and Clinical Psychology, 53,* 287–294.

LoPiccolo, J., & LoPiccolo, J. (1978). *Handbook of sex therapy.* New York: Plenum Press.

Marder, S. R., & Meibach, R. C. (1994). Risperidone in the treatment of schizophrenia. *American Journal of Psychiatry, 151,* 825–835.

Marks, I. M. (1981). Review of behavioral psychotherapy: 2. Sexual disorders. *American Journal of Psychiatry, 138,* 750–756.

Masters, W., & Johnson, V. (1966). *Human sexual response.* London: Churchill Livingstone.

Masters, W., & Johnson, V. (1970). *Human sexual inadequacy.* Boston: Little, Brown.

Maurice, W. (2005). Male hypoactive sexual desire disorder. In R. Balon & R. Segraves (Eds.), *Handbook of sexual dysfunction* (pp. 67–110). Boca Raton, FL: Taylor and Francis.

McCabe, M. P. (2001). Evaluation of a cognitive behavioral therapy program for people with sexual dysfunction. *Journal of Sex and Marital Therapy, 27,* 259–271.

McCarthy, B., & McCarthy, E. (1984). *Sexual awareness: Sharing sexual pleasure.* New York: Carroll and Graff.

McMahon, C. G. (1991). A comparison of the response to the intracavernosal injection of a combination of papaverine and phentolamine, prostaglandin E1 and a combination of all three in the management of impotence. *International Journal of Impotence Research, 3,* 113–121.

McMahon, C. G. (1998a). Treatment of premature ejaculation with sertraline hydrochloride. *International Journal of Impotence Research, 10,* 181–184.

McMahon, C. G. (1998b). Treatment of premature ejaculation with sertraline hydrochloride: A single-blind placebo controlled study. *Journal of Urology, 159,* 1935–1938.

McMahon, C. G., Stuckley, B., Andersen, M., & Purvis, K. (2005). Efficacy of sildenafil citrate (Viagra) in men with premature ejaculation. *Journal of Sexual Medicine*, 2, 368–375.

McMahon, C. G., & Touma, K. (1999). Treatment of premature ejaculation with paroxetine hydrochloride. *International Journal of Impotence Research*, 11, 241–245.

Mendels, J., Cameram, A., & Sikes, C. (1995). Sertraline treatment for premature ejaculation. *Journal of Clinical Psychopharmacology*, 15, 341–346.

Meston, C. M., & Heiman, J. R. (1998). Ephedrine-activated physiological sexual arousal in women. *Archives of General Psychiatry*, 55, 652–656.

Meyer, J. K. (1976). Psychodynamic treatment of the individual with a sexual disorder. In J. Meyer (Ed.), *Clinical management of sexual disorders* (pp. 120–135). Baltimore: Williams and Wilkins.

Miller, N. S., & Gold, M. S. (1988). The human sexual response and alcohol and drugs. *Journal of Substance Abuse Treatment*, 5, 171–177.

Minnen, A.V., & Kampman, M. (2000). The interaction between anxiety and sexual functioning in women with anxiety disorders. *Sex Relationship Therapy*, 15, 47–57.

Mohr, D. C. & Beuder, L. E. (1990). Erectile dysfunction: A review of diagnostic and treatment procedures. *Clinical Psychology Review*, 1, 123–150.

Monteiro, W. O., Noshivani, H. F., Marks, I. M., & Lelliott, P. T. (1987). Anorgasmia from clomipramine in obsessive-compulsive disorder: A controlled study. *British Journal of Psychiatry*, 51, 107–112.

Montejo, A. L., Llorca, G., Izquierdo, J. A., Ledesma, J., Iglesias, S. S., & Daniel, E. (1998). New antipsychotic induced sexual dysfunction: Comparative incidence of risperidone and olanzapine using a questionnaire. *American Psychiatric Association, New Research*, 152–153.

Morales, A., Surridge, D. H., & Marshall, P. G. (1987). Is yohimbine effective in the treatment of organic impotence? Results of a controlled trial. *Journal of Urology*, 137, 1168–1172.

Moreira, E., Brock, G., Galsser, D., Nicolosi, A., Laumann, E., Paik, A., et al. (2005). Help-seeking behavior for sexual problems: The global study of sexual attitudes and behavior. *International Journal of Clinical Practice*, 59, 6–16.

Mulhall, J. P., & Goldstein, I. (1999). Oral agents in the management of erectile dysfunction. In C. C. Carson, R. S. Kirby, & I. Goldstein (Eds.), *Textbook of erectile dysfunction* (pp. 317–322). Oxford, UK: ISIS.

Nemetz, G. H., Craig, K. D., & Reith, G. (1978). Treatment of female sexual dysfunction through symbolic modeling. *Journal of Consulting and Clinical Psychology*, 46, 62–73.

Nurnberg, H. G., Lauriello, J., Hensley, P. L., Parker, L. M., & Keith, S. J. (1999). Sildenafil for sexual dysfunction in women taking antidepressants. *American Journal of Psychiatry*, 156, 1664.

Obler, M. (1973). Systematic desensitization in sexual disorders. *Journal of Behavior Therapy and Experimental Psychiatry*, 4, 93–101.

O'Carroll, R. T., Segraves, M. D. F., & Bancroft, J. (1984). Testosterone for low sexual desire and erectile dysfunction in men. *British Journal of Psychiatry*, 145, 146–151.

Osterloh, L, Eardley, L, Carson, C., & Padma-Nathan, H. (1999). Sildenafil: A selective phosphodiesterase (PDE) inhibitor in the treatment of erectile dysfunction. In C. C. Carson, R. S. Kirby, & I. Goldstein (Eds.), *Textbook of erectile dysfunction* (pp. 285–308). Oxford, UK: ISIS.

O'Sullivan, J. D., & Hughes, A. J. (1998). Apomorphine-induced penile erections in Parkinson's disease. *Movement Disorders*, 13, 536–539.

Owen, J. A., Saunders, F., Harris, C., Fenemore, J., Reid, J., Surridge, D., et al. (1995). Modification of dysfunctional patterns of sexual response through autonomic arousal and false physiological feedback. *Journal of Consulting and Clinical Psychology*, 63, 604–613.

Padma-Nathan, H., Hellstrom, W. J. G., & Kaiser, F. E. (1997). Treatment of men with erectile dysfunction with transurethral aprostadil. *New England Journal of Medicine*, 33, 1–7.

Padma-Nathan, H., McCollough, A. R., Guiliano, F., Tolar, S., Wohlhuter, C., & Shpilsky, A. (2003, April). *Postoperative nightly administration of sildenafil citrate significantly improves the return of normal spontaneous erectile function after bilateral nerve-sparring radical prostatectomy*. Paper presented at the Annual Meeting of the American Urological Association, Chicago, IL.

Paick, J. S., Jeong, H., & Park, M. S. (1998). Penile sensitivity in men with premature ejaculation. *International Journal of Impotence Research*, 10, 247–250.

Palace, E. M. (1995). Modification of dysfunctional patterns of sexual response through autonomic arousal and false physiological feedback. *Journal of Consulting and Clinical Psychology*, 63, 604–615.

Palace, E. M., & Gorzalka, B. (1992). Differential patterns of arousal in sexually functional and dysfunctional women: Physiological and subjective components of sexual response. *Archives of Sexual Behavior, 21,* 135–159.

Parazzini, F., Menchini, F. F., Bortolottr, A., Calabro, A., Chatenoud, L., Col, E., et al. (2000). Frequency and determinants of erectile dysfunction in Italy. *European Urology, 37,* 43–49.

Perelman, M. (1976). *The treatment of premature ejaculation by time-limited, group sex therapy.* Unpublished doctoral dissertation, Columbia University, New York.

Perelman, M. (2005). Combination therapy for sexual dysfunction. In R. Balon & R. Segraves (Eds.), *Handbook of sexual dysfunction* (pp. 13–42). Boca Raton, FL: Taylor and Francis.

Perimenis, P., Markou, S., Gyftopoulas, K., Giannitsas, K., Athanasopoulos, A., Liatsikos, E., et al. (2004). Efficacy of apomorphine and sildenafil in men with nonarteriogenic erectile dysfunction: A comparative crossover study. *Andrologia, 36,* 106–110.

Persky, H., Lief, H. L., & Strauss, D. (1978). Plasma testosterone level and sexual behavior in couples. *Archives of Sexual Behavior, 7,* 157–162.

Pierini, A. A. & Nusimovich, B. (1981). Male diabetic sexual impotence: Effect of dopaminergic agents. *Archives of Andrology, 6,* 347–350.

Pinnock, C. B., Stapleton, A. M., & Marshall, R. (1999). Erectile dysfunction in the community: A prevalence study. *Medical Journal of Australia, 171,* 353–357.

Pukall, C. F., Payne, K. A., Kao, A., Khalife, A., & Binik, Y. (2005). Dyspareunia. In R. Balon & R. Segraves (Eds.), *Handbook of sexual dysfunction* (pp. 249–272). Boca Raton, FL: Taylor and Francis.

Rabo, S. (2000). Testosterone supplemental therapy after hysterectomy with or without concomitant oophorectomy: Estrogen is not enough. *Journal of Women's Health and Gender Based Medicine, 9,* 917–923.

Raboch, J., & Faltus, F. (1991). Sexuality of women with anorexia nervosa. *Acta Psychiatrica Scandinavica, 84,* 9–11.

Reid, K., Morales, A., Harris, C., Surridge, D. H., Condra, M., Owen, J., et al. (1987). Double-blind trial of yohimbine in the treatment of psychogenic impotence. *Lancet,* 421–424.

Reynolds, B. (1991). Psychological treatment of erectile dysfunction in men without partners: Outcome results and new direction. *Journal of Sex and Marital Therapy, 2,* 136–145.

Riley, A. J., Goodman, R. E., Kellet, J. M., & Orr, R. (1989). Double-blind trial of yohimbine hydrochloride in the treatment of erection inadequacy. *Sexual and Marital Therapy, 4,* 17–26.

Riley, A. J. & Riley, E. J. (1978). A controlled study to evaluate directed masturbation in the management of primary orgasmic failure in women. *British Journal of Psychiatry, 133,* 404–409.

Riley, A. J. & Riley, E. J. (1988). The effect of single dose diazepam on female sexual response induced by masturbation. *Sexual and Marital Therapy, 1,* 49–53.

Rosen, R. C. (1991). Alcohol and drug effects on sexual response: Human experiment and clinical studies. *Annual Review of Sex Research, 2,* 119–179.

Rosen, R. C., & Beck, J. G. (1988). *Patterns of sexual arousal: Psychophysiological processes and clinical applications.* New York: Guilford Press.

Rosen, R. C., & Kostis, J. B. (1991, July). *Sexual sequelae of antihypertensive drugs.* Paper presented at the 13th annual meeting of the Society of Behavioral Medicine, Washington, DC.

Rosen, R. C., & Leiblum, S. R. (1989). Assessment and treatment of desire disorders. In R. C. Rosen & S. R. Leiblum (Eds.), *Principles and practice of sex therapy: Update for the 1990s* (pp. 1–18). New York: Guilford Press.

Rosen, R. C., & Leiblum, S. R. (1995). Treatment of sexual disorders in the 1990s: An integrated approach. *Journal of Clinical and Consulting Psychology, 63,* 877– 990.

Rosen, R. C., Phillips, N. A., Gendrano, N. C., & Ferguson, D. M. (1999). Oral phentolamin and female sexual arousal disorder: A pilot study. *Journal of Sex and Marital Therapy, 25,* 137–144.

Rosen, R., Seidman, S. N., Menza, M. A., Roose, S. P., & Shabsign, R. (1999, March). *Effective treatment of erectile dysfunction improves symptoms of depression.* Poster presented at World Congress of Psychiatry, Hamburg.

Salerian, A. J., Deibler, W. E., Vittore, B. J., Geyer, S. D., Drell, L., Mimirani, N., et al. (2000). Sildenafil for psychotropic-induced sexual dysfunction. *Journal of Sex and Marital Therapy, 3,* 156–176.

Salonia, A., Maga, A., & Columbo, R. (2002). A prospective study comparing paroxetine alone to paroxetine plus sildenafil in patients with early ejaculation. *Journal of Urology, 168,* 2486–2490.

Sarrel, P. M. (1999). Psychosocial effects of menopause: The role of androgens. *American Journal of Obstetrics and Gynecology, 180,* 319–324.

Sarrel, P., Dobay, B., & Witta, B. (1998). Estrogen and estrogen-androgen replacement in postmenopausal women dissatisfied with estrogen only therapy: Sexual behavior and neuroendocrine responses. *Journal of Reproductive Medicine, 43,* 847–856.

Sarrel, P., & Sarrel, L. (1989). Dyspareunia and vaginismus. In *American Psychiatric Association Task Force on Treatments of Psychiatric Disorders* (Vol. 3, pp. 2291–2298). Washington, DC: American Psychiatric Press.

Sathre, R. S., Komisarul, B. R., Ladas, A. K., & Godbole, S. V. (2001). Naltrexone-induced augmentation of sexual response in man. *Archives of Medical Research, 32,* 221–226.

Scharf, D. E. (1985). *The sexual relationship: An object relations view of the family.* London: Routledge and Kegan Paul.

Schiavi, R. C. (1990). Chronic alcoholism and male sexual function. *Journal of Sex and Marital Therapy, 16,* 23–33.

Schiavi, R. C., Stimmel, B., Mandeli, J., & White, D. (1995). Chronic alcoholism and male sexual function. *American Journal of Psychiatry, 152,* 1045–1051.

Schmidt, W. C. (1995). Sexual psychopathology and DSM-IV. In J. Oldham & B. Riba (Eds.), *American Psychiatric Press review of psychiatry* (Vol. 14, pp. 719–733). Washington, DC: American Psychiatric Press.

Schnellen, T. (1968). Introduction of ejaculation by electrovibration. *Fertility and Sterility, 19,* 566–569.

Schover, L. R, Youngs, D., & Canata, R. (1992). Psychosexual aspects of the evaluation and management of vulvar vestibularis. *American Journal of Obstetrics and Gynecology, 167,* 630–638.

Schreiner-Engel, P., & Schiavi, R. (1986). Lifetime psychopathology in individuals with low sexual desire. *Journal of Nervous and Mental Disease, 174,* 646–651.

Schultz, W., & Van de Wiel, H. (2005). Vaginismus. In R. Balon & R. Segraves (Eds.), *Handbook of sexual dysfunction* (pp. 273–292). Boca Raton, FL: Taylor and Francis.

Segraves, R. T. (1988a). Drugs and sex. In S. R. Leiblum & R. C. Rosen (Eds.), *Sexual desire disorders* (pp. 313–347). New York: Guilford Press.

Segraves, R. T. (1988b). Hormones and libido. In S. R. Leiblum & R. C. Rosen (Eds.), *Sexual desire disorders* (pp. 271–312). New York: Guilford Press.

Segraves, R. T. (1989). Effects of psychotropic drugs on human erection and ejaculation. *Archives of General Psychiatry, 46,* 275–284.

Segraves, R. T. (1995a). Antidepressant-induced orgasm disorder. *Journal of Sex and Marital Therapy, 21,* 192–201.

Segraves, R. T. (1995b). Psychopharmacological influences on human sexual behavior. In J. M. Oldham & M. Riba (Eds.), *American Psychiatric Press review of psychiatry* (Vol. 14, pp. 697–718). Washington, DC: American Psychiatric Press.

Segraves, R. T. (1999). Two additional uses for sildenafil in psychiatric patients. *Journal of Sex and Marital Therapy, 25,* 265–266.

Segraves, R. T. (2002). Female sexual disorders: Psychiatric aspects. *Canadian Journal of Psychiatry, 47,* 419–425.

Segraves, R. T. (2003a). Emerging therapies for female sexual dysfunction. *Expert Opinion on Emerging Drugs, 8,* 515–522.

Segraves, R. T. (2003b). Recognizing and reversing sexual side effects of medications. In S. Levine, C. Risen, & S. Althof (Eds.), *Handbook of clinical sexuality for mental health professionals* (pp 377–392). New York: Brunner-Routledge.

Segraves, R. T., & Balon, R. (2004). *Sexual pharmacology: Fast facts.* New York: Norton.

Segraves, R. T., Bari, M., Segraves, K. B., & Spirnak, P. (1991). Effect of apomorphine on penile tumescence in men with psychogenic impotence. *Journal of Urology 145,* 1174–1175.

Segraves, R. T., Clayton, A., & Croft, H. (2004). Bupropion sustained release for the treatment of premenopausal women. *Journal of Clinical Psychopharmacology , 24,* 339–341.

Segraves, R. T., Croft, H., Kavoussi, R., Ascher, J., Batey, S., Foster, V., et al. (2001). Bupropion sustained release for the treatment of hypoactive sexual desire disorder in non-depressed women. *Journal of Sex and Marital Therapy, 27,* 303–306.

Segraves, R. T., Kavoussi, R., Hughes, A., Batey, S., Johnston, A., Donahue, R., et al. (2000). Evaluation of sexual functioning in depressed outpatients: A double-blind comparison of sustained-release bupropion and sertraline treatment. *Journal of Clinical Psychopharmacology, 20,* 122–128.

Segraves, R. T., Madsen, R., Carver, S. C., & Davis, J. (1985). Erectile dysfunction associated with pharmacological agents. In R. T. Segraves & H. W. Schoenberg (Eds.), *Diagnosis and treatment of erectile disturbances* (pp. 23–64). New York: Plenum Press.

Segraves, R. T., Saran, A., Segraves, K., & Meguire, E. (1993). Clomipramine versus placebo in the treatment of premature ejaculation: A pilot study. *Journal of Sex and Marital Therapy, 19,* 198–200.

Segraves, R. T., & Segraves, K. B. (1990). Categorical and multi-axial diagnosis of male erectile disorder. *Journal of Sex and Marital Therapy, 16,* 208–213.

Semans, J. H. (1956). Premature ejaculation: A new approach. *Southern Medical Journal, 49,* 353–357.

Sherwin, B. B., & Gelfand, M. M. (1984). Effects of parenteral administration of estrogen and androgen on plasma hormone levels and hot flushes in the surgical menopause. *American Journal of Obstetrics and Gynecology, 148,* 552–557.

Sherwin, B. B., & Gelfand, M. M. (1985). Differential symptom response to parental estrogen and/or androgen administration in the surgical menopause. *American Journal of Obstetrics and Gynecology, 151,* 153–160.

Sherwin, B. B., & Gelfand, M. M. (1987). The role of androgen in the maintenance of sexual functioning in oophorectomized women. *Psychosomatic Medicine, 49,* 397–409.

Sherwin, B., Gelfand, M. M., & Bender, W. (1985). Androgen enhances sexual motivation in females: A prospective, cross-over study of sex steroid administration in the surgical menopause. *Psychosomatic Medicine, 47,* 339–351.

Shifren, J., Braunstein, G., Simon, L, Casson, R., Buster, J., Redmond, G., et al. (2000). Transdermal testosterone treatment in women with impaired sexual function after oophorectomy. *New England Journal of Medicine, 343,* 682–688.

Shirai, M., Marui, E., Hayashi, K., Ishii, N., & Abe, T. (1999). Prevalence and correlates of erectile dysfunction in Japan. *International Journal and Clinical Practice Supplement, 102,* 36.

Siegel, R. K. (1982). Cocaine and sexual dysfunction. *Journal of Psychoactive Drugs, 14,* 71–74.

Snyder, S., & Karacan, I. (1981). Disulfiram and nocturnal penile tumescence in the chronic alcoholic. *Biological Psychiatry, 16,* 399–406.

Sommer, Engelmann, & the German Men's Health Study Group. (2005). Curing erectile dysfunction: Long-term effects (12 months) of taking PDE-5-inhibitors on a daily basis [Abstract no. P-082]. *Journal of Sex Medicine, 2*(Suppl. 1), 62–63.

Sondra, L. P., Mazo, R. T., Segraves, M. D., & Chanceler, M. D. (1990). The role of yohimbine for the treatment of erectile impotence. *Journal of Sex and Marital Therapy, 16,* 15–21.

Spector, I., & Carey, J. S. (1990). Incidence and prevalence of the sexual dysfunctions: A critical review of the literature. *Archives of Sexual Behavior, 9,* 389–408.

Spence, S. H. (1991). *Psychosexual therapy: A cognitive behavioral approach.* London: Chapman and Hall.

Strassberg, D. S., de Gouveia Brazao, C. A., Rowland, D. L., Tan, P., & Slob, A. K. (1999). Clomipramine in the treatment of rapid (premature) ejaculation. *Journal of Sex and Marital Therapy, 25,* 89–101.

Strassberg, D., Kelly, M., Carroll, C., & Kirchzer, J. (1987). The psychophysiological nature of prema-ture ejaculation. *Archives of Sexual Behavior, 16,* 327–336.

Susset, J. C., Tessier, C. D., Wincze, J., Banal, S., Malhtra, C., & Schwaba, M. G. (1989). Effect of yohimbine hydrochloride on erectile impotence: A double-blind study. *Journal of Urology, 141,* 1360–1363.

Tan, E. H., Johnson, R. A., Lambie, D. C., Vijayasenah, M. E., & Whiteside, E. A. (1984). Erectile impotence in chronic alcoholics. *Alcoholism: Clinical and Experimental Research, 8,* 297–301.

Tennett, G., Bancroft, J., & Cass, J. (1972). The control of deviant sexual behavior by drugs: A double-blind controlled study of benperidol, chlorpromazine and placebo. *Archives of Sexual Behavior, 3,* 216–271.

Thase, M. E., Reynolds, C. F., Jennings, J. R., Berman, R., Houch, P., Howell, J., et al. (1999). Diagnostic performance of NPT studies in healthy dysfunctional (impotent) and depressed men. *Psychiatric Research, 26,* 79–87.

Tiefer, L. (1995). *Sex is not a natural act and other essays.* Boulder, CO: Westview Press.

Tomlinson, J. (1999). Viagra and its use in cardiovascular disease. *Journal of Human Hypertension, 13,* 593–594.

Tran, P. U., Hamilton, S. H., Kuntz, A. J., Potvin, J. H., Andersen, S. W., Beasley, C., et al. (1997). Double-blind comparison of olanzapine versus risperidone in the treatment of schizophrenia. *Journal of Clinical Psychopharmacology, 17,* 402–418.

Trudel, G., Marchand, A., Ravart, M., Aubin, S., Turgeon, L., & Fortier, P. (2001). The effect of a cognitive behavioral group treatment program on hypoactive sexual desire in women. *Sexual Relationships Therapy, 16,* 145–164.

Tuiten, A., van Honk, J., Koppe, S., Chaar, H., Bernaars, C., Thijsen, J., et al. (2000). Time course of effects of testosterone administration on sexual arousal in women. *Archives of General Psychiatry, 57,* 149–153.

Turner, L., Althof, S., & Levine, S. (1992). A 12-month comparison of the effectiveness of two treatments for erectile failure: Self-injection versus external vacuum devices. *Urology, 39,* 139–144.

Turner, L., Althof, S., Levine, S., Risen, C., Bodner, D., Kursch, E., et al. (1989). Injection of papaverine and phentolamine in the treatment of psychogenic impotence. *Journal of Sex and Marital Therapy, 15,* 163–176.

Ugarte, F., and Hurtado-Coll, A. (2002). Comparison of the efficacy and safety of sildenafil citrate (Viagra) and oral phentolamine for the treatment of erectile dysfunction. *International Journal of Impotence Research, 14*(Suppl. 2), S48–S53.

Utian, W., Braunstein, G., Buster, J., Lucas, J., & Simon, J. (2004, October). *Testosterone transdermal patch and improved sexual activity and sexual desire in surgically menopausal women. Results from two phase III studies*. Annual meeting of the International Society for Study Women's Sexual Health, Atlanta, Georgia.

van Ahlen, H., Piechota, H. J., Kias, H. J., Brennemann, W., & Klingmuller, D. (1995). Opiate antagonists in erectile dysfunction: A possible new treatment option? Results of a pilot study with naltrexone. *European Urology, 28,* 246–250.

Waldinger, M. D., Hengeveld, M. Z., & Zwindman, A. H. (1994). Paroxetine treatment of premature ejaculation: A double-blind randomized placebo-controlled study. *American Journal of Psychiatry, 151,* 1377–1379.

Waldinger, M. D., Hengeveld, M. Z., & Zwindman, A. H. (1997). Ejaculation-retarding properties of paroxetine in patients with primary premature ejaculation: A double-blind randomized response study. *British Journal of Urology, 156,* 1631–1632.

Waldinger, M. D., Hengeveld, M. Z., Zwindman, A. H., & Olivier, S. (1998). Effect of SSRI antidepressant on ejaculation: A randomized placebo-controlled study with fluoxetine, fluvoxamine, paroxetine, and sertraline. *Journal of Clinical Psychiatry, 18,* 274–281.

Warnock, J. K., Bundren, J. C., & Morris, D. W. (1999). Female hypoactive sexual desire disorder: Studies of physiological androgen replacement. *Journal of Sex and Marital Therapy, 25,* 175–180.

Whalley, L. J. (1978). Sexual adjustment of alcoholics. *Acta Psychiatrica Scandinavica, 58,* 281–298.

Whitehead, A., & Mathews, A. (1986). Factors related to successful outcome in the treatment of sexually unresponsive women. *Psychological Medicine, 16,* 373–378.

Wise, T. H. (1999). Psychosocial side effects of sildenafil for erectile dysfunction. *Journal of Sex and Marital Therapy, 25,* 145–150.

Wolpe, J. (1958). *Psychotherapy by reciprocal inhibition.* Stanford, CA: Stanford University Press.

Wright, J., Perrault, R., & Mathieu, M. (1977). New treatment of sexual dysfunction. *Archives of General Psychiatry, 34,* 881–890.

Wylie, K., & MacInnes, I. (2005) Erectile dsyfunction. In R. Balon & R. Segraves (Eds.), *Handbook of sexual dysfunction* (pp. 155–191). Boca Raton, FL: Taylor and Francis.

Wyllie, M. G., & Anderson, K. E. (1999). Orally active agents: The potential of alpha-adrenergic antagonists. In C. C. Carson, R. S. Kirby, & I. Goldstein (Eds.), *Textbook of erectile dysfunction* (pp. 317–322). Oxford, UK: ISIS.

Xin, Z. C., Choi, Y., & Lee, W. (2000). Penile vibratory threshold changes with various doses of SS-cream in patients with premature ejaculation. *Yonsei Medical Journal, 41,* 29–33.

Xin, Z. C., Choi, Y. D., Rha, K. H., & Choi, I. K. (1997). Somatosensory evoked potentials in patients with primary premature ejaculation. *Journal of Urology, 158,* 451–455.

Yilmaz, U., Tatlisen, A., Turan, H., Arman, F., & Ekmekcioglu, O. (1999). The effects of fluoxetine on several neurophysiological variables in patients with premature ejaculation. *Journal of Urology, 161,* 107–111.

Zilbergeld, B. (1992). *The new male sexuality.* New York, Bantam.

Zilbergeld, B., & Evans, M. (1980, September). The inadequacy of Masters and Johnson. *Psychology Today,* 19–34.

20

Treatments for Pathological Gambling and Other Impulse Control Disorders

Jon E. Grant

Marc N. Potenza

Several controlled outcome studies (Type 1 and Type 2) suggest that specific behavioral (e.g., cognitive-behavioral therapy [CBT]) and pharmacological (e.g., naltrexone, nalmefene, lithium) treatments significantly reduce the symptoms of pathological gambling in the short term compared with wait-list or placebo. Although long-term effects of manual-based CBT have been observed in several small studies, the long-term benefits of pharmacological treatment have not been adequately tested. No studies combining behavioral and pharmacological therapies have been published to date. Thus, the potential benefit of combining behavioral and drug treatments for pathological gambling remains to be investigated systematically. Although several studies (Type 1 and Type 2) suggest that CBT is effective for trichotillomania, pharmacological treatment studies for this disorder have shown mixed results. Similarly, controlled pharmacological studies (Type 1 and Type 2) of compulsive buying have demonstrated mixed results. Limited treatment studies exist for other impulse control disorders (kleptomania, intermittent explosive disorder), although various pharmacological and psychological treatments have shown promise in uncontrolled studies.

In the *Diagnostic and Statistical Manual of Mental Disorders* (American Psychiatric Association [APA], 2000), the category of Impulse Control Disorders Not Elsewhere Classified currently includes intermittent explosive disorder, kleptomania, pyromania, pathological gambling, trichotillomania, and impulse control disorders not otherwise specified. Other specific disorders have been proposed for inclusion based on perceived phenomenological, clinical, and possibly biological similarities: psychogenic excoriation (skin picking), compulsive buying, compulsive Internet use, and nonparaphilic compulsive sexual behavior. The extent to which these impulse control disorders share clinical, genetic, phenomenological, and biological features continues to be debated.

Despite high prevalence rates in the general population (Kessler et al., 2005) and in psychiatric cohorts (Grant, Levine, Kim, & Potenza, 2005), impulse control disorders have been relatively understudied. Controlled treatment trials do not exist for many of the impulse control disorders. The disorder that has been arguably the most well researched (pathological gambling) has only recently been systematically investigated with respect to empirically supported behavioral and pharmacological treatments. Because rigorous research is particularly limited for several of the impulse control disorders (e.g., pyromania and compulsive computer use), this chapter reviews the available research on the treatment of pathological gambling, trichotillomania, compulsive buying, intermittent explosive disorder, and klepto-mania.

PATHOLOGICAL GAMBLING

Pathological gambling (PG), characterized by persistent and recurrent maladaptive patterns of gambling behavior, is associated with impaired functioning, reduced quality of life, and high rates of bankruptcy, divorce, and incarceration. PG usually begins in adolescence or early adulthood, with males tending to start at an earlier age (Ibanez, Blanco, Moreryra, & Saiz-Ruiz, 2003; Shaffer, Hall, & Vander Bilt, 1999). In epidemiological studies, women represent approximately 32% of the pathological gamblers in the United States (Volberg, 1994). Although prospective studies are largely lacking, PG appears to follow a similar trajectory as substance dependence, with high rates in adolescent and young adult groups, lower rates in older adults, and periods of abstinence and relapse (Grant & Potenza, 2004).

Male pathological gamblers appear more likely to report problems with strategic or "face-to-face" forms of gambling like blackjack or poker. Female pathological gamblers tend to report problems with nonstrategic, less interpersonally interactive forms of gambling like slot machines or bingo (Potenza et al., 2001). Both female and male gamblers report that advertisements are a common trigger of their urges to gamble, although females are more likely to report that feeling bored or lonely may also trigger their urges to gamble (Grant & Kim, 2001). Financial and marital problems are common (Grant & Kim, 2001). Many pathological gamblers engage in illegal behavior, such as stealing, embezzlement, and writing bad checks, to fund their gambling (Potenza et al., 2000). PG is associated with high rates of psychiatric comorbidity, including mood, anxiety, and substance use disorders (Bland, Newman, Orn, & Stebelsky, 1993; Ibanez, Blanco, Moreryra, & Saiz-Ruiz, 2001; Linden, Pope, & Jonas, 1986; Petry, Stinson, & Grant, 2005).

Pharmacological Treatment

Several medications have been investigated as treatments for PG (Table 20.1). These have included antidepressants (particularly serotonin reuptake inhibitors [SRIs]), mood stabilizers, and opioid antagonists.

Seven open-label studies using various medications (citalopram, escitalopram, carbamazepine, nefazodone, bupropion, valproate, naltrexone) for short periods of time (8 to 14 weeks) have demonstrated efficacy in 73% of the PG subjects. Nine double-blind, placebo-controlled pharmacotherapy studies have also been performed in PG, but the results of these studies have demonstrated mixed efficacy and tolerability.

Antidepressants

Hypotheses underlying the examination of antidepressant medications for PG are based on the neurobiology of PG and other impulse control disorders. Low levels of the serotonin metabolite 5-hydroxyindole acetic acid (5-HIAA) and blunted serotonergic response within the ventromedial prefrontal cortex (vmPFC) have been associated with impulsive behaviors (Coccaro, 1996; Linnoila, Virkkunen, George, & Higley, 1993; Mehlman, Higley, & Faucher, 1995; Rogers et al., 1999; Virkkunen, Goldman, & Nielsen, 1995). As compared with control comparison subjects, individuals with PG demonstrate diminished activation of the vmPFC when viewing gambling-related videotapes or during prepotent response inhibition when performing the Stroop color-word interference task (Potenza, Leung, et al., 2003; Potenza, Steinberg, et al., 2003). Individuals with PG also show relatively diminished activation of the vmPFC during a simulated gambling task, and severity of gambling problem correlated inversely with signal intensity within this brain region (Reuter et al., 2005). Together, the findings suggest that decreased serotonin function within vmPFC may engender disinhibition and contribute to PG. Thus, drugs targeting serotonin neurotransmission have been examined in the treatment of PG.

Of the nine double-blind, placebo-controlled pharmacological studies in PG, six have examined SRIs. Clomipramine, an SRI that also inhibits norepinephrine reuptake, was the first SRI tested in a controlled fashion in PG. Hollander and colleagues reported a response to clomipramine in a single PG subject using a double-blind, placebo-controlled design (Hollander, Frenkel, Decaria, Trungold, & Stein, 1992). After receiving placebo for 10 weeks without response, the woman reported a 90% improvement in gambling symptoms after being treated with 125 mg/day of clomipramine. There have been no fur-

TABLE 20.1 Double-Blind, Placebo-Controlled Pharmacotherapy Trials for Impulse Control Disorders

Impulse Control Disorder	Medication	Design/Duration	Subjects	Mean Daily Dose (+ SD)	Outcome
Pathological gambling (Hollander et al., 1992)	Clomipramine (Anafranil)	Parallel design 10 weeks	1 enrolled 1 completer	125 mg	90% improvement in gambling symptoms on medication
Pathological gambling (Saiz-Ruiz et al. 2005)	Sertraline (Zoloft)	Parallel design 6 months	60 enrolled 44 completers	95 mg	Similar improvement in both groups
Pathological gambling (Hollander et al., 2000)	Fluvoxamine (Luvox)	Crossover 16 weeks with a 1-week placebo lead-in	15 enrolled 10 completers	195 mg (± 50)	Fluvoxamine superior to placebo
Pathological gambling (Blanco et al., 2002)	Fluvoxamine (Luvox)	Parallel design 6 months	32 enrolled 13 completers	200 mg	Fluvoxamine not statistically significant from placebo
Pathological gambling (Kim et al., 2002)	Paroxetine (Paxil)	Parallel design 8 weeks with 1-week placebo lead-in	53 enrolled 41 completers	51.7 mg (± 13.1)	Paroxetine group significantly improved compared with placebo
Pathological gambling (Grant et al., 2003)	Paroxetine (Paxil)	Parallel design 16 weeks	76 enrolled 45 completers	50 mg (± 8.3)	Paroxetine and placebo groups with comparable improvement
Pathological gambling (Hollander et al., 2005)	Lithium carbonate SR (Lithobid SR)	Parallel design 10 weeks	40 Bipolar-spectrum patients enrolled 29 completers	1,170 mg (+ 221)	Lithium group significantly improved compared with placebo
Pathological gambling (Kim et al., 2001)	Naltrexone (ReVia)	Parallel design 12 weeks with 1-week placebo lead-in	89 enrolled 45 completers	188 mg (± 96)	Naltrexone group significantly improved compared with placebo
Pathological gambling (Grant et al., 2006)	Nalmefene	Parallel design 16 weeks	207 enrolled 73 completers	Fixed-dose study	Nalmefene 25 mg and 50 mg significantly improved compared with placebo
Compulsive buying (Black et al., 2000)	Fluvoxamine (Luvox)	Parallel design 9 weeks with 1-week placebo lead-in	23 enrolled 18 completers	220 mg	Fluvoxamine and placebo groups with comparable improvement
Compulsive buying (Ninan et al., 2000)	Fluvoxamine (Luvox)	Parallel design 13 weeks	37 enrolled 23 completers	215 mg (± 76.5)	Fluvoxamine and placebo groups with comparable improvement
Compulsive buying (Koran et al., 2003)	Citalopram (Celexa)	7 weeks open-label followed by 9 weeks randomized	24 enrolled 15 completers	42.1 mg (± 15.3)	Citalopram group significantly improved compared with placebo

(continued)

TABLE 20.1 (continued)

Impulse Control Disorder	Medication	Design/Duration	Subjects	Mean Daily Dose (+ SD)	Outcome
Trichotillo-mania (Swedo et al., 1989)	CMI vs. DMI	Crossover 5 weeks each agent	13 enrolled 13 completers	CMI: 180 mg (± 56) DMI: 173 mg (± 33)	CMI significantly greater improvement
Trichotillo-mania (Christenson et al., 1991)	Fluoxetine (Prozac)	Crossover 6 weeks fluoxetine and then placebo	21 enrolled 15 completers	Fixed titra-tion to 80 mg	Fluoxetine not signifi-cantly different from pla-cebo
Trichotillo-mania (O'Sullivan et al., 1999)	CMI vs. fluoxe-tine	Crossover 10 weeks each agent	12 enrolled No data on num-ber of completers	CMI: 200 mg ± 15; fluoxetine: 75 mg ± 5	Similar significant im-provement on both agents
Trichotillo-mania (Streichen-wein & Thornby, 1995)	Fluoxetine (Prozac)	Crossover 6 weeks on fluoxetine and placebo	23 enrolled 16 completers	70 mg	No differences between groups
Trichotillo-mania (Christenson et al., 1994)	Naltrexone (ReVia)	Parallel design 6 weeks	No data on num-ber enrolled 17 completers	50 mg	Naltrexone significant improvement on one measure
Intermittent explosive dis-order (Hol-lander et al., 2003)	Divalproex (Depakote)	Parallel design 12 weeks	109 subjects No data on num-ber of IED sub-jects who com-pleted	1,567 mg	Similar improvement in IED and placebo

CMI = clomipramine; DMI = desipramine

ther controlled studies of clomipramine, however, to confirm the limited results of this initial study. In addition to its more common side effects (dry mouth, constipation, blurred vision, sexual dysfunction, weight gain, fine tremor, muscle twitching), clomipramine may also cause cardiac conduction problems and has significant drug-drug interactions.

In a double-blind, placebo-controlled study using sertraline, 60 subjects with PG were treated for 6 months (mean dose = 95 mg/day; Saiz-Ruiz et al., 2005). At the end of the study, 23 sertraline-treated subjects (74%) and 21 placebo-treated subjects (72%) were rated as responders based on the primary out-come measure (Criteria for Control of Pathological Gambling Questionnaire), which assessed urges to gamble and gambling behavior. Sertraline did not demonstrate superiority to placebo. The authors pre-sented only limited data on the psychometrics of their primary outcome measure. Sertraline was gen-erally well tolerated, but, as with other antidepres-sants, sertraline may cause sedation, constipation, weight gain, headache, sexual dysfunction, and dry mouth.

Only two SRIs have been examined in at least two randomized, placebo-controlled trials of PG. A double-blind, 16-week crossover study of fluvoxa-mine in 15 PG subjects demonstrated a statistically significant difference compared with placebo (Hol-lander et al., 2000). Interpretation of the study is complicated, however, by a phase order treatment in-teraction (i.e., the medication did not separate from placebo during the first phase but did in the second phase). A 6-month double-blind, placebo-controlled trial of fluvoxamine in 32 gamblers failed to show statistical significance compared with placebo. The results of the latter study, however, are complicated by high rates of treatment discontinuation (only three subjects on medication completed the study) and a high placebo response rate (59%; Blanco, Petkova, Ibanez, & Saiz-Ruiz, 2002). Although differences in the results may be attributable to the temporal duration of each study, other design issues might also be important. For example, the Hollander et al. study used the Pathological Gambling Modification of the Yale Brown Obsessive Compulsive Scale (PG-YBOCS) as the primary outcome measure. The PG-YBOCS has demonstrated excellent validity and reliability in gambling treatment studies (Pallanti, DeCaria, Grant, Urpe, & Hollander, 2005). The Blanco et al. study, however, used amount of money spent weekly as the primary outcome measure. These differences in outcome measures complicate the comparisons one can make between these two studies. Although fluvoxamine is generally well tolerated, it may result in gastrointestinal distress, sedation, mild anxiety, headache, increased urinary frequency, and sexual dysfunction. Fluvoxamine is a potent P450 1A2 inhibitor, and drug-drug interactions should be considered before it is prescribed.

One randomized, blind-rater study of fluvoxamine and topiramate found that a greater percentage of responders were found in the group treated with topiramate, a drug that is thought to influence mesolimbic dopamine transmission indirectly through GABAergic and glutamatergic mechanisms (Dannon, Lowengrub, Gonopolski, Musin, & Kotler, 2005; Johnson, 2004).

As with fluvoxamine, studies have failed to demonstrate consistently the efficacy of paroxetine in treating PG. An initial double-blind, placebo-controlled study of paroxetine indicated its potential efficacy as a treatment for PG. Significant improvement was seen in subjects randomized to 8 weeks of treatment with paroxetine compared with those assigned to placebo (Kim, Grant, Adson, Shin, & Zaninelli, 2002). A larger multicenter, double-blind, placebo-controlled trial in PG, however, failed to reproduce the results (Grant et al., 2003). In this second study, a high placebo response rate ("very much improved" or "much improved" based on the Clinical Global Improvement scale) was observed: at study end, 48% of those assigned to placebo and 59% of those taking paroxetine were considered responders. Further study appears warranted to determine whether specific subgroups of individuals with PG (e.g., those with specific genetic characteristics) will respond preferentially to treatment with paroxetine or other SRIs.

Despite the high rates of co-occurring psychiatric disorders in association with PG (Petry et al., 2005), most pharmacotherapy studies performed to date have excluded people with co-occurring psychiatric conditions (Potenza, 2005). An open-label 12-week trial of escitalopram with an 8-week double-blind discontinuation period for responders was recently performed (Grant & Potenza, 2006). Of 13 subjects treated with a mean dose of 25.4 mg/day, 62% were considered responders in terms of both PG and anxiety symptoms. Four of six subjects who completed the study and were responders were entered into an 8-week double-blind discontinuation. Of the three assigned to escitalopram, improvement continued for the next 8 weeks in all three cases, whereas both gambling symptoms and anxiety returned within 4 weeks for the subject assigned to placebo.

Although the randomized, placebo-controlled trials of antidepressants in PG have focused on medications with primarily serotonergic properties, other antidepressants with different mechanisms of action have been tested in open-label designs. Bupropion (Black, 2004), a dopaminergic medication, and serzone (Pallanti, Baldini Rossi, Sood, & Hollander, 2002), a mixed serotonin/norepinephrine reuptake inhibitor, have shown initial promise in treating PG in small samples (10 and 12 subjects, respectively).

Mood Stabilizers

In one fluvoxamine study, two of three nonresponders worsened with active drug treatment and were observed to have symptoms of cyclothymia (Hollander et al., 1998). These findings suggested that alternate classes of drugs, such as mood stabilizers, might be helpful for specific individuals with PG. Although a case report and an open-label study, respectively, suggest that carbamazepine (Haller & Hinterhuber, 1994) and valproate (Pallanti, Quercioli, Sood, & Hollander, 2002) may be efficacious in the treatment of PG, there has been only one randomized, placebo-controlled trial of a mood stabilizer tested in PG. In a double-blind, placebo-controlled study of 40 PG subjects with bipolar spectrum disorders (bipolar type II, bipolar not otherwise specified, or cyclothymia), sustained-release lithium carbonate (mean lithium level 0.87 mEq/L) was shown to be superior to placebo in reducing PG symptoms during 10 weeks of treatment (Hollander, Pallanti, Allen, Sood, & Baldini Rossi, 2005). Although a majority (83%) of subjects in the treatment group displayed significant decreases in gambling urges, thoughts, and behaviors as measured by the PG-YBOCS, no differences were found in amount of money lost, episodes of gambling per week, or time spent per gambling episode. Active as compared with placebo drug was also superior in reducing symptoms of mania. Subjects in this study tolerated lithium without difficulty, but lithium may cause fine tremor, nausea, and diarrhea, and nephrotoxicity is possible when it is used chronically.

Opioid Antagonists

Mu-opioid receptor antagonists inhibit dopamine release in nucleus accumbens (NA) and ventral pallidum through the disinhibition of gamma-aminobutyric acid (GABA) input to the dopamine neurons in the ventral tegmental area (VTA; Broekkamp & Phillips, 1979; Phillips & LePiane, 1980; van Wolfswinkel & van Ree, 1985). Mu-opioid antagonists are thought to decrease dopamine neurotransmission in the NA and linked motivational neurocircuitry, thus dampening gambling-related excitement and cravings (Kim, 1998). As compared with control comparison subjects, individuals with PG show differences in NA activation during a simulated gambling task (Reuter et al., 2005). Although modulation of drive and subsequent behavioral output by dopamine, endorphin, and GABA have been investigated, the specific mechanisms underlying mu-opioid receptor antagonism in specific patient groups such as those with PG remain incompletely understood (Kalivas & Barnes, 1993; Koob, 1992).

A 12-week double-blind, placebo-controlled trial of naltrexone demonstrated superiority to placebo in 45 subjects with PG (Kim, Grant, Adson, & Shin, 2001). Naltrexone (mean dose of 188 mg/day) was effective in reducing the frequency and intensity of gambling urges, as well as gambling behavior. A separate analysis of those subjects with at least moderate urges to gamble revealed that naltrexone was more effective in gamblers with more severe urges to gamble. Naltrexone's clinical use, however, is limited by significant side effects, as well as the occurrence of liver enzyme elevations, especially in patients taking nonsteroidal anti-inflammatory drugs (Kim, Grant, Adson, & Remmel, 2001). More than 20% of sub-

jects receiving active naltrexone developed abnormal liver function tests during the 12-week study (Kim, Grant, Adson, & Shin, 2001). A recently completed multicenter study further demonstrated the efficacy of another opioid antagonist, nalmefene (25 mg/day), in the treatment of PG. In a sample of 207 subjects, nalmefene demonstrated statistically significant improvement in gambling symptoms compared with placebo in a 16-week double-blind trial (Grant et al., 2006). This latter study, however, suffered from high rates of treatment discontinuation (63%). One common side effect of opioid antagonists is nausea; these medications may also cause dizziness, insomnia, headaches, and loose stool. In addition, naltrexone, but not nalmefene, has been associated with a dose-dependent potential for hepatotoxicity.

Psychological Treatments

The majority of the psychosocial treatment literature for PG has focused on cognitive and behavioral therapy techniques (Table 20.2). The cognitive aspect includes psychoeducation, increased awareness of irrational cognitions, and cognitive restructuring. The behavioral techniques include identification of gambling triggers and the development of nongambling sources to compete with the reinforcers associated with gambling. There have been nine published randomized trials of CBT for PG. Motivational enhancement therapy in combination with CBT has been examined in a single randomized study. In addition, Gamblers Anonymous and self-exclusion programs have been examined, but not in controlled studies.

Cognitive-Behavioral Therapy

In one study of 40 subjects, individual cognitive therapy plus relapse prevention resulted in reduced gambling frequency and increased perceived self-control over gambling at 12 months when compared with a wait-list control group (Sylvain, Ladouceur, & Boisvert, 1997). Another study of cognitive therapy plus relapse prevention in 88 subjects also produced improvement in gambling symptoms compared with a wait-list group at 3 months that was maintained for 12 months (Ladouceur et al., 2001). Treatment discontinuation was high in both studies (37% and 47%, respectively), and the outcome analyses included only those subjects who completed the stud-

TABLE 20.2 Controlled Psychological Treatment Trials for Impulse Control Disorders

Impulse Control Disorder	Design/Duration	Subjects	Outcome
Pathological gambling (Echeburua et al., 1996)	Stimulus control, in vivo exposure, relapse prevention vs. cognitive restructuring vs. combined treatment vs. wait-list/6 weeks with 12-month follow-up	64 enrolled 50 completers	At 12 months, 69% abstinence or much reduced in the first condition compared with 38% for cognitive restructuring or combined treatment.
Pathological gambling (Sylvain et al., 1997)	Cognitive therapy with relapse prevention compared with wait-list/30 sessions with 6-month follow-up	40 enrolled 14/22 in treatment group completed	36% improved on five variables compared with 6% on wait-list.
Pathological gambling (Ladouceur et al., 2001)	Cognitive therapy plus relapse prevention compared with wait-list/20 sessions with 12-month follow-up	88 enrolled 35/59 in treatment group completed	32% improved on four variables compared with 7% on wait-list.
Pathological gambling (Ladouceur et al., 2003)	Group cognitive therapy plus relapse prevention compared with wait-list/10 weeks with 2-year follow-up	71 enrolled 34/46 in treatment group completed	65% no longer met PG criteria compared with 20% for wait-list group.
Pathological gambling (Petry et al. 2005)	Manualized CBT in individual counseling, vs. CBT workbook, vs. Gamblers Anonymous referral/8 sessions with 1-year follow-up	231 enrolled No data on completers	CBT was more effective than Gamblers Anonymous, and individual counseling more effective than workbook.
Pathological gambling (Hodgins et al., 2001)	CBT workbook vs. workbook plus motivational enhancement intervention via telephone vs. wait list	102 enrolled 85 available at 12 months	74% with motivational enhancement improved according to Clinical Global Impression compared with 61% with workbook and 44% on wait-list.
Pathological gambling (McConaghy et al., 1983)	Aversion therapy compared with imaginal desensitization	20 enrolled 20 completers	Improvement in both groups over 12 months.
Pathological gambling (McConaghy et al., 1991)	Aversion therapy vs. imaginal desensitization vs. in vivo desensitization vs. imaginal relaxation	120 enrolled 63 available 2 and 9 years later	Imaginal desensitization improved at 1 month and at 9 years.
Trichotillomania (Azrin et al., 1980)	Habit reversal therapy compared with negative practice	34 enrolled 34 completers	Habit reversal reduced hair pulling by more than 90% for 4 months, compared with 52 to 68% reduction for negative practice at 3 months.
Trichotillomania (Woods et al., 2005)	Acceptance and commitment therapy/habit reversal compared with wait-list	28 enrolled 25 completers	Improvement for acceptance and commitment therapy/habit reversal maintained at 3 months.
Trichotillomania (Ninan et al., 2000)	Cognitive behavior therapy compared with clomipramine compared with placebo	23 enrolled 16 completers	Cognitive behavioral therapy was significantly more effective in reducing the symptoms of trichotillomania than either clomipramine or placebo.
Trichotillomania (van Minnen et al., 2003)	Behavior therapy compared with fluoxetine compared with wait-list	43 enrolled 40 completers	Behavior therapy resulted in statistically significant reductions in trichotillomania symptoms compared with either fluoxetine or wait-list.

ies. Although the treatment was manualized, no measures of therapist competence and adherence were reported.

A randomized study of CBT in PG compared four groups: (a) individual stimulus control and in vivo exposure with response prevention, (b) group cognitive restructuring, (c) a combination of a and b, and (d) a wait-list control (Echeburua, Baez, & Fernandez-Montalvo, 1996). At 12 months, rates of abstinence or minimal gambling were higher in the individual treatment (69%) compared with group cognitive restructuring (38%) and the combined treatment (38%). The same investigators further assessed individual and group relapse prevention for completers of a 6-week individual treatment program. At 12 months, 86% of those receiving individual relapse prevention and 78% of those in group relapse prevention had not relapsed, compared with 52% with no follow-up.

Petry describes an eight-session manualized form of CBT where 231 subjects were randomized to weekly sessions with an individual counselor, the therapy in the form of a workbook, or referral to Gamblers Anonymous (Petry, 2005). Using an intent-to-treat analysis, the individual therapy and workbook reduced gambling behaviors to a greater degree than referral to Gamblers Anonymous. This study has been summarized by the author in various review articles, but the actual study methodology and results have not yet been published.

In one study of brief interventions, Dickerson, Hinchy, and England (1990) randomly assigned 29 subjects either to workbook or to workbook plus a single in-depth interview. The workbook included cognitive-behavioral and motivational enhancement techniques. Both groups reported significant reductions in gambling at 6 months (Dickerson et al., 1990). Another study assigned gamblers to a CBT workbook, a workbook plus a telephone motivational enhancement intervention, or a wait-list. Rates of abstinence at 6 months did not differ between groups, although the frequency of gambling and money lost gambling were lower in the motivational intervention group (Hodgins, Currie, & el-Guebaly, 2001). Compared with the workbook alone, those gamblers assigned to the motivational intervention and workbook reduced gambling throughout a 2-year follow-up period (Hodgins, Currie, el-Guebaly, & Peden, 2004).

Imaginal desensitization has been used in conjunction with CBT in the treatment of PG. Subjects are taught relaxation and then instructed to imagine experiencing and resisting triggers to gambling. McConaghy reported significant reduction in gambling behaviors in a comparison of imaginal desensitization to traditional aversion therapy in the randomized treatment of 20 compulsive gamblers (McConaghy, Armstrong, Blaszczynski, & Allcock, 1983). In a larger study of 120 subjects randomly assigned to aversion therapy, imaginal desensitization, in vivo desensitization, or imaginal relaxation, subjects assigned to imaginal desensitization reported better outcomes at 1 month and up to 9 years later (McConaghy, Blaszczynski, & Frankova, 1991). This latter study, however, failed to follow up on approximately half of the subjects.

Conclusions

Several conclusions can be drawn from the PG pharmacological and psychological treatment studies performed and published to date:

1. Although some pharmacotherapy and psychological treatment studies approximate a Type 1 study, the studies have generally lacked a large enough sample for adequate statistical power. One exception is the multicenter nalmefene study that was adequately powered at the time of enrollment. The nalmefene study, however, suffered from a large treatment discontinuation rate, which complicates the findings.
2. Although several different classes of medication have shown efficacy in treating PG in individual studies, no positive, randomized, placebo-controlled study of medication in PG has been successfully reproduced.
3. CBT has shown efficacy for PG, but no manualized CBT treatment has been examined in a confirmatory study by another independent investigator, and most published studies have relatively small sample sizes.
4. Manualized treatments of CBT for PG, with the exception of the Hodgins et al. study, have generally lacked published therapist adherence and competence measures.
5. Different classes of medication seem equally effective in PG. No comparison studies of medications have been performed in a randomized, placebo-controlled design.
6. Both drug and behavioral treatments appear effective for PG. Few studies have systematically compared interventions or examined

whether combinations of treatments are more beneficial. In addition, no study has examined whether certain individuals with PG would benefit differentially from specific pharmacotherapies or behavioral treatments.

7. Comparisons of treatment studies have generally been problematic due to the lack of consensus on appropriate outcome measure or measures (Walker et al., 2006).

8. With one exception, there have been no systematic dose-response studies for medication. The exception showed that 25 mg/day and 50 mg/day, but not 100 mg/day, of nalmefene was more effective than placebo (Grant et al., 2006).

9. CBT studies have shown that both brief interventions and longer term therapy are potentially effective, but no study has yet examined the optimal duration of CBT.

10. The long-term effects of medication for PG remain largely untested. Only two studies have examined pharmacological effects for 6 months, but these studies experienced dropout rates of 59% (Blanco et al., 2002) and 44% (Saiz-Ruiz et al., 2005). No study has examined pharmacological treatment effects for longer than 6 months or whether the effects of acute treatment last beyond the 8 to 16 weeks.

11. Predictors of a positive response to pharmacotherapy and CBT have largely yet to be identified. Preliminary findings suggest that PG subjects with more intense gambling urges respond better to naltrexone (Kim, Grant, Adson, & Shin, 2001), and males and younger PG subjects respond better to fluvoxamine (Blanco et al., 2002).

12. There are limited data concerning the effectiveness of pharmacotherapy or CBT for PG subjects with co-occurring psychiatric conditions. Preliminary data suggest that individuals with PG and bipolar symptoms respond to lithium (Hollander et al, 2005) and those with PG and anxiety respond to escitalopram (Grant & Potenza, 2006).

TRICHOTILLOMANIA

Pathological hair pulling, trichotillomania, has been defined as repetitive, intentionally performed pulling that causes noticeable hair loss and results in clinically significant distress or functional impairment (APA, 2000).

Although 17 to 23% of people with clinically meaningful hair pulling fail to meet the DSM criteria (which require either tension immediately before pulling or pleasure, gratification, or relief when pulling; Christenson, Mackenzie, & Mitchell, 1991), trichotillomania appears relatively common, with an estimated prevalence between 1 and 3% (Christenson, Pyle, & Mitchell, 1991).

The mean age of onset for trichotillomania is approximately 13 years (Christenson & Mansueto, 1999). Although prospective studies are lacking, the onset of trichotillomania has been associated with scalp disease and stressful life events (Christenson & Mansueto, 1999). Hair pulling is subject to great fluctuations in severity, with worsening of symptoms often related to stress. Trichotillomania has traditionally been considered a disorder predominantly affecting females (Swedo & Leonard, 1992) and is associated frequently with depression (39 to 65%), generalized anxiety disorder (27 to 32%), substance abuse (15 to 20%), and obsessive-compulsive disorder (13 to 23%; Christenson & Mansueto, 1999; Swedo & Leonard, 1992).

Pharmacological Treatments

Several controlled pharmacological trials have been performed in trichotillomania (see Table 20.1). Four of the five double-blind pharmacological studies published to date have examined antidepressants, particularly SRIs. One study examined clomipramine compared with desipramine in a 10-week double-blind, crossover (5 weeks for each agent) design (following 2 weeks of single-blind placebo lead-in; Swedo et al., 1989). Twelve of 13 subjects had significant improvement on clomipramine.

Fluoxetine has been studied in three randomized trials with conflicting results. In one study, fluoxetine was compared with placebo in a 6-week double-blind crossover study (with a 5-week washout period between treatment arms; Christenson, Mackenzie, Mitchell, & Callies, 1991). No significant differences were found between fluoxetine and placebo on measures of hair-pulling urges, frequency, or severity. In a study comparing fluoxetine with clomipramine, Pigott, L'Heueux, and Grady (1992) used a 2-week placebo lead-in followed by a double-blind, randomized 20-week crossover design (10 weeks on each agent). Both clomipramine and fluoxetine demonstrated a similar positive treatment effect (O'Sullivan, Christenson, & Stein, 1999). A third controlled study used a double-blind, placebo-controlled crossover design with 16 subjects treated with each agent for 12 weeks separated by a 5-week washout period (Streichenwein & Thornby, 1995). Fluoxetine failed to show significant improvement compared with placebo.

Christenson performed a placebo-controlled, 6-week, randomized, double-blind parallel arm study of the opioid antagonist naltrexone (O'Sullivan et al., 1999). Of 17 subjects completing the study, 10 received placebo and 7 received 50 mg/day of naltrexone. Significant improvement was noted for the naltrexone group on one measure of trichotillomania symptoms. However, although two other measures of symptom improvement showed change in the anticipated direction for the naltrexone group, they failed to reach statistical significance.

Psychological Treatments

Few controlled psychological treatment studies for trichotillomania have been published to date (see Table 20.2). Azrin and colleagues randomized 34 subjects to either habit reversal therapy or negative practice (where subjects were instructed to stand in front of a mirror and act out motions of hair pulling without actually pulling; Azrin, Nunn, & Frantz, 1980). Habit reversal reduced hair pulling by more than 90% for 4 months, compared with 52 to 68% reduction for negative practice at 3 months. No control group was included, and therefore time and therapist attention could not be adequately assessed.

A recent study examined 25 subjects randomized to 12 weeks (10 sessions) of either acceptance and commitment therapy/habit reversal or wait-list (Woods, Wetterneck, & Flessner, 2005). Subjects assigned to the therapy experienced significant reductions in hair pulling severity and impairment compared with those assigned to the wait-list, and improvement was maintained at 3-month follow-up.

Comparison Studies

Although the studies of either pharmacological or psychological treatment are too few to recommend specific treatment approaches, two studies have used controlled design to compare treatment interventions. Ninan and colleagues used a placebo-controlled, randomized, parallel treatment design to compare cognitive-behavioral therapy and clomipramine (Ninan, Rothbaum, Marsteller, Knight, & Eccard, 2000). Twenty-three subjects entered the 9-week

study. The cognitive-behavioral therapy was a modified manualized treatment based on the habit reversal therapy tested in a controlled study by Azrin and colleagues (1980). Cognitive-behavioral therapy was significantly more effective in reducing the symptoms of trichotillomania than either clomipramine or placebo. Although clomipramine resulted in greater symptom reduction than placebo, the difference was not statistically significant.

In a second comparison study, behavioral therapy was compared with fluoxetine in a 12-week randomized trial using a wait-list control (van Minnen, Hoogduin, Keijsers, Hellenbrand, & Hendriks, 2003). Forty-three subjects were enrolled (14 in behavior therapy, 11 in the fluoxetine group, and 15 in the wait-list). Behavior therapy resulted in statistically significant reductions in trichotillomania symptoms compared with either fluoxetine or wait-list.

Conclusions

Although there are many case reports on effective treatments for trichotillomania, the data from controlled trials are sparse. The one treatment that has shown potential promise in treating trichotillomania is habit reversal therapy, or some modification thereof. The manualized treatments using habit reversal, however, have not published therapist adherence and competence measures. In addition, no manualized treatment has been published in a confirmatory study by an independent investigator. Neither the Azrin et al. or Ninan et al. studies used control groups. The psychological and pharmacological studies have included small samples and have failed to provide power analyses. Although habit reversal appears promising in the short term, there are no controlled trials examining the long-term effects of this treatment. Clomipramine treatment may benefit individuals with trichotillomania, but there are conflicting data supporting the use of selective SRIs. Naltrexone appears to offer promise in treating trichotillomania, but further research (longer trials with larger samples) is needed before this and other pharmacological interventions can be recommended as a first-line treatment.

COMPULSIVE BUYING

Although not specifically recognized in the *DSM*, the following diagnostic criteria have been proposed for compulsive buying: (a) maladaptive preoccupation with or engagement in buying (evidenced by frequent preoccupation with or irresistible impulses to buy; or frequent buying of items that are not needed or not affordable; or shopping for longer periods of time than intended); (b) preoccupations or the buying lead to significant distress or impairment; and (c) the buying does not occur exclusively during hypomanic or manic episodes (McElroy, Keck, Pope, Smith, & Strakowski, 1994).

The onset of compulsive buying typically occurs during late adolescence or early adulthood (Black, 1996). The disorder appears more common among females (Black, 1996; Christenson et al., 1994). Individuals with compulsive buying report repetitive, intrusive urges to shop that are often triggered by being in stores and worsen during times of stress, emotional difficulties, or boredom. Compulsive buying regularly results in substantial financial debt, marital or family disruption, and legal consequences (Christenson et al., 1994). Guilt, shame, and embarrassment typically follow the buying episodes. Most items are not used or even removed from the packaging (Christenson et al., 1994).

Pharmacological Treatments

The effectiveness of pharmacotherapy in treating compulsive buying has been examined in three double-blind, randomized, placebo-controlled trials (see Table 20.1). In the first of two double-blind fluvoxamine studies, 37 subjects were treated for 13 weeks. Only 9 of 20 patients assigned to medication were responders (mean dose of 215 mg/day), and this rate did not differ significantly from that in the placebo group (8 of 17 were responders; Ninan et al., 2000). In the second double-blind study, Black and colleagues treated 23 patients for 9 weeks following a 1-week placebo lead-in phase. Using a mean dose of 200 mg/day, no differences in response rates were observed between the groups treated with active drug or placebo (Black, Gabel, Hansen, & Schlosser, 2000).

The third controlled study was a 7-week open-label study of citalopram that randomized the responders to 9 weeks of double-blind medication or placebo (Koran, Chuong, Bullock, & Smith, 2003). Subjects taking citalopram demonstrated statistically significant decreases in the frequency of shopping and the intensity of thoughts and urges concerning shopping.

Psychological Treatments

There are no formal studies of psychotherapy for compulsive buying. Several case reports suggest possible effective psychotherapeutic interventions might include exposure and response prevention, and supportive or insight-oriented psychotherapy (McElroy et al., 1994).

Conclusions

There is scant evidence concerning effective treatments for compulsive buying. Based on available data, citalopram may offer some benefit for this disorder, although the study suffers from several major limitations—small sample in the randomized phase ($n = 15$), a diagnostic instrument without sufficient psychometrics, and outcome measures that lack validity and reliability data. Current data do not support effective psychological treatments for compulsive buying.

INTERMITTENT EXPLOSIVE DISORDER

Intermittent explosive disorder (IED) is defined by recurrent, significant outbursts of aggression, often leading to assaultive acts against people or property, which are disproportionate to outside stressors and not better explained by another psychiatric diagnosis (APA, 2000). Recent research suggests IED may be common, with 6.3% of a community sample meeting criteria for lifetime IED (Coccaro et al., 2004).

IED symptoms tend to start in adolescence and appear to be chronic (Coccaro, Schmidt, Samuels, & Nestadt, 2004; McElroy, Soutullo, Beckman, Taylor, & Keck, 1998). Individuals suffering from IED regard their behavior as distressing and problematic (McElroy et al., 1998). Outbursts are generally short-lived (usually less than 30 minutes in duration) and frequent (multiple times per month; McElroy et al., 1998). Legal and occupational difficulties are common (McElroy et al., 1998).

Pharmacological Treatments

Pharmacological treatment data for IED are limited (see Table 20.1). Although pharmacotherapies have been studied in the treatment of aggression, impulsivity, and violent behavior, there is only one con-

trolled study specific to IED. In a randomized, double-blind, placebo-controlled study of 96 subjects
with Cluster B personality disorders, 116 subjects
with IED, and 34 subjects with posttraumatic stress
disorder were randomized to divalproex sodium or
placebo for 12 weeks of treatment. Using an intent-
to-treat analysis, the study found that divalproex had
no significant influence on aggression in the subjects
with IED (Hollander et al., 2003).

Psychological Treatments

Although case reports suggest that insight-oriented
psychotherapy and behavioral therapy may be beneficial, there are no controlled psychological treatment studies in IED (McElroy et al., 1998).

Conclusions

Given the paucity of Type 1 or 2 treatment studies
for IED, no treatment recommendations for IED can
be offered at present. The only pharmacological
study failed to demonstrate benefit, and there are
only case reports of psychological treatments. IED is
a disabling disorder with significant public health issues. Treatment studies for this disorder are needed.

KLEPTOMANIA

Kleptomania is characterized by repetitive, uncontrollable stealing of items not needed for personal
use. Kleptomania begins most often in late adolescence or early adulthood (McElroy, Pope, Hudson,
Keck, & White, 1991). The course of the illness is
generally chronic, with waxing and waning of symptoms. Women appear twice as likely to suffer from
kleptomania as do men (Grant & Kim, 2002a; Presta
et al., 2002; Sarasalo, Bergman, & Toth, 1996). Individuals with kleptomania frequently hoard, discard,
or return stolen items (McElroy et al., 1991).

Most individuals with kleptomania try unsuccess-
fully to stop stealing. The inability to stop the behavior often leads to feelings of shame and guilt (Grant
& Kim, 2002a). Many individuals with kleptomania
(64 to 87%) have been apprehended at some time
due to their stealing behavior (McElroy et al., 1991;
Presta et al., 2002), with a smaller percentage (15 to
23%) having been jailed (Grant & Kim, 2002a).

Pharmacological Treatments

There have been no randomized, placebo-controlled
studies of medication in the treatment of kleptomania. Other than case reports, there are data concerning effective pharmacotherapy. In a case series of
three patients treated with topiramate (100 mg/day to
150 mg/day), all three patients achieved remission of
kleptomania symptoms (Dannon, 2003). Two of the
patients were also taking a selective SRI concomitantly with topiramate, and two suffered from
comorbid diagnoses of attention-deficit/hyperactivity
disorder and panic disorder. In another case series
examining two subjects treated with naltrexone, both
responded to medication (Dannon, Iancu, & Grunhaus, 1999).

Ten subjects with kleptomania were treated over
12 weeks with escalating doses of naltrexone (50 mg/
day to 200 mg/day) in an open-label design (Grant
& Kim, 2002b). A mean dose of 150 mg/day resulted
in a significant decline in the intensity of urges to
steal, stealing thoughts, and stealing behavior in 9 of
the 10 subjects compared with baseline symptoms.
Unlike its use in pathological gambling, naltrexone
was well tolerated, with minimal nausea, and produced no elevated liver enzymes (due to controls on
concomitant nonsteroidal analgesic use) among kleptomania subjects. The lack of a randomized, placebo-controlled design, the small sample, and short
study duration complicate evaluation of the drug's
efficacy and tolerability in the treatment of kleptomania. A chart review study of 28 adult outpatients with
kleptomania treated with medication in a naturalistic
design for a mean of 378 days found that 72%
achieved significant symptom reduction (Grant, 2005).

Psychological Treatments

No controlled studies of psychological treatments exist for kleptomania. Case reports suggest that cognitive and behavioral therapies may be effective in
treating kleptomania. Undergoing seven sessions of
covert sensitization combined with exposure and response prevention over a 4-month period, a young
man was able to reduce his stealing frequency
(Guidry 1969). In addition, the man went to stores
and was asked to imagine that the store manager was
observing him. The young man reduced his stealing
behavior, although his urges to steal went unchanged.

In a case of covert sensitization, a young woman
underwent five weekly sessions wherein she was in-

structed to practice covert sensitization whenever she had urges to steal. She was able to then go 14 months with only a single lapse in behavior and with no reported urges to steal (Gauthier & Pellerin 1982). Similarly, another woman was instructed to have increasing nausea when tempted to steal with imagery of vomiting associated with actual stealing (Glover, 1985). After four sessions over 8 weeks, the woman was able to go with only a single lapse in behavior over the next 19 months. Aversive breath holding in combination with diary keeping of urges to steal and six weekly sessions of therapy resulted in significantly reduced stealing frequency in a single case (Keutzer 1972).

Imaginal desensitization in fourteen 15-minutes sessions over 5 days resulted in complete remission of symptoms for a 2-year period for two subjects (McConaghy & Blaszczynski, 1988). One case involved a woman treated weekly for 5 months to assist her in finding alternative sources of excitement, pleasure, and self-fulfillment. She was able to report a 2-year period of remitted symptoms (Gudjonsson, 1987).

Conclusions

The outcome data for the treatment of kleptomania are inconclusive. No controlled trials of either pharmacotherapy or psychosocial interventions have been reported. The current research is based primarily on case reports. Although there is slightly more evidence supporting pharmacotherapy in the treatment of kleptomania, those data are also severely limited.

The research on treatment outcome in kleptomania contrasts sharply with the quantity and quality of studies in PG. This state of affairs is probably attributable to the low prevalence of kleptomania and to clinical difficulties in treating individuals involved in illegal activities. Nevertheless, there is a substantial need for systematic studies of the treatment of this disorder. Such studies may need to involve collaboration across multiple treatment centers in view of the disorder's low prevalence. Given the existing data, it is not possible to propose evidence-based clinical recommendations regarding treatment.

RECOMMENDATIONS BASED ON TREATMENT OUTCOME LITERATURE

In the area of impulse control disorders, the systematic study of treatment efficacy and tolerability is in its infancy. With few studies published yet that even approximate a Type 1 study, it is not possible to make treatment recommendations with a substantial degree of confidence. No drugs are currently approved by the Food and Drug Administration (FDA) for the treatment of any of the formal impulse control disorders. Nonetheless, specific drug and behavioral therapies offer promise for the effective treatment of PG. However, treatment studies in PG are substantially limited. Most published studies have employed relatively small sample sizes, are of limited duration, and involve possibly nonrepresentative clinical groups (e.g., those without co-occurring psychiatric disorders). In addition, response measures have varied across studies, in part because the definition of "response" in PG treatment remains debated. Heterogeneity of treatment samples may also complicate identification of effective treatments. At present, issues such as which medication to use and for whom, or the duration of pharmacotherapy or CBT cannot be sufficiently addressed with the available data. Two consistent findings across treatment studies, the high placebo-response and study discontinuation rates, and identification of factors related to placebo response and treatment discontinuation, would help inform future studies and advance treatment strategies for the disorder.

For other impulse control disorders, there are fewer available data to generate empirically supported treatment recommendations. For trichotillomania, habit reversal therapy may be beneficial, but the evidence is based on only three studies with small samples, each using a different variation of habit reversal therapy and, in the cases of two studies, lacking a control group. There is even less evidence for effective treatments for compulsive buying, intermittent explosive disorder, or kleptomania. In conjunction with emerging epidemiological data supporting a relatively high prevalence of impulse control disorders, the small amount of empirical data in the area of effective treatments for impulse control disorders highlights the clinical need for additional research in this area.

REFERENCES

American Psychiatric Association. (2000). *Diagnostic and statistical manual of mental disorders* (4th ed., Text revision). Washington, DC: Author.

Azrin, N. H., Nunn, R. G., & Frantz, S. E. (1980). Treatment of hairpulling (trichotillomania): A comparative study of habit reversal and negative practice training. *Journal of Behavior Therapy and Experimental Psychiatry, 11,* 13–20.

Black, D. W. (1996). Compulsive buying: A review. *Journal of Clinical Psychiatry, 57*(Suppl. 8), 50–54.

Black, D. W. (2004). An open-label trial of bupropion in the treatment of pathologic gambling [Letter]. *Journal of Clinical Psychopharmacology, 24,* 108–110.

Black, D. W., Gabel, J., Hansen, J., & Schlosser, S. (2000). A double-blind comparison of fluvoxamine versus placebo in the treatment of compulsive buying disorder. *Annals of Clinical Psychiatry, 12,* 205–211.

Blanco, C., Petkova, E., Ibanez, A., & Saiz-Ruiz, J. (2002). A pilot placebo-controlled study of fluvoxamine for pathological gambling. *Annals of Clinical Psychiatry, 14,* 9–15.

Bland, R. C., Newman, S. C., Orn, H., & Stebelsky, G. (1993). Epidemiology of pathological gambling in Edmonton. *Canadian Journal of Psychiatry, 38,* 108–112.

Broekkamp, C. L., & Phillips, A. G. (1979). Facilitation of self-stimulation behavior following intracerebral microinjections of opioids into the ventral tegmental area. *Pharmacology, Biochemistry, and Behavior, 11,* 289–295.

Christenson, G. A., Faber, R. J., de Zwaan, M., Raymond, N. C., Specker, S. M., Ekern, M. D., et al. (1994). Compulsive buying: Descriptive characteristics and psychiatric comorbidity. *Journal of Clinical Psychiatry, 55,* 5–11.

Christenson, G. A., Mackenzie, T. B., & Mitchell, J. E. (1991). Characteristics of 60 adult chronic hair pullers. *American Journal of Psychiatry, 148,* 365–370.

Christenson, G. A., Mackenzie, T. B., Mitchell, J. E., & Callies, A. L. (1991). A placebo-controlled, double-blind crossover study of fluoxetine in trichotillomania. *American Journal of Psychiatry, 148,* 1566–1571.

Christenson, G. A., & Mansueto, C. S. (1999). Trichotillomania: Descriptive characteristics and phenomenology. In D. J. Stein, G. A. Christenson, & E. Hollander (Eds.), *Trichotillomania* (pp. 1–42). Washington, DC: American Psychiatric Publishing.

Christenson, G. A., Pyle, R. L., & Mitchell, J. E. (1991). Estimated lifetime prevalence of trichotillomania in college students. *Journal of Clinical Psychiatry, 52,* 415–417.

Coccaro, E. F. (1996). Neurotransmitter correlates of impulsive aggression in humans. *Annals of the New York Academy of Science, 794,* 82–89.

Coccaro, E. F., Schmidt, C. A., Samuels, J. F., & Nestadt, G. (2004). Lifetime and 1-month prevalence rates of intermittent explosive disorder in a community sample. *Journal of Clinical Psychiatry, 65,* 820–824.

Dannon, P. N. (2003). Topiramate for the treatment of kleptomania: A case series and review of the literature. *Clinical Neuropharmacology, 26,* 1–4.

Dannon, P., Iancu, I., & Grunhaus, L. (1999). Naltrexone treatment in kleptomanic patients. *Human Psychopharmacology: Clinical and Experimental, 14,* 583–585.

Dannon, P. N., Lowengrub, K., Gonopolski, Y., Musin, E., & Kotler, M. (2005). Topiramate versus fluvoxamine in the treatment of pathological gambling: A randomized, blind-rater comparison study. *Clinical Neuropharmacology, 28,* 6–10.

Dickerson, M., Hinchy, J., & England, L. S. (1990). Minimal treatments and problem gamblers: A preliminary investigation. *Journal of Gambling Studies, 6,* 87–102.

Echeburua, E., Baez, C., & Fernandez-Montalvo, J. (1996). Comparative effectiveness of three therapeutic modalities in psychological treatment of pathological gambling: Long-term outcome. *Behavioral and Cognitive Psychotherapy, 24,* 51–72.

Gauthier, J., & Pellerin, D. (1982). Management of compulsive shoplifting through covert sensitization. *Journal of Behavior Therapy and Experimental Psychiatry, 13,* 73–75.

Glover, J. H. (1985). A case of kleptomania treated by covert sensitization. *British Journal of Clinical Psychology, 24,* 213–214.

Grant, J. E. (2005). Outcome study of kleptomania patients treated with naltrexone: A chart review. *Clinical Neuropharmacology, 28,* 11–14.

Grant, J. E., & Kim, S. W. (2001). Demographic and clinical features of 131 adult pathological gamblers. *Journal of Clinical Psychiatry, 62,* 957–962.

Grant, J. E., & Kim, S. W. (2002a). Clinical characteristics and associated psychopathology of 22 patients with kleptomania. *Comprehensive Psychiatry, 43,* 378–384.

Grant, J. E., & Kim, S. W. (2002b). An open label study of naltrexone in the treatment of kleptomania. *Journal of Clinical Psychiatry, 63,* 349–356.

Grant, J. E., Kim, S. W., Potenza, M. N., Blanco, C., Ibanez, A., Stevens, L. C., et al. (2003). Paroxetine treatment of pathological gambling: A multi-center randomized controlled trial. *International Clinical Psychopharmacology, 18,* 243–249.

Grant, J. E., Levine, L., Kim, D., & Potenza, M. N. (2005). Impulse control disorders in adult psychiatric inpatients. *American Journal of Psychiatry, 162,* 2184–2188.

Grant, J. E., & Potenza, M. N. (2004). (Eds.). *Pathological gambling: A clinical guide to treatment.* Washington, DC: American Psychiatric Publishing.

Grant, J. E., & Potenza, M. N. (2006). Escitalopram in the treatment of pathological gambling with co-occurring anxiety: An open-label study with double-blind discontinuation. *International Clinical Psychopharmacology, 21,* 203–209.

Grant, J. E., Potenza, M. N., Hollander, E., Cunningham-Williams, R., Nurminen, T., Smits, G., et al. (2006). A multicenter investigation of the opioid antagonist nalmefene in the treatment of pathological gambling. *American Journal of Psychiatry, 163,* 303–312

Gudjonsson, G. H. (1987). The significance of depression in the mechanism of "compulsive" shoplifting. *Medicine, Science, and the Law, 27,* 171–176.

Guidry, L. S. (1969). Use of a covert punishing contingency in compulsive stealing. *Journal of Behavior Therapy and Experimental Psychiatry, 6,* 169.

Haller, R., & Hinterhuber, H. (1994). Treatment of pathological gambling with carbamazepine [Letter]. *Pharmacopsychiatry, 27,* 129.

Hodgins, D. C., Currie, S. R., & el-Guebaly, N. (2001). Motivational enhancement and self-help treatments for problem gambling. *Journal of Consulting and Clinical Psychology, 69,* 50–57.

Hodgins, D. C., Currie, S. R., el-Guebaly, N., & Peden, N. (2004). Brief motivational treatment for problem gambling: A 24-month follow-up. *Psychology of Addictive Behaviors, 18,* 293–296.

Hollander, E., DeCaria, C. M., Finkell, J. N., Begaz, T., Wong, C. M., & Cartwright, C. (2000). A randomized double-blind fluvoxamine/placebo crossover trial in pathological gambling. *Biological Psychiatry, 47,* 813–817.

Hollander, E., DeCaria, C. M., Mari, E., Wong, C. M., Mosovich, S., Grossman, R., et al. (1998). Short-term single-blind fluvoxamine treatment of pathological gambling. *American Journal of Psychiatry, 155,* 1781–1783.

Hollander, E., Frenkel, M., Decaria, C., Trungold, S., & Stein, D. J. (1992). Treatment of pathological gambling with clomipramine. *American Journal of Psychiatry, 149,* 710–711.

Hollander, E., Pallanti, S., Allen, A., Sood, E., & Baldini Rossi, N. (2005). Does sustained-release lithium reduce impulsive gambling and affective instability versus placebo in pathological gamblers with bipolar spectrum disorders? *American Journal of Psychiatry 162,* 137–145.

Hollander, E., Tracy, K. A., Swann, A. C., Coccaro, E. F., McElroy, S. L., Wozniak, P., et al. (2003). Divalproex in the treatment of impulsive aggression: Efficacy in cluster B personality disorders. *Neuropsychopharmacology, 28,* 1186–1197.

Ibanez, A., Blanco, C., Moreryra, P., & Saiz-Ruiz, J. (2003). Gender differences in pathological gambling. *Journal of Clinical Psychiatry, 64,* 295–301.

Johnson, B. A. (2004). Topiramate-induced neuromodulation of cortico-mesolimbic dopamine function: A new vista for the treatment of comorbid alcohol and nicotine dependence? *Addictive Behaviors, 29,* 1465–1479.

Kalivas, P. W., & Barnes, C. D. (1993). *Limbic motor circuits and neuropsychiatry.* Boca Raton, FL: CRC Press.

Kessler, R. C., Berglund, P., Demler, O., Jin, R., Merikangas, K. R., & Walters, E. E. (2005). Lifetime prevalence and age-of-onset distributions of DSM-IV disorders in the National Comorbidity Survey Replication. *Archives of General Psychiatry, 62,* 593–602.

Keutzer, C. (1972). Kleptomania: A direct approach to treatment. *British Journal of Medical Psychology, 45,* 159–163.

Kim, S. W. (1998). Opioid antagonists in the treatment of impulse control disorders. *Journal of Clinical Psychiatry, 59,* 159–162.

Kim, S. W., Grant, J. E., Adson, D. E., & Shin, Y. C. (2001). Double-blind naltrexone and placebo comparison study in the treatment of pathological gambling. *Biological Psychiatry, 49,* 914–921.

Kim, S. W., Grant, J. E., Adson, D. E., & Remmel, R. P. (2001). A preliminary report on possible naltrexone and nonsteroidal analgesic interactions [Letter]. *Journal of Clinical Psychopharmacology 21,* 632–634.

Kim, S. W., Grant, J. E., Adson, D. E., Shin, Y. C., & Zaninelli, R. M. (2002). A double-blind placebo-controlled study of the efficacy and safety of paroxetine in the treatment of pathological gambling. *Journal of Clinical Psychiatry, 63,* 501–507.

Koob, G. F. (1992). Drugs of abuse: Anatomy, pharmacology and function of reward pathways. *Trends in Pharmacological Science, 13,* 177–184.

Koran, L. M., Chuong, H. W., Bullock, K. D., & Smith, S. C. (2003). Citalopram for compulsive shopping disorder: An open-label study followed by double-blind discontinuation. *Journal of Clinical Psychiatry, 64,* 793–798.

Ladouceur, R., Sylvain, C., Boutin, C., Lachance, S., Doucet, C., & Leblond, J. (2003). Group therapy for pathological gamblers: A cognitive approach. *Behaviour Research and Therapy, 41,* 587–596.

Ladouceur, R., Sylvain, C., Boutin, C., Lachance, S., Doucet, C., Leblond, J., et al. (2001). Cognitive treatment of pathological gambling. *Journal of Nervous and Mental Disease, 189*, 774–780.

Linden, R. D., Pope, H. G., & Jonas, J. M. (1986). Pathological gambling and major affective disorder: Preliminary findings. *Journal of Clinical Psychiatry, 47*, 201–203.

Linnoila, M., Virkkunen, M., George, T., & Higley, D. (1993). Impulse control disorders. *International Clinical Psychopharmacology, 8*(Suppl. 1), 53–56.

McConaghy, N., Armstrong, M. S., Blaszczynski, A., & Allcock, C. (1983). Controlled comparison of aversive therapy and imaginal desensitization in compulsive gambling. *British Journal of Psychiatry, 142*, 366–372.

McConaghy, N., & Blaszczynski, A. (1988). Imaginal desensitization: A cost-effective treatment in two shoplifters and a binge-eater resistant to previous therapy. *Australian New Zealand Journal of Psychiatry, 22*, 78–82.

McConaghy, N., Blaszczynski, A., & Frankova, A. (1991). Comparison of imaginal desensitization with other behavioral treatments of pathological gambling: A two to nine year follow-up. *British Journal of Psychiatry, 159*, 390–393.

McElroy, S. L., Keck, P. E., Pope, H. G., Smith, J. M. R., & Strakowski, S. M. (1994). Compulsive buying: A report of 20 cases. *Journal of Clinical Psychiatry, 55*, 242–248.

McElroy, S. L., Pope, H. G., Hudson, J. I., Keck, P. E., & White, K. L. (1991). Kleptomania: A report of 20 cases. *American Journal of Psychiatry, 148*, 652–657.

McElroy, S. L., Soutullo, C. A., Beckman, D. A., Taylor, P., & Keck, P. E. (1998). DSM-IV intermittent explosive disorder: A report of 27 cases. *Journal of Clinical Psychiatry, 59*, 203–210.

Mehlman, P. T., Higley, J. D., & Faucher, I. (1995). Low CFS 5-HIAA concentrations and severe aggression and impaired impulse control in nonhuman primates. *American Journal of Psychiatry, 151*, 1485–1491.

Ninan, P. T., McElroy, S. L., Kane, C. P., Knight, B. T., Castor, L. S., Rose, S. E., et al. (2000). Placebo-controlled study of fluvoxamine in the treatment of patients with compulsive buying. *Journal of Clinical Psychopharmacology, 20*, 362–366.

Ninan, P. T., Rothbaum, B. O., Marsteller, F. A., Knight, B. T., & Eccard. M. B. (2000). A placebo-controlled trial of cognitive-behavioral therapy and clomipramine in trichotillomania. *Journal of Clinical Psychiatry, 61*, 47–50.

O'Sullivan, R. L., Christenson, G. A., & Stein, D. J. (1999). Pharmacotherapy of trichotillomania. In D. J. Stein, G. A. Christenson, & E. Hollander (Eds.), *Trichotillomania* (pp. 93–123). Washington, DC: American Psychiatric Press.

Pallanti, S., Baldini Rossi, N., Sood, E., & Hollander, E. (2002). Nefazodone treatment of pathological gambling: A prospective open-label controlled trial. *Journal of Clinical Psychiatry, 63*, 1034–1039.

Pallanti, S., DeCaria, C. M., Grant, J. E., Urpe, M., & Hollander, E. (2005). Reliability and validity of the Pathological Gambling Modification of the Yale-Brown Obsessive-Compulsive Scale (PG-YBOCS). *Journal of Gambling Studies, 21*, 431–443.

Pallanti, S., Quercioli, L., Sood, E., & Hollander, E. (2002). Lithium and valproate treatment of pathological gambling: A randomized single-blind study. *Journal of Clinical Psychiatry, 63*, 559–564.

Petry, N. M. (2005). *Pathological gambling: Etiology, comorbidity, and treatment.* Washington, DC: American Psychological Association.

Petry, N. M., Stinson, F. S., & Grant, B. F. (2005). Comorbidity of DSM-IV pathological gambling and other psychiatric disorders: Results from the National Epidemiologic Survey on Alcohol and Related Conditions. *Journal of Clinical Psychiatry, 66*, 564–574.

Phillips, A. G., & LePiane, F. G. (1980). Reinforcing effects of morphine microinjection onto the ventral tegmental area. *Pharmacology, Biochemistry, and Behavior, 12*, 965–968.

Pigott, T. A., L'Heueux, F., & Grady, T. A. (1992, December). *Controlled comparison of clomipramine and fluoxetine in trichotillomania* [Abstract]. Paper presented at the annual meeting of the American College of Neuropsychopharmacology Annual Meeting, San Juan, Puerto Rico.

Potenza, M. N. (2005). Advancing treatment strategies for pathological gambling. *Journal of Gambling Studies, 21*, 179–203.

Potenza, M. N., Leung, H. C., Blumberg, H. P., Peterson, B. S., Fulbright, R. K., Lacadie, C. M., et al. (2003) An fMRI Stroop study of ventromedial prefrontal cortical function in pathological gamblers. *American Journal of Psychiatry, 160*, 1990–1994.

Potenza, M. N., Steinberg, M. A., McLaughlin, S. D., Wu, R., Rounsaville, B. J., & O'Malley, S. S. (2000). Illegal behaviors in problem gambling: Analysis of data from a gambling helpline. *Journal of the American Academy of Psychiatry and the Law, 28*, 389–403.

Potenza, M. N., Steinberg, M. A., McLaughlin, S. D., Wu, R., Rounsaville, B. J., & O'Malley, S. S.

(2001). Gender-related differences in the characteristics of problem gamblers using a gambling helpline. *American Journal of Psychiatry, 158,* 1500–1505.

Potenza, M. N., Steinberg, M. A., Skudlarski, P., Fulbright, R. K., Lacadie, C. M., Wilber, M. K., et al. (2003). Gambling urges in pathological gamblers: An fMRI study. *Archives of General Psychiatry, 60,* 828–836.

Presta, S., Marazziti, D., Dell'Osso, L., Pfanner, C., Pallanti, S., & Cassano, G. B. (2002). Kleptomania: Clinical features and comorbidity in an Italian sample. *Comprehensive Psychiatry, 43,* 7–12.

Reuter, J., Raedler, T., Rose, M., Hand, I., Glascher, J., & Buchel, C. (2005). Pathological gambling is linked to reduced activation of the mesolimbic reward system. *Nature Neuroscience, 8,* 147–148.

Rogers, R. D., Everitt, B. J., Baldacchino, A., Blackshaw, A. J., Swainson, R., Wynne, K., et al. (1999). Dissociable deficits in the decision-making cognition of chronic amphetamine abusers, opiate abusers, patients with focal damage to prefrontal cortex, and tryptophan-depleted normal volunteers: Evidence for monoaminergic mechanisms. *Neuropsychopharmacology, 20,* 322–339.

Saiz-Ruiz, J., Blanco, C., Ibanez, A., Masramon, X., Gomez, M. M., Madrigal, M., et al. (2005). Sertraline treatment of pathological gambling: A pilot study. *Journal of Clinical Psychiatry 66,* 28–33.

Sarasalo, E., Bergman, B., & Toth, J. (1996). Personality traits and psychiatric and somatic morbidity among kleptomaniacs. *Acta Psychiatrica Scandinavica, 94,* 358–364.

Shaffer, H. J., Hall, M. N., & Vander Bilt, J. (1999). Estimating the prevalence of disordered gambling behavior in the United States and Canada: A research synthesis. *American Journal of Public Health, 89,* 1369–1376.

Streichenwein, S. M., & Thornby, J. I. (1995). A long-term, double-blind, placebo-controlled crossover trial of the efficacy of fluoxetine for trichotillo-mania. *American Journal of Psychiatry, 152,* 1192–1196.

Swedo, S. E., & Leonard, H. L. (1992). Trichotillomania: An obsessive compulsive spectrum disorder? *Psychiatric Clinics of North America, 15,* 777–790.

Swedo, S. E., Leonard, H. L., Rapoport, J. L., Lenane, M. C., Goldberger, E. L., & Cheslow, D. L. (1989). A double-blind comparison of clomipramine and desipramine in the treatment of trichotillomania (hair pulling). *New England Journal of Medicine, 321,* 497–501.

Sylvain, C., Ladouceur, R., & Boisvert, J. M. (1997). Cognitive and behavioral treatment of pathological gambling: A controlled study. *Journal of Consulting and Clinical Psychology, 65,* 727–732.

van Minnen, A., Hoogduin, K. A., Keijsers, G. P., Hellenbrand, I., & Hendriks, G. J. (2003). Treatment of trichotillomania with behavioral therapy or fluoxetine: A randomized, waiting-list controlled study. *Archives of General Psychiatry, 60,* 517–522.

van Wolfswinkel, L., & van Ree, J. M. (1985). Effects of morphine and naloxone on thresholds of ventral tegmental electrical self-stimulation. *Naunyn-Schmiedebergs Archives of Pharmacology, 330,* 84–92.

Virkkunen, M., Goldman, D., & Nielsen, D. A. (1995). Low brain serotonin turnover rate (low CSF 5-HIAA) and impulsive violence. *Journal of Psychiatry and Neuroscience, 20,* 271–275.

Volberg, R. A. (1994). The prevalence and demographics of pathological gamblers: Implications for public health. *American Journal of Public Health, 84,* 237–240.

Walker, M., Toneatto, T., Potenza, M. N., Petry, N., Ladouceur, R., Hodgins, D. C., et al. (2006). A framework for reporting outcomes in problem gambling treatment research: The Banff, Alberta Consensus. *Addiction, 101,* 504–511.

Woods, D. W., Wetterneck, C. T., & Flessner, C. A. (2006). A controlled evaluation of acceptance and commitment therapy plus habit reversal for trichotillomania. *Behaviour Research and Therapy, 44,* 639–656.

21

Treatments for Eating Disorders

G. Terence Wilson
Christopher G. Fairburn

A very substantial number of well-designed studies (Type 1 and Type 2) have shown that manual-based cognitive-behavioral therapy (CBT) is currently the treatment of choice for bulimia nervosa (BN); roughly half of patients receiving CBT cease binge eating and purging. Well accepted by patients, CBT is the most effective means of eliminating the core features of the eating disorder and is often accompanied by improvement in psychological problems such as low self-esteem and depression; long-term maintenance of improvement is reasonably good. A large number of good to excellent outcome studies (Type 1 and Type 2) suggest that different classes of antidepressant drugs produce significantly greater reductions in the short term for binge eating and purging in BN patients than a placebo treatment; the long-term effects of antidepressant medication on BN remain untested. There is little evidence that combining CBT with antidepressant medication significantly enhances improvement in the core features of BN, although it may aid in treating comorbid anxiety and depression.

The continuing paucity of controlled research on outcomes of treatment for anorexia nervosa (AN) contrasts sharply with the quantity and quality of research on outcomes of treatment for BN and binge-eating disorder (BED). Nevertheless, a specific form of family therapy, referred to as the Maudsley Model, has shown promising effects on AN in adolescent patients, although this remains to be shown to be a specific effect.

Several different psychological treatments appear equally effective in reducing the frequency of binge eating in the short term in BED; these treatments include CBT, interpersonal therapy (IPT), behavioral weight loss programs, and guided self-help based on cognitive-behavioral principles. To date, only CBT and IPT have been shown to have significant longer term effects in eliminating binge eating. Evidence on the specific effects of antidepressant medication on BED is mixed. As yet, there has been no research on the treatment of the most common eating disorder diagnosis, "eating disorder not otherwise specified."

There are two generally recognized eating disorders, bulimia nervosa (BN) and anorexia nervosa (AN). BN has been the subject of much research, whereas there have been relatively few studies of the treatment of AN. In clinical practice the majority of patients present with an "atypical eating disorder" (or an "eating disorder not otherwise specified" [EDNOS]; Fairburn & Bohn, 2005). These disorders resemble AN or BN but do not meet their diagnostic criteria because of their atypical form. Their treatment has not been studied other than some preliminary studies of a provisional subgroup labeled *binge-eating disorder* (BED).

In this chapter we review the research on the treatment of BN, AN, and BED focusing on randomized controlled treatment trials (RCTs). The treatment of obesity is not addressed, since obesity is not an eating disorder, although it may co-occur with one.

BULIMIA NERVOSA

Bulimia nervosa occurs mainly among young adult women, although it is seen in adolescence and middle age. It is characterized by a severe disturbance of eating in which determined attempts to restrict food intake are punctuated by episodes of uncontrolled overeating. These binges are commonly followed by self-induced vomiting or the misuse of laxatives, although some patients do not "purge." The effects of these behaviors on body weight tend to cancel each other out, with the result that most patients have a weight that is within the normal range. There are extreme concerns about shape and weight similar to those seen in AN, with self-worth being judged largely or even exclusively in terms of shape or weight or both. There is also a high level of psychosocial impairment. BN is associated with high rates of psychiatric comorbidity, including depression, anxiety disorders, substance abuse, and personality disorders (Bushnell et al., 1994; Grilo et al., 2003; Lilenfeld et al., 1997). Among cases that present for treatment, the disorder tends to run a chronic, unremitting course (Fairburn et al, 1995), and this is also true of cases in the community (Fairburn, Cooper, Doll, Norman, & O'Connor, 2000). For this reason, short-lived treatment effects are of limited clinical significance.

Psychological Treatments

Cognitive-Behavioral Therapy

The most intensively studied treatment for BN is cognitive-behavioral therapy (CBT). The use of CBT derives directly from Fairburn's first formulation of this approach in Oxford (Fairburn, 1981) and subsequently detailed in a treatment manual (Fairburn, Marcus, & Wilson, 1993). The evidence analyzed

below is based on this theory-driven and manual-based CBT treatment. Although there are differences in the ways in which cognitive-behavioral treatment has been implemented across different clinical and research settings, all are derived from the Oxford approach. More recently, Fairburn, Cooper, and Shafran (2003) have described an enhanced CBT treatment (CBT-E) that provides more individualized and expanded treatment derived from cognitive-behavioral therapy as a whole.

Manual-based CBT for BN is based on a model that emphasizes the critical role of both cognitive and behavioral processes in the maintenance of the disorder. It is described in detail by Fairburn (1997a). Of primary importance is the extreme personal value that is attached to an idealized body shape and low body weight and the associated low self-esteem. This results in an extreme and rigid restriction of food intake, which in turn makes patients physiologically and psychologically susceptible to periodic episodes of loss of control over eating (i.e., binge eating). The latter are in part maintained by negative reinforcement, since they temporarily reduce negative affect. Purging and other extreme forms of weight control are used in an attempt to compensate for the effects on weight of binge eating. Purging itself helps maintain binge eating by temporarily reducing the anxiety about potential weight gain and by disrupting the learned satiety that regulates food intake. In turn, binge eating and purging cause distress and lower self-esteem, thereby reciprocally fostering the conditions that will inevitably lead to more dietary restraint and binge eating. It follows from this model that treatment must address more than the presenting behaviors of binge eating and purging. The extreme dietary restraint must be replaced with a more normal pattern of eating, and the dysfunctional thoughts and attitudes about body shape and weight must also be addressed. To achieve these goals, manual-based CBT for BN uses an integrated sequence of cognitive and behavioral interventions. The treatment is conducted on an outpatient basis and is suitable for all patients bar the small minority who require hospitalization.

A meta-analysis by Whittal, Agras, and Gould (1999) included 26 studies that evaluated CBT. The total number of patients was 460. The studies that were included variously compared CBT with no treatment, delayed treatment, or an alternative form of psychological treatment. As in the meta-analysis of antidepressant medication, each effect size (ES) reflected within-treatment change using the formula described above. The respective ESs were as follows: binge eating = 1.28, purging = 1.22, depression = 1.31, and eating attitudes = 1.35. Planned comparisons showed that CBT was significantly more effective than antidepressant drugs on measures of both binge eating and purging.

Hay and Bacaltchuk (2000) compiled a systematic, quantitative review of psychotherapy for BN for the Cochrane Library. The rigorous search strategy they used identified 21 controlled studies of BN, 15 of which were limited to the purging subtype of BN. Specifically, what they identified as CBT was compared with no treatment, delayed treatment, some alternative form of psychotherapy, or a self-help form of CBT. Relative risk analyses were used to assess remission from binge eating, and standardized mean differences for continuous outcome variables. The analyses showed that CBT was significantly superior to delayed treatment in producing remission from binge eating and approached statistical significance from other psychotherapies. CBT was significantly more effective than comparison psychotherapies in reducing depression.

The strengths of this Cochrane review of controlled studies of BN are offset by several limitations. All the studies were coded for methodological quality. The criteria were the effectiveness of randomization, control of selection bias after randomization, and blinding of posttreatment assessment. As important as the methodological criteria in this review are, they are also limited. Vitally important methodological considerations were not considered in this quantitative review. For example, little if any attention is devoted to the adequacy of the CBT treatment. Indeed, at least one study is included that evaluates a form of treatment that cannot be viewed as CBT (Bachar, Latzer, Kreitler, & Berry, 1999). Nor is the adequacy of assessment evaluated. As we discuss below, studies vary widely not only in the adequacy of the method of assessment (e.g., interview vs. patient self-report) but also in the length of assessment period (e.g., 1 week vs. 4 weeks). Finally, unlike Whittal et al. (1999), Hay and Bacaltchuk (2000) did not report data on either purging, dietary restraint, or attitudes about body shape and weight.

The most comprehensive and objective analysis of treatment efficacy is the National Institute for Clinical Excellence (NICE; 2004) guideline, which includes a number of recommendations derived from a multidisciplinary and rigorous evaluation. The recommendations are based on data and are graded from A (strong empirical support from randomized controlled trials [RCTs]) to C (expert opinion without strong empirical data). The standard of evidence and its evaluation are consistent across medicine. The NICE (2004) guideline recommends CBT as the treatment of choice for adults with BN. The recommendation was given the grade of A, reflecting the numerous RCTs on the efficacy of CBT. This was the first time that NICE had recommended a psychological therapy as the treatment of choice for a psychiatric disorder. Specifically, CBT typically eliminates binge eating and purging in roughly 30 to 50% of all cases. Of the remaining patients, many show improvement, but some show no response. One measure of the clinical importance of treatment-induced change is the extent to which patients engage in normative levels of behavior after treatment. Fairburn et al. (1995) reported that at their 5.8 year follow-up, 74% of patients who had received CBT had global scores on the Eating Disorder Examination (EDE) within one standard deviation of the mean for young women in that community. CBT reliably produces changes across all four of the specific features of BN, namely, binge eating, purging, dietary restraint, and abnormal attitudes about body shape and weight.

Pharmacological Treatment

A number of different drugs have been investigated as possible treatments for BN. These drugs have included the anticonvulsant phenytoin, the opiate antagonist naltrexone, and the appetite suppressant fenfluramine (Mitchell & de Zwaan, 1993). The most intensively studied and commonly used drugs for BN are antidepressants.

Antidepressant Medication

The antidepressant drugs studied have included tricyclic drugs, monoamine oxidase inhibitors, and selective serotonin uptake inhibitors (SSRIs). Reviews of the literature have featured both meta-analyses and more traditional evaluations of individual studies.

In their meta-analysis, Whittal et al. (1999) included nine double-blind, placebo-controlled studies of antidepressant medication. The total number of patients in these studies was 870. The four outcome measures were frequency of binge eating, frequency of purging, depression, and what they labeled eating attitudes (i.e., self-reported dietary restraint, over-concern about body shape, and overconcern about body weight). Whittal et al. (1999) calculated within-treatment effect sizes (ESs), namely, posttreatment outcome minus pretreatment outcome divided by the pooled standard deviations. Weighted for sample sizes, the overall ESs were as follows: 0.66 for binge eating, 0.39 for purging, 0.73 for depression, and 0.71 for eating attitudes.

In a traditional review of the evidence on antide-pressant medication for BN, Devlin and Walsh (1995) listed 14 studies that yielded a mean reduc-tion in binge eating of 61.4% (range = 31 to 91%), with an average remission rate of 22% (range = 10 to 35%). The comparable figures for purging were a mean reduction of 58.9% (range = 34 to 91%), with an average remission rate of 34% (range = 23 to 44%). Several of the studies did not report remission rates. For example, only four studies reported remis-sion rates for purging. In some instances median re-ductions in binge eating and purging were reported, and in others the reduction rates were derived from examination of the graphs in the original articles. The average attrition rate was 27% (range = 13 to 42%). A major problem with all tallies of this nature is that averages compiled from studies differing widely in procedures, measurement, and method-ological rigor can be misleading. The NICE (2004) guideline rated the level of empirical support for an-tidepressant medication a B.

Several specific conclusions can be drawn from the antidepressant drug studies to date:

1. *Antidepressant drugs are more effective than a pill placebo in reducing binge eating and purging.*

2. *With one exception, there have been no system-atic dose-response studies.* The exception showed that 60 mg/day but not 20 mg/day of fluoxetine was more effective than a pill placebo (Fluoxetine Bulimia Nervosa Collaborative Study Group, 1992).

3. *Different classes of antidepressant drug seem to be equally effective.* However, there have been no di-rect comparisons of different drugs within the same study. At present, fluoxetine (60mg/day) would ap-pear to be the drug of choice because it produces fewer side effects than tricyclics.

4. *Patients who fail to respond to an initial antide-pressant drug may respond to another.* Walsh et al.

(1997) completed a controlled study in which treat-ment with desipramine (for 8 weeks) was followed by treatment with fluoxetine (60 mg/day for 8 weeks) if the patient's binge frequency had not declined by at least 75% or he or she experienced intolerable side effects. This two-stage regime was designed to more closely approximate actual clinical practice than con-ventional single-drug protocols. Of the patients ran-domized to active medication, two thirds were se-quentially administered the two drugs. Their average reduction in binge frequency was 69%, and 29% ceased binge eating. This compares with 47% and 13%, respectively, among patients treated with desi-pramine alone in an earlier placebo-controlled study conducted at the same center with a similar patient population (Walsh, Hadigan, Devlin, Gladis, & Roose, 1991).

5. *The long-term effects of antidepressant medica-tion still remain largely untested.* Walsh et al. (1991) required that patients in their study of desipramine versus placebo show a minimum reduction of 50% in binge eating after 8 weeks in order to be entered into a 16-week maintenance phase. Only 41% (29 of 71 patients) met this criterion. Of these patients, 8 declined to participate in the maintenance phase be-cause of lack of interest, intolerable side effects, or other problems. Therefore, just 21 patients entered the study maintenance phase. Eleven (52.4%) pa-tients completed the 16 weeks, 6 (28.6%) of whom relapsed (i.e., binged more than 50% of their base-line binge frequency), 2 (9.5%) dropped out to seek treatment elsewhere, and 2 (9.5%) were discontinued due to intolerable side effects. Patients who com-pleted the full 16 weeks of maintenance failed to show statistically significant improvement over this period. These results indicate that even over this modest period of follow-up, the outcome is poor among those who remain on active medication.

Romano, Halmi, Sarkar, Koke, and Lee (2002) compared fluoxetine with pill placebo in a 52-week, double-blind relapse prevention study. The drug was proved more effective than placebo in delaying time to relapse, but the primary finding of the study was that patients in both conditions fared poorly over the course of follow-up. Fully 83% of the patients receiving fluoxetine, and 92% of those on placebo, dropped-out.

The only other study of the longer-term effects of antidepressant drugs was by Agras, Rossiter, et al. (1994), described below. They found that 6 months of treatment with desipramine produced lasting improvement even after the medication was withdrawn. In contrast, treatment with desipramine for only 4 months was associated with substantial relapse. The mechanism(s) whereby 6 but not 4 months of treatment with desipramine reduces the probability of relapse is unknown.

6. *Few drug studies have evaluated the effects of antidepressant medication on aspects of BN other than binge eating and purging.* There is evidence that antidepressant drugs do not produce improvement in patients' eating between binge eating and purging episodes. One study found that desipramine actually increased rather than decreased dietary restriction between episodes of binge eating (Rossiter, Agras, Losch, & Telch, 1988). This failure to moderate the dieting of these patients may account for the poor maintenance of change with antidepressant medication, since the extreme and rigid form of dieting seen in BN is thought to encourage binge eating (Polivy & Herman, 1993; Fairburn, 1997a).

7. *Consistent predictors of a positive response to antidepressant medication have yet to be identified.* Pretreatment levels of depression appear not to be related to treatment outcome (Walsh et al., 1991).

8. *The mechanism(s) whereby antidepressant medication exerts its effects is unknown.*

Comparison of CBT With Antidepressant Medication

1. *CBT seems more acceptable to patients than antidepressant medication.* Patients with BN appear reluctant to take antidepressant medication and seem to prefer psychological treatment.

2. *The dropout rate is lower with CBT than with pharmacological treatments.*

3. *CBT seems to be superior to treatment with a single antidepressant drug .*

4. *Combining CBT with antidepressant medication is significantly more effective than medication alone.*

5. *Combining CBT and antidepressant medication produces few consistent benefits over CBT alone.*

6. *CBT plus medication has not been shown to be superior to CBT plus a pill placebo.*

7. *The combination of CBT and antidepressant medication may be more effective than CBT alone in reducing anxiety and depressive symptoms.*

8. *Longer-term maintenance of change is better with CBT than with antidepressant drugs.*

The Efficacy of Other Psychological Treatments

Interpersonal Psychotherapy

Other than CBT, the psychological treatment with most support is interpersonal psychotherapy (IPT), which was originally devised by Klerman, Weissman, Rounsaville, and Chevron (1984) as a short-term treatment for depression. IPT is a focal psychotherapy, the main emphasis of which is to help patients identify and modify current interpersonal problems. The treatment is both nondirective and noninterpretive and, as adapted for BN (Fairburn, 1997b), pays little attention to the patient's eating disorder. It is therefore very different from CBT. The findings of two major studies, discussed below, showed IPT was significantly less effective than CBT at posttreatment (Fairburn et al., 1991; Agras, Walsh, et al., 2000). However, neither at 1 year (Agras, Walsh, et al., 2000; Fairburn, Jones, et al., 1993) nor 6 year follow-up (Fairburn et al., 1995) was there any statistical difference between the two treatments.

In the Fairburn, Jones, et al. (1993) study, IPT was significantly more effective than the behavioral treatment that was equivalent in therapist contact and ratings of suitability and expectancy, indicating a specific effect of IPT. The study by Agras, Walsh, Fairburn, Wilson, and Kraemer (2000) lacked a third comparison treatment that controlled for nonspecific influences, making it impossible to conclude that IPT had specific effects. The NICE (2004) guidelines recommend that "interpersonal psychotherapy should be considered as an alternative to CBT but patients should be informed that it takes 8–12 months to achieve results" (p. 14). This recommendation receives a grade of B.

Psychodynamic Therapy

Controlled studies of the effectiveness of psychodynamic therapies are lacking. The exception is Garner et al.'s (1993) comparison of CBT with supportive-expressive psychotherapy (SET). Although equally effective in reducing binge eating, SET was inferior to CBT on other measures of BN, as well as associated psychopathology. The absence of a no-treatment control group and the lack of any follow-up make it difficult to interpret the findings of this study. Despite the continuing absence of data from RCTs to support the use of psychodynamic psychotherapy in the treatment of BN, it remains popular in the United States.

Family Therapy

A family approach to treating eating disorders has a long clinical tradition, yet only a single controlled study has evaluated the effectiveness of a family therapy approach (Russell, Szmukler, Dare, & Eisler, 1987). This study was marked by a high dropout rate (44%) and an unusually poor outcome (only a 9% abstinence rate), especially in adult patients. (It should be remembered that most patients with BN are adults.) However, since the patients in this study may have been a particularly recalcitrant group, given that they had been referred to a specialist treatment center, the generalizability of these findings could be questioned.

Comparisons of CBT With Alternative Psychological Treatments

1. *CBT is more effective than credible comparison treatments that control for the nonspecifics of therapy.*
2. *CBT is superior to behavioral versions of the treatment that omit cognitive restructuring and the focus on modifying attitudes toward body shape and weight.*
3. *CBT is significantly more effective than, or at least as effective as, any form of psychotherapy with which it has been compared.* Fairburn et al. (1991) compared CBT with two alternative treatments; the first was behavior therapy (BT), comprising the CBT treatment minus cognitive restructuring, and the behavioral and cognitive methods for modifying abnormal attitudes about weight and shape; the second treatment was an adaptation of interpersonal psychotherapy (IPT; described in more detail later). In the latter treatment, little attention was paid to the eating disorder per se. Each condition comprised 25 patients. All three treatments were manual-based, and their implementation was closely monitored. For the first time in the field, the EDE was used as the main measure of outcome.

At posttreatment, the three therapies were equally effective in reducing binge eating. The mean reduc-

tions were 71% for CBT, 62% for BT, and 62% for IPT. However, CBT was significantly more effective than IPT in reducing purging, dietary restraint, and attitudes to shape and weight, and superior to BT on the latter two variables, despite equivalent ratings of suitability of treatment and expectations of outcome. This pattern of results shows that CBT had specific effects on different measures of outcome consistent with its theoretical rationale. As in the previous study by the Oxford group, treatment was followed by a 1-year "closed" follow-up (i.e., it was treatment free). It showed that the effects of CBT were well maintained and significantly superior to BT but equal to IPT (Fairburn, Jones, et al., 1993). Thirty-six percent of CBT patients, 20% of BT patients, and 44% of IPT patients had ceased both binge eating and purging. The patients were followed up once more after an average of 5.8 (SD ± 2.0) years, thereby providing a unique perspective on the long-term impact of these three treatments. There was a clear difference between them, even after this long period of time. Those patients who had received CBT or IPT were doing equally well, with 63% and 72%, respectively, having no eating disorder diagnosis according to the fourth edition of the *Diagnostic and Statistical Manual* (*DSM-IV*) of the American Psychiatric Association (American Psychiatric Association, 2004) compared with 14% among those who had received BT (Fairburn et al., 1995).

Agras, Walsh, et al. (2000) compared the same CBT and IPT treatments in a much larger sample size ($n = 220$ patients). The findings essentially replicated those of the Fairburn, Jones, et al. (1993) study. At posttreatment, CBT was significantly superior to IPT in the number of patients who had ceased all binge eating and purging over the preceding 4 weeks as assessed by the EDE. The proportions were 29% versus 6% in the intent-to-treat analysis, and 45% versus 8% in the analysis of only those patients who completed treatment. Percentage reductions in frequency of binge eating and purging for completers were 86% and 84% for CBT versus 51% and 50% for IPT. CBT was also significantly superior to IPT in reducing dietary restraint but not in modifying dysfunctional attitudes about body shape and weight. There were no differences between the two treatments on measures of associated psychopathology (e.g., depression, self-esteem, or interpersonal functioning). At follow-up at 4 and 8 to 12 months, there were no statistically significant differences between the two therapies in terms of remission from binge eating and purging over the preceding 4 weeks.

The posttreatment course of patients in the two treatments was similar. For example, 66% of those who had recovered with CBT at the end of treatment remained recovered at follow-up, compared with 57% (4 of 7) of those treated with IPT. For those remitted at the end of CBT, 29% (6 of 21) recovered, compared with 33% (8 of 24) for the IPT group. Of the remaining participants, 7% (4 of 57) had recovered at follow-up in the CBT group, compared with 9% (7 of 79) in the IPT group. The percentages in each category at the end of treatment were similar for both treatments. These findings suggest that the absence of a statistically significant difference between CBT and IPT over follow-up may be more a function of their differential posttreatment status (such as a regression toward the mean effect) than any delayed "catch-up" property of IPT.

The Agras, Walsh, et al. (2000) study had several distinctive methodological strengths. First, in contrast to virtually all previous controlled studies of the treatment of BN, it had sufficient statistical power to detect differences between the two therapies. Second, the quality of the two therapies was rigorously controlled using manual-based treatment protocols. The study was conducted at two sites in the United States (Stanford and Columbia), where the therapists were closely monitored on a weekly basis throughout the study by two experienced supervisors. In addition, each treatment was independently and continually monitored by the investigator (Fairburn) who had originally developed each protocol and conducted the earlier study at Oxford. Third, assessment was detailed and comprehensive, using the EDE interview.

4. *CBT is comparatively quick-acting* (Wilson, Fairburn, Agras, Walsh, & Kraemer, 2002).

5. *CBT affects both the specific and the general psychopathology of BN.* Most studies have shown significant improvements in depression, self-esteem, social functioning, and measures of personality disturbance.

6. *CBT is associated with good maintenance of change at 6-month and 1-year follow-up.* The strongest findings have come from the Oxford group. After a 1-year follow-up, binge eating and purging (as assessed by the EDE) had declined by more than 90%. Thirty-six percent of patients had ceased all binge eating and purging. Given that the follow-up was

"closed," this ensured that patients seeking additional or different treatment did not confound evaluation of maintenance of change (Fairburn, Jones, et al., 1993). The subsequent 6-year follow-up showed that the effects of CBT were maintained (an abstinence rate of 50%; Fairburn et al., 1995). The 11-year follow-up of the Mitchell et al. (1990) study found that 67.6% of the original CBT plus medication group, and 70.8% of the CBT plus placebo group were in partial or full remission (Keel, personal communication, January 25, 2001). The good maintenance of change following CBT contrasts markedly with the natural course of the disorder, which is characterized by chronicity in the long term and flux in the short term (Keller, Herzog, Lavori, Bradburn, & Mahoney, 1992; Fairburn et al., 2000).

7. *Reliable pretreatment predictors of response to CBT have proved elusive.* Numerous pretreatment patient characteristics have emerged as predictor variables, including past history of anorexia nervosa or previous low body weight, low self-esteem, comorbid personality disorders, and severity of core eating disorder symptoms. The results across studies have been inconsistent, however, and of limited clinical value (Agras, Crow, et al., 2000). The NICE (2004) guideline tentatively identified impulsivity, borderline personality, concurrent substance misuse, and a history of obesity as potential predictors of outcome.

Much of the overall improvement achieved with CBT is evident after the first few weeks of treatment, and failure to respond early is a statistically and clinically significant predictor of ultimate outcome (Agras, Crow, et al., 2000). Fairburn, Agras, Walsh, Wilson, & Stice (2004) showed that reduction in purging at session 6 provided a better prediction of outcome than any pretreatment variable. This robust and replicated finding is of theoretical and practical importance. At the theoretical level it points to the early action of critical mechanisms of change in producing short-term and longer term effects. Among the clinical implications is the need to reevaluate the treatment plan should early response not be observed (see Fairburn et al., 2003).

Few studies have examined posttreatment predictors of longer term outcome. Available evidence suggests that both behavioral and attitudinal change during treatment are linked to longer term functioning. In a test of the cognitive model on which CBT is based, Fairburn, Peveler, Jones, Hope, and Doll (1993) found that among patients who had recovered in terms of behavioral change, 9% of those with the least dysfunctional concern with body shape and weight disturbance relapsed, compared with 29% and 75% among those with moderate and severe degrees of concern about body shape and weight. In a study of 143 BN patients who had received group CBT treatment, Mussell et al. (2000) found that symptom remission (total absence of binge eating and purging) during the final 2 weeks of treatment was the best predictor of outcome at a 6-month follow-up.

8. *The efficacy of manual-based CBT is mediated, in part, by the reduction of self-reported dietary restraint* (Wilson et al., 2002).

9. *Preliminary data indicate that the enhanced CBT approach of Fairburn et al. (2003) may be significantly more effective than the 1993 manual that has been tested in published RCTs to date.*

Less Intensive Treatments

Manual-based CBT was designed for use within specialist settings. It is time-consuming (involving about 20 sessions over 5 months), and to be implemented properly, expert training is required. Since there are unlikely ever to be sufficient specialist treatment resources for those with eating disorders, there is a need to develop simpler and briefer forms of CBT suitable for widespread use (Fairburn & Carter, 1997; Sysko & Walsh, in press).

Self-Help

Studies of self-help have varied widely in methodological quality (e.g., sample size, assessment of eating disorder psychopathology), clinical settings, and who administered the treatment. Variable outcomes have been reported. Three studies evaluated the use of a self-help manual based on cognitive-behavioral principles (Fairburn, 1995). Simply giving the manual to BN patients in what could be called unguided self-help did not produce a significantly better outcome than a "nonspecific" self-help manual or even a wait-list control condition (Carter et al., 2003). A second study compared four treatments in a primary care setting: fluoxetine, placebo, fluoxetine plus Fairburn's 1995 manual, and placebo plus the self-help manual. In the two self-help conditions, BN patients met with minimally trained nurses

for six to eight brief sessions of focused instruction in the implementation of the self-help manual (Walsh, Fairburn, Mickley, Sysko, & Parides, 2004). This guided self-help (GSH) approach was marked by a high dropout rate and had little therapeutic effect. A plausible explanation is that the nurses were inexperienced in eating disorders and their treatment, and received little training and no ongoing supervision. The nurses also did not collect patients' self-monitoring reports of their binge eating and purging, a key component of CBT that might have encouraged better treatment compliance. In sharp contrast to this study, however, four sessions of GSH administered by experienced nurses in a specialist eating disorders clinic resulted in marked improvement in 27% of eating disorder patients, the majority of whom had BN (Palmer, Birchall, McGrain, & Sullivan, 2002). GSH using the Fairburn (1995) book was significantly more effective than a wait-list control and unguided self-help. Using a similar self-help manual based on CBT principles, Banasiak et al. (2005) compared 10 sessions of GSH with a delayed treatment control group in the treatment of BN patients by general practitioners in a primary care setting. The practitioners were not specialists in eating disorders, but they received training and minimal supervision. GSH was significantly more effective than the delayed treatment, producing clinically impressive improvement that was maintained at a 6-month follow-up.

In their analysis of various self-help interventions for BN, Sysko and Walsh (in press) concluded that their use is associated with greater improvement compared with a waiting list control condition., but that the efficacy of self-help relative to more established interventions remains to be determined. The NICE guidelines recommendation regarding self-help is as follows: "As a possible first step, patients with bulimia nervosa should be encouraged to follow an evidence-based self-help program," and "Healthcare professionals should consider providing direct encouragement and support" to patients undertaking such a program in order to improve outcomes (NICE 2004, p. 14). These recommendations received a grade of B.

Psychoeducation in Groups

The goal of psychoeducation is the normalization of eating and body image concerns through didactic instruction. The content consists of education and cognitive-behavioral change strategies. Its advantages are that it is less costly than specialized therapy and more readily disseminable.

Davis, Olmsted, and Rockert (1990) developed a psychoeducation program ($n = 15$) comprising five 90-minute group sessions that produced significantly greater improvement than a wait-list control ($n = 26$). Compared with a longer course of 19 sessions of individual CBT, they found that the program was less effective overall (Olmsted et al., 1991). The abstinence rates for both binge eating and vomiting were 30% for CBT and 17% for psychoeducation. However, with the subset of patients with less severe specific eating disorder symptoms and associated psychopathology, the group psychoeducational program was equally effective. Higher frequency of vomiting and comorbid depression were significant predictors of poor treatment outcome.

In a subsequent sequential design study, patients who completed the group psychoeducation program were randomly assigned either to a 16-week trial of individual CBT or to no additional treatment (Davis, McVey, Heinmaa, Rockert, & Kennedy, 1999). The combined treatment resulted in greater improvement in binge eating and purging frequencies, and a higher abstinence rate (43.2% vs. 10.5%) than group psychoeducation alone at posttreatment. This pattern was maintained at follow-up. However, there were no significant differences between the treatments on measures of dietary restraint, shape and weight concern, or associated psychopathology such as depression. This study allows only the conclusion that subsequent therapeutic contact produces improvement beyond that obtained with group psychoeducation. It does not speak to the specific value of CBT as a second stage treatment. Collectively, these findings suggest that group psychoeducation may be effective for at least a subset of BN patients.

SUMMARY

Research Implications

The methodological quality of treatment outcome studies is uneven, although research has become increasingly rigorous. Assessment of outcome has been problematic in many studies. Too few studies, especially those of antidepressant medication, have used

valid interview-based methods that provide a comprehensive picture of eating disorder psychopathology. Whether the window of assessment is 4 weeks (as in the EDE) or only 1 week will significantly influence the results.

It is now imperative that follow-up evaluations of acute treatment effects be conducted. The absence of well-controlled follow-up of short-term drug effects remains a serious shortcoming. Despite its strong empirical base, CBT is relatively rarely implemented in routine clinical settings in the United States (Von Ranson & Robinson, 2006). Research on the more effective dissemination of evidence-based CBT should be a priority. Similarly, CBT should be extended to more diverse populations than those evaluated in the current literature. For example, there has been no controlled research on the adaptation of manual-based CBT in the treatment of adolescents with BN and related eating disorders (Wilson & Sysko, 2006).

Clinical Implications

Manual-based CBT is currently the first-line treatment of choice for BN. Well accepted by patients, it is the most effective means of eliminating the core features of the eating disorder and is usually accompanied by improvement in comorbid psychological problems such as low self-esteem and depression. Longer term maintenance of improvement appears to be good, although additional studies are needed. Early response to CBT is the best predictor of treatment outcome.

Antidepressant medication is another effective treatment, although its acute effects are inferior to those obtained with CBT. In the longer term, antidepressant medication appears to be associated with a high rate of relapse, although more data are needed. Medication is sometimes effective in cases where CBT has failed.

IPT is a promising alternative to CBT. It is not statistically different from CBT at 1-year follow-up. CBT should be preferred to IPT on the following grounds: First, numerous well-controlled studies in different countries have demonstrated the efficacy of manual-based CBT. The evidence for IPT derives from only two studies. Second, CBT is significantly quicker in producing improvement. Third, early response to treatment in CBT provides a clinically useful predictor of outcome. Predictors of success with IPT are lacking. The only advantage for IPT might be that it appears to be more acceptable and hence disseminable among clinical practitioners trained in traditional psychotherapeutic approaches (Wilson, 1998).

Manual-based CBT is currently the treatment of choice for BN, but its efficacy is limited. More broadly effective treatments are needed. An option popular with many practitioners would be to combine CBT with some other form of psychotherapy in an eclectic—often misleadingly called "integrative"—treatment, or with antidepressant medication (e.g., Walsh, et al., 2000). We argue that the preferred alternative is to expand and improve CBT itself (Wilson, 1999). Fairburn et al.'s (2003) CBT-Enhanced (CBT-E), which goes well beyond the 1993 manual in conceptual and clinical breadth, is a case in point. In brief, CBT-E is based on what is called a transdiagnostic model of eating disorders in general. The core cognitive-behavioral model that guides treatment has been broadened to include hypothesized maintaining mechanisms such as low self-esteem, clinical perfectionism, mood intolerance, and interpersonal difficulties. Each new mechanism is then addressed with a specific therapeutic module. The goal of treatment is to tailor the therapy to each patient's particular needs by employing the appropriate modules. CBT-E not only provides for greater flexibility and individualization of therapy, the advantages of which are know (Ghaderi, 2006), but also greatly expands the range of treatment strategies and techniques available to the therapist by drawing upon the state-of-the-art cognitive-behavioral approach as a whole (Wilson, 2004).

ANOREXIA NERVOSA

Anorexia nervosa (AN) is the least common of the eating disorder diagnoses. It affects a younger age-group than BN, most cases being female and aged between 10 and 30 years. It is therefore a disorder that straddles adolescent and adult psychiatric services. Like BN, AN is uncommon among males (about 10% of cases are male).

Diagnosis

The diagnostic criteria for AN are not entirely satisfactory. In principle, three features are required to make the diagnosis. The first is the presence of a characteristic set of attitudes concerning shape and weight, sometimes referred to as the *core psychopathology*. Various expressions have been used to describe these attitudes, including a "relentless pursuit of thinness" and a "morbid fear of fatness." The essential feature is that these people judge their self-worth almost exclusively in terms of their shape and weight. The second diagnostic feature is the active maintenance of an extremely low weight. The definition of what constitutes "low" varies: a widely used threshold is having a body mass index (BMI; weight in kg/(height in m)^2) below 17.5. The low weight is achieved by a variety of means, including marked dietary restriction, excessive exercising, and, in some cases, self-induced vomiting or the misuse of laxatives or diuretics. The third diagnostic feature is amenorrhea (in postmenarchal females who are not taking an oral contraceptive). The main problem with these diagnostic criteria is that they are too restrictive. As a result, patients with very similar clinical features are excluded from the diagnosis and relegated to the neglected diagnosis eating disorder not otherwise specified. For example, there are cases that closely resemble AN but, instead of there being over-evaluation of shape and weight, it is maintaining strict control over eating that is the basis for self-evaluation. Similarly, there are otherwise typical cases of AN that are not eligible for the diagnosis because menstruation has not ceased.

Clinical Features

The distinctive "core psychopathology" of AN and BN is essentially the same in females and males. Most of the other features of these disorders appear to be secondary to this psychopathology and to its consequences—for example, secondary to the state of starvation present in AN (Fairburn & Harrison, 2003). Thus, in AN there is a sustained and determined pursuit of weight loss, and to the extent that this is achieved, this behavior is not viewed as a problem. Indeed, these patients tend to regard their low weight as an "accomplishment rather than an affliction" (Vitousek, Watson, & Wilson, 1998); as a consequence, they have limited motivation to change. As in BN the core psychopathology has other expressions; for example, many patients mislabel certain adverse physical and emotional states as "feeling fat," and some repeatedly scrutinize aspects of their shape, which may contribute to them overestimating their size.

In AN the pursuit of weight loss is successful in that a very low weight is achieved. This is primarily the result of a severe and selective restriction of food intake, with foods viewed as fattening being excluded. In most cases there is no true "anorexia" as such. In some patients the restriction over food intake is also motivated by other psychological processes, including asceticism, competitiveness, and a wish to punish themselves. Many patients engage in a driven form of overexercising that can contribute to their low weight. Self-induced vomiting and other extreme forms of weight-control behavior (such as the misuse of laxatives or diuretics) are practiced by a minority. Some patients have times when they lose control over eating, although the amounts eaten may not be large (hence these episodes are sometimes termed *subjective binges*). Depressive and anxiety symptoms, irritability, lability of mood, impaired concentration, loss of sexual appetite, and obsessional features are frequent associated features. Typically they get worse as weight is lost and improve with weight regain. Interest in the outside world also declines as patients become underweight, with the result that most become socially withdrawn and isolated. This too is reversible.

Development and Course

AN typically starts in midteenage years with the onset of dietary restriction that proceeds to get out of control. In some cases the disorder is short-lived and self-limiting, or it requires only a brief intervention. This is most typical of young cases with a brief history. In others, the disorder becomes entrenched and necessitates more intensive treatment. In 10 to 20%, the disorder proves intractable and unremitting. This heterogeneity in course and outcome is often neglected in accounts of the disorder. The proportions with these outcomes vary according to the age of the sample and the treatment setting. Some residual features are common, particularly some degree of overconcern about shape, weight, and eating. A frequent occurrence is the development of binge eating and in many cases progression on to BN or eating disorder NOS. Most prominent among the favorable prognostic factors are an early age of onset and a short history, whereas unfavorable prognostic factors include a long history, severe weight loss, and binge

eating and vomiting. Anorexia nervosa is the one eating disorder to be associated with a raised mortality rate, the standardized mortality ratio over the first ten years from presentation being about 10. The majority of deaths are either a direct result of medical complications or due to suicide.

Research on Treatment

In principle, there are three elements to the treatment of AN. The first is engaging patients in treatment and maintaining their motivation thereafter; the second is achieving weight regain and establishing stable and healthy eating habits; and the third is ensuring that progress is maintained in the future by addressing the processes that were responsible for the energy deficit. How best to achieve these goals has been the subject of remarkably little research. What follows is a personal appraisal of the published research to date (March 2006) based largely on the studies identified in the context of the recent systematic review conducted by the United Kingdom National Institute for Clinical Excellence (NICE; 2004) supplemented with the limited amount of new data. As in the NICE systematic review, no meta-analysis has been possible due to the marked differences in the way treatment outcome has been reported.

Treatment Options

There is a range of treatment options for AN. There are various treatment settings, the main ones being outpatient, day patient (partial hospitalization), and inpatient treatment; within these settings a variety of interventions may be provided, pharmacological or psychological or both. To complicate matters, patients may move from one setting to another, and within any one setting often more than one treatment is employed.

There is limited empirical support for this plethora of options because there has been remarkably little research on the treatment of AN, and much of what has been done has been inconclusive. There are many reasons for the lack of research (Agras et al., 2004), a major one being that AN is uncommon. A consequence is that researchers often conduct treatment trials with inappropriately small sample sizes, with the result that there are frequently no statistically significant findings. This can tempt the researcher to conclude that the treatments in question were equivalent in their clinical effects, whereas the fact is that the sample sizes were too small to establish treatment equivalence.

There is no empirical evidence to support the use of any one treatment setting over any other in terms of patients' outcome. There has been just one attempt to randomize patients to different treatment settings (Crisp et al., 1991) and, unfortunately, the comparison was compromised by the unsurprising finding that many patients randomized to inpatient treatment did not want it.

Inpatient Treatment

Inpatient treatment is used differently in different places; for example, it is common in some countries but unusual in others, and length of stay also varies markedly (Maguire, Surgenor, Abraham, & Beumont, 2003). Such differences are intriguing but not evidence-based because inpatient treatment has received scant research attention. As Vandereycken (2003) has pointed out, even the most basic questions about inpatient treatment have not been adequately formulated, let alone addressed. For example, not only are the indications for hospitalization not established, but there is no agreement on specific goals, nor is it known how best to achieve them. Also, it is not clear whether the indications, goals, and treatments should differ for adolescents and adults. At best, there is modest evidence from cohort studies to support a focus on eating and an emphasis on weight regain (Herzog, Hartmann, & Falk, 1996). Comparisons of flexible behavioral programs with more rigid ones either have yielded no significant differences in the rate of weight regain (Touyz, Beumont, Glaun, Philips, & Cowie, 1984) or have favored the more flexible regime (Vandereycken & Pieters, 1978). A controlled evaluation of body warming yielded no significant differences (Birmingham, Gutierrez, Jonat, & Beumont, 2004). There is no evidence from RCTs that drug treatment significantly enhances weight regain in the hospital.

Day Patient Treatment

Even less is known about day patient treatment than inpatient treatment (Zipfel et al., 2002). Again, the indications are not agreed, and the goals not established. It is not clear whether day patient treatment is best viewed as a less expensive alternative to inpatient treatment, as an intensive form of outpatient treatment, or as a distinct modality with particular strengths and weaknesses.

Outpatient Treatment

Whatever the place of inpatient and day patient treatment, outpatient treatment is the mainstay of the treatment of AN. Outpatient treatment is the sole treatment for many patients, and even if patients receive inpatient or day patient treatment, it is usually preceded by and followed by outpatient treatment. The research on the effectiveness of outpatient treatment is therefore of particular importance.

Outpatient Treatment Studies

Drug Treatment

A small study of the use of fluoxetine following inpatient treatment (Kaye et al., 2001) suggested that outcome was improved. However, a larger, well-controlled trial showed no evidence that fluoxetine was superior to placebo or offered any incremental benefit to CBT (Walsh, et al., 2005).

Psychological Treatment of Adolescents

It is widely thought that there is good evidence regarding the treatment of adolescents with AN, the assumption being that family-based treatment (FBT) has a strong body of empirical support. This is not the case.

There have been three comparisons of FBT with another form of treatment. In the first, Russell and colleagues compared 1 year of FBT with 1 year of supportive psychotherapy in 21 patients (mean age 16.6 years, mean duration of disorder 1.2 years) who had just been discharged from a national specialist inpatient unit (Russell et al., 1987). The FBT has since come to be known as the *Maudsley method*, and it has been manualized (Lock, le Grante, Agras, & Dare, 2001). The results favored FBT; at the end of treatment, 6 out of the 10 patients who received FBT were judged to have a good outcome compared with 1 out of the 11 patients who received the comparison treatment. Five years later, although the patients in both conditions were found to have done well, the results continued to favor FBT (Eisler & Dare, 1997).

The second study involved the FCC comparison of a treatment similar to the Maudsley method with a psychodynamically oriented treatment in which the adolescent patients were seen individually with occasional supportive sessions for their parents (Robin et al., 1995). The outcome of both groups of patients (N = 19 and 18, respectively) was positive, both at the end of treatment and 1 year later. There was one statistically significant difference between them: In terms of increase in BMI, the patients in the FBT condition did better. It is not possible to attribute this finding to differences between the two psychotherapies, however, because many patients were hospitalized during their treatment, and this was especially common among those receiving FBT.

The most recent study was of a broader age range comprising 25 adolescent and young adult female patients (aged 13 to 23 years) currently living with their families (Ball & Mitchell, 2004). The patients received either FBT or CBT based on the principles described by Garner and Bemis (1982). Eighteen of the patients completed treatment, nine from each treatment condition. Outcome was generally good (60% of the total sample were categorized as having a good outcome), with there being no statistically significant differences (on completer analysis) between the two treatments on any of the variables studied. This was to be expected given the very small sample size.

In summary, there have been three comparisons of FBT with another form of treatment, the findings of the second and third studies being uninterpretable. Thus the case for favoring FBT over other forms of treatment rests on Russell and colleagues' study of 21 adolescent patients (just 10 of whom received FBT) who had recently been discharged from a specialist inpatient unit. This is a small body of data and one of questionable relevance to routine outpatient treatment. It is also worth noting that the superiority of FBT over supportive psychotherapy might not have been due to the involvement of the patient's family, since there was another important difference between the two treatments: FBT placed great emphasis on getting patients to eat well and maintain a healthy weight, whereas there was nothing like the same focus on eating and weight in the supportive psychotherapy condition.

There have been three main comparisons of different forms of FBT. The findings from the first two are also inconclusive. The first evaluated two ways of delivering the Maudsley method, one of which involved all the family being seen together, whereas the other involved separate sessions for the patient and the parents (Eisler, Dare, Hodes, & Russell, et al., 2000). In contrast with the Russell et al. study (1987), FBT was provided from the outset rather than after hospitalization. Forty patients (mean age 15.5 years, average duration of disorder just over 1 year) were randomized to the two approaches. Both groups of patients improved, with 37.5% achieving a good outcome and a further 25% improving substantially. Extensive testing for differences between the treatments revealed few statistically significant findings.

The second study involved a comparison of FBT with family education (Geist, Heinmaa, Stephens, Davis, & Katzman, 2000). Both treatments occurred in the context of considerable additional input, including an initial period of inpatient treatment and continuing medical and nursing contact following discharge. Not surprisingly given the amount of additional treatment and the small number of patients studied (N = 25), the two treatment conditions did not differ significantly in their effects.

The third study was the largest and most sophisticated to date. It compared two intensities of FBT, one involving 10 sessions over 6 months and the other involving 20 sessions over 1 year (Lock, Agras, Bryson, & Kraemer, 2005). No differences in outcome (at 12 months postrandomization) emerged despite the study being adequately powered.

Psychological Treatment of Adults

There has been somewhat more research on the outpatient psychological treatment of adults with AN. There have been eight studies of outpatient treatment in the absence of prior hospitalization. Hall and Crisp (1987) compared nutritional counseling with psychotherapy (individual and family) in 30 outpatients comprising both adolescents and adults. Channon, De Silva, Helmsley, and Perkins (1989) compared CBT, behavior therapy (BT), and a low-contact control condition in 24 adult patients. Crisp and colleagues (1991) compared one-to-one and group ways of delivering the combination of individual and family psychotherapy. And Treasure, Todd, Brolly, Nehmed, and Denman (1995) compared cognitive analytic therapy (CAT) with BT in 30 adult patients. In all four studies no statistically significant findings of note emerged. The fifth study, which was of CBT, was inconclusive because none of the patients in the nutritional counseling comparison condition completed treatment (Serfaty, Turkington, Heap, Ledsham, & Jolley, 1999).

The sixth study was larger than its predecessors in that 84 patients were studied (Dare, Eisler, Russell, Treasure, & Dodge, 2001). In common with most adult samples, the patients differed markedly from their adolescent counterparts; they were considerably older (mean age 26.3 years), and their disorder was well established (mean duration 6.3 years). The patients were randomized to four treatments, resulting once again in small groups being compared. The four treatments were focal psychoanalytic psychotherapy, CAT, FBT of the Maudsley style, and routine outpatient treatment involving brief sessions with a trainee psychiatrist. No statistically significant differences were found between the three psychotherapies, but all three were more effective than the routine treatment. Across the three psychotherapies 13.8% of the patients achieved a good outcome, and a further 18.5% improved substantially—note that the comparable figures for the same research center's adolescent sample were 37.5% and 25%, respectively. Although the authors attribute the difference between the psychotherapies and the routine treatment to the fact that these were "specialized psychotherapies," it seems just as plausible that it could have been due to the low "dose" of the routine treatment, which involved less than half the therapist-patient contact. In addition, the fact that the psychiatrists who delivered the treatment were trainees who changed every 6 months may also have been relevant.

The seventh study is an intriguing one. Thirty-three women with AN (ignoring the amenorrhea criterion) plus 23 with subthreshold "AN" (BMI 17.5 to 19.0) were randomized to 20 sessions of CBT, interpersonal psychotherapy (IPT), or supportive clinical management (McIntosh et al., 2005). At posttreatment the results favored the clinical management condition over the two specific psychotherapies, although none of the treatments was particularly effective. These findings are difficult to interpret for a number of reasons. First, a substantial proportion of the sample started treatment at a relatively high BMI for patients with "AN." This makes their outcome difficult to evaluate. Second, the forms of CBT and

IPT used appear to have been unusually focused, in marked contrast with the broader and more flexible clinical management condition. Third, the absence of follow-up data means that the findings must be considered interim. This is especially true of those who received IPT, since in BN it has been found to have a slow mode of action (Agras et al., 2000; Fairburn, Jones, et al., 1993).

The most recent study encountered major problems due to the failure of patients to complete treatment. It involved a multisite comparison of CBT, fluoxetine, and the two treatments combined (Halmi et al., 2005). In common with the McIntosh et al. (2005) study, the patients had a relatively high BMI (mean = 17.8) at the outset of treatment. Of 122 patients randomized, only 45 (37%) completed the 1 year of treatment. Of the remainder, 21 were withdrawn and 56 dropped out. The treatment noncompletion rate was particularly high in the fluoxetine alone condition (30/41 [73%]). The rates for the CBT alone and CBT plus fluoxetine conditions were 24/42 (57%) and 23/39 (60%), respectively. This high rate of attrition precluded the evaluation of the relative effects of the three treatments. However, it is a finding in its own right in that it highlights the difficulty clinicians face in engaging and retaining these patients.

Finally, there have been two studies of posthospitalization psychological treatment. The first was an arm of Russell et al.'s (1987) comparison of FBT with supportive psychotherapy. In addition to including adolescents, the study also included two groups of adults. In contrast with the adolescent findings, and hardly surprisingly given the small sample sizes, no statistically significant differences emerged. In the second study 33 patients were randomized to receive 12 months of CBT or nutritional counseling (Pike, Walsh, Vitousek, Wilson, & Bauer, 2003). Survival analysis showed that the patients who received CBT remained in treatment longer, and there was a trend for their relapse rate to be lower. In addition, significantly fewer of the CBT patients dropped out of treatment, and more met conventional criteria for a good outcome. Interestingly, 7 of the 8 CBT patients who had a good outcome were also receiving antidepressant medication compared with the 10 who did not. There was no suggestion of a medication effect within the nutritional counseling group. Thus the superiority of CBT over nutritional counseling could have been due in part to a synergism between CBT and antidepressant medication. One other point is also of note: Nutritional counseling is not a demanding comparison condition, nor is it a particularly informative one (Vitousek, 2002).

SUMMARY

Research Implications

The research on the treatment of AN is inferior in quantity and quality to that on BN. This is attributable in part to the low incidence of AN and the clinical and methodological difficulties inherent in studying the disorder. As matters stand, it is virtually impossible to construct evidence-based clinical recommendations regarding the treatment of AN (NICE, 2004; Fairburn, 2005). This is true with regard to the treatment of both adults and adolescents.

Turning to research priorities, three questions seem particularly pressing. First, in adolescents it needs to be established that FBT has a specific beneficial effect, for it is not clear that the effects of this treatment are due to its involvement of the family or indeed to any property of the treatment. The changes could simply reflect the good prognosis of AN in adolescence. Alternative treatment approaches (which will obviously involve the family to some extent) need to be tested and their short- and long-term outcome compared with that of FBT. Second, in adults two interesting findings have emerged from the posthospitalization studies, one being that CBT appears to be more effective than nutritional counseling, a difference that may have been due in part to a synergism between CBT and antidepressant medication, and the other being that fluoxetine may reduce the rate of relapse. A large-scale study of the posthospitalization effects of CBT, fluoxetine, and their combination has just been completed, but its findings are not yet available. Third, there is a need to develop more effective treatments for adults with AN, since outcome is at present poor. It has been argued that until promising new treatments have been developed (with preliminary data to support them), it would be premature to embark upon further costly and time-consuming randomized controlled trials (Fairburn, 2005; Halmi et al., 2005).

Clinical Implications

Treatment of Adolescent Patients

A general observation is worth making. This is that treatment outcome among adolescents with AN is generally good, whereas that among adults is poor. This may be more an inherent property of the disorder in these two age-groups than any reflection of the potency of the treatments available. Adolescent patients tend to have had AN for a short time — often little more than a year — whereas adults with AN have generally had the disorder for 5 or more years and often have been recipients of prior attempts at treatment. It is not unlikely that the explanation for adolescent AN being more treatment responsive than adult AN is that many of the maintaining mechanisms that obstruct change in the more enduring cases are not operating in younger patients.

Clinical experience and the limited research evidence support the use of FBT in the treatment of adolescents. This can be done with the family seen together or with the parents and patient being seen apart. Other permutations are also possible, but they have yet to be evaluated. There is also interest in treating groups of families together (Scholz & Asen, 2001). On the other hand, it must not be forgotten that it has not been established that family therapy has a specific beneficial effect. Rigorous adequately powered comparisons of FBT with appropriate alternative treatments are needed.

Treatment of Adult Patients

Given the marked overlap between the psychopathology of AN and BN, and the utility of CBT in the treatment of BN, it would seem likely that the same style of CBT might also benefit adults with AN. This is the premise underpinning the new "transdiagnostic" form of CBT for eating disorders (Fairburn et al., 2003). However, the effectiveness of this treatment with low-weight patients has yet to be established.

At present there appears to be no specific role for pharmacotherapy in the treatment of AN. This is not to say that drug treatment does not have a place in the treatment of conditions that coexist with AN: for example, it is important not to neglect the value of antidepressant drugs in treating those patients who have a comorbid clinical depression.

In some patients with AN, hospitalization is desirable or unavoidable. It is well established that inpatient treatment comprising dietary counseling with some behavioral elements can effectively restore body weight in the majority of cases. It is also clear that the behavioral component of hospital treatment can be simpler and much less restrictive than the regimes commonly used in the 1960s and 1970s (Touyz & Beumont, 1997). The challenge is how to minimize the high rate of relapse that follows inpatient treatment.

EATING DISORDER NOT OTHERWISE SPECIFIED

Eating disorder not otherwise specified (EDNOS) is the *DSM-IV* diagnostic category reserved for all eating disorders other than anorexia nervosa and bulimia nervosa. In most outpatient settings, more than 50% of the cases fall into this group (Fairburn & Bohn, 2005). Like most "NOS" diagnoses, EDNOS has attracted little research attention, an exception being binge-eating disorder (BED), for which provisional diagnostic criteria are available (American Psychiatric Association, 1994). The remaining clinical presentations consist primarily of mixed states in which the psychopathology of AN and BN is present but combined somewhat differently from that seen in AN and BN and a small number of subthreshold cases of AN and BN. A diagnosis of EDNOS is especially common in adolescents, who often do not report one or more of the clinical features of BN or AN (Commission on Adolescent Eating Disorders, 2005). The disorders within EDNOS are no less clinically severe than BN and AN.

With the exception of BED, there have been no controlled treatment trials of these disorders despite the prevalence and clinical severity of EDNOS. Yet existing evidence-based treatments seem readily adaptable to patients with EDNOS. The Fairburn et al. (2003) transdiagnostic model, with its emphasis on common mechanisms that maintain different eating disorders, provides the breadth and flexibility to address these various disorders.

BINGE-EATING DISORDER

Binge-eating disorder is characterized by recurrent episodes of binge eating in the absence of the extreme methods of weight control seen in BN. There is no regular purging and no overexercising, nor is there extreme and rigid dieting. Rather, the binge eating occurs against a background of a general tendency to overeat. The disorder is accompanied by concerns about shape and weight that are similar to those seen in BN (Allison et al., 2005; Wilfley, Schwartz, Spurrell, & Fairburn, 2000). Like BN, BED is associated with shame and self-recrimination and some degree of psychosocial impairment.

The prevalence of BED in the general population is 1.5 to 2.0% (Bruce & Agras, 1992; Gotestam & Agras, 1995), a figure similar to that of BN. BED differs from BN in a number of important respects. BED appears to affect an older age-group than BN, with many patients being in their 40s. Male cases are not uncommon in BED (Spitzer et al., 1993), whereas BN predominantly afflicts women. Unlike BN, BED is also significantly associated with obesity (Bruce & Agras, 1992; Striegel-Moore, Wilfley, Pike, Dohm, & Fairburn, 2000). As in BN, comorbid psychiatric disorders are common. As many as 75% of BED patients report a lifetime history of a psychiatric disorder, with more than half having suffered from major depressive disorder (MDD), and 20% of the patients were diagnosed with current MDD (Wilfley, Friedman, et al., 2000; Yanovski, Nelson, Dubbert, & Spitzer, 1993).

Research has focused not only on adaptations of pharmacological and psychological treatments for BN but also on behavioral weight loss interventions for obesity.

SPECIALIZED PSYCHOLOGICAL TREATMENTS

Cognitive-Behavioral Therapy

The NICE guidelines state that "cognitive behavior therapy for binge eating disorder (CBT-BED), a specifically adapted form of CBT, should be offered to adults with binge eating disorder" (NICE, 2004, p. 60), assigning a grade of A to the strength of evidence supporting CBT for BED. This evaluation reflects both the quantity and the quality of RCTs evaluating CBT for BED. Several RCTs have shown that CBT is significantly more effective than waiting list controls (e.g., Telch, Agras, Rossiter, Wilfley, & Kenardy, 1990; Wilfley et al., 1993). More important, CBT has been shown to be significantly superior both to fluoxetine 60 mg and to pill placebo (see Grilo, Masheb, & Wilson [2005] below), a finding that provides evidence of CBT's specific therapeutic effects.

In contrast to the literature on BN, however, CBT has not been shown to be more effective than IPT. Wilfley et al. (1993) studied the efficacy of a group adaptation of the IPT treatment, originally applied to BN by Fairburn et al. (1991), in a sample of 56 patients. The comparison treatments were CBT, as noted above, and a waiting list control (WL) condition. At the 16-week posttreatment assessment, IPT resulted in a 71% reduction in the number of days binged, with a remission rate of 44%. The comparable figures for CBT were 48% and 28%, and for the WL condition they were 10% and 0%. Both IPT and CBT were significantly more effective than the WL condition, but they did not differ from each other. The same pattern held true for measures of self-esteem and depression. IPT had an attrition rate of 11% compared with 33% in CBT, although this difference was not statistically significant. The two therapies did not differ from each other at 1-year follow-up. Patients showed a significant increase in binge eating over follow-up, although the rates remained below pretreatment levels.

Wilfley and her colleagues (2002) completed a second comparison of group CBT and IPT. The sample consisted of 162 overweight or obese men and women who met the DSM-IV criteria for BED and whose weight ranged from a BMI of 27 to 48. Treatment involved 20 sessions of group CBT or IPT. Comprehensive and rigorous assessment of treatment effects, including the use of the EDE, was completed at 4-, 8-, and 12-month follow-ups. Integrity checks revealed that both therapies were administered faithfully in accordance with their specifications. Ratings of nonspecific features of the therapies (e.g., empathy of the therapist) were highly positive and did not differ across treatments.

The dropout rates were 9.9% and 8.6% for CBT and IPT, respectively. An impressive 82% of patients completed all three follow-up assessments. Using intent-to-treat analyses, posttreatment abstinence rates were 79% for CBT and 73% for IPT. At 12-month follow-up the abstinence rates were 59% and 62%. Both therapies produced significant reductions in concerns about shape, weight, and eating as measured by the EDE, as well as psychiatric symptoms. Both treatments were also associated with a statistically significant but clinically small reduction in BMI, with the most weight loss occurring in patients who had ceased binge eating at posttreatment. The two treatments did not differ in their effects on any variable at any time point except with respect to dietary restraint at posttreatment. Despite the clinically important changes in binge eating and associated psychopathology, the absence of some form of control or comparison condition precludes drawing definitive conclusions about the specific efficacy of either CBT or IPT.

Wilfley, Friedman, et al. (2000) conducted a detailed analysis of the comorbid psychopathology of BED patients in this treatment outcome study. Despite the relatively large sample, few significant findings emerged. The presence of Axis I disorders was unrelated to the severity of the eating disorder at baseline. Nor did it predict outcome at posttreatment or follow-up. Axis II psychopathology, however, was significantly related to severity of binge eating at baseline. The presence of cluster B personality disorders predicted treatment outcome at 1-year follow-up but not at end of treatment.

Finally, group IPT has been evaluated as a treatment for those BED patients who failed to respond to CBT (Agras et al., 1995). Nonresponders to group CBT were given an additional 12 sessions of IPT delivered in a group format. Results showed that the secondary treatment produced no further improvement in binge eating or weight loss. The NICE guidelines assigned a grade of B to the evidence supporting the use of IPT for the treatment of BED.

CBT Compared With Behavioral Weight Loss Treatment

CBT has also been compared with behavioral weight loss (BWL) treatment. Marcus, Wing, and Fairburn (1995) compared an adaptation of CBT for BN with a BWL treatment and a delayed treatment condition (DT) in a sample of 115 BED patients. Both treatments lasted 6 months and were administered on an individual basis. Publication of the results of this well-designed study has been limited to a brief abstract. It suggests that at posttreatment both CBT and BWL BT produced significantly greater reductions than DT in days on which binge eating occurred during the previous month. Unlike CBT, BWL also resulted in substantial weight loss. The results of a second study of group CBT versus BWL, using a more complicated experimental design (Agras et al., 1994), is discussed below.

In a related study, Nauta, Hospers, Kok, and Jansen (2000) compared a form of cognitive therapy (CT) with behavioral treatment (BT) in the treatment of 37 overweight or obese BED patients. The CT, administered in 15 weekly group sessions, was a derivative of Beck's (1976) treatment in which the primary focus was on identifying and challenging "dysfunctional cognitions about shape, weight, eating, dieting or negative self-schemas" (p. 445). BT was aimed at developing healthy, regular eating patterns, increasing exercise, and restricting caloric consumption to a range of 1,500 and 1,800 kcal/day. The dropout rate was a low number of three patients in each group. The two treatments produced comparable reductions in binge eating at posttreatment in intent-to-treat analyses. However, at 6-month follow-up, the abstinence rate in the CT group (86%) was significantly higher than in the BT group (44%). CT also resulted in greater improvement in dysfunctional concerns about shape, weight, eating, and self-esteem than BT. Although BT produced greater weight loss at posttreatment than CT, there was no difference at follow-up because of rapid weight regain in the BT patients.

Conclusions

The research on CBT and IPT has included the most rigorously controlled studies of the treatment of BED to date. Comprehensive and valid assessment using the EDE and conservative intent-to-treat analyses of outcome has shown clinically significant improvement in binge eating and associated eating disorders psychopathology at both posttreatment and follow-up. The abstinence rates in the best controlled of these studies (Grilo, Masheb, & Wilson, 2005; Wilfley et al., 2002) are substantially higher than those obtained in BN.

Another treatment that has shown promise in treating BED is dialectical behavior therapy (DBT),

a primary goal of which is to teach patients how to use mindfulness and emotion regulation skills to cope with negative affect without resorting to binge eating. DBT has been shown to be significantly more effective than a delayed-treatment control group (Telch, Agras, & Linehan, 2001) and is given a B rating of supporting evidence in the NICE (2004) guidelines.

The apparent responsiveness of BED to different psychological therapies, plus the absence of any differences in outcome between such procedurally and conceptually distinctive interventions as CBT and IPT on the one hand, and the existing studies of CBT and BWL on the other, have fueled speculation about nonspecificity of treatment response in BED (e.g., Stunkard & Allison, 2003). As Wilfley, Wilson, and Agras (2003) point out, however, it would be premature to assume that BED patients respond equally well to most if not all forms of therapy. Comparisons of CBT with fluoxetine have provided evidence of CBT's specific treatment effects (Devlin et al., 2005; Grilo, Masheb, & Wilson, 2005). Moreover, comparisons of specialized psychological therapies such as CBT and IPT with BWL must await longer term follow-ups before meaningful conclusions can be drawn. Existing studies comparing CBT and BWL are methodologically limited in several respects (Wilfley et al., 2003).

Behavioral Weight Loss Treatments

Behavioral weight loss programs have been used to treat binge eating in overweight and obese BED patients. This form of treatment focuses on restricting caloric intake, improving nutrition, and increasing physical activity.

Moderate Caloric Restriction

As noted above, Marcus et al. (1995) found that both BWL and CBT produced striking and equal reductions in binge eating in obese BED patients. Similarly, Nauta et al. (2000) showed that a group BWL program resulted in improvement in binge eating comparable to that of a cognitive treatment aimed at binge eating. In this study, however, a 6-month follow-up indicated that the cognitive treatment was superior because it produced continued improvement in abstinence for binge eating.

Using an additive experimental design, Agras et al. (1994) compared a 9-month behavioral weight loss program with the two alternative treatments: one was an initial 3-month CBT treatment aimed at reducing binge eating, followed by the weight control program (CBT/BWL); the other was a combined CBT and behavioral weight loss program, supplemented by the addition of desipramine over the last 6 months of treatment (CBT/BWL/D), as noted earlier. Although the CBT treatment produced significantly greater reduction in binge eating at the 12-week stage, there were no significant differences among the three treatments at the end of 9 months on either binge eating frequency or weight loss. At posttreatment, 41% of the CBT/BWL/D treatment, 37% of the CBT/BWL treatment, and 19% of the BWL treatment had ceased binge eating. Weight losses for these three treatments were 6.0 kg, 1.6 kg, and 3.7 kg, respectively. Although patients who ceased binge eating lost more weight than their counterparts who did not at the 3- and 6-month assessments, this difference had disappeared by the end of treatment. Grilo, Masheb, and Wilson (2005) and Wilfley et al. (2002) similarly found that obese binge eaters who stop binge eating lose more weight than those who do not.

In contrast to studies of CBT and IPT for BED, assessment of eating disorder psychopathology in most studies of BWL has been problematic. For example, most studies have relied on the Binge Eating Scale (BES; Gormally, Black, Daston, & Rardin, 1982), which does not assess binge eating frequency and has low convergence with the interview-based EDE (Greeno, Marcus, & Wing, 1995). Nonetheless, these studies have consistently shown that BWL reduces binge eating. Porzelius, Houston, Smith, Arfken, and Fisher (1995) found no significant differences on BES scores between BWL and a group CBT program designed to reduce binge eating treatment at posttreatment and 1-year follow-up.

BWL has also resulted in improvements in measures of depression (Gladis et al., 1998; Sherwood, Jeffery, & Wing, 1999; Yanovski, Gormally, Lesser, Gwirtsman, & Yanovski, 1994). Foster, Wadden, Kendall, Stunkard, and Vogt (1996) showed that BWL produced improvement in depressive symptoms at 1-year follow-up despite total weight regain, although other research has indicated that depression returns commensurate with weight regain (Wadden, Stunkard, & Liebschutz, 1988).

BWL produces significant weight loss in obese BED patients—at least in the short term (Agras et al., 1994; Marcus et al., 1995; Nauta et al., 2000). Most studies have shown that obese binge eaters and obese non–binge eaters respond equally well to BWL treatment in terms of short-term weight loss (Gladis et al., 1998; Sherwood et al., 1999), whereas others have found that comorbid BED results in a less favorable outcome (Yanovski, et al., 1994).

Severe Caloric Restriction

Reduction of dietary restraint is an important goal of CBT for BN (Fairburn, Marcus, & Wilson, 1993). Extrapolating from these findings, several clinical investigators have warned against using treatments involving either moderate or severe caloric restriction in obese BED patients on the grounds that they might encourage binge eating (e.g., Garner & Wooley, 1991). The findings from the three studies summarized in the preceding section fail to support this prediction as it applies to moderate caloric restriction. The research on the effects of very-low-calorie diets (VLCDs) similarly provides no support for this assertion.

Telch and Agras (1993) identified binge eating in 20 obese patients who participated in a combined VLCD and behavioral weight loss program for obesity. The patients are very likely to have met the criteria for BED. During the 3 months of the VLCD, the frequency of binge eating declined substantially. Over the course of a subsequent 9-month phase of refeeding and behavioral treatment, the frequency of binge eating began to return to its baseline level but was no different from its rate of occurrence in those obese patients who had not reported binge eating prior to treatment. In a study of obese women with ($n = 21$) and without ($n = 17$) BED, Yanovski and Sebring (1994) found that a VLCD treatment resulted in significant reduction in the frequency and severity of binge eating by the end of treatment.

Conclusions

In general, the methodology of studies of BWL has not as been rigorous as that of research on the specialized therapies of CBT and IPT. One consistent problem has been the failure to use state-of-the-art assessment of eating disorder psychopathology such as the EDE. A second limitation is the lack of long-term follow-up. Treatment-induced weight loss is inexorably regained over follow-up, and the impact of this relapse in weight control on BED and associated psychopathology remains to be adequately studied.

Available evidence shows that the results of BWL are comparable to those of specialized therapies in reducing binge eating and associated eating disorder psychopathology. There is no evidence to date that the dietary restriction that is an integral part of BWL either initiates or exacerbates binge eating (National Task Force on the Prevention and Treatment of Obesity, 2000). The probable explanation for these findings is that BED patients differ from those with BN. In BN, binge eating represents periodic breakdowns in otherwise excessive dietary control. BED patients, however, show little dietary restriction between binge-eating episodes (Yanovski & Sebring, 1994). BWL appears to have similar results in producing weight loss in both obese BED and obese non-BED patients, at least in the short term. As in the treatment of obesity as a whole, the challenge is to develop methods for maintaining weight lost during treatment.

Pharmacological Treatments

Antiobesity Medication

Appetite suppressants are a logical class of drug to evaluate in the treatment of BED given the obvious overeating and association with obesity. In an 8-week, double-blind, placebo-controlled evaluation of d-fenfluramine (Stunkard, Berkowitz, Tanrikut, Reiss, & Young, 1996), 50 obese patients with BED participated in a 4-week placebo washout phase. Twenty-two patients improved to the point where they no longer met criteria for BED. The remaining 28 were randomized to d-fenfluramine or placebo. Three patients dropped out of the drug treatment, one from placebo. Analyses of the data from the 12 patients in each group who completed the 8-week treatment showed that d-fenfluramine was significantly more effective than placebo in reducing binge eating. No other statistically significant differences were found on a variety of measures including body weight. The strong placebo response is noteworthy. The subsequent finding that fenfluramine is associated with cardiac valvular insufficiency led to its withdrawal from the market (Jick, 2000).

Two drugs are currently approved by the Food and Drug Administration in the United States for treating obesity—sibutramine and orlistat. A 12-week study by Appolinario et al. (2003) found that sibutramine produced a significantly greater reduction in both binge eating and body weight than a placebo. In an intent-to-treat (ITT) analysis, the remission rates during the final week of treatment were 52% for the active drug versus 38% for placebo. Grilo, Masheb, and Salant (2005) compared a combination of orlistat plus guided self-help based on cognitive behavioral principles (GSHgsh) with CBTgsh and placebo. ITT analyses, using the EDE and hence a 28-day period of assessment, showed that CBTgsh plus orlistat was significantly more effective in producing remission in binge eating at posttreatment but not at a 3-month follow-up. Orlistat was more effective than the placebo in reducing body weight at both assessments.

A single study of topiramate, an anticonvulsant, has to date produced the most promising results of any medication. At the end of 14 weeks of treatment, McElroy et al. (2003) found that the ITT remission rate of topiramate was 64% compared with 30% for placebo. The drug was also associated with a clinically significant reduction in body weight. The dropout rate for topiramate was a high 47%. The drug has potentially serious side effects.

Antidepressant Medication

Tricyclic Antidepressants

Two studies evaluated the effects of desipramine. Using a 12 week, double-blind design, McCann and Agras (1990) compared desipramine ($n = 10$) with a pill placebo ($n = 13$) in the absence of any counseling regarding nutrition, weight loss, or psychological concerns. The average dose of desipramine was 188 mg/day. The desipramine resulted in a mean reduction in binge eating of 63%, whereas there was a 16% increase in binge eating in the placebo condition. Discontinuation of the drug after the 12-week treatment produced rapid relapse. A second study evaluated the effects of a trial of desipramine (285 mg/day) during the last 6 months of a 9-month cognitive-behavioral treatment for binge eating and weight loss in obese BED patients (Agras et al., 1994). The drug failed to improve on either the reduction of binge eating or weight loss at posttreatment.

Imipramine has been tested in two small studies. Alger, Schwalberg, Bigaouette, Michalek, and Howard (1991) compared imipramine (200 mg/day) with a pill placebo in obese binge eaters in an 8-week study of 41 obese binge eaters and 28 patients who met *DSM-III-R* criteria for bulimia nervosa. Clinical samples of obese binge eaters overlap with the diagnosis of BED but may not meet all the provisional research diagnostic criteria. Imipramine was not significantly superior to placebo in reducing the frequency of binge eating. In the second study, Laederach-Hoffman et al. (1999) randomly assigned 31 obese BED patients either to a low dose of imipramine (75 mg/day) or to pill placebo with concurrent diet counseling and psychological support over an 8-week period. All patients continued to receive diet counseling and psychological support for 6 months following the discontinuation of medication after 8 weeks. Imipramine resulted in significantly greater reduction in binge frequency and weight loss than placebo at posttreatment and at 32-week follow-up.

Selective Serotonin Reuptake Inhibitors

Fluvoxamine, sertraline, and fluoxetine have all been used to treat BED. De Zwaan and Mitchell (1992) compared fluvoxamine (100 mg/day) with a pill placebo in BED patients who were concurrently treated with either CBT or dietary management. There was no evidence of any specific effect of the fluvoxamine on binge eating. All treatment groups showed a modest and comparable weight loss during treatment, followed by weight regain at 1-year follow-up. In a second study, 85 obese BED patients were randomized to the drug (mean dose = 265 mg/day) or pill placebo for a period of 9 weeks (Hudson et al., 1998). Posttreatment results showed that fluvoxamine drug was significantly superior to placebo in reducing binge eating over the course of the study using a randomized regression analysis. However, there was no significant difference between fluvoxamine and pill placebo for either binge eating or depression in intent-to-treat analyses of response categories (i.e., remission, marked improvement, moderate response, no response). There was a significantly higher dropout rate in the fluvoxamine condition (31%) versus placebo (10%).

McElroy et al. (2000) compared sertraline with a pill placebo in a small, 6-week study of 34 BED patients, 8 of whom withdrew from treatment. The active drug resulted in a significantly more rapid reduction in binge eating than the placebo condition. The remission rates were 39% for sertraline and 13% for placebo.

Fluoxetine has received the most research attention. Marcus et al. (1990) evaluated the effectiveness over 52 weeks of fluoxetine (60 mg/day) versus a pill placebo in a double-blind study of obese binge eaters ($n = 22$) and non–binge eaters ($n = 23$). The fluoxetine treatment resulted in a significantly greater weight loss but reduced neither binge eating nor depressed mood in the binge eaters. A brief 6-week study by Arnold et al. (2002) found that fluoxetine was more effective in reducing frequency of binge eating than placebo, although the remission rates in both conditions were low.

In a large and rigorously controlled study, Grilo, Masheb, and Wilson (2005) randomly assigned 108 obese patients with BED to one of four 16-week treatments: fluoxetine, pill placebo, CBT plus fluoxetine, and CBT plus placebo. Based on 28-day EDE assessment, the IIT remission rates were 22%, 26%, 50%, and 61%, respectively, for the four treatment conditions. Both CBT conditions were significantly more effective than either fluoxetine or placebo. In contrast to the small Arnold et al. (2002) study, fluoxetine was not superior to placebo. Whereas CBT was more effective than fluoxetine, the results of the drug treatment in this study were comparable to those reported in previous studies (e.g., Arnold et al., 2002; Hudson et al., 1998). The efficacy of CBT was also comparable to prior findings (e.g., Wilfley, Welch, et al., 2000). Analyses of outcome using dimensional measures of binge eating and specific eating disorder psychopathology similarly revealed the significantly greater efficacy of CBT relative to fluoxetine. Weight loss was very modest and did not differ across the four treatments, although it was significantly associated with remission from binge eating. It is important to note that the patients in this study reported severe eating disorder psychopathology and exhibited high rates of psychiatric comorbidity. Finally, Devlin et al. (2005) failed to find any incremental benefit of adding fluoxetine to behavioral weight loss treatment (BWL). In contrast, combining CBT with BWL produced significantly greater improvement.

Conclusions

The findings on antidepressant medication are mixed at best. Some of the studies reviewed here failed to show the superiority of the active drug in comparison with a pill placebo. This pattern contrasts with that from the BN literature, where, as detailed earlier in this chapter, antidepressant medication has been shown to be consistently more effective than placebo in the short term. Other problems include a higher dropout rate than psychological treatments; the absence of any long-term follow-up, especially after discontinuation of the medication; and less rigorous assessment of treatment effects compared with psychological studies (see below). For example, earlier pharmacological studies have tended to focus on percentage reduction in binge eating frequency rather than the preferred outcome of complete remission of binge eating. Even in the more recent studies that have reported remission rates, these tend to be based on the last week of treatment. The two exceptions have been the Grilo, Masheb, and Salant (2005) and Grilo, Masheb, and Wilson (2005) studies using the EDE over a 28-day span.

Less Intensive Treatments

Self-Help Strategies

As in the treatment of BN, a cognitive-behavioral self-help treatment may be a cost-effective alternative to full CBT. Carter and Fairburn (1998) compared a pure self-help treatment (PSH), in which BED subjects were mailed a self-help book (Fairburn, 1995) and advised to follow its recommendations, with one in which they also received up to eight 25-minute supportive sessions (guided self-help [GSH]). There were 24 participants in each condition. The therapist's role was to encourage the patients to follow the advice in the self-help book (which was a direct translation of full CBT). A primary aim of this study was to evaluate self-help as it would be used in primary care settings or in the general community. Thus, the guided self-help treatment was conducted by nonspecialist therapists with no formal clinical qualifications. Treatment lasted 12 weeks. Both treatments were compared with a delayed-treatment control condition (DT). Wait-list control patients were randomized at 12 weeks to one of the two treatment conditions and were included in the longer term comparisons of the two self-help groups. Patients were followed up for 6 months.

The two interventions produced significant and lasting improvements in binge eating. The remission rates for PSH and GSH were 43% and 50%, respectively, in intent-to-treat analyses. Both were superior to the control group but similar to one another in

reducing binge eating frequency and general psychopathology over the 12 weeks. Binge eating results for the full sample across the 9 months of the study, however, favored guided self-help. Patients who demonstrated more knowledge of the manual's psychoeducational material at posttreatment fared better at 6-month follow-up.

Loeb, Wilson, Gilbert, and Labouvie (2000) compared guided and unguided use of the Fairburn (1995) self-help manual in a randomized trial with 40 female binge eaters, 83% of whom met diagnostic criteria for BED. In contrast to the Carter and Fairburn (1998) study, these experimental conditions were designed to mimic the two least intensive interventions in a stepped-care-based specialty treatment setting. The GSH therapists were well experienced in the treatment of eating disorders. In addition, patients in the unguided self-help (USH) condition maintained regular contact with the clinic by mailing weekly self-monitoring forms. If records revealed major problems or if no records were received, participants were telephoned. Over the 3 months, both the USH and GSH groups experienced significant reductions in binge eating frequency, shape and weight concerns, other symptoms of eating-related psychopathology, and general psychopathology. In intent-to-treat analyses, binge eating remission rates were 30% for USH and 50% for GSH. Similar to the results obtained by Carter and Fairburn (1998), the GSH condition was superior to USH in reducing binge eating and its associated symptomatology, such as dietary restraint. A limitation of this study is the lack of adequate long-term follow-up.

In a more recent study in a specialty setting, Grilo and Masheb (2005) found that GSH was significantly superior to BWL administered as a self-help treatment (BWLgsh) using the LEARN manual (Brownell, 2000). GSH resulted in a 50% remission rate compared to less than 20% in the BWL condition. Additionally, across broad outcomes measures, CBTgsh was significantly superior to BWL. These findings provide further support for the specificity of CBTgsh for BED. As in all other studies of self-help for BED, no weight loss occurred.

Psychoeducation in Groups

Little is known about psychoeducation for BED. In the sole controlled trial, 61 women with BED were randomized to one of three 8-week group interventions or to a waiting list control condition (WL; Peterson et al., 1998). The three active treatments all consisted of psychoeducation plus group discussion. In the therapist-led condition (TL), a specialty therapist led both components. In the partial self-help condition (PSH), the psychoeducational component was administered by videotape followed by a therapist-led discussion. In the full self-help condition (SH), the psychoeducational videotape was followed by a group-led discussion. The three treatments were all superior to the control condition but did not differ from each other. The abstinence rates were 69%, 68%, and 87%, respectively. Conclusions about the value of psychoeducation for BED must await additional research.

Summary

Research Implications

Research on the treatment of BED is still at a relatively early stage. Sample sizes in most studies have been small. Other methodological shortcomings include inadequate assessment of outcome. Assessment of binge eating and associated eating disorder psychopathology is typically limited. Assessment using a comprehensive and valid measure of BED, such as the EDE, which also covers a more extensive 4-week period, is a research priority. The lack of long-term evaluation is a major problem, especially given the high rate of spontaneous remission in a study of the natural course of BED (Fairburn et al., 2000).

Although CBT has shown specific treatment effects, the evidence indicates more nonspecificity of response to treatment in BED than BN. Accordingly, future comparative outcome studies need to control for nonspecific therapeutic influences and the passage of time in the short and long term.

It is clear that binge eating, specific eating disorders psychopathology, and associated psychopathology can all be treated effectively in BED patients. The challenge that remains is to find an effective intervention for obesity, which is strongly associated with BED.

Clinical Implications

Consistent with the NICE (2004) guidelines, CBT or IPT would seem to be the initial treatment of choice. Nevertheless, a case can also be made for

BWL (Gladis et al., 1998). First, it appears to be as effective as specialized therapies for BED (CBT and IPT) in reducing binge eating and other eating disorder psychopathology. Second, it produces weight loss, at least in the short term. Third, it is more disseminable than either CBT or IPT because it does not require the same professional training and expertise. BWL can be administered by a wider range of health care professionals.

GSH, using a cognitive-behavioral self-help program, can also be recommended as a less costly and more efficient treatment than CBT or IPT. Initial results with GSH are promising and encourage future studies with larger samples and longer followups. BED patients who do not respond to BWL or GSH should be referred for more intensive treatment with either CBT or IPT.

Evidence on antidepressant medication is mixed at best. These drugs cannot be recommended as the first treatment for BED, although they may prove useful in treating serious psychiatric comorbidity in specific cases.

CLINICAL UTILITY OF RESEARCH FINDINGS

This chapter is based on the findings of randomized control trials. Critics of RCTs have questioned their relevance to clinical practice, arguing that they do not reflect psychological therapy as it is implemented in the field (Westen, Novotny, & Thompson-Brenner, 2004). This skepticism about the clinical value of RCTs may partly explain why CBT has not been adopted more widely by practitioners (Crow, Mussell, Peterson, Knopke, & Mitchell, 1999; Wilson, in press).

RCTs are designed to establish the causal effect of a specific treatment under controlled conditions. These investigations, in which it is essential to establish internal validity by eliminating alternative explanations of the results, are now commonly referred to as *efficacy studies*. Of course we also need so-called effectiveness studies to evaluate external validity, or the generalizability of the findings of efficacy studies to diverse settings, therapists with varying degrees of experience and expertise, and heterogeneous patient groups. RCTs can—and should—be adapted to investigate questions of clinical utility as Jacobson and Christensen (1996) and others have argued.

A common objection to RCTs is that they allegedly select patients for one diagnosis only using a large number of exclusion criteria, whereas in "real-world" clinical practice patients have multiple problems. The inclusion and exclusion criteria for patients vary from study to study. But even a cursory examination of the major RCTs on BN and BED will show that they include patients with a severe eating disorder, high rates of psychiatric comorbidity, and frequent histories of previously failed therapy (Wilson, 1998). In their quantitative review, Hay and Bacaltchuk (2000) concluded that the nature of RCTs of CBT "increases the generalizability of the findings, supporting the effectiveness as well as efficacy of [treatment]" (p. 11). One of the features of the RCTs that led them to this conclusion was the relatively low exclusion rate of patients.

An analysis by Mitchell, Maki, Adson, Ruskin, and Crow (1997) directly examined the selectivity of exclusion criteria in a number of RCTS on BN. These exclusion criteria were applied to a series of patients seeking treatment at a university-based clinic. Of the patients, 21.6% would have been excluded from 39% of the RCTs because of age (greater than 30 years); 16% from 32% of the studies because of weight (greater than 110% of expected body weight); and 26% from 54% of the studies because of active psychotropic drug use.

Discussions of the limited external validity of RCTs often overlook the marked heterogeneity of clinical service settings to which research results are generalized. The crucial question in evaluating any research finding is how closely do the study sample and methods (therapists and therapies) resemble the situation to which one wants to generalize (Kazdin & Wilson, 1978)? Mitchell et al.'s (1997) sample of patients were treated in a specialty outpatient treatment clinic at the University of Minnesota. It can be argued that this hospital/facility clinic, well known as a major clinical research center for eating disorders and substance abuse, might draw an unrepresentative sample of cases. Most practitioners, however, do not predominantly see BN patients who are drug or alcohol dependent, suicidal, or psychotic.

Studies of anxiety and mood disorders have directly evaluated the application in routine clinical service settings of the same manual-based therapy that had been tested in RCTs (e.g., Franklin, Abramowitz, Kozak, Levitt, & Foa, 2000; Wade, Treat, & Stuart, 1998; Weisz, Weersing, & Henggeler, 2005).

The results, using the same measure of outcome as in the RCTS, were very similar. Research of this kind is needed with eating disorders. Two studies are relevant in this connection. First, only one published study of BN has addressed this issue directly, with results that suggest findings from efficacy studies may generalize to unselected BN patients treated in a clinical setting (Tuschen-Caffier, Pook, & Frank, 2001). Second, Fairburn (2004) has described an ongoing RCT of the treatment of eating disorders that has very few exclusion criteria. Virtually all patients seeking treatment at two community psychiatric centers offering specialty treatment for eating disorders are randomly assigned to two forms of the enhanced version of CBT (Fairburn et al., 2003). Any eating disorder of clinical severity merits inclusion; the sample is not limited to any specific *DSM-IV*-defined diagnosis (e.g., BN). A major advantage of this innovative study of unselected patients is that it includes individuals with EDNOS, who constitute the majority of patients in routine clinical settings but who have previously been excluded from efficacy research. The patients in this study exemplify a clinically representative and relevant sample. The therapists, however, are specifically trained and supervised in the administration of the treatments.

Contrary to Westen et al. (2004), there is good reason to believe that the findings of RCTs are likely to have external validity and should guide clinical practice (Wilson, in press).

ACKNOWLEDGMENTS

Dr. Fairburn is supported by a Principal Research Fellowship (046386) from the Wellcome Trust. The section of this chapter on AN was adapted from "Evidence-Based Treatment of Anorexia Nervosa," by C. G. Fairburn, 2005, *International Journal of Eating Disorders*, 7, pp. S26–S30. Dr. Wilson was supported by NIMH Grant MH63862.

REFERENCES

Agras, W. S., Brandt, H. A., Bulik, C. M., Dolan-Sewell, R., Fairburn, C. G., Halmi, K. A., et al. (2004). Report of the National Institutes of Health Workshop on Overcoming Barriers to Treatment Research in Anorexia Nervosa. *International Journal of Eating Disorders, 35,* 509–521.

Agras, W. S., Crow, S. J., Halmi, K. A., Mitchell, J. E., Wilson, G. T., & Kraemer, H. C. (2000). Outcome predictors for the cognitive-behavioral treatment of bulimia nervosa: Data from a multisite study. *American Journal of Psychiatry, 157,* 1302–1308.

Agras, W. S., Rossiter, E. M., Arnow, B., Schneider, J. A., Telch, C.F., Raeburn, S. D., et al. (1992). Pharmacologic and cognitive-behavioral treatment for bulimia nervosa: A controlled comparison. *American Journal of Psychiatry, 149,* 82–87.

Agras, W. S., Rossiter, E. M., Arnow, B., Telch, C. F., Raeburn, S. D., Bruce, B., et al. (1994). One-year follow-up of psychosocial and pharmacologic treatments for bulimia nervosa. *Journal of Clinical Psychiatry, 55,* 179–183.

Agras, W. S., Telch, C. F., Arnow, B., Eldredge, K., Detzer, M. J., Henderson, J., et al. (1995). Does interpersonal therapy help patients with binge eating disorder who fail to respond to cognitive-behavioral therapy? *Journal of Consulting and Clinical Psychology, 63,* 356–360.

Agras, W. S., Telch, C. F., Arnow, B., Eldredge, K., Wilfley, D. E., Raeburn, S. D., et al. (1994). Weight loss, cognitive-behavioral, and desipramine treatments in binge eating disorder: An additive design. *Behavior Therapy, 25,* 209–224.

Agras, W. S., Walsh, B. T., Fairburn, C. G., Wilson, G. T., & Kraemer, H. C. (2000). A multicenter comparison of cognitive-behavioral therapy and interpersonal psychotherapy for bulimia nervosa. *Archives of General Psychiatry, 57,* 459–466.

Alger, S. A., Schwalberg, M. D., Bigaouette, J. M., Michalek, A. V., & Howard, L. J. (1991). Effect of tricyclic antidepressants and opiate agonist on binge-eating behavior in normal weight bulimic and obese, binge-eating subjects. *American Journal of Clinical Nutrition, 53,* 865–871.

Allison, K. C., Grilo, C. M., Masheb, R. M., & Stunkard, A. J. (2005). Binge eating disorder and night eating syndrome: A comparative study of disordered eating. *Journal of Consulting and Clinical Psychology, 73,* 1107–1115.

American Psychiatric Association. (1994). *Diagnostic and statistical manual of mental disorders* (4th ed.). Washington, DC: Author.

Appolinario, J. C., Bacaltchuk, J., Sichieri, R., Claudino, A. M., Gody-Matos, A., Morgan, C., et al. (2003). A randomized, double-blind, placebo-controlled study of sibutramine in the treatment of binge eating disorder. *Archives of General Psychiatry, 60,* 1109–1116.

Arnold, L. M., McElroy, S. L., Hudson, J., Welge, J., Bennett, A. J., & Keck, P. (2002). A placebo controlled, randomized trial of fluoxetine in the treatment of binge-eating disorder. *Journal of Clinical Psychiatry, 63,* 1028–1033.

Bachar, E., Latzer, Y., Kreitler, S., & Berry E. M. (1999). Empirical comparison of two psychological therapies. *Journal of Psychotherapy Practice and Research, 8,* 115–128.

Ball, J., & Mitchell, P. (2004). A randomized controlled study of cognitive behavior therapy and behavioral family therapy for anorexia nervosa patients. *Eating Disorders, 12,* 303–314.

Banasiak, S. J., Paxton, S. J., & Hay, P. (2005). Guided self-help for bulimia nervosa in primary care: A randomized controlled trial. *Psychological Medicine, 35,* 1283–1294.

Beck, A. T. (1976). *Cognitive therapy and the emotional disorders.* New York: International Universities Press.

Birmingham, C. L., Gutierrez, E., Jonat, L, & Beumont, P. (2004). Randomized controlled trial of warming in anorexia nervosa. *International Journal of Eating Disorders, 35,* 234–238.

Brownell, K. D. (2000). *The LEARN program for weight management.* Dallas, TX: American Health.

Bruce, B., & Agras, W. S. (1992). Binge eating in females: A population-based investigation. *International Journal of Eating Disorders, 12,* 365–373.

Bushnell, J. A., Wells, J. E., McKenzie, J. M., Hornblow, A. R., Oakley-Browne, M. A., & Joyce, P. R. (1994). Bulimia comorbidity in the general population and in the clinic. *Psychological Medicine, 24,* 605–611.

Carter, J. C., & Fairburn, C. G. (1998). Cognitive-behavioral self-help for binge eating disorder: A controlled effectiveness study. *Journal of Consulting and Clinical Psychology, 66,* 616–623.

Carter, J. C., Olmsted, M. P., Kaplan, A. S., McCabe, R. E., Mills, J. S., & Aime, A. (2003). Self-help for bulimia nervosa: A randomized controlled trial. *American Journal of Psychiatry, 160,* 973–978.

Channon, S., De Silva, P., Helmsley, D., & Perkins, R. (1989). A controlled trial of cognitive behavioural and behavioural treatment of anorexia nervosa. *Behaviour Research and Therapy, 27,* 529–535.

Commission on Adolescent Eating Disorders. (2005). Eating disorders. In D. L. Evans, E. B. Foa, R. E. Gur, H. Hendin, C. P. O'Brien, M. E. P. Seligman, et al. (Eds.), *Treating and preventing adolescent mental health disorders: What we know and what we don't know.* New York: Oxford University Press, the Annenberg Foundation Trust at Sunnylands, and the Annenberg Public Policy Center of the University of Pennsylvania.

Crisp, A. H., Norton, K., Gowers, S., Halek, C., Bowyer, C., Yeldham, D., et al. (1991). A controlled study of the effect of therapies aimed at adolescent and family psychopathology in anorexia nervosa. *British Journal of Psychiatry, 159,* 325–333.

Crow, S. J., Mussell, M. P., Peterson, C. B., Knopke, A., & Mitchell, J. E. (1999). Prior treatment received by patients with bulimia nervosa. *International Journal of Eating Disorders, 25,* 39–44.

Dare, C., Eisler, I., Russell, G., Treasure, J., & Dodge, L. (2001). Psychological therapies for adults with anorexia nervosa: Randomised controlled trial of out-patient treatments. *British Journal of Psychiatry, 178,* 216–221.

Davis, R., McVey, G., Heinmaa, M., Rockert, W., & Kennedy, S. (1999). Sequencing of cognitive-behavioral treatments for bulimia nervosa. *International Journal of Eating Disorders, 25,* 361–374.

Davis, R., Olmsted, M. P., & Rockert, W. (1990). Brief group psychoeducation for bulimia nervosa. *Journal of Consulting and Clinical Psychology, 58,* 882–885.

Devlin, M. J., Goldfein, J. A., Petkova, E., Jiang, H., Raizman, P. S., Wolk, S., et al. (2005). Cognitive behavioral therapy and fluoxetine as adjuncts to group behavioral therapy for binge eating disorder. *Obesity Research, 13,* 1077–1088.

Devlin, M. J., & Walsh, T. (1995). Medication treatment for eating disorders. *Journal of Mental Health, 4,* 459–469.

de Zwaan, M., & Mitchell, J. E. (1992). Binge eating in the obese. Special Section: Eating disorders. *Annals of Medicine, 24,* 303–308.

Eisler, I., & Dare, C. (1997). Family and individual therapy in anorexia nervosa. A 5-year follow-up. *Archives of General Psychiatry, 54,* 1025–1030.

Eisler, I., & Dare, C. (2000). Family therapy for adolescent anorexia nervosa: The results of a controlled comparison of two family interventions. *Journal of Child Psychology and Psychiatry, 41,* 727–736.

Eisler, I., Dare, C., Hodes, M., Russell, G., Dodge, E., & le Grange, D. (2000). Family therapy for adolescent anorexia nervosa: the results of a controlled comparison of two family interventions. *Journal of Child Psychology and Psychiatry, 41,* 727–736.

Fairburn, C. G. (1981). A cognitive behavioural approach to the management of bulimia. *Psychological Medicine, 11,* 707–711.

Fairburn, C. G. (1985). Cognitive-behavioral treatment for bulimia. In D. M. Garner & P. E. Garfinkel (Eds.), *Handbook of psychotherapy for anorexia nervosa and bulimia* (pp. 160–192). New York: Guilford Press.

Fairburn, C. G. (1995). *Overcoming binge eating.* New York: Guilford Press.

Fairburn, C. G. (1997a). Eating disorders. In D. M. Clark & C. G. Fairburn (Eds.), *The science and practice of cognitive behaviour therapy* (pp. 209–242). Oxford, UK: Oxford University Press.

Fairburn, C. G. (1997b). Interpersonal psychotherapy for bulimia nervosa. In D. M. Garner & P. E. Garfinkel (Eds.), *Handbook of treatment for eating disorders* (pp. 278–294). New York: Guilford Press.

Fairburn, C. G. (2004, April). *The relationship between treatment research and clinical practice.* Paper presented at the International Conference on Eating Disorders of the Academy of Eating Disorders, Orlando, Florida.

Fairburn, C. G. (2005). Evidence-based treatment of anorexia nervosa. *International Journal of Eating Disorders, 37,* S26–S30.

Fairburn, C. G., Agras, W. S., Walsh, B.T., Wilson, G. T., & Stice, E. (2004). Prediction of outcome in bulimia nervosa by early change in treatment. *American Journal of Psychiatry, 161,* 2322–2324.

Fairburn, C. G., & Bohn, K. (2005). Eating disorder NOS (EDNOS): An example of the troublesome "Not Otherwise Specified" (NOS) category in *DSM-IV. Behaviour Research and Therapy, 43,* 691–701.

Fairburn, C. G., & Carter, J. C. (1997). Self-help and guided self-help for binge eating problems. In D. M. Garner & P. E. Garfinkel (Eds.), *Handbook of treatment for eating disorders* (pp. 494–500). New York: Guilford Press.

Fairburn, C. G., & Cooper, Z. (1993). The eating disorder examination. In C. G. Fairburn & G. T. Wilson (Eds.), *Binge eating: Nature, assessment, and treatment* (pp. 361–404). New York: Guilford Press.

Fairburn, C. G., Cooper, Z., Doll, H. A., Norman, P., & O'Connor, M. (2000). The natural course of bulimia nervosa and binge eating disorder in young women. *Archives of General Psychiatry, 57,* 659–665.

Fairburn, C. G., Cooper, Z., & Shafran, R. (2003). Cognitive behaviour therapy for eating disorders: A "transdiagnostic" theory and treatment. *Behaviour Research and Therapy, 41,* 509–529.

Fairburn, C. G., & Harrison, P. J. (2003). Eating disorders. *Lancet, 361,* 407–416.

Fairburn, C. G., Hay, P. J. & Welch, S. L. (1993). Binge eating and bulimia nervosa: Distribution and determinants. In C. G. Fairburn & G. T. Wilson (Eds.), *Binge eating: Nature, assessment, and treatment* (pp.123–143). New York: Guilford Press.

Fairburn, C. G., Jones, R., Peveler, R. C., Carr, S. J., Solomon, R. A., O'Connor, M. E., et al. (1991).

Three psychological treatments for bulimia nervosa. *Archives of General Psychiatry, 48*, 463–469.

Fairburn, C. G., Jones, R., Peveler, R. C., Hope, R. A., & O'Connor, M. (1993). Psychotherapy and bulimia nervosa: The longer-term effects of interpersonal psychotherapy, behaviour therapy and cognitive behaviour therapy. *Archives of General Psychiatry, 50*, 419–428.

Fairburn, C. G., Marcus, M. D. & Wilson, G. T. (1993). Cognitive behaviour therapy for binge eating and bulimia nervosa: A comprehensive treatment manual. In C. G. Fairburn & G. T. Wilson (Eds.), *Binge eating: Nature, assessment and treatment* (pp. 361–404). New York: Guilford Press.

Fairburn, C. G., Norman, P. A., Welch, S. L., O'Connor, M. E., Doll, H. A., & Peveler, R. C. (1995). A prospective study of outcome in bulimia nervosa and the long-term effects of three psychological treatments. *Archives of General Psychiatry 52*, 304–312.

Fairburn, C. G., Peveler, R. C., Jones, R., Hope, R. A., & Doll, H. A. (1993). Predictors of twelve-month outcome in bulimia nervosa and the influence of attitudes to shape and weight. *Journal of Consulting and Clinical Psychology, 61*, 696–698.

Fairburn, C. G., & Wilson, G. T. (Eds.). (1993). *Binge eating: Nature, assessment, and treatment.* New York: Guilford Press.

Fluoxetine Bulimia Nervosa Collaborative Study Group. (1992). Fluoxetine in the treatment of bulimia nervosa: A multicenter, placebo-controlled, double-blind trial. *Archives of General Psychiatry, 49*, 139–147.

Foster, G. D., Wadden, T. A., Kendall, P. E., Stunkard, A., & Vogt, R. A. (1996). Psychological effects of weight loss and regain: A prospective evaluation. *Journal of Consulting and Clinical Psychology, 64*, 752–757.

Franklin, M. E., Abramowitz, J. S., Kozak, M. J., Levitt, J. T., & Foa, E. B. (2000). Effectiveness of exposure and ritual prevention for obsessive-compulsive disorder: Randomized compared with nonrandomized samples. *Journal of Consulting and Clinical Psychology, 68*, 594–602.

Garner, D. M., & Bemis, K. M. (1982). A cognitive-behavioral approach to anorexia nervosa. *Cognitive Therapy and Research, 6*, 123–150.

Garner, D. M., Rockert, W., Davis, R., Garner, M. V., Olmsted, M. P., & Eagle, M. (1993). Comparison of cognitive-behavioral and supportive-expressive therapy for bulimia nervosa. *American Journal of Psychiatry, 150*, 37–46.

Garner, D. M., & Wooley, S. C. (1991). Confronting the failure of behavioral and dietary treatments for obesity. *Clinical Psychological Review, 11*, 729–790.

Geist, R., Heinmaa, M, Stephens, D., Davis, R., & Katzman, D. K. (2000). Comparison of family therapy and family group psychoeducation in adolescents with anorexia nervosa. *Canadian Journal of Psychiatry, 45*, 173–178.

Ghaderi, A. (2006). Does individualization matter? A randomized trial of standardized (focused) versus individualized (broader) cognitive behavior therapy for bulimia nervosa. *Behaviour Research and Therapy, 44*, 273–288.

Gladis, M. M., Wadden, T. A., Vogt, R., Foster, G., Kuehnel, R. H., & Bartlett, S. J. (1998). Behavioral treatment of obese binge eaters: Do they need different care? *Journal of Psychosomatic Research, 44*, 375–384.

Gormally, J., Black, S., Daston, S., & Rardin, D. (1982). The assessment of binge eating severity among obese persons. *Addictive Behaviors, 7*, 47–55.

Gotestam, K. G., & Agras, W. S. (1995). General population-based epidemiological study of eating disorders in Norway. *International Journal of Eating Disorders, 18*, 119–126.

Greeno, C. G., Marcus, M. D., & Wing, R. R. (1995). Diagnosis of binge eating disorder: Discrepancies between a questionnaire and clinical interview. *International Journal of Eating Disorder, 17*, 153–160.

Grilo, C. M., & Masheb, R. M. (2005). A randomized controlled comparison of guided self-help cognitive behavioral therapy and behavioral weight loss for binge eating disorder. *Behaviour Research and Therapy, 43*, 1509–1525.

Grilo, C. M., Masheb, R. M., & Salant, S. L. (2005). Cognitive behavioral therapy guided self-help and orlistat for the treatment of binge eating disorder: A randomized, double-blind, placebo-controlled trial. *Biological Psychiatry, 57*, 1193–1201.

Grilo, C. M., Masheb, R. M., & Wilson, G. T. (2005). Efficacy of cognitive behavioral therapy and fluoxetine for the treatment of binge eating disorder: A randomized double-blind placebo-controlled comparison. *Biological Psychiatry, 57*, 301–309.

Grilo, C., Masheb, R., & Wilson, G. T. (2006). Rapid response to treatment for binge eating disorder. *Journal of Consulting and Clinical Psychology, 74*, 602–612.

Grilo, C. M., Sanislow, C. A., Shea, M. T., Skodol, A. E., Stout, R. L., Pagano, M. E., et al. (2003). The natural course of bulimia nervosa and eating disorder not otherwise classified is not influenced by personality disorders. *International Journal of Eating Disorders, 34,* 319–330.

Hall, A., & Crisp, A. H. (1987). Brief psychotherapy in the treatment of anorexia nervosa. *British Journal of Psychiatry, 151,* 185–191.

Halmi, K. A., Agras, W. S., Crow, S., Mitchell, J., & Wilson, G. T., Bryson, S. W., et al. (2005). Predictors of treatment acceptance and completion in anorexia nervosa: Implications for future study designs. *Archives of General Psychiatry, 62,* 776–781.

Hay, P. J., & Bacaltchuk, J. (2000). Psychotherapy for bulimia nervosa and binging (Cochrane Review). In *The Cochrane Library, Issue 4,* 2000. Oxford: Update Software.

Herzog, T., Hartmann, A., & Falk, C. (1996). The short-term effects of psychodynamic inpatient treatment of anorexia nervosa with and without an explicit focus on eating pathology: A controlled study. *Psychotherapy, Psychosomatics, Medical Psychology, 46,* 1–22.

Hudson, J. I., McElroy, S. L., Raymond, N. C., Crow, S., Keck, P. E., Carter, W. P., et al. (1998). Fluvoxamine in the treatment of a binge-eating disorder: A multicenter placebo-controlled, double-blind trial. *American Journal of Psychiatry, 155,* 1756–1762.

Jacobson, N. S., & Christensen, A. (1996). Studying the effectiveness of psychotherapy: How well can clinical trials do the job? *American Psychologist, 51,* 1031–1039.

Jick, H. (2000). Heart valve disorders and appetite-suppressant drugs. *Journal of the American Medical Association, 283,* 1738–1740.

Kaye, W. H., Nagata, T., Weltzin, T. E., Hsu, G. L. K., Sokol, M. S., McConaha, C., et al. (2001). Double-blind placebo-controlled administration of fluoxetine in restricting and restricting-purging-type anorexia nervosa. *Society of Biological Psychiatry, 49,* 644–652.

Kazdin, A. E., & Wilson, G. T. (1978). *Evaluation of behavior therapy: Issues, evidence, and research strategies.* Cambridge, MA: Ballinger.

Keller, M. B., Herzog, D. B., Lavori, P. W., Bradburn, I. S., & Mahoney, E. M. (1992). The naturalistic history of bulimia nervosa: Extraordinarily high rates of chronicity, relapse recurrence, and psychosocial morbidity. *International Journal of Eating Disorders, 12,* 1–10.

Klerman, G. L., Weissman, M. M., Rounsaville, B. J., & Chevron, E. S. (1984). *Interpersonal psychotherapy of depression.* New York: Basic Books.

Laederach-Hoffman, K., Graf, C., Horber, F., Lippuner, K., Lederer, S., Michel, R., et al. (1999). Imipramine and diet counseling with psychological support in the treatment of obese binge eaters: A randomized, placebo-controlled double-blind study. *International Journal of Eating Disorders, 26,* 231–244.

Lilenfeld, L. R., Kaye, W. H., Greeno, C. G., Merikangas, K. R., Plotnicov, K., Pollice, C., et al. (1997). Psychiatric disorders in women and bulimia nervosa and their first-degree relatives: Effects of comorbid substance dependence. *International Journal of Eating Disorders, 22,* 253–264.

Lock, J., Agras, W. S., & Bryson, S., & Kraemer, H. C. (2005). A comparison of short- and long-term family therapy for adolescent anorexia nervosa. *Journal of the American Academy of Child and Adolescent Psychiatry, 44,* 632–639.

Lock, J., le Grange, D., Agras, W. S., & Dare, C. (2001). *Treatment manual for anorexia nervosa: A family-based approach.* New York: Guilford Press.

Loeb, K. L., Wilson, G. T., Gilbert, J. S., & Labouvie, E. (2000). Guided and unguided self-help for binge eating. *Behaviour Research and Therapy, 38,* 259–272.

Maguire, S., Surgenor, L. J., Abraham, S., & Beumont, P. (2003). An international collaborative database: Its use in predicting length of stay for inpatient treatment of anorexia nervosa. *Australian and New Zealand Journal of Psychiatry, 37,* 741–747.

Marcus, M. D., Wing, R. R., Ewing, L., Kern, E., Gooding, W., & McDermott, M. (1990). A double-blind, placebo-controlled trial of fluoxetine plus behavior modification in the treatment of obese binge eaters and non–binge eaters. *American Journal of Psychiatry, 147,* 876–881.

Marcus, M. D., Wing, R. R., & Fairburn, C. G. (1995). Cognitive behavioral treatment of binge eating vs. behavioral weight control on the treatment of binge eating disorder. *Annals of Behavioral Medicine, 17,* S090.

McCann, U. D., & Agras, W. S. (1990). Successful treatment of nonpurging bulimia nervosa with desipramine: A double-blind, placebo-controlled study. *American Journal of Psychiatry, 147,* 1509–1513.

McElroy, S. L., Casuto, L. S., Nelson, E. B., Lake, K. A., Soutullo, C. A., Keck, P. E., Jr., et al. (2000). Placebo-controlled trial of sertraline in the treatment of binge eating disorder. *American Journal of Psychiatry, 157,* 1004–1006.

McElroy, S. L., Arnold, L. M., Shapira, N. A., Keck, P. E., Rosenthal, N. R., Karim, M. R., et al. (2003). Topiramate in the treatment of binge eating disorder associated with obesity: A randomized placebo-controlled trial. *American Journal of Psychiatry, 160,* 255–261.

McIntosh, V. V. W., Jordan, J., Carter, F. A., Luty, S. E., McKenzie, J. M., Bulik, C. M., et al. (2005). Three psychotherapies for anorexia nervosa: A randomized, controlled trial. *American Journal of Psychiatry, 162,* 741–747.

Mitchell, J. E., & de Zwaan, M. (1993). Pharmacological treatments of binge eating. In C. G. Fairburn & G. T. Wilson (Eds.), *Binge eating: Nature, assessment and treatment* (pp. 250–269). New York: Guilford Press.

Mitchell, J. E., Maki, D. D., Adson, D. E., Ruskin, B. S., & Crow, S. (1997). The selectivity of inclusion and exclusion criteria in bulimia nervosa treatment studies. *International Journal of Eating Disorders, 22,* 219–230.

Mitchell, J. E., Pyle, R. L., Eckert, E. D., Hatsukami, D., Pomeroy, C., & Zimmerman, R. (1990). A comparison study of antidepressants and structured intensive group psychotherapy in the treatment of bulimia nervosa. *Archives of General Psychiatry, 47,* 149–157.

Mussell, M. P., Mitchell, J. E., Crosby, R. D., Fulkerson, J. A., Hoberman, H. M., & Romano, J. L. (2000). Commitment to treatment goals in prediction of group cognitive-behavioral therapy treatment outcome for women with bulimia nervosa. *Journal of Consulting and Clinical Psychology, 68,* 432–437.

National Institute for Clinical Excellence. (NICE). (2004). *Eating disorders: Core interventions in the treatment and management of anorexia nervosa, bulimia nervosa and related eating disorders.* NICE Clinical Guideline No. 9. London: NICE.

National Task Force on the Prevention and Treatment of Obesity. (2000). Dieting and the development of eating disorders in overweight and obese adults. *Archives of Internal Medicine, 160,* 2581–2589.

Nauta, H., Hospers, H., Kok, G., & Jansen, A. (2000). A comparison between a cognitive and a behavioral treatment for obese binge eaters and obese non–binge eaters. *Behavior Therapy, 31,* 441–462.

Olmsted, M. P., Davis, R., Garner, D. M., Eagle, M., Rockert, W., & Irvine, M. J. (1991). Efficacy of a brief group psychoeducational intervention for bulimia nervosa. *Behaviour Research and Therapy, 29,* 71–84.

Palmer, R. L., Birchall, H., McGrain, L., & Sullivan, V. (2002). Self-help for bulimic disorders: A randomised controlled trial comparing minimal guidance with face-to-face or telephone guidance. *British Journal of Psychiatry, 181,* 230–235.

Peterson, C. B., Mitchell, J. E., Engbloom, S., Nugent, S., Mussell, M. P., & Miller, J. P. (1998). Group cognitive-behavioral treatment of binge eating disorder: A comparison of therapist-led versus self-help formats. *International Journal of Eating Disorders, 24,* 125–136.

Pike, K. M., Walsh, B. T., Vitousek, K., Wilson, G. T., & Bauer, J. (2003). Cognitive behavior therapy in the posthospitalization treatment of anorexia nervosa. *American Journal of Psychiatry, 160,* 2046–2049.

Polivy, J., & Herman, C. P. (1993). Etiology of binge eating: Psychological mechanisms. In C. G. Fairburn & G. T. Wilson (Eds.), *Binge eating: Nature, assessment and treatment* (pp. 173–205). New York: Guilford Press.

Porzelius, L. K., Houston, C., Smith, M., Arfken, C., & Fisher, E., Jr. (1995). Comparison of a standard behavioral weight loss treatment and a binge eating weight loss treatment. *Behavior Therapy, 26,* 119–134.

Robin, A. L., Siegel, P. T., & Moye, A. (1995). Family versus individual therapy for anorexia: Impact on family conflict. *International Journal of Eating Disorders, 17,* 313–322.

Romano, S. J., Halmi, K .A., Sarkar, N. P., Koke, S. C., & Lee, J. S. (2002). A placebo-controlled study of fluoxetine in the continued treatment of bulimia nervosa after successful treatment. *American Journal of Psychiatry, 159,* 96–102.

Rossiter, E. M., Agras, W. S., Losch, M., & Telch, C. F. (1988). Dietary restraint of bulimic subjects following cognitive-behavioral or pharmacological treatment. *Behaviour Research and Therapy, 26,* 495–498.

Russell, G. F. M., Szmukler, G. I., Dare, C., & Eisler, I. (1987). An evaluation of family therapy in anorexia nervosa and bulimia nervosa. *Archives of General Psychiatry, 44,* 1047–1056.

Scholz, M., & Asen, E. (2001). Multiple family therapy with eating disordered adolescents: Concepts and preliminary results. *European Eating Disorders Review, 9,* 33–42.

Serfaty, M. A., Turkington, D., Heap, M., Ledsham, L., & Jolley, E. (1999). Cognitive therapy versus dietary counselling in the outpatient treatment of anorexia nervosa: Effects of the treatment phase. *European Eating Disorders Review, 7,* 334–350.

Sherwood, N. E., Jeffery, R. W., & Wing, R. R. (1999). Binge status as a predictor of weight loss treatment outcome. *International Journal of Obesity, 23,* 485–493.

Spitzer, R. L., Yanovski, S., Wadden, T., Wing, R., Marcus, M. D., Stunkard, A., et al. (1993). Binge eating disorder: Its further validation in a multisite study. *International Journal of Eating Disorders, 13,* 137–154.

Striegel-Moore, R. H., Wilfley, D. E., Pike, K. M., Dohm, F. A., & Fairburn, C. G. (2000). Recurrent binge eating in Black American women. *Archives of Family Medicine, 9,* 83–87.

Stunkard A. J., & Allison K. C. (2003). Binge eating disorder: Disorder or marker? *International Journal of Eating Disorders, 34*(Suppl.), S107–S116

Stunkard, A. J., Berkowitz, R., Tanrikut, C., Reiss, E., & Young, L. (1996). d-Fenfluramine treatment of binge eating disorder. *American Journal of Psychiatry, 153,* 1455–1459.

Sysko, R., & Walsh, B. T. (in press). Guided self-help for bulimia nervosa. In J. Latner & G. T. Wilson (Eds.), *Self-help for obesity and eating disorders.* New York: Guilford Press.

Telch, C. F. & Agras, W. S. (1993). The effects of a very low calorie diet on binge eating. *Behavior Therapy, 24,* 177–194.

Telch, C. F., Agras, W. S., & Linehan, M. M. (2001). Dialectical behavior therapy for binge eating disorder. *Journal of Consulting and Clinical Psychology, 69,* 1061–1065.

Telch, C. F., Agras, W. S., Rossiter, E. M., Wilfley, D., & Kenardy, J. (1990). Group cognitive-behavioral treatment for the non-purging bulimic: An initial evaluation. *Journal of Consulting and Clinical Psychology, 58,* 629–635.

Touyz, S. W., & Beumont, P. J. V. (1997). Behavioral treatment to promote weight gain in anorexia nervosa. In D. M. Garner & P. E. Garfinkel (Eds.), *Handbook of treatment for eating disorders* (2nd ed., pp. 361–371). New York: Guilford Press.

Touyz, S. W., Beumont, P. J . V., Glaun, D., Philips, T., & Cowie, I. (1984). A comparison of lenient and strict operant conditional conditioning programmes in refeeding patients with anorexia nervosa. *British Journal of Psychiatry, 144,* 517–520.

Treasure, J., Todd, G., Brolly, J., Nehmed, A., & Denman, F. (1995). A pilot study of a randomised trial of cognitive analytical therapy vs. educational behavioral therapy for adult anorexia nervosa. *Behaviour Research and Therapy, 33,* 363–367.

Tuschen-Caffier, B., Pook, M., & Frank, M. (2001). Evaluation of manual-based cognitive-behavioral therapy for bulimia nervosa in a service setting. *Behaviour Research Therapy, 39,* 299–308.

Vandereycken, W. (2003). The place of inpatient care in the treatment of anorexia nervosa: Questions to be answered. *International Journal of Eating Disorders, 34,* 409–422.

Vandereycken, W., & Pieters, G. (1978). Short-term weight restoration in anorexia nervosa through operant conditioning. *Scandinavian Journal of Behavior Therapy, 7,* 221–236.

Vitousek, K. (2002). Cognitive behaviour therapy in the treatment of anorexia nervosa. In C. G. Fairburn & K. D. Brownell (Eds.), *Eating disorders and obesity: A comprehensive handbook* (2nd ed., pp. 308–313). New York: Guilford Press.

Vitousek, K. M., Watson, S., & Wilson, G. T. (1998). Enhancing motivation for change in treatment-resistant eating disorders. *Clinical Psychology Review, 18,* 391–420.

Von Ranson, K., & Robinson, K. (2006). Who is providing what type of psychotherapy to eating disorder clients? A survey. *International Journal of Eating Disorders, 39,* 27–34.

Wadden, T. A., Foster, G. D., & Letizia, K. A. (1994). One-year behavioral treatment of obesity: Comparison of moderate and severe caloric restriction and the effects of weight maintenance therapy. *Journal of Consulting and Clinical Psychology, 62,* 165–171.

Wadden, T. A., Stunkard, A. J., & Liebschutz, J. (1988). Three-year follow-up of the treatment of obesity by very low calorie diet, behavior therapy, and their combination. *Journal of Consulting and Clinical Psychology, 56,* 925–928.

Wade, W. A., Treat, T. A., & Stuart, G. L. (1998). Transporting an empirically supported treatment for panic disorder to a service clinic setting: A benchmarking strategy. *Journal of Consulting and Clinical Psychology, 66,* 231–239.

Walsh, B. T., Agras, W. S., Devlin, M. J., Fairburn, C. G., Wilson, G. T., Kahn, C., et al. (2000). Fluoxetine in bulimia nervosa following poor response to psychotherapy. *American Journal of Psychiatry, 157,* 1332–1333.

Walsh, B. T., Fairburn, C. G., Mickley, D., Sysko, R., & Parides, M. K. (2004). Treatment of bulimia nervosa in a primary care setting. *American Journal of Psychiatry, 161,* 556–561.

Walsh, B. T., Hadigan, C. M., Devlin, M. J., Gladis, M., & Roose, S. P. (1991). Long-term outcome of antidepressant treatment for bulimia nervosa. *American Journal of Psychiatry, 148,* 1206–1212.

Walsh, B. T., Kaplan, A., Attia, E., Carter, J., Devlin, M. J., Olmstead, M., et al. (2005, September). *Fluoxetine vs placebo to prevent relapse in anorexia nervosa.* Paper presented at the Eating Disorders Research Society, Toronto, Canada.

Walsh, B. T., Wilson, G. T., Loeb, K. L., Devlin, M. J., Pike, K. M., Roose, S. P., et al. (1997). Medication and psychotherapy in the treatment of bulimia nervosa. *American Journal of Psychiatry, 154,* 523–531.

Weisz, J. R., Weersing, V. R., & Henggeler, S. W. (2005). Jousting with straw men: Comment on

Westen, Novotny, and Thompson-Brenner (2004). *Psychological Bulletin, 131,* 418–426.

Westen, D., Novotny, C. M., & Thompson-Brenner, H. (2004). The empirical status of empirically supported psychotherapies: Assumptions, findings, and reporting in controlled clinical trials. *Psychological Bulletin. 130,* 631–663.

Whittal, M. L., Agras, W. S., & Gould, R. A. (1999). Bulimia nervosa: A meta-analysis of psychosocial and pharmacological treatments. *Behavior Therapy, 30,* 117–135.

Wilfley, D. E., Agras, W. S., Telch, C. F., Rossiter, E. M., Schneider, J. A., Cole, A. G., et al. (1993). Group cognitive-behavioral therapy and group interpersonal psychotherapy for the nonpurging bulimic: A controlled comparison. *Journal of Consulting and Clinical Psychology, 61,* 296–305.

Wilfley, D. E., Friedman, M. A., Dounchis, J. Z., Stein, R. I., Welch, R., & Ball, S. A. (2000). Comorbid psychopathology in binge eating disorder: Relation to eating disorder severity at baseline and following treatment. *Journal of Consulting and Clinical Psychology, 68,* 296–305.

Wilfley, D. E., Schwartz, M. B., Spurrell, E. B., & Fairburn, C.G. (2000). Using the Eating Disorder Examination to identify the specific psychopathology of binge eating disorder. *International Journal of Eating Disorders, 27,* 259–269.

Wilfley, D. E, Welch, R. R., Stein, R. I., Spurrell, E. B., Cohen, L. R, Ceylonese, B. E., et al. (2002). A randomized comparison of group cognitive-behavioral therapy and group interpersonal psychotherapy for the treatment of overweight individuals with binge-eating disorder. *Archives of General Psychiatry, 59,* 713–721.

Wilfley, D. E., Wilson, G. T. & Agras, W. S. (2003). The clinical significance of binge eating disorder. *International Journal of Eating Disorders, 34,* 596–606.

Wilson, G. T. (1998). Manual-based treatment and clinical practice. *Clinical Psychology: Science and Practice, 5,* 363–375.

Wilson, G. T. (1999). Cognitive behavior therapy for eating disorders: Progress and problems. *Behaviour Research and Therapy, 37,* 579–596.

Wilson, G. T. (2004). Acceptance and change in the treatment of eating disorders: The evolution of manual-based cognitive behavioral therapy (CBT). In S. C. Hayes, V. M. Follette, & M. Linehan, (Eds.), *Acceptance, mindfulness, and behavior change* (pp.243–260). New York: Guilford Press.

Wilson, G. T. (in press). Manual-based treatment: Evolution and evaluation. In T. A. Treat, R. R. Bootzin, & T. B. Baker (Eds.), *Psychological clinical science: Papers in honor of Richard M. McFall.* Mahwah, NJ: Erlbaum.

Wilson, G. T., Fairburn, C. G., Agras, W. S., Walsh, B. T., & Kraemer, H. D. (2002). Cognitive behavior therapy for bulimia nervosa: Time course and mechanisms of change. *Journal of Consulting and Clinical Psychology, 70,* 267–274.

Wilson, G. T., & Shafran, R. (2005). Eating disorders guidelines from NICE. *Lancet, 365,* 79–81.

Wilson, G. T., & Sysko, R. (2006). Cognitive-behavioral therapy for adolescents with bulimia nervosa. *European Eating Disorders Review, 14,* 8–16.

Wonderlich, S. A., de Zwaan, M., Mitchell, J. E., Peterson, C., & Crow, S. (2003). Psychological and dietary treatments of binge eating disorder: Conceptual implications. *International Journal of Eating Disorders, 34*(Suppl.), S58–S73.

Yanovski, S. Z., Gormally, J. F., Leser, M. S., Gwirtsman, H. E., & Yanovski, J. A. (1994). Binge eating disorder affects outcome of comprehensive very-low-calorie diet treatment. *Obesity Research, 2,* 205–212.

Yanovski, S. Z., Nelson, J. E., Dubbert, B. K., & Spitzer, R .L. (1993). Association of binge eating disorder and psychiatric comorbidity in obese subjects. *American Journal of Psychiatry, 150,* 1472–1479.

Yanovski, S. Z., & Sebring, N. G. (1994). Recorded food intake of obese women with binge eating disorders before and after weight loss. *International Journal of Eating Disorders, 15,* 135–150.

Zipfel, S., Reas, D. L., Thornton, C., Olmsted, M. P., Williamson, D. A., Gerlinghoff, M., et al. (2002). Day hospitalization programs for eating disorders: A systematic review of the literature. *International Journal of Eating Disorders, 31,* 105–117.

22

Treatments for Insomnia and Restless Legs Syndrome

Douglas E. Moul

Charles M. Morin

Daniel J. Buysse

Charles F. Reynolds III

David J. Kupfer

Treating a chief complaint of inability to sleep is a core problem in psychiatric practice, together with treating other comorbid physical or mental disorders. The treatments for insomnia and restless legs syndrome (RLS) are well within the scope of psychiatric practice. Treatments for insomnia have been controversial over the past several decades, with practice patterns being driven partly by nonmedical influences operating in the setting of limited data. In recent years, the need to consider both cognitive-behavioral and pharmacological approaches together has become more apparent, with less insistence on strict either-or approaches. Clinical trial data clearly point to the efficacy of cognitive-behavioral approaches such as stimulus control, bed restriction, and related approaches. The literature on the short-term efficacy of benzodiazepine receptor agonists (BZRAs) as hypnotics has strengthened. There is a great amount of use of non-BZRAs as hypnotics, even though there are limited studies supporting their use. For RLS, the use of low-dose dopamine agonists has been substantially supported in Type 1 clinical trials. For iron-deficiency-induced RLS, iron replacement is strongly encouraged. Approaches such as using benzodiazepines are second-line treatments. Limited support for the use of gabapentin and carbamazepine is available, but the centuries-old approach of using opiates for the treatment of RLS remains a third-line approach.

Psychiatry is the practical discipline of managing impairments in mindfulness and motivation throughout wakefulness and sleep. It is concerned not only with abnormal mental and emotional phenomena during wakefulness, but also with those that occur during sleep, that impair sleep, or that are caused by impairments of sleep. One's mind has many intercoordinated modes, and sleep is among them, so managing sleep is an integral part of everyone's daily mental health self-care. However, sleep requirements vary across individuals and the life span, and identical impairments of sleep affect individuals differently. How poor sleep leads to daytime consequences remains uncertain, and to hedge the uncertainties, interventions to correct sleep have had many foci. Some approaches attempt to focus on the core biology of sleep/wake functioning. Other approaches attempt just to compensate to aid daytime mindfulness and motivation even in the presence of sleep abnormalities. Still other approaches attempt to change the modes of daytime mindfulness and motivation, in order to improve sleep. Both behavioral/cognitive and pharmaceutical techniques have been conceptualized in all three ways. In light of the uncertainties and types of intervention, the causal interface between wakefulness and sleep remains a core research problem in psychiatry.

Sleep disorders comprise a broad collection of more than 90 separate diagnoses in the second edition of the *International Classification of Sleep Disor-*

ders (ICSD-2; American Academy of Sleep Medicine, 2005). Although not as elaborate in its sleep disorders classification, the fourth edition of the *Diagnostic and Statistical Manual of Mental Disorders* (American Psychiatric Association [APA], 2000) recognizes the main classes of sleep disorder as well. Sleep disturbances, if not primary complaints themselves, are often important for how they complicate many medical and psychiatric illnesses. Sleep/wake disturbances fall into the classes of excessive daytime sleepiness, circadian rhythm disorders, parasomnias, and insomnias, with a number of additional diagnoses not easily classified. Excessive daytime sleepiness is a major mental health problem. Within sleep medicine clinics, obstructive sleep apnea is the most prevalent diagnosis related to excessive sleepiness (Partinen & Hublin, 2005). Other causes of excessive sleepiness, such as narcolepsy and periodic limb movement disorder, are much less common. However, in the broader population, excessive sleepiness is often due to the lifestyle-associated restriction of time available for sleep. Circadian rhythm disorders include shift work disorder, jet lag syndrome, delayed sleep phase syndrome, and advanced sleep phase syndrome, all noted within *DSM-IV-TR* (APA, 2000). Parasomnias are "undesirable physical events or experiences that occur during entry into sleep, within sleep, or during arousals from sleep" (American Academy of Sleep Medicine, 2005, 137), and include sleepwalking, REM behavior disorder, sleep bruxism, and sleep eating. For the treating psychiatrist and primary care physician, the disorders involving excessive daytime sleepiness, circadian phase disorders, and parasomnias will be seen in clinical practice. When they occur, referrals to a sleep physician, medication adjustment, or lifestyle counseling are options for treatment. Treatments for the broad spectrum of sleep disorders can be found elsewhere (Chokroverty, 1999; Kryger, Roth, & Dement, 2005).

The present chapter will discuss treatments for insomnia, for which primary insomnia is an archetype, and restless legs syndrome, for which the inability to sleep is a primary complaint. In composing a treatment plan for either condition, one should take into account the composite medical, psychiatric, psychological, developmental, social, or financial aspects of the patient's circumstances. A few are worth highlighting here. First, sleep tends to lighten and become more fragmented with advancing age, often beginning in midlife. Research suggests that sleep time requirements may lessen to a degree as one ages, limiting the amount of sleep that may be obtained with any treatment. So some realism is needed about this aging effect when the doctor, nurse, psychologist, caregiver, or patient plans for improvements in sleep. Second, in some cases, the patient may suffer from a life-skills deficit or adverse social conditions, and benefit from a social services referral to address these. Addressing psychosocial stressors, for example, in caregivers of spouses with Alzheimer's dementia, is an indirect yet important aspect of overall treatment. Finally, additional clinical time and attention may be required in treating the very old, very ill, and very comorbid. There is wide variability in the kinds of circumstances fostering sleep difficulties.

Two considerations arise immediately when a patient presents with an insomnia complaint. First, many kinds of insomnia occur in direct association with other psychiatric or medical conditions, so that the insomnia complaint often must be considered in direct conjunction with other pathologies. Second, polysomnography (PSG) is not recommended for the routine differential diagnosis of an initial complaint of insomnia (Chesson et al., 2000), whether transient or chronic. Thus, effective treatments for an insomnia-like complaint are often context dependent, individualized, and interview based. So careful interviewing is a hallmark of evaluating any insomnia complaint. Obtaining the proper diagnosis can determine a treatment's effectiveness. Since the population 1-year prevalence of any insomnia complaint is approximately 30% (Ohayon, 2002) and not uniquely comorbid with any one other disorder, evaluating an insomnia complaint naturally involves assessing patients for the treatment of other somatic and mental disorders that may be present. Evaluating for a psychiatric disorder is treated elsewhere in this book. One potential pitfall in treating insomnia would be to fail to diagnose restless legs syndrome (population prevalence of 2.5 to 15%; Zucconi & Ferini-Strambi, 2004) when it is present, as it may be a sole or a complicating factor in the presentation of an "insomnia" complaint. Restless legs syndrome is a treatable sleep disorder rather than a psychiatric disorder. Treatments for insomnia will not necessarily be optimal for restless legs syndrome. Insomnia and restless legs syndrome are both diagnosed and treated clinically and fall within the scope of practice for psychiatrists.

One of the ironies in reviewing "what works" for insomnia is the systems framework used for the assessment of effectiveness. This is especially true in everyday clinical practice. In a "hard systems" perspective, treatment effectiveness is assessed in relation to clear, fixed, and specifically predetermined target goals (Checkland, 1981). An example of a hard goal would be obtaining an increase in total sleep time as measured with polysomnography. Ironically, PSG-derived parameters such as PSG-assessed total sleep time, percent stages 3 and 4 sleep, and even number of awakenings, may not be unequivocal in meaning for the patient. For example, as discussed later concerning assessing benefits in the use of medications, the percent of stages 3 and 4 may be extolled commercially as a metric for deep, restorative sleep, and there may be reasons for supposing sleep stages 3 and 4 may be restorative in some sense, yet it is not at all clear that these or other PSG sleep parameters have good, direct one-to-one relationships to clinical effects.

By contrast, with a "soft systems" perspective, the goals embodying treatment effectiveness are considered as existential (i.e., how one sees oneself right now) for each patient and also may change as the attempts at treatment unfold. With this perspective, it may be more important to know how the patient feels about sleep now in relation to his or her beliefs about sleep, his or her sleep-related behaviors, taking medications, and other behaviors. More than 30 years ago, one report noted, "In the present state of knowledge, for the evaluation of any drug with psychic effects, the final court of appeal must be based upon the subjective response of the patient" (Teutsch et al., 1975, p. 201). For the prescriber, the process of deciding what to do for a particular patient stands on the horizon of "hard" versus "soft" treatment goals and risks. While mention will be made during this chapter to Type 1 (best) or lower grades of research evidence, in many cases even Type 1 studies concerning insomnia treatments choose self-report data, rather than PSG data, as metrics of efficacy. This reflects the fact that there is no validated medical model for chronic insomnia, so that even objective signs of sleep cannot be taken as a gold standard of sleep state.

INSOMNIA

Insomnia is a complaint of inadequate or nonrestorative sleep when the patient has had the adequate time and opportunity to sleep. The essential impair-

ment is an inability to sleep as desired. Insomnia is not present in "short sleepers," who naturally require less sleep than others. People may not be distressed by poor sleep, or even be dissatisfied with their sleep, but not complain, or not have daytime consequences, and not fulfill the definition of clinical insomnia (McCrae et al., 2003; Ohayon, 2002). Many persons have transient insomnia complaints associated with stressors, changes in sleep schedule, or changes in sleep environment that may be important to treat with a hypnotic medication for short periods of time.

By contrast, primary insomnia is a disorder defined in the *DSM-IV-TR* as an insomnia lasting 1 month or more in which there is difficulty initiating or maintaining sleep, or nonrestorative sleep, in the absence of other medical or mental disorders producing the insomnia (APA, 2000) Thus the term *chronic insomnia* includes both insomnia related to another medical or mental disorders as well as primary insomnia. The prevalence of primary insomnia is estimated at between 5 and 10% of the general population (Ohayon, 2002). *DSM-IV-TR* primary insomnia embodies three identified insomnias within the *ICSD-2*: psychophysiological insomnia, paradoxical insomnia, and idiopathic insomnia (American Academy of Sleep Medicine, 2005). In psychophysiological insomnia there is evidence of conditioned sleep difficulty or heightened arousal in bed. With paradoxical insomnia the insomnia complaint exists alongside some external evidence or presumption that adequate sleep length actually occurred. Idiopathic insomnia originates in childhood and extends into adulthood. Without considering restless legs syndrome (discussed later), these classifications imply that the differential diagnostic process should take into account the *DSM-IV-TR* and the *ICSD-2* classifications. Those for the *DSM-IV-TR* are discussed elsewhere in this volume. The importance of diagnosing subtypes of primary insomnia according to the *ICSD-2* classification rests with the implications for case formulation and direction of treatment. If psychophysiological insomnia is suspected, then greater effort is best directed at uncovering the stimulus conditions associated with sleeping in the patient, so that those conditions may be changed to improve sleep. If paradoxical insomnia is suspected, then the clinician may focus efforts on seeking to find and correct key cognitive distortions that the patient may have about his or her sleep, but not with the absolute assumption that our current means of measuring sleep are sacrosanct or purely representative of sleep.

If idiopathic insomnia is suspected, then finding changes in stimulus conditions remains relevant, but the case may be conceptualized as perhaps having a genetic or temperamental basis, so pharmaceutical interventions may be more relevant. In practical terms, the *ICSD-2* insomnia subtypes represent a family-resemblance approach to classification.

General Characteristics of Treatment for an Insomnia Complaint

There are several generic aspects (see Table 22.1) to treating an insomnia complaint (Hauri & Linde, 1990; Lacks, 1987; Morin, 1993) that are also relevant for patients with restless legs syndrome. First among these is patient education about sleep. Misconceptions about sleep may be at least partly the cause of some of the patient's complaint severity. As with any medical condition, explaining the normal physiological processes involved that are relevant for the patient's sleep problem is an important way to reduce apprehension and worry and to enhance treatment compliance by providing a rationale for the intervention prescribed. Second, encouraging patients to complete a sleep log or diary will be helpful in providing a means for them to review their sleep patterns from a more objective perspective. In completing a clinical sleep log (see Figure 22.1 for an example), patients should do so only in the morning and without having clock-watched during the previous night (i.e., they should complete the log based on their subjective impressions rather than on a worry-dominated process of obtaining exact clock

times). The log data help with clinical problem solving when reviewed interactively with the patient. Third, whether the intervention is with medication, with behavior-based changes, or with their use in combination, the patient should be encouraged to conceptualize treatment effectiveness trials over spans of 2 to 3 weeks at a minimum. Medication treatments may work well initially but may later fade in effectiveness or lose all effectiveness (Kales, Kales, Bixler, & Scharf, 1975). Behavior-based approaches will usually not work instantly, but require consistency over several weeks to show or fail to show their effectiveness (Morin, 1993). This several-week time frame of patient self-evaluation encourages the patient to avoid any fretful day-to-day adjustments that may have encouraged insomnia to continue. Fourth, it is important to communicate a realism about intervention effectiveness: Some patients expect a cure or, in its absence, no benefit whatsoever. Realistic optimism will help the patient benefit as much as possible. Fifth, insomnia usually requires a number of follow-up visits to assess progress and make adjustments until treatment benefits are maximized. Sixth, even when good results are obtained in the short run, it happens often enough that insomnia recurs after a longer period of time, occasioning the need to revisit the adequacy of treatment compliance or other factors that may have affected the longer term stability of treatment effectiveness.

Pharmacological treatments for insomnia are generally appropriate for treating an insomnia that is expected to be short-lived. Here treatment is directed at reducing unwanted nighttime wakefulness, and

TABLE 22.1 Core Concepts for Insomnia Treatment

Concept	Rationale
Educate patient about sleep and address any sense of "being all alone" with the problem.	Misconceptions or alienation will lead to undue worry, which will impair sleep.
Patient should do sleep logging but without clock watching.	Approximate sleep logging provides self-verified feedback and helps clinical review.
Adopt a habit-formation perspective, with follow-up periods of several weeks.	Avoiding obsessions about daily variability will foster treatment benefit and objective review.
Patient should have realistic expectations about treatment benefit.	All-or-none thinking will get in the way of seeing actual benefits, risks, and limitations.
Adopt the perspective of progressively optimizing treatment.	Often the causes of insomnia are multiple or may change.
Be available for long-term follow-up.	Circumstances, preferences, or habits may change, yet basic need for treatment may not.

Note: A variety of texts are available exemplifying these concepts (see Hauri & Linde, 1990; Laccks, 1997; Morin, 1993).

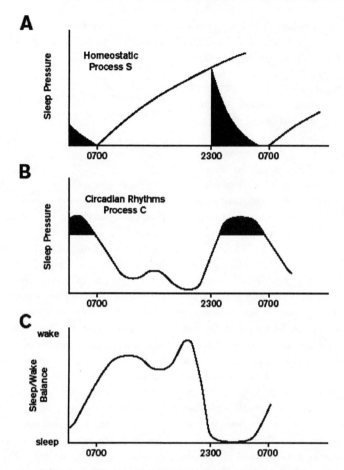

FIGURE 22.1 Illustration of the two-process model (Borbély, 1982, 2005) of sleep regulation. **A.** The homeostatic Process S builds up continuously throughout daytime wakefulness, dissipating more rapidly with sleep than it builds up with wakefulness. Process S is thought to be related to the extracellular buildup of adenosine in the preoptic area of the brain concerned with initiating sleep. **B.** The circadian Process C has a daily maxima for sleepiness during predawn hours, but also an afternoon minor increase. Process C is time governed by the daily rhythm of the suprachiasmatic nucleus, which itself is time corrected by light at dawn, as mediated through retinohypothalamic tract pathways. **C.** The combined inputs of process S and Process C create a sleep-wake balance that varies in a curvilinear pattern across 24 hours. Paradoxically, there is a period of maximal alertness in the evening hours before bedtime.

presumably to reduce the effects of sleep deprivation (Toussaint et al., 1997).

Because a patient's insomnia may evolve into primary insomnia, however, it is less useful to conceptualize the insomnia problem simply in terms of preventing "sleep deprivation," because doing so will often misconstrue the patient's actual clinical situation. The clinical problem in chronic insomnia is much more involved than simple sleep deprivation (although undoubtedly aspects of sleep deprivation also apply; Bonnet & Arand, 1998a). Normally, sleep

deprivation increases the likelihood of sleep quite substantially (Van Dongen, Maislin, Mullington, & Dinges, 2003), but this does not happen to the same degree with the chronic insomnia patient (Bonnet & Arand, 1998a). The chronic insomnia patient is not able to sleep normally even if significantly sleep deprived. The chronic insomnia patient appears to have a stable neuropathological basis for difficulties with initiating and sustaining sleep, as reflected in changes in regional abnormalities in brain glucose metabolism during the night (Nofzinger et al., 2004), abnormal amounts of beta-band EEG frequencies during sleep (Perlis, Merica, Smith, & Giles, 2001), and other biological markers suggesting a persisting wake-prone ("hyperaroused") brain state in these patients (Bonnet & Arand, 1995, 1998b, 2000). This wake-proneness may be driven by excessive cognitive activity and monitoring (A. G. Harvey, 2002) in some patients. At present, no biological variable has been identified to assist in guiding the selection of treatments for any putative subtype of primary insomnia. Classifying insomnia patients by whether they have a problem with sleep onset versus sleep maintenance would seem to offer such an approach. However, such typing appears to be unstable over time (Hohagen et al., 1994).

Both pharmacological and behavioral treatments have demonstrated efficacy for primary insomnia, but it has not been established that there is a differential diagnostic test to distinguish the "best" treatments for particular patients. Because benefits may occur without medication use in many patients, where possible it is preferable to emphasize the possible benefits of psychological and behaviorally based approaches initially *while* presenting the entire approach to the patient (see comments above). Many patients will prefer not to use medications if at all possible (Morin, Gaulier, Barry, & Kowatch, 1992), but others, either for reasons of personal philosophy or because of lifestyle demands, may prefer or require a pharmacological approach. Thus, pharmacological approaches should probably be considered as secondary approaches, but nonetheless ones that have increasing evidence for longer term effectiveness (see below). From a theoretical perspective, both psychological and neurobiological perspectives about chronic insomnia may have applications in the diagnosis and treatment of chronic insomnia patients. Yet often the practical decisions (Yaniv, 2004) about the best treatment(s) depend on the patient's psychology, lifestyle demands, medical/psychiatric comorbidities, history of drug dependency, frailty, age, and treatment preferences, as well as the provider's training itself. These practical aspects highlight the difference between the efficacy question ("Has the intervention been shown to have therapeutic effects under ideal study conditions?") and the effectiveness question ("Does the intervention work in usual practice settings?"). Additionally, even Type 1 clinical trials mostly cannot address whether the studied intervention, even if efficacious, would be appropriate to use in most or only in particular clinical circumstances.

Behavioral and Psychological Treatments for Insomnia

General Rationale

The generic applicability of the behavioral/psychological approaches rests with their basis in the two-process model of normal sleep regulation (see Figure 22.1; Borbély, 1982; Borbély & Achermann, 2005), along with an understanding that stimulus-linked conditions (Lacks, Bertelson, Gans, & Kunkel, 1983) or sleep-related beliefs (Morin, 1993) that foster wakefulness are often good targets for potential modification. These concepts apply to a broad range of clinical situations. Substantial data support the process of sleep propensity being normally governed by the length of time a person is *continuously* (i.e., not napping) awake ("Process S") *and* by the biological time of day as set by the suprachiasmatic nuclei governing the body's circadian rhythms ("Process C"). It is Process C that makes it more difficult to remain awake between 3:00 A.M. and 5:00 A.M. Concepts of sleep hygiene generally address these processes, along with control of substances (e.g., caffeine, alcohol) having some bearing on sleep propensity and regulation. The behaviorally based interventions also postulate pathological processes that foster wake-promoting neuronal activities occurring in temporal or psychological association with sleep. These wake-promoting neuronal activities are associated with habitual environmental stimulus conditions (e.g., habitual wake-promoting activities occurring in bed) and with neuropsychological events (e.g., worries, thoughts, images, anticipations, affects, perceived threats, nightmares) available to self-consciousness. Removing these wake-promoting neuronal activities is postulated to restore normal sleep/wake regulation as expressed in the two-process model, in accordance with the individual's actual underlying "brain aptitude" for producing sleep across 24 hours. This concept is coherent with the wake-biased functioning in insomnia patients of the thalamic reticular neurons that normally facilitate sleep spindles and other phenomena associated with non-REM sleep under conditions of lower neural activity (Steriade, Jones, & Llinás, 1990).

Evidence for Efficacy and Effectiveness

Behavioral and psychological treatments have demonstrated efficacy in Type 1 clinical trials for primary insomnia in middle-aged and aged adults (Morin, Culbert, & Schwartz, 1994; Murtagh & Greenwood, 1995; Pallesen et al., 2003) and for insomnia associated with a number of medical and psychological comorbidities, including pain (Currie, Wilson, Pontefract, & deLaplante, 2000; Lichstein, Wilson, & Johnson, 2000; Quesnel, Savard, Simard, Ivers, & Morin, 2003; Rybarczyk, Lopez, Benson, Alsten, & Stepanski, 2002). Behavioral treatments appear to be effective in many insomnia subtypes regardless of whether the problem concerns sleep latency, sleep awakenings, total sleep time, or general sleep quality (Morin, Hauri, et al., 1999). This general statement may or may not apply as well for patients with particular diagnostic subtypes or comorbidities, but the generalizability of behavioral and psychological treatments is suggested by studies pointing to their usefulness and cost-effectiveness in weaning patients from the use of nightly hypnotics (Morgan, Dixon, Mathers, Thompson, & Tomeny, 2004; Morin et al., 2004).

Table 22.2 presents key elements of various behavioral/psychological approaches to treating insomnia. More than 50 clinical trials using behavioral modalities of therapy have been reviewed in two independent meta-analyses in middle-aged adults (Morin et al., 1994; Murtagh & Greenwood, 1995; Smith et al., 2002) and one in older adults (Pallesen, Nordhus, & Kvale, 1998), along with a qualitative review (American Academy of Sleep Medicine Standards of Practice Committee, 2006). In statistical terms, these data point to large or moderate statistical effects in measures of sleep latency, sleep quality, and other sleep parameters. In practical terms, these reviews point to predictable reductions in sleep latency from perhaps 60 minutes to 35 minutes in the average insomnia patient, with middle-of-the-night wakefulness dropping from 70 minutes to an average 38 minutes. A realistic thing to say to patients is, "The average patient gets some real benefit, and some can get very good benefit, from behavioral approaches alone."

Among the specific approaches, stimulus control therapy has the most data supporting its effectiveness generally (Edinger, Wohlgemuth, Radtke, Marsh, & Quillian, 2001; Engle-Friedman, Bootzin, Hazlewood, & Tsao, 1992; Morin et al., 1994; Murtagh & Greenwood, 1995), even though the specific fine points of its theoretical rationale have not been demonstrated. The related sleep/bed restriction therapy is thematically similar to stimulus control (Friedman, Bliwise, Yesavage, & Salom, 1991), involving restricting the single-bout time in bed to the time that the brain can produce sleep over 24 hours. Stimulus control and sleep/bed restriction therapies generally have greater effectiveness than relaxation or sleep hygiene education. It is probably a standard of practice that sleep hygiene education be incorporated into all modalities, including pharmacological modalities. Sleep hygiene education, though, is not sufficient for most insomnia patients (Edinger & Sampson, 2003). Additionally, relaxation therapies and paradoxical intention therapies are superior to inactive treatments (American Academy of Sleep Medicine Standards of Practice Committee, 2006). Solely cognitive therapies have not been evaluated, but the cognitive aspects of the patient's functioning are increasingly seen as contributing factors in sustaining many patients' insomnia. Thus cognitive therapies are increasingly added to newer, synergistic approaches. CBT therapies generally have more durability than medications (American Academy of Sleep Medicine Standards of Practice Committee, 2006). In one review (L. Harvey, Inglis, & Espie, 2002), the order of effectiveness appears to be first stimulus control, followed by sleep restriction, then cognitive restructuring.

The method of paradoxical intention is a less-researched but intriguing modality within the overall cognitive-behavioral spectrum of treatments (Broomfield & Espie, 2003). This treatment asks patients to lie quietly in bed with eyes open, gently (not reading, etc.) but persistently resisting sleep onset. This method hypothesizes that the sleep-onset insomniac carries performance anxiety and monitoring about sleep that gets in the way of sleep onset through the use of countertherapeutic mental efforts at sleep. This model is generally consonant with the cognitive model of insomnia, which also incorporates the role of counterproductive mental strategies during the daytime (A. G. Harvey, 2002).

TABLE 22.2 Behavioral and Psychological Treatments for Insomnia

Therapy	Rationale	Components/Options	Practical Issues
Stimulus control (Bootzin & Perlis, 1992)	The sleep habit system has linked the stimuli normally cueing sleep instead to responses favoring wakefulness. Therapy tries to revert to the normal stimulus control response.	Going to bed only when sleepy, not when fatigued. Getting out of bed when unable to sleep and going to another room until sleepy. Curtailing sleep-incompatible activities (e.g., watching TV) in bed. Fixed wake-up time, no matter what. Avoid daytime napping.	Patients need to identify their sleepiness. Some incompatible activities may be lifestyle choices. Many patients like to sleep late on weekends. Napping may be hard to relinquish.
Sleep restriction (Lichstein, Riedel, Wilson, & Lester, 2001)	Restricting time in bed nearly to only that that the brain can produce. Some modest sleep deprivation may help to consolidate sleep, improving sleep quality overall.	Avoid awake-in-bed time. One bout of sleep permitted at night. Shortened time in bed, but no less than 5.5 hours.	Early sleep deprivation needs working through. Take patient's self-discipline. Harder to explain therapy rationale.
Relaxation training (Borkovec, Grayson, O'Brien, & Weerts, 1979)	Somatic tension or intrusive thoughts are states fostering wakefulness. Reducing them will remove a barrier to sleep onset.	Progressive muscle relaxation. Autogenic training. Calm image immersion. Medication.	Often requires overlearning the skill. Variable results. Patients have variable skills in different techniques.
Paradoxical intention (Broomfield & Espie, 2003)	The forced suppression of mental activities paradoxically increases mental activities. Patients try to force sleep or try to stop thoughts at bedtime, only increasing their mental activity, inhibiting sleep.	Instruction to lie quietly with eyes open, gently resisting sleep onset. Proscribing grossly activating activities (e.g., reading, exercising, angry or phobic forcing behaviors) around bedtime. Sleep education probably helpful in providing faith about sleep processes.	Fostering the inattention to body or mental phenomena may be helpful. Providing nonphobic expectancy about not sleeping may be an important aspect of instruction delivery.
Cognitive therapy (Morin, 1993)	Faulty/distorted beliefs or attitudes about sleep create unwarranted expectations. Reducing unwarranted expectations reduces the frustrations that themselves impede sleep.	Correct faulty assumptions about sleep. Reduce either-or black-or-white thinking about sleep. Deamplify exaggerations about consequences of suboptimal sleep. Entitle other problem-solving approaches. Avoid self-fulfilling prophecies.	Time-consuming to ferret out beliefs and their ramifications for the patient. May be linked to other worldviews that are refractory to change.
Sleep hygiene education (Hauri & Linde, 1990)	Some patients may simply not know basic facts, rules, or practices about sleep. Simple corrections in sleep habits may be needed.	Avoiding stimulants (e.g., caffeine) before bedtime. Avoiding alcohol before bedtime—it will fragment sleep later toward the morning. Regular exercise, but not near bedtime. Allow 1 hour of wind-down before bedtime. Ensure bed situation is quiet, comfortable, and dark. Keep a regular sleep schedule.	This is education, not training. Education involves more clinic time for explaining. Actual focus on training the sleep system may be a key component for change. By itself, may not engage the patient with a practical discussion about real lifestyle changes.

TABLE 22.2 (continued)

Therapy	Rationale	Components/Options	Practical Issues
Cognitive-behavioral (Morin, 1993; Edinger et al., 2001)	Effectiveness of therapy might be maximized if synergy of treatment modalities can be coordinated.	Included elements of stimulus control, sleep restriction, cognitive therapy, and sleep hygiene education.	Targets multiple facets of insomnia (sleep habits, misconceptions about sleep, and inadequate sleep hygiene). More complex in conception and execution. Higher therapist skill needed. May not be able to tell what is the key component of treatment.

Only a minority of patients (20 to 30%) return to normal sleep, whereas most patients will sleep better but not have fully normal sleep (Espie, Inglis, & Harvey, 2001; Morin, Hauri, et al., 1999). Avoiding the expectation of strictly either continuing bad sleep or attaining perfect sleep as the exclusive outcomes lowers the risk that less-than-perfect sleep will be interpreted as a bad outcome. When this all-or-none expectation is present, there is the risk that the patient will become alienated from the potential benefits of cognitive-behavioral changes and lose a therapeutic opportunity. Avoiding this alienation is critical, since it is only with consistent practice that the behavioral modalities can provide their benefits.

Expectations and Risks

Behavioral/psychological treatments will be more difficult to implement in the cognitively limited or in those with currently severe psychiatric or substance abuse disorders. For example, the insomnia associated with severe psychosis is harder, if not impossible, to treat with behavioral treatments alone. Additionally, some patients may appear to implement all suggested behavioral treatments, but do not improve in their sleep. Thus, it is best to think of the behavioral therapies for insomnia as a collection of generally useful and effective techniques that can be tried in any clinical situation, but without supposing that they will be universally applicable or fully effective. Exact percentages of primary care patients favoring the behavioral approach over the pharmaceutical approach are unknown but are suspected to be high because the long-term expense of medications could thus be avoided (Morgan, Dixon, Mathers, Thompson, & Tomeny, 2003) and, possibly, the durability

of effectiveness for such behavioral approaches could be superior (Edinger et al., 2001; Engle-Friedman et al., 1992; Morin, Colecchi, Stone, Sood, & Brink, 1999).

The side effects of behavioral modalities concern the changes that patients may need to make in their behavioral patterns. Improvements in sleep hygiene may mean avoidance of preferred behaviors, such as reducing caffeine consumption or regulating bedtimes. As with using medications, discussion of side effects beforehand often can be the key to the patient feeling in control of the intervention. Some clinical time may be needed in order to iron out how the patient will adjust to the loss of a favorite component of current sleep/wake behavior or thinking, or how to think through the rearrangement of daily sleep/wake scheduling. Individualized problem solving will usually be needed in addition to sleep education.

In the case of bed restriction, the patient can expect that he will experience some actual sleep deprivation during the transition phase when the new bed restriction is imposed and naps are *proscribed*. If the patient is not warned to expect this, he or she may infer prematurely that the intervention is a failure, when it may only be the case that a difficult period (approximately 2 weeks) may need to be breached before the actual therapeutic benefits can appear or be properly evaluated.

The composite cognitive-behavioral philosophical approach to treatment is probably best when used flexibly and creatively with each patient in a prospective way, over time, in follow-up. The cognitive side effects of this therapy can mean for some patients that they must change their cognitive appraisal of sleep or daytime consequences, which may also reflect their cognitive styles generally—so for some cases, changing how one thinks about one's sleep may risk needing to change how one generally thinks about other life problems. For example, the psychological insight that clock watching at night can cause a cascade of intrusive thoughts to inhibit sleep could be extended to how other excessive self-monitoring during the daytime might interfere with other life activities (A. G. Harvey, 2002). For such "arousable" patients, transitions to new forms of psychological functioning may be useful even if such forms of functioning may be alien to them.

The costs associated with paying for behavioral therapy sessions that lead to a durable benefit in the long run will be lower than paying for a nightly hypnotic medication for a prolonged, indefinite period. This truism, though, cannot overcome the limitation that the behavioral therapies realistically require more clinician-patient contact time and interpersonal effort. In practical terms, delivering these modalities effectively usually requires a psychologist, specially trained nurse (Espie, Inglis, Tessier, & Harvey, 2001), or other behavioral specialist who has training with these modalities. These specialists are often in short supply in metropolitan regions and absent in rural areas. Clearly one of the limitations in many practice locations is the absence of clinicians with this training. Other approaches such as group treatment, abbreviated treatment, bibliotherapy with phone consultation, and Internet-based approaches are under active investigation. However, when specialists are not available, selecting a pharmacological approach to treating insomnia may be the only practical choice, even when it might not be the ideal or preferred choice.

Pharmacological Treatments for Insomnia

The Ideal Hypnotic, Alcohol, and the Not-So-Ideal Historical Context

The properties of an ideal hypnotic are presented in Table 22.3; they are characteristic of no currently available medication. If pharmacotherapy is chosen, then some consideration should be given to the patient's particular clinical circumstances. All hypnotics should have a reasonably short absorption phase and onset of action (less than 2 hours) so that when

they are taken, their effects will be available promptly and only during the desired sleep period. In some cases, patients may have particular difficulty only with a long sleep latency (i.e., taking a long time to initially fall asleep), in which case selecting an agent with an especially short onset of action would be better. In cases where sleep latency is satisfactory but waking up after going to sleep is the problem, an agent with a longer action may be a better initial choice.

As a nonideal hypnotic, beverage alcohol warrants brief discussion. Ethanol is a hypnotic drug, with known properties of decreasing sleep latency and initially increasing the amount of non-REM sleep, while suppressing REM sleep (Yules, Lippman, & Freedman, 1967). Because ethanol is metabolized rather rapidly, its paradoxical effects toward morning are to lighten sleep and to increase the number of awakenings later in the sleep period. Ethanol also increases snoring and prolongs obstructive sleep apneas. Chronic severe alcoholism is associated with long-term insomnia postsobriety (Gillin, Smith, Irwin, Kripke, & Schuckit, 1990). Thus using ethanol as a hypnotic is irrational.

"Which medications work for insomnia?" is also a medical question separate and apart from the socio-legal question, "Which hypnotics are popular or stigmatized?" Ironically, we still do not know the exact reasons that sleep is needed. Historically, benzodiazepines became popular and rational in the 1970s for insomnia compared with barbiturates and other older medications because of their comparative safety. However, during the 1970s it became known that some patients developed a benzodiazepine dependency syndrome (Salzman, 1991) with around-the-clock use, and a limited number of publications described the fall-off, after about 3 weeks, of benzodiazepines' effectiveness for insomnia in some patients (Kales, Bixler, Tan, Scharf, & Kales, 1974), as well as the fact that some patients will respond to placebo treatments. As documented by Balter and colleagues (Mellinger, Balter, & Uhlenhuth, 1985), this led to a period when insomnia was not treated, despite epidemiological evidence that chronic insomnia had significant prevalence. During that period, use of controlled substances such as benzodiazepines in clinical practice was avoided. However, the problem of insomnia did not go away, and epidemiological data began to show that there may be significant se-

TABLE 22.3 Properties of an Ideal Hypnotic Medication

Pharmacology	Quickly absorbed to provide prompt sleep onset
	Pharmacodynamic actions last as long as sleep needed, with no morning aftereffects
	No pharmacologically active metabolites
	No cross-reaction with other medications that the patient may be taking
	Does not increase risks if taken with alcohol
	Nonlethal in overdose
	Comes in defined dosing and with good quality control
Patient perceptions	Provides full, normally restorative sleep experience
	No annoying sideeffects
	No delayed sideeffects (e.g., daytime sedation, memory problems)
	Nonstigmatizing for patient
	Easy to discontinue use if discontinuation is desired
Evidence	Has clear-cut published efficacy data supporting its use
	Does not influence circadian rhythms
	Does not cause rebound insomnia when discontinued
	Resets sleep system to normal sleep physiology even when discontinued
	Useful in the comorbid conditions other than primary insomnia
	Treats restless legs syndrome as well as insomnia
	Maintains effectiveness indefinitely if taken nightly
	Restores all polysomnographic parameters to normal
Medical risks	Low risk for physiological dependency
	Does not increase risks for sleep apnea, other sleep disorders, or falls during the night
	Safe and appropriate in patients with histories of substance dependence disorders
Polysomnography	Does not influence polysomnographic interpretation
	Causes no polysomnographic abnormalities or peculiarities
Availability	Available at an affordable price
	Provided by formularies without special authorization procedures
Regulatory	Nonstigmatizing for prescriber and does not require special prescribing vigilance
	Has FDA approval without the need for DEA scheduling

Elaborated from Mendelsohn et al., 2004.

quelae of chronic insomnia to mental health (Breslau, Roth, Rosenthal, & Andreski, 1996; Chang, Ford, Mead, Cooper-Patrick, & Klag, 1997; Ford & Kamerow, 1989). Clinicians continued to try to treat insomnia, in ways to avoid the stigma of using sleeping pills that are approved by the Food and Drug Administration (FDA) but nonetheless controlled substances—even though these agents had the best Type 1 studies. So agents such as tricyclics and trazodone were used to treat chronic insomnia, at least partly because they were more socially acceptable and seemed to pose low risks. In recent years, benzodiazepine receptor agonists (i.e., zolpidem, zaleplon, and eszopiclone) without the specific benzodiazepine chemical structure have been marketed that have more insomnia-specific action, but possibly without the muscle-relaxant properties of conventional benzodiazepines (although this is not proven).

The availability of newer BZRAs has undoubtedly reduced the stigma of prescribing sleeping pills. In addition, the American Psychiatric Association and the American Academy of Sleep Medicine have produced clearer definitions of essential chronic insomnias, thus better "medicalizing" them. Clarity of definition has encouraged study designs on the insomnias to be more rigorous, but the number of research studies remains limited. Previous conclusions drawn about insomnia treatment have been historically confounded by irrational, nonempirical influences (e.g., both pro-drug and antidrug marketing), leaving open the question of which behavioral or pharmacological treatments will work for whom, for how long, and under what circumstances. Even with rigorous research studies, prescribing for insomnia will always face the problem of working with patients' preferences when deciding about treatments.

In day-to-day practice, these preferences complicate the assessment of treatment effectiveness and safety in individual circumstances.

Evidence of Efficacy and Effectiveness

Table 22.4 presents a nonexhaustive list of pharmacological interventions for insomnia. Aside from benzodiazepine receptor agonists with FDA approval, many pharmacological treatments that prescribers currently use have no formal FDA indication for insomnia. Newer FDA-approved medications are supported by Type 1 clinical study data. For many agents lacking such an indication, the medication's "side effect" of sedation relative to the FDA indication is what is used clinically to treat an insomnia complaint. In situations where the medication is used also for another purpose and might be prescribed anyway for another condition, for example, major depression, the advantage of selecting a particular agent lies in its overall utility in addressing both comorbidities adequately. Naturally, being sure the patient takes the medication before bedtime maximizes the hypnotic benefit and minimizes daytime sedation. For all agents, there may be some risk of return to baseline levels of sleep difficulty if the agent is discontinued ("relapsing insomnia"), although worse insomnia after discontinuation than before baseline ("rebound insomnia"; Gillin, Spinweber, & Johnson, 1989) is usually short-lived.

Research data point to the clinical priority of treating insomnia in conditions such as major de-

TABLE 22.4 Pharmacologic Approaches to Treating Insomnia

Class	Subclass	Generic Name	Usual Dose (mg)	Onset (min)	Half-Life (hrs)	Comment
Benzodiazepine receptor agonists (BZRAs)	Benzodiazepines	Triazolam	0.125–0.250	2–30	2–6	Helps sleep onset more
		Temazepam	7.5–30	60–90	8–20	Helps sleep maintenance
		Estazolam	1–2	8–24	8–24	
		Lorazepam[b]	0.5–2	30	10–20	Familiar to psychiatrists
		Clonazepam[a,b]	0.5–2	60–90	30–40	Suppresses arousals
		Flurazepam[d]	15–30	15–30	48–120	Older, very long half-life
	Nonbenzodiazepines	Zolpidem	5–10	30	1.5–2.4	
		Ambien CR	6.25–12.5		2.5–2.8	No FDA-given timelimit;
		Zaleplon	5–10	30	1	Very short acting
		Eszopiclone	1–3	30	5–7	No FDA-given timelimit
GABA Precursor		Sodium oxybate[c]	4,500–9,000	15–45	0.5–1	Given for cataplexy
Antidepressants[b]	Tricyclics[b]	Amitriptyline[b]	25–100	30–60	10–25	Often used; inexpensive
		Doxepin[b]	25–100	30–60	8–24	Studied in insomniacs
		Trimipramine[b]	25–100	30–60	15–40	Studied in Insomniacs
		Clomipramine[a,b]	25–100	30–60	15–60	If with OCD Rx
	Nontricyclics[b]	Trazodone[b]	25–100	60–120	3–14	For primary insomnia?
		Mirtazepine[a,b]	15	30–120	13–40	Low dose better for sleep
Atypical antipsychotics[b]		Quetiapine[a,b]	25–200	60	6	Expensive
		Olanzepine[a,b]	5	120	20–54	Expensive
Anticonvulsants[b]		Valproate[a,b]	500–1,000	3–8	9–16	In epilepsy or bipolar
		Tiagabine[b]	4–12	60–90	8	Third-line choice
		Gabapentin[a,b]	100–500	60–120	5–7	Better with neuropathies
Sedating antihistamines		Diphenhydramine	25–50	30–60	4–8	Dose ceiling of 50 mg
		Doxylamine	6.25	–	10	In Nyquil, etc.
Melatoninergics		Melatonin[b]	0.5–3	30–60	1	A "dietary supplement"
		Ramelteon	8	30–69	1–2	Very new

Note: The medications listed here are representative, so this list is not exhaustive and is not limited to treatments for primary insomnia. See *Diagnostic and Coding Manual*, 2005; Mendelsohn, 2005; Buysse, Schweitzer, & Moul, 2005; Walsh, Roehrs, & Roth, 2005.
[a] Most used in association when another psychiatric or sleep diagnosis also present.
[b] Class or agent does not have an FDA-approved indication for treating insomnia.
[c] Requires unique prescribing procedures, Schedule III as FDA-approved for cataplexy, Schedule I otherwise.
[d] Has long half-life active metabolite.

pression and bipolar disorder. Increasingly, literature is pointing to the benefits of treating insomnia or difficulty sleeping in these conditions, as doing so may affect a patient's prognosis for remission substantially. For extremely ill patients with these disorders, psychological or behavioral approaches are unlikely to be immediately useful, in which circumstance pharmaceutical approaches to treating insomnia should be actively considered.

Among experts on insomnia, use of BZRAs is considered as a first-line pharmacotherapy of primary insomnia. BZRAs act by binding to $GABA_A$ Type 1 receptors to enhance chloride inflow into inhibitory neurons when GABA activates its receptor (Mendelson, 2005a). BZRAs have been demonstrated in several meta-analyses (Nowell et al., 1997; Smith et al., 2002) to provide statistically significant improvements in short-term (less than 3 weeks) studies of patient-reported and PSG-derived parameters such as sleep latency, number of awakenings, wake after sleep onset, and total sleep time. Formerly, it was believed that short-acting compounds such as triazolam produced morning anxiety, but this belief is questionable (Jonas, Coleman, Sheridan, & Kalinske, 1992). It is probably true that short-acting compounds have more liability for rebound after discontinuation (Gillin et al., 1989), which might be addressed by tapering the dose over a number of nights.

There are relatively few studies examining BZRA efficacy versus placebo for as long as 1 month (Asnis et al., 1999; Elie, Ruther, Farr, Emilien, & Salinas, 1999; Krystal et al., 2003; Mitler, Seidel, van den Hoed, Greenblatt, & Dement, 1984; Monti, Monti, Estevez, & Giusti, 1996; Morin, Colecchi, et al., 1999; Oswald, French, Adam, & Gilham, 1982; Reeves, 1977; Scharf, Roth, Vogel, & Walsh, 1994; Walsh, Vogel, et al., 2000; Ware et al., 1997), and they vary widely in their metrics of PSG and self-reported outcomes. A few longer term studies exist in drug-to-drug comparisons (Allen, Mendels, Nevins, Chernik, & Hoddes, 1987; Kales et al., 1982; Leibowitz & Sunshine, 1978; Tamminen & Hansen, 1987). The rather recent study of eszopiclone in a Type 1 randomized, blinded, placebo-controlled trial using patient-reported data was well designed and showed continued efficacy over 6 months (Krystal et al., 2003). These data allowed the FDA to issue an indication for eszopiclone as a hypnotic, but without a length-of-use stipulation. The new controlled-release preparation of zolpidem also lacks a length-of-use

stipulation. Despite these exceptions, solid research data are inadequate to allow a comprehensive assessment of the wisdom of using sleeping pills over the long term.

Currently the most widely prescribed non-BZRA, non-FDA-approved "hypnotic" is trazodone, even though the research supporting its use is limited largely to Type 3 studies (State-of-the-Science Panel, 2005). Ironically, diphenhydramine has an FDA over-the-counter indication for use with insomnia but likewise has limited research supporting its use (due to its early acceptance by the FDA decades ago using mostly Type 2 studies). It is desirable that we know more about these agents' efficacy in clinical trials, since they may have risks or benefits that are underappreciated; however, often the reason that we know less about particular "off-label" uses of medications for sleep is that pharmaceutical companies have no commercial incentive to fund the research needed once they are able to put a drug on the market (or certainly after the drug patent expires), and that national research funding agencies have not seen the need to formally research these medications as hypnotics. Thus, Which medications work for insomnia? is a medical practice question separate and apart from the commercial question Which medications have FDA approval for treating insomnia? What can be said, however, is that if the FDA approved a medication for insomnia after 1980, there has been at least one Type 1 clinical trial that has established its efficacy.

Since studies of other classes of agents are poorly funded, their overall effectiveness is less well understood. Diphenhydramine is an over-the-counter drug that has been available as a hypnotic for many decades. A few limited Type 2 studies using self-report have suggested that it improves sleep latency, continuity, and duration (Kudo & Kurihara, 1990; Meuleman, Nelson, & Clark, 1987; Sunshine, Zighelboim, & Laska, 1978; Teutsch et al., 1975). Its dose-response appears to be flat after 50 mg (Kudo & Kurihara, 1990; Sunshine et al., 1978; Teutsch et al., 1975), but it is not preferred by patients compared with triazolam (Rickels et al., 1983) and presumably other BZRAs. Patients will often try to use formulations with diphenhydramine prior to seeking clinical attention, and many who do not seek care may use it in the community (Basu, Dodge, Stoehr, & Ganguli, 2003). Clinically, data suggest that the sedative responses abate after several days (Richardson, Roehrs,

Rosenthal, Koshorek, & Roth, 2002). Other antihistaminic agents probably work similarly, although perhaps without the identical anticholinergic and other effects of diphenhydramine (e.g., residual daytime sleepiness) that are of particular concern in the elderly (McCall, 2004).

Antidepressants are popular as sleep aids when taken in less-than-antidepressant dosage at bedtime. The most popular, trazodone, has been studied in normals (Ware & Pittard, 1990; Yamadera, Nakamura, Suzuki, & Endo, 1998) and as an add-on hypnotic (Haffmans & Vos, 1999; Jacobsen, 1990; Kaynak, Kaynak, Gozukirmizi, & Guilleminault, 2004; Metz & Shader, 1990; Nierenberg, Adler, Peselow, Zornberg, & Rosenthal, 1994; Nierenberg, Cole, & Glass, 1992; Nierenberg & Keck, 1989) or as sole agent (Parrino, Spaggiari, Boselli, Di Giovanni, & Terzano, 1994; Saletu-Zyhlarz et al., 2002; Saletu-Zyhlarz et al., 2001; Saletu-Zyhlarz, Anderer, Arnold, & Saletu, 2003; Scharf & Sachais, 1990) in depressed patients, in alcoholic patients with sleep disturbances (Karam-Hage & Brower, 2003; Le Bon et al., 2003), and in patients with posttraumatic stress disorder (Liebowitz & el-Mallakh, 1989; Warner, Dorn, & Peabody, 2001). Its study in primary insomnia has been quite limited (Montgomery, Oswald, Morgan, & Adam, 1983; Walsh et al., 1998). The most consistent finding overall is an increase the amount of stages 3 and 4 sleep (Mendelson, 2005b), suggesting that it may deepen sleep. A number of studies suggest overall benefit for sleep quality, duration, and continuity. Variation in assessments of risk of trazodone use for insomnia can be found. In summary, good clinical trials data are limited in quality for insomnia, but much better for depression, with the sleep disorders literature being more skeptical (Mendelson, 2005b) of its use than the depression literature. Tricyclics such as amitriptyline, doxepin, and trimipramine are also popular choices, since they have complex receptor pharmacodynamics that can produce sedation. Trimipramine and doxepin have been studied in patients with primary insomnia, with some data supporting effectiveness (Hajak et al., 2001; Riemann et al., 2002). Rebound insomnia has been reported after discontinuation of tricyclic antidepressants and trazodone. One Type 2 study (limited sample size) of paroxetine in primary insomnia suggested benefit for primary insomnia (Nowell, Reynolds, Buysse, Dew, & Kupfer, 1999) despite the usual finding that serotonin-specific reuptake inhibitors impair sleep. Mirtazepine has sedation as a side effect at lower doses, but not at higher doses (Fawcett & Barkin, 1998).

Melatonin is a nocturnal hormone influencing a variety of physiological systems at night, probably through a cyclic GMP mechanism (Dubocovich, Masana, & Benloucif, 1999) and has effects on suprachiasmatic melatonin receptors (Hunt, Al-Ghoul, Gillette, & Dubocovich, 2001). Physiological oral doses of melatonin are less than 3 mg. Melatonin has two possible uses. Its more predictable use is as a chronobiotic (time-setting) compound when it is taken in the evening as a neurochemical signal of dusk. This would be a use considered when the patient has a circadian phase disorder. The second use, as a hypnotic, is more controversial, with skeptical (Mendelson, 1997), neutral (Olde Rikkert & Rigaud, 2001), or positive (Zhdanova & Wurtman, 1997) reviews for its overall effectiveness. Some patients may respond to melatonin as a hypnotic. Type 1 evidence for the efficacy of ramelteon (Roth, Stubbs, & Walsh, 2005), a new melatoninergic agent, suggests it may be useful, but its overall effectiveness across the range of insomnia subtypes remains to be clarified.

Less-researched approaches are also used by clinicians, often based on individual practice experience and reasoning from side effects. Antipsychotics are generally to be avoided in nonpsychotic patients due to their potential risk of akathisia, dystonia, tardive dyskinesia, postural hypotension, daytime mental impairment, and metabolic syndrome. However, both quetiapine and olanzepine given at bedtime generally increase sleep. Olanzapine increases stage 3 and 4 sleep (Lindberg et al., 2002; Salin-Pascual, Herrera-Estrella, Galicia-Polo, & Laurrabaquio, 1999; Sharpley, Vassallo, & Cowen, 2000). Quetiapine is now popular, but controversial, as a hypnotic when from 25 to 200 mg are given at bedtime. In healthy controls, it increased stage 2 sleep and reduced sleep latency (Cohrs et al., 2004). Its duration of action for sleep probably does not exceed 4 hours. No well-controlled trials of antipsychotics as hypnotics for primary insomnia are known. Anticonvulsants also produce sedation. With seizure disorders or with bipolar disorder, for which valproic acid is well established as an independent indication, it is often useful to dose the medication at bedtime to encourage sleep. Valproic acid is not used as a stand-alone hypnotic. Gabapentin is another anticonvulsant that may be useful for insomnia in the settings of restless legs

(Garcia-Borreguero et al., 2002), substance abuse (Freye, Levy, & Partecke, 2004; Karam-Hage & Brower, 2003), neuropathic pain, or hot flashes (Guttuso, Kurlan, McDermott, & Kieburtz, 2003) based on Type 3 studies

There have been recent publications suggesting that tiagabine in doses of 4 to 12 mg given at bedtime might serve as a hypnotic in some patients (Mathias, Wetter, Steiger, & Lancel, 2001). However, well-controlled studies are needed for these off-label uses of non-BZRAs for insomnia.

One very sedating compound of interest in particular situations is sodium oxybate. It has not yet been studied for primary insomnia but is mentioned here because it is important for clinicians to know about it. This is a drug otherwise known as "G" (for gamma-hydroxybutyrate) among drug abusers, but it has an FDA indication for the treatment of cataplexy in narcolepsy. Because of the abuse potential, only one pharmacy in the United States is licensed to dispense it, and then with rather elaborate prescribing procedures. For the narcoleptic, this medication is consumed in two liquid doses *while in bed*, once initially at bedtime and then 3 hours later. It is very sedating. It treats the insomnia of narcolepsy as well as cataplexy. Sodium oxybate apparently increases stage 3 and 4 sleep during its short duration of action (Scharf, Baumann, & Berkowitz, 2003). Because of its "sleep-deepening" effects, it has also been studied in fibromyalgia, where early data suggest drug benefit (Scharf et al., 2003). Other contexts of use of this compound may appear. Its withdrawal is dangerous when abused (Dyer, Roth, & Hyma, 2001), but not when taken as prescribed (U.S. Xyrem Multi-Center Study Group, 2003). Its prescription involves very specialized procedures, as it is only dispensed by one pharmacy in the United States.

Expectations and Risks

There are no precise data about treatment expectations across patients, but the following can probably be offered by way of clinical experience (see also Table 22.5): a minority of hypnotic responders will report that they sleep well, sleep deeply, and will be entirely pleased with a medication. Many patients will report some noticeable benefit, but also report that they feel the sleep they get is still light, not normal, or not fully restorative. Among the medication responders, some will find that the medication loses its effectiveness entirely after a few weeks of nightly use, some will require an upward dose adjustment after a few weeks, and some will not want or need a dose adjustment. Among those losing effectiveness, a trial of using the hypnotic only on some nights of the week may preserve some effectiveness (Hajak, Bandelow, Zulley, & Pittrow, 2002; Walsh, Roth, et al., 2000). A minority of patients will find that one or more agents do not work at all or "wake them up." Among these complete nonresponders, trying another medication — even within drug class — may prove useful. However, for some patients no plausible sedating medication of any kind will work: the first author had one patient who had been tried on 23 different agents, all ineffective!

The side effects experienced will govern the patient's continued use of a particular hypnotic. Diphenhydramine available over the counter can be used often for short periods, but patients can find it difficult to continue, due to its persisting daytime sedating effects and tendency to promote weight gain. The elderly are more vulnerable to its anticholinergic, cognitive side effects.

The benzodiazepine receptor agonists as a group share many common side effects. Benzodiazepines in general acutely impair memory consolidation (as do sleep inertia and sleepiness). It takes some time for an arousal to be processed by the long-term memory systems of the brain to register the arousal as an arousal, and it appears that BZRAs interfere in some way with this process. This drug action may be one way in which they are useful in treating anxiety conditions. Longer acting benzodiazepines (e.g., clonazepam, flurazepam) may be selected to dually treat a comorbid anxiety disorder. Longer acting agents will produce more morning "hangover" effects. All BZRAs can also impair balance, of concern in the elderly at risk for falls (Leipzig, Cumming, & Tinetti, 1999; Ray, Thapa, & Gideon, 2000), and they may impair concentration, of concern in workers. However, this statement is confounded by evidence that insomnia itself, even without the use of medications, increases the risk of falls as well (Avidan et al., 2005; Brassington, King, & Bliwise, 2000). The exact magnitude of the two fall risks remains to be quantified in relative terms. Some patients may report memory impairment extending into early afternoon even with short-acting BZRAs. Paradoxically, short-acting medications such as triazolam may cause morning sedative hangover effects in some patients; whereas others

TABLE 22.5 Types of Response to the Use of a Hypnotic Medication

No effect	The particular hypnotic medication paradoxically wakes the patient up, or does nothing.
Side effects	Acute intolerable side effects occur (e.g., sedation, rebound anxiety, GI disturbance).
	It is effective, but chronic side effects (e.g., memory problems, clumsiness, disinhibition, mania, depression, personality changes) develop.
	Patient falls after taking medication.
Temporary effect	It is effective in the short term but loses effectiveness after a few weeks of use.
Durable effects	It provides continued stable benefit with nightly use, with no dose increase required.
Decreased effects	It provides continued benefit with nightly use, but a modest dose increase is needed.
	The patient may need an additional medication from another class of compound.
	The medication loses nightly effectiveness but can be used 3–4 nights per week with benefit.
Change in preferences	The patient decides to try coming off or reducing the use of the medication.
Addiction risks	Clinically it becomes obvious that the patient will escalate the dose of a benzodiazepine receptor agonist unsafely, without consulting the prescriber, and functionally is a substance abuse patient who cannot be safely prescribed any controlled substance.
	Clinically it becomes obvious that the patient will escalate the dose of any sedative-hypnotic substance unsafely, without consulting the prescriber, and functionally is a substance abuse patient who cannot be safely prescribed *any* medication (e.g., even chlorpromazine) for sleep.
Overdose	The patient overdoses on the medication "to get one good night's sleep" or to attempt suicide.

Note: These are the types of responses that the authors have seen at one time or another with hypnotic medications. The exact rate of each response may vary depending on patient population and/or referral pattern and remains a topic for future research.

may report increased morning anxiety. Headache is a common side effect. Some patients develop intolerable GI disturbances. Psychological disinhibition may occur in a minority, as well as other psychiatric side effects.

BZRAs are Schedule IV drugs, which by definition have some risk of physiological and/or psychological dependency. Physiological dependency is more of a consideration for those medications that have especially long half-lives (in the absence of BZRA use during the daytime). Patients taking these long-duration drugs are never free of the drug's effects throughout the day or night, may become physiologically regulated to the drug's presence, and may thus become at risk for physiological dependency. However, such long-acting compounds are self-tapering, and so are less likely to cause physiologically reinforced pill taking. Physiological dependence can be predicted if the patient begins taking a shorter acting hypnotic medication in escalating doses throughout the day and night. This generalized physical dependence would raise the concern of delirium tremens — but this pattern of use for hypnotics is rare in patients without a drug abuse history (Hajak, Muller, Wittchen, Pittrow, & Kirch, 2003).

Psychological dependency, on the other hand, is a problem seen in the use of any hypnotic, whether it is a controlled substance or not. The malignant presentation of psychological dependency is when the patient takes more and more of a sedating compound (e.g., BZRA, trazodone, clonidine, chlorpromazine) in the semimaniacal quest for a good night's sleep. A more benign form of such dependency is when a patient clings to the use of a hypnotic rather than consider behavioral measures that might improve sleep. It is easy to identify extreme cases of psychological dependency, but often the issues fall along the spectrum between psychological dependency and patient preference, rather than a strict either-or dichotomy. For this reason, the astute clinician always looks for opportunities to promote nonpharmaceutical treatment trials in the management of insomnia: if the behavioral treatments work, they will provide more freedom, fewer risks, and lower long-term costs (Morgan et al., 2003).

Starting doses for trazodone should begin at 25 to 50 mg 30 to 60 minutes before bedtime, since this agent is well known to provide significant morning hangover in many patients. The sedative effects are believed to be due to alpha-1, 5HT1a, and 5HT2c receptor blockade, but trazodone is largely free of anticholinergic effects. Orthostatic hypotension can occur, along with lightheadedness, weakness, and weight gain. Priapism is a risk in males. Case reports have suggested risks of cardiac dysrhythmias, but overall, trazodone is generally safe, even in overdose.

Popular tricyclics such as trimipramine, doxepin, and amitriptyline are side-effect laden owing to their anticholinergic, antihistaminergic, anti-alpha-1, and quinidine-like effects. These are especially problematic in the elderly, involving risks of persistent daytime memory impairment, orthostatic hypotension (with falling), glaucoma event, constipation, urinary retention, weight gain, dry mouth, and cardiac conduction effects. At the hypnotic doses used (10 to 100 mg before bedtime), in otherwise healthy middle-aged adults, these side effects may not be especially dangerous, only annoying.

Melatonin in nonprimates is known directly to cause changes in pelage, to regulate seasonal behavior, and to affect reproductive cycles. In humans such effects have not been reported. More recently, controversy has emerged whether increased melatonin helps sleep in asthmatics (Campos, da Silva-Junior, de Bruin, & de Bruin, 2004) or poses added immunological risks to asthmatics (Sutherland, Ellison, Kraft, & Martin, 2003).

Realistic considerations in the use of hypnotics focus on selecting those patients who may benefit, and managing their insomnia illness prospectively as one would any other ailment. One key concern about the use of hypnotics is that they may complicate the course of a substance abuse disorder patient with insomnia. Yet insomnia is a risk factor for relapse in alcoholism (Brower, Aldrich, Robinson, Zucker, & Greden, 2001) and possibly other substance use disorders. The choice of a particular sedative-hypnotic is usually governed by whether the patient has a substance abuse disorder: BZRAs are proscribed for all substance-dependent patients (except the just-nicotine dependent). This proscription is a generally wise, but perhaps overdrawn, policy. Little formal data are available to support this absolutist proscriptive policy, and there is very limited support for using trazodone or gabapentin in this kind of circumstance (Karam-Hage & Brower, 2003; Le Bon et al., 2003; Liebowitz & el-Mallakh, 1989).

In the frail elderly, the issue of treating the inability to sleep is confounded with a number of other issues that affect prescribing choices. First, the elderly do not metabolize drugs with the efficiency of younger adults, so the dosing of hypnotics, if used, should begin at one third or less of the usual adult dose, to avoid acute toxicity. Second, the elderly brain produces less, more shallow, and more fragmented sleep compared with middle-aged adults, so "hard-system" treatment goals are more modest. Third, the prescriber needs to be clear about who needs the hypnotic and the exact indication. For example, if a nurse wants an elderly patient prescribed a hypnotic in order that the patient should sleep from 9:00 P.M. until 7:00 A.M. to allow the night shift to go smoothly, this request is at odds both with sleep biology and with clinical safety. Ray and colleagues (2000) demonstrated epidemiologically that benzodiazepines used in the 1980s in nursing homes were associated with an increased risk of hip fractures, presumably from falls. However, Avidan (Avidan et al., 2005) provided evidence that insomnia caused falls as well, so the matter of fall risks appears to be one of competing, rather than absolute, risks. All hypnotics bear some risk of patients' falling. Many sedating medications come with receptor effects (e.g., anticholinergic) that are irrelevant to the directly intended hypnotic action, so short-acting, nonbenzodiazepine BZRAs may be preferred in the elderly insomnia patient for this reason. Yet the relevant research data are not well developed.

Long-term exposure to a medication may raise risks in ways that short-term exposure does not. For some agents such as antihistamines, antidepressants, and antipsychotics, weight gain and associated metabolic syndrome can be important issues, with their attendant risks. One limitation inherent in selecting a hypnotic medication is its ongoing cost. Older medications are inexpensive and possibly cause more side effects; whereas newer nonbenzodiazepine BZRAs may be more than 10 times as expensive and are less likely to be covered by a patient's pharmacy benefit plan.

Thoughtful, prospective consideration of the benefits and limitations of behavioral and pharmacological treatments for each insomnia patient will ensure that the patient is provided an optimal treatment—provided that the patient actually has insomnia and not restless legs syndrome, or numbers among the minority of patients who have both problems.

RESTLESS LEGS SYNDROME:
A NEUROPHYSIOLOGICAL
DISTURBANCE RESEMBLING
INSOMNIA

Description and Differential Diagnosis

Restless legs syndrome (RLS) is characterized by the symptom of the urge to move the legs, or less frequently the arms, when they are kept immobile (Allen & Earley, 2001; Earley, 2003). More complete reviews are found elsewhere (Allen et al., 2003). For most patients, this symptom appears solely during the evening and early night during sedentary activities, making it a disorder associated with a particular circadian time of day. The urge to move the legs is often accompanied by a difficult-to-describe paresthesia in the calves or legs. Patients use "internal itch," "creepy-crawly," "shooting," and similar descriptions. RLS can begin in childhood but often starts during adulthood. It tends to have a waxing and waning course over days to months, and tends to become more severe with age. Risk factors include iron deficiency (ferritin less than 50 mcg/L) conditions (e.g., iron malabsorption, chronic blood loss), uremia requiring renal dialysis (Gigli et al., 2004), female gender (Zucconi & Ferini-Strambi, 2004), and genetic diathesis. Iron is a cofactor required in the biosynthesis of dopamine, and RLS is believed to be linked to defects in dopamine neurotransmission (Allen & Earley, 2001). Pregnancy illustrates this relationship well. During pregnancy, iron transfer to the developing fetus lowers the mother's iron stores and occasions the RLS symptoms that later tend to abate after delivery.

RLS is underdiagnosed (Zucconi & Ferini-Strambi, 2004). Its differential diagnosis includes periodic limb movement disorder (PLMD), with which is it often comorbid. PLMD is a sleep disorder in which the patient produces brief but periodic leg movements that cause arousals from sleep, leading to daytime sleepiness or other symptoms in much the same way that obstructive sleep apnea does so. However, many persons have nocturnal periodic limb movements, but without PLMD. PLMD may be diagnosed with polysomnography yet may also respond to treatments for RLS. Diabetic neuropathy also occurs in the legs, but usually in the distal extremities, and does not have a circadian timing. Leg movements can occur in congestive heart failure due to

poor circulation (Cheshire, 2000). Prolonged daytime exercise of the leg muscles may give rise to nighttime leg parasthesias, but this is related to the exercise intensity rather than to circadian timing.

Medications may also affect RLS symptom levels. For patients who are taking neuroleptics (Catalano, Grace, Catalano, Morales, & Cruse, 2005; Wetter, Brunner, & Bronisch, 2002) that antagonize dopamine neurotransmission, review of the need for these agents is advised, because their discontinuance may reduce RLS symptoms. Patients using lithium, serotonin specific reuptake inhibitors (SSRIs), central-acting antihistamines, or tricyclic antidepressants in significant dosage may be at increased risk of RLS symptoms (Agargün, Kara, Ozbek, Tombul, & Ozer, 2002; Bakshi, 1996; Bonin, Vandel, & Kantelip, 2000; Heiman & Christie, 1986; Lipinski, Mallya, Zimmerman, & Pope, 1989; Markkula & Lauerma, 1997; Terao, Terao, Yoshimura, & Abe, 1991; Ware, Brown, & Moorad, 1984), although a recent report questions whether these risks are idiosyncratic (Brown, Dedrick, Doggett, & Guido, 2005). Akathisia (Blaisdell, 1994), a general urge to move the entire body, is a side effect of dopamine antagonists and of SSRIs and does not have a circadian pattern of symptom presence. Occasionally, particularly a heroin-dependent or illicit opiate–dependent patient, but also patients withdrawing from benzodiazepines or anticonvulsants, may experience RLS during or after detoxification (American Sleep Disorders Association, 1990). Among them, there are some patients who became "opiate dependent" after a postsurgical course of opiates for pain relief made it obvious to them that opiates treat RLS as well. Undiagnosed for RLS, they may have sought opiates for bedtime use only. With these points in mind, patients admitted to a psychiatric or drug detoxification facility with a complaint of inability to sleep should be asked about restless legs symptoms. For the untreated, the experience of RLS can significantly impair mental health by itself (Phillips et al., 2000). Improperly diagnosed, this illness might be confused with major psychiatric illness, severe primary insomnia, or manipulative drug-seeking behavior.

Evidence for Efficacy and Effectiveness

Table 22.6 presents a list of effective treatments for RLS. Oral iron replacement is effective in the iron-deficient patient but usually takes 6 months to work

TABLE 22.6 Approaches to Treating Restless Legs Syndrome

Class	Subclass	Generic Name	Dosing (mg)	Onset (hours)	Half-Life (hours)	Comment
Dopaminergic agents	Precursor	Carbidopa/ levodopa	10/100 to 50/ 200 SR	1.2	3–5	Older, more risk of augmentation
	Agonist (first-line therapy)	Pramipexole	0.125–1	1–2	8–12	First line, well tolerated
		Ropinerole	0.25–4	1–2	6	First line, FDA approved
		Pergolide	0.5–5	1–2	–	
An ergot with more side effects		Cabergoline	0.5–2 mg/week	2–3	65	Expensive, but once weekly
	Antidepressant	Bupropion	75–450	2–4 weeks	8–24	+ depression and smoking cessation
Benzodiazepine receptor agonists (generally second-line therapy)		Clonazepam Other hypnotics (see Table 22.1)	0.5–2	1–3	30–40	Daytime sedation Used, but no efficacy trials
Opiate agonists (third- to fourth-line therapy)		Oxycodone	15–30	0.5–1	3–5	Third line
		Codeine	15–120	0.5–2	3–4	Third line
Alpha$_2$ agonist		Clonidine	0.1	0.5–1	12–16	Fourth line, drops blood pressure
Anticonvulsants		Carbamazepine	200–400	1–2	12–54	Third line, complex pharmacodynamics
		Gabapentin	100–1,800	60–120	5–7	Good side-effect profile, if effective
Iron replacement (if needed)	Oral	Ferrous gluconate + vitamin C	325 qd to tid	6 months	N/A	If ferritin <50, GI side effects
	Intravenous	Iron dextran	Grams	Days	N/A	Anaphylaxis risk

Note: The medications listed here are representative, so this list is not exhaustive.

and may involve side effects from the oral iron supplements. There is increased interest in the use of intravenous iron replacement (Earley, Heckler, & Allen, 2005), initially documented in the 1950s by Nordlander (1953a, 1953b); however, its exact role in the treatment remains unsettled. The first author had one RLS patient with a ferritin level of 4 mcg/L whose internist gave her intravenous replacement, with rather prompt symptom relief. Magnesium (Hornyak, Voderholzer, Hohagen, Berger, & Riemann, 1998) or thyroid replacements (Tan, Ho, Eng, et al., 2004; Tan, Ho, Koh, & Pavanni, 2004) also may be useful.

Randomized, blinded, placebo-controlled Type 1 clinical trials have established the efficacy of levodopa (Hening et al., 1999), pramipexole (Mont-plaisir, Nicolas, Denesle, & Gomez-Mancilla, 1999), ropinirole (Bliwise et al., 2005), pergolide, and cabergoline (Zucconi, Oldani, Castronovo, & Ferini-Strambi, 2003) for RLS. This collection of studies is a proof-of-concept for the use of dopamine agonists generally. The usual dosages of these dopaminergic agents are well below those used for the treatment of Parkinson's disease. Even when an iron deficiency may be present, most patients should be encouraged to try these first-line treatments, if such are feasible and safe in the patient's circumstances. The direct dopamine agonists are considered first-line treatments because of their general effectiveness, low dosing, tolerability, nonaddictiveness, and suspected lower rates of causing symptom augmentation compared with levodopa. Benzodiazepines are favored as second-line treatments (Littner et al., 2004), with utility demonstrated for clonazepam, but other benzodiazepines are likely to be useful as well due to similarity of mechanism. Among these agents, clonazepam is often preferred because of its long duration of action. The use of nonbenzodiazepine BZRAs has not been studied and may be less relevant for the treatment of RLS because of their lower muscle-relaxant properties. However, the mechanism by which BZRAs act favorably for RLS may be due more to their wake-suppression properties than to suppression of any dopamine-related abnormality (Allen & Earley, 2001). Patients will generally favor using dopamine agonists and benzodiazepines over opiates or anticonvulsants.

Gabapentin has been reported in case reports and in one clinical trial (Garcia-Borreguero et al., 2002) to be an effective agent for RLS. It is a relatively safe medication and may be worth trying in situations where treatment for RLS is desirable, but without using either a controlled medication or a dopamine agonist. Gabapentin may be more relevant in those RLS patients who have small sensory fiber loss neuropathy (Polydefkis et al., 2000). In a similar way, there is a clinical trial suggesting that carbamazepine is an effective treatment (Telstad et al., 1984).

Opiates were among the first known treatments for RLS and can be used in more severe cases or where first- or second-line medications may have relative contraindication or when opiates are used for another condition (Walters et al., 1993).

Expectations and Risks

For most noncomplicated cases of RLS, the use of a dopamine agonist in the evening, either with one dose or with two spaced doses, provides swift and decisive relief. A minority of patients have more severe illness, which may require the use of multiple therapies or the extension of therapies to other times of day. For this minority, some relief will be possible, yet some symptoms may break through. It is unusual for a RLS patient receiving treatment to be severely disabled from RLS. Most of the time, treating RLS is straightforward and successful.

Levodopa and dopamine agonists have typical side effects of headache and nausea, along with sleepiness in higher dosages. Pergolide has the disadvantage of lowering blood pressure more with the first dose. All agents can cause a small minority of patients to have nausea with vomiting until the medication effect wears off. For this reason, it is wise to begin with the smallest pill size in initial dosing before further dose increases. With the dopaminergic agents, after some use the phenomena of augmentation may occur, where the symptoms paradoxically worsen, migrate to the arms, or expand to times of the day other than the nighttime. If this occurs, careful review is needed concerning the overall approach because further dose increases may only yield further augmentation. Excessive daytime sleepiness has also been described as a side effect for dopamine agonists, particularly in dosages used to treat parkinsonism, but may be an issue at lower doses in some patients. Buproprion, a dopaminergic antidepressant, has been shown to reduce periodic limb movements (Nofzinger, Fasiczka, Berman, & Thase, 2000) and so might be a choice in the setting where another of its indications for use is present.

Benzodiazepines as treatments for RLS have the same side effects, cautions, and limitations of use as when given for insomnia, discussed previously.

Opiates as treatments for RLS have the typical side effects of sedation, nausea with potential emesis, constipation, and miosis, with considerably more liability to development of drug abuse and psychological effects in susceptible patients. The usual pattern of prescribed use focuses on using low doses in the evening for symptom coverage only. This medication class is considered an acceptable third-tier strategy after the benefits and limitations of dopaminergic and benzodiazepine-type medications have been adequately tested.

Carbamazepine, gabapentin, and clonidine are usually fourth-tier medications for RLS, since the predictability of their effectiveness is more uncertain. Carbamazepine may cause a leukopenia in very rare patients; however, a more usual concern is its complex pharmacokinetics and effects on the metabolism of other medications the patient may be taking. Gabapentin is rather safe pharmacologically but comes with sedation and some mental fogginess as side effects. Clonidine is used in opiate detoxification, and so may have use for RLS symptoms with that condition, but has the liability that it can reduce blood pressure dangerously. It should be prescribed cautiously because it could occasion a fatality if the patient attempts to "get a good night's sleep" and uses too much of the medicine.

CASE PRESENTATION

K.S. was a 62-year-old married woman who presented to the sleep clinic in the company of her husband with a chief complaint of comorbid insomnia and restless legs. Her sleep difficulties went back 18 years. About 10 years ago, she saw a psychiatrist, who diagnosed depression and put her on trimipramine 50 mg before bedtime. She had not been sure she was really depressed, but the trimipramine appeared to help her sleep for a number of years. About 5 years previously, she began having restless legs symptoms, in which she felt she needed to move her legs if they were kept still in the evening. Over time she found that reading in bed helped her deal with the symptoms enough to permit her to sleep. Her doctor tried ropinirole, which she felt made her "unconscious." The husband thought the dose had just been too high. Clonazepam did not work well. Recently she had been taking carbidopa/levodopa 10/100, with satisfactory symptom suppression on problem nights. Her other medicines were calcium supplement, 80 mg aspirin, and occasional doses of naproxen 400 mg. She exercised regularly.

Her daytime fatigue and memory difficulties were demoralizing her, almost to the point of depression. She was "no good anymore" with her golf game. She would have long periods of fatigue around late morning and late afternoon. Her sleep log indicated a range of bedtimes from 9:30 P.M. until 11:30 P.M., with out-of-bedtimes of 6:30 A.M. until 9:00 A.M. She took as long as several hours to get to sleep, with a later bout of 3 hours' continuous sleep followed by choppy sleep until she arose from bed. She had normal thyroid and CBC studies. She typically drank one to two glasses of wine nightly.

Family history indicated that K.S.'s brother took temazepam for insomnia. She had a good marriage and retirement security. Her Beck Depression Inventory score was 9, and her Epworth Sleepiness Scale score was 0. Her score on the Pittsburgh Insomnia Rating Scale (Moul, 2001; Moul, Pilkonis, Miewald, Carey, & Buysse, 2002), a local instrument, was 103. These scores indicate scant depression, no tendency to doze unintentionally, and high symptom burden from insomnia-type symptoms. Her physical and mental status findings were otherwise unremarkable.

After assessment, she was educated about realistic expectations and timing of sleep. After negotiation concerning what she could change or prefer, zolpi-

dem 5 mg was chosen as a nightly hypnotic, yet at the same time a fixed morning out-of-bed time was targeted, and the use of stimulus control procedures prescribed. Sleep logging was to continue. After several weeks, the patient reported back that the zolpidem was of limited benefit, and the sleep was mostly unchanged. In keeping with a clinical report suggesting possible benefit, tiagabine 4 to 12 mg before bedtime was tried next. After several weeks, the patient reported some benefit, possibly with increased daytime energy, but still sleep was suboptimal. The patient and her husband went on a vacation. During that time, the tiagabine lost its benefit. Later during that vacation she experienced three nights of solid, restorative sleep lasting 8 hours each, but this reverted to her usual sleep pattern when she returned home. These new data suggested that the patient's sleep biology probably worked well, but that something additional was interfering with the sleep process, unrelated to medications. After some discussion, the patient agreed to try, "but not marry," the idea of *not* initially reading in bed for 3 weeks. After 3 weeks, patient and her husband returned to report that her sleep difficulties were largely solved with the combination of not reading and using the trimipramine nightly and the carbidopa/levodopa occasionally. She was relieved of depressive feelings and was again a competitive threat on the golf course.

Comments About Case

This patient had evidently experienced primary insomnia for some time and had found some benefit from the use of a tricyclic prescribed, ironically, for the wrong diagnosis. Although one cannot say for sure, use of the drug may have caused or exacerbated her restless legs symptoms, which also had contributed to her problems with getting to sleep. She had stumbled onto a behavior (reading) that in the long run was stimulus paired with the difficulties of getting to sleep, even after getting carbidopa/levodopa for her restless legs symptoms. Her ferritin level might have been checked, but her restless legs symptoms were not the patient's main focus of concern, and she had no overt reason for iron loss with eating a normal amount of meat in her diet. Carbidopa/levodopa poses more risk of restless legs syndrome augmentation than other dopaminergic agents, but her dose was limited, occasional, and what she preferred after having had a misadventure with ropinir-

SLEEP LOG Name:

	Date	Noon	P.M.												Midnight	A.M.												Sleep Quality
			Afternoon						Evening							Morning												
		12	1	2	3	4	5	6	7	8	9	10	11	12	1	2	3	4	5	6	7	8	9	10	11	
M																											
T																											
W																											
Th																											
F																											
Sa																											
Su																											
M																											
T																											
W																											
Th																											
F																											
Sa																											
Su																											

Instructions: Use the symbols below to indicate your sleep times in the grid. Rate your sleep quality each night from 0 (poor) to 10 (excellent).
□ = Go to bed
□ = Get out of bed
□ = Actual sleep

Comments
_____
_____
_____
_____
_____

ole. Her profile of sleep hygiene defects was rich with potential therapeutic targets, but like many patients, she was willing to modify only some of her lifestyle choices. With follow-up, the chance nights of good sleep helped motivate her to understand that she might benefit from further behavioral modifications. The nights of good sleep away from home suggested psychophysiological insomnia, with some stimuli associated with the bed linked to an arousal pattern. Feeding back the self-report of several good nights' sleep may have addressed sleep anxiety ("Something's wrong with my brain") related to her pessimism about possible benefit with behavioral change. The maneuver of not doing an antitherapeutic sleep-forcing activity (here: light reading in bed) may have reduced performance anxiety related to sleep, to allow sleep to occur—according to the rationale of paradoxical intention therapy. The final regimen proved to be a continuing compromise between behavioral (i.e., not reading in bed) and pharmacological (i.e., trimipramine, carbidopa/levodopa) measures that she was perfectly happy with. She has an open invitation to return to the sleep clinic if problems arise again. If she does return, a review will be needed to examine any possible interplay between her primary insomnia, her restless legs syndrome, and any new medical, psychiatric, or psychosocial developments in the setting of her advancing age.

CONCLUSION

Patients may describe "insomnia" on initial presentation but may have another sleep disorder, among them restless legs syndrome. As the case just discussed illustrates, finding an effective treatment for a patient with an insomnia-like complaint often requires diagnostic acuity. This case was selected because the coincidental comorbidity between a psychophysiological insomnia and restless legs syndrome afforded an opportunity to illustrate a general reasoning process in a case needing consideration of different treatment modalities. Insomnia properly defined is more prevalent than restless legs syndrome and is often comorbid with other conditions too numerous to have been discussed here. Similarly, restless legs syndrome can be comorbid with many conditions other than insomnia. Both problems are worth identifying and treating, because doing so will increase a patient's mental health and quality of life, if not reduce risks of other psychiatric conditions. Treating uncomplicated cases of insomnia or restless legs syndrome can be quite professionally gratifying because "cures" are sometimes possible and much appreciated by patients. By and large, though, obtaining acceptable outcomes will require the clinician to diagnose carefully, to carry out personalized treatment trials, and to follow patients prospectively.

There is currently a broad domain of research questions concerning insomnia under investigation, in keeping with the likelihood that "primary insomnia" comprises not one syndrome but many. One key question is the mechanism by which insomnia has genetic predeterminants and how it becomes chronic. The relation between symptoms and neurophysiology remains a key focus. In the treatment domain, questions about treatment selection, treatment modality (e.g., individual vs. group), and the core aspects of psychotherapy are continuing issues. National research goals are published (National Center on Sleep Disorders Research, 2003). Of particular usefulness would be studies of head-to-head comparisons of one treatment versus another, including non-BZRA treatments. For RLS, studies continue to probe its genetic and neurophysiological basis. In the treatment domain, key questions remain concerning how to manage the risks of augmentation with dopamine agonists, and whether intravenous iron therapy might be used more regularly for more severe cases.

REFERENCES

Agargün, M. Y., Kara, H., Ozbek, H., Tombul, T., & Ozer, O. A. (2002). Restless legs syndrome induced by mirtazapine. *Journal of Clinical Psychiatry, 63,* 1179.

Allen, R. P., & Earley, C. J. (2001). Restless legs syndrome: A review of clinical and pathophysiologic features. *Journal of Clinical Neurophysiology, 18,* 128–147.

Allen, R. P., Mendels, J., Nevins, D. B., Chernik, D. A., & Hoddes, E. (1987). Efficacy without tolerance or rebound insomnia for midazolam and temazepam after use for one to three months. *Journal of Clinical Pharmacology, 27,* 768–775.

Allen, R. P., Picchietti, D., Hening, W. A., Trenkwalder, C., Walters, A. S., & Montplaisi, J. (2003). Restless legs syndrome: Diagnostic criteria, special considerations, and epidemiology. A report from the restless legs syndrome diagnosis and epidemiology workshop at the National Institutes of Health. *Sleep Medicine, 4,* 101–119.

American Academy of Sleep Medicine. (2005). *International Classification of Sleep Disorders: Diagnostic and coding manual* (2nd ed.). Westchester, IL: Author.

American Academy of Sleep Medicine Standards of Practice Committee. (2006). Psychological and behavioral treatment of insomnia. *Sleep.* Manuscript submitted for publication.

American Psychiatric Association. (2000). *Diagnostic and statistical manual of mental disorders* (4th ed., Text revision). Washington, DC: Author.

American Sleep Disorders Association. (1990). *The International Classification of Sleep Disorders: Diagnostic and coding manual.* Rochester, MN: Author.

Asnis, G. M., Chakraburtty, A., DuBoff, E. A., Krystal, A., Londborg, P. D., Rosenberg, R., et al. (1999). Zolpidem for persistent insomnia in SSRI-treated depressed patients. *Journal of Clinical Psychiatry, 60,* 668–676.

Avidan, A. Y., Fries, B. E., James, M. L., Szafara, K. L., Wright, G. T., & Chervin, R. D. (2005). Insomnia and hypnotic use, recorded in the minimum data set, as predictors of falls and hip fractures in Michigan nursing homes. *Journal of the American Geriatrics Society, 53,* 955–962.

Bakshi, R. (1996). Fluoxetine and restless legs syndrome. *Journal of the Neurological Sciences, 142,* 151–152.

Basu, R., Dodge, H., Stoehr, G. P., & Ganguli, M. (2003). Sedative-hypnotic use of diphenhydramine in a rural, older adult, community-based cohort: Effects on cognition. *American Journal of Geriatric Psychiatry, 11,* 205–213.

Blaisdell, G. D. (1994). Akathisia: A comprehensive review and treatment summary. *Pharmacopsychiatry, 27,* 139–146.

Bliwise, D. L., Freeman, A., Ingram, C. D., Rye, D. B., Chakravorty, S., & Watts, R. L. (2005). Randomized, double-blind, placebo-controlled, short-term trial of ropinirole in restless legs syndrome. *Sleep Medicine, 6,* 141–147.

Bonin, B., Vandel, P., & Kantelip, J. P. (2000). Mirtazapine and restless leg syndrome: A case report. *Therapie, 55,* 655–656.

Bonnet, M. H., & Arand, D. L. (1995). 24-hour metabolic rate in insomniacs and matched normal sleepers. *Sleep, 18,* 581–588.

Bonnet, M. H., & Arand, D. L. (1998a). The consequences of a week of insomnia: II. Patients with insomnia. *Sleep, 21,* 359–368.

Bonnet, M. H., & Arand, D. L. (1998b). Heart rate variability in insomniacs and matched normal sleepers. *Psychosomatic Medicine, 60,* 610–615.

Bonnet, M. H., & Arand, D. L. (2000). Activity, arousal, and the MSLT in patients with insomnia. *Sleep, 23,* 205–212.

Bootzin, R. R., & Perlis, M. L. (1992). Nonpharmacologic treatments of insomnia. *Journal of Clinical Psychiatry, 53*(Suppl.), 37–41.

Borbély, A. A. (1982). A two process model of sleep regulation. *Human Neurobiology, 1,* 195–204.

Borbély, A. A., & Achermann, P. (2005). Sleep homeostasis and models of sleep regulation. In M. H. Kryger, T. Roth, & W. C. Dement (Eds.), *Principles and practices of sleep medicine* (4th ed., pp. 405–417). Philadelphia: Elsevier.

Borkovec, T. D., Grayson, J. B., O'Brien, G. T., & Weerts, T. C. (1979). Relaxation treatment of pseudoinsomnia and idiopathic insomnia: An electroencephalographic evaluation. *Journal of Applied Behavior Analysis, 12,* 37–54.

Brassington, G. S., King, A. C., & Bliwise, D. L. (2000). Sleep problems as a risk factor for falls in a sample of community-dwelling adults aged 64–99 years. *Journal of the American Geriatrics Society, 48,* 1234–1240.

Breslau, N., Roth, T., Rosenthal, L., & Andreski, P. (1996). Sleep disturbance and psychiatric disorders: A longitudinal epidemiological study of young adults. *Biological Psychiatry, 39,* 411–418.

Broomfield, N. M., & Espie, C. A. (2003). Initial insomnia and paradoxical intention: An experimental investigation of putative mechanisms using subjective and actigraphic measurement of sleep. *Behavioural and Cognitive Psychotherapy, 31,* 313–324.

Brower, K. J., Aldrich, M. S., Robinson, E. A., Zucker, R. A., & Greden, J. F. (2001). Insomnia, self-medication, and relapse to alcoholism. *American Journal of Psychiatry, 158,* 399–404.

Brown, L. K., Dedrick, D. L., Doggett, J. W., & Guido, P. S. (2005). Antidepressant medication use and restless legs syndrome in patients presenting with insomnia. *Sleep Medicine, 6,* 443–450.

Buysse, D. J., Schweitzer, P. K., & Moul, D. E. (2005). Clinical pharmacology of other drugs used as hypnotics. In M. H. Kryger, T. Roth, & W. C. Dement (Eds.), *Principles and practice of sleep medicine* (4th ed., pp. 452–467). Philadelphia: Saunders.

Campos, F. L., da Silva-Junior, F. P., de Bruin, V. M., & de Bruin, P. F. (2004). Melatonin improves sleep in asthma: A randomized, double-blind, placebo-controlled study. *American Journal of Respiratory and Critical Care Medicine, 170,* 947–951.

Catalano, G., Grace, J. W., Catalano, M. C., Morales, M. J., & Cruse, L. M. (2005). Acute akathisia associated with quetiapine use. *Psychosomatics, 46,* 291–301.

Chang, P. P., Ford, D. E., Mead, L. A., Cooper-Patrick, L., & Klag, M. J. (1997). Insomnia in young men and subsequent depression: The Johns Hopkins Precursors Study. *American Journal of Epidemiology, 146,* 105–114.

Checkland, P. (1981). *Systems thinking, systems practice.* New York: Wiley.

Cheshire, W. P., Jr. (2000). Hypotensive akathisia: Autonomic failure associated with leg fidgeting while sitting. *Neurology, 55,* 1923–1926.

Chesson, A., Jr., Hartse, K., Anderson, W. M., Davila, D., Johnson, S., Littner, M., et al. (2000). Practice parameters for the evaluation of chronic insomnia. An American Academy of Sleep Medicine report. Standards of Practice Committee of the American Academy of Sleep Medicine. *Sleep, 23,* 237–241.

Chokroverty, S. (1999). *Sleep disorders medicine* (2nd ed.). Boston: Butterworth-Heinemann.

Cohrs, S., Rodenbeck, A., Guan, Z., Pohlmann, K., Jordan, W., Meier, A., et al. (2004). Sleep-promoting properties of quetiapine in healthy subjects. *Psychopharmacology (Berlin), 174,* 421–429.

Currie, S. R., Wilson, K. G., Pontefract, A. J., & deLaplante, L. (2000). Cognitive-behavioral treatment of insomnia secondary to chronic pain. *Journal of Consulting and Clinical Psychology, 68,* 407–416.

Dubocovich, M. L., Masana, M. I., & Benloucif, S. (1999). Molecular pharmacology and function of melatonin receptor subtypes. *Advances in Experimental Medicine and Biology, 460,* 181–190.

Dyer, J. E., Roth, B., & Hyma, B. A. (2001). Gammahydroxybutyrate withdrawal syndrome. *Annals of Emergency Medicine, 37,* 147–153.

Earley, C. J. (2003). Clinical practice: Restless legs syndrome. *New England Journal of Medicine, 348,* 2103–2109.

Earley, C. J., Heckler, D., & Allen, R. P. (2005). Repeated IV doses of iron provides effective supplemental treatment of restless legs syndrome. *Sleep Medicine, 6,* 301–305.

Edinger, J. D., & Sampson, W. S. (2003). A primary care "friendly" cognitive behavioral insomnia therapy. *Sleep, 26,* 177–182.

Edinger, J. D., Wohlgemuth, W. K., Radtke, R. A., Marsh, G. R., & Quillian, R. E. (2001). Cognitive behavioral therapy for treatment of chronic primary insomnia: A randomized controlled trial. *Journal of the American Medical Association, 285,* 1856–1864.

Elie, R., Ruther, E., Farr, I., Emilien, G., & Salinas, E. (1999). Sleep latency is shortened during 4 weeks of treatment with zaleplon, a novel nonbenzodiazepine hypnotic. Zaleplon Clinical Study Group. *Journal of Clinical Psychiatry, 60,* 536–544.

Engle-Friedman, M., Bootzin, R. R., Hazlewood, L., & Tsao, C. (1992). An evaluation of behavioral treatments for insomnia in the older adult. *Journal of Clinical Psychology, 48,* 77–90.

Espie, C. A., Inglis, S. J., & Harvey, L. (2001). Predicting clinically significant response to cognitive behavior therapy for chronic insomnia in general medical practice: Analysis of outcome data at 12 months posttreatment. *Journal of Consulting and Clinical Psychology, 69,* 58–66.

Espie, C. A., Inglis, S. J., Tessier, S., & Harvey, L. (2001). The clinical effectiveness of cognitive behaviour therapy for chronic insomnia: Implementation and evaluation of a sleep clinic in general medical practice. *Behaviour Research and Therapy, 39,* 45–60.

Fawcett, J., & Barkin, R. L. (1998). Review of the results from clinical studies on the efficacy, safety and tolerability of mirtazapine for the treatment of patients with major depression. *Journal of Affective Disorders, 51,* 267–285.

Ford, D. E., & Kamerow, D. B. (1989). Epidemiologic study of sleep disturbances and psychiatric disorders: An opportunity for prevention? *Journal of the American Medical Association, 262,* 1479–1484.

Freye, E., Levy, J. V., & Partecke, L. (2004). Use of gabapentin for attenuation of symptoms following rapid opiate detoxification (ROD): Correlation with neurophysiological parameters. *Neurophysiologie Clinique, 34,* 81–89.

Friedman, L., Bliwise, D. L., Yesavage, J. A., & Salom, S. R. (1991). A preliminary study comparing sleep restriction and relaxation treatments for insomnia in older adults. *Journal of Gerontology, 46,* P1–8.

Garcia-Borreguero, D., Larrosa, O., de la Llave, Y., Verger, K., Masramon, X., & Hernandez, G. (2002). Treatment of restless legs syndrome with gabapentin: A double-blind, cross-over study. *Neurology, 59,* 1573–1579.

Gigli, G. L., Adorati, M., Dolso, P., Piani, A., Valente, M., Brotini, S., et al. (2004). Restless legs syndrome in end-stage renal disease. *Sleep Medicine, 5,* 309–315.

Gillin, J. C., Smith, T. L., Irwin, M., Kripke, D. F., & Schuckit, M. (1990). EEG sleep studies in "pure" primary alcoholism during subacute withdrawal: Relationships to normal controls, age, and other clinical variables. *Biological Psychiatry, 27,* 477–488.

Gillin, J. C., Spinweber, C. L., & Johnson, L. C. (1989). Rebound insomnia: A critical review. *Journal of Clinical Psychopharmacology, 9,* 161–172.

Guttuso, T., Jr., Kurlan, R., McDermott, M. P., & Kieburtz, K. (2003). Gabapentin's effects on hot flashes in postmenopausal women: A randomized controlled trial. *Obstetrics and Gynecology, 101,* 337–345.

Haffmans, P. M., & Vos, M. S. (1999). The effects of trazodone on sleep disturbances induced by brofaromine. *European Psychiatry, 14,* 167–171.

Hajak, G., Bandelow, B., Zulley, J., & Pittrow, D. (2002). "As needed" pharmacotherapy combined with stimulus control treatment in chronic insomnia: Assessment of a novel intervention strategy in a primary care setting. *Annals of Clinical Psychiatry, 14,* 1–7.

Hajak, G., Muller, W. E., Wittchen, H. U., Pittrow, D., & Kirch, W. (2003). Abuse and dependence potential for the non-benzodiazepine hypnotics zolpidem and zopiclone: A review of case reports and epidemiological data. *Addiction, 98,* 1371–1378.

Hajak, G., Rodenbeck, A., Voderholzer, U., Riemann, D., Cohrs, S., Hohagen, F., et al. (2001). Doxepin in the treatment of primary insomnia: A placebo-controlled, double-blind, polysomnographic study. *Journal of Clinical Psychiatry, 62,* 453–463.

Harvey, A. G. (2002). A cognitive model of insomnia. *Behaviour Research and Therapy, 40,* 869–893.

Harvey, L., Inglis, S. J., & Espie, C. A. (2002). Insomniacs' reported use of CBT components and relationship to long-term clinical outcome. *Behaviour Research and Therapy, 40,* 75–83.

Hauri, P., & Linde, S. M. (1990). *No more sleepless nights.* New York: Wiley.

Heiman, E. M., & Christie, M. (1986). Lithium-aggravated nocturnal myoclonus and restless legs syndrome. *American Journal of Psychiatry, 143,* 1191–1192.

Hening, W., Allen, R., Earley, C., Kushida, C., Picchietti, D., & Silber, M. (1999). The treatment of restless legs syndrome and periodic limb movement disorder: An American Academy of Sleep Medicine review. *Sleep, 22,* 970–999.

Hohagen, F., Kappler, C., Schramm, E., Riemann, D., Weyerer, S., & Berger, M. (1994). Sleep onset insomnia, sleep maintaining insomnia and insomnia with early morning awakening: Temporal stability of subtypes in a longitudinal study on general practice attenders. *Sleep, 17,* 551–554.

Hornyak, M., Voderholzer, U., Hohagen, F., Berger, M., & Riemann, D. (1998). Magnesium therapy for periodic leg movements-related insomnia and restless legs syndrome: An open pilot study. *Sleep, 21,* 501–505.

Hunt, A. E., Al-Ghoul, W. M., Gillette, M. U., & Dubocovich, M. L. (2001). Activation of MT_2 melatonin receptors in rat suprachiasmatic nucleus phase advances the circadian clock. *American Journal of Physiology: Cell Physiology, 280,* C110–C118.

Jacobsen, F. M. (1990). Low-dose trazodone as a hypnotic in patients treated with MAOIs and other psychotropics: A pilot study. *Journal of Clinical Psychiatry, 51,* 298–302.

Jonas, J. M., Coleman, B. S., Sheridan, A. Q., & Kalin-ske, R. W. (1992). Comparative clinical profiles of triazolam versus other shorter-acting hypnotics. *Journal of Clinical Psychiatry, 53*(Suppl.), 19–31; discussion 32–13.

Kales, A., Bixler, E. O., Soldatos, C. R., Vela-Bueno, A., Jacoby, J., & Kales, J. D. (1982). Quazepam and flurazepam: Long-term use and extended with-drawal. *Clinical Pharmacology and Therapeutics, 32,* 781–788.

Kales, A., Bixler, E. O., Tan, T. L., Scharf, M. B., & Kales, J. D. (1974). Chronic hypnotic-drug use: In-effectiveness, drug-withdrawal insomnia, and de-pendence. *Journal of the American Medical Associ-ation, 227,* 513–517.

Kales, A., Kales, J. D., Bixler, E. O., & Scharf, M. B. (1975). Effectiveness of hypnotic drugs with pro-longed use: Flurazepam and pentobarbital. *Clini-cal Pharmacology and Therapeutics, 18,* 356–363.

Karam-Hage, M., & Brower, K. J. (2003). Open pilot study of gabapentin versus trazodone to treat in-somnia in alcoholic outpatients. *Psychiatry and Clinical Neurosciences, 57,* 542–544.

Kaynak, H., Kaynak, D., Gozukirmizi, E., & Guillemi-nault, C. (2004). The effects of trazodone on sleep in patients treated with stimulant antidepressants. *Sleep Medicine, 5,* 15–20.

Kryger, M. H., Roth, T., & Dement, W. C. (Eds.). (2005). *Principles and practice of sleep medicine* (4th ed.). Philadelphia: Elsevier.

Krystal, A. D., Walsh, J. K., Laska, E., Caron, J., Amato, D. A., Wessel, T. C., et al. (2003). Sustained effi-cacy of eszopiclone over 6 months of nightly treat-ment: Results of a randomized, double-blind, pla-cebo-controlled study in adults with chronic insomnia. *Sleep, 26,* 793–799.

Kudo, Y., & Kurihara, M. (1990). Clinical evaluation of diphenhydramine hydrochloride for the treatment of insomnia in psychiatric patients: A double-blind study. *Journal of Clinical Pharmacology, 30,* 1041–1048.

Lacks, P. (1987). *Behavioral treatment for persistent in-somnia.* New York: Pergamon Press.

Lacks, P., Bertelson, A., Gans, L., & Kunkel, J. (1983). The treatment of sleep-maintenance insomniac with stimulus control techniques. *Behaviour Re-search and Therapy, 21,* 291–295.

Le Bon, O., Murphy, J. R., Staner, L., Hoffmann, G., Kormoss, N., Kentos, M., et al. (2003). Double-blind, placebo-controlled study of the efficacy of trazodone in alcohol post-withdrawal syndrome: Polysomnographic and clinical evaluations. *Jour-nal of Clinical Psychopharmacology, 23,* 377–383.

Leibowitz, M., & Sunshine, A. (1978). Long-term hyp-notic efficacy and safety of triazolam and fluraze-pam. *Journal of Clinical Pharmacology, 18,* 302–309.

Leipzig, R. M., Cumming, R. G., & Tinetti, M. E. (1999). Drugs and falls in older people: A system-atic review and meta-analysis: I. Psychotropic drugs. *Journal of the American Geriatrics Society, 47,* 30–39.

Lichstein, K. L., Riedel, B. W., Wilson, N. M., Lester, K. W., & Aguillard, R. N. (2001). Relaxation and sleep compression for late-life insomnia: A pla-cebo-controlled trial. *Journal of Consulting and Clinical Psychology, 69,* 227–239.

Lichstein, K. L., Wilson, N. M., & Johnson, C. T. (2000). Psychological treatment of secondary in-somnia. *Psychology and Aging, 15,* 232–240.

Liebowitz, N. R., & el-Mallakh, R. S. (1989). Trazodone for the treatment of anxiety symptoms in substance abusers. *Journal of Clinical Psychopharmacology, 9,* 449–451.

Lindberg, N., Virkkunen, M., Tani, P., Appelberg, B., Virkkala, J., Rimon, R., et al. (2002). Effect of a single-dose of olanzapine on sleep in healthy fe-males and males. *International Clinical Psycho-pharmacology, 17,* 177–184.

Lipinski, J. F., Jr., Mallya, G., Zimmerman, P., & Pope, H. G., Jr. (1989). Fluoxetine-induced akathisia: Clinical and theoretical implications. *Journal of Clinical Psychiatry, 50,* 339–342.

Littner, M. R., Kushida, C., Anderson, W. M., Bailey, D., Berry, R. B., Hirshkowitz, M., et al. (2004). Practice parameters for the dopaminergic treat-ment of restless legs syndrome and periodic limb movement disorder. *Sleep, 27,* 557–559.

Markkula, J., & Lauerma, H. (1997). Mianserin and restless legs. *International Clinical Psychopharma-cology, 12,* 53–58.

Mathias, S., Wetter, T. C., Steiger, A., & Lancel, M. (2001). The GABA uptake inhibitor tiagabine pro-motes slow wave sleep in normal elderly subjects. *Neurobiology and Aging, 22,* 247–253.

McCall, W. V. (2004). Sleep in the elderly: Burden, diagnosis, and treatment. *Primary Care Companion to the Journal of Clinical Psychiatry, 6,* 9–20.

McCrae, C. S., Wilson, N. M., Lichstein, K. L., Dur-rence, H. H., Taylor, D. J., Bush, A. J., et al. (2003). "Young old" and "old old" poor sleepers with and without insomnia complaints. *Journal of Psychosomatic Research, 54,* 11–19.

Mellinger, G. D., Balter, M. B., & Uhlenhuth, E. H. (1985). Insomnia and its treatment: Prevalence and correlates. *Archives of General Psychiatry 42,* 225–232.

Mendelson, W. B. (1997). A critical evaluation of the hypnotic efficacy of melatonin. *Sleep, 20,* 916–919.

Mendelson, W. B. (2005a). Hypnotic medications: Mechanisms of action and pharmacological effects. In M. H. Kryger, T. Roth, & W. C. Dement (Eds.), *Principles and practice of sleep medicine* (4th ed., pp. 444–451). Philadelphia: Saunders.

Mendelson, W. B. (2005b). A review of the evidence for the efficacy and safety of trazodone in insomnia. *Journal of Clinical Psychiatry, 66,* 469–476.

Mendelson, W. B., Roth, T., Cassella, J., Roehrs, T., Walsh, J. K., Woods, J. H., et al. (2004). The treatment of chronic insomnia: Drug indications, chronic use and abuse liability. Summary of a 2001 New Clinical Drug Evaluation Unit meeting symposium. *Sleep Medicine Reviews, 8,* 7–17.

Metz, A., & Shader, R. I. (1990). Adverse interactions encountered when using trazodone to treat insomnia associated with fluoxetine. *International Clinical Psychopharmacology, 5,* 191–194.

Meuleman, J. R., Nelson, R. C., & Clark, R. L., Jr. (1987). Evaluation of temazepam and diphenhydramine as hypnotics in a nursing-home population. *Drug Intelligence and Clinical Pharmacy, 21,* 716–720.

Mitler, M. M., Seidel, W. F., van den Hoed, J., Greenblatt, D. J., & Dement, W. C. (1984). Comparative hypnotic effects of flurazepam, triazolam, and placebo: A long-term simultaneous nighttime and daytime study. *Journal of Clinical Psychopharmacology, 4,* 2–13.

Montgomery, I., Oswald, I., Morgan, K., & Adam, K. (1983). Trazodone enhances sleep in subjective quality but not in objective duration. *British Journal of Clinical Pharmacology, 16,* 139–144.

Monti, J. M., Monti, D., Estevez, F., & Giusti, M. (1996). Sleep in patients with chronic primary insomnia during long-term zolpidem administration and after its withdrawal. *International Clinical Psychopharmacology, 11,* 255–263.

Montplaisir, J., Nicolas, A., Denesle, R., & Gomez-Mancilla, B. (1999). Restless legs syndrome improved by pramipexole: A double-blind randomized trial. *Neurology, 52,* 938–943.

Morgan, K., Dixon, S., Mathers, N., Thompson, J., & Tomeny, M. (2003). Psychological treatment for insomnia in the management of long-term hypnotic drug use: A pragmatic randomised controlled trial. *British Journal of General Practice, 53,* 923–928.

Morgan, K., Dixon, S., Mathers, N., Thompson, J., & Tomeny, M. (2004). Psychological treatment for insomnia in the regulation of long-term hypnotic drug use. *Health Technology Assessment, 8,* iii–iv, 1–68.

Morin, C. M. (1993). *Insomnia: Psychological assessment and management.* New York: Guilford Press.

Morin, C. M., Bastien, C., Guay, B., Radouco-Thomas, M., Leblanc, J., & Vallieres, A. (2004). Randomized clinical trial of supervised tapering and cognitive behavior therapy to facilitate benzodiazepine discontinuation in older adults with chronic insomnia. *American Journal of Psychiatry, 161,* 332–342.

Morin, C. M., Colecchi, C., Stone, J., Sood, R., & Brink, D. (1999). Behavioral and pharmacological therapies for late-life insomnia: A randomized controlled trial. *Journal of the American Medical Association, 281,* 991–999.

Morin, C. M., Culbert, J. P., & Schwartz, S. M. (1994). Nonpharmacological interventions for insomnia: A meta-analysis of treatment efficacy. *American Journal of Psychiatry, 151,* 1172–1180.

Morin, C. M., Gaulier, B., Barry, T., & Kowatch, R. A. (1992). Patients' acceptance of psychological and pharmacological therapies for insomnia. *Sleep, 15,* 302–305.

Morin, C. M., Hauri, P. J., Espie, C. A., Spielman, A. J., Buysse, D. J., & Bootzin, R. R. (1999). Nonpharmacologic treatment of chronic insomnia. An American Academy of Sleep Medicine review. *Sleep, 22,* 1134–1156.

Moul, D. E. (2001). The Pittsburgh Insomnia Rating Scale (PIRS), University of Pittsburgh. Available at http://www.wpic.pitt.edu/research/pirs.pdf

Moul, D. E., Pilkonis, P. A., Miewald, J. M., Carey, T. J., & Buysse, D. J. (2002). Preliminary study of the test-retest reliability and concurrent validities of the Pittsburgh Insomnia Rating Scale (PIRS). *Sleep, 25*(Abstract suppl.), A246–247.

Murtagh, D. R., & Greenwood, K. M. (1995). Identifying effective psychological treatments for insomnia: A meta-analysis. *Journal of Consulting and Clinical Psychology, 63,* 79–89.

National Center on Sleep Disorders Research. (2003). *2003 National Sleep Disorders Research Plan.* Bethesda, MD. Author.

Nierenberg, A. A., Adler, L. A., Peselow, E., Zornberg, G., & Rosenthal, M. (1994). Trazodone for antidepressant-associated insomnia. *American Journal of Psychiatry, 151,* 1069–1072.

Nierenberg, A. A., Cole, J. O., & Glass, L. (1992). Possible trazodone potentiation of fluoxetine: A case series. *Journal of Clinical Psychiatry, 53,* 83–85.

Nierenberg, A. A., & Keck, P. E., Jr. (1989). Management of monoamine oxidase inhibitor-associated insomnia with trazodone. *Journal of Clinical Psychopharmacology, 9,* 42–45.

Nofzinger, E. A., Buysse, D. J., Germain, A., Price, J. C., Miewald, J. M., & Kupfer, D. J. (2004). Functional neuroimaging evidence for hyperarousal in insomnia. *American Journal of Psychiatry, 161,* 2126–2128.

Nofzinger, E. A., Fasiczka, A., Berman, S., & Thase, M. E. (2000). Bupropion SR reduces periodic limb movements associated with arousals from sleep in depressed patients with periodic limb movement disorder. *Journal of Clinical Psychiatry, 61,* 858–862.

Nordlander, N. B. (1953a). Restless legs. *British Journal of Physiological Medicine, 17,* 160–162.

Nordlander, N. B. (1953b). Therapy in restless legs. *Acta Medica Scandinavica, 145,* 453–457.

Nowell, P. D., Mazumdar, S., Buysse, D. J., Dew, M. A., Reynolds, C. F., & Kupfer, D. J. (1997). Benzodiazepines and zolpidem for chronic insomnia: A meta-analysis of treatment efficacy. *Journal of the American Medical Association, 278,* 2170–2177.

Nowell, P. D., Reynolds, C. F., Buysse, D. J., Dew, M. A., & Kupfer, D. J. (1999). Paroxetine in the treatment of primary insomnia: Preliminary clinical and electroencephalogram sleep data. *Journal of Clinical Psychiatry, 60,* 89–95.

Ohayon, M. M. (2002). Epidemiology of insomnia: What we know and what we still need to learn. *Sleep Medicine Reviews, 6,* 97–111.

Olde Rikkert, M. G., & Rigaud, A. S. (2001). Melatonin in elderly patients with insomnia: A systematic review. *Zeitschrift für Gerontologie und Geriatrie, 34,* 491–497.

Oswald, I., French, C., Adam, K., & Gilham, J. (1982). Benzodiazepine hypnotics remain effective for 24 weeks. *British Medical Journal, 284,* 860–863.

Pallesen, S., Nordhus, I. H., & Kvale, G. (1998). Nonpharmacological interventions for insomnia in older adults: A meta-analysis of treatment efficacy. *Psychotherapy, 35,* 472–482.

Pallesen, S., Nordhus, I. H., Kvale, G., Nielsen, G. H., Havik, O. E., Johnsen, B. H., et al. (2003). Behavioral treatment of insomnia in older adults: An open clinical trial comparing two interventions. *Behaviour Research and Therapy, 41,* 31–48.

Parrino, L., Spaggiari, M. C., Boselli, M., Di Giovanni, G., & Terzano, M. G. (1994). Clinical and polysomnographic effects of trazodone CR in chronic insomnia associated with dysthymia. *Psychopharmacology (Berlin), 116,* 389–395.

Partinen, M., & Hublin, C. (2005). Epidemiology of sleep disorders. In M. H. Kryger, T. Roth, &

W. C. Dement (Eds.), *Principles and practice of sleep medicine* (4th ed., pp. 626–647). Philadelphia: Saunders.

Perlis, M. L., Merica, H., Smith, M. T., & Giles, D. E. (2001). Beta EEG activity and insomnia. *Sleep Medicine Reviews, 5,* 365–376.

Phillips, B., Young, T., Finn, L., Asher, K., Hening, W. A., & Purvis, C. (2000). Epidemiology of restless legs symptoms in adults. *Archives of Internal Medicine, 160,* 2137–2141.

Polydefkis, M., Allen, R. P., Hauer, P., Earley, C. J., Griffin, J. W., & McArthur, J. C. (2000). Subclinical sensory neuropathy in late-onset restless legs syndrome. *Neurology, 55,* 1115–1121.

Quesnel, C., Savard, J., Simard, S., Ivers, H., & Morin, C. M. (2003). Efficacy of cognitive-behavioral therapy for insomnia in women treated for nonmetastatic breast cancer. *Journal of Consulting and Clinical Psychology, 71,* 189–200.

Ray, W. A., Thapa, P. B., & Gideon, P. (2000). Benzodiazepines and the risk of falls in nursing home residents. *Journal of the American Geriatrics Society, 48,* 682–685.

Reeves, R. L. (1977). Comparison of triazolam, flurazepam, and placebo as hypnotics in geriatric patients with insomnia. *Journal of Clinical Pharmacology, 17,* 319–323.

Richardson, G. S., Roehrs, T. A., Rosenthal, L., Koshorek, G., & Roth, T. (2002). Tolerance to daytime sedative effects of H1 antihistamines. *Journal of Clinical Psychopharmacology, 22,* 511–515.

Rickels, K., Morris, R. J., Newman, H., Rosenfeld, H., Schiller, H., & Weinstock, R. (1983). Diphenhydramine in insomniac family practice patients: A double-blind study. *Journal of Clinical Pharmacology, 23,* 234–242.

Riemann, D., Voderholzer, U., Cohrs, S., Rodenbeck, A., Hajak, G., Ruther, E., et al. (2002). Trimipramine in primary insomnia: Results of a polysomnographic double-blind controlled study. *Pharmacopsychiatry, 35,* 165–174.

Roth, T., Stubbs, C., & Walsh, J. K. (2005). Ramelteon (TAK-375), a selective MT1/MT2-receptor agonist, reduces latency to persistent sleep in a model of transient insomnia related to a novel sleep environment. *Sleep, 28,* 303–307.

Rybarczyk, B., Lopez, M., Benson, R., Alsten, C., & Stepanski, E. (2002). Efficacy of two behavioral treatment programs for comorbid geriatric insomnia. *Psychology and Aging, 17,* 288–298.

Saletu-Zyhlarz, G. M., Abu-Bakr, M. H., Anderer, P., Gruber, G., Mandl, M., Strobl, R., et al. (2002). Insomnia in depression: Differences in objective and subjective sleep and awakening quality to normal controls and acute effects of trazodone. *Progress in Neuropsychopharmacology and Biological Psychiatry, 26,* 249–260.

Saletu-Zyhlarz, G. M., Abu-Bakr, M. H., Anderer, P., Semler, B., Decker, K., Parapatics, S., et al. (2001). Insomnia related to dysthymia: Polysomnographic and psychometric comparison with normal controls and acute therapeutic trials with trazodone. *Neuropsychobiology, 44,* 139–149.

Saletu-Zyhlarz, G. M., Anderer, P., Arnold, O., & Saletu, B. (2003). Confirmation of the neurophysiologically predicted therapeutic effects of trazodone on its target symptoms depression, anxiety, and insomnia by postmarketing clinical studies with a controlled-release formulation in depressed outpatients. *Neuropsychobiology, 48,* 194–208.

Salin-Pascual, R. J., Herrera-Estrella, M., Galicia-Polo, L., & Laurrabaquio, M. R. (1999). Olanzapine acute administration in schizophrenic patients increases delta sleep and sleep efficiency. *Biological Psychiatry, 46,* 141–143.

Salzman, C. (1991). The APA Task Force report on benzodiazepine dependence, toxicity, and abuse. *American Journal of Psychiatry, 148,* 151–152.

Scharf, M. B., Baumann, M., & Berkowitz, D. V. (2003). The effects of sodium oxybate on clinical symptoms and sleep patterns in patients with fibromyalgia. *Journal of Rheumatology, 30,* 1070–1074.

Scharf, M. B., Roth, T., Vogel, G. W., & Walsh, J. K. (1994). A multicenter, placebo-controlled study evaluating zolpidem in the treatment of chronic insomnia. *Journal of Clinical Psychiatry, 55,* 192–199.

Scharf, M. B., & Sachais, B. A. (1990). Sleep laboratory evaluation of the effects and efficacy of trazodone in depressed insomniac patients. *Journal of Clinical Psychiatry, 51*(Suppl.), 13–17.

Sharpley, A. L., Vassallo, C. M., & Cowen, P. J. (2000). Olanzapine increases slow-wave sleep: evidence for blockade of central 5-HT(2C) receptors in vivo. *Biological Psychiatry, 47,* 468–470.

Smith, M. T., Perlis, M. L., Park, A., Smith, M. S., Pennington, J., Giles, D. E., et al. (2002). Comparative meta-analysis of pharmacotherapy and behavior therapy for persistent insomnia. *American Journal of Psychiatry, 159,* 5–11.

State-of-the-Science Panel. (2005, June 13–15). *Report of the NIH State-of-the Science Conference on Manifestations and Management of Chronic Insomnia in Adults.* Retrieved from http://consensus.nih. gov/2005/2005InsomniaSOS026html.htm

Steriade, M., Jones, E. G., & Llinás, R. R. (1990). *Thalamic oscillations and signaling.* New York: Wiley.

Sunshine, A., Zighelboim, I., & Laska, E. (1978). Hypnotic activity of diphenhydramine, methapyrilene, and placebo. *Journal of Clinical Pharmacology, 18,* 425–431.

Sutherland, E. R., Ellison, M. C., Kraft, M., & Martin, R. J. (2003). Elevated serum melatonin is associated with the nocturnal worsening of asthma. *Journal of Allergy and Clinical Immunology, 112,* 513–517.

Tamminen, T., & Hansen, P. P. (1987). Chronic administration of zopiclone and nitrazepam in the treatment of insomnia. *Sleep, 10*(Suppl. 1), 63–72.

Tan, E. K., Ho, S. C., Eng, P., Loh, L. M., Koh, L., Lum, S. Y., et al. (2004). Restless legs symptoms in thyroid disorders. *Parkinsonism and Related Disorders, 10,* 149–151.

Tan, E. K., Ho, S. C., Koh, L., & Pavanni, R. (2004). An urge to move with L-thyroxine: Clinical, biochemical, and polysomnographic correlation. *Movement Disorders, 19,* 1365–1367.

Telstad, W., Sorensen, O., Larsen, S., Lillevold, P. E., Stensrud, P., & Nyberg-Hansen, R. (1984). Treatment of the restless legs syndrome with carbamazepine: A double blind study. *British Medical Journal (Clinical Research Edition), 288,* 444–446.

Terao, T., Terao, M., Yoshimura, R., & Abe, K. (1991). Restless legs syndrome induced by lithium. *Biological Psychiatry, 30,* 1167–1170.

Teutsch, G., Mahler, D. L., Brown, C. R., Forrest, W. H., Jr., James, K. E., & Brown, B. W. (1975). Hypnotic efficacy of diphenhydramine, methapyrilene, and pentobarbital. *Clinical Pharmacology and Therapeutics, 17,* 195–201.

Toussaint, M., Luthringer, R., Schaltenbrand, N., Nicolas, A., Jacqmin, A., Carelli, G., et al. (1997). Changes in EEG power density during sleep laboratory adaptation. *Sleep, 20,* 1201–1207.

U.S. Xyrem Multi-Center Study Group. (2003). The abrupt cessation of therapeutically administered sodium oxybate (GHB) does not cause withdrawal symptoms. *Journal of Toxicology, Clinical Toxicology, 41,* 131–135.

Van Dongen, H. P., Maislin, G., Mullington, J. M., & Dinges, D. F. (2003). The cumulative cost of additional wakefulness: Dose-response effects on neurobehavioral functions and sleep physiology from chronic sleep restriction and total sleep deprivation. *Sleep, 26,* 117–126.

Walsh, J. K., Erman, M., Erman, C. W., Jamieson, A., Mahowald, M. W., Regestein, Q. R., et al. (1998). Subjective hypnotic efficacy of trazodone and zolpidem in *DSMIII-R* primary insomnia. *Human Psychopharmacology, 13,* 191–198.

Walsh, J. K., Roehrs, T., & Roth, T. (2005). Pharmacological treatment of primary insomnia. In M. H. Kryger, T. Roth, & W. C. Dement (Eds.), *Principles and practice of sleep medicine* (4th ed., pp. 749–760). Philadelphia: Saunders.

Walsh, J. K., Roth, T., Randazzo, A., Erman, M., Jamieson, A., Scharf, M., et al. (2000). Eight weeks of non-nightly use of zolpidem for primary insomnia. *Sleep, 23,* 1087–1096.

Walsh, J. K., Vogel, G. W., Scharf, M., Erman, M., Erwin, C. W., Schweitzer, P. K., et al. (2000). A five week, polysomnographic assessment of zaleplon 10 mg for the treatment of primary insomnia. *Sleep Medicine, 1,* 41–49.

Walters, A. S., Wagner, M. L., Hening, W. A., Grasing, K., Mills, R., Chokroverty, S., et al. (1993). Successful treatment of the idiopathic restless legs syndrome in a randomized double-blind trial of oxycodone versus placebo. *Sleep, 16,* 327–332.

Ware, J. C., Brown, F. W., & Moorad, P. J., Jr. (1984). Nocturnal myoclonus and tricyclic antidepressants. *Sleep Research, 13,* 72.

Ware, J. C., & Pittard, J. T. (1990). Increased deep sleep after trazodone use: A double-blind placebo-controlled study in healthy young adults. *Journal of Clinical Psychiatry, 51*(Suppl.), 18–22.

Ware, J. C., Walsh, J. K., Scharf, M. B., Roehrs, T., Roth, T., & Vogel, G. W. (1997). Minimal rebound insomnia after treatment with 10-mg zolpidem. *Clinical Neuropharmacology, 20,* 116–125.

Warner, M. D., Dorn, M. R., & Peabody, C. A. (2001). Survey on the usefulness of trazodone in patients with PTSD with insomnia or nightmares. *Pharmacopsychiatry, 34,* 128–131.

Wetter, T. C., Brunner, J., & Bronisch, T. (2002). Restless legs syndrome probably induced by risperidone treatment. *Pharmacopsychiatry, 35,* 109–111.

Yamadera, H., Nakamura, S., Suzuki, H., & Endo, S. (1998). Effects of trazodone hydrochloride and imipramine on polysomnography in healthy subjects. *Psychiatry and Clinical Neurosciences, 52,* 439–443.

Yaniv, G. (2004). Insomnia, biological clock, and the bedtime decision: An economic perspective. *Health Economics, 13,* 1–8.

Yules, R. B., Lippman, M. E., & Freedman, D. X. (1967). Alcohol administration prior to sleep: The effect on EEG sleep stages. *Archives of General Psychiatry, 16,* 94–97.

Zhdanova, I. V., & Wurtman, R. J. (1997). Efficacy of melatonin as a sleep-promoting agent. *Journal of Biological Rhythms, 12,* 644–650.

Zucconi, M., & Ferini-Strambi, L. (2004). Epidemiology and clinical findings of restless legs syndrome. *Sleep Medicine, 5,* 293–299.

Zucconi, M., Oldani, A., Castronovo, C., & Ferini-Strambi, L. (2003). Cabergoline is an effective single-drug treatment for restless legs syndrome: Clinical and actigraphic evaluation. *Sleep, 26,* 815–818.

23

Psychological Treatments
for Personality Disorders

Paul Crits-Christoph
Jacques P. Barber

A Type 2 randomized clinical trial (RCT) of psychosocial treatment for avoidant personality disorder compared three group-administered behavioral interventions (graded exposure, standard social skills training, intimacy-focused social skills training) with a wait-list control; although all three treatments were more efficacious than the control condition, no differences among the treatments were identified either after the 10-week treatment or at follow-up. For the treatment of borderline personality disorder, a Type 1 RCT randomized 101 women with recent suicidal and self-injurious behaviors and borderline personality disorder to either dialectical behavior therapy (DBT) or community-treatment-by-experts psychotherapists (CTBE). Over the 2-year treatment and follow-up period, DBT was superior to CTBE on rates of suicide attempt, hospitalization for suicide ideation, and overall medical risk (combining suicide attempts and self-injurious acts). Patients in the DBT group were also less likely to drop out of treatment and had fewer psychiatric emergency room visits and fewer psychiatric hospitalizations. There were no significant group differences on measures of depression, reasons for living, and suicide ideation, with patients in both treatment groups improving significantly on these measures. Four additional Type 2 and Type 3 studies support the efficacy of DBT as a treatment for borderline personality disorder with or without comorbid substance abuse or dependence. No RCTs of psychological treatment for other personality disorders have been reported. Several review articles have found a consistent adverse impact of personality disorders on outcomes of treatment for a wide range of Axis I disorders.

DEFINITION, EPIDEMIOLOGY, AND ETIOLOGY OF PERSONALITY DISORDERS

The fourth edition of the *Diagnostic and Statistic Manual of Mental Disorders* (American Psychiatric Association [APA], 1994) defines personality traits in terms of enduring patterns of thinking about, perceiving, and relating to the environment and oneself. A personality disorder (PD), or Axis II diagnosis, is present when such personality traits result in impair- ment in social or occupational functioning or distress to the person. The *DSM-IV* describes 10 specific Axis II diagnoses. These are grouped into three clusters: (a) the "odd" cluster (paranoid, schizoid, and schizotypal), (b) the dramatic cluster (histrionic, narcissistic, antisocial, and borderline), and (c) the anxious cluster (avoidant, dependent, obsessive-compulsive). The final PD, personality disorder not otherwise specified (NOS), is not in a cluster. This disorder is defined as either (a) the pattern meets general criteria for a PD and traits of several PDs are evident, but the criteria for any one specific disorder are not met, or (b) the pattern meets the general criteria for a PD, but the type of PD is not included in the classification. In terms of this latter criterion, two PDs, passive-aggressive and depressive, are listed in the appendix as potential diagnoses requiring further study but can be used to assign a PD NOS diagnosis

Although PDs are relatively common compared with many other psychiatric disorders, estimates of the prevalence of different PDs have been hampered by difficulty in reliably assessing these disorders. Strides have been made in the development of structured clinical interviews for assessing Axis II disorders, but to date these instruments have displayed modest and variable convergence (Clark, Livesley, & Morey, 1997, Perry, 1992; Widiger & Samuel, 2005) among themselves or with other measures. Poor convergent validity in assessing PDs suggest that one cannot necessarily treat similarly results from studies that use different instruments, thus limiting the validity of these measures (Perry, 1992). However, advances have been reported in the reliability of these measures. Maffei et al. (1997), for example, reported acceptable interrater reliability coefficients of .49 to .98 (kappas) for DSM-IV categorical diagnoses and excellent intraclass correlation coefficients from .90 to .98 for dimensional judgments. The Collaborative Longitudinal Personality Disorders Study (CLPS), which focused on schizotypal, borderline, avoidant, and obsessive-compulsive PD, also reported relatively good median interrater reliability kappa coefficients (.40 to .75) for all Axis II disorders diagnosed five times or more, and excellent reliability for the diagnosis of antisocial PD (kappa = 1.0; Zanarini et al., 2000). This study also found excellent inter-rater reliability (>.75) when dimensional scores were utilized.

Community-based epidemiological studies have put the overall prevalence of DSM-IV PDs at about 9% (Samuels et al., 2002). For individual PDs, Samuels et al. (2002) report the following prevalences: paranoid, 0.7%; schizoid, 0.9%; schizotypal, 0.6%; borderline, 0.5%; histrionic, 0.2%; narcissistic, 0.03%; antisocial, 4.1%; obsessive-compulsive, 0.9%; avoidant, 1.8%; dependent, 0.1%. Torgersen, Kringlen, and Cramer (2001) reported a similar prevalence rate of 13.4% in a representative sample of 2,053 adult Norwegians. However, there are reasons to believe that some PDs such as narcissistic PD are difficult to diagnose using current structured interviews, which basically require the patient to be aware of and

to be willing to report behaviors that are not always socially acceptable. Therefore, the prevalence rate for avoidant and obsessive-compulsive PDs is likely to be closer to reality than the prevalence rate for disorders such as narcissistic, paranoid, or histrionic.

The presence/absence of a PD has been found to be stable over 2 years among adolescents in a psychiatric setting (Chanen et al., 2004). However, a recent study examining stability of PDs in adults over a 4-year period found statistically significant variation in PD features over time, suggesting that such features are not always enduring (Lenzenweger, Johnson, & Willet, 2004). The impairment in functioning that is commonly seen in those individuals with PDs does appear to be a relatively enduring aspect of these disorders (Skodol et al., 2005).

There is also an extensive amount of comorbidity with PDs, that is, having one disorder tends to be associated with having one or more additional Axis II diagnoses. For example, Widiger and Rogers (1989) reported that the average number of multiple diagnoses was 85% in a group of 568 patients. In some disorders such as borderline PD, comorbidity rate ranges from 90 to 97% (Gunderson, Zanarini, & Kisiel, 1991). In the CLPS, patients in their four PD study groups ($N = 571$) received a mean of 1.4 additional PD diagnoses. The schizotypal group (mean = 2.4) had a higher rate of comorbid PD than the borderline personality disorder (BPD) group (mean = 1.9), which had more PD diagnoses than the avoidant personality disorder (AVPD; mean = 1.0) and obsessive-compulsive personality disorder (OCPD; mean = 0.9) groups. Whereas about half of the AVPD and OCPD patients had no other PD, the majority of schizotypal and BPD patients had at least two additional PD diagnoses (McGlashan et al., 2000).

Comorbidity of Axis II with Axis I disorders is especially important for treatment planning. In particular, individuals with a PD are highly likely to have a mood disorder as well, and those with a mood disorder often have a PD. In terms of the former, Skodol et al. (1999) and McGlashan et al. (2000) reported rates of co-occurrence of mood disorders and PDs in the multisite CLPS. Of the 571 patients with Axis II diagnoses (schizotypal, borderline, avoidant, and obsessive-compulsive), 61.3% had a current mood disorder based on the Structured Clinical Interview for DSM-IV-Axis I (SCID-I). More specifically, 39% had a current major depressive disorder (MDD), and

74% had a lifetime MDD. MDD most often co-occurred with avoidant (32%), borderline (31%), depressive (29%), and obsessive-compulsive (24%) PD. Regarding PDs among individuals with depressive disorders, a multinational community study in Europe found PDs to be present in 22% of individuals with depressive disorders (Casey et al., 2004). However, earlier figures suggested a comorbidity rate of about 50% for PD among depressed patients (Charney, Nelson, & Quinlan, 1981; Friedman, Aronoff, Clarkin, Corn, & Hurt, 1983).

Comorbidity of Axis II disorders with other Axis I disorders besides depression is also common. Of patients with bulimia, in two studies, 39% (Fahy, Eisler, & Russell, 1993) and 38% (Ames-Frankel et al., 1992) had PDs. Ruegg and Frances (1995) reported high percentages of patients with anxiety disorders (36 to 76%; six studies) also have a PD. Patients with obsessive-compulsive disorder were found to have high rates of compulsive PD and other PDs, particularly avoidant (Ruegg & Frances, 1995). Zimmerman and Mattia (1999) found that borderline PD patients were more likely to have multiple Axis I disorders than patients without borderline PD. In the CLPS study, McGlashan et al. (2000) reported high levels of anxiety comorbidities in their four groups of PD patients. For example, social phobia, which had an overall base rate of 23%, was diagnosed significantly more often in AVPD patients (38%) than in the borderline, schizotypal, and obsessive-compulsive (21%) groups. Posttraumatic stress disorder (PTSD) was also quite meaningful in this sample, with an overall base rate of 30%. PTSD, as expected, was more frequent among BPD (53%) than among the other three PD groups (25%). These differences were found across mood, anxiety, substance use, eating, and somatoform disorder categories.

Comorbidity of Axis II with substance use disorders has been studied extensively and has been found to be particularly high. Weiss, Mirin, Griffin, Gunderson, and Hufford (1993) found that 74% of hospitalized cocaine-dependent patients had at least one Axis II diagnosis. Similarly, Haller, Knisely, Dawson, and Schnoll (1993) found that 75% of perinatal substance abusers also received an Axis II diagnosis. In a sample of outpatient cocaine-dependent patients who participated in the pilot phase of a large multisite treatment study, Barber et al. (1996) found that 48% of the patients had at least one personality disorder and 18% had two or more. Looking at it the other way, incidence of drug use or drug dependence and alcohol use or alcohol dependence is relatively prevalent among PD patients. Overall, 37% of the PD patients included in the CLPS reported drug use disorder. Borderline personality disorder patients were more often (53%) diagnosed with drug use or dependence than were patients with other PDs (37%; McGlashan et al., 2000). Similar rates were found for alcohol/drug use and dependence (McGlashan et al., 2000, Haaga, Hall, & Haas, in press). Dinwiddle, Reich, and Cloninger (1992) found that injecting drugs increased the odds of a diagnosis of comorbid antisocial PD 21-fold, and that the diagnosis of antisocial PD increased the odds of injecting drugs by 27-fold.

Little is known about the etiology of PDs. A number of studies have documented high rates of physical and sexual abuse or other trauma during childhood in patients later diagnosed as having borderline PD (Herman, Perry, & van der Kolk, 1989; Ogata, Silk, Goodrich, Lohr, Westen, & Hill, 1990; Westen, Lundolph, Misle, Ruffins, & Block, 1990). Fossati, Madeddu, and Maffei (1999) conducted a meta-analysis of the relationship between childhood sexual abuse and borderline PD based on 21 studies. They found a moderate correlation of .28. Because the correlation was modest and because they found that larger effect sizes were related to smaller, less representative samples, the authors concluded that their results do not support the view that childhood sexual abuse is a major psychological risk factor or causal antecedent of borderline PD. Paris (2000) concluded that "none of the risk factors for borderline PD fully explain its development" (p. 86).

Other studies have found evidence for familial transmission of borderline PD (Baron, Gruen, Asnis, Asnis, & Lord, 1985; Loranger, Oldham, & Tullis, 1982) and schizotypal PD (Baron et al., 1985). Twin studies have supported a genetic component for schizotypal PD but not borderline PD (Torgersen, 1984). There is also a rich literature on the childhood precursor (most important, presence of conduct disorder in childhood and behavioral disinhibition) of antisocial PD (Paris, 2000).

HISTORICAL PERSPECTIVE

Early psychoanalytic writings devoted a considerable amount of attention to the treatment of "characterological" problems (Alexander, 1930; Fenichel, 1945). Although some of this literature informs modern approaches, particularly modern psychodynamic approaches, it is difficult to know of the relevance of these early writings to the current classification system for psychiatric disorders. For example, the distinction between obsessive-compulsive disorder and obsessive-compulsive PD was not made in early writings on "obsessive-compulsive" character, and this distinction is likely to be important for treatment selection.

Within the psychodynamic literature, there has been voluminous writing on the nature and treatment of narcissistic and borderline personality types in particular (Kernberg, 1984; Kohut, 1984; see review by Aronson, 1989). Even in these more recent writings, however, there has remained a lack of use of a consensual definition of the target patient population. As a consequence of the varying definitions of "characterological" conditions, the research literature on the treatment of PDs begins with the advent of the *DSM-III* and *DSM-III-R* classification system for Axis II disorders.

This is not to say that the *DSM* definition of personality pathology is not without problems. A number of authors have described various problems with the *DSM* classification, including lack of discrimination of many of the *DSM* criteria (Svrakic & Divac-Jovanovic, 1994), problems in distinguishing normal from deviant personality (Lively, Schroeder, Jackson, & Jang, 1994), and general lack of empirical support (Widiger, 1993). Alternatives to the *DSM* system have been reviewed by Dyce (1994). These alternatives include interpersonal circumplex models, neurobiological learning theory, biosocial learning theory, and the five-factor model of personality. Although these alternatives appear promising, they have not yet been developed to the extent that they have guided treatment research. It seems likely that *DSM* system will not be modified or replaced until adequate data justifying an alternative system exists.

REVIEW OF TREATMENT OUTCOME LITERATURE

Despite the relatively high prevalence of Axis II disorders, there have been very few outcome studies using patients with these disorders. Since the second edition of *Treatments That Work* (Nathan & Gor-

man, 2002), additional important research on the treatment of borderline PD has been published, but there continues to be little attention to other PDs.

The first meta-analysis on the effectiveness of psychotherapy for PDs was published by Perry, Banon, and Ianni (1999). These authors found 15 studies that attempted to systematically diagnose their patients and evaluate outcome. Since most of these studies were not randomized trials, Perry et al. calculated within-treatment change effect size, which ranged between 1.1 and 1.3 depending on the measure. In addition, they compared results from four studies that reported the percentage of patients who no longer met Axis II criteria at follow-up with studies that examined the natural history of recovery of borderline PD patients. They showed that, in comparison to the natural history of the latter, PD patients who received psychotherapy had a sevenfold faster rate of recovery. Unfortunately, only half of the patients in the four studies had a diagnosis of borderline PD, thus limiting the validity of the comparison.

Another more recent meta-analysis compared psychodynamic therapy ($n = 14$ studies) and cognitive-behavioral therapy ($n = 11$ studies) in the treatment of various PDs (Leichsenring & Leibing, 2004). Because many of the studies were uncontrolled, the authors relied on within-group effect sizes and concluded that there was evidence that both treatments are effective. However, many of the studies did not standardize treatment, and therefore it is difficult to know what interventions were actually provided. Because of this problem and the lack of controlled comparisons, these results cannot be used to provide empirical support for the use of specific treatment modalities with specific patient disorders or problems.

Below, we summarize the existing literature on the treatment of PDs, using the Type 1 to Type 6 classification of studies employed in this volume. Our emphasis in on Type 1 and Type 2 studies with patients who meet *DSM-III*, *DSM-III-R*, or *DSM-IV* criteria. Type 3 through Type 6 studies, including any study using pre-*DSM-III* criteria, are mentioned only when no Type 1 or 2 studies are available.

Avoidant PD

The only randomized controlled trial on *DSM-III* avoidant PD compared graded exposure, standard social skills training, intimacy-focused social skills training, and a wait-list control (Alden, 1989). The behavioral treatments were all administered in group format. All of the active treatments were better than the wait-list, but no differences among the behavioral treatments were found at the end of the 10-week treatment period or at follow-up. Examination of the clinical significance of the outcomes revealed that although positive changes had occurred in the active treatment conditions, patients were not functioning at the level of normative comparison samples. This study, however, had minimal statistical power for detecting differences among the treatments (fewer than 20 patients per group) and therefore is a Type 2 study.

One Type 3 study (not controlled) has been reported on *DSM-III-R* avoidant PD (Renneberg, Goldstein, Phillips, & Chambless, 1990). This study evaluated an intensive (4 full days) group behavioral treatment program with 17 patients. The treatment included group systematic desensitization, behavioral rehearsal, and self-image work. Outcome was evaluated at posttreatment and 1-year follow-up. The results evidenced positive changes, especially in terms of fear of negative evaluation. Gains were maintained over the follow-up period.

In a comparative study without a control group, Stravynski, Lesage, Marcouiller, and Elie (1989) compared social skills training with group discussion plus homework in a crossover design for patients with *DSM-III* avoidant PD. Although significant improvements on most measures were found in general, no differences between the treatment modalities were found, questioning the centrality of skills acquisition as the mechanism of action of social skills training. Treatment, however, may have been too brief (five sessions of each modality) to detect an effect. More recently, Stravynski, Belisle, Marcouiller, and Lavallee (1994) examined whether a combination of office-based and in vivo (real-life interactions with people in shopping malls, a cafeteria, etc.) enhanced the outcome of office-based social skills training for 28 patients with *DSM-III* avoidant PD. Outcomes were generally equal in the two conditions, although the in vivo condition had a greater attrition rate.

Because avoidant PD appeared to be equally responsive to different kinds of behavioral treatments, Alden and Capreol (1993) examined the hypothesis that different kinds of interpersonal problems would moderate treatment response to various therapies. To test this hypothesis, data from the Alden (1989) proj-

ect described above were used. Several findings emerged. Avoidant PD patients who had greater problems related to distrustful and angry behavior benefited more from structured exercises that required them to approach and talk to others (graded exposure). Patients with problems resisting others' demands benefited from both graded exposure and social skills training but were particularly responsive to intimacy-focused social skills training. The results suggest that a comprehensive assessment of interpersonal problems may be important in planning what type of treatment intervention is most likely to be beneficial to patients with avoidant PD.

In a quantitative case study, Coon (1994) has reported on the successful treatment of avoidant PD using a schema-focused cognitive therapy. Positive outcomes were evidenced not only at termination but also at 1-year follow-up.

In an uncontrolled pilot (Type 3) study of 52 weeks of supportive-expressive dynamic therapy (SE), Barber, Morse, Krakauer, Chittams, and Crits-Christoph (1997) showed that by the end of treatment (up to 52 sessions), 61% of carefully diagnosed avoidant PD patients had lost their avoidant PD diagnosis.

Obsessive-Compulsive PD

Barber et al. (1997) also conducted an open trial of SE for obsessive-compulsive PD (Type 3 study). Obsessive-compulsive PD patients lost their PD diagnoses significantly faster than did avoidant PD patients. By the end of treatment, 39% of avoidant PD patients retained their diagnosis, whereas only 15 percent of obsessive-compulsive PD patients (1 out of 13) did so. Most obsessive-compulsive PD patients lost their diagnoses, assessed via the Structured Clinical Interview for *DSM-IV*-Axis II (SCID-II), within the first 17 sessions of treatment. Both avoidant PD and obsessive-compulsive PD patients improved significantly across time on measures of PDs, depression, anxiety, general functioning, and interpersonal problems.

Borderline PD

The most widely investigated treatment for any PD has been dialectical behavior therapy (DBT) for borderline PD. Several randomized trials with DBT have been published. Linehan, Hubert, Suarez, Douglas, and Heard (1991) reported on 44 women with borderline PD and parasuicidal behavior who were randomized to either DBT or treatment as usual in the community. DBT is actually a complex treatment modality that is more accurately described as eclectic rather than a traditional behavior therapy per se. The treatment consists of weekly group and individual sessions for 1 year. The group component includes psychoeducational, teaching interpersonal skills, distress tolerance/reality acceptance, and emotion regulation skills. The individual therapy sessions involve directive, problem-solving techniques, as well as supportive techniques such as empathy and acceptance. Behavioral goals serve as the focus of the individual sessions and are addressed in a sequential order, but previous goals are readdressed if the problem returns. These goals include decreasing suicidal behaviors, decreasing therapy-interfering behaviors, decreasing behaviors that interfere with quality of life, increasing behavioral skills, decreasing behaviors related to posttraumatic stress, increasing respect for self, and achieving individual goals. More details about DBT can be found in the published treatment manual (Linehan, 1993).

The Linehan et al. (1991) study found that DBT resulted in relatively fewer and less severe episodes of parasuicidal behavior and fewer days of hospitalization compared with treatment as usual, but no differences in depression, hopelessness, or suicidal ideation were found. The attrition rate for DBT (16.7%) was much lower than that for treatment as usual (58.3%). Treatment gains were, for the most part, maintained relative to the control condition during the 1-year follow-up (Koerner & Linehan, 1999). Although this important study yielded very promising information on DBT as a treatment for parasuicidal patients with borderline PD, several aspects of the study lead to a Type 2 classification. These limitations include the fact that the therapists in the treatment-as-usual condition were not equated with the DBT therapists in terms of their experience in treating patients with borderline PD and the fact that 27% of the control patients never actually began therapy, although they were referred to a therapist.

These limitations were addressed in a recent Type 1 RCT (Linehan et al., 2006). A total of 101 women with recent suicidal and self-injurious behaviors meeting criteria for *DSM-IV* borderline personality disorder were randomized to 1 year of DBT or community treatment-by-experts psychotherapists (CTBE). The CTBE condition was designed to ad-

dress the limitations of the previous study by controlling for therapist availability, expertise, allegiance, gender, training and experience, consultation availability, and institutional prestige. The results of the study provided strong support for the efficacy of DBT: over the 2-year treatment and follow-up period, patients in the DBT group, compared with the CTBE group, were half as likely to make a suicide attempt, were significantly less likely to be hospitalized for suicide ideation, and had significantly lower medical risk (combining suicide attempts and self-injurious acts). Patients in the DBT group were also less likely to drop out of treatment, had fewer psychiatric emergency room visits, and had fewer psychiatric hospitalizations. There were no significant group differences on measures of depression, reasons for living, and suicide ideation, with patients in both treatment groups improving significantly on these measures.

Additional randomized clinical trials have also lent further empirical support to DBT as a treatment for borderline PD. Verheul et al. (2003) found DBT to be better than treatment as usual in terms of treatment retention and reductions of self-mutilating and self-damaging impulsive behaviors. Linehan et al. (1999) reported on a randomized clinical trial comparing DBT to treatment as usual for drug-dependent women with borderline PD. DBT patients had significantly greater reductions in drug abuse throughout the 1-year treatment and at follow-up than did treatment-as-usual patients. Another randomized trial, however, found that although 1 year of DBT was significantly better than treatment as usual in reducing symptoms of borderline PD, DBT had no effect on substance abuse problems at termination (van den Bosch, Verheul, Schippers, & van den Brink, 2002) or 18-month follow-up (van den Bosch et al., 2005).

Whether DBT is uniquely effective for borderline PD or for suicidal borderline PD has not been established. Using opiate-dependent patients with comorbid borderline PD who were being treated with concurrent opiate agonist therapy, Linehan et al. (2002) compared DBT to another psychotherapy treatment (comprehensive validation therapy with 12-step) that consisted of the nonspecific elements of DBT (therapeutic warmth, responsiveness, and empathy) in combination with participation in 12-step programs. On most outcomes, there were no significant differences between the treatment groups, although the sample size was limited (Type 2 study). In addition, preliminary results of a large randomized clinical trial indicate that, in the treatment of borderline PD, outcomes for DBT were no better than those for transference-focused psychotherapy or supportive psychotherapy (Levy, 2005).

Nonrandomized (Type 3) studies of DBT with special populations have also been reported. In an adaptation of DBT for suicidal adolescents with borderline personality features, DBT was found to yield better treatment retention and fewer hospitalizations than a nonrandomized treatment-as-usual control group (Rathus & Miller, 2002). In another nonrandomized comparison, Evershed et al. (2003) reported that DBT was superior to treatment as usual for male forensic patients with borderline PD in a high-security hospital, especially in reducing the seriousness of violence-related incidents and self-report of anger. Uncontrolled studies reporting favorable outcomes for DBT adapted for patients with eating disorders and borderline PD (Palmer et al., 2003) and post-traumatic stress disorder and borderline PD (Lanius & Tuhan, 2003) have also been published.

DBT has also been extended to the treatment of inpatients with a diagnosis of borderline PD. In one study, the implementation of DBT on an inpatient unit decreased the rates of incident reports of self-inflicted injuries and overdoses (Barley et al., 1993). No information on the assessment of patient diagnosis, however, was presented in that report. In a small ($N = 20$) pilot, randomized study, Koons et al. (2001) evaluated women veterans with borderline PD who were treated with DBT or treatment as usual for 6 months. The DBT group had significantly greater decreases in suicidal ideation, hopelessness, depression, and anger expression. Bohus et al. (2004) conducted a nonrandomized comparison of inpatient DBT to a wait-list control. The DBT group improved significantly more than the wait-list on most outcomes, including depression, anxiety, interpersonal functioning, social adjustment, global psychopathology, and self-mutilation.

An intensive (3-week) version of DBT has also been evaluated as crisis intervention for outpatients with borderline PD. The intensive program appeared to retain patients well and reduced symptoms of depression and hopelessness (McQuillan et al., 2005).

Psychodynamic therapy was evaluated as a treatment of borderline PD by Stevenson and Meares (1992; Type 3 study). The treatment was, broadly speaking, based on self-psychology. Therapy had a maturational goal accomplished through helping the patient discover and elaborate his or her inner life, with empathy and attention to disruptions in empathy central aspects of the process of therapy (Meares, 1987). Thirty patients with *DSM-III* borderline PD were treated with twice-per-week therapy for 1 year. Outcome was assessed 1 year after termination of treatment. Substantial reductions in violent behavior, drug use, medical visits, episodes of self-harm, time away from work, and symptoms were found. Thirty percent of patients no longer met criteria for borderline PD. Improvement was maintained at 1- and 5-year follow-ups, with substantial saving in health care costs (Stevenson & Meares, 1999; Stevenson, Meares, & D'Angelo, 2005).

Munroe-Blum and Marziali (1995) compared open-ended individual psychodynamic therapy with a manualized interpersonal group therapy for 110 patients with borderline PD (Type 1 study). The group treatment lasted 30 sessions. No differences at 1 year (termination) or 2 years were found, although patients in general benefited from both treatments. Bateman and Fonagy (1999) reported on the treatment of borderline PD patients randomized to either partial hospitalization ($n = 19$) or to standard care ($n = 19$; Type 2 study). The treatment included individual and group psychoanalytic psychotherapy (not standardized) for a maximum of 18 months. Results indicated that patients in the partial hospitalization group improved significantly more than controls in decreased number of suicidal attempts, acts of self-harm, psychiatric symptoms, inpatient days, and better social and interpersonal functioning at 6 months and 18 months (Bateman & Fonagy, 1999, 2001).

A recently manualized form of dynamic therapy, transference-focused therapy (Kernberg, Selzer, Koenigsberg, Carr, & Appelbaum, 1989), has also been investigated as a treatment for borderline PD. An uncontrolled study of 23 female patients with borderline PD treated with a year of transference-focused psychotherapy demonstrated improvements in the severity of self-injurious behavior, fewer hospitalizations, and fewer suicide attempts in the year following treatment compared with the year prior to therapy (Clarkin et al., 2001). In another uncontrolled study of 19 patients with borderline PD evaluated after 48 sessions of transference-focused psychotherapy, positive changes in impulsivity and affective instability were observed (Lopez, Cuevas, Gómez, &

Mendoza, 2004). As mentioned, preliminary results of a large, randomized (Type 1) clinical trial indicate that, in the treatment of borderline PD, transference-focused therapy yields outcomes equivalent to DBT and supportive psychotherapy (Levy, 2005; Clarkin, Lenzenweger, & Kernberg, 2004). Another randomized clinical trial comparing transference-focused therapy, DBT, and treatment as usual is ongoing at the Karolinska Institute in Stockholm, Sweden.

In a small (N = 5) uncontrolled study, brief cognitive analytic therapy (an integration of cognitive theory and some facets of psychodynamic therapy) was found to result in improvements in the severity of borderline PD (Wildgoose, Clarke, & Waller, 2001).

Cognitive therapy has also been adapted to the treatment of borderline PD (Layden, Newman, Freeman, & Byers Morse, 1993). Results from an open trial (single treatment group; Type 3 study) investigation of cognitive therapy for borderline PD were recently reported (Brown, Newman, Charlesworth, Crits-Christoph, & Beck, 2004). In this study of 32 borderline patients who reported suicidal ideation or engaged in self-injurious behavior, clinically important decreases in suicidal ideation, depressive symptoms, and number of borderline symptoms were evident at termination (1-year) and 18-month follow-up assessments. Young (1994) has developed a version of cognitive therapy ("schema therapy") that integrates a focus on maladaptive beliefs or schemas with experiential techniques. A case series of six patients showed that the approach has some promise in the treatment of borderline PD (Nordahl & Nysæter, 2005). In addition, an unpublished randomized study of patients with borderline PD found that schema therapy was superior to transference-focused psychotherapy on measures of quality of life and retention in treatment (Giesen-Bloo et al., 2006)

A cognitive-behavioral based treatment program (Systems Training for Emotional Predictability and Problem Solving [STEPPS]) that combines cognitive-behavioral techniques and skills training with a systems component has been described (Blum, Pfohl, St. John, Monahan, & Black, 2002). The systems component includes the involvement of other patients with borderline PD (in 20 weekly 2-hour group meetings), as well as other people in the patient's support system (e.g., family members, significant others, health care professionals). An uncontrolled study (Type 3) found that this treatment program was effective at reducing

negative behaviors and affect and borderline PD symptoms (Blum et al., 2002).

Other PDs

No controlled treatment outcome studies have yet been performed for histrionic, dependent, schizotypal, schizoid, narcissistic, passive-aggressive, antisocial, or paranoid PD. A case study with quantitative outcome data has been published showing positive effects of cognitive therapy for a paranoid PD patient (Williams, 1988). Another quantitative case study reported that functional analytic therapy produced positive outcomes in a patient with histrionic and narcissistic PD diagnoses (Callaghan, Summers, & Weidman, 2003).

Mixed Axis II Samples

There have been several controlled studies using a sample of mixed PDs. Winston et al. (1991, 1994) randomized 81 patients with PDs to two forms of brief dynamic therapy, one more cognitively oriented (brief adaptive therapy) and one more oriented toward confronting defenses and eliciting affect (modeled after Davanloo, 1980), and to a wait-list control condition. The sample consisted mostly of Cluster B and C PD types, as well as patients diagnosed as PD not otherwise specified (mostly with Cluster C features). However, paranoid, schizoid, schizotypal, narcissistic, and borderline PDs were excluded. Treatment lasted on average 40 weeks, although the wait-list was on average only 15 weeks. Because of this confound of treatment condition with time, this study is classified as a Type 2 study. The results showed that both forms of brief dynamic therapy produced substantial improvements across multiple outcome measures, including general psychiatric symptoms, social adjustment, and target complaints. At follow-up assessments, obtained at 1.5 years on average after the end of therapy, the gains in improvement were maintained on target complaints (the only outcome measured).

In another study by the same group, Hellerstein et al. (1998) described the results of a study involving mixed PD patients who received 40 sessions of supportive therapy (n = 24) or short-term dynamic psychotherapy (n = 25). Thirty-five percent of the patients dropped out from treatment. There were no differences between the treatment modalities at mid-phase (week 20), termination, or 6-month follow-up. However, within-group effect sizes (intake to termination) were large on all outcome measures.

A recent randomized clinical trial (Type 1) compared the efficacy of 40 sessions of supportive-expressive psychoanalytic psychotherapy (*n* = 80) with that of community-delivered psychodynamic therapy (*n* = 76) for patients diagnosed with any *DSM-IV* PD (Vinnars et al., 2005). In both treatment conditions, the global level of functioning improved, and there were decreases in the prevalence of patients fulfilling criteria for a PD diagnosis, PD severity, and psychiatric symptoms. There were no outcome differences between the two treatments. During the 1-year follow-up, patients who received supportive-expressive psychotherapy made significantly fewer visits to the community mental health centers than the patients who received community-delivered psychodynamic therapy.

Hardy et al. (1995) reported on the 27 Cluster C PD patients out of the 114 depressed patients included in the Sheffield 2 study (Shapiro et al., 1994). Cluster A and B were not assessed in that study. In this Type 2 study, white-collar, employed patients received either 8 or 16 sessions of either cognitive or psychodynamic psychotherapy. At the end of treatment, Cluster C PD patients continued to display significantly more severe symptoms than non–Cluster C PD patients if they received dynamic therapy, but not if they received cognitive therapy. Karterud et al. (1992) present the results of the effectiveness of day hospital community treatment for decompensated PD patients. In this Type 3 study, 97 patients were prospectively followed, 74 had a PD diagnosis (34 were borderline PD, 13 were schizotypal PD, and 27 with other PD, two thirds of which were cluster C PD patients). All but the schizotypal PD patients improved significantly on the SCL 90 and Health Sickness Rating Scale at discharge (mean stay was 171 days with a standard deviation of 109).

Monsen, Odland, Faugli, Daae, and Eilertsen (1995) reported on the results of treating 25 patients (23 of whom had a diagnosis of a PD) with psychodynamic therapy based on object relations theory and self-psychology. Treatment lasted on average a little bit more than 2 years. Patients were assessed at termination and again 5 years after termination. At the end of treatment, substantial change was found on measures of symptoms, affect consciousness, and defenses. In addition, 75% of the patients who had an Axis I disorder at intake no longer qualified for an Axis I disorder at termination. Seventy-two percent of the patients with Axis II disorders no longer qualified for the disorder at termination. The gains were maintained at the 5-year follow-up.

Høglend (1993) compared 15 patients with PDs in comparison to 30 patients without Axis II disorders (Type 2 study). The treatment was psychodynamic therapy of brief to moderate length (9 to 53 sessions) that was based on the approaches of Sifneos (1979) and Malan (1976). At termination, the Axis II patients evidenced less change than the patients without Axis II diagnoses, but at 4-year follow-up there was no difference. For the Axis II patients, the number of treatment sessions was significantly related to the acquisition of insight and dynamic change at follow-up. Thus, length of treatment appeared to be a crucial factor in producing positive outcomes for the Axis II patients (but not the patients without PDs).

In a nonrandomized (Type 2) comparison using a mixed PD sample, Chiesa and Fonagy (2000) compared the effectiveness of a residential treatment based on a combination of a sociotherapeutic intervention (daily unit meetings, community meetings, structured activities, coresponsibility planning of the running of the therapeutic community, dance therapy, etc.) and formal psychoanalytical psychotherapy (individual and in small groups) to a step-down program that consisted of a short-term residential stay followed by outpatient group psychoanalytic psychotherapy. At 1 year, and continuing through a 3-year follow-up, the stepped-care model was significantly more effective than the pure inpatient model (Chiesa & Fonagy, 2000). In another nonrandomized (Type 2) study of mixed PDs, the step-down program was compared again with a long-term residential program and with general community psychiatric care (medications, supportive outpatient therapy, hospitalization as needed; Chiesa, Fonagy, Holmes, & Drahorad, 2004). The results again favored the stepped-down approach. Similarly, a program model of outpatient group psychodynamic therapy following a brief period of more intensive treatment (day treatment) was also supported by an uncontrolled (Type 3) study in Norway (Wilberg et al., 2003). The treatment program in these studies, however, was not standardized, so the exact nature of the programs is unclear.

Axis II as Moderator of Treatment of Axis I Disorders

Reich (2003), Reich and Vasile (1993), and Reich and Green (1991) have reviewed studies of the relation of personality traits and Axis II PDs to the outcome of treatments (both psychosocial and psychopharmacological) for Axis I conditions. Examination of the studies in these reviews, plus some more recent studies that investigate specific PDs and specific psychosocial treatments, reveals the following findings: (a) Antisocial PD (without a co-occurring diagnosis of depression) predicted poor outcome from cognitive therapy and psychodynamic therapy for opiate addiction (Woody, McLellan, Luborsky, & O'Brien, 1985); (b) avoidant PD was associated with relatively poorer outcome for agoraphobia from exposure therapy (Chambless, Renneberg, Goldstein, & Gracely, 1992) or from exposure therapy and additional anxiety management and group and individual therapy (Chambless, Renneberg, Gracely, Goldstein, & Fydich, 2000); (c) schizotypal PD was associated with poor outcome of behavior therapy for obsessive-compulsive disorder (Minichiello, Baer, & Jenike, 1987); (d) presence of a PD predicted poor outcome of cognitive-behavioral group therapy for social anxiety (Turner, 1987) and panic disorders (Mennin & Heimberg, 2000); (e) patients with PDs show slower response to imipramine plus interpersonal psychotherapy for recurrent unipolar depression (Frank, Kupfer, Jacob, & Jarrett, 1987); (f) patients with a diagnosis in the anxious cluster of PDs evidenced much poorer outcome with imipramine plus interpersonal therapy for recurrent unipolar depression (Pilkonis & Frank, 1988); (g) a comorbid PD was associated with higher rates of recurrence of depressive episodes and shorter time to recurrence over 2 years of maintenance interpersonal psychotherapy for patients with a recurrent depression who were initially treated to remission (Cyranowski et al., 2004); (h) patients with a borderline PD have relatively poorer outcomes, and incur higher treatment costs, following brief cognitive therapy for recurrent self-harm, than those without this diagnosis (Tyrer et al., 2004); (i) combined medication plus psychotherapy (brief psychodynamic therapy) is more effective than medication alone for depressed patients with comorbid PDs, but not more effective for those without PDs (Kool, Dekker, Duijsens, de Jonghe, & Puite,

2003); and (j) number of PDs rather than presence or absence of any PD was predictive of the outcomes of brief interpretive and brief supportive psychotherapies (Ogrodniczuk et al., 2001).

In group therapy, the presence of a patient with borderline PD may be detrimental to treatment outcome for other patients. Cloitre and Koenen (2001) found that, in interpersonally oriented group therapy for women with PTSD, groups that had at least one member with borderline PD showed less change than did groups that did not have any members with borderline PD.

Presence of a PD, however, does not always lead to poor outcomes. Presence of a PD did not predict outcome of behavioral treatment of panic disorder in one study (Ramnero & Ost, 2004), but it did predict relapse following behavioral treatment in another (Fava et al., 2001). Presence of a PD also did not impact outcome (prevalence of posttraumatic stress disorder) among women with chronic posttraumatic stress disorder who received prolonged exposure therapy (Hembree, Cahill, & Foa, 2004). In long-term group psychoanalytic therapy, presence of a PD was not related to outcome (Lorentzen & Høglend, 2004). Kuyken, Kurzer, DeRubeis, Beck, and Brown (2001) reported that it was not PD status per se but rather the presence of maladaptive and paranoid beliefs that predicted the outcome of cognitive therapy for depression.

In some studies, patients with selected PDs fared better in certain types of treatments. For example, Longabaugh et al. (1994) recently investigated the extent to which antisocial PD moderated the treatment of alcohol abuse. Thirty-one patients with antisocial PD were compared with 118 non-antisocial PD alcohol abusers randomly assigned either to a group extended cognitive-behavioral treatment (which included stimulus control, rearranging consequences, restructuring cognitions, assertion training, problem solving for alternatives to drinking, and dealing with slips/relapses) or to relationship-enhanced cognitive-behavioral treatment (involving functional analysis, enhancing reinforcements in relationships with partners, using partners' relationship to reinforce abstinence, and educational/didactic sessions for partners). A significant interaction was found for antisocial PD by treatment modality for the average number of drinks consumed on a drinking day, with patients with antisocial PD in the extended cognitive-behavioral treatment having the fewest drinks (about two on a drinking day) and patients with anti-social PD in the relationship enhancement condition having the most (about eight). Non-antisocial PD patients had an intermediate level of drinking on a drinking day in both treatment conditions. This interaction, however, was not found for percent of days abstinent. At 13- to 18-month follow-up, a main effect for antisocial PD emerged, with antisocial PD patients showing more days abstinent than non-antisocial PD patients.

Rosenblum et al. (2005) also found an interaction of antisocial PD and treatment type. In this study, substance-abusing patients with antisocial PD had relatively better outcomes in group cognitive-behavioral therapy than in group motivational therapy. Similarly, Messina, Farabee, and Rawson (2003) found that cocaine-dependent patients with antisocial PD were more likely to be abstinent following treatment, particularly contingency management, than those without antisocial PD.

Barber and Muenz (1996) reported that features of two PDs, avoidant and obsessive-compulsive, interact with type of psychotherapy in the treatment of depression. Using data from the Treatment of Depression Collaborative Study (Elkin et al., 1989), Barber and Muenz (1996) found that interpersonal psychotherapy produced better outcomes for depressed patients with features of obsessive-compulsive PD, but cognitive therapy produced better outcomes for depressed patients with features of avoidant PD (Type 2 study).

In the treatment of public speaking anxiety among patients with social phobia, the presence of avoidant PD did not predict outcome (i.e., treatment was equally successful in those with and without avoidant PD) in one study (Hofmann, Newman, Becker, Taylor, & Roth, 1995).

There may be ways in which standard treatment can be enhanced or improved to more effectively treat Axis I patients who have a comorbid Axis II condition. For example, a case study by Walker, Freeman, and Christensen (1994) used restricted environmental stimulation to successfully enhance the exposure treatment of obsessive-compulsive disorder in a patient with schizotypal PD. Although this treatment focused on the obsessive-compulsive disorder and not the schizotypal PD per se, restricted environmental stimulation therapy was incorporated because

of the attentional problems found with patients with schizotypal personality. Thus, this treatment may have other applications for schizotypal PD as a means of increasing attentional focus.

SUMMARY OF RECOMMENDATIONS BASED ON TREATMENT OUTCOME LITERATURE

It is obvious that the systematic study of treatment efficacy with PDs remains in its infancy. With few Type 1 studies published yet, it is difficult to make recommendations with a high degree of confidence. Linehan's dialectical behavior therapy is the most well-established treatment, with several randomized clinical trials documenting its efficacy. However, recent studies appear to question whether DBT is uniquely efficacious, in that other credible psychotherapies have yielded similar results. Recent results from the United Kingdom also seem to indicate that psychodynamically oriented treatment is also effective for borderline PD. Other promising treatments for borderline PD include adaptations of cognitive therapy and schema-focused therapy. Behavior therapy is promising in the treatment of avoidant PD, but the specific form of behavior therapy may need to be tailored to patients' types of interpersonal problems, with graded exposure better when distrust is an issue and intimacy-focused social skills training preferable when resisting others' demands is the major interpersonal problem in patients with avoidant PD. A structured cognitive-behavioral treatment appears to be best for patients with antisocial PD. Psychodynamic therapy, particularly longer term and involving stepped-down care beginning with residential care and then moving to outpatient treatment, appears useful for the treatment of mixed PDs. One clear recommendation can be made based on a consistent finding across many studies: Standard brief treatments for Axis I conditions often fail when Axis II pathology is also present, and therefore the clinician should be alert to the presence of a comorbid Axis II disorder and reevaluate the selection of treatment modality if progress is not made within the period of brief therapy. Consistent with this recommendation are the results of Kopta, Howard, Lowry, and Beutler (1994), who found that characterological symptoms that are typical of PDs improve slowly, with only 59% of outpatients achieving clinically significantly change on such symptoms after 52 treatment sessions.

FUTURE DIRECTIONS IN THE TREATMENT OF PDS

The studies reviewed above begin to point to some promising likely developments in the treatment of PDs. First, we can predict that there will likely need to be modification of the existing Axis I treatments to take into account the Axis II pathology. These modifications should include the lengthening of brief treatments and greater attention to the long-standing rigid belief systems and maladaptive interpersonal patterns of Axis II patients, rather than a focus only on symptoms or recent triggers. A second major direction will be the matching of patients to treatment modalities. This matching may occur at the level of the PD syndrome in view of Barber and Muenz's (1996) finding that depressed patients with features of avoidant PD do better in cognitive therapy, but depressed patients with features of obsessive-compulsive PDs fare better in interpersonal therapy. These authors have shown that using these two diagnostic categories (either dimensionally or categorically) could be helpful in matching patients to either cognitive or interpersonal psychotherapy. Alternatively, matching patients to treatment according to patient attributes that either underlie the distinctions between PDs or are other salient patient variables not captured in the current system may also take place. For example, Beutler, Mohr, Grawe, and Engle (1991) suggest that impulsivity/external coping style and resistance/reactance are two important dimensions for which there is preliminary evidence for the matching of patients to treatments. Thus, rather than use the diagnosis of antisocial PD as a basis for recommending a more structured treatment modality, the underlying dimensions of impulsivity and low socialization that characterize but do not uniquely define antisocial PD might be more salient for treatment selection. Whether these patient dimensions are examined in addition to the *DSM* categories or eventually replace them in some form remains to be seen.

Another direction for the future is the movement toward psychotherapy integration. In fact, Linehan's dialectical behavior therapy already integrates techniques from a wide variety of approaches. With PDs, such integration might be especially necessary because of the diverse set of problems that characterize these patients. Thus, a successful treatment might need elements of exposure therapy, understanding and modification of long-standing cognitive/interpersonal patterns, practice in new behaviors, and attention to disruptions in the therapeutic relationship (transference). Psychosocial and psychopharmacological interventions will also be examined in combination for PDs as a way of managing the symptoms while also treating the underlying psychological processes. Significant advances in the treatment of PDs can be expected to have important public health impacts, given the prevalence of these disorders and the impairment in social and occupational functioning associated with them.

ACKNOWLEDGMENT

The preparation of this manuscript was funded in part by National Institute of Mental Health Grants P30-MH-45178 and R01-MH61410. Address reprint request to Paul Crits-Christoph, Ph.D., Room 650, 3535 Market St., Philadelphia, PA 19104.

REFERENCES

Alden, L. E. (1989). Short-term structured treatment for avoidant personality disorder. *Journal of Consulting and Clinical Psychology, 57,* 756–764.

Alden, L. E., & Capreol, M. J. (1993). Avoidant personality disorder: Interpersonal problems as predictors of treatment response. *Behavior Therapy, 24,* 357–376.

Alexander, F. (1930). The neurotic character. *International Journal of Psychoanalysis, 11,* 292–311.

American Psychiatric Association. (1994). *Diagnostic and statistical manual of mental disorders* (4th ed.). Washington, DC: Author.

Ames-Frankel, J., Devlin, M. J., Walsh, B. T., Strasser, T. J., Sadik, C., Oldham, J. M., et al. (1992). Personality disorder diagnoses in patients with bulimia nervosa: Clinical correlates and changes with treatment. *Journal of Clinical Psychiatry, 53,* 90–96.

Aronson, T. A. (1989). A critical review of psychotherapeutic treatments of the borderline personality: Historical trends and future directions. *Journal of Nervous and Mental Disease, 177,* 511–527.

Barber, J. P., Frank, A., Weiss, R. D., Blaine, J., Siqueland, L., Moras, K., et al. (1996). Prevalence of personality disorder diagnoses among cocaine/crack dependents in the NIDA study. *Journal of Personality Disorders, 10,* 297–311.

Barber, J. P., Morse, J. Q., Krakauer, I., Chittams, J., & Crits-Christoph, K. (1997). Change in obsessive-compulsive and avoidant personality disorders following time-limited supportive-expressive therapy. *Psychotherapy, 34,* 133–143.

Barber, J. P., & Muenz, L. R. (1996). The role of avoidance and obsessiveness in matching patients to cognitive and interpersonal psychotherapy: Empirical findings from the Treatment for Depression Collaborative Research Program. *Journal of Consulting and Clinical Psychology, 64,* 951–958.

Barley, W. D., Buie, S. E., Peterson, E. W., Hollingsworth, A. S., Griva, M., Hickerson, S. C., et al. (1993). Development of an inpatient cognitive-behavioral treatment program for borderline personality disorder. *Journal of Personality Disorders, 7,* 232–240.

Baron, J., Gruen, R., Asnis, L., & Lord, S. (1985). Familial transmission of schizotypal and borderline personality disorders. *American Journal of Psychiatry, 142,* 927–934.

Bateman, A., & Fonagy, P. (1999). Effectiveness of partial hospitalization in the treatment of borderline personality disorder: A randomized controlled trial. *American Journal of Psychiatry, 156,* 1563–1569.

Bateman, A., & Fonagy, P. (2001). Treatment of borderline personality disorder with psychoanalytically oriented partial hospitalization: An 18-month follow-up. *American Journal of Psychiatry, 158,* 36–42.

Beutler, L. E., Mohr, D. C., Grawe, K., & Engle, D. (1991). Looking for differential treatment effects: Cross-cultural predictors of differential psychotherapy efficacy. *Journal of Psychotherapy Integration, 1,* 121–141.

Blum, N., Pfohl, B., St. John, D., Monahan, P., & Black, D. W. (2002). STEPPS: A cognitive-behavioral systems-based group treatment for outpatients with borderline personality disorder: A preliminary report. *Comprehensive Psychiatry, 43,* 301–310.

Bohus, M., Haaf, B., Simms, T., Limberger, M. F., Schmahl, C., Unckel, C., et al. (2004). Effectiveness of inpatient dialectical behavioral therapy for borderline personality disorder: A controlled trial. *Behaviour Research and Therapy, 42,* 487–499.

Brown, G. K., Newman, C. F., Charlesworth, S. E., Crits-Christoph, P., & Beck, A. T. (2004). An open trial of cognitive therapy for borderline personality disorder. *Journal of Personality Disorders, 18,* 257–271.

Callaghan, G. M., Summers, C. J., & Weidman, M. (2003). The treatment of histrionic and narcissistic personality disorder behaviors: A single-subject demonstration of clinical improvement using functional analytic psychotherapy. *Journal of Contemporary Psychotherapy, 33,* 321–339.

Casey, P., Birbeck, G., McDonagh, C., Horgan, A., Dowrick, C., Dalgard, O., et al. (2004). Personality disorder, depression, and functioning: Results from the ODI study. *Journal of Affective Disorders, 82,* 277–283.

Chambless, D. L., Renneberg, B., Goldstein, A., & Gracely, E. J. (1992). MCMI-diagnosed personality disorders among agoraphobic outpatients: Prevalence and relationship to severity and treatment outcome. *Journal of Anxiety Disorders, 6,* 193–211.

Chambless, D. L., Renneberg, B., Gracely, E. J., Goldstein, A., & Fydich, T. (2000). Axis I and II comorbidity in agoraphobia: Prediction of psychotherapy outcome in a clinical setting. *Psychotherapy Research, 10,* 279–295.

Chanen, A. M., Jackson, H. J., McGorry, P. D., Allot, K. A., Clarkson, V., & Yuen, H. P. (2004). Two-year stability of personality disorder in older adolescent outpatients. *Journal of Personality Disorders, 18,* 526–541.

Charney, D., Nelson, J. C., & Quinlan, D. M. (1981). Personality traits and disorder in depression. *American Journal of Psychiatry, 138,* 1601–1604.

Chiesa, M. & Fonagy, P. (2000). Cassel Personality Disorder Study: Methodology and treatment effects. *British Journal of Psychiatry, 176,* 485–491.

Chiesa, M., Fonagy, P., Holmes, J., & Drahorad, D. (2004). Residential versus community treatment of personality disorders: A comparative study of three treatment programs. *American Journal of Psychiatry, 161,* 1463–1470.

Clark, L. E., Livesley, J., & Morey, L. (1997). Special feature: Personality disorder assessment: The challenge of construct validity. *Journal of Personality Disorders, 11,* 205–231.

Clarkin, J. F., Foelsch, P. A., Levy, K. N., Hull, J. W., Delaney, J. C., & Kernberg, O. F. (2001). The development of a psychodynamic treatment for patients with borderline personality disorder: A preliminary study of behavioral change. *Journal of Personality Disorders, 15,* 487–495.

Clarkin, J., Levy, K. N., Lenzenweger, M. F., & Kernberg, O. F. (2004). The Personality Disorders Institute/Borderline Personality Disorder Research Foundation randomized controlled trial for borderline personality disorder: Rationale, methods, and patient characteristics. *Journal of Personality Disorders, 18,* 52–72.

Cloitre, M., & Koenen, K. C. (2001). The impact of borderline personality disorder on process group outcome among women with posttraumatic stress disorder related to childhood abuse. *International Journal of Group Psychotherapy*, 51, 379–398.

Coon, D. W. (1994). Cognitive-behavioral interventions with avoidant personality: A single case study. *Journal of Cognitive Psychotherapy: An International Quarterly*, 8, 243–253.

Cyranowski, J. M., Frank, E., Winter, E., Rucci, P., Novick, D., Pilkonis, P., et al. (2004). Personality pathology and outcome in recurrently depressed women over 2 years of maintenance interpersonal psychotherapy. *Psychological Medicine*, 34, 659–669.

Davanloo, H. (1980). *Short-term dynamic psychotherapy*. New York: Jason Aronson.

Dinwiddle, S. H., Reich, T., & Cloninger, C. R. (1992). Psychiatric comorbidity and suicidality among intravenous drug users. *Journal of Clinical Psychiatry*, 53, 364–369.

Dyce, J. A. (1994). Personality disorders: Alternatives to the official diagnostic system. *Journal of Personality Disorders*, 8, 77–88.

Elkin, I., Shea, T., Watkins, J. T., Imber, S. D., Sotsky, S. M., Collins, J. F., et al. (1989). NIMH Treatment of Depression Collaborative Research Program: General effectiveness of treatments. *Archives of General Psychiatry*, 46, 971–982.

Evershed, S., Tennant, A., Boomer, D., Rees, A., Barkham, M., & Watsons, A. (2003). Practice-based outcomes of dialectical behaviour therapy (DBT) targeting anger and violence, with male forensic patients: A pragmatic and non-contemporaneous comparison. *Criminal Behaviour and Mental Health*, 13, 198–213.

Fahy, T. A., Eisler, I., & Russell, G. F. (1993). Personality disorder and treatment response in bulimia nervosa. *British Journal of Psychiatry*, 162, 765–770.

Fava, G. A., Rafanelli, C., Grandi, S., Conti, S., Ruini, C., Mangelli, L., et al. (2001). Long-term outcome of panic disorder with agoraphobia treated by exposure. *Psychological Medicine*, 31, 891–898.

Fenichel, O. (1945). *The psychoanalytic theory of neurosis*. New York: Norton.

Fossati, A., Madeddu, F., & Maffei C. 1999). Borderline personality disorder and childhood sexual abuse: A meta-analytic study. *Journal of Personality Disorders*, 13, 268–280.

Frank, E., Kupfer, D. J., Jacob, M., & Jarrett, D. (1987). Personality features and response to acute treatment in recurrent depression. *Journal of Personality Disorders*, 1, 14–26.

Friedman, R. C., Aronoff, M. S., Clarkin, J. F., Corn, R., & Hurt, S. W. (1983). History of suicidal behavior in depressed borderline inpatients. *American Journal of Psychiatry*, 140, 1023–1026.

Giesen-Bloo, J., van Dijck, R., Spinhoven, P., & van Tilburg, W., Dirksen, C., van Asselt, T., et al. (2006). Outpatient psychotherapy for borderline personality disorder: Randomized trial of schema-focused therapy vs transference-focused psychotherapy. *Archives of General Psychiatry*, 63, 649–658.

Gunderson, J. G., Zanarini, M. C., & Kisiel, C. L. (1991). Borderline personality disorder: A review of data on DSM-III-R descriptions. *Journal of Personality Disorders*, 5, 340–352.

Haaga, D. A. F., Hall, S. M., & Haas, A. (2006). Participant factors in treating substance use disorders. In L. G. Castonguay & L. E. Beutler & (Eds.), *Principles of therapeutic change that work* (pp.275–292). New York: Oxford University Press.

Haller, D. L., Knisely, J. S., Dawson, K. S., & Schnoll, S. H. (1993). Perinatal substance abusers: Psychological and social characteristics. *Journal of Nervous and Mental Disease*, 181, 509–513.

Hardy, G. E., Barkham, M., Shapiro, D. A., Stiles, W. B., Rees, A., & Reynolds, S. (1995). Impact of Cluster C personality disorders on outcomes of contrasting brief psychotherapies for depression. *Journal of Consulting and Clinical Psychology*, 63, 997–1004.

Hellerstein, D. J., Rosenthal, R. N., Pinsker H., Samstag L. W., Muran, J. C., & Winston, A. (1998). A randomized prospective study comparing supportive and dynamic therapies. *Journal of Psychotherapy Practice and Research*, 7, 261–271.

Hembree, E. A., Cahill, S. P., & Foa, E. B. (2004). Impact of personality disorders on treatment outcome for female assault survivors with chronic posttraumatic stress disorder. *Journal of Personality Disorders*, 18, 117–127.

Herman, J. L., Perry, J. C., & van der Kolk, B. A. (1989). Childhood trauma in borderline personality disorder. *American Journal of Psychiatry*, 146, 490–495.

Hofmann, S. G., Newman, M. G., Becker, E., Taylor, C. B., & Roth, W. T. (1995). Social phobia with and without avoidant personality disorder: Preliminary behavior therapy outcome findings. *Journal of Anxiety Disorders*, 9, 427–438.

Høglend, P. (1993). Personality disorders and long-term outcome after brief dynamic psychotherapy. *Journal of Personality Disorders*, 7, 168–181.

Hwu, H. G., Yeh, E. K., & Chang, L. Y. (1989). Prevalence of psychiatric disorders in Taiwan defined by the Chinese Diagnostic Interview Schedule. *Acta Psychiatrica Scandinavica, 79*, 136–147.

Karterud, S., Vaglum, S., Friis, S., Irion, T., Johns, S., & Vaglum, P. (1992). Day hospital therapeutic community treatment for patients with personality disorders. An empirical evaluation of the containment function. *Journal of Nervous and Mental Disease, 180*, 238–243.

Kernberg, O. (1984). *Severe personality disorders: Psychotherapeutic strategies.* New Haven, CT: Yale University Press.

Kernberg, O., Selzer, M. A., Koenigsberg, H. W., Carr, A. C., & Appelbaum, A. H. (1989). *Psychodynamic psychotherapy of borderline patients.* New York: Basic Books.

Koerner, K., & Linehan, M. M. (1999) Research on dialectical behavior therapy for patients with borderline personality disorder. *Psychiatric Clinics of North America, 23*, 151–167.

Kohut, H. (1984). *How does analysis cure?* Chicago: University of Chicago Press.

Kool, S., Dekker, J., Duijsens, I. J., de Jonghe, F., & Puite, B. (2003). Efficacy of combined therapy and pharmacotherapy for depressed patients with or without personality disorders. *Harvard Review of Psychiatry, 11*, 133–141.

Koons, C. R., Robins, C. J., Tweed, J. L., Lynch, T. R., Gonzalez, A. M., Morse, J. Q., et al. (2001). Efficacy of dialectical behavior therapy in women veterans with borderline personality disorder. *Behavior Therapy, 32*, 371–390.

Kopta, S. M., Howard, K. I., Lowry, J. L., & Beutler, L. E. (1994). Patterns of symptomatic recovery in psychotherapy. *Journal of Consulting and Clinical Psychology, 62*, 1009–1016.

Kuyken, W., Kurzer, N., DeRubeis, R. J., Beck, A. T., & Brown, G. K. (2001). Response to cognitive therapy in depression: The role of maladaptive beliefs and personality disorders. *Journal of Consulting and Clinical Psychology, 69*, 560–566.

Lanius, R. A., & Tuhan, I. (2003). Letters to the editor: Stage oriented trauma treatment using dialectical behaviour therapy. *Canadian Journal of Psychiatry, 48*, 126–127.

Layden, M. A., Newman, C. F., Freeman, A., & Byers Morse, S. (1993). *Cognitive therapy of borderline personality disorders.* Boston: Allyn and Bacon.

Leichsenring, F., & Leibing, E. (2004). The effectiveness of psychodynamic therapy and cognitive behavior therapy in the treatment of personality disorders: A meta-analysis. *American Journal of Psychiatry, 160*, 1223–1232.

Lenzenweger, M. F., Johnson, M. D., & Willet, J. B. (2004). Individual growth curve analysis illuminates stability and change in personality disorder features: The longitudinal study of personality disorders. *Archives of General Psychiatry, 61*, 1015–1024.

Levy, K. (2005, June). *Clinical outcome and mechanism of change.* Part of panel presentation on A *Modified Dynamic Treatment for Borderline Personality Disorder: Treatment Model, Outcome Data, and Case Illustration.* Paper presented at the annual meeting of the Society for Psychotherapy Research, Montreal, Canada.

Linehan, M. M. (1993). *Cognitive-behavioral treatment of borderline personality disorder.* New York: Guilford Press.

Linehan, M. M., Comtois, K. A., Murray, A. M., Brown, M. Z., Gallop, R. J., Heard, H. L., et al. (2006). Two-year randomized trial and follow-up of dialectical behavior therapy vs. therapy by experts for suicidal behaviors and borderline personality disorder. *Archives of General Psychiatry, 63*, 757–766.

Linehan, M. M., Dime., L. A., Reynolds, S. K., Comtois, K. A., Welch, S. S., Heagerty, P., et al. (2002). Dialectical behavior therapy versus comprehensive validation therapy plus12-step for the treatment of opioid dependent women meeting criteria for borderline personality disorder. *Drug and Alcohol Dependence, 67*, 13–26.

Linehan, M. M., Hubert, A. E., Suarez, A., Douglas, A., & Heard, H. L. (1991). Cognitive-behavioral treatment of chronically parasuicidal borderline patients. *Archives of General Psychiatry, 48*, 1060–1064.

Linehan, M. M., Schmidt, H., Dimeff, L. A., Craft, J. C., Kanter, J., & Comtois, K. A. (1999). Dialectical behavior therapy for patients with borderline personality disorder and drug-dependence. *American Journal on Addictions, 8*, 279–292.

Lively, W. J., Schroeder, M. L., Jackson, D. N., & Jang, K. L. (1994). Categorical distinctions in the study of personality disorder: Implications for classification. *Journal of Abnormal Psychology, 103*, 6–17.

Longabaugh, R., Rubin, A., Malloy, P., Beattie, M., Clifford, P. R., & Noel, N. (1994). Drinking outcomes of alcohol abusers diagnosed as antisocial personality disorder. *Alcoholism: Clinical and Experimental Research, 18*, 778–785.

López, D., Cuevas, P., Gómez, A., & Mendoza, J. (2004). Transference-focused psychotherapy for borderline personality disorder: A study with female patients/Psicoterapia focalizada en la transferencia para el trastorno límite de la personalidad. un estudio con pacientes femeninas. *Salud Mental, 27*(4), 44–54.

Loranger, A., Oldham, J., & Tullis, E. (1982). Familial transmission of DSM-III borderline personality disorder. *Archives of General Psychiatry, 39,* 795–799.

Lorentzen, S., & Høglend, P. (2004). Predictors of change during long-term analytic group psychotherapy. *Psychotherapy and Psychosomatics, 73,* 25–35.

Maffei, C., Fossati, A., Agostoni, I., Barraco, A., Bagnato, M., Deborah, D., et al. (1997). Interrater reliability and internal consistency of the structured clinical interview for *DSM-IV* Axis II personality disorders (SCID-II), version 2.0. *Journal of Personality Disorders, 11,* 279–284.

Malan, D. H. (1976). *The frontier of brief psychotherapy.* New York: Plenum Press.

McGlashan, T. H., Grilo, C. M., Skodol, A. E., Gunderson, J. G., Shea, M. T., Morey, L. C., et al. (2000). The Collaborative Longitudinal Personality Disorders Study: Baseline Axis I/II and II/II diagnostic co-occurrence. *Acta Psychiatrica Scandinavica, 102,* 256–264.

McQuillan, A., Nicastro, R., Guenot, F., Girard, M., Lissner, C., & Ferrero, F. (2005). Intensive dialectical behavior therapy for outpatients with borderline personality disorder who are in crisis. *Psychiatric Services, 56,* 193–197.

Meares, R. (1987). The secret and the self: On a new direction in psychotherapy. *Australian and New Zealand Journal of Psychiatry, 21,* 545–559.

Mennin, D. S., & Heimberg, R. G. (2000). The impact of comorbid mood and personality disorders in the cognitive-behavioral treatment of panic disorder. *Clinical Psychology Review, 20,* 339–57.

Messina, N., Farabee, D., & Rawson, R. (2003). Treatment responsivity of cocaine-dependent patients with antisocial personality disorder to cognitive-behavioral and contingency management interventions. *Journal of Consulting and Clinical Psychology, 71,* 320–329.

Minichiello, W. E., Baer, L., & Jenike, M. A. (1987). Schizotypal personality disorder: A poor prognostic indicator for behavior therapy in the treatment of obsessive-compulsive disorder. *Journal of Anxiety Disorders, 1,* 273–276.

Monsen, J., Odland, T., Faugli, A., Daae, E., & Eilertsen, D. E. (1995). Personality disorders: Changes and stability after intensive psychotherapy focusing on affect consciousness. *Psychotherapy Research, 5,* 33–48.

Munroe-Blum, H., & Marziali, E. (1995). A controlled trial of short-term group treatment for borderline personality disorder. *Journal of Personality Disorders, 9,* 190–198.

Nace, E. D., Davis, C. W., & Gaspari, J. P. (1991). Axis II comorbidity in substance users. *American Journal of Psychiatry, 148,* 118–120.

Nathan, P. E., & Gorman, J. M. (2002). *A guide to treatments that work* (2nd ed.). New York: Oxford University Press.

Nordahl, H. M., & Nysæter, T. E. (2005). Schema therapy for patients with borderline personality disorder: A single case series. *Journal of Behavior Therapy and Experimental Psychiatry, 36,* 254–264.

Ogata, S. N., Silk, K. R., Goodrich, S., Lohr, N., Westen, D., & Hill, E. M. (1990). Childhood sexual and physical abuse in adult patients with borderline personality disorder. *American Journal of Psychiatry, 147,* 1008–1013.

Ogrodniczuk, J. S., Piper, W. E., Joyce, A. S., & McCallum, M. (2001). Using *DSM* Axis II information to predict outcome in short-term individual psychotherapy. *Journal of Personality Disorders, 15,* 110–122.

Palmer, R. L., Birchall, H., Damani, S., Gatward, N., McGrain, L., & Parker, L. (2003). A dialectical behavior therapy program for people with an eating disorder and borderline personality disorder: Description and outcome. *International Journal of Eating Disorders, 33,* 281–286.

Paris, J. (2000). Childhood precursors of borderline personality disorders. *Psychiatric Clinics of North America, 23,* 77–88.

Perry, J. C. (1992). Problems and considerations in the valid assessment of personality disorders. *American Journal of Psychiatry, 149,* 1645–1653.

Perry, J. C., Banon, E., & Ianni, F. (1999). Effectiveness of psychotherapy for personality disorders. *American Journal of Psychiatry, 156,* 1312–1321.

Pilkonis, P. A., & Frank, E. L. (1988). Personality pathology in recurrent depression: Nature, prevalence, and relationship to treatment response. *American Journal of Psychiatry, 145,* 435–441.

Ramnero, J., & Ost, L. G. (2004). Prediction of outcome in the behavioral treatment of panic disorder with agoraphobia. *Cognitive Behaviour Therapy, 33,* 176–180.

Rathus, J. H., & Miller, A. L. (2002). Dialectical behavior therapy adapted for suicidal adolescents. *Suicide and Life-Threatening Behavior, 32,* 146–157.

Reich, J. (2003). The effect of Axis II disorders on the outcome of treatment of anxiety and unipolar depressive disorders: A review. *Journal of Personality Disorders, 17,* 387–405.

Reich, J. H., & Green, A. I. (1991). Effect of personality disorders on outcome of treatment. *Journal of Nervous and Mental Disease, 179,* 74–82.

Reich, J. H., & Vasile, R. G. (1993). Effect of personality-disorders on the treatment outcome of Axis-I conditions: An update. *Journal of Nervous and Mental Disease, 181*, 475–484.

Renneberg, B., Goldstein, A. J., Phillips, D., & Chambless, D. L. (1990). Intensive behavioral group treatment of avoidant personality disorder. *Behavior Therapy, 21*, 363–377.

Rosenblum, A., Foote, J., Cleland, C., Magura, S., Mahmood, D., & Kosanke, N. (2005). Moderators of effects of motivational enhancements to cognitive behavioral therapy. *American Journal of Drug and Alcohol Abuse, 31*, 35–58.

Ruegg, R., & Frances, A. (1995). New research on personality disorders. *Journal of Personality Disorders, 9*, 1–48.

Samuels, J., Eaton, W. W., Bienvenu, O. J., Brown, C. H., Costa, P. T., & Nestadt, G. (2002). Prevalence and correlates of personality disorders in a community sample. *British Journal of Psychiatry, 180*, 536–542.

Shapiro, D. A., Barkham, M., Rees, A., Hardy, G. E., Reynolds, S., & Startup, M. (1994). Effects of treatment duration and severity of depression on the effectiveness of cognitive-behavioral and psychodynamic-interpersonal psychotherapy. *Journal of Consulting and Clinical Psychology, 62*, 522–534.

Sifneos, P. E. (1979). *Short-term dynamic psychotherapy.* New York: Plenum Press.

Skodol, A. E., Pagano, M. E., Bender, D. S., Shea, M. T., Gunderson, J. G., Yen, S., et al. (2005). Stability of functional impairment in patients with schizotypal, borderline, avoidant, or obsessive-compulsive personality disorder over two years. *Psychological Medicine, 35*, 443–451.

Skodol, A. E., Stout, R. L., McGlashan, T. H., Grilo, C. M., Gunderson, J. G., Shea, M. T., et al. (1999). Co-occurrence of mood and personality disorders: A report from the Collaborative Longitudinal Personality Disorders Study (CLPS). *Depression and Anxiety, 10*, 175–182.

Stevenson, J., & Meares, R. (1992). An outcome study of psychotherapy for patients with borderline personality disorder. *American Journal of Psychiatry, 149*, 358–362.

Stevenson, J., & Meares, R. (1999). Psychotherapy with borderline patients: II. A preliminary cost benefit study. *Australian and New Zealand Journal of Psychiatry, 33*, 473–477.

Stevenson, J., Meares, R., & D'Angelo, R. (2005). Five-year outcome of outpatient psychotherapy with borderline patients. *Psychological Medicine, 35*, 79–87.

Stravynski, A., Belisle, M., Marcouiller, M., & Lavallee, Y. (1994). The treatment of avoidant personality disorder by social skills training in the clinic or in real-life settings. *Canadian Journal of Psychiatry, 39*, 377–383.

Stravynski, A., Lesage, A., Marcouiller, M., & Elie, R. (1989). A test of the therapeutic mechanism in social skills training with avoidant personality disorder. *Journal of Nervous and Mental Disease, 177*, 739–744.

Svrakic, D., & Divac-Jovanovic, M. (1994). Personality disorders: Model for conceptual approach and classification: II. Proposed classification. *American Journal of Psychotherapy, 48*, 562–580.

Torgersen, S. (1984). Genetic and nosological aspects of schizotypal and borderline personality disorders. *Archives of General Psychiatry, 41*, 546–554.

Torgersen, S., Kringlen, E., & Cramer, V. (2001). The prevalence of personality disorders in a community sample. *Archives of General Psychiatry, 58*, 590–596.

Turner, R. M. (1987). The effects of personality disorder diagnosis on the outcome of social anxiety symptom reduction. *Journal of Personality Disorders, 1*, 136–144.

Tyrer, P., Tom, B., Byford, S., Schmidt, U., Jones, V., Davidson, K., et al. (2004). Differential effects of manual assisted cognitive behavior therapy in the treatment of recurrent deliberate self-harm and personality disturbance: The POPMACT study. *Journal of Personality Disorders, 18*, 102–116.

van den Bosch, L. M., Koeter, M. W. J., Stijnen, T., Verheul, R., & van der Brink, W. (2005). Sustained efficacy of dialectical behaviour therapy for borderline personality disorder. *Behaviour Research and Therapy, 43*, 1231–1241.

van den Bosch, L. M., Verheul, R., Schippers, G. M., & van den Brink, W. (2002). Dialectical behavior therapy of borderline patients with and without substance use problems: Implementation and long-term effects. *Addictive Behaviors, 27*, 911–923.

Verheul, R., van den Bosch, L. M., Koeter, M. W., De Ridder, M. A., Stijnen, T., & van den Brink, W. (2003). Dialectical behavior therapy for women with borderline personality disorder: 12-month, randomized clinical trial in the Netherlands. *British Journal of Psychiatry, 182*, 135–140.

Vinnars, B., Barber, J. P., Norén, K., Thormählen, B., Gallop, R., & Weinryb, R. M. (2005). Manualized supportive-expressive psychotherapy versus non-manualized community-delivered psychodynamic therapy for patients with personality disorders: Bridging efficacy and effectiveness. *American Journal of Psychiatry, 162*, 1933–1940.

Walker, W. R., Freeman, R. F., & Christensen, D. K. (1994). Restricting environmental stimulation (REST) to enhance cognitive behavioral treatment for obsessive compulsive disorder with schizotypal personality disorder. *Behavior Therapy, 25,* 709–719.

Weiss, R. D., Mirin, S. M., Griffin, M. L., Gunderson, J. G., & Hufford, C. (1993). Personality disorders in cocaine dependence. *Comprehensive Psychiatry, 34,* 145–149.

Weissman, M. M. (1993). The epidemiology of personality disorders: A 1990 update. *Journal of Personality Disorders, 7,* 44–62.

Westen, D., Lundolph, P., Misle, B., Ruffins, S., & Block, J. (1990). Physical and sexual abuse in adolescent girls with borderline personality disorder. *American Journal of Orthopsychiatry, 60,* 55–66.

Widiger, T. (1993). The *DSM-III-R* categorical personality disorder diagnoses: A critique and an alternative. *Psychological Inquiry, 4,* 75–90.

Widiger, T., & Rogers, J. H. (1989). Prevalence and comorbidity of personality disorders. *Psychiatric Annals, 19,* 132–136.

Widiger, T. A., & Samuel, D. B. (2005). Evidence-based assessment of personality disorders. *Psychological Assessment, 17,* 278–287.

Wilberg, T., Karterud, S., Pedersen, G., Urnes, O., Irion, T., Brabrand, J., et al. (2003). Outpatient group psychotherapy following day treatment for patients with personality disorders. *Journal of Personality Disorders, 17,* 510–521.

Wildgoose, A., Clarke, S., & Waller, G. (2001). Treating personality fragmentation and dissociation in borderline personality disorder: A pilot study of the impact of cognitive analytic therapy. *British Journal of Medical Psychology, 74,* 47–55.

Williams, J. G. (1988). Cognitive intervention for a paranoid personality disorder. *Psychotherapy, 25,* 570–575.

Winston, A., Laikin, M., Pollack, J., Samstag, L. W., McCullough, L., & Muran, J. C. (1994). Short-term psychotherapy of personality disorders. *American Journal of Psychiatry, 151,* 190–194.

Winston, A., Pollack, J., McCullough, L., Flegenheimer, W., Kestenbaum, R., & Trujillo, M. (1991). Brief psychotherapy of personality disorders. *Journal of Nervous and Mental Disease, 179,* 188–193.

Woody, G. E., McLellan, A. T., Luborsky, L., & O'Brien, C. P. (1985). Sociopathy and psychotherapy outcome. *Archives of General Psychiatry, 42,* 1081–1086.

Young, J. E. (1994). *Cognitive therapy for personality disorders: A schema-focused approach* (rev. ed.). Sarasota FL: Professional Resource Press.

Zanarini, M. C., Skodol, A. E., Bender, D., Dolan, R., Sanislow, C., Schaefer, E., et al. (2000). The Collaborative Longitudinal Personality Disorders Study: Reliability of Axis I and II diagnoses. *Journal of Personality Disorders, 14,* 291–299.

Zimmerman, M., & Mattia, J. I. (1999). Axis I diagnostic comorbidity and borderline personality disorder. *Comprehensive Psychiatry, 40,* 245–252.

24

Psychopharmacological Treatment
of Personality Disorders

Harold W. Koenigsberg

Ann Marie Woo-Ming

Larry J. Siever

Evidence is emerging that medications have a valuable role in the treatment of borderline, schizotypal, and avoidant personality disorders, although that role appears to be limited, since the degree of improvement associated with the addition of medication is moderate and is typically limited to some but not all of the symptom domains of the disorder. Strong evidence is emerging that supports the efficacy of the atypical antipsychotic medication olanzapine in reducing anger, impulsivity/aggression, and possibly depression and interpersonal sensitivity in borderline personality disorder.

The use of medication to treat personality disorders has become more widespread in recent years as anecdotal clinical reports have been supplanted by well-designed trials and as the body of evidence identifying biological correlates in the personality disorders has grown. Pharmacotherapy for some personality disorders has been studied extensively, and for others hardly at all. Personality disorders are commonly divided into three clusters: Cluster A disorders (odd cluster), Cluster B disorders (dramatic cluster), and Cluster C disorders (anxious cluster). The most extensive studies of the pharmacotherapy of personality disorders have examined the Cluster B disorders, particularly borderline personality disorder (BPD), and schizotypal personality disorder (SPD) in Cluster A. Several studies of the treatment of Cluster C avoidant personality disorder have also been reported.

The pharmacotherapy of personality disorders represents a relatively new frontier of psychopharmacology. Traditionally, personality-disordered patients have been treated with psychotherapy and have not been thought responsive to pharmacological intervention. However, advances in the field over the past two decades have challenged that perspective. A biological approach to the personality disorders questions the traditional separation of Axis I and Axis II diagnoses. However, clinical research investigations seeking to clarify the biological substrates of those disorders also pose some logistic difficulties. What follows is a summary of some of these methodological problems and a description of the more well-documented clinical strategies in current use.

Attempts to investigate biological etiologies and treatments systematically for these disorders have been in part limited by the overlap in symptomatology among the various personality disorder diagnoses. Other conceptual problems include (a) the existence of significant clinical heterogeneity even within one personality disorder diagnosis, (b) the relationship between Axis I and Axis II disorders, and (c) limited reliability assessment of the diagnoses of personality disorders.

CLINICAL HETEROGENEITY AND OVERLAP OF AXIS II DISORDERS

Within each Axis II category, many combinations of clinical presentations are possible, and it is possible to have a clinically heterogeneous group of patients in any one study even though the patients may technically meet criteria for the same personality disorder. For example, some schizotypal patients have marked borderline features, whereas others appear more emotionally restricted. Different Axis II diagnoses may share similar criteria under the fourth edition of the *Diagnostic and Statistical Manual of Mental Disorders* (American Psychiatric Association, 1994) categorization, and often patients meet criteria for more than one type of personality disorder (Hyler et al., 1990), adding to the potential for clinical heterogeneity within a given study sample.

RELATIONSHIPS BETWEEN AXIS I AND AXIS II DISORDERS

Overlap in symptomatology also exists between the Axis I and Axis II disorders. For example, in the Cluster B disorders in which depressive and labile mood are often found, distinction between these Axis II symptoms and the symptoms of bipolar spectrum disorders, dysthymia, or major depression is often unclear. In the Cluster C disorders, avoidant personality disorder shares many criteria of Axis I's social phobia disorder, and some authors feel that they are actually the same disorder.

Frequent comorbidity is seen between Axis I and Axis II syndromes; for example, up to 50% of patients with borderline personality disorder (BPD) or schizotypal personality disorder (SPD) are found to have concurrent diagnoses of a depressive disorder. Thus, evaluating a personality-disordered patient's response to drug treatment can be confounded by drug effects on a comorbid Axis I disorder.

RELIABILITY OF ASSESSMENT TOOLS

Methodological problems in designing studies of personality-disordered patients include limited reliability assessment of the diagnoses and limited longitudinal stability with this population. Questionable efficacy exists for our assessment instruments, as seen by mediocre retest and intratest reliability (Gitlin, 1993). Many of these difficulties are related to our limited understanding of how a personality disorder trait differs from adaptive personality traits. Measuring or standardizing change in personality disorder symptoms poses a challenge given the "persistently transient" nature of many of these symptoms (e.g., mood lability in the borderline patient). Because of the environmental responsiveness of the symptoms, a cardinal feature of most of these disorders, nonpharmacological variables such as milieu of the research setting and interactions with the research team should ideally be consistent.

Due to the episodic nature of some personality traits, such as mood lability, studies spanning a greater length of time would ideally allow investigation of these traits over their natural course. However, chaotic interpersonal relationships or suspiciousness of others may interfere with the sometimes lengthy treatment alliance required to complete a research study, leading to high dropout rates.

THE NEED FOR MULTIPLE APPROACHES TO DEFINING AND TREATING PERSONALITY DISORDERS

Attempts to avoid the overlap in diagnoses inherent in *DSM-IV* categorization have led to dimensional models of personality disorders in the context of which psychobiological findings can be understood (Siever & Davis, 1991; Cloninger, Svrakic, & Przybeck, 1993; Skodol et al., 2002). Such models derive from studies of biological correlates of personality traits, and family studies that point to heritability of these dimensions (Torgersen et al., 2000; Trestman, deVegvar, & Siever, 1995). One model that identifies dimensions on the basis of their prominence in particular personality disorders and their presumed underlying biological substrates conceptualizes the target dimensions of personality in terms of cognitive/perceptual distortions, affective lability and impulsivity/aggression, and anxiety. These categories correspond to the odd, dramatic, and anxious clusters, respectively, in *DSM-IV*. One challenge in studying a particular personality dimension is that abnormalities in more than one neurotransmitter system may converge to provide the substrate for a specific dimension (Gurvits, Koenigsberg, & Siever, 2000). Also, targeting one core dimension still leaves unaddressed the complex clinical syndrome that encompasses a personality disorder. Finally, in defining a core dimension in the personality-disordered patient, a distinction must be made between a trait and a state symptom. Despite these hurdles, the dimensional approach allows consideration of the fluidity that is clinically recognized between Axis I and Axis II symptoms and provides a framework for inquiry into the interrelationships among types of behavior, their modulatory neurotransmitters, and pharmacological interventions.

In summary, categorical (i.e., Axis II categories) and dimensional approaches can be used for investigating psychopharmacological treatments for personality disorders. A categorical approach allows a more clinical conceptualization of the personality disorders but may not allow for meaningful measurements of change in response to medication given the broad overlap of symptoms within Axis II, comorbidity with Axis I disorders, and an incomplete distinction between state versus trait phenomena. A dimensional approach allows for more precise "targeting" of phenomena to be examined, yet it may fail to wholly capture the complex entity of human personality. Although each approach has recognized limitations, each can also offer valuable frameworks within which these disorders can be further investigated.

We now turn to a review of the pharmacological treatments of personality disorders and the psychobiological findings that prompted the use of such treatments.

CLUSTER A DISORDERS (ODD CLUSTER)

Schizotypal personality disorder has been the most carefully studied of the odd cluster (Cluster A) disorders. Clinical, genetic, and psychophysiological studies have established its place within the schizophrenia spectrum disorders (Siever et al., 2002). Phenomenologically, the SPD patient can be described as having both the deficit-like and psychotic-like symptoms seen in schizophrenia but in an attenuated form. Family studies have revealed significantly higher rates of SPD in the relatives of schizophrenic patients in comparison to control patients (Silverman et al., 1993), and siblings of probands with schizophrenia have been found to be at higher risk for both

SPD and schizophrenia if either one or both parents had SPD (Baron, Gruen, & Asnis, 1985).

Psychophysiological testing reveals abnormal performance on smooth pursuit eye movements, backward masking tests, and continuous performance tasks associated with both schizophrenia and SPD (Siever, 1991). Recent magnetic resonance imaging studies have identified structural similarities common to both disorders, and functional imaging has identified similarities in regional brain activity during cognitive task performance in both (Koenigsberg et al., 2005; Siever et al., 2002; Kirrane & Siever, 2000). These findings have strengthened the concept of a spectrum of schizophrenia-like disorders that span both Axis I and Axis II categories. Psychobiological investigations into SPD, based on a dimensional model of symptoms, have also supported the relationship between SPD and schizophrenia and provide a logical starting point for psychopharmacological interventions for this personality disorder.

Schizotypal personality disorder can be characterized by disturbances in the cognitive/perceptual domain, manifested by impairment in attending to the environment, discriminating among stimuli, or processing information. Clinically, this may translate into psychotic-like symptoms (such as magical thinking, ideas of reference, or perceptual distortion), deficit-like symptoms (such as poor interpersonal relatedness or social detachment), and cognitive disorganization (such as deficient performance on cognitive, psychophysiological, and attentional testing).

Psychotic-Like Symptoms in Schizotypal Personality Disorder

The commonalities between SPD and schizophrenia and the role of dopamine in psychotic symptoms spurred interest into dopaminergic function in SPD. Cerebrospinal fluid homovanillic acid (HVA; the major dopamine metabolite) concentrations in SPD patients correlate significantly with psychotic-like symptoms and were significantly elevated compared with levels in other types of personality-disordered patients in one study from our center (Siever, 1991). Similarly, plasma HVA concentrations also correlated significantly with psychotic-like symptoms in SPD and were elevated compared with normal subjects in an overlapping sample (Siever et al., 1991).

These findings suggest the possibility that dopamine antagonism might be beneficial in these disorders. Given the known efficacy of antipsychotic medications in the schizophrenia spectrum disorders, their effect on SPD psychotic-like symptoms has also been investigated (see Table 24.1). However, the majority of these studies primarily targeted subjects with borderline personality disorder and described findings for patients who also met criteria for SPD. The single study of traditional neuroleptics involving only SPD patients (Hymowitz et al., 1986) did find an improvement in psychotic-like symptoms following treatment with haloperidol; however, a single-blind design was used. The three double-blind, placebo-controlled studies of mixed populations of SPD and BPD patients (Cowdry & Gardner, 1988; Goldberg et al., 1986; Soloff et al., 1989) show an association between low-dose antipsychotic use and broad improvements in symptomatology, including scales of psychoticism, anxiety, depression, hostility, and rejection sensitivity. However, one study (Cowdry & Gardner, 1988) involved patients characterized by severe affective instability, so that the applicability of these findings to the more typically emotionally constricted SPD subjects is in question. Other non-placebo-controlled studies (Jensen & Andersen, 1989; Serban & Siegel, 1984) described moderate, global improvements in mixed BPD and SPD populations with the use of antipsychotic medication.

The atypical antipsychotic medications are attractive candidates for the treatment of SPD because of their low incidence of side effects and the possibility that they may particularly target negative symptoms (Javitt, 1999; Lane, Liu, & Chang, 1999). A favorable side effect profile is especially important for medications used to treat SPD because this disorder is characterized by a tendency toward somatic preoccupation, which can lead to an unusual sensitivity to side effects. One open-label study of the atypical antipsychotic olanzapine in the treatment of dysthymic borderline patients, most of whom also met criteria for SPD, has been published (Schulz et al., 1999). The authors report robust improvement over the 8-week treatment period in global scores in the five rating scales they employed (see Table 24.1). Our group (Koenigsberg et al., 2003) has completed a 9-week placebo-controlled, double-blind study of low-dose risperidone in the treatment of nondepressed SPD patients, only 20% of whom had comorbid BPD. We found statistically significant reductions in Positive and Negative Syndrome (PANSS) negative and general symptom scores by week 3 and

PANSS positive score by week 7 in the risperidone group compared with the placebo-treated group.

Conversely, a state of dopamine agonism might be expected to exacerbate the psychotic-like symptoms of SPD. Indeed, a study of eight SPD/BPD and eight BPD patients selected by virtue of affective lability showed that, when administered amphetamine, SPD subjects had significantly increased Brief Psychiatric Rating Scale scores of thought disturbance and self-rated psychoticism compared with BPD subjects (Schulz, Cornlius, Schulz, & Soloff, 1988). The authors concluded that this finding supported the hypothesis that SPD is included in the psychotic spectrum disorders. In contrast, 20 patients selected solely on the basis of meeting SPD criteria demonstrated no increase in psychotic-like symptoms with amphetamine administration (Siever et al., 1994). Thus, it may be that certain SPD subjects with hyperdopaminergic states may be more responsive to treatment with dopamine antagonist agents and respond negatively to dopamine agonism, whereas those with normal or reduced dopaminergic activities (see below) may respond beneficially to dopamine agonism.

Thus, it appears that schizotypal symptomatology in mixed SPD/BPD populations is responsive, in modest and generalized ways, to low-dose antipsychotic medication. Given the state of dopamine antagonism induced by these medications and correlations between increased plasma and cerebrospinal fluid (CSF) HVA and psychotic-like symptoms in SPD, it is tempting to hypothesize that psychotic-like symptoms in SPD would be particularly responsive to antipsychotic medications. Future trials with primarily SPD subjects in double-blind, placebo-controlled settings would help to refine further the role for these agents in SPD.

Deficit-Like Symptoms and Cognitive Disorganization in Schizotypal Personality Disorder

Neurobiological studies of the deficit-like symptoms of SPD have investigated their relationship to psychophysiological, neuroanatomic, and monoaminergic indices. Abnormal performance on smooth pursuit eye movements, backward masking tests, and continuous performance tasks correlate with deficit symptoms of SPD (Siever, 1991). Cognitive disorganization, as measured by performance on psychologi-

TABLE 24.1 Table of Antipsychotic Studies: Borderline Personality Disorder and Schizotypal
Personality Disorder

Study	Diagnosis	Study Design	Comment
Goldberg et al. (1986)	N = 50 BPD and/or SPD patients (BPD with at least one prior psychotic episode)	Type 1 study: thiothixene (average 8.6 mg), 12 weeks, double-blind, placebo-controlled	Thiothixene led to improvement of psychotic-like/obsessive/phobic anxiety symptoms; no effect on depression.
Cowdry & Gardner (1988)	N = 16, female BPD outpatients; all characterized as "seriously ill with severe dysphoria in setting of rejection, and dyscontrol behavior such as assaultiveness, cutting, overdose"; of these, 6 patients also SPD	Type 1 study: tranylcypromine, trifluoperazine, carbamazepine, alprazolam; 6 weeks; double-blind, placebo-controlled	Tranylcypromine led to improved global and mood scores, improved impulsivity, but no effect on behavioral dyscontrol; trifluoperazine showed a trend toward broad symptomatic improvement; carbamazepine showed improvement of impulsivity and behavioral dyscontrol; alprazolam led to increases in suicidality and dyscontrol.
Soloff et al. (1989)	N = 90 inpatients with BPD, mixed SPD/BPD symptoms, and a small number of SPD patients	Type 2 study: amitriptyline (100–175 mg) or haloperidol (4–16 mg); 5 weeks; placebo-controlled	Haloperidol led to global improvements, including hostile depression and impulsive ward behavior, especially if patient had severe schizotypal symptoms, hostility, or suspiciousness. Amitriptyline not as effective as haloperidol for anxiety and hostility; not effective on core depressive symptoms.
Serban & Siegel (1984)	N = 52 outpatients with SPD (14), BPD with prior psychotic episode (16), mixed SPD/BPD (16)	Type 2 study: haloperidol or thiothixene (4–12 mg), 6 weeks to 3 months, double-blind	Thiothixene > haloperidol led to moderate to marked improvements in all patients for general symptoms, paranoid ideation, anxiety, ideas of reference, and depression regardless of diagnosis.
Hymowitz et al. (1986)	N = 17 SPD outpatients	Type 2 study: haloperidol (up to 12 mg, average 3.6 mg); 6 weeks; single-blind, 2-week placebo washout	Drug led to mild to moderate improvement in ideas of reference, social isolation, odd communication, and thought disorder; also GAS scores increased.
Jensen & Andersen (1989)	N = 5 SPD, 5 BPD inpatients	Type 3 study: amoxapine (up to 300 mg); 3 weeks minimum; open label, no placebo; oxazepam prn agitation (36–42 mg qd)	SPD subjects showed broad improvement in BPRS (schizophrenia subscale) and HDRS scores. BPD subjects showed no improvement.
Chengappa et al. (1999)	N = 7 inpatients with BPD, 6 with Axis I psychotic disorders	Type 3 study: clozapine; chart audit with mirror image design; mean dose 421 mg/day.	Decrease in number of seclusion and restraint incidents, modest improvement in GAF.

(continued)

TABLE 24.1 (continued)

Study	Diagnosis	Study Design	Comment
Schulz et al. (1999)	N = 11 community-based referrals meeting criteria for BPD and dysthymia (7 of whom also met SPD criteria)	Type 3 study: olanzapine (up to 10 mg, average 7.7 mg); open label no placebo; 8-week study.	Olanzapine led to improvement in global scores on BPRS, BDHI, BIS11, GAF, SCL-90.
Koenigsberg et al (2003)	N = 25 community and clinic referrals meeting criteria for SPD (only 20% also meet BPD criteria)	Type 1 study: risperidone (up to 2 mg) 9-week double-blind, placebo-control; 2-week placebo wash-out	Risperidone led to significantly lower PANSS negative and general score by week 3 and PANSS positive score by week 7.
Rocca et al. (2002)	N = 15 outpatients meeting criteria for BPD (4 were comorbid for ASPD)	Type 3 study: risperidone (mean dose 3.3 mg/day); 8-week open-label no placebo trial	Significant improvement in BPRS total, hostility/suspicion, and anergia scales; HDRS; GAF; AQ.
Zanarini & Frankenburg (2001)	N = 28 females meeting criteria for BPD recruited by advertisement (1 comorbid for SPD)	Type 1 study: olanzapine (mean dose 5.3 mg/day). 6-month randomized placebo-controlled double-blind	Olanzapine significantly superior to placebo in SCL-90 anger/hostility, anxiety. paranoia, interpersonal sensitivity. Few dropouts.
Zanarini et al.(2004)	N = 45 females meeting criteria for BPD recruited by advertisement	Type 2 study: randomized double-blind non-placebo-controlled 8-week parallel comparison of olanzapine (3.3 mg), fluoxetine (15 mg), and olanzapine fluoxetine combination (OFC) (3 mg/ 13 mg)	OFC is more effective than fluoxetine in treating impulsivity-aggression and dysthymia. Olanzapine is more effective than OFC in treating dysthymia and equally effectve in impulsivity aggression. Few dropouts.
Soler et al. (2005)	N = 60 clinically referred BPD patients	Type 2 study: 12-week randomized double-blind, placebo-controlled trial of olanzapine (8.8 mg/day). Both groups received DBT	Olanzapine + DBT superior to DBT alone in impulsive-aggressive behaviors, ED visits, depression, anxiety, and CGI score.
Villeneuve & Lemelin (2005)	N = 34 BPD patients with GAF < 55	Type 3 study: 12-week open-label trial of quetiapine (mean dose 251 mg)	Significant improvement in impulsivity, hostility, anxiety depression, GAF score, and for points with psychotic symptom at baseline, micropsychotic symptoms.

AMI = amitriptyline; AQ = Aggression Questionnaire; BPD = borderline personality disorder; BDHI = Buss-Durkee Hostility Inventory; BIS11 = Baratt Impulsivity Scale version 11; BPRS = Brief Psychiatric Rating Scale; CGI-BPD = Clinical Global Impression Scale for BPD; DBT = dialectical behavior therapy; ED = emergency department; GAF = Global Assessment of Function; HDRS = Hamilton Depression Rating Scale; OFC = olanzapine/fluoxetine combination; PANSS = Positive and Negative Syndrome Scale; SCL-90 = Hopkins Symptom Check List 90; SPD = schizotypal personality disorder.

cal testing, has also been described among SPD patients. These subjects have been shown to make significantly increased numbers of errors on the Wisconsin Card Sort Test (WCST) and the California Verbal Learning Test compared with normal subjects and other non–Cluster A personality-disordered patients (Bergman et al., 1996). These indices

suggest roles for the frontal and temporal cortices in the deficit symptoms of SPD.

Correlations between neurotransmitter levels and deficit-like symptoms in SPD have been investigated. Whereas increased plasma HVA levels have been shown to correlate with psychotic-like symptoms in personality-disordered patients, decreased plasma HVA levels may be associated with deficit-like symptoms in relatives of schizophrenic patients and cognitive deficits in SPD patients (Siever, Kalus, & Keefe, 1993). Investigations of cholinergic indices in schizophrenic patients have yielded mixed results (Karson, Casanova, Kleinman, & Griffin, 1993; Tandon & Greden, 1989); however, preliminary data from our laboratory suggest that the cholinergic agent physostigmine may improve visuospatial delayed-response attentional performance in SPD patients.

Thus, an interrelationship may exist among deficit-like symptoms, cognitive deficits as measured by psychological and psychophysiological tests, and decreased plasma HVA concentrations. The above findings raise the possibility that dopaminergic agents may lead to improvement of deficit symptoms and cognitive disorganization in SPD subjects. One double-blind, placebo-controlled study of amphetamine in SPD/BPD patients found that in addition to worsening of psychotic-like symptoms among the SPD group, all subjects had increased activation scores on the Brief Psychiatric Rating Scale (BPRS) in response to amphetamine (Schulz et al., 1988). This might suggest an improvement in such deficit symptoms as anergia and withdrawal. Further, a preliminary study of amphetamine use in SPD patients showed improved performance on the Wisconsin Card Sort Test (Siever et al., 1995).

An important body of preclinical work (Franowicz & Arnsten, 2002) has demonstrated the role of noradrenergic agonists, particularly alpha-2 agonists, in enhancing working memory. Our group has carried out a pilot trial of the alpha-2A agonist guanfacine in a group of SPD patients and patients with other non-SPD personality disorders (OPD). Guanfacine produced improvement in a number of cognitive domains, including visuospatial working memory and executive function, in the SPD subjects but not the OPD controls.

The monoamine oxidase inhibitor (MAOI) tranylcypromine has been associated with broad-based behavioral effects in one mixed SPD/BPD group (see Table 24.1). Among the changes observed was an increased capacity for pleasure. Although this may reflect an improvement of deficit-like symptoms, the effect of comorbidity of affective symptoms for both groups is unclear in the study. The continued investigation of catecholaminergic agents for SPD patients would be of value, with special focus on their effect on cognitive performance, as well as deficit-like symptoms.

Treatment of Comorbid Diagnoses in Schizotypal Personality Disorder

The use of antidepressant agents for SPD has a basis in the observation that high rates of comorbidity exist between SPD and the depressive disorders: 30 to 50% of SPD patients seen in clinical settings have been found to have a concurrent major depressive disorder, and 50% of patients have a history of major depressive disorder (Kaplan & Sadock, 1995). So far, however, trials with antidepressant agents in SPD have only been conducted in groups of mixed SPD/BPD patients (see Tables 24.1 and 24.2). The use of fluoxetine, up to 80 mg over a 12-week period, was investigated in a mixed group and was found to decrease obsessive symptoms, rejection sensitivity, depressive symptoms, anxiety, and psychoticism (Markovitz et al., 1991). These improvements occurred regardless of whether subjects had a concurrent diagnosis of major depressive disorder. Such findings are limited by the fact that the study was open label and again by the heterogeneity of the subjects.

There have been attempts to "pharmacologically distinguish" between affective and psychotic-like symptoms, primarily in BPD groups with some SPD patients included. In one large, mixed sample, amitriptyline led to a significant improvement in anxiety and hostility for the whole group, although less effectively than haloperidol (Soloff et al., 1989). Tranylcypromine was used in a primarily BPD group with a small subset of SPD patients and was found to decrease significantly a broad array of symptoms, including depressive scores, anxiety, rejection sensitivity, and impulsivity (Cowdry & Gardner, 1988). However, the generalized response of symptoms has failed to elucidate a differential response of affective symptoms or psychotic-like symptoms to antidepressants in these patient populations. Thus, in order to determine the efficacy of antidepressants for SPD symptomatology, replication studies using double-blind, placebo-controlled methods in homogeneous groups of SPD patients are needed.

CLUSTER B (DRAMATIC CLUSTER)

The disorders seen in Cluster B (dramatic cluster) have been defined dimensionally as being composed of impulsivity/aggression and affective lability. The prototype diagnoses involving these traits are borderline personality disorder and antisocial personality disorder. There are numerous investigations into the neurobiological substrates that may underlie each of these dimensions and corresponding implications for pharmacological management of the disorders that incorporate these dimensions.

Psychobiology of Impulsivity/Aggression

Impulsivity/aggression has been associated with a number of determinants, including familial inheritance, disturbances of the serotonergic and noradrenergic systems, and nonspecific cerebral dysfunction.

Family Studies for Impulsivity/Aggression

First-degree relatives of BPD patients have been shown to have significantly greater prevalences of both impulsive/aggressive behaviors and affective lability than relatives of other personality-disordered or schizophrenic patients (Silverman & Pinkham, 1991). Furthermore, relatives of borderline probands appear to be at greater risk for BPD than the relatives of normal control subjects (Baron et al., 1985). Although such findings do not distinguish the role of environmental versus genetic influences on familial inheritance, preliminary results from a twin study show that individual BPD criteria may be genetically determined. These criteria include instability in relationships, impulsivity, anger, and affective instability (Torgersen, 1992).

Serotonergic and Noradrenergic Indices in Impulsivity/Aggression

Diminished serotonergic indices have been implicated in impulsive/aggressive behavior directed toward the self (i.e., suicide attempts) and others. This association exists across diagnostic categories, lending support to the conceptualization of impulsivity/aggression as a dimensional trait. For example, CSF 5-hydroxyindoleacetic acid (5-HIAA) levels have been shown to correlate inversely with a history of aggressive behavior and with rating scales of aggressive behavior. Decreased CSF 5-HIAA levels are also associated with depressed patients who had made suicide attempts compared either with depressed patients who had never attempted suicide or with healthy controls (Brown et al., 1982).

Central serotonergic function is also diminished in association with impulsivity/aggression in affective disorders, BPD, and other personality disorders. Decreased central 5-hydroxytryptophan (5-HT) function appears to be associated with self- and other-directed aggression in personality-disordered patients and associated with a history of suicide attempts in patients with major depression. One study compared subjects with major affective disorder (acute or remitted depression or bipolar type), personality disorders, and normal controls on subscales of impulsivity, history of alcohol abuse, and history of suicide attempts (Coccaro et al., 1991). Central serotonergic function was assessed using fenfluramine; a blunted prolactin response to fenfluramine is thought to reflect decreased central serotonergic function. Results showed that among all the personality-disordered patients, those with BPD had significantly blunted peak prolactin response compared with the others, and that this was associated with the impulsive/aggressive features of this disorder. Similarly, among all PD patients, impulsive/aggressive scores were negatively correlated with peak prolactin values. For subjects with PD or major depression, a history of a suicide attempt was associated with a significant blunting of prolactin when compared with patients who had never attempted suicide. More recently, positron-emission tomography (PET) imaging has made it possible to measure cerebral glucose metabolic rates in those frontal regions believed to play a role in inhibiting impulsive behavior. Borderline patients with impulsivity/aggression show a decreased metabolic response to serotonin agonists compared with healthy controls in the orbital and medial frontal cortices (New et al., 2002; Siever et al., 1999; Soloff, Meltzer, Greer, Constantine, & Kelly, 2000), demonstrating a decrease in serotonin responsiveness of brain regions involved in the inhibition of impulsive behavior. A recent PET study of the effect of 12 weeks of treatment with fluoxetine in a group of impulsive aggressive borderline patients (New et al., 2004) showed that as fluoxetine treatment reduced impulsive aggression, it also normalized the decreased metabolic rate in the orbitofrontal cortex. These studies provide strong support from the domain of clinical neurobiology for the use of selective serotonin reuptake inhibitors (SSRIs) to treat impulsivity/aggression in BPD.

Noradrenergic function, in contrast to serotonergic indices, may be elevated in association with impulsivity/aggression across such diagnostic categories as pathological gambling, major affective disorders, and personality disorders. The CSF and plasma levels of the norepinephrine metabolite 3-methoxy 4-hydroxy phenylglycol were found to be increased and associated with extraversion scores in pathological gamblers. The scores also correlated positively with urine concentrations of vanillylmandelic acid, a nor-adepinephrine metabolite, and the sum of urinary output of norepinephrine and its major metabolites (Roy, De Jon, & Linnoila, 1989).

Cerebral Dysfunction in Impulsivity/Aggression

Electroencephalogram (EEG) measures have been the focus of several investigations, with equivocal results, into cerebral dysfunction as another possible biologic substrate of impulsivity and aggression. For example, episodic/dyscontrol patients (defined as having impulsive, aggressive, and violent behavior) were shown in one study to have a significant increase in nonspecific EEG changes when contrasted with subjects with depression or headaches (Drake, Hietter, & Pakalnis, 1992). However, a comparison of BPD and other personality-disordered patients has shown no significant differences in the number of EEG abnormalities, and no associations between EEG abnormalities and impulsivity (Cornelius et al., 1986).

Further evidence for generalized cerebral dysfunction in impulsive/aggressive traits was found in a study of neurological soft signs in BPD and antisocial PD patients (Stein, Hollander, Cohen, & Frenkel, 1993). Compared with control subjects, the personality-disordered patients displayed a significantly greater number of left-sided neurological soft signs. Among the patients, nine were identified as "aggressive" based on the Brown-Goodwin Lifetime Aggression Scale. Compared with the nonaggressive PD patients, those with aggression showed significantly greater right-sided soft signs. Patients also underwent neuropsychological testing. Left-sided neurological soft signs were found to correlate with errors on Trails A and B tests, as well as on the Matching Familiar Faces Test, which may indicate an impairment of complex information processing. Right-sided soft signs correlated with errors on the Wisconsin Card Sort Test, a measure of frontal lobe functioning. Thus, in this study, lateralized neurological soft signs that correlated with specific neuropsychological deficits were found to be significantly associated with impulsive/aggressive traits in personality-disordered patients.

Psychobiology of Affective Lability

The cluster of traits thought to define affective instability in BPD subjects includes marked shifts between baseline and depressed moods, irritability, and anxiety that may persist from a few hours to a few days (Steinberg, Trestman, & Siever, 1994). Knowledge of the biological correlates of Axis I mood disorders provided a foundation for investigations into the psychobiology of affective-related traits in personality-disordered patients. However, the state-dependent markers associated with major affective disorder, such as blunted thyroid-stimulating hormone (TSH) response to thyrotropin-releasing hormone (TRH) and lack of plasma cortisol suppression in response to dexamethasone, have not been found to correlate consistently with affective-related traits in personality-disordered patients (Coccaro & Siever, 1995). Noradrenergic and cholinergic systems, which appear to play pivotal roles in Axis I mood disorders, have also been a logical area of study for the personality disorders.

Cholinergic agents are known to create a depressive-like picture in animal and human studies and can increase the rapid eye movement sleep latency associated with depression (Steinberg et al., 1994). Physostigmine, a centrally active cholinergic agent, has been shown to produce greater depressive responses in BPD subjects than in normal controls (Steinberg et al., 1997). The depressive responses correlated with affective instability and were independent of a past or present history of major depressive disorder. Thus, the dysphoric response seen with physostigmine infusion in BPD subjects appears to be specifically associated with affective lability and not due to comorbid major depression.

The role of noradrenergic and dopaminergic systems in affective lability has been investigated using dextroamphetamine (d-Amp), which releases and prevents reuptake of norepinephrine and dopamine. Following administration of d-Amp, a significant correlation between dysphoric/irritable mood response to the drug and measures of lifetime history of mood instability was observed in healthy volunteers (Kavoussi & Coccaro, 1993). However, neither of these variables correlated with plasma levels of homovanillic acid or 3-methoxy 4-hydroxyphenylglycol, metabolites of dopamine and norepinephrine, respectively. Irritability, another symptom associated with affective lability, has been shown to correlate with increased growth hormone (GH) response to clonidine in personality-disordered patients and normal controls (Coccaro et al., 1991). The growth hormone response to clonidine is thought to reflect activity of postsynaptic alpha-2-adrenergic receptors. The number of alpha-2 platelet binding sites has been shown to be reduced in borderline patients (Southwick, Yehuda, Giller, & Perry, 1990), consistent with increased noradrenergic activity. Thus, increased responsiveness of the central adrenergic system may be involved in affective instability in BPD and other personality-disordered subjects.

In summary, initial investigations have suggested that excessive cholinergic availability may play a role in the transient dysphoria seen in borderline patients, and that a hyperresponsive noradrenergic system may contribute to irritability/mood instability among healthy volunteers and personality-disordered subjects.

Pharmacology of Borderline Personality Disorder: Antidepressant Agents

The evidence implicating hyporesponsive serotonergic systems in impulsivity/aggression in BPD suggests that antidepressant medications that enhance serotonergic function may play an important role in the treatment of BPD. The investigation of antidepressant agents for the treatment of borderline symptomatology poses particular methodological challenges. First, the rates of comorbidity between BPD and Axis I depressive disorders may be as high as 50%. Although there is evidence to suggest that the affective picture in BPD can be conceptualized as a distinct entity from comorbid Axis I depressive disorders (Kavoussi & Coccaro, 1993; Koenigsberg et al., 1999; Silverman & Pinkham, 1991), the depressive symptomatology of BPD may be so heterogeneous as to defy further definition. In studies of antidepressant effects on symptoms or traits of BPD, it is important to acknowledge that we are limited in our knowledge of how dimensions or symptom clusters overlap and impinge on each other. For example, a drug's effect on depressive symptoms may in turn affect impulsive/aggressive traits. Several recent randomized double-blind, placebo-controlled studies of SSRIs have helped better define the efficacy of these medications

in treating BPD. A summary of antidepressant trials in the treatment of BPD can be found in Table 24.2.

In a double-blind, placebo-controlled study (Coccaro & Kavoussi, 1995), fluoxetine was shown to be effective in decreasing impulsivity/aggression and depression scores and in improving a broad array of symptoms such as rejection sensitivity, anxiety, psychoticism, and obsessive-compulsive symptoms in BPD subjects. A second controlled study (Salzman et al., 1995) found that fluoxetine had a clinically and statistically significant effect in reducing anger and depression in a sample of patients with mild to moderate BPD. The effect on anger was independent of the antidepressant effect. A third double-blind, placebo-controlled study of fluoxetine, limited by the small number of placebo completers, showed an improvement in aggression and irritability in the fluoxetine group but no change in suicidality or depression (New et al., 2004). Fluoxetine appeared to be more effective in reducing impulsive aggression in men than in women. A randomized, placebo-controlled study of the SSRI fluvoxamine in a clinically representative sample of moderate to severely symptomatic female BPD patients, which did not exclude patients with concurrent major depression or PTSD (Rinne, van den Brink, Wouters, & van Dyck, 2002), did not replicate the finding of an improvement in anger or impulsivity (independent of the presence or absence of an affective disorder). This study did, however, find a reduction in affective instability with fluvoxamine. A study of female BPD patients who were all receiving dialectical behavior therapy (DBT) concurrently found no added benefit from fluoxetine compared with placebo in aggression, self-injury, suicidality, depression, dissociation, or global functioning (Simpson et al., 2004). This study, however, was limited by the possibility that the sample was biased toward drug nonresponders and by the absence of a psychotherapy control condition. A study comparing three active medication treatments, without a placebo control, found no advantage of fluoxetine over either olanzapine alone or olanzapine plus fluoxetine in treating female BPD patients who did not have a concurrent major depression (Zanarini, Frankenburg, & Parachini, 2004). Taken together, the studies of SSRI treatment of BPD provide strongest support for its efficacy in treating impulsivity/aggression, particularly in male borderline patients. The findings on its effectiveness in treating suicidality and depression are more mixed.

TABLE 24.2 Pharmacology of Borderline Personality Disorder: Antidepressants

Study	Diagnosis	Study Design	Comment
Coccaro & Kavoussi (1995)	$N = 40$ PD patients with histories of impulsive aggression	Type 1 study: fluoxetine 20–60 mg; double-blind, placebo-controlled; 12 weeks	Overt aggression scores reduced at weeks 4, 10, 12, and end point; irritability scores reduced at weeks 6–12 and end point.
Salzman et al. (1995)	$N = 22$ patients recruited from the community (13 met BPD criteria and 9 had BPD traits); mild to moderate severity	Type 1 study: fluoxetine 20–60 mg; double-blind, placebo-controlled; 13 weeks including 1-week placebo lead-in	Anger and depression significantly declined more in the fluoxetine group than in the placebo group. Measures included PDRS anger and depression, POMS anger and depression, OAS anger against objects, and HAM-D scales.
Norden (1989)	$N = 12$ BPD patients, all except 1 with histories of suicidality	Type 3 study: fluoxetine; open label	Very much or much improved; irritability and suicidality among the most responsive symptoms.
Comelius et al. (1991)	$N = 5$, BPD inpatients who had failed phenelzine and at least one neuroleptic	Type 3 study: fluoxetine; open label	Decreases in impulsivity and suicidality
Markovitz et al. (1991)	$N = 22$ outpatients: 8 BPD, 10 SPD/BPD with mixed symptoms, 4 SPD; 13 patients also with MDD	Type 3 study: fluoxetine; open label; 20–80 mg over 12 weeks sensitivity, psychoticism, anxiety, and obsessive-compulsive symptoms regardless of comorbid diagnosis of MDD	Decrease in 50% of patients' self-mutilatory behavior; significant decrease in depression, rejection.
Rinne et al. (2002)	$N = 38$ BPD patients; moderate to severe pathology from outpatient clinic and newspaper referral	Type 1 study: fluvoxamine (150–200 mg/day); randomized placebo-controlled double-blind for 6 weeks; followed by single-blind half-crossover for 6 weeks and open label for next 12 weeks	Significant improvement in rapid-mood shift subscale of BPD-SI (independent of comorbid affective disorders or PTSD). No significant medication effect upon BPD-SI anger or impulsivity.
Simpson et al. (2004)	$N = 25$ female BPD patients in treatment in a 5-day DBT-based partial hospital program, dissociation or GAF.	Type 1 study: fluoxetine (40 mg/day); randomized double-blind 12-week comparison of DBT+Fluoxetine to DBT+Placebo	No added benefit of fluoxetine over placebo in aggression, self-injury, suicidality, depression.
New et al. (2004)	$N = 20$ BPD patients recruited from advertisements and clinic referral	Type 3 study: fluoxetine (20 mg/day); randomized double-blind placebo-controlled. Only 3 placebo subjects completed.	Significant improvement from baseline to completion in OAS-M aggression and irritability scores, but not suicidality or depression.
Soloff et al. (1986)	$N = 52$, BPD inpatients	Type 2 study: amitriptyline; placebo-controlled	AMI nonresponders showed significantly more impulsive/assaultive behavior than placebo nonresponders; AMI responders showed improvement in impulsive behavior and depression scores.

(continued)

TABLE 24.2 (continued)

Study	Diagnosis	Study Design	Comment
Soloff et al. (1993)	N = 92, BPD and mixed BPD/SPD features	Type 1 study: comparison between haloperidol and phenelzine; double-blind, placebo controlled	Phenelzine less effective than haloperidol in decreasing impulsivity/hostile-belligerence; phenelzine did not improve atypical depressive symptoms but did decrease scores on Buss-Durkee Hostility Inventory.
Parsons et al. (1989)	All patients had symptoms of atypical depression; Group 1: n = 40 patients with >5 DSM-III BPD criteria, n = 61 patients with >4 criteria; Group 2: n = 19 patients, BPD to a considerable extent, n = 29, patients BPD to only some extent as measured by the Personality Assessment Form	Type 1 study: double-blind, placebo-controlled; random assignment to phenelzine 60 mg or imipramine 200 mg for 3–6 weeks each medication	BPD patients with symptoms of atypical depression had significant improvement in CCI scores due to phenelzine, as compared with imipramine and placebo; imipramine felt to be minimally effective.

AMI = amitriptyline; BPD = borderline personality disorder; BPD-SI = Borderline Personality Disorder Severity Scale; CGI = Clinical Global Impression; DBT = dialectical behavior therapy; GAF = Global Assessment of Functioning; HAM-D = Hamilton Depression Rating Scale; MDD = major depressive disorder; OAS = McLean Hospital Overt Aggression Scale; PDRS = Personality Disorders Rating Scale; POMS = Profile of Mood States; SPD = schizotypal personality disorder.

There is some evidence that SSRIs may reduce affective instability and self-harming behaviors.

There is a trend for noradrenergic agents to improve mood but to be inconsistent in treating irritability and dyscontrol in BPD. Amitriptyline, for example, while significantly decreasing depression scores and impulsive behaviors in a group of BPD patients, was found to paradoxically worsen impulsivity, assaultiveness, paranoid ideation, and global functioning in a subset of patients compared with normal controls (Soloff et al., 1986). The authors concluded that the paradoxical worsening of the amitriptyline nonresponders was due to its effect on impulsive behaviors rather than on depressive symptoms. Desipramine was also shown to have no effect or actually to worsen anger and suicidality in comparison to lithium among a cohort of borderline subjects (Links, Steiner, Boiago, & Irwin, 1990). Similarly, the noradrenergic agent maprotiline may be associated with an increase in suicide-provoking potential in patients with histories of repeated suicidal behavior (Montgomery et al., 1992). The monoamine oxidase inhibitor phenelzine has been shown to have a good effect on BPD patients with atypical depressive features such as leaden paralysis, rejection sensitivity, and mood reactivity (Parsons et al., 1989). Tranylcypromine was also found to improve physi-

cian-rated mood scores, impulsivity, and global functioning in a cohort of primarily BPD patients, yet no improvement of behavioral dyscontrol was noted (Cowdry & Gardner, 1988). Thus, while these medications were found to improve depressive features and, in the case of amitriptyline responders, impulsive behavior, there may also be the risk of worsening anger and impulsivity in a subset of BPD patients (amitriptyline and desipramine), worsening suicidality in other patients (maprotiline), or having no effect on dyscontrol (tranylcypromine).

Thus, it appears that for both features of impulsivity, aggression, and possibly depressive spectrum symptomatology, serotonergic agents would be reasonable first-line agents. Noradrenergic agents such as the tricyclic antidepressants or MAOIs are less desirable; although they may have an effect on depressive or atypical depressive features, results have been inconsistent in the trials conducted so far. If they are used, patients should be carefully monitored for the appearance of increased impulsivity.

Pharmacology of Borderline Personality Disorder: Antipsychotic Agents

Early studies of typical antipsychotic medication use for BPD (see Tables 24.1 and 24.2) have shown global, but modest, improvement in symptoms. Among the symptoms described, improvements have been shown in depression, suicidal ideation, rejection sensitivity, and psychotic-like symptoms, including paranoid ideation, ideas of reference, and derealization. One study also noted an effect for haloperidol in reducing impulsive ward behavior (Soloff et al., 1989).

These studies provide information about the clinical predictors of greater response, which can guide treatment selection for a given patient. Although one study of BPD and SPD subjects found no difference in response to neuroleptics among diagnoses (Serban & Siegel, 1984), another study found that in its sample of BPD and/or SPD subjects, those who did respond to thiothixene were likely to be more severely ill at baseline, with psychoticism, illusions, ideas of reference, phobic anxiety, and obsessive compulsivity (Goldberg et al., 1986). Further, schizotypal symptoms, hostility, and suspiciousness seemed to predict a good response to haloperidol in another study (Soloff et al., 1989). Thus, it may be reasonable to choose an antipsychotic medication for a borderline patient who has a predominance of psychotic-like features, such as transient paranoid ideation. Consideration of extrapyramidal side effects, including tardive dyskinesia, must also be weighed before instituting a trial with these agents.

More recently, several studies have examined the effectiveness of atypical antipsychotic medications, a potentially important class of drugs for this population because of better tolerability and fewer side effects. Olanzapine has now been studied in several randomized, double-blind trials (Soler et al., 2005; Zanarini & Frankenburg, 2001; Zanarini et al., 2004). All of these studies find that olanzapine is effective in treating anger/aggression in BPD, and several studies report that olanzapine treats depression and anxiety as well. Olanzapine also appears to reduce interpersonal sensitivity and paranoia (Zanarini & Frankenburg, 2001). One study found that the combination of olanzapine and fluoxetine was less effective than olanzapine alone in treating the dysthymia characteristic of BPD (Zanarini et al., 2004). All studies reported weight gain with olanzapine, and two recorded mean gains of greater than 6 pounds over a period of 12 weeks. These weight gains are likely to be troublesome to many borderline patients and may reduce their acceptance of the drug. Zanarini et al. (2004) reported less weight gain from olan-

zapine/fluoxetine combined treatment than from olanzapine alone. An open-label, uncontrolled trial of risperidone found it to be effective in reducing hostility, suspicion, and depression in borderline patients and did not report weight gain as a side effect (Rocca, Marchiaro, Cocuzza, & Bogetto, 2002). Recently an open-label trial of quetiapine has reported significant improvement from baseline levels in impulsivity, hostility, anxiety, depression, and social and global functioning, but not hopelessness, in a group of marked to severely symptomatic BPD clinic outpatients (Villeneuve & Lemelin, 2005). The dropout rate was 33%. The patients who dropped out had significantly lower perseverance scores at baseline on the Temperament and Character Inventory (Cloninger et al., 1993).

Two open-label studies have examined the effect of the atypical antipsychotic medication clozapine. In a study of 12 BPD inpatients with severe psychotic-like symptoms (Benedetti et al., 1990), low-dose clozapine treatment was associated with a decrease in psychotic-like symptoms, suicide attempts, physical fights, and depression. A retrospective mirror-image open-label chart review study (Chengappa, Ebeling, Kang, Levine, & Parepally, 1999) of the treatment of seven inpatients meeting criteria for BPD, six of whom had Axis I psychotic disorders, found a decrease in self-mutilation, seclusion, and use of antianxiety medications and an increase in GAF score. It is not possible to determine whether the improvements were due to the effect of clozapine upon BPD or upon the Axis I disorder. Because of the risk of agranulocytosis, it is prudent to reserve trials of clozapine at present for the most severely symptomatic BPD patients who have psychotic symptoms and have not responded to other atypicals.

Pharmacology of Borderline Personality Disorder: Mood-Stabilizing Agents

The prominence of impulsive aggression and mood instability in BPD suggests that mood stabilizers may be valuable treatment options. Lithium has been used to treat aggressive behavior in various patient populations (Wickham & Reed, 1987), and several case reports describe the efficacy of both carbamazepine (CBZ) and divalproex sodium (VPA) for episodic dyscontrol and violence and dyscontrol in organic mental syndromes or dementia (Giakas, Seibyl, & Mazure, 1990; Keck, McElroy, & Friedman, 1992).

Lithium has been shown to decrease irritability, suicidality, and angry behavior, as rated by the treating therapist, in a cohort of borderline subjects (Links et al., 1990). Interestingly, there was a clear trend in this study for lithium to be more effective than desipramine (a noradrenergic agent) in decreasing anger and suicidality, as well as depression.

The use of carbamazepine for patients with behavioral dyscontrol/impulsivity or borderline patients has yielded mixed results in placebo-controlled trials. Carbamazepine has been found to decrease assaultiveness and depression significantly in patients with frontal lobe dysfunction (Foster, Hillbrand, & Chi, 1989) and was initially found to improve impulsivity and behavioral dyscontrol among borderline patients (Cowdry & Gardner, 1988). However, this finding was not replicated in a later study, which suggested that CBZ may have no effect on dyscontrol and may in fact be associated with an increase in impulsive, violent behavior in some borderline subjects (de la Fuente & Lotstra, 1994). In comparison to propranolol, use of CBZ may be associated with a decrease in aggression in patients with intermittent explosive disorder (Mattes, 1990), although both medications tend to lead to fewer aggressive outbursts. In this study, however, subjects also received antipsychotic agents, other anticonvulsants, and antidepressants, limiting the applicability of the findings.

The mood stabilizer most extensively studied in the borderline population is divalproex sodium. An early open-label 8-week trial (Stein, Simeon, Frenkel, Islam, & Hollander, 1995) of divalproex in 11 patients meeting *DSM-III-R* criteria for BPD showed an overall improvement in half of the sample, with modest beneficial effects upon anger, impulsivity, irritability, and rejection sensitivity. A subsequent small, 10-week, double-blind, placebo-controlled study of divalproex sodium (Hollander et al., 2001) found a significant improvement in Clinical Global Impression (CGI) score and Global Assessment Scale (GAS) scores among the 6 patients who completed treatment. The study was limited by the premature dropout of all 4 placebo-treated patients and 50% of the divalproex-treated patients. Impulsiveness in this patient population contributed to the high dropout rate, rather than medication side effects, highlighting the challenge in conducting treatment studies of impulsive patients. A somewhat larger placebo-controlled, double-blind study of female borderline patients with comorbid bipolar disorder (Frankenburg & Zanarini,

2002) found divalproex sodium superior to placebo in reducing anger, hostility, aggression, and interpersonal sensitivity. Because these patients all met criteria for bipolar disorder, it remains unclear whether the divalproex was treating the borderline condition or the bipolar disorder. A recent Type 1 multisite, randomized, double-blind, placebo-controlled study of the efficacy of divalproex sodium in treating aggression in Cluster B personality disorders (including BPD), intermittent explosive disorder, and PTSD represents the largest study of this medication in the treatment of BPD (Hollander et al., 2003). Although no effect of divalproex sodium in reducing aggression was reported for the sample taken as a whole, a post hoc analysis of the 96 Cluster B personality disorder patients (52 of whom met criteria for BPD) showed that divalproex sodium was superior to placebo in reducing aggression, verbal assault, assault against objects, and irritability and in improvement on the clinical global impression severity scale. In this study, too, the dropout rate among the Cluster B personality disorders was close to 50% for both the placebo and divalproex groups. In a post hoc follow-on report, Hollander, Swan, Coccaro, Jiang, and Smith (2005) examined the response of the 52 individuals with BPD in more detail. They found that divalproex sodium was superior to placebo in reducing Overt Aggression Scale aggression score when baseline aggression, impulsiveness, hypomania, and depression were entered as covariates. Moreover, baseline trait impulsivity and state aggression, but not trait aggression or hypomania, predicted treatment response to divalproex sodium.

Two studies of the efficacy of topiramate in female and male BPD patients, respectively, have been reported (Nickel et al., 2004; Nickel et al., 2005). For both female and male patients, topiramate was superior to placebo in reducing state anger, trait anger, and outwardly directed anger and in improving anger control. There was no effect on the tendency to repress anger. Topiramate is an attractive candidate for treating BPD because, unlike many of the other promising medications for BPD, which are associated with weight gain, topiramate was associated with modest weight loss. This should increase its acceptability in this population. A 12-week open-label trial of oxcarbamazepine, a chemical analog of carbamazepine that is less likely to cause blood dyscrasias, autoinduce its own metabolism, or interact with other drugs, found a statistically significant improvement in ratings of impulsivity, anger outbursts, affective instability, interpersonal sensitivity, anxiety, Brief Psychotic Rating Scale (BPRS) score, and Clinical Global Impression-Severity score (Bellino, Paradiso, & Bogetto, 2005; Table 24.3). Twenty-five percent of patients dropped out by the 4th week for noncompliance.

A case report series (Pinto & Akiskal, 1998) describes the open-label use of lamotrigine, the anticonvulsant and putative mood stabilizer, in eight severely disabled BPD patients who did not meet criteria for any concurrent major mood disorder. Three of the eight patients showed a dramatic improvement, with disappearance of suicidal, impulsive, sexual, and drug-taking behaviors, and no longer met BPD criteria at an average follow-up of 1 year. A single randomized, double-blind, placebo-controlled study of lamotrigine in female BPD patients has been reported (Tritt et al., 2005). Lamotrigine was superior to placebo in reducing state anger, trait anger, and outwardly directed anger and in improving anger control and did not cause clinically significant weight gain.

Pharmacotherapy of Borderline Personality Disorder: Novel Agents

Despite evidence of increased noradrenergic activity in irritable or emotionally unstable patients with BPD, there are few BPD treatment studies of medications that directly target this system. One recently reported study examined the acute effect of clonidine, an alpha-2 agonist with peripheral and central activity that reduces norepinephrine release, in 22 female symptomatic borderline inpatients (Philipsen et al., 2004). Patients were instructed to notify staff at times of "strong aversive inner tension," at which point they would be administered clonidine 75 mcg or 150 mcg in a single-blind, randomized design. On the next occasion that they notified staff of high tension, they received 150 mcg or 75 mcg of clonidine, whichever dose they had not received on the first occasion. Self-report ratings of aversive inner tension, the urge to commit self-injurious behavior, dissociative symptoms, and suicidal ideation were obtained prior to drug administration and at 30-minute intervals for the next 2 hours. Repeated measures ANOVAs showed a significant effect for time in all four measures. There was no main effect for dose (75 mcg vs. 150 mcg). Although this study is strongly

limited by the lack of a placebo control or a blind to active treatment, it provides support for further investigation of alpha-2 agonists in the treatment of BPD.

Following reports that omega-3 fatty acids may be effective adjunctive treatments for bipolar disorder or depression, Zanarini and Frankenburg (2003) administered 1,000 mg of the omega-3 fatty acid ethyleicosapentaenoic acid (E-EPA) or placebo in an 8-week randomized, double-blind design to 30 female BPD subjects recruited by newspaper advertisement. E-EPA was superior to placebo at the 8-week point in improvement in scores on the Modified Overt Aggression Sale and the Montgomery-Asberg Depression scale. There were no clinically significant side effects, and 90% of the subjects in both groups completed the study.

Overview of the Pharmacotherapy of Borderline Personality Disorder

In the last several years there has been an advance in the quality of studies of the pharmacotherapy of BPD, with the publication of a body of Type 1 randomized, placebo-controlled, double-blind studies of reliably defined and well-characterized patient populations. Placebo-controlled trials are particularly important in this area because of the high placebo response rate of borderline patients.

Strong evidence is emerging that supports the efficacy of the atypical antipsychotic medication olanzapine in reducing anger, impulsivity/aggression, possibly depression, and interpersonal sensitivity. Unfortunately, weight gain with this medication may be problematic for some patients and may affect patient acceptability. Dropout rates tend to be high but are similar in both olanzapine and placebo groups, suggesting that dropping out has less to do with side effects than with personality characteristics such as perseverance or a tendency to somatize. Although there are no placebo-controlled, double-blind studies of other atypicals, open-label trials of risperidone and quetiapine suggest they may have similar efficacy.

Anticonvulsant mood stabilizers also appear to be quite promising. Two double-blind, placebo-controlled studies and two additional studies lacking analyzable placebo groups demonstrate the efficacy of divalproex sodium in reducing anger and impulsivity/aggression. One double-blind study (Frankenburg & Zanarini, 2002) also found divalproex superior to placebo in reducing interpersonal sensitivity,

TABLE 24.3 Pharmacology of Borderline Personality Disorder: Mood Stabilizers/Anticonvulsants

Study	Diagnosis	Study Design	Comment
Sheard et al. (1976)	N= 66, inmates characterized by extreme impulsivity, aggression, and hostility	Type 2 study: lithium vs. placebo	Decrease in number of major prison infractions.
Links et al. (1990)	N = 15 BPD	Type 1 study: lithium vs. desipramine; double-blind, placebo controlled	Lithium led to decrease in therapist's perception of patient irritability, anger, and suicidal symptoms; trend for desipramine to have no effect or to worsen symptoms of anger/suicide and to be less effective than lithium in decreasing depression scores.
Hollander et al. (2001)	N = 16 BPD patients referred clinically and from advertisements	Type 2 study: divalproex (mean blood level 64.6) 10-week randomized double-blind placebo-controlled	50% dropout rate in divalproex group, 100% in placebo group; among completers 5/6 were responders based on CGI.
Frankenburg & Zanarini (2002)	N = 20 female BPD patients who also met *DSM-IV* criteria for bipolar II disorder	Type 2 study: divalproex (mean dose 850 mg/day); 6-month randomized double-blind placebo-controlled	Divalproex superior to placebo for SCL-90 anger/hostility and interpersonal sensitivity and MOAS aggression; 50% dropout in divalproex group by week 12.
Hollander et al. (2003, 2005)	N = 96 Cluster B personality disorder patients (including 52 with BPD); *n* = 34 PTSD and *n* = 116 IED patients	Type 1: divalproex (mean dose 1,404 mg, blood level 65.5); randomized multicenter 12-week double-blind placebo-controlled	For Cluster B, divalproex superior to placebo in OAS-M aggression, verbal assault, assault against objects, assault against others, irritability scales, and CGI-S; no significant effect of diavalproex on aggression for the IED or PTSD patients.
Nickel et al. (2004)	N = 29 female BPD patients recruited by advertisement who had subjective feelings of "constantly increasing anger"	Type 1: topiramate (dose titrated to 250 mg/day by week 6); 8-week randomized double-blind placebo-controlled	Topiramate superior to placebo on STAXI anger-out, anger-control, state anger, and trait anger, but not anger-in scales.
Nickel et al. (2005)	N = 42 male BPD patients meeting criteria of Nickel et al., 2004, above	Type 1: topiramate same as Nickel et al., 2004, above	Topirimate superior to placebo on STAXI anger-out, anger-control, state anger, and trait anger, but not anger-in scales.
Tritt et al. (2005)	N = 24 female BPD patients	Type 2: lamotrigine 8-week double-blind placebo-controlled	Lamotrigine superior to placebo on STAXI anger-out, anger-control, state anger, and trait anger, but not anger-in scales.
Bellino et al. (2005)	N = 17 clinic outpatients meeting criteria for BPD	Type 3: oxcarbamazepine (mean dose 1,315 mg) 12-week open-label design	Repeated measures ANOVA showed significant improvement in impulsivity, affective instability, anger outbursts, interpersonal sensitivity, anxiety, CGI-S, but not depression or social-occupational functioning.

CGI-S = Clinical Global Impression-Severity; IED = Intermittent Explosive Disorder; OAS-M = Overt Aggression Scale Modified; PTSD = posttraumatic stress disorder; STAXI = State-Trait Anger Expression Inventory.

but not in reducing depression. Two double-blind, placebo-controlled studies show efficacy for topiramate, and one similar study by the same group shows efficacy for lamotrigine in reducing outwardly directed anger and state and trait anger and enhancing anger control. Topiramate may have particularly high patient acceptability because it is not associated with weight gain, but rather with modest weight loss.

Although there is empirical support for the use of SSRIs in treating BPD, only three Type 1 randomized, double-blind, placebo-controlled studies of a pure well-defined BPD population have been published, and they show some conflicting findings. One study, in which all subjects received concurrent psychotherapy (DBT), showed no increased benefit from the addition of an SSRI over placebo (Simpson et al., 2004). One study found an improvement in affective instability, but not in anger or impulsivity (Rinne et al., 2002), and the remaining study found that the SSRI reduced aggression and irritability but not depression or suicidality (New et al., 2004). Additional studies in this area are needed.

CLUSTER C (ANXIOUS CLUSTER)

The psychobiology of anxiety (Cluster C) has been investigated in greater depth recently. The guiding principle for much of the research is the assumption that the biological factors regulating anxiety provide a common basis for the anxiety spectrum disorders, superseding Axis I and Axis II distinctions.

This assumption is supported by the comorbidity seen clinically between avoidant personality disorder (APD) and social phobia (SP). A number of authors have demonstrated that there are high rates of association between these two disorders (Schneier, Spitzer, & Gibbon, 1991; Stein & Hollander, 1993). Specifically, generalized social phobia, which involves pervasive fear in most social situations, is felt to be more closely linked to APD than discrete social phobia, which involves fear in one or two specific social situations. One recent study of 50 patients diagnosed with SP found rates of APD in 89% of patients diagnosed with generalized social phobia (Schneier et al., 1991). Some investigators feel that these findings suggest that APD and SP are variations of a similar underlying pathophysiology.

Thus, a review of the psychobiology of anxiety spectrum personality disorders may be best represented by studies of SP and APD. Early studies have

established the role of the noradrenergic system in arousal and anxiety. Investigations of the growth hormone (GH) response to clonidine, a marker of postsynaptic alpha-2-adrenergic function, have consistently shown a blunted GH response in panic disorder patients (Uhde, 1994). A logical outgrowth of these findings was to study the clonidine-GH response in patients with social phobia. Two studies, one using intravenous clonidine and one using oral clonidine, found contrasting results. The first study of GH response to intravenous clonidine in normal controls, SP, and panic disorder patients found significant blunting in SP patients compared with normal controls. There was no difference in the blunting between SP subjects and the panic disorder group (Uhde, 1994). The second study found no GH response difference for 21 subjects with SP when compared with 22 healthy controls in a double-blind, placebo-controlled study (Tancer, 1993). Thus, replication studies are needed to establish whether the clonidine-GH response is an index of abnormal noradrenergic activity in social phobia.

There have been few other positive findings with the use of chemical probes or challenge studies to define a biological basis for social phobia. Studies using lactic acid, norepinephrine, and caffeine (chosen because of their use as chemical probes in panic disorder) failed to induce symptoms of social phobia in patients with social phobia (Tancer, 1993). Investigations into the hypothalamic-pituitary-adrenal axis, via measures of urinary free cortisol and response to the dexamethasone suppression test, showed no abnormalities (Uhde, 1994). Challenge studies examining neurotransmitter systems revealed no abnormality in prolactin response to l-dopamine or fenfluramine; however, an increased cortisol response to fenfluramine differentiated social phobia patients from normal controls in one study (Uhde, 1994). Thus, the serotonergic system may play a role in the etiology of fear and avoidance responses of SP subjects. Interestingly, in contrast to impulsive borderline patients, avoidant personality-disordered patients demonstrate some suggestions of increased serotonergic activity and reduced noradrenergic activity.

Pharmacotherapy Trials for Social Phobia and Avoidant Personality Disorder

There have been few pharmacotherapy trials involving the anxious cluster disorders. A limited number of controlled studies have looked at avoidant personality traits in patients with SP, whereas the use of medications for APD alone has been documented only in reports. Several medications have been tested and shown to be effective for social phobia, including MAOIs, the benzodiazepine clonazepam, and antidepressants. Among the latter, paroxetine, sertraline, and extended-release venlafaxine are approved by the Food and Drug Administration for the treatment of social phobia.

Case reports have described the usefulness of the MAOIs phenelzine and tranylcypromine for subjects with APD: After 4 to 6 weeks of treatment, patients experienced marked improvements in their abilities to socialize. These gains were maintained at a 1-year follow-up when the patients continued to take the medications (Deltito & Stamm, 1989). Two case reports document the efficacy of fluoxetine for APD (Deltito & Stamm, 1989; Goldman & Grinspoon, 1990). Within several weeks of initiating treatment, subjects reported decreases in social sensitivity and improvements in socialization, self-confidence, and assertiveness. Further controlled studies with well-defined groups of APD and other anxious cluster subjects are needed to establish the clinical indications for pharmacotherapy in this group of patients.

CONCLUSION

The search for pharmacological treatments for personality-disordered patients has led to an exciting expansion of our views of the Axis II disorders. Attempts to find a biological dimension that could be targeted by such treatments have enhanced the notion of a fluid boundary between Axis I and Axis II symptomatology. Future research should be aimed toward clearer descriptions, either categorically or psychobiologically, of personality disorders. Although further controlled clinical trials are needed to create and test hypotheses concerning the efficacy of medications in these disorders, evidence is emerging that medications have a valuable role in the treatment of borderline, schizotypal, and avoidant personality disorders. By the same token, it appears that the role of medication is limited, since the degree of improvement associated with the addition of medication is moderate and is typically limited to some but not all of the symptom domains of the disorder. In addition, securing long-term medication compliance is often a challenge in the personality disorder population.

Finally, there is a great need to examine the role of medications in the many personality disorders that that have not yet been studied.

REFERENCES

American Psychiatric Association. (1994). *Diagnostic and statistical manual of mental disorders* (4th ed.). Washington, DC: Author.

Baron, M., Gruen, R., & Asnis, L. (1985). Familial transmission of schizotypal and borderline personality disorders. *American Journal of Psychiatry, 142,* 927–933.

Bellino, S., Paradiso, E., & Bogetto, F. (2005). Oxcarbamazepine in the treatment of borderline personality disorder: A pilot study. *Journal of Clinical Psychiatry, 66,* 1111–1115.

Benedetti, F., Sforzini, L., Coccaro, E. F., Astill, J. L., Herbert, J. A., et al. (1990). Fluoxetine treatment of impulsive aggression in *DSM-III-R* personality disorder patients. *Journal of Clinical Psychopharmacology, 10,* 373–375.

Brown, G. L., Ebert, M. H., Goyer, P. F., et al. (1982). Aggression, suicide and serotonin: Relationships to CSF amine metabolites. *American Journal of Psychiatry, 139,* 741–746.

Chengappa, K. N. R., Ebeling, T., Kang, J. S., Levine, J., & Parepally, H. (1999). Clozapine reduces severe self-mutilation and aggression in psychotic patients with borderline personality disorder. *Journal of Clinical Psychiatry, 60,* 477–484.

Cloninger, C. R., Svrakic, D. M., & Przybeck, T. R. (1993). A psychobiological model of temperament and character. *Archives of General Psychiatry, 50,* 975–990.

Coccaro, E. F., & Kavoussi, R. J. (1995, May). *Fluoxetine in aggression in personality disorders* [New research abstracts]. Presented at the 148th annual meeting of the American Psychiatric Association, Miami, Florida.

Coccaro, E. F., Lawrence, T., Trestman, R. L., et al. (1991). Growth hormone response to IV clonidine challenge correlates with behavioral irritability in psychiatric patients and healthy volunteers. *Psychiatric Research, 39,* 129–139.

Coccaro, E. F., & Siever, L. J. (1995). The neuropsychopharmacology of personality disorders. In F. E. Bloom & D. J. Kupfer (Eds.), *Psychopharmacology: The fourth generation of progress.* New York: Raven Press.

Cornelius, J. R., Brenner, R. P., Soloff, P. H., Schulz, S. C., & Tumuluru, R. V. (1986). EEG abnormalities in borderline personality disorder: Specific or nonspecific? *Biological Psychiatry, 21,* 977–980.

Cornelius, J. R., Soloff, P. H., Perel, J. M., & Ulrich, R. F. (1991). A preliminary trial of fluoxetine in refractory borderline patients. *Journal of Clinical Psychopharmacology, 11,* 116–120.

Cowdry, R. W., & Gardner, D. L. (1988). Pharmacotherapy of borderline personality disorder: Alprazolam, carbamazepine, trifluoperazine, and tranylcypromine. *Archives of General Psychiatry, 45,* 111–119.

de la Fuente, J. M., & Lotstra, F. (1994). A trial of carbamazepine in borderline personality disorder. *European Neuropsychopharmacology, 4,* 479–486.

Deltito, J. A., & Stamm, M. (1989). Psychopharmacological treatment of avoidant personality disorder. *Comprehensive Psychiatry, 30,* 498–504.

Drake, M. E., Hietter, S. A., & Pakalnis, A. (1992). EEG and evoked potentials in episodic- dyscontrol syndrome. *Neuropsychobiology, 26,* 125–128.

Foster, H. G., Hillbrand, M., & Chi, C. C. (1989). Efficacy of carbamazepine in assaultive patients with frontal lobe dysfunction. *Progress in Neuropsychopharmacology and Biological Psychiatry, 13,* 865–874.

Frankenburg, F. R., Zanarini, M. C. (2002). Divalproex sodium treatment of women with borderline personality disorder and bipolar II disorder: A double-blind placebo-controlled pilot study. *Journal of Clinical Psychiatry, 63,* 442–446.

Franowicz, J. S., & Arnsten, A. F. (2002). Actions of alpha-2 noradrenergic agonists on spatial working memory and blood pressure in rhesus monkeys appear to be mediated by the same receptor subtype. *Psychopharmacology (Berlin), 162,* 304–312.

Giakas, W. J., Seibyl, J. P., & Mazure, C. M. (1990). Valproate in the treatment of temper outbursts. *Journal of Clinical Psychiatry, 51,* 525.

Gitlin, M. J. (1993). Pharmacotherapy of personality disorders: Conceptual framework and clinical strategies. *Journal of Clinical Psychopharmacology, 13,* 343–353.

Goldberg, S., Schulz, S., et al. (1986). Borderline and schizotypal personality disorder treatment with low-dose thiothixene versus placebo. *Archives of General Psychiatry, 43,* 680–686.

Goldman, M. J., & Grinspoon, L. (1990). Ritualistic use of fluoxetine by a former substance abuser. *American Journal of Psychiatry, 147,* 1377.

Gurvits, I. G., Koenigsberg, H. W., & Siever, L. J. (2000). Neurotransmitter dysfunction in patients with borderline personality disorder. *Psychiatric Clinics of North America, 23,* 27–40.

Hollander, E., Allen, A., Lopez, R. P., Bienstock, C. A., Grossman, R., Siever, L. J., et al. (2001). A preliminary double-blind, placebo-controlled trial of dival-proax sodium in borderline personality disorder. *Journal of Clinical Psychiatry, 62,* 199–203.

Hollander, E., Swann, A. C., Coccaro, E. F., Jiang, P., & Smith, T. B. (2005). Impact of trait impulsivity and state aggression on divalproex versus placebo response in borderline personality disorder. *American Journal of Psychiatry, 162,* 621–624.

Hollander, E., Tracy, K. A., Swann, A. C., Coccaro, E. F., McElroy, S. L., Wozniak, P., et al. (2003). Divalproex in the treatment of impulsive aggression: Efficacy in Cluster B personality disorders. *Neuropsychopharmacology, 28,* 1186–1197.

Hyler, S. E., Skodol, A. E., Kellman, H. D., Oldham, J. M., & Rosnick, L. (1990). Validity of Personality Diagnostic Questionnaire-Revised: Comparison with two structured interviews. *American Journal of Psychiatry, 147,* 1043–1048.

Hymowitz, P., Frances, A., Jacobsberg, L. B., et al. (1986). Neuroleptic treatment of schizotypal personality disorder. *Comprehensive Psychiatry, 27,* 267–271.

Javitt, D. C. (1999). Treatment of negative and cognitive symptoms. *Current Psychiatry Reports, 1,* 25–30.

Jensen, H. V., & Andersen, J. (1989). An open, noncomparative study of amoxapine in borderline disorders. *Acta Psychiatrica Scandinavica, 79,* 89–93.

Kaplan, H. I., & Sadock, B. J. (Eds.). (1995). *Comprehensive textbook of psychiatry* (Vol. 6). Baltimore: Williams and Wilkins.

Karson, C. N., Casanova, M. F., Kleinman, J. E., & Griffin, W. S. (1993). Choline acetyltransferase in schizophrenia. *American Journal of Psychiatry, 150,* 454–459.

Kavoussi, R. J., & Coccaro, E. R. (1993). The amphetamine challenge test correlates with affective lability in healthy volunteers. *Psychiatry Research, 48,* 219–228.

Keck, P. E., McElroy, S. L., & Friedman, L. M. (1992). Valproate and carbamazepine in the treatment of panic and posttraumatic stress disorders, withdrawal states, and behavioral dyscontrol syndromes. *Journal of Clinical Psychopharmacology, 12*(Suppl.), 36–41.

Kirrane, R. M., & Siever, L. J. (2000). New perspectives on schizotypal personality disorder. *Current Psychiatry Reports, 2,* 62–66.

Koenigsberg, H. W., Anwunah, I., New, A. S., Mitropoulou, V., Schopick, F., & Siever, L.J. (1999). Relationship between depression and borderline personality disorder. *Depression and Anxiety, 10,* 158–167.

Koenigsberg, H. W., Buchsbaum, M. S., Buchsbaum, B. R., Schneiderman, J. S., Tang, C. Y., New, A. S., et al. (2005). Functional MRI of visuospatial working memory in schizotypal personality disorder: A region-of-interest analysis. *Psychological Medicine, 35,* 1019–1030.

Koenigsberg, H. W., Reynolds, D., Goodman, M., New, A. S., Mitropoulou, V., Trestman, R. L., et al. (2003). Risperidone in the treatment of schizotypal personality disorder. *Journal of Clinical Psychiatry, 64,* 628–634.

Lane, H. Y., Liu, C. C., & Chang, W. H. (1999). Risperidone for exclusively negative symptoms. *American Journal of Psychiatry, 156,* 1999.

Links, P. S., Steiner, M., Boiago, I., & Irwin, D. (1990). Lithium therapy for borderline patients: Preliminary findings. *Journal of Personality Disorders, 4,* 173–181.

Markovitz, P. J., Calabrese, J. U., Schulz, S. C., & Meltzer, H. Y. (1991). Fluoxetine in the treatment of borderline and schizotypal personality disorders. *American Journal of Psychiatry, 148,* 1064–1067.

Mattes, J. A. (1990). Comparative effectiveness of carbamazepine and propranolol for rage outbursts. *Journal of Neuropsychiatry and Clinical Neuroscience, 2,* 159–164.

Montgomery, S. A., Montgomery, D. B., Green, M., Bullock, T., & Baldwin, D. (1992). Pharmacotherapy in the prevention of suicidal behavior. *Journal of Clinical Psychopharmacology, 12*(Suppl.), 27S–31S.

New, A. S., Buchsbaum, M. S., Hazlett, E. A., Goodman, M., Koenigsberg, H. W., Lo, J., et al. (2004). Fluoxetine increases relative metabolic rate in prefrontal cortex in impulsive aggression. *Psychopharmacology (Berlin) 176,* 451–458.

New, A. S., Hazlett, E. A., Buchsbaum, M. S., Goodman, M., Reynolds, D., Mitropoulou, V., et al. (2002). Blunted prefrontal cortical 18fluorodeoxyglucose positron emission tomography response to meta-chlorophenylpiperazine in impulsive aggression. *Archives of General Psychiatry, 59,* 621–629.

Nickel, M. K., Nickel, C., Kaplan, P., Lahmann, C., Muhlbacher, M., Tritt, K., et al. (2005). Treatment of aggression with topiramate in male borderline patients: A double-blind, placebo-controlled study. *Biological Psychiatry, 57,* 495–499.

Nickel, M. K., Nickel, C., Mitterlehner, F. O., Tritt, K., Lahmann, C., Leiberich, P. K., et al. (2004). Topiramate treatment of aggression in female borderline personality disorder patients: A double-blind, placebo-controlled study. *Journal of Clinical Psychiatry, 65,* 1515–1519.

Norden, M. J. (1989). Fluoxetine in borderline personality disorder. *Progress in Neuropsychopharmacology and Biological Psychiatry, 13,* 885–893.

Parsons, B., Quitkin, F. M., McGrath, P. J, Stewart, J. W., Tricamo, E., Ocepek-Welikson, K., et al. (1989). Phenelzine, imipramine, and placebo in borderline patients meeting criteria for atypical depression. *Psychopharmacology Bulletin, 25,* 524–534.

Philipsen, A., Richter, H., Schmahl, C., Peters, J., Rusch, N., Bohus, M. et al. (2004). Clonidine in acute aversive inner tension and self-injurious behavior in female patients with borderline personality disorder. *Journal of Clinical Psychiatry, 65,* 1414–1419.

Pinto, O. C., & Akiskal, H. S. (1998). Lamotrigine as a promising approach to borderline personality: An open case series without concurrent *DSM-IV* major mood disorder. *Journal of Affective Disorders, 51,* 333–343.

Rinne, T., van den Brink, W., Wouters, L., & van Dyck, R. (2002). SSRI treatment of borderline personality disorder: A randomized, placebo-controlled clinical trial for female patients with borderline personality disorder. *American Journal of Psychiatry, 159,* 2048–2054.

Rocca, P., Marchiaro, L., Cocuzza, E., & Bogetto, F. (2002). Treatment of borderline personality disorder with risperidone. *Journal of Clinical Psychiatry, 63,* 241–244.

Roy, A., De Jon, J., & Linnoila, M. (1989). Extroversion in pathological gamblers correlates with indices of noradrenergic function. *Archives of General Psychiatry, 46,* 679–681.

Salzman, C., Wolfson, A. N., Schatzberg, A., Looper, J., Henke, R., Albanese, M., et al. (1995). Effects of fluoxetine on anger in symptomatic volunteers with borderline personality disorder. *Journal of Clinical Psychopharmacology, 15,* 23–29.

Schneier, F. R., Spitzer, R. L., & Gibbon, M. (1991). The relationship of social phobia subtypes and avoidant personality disorder. *Comprehensive Psychiatry, 32,* 496–502.

Schulz, S. C., Camlin, K. L., Berry, S. A., & Jesberger, J. A. (1999). Olanzapine safety and efficacy in patients with borderline personality disorder and comorbid dysthymia. *Biological Psychiatry, 4,* 1429–1435.

Schulz, S. C., Cornelius, J, Schulz, P. M., & Soloff, P. H. (1988). The amphetamine challenge test in patients with borderline personality disorder. *American Journal of Psychiatry, 145,* 809–814.

Serban, G., & Siegel, S. (1984). Response of borderline and schizotypal patients to small doses of thiothixene and haloperidol. *American Journal of Psychiatry, 141,* 1455–1458.

Sheard, M. J., Marini, J. L., Bridges, C. I., & Wagner, E. (1976). The effect of lithium on impulsive aggressive behavior in man. *American Journal of Psychiatry*, *133*, 1409–1413.

Siever, L. J. (1991). The biology of the boundaries of schizophrenia. In C. A. Tamminga & S. C. Schulz (Eds.), *Schizophrenia: Advances in neuropsychiatry and neuropsychopharmacology: Vol. 4, Schizophrenia research*. New York: Raven Press.

Siever, L. J. (1995). Brain structure/function and the dopamine system in schizotypal personality disorder. *Schizotypal Personality*, *12*, 272–286.

Siever, L. J., Amin, F., Coccaro, E. F., et al. (1991). Plasma HVA in schizotypal personality disorders. *American Journal of Psychiatry*, *148*, 1246–1248.

Siever L. J., Buchsbaum, M. S., New, A. S. Spiegel-Cohen, J., Wei, T., Hazlett, E. A., et al. (1999): d,1-fenfluramine response in impulsive personality disorder assessed with [18F]flourodeoxyglucose positron emission tomography. *Neuropsychopharmacology*, *20*, 413–423.

Siever, L. J., & Davis, K. L. (1991). A psychobiological perspective on the personality disorders. *American Journal of Psychiatry*, *148*, 1647–1658.

Siever, L. J., Kalus, O. F., & Keefe, R. S. (1993). The boundaries of schizophrenia. *Psychiatric Clinics of North America*, *16*, 217–244.

Siever, L. J., Koenigsberg, H. W., Harvey, P., Mitropoulou, V., Laruelle, M., Abi-Dargham, A., et al. (2002). Cognitive and brain function in schizotypal personality disorder. *Schizophrenia Research*, *54*, 157–167.

Silverman, J. M., & Pinkham, L. (1991). Affective and impulsive personality disorder traits in the relatives of patients with borderline personality disorder. *American Journal of Psychiatry*, *148*, 1378–1385.

Silverman, J. M., Siever, L. J., Horvath, T. B., Coccaro, E. F., Klar, H., Davidson, M., et al. (1993). Schizophrenia related and affective personality disorder traits in relatives of probands with schizophrenia and personality disorders. *American Journal of Psychiatry*, *150*, 435–442.

Simpson, E. B., Yen, S., Costello, E., Rosen, K., Begin, A., Pistorello, J., et al. (2004). Combined dialectical behavior therapy and fluoxetine in the treatment of borderline personality disorder. *Journal of Clinical Psychiatry*, *65*, 379–385.

Skodol, A. E., Gunderson, J. G., Pfohl, B., Widiger, T. A., Livesley, W. J., & Siever, L. J. (2002). The borderline diagnosis I: Psychopathology, comorbidity, and personality structure. *Biological Psychiatry*, *5*, 936–950.

Soler, J., Pascual, J. C., Campins, J., Barrachina, J., Puigdemont, D., Alvarez, E., et al. (2005). Double-blind, placebo-controlled study of dialectical behavior therapy plus olanzapine for borderline personality disorder. *American Journal of Psychiatry*, *162*, 1221–1224.

Soloff, P. H., Corneluis, J. R., George, A., Nathan, S., Perel, M. J., & Ulrich, R. F. (1993). Efficacy of phenelzine and haloperidol in borderline personality disorder. *Archives of General Psychiatry*, *50*, 377–385.

Soloff, P. H., George, A., Nathan, R. S., Schulz, P. M., & Percel, J. M. (1986). Paradoxical effects of amitriptyline in borderline patients. *American Journal of Psychiatry*, *143*, 1603–1605.

Soloff, P. H., George, A., Nathan, R. S., Schulz, P. M., Covnelius, J. R., Herring, J., et al. (1989). Amitriptyline versus haloperidol in borderlines: Final outcomes and predictors of response. *Journal of Clinical Psychopharmacology*, *9*, 238–246.

Soloff, P. H., Meltzer, C. C., Greer, P. J., Constantine, D., & Kelly, T. M. (2000). A fenfluramine-activated FDG-PET study of borderline personality disorder. *Biological Psychiatry*, *47*, 540–547.

Southwick, S. M., Yehuda, R., Giller, E. L., Jr., & Perry, B. D. (1990). Altered platelet alpha 2-adrenergic receptor binding sites in borderline personality disorder. *American Journal of Psychiatry*, *147*, 1014–1017.

Stein, D. J., & Hollander, E. (1993). Anxiety disorders and personality disorders. *Journal of Personality Disorders*, *7*, 87–104.

Stein, D. J., Hollander, E., Cohen, L., & Frenkel, M. (1993). Neuropsychiatric impairment in impulsive personality disorders. *Psychiatry Research*, *48*, 257–266.

Stein, D. J., Simeon, D., Frenkel, M., Islam, M., & Hollander, E. (1995). An open trial of valproate in borderline personality disorder. *Journal of Clinical Psychiatry*, *56*, 506–510.

Steinberg, B. J., Trestman, R., Mitropolous, V., Serby, M., Silverman, J., Coccaro, E., et al. (1997). Depressive response to physostigmine challenge in borderline personality disorder patients. *Neuropsychopharmacology*, *17*, 264–273.

Steinberg, B. J., Trestman, R. L., & Siever, L. J. (1994). The cholinergic and noradrenergic neurotransmitter systems: Affective instability in borderline personality disorder. In K. R. Silk (Ed.), *Biological and neurobehavioral studies in borderline personality disorder* (pp. 41–62). Washington, DC: American Psychiatric Association.

Tancer, M. E. (1993). Neurobiology of social phobia. *Journal of Clinical Psychiatry*, *54*(Suppl.), 26–30.

Tandon, R., & Greden, J. F. (1989). Cholinergic hyperactivity and negative schizophrenic symptoms: A model of cholinergic/dopaminergic interactions in schizophrenia. *Archives of General Psychiatry, 46,* 745–753.

Torgersen, S. (1992, December). *The genetic transmission of borderline personality features displays multidimensionality* [New abstracts]. Presented at the annual meeting of the American College of Neuropsychopharmacology, San Juan, Puerto Rico.

Torgersen, S., Lygren, S., Oien, P. A., Skre, I., Onstad, S., Edvardsen, J., et al. (2000). A twin study of personality disorders. *Comprehensive Psychiatry, 41,* 416–425.

Trestman, R. L., deVegvar, M., & Siever, L. J. (1995). Treatment of personality disorders. In C. B. Nemeroff & A. F. Schatzberg (Eds.), *The APA textbook of psychopharmacology.* Washington, DC: American Psychiatric Press.

Tritt, K., Nickel, C., Lahmann, C., Leiberiche, P. K., Rother, W. K., Loew, T. H., et al. (2005). Lamotrigine treatment of aggression in female borderlinepatients: A randomized, double-blind, placebo-controlled study. *Journal of Psychopharmacology, 1,* 287–291.

Uhde, T. W. (1994). A review of biological studies in social phobia. *Journal of Clinical Psychiatry, 55* (Suppl.), 17–27.

Villeneuve, E., & Lemelin, S. (2005). Open-label study of atypical neuroleptic quetiapine for treatment of borderline personality disorder: Impulsivity as main target. *Journal of Clinical Psychiatry, 66,* 1298–1303.

Wickham, E. A., & Reed, J. V. (1987). Lithium for the control of aggressive and self-mutilating behaviour. *International Clinical Psychopharmacology, 2,* 181–190.

Zanarini, M. C., & Frankenburg, F. R. (2001). Olanzapine treatment of female borderline personality disorder patients: A double-blind, placebo-controlled pilot study. *Journal of Clinical Psychiatry, 62,* 849–854.

Zanarini, M. C., & Frankenburg, F. R. (2003). Omega-3 fatty acid treatment of women with borderline personality disorder: A double-blind, placebo-controlled pilot study. *American Journal of Psychiatry, 160,* 167–169.

Zanarini, M. C., Frankenburg, F. R., & Parachini, E. A. (2004). A preliminary, randomized trial of fluoxetine, olanzapine, and the olanzapine-fluoxetine combination in women with borderline personality disorder. *Journal of Clinical Psychiatry, 65,* 903–907.

25

Combination Pharmacotherapy and Psychotherapy for the Treatment of Major Depressive and Anxiety Disorders

Cindy J. Aaronson

Gary P. Katzman

Jack M. Gorman

Numerous randomized clinical trials (RCTs) have compared the effectiveness of pharmacotherapy to psychosocial treatments for major depressive disorder (MDD) and the anxiety disorders, yet there are far fewer comparing the combination of medication and psychosocial treatments to each treatment individually. Clinical wisdom suggests that combining two efficacious treatments would be superior to either treatment alone. The few data that have been gathered employing RCTs for MDD and for anxiety disorders do not completely support that assertion. A review of RCTs conducted since 1990 in which monotherapy is compared with combined treatment for MDD has shown that combined treatment is more effective than either individual treatment for the chronically and recurrently depressed patients. Overall, in the anxiety disorders, there are no data supporting the superiority of combined treatment over either individual treatment with the exception of studies involving adolescents and children.

Clinical wisdom and intuition suggest that when treating major depression and/or anxiety disorders, combining two documented efficacious treatments such as antidepressants and psychotherapy would improve outcome. However, the data do not completely support this conclusion. In this chapter we review randomized clinical trials (RCTs) comparing combined pharmacotherapy and psychotherapy with monotherapy for the treatment of major depressive disorder (MDD), panic disorder (PD), obsessive-compulsive disorder (OCD), posttraumatic stress disorder (PTSD), generalized anxiety disorder (GAD), and social anxiety disorder (SAD) in adults.

MAJOR DEPRESSIVE DISORDER

The research literature on MDD is divided into three types of studies: acute treatment of nonspecific MDD, acute treatment of specific groups such as the chronically depressed or the elderly, and relapse prevention or maintenance therapy. There are four review articles of RCTs of combined treatment for MDD since 1997 (Arnow & Constantino, 2003; Hegerl, Plattner, & Möller, 2004; Pampallona, Bollini, Tibaldi, Kupelnick, & Munizza, 2004; Segal, Vincent, & Levitt, 2002) and one meta-analysis (Thase et al., 1997), which conclude that combined treatment is superior to monotherapy for the severely and chronically depressed. Hegerl and colleagues (2004) determined that reviews of studies published before the 1990s are based on small sample sizes that limit the generalizability to other populations, so in their review they included only studies published since 1990.

Acute Treatment for Unspecified Depression

An acute treatment study for nonspecific MDD was conducted by Hollan and colleagues (1992) on 107 outpatients. They compared imipramine with CBT and their combination for 12 weeks. The results were that all groups showed significant symptom reduction on the Hamilton Rating Scale for Depression (HRSD), but there were no differences in response between combination and each single treatment. It is difficult to interpret these results because only 64 of the 107 subjects completed the treatment, and no intent-to-treat analysis was performed. The overall attrition rate was 40%, without any mention of breakdown by group. Perhaps the high attrition rate was due to the side effects of imipramine.

In a European trial comparing amitriptyline with clinical management, CBT alone, and the combination of CBT and amitriptyline for 8 weeks, Hautzinger, deJong-Meyer, and Treiber (1996) studied 191 inpatients and outpatients. Their results were based on an intent-to-treat analysis with a 30% dropout rate, which was seen more frequently in the amitriptyline-only group. Dropouts occurred least frequently in the CBT-alone group, significantly later in the study (during the follow-up period) than in the combination group. Hautzinger's group only found a trend toward combination treatment demonstrating a higher response than either single modality alone.

We include one study that compared the tricyclic clomipramine with psychodynamic psychotherapy (Burnand, Andreoli, Kolatte, Venturini, & Rosset, 2002) in 95 patients (aged 20 to 65) recruited from a community mental health center. The patients (45 females, mean age 36, mean HRSD score 24) were randomly assigned to clomipramine alone ($n = 48$) or to combined medication with psychodynamic psychotherapy ($n = 47$). More than half the participants had a previous MDD episode, and 46% had a personality disorder (although it was not stated how this was diagnosed). Of the initial 95 who were randomized, 74 completed the study (22% dropout rate, 12 in the combined group and 9 in the clomipramine-only group). The psychotherapy lasted 10 weeks, conducted by nurses with 5 years' experience working with depressed patients, and covered therapeutic alliance, past and current crises, conflict resolution especially of those involving disruptions of emotional bonds, maladaptive interpersonal relationships, and attachment style. The therapists were supervised weekly by a psychoanalyst. Results showed that the combined group had significantly lower HRSD scores at 10 weeks and less treatment failure. The combined

group had a lower hospitalization rate and spent fewer days in the hospital than the medication-only group.

A recent Amsterdam study (Dekker et al., 2005) randomized 103 depressed outpatients to one of two conditions: medication and 8 or 16 weeks of psychodynamic supportive psychotherapy. The medication treatment included fluoxetine (20 mg/day) that could then be changed to nortriptyline (50 mg/day up to 150 mg/day) if fluoxetine was not tolerated or was ineffective. A further medication switch was allowed to mirtazapine (15 mg/day up to 45 mg/day) if nortriptyline was either intolerable or ineffective. All medications were maintained for 6 months. The short-term psychotherapy was based on treatment guidelines. Adherence was measured by review of audiotape sessions.

Measures used to determine outcome were the Hamilton Rating Scale for Depression (HRSD), the Clinical Global Impression (CGI), the Symptom Checklist (SCL-90), and the Quality of Life Depression Scale. All subjects were moderately depressed with a history of previous depressive episodes, and no current episode lasting longer than 2 years. Although the results showed that both treatments were effective in reducing symptoms over 6 months, the 8-session group achieved remission faster than the 16-session group. There are several limitations to this study, but the most important one is the lack of a control group. Both groups received medication and the same type of psychotherapy, only varying in the duration of treatment. It is difficult to determine how much improvement would be accounted for by the medication and how much by the psychotherapy, since medications were changed for efficacy or intolerance. This study was included in this review because the flexibility of medication treatment more closely resembles clinical practice than usual RCTs and may provide some usefulness to clinicians.

Another Dutch group (de Jonghe, Kool, van Aalst, Dekker, & Peen, 2001) conducted an earlier study comparing pharmacotherapy alone to the combination of pharmacotherapy and short-term psychodynamic supportive psychotherapy (SPSP) in 167 MDD patients. Most of the patients had been depressed for less than 2 years, and just fewer than half were recurrently depressed. The medication protocol was similar to that of the Dekker study in which patients were first treated with a fixed dose of fluoxetine, then switched to amitriptyline at a flexible dose if fluoxetine was found to be intolerable or ineffective, then to a flexible dose of moclobemide if amitriptyline was found to be intolerable or ineffective. The psychotherapy consisted of 16 sessions (each lasting 45 minutes), weekly for the first 8 weeks then once every 2 weeks for the last 8 sessions for a total of 24 weeks of treatment. The SPSP focused primarily on thoughts, feelings, and behaviors concerning the patients' relationships. Supportive interventions made by the therapist included being empathic, reducing anxiety, clarification, enhancing self-esteem, problem solving, and modeling.

Outcome measures used were HDRS score, CGI score, and SCL-90. There were 84 patients in the medication-only group and 83 in the combined group. After randomization, 27 patients from the medication group and 11 from the combined group refused to continue participating; these dropout rates are significantly different.

Results are based on a sample of 129 who began treatment and 92 who completed treatment, as well as the intent-to-treat sample ($n = 167$). Based on HRSD, at 16 weeks, 30% ($n = 37$) of the medication-only group and 42% ($n = 59$) of the combined group were remitted, although these results were not significantly different. At 24 weeks, 21% ($n = 33$) of the medication-only group and 44% ($n = 59$) of the combined group were remitted, a significant difference between the groups. What is also significantly different is the higher dropout rate in the medication-only group (26% at 16 weeks vs. 13% in the combined group; 40% at 24 weeks vs. 22% in the combined group). Patients in the combined group were allowed to drop out from one of the two treatments without withdrawing completely from the study. More patients discontinued the medication than dropped out of psychotherapy (22% at 24 weeks vs. 10%). In this study, combined therapy was more effective than monotherapy only at week 24, but the addition of psychotherapy was clearly more tolerable to patients as evidenced by the high dropout rate for pharmacotherapy alone.

Acute Treatment for Chronic Depression

One of the premier trials included in all the above reviews was conducted by Keller and colleagues (2000), who compared nefazodone alone, a hybrid serotonin antagonist/reuptake inhibitor, a form of CBT called cognitive-behavioral analysis system of psychotherapy (CBASP), and their combination. For the 12-week trial the researchers recruited 681 outpatients with either MDD for 2 years or longer, current MDD superimposed on dysthymia, or partially remitted recurrent MDD in a current episode who were randomized to one of three conditions. From that initial sample, 519 completed the multicenter study. Any patients who had a history of seizures or abnormal EEG findings, severe head trauma, or stroke were excluded. In addition, patients who were suicidal or psychotic, who had schizophrenia, bipolar disorder, antisocial personality disorder, schizotypal personality disorder, or severe borderline personality, or who met criteria for any Axis I anxiety, eating, or substance use disorder were not included. Any individuals who had a history of nonresponse to nefazodone, CBASP, ECT, or adequate trials of two different classes of antidepressants were also excluded.

CBASP, developed for chronic MDD, is based on aspects of cognitive, behavioral, and interpersonal treatment techniques but is more directive and structured than interpersonal psychotherapy (IPT). The treatment emphasizes social problem-solving methods for dealing with interpersonal problems, and the cognitive work focuses more attention on thoughts about interpersonal interactions, including those with the therapist. The goal of CBASP is to help patients understand how their maladaptive patterns of interactions with others foster interpersonal problems.

The manualized psychotherapy was conducted by clinicians who had between 2 and 5 years of experience. The therapists attended training workshops on CBASP and were evaluated for competency on two videotaped sessions. Adherence was maintained by regular videotaping of all sessions. Sessions occurred twice a week during the first 4 weeks, then weekly for 8 weeks. If deemed necessary, the twice-weekly meeting schedule could be continued until week 8.

All patients receiving medication were seen for 15 to 20 minutes weekly, and clinical management was based on a manual. Pharmacotherapists were instructed to inquire about symptoms, side effects, and other medication use but were not allowed to make any psychotherapeutic interventions. The initial dose of nefazodone was 200 mg/day for week 1 and was increased to 300 mg/day at week 2 with incremental increases of 100 mg/day to a maximum dose of 600 mg/day. Patients had to be maintained on at least 300 mg/day by week 3 to stay in the trial.

After randomization of the 681 patients, 226 were assigned to the nefazodone-only group, 228 to the CBASP group, and 227 to the combined group. There were no significant differences among the groups on demographic and baseline clinical measures. Outcome was measured by the 24-item HRSD; response was defined as a 50% reduction in HRSD score from baseline at weeks 10 and 12, and remission was defined as a score of 8 or less at both weeks 10 and 12.

Results showed significant reduction in HRSD scores after 12 weeks of treatment both in the completers and in the intent-to-treat analysis. Using both completer and intent-to-treat analysis, the combined treatment group had a significantly higher response rate than either of the monotherapy groups. The intent-to-treat response rates were 73% for the combined group, 48% for the CBASP group, and 48% for the nefazodone group. The completer response rates were 85% for the combined group, 52% for the CBASP group, and 55% for the nefazodone group. The dropout rate was 24%, with no significant differences among groups. In summary, for chronic depression, combined nefazodone and CBASP was significantly better for achieving response than either therapy alone.

In the same sample as above, Thase and colleagues (2002) analyzed the effectiveness of each treatment on insomnia. A subgroup of 597 of the sample of 681 chronically depressed outpatients had at least one symptom of insomnia as measured by HRSD (24 items) and Inventory of Depressive Symptoms-Self Report (IDS-SR; 30 items). Nefazodone, in combination and alone, was superior to CBASP at all time points, but the combined treatment was superior to nefazodone alone at the end of 12 weeks of treatment (there was no difference at 4 weeks between the two nefazodone groups).

Another substudy of the Keller et al. trial involved assessing the independence of psychosocial functioning from depressive symptoms after treatment (Hirschfeld et al., 2002). Psychosocial functioning was measured by the Social Adjustment Scale Self-Report (SAS-SR), the Endicott Work Productivity Scale (EWPS), and the Medical Outcome Study 36-item Short Form (SF-36). These instruments measured overall psychosocial, interpersonal, and work functioning and general health in the 681 depressed patients.

Before treatment, the sample demonstrated very low or impaired psychosocial functioning in comparison to community norms. After treatment, although there was substantial improvement, some impairment remained independent of depressive symptoms. Combined treatment had a greater impact on psychosocial improvement than either treatment alone. When depressive symptoms were controlled, all the change in psychosocial functioning was predicted from changes in depressive symptoms for the nefazodone-only group, but in the CBASP group, one third to one half of the improvement in overall psychosocial functioning remained after controlling for depressive symptoms. The combined group fell in between the two monotherapy groups, with one fourth the overall improvement in psychosocial functioning remaining after controlling for depressive symptoms.

This study demonstrates the significant impact MDD has on overall, work, and social functioning, especially in the chronically and severely depressed population even after successful treatment. Combined nefazodone and CBASP were more effective in improving psychosocial functioning than either treatment alone, independent of depressive symptomology.

In the final substudy of the Keller et al. trial presented here, sexual functioning and satisfaction were considered before and after treatment (Zajecka et al., 2002). Sexual interest, satisfaction, and functioning were measured using the Modified Rush Sexual Inventory (MRSI) self-report, in which sexual interest and satisfaction over the previous month were rated from 0 to 100 for five items: (a) frequency of pleasurable sexual thoughts, (b) ability to become sexually excited, (c) desire to initiate sexual activity, (d) frequency of initiating sexual activity, and (e) overall degree of sexual satisfaction. The items were summed to yield a total sexual interest/satisfaction score. In addition to these five items, the MRSI also assesses sexual functioning in the previous month through yes/no items (i.e., for men: erectile function — both achieving and maintaining, decreased genital sensitivity, delay in reaching or inability to reach orgasm, and premature orgasm; for women: decreased genital sensitivity, difficulty or inability to achieve orgasm).

Of the 681 patients in the study, 65% of the men and 48% of the women had experienced some sexual dysfunction at baseline. After treatment, all patients experienced significant improvement in sexual interest and satisfaction. After controlling for gender and depressive symptoms, the combined treatment group demonstrated significantly greater improvement in sexual interest and satisfaction than the CBASP-only group, but there was no difference compared with the nefazodone-only group. For both men and women, improvement in sexual interest and satisfaction was associated with improvement in depressive symptoms. For men, improvement in sexual functioning was associated with improvement in depressive symptoms.

This study points out the high degree of impairment in sexual interest and functioning experienced by chronically and severely depressed patients. Treatment of the depressive symptoms also improves sexual impairment, but combined treatment, because it was more effective than either individual therapy, was more efficacious in this MDD sample.

One meta-analysis of combination treatment for MDD (Thase et al., 1997) lasting 16 weeks compared CBT alone, IPT alone, and both combined with antidepressant medication (imipramine or nortriptyline). The analysis included 595 subjects from six protocols with unipolar depression and was based on a semistructured assessment using *DSM-III* or *DSM-III-R* criteria. All six studies were conducted at the authors' research center between 1982 and 1992. One was a maintenance study of recurrent MDD, a second was a maintenance study for late-life MDD, and the others focused on a specific area such as psychobiology or social factors. Three of the studies included chronically depressed patients whose episode duration lasted 2 or more years. The researchers concluded that combined therapy was superior to psychotherapy alone for recurrent, severe MDD (43% recovery for combined treatment vs. 25% for psychotherapy alone), but there was no difference in less severe depression (48% recovery for combination treatment vs. 37% for psychotherapy alone). In recurrently depressed patients, a shorter duration of illness (time to remission) resulted from combination treatment.

Acute Treatment of MDD in Primary Care

One RCT of MDD in primary care (Mynors-Wallis, Gath, Day, & Baker, 2000) was conducted in England, where 151 subjects were randomized into four treatment groups. The first group (n = 39) was treated by research medical practitioners using a problem-solving technique, the second (n = 41) was treated by research nurses using a problem-solving technique, the third (n = 36) was treated by research medical practitioners with antidepressant medication (selective serotonin reuptake inhibitor [SSRI]), and the fourth group (n = 25) was treated by research medical practitioners with medication and by the research nurse, with a problem-solving technique.

The problem-solving treatment was based on the premise that depressive symptoms may be associated with psychosocial problems and that resolving those problems will improve the depressive symptoms. There are six stages to this technique: (a) clarification and problem definition, (b) choice of achievable goals, (c) generation of solutions, (d) choice of solution preference, (e) implementation of chosen solutions, and (f) evaluation. The SSRIs chosen were first fluvoxamine, then paroxetine, and dosage was flexible. The medication treatment followed manualized guidelines and did not include any psychological interventions. The monotherapy groups met six times over 12 weeks, weekly, for the first 3 weeks (sessions 1 through 3) then intermittently (weeks 5, 7, and 11) for the next 9 weeks. The combined therapy group met with each therapist on the same day. Any patient could receive an extra session if necessary. All treatment occurred in the local health center or in the patient's home.

Outcome was measured by HRSD and the Beck Depression Inventory (BDI), with clinical interviews and assessments conducted before treatment and at 6 weeks, 12 weeks, and 1 year by blinded raters. In this study, there was no significant difference among treatment groups in outcome at any time point. Only 77% of patients completed treatment, but the investigators managed to collect 12-week data on patients who did not complete treatment. The problem-solving-only group experienced the most dropouts (n = 14), while the medication-only and combined treatment groups experienced the fewest dropouts (n = 6). At 12 weeks, the response rates ranged between 51% and 67%, perhaps a slightly lower overall response rate than found in other studies using CBT or IPT in combination with medication.

Acute Treatment With Adolescents

Prior to the Treatment for Adolescents with Depression Study (TADS, 2004), there were few data testing the efficacy of combined CBT and medication for depressed adolescents. This large RCT conducted at 13 academic and community centers treated 439 adolescents between ages 12 and 17 who met criteria for *DSM-IV* MDD and did not meet criteria for bipolar, conduct, substance, thought, or pervasive developmental disorders. Current use of any antidepressant, failure to respond to two SSRIs, poor past response to CBT for MDD, and intolerance of fluoxetine were exclusion criteria for study participation. In addition, medical conditions that would interfere with safe administration of fluoxetine, high risk for suicide, and inability to speak English were also exclusion criteria. Current treatment with psychostimulants for attention-deficit/hyperactivity disorder (ADHD) was allowed if the dosages remained stable throughout the study.

Those participants who screened positive and consented ($n = 439$) were randomized to one of four treatment groups: fluoxetine alone ($n = 109$), CBT alone ($n = 111$), combined CBT and fluoxetine ($n = 107$), and placebo ($n = 112$). Clinicians and patients were blind in both the fluoxetine-alone and placebo groups, and all knew that the combined and CBT-only groups involved active treatments. Assessments were made by blind independent evaluators, and outcome was measured by the Children's Depression Rating Scale (CDRS) and the Clinical Global Impressions Improvement (CGI-I) score.

Pharmacotherapy was manualized and monitored; it consisted of six sessions of 20 to 30 minutes spread over 12 weeks. Pharmacotherapists used a flexible dose of fluoxetine or placebo beginning at 10 mg, increasing to 20 mg after 1 week to a maximum dose of 40 mg by the 8th week. CBT consisted of 15 sessions of 50 to 60 minutes over 12 weeks with the adolescents alone, at times with parents and family, or parents alone. Beginning sessions (1 through 6) covered psychoeducation about depression, monitoring of mood, setting of goals, increasing participation in pleasurable activities, cognitive restructuring, and problem solving of social concerns. The second half of treatment focused on improving social skills (e.g., problems in social engagement, communication, negotiation, compromise, or assertiveness). Combined treatment was conducted by two clinicians, each following the manual for the treatment as conducted in monotherapy, but was integrated for partial response and dose increases.

Of the 439 participants who began the trial, 359 completed the 12 weeks of treatment, though the outcome data were based on the 351 participants who were assessed at the end of the treatment period (80% of the total). There were no significant differences between groups for dropouts or early terminators. There were no significant differences between the groups on any baseline characteristics, including demographics and illness severity. The sample was representative of the general depressed adolescent population in clinical practice, with a mean illness severity of moderate to severe.

Outcome results using CDRS showed that combined treatment of fluoxetine and CBT was superior to placebo ($p = .001$) and to either monotherapy ($p = .02$ for fluoxetine alone and $p = .01$ for CBT alone). Fluoxetine alone was superior to CBT alone ($p = .01$). The completer response rate for combined treatment was 71% compared with 60.6% for fluoxetine alone, and 43.2% for CBT alone. The placebo response rate was 34.8%. The intent-to-treat analysis yielded the same findings: Combined treatment was superior to all other groups, and fluoxetine alone was superior to CBT alone. In this sample, CBT was not superior to placebo, in contrast to other findings. However, the authors suggest that their sample may have been a more severely ill group both in MDD severity and in comorbidity, which may account for the poorer outcome in the CBT-alone group. The data from this study are consistent with findings on adult populations: combined treatment is more effective than monotherapy in more severely depressed patients.

Acute and Maintenance Treatment in the Elderly

Comparing combined pharmacotherapy and psychotherapy in the elderly with those in midlife with recurrent MDD, Reynolds et al. (1996) presented the response rates in acute and continuation treatment conducted in two separate clinical trials with the goal of achieving the maximum number of remitted patients to be eligible for inclusion in an RCT of maintenance treatment. The first study involved 148 depressed patients aged 60 and over, considered the elderly group. During the acute treatment phase, patients were treated with nortriptyline and weekly IPT modified for the needs of the elderly. Acute treatment lasted until the patient achieved a score of 10 or lower on HRSD for 3 weeks, a remission score consistent with other studies of the elderly. The remission rate was 78.4% ($n = 116$) for the elderly. The number of dropouts was low, 12.2% ($n = 18$). After acute treatment, remitters entered continuation treatment for 16 weeks consisting of pharmacotherapy (same dose) and biweekly IPT to ensure complete remission and prevent relapse.

The midlife study included 214 recurrently depressed patients between ages 21 and 59 (mean age 38.5) who were treated with imipramine and IPT. Acute treatment in this group lasted until an HRSD score of 7 or lower was maintained for 3 weeks. The midlife remission rate was 69.6% ($n = 149$) with a dropout rate of 11.2% ($n = 24$). In the midlife group, remitters entered continuation treatment for 20 weeks, also consisting of same-dose pharmacotherapy and biweekly IPT. There were no significant differences in remission rates between the elderly and midlife groups for acute treatment.

The researchers analyzed the temporal course of response to treatment in both groups and found that the two groups were similar in that both showed a significant reduction in HRSD scores at 8 weeks. The slope of the regression differed in that the midlife patients experienced a faster reduction than the elderly patients.

There was a significant difference in relapse rates, with 15.5% of the elderly group ($n = 18$) and 6.7% of the midlife group ($n = 10$) relapsing. In addition, the elderly group experienced a shorter time to relapse than the midlife group (7.4 weeks in the elderly group and 16.6 weeks in the midlife group). Due to the uneven length of continuation treatment, the researchers reanalyzed the data eliminating any midlife subjects who relapsed after the 16th week and found that 3.4% ($n = 5$) of the midlife group relapsed during the first 16 weeks of continuation treatment. In comparison, 13.8% of the elderly group relapsed during the 16 weeks ($n = 16$), a significant difference. At the end of the study, 66.2% ($n = 98$) of the elderly patients and 57% ($n = 122$) of the midlife patients were eligible to enter the maintenance therapy condition. The maintenance data were not reported in this manuscript.

This study is included here even though it did not employ a monotherapy or placebo group, since there are few data on outcomes using combined

treatment with the elderly. In addition, there is value in comparing treatment results in the elderly with those in a younger population, especially one in which much research information has been collected.

Reynolds and colleagues (1999) conducted a maintenance trial on 187 recurrently depressed patients aged 59 or older. These patients were not demented, had a mean number of previous episodes of 5.3, and had no period of remission longer than 3 years.

Acute treatment included open-label nortriptyline combined with weekly IPT for 9 weeks (50% received some adjunctive pharmacotherapy). After the 9-week acute treatment period, those who were responders were continued on the combined nortriptyline and IPT treatment every other week for an additional 16 weeks to ensure stability of remission. Those able to sustain remission for 6 months were randomized for maintenance treatment. The 107 such patients were placed in one of four groups: monthly clinic visits with full-dose nortriptyline, placebo with clinical management, monthly maintenance IPT with pill placebo, and monthly maintenance IPT with nortriptyline. Maintenance therapy lasted for 3 years, but relapse or recurrence of MDD symptoms caused subjects to be dropped from the study.

Results of the maintenance trial showed that all active treatments were superior to placebo. The combined nortriptyline plus IPT was superior to IPT plus placebo, with a recurrence rate of only 20%. The combined treatment showed a trend toward significance ($p = .06$) over nortriptyline plus clinical management, with a 43% recurrence rate. The recurrence rate for IPT plus pill placebo was 64%, and the recurrence rate for pill placebo plus clinical management was 90%. The authors point out that 53% of recurrence was associated with medication noncompliance. The strength of this study is the inclusion of a placebo arm. In addition, open-label treatment and the allowance of adjunctive medications make the results more generalizable to clinical practice.

Blackburn and Moore (1997) conducted both an acute and a maintenance treatment study of 75 recurrently depressed outpatients to determine whether cognitive therapy (CT) would be more effective than medication when used for maintenance treatment. Technically, this trial did not combine the two treatments at the same time. Rather, it used a crossover-type design, but it is included in this chapter because it is often cited and presents some important findings.

The MDD patients were randomized into one of three groups for 16 weeks of acute treatment followed by 2 years of maintenance treatment: antidepressants alone ($n = 26$), antidepressant first followed by CT ($n = 22$), and CT alone ($n = 27$). Medication treatment, conducted by general practitioners or psychiatrists, was determined by the clinician's choice, prescribed at or above therapeutic dose and changed as needed. Meetings occurred once every 3 weeks for 30 minutes during acute treatment, but maintenance therapy meeting times were not mentioned. Cognitive therapy was conducted by trained clinicians weekly during the 16-week acute treatment and less frequently during maintenance (three sessions during month 1, two sessions during month 2, and once per month throughout the 2-year period).

Measures used were HRSD and BDI. There were no significant differences between the three treatment groups on demographic variables, baseline HRSD and BDI measures, number of past depressive episodes, or number of hospitalizations or suicide attempts. The only significant difference was that the antidepressant first followed by CT group had lower functioning prior to entering the study.

Thirteen patients were dropped from the acute phase results (11 who dropped out and 2 who received inadequate medication dosages). Of the 65 who completed treatment, there was significant improvement for all groups; 24% of the medication groups achieved remission, and 33% of the CT group remitted. There was no difference among the three groups on HRSD scores. In addition, the authors analyzed whether depression severity accounted for any treatment differences in their sample and found that it did not, contrary to other findings.

After 24 months of maintenance treatment, there was no significant difference among the groups on either outcome measure. It should be noted that only 20 patients were assessed at 24 months. Some were dropouts, but the majority were still in the maintenance phase when the analysis was performed (subjects were recruited late in the study and did not have time to complete the 24 months of maintenance). Even during the periodic assessments made earlier in the maintenance phase, there were no significant differences among the groups. It is important

to note that all patients continued to improve with maintenance therapy. The relapse rates during the 2-year period were significant, with the CTonly group demonstrating the lowest rates (24%) compared with the medication-only group (31%) and the medication first then CT group (36%). When the cognitive therapy maintenance groups were combined, the relapse rate was 26%, compared with 31% for the medication-only group.

The acute treatment phase showed no difference in outcome rates (remission) for medication only and cognitive therapy only, with mixed severity levels among the participants. The groups remained similar during the maintenance phase and only demonstrated significance in prevention of relapse when the CT-only treatment group had a lower relapse rate than the medication-only and the medication followed by CT group.

Frank et al. (1990) conducted a continuation treatment study of recurrently depressed patients aged 21 to 65 who had experienced at least three episodes of MDD, the prior episode lasting no longer than 2.5 years. Initially, 230 patients were treated with imipramine (150 to 300 mg) and weekly IPT for 12 weeks. For the next 8 weeks, patients were seen biweekly, then treated monthly until response was achieved (HRSD score of 7 or lower and a Raskin Severity of Depression score of at least 7). All patients continued in treatment for an additional 17 weeks at the same dosage ($n = 157$). In order to be entered into the maintenance protocol, patients were required to maintain a HRSD score of 7 or lower. Of the 230 who entered the acute treatment phase, 128 patients (30 males, 98 females) were randomized to one of five maintenance conditions: imipramine plus clinic visits ($n = 28$), IPT plus imipramine ($n = 25$), placebo plus clinic visits ($n = 23$), IPT alone ($n = 26$), and IPT plus placebo ($n = 26$), for 3 years.

The maintenance IPT involved monthly sessions conducted by a social worker, psychologist, or nurse-practitioner. IPT therapists were highly trained and supervised by clinicians who had developed IPT (Bruce Rounsaville, Eve Chevron, Gerald Klerman, and Myrna Weissman). The imipramine dose averaged 200 mg and was administered by a psychiatrist who met with patients monthly. For those patients receiving placebo or IPT alone, medication was withdrawn over 3 weeks.

The attrition rate of the maintenance phase was 17% ($n = 22$), leaving 106 patients who completed the 3-year trial. Fifteen of the 22 dropped out due to noncompliance with the protocol, but only 4 complained of side effects as the reason. The others who dropped out did so due to medical problems that interfered with continuation of treatment, moving out of the area, or other reasons.

The research showed that the likelihood of experiencing recurrence from not receiving imipramine was 4.9, whereas the likelihood of experiencing recurrence from not receiving IPT was 1.7 in the 3-year period following successful treatment of recurrent depression. Imipramine and clinic visits were as effective in preventing recurrence as combined imipramine and IPT, although both were more effective than IPT alone, IPT and placebo, and placebo with clinic visits. As a means of recurrence prevention, imipramine was the most effective treatment, more than combined treatment in this recurrently depressed sample. IPT alone had significant benefit in preventing recurrence.

Summary

The consistent finding from all these studies of treatment for depression is that combined treatment is superior to monotherapy when used to treat chronic or severe major depression. Relapse prevention is most effective when medication is combined with psychotherapy (CBT or IPT). Patients with milder severity or a first episode of depression seem to benefit from either treatment at about the same rate, but one advantage of combining psychosocial treatment with medication may be in treatment adherence. Attrition rates are often higher in the medication-only groups (Hautzinger et al., 1996; de Jonghe et al., 2001); patients may drop out due to side effects or dissatisfaction with taking medication.

Most of the combined treatment studies that included an evidenced-based treatment (CBT or IPT) used a tricyclic or a monoamine oxidase inhibitor rather than an SSRI with the exception of the TADS (adolescents) trial, which employed fluoxetine and CBT with the result that combination treatment was more effective than monotherapy. It was suggested that the participants in the TADS trial were more severely ill, thus the higher response rate with combined treatment. Since SSRIs are frequently prescribed in clinical practice, more RCTs using SSRIs in combination with CBT or IPT in MDD are needed.

In the primary care study (Mynors-Wallis et al., 2000), combined treatment did employ SSRI medication, but the psychosocial treatment chosen was problem-solving therapy, not CBT or IPT. The problem-solving therapy was not well received by patients (highest attrition rate), nor has it been demonstrated as particularly effective. In this study, combined treatment was no more effective than medication alone or the problem-solving therapy alone.

One last issue to consider when evaluating the results of clinical trials for MDD that use the HRSD as the primary outcome measure is rater training and reliability testing. Some of the older studies did not describe training of raters, and reliability tests were not mentioned. The HRSD, in its original format, has very few probes for each item, leaving it to the interviewer to know what to ask in order to rate the item. Frequently, independent raters are not highly experienced clinicians and are not necessarily familiar with scoring guidelines and rules of administration (Lipsitz et al., 2004). Williams (1988) developed the Structured Interview Guide for Hamilton Depression Scale (SIGH-D), where gate and follow-up questions are provided so that interviewers systematically gather the same material over time, increasing the reliability of the data. Use of such structured guides and attention to rater training could significantly affect the results of treatment trials (Lipsitz et al., 2004).

PANIC DISORDER

There have been many RCTs of treatments for PD, but almost all have compared medication alone to psychotherapy alone, and both to placebo; little has been conducted on combined treatment.

The gold standard RCT for PD was a multicenter study conducted by Barlow, Gorman, Shear, and Woods (2000). This four-site study (Boston, New York, Pittsburgh, and New Haven) compared imipramine plus medical management, CBT alone, their combination, placebo plus CBT, and placebo plus clinical management in the treatment of 312 patients with panic disorder. There were three phases to the study: acute treatment, maintenance treatment, and follow-up.

All patients met criteria for PD using the Anxiety Disorders Interview Schedule Revised (ADIS-R) and had experienced at least one full or limited panic attack in the 2 weeks prior to starting treatment. Most Axis I disorders were excluded except major depression, and some agoraphobia (mild) was acceptable. After passing the screening procedures, 326 PD patients without agoraphobia were randomized to one of the five acute treatment groups: CBT alone ($n = 77$), imipramine alone ($n = 83$), placebo alone ($n = 24$), CBT plus imipramine ($n = 65$), or CBT plus placebo ($n = 63$).

In the acute phase, patients were seen weekly for 12 weeks. The CBT used in this study is called Panic Control Therapy, developed by Barlow and Craske, and focuses on psychoeducation, breathing retraining, relaxation exercises, cognitive restructuring, interoceptive exposure (exposure to bodily sensations that are similar to those experienced during a panic attack), and situational exposure. Imipramine and placebo were both double-blind administered in a fixed, flexible dose beginning at 10 mg titrated by 10 mg up to 50 mg in 4 to 5 days, then increasing more rapidly to 200 mg by week 5, with a maximum dose of 300 mg. Medical management involved monitoring adverse effects, clinical state, and symptoms with a goal of increased compliance with medication use. It should be noted that patients were allowed some benzodiazepine use through the acute treatment phase.

CBT- and pharmaco-therapists were well trained, experienced clinicians, and each conducted treatment according to a manual, with adherence monitored regularly. All assessments were conducted by independent evaluators. Primary outcome measures included Panic Disorder Severity Scale (PDSS), a 7-item, clinician-administered scale that measures panic frequency, severity, anticipatory anxiety, avoidance, and impairment; and the Clinical Global Impression-Improvement Scale (CGI-I). Response was calculated by a 40% decrease in PDSS score from baseline and a CGI-I of 1 or 2 (much improved).

Ninety-nine participants dropped out after randomization, with no significant difference in attrition rates among the five groups. At the end of the acute phase, all three treatment groups were superior to placebo but not different from each other. Improvement was faster for patients treated with medication. The PDSS response rate for those who completed treatment in the imipramine group was 74.5%, whereas the CBT-only group's response rate was 67.3%. The imipramine plus CBT group had a response rate of 84.4%, and the CBT plus placebo

group response rate was 80%. The placebo-only response rate was 38.5%. Using an intent-to-treat analysis, the PDSS response rates for the five groups were as follows: CBT alone 48.7%, imipramine alone 45.8%, CBT plus imipramine 60.3%, CBT plus placebo 57.1%, and placebo alone 21.7%. There was some evidence for a slightly better outcome with medication than psychotherapy and no evidence that combination therapy was better than monotherapy.

In the maintenance phase, responders to acute therapy (including placebo responders) were continued on the original treatment assigned, still under blinded conditions, and seen monthly for the next 6 months ($N = 170$). Imipramine- and placebo-treated patients continued on medication, and CBT-treated patients were given monthly booster sessions. The results after the maintenance phase showed that placebo-treated patients who had responded during acute treatment had a poor outcome during the maintenance phase. Patients assigned to CBT alone, imipramine alone, and combination therapy continued to be responders. The maintenance phase PDSS response rates by group were as follows for completers: CBT alone 73.2%, imipramine alone 79.5%, CBT plus imipramine 90%, CBT plus placebo 76.3%, and placebo only 37.5%. The intent-to-treat PDSS response rates were CBT alone 39.5%, imipramine alone 37.8%, CBT plus imipramine 57.1%, CBT plus placebo 46.8%, and placebo only 13%.

Results after this phase showed that combined treatment was better than monotherapy. The PDSS response rate was significantly higher in the combined group when compared with each individual treatment (CBT plus imipramine vs. CBT $p = .04$; CBT plus imipramine vs. imipramine $p = .03$).

The last phase of this study was the follow-up phase, lasting 6 months after treatment was completed. The number of patients who were assessed during follow-up was 116. It is at this point that significant differences emerged among the groups in outcome. The PDSS completer response rate for the CBT-only group was 85.2%, imipramine-only group was 60%, CBT plus imipramine was 50%, CBT plus placebo was 83.3%, and placebo alone was 100% (there were only three participants in the placebo group after this phase). The intent-to-treat response rates were CBT only 32.4%, imipramine only 19.7%, CBT plus imipramine 25%, CBT plus placebo 41%, and placebo only 9.1%. The CBT without imipramine groups had fewer patients relapse than the imipramine-alone and combined treatment groups.

This study demonstrates the effectiveness of imipramine, CBT, and their combination for acute treatment of PD. Medication (imipramine) works more quickly than CBT but is not tolerated as well, and at the end of treatment, both are quite effective. The combined treatment was not as durable as CBT alone in the follow-up period; in fact, the relapse rates were about the same as for imipramine alone.

Another RCT involving combined treatment for PD was conducted by de Beurs, van Balkom, Lange, Koele, and van Dyck (1995) in Amsterdam comparing fluvoxamine and exposure therapy, monotherapy and placebo in panic disorder with agoraphobia (PDA). After screening for panic disorder using the ADIS, 96 PD patients with moderate or severe agoraphobia, who were between the ages of 18 and 65, were medically healthy, and did not have any history of psychosis, organic mental disorder, or substance use disorder, were randomized to one of four treatment groups ($n = 24$ per group). All psychoactive medications except benzodiazepines were discontinued before subjects entered the protocol.

The four treatment groups were fluvoxamine plus exposure therapy, placebo plus exposure therapy, psychological panic management plus exposure therapy, and exposure therapy alone. The fluvoxamine and placebo treatments began at 50 mg, administered by a psychiatrist or psychiatric resident over 12 weekly sessions, and titrated to 100 mg in week 2 and 150 mg in week 3. Patients were told about the effects of fluvoxamine and the serotonergic pathways in the brain of PD patients. Their medication dose was kept stable at 150 mg unless side effects necessitated a reduction. No exposure therapy was conducted until after 6 weeks of medication treatment, and patients were told to avoid exposing themselves to feared situations until the medication started working.

Psychological panic management was conducted by clinicians experienced in behavior therapy. Sessions were held weekly and focused on psychoeducation about panic, the hyperventilation process (its role in panic attacks), and the cognitive process whereby bodily sensations provoke fear thoughts and fear thoughts further provoke bodily sensations. Patients were then encouraged to bring on paniclike sensations by hyperventilation, first in the session and then later at home. Patients were trained to breathe into a paper bag to counteract the hyperventilation process and later to breathe from the abdomen.

The exposure therapy (in vivo) began after 6 weeks of treatment (fluvoxamine, placebo, or panic management). The therapists conducting exposure therapy were the same as the panic management therapists. Patients were told to practice their techniques (those in panic management) in situations that they feared or avoided and were encouraged to gradually expose themselves to those situations. During the sessions they constructed a hierarchy of agoraphobic situations. Homework was then assigned to practice going into those situations for at least 90 minutes, three times per week.

Measures were self-report scales including the Fear Questionnaire (FQ), the Mobility Inventory (MI), the Agoraphobia Cognitions Questionnaire, the Bodily Sensations Questionnaire, the SCL-90, the Beck Depression Inventory (BDI), and the Depression Adjective Checklist. The authors created a composite score from subscales of these instruments that measure the same construct. The agoraphobia composite score combined the agoraphobia subscales of the FQ, the SCL-90, and the MI avoidance when alone scale. The composite for depression combined the BDI, the Depression Adjective Checklist, and the SCL-90. The last composite score measured bodily sensations and combined the Bodily Sensations Questionnaire and a subscale of the Agoraphobia Cognitions Questionnaire. All composite scores ranged from 1 to 10, with the higher score reflective of more symptomatology.

All patients underwent a behavioral avoidance test that included three tasks: walking 3 miles from the clinic toward town, supermarket shopping, and riding on a streetcar, which is usually crowded, for a short period of time. Evaluations of the patients' ability to perform the tasks and the amount of anxiety experienced during the tasks were rated and averaged to yield one score from 1 to 10, with the higher score indicating poor performance.

Before being assigned to a treatment group, each patient was interviewed by an independent evaluator who devised four treatment goals for the patient. Using a 5-point scale, these goals were reformulated into a goal attainment scale and became another measure of treatment outcome. During the treatment, patients were asked to monitor their panic attacks on a registration form.

Of the 96 patients who began treatment, only 76 completed the full course. Six patients dropped out due to treatment-related problems and six due to other reasons. There were no significant differences between the dropouts and the completers.

The authors tested whether blindness or the use of benzodiazepines affected the results, and neither was found to be significant. All treatment groups experienced significant improvement on the three composite scores from baseline to end of treatment. The fluvoxamine plus exposure group experienced superior effects compared with the other three groups. There were no significant differences among the placebo plus exposure group, the psychological panic management plus exposure group, and the exposure alone group. On the behavioral avoidance test, all patients experienced significant improvement on performance after treatment. The intent-to-treat analysis did not yield different results from the completer analysis.

Using the panic attack registers, the researchers analyzed panic-free status as well as increase in panic in the four groups over time. They found that there was a significant difference: the participants in the psychological panic management group had poorer outcome than the other three groups, who were not different from each other on presence of panic attacks.

Effect sizes for the four groups on each composite score were calculated. Agoraphobia: fluvoxamine plus exposure was 2.00, placebo plus exposure was 1.29, psychological panic management plus exposure was 0.99, and exposure alone was 1.32. Depression: fluvoxamine plus exposure was 1.28, placebo plus exposure was 0.75, psychological panic management plus exposure was 0.24, and exposure alone was 0.66. Bodily sensations: fluvoxamine plus exposure was 1.22, placebo plus exposure was 0.82, psychological panic management plus exposure was 0.73, and exposure alone was 0.75.

The conclusion drawn from this study is that combined treatment of fluvoxamine plus exposure therapy was more effective than exposure alone (with or without placebo). The psychological panic management was not very effective in decreasing panic attacks. This is not surprising, since breathing retraining alone is not very effective in preventing panic attacks (Schmidt et al., 2000). It is important to note that these data did not measure response with a particular criteria set, such as CGI, making the data difficult to compare with those from other trials. Combined treatment may have been superior to the other treatment, but not all patients were panic free. Nonresponders in the Barlow et al. (2000) trial demonstrated improvement after treatment. However, just demonstrating some improvement is not adequate.

Loerch and colleagues (1999) used moclobemide and CBT to treat PD with agoraphobia patients for 8 weeks. They randomized 55 patients to three conditions: placebo plus CBT, moclobemide plus clinical management (psychological placebo), and placebo plus clinical management. In this trial, moclobemide plus clinical management was not more effective than placebo, so it is not surprising that the combination of moclobemide and CBT was not superior to CBT plus placebo.

A study of combined medication and CBT for PD in primary care was conducted by Roy-Byrne and colleagues (2005) in six academic medical centers in Seattle, San Diego, and Los Angeles. The Collaborative Care for Anxiety and Panic study aimed to determine whether evidenced-based treatments could be generalized to primary care. Patients met study criteria if they had PD and had experienced a panic attack in the week prior to study entry, spoke English, and were willing to take medication in addition to receiving CBT treatment. After intensive screening procedures (diagnostic evaluation was determined by use of the Composite International Diagnostic Interview [CIDI]), 232 panic patients were enrolled and randomly assigned to the intervention group ($n = 119$) or usual care ($n = 113$).

The intervention consisted of six sessions of CBT in person over a 3-month period and six telephone contacts lasting between 15 and 30 minutes every 6 to 12 weeks over the next year. The CBT was conducted by the "behavioral health specialist" (a master's-level or recent doctoral-level individual with little previous CBT experience) who was trained to deliver the shorter treatment. An instructional videotape explaining about panic disorder and the treatment was also given to patients. Medication was administered by the primary care physician (PCP) under the supervision of a psychiatrist. The PCPs had received an hour-long didactic training on medication treatment for panic. SSRIs were given first if there was no history of two previous failed trials; otherwise the PCP may have chosen a different antidepressant such as a tricyclic, nefazodone, or mirtazapine for 6 weeks. Clinical care was managed by the behavioral health specialist who was in contact with the PCT regularly via telephone, fax, or e-mail.

Measures included diagnostic assessment (CIDI), panic frequency and severity, agoraphobic avoidance, other fears and anxiety using the Fear Questionnaire (FQ) and the Anxiety Sensitivity Index (ASI), and assessment of pharmacological and psychotherapeutic help received (amount and type), all administered at baseline and every 3 months throughout participation in the study. Outcome was measured by a subscale of the World Health Organization Disability Scale, the Global Physical and Mental Health Scale short form (SF-12), the Center for Epidemiologic Studies-Depression Scale, and ASI. Response criteria or "high end-state functioning" was based on a composite score of the above measures: no panic attacks in the previous month, minimal anticipatory anxiety about having a panic attack (one or less on a 0- to 3-point scale), and a score of less than 10 on an agoraphobia subscale.

There were no significant differences between the two treatment groups at baseline. The sample was primarily female (67%), with a mean age of 41.2, mostly educated (76% graduated high school, 39% had some college or more) and predominantly Caucasian (65.5%; Hispanic 13%, African American 13.8%). Comorbidity of a medical condition occurred in almost two thirds of the sample; 55.6% had comorbid MDD, 45.7% had generalized anxiety disorder, 29.3% had posttraumatic stress disorder, and 39.7% had social anxiety disorder. Very few had received two or more sessions of CBT-type treatment previously (3.5%), and only 28% had received any antipanic medication for at least 6 weeks before entering the trial.

Of those who were assigned to the CBT intervention group (N = 119), 81 (68%) received four to six sessions of CBT, 24 (20.1%) received one to three sessions, and 14 (11.8%) received no sessions. Adherence to the treatment was measured by independent clinical raters employing the same method as used in the Barlow et al. multicenter study (2000), resulting in adequate adherence to the treatment manual. The study investigators were concerned that a "spillover" effect might occur. Since some PCPs had patients in the intervention group and others in usual care, they might use the knowledge gained from the intervention training to influence their treatment in usual care. However, there were no differences

found between the PCPs who had patients in both groups and the PCPs who had patients only in the usual care group.

Attrition from the study was as follows: at the 3-month assessment only 1 participant had dropped out (from the intervention group), at the 6-month assessment there were 2 dropouts from the usual care group and 8 dropouts from the intervention group, at the 9-month follow-up there were 4 dropouts from the usual care group and 10 dropouts from the intervention group, and at the final 12-month follow-up assessment there were 5 dropouts from the usual care group and 11 dropouts from the intervention group.

Although 6 months of CBT treatment (consisting of six sessions encompassing all seven techniques) was offered to the intervention group, only 63% actually received three or more sessions consisting of four of the seven techniques at the 3-month assessment and only 17% at the 6-month assessment. In the usual treatment group, 14% had received three or more sessions consisting of four of seven techniques at the 3-month assessment, and 9% had at the 6-month assessment, a highly significant difference. At the 9-month assessment, there was no difference between the groups, but significance was found at the 12-month assessment period, with 6% of the intervention group and 11% of the usual care group having received three or more sessions of four of seven CBT techniques.

The results of the medication treatment were nonsignificant. In the intervention group (which was offered appropriate antipanic pharmacotherapy for at least 6 weeks), 44% actually received appropriate antipanic medication at the 3-month assessment, and 40% of the usual care group received appropriate antipanic medication. The number of participants who actually received appropriate antipanic medication throughout the follow-up period was about the same for both groups: 42% at 6 months, 41% at 9 months, and 41% at 12 months in the intervention group; and 39% at 6 months, 39% at 9 months, and 39% at 12 months in the usual care group.

The difference between the two groups becomes clear when looking at high end-state functioning as the outcome. The intervention group demonstrated a superior proportion of patients who achieved high end-state functioning at all assessment points. At the 3-month assessment, 20% of the intervention group was considered remitted, whereas only 12% of the usual care group remitted. At the 12-month assessment, 29% of the intervention group and 16% of the usual care group were responders. Using the ASI as the outcome measure, 66% of the intervention group versus 38% of the usual care group were responders at the 12-month assessment period. The study showed trends toward significance in dose response for both CBT and antipanic medication. Those who received at least four CBT technique components while attending at least six sessions showed better response than those who received at least four CBT components while attending three to five sessions (56% vs. 40%). Those who took appropriate medication for 3 months showed better response than those who took appropriate medication for 6 to 11 weeks (35% vs. 29%). The power was limited in these analyses, contributing to the lack of significance.

One other measure of importance showed significant improvement between the two groups. At all assessment points, the usual care group demonstrated more improvement in depression (23%) than the intervention group (19%).

In this trial, conducted in the primary care setting, the combination of CBT and medication delivered by PCPs and behavior specialists was superior to usual care in achieving high end-state functioning and response in panic disorder patients. Since the medication component of the treatment did not differ between the two groups, the CBT treatment accounts for most of the improvement experienced by the patients. Only 40% of the intervention group actually completed the entire course of CBT, whereas 72% in the Barlow et al. (2000) trial completed 11 sessions of CBT. This study did not exclude subjects who failed to continue treatment, as usually is the case in clinical trials. There was no placebo group for comparison of the efficacy of combined treatment, but the utility of including this trial here is to demonstrate treatment effectiveness in the primary care setting.

The only other combined treatment RCT in panic disorder was conducted by Marks and colleagues (1993) in London and Toronto using alprazolam, placebo, situational exposure, and relaxation therapy. The 154 panic patients were randomly assigned to one of four groups: alprazolam plus situational exposure (considered the combined treatment group, $n = 40$), alprazolam plus relaxation therapy (considered a medication plus psychological placebo, $n = 37$), placebo plus situational exposure (considered placebo plus psychological treatment,

$n = 38$), and placebo plus relaxation therapy (considered a double placebo, $n = 39$).

All participants were screened using the SCID for DSM-III; they were adults between the ages of 18 and 65 who had PD, had experienced some attacks in the previous 4 weeks, did not have other Axis I disorders, and were not on any medication when entered into the protocol. In addition, patients underwent a physical examination and laboratory tests to determine medical status.

For the medication groups, the beginning dose of alprazolam was 1 mg, then titrated to a maximum dose of 10 mg, with a mean dose of 6 mg. All patients before randomization met with an evaluator who assessed which situations were feared and/or avoided. The exposure therapy involved first reading a chapter from the manual Living With Fear. With the therapist, the patient planned exposures to situations that were listed with the evaluator. The therapist accompanied the patient for the first two sessions. During the exposures, the patient rated his or her level of anxiety every 30 minutes of the two exercises. The relaxation therapy involved giving patients audiotapes of instructions to be used at home for 1 hour daily. During sessions, the therapist reviewed the patients' weekly diaries and checked progress. No instructions for exposure were given, and patients were told to "do whatever you wish" if they asked about exposure. All treatment lasted for 8 weeks.

Measures for outcome were ratings on the phobia list (0 to 8) by the patient and the independent evaluator, Phobia Questionnaire (PQ), Attack and Anticipatory Anxiety Scale, HRSD, Beck Depression Inventory (BDI), and CGI-Improvement. Ratings occurred at baseline, 4 weeks, and 8 weeks (posttreatment), and at 43 weeks for follow-up.

There were no significant differences among the four groups at baseline and no differences between the two sites, so all the results were pooled. Results for the alprazolam groups showed that patients improved during the first 4 weeks on a measure of panic attack frequency but remained steady until week 8. The exposure groups improved by the 2nd week and continued to steadily improve until the 8th week. Using the CGI data at 8 weeks, the percentage of patients who were considered improved (rating of 1 or 2) by group were 71% in the alprazolam plus exposure group, 71% in the placebo plus exposure group, 51% in the alprazolam plus relaxation group, and 25% in the placebo plus relaxation group. After medication taper, only 36% of the alprazolam plus exposure group, 29% of the alprazolam plus relaxation group, and 18% of the placebo plus relaxation group stayed well, and 62% of the placebo plus exposure group stayed well.

The combination treatment was only slightly better than the other treatments at the end of the 8 weeks. The alprazolam groups relapsed more frequently than the exposure therapy group, so that exposure alone was the most effective treatment after medication was discontinued. Some of the difficulty in this trial with relapse after medication discontinuation may be attributed to the very rapid withdrawal of alprazolam, which may have produced severe withdrawal symptoms in the patients.

In summary, there is no advantage to combined treatment in panic disorder. The use of imipramine combined with CBT is no more effective than imipramine alone. The combination of a benzodiazepine and CBT is also no more effective than either treatment alone, and may even be relatively contraindicated, with data suggesting poor long-term outcome when compared to CBT alone.

OBSESSIVE-COMPULSIVE DISORDER

The growing research literature on the combined treatment of pharmacotherapy and psychotherapy for the treatment of obsessive-compulsive disorder (OCD) lends itself nicely to being grouped into three main categories: acute treatment, long-term outcome/maintenance, and treatment discontinuation. Combination treatment studies are included when delivered concomitantly as well as sequentially.

Acute Concomitant Combined Treatment for OCD

Foa and colleagues (2005) conducted a randomized, placebo-controlled trial comparing clomipramine, exposure, and response prevention (a form of CBT) and their combination in the treatment of obsessive-compulsive disorder. Patients were randomized to one of four conditions: clomipramine alone ($n = 47$), exposure and response (ritual) prevention alone ($n = 37$), exposure and response prevention plus clomipramine ($n = 33$), and pill placebo ($n = 32$). The authors did not include a placebo psychotherapy group in this study, other investigators having previously de-

termined that exposure and response prevention was superior to matched psychosocial comparison conditions in length and treatment intensity. After randomization, the overall dropout rate was 18%, with 22% from the exposure and response prevention group, 23% from the clomipramine group, only 6% from the combined group, and 19% from the placebo group.

The exposure sessions lasted 2 hours each daily, for the first 3 weeks, and 45 minutes weekly for the final 8 weeks. Daily homework assignments of up to 2 hours per day were given. During week 4, two 2-hour sessions took place in the patients' homes to promote generalizability.

Patients in the clomipramine and pill placebo arms received 30-minute, weekly medication management sessions. Patients in these groups were also encouraged to engage in exposure and ritual prevention, but without systematic instructions or homework assignments.

Blinded raters assessed OCD symptoms at weeks 0, 4, 8, and 12. The primary outcome measure was the mean total score on the Yale-Brown Obsessive Compulsive Scale (Y-BOCS). Other assessments included the Clinical Global Impression Scale (CGI), the NIMH Global Obsessive Compulsive Scale, and the HRSD.

After 12 weeks, the results showed that exposure and response prevention was superior to clomipramine and to pill placebo on all measures. The combination of exposure and response prevention plus clomipramine was also superior to clomipramine on all measures. However, no difference was found between the combination and exposure and response prevention alone groups.

The authors suggest that the combination treatment may have failed to show superiority to the exposure and response prevention alone group because the intensive phase of exposure and response prevention (first 3 weeks of the study) was over by the time the clomipramine would have generated an effect. The exposure and response prevention was so successful it may have left little room for further improvement by the addition of clomipramine. We also cannot exclude the possibility that the exposure and response prevention effect was so robust because of the unusual intensity in the treatment design.

Cottraux et al. (1990) compared the combinations of fluvoxamine plus exposure therapy, pill placebo plus exposure therapy, and fluvoxamine with antiexposure therapy. There was no pill placebo plus antiexposure group, which was considered to be an unethical control group. Twenty patients were randomized to each of the three groups. The fluvoxamine plus antiexposure group was single-blind; the other two groups were double-blind. Prior to study entrance, 58 patients had received medications, 12 had received psychodynamic or psychoanalytic psychotherapy, and 3 had received behavior therapy; all had failed treatment.

Medication was titrated to a dose of up to 300 mg and was continued for 24 weeks. Over this time course, patients met with the psychiatrist nine times. Patients were permitted "occasional use" of the benzodiazepine bromazepam. Exposure sessions consisted of 8 weeks of exposure homework assignments, followed by 16 weeks of guided exposure and response prevention. The sessions were not standardized and for some patients included couples counseling, cognitive restructuring, and/or assertiveness training. Antiexposure instructions involved avoiding fearful stimuli and engaging in ritualized behaviors to relieve anxiety.

Assessment measures included self-rated and assessor-rated scales to measure severity, frequency, and duration of obsessive-compulsive symptoms, the Behavioral Avoidance Test (BAT), the Compulsion Checklist, the BDI, and the HRSD.

Of the 60 patients who began the trial, 17% dropped out by week 8, 27% dropped out by week 24, and 38% dropped out by week 48. Dropouts were fairly evenly distributed among the three groups. Fifty percent of the patients in the fluvoxamine groups used the benzodiazepine, whereas only 30% did in the pill placebo group.

Results showed that all three groups improved on measures of rituals and depression, at weeks 24 and 48. There was a small but nonsignificant superiority for combined treatment up to week 24.

The sample size in each group was somewhat small, and there is no indication that an intent-to-treat analysis was used. The high baseline levels of depression, with a mean and median of 19 on the HRSD, the possible confounding use of a benzodiazepine, the loosely standardized exposure therapy sessions, and the very high noncompliance in the antiexposure group make it difficult to draw conclusions from this study. However, the data do not seem to point toward superiority for combined treatment.

Acute Sequentially Combined Treatment for OCD

Van Balkom et al. (1998) examined the sequential combination of fluvoxamine with CBT in the treatment of OCD, compared with CBT alone. Patients were randomized to one of five groups: cognitive therapy alone, exposure with response prevention alone, 8 weeks of fluvoxamine followed by 8 weeks of cognitive therapy, 8 weeks of fluvoxamine followed by 8 weeks of exposure with response prevention, or a wait-list control for 8 weeks.

The cognitive therapy (CT) and exposure with response prevention (CBT) consisted of 45-minute sessions (6 during the first 8 weeks, 10 during the following 8 weeks). The CBT therapists were all experienced in using exposure and response prevention techniques; however, they were specifically trained to provide cognitive therapy for the purpose of this study. The fluvoxamine plus CBT groups consisted of 30-minute medication management sessions (six during the first 8 weeks). Fluvoxamine was titrated to a maximum dose of 300 mg. Once the CBT started at week 9, brief medication management sessions commenced monthly. Plasma levels of fluvoxamine were ascertained at weeks 8 and 16, and homework diaries were kept to monitor treatment compliance. The mean doses of fluvoxamine at weeks 8 and 16 were 235.3 mg ($SD = 73.4$ mg) and 197.1 mg ($SD = 82.0$ mg), respectively. Outcome measures included the Y-BOCS, the Anxiety Discomfort Scale (ADS), the Padua Inventory-Revised (PI-R), the BDI, and the Symptom Checklist (SCL).

Of the 152 patients who met inclusion and exclusion criteria, 35 patients refused to participate, mostly due to unwillingness to be randomized to either the medication or wait-list groups. Of the 117 patients who agreed to participate, 9 patients dropped out of the two CBT-alone groups, and 20 dropped out of the two fluvoxamine plus CBT groups. All the CBT dropouts were due to noncompliance at the treatment and assessment sessions. Half the dropouts in the fluvoxamine plus CBT groups were due to treatment and assessment noncompliance, and half were attributed to side effects. No significant difference in dropout rates was noted across treatment groups. Although the majority of participants had received treatments in the past for OCD, the types of treatment were evenly distributed over the five treatment conditions in this study.

At 8 weeks, both the cognitive therapy and the exposure with response prevention groups did significantly better than the wait-list control group on measures from the Y-BOCS and ADS. At week 16, the sequential combination of fluvoxamine plus CBT groups did not show any significant difference from the CBT-alone treatments on all measures. The same results were obtained with an intent-to-treat analysis of the data.

The participants in this study were not blind to their respective groups at randomization, which may have influenced their outcome. This study also had a relatively high dropout rate (41% for the fluvoxamine plus CT group, 36% for the fluvoxamine plus exposure with response prevention group, 24% for the CT group, and 15% for the exposure therapy group, although there was no statistically significant difference among these dropout rates). One possible explanation for the combination groups' failure to demonstrate better outcome than the CBT-alone groups may be due to the combination groups having received 8 weeks less CBT than did the CBT-alone groups. This was due to the need to balance the duration of total treatment, so the sequential combination treatment group received the same 16 weeks of treatment but less of one in favor of the other. Since there was no fluvoxamine-alone group, this study does not allow us to make inferences about the efficacy of combination treatment compared with fluvoxamine alone.

Hohagen et al. (1998) studied the interaction of CBT plus fluvoxamine compared with CBT plus placebo. They also looked at treatment outcome of OCD symptoms after treatment of secondary depressive symptoms. In this multicenter study conducted in Germany, 60 patients were randomized to receive CBT plus fluvoxamine or CBT plus placebo. Assessment measures were the SCID, Y-BOCS, HRSD, the Clinical Anxiety Scale (CAS), the Global Assessment Scale (GAS), the Clinical Global Impression Scale (CGI), and the Symptom Check List (SCL-90-R). Because the groups differed significantly on Y-BOC scores at baseline, outliers were dropped, and the sample was reduced to 49 patients. Response criteria were defined as a reduction in Y-BOC scores by more than 35%.

Prior to entering the study, almost all patients had received outpatient treatment for OCD (92%), 41% had received inpatient treatment, and 84% had been on medication. All the patients who had received CBT prior to the study had either relapsed or been treatment nonresponders, but the article did not describe those details.

During the first 3 weeks, patients received fluvoxamine or pill placebo and an introduction to CBT with evaluation of their symptoms ("behavioral analysis"). The fluvoxamine was titrated over the course of 5 weeks with a mean dose of 288 mg. During weeks 4 and 5, patients received therapist-aided exposure sessions, lasting at least 3 hours each. Each day during the remaining 3 weeks patients received cotherapist aided and self-management CBT sessions. Cognitive restructuring was an integral part of the CBT treatments.

Both groups showed significant response, as measured by change in the Y-BOCS. Obsessions were significantly reduced in those receiving CBT plus fluvoxamine, as compared with CBT plus pill placebo. However, no significant differences were noted with regard to compulsions. The study authors suggest that CBT may be an adequate treatment for compulsions, and medications are necessary for successful treatment of obsessions. The lack of therapeutic efficacy in treating obsessions with CBT in this study may be a reflection of the techniques used. We now know that although often difficult to treat, obsessions are amenable to a variety of techniques in the CBT armamentarium. The treatment of OCD symptoms in patients who suffered from comorbid depression was enhanced by the addition of fluvoxamine to CBT.

The latest combined treatment studies typically use more regimented protocols and more standardized assessment measures for the evaluation of OCD severity, such as the Y-BOCS, than did the initial combination studies. However, it is important to briefly mention two of the early RCTs, from around 25 years ago, because they helped to set the stage for the more current rigorous designs.

Marks (1980) conducted a double-blind RCT consisting of 4 weeks of outpatient clomipramine or pill placebo, followed by 6 weeks of inpatient exposure (with modeling and self-imposed response prevention) or relaxation (progressive muscle relaxation) therapy. From weeks 7 through 10 the relaxation groups were switched to receive exposure therapy.

Exposure and relaxation sessions were conducted 5 days per week, for 45 minutes each. Mean dosage of medication was 183 mg for the first 10 weeks and then 145 mg during the remainder of the study. Medications were continued until week 36, and then tapered off over the course of 4 weeks.

Assessment measures included a compulsion checklist, a behavioral avoidance test, an anxiety scale, the Wakefield Inventory to measure depression, and the HRSD.

The results showed clomipramine alone produced transient beneficial effects, primarily in those who had comorbid depression. Progressive muscle relation did not provide much benefit. The combination of clomipramine plus exposure had only a slight additive effect.

Marks el al (1988) conducted another randomized, double-blind study comparing clomipramine, pill placebo, and clomipramine in combination with three different exposure conditions. Of 145 participants screened, 119 were offered treatment, 55 entered the study, and 49 completed the study. Clomipramine was titrated over the course of 3 weeks, and patients were given homework assignments for weeks 1 through 8. They attended 40-minute sessions at weeks 1, 2, 4, and 6 and had telephone contact during the other weeks of the study. Homework assignments were designed to last 3 hours per day; however, compliance was poor, with great variability among individuals. The three exposure conditions consisted of (a) an exposure and response prevention group, (b) an antiexposure condition, where patients were told to avoid contact with anxiety- or ritual-evoking stimuli and were encouraged to engage in their rituals, and (c) a group that included therapist-aided exposure, with occasional home visits if necessary. The number of exposure sessions and the option of home visits were quite flexible and clinically based, not randomly determined, or standardized.

Raters, who were blind to treatment groups, guessed correctly the medication group 90% of the time based on side effects alone, particularly those that were anticholinergic in nature. Assessments included various scales for OCD symptoms, mood, functioning, compliance, and physical symptoms.

The results showed that self-exposure was significantly more effective than antiexposure instructions. The data suggest that self-exposure, via homework assignments, in combination with clomipramine, leads to transient improvement over exposure plus pill placebo. This difference disappeared as treatment continued after the 7-week assessment period. Therapist-aided exposure did not seem to add much benefit to self-guided exposure.

Although there were some limitations to both of Marks's studies, they set the groundwork for later studies and suggest that patients have the ability to employ self-therapy techniques for the treatment of their OCD symptoms.

Long-Term Outcome

There is a dearth of data investigating the long-term outcome of combined pharmacology and psychotherapy for the treatment of OCD. The available studies have been uncontrolled and naturalistic in design, with relatively small sample sizes. They still provide valuable insight, although they raise more questions than they answer.

The results of naturalistic 6-month and 5-year follow-ups, with pooled data from the van Balkom et al. (1998) RCT and from another RCT (van Oppen et al., 1995) comparing cognitive therapy with exposure-based therapy, were published by de Haan et al. (1997) and van Oppen, van Balkom, de Haan, and van Dyck (2005), respectively. The two original studies, from where the data were pooled, used the same inclusion and exclusion criteria, identical treatment protocols, therapists, clinics, assessment methods, and measurement intervals.

Of the participants in the original two studies, 12.9% of the treatment completers and 16.4% of the dropouts did not have data collected at the 6-month and 5-year follow-ups; however, they were included in the intent-to-treat analyses. Of note, the nonparticipants were significantly younger and had lower educational levels than did the participants. The interviewers were blind to the original group assignment. Assessments collected included the Y-BOCS, information on poststudy treatments, and the self-report scales: the Padua Inventory Revised (PI-R), the Anxiety Discomfort Scale (ADS), the SCL-90-R, and the Beck Depression Inventory (BDI).

Results of the 6-month follow-up showed that 17 of the 45 nonresponders in the original studies became responders. The 5-year follow-up showed no significant difference in clinical outcome, on the Y-BOCS measure, among the cognitive therapy, exposure with response prevention, and fluvoxamine in combination with the CBT groups.

It is important to note that, as naturalistic studies, there were no control conditions for the treatments during the follow-up periods. Most of the patients who responded by 6 months had received further treatment after the initial study period. At the 5-year follow-up, more than half the patients who had received combined CBT and fluvoxamine in the original RCT were using an antidepressant. Nineteen percent and 33% of those who had received only cognitive therapy or exposure with response prevention, respectively, were using an antidepressant. Antidepressant use at 5-year follow-up among these groups did not actually meet statistical significance, most likely because the numbers in each group were quite small. Overall, 63% of patients received additional psychotherapy during the 5-year follow-up period, with no statistical difference among groups.

The high use of both psychotherapy and pharmacotherapy during the 5-year follow-up period may partially explain why the treatment dropouts from the original study showed significant improvement on Y-BOCS scores as well, albeit less so than treatment completers. Although the numbers in the subgroups were small, and many of the patients who received antidepressant medication during the 5-year follow-up had also received additional psychotherapy during that time, the data suggest that those who had received medication in the original RCTs may have found it difficult to discontinue the use of the antidepressant in the long term.

Cottraux, Mollard, Bouvard, and Marks (1993) conducted a 1-year naturalistic follow-up of the Cottraux et al. (1990) RCT discussed above. Fifty-five percent of the patients who began the initial study were available for testing at the 1-year follow-up period. Between the end of the initial study and the 1-year follow-up, roughly 20% of the patients who had received exposure therapy, and 60% of those who had received antiexposure therapy, had used an antidepressant.

Assessment measures included self-rating and assessor-rated scales to measure severity, frequency, and duration of obsessive-compulsive symptoms, the Behavioral Avoidance Test (BAT), the Compulsion Checklist, the BDI, and the HRSD.

Although an intent-to-treat analysis does not appear to have been performed, the 27 dropouts differed from the 33 completers only with a greater avoidance score on the Behavioral Avoidance Test. The results suggest that all patients, regardless of

treatment, improved at 1-year follow-up. However, those who received exposure therapy were less likely to have reported antidepressant treatment.

Treatment Discontinuation

Fairly recently, the effects of treatment discontinuation in those who have responded to OCD treatment have been studied. Simpson et al. (2004) published data from the discontinuation phase of the Foa et al. (2005) RCT, discussed above, which compared exposure with response prevention, clomipramine, their combination, and pill placebo. The methods for the acute phase of the study (Foa et al., 2005) were discussed above. Those who were treatment responders in the acute phase were eligible to enter the discontinuation phase.

During the discontinuation phase, which lasted 12 weeks, the exposure with response prevention was stopped and the medication was tapered off. Patients still continued to see their therapist or pharmacotherapist for supportive/evaluative meetings, lasting up to 20 minutes each, at regular intervals. Those who relapsed were removed from the study and offered open treatment. Relapse was determined by CGI-S scores at or below those at the beginning of the acute phase of the study, or sufficient impairment to be unable to continue with the assessment. Raters were blind to the original treatment.

Of the 87 patients who completed phase 1 of the initial trial, 48 were responders and were eligible to enter the discontinuation phase of the study. All but 2 of the responders actually participated in the discontinuation phase. Nine of the participants relapsed during the discontinuation phase.

Although the sample size was small in the 12-week discontinuation phase, and there was no randomization or control group, the following trends were highly suggestive. Responders who originally received either CBT alone or in combination with clomipramine had less severe OCD symptoms at the beginning of the discontinuation phase, were less likely to relapse during the discontinuation phase, and, if they did relapse, had a longer time to relapse following treatment discontinuation.

Special Populations

One third to one half of adults with OCD develop the disorder during childhood or adolescence. The

Pediatric OCD Treatment Study (POTS) Team recently published the first RCT exploring treatment efficacies of combined treatment in child and adolescent OCD patients (March et al., 2004). The multicenter study included 112 patients, aged 7 through 17, who were randomized to CBT, sertraline, combined treatment, or pill placebo groups for 12 weeks. Responders to any active treatment were eligible for entry into a discontinuation phase of the study (unpublished as of this date). Patients receiving sertraline or pill placebo were blind to treatment group. However, those receiving either CBT alone or in combination with sertraline were not.

Patients receiving sertraline or pill placebo had weekly medication management sessions, lasting roughly 30 minutes each, and were given supportive encouragement to resist their obsessions and compulsions. Patients receiving CBT also had weekly sessions, lasting roughly 1 hour each. Three of the sessions included the parents for the entire session.

Assessment measures included the ADIS-C and the CY-BOCS, a clinician-rated tool that incorporates data from clinical observation and parent and child report. Overall, only 13% of the participants dropped out of the study. In each of the active treatment groups, which consisted of 28 assigned patients, only 2 per group dropped out; in the pill placebo group, 6 dropped out, mostly due to nonresponse at 8 weeks. All of the 112 patients assigned to groups were included in an intent-to-treat analysis.

This study had minimal inclusion and exclusion criteria, designed to recruit a population representative of those who generally seek OCD treatment. By age, 46% of the patients were 11 or younger, and 54% were adolescents, aged 12 or older. Comorbid disorders were included: 63% had a comorbid affective or anxiety disorder; 27% had a comorbid ADHD, oppositional defiant disorder, or conduct disorder (10% of the total study population was taking a psychostimulant for ADHD); and 16% had a comorbid tic disorder. The mean doses of medication in the sertraline-alone group and the pill-placebo group were 170 mg and 176 mg, respectively, whereas the mean dose in the combined treatment was only 133 mg.

No child or adolescent experienced any episode of mania, hypomania, depression, suicidal ideation, or suicide attempts while on sertraline. Seven patients treated with sertraline experienced increased hyperactivity, two of them with an associated increased impulsivity who responded well to a decrease in medication dose.

Results showed that patients in the combined treatment group did better than either the CBT- or sertraline-alone groups, which did not differ from each other. Remission rates, as defined by a CY-BOCS score of less than 10, were 54% in the combined group, 39% in the CBT-alone group, 21% in the sertraline-alone group, and 4% in the pill-placebo group. The difference between the combined and CBT-alone groups did not reach statistical significance.

Foa, Kozak, Steketee, and McCarthy (1992) sought to determine whether behavior therapy (exposure and response prevention) for the treatment of OCD was enhanced by prior treatment of comorbid depression. Patients ($N = 38$) were divided into highly depressed (BDI greater than 21) and mildly depressed (BDI less than 20) groups, then randomly assigned to imipramine or pill placebo. Patients received medication for 6 weeks, which was continued while they began the behavior therapy sessions. These daily sessions were 2 hours each, lasting 3 weeks. Patients then had two home visits, each of 4 hours' duration. Participants then received 12 weekly, 45-minute supportive behavior therapy sessions. Medication was discontinued at 22 weeks.

Assessment measures included an obsessive-compulsive severity scale, the Compulsive Activity Checklist (CAC), BDI, HRSD, and the Social Adjustment Scale-Self Report (SAS-SR). The results showed that imipramine did decrease depressive symptoms but did not seem to increase the likelihood of successful behavior therapy for OCD, a finding that differs from the study by Marks, Stern, Mawson, Cobb, and McDonald (1980), where clomipramine was used. Behavior therapy was shown to decrease both depressive and OCD symptoms.

Although much further research is needed, the general consensus at present seems to advocate for either combined CBT with medication management or CBT alone for the treatment of OCD. There are data that suggest that combination therapy is somewhat better than CBT alone, especially in children and adolescents, and there are data suggesting otherwise. The data suggesting superiority in combination treatment or with CBT alone are based on better long-term outcomes than medication alone.

POSTTRAUMATIC STRESS DISORDER

While there have been numerous studies showing the efficacy of both pharmacological and psychosocial therapies in the treatment of PTSD, few studies have directly compared the two, and apparently no RCTs explored their combination. However, expert recommendations and common practice often espouse the usefulness of this combination.

One recent randomized pilot study (Otto et al., 2003) did compare the combination of CBT plus sertraline with use of sertraline alone in pharmacotherapy-refractory PTSD patients among Cambodian refugees. All 10 women in this study had previously failed combined treatment of clonazepam plus an SSRI other than sertraline. It is unclear what the inclusion and exclusion criteria were, but patients had significant psychiatric comorbidities that were comparable between the two groups of five patients.

The primary assessment measure was the Clinician-Administered PTSD Scale (CAPS). Other measures sought to assess anxiety and depressive severity, with particular attention and modifications to account for culture-specific somatizations and autonomic arousal.

Patients appear to have been continued on their dose of clonazepam while open dosing of sertraline was added. The mean doses of sertraline in the combined and alone groups were 100 mg and 125 mg, respectively. CBT sessions, conducted in a group format in a Buddhist temple, were a combination of exposure-based treatment, progressive muscle relaxation, diaphragmatic breathing, and cognitive restructuring.

This pilot study suggests an improved outcome for those patients who received combined treatment of CBT plus sertraline, compared with sertraline alone, on all measures except depressive severity. The combined treatment seemed to be particularly helpful in reducing catastrophic misinterpretations of culturally relevant somatic symptoms.

Marshall, Cárcamo, Blanco, and Liebowitz (2003) reported three case studies of partial responders to pharmacotherapy who subsequently received prolonged exposure therapy. Apart from the very small number of patients, we cannot draw any statistical inferences from these cases. The medications given and even the assessment measures were not standardized, and there were very significant differences among the patients. It was reported, however, that the three patients seemed to exhibit some further improvement with the addition of exposure-based therapy.

An RCT is in progress (Simon) exploring the use of paroxetine following exposure therapy in PTSD. No data were yet available for inclusion in this review. Perhaps future studies will shed more light on the efficacy of combined treatment for PTSD; however, for the time being, we will have to make inferences from studies that explore the combined treatment for other anxiety disorders.

GENERALIZED ANXIETY DISORDER

There are hardly any RCTs comparing combined treatment with monotherapy in generalized anxiety disorder (GAD). Bond and colleagues (Bond, Wingrove, Curran, & Lader, 2002) studied 60 patients with GAD in London by randomly assigning them to one of four treatment conditions: buspirone and anxiety management training, buspirone and nondirective therapy, placebo and anxiety management training, and placebo and nondirective therapy for 8 weeks. The anxiety management and the nondirective therapy were conducted by the same clinician (a psychologist). The clinician administering the buspirone was not mentioned in this article.

Nondirective therapy involved the patients talking freely with the therapist, acknowledging and reflecting back feelings discussed, using open-ended questions in a nonjudgmental manner. Anxiety management training incorporated some elements of CBT: psychoeducation, progressive muscle relaxation, and homework assignments. In addition, avoidance behaviors and anxiety triggers were explored, as well as the relationship between thoughts, feelings, and symptoms. Negative thoughts were recorded and challenged, possibly in a similar manner to cognitive therapy, but no further elaboration of the technique was presented. Both types of psychotherapy continued weekly, consisting of 45-minute sessions for 7 weeks.

The medication and placebo were administered with flexible dosing, beginning at 5 mg in three daily capsules, with an increase if necessary to six capsules for the duration of the 8 weeks. Whether the clinicians and patients were blind to placebo versus buspirone was not mentioned. Outcome was measured using the HRSA, administered by a blind evaluator. Self-reports included the Hospital Anxiety and Depression Scale, the Zung Self Rating Anxiety Scale, the General Health Questionnaire, the Cognitive Checklist, and the Mood Rating Scale.

Of the 60 patients who began the trial, 44 completed treatment. Patients in the buspirone groups were more likely to drop out than those in the placebo groups, often due to adverse effects. After treatment, there was no significant difference in outcome among the groups; all showed a 50% reduction on HRSA, indicating some improvement. When comparing the completer analysis to the intent-to-treat analysis, similar results occurred.

This study makes the case that psychotherapy is helpful in the treatment of GAD with or without the addition of buspirone. It is difficult to compare the results of this research to other studies of GAD using CBT, since only improvement on HRSA and self-reports were measured. Most other studies institute remission or response criteria and measure rate of response. Many clinicians also agree that dosages of 30 mg or less per day of buspirone, such as used in their study, are grossly subtherapeutic.

The duration of treatment in this trial was rather short (only 8 weeks), whereas other studies using CBT have been conducted for a minimum of 12 weeks (Borkevec, Newman, Pincus, & Lytle, 2002). The major hallmark of GAD is uncontrollable worry. The HRSA measures worry but not exclusively; rather, the items combine anxious mood, worry, fearful anticipation, and irritability. Other instruments have been used that focus primarily on worry (e.g., Penn State Worry Questionnaire; Meyer, Miller, Metzger, & Borkovec, 1990) and make comparisons between studies easier.

Clearly, more research is needed for efficacy testing of combined treatment of GAD, especially involving SSRIs and a full course of CBT that includes cognitive restructuring, worry reduction, and progressive muscle relaxation techniques.

SOCIAL ANXIETY DISORDER

There is a paucity of RCTs for social anxiety disorder (SAD) comparing medication, psychotherapy, and their combination, whereas the number of such trials for monotherapy comparisons abound. Of the three RCTs that exist, two were conducted in an academic psychiatric setting employing trained clinicians; the other was conducted in a primary care setting with medical practitioners.

Davidson and colleagues (2004) conducted a large RCT for generalized SAD using fluoxetine, CBT, their combination, and placebo to test treatment effectiveness at two sites. After 722 subjects were screened, 295 were randomized to 14 weeks of treatment in one of five groups. The groups included fluoxetine alone ($n = 57$), comprehensive group CBT alone ($n = 60$), fluoxetine and comprehensive group CBT combined ($n = 59$), placebo plus comprehensive group CBT ($n = 59$), and placebo alone ($n = 60$). Exclusion criteria were similar to those for other RCTs for anxiety disorders: schizophrenia, bipolar disorder, current substance use disorder, cognitive impairment or organic brain syndrome, any unstable medical condition, MDD within the last 6 months, and another primary anxiety disorder (one that causes more impairment than SAD).

Fluoxetine treatment and placebo, both administered double-blind by a psychiatrist following a manual, were initiated at 10 mg, increased to 20 mg on day 8, to 30 mg on day 15, and to 40 mg on day 29 (the target dose). If patients failed to achieve response at 40 mg, the dose was raised to 50 mg on day 43 and to 60 mg on day 57. Patients were seen weekly for 4 weeks, then every other week for the rest of the 10 weeks. The comprehensive group CBT (CCBT) involved psychoeducation, social skills training, cognitive restructuring, and in vivo exposure during the 14 weekly sessions. This type of CBT differs from that based on Heimberg by the addition of social skills training and two sessions in which the patients were taught how to begin a conversation with a stranger and how to make eye contact. Group sessions were led by two extensively trained therapists and comprised five or six patients; length of group sessions was not discussed.

Outcome was measured using the Brief Social Phobia Scale and the CGI, both rated by an independent evaluator. A videotaped role-play test of social skills was conducted before and after treatment and served as a secondary outcome measure. Of the 295 randomized patients, 211 (72%) completed the 14 weeks of treatment, with 5% ($n = 16$) dropping out before treatment began. In pairwise comparisons, the placebo-only group experienced more dropouts than the CCBT-only group and the CCBT plus placebo group.

Based on CGI scores as the response criterion, the intent-to-treat response rates were 50.9% for fluoxetine alone, 51.7% for CCBT alone, 54.2% for combined fluoxetine and CCBT, 50.8% for CCBT plus placebo, and 31.7% for placebo only, demonstrating only a trend for significance ($p = .09$). When pairwise comparisons were tested, all treatments were significantly more effective than placebo, with combined treatment demonstrating slightly greater significance ($p = .01$; $p = .03$ for all comparisons). The completer response rates were higher: fluoxetine 64.1%, CCBT 64.6%, combined treatment 66.7%, CCBT plus placebo 59.6%, and placebo 40.5%. Again, overall, there was a trend toward significance ($p = .09$), but the pairwise comparisons demonstrated that active treatment was more effective than placebo except that the CCBT plus placebo group only showed a trend toward significance ($p = .08$). The combined treatment group demonstrated the greatest significance ($p = .01$), with CCBT next ($p = .02$), and fluoxetine alone last ($p = .03$).

The two phobia measures demonstrated a significant difference in outcome between the active treatments and placebo, but in pairwise comparisons, fluoxetine alone followed by CCBT alone demonstrated the fastest onset of action. In this very well conducted RCT, there was no significant benefit to combined CBT and medication for SAD.

The second RCT for SAD that compared a combination of medication and psychotherapy with both psychotherapy alone and placebo was conducted by Clark et al. (2003) in England. Patients aged 18 to 60 with generalized social phobia of at least 6 months' duration as the primary problem without current MDD, bipolar disorder, psychosis, or substance use disorder were included. No participants were accepted if they had previous treatment experience with cognitive or exposure therapy or an SSRI.

Using stratified random assignment, 60 SAD patients were evenly allocated to one of three treatment conditions: cognitive therapy (CT) alone, fluoxetine plus self-exposure, and placebo plus self-exposure. Acute treatment lasted for 16 weeks followed by a 3-month maintenance period. All patients were assessed at 12 months for follow-up.

The cognitive therapy treatment was based on the model of Clark and Wells and was conducted by psychologists experienced in CBT for anxiety, and su-

pervised regularly by Dr. Clark. The CT focused on the ways that social phobia is maintained through thoughts and safety behaviors. One of the treatment components involved helping patients change their self-focus (constant monitoring of their own sensations and worry about how others perceive them) to an external one (e.g., the social situation in which they are engaged). The treatment also incorporated videotape feedback to correct distorted self-images frequently held by socially phobic patients. In addition to receiving exposure therapy, patients were prepared in advance for what they feared would occur and then were tested for whether the feared event actually occurred. Cognitive restructuring was implemented to change dysfunctional assumptions and anticipatory as well as postevent processing.

Pharmacotherapists were psychiatrists with experience using SSRIs but with little formal CBT training. Prior to beginning the study, pharmacotherapists conducted two practice cases under the supervision of Dr. Clark. The fluoxetine or placebo treatment groups received 20-mg capsules, with the first dosage increase to 40 mg at week 2 or 3, increasing to a maximum of 60 mg if needed. Patients were told that fluoxetine would make them more confident in social situations by correcting a neurochemical disturbance and were advised to systematically expose themselves to social situations to derive maximum benefit from the medication.

Measures of social anxiety in this study were the Social Phobia Scale, the Social Interaction Anxiety Scale, the Liebowitz Social Anxiety Scale, the Fear Questionnaire Social Phobia subscale, the Fear of Negative Evaluation Scale, and the Social Phobia Weekly Summary Scale (a self-report of social anxiety, social avoidance, self-focused versus external attention, anticipatory processing, and postevent rumination). The Beck Anxiety Inventory and the Beck Depression Inventory were used to assess mood.

The sample was 52% female. Half of participants were married or living with a partner, 72% were working, with a mean age of 33.2 years and a mean duration of illness of 13.3 years ($SD = 11.3$). In addition, 43% met criteria for avoidant personality disorder. There were no significant differences between the treatment groups on these demographic variables.

Six patients did not complete the treatment phase: two dropped out due to side effects (one was in the placebo group), one in the placebo group sought treatment elsewhere, one moved out of the area, one became pregnant, and the last became severely depressed and required additional treatment. Of the 54 completers, 20 were in the CT group, 17 in the fluoxetine plus exposure group, and 17 in the placebo plus exposure group.

At the end of the 16-week treatment phase, cognitive therapy was significantly more effective on a composite measure of social anxiety than either combined treatment or placebo. The combined fluoxetine and exposure was not significantly different than the placebo plus exposure group on this composite measure. All three treatment groups demonstrated a significant decrease in all measures, composite and individual, from baseline to posttreatment. All three treatment groups demonstrated significant improvement in mood measures from baseline to posttreatment, but there was no difference among the groups. These results are based on an intent-to-treat analysis.

Patients in the CT and fluoxetine plus exposure groups were entered into the maintenance phase after the 16-week, acute-treatment phase. The placebo plus exposure group patients were withdrawn from the study. During the maintenance treatment phase, CT patients received three monthly booster sessions. The fluoxetine patients continued on their full dose for 3 months, which was then gradually tapered over 3 to 6 weeks. Measures of composite social anxiety were again taken, and the results showed that CT patients maintained their treatment gains, and fluoxetine plus exposure patients continued to improve. The CT group continued to demonstrate significantly better outcome after the maintenance phase. These differences were also found at the 12-month follow-up: cognitive therapy was superior to fluoxetine plus exposure on both composite and individual social anxiety measures.

The study authors also calculated effect sizes for the treatment groups by taking the mean social phobia composite score at pretreatment and subtracting the mean social phobia composite score at posttreatment, end of maintenance, and follow-up. The effect size was 2.14 for the CT group at posttreatment, compared with 0.92 for the fluoxetine group and 0.56 for the placebo group. The end of maintenance effect size was 2.57 for the CT group and 1.14 for the fluoxetine group. The 12-month follow-up effect size was 2.53 for the CT group and 1.36 for the fluoxetine group.

In this trial, combined treatment was not better than monotherapy (cognitive therapy or exposure) in the treatment of generalized social anxiety disorder, although significant improvement was demonstrated. Cognitive therapy was greatly more effective than self-directed exposure.

The primary care RCT for social anxiety was conducted by Blomhoff and colleagues (2001) in Norway and Sweden. They randomly treated 387 socially anxious patients with sertraline or placebo. Half of those patients were randomly assigned to exposure therapy or general medical care. There were 98 patients in the sertraline plus exposure therapy group, 98 in the placebo plus exposure therapy group, 96 in the sertraline plus general care group, and 95 in the placebo plus general care group. All treatment was provided by medical practitioners who received training in diagnostic interviewing and exposure therapy.

The study sample was predominantly female ($n = 234$), with a mean age of 40.4; 67% of participants were married or living with a partner, and their mean duration of illness was 23.6 years. One hundred thirty-five subjects from the sample had a comorbid diagnosis, but only 2% had comorbid dysthymia. Excluded diagnoses were history of bipolar disorder, psychosis, or panic disorder that began before social phobia, as well as current MDD, any other anxiety disorder, eating disorder, or substance use disorder.

Measures used to determine outcome were the Social Phobia Scale (SPS), the Clinical Global Impression-Social Phobia Scale (CGI-SP), and the Montgomery Asberg Depression Rating Scale (MADRS). Diagnosis was assessed using the Mini International Neuropsychiatric Interview (MINI). Clinicians in this study included 50 physicians who underwent a 30-hour training program in order to conduct the MINI and other rating scales, to make a reliable diagnosis of social phobia, and to conduct the exposure therapy component of the treatment. Training involved lectures, videotapes, manuals, and group supervision.

The sertraline treatment or placebo began with one pill daily (50-mg dose) for 4 weeks. If there was no minimal improvement (CGI-SP less than 3), the dosage then was increased to 100 mg daily (two pills). At weeks 8 and 12, if minimal improvement had not occurred, the dosage was again increased to a maximum of 150 mg. The dosage at 12 weeks was maintained through the 16th week if no difficulty with tolerance was noted. Patients were seen for nine visits over the 16 weeks of the study. Pharmacotherapy adherence was evaluated regularly through blood levels, as well as through pill counts.

The general medical care component of the study was based on National Institute of Mental Health guidelines for clinical management of mood disorders: general therapeutic support, reassurance and encouragement with some advice, and allowing the patient to express fears and concerns. No interpretations of patient behavior or specific behavioral instructions were allowed.

The exposure therapy component was conducted during eight sessions over the first 12 weeks of the study, with each session lasting between 15 and 20 minutes. During the first session, psychoeducation was the focus, with explanations of the treatment and the identified problems; homework assignments were covered during the second session. Sessions 3 through 8 involved instructions for the patient to gradually expose him- or herself to feared situations outside the session meeting, using rating scales to measure the level of anxiety. The goal was for the patient to slowly decrease his or her anxiety as each exposure occurred. The physician's role throughout the 12 weeks of exposure therapy was to identify goals, to explore new coping strategies, and to support self-exposure.

Outcome was measured on three levels: responder, partial responder, and nonresponder, based on the CGI-SP and the SPS (self-report). Ratings were made at weeks 4, 8, 12, 16, and 24. Response criteria were a 50% reduction on SPS from baseline and a CGI-SP severity rating of not mentally ill or mildly ill (1 or 2) and a CGI-SP improvement rating of very much improved or much improved (1 or 2). Nonresponse criteria were a less than 25% reduction on SPS from baseline and a CGI-SP improvement rating of no change or worse (4 or higher). Partial response criteria were scores between response and nonresponse.

The protocol called for treatment withdrawal after 16 weeks if nonresponse occurred, and 44 (11%) patients were withdrawn. The intent-to-treat group consisted of 354 patients. There was a significant difference in response between those patients receiving sertraline and those receiving placebo, but no significant difference between patients in the exposure group compared with the general care group ($p = 0.08$). The combined sertraline and exposure group had an intent-to-treat response rate of 40.8% ($n = 40$) and a completer response rate of 45.5%. The sertraline-only group had an intent-to-treat response rate of 36.4% and a completer response rate of 40.2%. The intent-to-treat response rate for both sertraline groups was 38.6%, and the completer response rate was 48.4%. The exposure-only intent-to-treat response rate was 30.6%, and the completer response rate was 33%. The combined treatment group had a trend toward significance compared with the exposure-only group ($p = 0.059$). In this primary care trial, treatment with sertraline, with or without exposure therapy, was effective in treating generalized social anxiety disorder, and combined treatment was not more effective than sertraline alone.

The London group conducted a 1-year follow-up after the termination of the 24-week treatment (Haug et al., 2003). Of the 354 patients who were assessed at the 24-week period, 328 were evaluated 1 year later, 83 in the sertraline plus exposure group, 85 in the sertraline plus general care group, 78 in the exposure only group, and 82 in the placebo plus general care group.

All groups demonstrated a significant decrease from their baseline measures at the 1-year follow-up. The exposure-only group continued to improve from the 24-week assessment to the 1-year follow-up, with a significant change on the CGI-SP. The placebo group also showed improvement from the 24-week period to the 1-year follow-up on the CGI-SP. For the sertraline plus exposure and the sertraline plus general care groups, there was a nonsignificant worsening on the CGI-SP at follow-up. On individual scales measuring aspects of social fear and avoidance, the exposure-only group also demonstrated continued improvement from the end of treatment to the 1-year follow-up. In addition, the placebo group also demonstrated some of the same improvement, whereas there was again slight deterioration in the sertraline groups (nonsignificant).

One very important note must be considered when evaluating these data: 66 patients (20.5% of the sample) received some SSRI during the follow-up period. There were 13 (15.5%) in the sertraline plus exposure group, 18 (21.6%) in the sertraline plus general care group, 14 (19.2%) in the exposure-only group, and 21 (19.5%) in the placebo group. This may account for the high rate of improvement in the placebo group and the lack of significance in decreased improvement in the sertraline groups.

This RCT of generalized SAD in primary care has demonstrated no greater efficacy for combined treatment than for monotherapy. There are some limitations to this research. The design did not allow for blinded evaluations of outcome; therefore, there may be some rater bias given the fact that the clinicians who conducted the treatments also made the response determinations. The exposure therapy, as conducted by physicians, differs somewhat from that conducted by trained psychiatric clinicians — the physicians directed the patients to do the exposures on their own, whereas psychiatric clinicians generally accompany the patients on many or at least some exposures, offering support and encouragement throughout the process. This often facilitates further exposures, many of which are self-directed in between sessions. This may have accounted for the lower efficacy of the exposure-only results.

SUMMARY

According to an analysis of the national trends for outpatient treatment of anxiety disorders (Olafson, Marcus, Wan, & Geissler, 2004), the community rate of combined medication and psychotherapy treatment for any anxiety disorder was 27%, whereas the rate of combined antidepressant and psychotherapy treatment was 21%. Although combining medication and a psychotherapy such as cognitive therapy, CBT, exposure therapy, or relaxation therapy is ubiquitous in clinical practice for the treatment of anxiety disorders, the data show that there is little or no benefit over either medication alone or CBT alone. In PD, although combined imipramine and CBT was slightly superior initially, the treatment gains leveled over time and in the long term, and outcome was actually no different from imipramine alone in relapse rates.

There are several hypotheses to explain this troubling finding that combined treatment has a similar relapse rate as medication alone in PD. According to Otto (2002), the medication forms a context in which learning occurs. In this case, the learning involves the gradual exposure to bodily sensations (interoceptive exposure) whereby the patient learns to be less fearful of these sensations. When the context is withdrawn, the benefit of what was learned may be diminished as well.

Another explanation involves the concept of extinction of fear that has been tested in animal studies and is applicable to treatment of phobic disorders. Through experiments in rats (LeDoux, 2000) in which a loud tone is played (conditioned stimulus) and then a foot shock is repeatedly paired with the tone, the rat learns to fear the tone (unconditioned stimulus). When the shock is no longer given but the

tone is sounded, the rats respond physiologically with freezing, rapid heart rate, and shallow breathing as if the shock were given (conditioned response). This process is known as *fear conditioning*. In order to diminish the fear, the tone is played repeatedly without the foot shock, so the rat learns to uncouple the conditioned stimulus from the unconditioned stimulus, and the conditioned response diminishes. This process of learning is known as extinction (Myers & Davis, 2002). If the foot shock is again paired with the tone, the rat responds as before (freezing, heart racing, breathing rapidly) even when the tone is played alone. This process is known as *reinstatement*.

Bouton (2002) categorized four types of reversal of extinction: reinstatement, spontaneous recovery, renewal, and reacquisition. These are clearly reminiscent of clinical relapse and recurrence in patients with PD and other phobic disorders. Reinstatement refers to recovery of behavior that occurs when the subject is exposed to the unconditioned stimulus after extinction. This type of extinction reversal is highly controlled by the context in which the unconditioned stimulus is presented. As reviewed by Bouton (2002), but probably first proposed by Rachman (1979), is the idea that CBT creates a kind of context-dependent form of new learning. Patients with a phobic disorder, like PD, are subject to relapse under a variety of circumstances that map onto Bouton's extinction reversal.

An important feature of extinction is that it is highly context specific (Westbrook, Iordanova, McNally, Richardson, & Harris, 2002). For example, the rat that has undergone conditioning (foot shock with tone) and then extinction (tone without shock until no anxiety occurs) in a specific chamber will no longer evince freezing behavior (conditioned response) in that environment, when exposed to that tone (conditioned stimulus). If the rat were then placed in a different chamber, and the tone was played, a strong conditioned response (freezing behavior) occurs. Although the conditioned response had been extinguished, extinction does not generalize to a new context, whereas conditioned fear does.

If medication does indeed form a context for learning, then a potential means of delivering improved care in anxiety disorders with phobic avoidance may be in sequential treatment. If medication was to be given first, allowing for the rapid response known with SSRIs, then CBT begun later, perhaps at the point of medication taper, long-term outcome may be improved. Whittal, Otto, and Hong (2001) instituted a manualized CBT treatment for withdrawal from an SSRI based on earlier work used in benzodiazepine withdrawal (Otto, Pollack, & Barlow, 1995; Otto et al., 1993), in eight PDA patients with favorable results at 3-month follow-up. Schmidt, Wollaway-Bickel, Trakowski, Santiago, and Vasey (2002) also tested discontinuation of SSRI during treatment with group CBT compared with combined treatment and found no outcome difference at posttreatment and 6-month follow-up. Although the principles of extinction and reinstatement have been applied to PD, they are applicable to other anxiety disorders as well. Long-term outcome RCTs comparing monotherapy, combined treatment, and sequential treatment are needed to test which are most effective for which patients not only in PD but in all the anxiety disorders.

REFERENCES

Arnow, B. A., & Constantino, M. J. (2003). Effectiveness of psychotherapy and combination treatment for chronic depression. *Journal of Clinical Psychology, 59,* 893–905.

Barlow, D. H., Gorman, J. M., Shear, M. K., & Woods, S. W. (2000). Cognitive-behavioral therapy, imipramine, or their combination for panic disorder: A randomized controlled trial. *Journal of the American Medical Association, 283,* 2529–2536.

Blackburn, I. M., & Moore, R. G. (1997). Controlled acute and follow-up trial of cognitive therapy and pharmacotherapy in out-patients with recurrent depression. *British Journal of Psychiatry, 171,* 328–334.

Blomhoff, S., Haug, T. T., Hellstrom, K., Holme, I., Humble, M., Madsbu, H. P., & Wold, J. E. (2001). Randomized controlled general practice trial of sertraline, exposure therapy and combined treatment in generalized social phobia. *British Journal of Psychiatry, 179,* 23–30.

Bond, A. J., Wingrove, J., Curran, H. V., & Lader, M. H. (2002). Treatment of generalized anxiety disorder with a short course of psychological therapy, combined with buspirone or placebo. *Journal of Affective Disorders, 72,* 267–271.

Borkovec, T. D., Newman, M. G., Pincus, A. L., & Lytle, R. (2002). A component analysis of cognitive-behavioral therapy for generalized anxiety disorder and the role of interpersonal problems. *Journal of Consulting and Clinical Psychology, 70,* 288–298.

Bouton, M. E. (2002). Context, ambiguity, and unlearning: Sources of relapse after behavioral extinction. *Biological Psychiatry, 52,* 976–986.

Burnand, Y., Andreoli, A., Kolatte, E., Venturini, A., & Rosset, N. (2002). Psychodynamic psychotherapy and clomipramine in the treatment of major depression. *Psychiatric Services, 53,* 585–590.

Clark, D. M., Ehlers, A., McManus, F., Hackmann, A., Fennell, M., Campbell, H., et al. (2003). Cognitive therapy versus fluoxetine in generalized social phobia: A randomized placebo-controlled trial. *Journal of Consulting and Clinical Psychology, 71,* 1058–1067.

Cottraux, J., Mollard, E., Bouvard, M., & Marks, I. (1993). Exposure therapy, fluvoxamine, or combination treatment in obsessive-compulsive disorder: One-year follow-up. *Psychiatry Research, 49,* 63–75.

Cottraux, J., Mollard, E., Bouvard, M., Marks, I., Sluys, M., Nury, A. M., et al. (1990). A controlled study of fluvoxamine and exposure in obsessive-compulsive disorder. *International Clinical Psychopharmacology, 5,* 17–30.

Davidson, J. R. T., Foa, E. B., Huppert, J. D., Keefe, F. J., Franklin, M. E., Compton, J. S., et al. (2004). Fluoxetine, comprehensive cognitive behavioral therapy, and placebo in generalized social phobia. *Archives of General Psychiatry, 61,* 1005–1013.

de Beurs, E., van Balkom, A. J. L. M., Lange, A., Koele, P., & van Dyck, R. (1995). Treatment of panic disorder with agoraphobia: Comparison of fluvoxamine, placebo, and psychological panic management combined with exposure and of exposure in vivo alone. *American Journal of Psychiatry, 152,* 683–691.

de Haan, E., van Oppen, P., van Balkom, A. J. L. M., Spinhoven, P., Hoogduin, K. A. L., & Van Dyck, R. (1997). Prediction of outcome and early vs. late improvement in OCD patients treated with cognitive behaviour therapy and pharmacotherapy. *Acta Psychiatrica Scandinavica, 96,* 354–361.

de Jonghe, F., Kool, S., van Aalst, G., Dekker, J., & Peen, J. (2001). Combining psychotherapy and antidepressants in the treatment of depression. *Journal of Affective Disorders, 64,* 217–229.

Dekker, J., Molenaar, P. J., Kool, S., van Aalst, G., Peen, J., & de Jonghe, F. (2005). Dose-effect relations in time-limited combined psycho-pharmacological treatment for depression. *Psychological Medicine, 35,* 47–58.

Foa, E. B., Kozak, M. J., Steketee, G. S., & McCarthy, P. R. (1992). Treatment of depressive and obsessive-compulsive symptoms in OCD by imipramine and behaviour therapy. *British Journal of Clinical Psychology, 31,* 279–292.

Foa, E. B., Liebowitz, M. R., Kozak, M. J., Davies, S., Campeas, R., Franklin, M. E., et al. (2005). Randomized, placebo-controlled trial of exposure and ritual prevention, clomipramine, and their combination in the treatment of obsessive-compulsive disorder. *American Journal of Psychiatry, 162,* 151–161.

Frank, E., Kupfer, D. J., Perel, J. M., Cornes, C., Jarrett, D. B., Mallinger, A. G., et al. (1990). Three year outcomes for maintenance therapies in recurrent depression. *Archives of General Psychiatry, 47,* 1093–1099.

Haug, T. T., Blomhoff, S. Hellstrom, K., Holme, I., Humble, M., Madsbu, H. P., et al. (2003). Exposure therapy and sertraline in social phobia: 1-year follow-up of a randomized controlled trial. *British Journal of Psychiatry, 182,* 312–318.

Hautzinger M., de Jong-Meyer, R., & Treiber, R (1996). Effectiveness of cognitive behavior therapy, pharmacotherapy, and the combination of both in nonendogenous unipolar depression. *Zeitschrift für klinische Psychologie und Psychotherapie, 25,* 130–145.

Hegerl, U., Plattner, A., & Möller, H.-J. (2004). Should combined pharmaco- and psychotherapy be offered to depressed patients? A qualitative review of randomized clinical trials from the 1990s. *European Archives of Psychiatry and Clinical Neuroscience, 254,* 99–107.

Hirschfeld, R. M. A., Dunner, D. L., Keitner, G., Klein, D. N., Koran, L. M., Kornstein, S. G., al. (2002). Does psychosocial functioning improve independent of depressive symptoms? A comparison of nefazodone, psychotherapy, and their combination. *Biological Psychiatry, 51,* 123–133.

Hohagen, F., Winkelmann, G., Rasche-Räuchle, H., Hand, I., König, A., Münchau, N., et al. (1998). Combination of behaviour therapy with fluvoxamine in comparison with behaviour therapy and placebo. *British Journal of Psychiatry, 17*(Suppl. 35), 71–78.

Hollan, S. D., DeRubeis, R. J., Evans, M. D., Wiemer, M. J., Garvey, M. J., Grove, W. M., et al. (1992). Cognitive therapy and pharmacotherapy for depression: Singly and in combination. *Archives of General Psychiatry, 49,* 774–781.

Keller, M. B., McCullough, J. P., Klein, D. N., Arnow, B., Dunner, D. L, Gelenberg, A. J., et al. (2000). A comparison of nefazodone, the cognitive behavioural-analysis system of psychotherapy and their combination therapy for the treatment of chronic depression. *New England Journal of Medicine, 342,* 1462–1470.

LeDoux, J. E. (2000). Emotion circuits in the brain. *Annual Review of Neuroscience, 23,* 155–184.

Lipsitz, J., Kobak, K., Feiger, A., Sikich, S., Moroz, G., & Engelhardt , N. (2004). The rater applied performance scale: Development and reliability. *Psychiatry Research, 127,* 147–155.

Loerch, B., Graf-Morgenstern, M., Hautzinger, M., Schlegel, S., Hain, C., Sandmann, J., et al. (1999). Randomized placebo-controlled trial of moclobemide, cognitive-behavioural therapy and their combination in panic disorder with agoraphobia. *British Journal of Psychiatry, 174,* 205–212.

March, J. S., Foa, E., Gammon, P., Chrisman, A., Curry, J., Fitzgerald, D., et al. (2004). Cognitive-behavior therapy, sertraline, and their combination for children and adolescents with obsessive-compulsive disorder: The pediatric OCD treatment study (POTS) randomized controlled trial. *Journal of the American Medical Association, 292,* 1969–1976.

Marks, I. M., Lelliott, P., Basoglu, M., Noshirvani, H., Monteiro, W., Cohen, D., et al. (1988). Clomipramine, self-exposure and therapist-aided exposure for obsessive-compulsive rituals. *British Journal of Psychiatry, 152,* 522–534.

Marks, I. M., Stern, R. S., Mawson, D., Cobb, J., & McDonald, R. (1980). Clomipramine and exposure for obsessive-compulsive rituals. *British Journal of Psychiatry, 136,* 1–25.

Marks, I. M., Swinson, R. P., Basoglu, M., Kuch, K., Noshirvani, H., O'Sullivan, G., et al. (1993). Alprazolam and exposure alone and combined in panic disorder with agoraphobia: A controlled study in London and Toronto. *British Journal of Psychiatry, 162,* 776–787.

Marshall, R. D., Cárcamo, J. H., Blanco, C., & Liebowitz, M. (2003). Trauma-focused psychotherapy after a trial of medication for chronic PTSD: Pilot observations. *American Journal of Psychotherapy, 57,* 374–383.

Meyer, T. J., Miller, M. L., Metzger, R. L., & Borkovec, T. D. (1990). Development and validation of the Penn State Worry Questionnaire. *Behaviour Research Therapy, 28,* 487–495.

Myers, K. M., & Davis, M. (2002). Behavioral and neural analysis of extinction. *Neuron, 36,* 567–584.

Mynors-Wallis, L. M., Gath, D. H., Day, A., & Baker, F. (2000). Randomized controlled trial of problem-solving treatment, antidepressant medication, and combined treatment for major depression in primary care. *British Medical Journal, 320,* 26–30.

Olafson, M., Marcus, S. C., Wan, G. J., & Geissler, E. C. (2004). National trends in the outpatient treatment of anxiety disorders. *Journal of Clinical Psychiatry, 65,* 1166–1173.

Otto, M. W. (2002). Learning and "unlearning" fears: Preparedness, neural pathways, and patients. *Biological Psychiatry, 52,* 917–929.

Otto, M. W., Hinton, D., Korbly, N. B., Chea, A., Phalnarith, B, Gershuny, B. S., et al. (2003). Treatment of pharmacotherapy-refractory posttraumatic stress disorder among Cambodian refugees: A pilot study of combination treatment with cognitive-behavior therapy vs. sertraline alone. *Behaviour Research and Therapy, 41,* 1271–1276.

Otto, M. W., Pollack, M. H., & Barlow, D. H. (1995). *Stopping anxiety medication: A workbook for patients wanting to discontinue benzodiazepine treatment for panic disorder.* New York: Psychological Corporation.

Otto, M. W., Pollack, M. H., Sachs, G. S., Reiter, S. R., Meltzer-Brody, S., & Rosenbaum, J. F. (1993). Discontinuation of benzodiazepine treatment: Efficacy of cognitive-behavioral therapy for patients with panic disorder. *American Journal of Psychiatry, 150,* 1485–1490.

Pampallona, S., Bollini, P., Tibaldi, G., Kupelnick, B., & Munizza, C. (2004). Combined pharmacotherapy and psychological treatment for depression: A systematic review. *Archives of General Psychiatry, 61,* 714–719.

Rachman, S. (1979). The return of fear. *Behavior Research Therapy, 17,* 164–166.

Reynolds, C. F., III, Frank, E., Kupfer, D. J., Thase, M. E., Perel, J. M., Mazumdar, S., et al. (1996). Treatment outcome in recurrent major depression: A post hoc comparison of elderly ("young old") and mid-life patients. *American Journal of Psychiatry, 153,* 1288–1292.

Reynolds, C. F., III, Frank, E., Perel, J. M., Imber, S. D., Cornes, C., Miller, M. D., et al. (1999). Nortriptyline and interpersonal psychotherapy as maintenance therapies for recurrent major depression: A randomized controlled clinical trial in patients older than 59 years. *Journal of the American Medical Association, 281,* 39–45.

Roy-Byrne, P. P., Craske, M. G., Stein, M. B., Sullivan, G., Bystritsky, A., Katon, W., et al. (2005). A randomized effectiveness trial of cognitive-behavioral therapy and medication for primary care panic disorder. *Archives of General Psychiatry, 62,* 290–298.

Schmidt, N. B., Wollaway-Bickel, K., Trakowski, J., Santiago, H., Storey, J., Koselka, M., et al. (2000). Dismantling cognitive-behavioral treatment for panic disorder: Questioning the utility of breathing retraining. *Journal of Consulting and Clinical Psychology, 68,* 417–424.

Schmidt, N. B., Wollaway-Bickel, K., Trakowski, J. H., Santiago, H. T., & Vasey, M. (2002). Antidepressant discontinuation in the context of cognitive behavioral treatment for panic disorder. *Behaviour Research and Therapy, 40,* 67–73.

Segal, Z., Vincent, P., & Levitt, A. (2002). Efficacy of combined, sequential and crossover psychotherapy and pharmacotherapy in improving outcomes in depression. *Journal of Psychiatry and Neuroscience, 27,* 281–290.

Simpson, H. B., Liebowitz, M. R., Foa, E. B., Kozak, M. J., Scmidt, A. B., Rowan, V., et al. (2004). Post-treatment effects of exposure therapy and clomipramine in obsessive-compulsive disorder. *Depression and Anxiety, 19,* 225–233.

Thase, M. E., Greenhouse, J. B., Frank, E., Reynolds, C. F., III, Pilkonis, P. A., Hurley, K., et al. (1997). Treatment of major depression with psychotherapy or psychotherapy-pharmacotherapy combinations. *Archives of General Psychiatry, 54,* 1009–1015.

Thase, M. E., Rush, A. J., Manber, R., Kornstein, S. G., Klein, D. N., Markowitz, J. C., et al. (2002). Differential effects of nefazodone and cognitive behavioral analysis system of psychotherapy on insomnia associated with chronic forms of major depression. *Journal of Clinical Psychiatry, 63,* 493–500.

Treatment for Adolescents with Depression Study (TADS) randomized controlled trial. (2004). Fluoxetine, cognitive-behavioral therapy, and their combination for adolescents with depression. *Journal of the American Medical Association, 292,* 807–820.

van Balkom, A. J. L. M., de Haan, E., van Oppen, P., Spinhoven, P., Hoogduin, K. A. L., & van Dyck, R. (1998). Cognitive and behavioral therapies alone and in combination with fluvoxamine in the treatment of obsessive compulsive disorder. *Journal of Nervous and Mental Disease, 186,* 492–499.

van Oppen, P., de Haan, E., van Balkom, A. J. L. M., Spinhoven, P., Hoogduin, K. A. L., & van Dyck, R. (1995). Cognitive therapy and exposure in vivo in the treatment of obsessive compulsive disorder. *Behaviour Research and Therapy, 33,* 379–390.

van Oppen, P., van Balkom, A. J. L. M., de Haan, E., & van Dyck, R. (2005). Cognitive therapy and exposure in vivo alone and in combination with fluvoxamine in obsessive-compulsive disorder: A 5-year follow-up. *Journal of Clinical Psychiatry, 66,* 1415–1422.

Westbrook, R. F., Iordanova, M., McNally, G., Richardson, R., & Harris J. A. (2002). Reinstatement of fear to an extinguished conditioned stimulus: Two roles for context. *Journal of Experimental Psychology: Animal Behavior Processes, 28,* 97–110.

Whittal, M. L., Otto, M. W., & Hong, J. J. (2001). Cognitive-behavior therapy for discontinuation of SSRI treatment of panic disorder: A case series. *Behavior Research and Therapy, 39*, 939–945.

Williams, J. B. W. (1988). A structured interview guide for the Hamilton Depression Rating Scale. *Archives of General Psychiatry, 45*, 742–747.

Zajecka, J., Dunner, D. L., Gelenberg, A. J., Hirschfeld, R. M. A., Kornstein, S. G., Ninan, P. T., et al. (2002). Sexual function and satisfaction in the treatment of chronic major depression with nefazodone, psychotherapy, and their combination. *Journal of Clinical Psychiatry, 63*, 709–716.

Author Index

Subject Index